CLASSIC
CHRISTIANITY

A SYSTEMATIC THEOLOGY

Previously Published in Three Volumes

THOMAS C. ODEN

HarperOne
An Imprint of HarperCollinsPublishers

For Clark, Edward, and Laura

HarperOne

The previous three-volume edition of *Systematic Theology* condensed in consultation with John Tyson, Stephen A. Seamands, Alan Padgett, David Eaton, Sang Hoon Lee, Thomas Buchan, Neil Anderson, and Thomas Clark Oden II

Editorial Advisory Committee for the revision of this edition:

John R. Tyson

Stephen A. Seamands

Alan G. Padgett

David E. Eaton

Sang Hoon Lee

Thomas N. Buchan

Neil D. Anderson

Thomas Clark Oden II

Systematic Theology, Three Volumes. Copyright © 1987, 1989, 1992 by Thomas C. Oden.

First HarperCollins paperback edition published in 1992

HarperCollins Web site: http://www.harpercollins.com

HarperCollins®, ■®, and HarperOne™ are trademarks of HarperCollins Publishers

Library of Congress Cataloging-in-Publication Data is available upon request.

ISBN 978–0–06–144971–0

18 19 20   LSC(H)   10 9 8 7

CONTENTS

BOOK ONE
THE LIVING GOD

PART I
THE LIVING GOD

PART II
THE REALITY OF GOD

PART III
THE WORK OF GOD

PART IV
THE STUDY OF GOD

BOOK TWO
THE WORD OF LIFE

PART I
WORD MADE FLESH

PART III
HE DIED FOR OUR SINS

PART IV
EXALTED LORD

BOOK THREE
LIFE IN THE SPIRIT

PART I
THE PERSON OF THE HOLY SPIRIT

PART II
SALVATION

PART III

THE CHURCH

PART IV

HUMAN DESTINY

PREFACE:
GETTING STARTED

Classic Consensual Ecumenical Teaching

My basic purpose is to set forth an ordered view of the faith of the Christian community upon which there has generally been substantial agreement between the traditions of East and West, including Catholic, Protestant, and Orthodox. My intent is not to present the views of a particular branch of modern Christian teaching, such as Roman Catholic or Reformed, but to listen single-mindedly for the voice of that deeper consensus that has been gratefully celebrated as received teaching by believers of vastly different cultural settings, whether African or Asian, Eastern or Western, sixth or sixteenth century.

My intention may be simply put: I hope to set forth what is most commonly stated in the central Christian tradition concerning God. This effort is therefore ecumenical in a larger sense than is usually assumed in the modern ecumenical movement. It proposes to follow that ancient ecumenical consensus of Christian teaching of God as seen in earliest creedal summaries of Irenaeus, c. AD 190; Tertullian, c. 200; Hippolytus, c. 215; Council of Caesarea, 325; Council of Nicaea, 325; Marcellus, 340; Cyril of Jerusalem, 350; Council of Constantinople, 381; Rufinus, 404; Council of Chalcedon, 451. These confessions still embrace and empower not only centrist Protestants and traditional Roman Catholics and Orthodox but also great numbers of evangelicals, liberals, and charismatics.

Hence I am seeking to set forth key constructive arguments of two millennia of ecumenical Christian thinking—*that* God is, *who* God is, and what that *means* for us today. I seek an internally consistent statement of classical Christian thinking about God so as to provide a reliable foundation for baptism, the life of prayer, scripture studies, and for the living of Christian life.

No attempt has been made to avoid the classical language of the church. The study of God does better by letting tested classical Christian language speak for itself in its own directly powerful way to modern minds and hearts wrestling with the limits and failures of modern consciousness. The faithful have no dread of using the traditional language of the church. Terms like incarnation and resurrection need to be explained, not avoided.

Contemporary cultures present no tougher challenges to Christianity than did the fall of Rome, the collapse of the medieval synthesis, the breakup of the unity of Christendom in the sixteenth century, or the French Enlightenment. Christian teaching today must be pursued amid a similar collapse of modern assumptions. I will not try to offer classic Christianity artificial crutches to assist it in catching up with the frenzied pace of modernity. My premise is that modernity has more catching up to do with classic Christianity. My passion is in the closest possible adherence to the texts of classic Christian teaching.

Modest Reaffirmations

In reworking the earlier three-volume edition (1987–92) into a single volume, I reaffirm solemn commitments made at its beginning:

- to make no new contribution to theology

- to resist the temptation to quote modern writers less schooled in the whole counsel of God than the best ancient classic exegetes

- to seek quite simply to express the one mind of the believing church that has been always attentive to that apostolic teaching to which consent has been given by Christian believers everywhere, always, and by all. This is what I mean by the Vincentian method (Vincent of Lérins, *Commonitory*).

I have listened closely for the historic ecumenical consensus received by believers of widely varied languages, social locations, and cultures, whether of East or West, African, or Asian, whether expressed by women or men of the second or first Christian millennium, whether European or decisively pre-European, post- or pre-Constantinian.

My goal has not been to survey the bewildering varieties of *dissent*, but to identify and plausibly set forth the cohesive central tradition of general lay *consent* to apostolic teaching, seen not through its centrifugal aberations but in its centripetal centering. I will spend little time trying to knock down others' cherished views. The focus is upon setting forth plausible layers of argument traditionally employed while presenting in connected order the most commonly held points of biblical teaching as classically interpreted by the leading teachers of the earliest centuries of Christianity.

My intention is not to try to satisfy the finicky appetites of naturalistic skeptics who will always remain hungry. Nor is it to find a clever way of making the way of salvation conveniently acceptable to the prejudices of modernity. I am pledged not to become fixated upon the ever-spawning species of current critical opinions, but instead to focus single-mindedly upon early consensual assent to apostolic teaching of how God the Spirit works to fulfill the mission of God the Son on behalf of God the Father.

I do not assume that my reader already affirms classic Christian teaching. I wish only to give a fair hearing to the way in which classical Christian teachers have always understood their own grounding and empowerment.

I will not dodge or explain away the time-honored vocabulary of the church, or seek constantly to substitute diluted terms congenial to modernity. The witness to God's saving action is best served by letting the tested language of the Christian tradition, as refined through countless historical and political mutations, speak for itself out of its own power to modern minds struggling with the follies and limits of modernity. Only those who give traditional Christianity a fair hearing can fairly decide whether it makes sense. Deteriorating modern ideologies must now catch up with the ever-new forgings of classic Christianity, not the other way around.

Those who are at home with liturgy and those who prefer a down-to-earth, socially engaged, pragmatic level are inheritors of the same consensus. Both can dive deeply into the stream of classic Christian language without a sacrifice of conscience. Some will bring an imagination awakened by theoretical interests, other by practical ethics. All of these varied partners will recognize the best of their own recent traditions as already at home and included within the embrace of classical Christian thought. The beautiful species known as Christian orthodoxy deserves advocates who try to do what Rachel Carson did for birds or what Archie Carr did to advocate the cause of endangered sea turtles.

The Promise of Unoriginality

The only promise I intend to make, however inadequately carried out, is that of unoriginality. I plan to present nothing new or original in these pages. Nothing of my own that would have my initials stamped upon it is important in this discussion. Admittedly the classic language must be reappropriated and articulated in sentences written and ordered by some particular person. Yet I hope my own voice does not intrude upon the radiant voices of Paul, Irenaeus, Anthony, and Athanasius.

I wish to provide neither a new interpretation of old ideas, nor a new language that is more acceptable for modern sensibilities. Rigorous accountability to the ancient teachers themselves is a large enough task, without adding to it other heavy burdens. If that seems irregular, it can be viewed as a response to a prevailing excess, one that inordinately emphasizes self-expression, often exaggerated in current self-importance. I do not pretend to have found a comfortable way of making Christianity tolerable to vanishing forms of modernity. I present no revolutionary new ideas, no new way to salvation. The road is still narrow (Matt. 7:14).

I do not have the gift of softening the sting of the Christian message, of making it seem light or easily borne or quickly assimilated into prevailing modern ideas (Clement of Alex., *Exhort to the Heathen*; Hippolytus, *Refutation of All Her.* 4.47–51; Origen, *Ag. Celsus* 6.16). I do not wish to make a peace of bad conscience with dubious "achievements of modernity" or pretend to find a comfortable way of making Christianity expediently acceptable to modern assumptions (Kierkegaard, *Judge for Yourselves!*; *Prefaces*). If Paul found that "the Athenians in general and foreigners there had no time for anything but talking or hearing about the latest novelty" (Acts 17:21; Basil, Hom. on Ps. 45), so have I found too much talk of religion today obsessed with novelty.

I am dedicated to unoriginality. My aim is to present classical Christian teaching of God on its own terms, undiluted by modern posturing. I take to heart Paul's admonition: "But even if we or an angel from heaven should preach a gospel *other than* the one we preached to you, let him be eternally condemned! As we had already said, so now I say again: If anybody is preaching to you a gospel other than what you accepted [*par o parelabete*, other than what you received from the apostles], let him be eternally condemned [*anathema esto*]!" (Gal. 1:8, 9, italics added).

I have not focused upon answering contrary or odd opinions except when they have served to make ancient ecumenical reasoning more transparent. I have tried to keep out petty local viewpoints in the interest of clarifying only those teachings upon which the central streams of classical Christian theologians have textually agreed as expressing the mind of the believing church. At points where that agreement is not fully evident, I either leave the subject for further debate or try to state the principal viewpoints remaining in tension within classic voices. I hope to constrain my own particular idiosyncratic way of looking at things. My mission is to deliver as clearly as I can that core of consensual belief that has been shared for almost two millennia of Christian teaching. Vincent of Lérins described this core as that which has always, everywhere, and by all Christians been believed about God's self-disclosure.

The modern rules of authorship insist that every author strive for originality. The classic Christian rule is opposite. Its writings value the most faithful replication of the most ancient sacred texts and resist vain pretenses of originality. So brace yourself. There is hardly a sentence ahead that is not accompanied by a classic reference or quote, most from the period before the fall of Rome.

The Consensual Doctors and Documents

The principal classical interpreters of scripture are those usually designated as the four great ecumenical Doctors of the Church of the Eastern tradition (Athanasius, Basil, Gregory of Nazianzus, and Chrysostom) and the four Doctors of the Church of the West (Ambrose, Augustine, Jerome, and Gregory the Great).

Among others who have been perennially valued for accurately stating points of ecumenical consensus are Hilary of Poitiers, Cyril of Alexandria, Leo I, John of Damascus, Thomas Aquinas, and among Protestants especially Luther, Calvin, and Cranmer. "Classic" in our definition includes classic Reformation sources in so far as they reflect the ancient ecumenical consensus.

Consensual documents widely received by the consenting church over a long period of time are valued above statements of individuals. Most important of consensual documents are the decisions of ecumenical councils and the most widely received synods and councils. The method of consensus hinges on the fact of wide consent (*consentio*, "to be of one mind, to agree," from *con-*, "with," and *sentire*, "feel" or "sense"). Who gives consent in this consensus? The whole church, the cloud of witnesses. How is this consent defined? In correspondence with ancient ecumenical consent as found textually in the ecumenical councils.

The term traditionally applied to the classic Christian teachers of the first five centuries is "patristic" (from *pater*), in reference to the fathers of the church. Yet since there were also influential women and not men alone, we will also be hearing from the matristic (from *mater*) exegetes and saints such as Macrina, Perpetua, Caecilia of Rome, Agatha of Sicily, Margaret of Antioch, Paula, Eustochium, and Amma Theodora. When the generic term "patristic" is used, it refers mainly to those whose writings have most shaped the tradition, the fathers and mothers in the faith, whether they write or die to attest the faith.

I do not quote these interpreters in order to make intellectual heroes of them or to treat them as geniuses or creative innovators. Oddly enough, most of them, insofar as they were consensually received, thought of themselves as unoriginal in desiring especially *not to add anything to an already sufficient apostolic faith*, but only to receive and reappropriate that faith accurately and honestly in their particular social and historical setting. They were not seeking to invent new ideas but simply and plainly to understand God's actual goodness and purpose as revealed in universal history.

There was indeed creative genius at work in the communities of orthodoxy, but the individual teachers who best served those communities did not think of themselves as creative geniuses. They knew that it was the community itself that was brilliant, and made brilliant by the power of the Spirit. The most powerful writers, such as Gregory of Nazianzus and Augustine, were those who most accurately gave expression to the faith that was already well understood generally by the community they served.

Hence I will constrain the impulse to tangle with detailed controversies in modern sources. That is not my purpose. Each doctrine has a lengthy history of controversy. That history is the subject of historical theology, but that differs from the method of a compendium of classic Christianity, which assumes that it is useful to set forth classic Christian thinking cohesively without becoming disrupted or preoccupied with each successive stage of development through which each teaching has passed in various contexts, traditions, symbol systems, and periods. The teacher of classic Christianity must be thoroughly informed about these developments but need not always burden readers with their details.

Readers may be helped by assuming that before each and every paragraph is an implicit phrase: "The principal classical exegetes say . . ." It would be tedious to repeat such a reference constantly, so I ask your indulgence in my saying it only once.

Rediscovering Early African Voices in Classic Christianity

The earliest forms of classic Christian teaching bear a distinctly African stamp. The common perception is that Christianity in Africa is a relatively recent arrival from the West. This classic consensus shows the opposite: Christian intellectual formation is oldest in Africa. The contributions made by African Christian thinkers had decisive effects on the formation of world Christianity, and especially European Christianity. The editorial and translation teams that produced the twenty-nine volumes of the Ancient Christian Commentary on Scripture were amazed to find such a large proportion of texts from the African continent in the earliest comments on scripture.

African Christianity is foundational for classic Christian teaching. This serves as the potential basis for a new African ecumenism that promises to reshape the recovery of apostolic teaching in world Christianity. In the years between the publication of *Systematic Theology* and that of *Classic Christianity*, these African texts were being heavily mined in primary sources. Many of these appear prominently in these pages: Tertullian, Origen, Cyprian, Athanasius, Didymus the Blind, Augustine, and the great Cyril. Christianity is often portrayed as an essentially European religion. This is regrettable because classic Christianity has its pre-European roots in cultures that are far distant from Europe and that preceded the development of early modern European identity, and some of its greatest minds have been African, as I have set forth in *How Africa Shaped the Christian Mind: Rediscovering the African Seedbed of Western Christianity*.

The System of References

Embedded in almost every paragraph of these pages are references to leading classical Christian sources. They point modern readers to a textual history of dialogue that rightly informs contemporary discussion. The most important service I can render readers is manifested in these quotations and embedded annotations. This follows the method of reference in classic Christianity, with constant orientation to scripture and the tradition of exegesis of scripture.

To some it may seem amusing—to me it remains a sober, ironic fact—that this volume is written as *an introduction to its annotations*. If the text invites readers to search out the original sources that called it forth, the arrow will have struck its mark. Only if it succeeds in pointing believers back to Cyprian, Chrysostom, and Macrina has it fulfilled my expectation. This kind of textual accountability hopes to point beyond itself to the texts out of which its argument lives.

Among eccentricities I ask the reader to tolerate is my sincere opinion that the most valuable aspect of this compendium of classic Christianity is its parenthetical references. If it is possible for an author sincerely to ask a reader to rivet attention upon the sources to which he points and relatively less to his own inventions, I would indicate that as my true intention. Picture me as on my knees begging you to do just this one thing.

My concern is not primarily with knocking down beliefs but with upbuilding, not with polemics but with peacemaking, not with differences but with consensus, not with development of doctrine but with the unity of the Christian tradition, which has so astutely and imaginatively addressed so many different cultural environments. Hence I have preferred primary biblical and early Christian sources to recent secondary sources.

My criteria for textual citations need to be candidly stated. I have preferred citing:

- biblical texts with clear teaching values, rather than those containing ambiguities or requiring clarification of complex historical conditions and assumptions;

- the most widely received classical teachers rather than ancillary or non-consensual exhibits;

- earlier rather than later classical writers; and

- those writings that most clearly reflect ancient apostolic teaching rather than those dealing with special viewpoints and controversial themes.

Clear Models of Consensus Versus Disputable Figures

I am less prone to quote Origen than Augustine, but I quote Origen on points on which he was generally received by the ancient church consensus and do not quote Augustine on those points on which he was not generally received. On those particular points on which respected patristic writers tended to diverge from the central ancient ecumenical consensus (e.g., Origenist views that the power of God is limited or that stars have souls, or Novatian's view of the permanent exclusion of the lapsed, or Gregory of Nyssa's universalism, or some of Augustine's views of election and reprobation), I will be less prone to quote them, but I will quote freely from their writings that have been widely received.

Some may think it odd that I have sometimes quoted classic Christian teachers who have been declared anathema on some particular points by the councils or condemned by various consensual teachers. Examples among our referees are selected appreciative citations from Tertullian, Novatian, Theodoret, and Ambrosiaster, whose doctrinal aberations have been limited to specific points, but whose teachings beyond these are freely quoted within orthodox teaching. The points on which they are quoted here are only those in which their orthodoxy was not questioned or those on which they may have expressed the consensus better than many others. Among those regarded by most as profoundly orthodox but who suffered on some particular point from temporary excommunication are Maximus the Confessor, who lost his tongue for what he said, Chrysostom, who was expelled from Constantinople and died in exile, and the brilliant Origen, who was rejected by Jerome and Cyril but used extensively by both of them.

I will take this story step by step, avoiding technical phrases, striking for the heart of the matter. For models of the theological clarity, precision, and cohesion that all do well to emulate, see Gregory of Nazianzus, *Theological Orations*, and John of Damascus, *Orthodox Faith*. Models for this ancient ecumenical method may be seen in Cyril of Jerusalem, *Catech. Lect.*; Vincent of Lérins, (*Commonit.* 1–3), and Gregory the Great (*Epis.* 25). Watching them play theology is like watching Willie Mays play centerfield or Duke Ellington play "Sophisticated Lady."

As you go, bear in mind Kierkegaard's axiom: everything about religion is amusing, and especially Christianity, where everything hinges on the incarnation. So cool it, relax, breathe, and swim to the deep fathoms.

Interlude: Seven Reasons Why this Exploration is Distinctive

Several features of this compendium make it unusual and in some ways distinctive. If asked to write an honest description of what is atypical and unusual about this volume, I would note the following:

1. This compendium is the first in many years to view systematic theology as a classic treasury of scriptural and widely received patristic texts that point toward this *distinctive work of the Spirit*: These texts all share a common classic premise that *it is the same Spirit who inspired the canonical text who is actively creating the unity and cohesion of the whole doctrinal effort amid changing historical circumstances.* This cohesion is not the product of the work of modern scholars, but of the work of the Spirit throughout twenty centuries of intensive, critical scriptural exegesis. Note how different this premise is from those that have prevailed in most theologies written since Schleiermacher early in the nineteenth century.

2. This volume is the first in the modern period to present the *whole range of issues of classic Christian teaching with constant reference to the much wider range of patristic texts now available.* Many of these were not available to premodern writers.

3. This volume is the first in recent decades to attempt to present a *text-based consensus* of early Christian thought that embraces the whole range of issues of systematic theology. It presents a consensual argument that appeals to authoritative texts shared by Protestants, Catholics, Orthodox, classic liberal, evangelical, and charismatic believers. Most comparable attempts address only one or two of these audiences.

4. The reason for presenting these texts in systematic order in one volume is to offer the opportunity to *see their intrinsic interconnections.* Where repetitions occur, they are necessary to demonstrate the connections textually. I want only to provide clear evidences of the unity of classic Christian teaching by presenting discrete, convincing, and authoritative examples of it. This is the task of the science of theological reasoning as viewed classically. I know of no better place to glimpse the spirit and method that pervaded the forms of theological reasoning modeled notably by Cyprian, Augustine, Cyril of Alexandria, and Bede. They all showed these textual interconnections. They focused on delivering accurately the authoritative texts in a plausible, thoughtful arrangement and in an uncomplicated, readable style in order to show forth their cohesiveness as a demonstration of the work of the Spirit. There was no accent on the individual virtuosity of individual thinkers or on those who were putting the pattern together. The pattern arose out of a worshiping community. The important thing was not the brilliance of any individual's arguments but the shared pattern formed by the conflation of texts themselves, radiating the power of the Spirit.

   The purpose of extensive consensual reference is not to set forth all the conceivable interpretations of scripture. Rather it is highly selective: to present only those that *best convey the consensus* of faith. No other work focuses deliberately on this criterion to my knowledge. In fact this whole standard classic procedure is viewed with alarm by many academicians as an incongruous act of proof-texting. It is deemed incongruous because many in the academy have already decided before making the investigation that there can never be any consensus among such varieties. Meanwhile the truth of the consensus and its durability have remained unexplained and ignored in the academy. The cost is that the modern laity is deprived of the authoritative texts upon which classic Christianity is built. The selection of these references is very deliberate. They all hinge on canonical and authoritative classic texts—scripture texts first, and the most widely received interpreters of scripture worldwide over the centuries next. They beg to be read. They plead to be placed within an overarching argument of the whole sequence of topics of classic Christian teaching, as they have been so often in the history of classic Christian teaching.

5. My particular way of arranging and titling the headings of the compendium has little importance other than to introduce these more important voices in due order. *The order is entirely borrowed from the consensus.* If anything makes this book a little different from most popular modern theologies, it is this. I have exercised the freedom to reference a few modern texts, but only in those cases where a modern text gathers up the wisdom of the classic consensual texts most aptly.

6. This compendium is *the first comprehensive attempt to carry out the ecumenical method proposed by Vincent of Lérins* in the fifth century. Its classic medieval form is found in Thomas Aquinas' *Compendium of Theology* and its best modern representative is William Burt Pope.

For these reasons this compendium is unique.

This Treasury

What I most want my reader to grasp is that the worshiping community has this treasury of sacred texts to deal with in constructing a pattern of Christian teaching. They are not merely speculation, and not the result of autonomous creative thinking, but wise texts that have proven important and valuable to the community of prayer for generations. This compendium consists primarily of the sequential presentation of those texts, both from scripture and tradition, with minimal claim of any originality of arrangement. Both the texts and their arrangement have been available for centuries. But they have been too long ignored.

This is a tested way of teaching introductory classic Christianity. Since so long ignored, it is perceived as a very *unexpected way of teaching basic theology today.* It is new only because it has been forgotten for many decades as a valid method of teaching. I want to show that the return to the method of classical Christian teaching is just as illuminating and fresh and edifying today as it has been for dozens of previous generations. I can only do this by presenting it point by point, in the order in which it has been most commonly presented over two millennia.

Classic Christian thinking can be grasped by contemporary critical minds if they can learn to think historically within a community, rather than individualistically. Only when each one hears his or her own individual experience illuminated by the wisdom of the historical Christian community is it then possible to contribute that illumined personal experience back to the community (Cyril of Jerusalem, *Procatechesis*, prologue:1–6).

The Storehouse of Sources

The references in this book represent consensual Christianity, not because I say so but because a history of widely recognized consensual advocates says so. These are not just my opinions and choices. They are choices made by thousands, millions, of believers from multiple cultures over multiple centuries. Most of the references are from those sources most widely recognized by the classical tradition, especially through the councils and the Great Doctors of the Church. Ancillary voices that have received less attention may just as accurately express the mind of the believing church. They include great teachers of widely different cultures—like Ephrem the Syrian, Pachomius of Tabennisi on the Nile, Optatus of Numidia, Didymus the Blind, and Dorotheus of Gaza. They show that the consensus can be expressed by marginalized or minority voices who have not often been heard within the majority traditions.

The historic church does not depend upon modern cultural sources to legitimize it. Its sources are mature and made sufficient by the ways that the Holy Spirit has brought centrifugal unity to Christian teaching in the earliest centuries of Christianity. And do not get angry at me if I report what classic Christianity says. If I represent it wrongly, yes, let's hear it. If I insert my own biases, tell me. But in most cases the problem is not with me but with classic Christianity, especially if I am telling the same truth held by the great tradition. You are confronted with a decision. Those who flatly disagree with classic Christianity have a basic decision to make, especially if they seek ordination. Is it right to pretend to ignore this teaching? Better to work it out by further counsel with people you trust. Better yet to go back to the texts and see if I am telling the truth.

Subjective judgments on whether these texts are intriguing or irrelevant, exciting or boring are entirely for the reader to decide. There is no doubt that they have been regarded as life-changing to many. But it remains a subjective judgment as to their ability to enliven a given reader. I prefer allowing them to be freely given permission to speak in their own language, even if it means that modern ears will stereotype them as old-fashioned and traditional. Being traditional is what makes them worth returning to again and again. Their longevity and the multicultural breadth of their authority is precisely what commends them. It is more relevant to ask why this extraordinary power of endurance still persists. The perception of classic Christian wisdom as if it were tedious may say more about the perceiver than about the truth of what is perceived. Even if they are perceived as dusty and dull, that does not change the objective fact that these texts have spoken powerfully for Christian teaching for hundreds of years, and in most cases more than a thousand years. They have changed thousands of lives. The reason why they are quoted directly is to allow the reader to encounter openly the texts that modern chauvinism has already decided are boring and dated, letting the reader make the call.

A Guide for Locating Parenthetical References

Those who wish to pursue a more concentrated investigation of classic works cited in this compendium will be able to do so through the parenthetical references. The key to the abbreviations is provided on page 865. Section numbers have been preferred to page numbers in citing references because this is common practice in patristic reference, and it more accurately points to the ancient text in its original language as found in commonly received editions. Patristic references provide information on the author and title, either by section number (ordinarily inserting periods between section and subsection numbers) or by page number (ordinarily inserting a colon before a page number). A colon in a parenthetical reference may point either to a page number or, in the case of a scripture text, a verse number. A period within a reference points to a section or subsection number. For example, Augustine, *Confessions* 10.1 means Book 10, Section 1 of the *Confessions*. References to scriptural commentaries by ancient writers typically follow the convention of including book, chapter, homily, section, or part number (then period), then section number or biblical chapter (period), then verse number (for example: Chrysostom, *Hom. on Acts* 11.4.31 means Homily 11 at the specific point of commenting on Acts 4.31, because that is how the commentary is arranged). Whether the first digit refers to a book, chapter, homily, section, or part number depends on the way the received source text or original language text is separated into segments. Anomalies persist because original language editions may vary in their systems of numbering or sectioning. Some texts are divided by book, chapter, section, and subsection, and others in other ways, such as volume, part, or division. A reference to Chrysostom, *Hom. on John* 88.2 does not refer to Chapter 88 of John, but Homily 88 written by Chrysostom on John, quoted from Section 2.

The comments on scripture by Origen, Chrysostom, Ambrosiaster, and others are commonly noted either as homilies or as commentary. We are forced by the standard literature to employ both forms. Homilies were normally presented as instruction to a worshiping community, while commentaries were line-by-line analyses of problems and issues in the text. While some prefer to distinguish these approaches sharply, we see them flowing together quietly in most ancient Christian writers. Chrysostom's work is most variably referenced as homily, commentary, or simply epistle or gospel, but our preference is homily.

Since each original source may discuss varied topics in a single section or page, it is best not to expect the section reference to deal solely with the specific point the reader desires to see in context. Work through the flow of reasoning in the reference. Where some difficulty persists in locating a classic passage, it is wise to read sequential pages immediately following (or for context, preceding) the portion referenced, or consult the Latin, Greek, or Syriac text or another English translation (see list of abbreviations). Many difficulties will be avoided by remembering the distinction between colons and periods in the citations. The rule: where page numbers occur, they are preceded by a colon.

In order to standardized spelling and make grammatical idioms more uniform, the English references will not reflect odd alternative spelling variations of older translations. In cases where Greek, Latin, Syriac, and Coptic texts have not been previously translated into suitable English, we provide new translations. The references point to the best and most accessible translations of biblical and patristic texts. Recent translations have been preferred to older ones, and many have been newly translated. We intend to present dynamic equivalency translations of long-neglected texts which historically have been regarded as authoritative models of biblical interpretation. Where current English translations are already well rendered, they will be used, but if necessary their language will be brought up to date or amended for easier reading. For ease of reading we have in some cases edited out superfluous conjunctions.

Where a scripture reference is followed by a classic patristic reference, my intention is to refer the reader to further insights from the consensual tradition of exegesis into that scripture text. The reason I have not limited the scripture references to a single translation from a single original language version is because the patristic writers themselves were quoting from various original Hebrew, Greek, or Old Latin texts. The Septuagint was their most frequent source for the Old Testament and Apocrypha, which they then translated into Latin or Greek or Syriac, from which the modern English translator of the patristic source has to search for the way in which that writer understood the scripture text. Since they did not always work out of the same original text, we cannot arbitrarily impose upon them a modern translation from the Hebrew Bible or Greek original. Most patristic writers were working out of the Greek Septuagint and New Testament, and some fewer out of a version of the Old Latin or Peshitta or Syriac text. The task of the modern translator is to follow the intent of the classic exegete rather than to provide a translation that would assume that the ancient writer who was using the Septuagint had access to the Hebrew Bible or the accepted modern critical text of the New Testament. In accord with the criteria used by the Ancient Christian Commentary on Scripture (*ACCS*), we have either made our own translations in accordance with the patristic writer's intent, or used or modified a reliable contemporary translation in accord with that intent. Since this is not a work for philological professionals, we have not cluttered up the text by seeking to speculate on which original source text the author was using or which modern translator comes closest to approximating that author's intent in interpreting it. We prefer to use those translations that we have worked on together as an international translation team in the *ACCS* and its successive projects, and to use the norms of abbreviations that have been established there. The reader can search out page numbers of references in further detail by going directly to the extract as it is found in the *ACCS* or in the original edition of *Systematic Theology*. The central rule of translation has been clarity of intent and brevity of reference, so as not to load up the sentences with unnecessary subsequent or modern references. Intrinsically an ecumenical project, this study hopes to serve Protestant, Catholic, and Orthodox lay, pastoral, and scholarly audiences.

The Pyramid of Sources

Following these criteria, it is evident that only a few of the most important contemporary contributors will be noted, whereas a much broader spectrum of ancient sources will be recalled. Over fifteen thousand specific primary source references to consensus-bearing teachers are here offered, most of which are ancient.

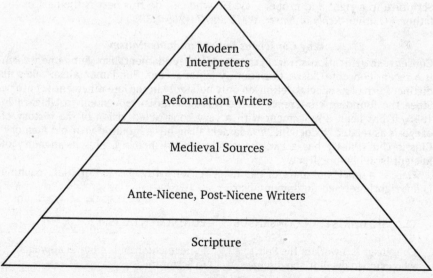

PYRAMID OF SOURCES

The weighting of references may be compared to a pyramid of sources, with scripture at the base, then the early Christian writers, first pre-Nicene then post-Nicene, as the central mass, then the best of medieval followed by centrist Reformation writers at the narrowing upper mass, and more recent interpreters at the smaller, tapering apex—but only those who grasp and express the prevailing mind of the believing historical church. Modern trends in systematic theology have been prone to turn that pyramid of texts upside down, quoting mostly modern sources and few earlier ones. I am pledging not to turn that pyramid upside down, as have those guild theologians who have most valued what is least tested.

I intend to set forth in consistent order those points most commonly held on all major affirmations of classic Christian teaching. The most authoritative affirmations of classic Christian doctrine hinge on the best and most widely received scripture interpretations of the classic exegetes. These are the views that have been happily received by the *consensus fidelium*. Medieval and Reformation exegesis stands upon the shoulders of the ancient Christian writers. The accompanying diagram (on page xxvii) represents this priority ordering of sources.

Hence primary biblical and classical Christian sources are consistently cited in preference to recent and secondary sources of all kinds. Among classic exegetes, those who have gained the widest consensus are quoted more often than those who have tended to elicit division, speculation, individual creativity, and controversy. Earlier rather than later sources are cited where possible, not because older is sentimentally prized, but because they have had longer to enrich and sculpt the historic consensus.

These classic Christian writers must not be pitted against scripture, since their deliberate purpose was to illuminate, order, and explicate the truth of scripture. In Luther's view, that was precisely what made them authoritative sources: "All the fathers concede their own obscurity and illuminate Scripture by Scripture alone. And, indeed, that is the right method. Scripture should be placed alongside Scripture in a right and proper way. He who can do this best is the best of the fathers" (Luther, *Reply to Emser*, WML 3:277; WLS 1:88).

Why Consensus Is Not Fundamentalism

Consensus clarification is a far cry from peddling fundamentalism. Fundamentalism is a recent concept. Classic Christianity is not recent. Fundamentalism takes its distinct form of its special definition only belatedly in the late nineteenth century. Since the founding conference of the fundamentalist movement in Niagara in 1895, it has been a movement with a very constricted vision of the history of exegesis as related to doctrine. Fundamentalism has a hundred-year-old memory. Classic Christianity has a two-thousand-year-old memory, plus its memory of ancient Israel before Jesus.

Here is a quick summary of ten major reasons why classic Christian teaching is not rightly termed fundamentalism.

CLASSIC CHRISTIAN CONSENSUS	FUNDAMENTALISM
Consensus is a work of the Spirit who came to dwell in the disciples after the resurrection	Fundamentalism is a literal approach to Scripture
Focuses on the meaning of the resurrection	Focuses on the historicity of the resurrection

Longevity: two millennia	Longevity: since the 1895 Niagara Conference
A faith shared worldwide by believers of twenty centuries of diverse generations and cultures	A particular crisis between parties within North American Protestantism
Has lived through and beyond hundreds of alleged "modernities"	A defensive response to particular challenges of nineteenth-century "modernity," especially Darwin and rising secular humanism
Scriptural authority received and tested by lay consensus of believers	Scriptural authority asserted against tradition
A catholic and orthodox faith is established through authoritative texts tested in many cultures	A truncated orthodoxy is cast in terms of the crises of modernity, lacking in the whole fabric of historic orthodox belief
Confident through historical change based on historic experience	Often expecting the worst from the human future
Recognition of metaphor and varieties of expression of inspired doctrine in Scripture	Single legitimate interpretation of each text
Texts viewed within historic contexts	Texts viewed apart from historic contexts

This is merely recapped in ten points that could themselves constitute a book. But this is not what this book is about. Nonetheless it is necessary to say because some might misread my intent or mistake the catholicity and evangelical depth of classic Christianity. I cannot allow you to have an easy excuse to put down the great forms of reasoning in classic Christianity by pigeonholing it with an entirely wrong designation. "Those who handle the text in too literal a manner have a veil cast over their eyes, whereas those who turn to contemplate the God of whom the Scriptures speak receive the revelation of divine glory which lies behind the letter of the text" (Gregory of Nyssa, *Against Eunomius,* 7.1).

Re-Establishing the Scriptural Foundation of Classic Christian Teaching

Classic exegetes cite scripture not as wooden, lifeless proof-texts, but as vital landmark affirmations of a worshiping community, where the church has found consolation and wisdom, and upon which ancient teachers have repeatedly reasoned and commented.

The history of classic Christianity is primarily a history of exegesis. If so, today's readers cannot be denied the right to examine the verbatim biblical texts upon which classic Christian teaching is largely a comment. It would be absurd to provide references to early exegetes but fail to mention the texts themselves. Yet this absurdity prevails in much contemporary theology. Most common points of consensual Christian exegesis were reasonably well formulated by the fifth century. Upon these we will focus.

A theology bent upon avoiding its textuary is inordinately self-inhibited. It ends in finally cutting itself off from its own vital sources. A theology that limits its referrals only to those texts that are elaborately placed in historical context will finally mutate into a historical report, not a systematic theology.

Literalist practices of proof-texting or stacking references relentlessly are rightly rejected. Yet the ancient ecumenical tradition requires theology to show how it bases its conclusions upon canonical texts. Disapproval of proof-texting must not lead to ignoring the very canonical texts upon which classic Christian teaching thrives. When modern forms of historical exegesis compulsively attempt to place every scriptural reference in its historical context, they risk becoming a long string of historical digressions on modern commentators so as to inadvertently forget the sacred text itself. This is another way for the interpreter to exercise silent control over the text. In this way the well-meaning attempt at historical critical exegesis may take a heavy toll on actually hearing the text, contrary to its intention.

The faithful are drawn to the living tradition, not dead archaisms. The affirmations most alive in Christian teaching are those that are most widely shared through all the times and contexts in which they have been celebrated. The faithful value the practiced wisdom of Christian tradition. Where highly imaginative forms of Christian tradition have received general lay consent, they are typically grounded in the preceding consensus of apostolic testimony.

The classic exegetes treated conserving forms of Christian tradition with lively imagination, and imaginative forms of Christian experience with a celebration of their antecedents. They have discovered through experience that there is nothing more forward-looking than taking the risk of allowing themselves to be addressed by the texts of holy scripture and tested tradition.

ACKNOWLEDGMENTS

In making these extensive revisions, I have sought rigorous criticism and advice from eight of my closest long-term associates. To these esteemed colleagues, my Editorial Advisory Group, I am profoundly grateful:

Prof. John R. Tyson of Houghton College

Prof. Stephen A. Seamands of Asbury Theological Seminary

Prof. Alan Padgett of Luther Theological Seminary

Dean David Eaton of Wesleyan Bible College

Prof. Sang Hoon Lee of the Academy of Korean Studies

Prof. Thomas Buchan of Asbury Theological Seminary (Orlando)

Prof. Neil Anderson of Asbury College

and my son Thomas Clark Oden II.

Each one of these editorial partners participated in a thorough review and critique of these classic arguments. Each one gave me invaluable advice on revisions and refinements. Innumerable hours have been selflessly devoted by these colleagues.

The last seventeen years of my academic life have been spent in close dialogue with colleagues in the research and writing of the Ancient Christian Commentary on Scripture (*ACCS*). Special thanks in this effort go to all my fellow volume editors of the *ACCS*. Digital searches for producing each of its twenty-nine volumes were actively utilized in the refashioning and strengthening of this inquiry. It would have been almost impossible to amass the exegetical and textual depth to accomplish this revision without the extensive research that went into the *ACCS*. My life has been enriched by my three closest colleagues in particular: Christopher Hall, Joel Elowsky, and Michael Glerup. To Howard and Roberta Ahmanson, I am forever grateful for their encouragement, as well as to the editors at Harper Collins for their helpful editorial judgment over the years since my first Harper book thirty-four years ago (1975).

For rabbinic partners in dialogue, especially Rabbi Judah Goldin, my former colleagues Peter Ochs and the late Will Herberg, and David Novak, I am inexpressibly grateful. To superb Protestant, Catholic, and Jewish partners in dialogue in the New York circle of theologians in the Avery Dulles Group, I am truly appreciative. Especially for the extended ministry of friendship of Richard John Neuhaus, James M. O'Kane, and John Ollom, I give grateful thanks. Orthodox theologians to whom I am most deeply indebted include John Breck, Vigen Guroian, and David Ford.

To Joseph Ratzinger (Pope Benedict XVI) I have remained especially indebted since 1988 for his theological wisdom and empathic concern for my struggles from the time when we first met in a New York symposium of theologians, and then through subsequent dialogues in Rome during the 1990s on my sabbatical leave and other research visits. Among Catholic thinkers to whom I owe an incalculable debt are Avery Dulles, Michael Novak, George Weigel, Robert Wilken, C. John McCloskey, and Louis Bouyer. Evangelical scholars to whom I continue to be indebted include Carl F. H. Henry, Timothy Smith, and James I. Packer. Other Protestant partners in dialogue upon whom I have long depended are Reinhold and H. Richard Niebuhr, Wolfhart Pannenberg, and Albert C. Outler. Special thanks are due to William Burt Pope of Didsbury College, Manchester, the most brilliant of Methodist theologians, whose ignored but classic 1875 three-volume *Compendium of Christian Theology* has inspired my vision throughout. Among those who have most deeply enriched my awareness of classic Reformed and Baptist exegesis are John Leith and Timothy George. Among charismatic and Pentecostal theologians, I am beholden to H. Vinson Synon, W. J. Hollenweger, and Frederick Dale Bruner. I have been blessed by many superb graduate school students at Drew University who have challenged me on virtually every issue broached in this study. This far-flung circle of collaborators stretching from Africa to the Far East and to Oxford, Tübingen, and Rome means all the world to me. I have been rescued from innumerable blunders by these wonderful colleagues.

The overarching theme of classic Christianity is *life*—life with God, life in Christ, life in the Spirit. If Michelangelo could invest eleven years of his life on the Rondanini *Pietà*, I do not regret spending three decades hammering, chipping, and polishing away intermittently at this endeavor, and now revising it for a new generation of partners. I did not know when I began this work that my own life would be gravely threatened after bypass heart surgery. I am especially thankful for superb physicians (Carlos Garces, Stephen Guss, Carl Rubenstein, and Philip Adamson), who have kept this heart beating under challenging circumstances. Ensuing limitations have deepened my awareness of how God's strength is made perfect through human weakness. Paul expressed his ongoing confidence that "he who began a good work in you will carry it on to completion" (Phil. 1:6).

No words can adequately express my enduring affection for Edrita, my life partner of blessed memory, now much missed, and our sons and daughter, Clark, Edward, and Laura, to whom this book is affectionately dedicated.

Classic Christianity remains, like Keats's urn, a "still unravish'd bride of quietness," a "foster-child of silence and slow time" ("Ode on a Grecian Urn"). I feel the eccentric longing of Henry Vaughan's "Retreat":

O how I long to travel back,
and tread again that ancient track! . . .
Some men a forward motion love,
But I by backward steps would move.

BOOK ONE

THE LIVING GOD

B ECAUSE OF PIETY'S PENCHANT for taking itself too seriously, theology does well to nurture a modest, unguarded sense of comedy. Some droll sensibility is required to keep in due proportion the pompous pretensions of the study of divinity.

I invite the kind of laughter that wells up not from cynicism about reflection on God but from the ironic contradictions accompanying such reflection. Theology is intrinsically funny. This comes from glimpsing the incongruity of humans thinking about God. I have often laughed at myself as these sentences went through their tortuous stages of formation. I invite you to look for the comic dimension of divinity that stalks every page. It is not blasphemy to grasp the human contradiction for what it is. The most enjoyable of all subjects has to be God, because God is the source of all joy.

Working Assumptions

The Subject

The subject matter that we cannot finally evade if we pursue a reflection on faith's understanding, is the incomparable Subject, the Living God, the insurmountably alive reality whom Moses heard addressing him as "Yahweh."

Yahweh is a name—significantly, a personal noun, not an impersonal noun describing an object. Yahweh is the name used to address an incomparably encountering personal Subject who breaks through and circumscribes all our category systems (Gregory of Nazianzus, *First Theol. Orat.* 27; Calvin, *Inst.* I.13). The Christian community speaks of a conscious, personal reality who meets us in personal terms as companionable divine Subject, as Thou, or in familiar terms: You. The reason you do not say you-all in triune teaching is that God is one.

If we must use some pronoun to point to this reality, it can only be

- *Thou,* the solemn personal form of the second person singular address, or the more problematic

- *him* or

- *her*

Note carefully the limited choices: *Thou, you, him, her, he, she*—all fundamentally based on three forms: *Thou, him,* and *her.* The neuter, *it* or *It,* cannot adequately convey personhood. We must say either Thou, Him, or Her because we cannot say *It* if the One with whom we finally must deal is indeed incomparably personal, and if that One's Word speaks to us as a personal address (John 4:1–26; 9:1–12; Augustine, *Tractates on John* 44.5–6; Tho. Aq., *ST* 1 Q. 13).

This makes it difficult to use language in an ordinary way about Yahweh. It would be as if one looked at a list of three courses called mathematics, political science, and George. Instantly you can tell that you cannot study a person as you would a thing. The names we have for God (*Gott* in Teutonic languages and, before that, *Adōnaī, El, Theos, Deus*) all point to a personal reality that cannot finally be reduced to objective, descriptive sentences or abstract ideas, just as George is always something more than our sentences or ideas about George.

This is why Christian teaching about God is a different sort of study than any empirical science that deals with measurable objects. Yet theology is not thereby less organized; nor is it lacking in method or wholly without language (Augustine, *On Chr. Doctrine* 1; Calvin, *Inst.* 1.6), any more than our interpersonal relations are without language when we are speaking to Miriam or George—for this is where we need language most.

God has left a trail of language behind a stormy path of historical activities. That language is primarily the evidence with which theology has to deal—first with Scripture, then with a long history of interpretation of Scripture called church history and tradition, and finally with the special language that emerges out of each one's own personal experience of meeting the living God (Augustine, *On Chr. Doctrine, I*; John of Damascus, *OF* 4.17; Catherine of Siena, *Prayers*, 6; Thirty-nine Articles 6, 20, 21, 34). This free and personally revealing God is the unavoidable subject matter of Christian teaching. The object investigated is *faith's view of God*. But to say that alone may be to neglect the more decisive point: the divine Subject who is constantly confronting us in this study is none other than the holy One present in our midst, the living God who calls forth and enables our responses.

What the Study of God Studies

The object of study in theology must be carefully stated. It is God as known in the faith of the worshiping Christian community. This study seeks to know an investigatable reality and thus is not merely speculation. For there actually exists in history a community of persons who hold steadfastly to faith in God. Yet since God is not an object, it is inexact to assert that God is directly, flatly, or empirically viewable as an object of theology. God does not, for our convenience, become a direct object of scientific investigation, since God by definition is not finite and thus not subject to the measurements required by empirical sciences (Gregory of Nyssa, *Answer to Eunomius' Second Book*; Augustine, *CG* 10.13; Tho. Aq., *ST* 1 Q1).

Nonetheless, Christian theology has a definite subject matter to which it devotes disciplined and sustained reflective attention: that knowledge of God as understood in the faith of the community that lives out of Christ's resurrection (Cyril of Jerusalem, *Catech. Lect.* 4.1–17). The basis for the study of God becomes confused if theology is presented strictly as a privatized, individual credo, or as a limited confessional statement of a particular faction that views itself as the arbiter of Christian truth for all other communions. Theology is not primarily the repeating of confessional assertions but, rather, the investigation and clarification of the internal consistency of those assertions, their reasoning about their ground, and the way they relate to the problems of daily life. Hence Christian theology has a particular area of research: the worshiping community's understanding of God, viewed consensually from its earliest beginnings and sources. The subject of investigation is not God as such or God as viewed by himself. Rather it is *God as known in the faith of the worshiping Christian community*.

In this sense the study of God attempts to sustain the greatest possible objectivity insofar as it seeks to understand its object (God as known by faith). The goal is to know God as accurately as possible without emotive distortions or hidden projections (Tho. Aq., *ST* 1 Q1). God, as viewed by Christian teaching and worship, can and has become the central interest and concern of an academic inquiry. Christian faith as classically understood inquires into its own practical self-understanding, as attested by texts of Scripture and tradition. The modern university was spawned in the medieval period by the all-inclusive seriousness of this inquiry (Bonaventure, *Breviloquium*; J. H. Newman, *The Idea of a University*; H. Rashdall, *UEMA*). There is no history of the university that can fail to name Alexandria, Padua, Paris, Oxford and Heidelberg. Faith's inquiry is not merely into itself but also into its ground and enabler—God, the source, subject, and end of faith's understanding of itself—and into all things as they relate to God (Augustine, *Enchiridion*; Calvin, *Inst.* 1. 1.1).

Only God can reveal God (Hilary, *Trin.* 1. 18), just as a person can only become known when that person decides to reveal his or her inner feelings, spirit, will, or intention to another. For who among us knows the thoughts of another, Paul asked, except as that person chooses to reveal him or herself: "In the same way no one knows the thoughts of God except the Spirit of God. We have not received the spirit of the world but the Spirit who is from God, that we may understand what God has freely given us. This is what we speak, not in words taught us by human wisdom but in words taught by the Spirit" (1 Cor. 2:10–13). Yet even prior to hearing the gospel of God in Jesus, "what may be known about God" through human reasoning and moral awareness was plain to everyone because "God has made it plain" (Rom. 1:19). "If something is revealed it must be brought to our notice from something we have not yet noticed" (Origen, *Comm. on Rom.* 1.19).

Paul was convinced that "the wisdom of this age," which "comes to nothing," must be sharply distinguishable from the "message of wisdom among the mature" who know of "God's secret wisdom" (1 Cor. 2:6,7). He implied that a profound inquiry was proceeding among the faithful in Corinth concerning the "deep things of God" (*ta tou theou*, 1 Cor. 2:11; the "thoughts of God") as understood by faith (1 Cor. 2:9–11; Tertullian, *Ag. Marcion* 2.2). "Only the Spirit can search everything. The human soul cannot do this, which is why it needs to be strengthened by the Spirit if it is ever going to penetrate the depths of God" (Origen, Comm. on 1 Cor. 1.10.6–10).

In these passages, Paul suggests and anticipates the complex relationship that would later develop between these two tendencies in theology: *revealed* theology, which speaks of God's revelation in history, and *natural* theology, which is given by divine grace as a longing for divinity that develops out of human natural reasoning and moral awareness (Clement of Alex., *Stromata* 2.1–4; Origen, *Ag. Celsus* 6; Augustine, *CG* 10.32). Following the classical Christian consensus, we will be primarily concerned in this study with revealed theology, yet always with respect for human reasoning.

Defining the Study of God

The study of God is an attempt at orderly, consistent, and reasoned discussion of the Source and End of all things (John of Damascus, *OF* 1.1–5). The term theology is itself a rudimentary definition, indicating discourse about God.

Theology (from the Latin *theologia*, which comes from two crucial Greek root words: *theos*, God, and *logos*, discourse, language, study), is reasoned discourse about God gained either by rational reflection or by response to God's self-disclosure in history (Augustine, *CG* 11.2; *Conf.* of Saxony 9). *Christian theology* is the orderly exposition of Christian teaching. It sets forth that understanding of God that is made known in Jesus Christ (Augustine, *On Faith and the Creed 2*;

Concerning Faith of Things Not Seen 5). It seeks to provide a coherent reflection on the living God as understood in the community whose life is "in Christ."

Theology presupposes the study of Scripture and of the history of the community's reflection upon Scripture. It seeks to provide a fit ordering of scriptural teachings and of central themes of the history of Scriptural interpretation (Jerome, *Ag. Rufinus* 12–16; Calvin, *Inst.* 1.13). Systematic theology provides resources for apologetics, Christian ethics, pastoral theology, and the study of comparative religion (Irenaeus, *Ag. Her.* 3.24, 4. 20), but in no case may it be reduced to these disciplines. Subsequently when we use the term *theology* we will refer to Christian theology.

The essential purpose of theology is to study and bring into a fitting, consistent expression the truth of the Christian faith (Jn 1:14–17; Theodore of Mopsuestia, *Comm. on John* 1.1.14). The primary task is neither logical demonstration nor normative proclamation of established truth, nor the refining of rigorous proofs for faith, but rather clarification of faith's understanding of itself and its ground (Anselm, *Monologium*; Belgic *Conf.*). This clarification asks for fair-minded analysis, critical reasoning, tolerance, and logical coherence, as well as active listening to Scripture and tradition (Jn 16:13; Hilary, On *Trin.* 12:55–57; Tho. Aq., *ST* 1 Q1).

If we begin by assuming the existence of God and the authority of Scripture, we are open to the charge that we have not credibly established those assumptions. Hence the first chapter will take only those necessary preliminary steps that are required in order to begin naming God. For classical treatments that provide models for the sequence of topics that we will follow, see Cyril of Jerusalem (*Catech. Lect.* 4.15, 5.12), John of Damascus (*OF* 1.1–3), Thomas Aquinas (*ST* 1 Q1), and Calvin (*Catechism of the Church of Geneva*, SW:245–66).

Natural and Revealed Theology

Revealed theology focuses on God's search for humanity; natural theology focuses on the human search for God. We will follow the central ecumenical stream found in Irenaeus, Gregory of Nazianzus, Chrysostom, Ambrose, Augustine, John of Damascus, Melanchthon, Calvin, and Wesley. It does not rule out all possibility of natural reasoning concerning God, yet focuses on consistent reasoning out of Scripture's revelation.

Classical Christianity teaches that by grace God has provided a natural inclination in human consciousness to seek God (Lactantius, *Div. Inst.* 4.1–4; John of Damascus, *OF* 2.30). Humanity has a natural hunger for God and a tendency to religious awareness (Minucius Felix, *Octavius* 17–19; Tertullian, *Apol.* 17; Fulgence, *Letters To Theodore*). A limited reasoning toward God can proceed without direct reference to the history of revelation on the basis of natural human intuition, moral insight, and reasoning, whether it is called natural theology or the philosophy or psychology of religion (Ps 19:1; Rom 1:20).

The term theology had been in use prior to its being adopted by Christian teaching, as is evident from ancient writings (Aristotle, *Metaphysics* 1.3; Cicero, *De Natura Deorum* 3.212; Augustine, *CG* 6.5). Such natural reasoning about God is distinguishable from that knowledge of God that lives out of God's own self-disclosure, God's self-manifestation in the history of Israel and Jesus (Irenaeus, *Ag. Her.* 2,3I; Calvin, *Inst.* 1.14; Chemnitz, *LT* 1.20–22; Belgic *Conf.* 9).

Jewish and Christian forms of theology proceed as a reflection upon God's own self-disclosure as God becomes known through historical events. Such an inquiry in the Christian tradition has usually been called *revealed theology*, in so far as it responds to the ways in which God chooses to become self-revealed. In some established Christian traditions this is called *symbolic* or confessional theology, because it grounds itself in the symbols and confessional statements of the community of faith, or *dogmatics* because it states the *dogmata*, the irreducible tenets of Christian religion.

The truth, wherever it is to be found, is God's truth (Justin Martyr, *Address to the Greeks* 7–9; Clement of Alex., *Inst.* 10; Augustine, *On Chr. Doctrine* 2.40). God is revealed in history in a way that corresponds to the fundamental hungers of the human soul (Cyril of Jerusalem, *Catech. Lect.* 6.6; Gregory of Nazianzus, *Orat.* 38.17, 31; Augustine, *CG* 11.29).

The Fairness Issue

There is one sensitive issue in current Christian theology that merits special preliminary attention. This concerns the frequent use by traditional Christian teaching of masculine names and pronouns in referring to God. I am treating that question deliberately at numerous points along the way (especially on the question of naming God, on analogy, on the Holy Spirit, and on human existence). I intend to hold as closely as possible to the classical Christian affirmation that neither of the gender types—"He" or "She,"—adequately reflects the fullness of the divine being (Gregory of Nazianzus, First *Theol. Orat., Orat.* 27; John of Damascus, *OF* 1.4–8).

Yet it is not possible to speak of God as if the distinction between male and female could be ignored. That would require giving up personal pronouns which are necessary to express the intensely personal reality of God as known in the faithful community. There are times when the tradition has thought it fitting to transcend personal metaphors with terms like *the Eternal* or *the Holy One*. While this pattern is available within the ecumenical consensus, it is not followed at the price of forgoing all personal pronouns, since God is so much more frequently viewed through personal metaphors in Scripture (Cyril of Jerusalem, *Catech. Lect.* 6.8, 9.1). Since naming conveys power, the naming of God normatively or exclusively as "he" tends to limit the idea of God by human sexual categories. Even when its intent may have been generic, the tradition's language has sounded exclusionary to many, who regrettably may then too readily dismiss the tradition on the grounds of language alone before allowing the tradition's reasoning a fair hearing. I can only ask that the reader not prejudge the fairness of classical Christian language without seeking to understand it. These are not problems that can or should be addressed in detail in an introduction, but I appeal to the reader to withhold predisposing judgment, letting each of the language issues develop organically. Meanwhile I remain indebted to both male and female partners in dialogue who have carefully combed this text both for unbalanced language and fidelity to ancient ecumenical Christian teaching.

One way I have sought to redress the balance practically is by not neglecting to quote, where texts have been preserved, those important women contributors to the classic Christian theological tradition. There are many: Melania the Elder and Melania the Younger (in Palladius, *Lausaic History, ACW*), Amma Theodora, Amma Sarah (among the Desert Ascetics, *SDF*), Macrina (sister of Basil, whom Gregory of Nyssa called "the Teacher"), Paula of Bethlehem, Clare of Assisi, Hildegard of Bingen, Catherine of Genoa, Julia of Norwich, Catherine of Siena, and Teresa of Avila. By this means it is evident that the voices and writings of astute, learned, and faithful women have been important in the life and witness of classic Christianity (Amma Sarah 4, *SCD*:193).

The crux of the language fairness issue hinges on whether Father-Son language, with the reference to God as "he," is primarily the result of male-dominated social structures, and is therefore degrading to the dignity of women and men, or whether such language is a part of the scandal of particularity that accompanies all claims of historical revelation —that is, that God is made known through a particular history, and that the Word of God is spoken through the life of *a man born of woman* (Gal. 4:4; Theodoret, Epist. Gal. 4.4–5) This incarnational event remains an intrinsic feature of God's historical self-disclosure honoring both men and women as participants in the history of salvation. In view of our central purpose and method (allowing the classical Christian tradition to speak for itself), we will maintain faithfulness to the historic language of the church but, in doing so, seek fairness and balance in our contemporary use of language.

Knowing from the Heart

The study of God and delight in knowing God requires a depth of understanding that surpasses simple empirical data gathering, logical deduction, or dutiful organization of scriptural or traditional texts into a coherent sequence. The Christian study of God intrinsically involves a mode of knowing from the heart that hopes to make the knower "wise unto salvation" (2 Tim. 3:15—a knowing grounded in the "sacred writings which have power to make you wise and lead you to salvation,"), to save the soul, to teach the sinner all that is needed to attain saving knowledge of God (Clement of Alex., *Who Is the Rich Man That Shall Be Saved?;* Catherine of Siena, Prayers 7; Baxter, *PW* 2: 23–25; Wesley, *WJW* 8:20).

Faith's knowing is distinguishable from objective, testable, scientific knowledge, although not necessarily inimical to it. It is a form of knowing that embraces the practical question of how we choose to live in the presence of this Source and End of all (Clement of Alex., *Exhort. to the Heathen* 9; Teresa of Avila, *CWST*, 3:219–22; Calvin, *Inst.* 1.11–13).

It need not be demeaning to faith that it humbly remains a *logos*, a word, a way of speaking and reasoning through words—"just talk," in a sense, yet talk concerning almighty God. These are our human words—limited, fragile, inadequate—pointing beyond themselves to nothing less than *Theos*, the Source and End of all things. Christian teaching lives out of a conversation that is found in a living community of people who pray to this incomparable One. It is our reasoning about the mystery of the One from whom we come and to whom we return (Chrysostom, Comm. on 2 Tim. 8; Augustine, *On the Profit of Believing*; H. R. Niebuhr, *RMWC*:122).

Credo

Christians who first said credo ("I believe") did not do so lightly, but at the risk of their lives under severe persecution. We listen carefully to those who are prepared to sacrifice their lives for their belief. To say credo genuinely is to speak from the heart, to reveal who one is by confessing one's essential belief, the faith that makes life worth living. One who says credo without willingness to suffer, and if necessary die, for the faith has not yet genuinely said credo.

Christians have a right and a responsibility to know the meaning of their baptism. This is the purpose of Christian theology and of this study: to clarify the ancient ecumenical faith into which Christians of all times and places are baptized. It is expected of all who are baptized that they will understand what it means to believe in God the Father Almighty, in God the Son, and in God the Spirit (Gregory of Nyssa, *The Great Catech.*, prologue; Luther, *Sermons on the Catech.*).

The Apostles' Creed is the most common confession of Christians. This ancient confession will serve as the scaffold for the architecture of this book. Like other ancient baptismal confessions, it is divided into three parts, corresponding with the three Persons of the one God (Luther, *Small Catech.* 2.44; *Brief Expl.*, *WML* 2:368). The first part confesses trust in God the Father Almighty, maker of heaven and earth, the subject of this first phase of this *Systematic Theology*.

Other early ecumenical confessions, such as the Nicene Creed (325), the Constantinopolitan Creed (351), and the Athanasian Creed (c. 500) were organized in the same three-part way, to teach inquirers and the faithful the significance of baptism in the name of the Father, Son, and Spirit. Earlier creedal prototypes, such as the Letter of the Apostles (c. 150), the rule of faith known to Justin Martyr (c. 165; *CC*:18), the Balyzeh Papyrus (c. 200 or later), the Interrogatory Creed of Hippolytus (c. 214), the Oriental Creed, and the Creed of Caesarea all follow this threefold pattern. As early as about 190, Irenaeus of Lyons (fl. c. 175 to c. 195) summarized the faith of Christians in the following concise way, which plots the trajectory of this entire volume:

The Church, though dispersed throughout the whole world, even to the ends of the earth, has received from the apostles, and their disciples, this faith:

- [She believes] in one God, the Father Almighty, Maker of heaven, and earth, and the sea, and all things that are in them;

- and in one Christ Jesus, the Son of God, who became incarnate for our salvation;

- and in the Holy Spirit, who proclaimed through the prophets the dispensations of God. (*Ag. Her.* 1. 10.1)

Scripture itself provides the structural basis for the organization of the baptismal teaching, and of that basic Christian instruction (*catechesis*) preparing for baptism. The same sequence for summarizing Christian teaching appeared in Matthew 28:19, the climactic point of Matthew's Gospel, in the formula for baptism. There the resurrected Lord concluded His earthly teaching with this summary charge: "Therefore go and make disciples of all nations, baptizing them in the name of the Father and of the Son and of the Holy Spirit, and teaching them to obey everything I have commanded you. And surely I will be with you always, to the very end of the age" (Matt. 28:19, 20).

In this way, Jesus forever linked the two key actions of *baptizing* and *teaching*. In subsequent periods of Christian history they have remained intimately interwoven. Implicitly included in the instructions for baptism is the charge to teach its significance. This is why the Christian study of God has been so often organized into these three triune divisions. Christian teaching is baptismal teaching. Christian baptism has required clarification of itself as faith in God the Father, Son, and Spirit. Christian theology came into being to explain Christian baptism.

Topics of Christian teaching are not taken up in a disconnected way: "The teaching of all doctrine has a certain order, and there are some things which must be delivered first, others in the second place, and others in the third, and so all in their order; and if these things be delivered in their order, they become plain," so that "he who enters rightly upon the road, will observe the second place in due order, and from the second will more easily find the third" (Clementina, *Recog.* 3.34). The classic way to "enter the road" is by dealing first with the opening affirmation of the creed—"God Almighty, Maker of heaven and earth."

The earliest summaries of Christian teaching were lectures to put feet firmly on this road, to prepare people for baptism. Our organization of key themes of Christian teaching will depend heavily upon the thought-sequence of those most influential early summaries by Cyril of Jerusalem (*Catechetical Lectures*), Gregory of Nyssa (*The Great Catechism*), Chrysostom (*Baptismal Instructions*), and Augustine (*Catech. Instr.* and *On Faith and the Creed*).

Classic teachers as varied as Augustine, Thomas Aquinas, and Luther have held that the Apostles' Creed remains the best condensed statement of Christian faith and the most reliable way to learn the heart of faith. In professing the Creed, Cyril explained, the believer is helped to keep closely to the center of faith as delivered by the apostles, "which has been built up strongly out of all the Scriptures":

> *For since all cannot read the Scriptures, some being hindered from the knowledge of them by lack of learning, and others because they lack leisure to study, in order that the soul should not be starved in ignorance, the church has condensed the whole teaching of the Faith in a few lines. This summary I wish you both to commit to memory when I recite it, and to rehearse it with all diligence among yourselves, not writing it out on paper, but engraving it by the memory upon your heart, taking care while you rehearse it that no catechumen may happen to overhear the things which have been delivered to you. I wish you also to keep this as a provision through the whole course of your life, and beside this to receive no alternative teaching, even if we ourselves should change and contradict our present teaching.* (Catech. Lect. 5.12, is here slightly amended)

During the perilous times prior to Cyril, there was an evident reason for memorizing the creed: persecution, torture, imprisonment, including the seizure of the sacred books by the authorities, and the lethal prosecution of those who followed them. Thus a tight summary of scripture had to be memorized before baptism.

Throughout the succeeding generations, key scriptural teachings have ordinarily been grouped by classical Christian exegetes under these three triune headings: The first article teaches of God the Father Almighty, creation, and providence. The second deals with Christ's redeeming person and work. The third teaches of the Spirit that enlivens the church and the Christian life (Cyril of Jerusalem, *Catech. Lect.* 6–18; Hilary, *On Trin.* 1–13; Luther, *Sermons on the Catech.*; Anglican Thirty-nine Articles of Religion; Helvetic *Conf.* 1,2).

The creed in all its classic forms is a "short word" summarizing biblical faith, approved by the apostles as "standard teaching to converts," "a badge for distinguishing" those who preach Christ according to apostolic rule, constructed "out of living stones and pearls supplied by the Lord" (Rufinus, *Comm. on Apostles' Creed*, Intro.). Rufinus (345–410 AD), among the earliest of many commentators on the Creed, taught that the Holy Spirit had superintended its transmission in order that it "contain nothing ambiguous, obscure, or inconsistent." Poignantly, he explained why it must be committed to memory: "The reason why the creed is not written down on paper or parchment, but is retained in the believers' hearts, is to ensure that it has been learned from the tradition handed down from the Apostles, and not from written texts, which occasionally fall into the hands of unbelievers." That sentence echoes directly from the tragic horrors of the Diocletian persecution. Rufinus based his commentary on the personally remembered "text to which I pledged myself when I was baptized in the church of Aquileia."

The ancient creeds all begin with "I believe" (*credo*) or "We believe" (*credimus*). What does it mean to believe? "And what is faith?" the Letter to Hebrews asked. "Faith gives substance to our hopes, and makes us certain of realities we do not see" (Heb. 11:1). "Without faith it is impossible to please God, because anyone who comes to him must believe that he exists and that he rewards those who earnestly seek him" (Heb. 11:6; Chrysostom, *Comm. on Hebrews*, 22.6–7). Just as no farmer sweats to plant a field without some faith that the seeds will grow, and no one sets out to sea without some confidence of being able to survive, so: "In fact, there is nothing in life that can be transacted without a preliminary readiness to believe" (Rufinus, *Comm. ACW 20:32*). In entering the pathway of belief, the inquirer must first listen with empathy to what the worshiping community is saying about the One who makes belief possible.

The Living God is the first of three major divisions of this study. Succeeding divisions deal with *The Word of Life* and *Life in the Spirit*, so as to reveal the inner structure of theology as triune.

PART I

THE LIVING GOD

1

THE NAME OF GOD

E VERY INQUIRY HAS ITS POSTULATES. No scientific inquiry proceeds altogether without assumptions. Nothing can be studied scientifically without postulating the intelligibility of the universe—an assumption that itself is, strictly speaking, not subject to empirical verification.

Like every other inquiry, theology proceeds with postulates, out of which its data gathering and induction of facts proceed (Origen, *OFP* 2.1–4). Chief among the postulates of Christian teaching is the assumption that God has taken initiative to encounter humanity in and through human history (Origen, *Ag. Celsus* 1.11). "Therefore as is only reasonable, we grasp the undemonstrable first principle by faith, and then we receive abundant proof of the truth of the first principle from the first principle itself" (Clement of Alex., *Stromata* 7.16).

The shorthand term for this primary postulate is *revelation*. Revelation may be viewed either in a general or a specific sense.

The Joy of Studying God

You are invited to the quiet joy of the study of God—God's being, God's power, God's insurmountable goodness, and God's unfailing care of creation. Over centuries this subject has been the source of contemplative happiness, intellectual fascination, and moral guidance. (On joy in the contemplation of divinity, see Cyril of Jerusalem, *Procatechesis,* Prologue; Bonaventure, *Breviloquium*, prologue; Tho. Aq., *SCG* 2.1; 2 Richard Baxter, *PW* 17:157).

The most intriguing questions of the introductory study of God can be stated in plain, uncomplicated words:

In what way is God able to be known?

Is God uncreated?

Is God free?

Is God personal?

Is God compassionate?

Does God exist?

Does Jesus reveal God?

Does God care about us?

Why are we born? Why do we die?

How do we draw closer to God?

How may we participate in God's life?

Does scripture reveal God?

Does the reception of revelation call for reasoning?

These are among the questions that will occupy us in the first leg of this journey (Book One on The Living God). Chapters 1, 2, and 3 seek to answer honestly what we mean when we say "God." Chapter 4 asks upon what reasonable grounds we may conclude that God exists in reality and not in our minds only. Chapter 5 asks whether Christianity's most distinctive contribution to the idea of God might be the teaching that God is Father, Son, and Spirit. Chapters 6 and 7 discuss the work of God as creator and whether God provides for the created order as sustainer, as enabler of natural causality, and as guide of errant human history. Chapter 8 concludes with a discussion of the appropriate method in the study of God: Whether Scripture is trustworthy for Christian teaching and to what extent Christian tradition, experience, and reason are valued sources in the study of God.

Whether God Is Revealed

The Meaning of Revelation

The word revelation unites the two biblical ideas of an unveiling (*apokalypsis*, disclosure, appearing, coming) of God and a making known (*phanerōsis*, exhibition, manifestation, expression) of divine mysteries previously concealed (Eph. 3:3; Job 12:22; Dan. 2:22–29). When we say God is revealed we mean that the mystery of God's presence is unveiled in history (John 9:5; Theodore of Heraclea, Fragments on John 71). God's redemptive purpose toward humanity is made known (Augustine, *CG* 11.2). The revelation of God has its central locus in a single personal history—that of Jesus the Christ. Yet the shock waves from that center resound in the farthest reaches of the cosmos (Rom. 8:18–30; 11:15; Calvin, *Inst.* 1:1–6; Quenstedt, *TDP* 1:32).

Revelation includes manifestations of God to humanity through reason, conscience, and history. The term *general revelation* (sometimes called common revelation) encompasses all these forms of divine disclosure (Origen, *OFP* 1.1–9; Augustine, *Conf.* 7.10; *CG* 5.11). Scripture reports revelation as occurring in dreams, visions, and in the divine illumination of the intellect (Tho. Aq., *ST* 1 Q57).

In the maturing religion of the early Hebrew covenant, the focus was upon the divine requirement, human destiny, and the divine-human covenant:

- the law set forth the divine command
- the prophets interpreted the meaning of history
- the priestly tradition provided a ritual order of atoning for sin.

In the consummate revelation proclaimed in the New Testament, God the Revealer appeared *in person* as the central datum of Christian experience to which the apostolic witness bears testimony (Cyril of Alex., Comm. on Hebr. 1.1; Tho. Aq., *ST* 1 Q57).

Revelation is not primarily the imparting of information but rather the self-giving and self-evidencing of God. Rightly known, God illumines all reality, all human experience, all revelation, and all religion (Sir. 1.1; Clement of Alex., *Stromata* 1.4; Julia of Norwich, *Showings*). In this general sense, revelation is present in the history of all religions and is a familiar theme in the study of religions. Judaism and Christianity participate in that history of religions, yet in a special way in that they have understood themselves to be fulfilling the promise of that history (Justin Martyr, *Dialogue with Trypho, 1–8,* Athanasius, *On the Incarnation,* 9.1).

General revelation is sharply distinguished from the laborious process of scientific inquiry. In science the subject self works toward discovering the truth; in revelation the truth works toward discovering the subject self. In scientific work, enigmas are gradually unveiled about physics, space, time, atomic structures, DNA, and biological processes through empirical investigation. But these discoveries are not typically viewed as divine revelation. The very character of revelation, on the other hand, implies that God is freely on God's own initiative allowing the divine intention to become known (Gal. 1:12; 2:2, Chrysostom, Comm. on Gal. 2.2). Previously obscure, the truth is reaching out to become knowable through events in finite history.

The consensual reception of revelation is a highly social process that occurs through the extended generations of communities of prayer and teaching (Eph. 3:3; Lev. 4:13–27; Num. 16). The memory of God's becoming recognizable is mediated through families, rites, archetypal memories, and intricate modes of institutional influence (Exod. 16; Basil, *On the Spirit* 27.65–68; Anglican Thirty-nine Articles 20).

General Revelation in Scripture

Scripture often speaks of the general revelation of God to all humanity. The covenant with Noah signals the intention of God to care for all humanity (Gen. 9:8–11), for the covenant was with all the descendants of Noah, that is, all humanity. 2 Pet. 2:5 viewed Noah as a "herald of righteousness" prior to Abraham, and inclusive of all surviving humanity. God has not left himself without witness in any corner of human affairs (1 Kings 19:18; Acts 14:17; Chrysostom, *Comm. on Acts*, 31). Revelation may be known by some, yet be awaiting the appointed time to be revealed to others (Hab. 2:2).

The New Testament witnesses to a general revelation of God in creation and providence, discernible through conscience, prior to the coming of Jesus and outside the covenant with Israel (Rom. 1:13–2:16; 1 Cor. 10:18–11:1; John 1:9; 2 Tim. 1:3). God can make himself known in creation at any time, anywhere, at any point in history. The revelation in Christ does not limit these broader disclosures, but completes and culminates them. God has spoken "at sundry times and in diverse manners" (not only in one time or in one manner) in a way that prepares humanity for the coming of the Son, the Revealer, God himself (Heb. 1:1).

At the least, this general revelation performs the negative function of leaving humanity without excuse if any should ever claim that they never knew God existed. "When Gentiles who do not possess the law carry out its precepts by the light of nature, then, although they have no law, they are their own law, for they display the effect of the law inscribed on their hearts. Their conscience is called as a witness, and their own thoughts argue the case on either side, against them or even for them, on the day when God judges the secrets of human hearts through Christ Jesus" (Rom. 2:14–16). The light that in due time appeared in Jesus was a light "which enlightens every human being" that "was even then coming into the world" (John 1:9, Cyril of Alex. *Comm. on John* 1.9).

Special Revelation in the History of Israel

Although God is generally knowable indistinctly throughout all nature and history, God has become specially and conspicuously known through a particular history, the history of a people set aside, a holy place, and a salvation history (Esther 3:8; Ps. 122; Matt. 20:17; Augustine, First Catech. *Instr.* 6). There remains a "scandal of particularity" in all historical revelation. If God is to become known in history, then that must occur at some time and some place in history. The history of salvation is about those particular times and places and events (Deut. 6:20–25; First Helvetic *Conf.* V; New Hampshire *Conf.* 6) where the whole of history is revealed through some eventful part. Scripture tells the story of this people of Israel, a set-apart kingdom of priests, called to be a holy nation (Exod. 19:6). Holy Writ tells the story of these times and places (Ps. 145:1–12; Edwardian Hom., *CC*:239).

God became fully self-revealed in the life of a particular man born of a particular woman (Matt. 1:16; Luke 1:5–2:40). This particularity is a scandal or offense in the sense that God condescends to become human not generally in all but particularly in one (Athanasius, *Four Discourses Ag. Arians* 3.27, 28; Kierkegaard, *Training in Christianity*).

That the Messiah is born male, according to Jewish expectation, is a less crucial point than that the Messiah was *born* at all, and was born as a single *individual* (hence not male *and* female), and was born as a *Jew* (among whom the Expected One was a male heir of the Davidic line; Matt. 1:1–20; Luke 2:4; Rom. 1:3; Rev. 22:16; Augustine, *CG* 17.8–9).

The worshiping community takes it as a premise that God makes himself known in actual history. Thereafter consequences abound everywhere for the study of God. They pay attention to these events in which God has become known (Acts 10:42; 26:16; Lactantius, *Div. Inst.* 3.27; Calvin, *Inst.* 1.6; 1.16). Their importance to the community is not due to their merit but to their attentiveness—their eyes are open to unfolding history.

In the history of revelation, God does not merely speak to himself but to ordinary human beings—particular human beings, persons with names like Abraham, Isaac, Miriam, Amos, Naomi, Jeremiah, Paul, John, and Mary. In prayer humans speak and God listens. In revelation God speaks to human hearers. In this way scripture and prayer feed the dialogue between humanity and God.

The Revealer

Christian revelation refers to the disclosure of God in the person and work of Christ. Christ himself is God's own revelation, God's Word. Through Christ all the other moments of divine disclosure draw closer to being more understandable. All of God's other manifestations, past and future, become better received, remembered, and defined. Christ is the One whom the angels have longed to see, "the desire of all nations," the goal toward which all the history of revelation prior to Christ had been tending (Hag. 2:7; John 1; Eph. 1).

In Christ the eternal purpose of God, the mystery hidden for ages, the incomparable secret of God, is revealed (1 Cor. 2:7; 4:1; Eph. 3:1–5). Christ is the singular embodiment of truth, infinitely plural in meaning. Christ is the sum and hidden interior meaning of all other genuine revelations of God (Theodoret, Epistle to the Ephesians, 3.5).

In Christ all who behold attentively are able to "grasp God's secret. That secret is Christ himself; in him lie hidden all God's treasures of wisdom and knowledge" (Col. 2:2, 3). "Great beyond all question is the mystery of our religion: 'He who was manifested in the body, vindicated in the spirit, seen by angels; who was proclaimed among the nations, believed in throughout the world, glorified in high heaven'" (1 Tim. 3:16). Even as Christ became for Christians the inner meaning of the Old Testament history, so does the Old Testament history bestow otherwise hidden meaning upon the history of Jesus who did not come to destroy, but to fulfill, the covenant people and the law (Matt. 5:7). "Our knowledge and our prophecy alike are partial, and the partial vanishes when wholeness comes" (1 Cor. 13:9).

Human beings do not set the conditions for what God can or cannot do. But Christian faith has gained confidence that God will not reveal himself in a way contrary to the way he has revealed himself in Jesus Christ (Augustine, *Enchiridion* 1.5; Calvin, *Inst.* 2.10). Christianity does not limit revelation to Christ, but through Christ sees God's revelation as occurring elsewhere and finally, echoing everywhere.

The more clearly God is seen in Christ, the less ambiguously God is seen everywhere else. This does not result in a syncretism that then quickly forgets that God was made known in Christ and looks for God independently elsewhere (Basil, *Letters,* 234). For the general revelation of God everywhere is now all the more knowable through the Revealer. Christ is the unparalleled and unrepeatable Revealer through whom other revelations are best understood (Justin, *Hortatory Address*; Calvin, *Inst.* 1.14–17; 3.20).

Christianity stands in a unique relation to the Hebrew Bible and Judaism. Judaism is not viewed by Christianity as one among other religions that emerge out of human striving for God. Rather, the God and Father of Jesus Christ freely and sovereignly allows himself to be known in the history of Israel. The Holy Writ of Israel is also the church's Holy Writ. The salvation history of the people of Israel is indispensable to the salvation history of Christians. The two covenants need each other; one to promise, the other to fulfill (Acts 7:17; Luke 4:21; Matt. 26:54–56; John 19:24–37).

The Word spoken in Jesus is addressed to all humanity (Rom. 5; Col. 1). Attention is riveted upon the meaning of the whole of human history as seen through a particular history. This Word was spoken in a particular time and place and through the life of a particular person who taught, did good, died, and was raised (Matt. 1:18; Luke 1:1–4; Luther, *Brief Expl.*). The New Testament does not assert the universal against the particular or the particular against the universal, but both in relation. Christianity celebrates no other Source and End than the One who makes himself known in Jesus (Basil, *Letters* 233; Gregory of Nyssa, *Ag. Eunomius* 2.1).

The Human Recipient of Revelation

Since God's care for the world focuses on God's care for human beings, the study of God necessarily includes the study of humanity, our plight and our destiny

(Lactantius, On the Workmanship of God). Rightly used, the word theology therefore embraces all that pertains to the study of humanity (Gregory of Nyssa, On the Making of Man 5). There is nothing in humanity or the cosmic setting of human history that is foreign to God. Theology therefore seeks an integral understanding of the human situation before God (Augustine, CG 5.11). This explains why, viewed historically, the university sprang directly and organically out of the study of God (H. Rashdall, UEMA, I).

Humanity is God's constant preoccupation throughout the Bible. The Christian study of God cannot neglect God's own prevailing interest—the redemption of humanity. No Christian theology can speak only of God and never of human beings. There is no part of Christian teaching that does not touch upon good news for humanity. In the Genesis narrative, the creation of human beings is the decisive act of divine creation, in which persons are provided with a capacity for communion with God exceeding that of all other earthly creatures. Christ the Redeemer is completely human while not ceasing to be truly God. The Holy Spirit speaks to human hearts.

From beginning to end, the biblical story is the story of the creation of humanity, the fall of humanity, and the redemption of humanity. Revelation is for human salvation, the mending of human brokenness (Athanasius, On the Incarnation of the Word 3). Early ecumenical theology seldom offers a separate section labeled "anthropology" because humanity is God's constant concern. When Gregory of Nyssa wrote On the Making of Man, he places the study of man within the study of God, not vice versa.

God pays a high cost (the death of his beloved Son) to become revealed to human beings. That implies that humans are of incomparable value in God's eyes. When God becomes incarnate, he becomes a human being, not a grasshopper. Why? Human beings are assumed to have a distinctly grace-bestowed capacity to receive revelation. Why would God bother to speak to a grasshopper who could not meaningfully hear?

Humanity is—more than trees or animals—uniquely able to hear, hence the intended recipient of revelation. Human reasoning is created by God with a capacity for reaching toward God by thinking, choosing, and speaking. Human freedom is created by God with a capacity for responsiveness to God. Human personality is created with the restless yearning for communion with the unseen but present personal God (Augustine, Conf. 1.1). Human love is created with some capacity, however distorted, to love God and to love creatures through God. If any creature exists that is more than others prepared for the divine self-disclosure, it surely must be the human creature (Lactantius, Div. Inst. 2.9). God comes as incomparably personal Visitor into interpersonal meeting with men and women.

Faith Seeking Intelligibility

In faith revelation becomes a matter of inner certitude and assurance. Revelation bears testimony to God's action. Faith receives and believes and thereby transforms the knowing process. Faith then shapes reasoning (Origen, Ag. Celsus 1. 9). "By faith we perceive that the universe was fashioned by the word of God, so that the visible came forth from the invisible" (Heb. 11:3). Reason judges according to what the mind can see and know by sense experience. Faith nurtures reason's seeing. Its evidences are attested in a community in order that faith may become consensually received and its joy known (Heb. 11:1; Clement of Alex., Stromata 2). Faith is that response which trusts that God speaks truly and reliably.

Classic Christian teaching seeks to understand in a reflective and orderly way what God has revealed (Cyril of Jerusalem, Catech. Lect. 5). It seeks to put the many sentences, episodes, and maxims of the Bible into a whole, orderly, consistent statement about the overarching meaning of the message revealed in Holy Writ (Cyril of Jerusalem, *Catech. Lect.* 4.33–36). There is no Christian theology without the Bible. There is no Bible without an inspirited community to write, remember, and translate it, to guard it and pass it on, study it, live by it, and invite others to live by it. The Bible provides means by which the Christian message can be received into the minds and hearts of each new generation. It is from the Bible that Christianity learns how God is revealed.

The Christian study of God is faith seeking understanding (*fides quaerens intellectum*; Anselm, *Proslog.* 1), a branch of learning in which the faith of the Christian community is seeking to make itself intelligible. Faith has learned from experience to trust that God's self-disclosure in history as attested by Scripture is true, reliable, and worthy of trust. Faith reasons as far as it may behold the mysteries of God revealed in history (Eph. 1:9). These mysteries are greater than human intellect, yet if reason studies the history of God's self-disclosures in a thoroughgoing and receptive way, faith grows toward understanding, since understanding is susceptible to growth (Augustine, *Answer to Skeptics*).

It is this sort of emergent, maturing understanding that the study of God (theology) seeks to nurture. It is a knowledge that is not to be equated with faith, but that emerges out of faith. It is not a form of knowing that is simply infused or given directly to the recipient by God, but acquired only with human effort enabled by grace. It is a knowledge that differs from philosophical inquiry about God because it exists as a response to revelation (Hab. 2:2, 3). Its reasoning is not self-sufficient, but lives out of its being illumined by the history of revelation (Augustine, *Enchiridion* 30, 31; Calvin, *Inst.* 3.2; 4.8).

Whether God Can Be Defined

A simple organization is fitting to the study of One who is adored as the most simple of all realities. This chapter focuses upon a question so plain that it cries out for a plain answer: What do we mean when we say "God"? Are any of the words we use to speak of God actually appropriate to the reality of God?

Can God Be Defined?

If definition means clarifying the boundaries of a thing so that it is placed in a known category and compared to other species, then God cannot be defined. For God is not an object that can fit into our categories of objects (John of Damascus, *OF* 1. 1; Tho. Aq., *ST* 1 Q1.7). Our minds and language cannot specify accurately the limits of that reality which transcends measurement in space and time (Augustine, *On Chr. Doctrine* 4.2). God "surpasses human wit and speech. He knows God best who recognizes that whatever he thinks and says falls short of what God really is" (Tho. Aq., TAPT:89).

Hence Gregory the Theologian cautioned: "It is difficult to conceive God, but to define Him in words is an impossibility." "It is impossible to express Him, yet even more impossible to conceive Him. For that which may be conceived may perhaps be made clear by language, if not fairly well, at any rate imperfectly, to any one who is not quite deprived of hearing or slothful of understanding. But to comprehend the whole of so great a Subject as this is quite impossible and impracticable, not merely to the utterly careless and ignorant, but even to those who are highly exalted, and who love God" (Gregory of Nazianzus, *Orat.* 38.4)

Classic Christian teaching has often acknowledged that the being of God is ultimately indefinable because God sees all with eternal simultaneity while we see parts only within time. This is why Scripture speaks of God as "dwelling in unapproachable light" (1 Tim. 6:16a), as "the one whom no mortal eye has ever seen or ever can see" (1 Tim. 6:16b). Only the infinite God can fully comprehend the infinite (Augustine, *On Chr. Doctrine* 1.6; Hilary, *Trin.* 1.6).

Must God then remain completely undefined? If so, this book must end here, for it is about God, and one cannot write a book about a Subject that is in every sense unknowable. No. Even within its temporal limits, the human mind can take small steps toward thinking precisely about God. What steps?

Defining by Negation

It is possible to distinguish God from everything else that exists (Clement of Alex., *Stromata* 8.2; Augustine, *On Chr. Doctrine* 1.6). In this sense it is not only possible but surprisingly easy to define God, for God is not finite, not time-bound, not partial, not dependent, not this thing, not that thing, and so on. Not . . . not . . . not. This approach is sometimes called apophatic theology (meaning that it proceeds by negation, from the Greek apophanai, "to say no," refers to "mentioning by not mentioning"), denying that God can be equated with anything finite. This "negative way" defines God by what God is not, namely, any thing, any created being.

It is on this basis that short definitions such as that of the Augsburg Confession are formed, largely showing what God is not, and distinguishing God from all created things. There God is defined as "*without* body, *without* parts, of *infinite* power, wisdom and goodness" (italics added). At least we can reason that God is not a material body, not measurable in divisible parts, not limited in power, not partial in wisdom or goodness. This negative form of definition sets forth a series of terms that are properly ascribed in their fullness only to God.

The preliminary definition of God in classic Christian reasoning hinges primarily upon the clarification of a series of terms, called the attributes of God. They usually begin by showing what God is *not* in the slightest degree, and only then what God *is* to the largest possible degree (Maimonides, *Guide for the Perplexed* 1. 58; Tho. Aq., *ST* 1 Q13.2).

One of the most influential of classical Protestant attempts at such a definition is the Westminster Larger Catechism, whose leading definition of God brings together many of the terms that the worshiping community lifts up in prayer: "God is a Spirit in and of Himself infinite in being, glory, blessedness and perfection; all-sufficient, eternal, unchangeable, incomprehensible, everywhere present, almighty, knowing all things, most wise, most holy, most just, most merciful and gracious, long-suffering, and abundant in goodness and truth" (for similar short definitions, examine the Creed of Dositheus, art. I; New Hampshire *Conf.*, art. 2; Batak *Conf.*, art. 1, in *CC*:486, 335, 556). These terms are all viewed as attributes of God, defining who God is by what God is not.

While acknowledging the indescribable divine mystery, it *is* nonetheless possible to say more, as did Paul: "For (in the words of Scripture) 'who knows the mind of the Lord? Who can advise him?' We, however, possess the mind of Christ" (1 Cor. 2:16). The next step asks: How did the ecumenical consensus speak, beyond simply asserting negations?

A Classical Approach to Defining God

The apostles taught that we understand God best by looking at Jesus. "Anyone who has seen me has seen the Father" (John 1:9b). If God is made known in Jesus, then we do well to define God in relation to what we know of Jesus. Classic exegesis has sought to define God's character by beholding the character, teaching, life, ministry, death, and resurrection of Jesus the Christ (Athanasius, *Letter 60 to Adelphius*).

Christian teaching does not view God as one among the class of objects called gods, for there is "none like him" (Isa. 46:9). Of this reality there can only be one (Tho. Aq., *ST* 1 Q45–48). No finite being has the insurmountably good qualities that are uniquely ascribed to God. Although the uncapitalized term *god* (meaning idol, a created object that is worshiped) may be rightly used as a noun to speak of a class of projected or assumed divinities, the word *God* as expressed in the prayers of Christian worship is the *name* of the One worthy of true worship, distinguishable from all created objects.

A personal noun is distinguished from a common noun, which indicates what an individual object has in common with other objects of its class. *God* cannot be a common noun because there is nothing else in God's class (Justin Martyr, *Second Apol.* 6; Luther, *Bondage of the Will*; Calvin, *Inst.* 1.10; 3.20). We make our first mistake if we think of *God* as a common noun rather than a personal noun. *God* is a *name*, used in the way we address a person—with a name (Hilary, *On Trin.* 1.5). We do not ordinarily name our houseplants unless they come to display qualities that remind us of actual persons (and in that case we know we are doing something a bit zany).

Unlike a houseplant, *God* is a personal noun, more like *David* or *Mary*, because *God* names an incomparably personal being having consciousness and freedom (Chrysostom, *Comm. on Philippians* 7 Bonaventure, *Soul's Journey into God* 6).

When we speak of God as the Source and End of all things, we are already indicating that God is different from everything else. To express that difference in a careful way is the subject matter classically discussed under the heading of "God's names and attributes" (John of Damascus, *OF* 1.2–3; Calvin, *Inst.* 1.10.3; 1.13–16).

If ten believers got together and wrote a definition of God and then approved it by a seven-to-three vote, this would not make it normative for Christian teaching. It becomes true for Christian teaching not by changing styles of popular consensus but by resonance with the consensus of apostolic teaching and ancient ecumenical clarification confirmed by all subsequent centuries of faithful consent (Irenaeus, *Ag. Her.* 3.1–4; Vincent of Lérins, *Comm.* 2).

Consensual Definition

The classic consensual definition of God is true not because it tallies votes exhaustively, but because it corresponds truthfully to what the worldwide intergenerational worshiping community knows of God revealed in history. Christians have a true definition of God only if Christ's revelation of God is true, and truly remembered (Augustine, *On Chr. Doctrine* 1. 6). It can be stated in a concise sentence:

> *God is the uncreated source and end of all things; one; incomparably alive;*
> *insurmountable in presence, knowledge, and power; personal, eternal*
> *spirit, who in holy love freely creates, sustains, and governs all things.*

Many alternative forms of language are possible, but these terms are among the most familiar in the classic Christian tradition. Four essential features are condensed in this spare sentence that form the backbone of classic deliberations on the right naming of God:

The Transcendent Nature of God—God alone is One, eternal, infinite, necessary, sufficient, independent, uncreated, Source of all.

The Outreaching Majesty of God—God in relation to creatures is almighty, all-knowing, and everywhere present.

The Free Personal Spirit of God—God is incomparably free and irreducibly Spirit, while remaining personally addressable.

The Moral Character of God—is holy Love.

Every discrete word and category of these four groups of terms is implicit in the classic consensus. Only a fuller clarification of these four levels will constitute a convincing account of the meanings associated with the name God as known in Christian worship.

All of these descriptive terms are valid only insofar as the Holy One allows the divine life to be expressed through limited human language. Christian teaching can thus be saved the embarrassment of always needing to resort to vague claims and subjective feelings. This becomes plausible only by explaining these attributes in their intrinsic connection.

Naming God

God in Scripture does not deal with humanity anonymously (as if without a personal name). God is willing to let the recipients of divine mercy know the divine name, Yahweh (He who is, Gen. 2:4–9; Exod. 4:1; Ps. 23:1).

Indeed, many names have emerged in the history of salvation to speak of this incomparable personal reality. Among Scripture's names for God are *Yahweh* (Lord, Isa. 6:3), *Yah* (a contraction of *Yahweh*, Exod. 15:2); *El* (Mighty One, Gen. 14:18–19; Ps. 90:2), *Elōhīm* (Gen. 1:1), *Elōah* (Job 33:12), *Adōnai* (Lord, Ps. 38:22), *Ādōn* (Lord, Ps. 8:1, 9), *El Shaddai* (God Almighty, All-sufficient, Gen. 28:3), *Theos* (God, Mark 1:24), and *Kyrios* (Lord, Mark 1:3). Though different, these names point to a single reality, God. God is the Teutonic languages' way (also *Gott, Gud* from the Gothic *gheu,* to invoke or to sacrifice) of calling the name of the One who in Scripture is called Yahweh, El, and Theos (Jerome, *Letters*, To Pamachius 57.9; *TDOT* I:242–61; Calvin, *Inst.* 1.10.3; *TDNT* on "*theos*").

The revelation of God's personal character is closely connected with these names that reveal God's nature. Characteristically in Hebraic Scripture, God's very being is revealed to us through these sublime names. Their meanings are not able to be exhaustively analyzed, but are able to be humbly contemplated. The classic discussion of divine *attributes* is best viewed as a secondary development of scriptural *names* for God. They assist Christian teaching in ordering, limiting, and regulating Christian language about God (Origen, *Ag. Celsus* 1. 24; Gregory of Nyssa, *On the Holy Trin.*; Calvin, *Inst.* 1.5).

In no case do these scriptural names imply that God can be fully comprehended in essence (as God is known to himself) merely by being named (Gregory of Nazianzus, *First Theol. Orat., Orat.* 27; Hilary, *On Trin.* 4.2). For God is the "King of kings and Lord of lords" (Rev. 19:16) "whom no one has ever seen or can see" objectively (1 Tim. 6:16), but who is beheld in the mind and heart (Augustine, *Sermons* 7.4; WSA 3/1:235). This does not imply that God is wholly unnameable. When Moses prayed that God would reveal his glory, "The Lord answered, 'I will make all my goodness pass before you, and I will pronounce in your hearing the name Jehovah. . . .' But he added, 'My face you cannot see, for no mortal man may see me and live'" (Exod. 33:18–20). Thus, though invisible, God is not nameless or in all ways unknowable (Tertullian, *Ag. Praxeas* 4–5; Chrysostom, *Comm. on John* 15.1–2).

Two of these names in particular—Yahweh (Lord) and Elōhīm (God)—point succinctly to the divine reality. They are especially laden with meaning when combined in the condensed ascription: Lord God (Yahweh Elohim, Gen. 2:4).

The name Yahweh (Jahweh or Jehovah or YHWH) is closely connected with the intensification of the Hebrew verb *to be*. YHWH has more "be" than all other conceivable forms of "be." His is a form of "to be" that will still be when all other forms of being are no longer anywhere.

"Then Moses said to God: 'If I go to the Israelites and tell them that the God of their forefathers has sent me to them, and they ask me his name, what shall I say?' God answered, 'I AM, that is who I am. Tell them I AM has sent you to them'" (Exod. 3:13–14). Yahweh (I AM) suggests the awesome meaning: "HE WHO IS" or "HE WHO IS WHAT HE IS" (NRSV alternatively translates: "I WILL BE WHAT I WILL BE"). Yahweh incomparably IS.

One named "I am because I am," suggests that there is no external cause for God's existence outside himself. The name Yahweh unites the notion of *One who purely is* with the notion of One who is in the process of continually becoming disclosed through historical revelation (Justin Martyr, *First Apol.* 58; Gregory of Nyssa, *FGG*: 87). In a remarkable passage, John's Gospel recalled that Jesus said of himself: "In very truth I tell you, before Abraham was born, I am" (John 8:58), in a way that suggests that in Jesus we meet nothing less than the personal self-disclosure of YHWH, "I am" (Irenaeus, *Ag. Her.* 4.13; Athanasius, *Incarnation of the Word* 11).

El, the most frequent name by which God is called in Scripture and by the Semites in general, has the root meaning of "Strong and Mighty One," the One whose incomparable power elicits reverent fear or awe (Ignatius, *Ephesians* 11,; John Cassian, *Conferences*, 2d pt., 11.11–13; Tho. Aq., *ST* 1–2 Q41–44; Calvin, *Inst.* 3.1; 3.4.31; 3.12.1). *Elōah* and *Elōhīm* are related terms referring to this unspeakably powerful One whose awesome presence instantly inspires reverential awe. *Elōhīm* is plural in form—a Hebraic way of saying that this name points to the fullness or glory of all the powers of the divine nature. When Yahweh and El are united, as in Lord God, Elōhīm is the generic name for God and Yahweh is the personal or proper name.

Among complementary names are *El Shaddaī*, "God Almighty" (NT: *Pantokratōr*); *El Elyōn*, "God Most High" (Greek Septuagint: *Hypsistos*); *El Ōlām*, "the Everlasting God" (*Aiōnios*, Rom. 16:26); *Yahweh Sābāōth*, "Lord of Hosts" (Ps. 46:7). These primitive, personalized *names* of God suggest *attributes* (such as almighty power, omnipresence, infinite wisdom) and have in time become the nucleus of the tradition's more deliberate reflection on the divine attributes (Justin Martyr, *Second Apol.* 6; *Dialogue with Trypho*; Irenaeus, *Ag. Her.* 2.30). These names correlate closely with the attributes we will be discussing: majesty, eternity, omnipotence, and holiness.

The special name *Adōnai*, "my Lord," arose about 300 BC out of the reluctance of pious Jews to pronounce the divine name, later translated into Greek as *Kyrios*. The testimony of Thomas to the lordship of Christ, "my Lord and my God" (John 20:28), brings together in the New Testament the two earlier traditions of naming God as Adōnai (for Yahweh) and *Elōhīm* (God). The single New Testament text that best draws together in Greek these key Hebraic names for God (Elōhīm, Yahweh, Adōnai, and Shaddaī) is the remarkable ascription in Revelation 1:8, where the divine Word declares: "'I am the Alpha and the Omega,' says the Lord [*Kyrios*, i.e., Adōnai] God [*Theos*, i.e., El], who is and who was and who is to come, the sovereign Lord of all [*Pantokratōr*, i.e., El Shaddaī]." It is through the historical activity of the One thus named that God's character has been made known to the remembering community (Tertullian, *Ag. Praxeas* 22; *Ag. Marcion*, 1.6).

Father (*patēr, abba*) suggests a caring parental relationship of generativity and guardianship. In intention the term may apply to analogies of both mother-ing and fathering, both nurturing and protecting (Chrysostom, *Comm. on John*, 25–26). Scripture views God as the one who engenders all things by creation (Gen. 2:4; James 1:17), especially of human beings, as their personal guide and protector (Isa. 63:16; Acts 23:28), but even more so of those who have through baptism become God's children by adoption and grace (Luke 11:2; John 3:3–10; Chrysostom, *Comm. on John* 24.2; Rom. 8:15). God as Father is most fully beheld and understood in the light of God coming as Son (John 10:15). So decisive is this parental metaphor that it becomes the leading contribution of Christianity to the Hebraic understanding of God, and the central feature of triune teaching.

Whether God's Character Can Be Ascertained

Five Methods of Knowing God's Character

In classical Christian teaching five methods of knowing God's character converge:

1. It is essentially from God's own self-disclosure that God's character has become known. Thus the *revelation* set forth in Scripture and fulfilled in Jesus is crucial to all Christian speech about God's qualities (Irenaeus, *Ag. Her.* 3). These characteristics of God are revealed and discovered in the events of the history of revelation. They cannot be abstracted, as if separable, from the events of the history of covenant.

2. Nonetheless, some attributes can be partially inferred through reasoning about causality, that is, from effect to cause (the way of causality, *via causalitatis*), by carefully and rightly attributing to God the cause (original, virtual, or permissive) of every effect (Tho. Aq., *ST* 1 Q44).

3. Other attributes may be derived through reasoning by way of negation (*via negativa*), denying as applicable to God the limits and defects we find in creaturely things (Novatian, *On Trin.* 4).

4. Oppositely some attributes of God may be derived through reasoning by way of heightening, or eminence (*via eminentiae*), ascribing to God in the highest degree all the best that we behold in creaturely life (Tho. Aq., *ST* 1 Q5).

5. Finally, there are qualities of the divine character that can be inferred *a priori* or deductively by means of thinking consistently about the consequences of the very idea of God—for whatever is essential to the idea of perfect being we may reliably know to be characteristic of God alone (Anselm, *Proslog.* 2–5; for alternative views of these varied approaches, see Dionysius, *Div. Names* 1.5; Bonaventure, *Soul's Journey into God*; Tho. Aq., *ST* 1 Q12.12; Q13.1; Calvin, *Inst.* 1.14–16).

The rest of this chapter will assess all these approaches to knowing God, be-ginning with knowing God's character through revelation as declared in Scrip-ture—the primary mode found in the classic Christian writers.

What Are Attributes?

Attributes of God are qualities that belong to God's essential nature and that are found wherever God becomes self-revealed. They are those reliable character patterns that belong to God as God. We attribute these to God based upon what we as a community know of God's self-disclosure in history. Only God has these qualities (John of Damascus; *OF* 1. 14; Calvin, *Inst.* 1.5). If in the fullest conceivable measure God is rightly understood as the Source and End of all things, full of goodness and truth, then God may be said to have a definable character, and may be counted upon to act in ways consistent with the most merciful, just, loving, almighty, good character conceivable.

God's way of knowing which knows *all* is a quality attributable only to God. All human beings have a will, but having a will that is perfect in holy love and able to perform all that it desires is an attribute of God. All living things have life, but having life in such an incomparable way that all things live through that unique life is an attribute of God (Tertullian, *Ag. Praxeas* 25–27; Tho. Aq., *ST* 1 Q18; Chemnitz, *LT* 1).

The essence of something is understandable from its abiding attributes—its defining qualities. Similarly, the nature of God is made understandable to us by our looking at the qualities that are intrinsic to God's being and therefore always present in God's revealed activity. God would be completely unknowable if there were no energies, characteristics, or qualities attributable to him, but solely an essence known only to himself (Novatian, *Trin.* 1).

These attributes are distinguishable from the actions of God. The particular act of a person is not in the fullest sense the same as that person over time moving with continuity through numerous situations. So God's character over the whole of time is more fully definitive of God than is a single action of God. God's particular acts arise out of God's essential nature and character (Hilary, *On Trin.* 7.21; Calvin, *Inst.* 1.13; 2.3.10).

To attribute to God such qualities as infinity or mercy is to concede them as belonging rightfully to God as an essential and permanent feature of God's character. The divine attributes are those belonging only to God in their fullest sense. They are essential to the divine nature. Hence they are not subject to being gained or lost by God.

Why Attributes Are Possible and Necessary in Speaking of God

It would be absurd to try to worship God without implicitly thinking of some divine attributes, such as holiness, love, presence, or power. Every thought of God or prayer to God assumes something about God's attributes. There is no way to speak to, of, or about God without speaking in some way of God's defining qualities or abiding attributes. Only by clarifying these can one arrive at an acceptable statement of what is meant in Christian teaching by the proper name God (John of Damascus, *OF* 1. 1–3).

Christian teaching has a duty to say straightforwardly just what is meant by the word *God* in order to speak at all about its major subject: God as understood by the community of faith. Christian teaching builds upon the modest awareness that God is truly and sufficiently revealed to us through an actual history. God has not misrepresented himself through revealing to us in scripture these names and characteristics (Ambrosiaster, Comm. on Paul, 1 Cor. 2:10; Calvin, *Inst.* 1.10; Chemnitz, *LT* I:43; Quenstedt, I:300, 320).

Why We Ask Who God Is Before We Ask Whether God Exists

Why are God's attributes taken into account before discussing God's existence? My intention is first to set forth that understanding of God that arises in Christian worship and then inquire whether the classic exegetes provide plausible reasons for believing that this incomparable reality exists. Note that this classical sequence is typically reversed in almost all modern discussions. But here I am following the classical order: setting forth the characteristics of God as understood by the worshiping community, and only then seeing if it is reasonable to believe that such a God does indeed exist as claimed.

This is why some of Christianity's earliest teachers deferred the question of the reality or existence of God until the being of God had been sufficiently clarified (Novatian, *Trin.* I–9; Cyril of Jerusalem, *Catech. Lect.* 4.4, 5.1). They began their discussion of God with a clarification of the divine attributes (Irenaeus, *Ag. Her.* 2. 1–2; Gregory of Nazianzus, *Second Theol. Orat.* 1–4) and subsequently spoke of reasons for proclaiming that such an incomparable One truly exists (Theophilus, *To Autolycus*, Bks. 1. 3–6, 2.3 , Irenaeus, *Ag. Her.* 4.15; Gregory of Nazianzus, *Second Theol. Orat.* 5–7).

Thus it is fitting first to consider the question of *who* God is (God's being), and then to ask *whether* God is (God's existence), for it seems idle to ask whether something exists until one has first defined, envisioned, or imagined it.

The Unity of Diverse Attributes

The qualities intrinsic to God are one in God, yet many in our perception. In their unity they reveal God's singular character and personality. In their variety they allow us to behold and praise various aspects of the divine activity, and to name the one God by different names using guarded metaphors. "The diverse names we give to God are not synonyms, for they convey diverse meanings, though everything is one in his reality" (Tho. Aq., *Compend.* 25, TAPT:94). The beauty of God's holiness blends all attributes into a single unified effulgence of the divine glory (Ps. 29:2; Gregory of Nyssa, *On the Holy Spirit*).

Classic Christian teachers warned against emphasizing one attribute at the expense of another. A good person will manifest good behavior. That behavior varies in situations where different responses are called for. God is the infinitely good One with the most varied conceivable qualities that are wonderfully unified in the divine character (Hilary, *On Trin.* 4.15:71–75; Anselm, *Monologium* 17; Wesley, *Sermons*, "The Unity of the Divine Being"). God's perfectly integrated character is precisely the appropriate balance of these excellences or insurmountably good qualities (sometimes rendered "perfections"; Tho. Aq., *ST* 1, Q19). As history unfolds there may be one occasion when one of the attributes (such as justice or holiness) may seem to the believing community to be relatively more recognizable or dominant; at another time another attribute (eternality or mercy) may come more clearly into view. But regardless of which attribute may be recognizable at any given moment, all attributes are unified in an appropriate integration in the eternal being of God. What appears to be divided within a temporal perspective is simple and united in God (Hilary *Trin.* 7.1; Tho. Aq., *ST* 1 Q13.4, Calvin, *Inst.* 1.13; Chemnitz, *LT* 1.43).

The history of theism is plagued by mistakes caused by overemphasizing a single one or set of attributes while neglecting others. Aristotle stressed God's absolute essence, aseity (underived existence), self-contemplation, transcendence, and immutability, yet failed to grasp God's relationality, closeness, and covenant love toward humanity. Kant rightly grasped God's justice as it impinges upon human reason and conscience but did not fully acknowledge God's mercy, grace, and power. Wieman understood God's relationality but did not sufficiently affirm God's sovereign freedom (Aristotle, *Metaphy.*; Kant, *Fundamental Principles of the Metaphy of Morals*; H. N. Wieman, *Source of the Human Good*).

A healthy equilibrium in the Christian teaching of God grows as the faithful become firmly grounded in the interpenetrating qualities of the divine attributes so as to not exaggerate one to the neglect of others (Tho. Aq., *ST* 1 Q12, 1:48; Pearson, *Apostles' Creed:*40). Each attribute complements the others so that taken together the glory of God embraces and manifests all attributes in perfect tension, correspondence, and complementarity (Cyril of Jerusalem, *Catech. Lect.* 6; Tho. Aq., *ST* 1 Q15, Q31). All the attributes fitting to God are united and inseparable in God's being.

Scripture shows how God's name (hence character) is known precisely through *events* in which God's activity has been recognized and received by the community of faith. It is not an abstract idea or speculation that God is incomparably just, good, powerful, and present. For God has revealed himself as such through historical activity, through the whole length of the divine-human encounter (*Letter to Diognetus*, 6–12; Athanasius, *Ag. Heathen* 38–40).

It is nonetheless possible to *distinguish* these attributes conceptually, even though in God's unitary being they remain *inseparable*. For God's presence, for example, is not the same as God's knowing. Though distinguishable in language, they are united in God. God's being is integral, self-congruent, expressing over time each of these distinguishable attributes.

In God, to *be* is to be incomparably strong. To be God is to be unfailingly merciful. No single characteristic can be viewed independently, as if separable from the rest. God is not at one moment unmercifully strong and at another moment unwisely omnipotent. God is always mercifully strong and wisely omnipotent. Nor is God at one time just, at another time loving, and at another time all-knowing. God's whole being, inclusive of all attributes, is present in each of the discrete attributes that faith recognizes and celebrates. God is fully and simultaneously all these attributes, and more than any language could attribute (Novatian, *On Trin.* 2, Gregory of Nazianzus, *Orat.* 5). This notion is interwoven with faith's affirmation of God's simplicity. God is not divided up into our petty conceptions of God's attributes. In all attributes, God is, and remains, simply and completely God (John of Damascus, *OF* 1.9; Hilary, *On Trin.* 9.1; Tho. Aq., *ST* 1 Q3; Calvin, *Inst.* 1.10.3).

The Biblical Revelation of the Character of God

In Hebraic religion, God is known by what God does. What God does is remembered and recollected as history—the history of God's encounter with humanity. In these encounters, God is remembered as having a definable, discernible character by those whom God has met: "He made known his ways to Moses and his acts to the people of Israel" (Ps. 103:7; Irenaeus, *Ag. Her.* 4.9). It is through that story of God's actions that we come to say something in language about God's character, reliability, and personhood (Julia of Norwich, SGL 6; Calvin, *Inst.* 1.8).

The ways of this One are disclosed for our enjoyment, celebration, salvation, and instruction (Pss. 25:4; 119:3). The Jewish-Christian study of God inquires into a history (the history of Israel and universal history) to get the picture of how God has become known (Deut. 5:6). Yet history is a highly complex cacophony of many generations of human experience. It seems virtually impossible to condense all that experience into a single, central, revealing insight or meaning. Yet in the events surrounding the ministry of Jesus, Christianity understands and proclaims that God has become self-disclosed so as to reveal the inner meaning, direction, and end of universal history (Augustine, *CG* 16–18).

The biblical history resists systematization. Yet since the Bible wishes to address each hearer as a whole person, it invites and requires that each believer seek to bring its loose ends together, to listen for its unity, and to try to see it integrally. It calls for systematic, cohesive thinking about its varied events and

messages. History does not readily lend itself to systematic statement or definition, yet Christian teaching rightly persists in modestly seeking internal consistency and clear definition concerning God's self-disclosure in history (Justin
Martyr, *Dialogue with Trypho* 6; John of Damascus, *OF* 4.17).

Whether or in what sense God "exists" must indeed remain a major concern
of Christian apologetics, which seeks to make God plausible to those who do not
participate in the community of faith. But biblical writers were far more concerned with polytheism than with atheism, and with idolatry than with formal
theism. Their central problem was not *whether* God is, but rather *who* God is
(Gen. 28:10–22; Ps. 20:1; Isa. 9:6; Jerome, Comm. on Is. 3.9.16–17).

What is the character of God? To Whom do we address our prayers? What sort
of language can one ascribe to this transcendent reality? (Exod. 3:13–16; Gregory
of Nazianzus, *Theol. Orat.* 4.18). If God has become self-revealed in history, just
as human beings make themselves known by their self-disclosure, what kind of
character can we say God has? (Gen. 22:1–18; Gen. 37–50).

The Role of Doubt in Faith

There is still room for doubt in biblical faith. The exodus wanderers were
subjected to despair and anxiety that God might not fulfill his promises ("Is the
Lord in our midst or not?" Exod. 17:7). Jeremiah complained that God was like a
deceitful wadi, as if God occasionally came in like rain on the desert and swept
everything away, and then did not appear for a long while (Jer. 15:16). Job was
tormented by questions about the fairness of God and the remoteness of God
(Gregory I, *Morals on Job* 9.27–28).

Some say, "God has forgotten; he has hidden his face and has seen nothing"
(Ps. 10:11; Jer. 5:12). Doubts of this type are intensely present in key moments reported by Scripture, but they have emerged precisely out of a radical sense of the
sovereignty of God and the providential presence of the almighty God—precisely
because God *has* appeared at some points in history.

Worshipers who today experience profound doubts about God can at least
know that they belong to a community whose greatest minds have from time to
time experienced such doubts (Job 3:1; Jer. 2:4–37; Augustine, *Conf.* 2.9).

Knowing God by Negation and by Analogy

God is known by stating what God is not, and by stating what God most surely is.
This involves two ways of reasoning: by limiting and by heightening. These two
ways are among the most recurrent of classic Christian attempts to speak clearly
of God according to the ecumenical consensus:

the way of negation (*via negativa*)

the way of heightening or intensifying (*via eminentiae*).

In order to prepare the way for speaking discretely in these two ways, it is first
necessary to show how analogies may function prudently in theological reasoning—how they are used and sometimes abused.

The Usefulness of Analogy

The self-constrained use of analogy has helped Christian teaching think in a
disciplined way about the qualities characteristic of God. The proper use of
analogy is distinguished from rigid, univocal language which allows only a single
meaning to a word. Analogy is also distinguished from evasive, ambiguous,

uncertain language called equivocation. Equivocal language too loosely allows words to have multiple meanings and thereby makes definite statements impossible. Finding the path on the high ground between these two gullies is the modest task of thinking cautiously by analogy.

Every language has the word *good* or its equivalent in its vocabulary. All users of the word *good* know that there are degrees of goodness. When Christian teachers have cautiously applied this ordinary human word (*good*) to God, they have applied it cautiously by analogy, i.e., by some proportional comparison to what we know to be *like* human goodness, remaining aware that God's goodness is also vastly *unlike* human goodness (Gregory of Nyssa, *Ag. Eunomius* 11.1, 2). Although God is insurmountably good, we know that even our best conceptions of goodness do not do full justice to the infinitely wise, eternal goodness of God. We do well to avoid using the word *good* univocally, as if the word had only one strict meaning that applied in exactly the same way to our goodness and God's goodness (Novatian, *On Trin.* 2). Yet in avoiding this extreme we must not bend so far as to apply language too ambiguously or equivocally, which would suppose that human goodness is in every respect different from God's goodness. In this case we would equivocate on two completely different meanings of the word *good*. Rather, we rely upon a constrained *analogy* (which is neither univocal nor equivocal) that says that God's goodness is in some ways akin to and in other ways distinct from what we know of human goodness (Luke 13:18–21; Maximus of Turin, Sermon 2.2; Tho. Aq.; *ST* 1 Q13, 1:59; Calvin, *Inst.* 4.17.21, 32).

A prudent analogy proportionally compares God's insurmountable goodness with our limited but real goodness, so that what we know of human goodness is in some sense really correlated, though modestly and self-critically, with what we know about God. Thus we can say with some confidence, in recollecting the history of language about the divine-human encounter, that *God is good*, although God's goodness is not to be finally constricted univocally in terms of our limited, culturally shaped, class-oriented conceptions of goodness (Origen, *OFP* 2.5; Tho. Aq., *ST* 1 Q6, I). Analogy is a most important intellectual tool in Christian teaching, yet is best used modestly and self-critically.

God transcends every human picture of God. Though God is sufficiently revealed to the apostles in Christ, much remains as yet unrevealed: "No eye has seen, no ear has heard, no mind has conceived what God has prepared for those who love him" (1 Cor. 2:9; Isa. 64:4). Neither the way of negation or of analogy reveals how the divine is perceived from God's own perspective. That is impossible to state, since the only competent perceiver is God.

The Christian community proceeds on the confident assumption that the ultimate Source and End of being desires to become known by us. For this reason God is becoming intentionally revealed to us: "Now we see in a mirror dimly, but then face to face. Now I know in part; then I shall know fully, even as I have been fully known" (1 Cor. 13:12). Now I see from within the frail limitations of human perception, listening, intelligence, intuition, language, and egocentric willing. But I live in hope that a full disclosure awaits the end of history in a way that will be consistent with what we know of the Father through the Son (Origen, *De Princip.* 1. 6; Augustine, *CG* 22.29).

Clarifying What God Is Not: The Negative Way

Classic Christianity has found it easier to say what God is not than what God is. There are two major, complementary ways that classical theism has found to attribute human, descriptive language to God: The first is by constantly saying No: "God is not this, not that, not anything finite, limited, dependent, caused, or created."

This is the negative way (*via negativa*) of reasoning toward God. This way seeks to form an appropriate idea of the greatness of God by removing from thought and language everything that would make God small or limited, or less wise or less holy than we already know God to be.

We know with certainty that there are some things that God clearly is *not*, such as air, earth, fire, and water, fireflies, comets, and buzzards (although God may at some time be metaphorically described as something like any of these). The negative way tries to trim from our language about God all those words that imply limitation and imperfection (Dionysius, *Myst. Theol.* 2). Thomas wrote: "What manner of being God is not may be known by eliminating characteristics that cannot apply to him, such as composition, change, and so forth" (Tho. Aq., *ST* 1 Q3).

This is the simpler, and probably more ancient, way to speak safely of God without misrepresentation. Rooted in a long tradition influenced by Greek, Talmudic, and patristic thought, Philo, Dionysius, and Maimonides have been among the most influential exponents of the negative way, which has doggedly argued: "God is not like that." "God is more than that." In fact, God is not *anything* to which one can point objectively, for God is no object. In this way one *can* derive some reliable knowledge of God (if only by negation), in the sense that one can know what God is not (Dionysius, *Myst. Theol.* 2, 3).

Even on this narrow basis it is surprising the extent to which classic writers could speak of God. For if it is apparent that God is *not* anything finite, then one may speak rightly of God's *infinity*, ruling out from the reference to God anything that is limited, countable, and measurable. If one can know that God is not visible, then we can speak of God's *invisibility*, ruling out from the being of God anything capable of being seen or objectified. Insofar as God is not circumscribed by any particular space or restricted to the changing temporal order, it is possible to speak of God as *im*measurable and *im*mutable. These prefixes beginning with *in* or *im* or *un* (implying negation) therefore may help clarify many characteristics of the divine life: incomprehensible, incorporeal, immeasurable, immortal, immutable, and infinite. All belong to the negative way, where we sing: "Immortal, invisible, God only wise, in light inaccessible hid from our eyes."

Psalm 139 fittingly declared the personally present transcendence of God exceeding all our categories of understanding:

> O Lord, you have searched me, and you know me. You know when I sit and
> when I rise; you perceive my thoughts from afar. You discern my going out
> and my lying down; you are familiar with all my ways. Before a word is on
> my tongue you know it completely, O Lord. You hem me in behind and before;
> you have laid your hand upon me. Such knowledge is too wonderful for me,
> too lofty for me to attain. Where can I go from your Spirit? Where can I flee
> from your presence? (Ps. 139:1–7)

Apart from the incarnation, there is in God no finitude, no temporal restriction, no limited locality. There are no limits to God's knowledge of the world and humanity. There is no way to escape the presence of the living God. God knows our human downsittings and uprisings, actions and movements. God is acquainted with our habits, ways, plans, and despairs. If at times we may deceive our fellow creatures, we cannot deceive this One.

To speak rightly of God, we must first rule out all conceptions that imply limitation. The negative way attempts to do this in a disciplined and deliberate way. It is a way of knowing what God is not, which becomes an important avenue toward reliable but limited knowledge of who God is (Novatian, *On Trin.* 4–8; Tho. Aq., *ST* 1 Q12).

The Way of Heightening: Attributions from Proximate Creaturely Perfections

The other way of thinking analogically is classically called the way of heightening or eminence (Latin: via eminentiae). Unlike the negative way, it does not remove comparisons, but offers language to show that God is like the best we can envision. God is the eminent or highest degree of the most perfect things we know (Dionysius the Areopagite, *Myst. Theol.* 3; Hollaz, ETA:190; Gerhard, LT 3:86). This way of reasoning proceeds by comparing God with desirable qualities of creatures which are already known and universally conceded to be good, great, noble, just, or worthy of adoration. We compare God with the observed excellence of powers and virtues we regard as most highly valued and adored. This positive way proceeds by intensifying observed human excellences to their highest conceivable degree and positing them of God (Augustine, *CG* 11.24).

The way of eminence beholds something that we know to be good and attributes that correspond in their fullest dimension or proportion to God (Tho. Aq., *ST* 1 Q5, 6). The argument begins by looking at limited creaturely things, interpersonal relationships, ourselves, and our societies. There we see striking evidences of justice, goodness, beauty, and other excellent qualities. By this means we come to speak of God as the fullest measure of the best that we know, even if known in an imperfect way (Cyril of Jerusalem, *Catech. Lect.* 6.4–9). Note that we are not here referring to immanence (to indwell, from *in manere*), but to eminence as height.

Who does not know what it means to be treated unjustly? Everyone implicitly knows this about justice: It is better to be treated fairly than unfairly. In this way God becomes conceivable as that One who is fair in the highest degree imaginable, that is, perfectly just (Acts 7:52; Anselm, *Monologium*; Tho. Aq., *ST* 2–2ae Q58).

The Supremely Good Being: From Degrees of Goodness

This positive way of reasoning by height (eminence) can be illustrated in the term Supreme Good, by picturing a scale of degrees of excellence:

1. Better than the best we know

2. The best we know

3. Known by general consent to be something good

4. Known to be lacking in some good

5. Lacking good altogether

Anyone can see that 4 is better than 5, and that 3 is not as good as 2. But is there a distinction between 1 and 2? If you answer 1 is better than 2, you have made a theological decision: Something is better than the best we know. This is what Christian theistic reasoning has meant by the way of eminence: the attribution to God of the height of goods and perfections, analogous to what is in part known, but beyond complete knowing (Tho. Aq., *ST* 1 Q12).

Traditionally the term *perfections of God* has been reserved to those qualities that intrinsically belong to the divine essence. Divine attributes are qualities that our language attributes to God that seek to do proximate justice to the divine perfections (Didymus the Blind, Comm. *on 1 John* 4.12; Tho. Aq., *ST* 1 Q4).

This attribution of language is not in itself a mystery. It is an ordinary fact of human speech. Degrees of goodness are recognizable in all human experience. Everyone knows how to say better or worse in their own native language. Though we may disagree on how to rank some created good, no one is foolish enough to deny *that* there is a difference between some things that are fairly good, some a little better, some really and invariably good, and some are indescribably good, even beyond our imagination. God belongs to the highest category in the scale.

The Supreme Being: Reasoning from Degrees of Being

This same positive way of reasoning "by heightening" (eminence) can also be illustrated in the term Supreme Being by picturing a scale of degrees of conscious participation in being:

1. That which most completely *is* and always will be

2. Human life, consciousness, and freedom

3. Animal life, limited consciousness, and movement

4. Plant life, vegetative growth, and reproductive life

5. Lifeless, inorganic matter

6. That which never has been

7. That which never has been or can be

Anyone can easily see that 6 participates in the fullness of being less than 5, and that 3 does not share in being as fully as 2. But is there a distinction between 1 and 2? If you answer that 1 more completely exists than 2, you have made a theological decision: Something can be conceived which is, as Anselm famously said: "That than which nothing greater can be conceived" (*Proslogion* 1). This is what Christian theistic reasoning has meant by the way of eminence applied to being, or that which most is. The argument ascribes to God of the height of being, even if it is beyond what we can know within our form of being in time (Gregory of Nyssa, *Catechetical Oration*, 1; Tho. Aq., *ST* 1 Q12).

Begin reflecting at the bottom of the scale: Some things can be imagined that never can be, and have never been. Others could have been but were not. Some things participate in being at a very low level of awareness. The capacity for plants to participate interactively in their environments is greater than that capacity of rocks, yet rocks are participants in being in an important sense, inasmuch as they last much longer than plants, even though without life. Human intelligence is far more capable of self-consciously participating in being than is instinctual animal consciousness.

By analogy it is reasonable to posit another reality at the apex of the scale: One who insurmountably *is* more than anything else thinkable, who more fully shares in being, grounds being and embraces all being. This One *is* more fully than any other being, and is more fully conscious of being than any other conceivable being. To posit that One who supremely *is*, by the way of heightening or eminent thinking, is to reliably know, learn, and affirm something about God: God supremely *is* (i.e., Supremely Being, or the Supreme Being). For how is it reasonable to have a scale of degrees of perfection without also positing the apex of that scale? Leaving it blank does not solve this dilemma. The scale itself requires that it be completed, with null at one end and infinity at the other end, with nonbeing at one end and supreme being at another end; otherwise the scale itself is defective and incomplete (Augustine, *Trin.* 5.16.17; Tho. Aq., *ST* 1 Q4, 5, 12).

I AM as God's Name in Hebrew Scripture

This is an appropriate point at which to note that, rightly understood, the word being (cognate with the direct name "I AM") is a more intensive word than the flat word existence (even in English, but more so in its Hebraic, Greek, and Latin roots). Existence, as its root meaning (*existere*) suggests, includes an ex, a standing-out, a coming out of being into definite manifestations. Existence requires a "standing" (*sistere*) "out from" (*ex*) being. The English language has to stretch in order to say that being in this sense may be thought of as the ground of existing, but the Greek and Latin terms that were familiar to the early church teachers made this point more transparent. For one cannot exist (stand out) without something to stand upon (being), just as one cannot subsist (stand firm, from *sub + sistere*) without having something (being, *esse*) to support one's subsistence.

Even in modern speech, *existing* seems a less full term than *being*, and "merely to exist" less weighty than "to be." One would never render Shakespeare's "To be or not to be" by saying, "To exist or not to exist." In English we freely use both terms (*being* and *existence*) interchangeably of God, for it is no less fitting to say that God exists than that God has being or simply *is*. But God *is* (sing it *fortissimo*: IS) more fully, completely than any creature could be. Thus the term *existence* does not pertain to God in precisely the same way that it pertains to creatures. For God *is*—immeasurably, necessarily, and eternally—whereas creatures exist measurably, contingently, and temporally (Tertullian, *Against Marcion*, 1.3.; Tho. Aq., *ST* 1 Q2; *SCG* 1. 13). Hebrew Scriptures did not use terms like God's *essence* or *substance*, but they did speak often of God as Yahweh (the incomparable "I AM"), the One who insurmountably *is*.

The Sequence of Attributes

We now turn from preparing the way to speak to speaking clearly and descriptively of God's attributes: How might the characteristics of the divine life be properly ordered into a whole mosaic that brings them fittingly together, or into a sequential argument that moves from one point to another?

The most satisfactory classical classification distinguishes four types of attributes of God: *primary, relational, interpersonal*, and *moral* attributes. These four are (a) those attributes that belong to God's essence apart from God's creative work; (b) those that arise necessarily out of the relation of God with the created order; (c) those that arise out of personal and interpersonal analogies, inasmuch as the revelation of God is personal, and human beings, the recipients of revelation, are persons; and (d) those that arise necessarily out of the relation of free personal beings capable of moral choices.

These four levels may be distinguished as follows:

1. The primary or essential attributes (sometimes called absolute, incommunicable, quiescent, or prerelational) are intrinsic to God prior to any possible connection or relation with creatures.

2. The relational attributes (sometimes called relative, communicable, operative, or postrelational) are also intrinsic to God, but can only be conceived in relation with creatures in time and space.

3. The interpersonal and personal attributes are also intrinsic to God, but can be conceived only by analogies from personal existence and from interpersonal excellences.

4. The moral attributes (sometimes called axiological—value based, or areteological—virtue based, or teleological—purpose based), like all attributes, are intrinsic to God, but these may be conceived only in the moral sphere of a relationship between responsible and free beings.

These four levels will be set forth in the next two chapters (primary and relational in Chapter 2, and personal and moral in Chapter 3).

Some arrangement or organization is required. It is not aesthetically, psychologically, or logically satisfactory merely to list the attributes alphabetically or arbitrarily. Scripture itself does not provide a specific or definitive order, although it does provide terms that tend to fall into a certain sequence that reason can reflect upon, aesthetically arrange, and logically place in symmetrical order. The sequence that will follow is derived not from any single classic Christian biblical teacher but from many in combination, which ecumenical teaching seeks to harmonize. Most important are the ordered discussions of divine attributes by Novatian, Cyril of Jerusalem, Hilary of Poitiers, Gregory of Nazianzus, Augustine, and John of Damascus. Their teaching helps provide a way of looking synoptically at the characteristics of the divine life.

This organization of terms provides key building blocks for a preliminary clarification of the meaning of the biblical name Yahweh Elōhīm, or the Lord God, to whom Christian worship is addressed. This classification seeks to be consistent with scriptural priorities and church tradition, rational in its conception and sequence, meaningful to experience, and aesthetically appropriate to a sense of rational design:

Attributes of God

I: THE NATURE OF GOD (Chapter 2):

The Divine Sufficiency: Primary and Essential Attributes of God Inapplicable to Creatures and Not Communicable to Creatures

The Uncreated One (Aseity, Independence, Necessity)

The Unity of God (Oneness and Simplicity)

The Infinity of God (in relation to space, Immensity; in relation to time, Eternality)

The Living God (Incomparable Aliveness, "I Am–ness")

The Divine Majesty: Relational Attributes Displaying God's Way of Being Present, Knowing and Influencing the World

God's Way of Being Present (Omnipresence)

God's Way of Knowing (Omniscience, Prescience, Foreknowledge, Wisdom)

God's Way of Influencing (Almighty Omnipotence, All-Powerful and All-Empowering)

II: THE CHARACTER OF GOD (Chapter 3):

The Divine Thou: Active and Interpersonal Attributes Belonging to the Divine-Human Relationship and Analogous to Personal Experience

God as Incomparably Personal (the Divine Thou; Personal Agent; All-Experiencing One; Congruent in Feeling, Sensibility, Emotivity, Affection)

The Spiritual Nature of God (Spirituality, Invisibility)

The Freedom of God (Radically Free, Choosing, Electing Will;

Interpersonally Interactive, All-Encountering One)

The Divine Goodness: Moral Qualities Intrinsic to the Divine Character

The Holiness of God (Moral Purity: Holiness, Righteousness, Justice)

The Goodness of God (Benevolence and Integrity: Congruence, Veracity, Faithfulness, Persistence)

The Compassion of God (Love: Grace, Mercy, Forbearance)

Conclusion: *The Blessedness of God*

No conceptualization of God, however careful, can be adequate to its incomparable Subject (Chrysostom, On the Incomprehensible, 3.1). Even if God is revealed, yet God may have characteristics that remain unknown to us. Nevertheless, though our knowledge of God's attributes is admittedly incomplete, that limitation does not dislodge the confidence of Christian teaching that the revelation of God in Scripture is sufficient for salvation. The worshiping community affirms that whatever characteristics God has that remain *unknown* must be in harmony with what God has made *known* and accessible through the history of revelation, the historical experience of the believing community, and rational reflection.

2

THE NATURE OF GOD

CHRISTIAN SCRIPTURES AND TRADITION view God as independent of all else that exists, that is, as:

- uncreated
- underived
- necessary
- one
- simple
- infinite
- immeasurable
- eternal
- self-sufficient
- necessary being
- the life of all that lives

To grasp these crucial terms, we show them in slow motion, making clear precisely how they are attested in Scripture, interpreted by tradition, organized by reason, and celebrated in a worshiping community. These are defining characteristics of the divine life.

God Is Before Time

God does not need a world to be God, at least not a particular world. But, as the ancient ecumenical exegetes well knew, to imagine God as prior to creation is

exceptionally difficult for minds that are themselves the products of creation
(Novatian, On *Trin.* 3; Augustine, *Conf.* 7.17). To think of God as originator of
time is mind-boggling to finite minds who think only within the confines of time
and space (Augustine, *Conf.* 11.11–13; Cassiodorus, Expos. Pss., 49.7).

God minus the world is God. The world minus God is nothing. This is essential
to any teaching of creation or of the Creator. If so, what can we say about God
prior to creation? What characteristics might God be said to have even *before*
positing of any world or any time. Here we are reflecting upon what might be
knowable about the "primordial nature of God," that pre-temporal nature of God
that preconditions any activity in or relationship with the world.

The attributes or qualities implied in such a hypothesized pre-relational, pre-
time, pre-space, pre-world being are called attributes of God's absolute essence.
They are primary attributes of God inapplicable to creatures.

All of these have traditionally been called *incommunicable* attributes, in the
sense that they cannot be communicated from God to creatures, or ascribed to
creatures, or bestowed upon or even shared with creatures. For no creature is or
can ever become uncreated or utterly self-sufficient (Gregory of Nazianzus, *First
Theol. Orat.*; Calvin, *Inst.* 1.10–13; Anglican Thirty-nine Articles).

The Divine Sufficiency

The Uncreated One: God Is Self-sufficient,
Independent, Necessary, Underived

Scripture attests that God is the Uncreated One, underived, the Source and End
of all things (Ps. 90; Isa. 40:28; Theodoret, Comm. on Is. 12.40.25; 1 Cor. 1:30).
"Before me there was no god fashioned nor ever shall be after me. I am the Lord,
I myself" (Isa. 43:10; Calvin, *Inst.* 1.7). God is by definition self-sufficient, in the
sense that this One cannot be dependent upon any other being, since all things
have their beginning and end in this One (Augustine, *Conf.* 2.5, 11.2; *Trin.* 1. 6;
Anselm, Monologium 5–6).

The most telling Hebraic name for God, "I AM" (Yahweh), suggests that God
simply and incomparably *is*. If anyone should try to speak of some "cause of God,"
that would demonstrate the folly of the speaker. That would mean that the alleged cause of God would displace God as the cause of all things, tantamount to
discarding God and ascribing deity to whatever that prior cause might conceived
to be (Novatian, *Trin.* 3).

This uncreated cause of all things is addressed personally, unlike the "other
gods": "O Lord our God, other lords than you have been our masters, but you
alone do we invoke by name" (Isa. 26:13; Augustine, EDH, Question 69.4). To this
independent, self-sufficient being "everything is possible" (Mark 10:27). Isaiah
prophesied of God: "I am the first and I am the last, and there is no god but me"
(Isa. 44:6; Theophilus, *To Autolycus* 1. 1–5; Tho. Aq., *ST* 1 Q5). Job is asked by
Yahweh: "Where were you when I laid the earth's foundations?" (Job 38:4).

To affirm that God is underived or independent or necessary means that God
depends on no cause external to God. God's life is contingent upon nothing else.
This is sometimes called aseity (from *a se*, from itself) or self-existence, or underived existence. To say that God is uncreated or self-existent means that God
is without origin, that God is the only ground of God's being, and that there is
no cause prior to God (Tho. Aq., *ST* 1 Q7, 8). This teaching arises necessarily out
of the awareness that if any outcomes or effects exist at all, then there must be
causes, and consequently some reality must ultimately be uncaused, or have the
cause in itself. Such a being must exist in itself, requiring no antecedent cause.

This eternal One has not at some point in time *become* the Supreme Being, but simply *is*, and has never been otherwise. This being whose nature is to be, the Hebrews called Yahweh ("I am Who I am," Exod. 3:14) and Teutonic languages have called God. God has no cause external to God, and this is precisely what makes God God and not something else (Hilary, *On Trin.* 1. 5).

Some may object that this self-existence by its very language shuts out creatures and points to a being who needs no one to "complete himself," and "nothing but himself" in order to be. In the coming discussion of creation we will correct the impression left by some natural theology that God could have been happy and better blessed without creation. At this point, however, we have a much less ambitious aspiration: simply to establish the primordial independence of God that preconditions God's engagement with the world (Gregory of Nazianzus, *Orat.* 30; Hilary, *On Trin.* 2.2, 2.6).

The Difference Between God and Anything Else

Essential attributes are those that are intrinsic to God. They belong to God apart from and, so to speak "prior to" any expression of God's activity or energies in the created order (Gregory Nyssa, To Eunomius 3.5). "Prior to" is used hypothetically, because time begins with creation strictly speaking. So chronologically there is no time prior to creation, but logically God may rightly be said to be prior to and the ground of creation (Augustine, *Conf.* 13.34).

The relations that God creates and enables are not necessary to God's being, for God alone created them. No relation in which the necessary being freely engages can place a final limit on God's own primordial being.

God's freely chosen relationships do not fundamentally displace or frustrate this divine sufficiency (Deut. 28:3; Ps. 119:12; Rom. 4:6, 9; 9:5; Chrysostom, *Comm. on Rom.* 16; Calvin, *Inst.* 2.8). The freedom of God has no limit except whatever limit God chooses freely to permit. God's gracious choice to create and share being with other beings is an expression of God's unfettered freedom. God's underived existence is not conditioned by anything except that which God elects to provide and permit through a world in which other beings temporarily are empowered through God's unlimited power (Job 21:15; Ps. 91:1; Heb. 6:3; Rev. 21:22; Apringius of Beja, Tractate on the Apoc. 21.24–26; Calvin, *Inst.* 1.17–18).

The Unity of God

One God

The Source and End of all things is One, not divisible into parts. "Hear, O Israel, the Lord our God is one Lord" (Deut. 6:4). This reality—God, Yahweh, Elōhīm, Theos—the central subject of all Jewish-Christian Scripture, is one, not many. Any polytheistic conception is by definition inadequate (Arnobius, Ag. the Heathen 3 : Tertullian, Ag. Hermogenes 3). "Is there any God beside me?" (Isa. 44:8; Jerome, Comm. on Is. 12.18).

There is no pantheon. "I am God, there is no other" (Isa. 45:22). There are no gradations of divinity. God is the one and only incomparable divine being. Jesus affirmed the ancient way of Israel that maintained: "The Lord our God is the only Lord" (Mark 12:29). "Among the gods not one is like you, O Lord, no deeds are like yours. . . . You alone are God" (Ps. 86:8, 10). "Among the gods" is not a tacit concession to polytheism, but a way of exposing the futility of faith in claims made for other alleged deities. Similarly, Paul: "For us there is one God, the Father, from whom all being comes, towards whom we move" (1 Cor. 8:6).

There is no other "god" to which God can be compared (Origen, *De Princip.* 1. 1; Jerome *Letters* 15.4).

A statue or graven image of God must not be made since God cannot be reduced to creaturely matter, even though God's glory may shine through creaturely beings (Second Council of Nicaea, session 1). In the Old Testament there is a symbolic visualization of seraphim and cherubim in the holy of holiest; however, they are not worshiped as God but only as pointing beyond themselves, an expression of the aura of God's presence, a reflection of the manifold glory of the one God (Basil, *Letters* 8; Calvin, *Inst.* 1.10.3; Pearson, *Expos. of the Creed* 1).

With his usual precision, John of Damascus summarized the point: "If there are many Gods, how can one maintain that God is uncircumscribed? For where the one would be, the other could not be" (John of Damascus, *OF* 1. 5; Tho. Aq., *ST* 1 Q15).

Simplicity

Simplicity is the opposite of composition. God is one, not composed of parts. The fullness of God is present in each of God's discrete actions (Clement of Alex., *Stromata* 5.12; Hilary, On *Trin.* 1.6; Tho. Aq., *ST* 1 Q3). In God all the diversity of creation is unified (Augustine, *CG* 11.10; Anselm, Monologium 17; Julia of Norwich, SGL; Wesley, "Unity of the Divine Being"). To assert that God is absolutely simple is to stand against the proposition that God could be divisible into parts (Ambrose, *On Chr. Faith* 1. 16; Augustine, *Trin.* 5.5; Basil, *Letters* 234). The triune teaching strongly affirms the unity of God, for God is "not three gods," but Three-in-One (Gregory of Nyssa, On "Not Three Gods").

This One simply *is*. There is no "has been" or "will be" for God, for whom all temporal events are simultaneously experienced. Whatever God has been, God is eternally. Whatever God can be, God is eternally (Augustine, Conf 7.10; *CG* 8.6, 11.10). And whatever distinctions human imagination might apply to God, God remains *one* through and beyond such distinctions (Athanasius, *Ag. the Heathen* 38, 39). The essence of God is simply to exist in the uniquely simple way that only God can exist—as God (Athanasius, *Defense of Nicaea:* 22; Tho. Aq., *ST* 1 Q3).

Infinity

The infinite is that which has no end, no limit, no finite boundary, and thus cannot be measured or timed by any finite standard (Catherine of Siena, Prayers 12). The infinite cannot be reached by successive addition or exhausted by successive subtraction of finite numbers, parts, or qualities (Gregory of Nazianzus, On Theophany 7).

Worshipers acknowledge their human, natural, and historical limitations in time and space, yet their petitions implicitly point beyond all times and spaces toward that unsurpassable One who transcends and embraces all times, all spaces (Gregory of Nazianzus, *Orat.* 45.3; Anselm, *Monologium* 15; Teresa of Avila, *Life* 39).

It is only when infinity is attributed to God that the concept has precise, plausible, and consistent meaning (John of Damascus, *OF* 1.13). All of God's good qualities are said to be without end or limit (Hilary, *On Trin.* 2.6), so infinity applies to every divine attribute, for God is infinitely merciful, infinitely holy, infinitely just (Calvin, *Inst.* 1.13).

Immeasurability

God is clearly not any thing that can be measured. Every creaturely being can be measured—even galaxies, if we had a big enough measuring device (Ambrose, Of the *Chr. Faith* 2.8.59–73). By this means we are walking on a negative path (via negativa) toward knowledge of God, where limitations and imperfections are, one by one, removed from the character of God.

The divine immensity is the divine infinity regarded from the point of view of space. "Great is the Lord, and greatly to be praised; and of His greatness there is no end" (Ps. 145:3; Tho. Aq., *SCG* 1.43). The medieval scholastics taught that "God's center is everywhere, God's circumference nowhere" (Bonaventure, *Soul's Journey into God* 2). God transcends all spatial relations, while remaining their ultimate cause and ground (Hermas, *The Pastor* 2.1; Irenaeus, *Ag. Her.* 4.20; Tertullian, *Ag. Praxeas* 16).

Having built the temple, Solomon humbly asked: "But can God indeed dwell on earth? Heaven itself, the highest heaven, cannot contain thee; how much less this house that I have built" (1 Kings 8:27). How is human imagination and reason to measure God? After Job had inquired of God, being unable to fathom the divine purpose, God then inquired of Job: "Have you comprehended the vast expanse of the world? Come, tell me all this, if you know" (Job 38:18). "Can you bind the cluster of the Pleiades or loose Orion's belt?" (Job 38:31; Gregory I, *Morals on Job* 29.77). "Tell me, if you know and understand" how the earth's foundations were laid. "Who settled its dimensions? Surely you should know. Who stretched his measuring-line over it?" (Job 38:4, 5). Human imagination stands in meek silence in the presence of the Measurer of all our measurements (Julia of Norwich, *Showings*).

As time cannot circumscribe eternity, so the totality of space cannot encompass the divine immensity. God is not containable or measurable by even the most extensive schemes of measurement (John of Damascus, *OF* 1.13). God is so boundless that our very word *immensity* remains a weak and inexact way of pointing to the relation of God and space. It is only of God that one can rightly speak of infinite immensity (Tho. Aq., *ST* 1 Q7), for only God is neither measured nor measurable.

The attributes of infinity, immensity, eternity, and omnipresence are closely intertwined. For *immensity* is infinity regarded from the viewpoint of space, whereas *eternity* is infinity regarded from the viewpoint of time. God's infinity is eternal in relation to time and immeasurable in relation to space. *Omnipresence* is God's mode of being present to all aspects of both space and time. Although God is present in all time and space, God is not locally limited to any particular time or space. God is everywhere and in every now (Calvin, *Inst.* 1.13.1, 21; Quenstedt, *TDP* 1:288). At first glance it may seem that talk of the divine immensity is far removed from Christian worship, yet rightly viewed this divine perfection powerfully lifts human thoughts toward a necessary being above all creaturely measurement (Teresa of Avila, *Way of Perfection* 19).

Eternity

That which is eternal is without beginning and without ending (Clement of Alexandria, *Stromata* 5.14). According to Boethius, divine eternity is "simultaneous and perfect possession of interminable life" (Consolation of Phil., 5.6; Augustine, True Religion, 40).

For God, the whole of time is viewed as *now* (Tho. Aq., *ST* 1 Q10.; Kierkegaard, *Phil. Frag.* 2). "With the Lord one day is like a thousand years and a thousand years like one day" (2 Pet. 3:8; Eusebius of Emesa, Cramer, CEC 99–100; Ps. 90:4).

God does not grow older with time. For humans who are time-bound, it is difficult to imagine that all time is present, as if now, to this divine consciousness. God is the inexorable one who outlasts every time. "You are the same, and your years have no end" (Ps. 102:27; Isa. 40:28, Rev. 1:4). "The guardian of Israel never slumbers, never sleeps" (Ps. 121:4). "'I am the Alpha and the Omega' says the Lord God, who is and who was and who is to come, the sovereign Lord of all" (Rev. 1:8). "The eternal God is your refuge, and underneath are the everlasting arms" (Deut. 33:27; Athenagoras, *A Plea for Chr.* 31).

God had no beginning, for who would be there to begin God? "From age to age everlasting thou art God" (Ps. 90:2). If God were imagined as a temporal being, God would have to have had a beginning. But God wholly transcends time without ceasing to be present to time. "The Lord, the everlasting God, creator of the wide world, grows neither weary nor faint" (Isa. 40:28). Abraham at Beersheba "invoked the Lord, the everlasting God, by name" (Gen. 21:33). The benediction of Jude prayed to One who is "before all time": "Now to the One who can keep you from falling and set you in the presence of his glory, jubilant and above reproach, to the only God our Savior, be glory and majesty, might and authority, through Jesus Christ our Lord, before all time, now, and for evermore. Amen" (Jude 25; Hilary of Arles, *Intro. Comm.* on Jude 25).

The faithful share in God's eternal life, but not in the same unbeginning sense that God lives eternally. The eternal I AM is before and after every space and time. God is the incomparable One present in every time. The eternity of God is not adequately described as an indefinite extension of temporal duration. Eternity is an attribute intrinsic to God and to God alone.

The same eternal One who is giver of time sovereignly chooses to enter into relationships with finite creatures, freely willing to participate in time, ordering and guiding the temporal process, not as if it were necessary to God's essential being, but as utterly contingent upon the divine (Cyril of Jerusalem, *Catech. Lect.* 4.5; Gregory of Nyssa, *Ag. Eunomius* 8.1; Wesley, *On Eternity*).

Those who are time-bound in every moment of consciousness may tend understandably to think of eternity as infinite duration, but this is an inexact idea. Since human reason and experience are so saturated with the assumption of time, it is difficult for the time-bound to fathom this mystery.

Only by feeble analogies can humans think of time as God thinks of time: Eternity is like a circle that continues endlessly in the same line, yet its circumference can be divided and measured. It is as if God were on a mountain watching a river. Humans see the flow of this river only from a particular point on the bank, but God, as if from high above, sees the river in its whole extent, at every point, simultaneously (Hilary, *On Trin.* 12.39; Calvin, *Inst.* 2.8–10).

The incarnation of God in the flesh bestows decisive significance upon all time. God the Son inhabits human flesh without ceasing to be eternal (Hilary, *On Trin.* 3; Nemesius, *On Nature of Man* 3). As in creation God is manifested in time, so in the incarnation God is manifested bodily in the flesh. Just as the Son does not stop being God while becoming human—feeling, experiencing, and acting as a human being—so does the Father not cease to be God while engaging in active relationship with unfolding time, acting as God in and through the conditions of time (Augustine, *Trin.* 14; *Letters* 143.7; Tho. Aq., *ST* 1 Q10).

God's Joy in Simply Being

God finds eternal joy in being. There can be no desire to "cease to be" in One who is insurmountably blessed and wise. God could never wish to end God's own life. That would be unthinkable, since inconsistent with God's blessed enjoyment of life. God exists in the fullest imaginable sense.

Simply being is a source of infinite enjoyment to one who incomparably *is*. God would never yearn to be less than God in full plenitude. God would never despair over simply being God in the fullest sense conceivable. The joy that comes from being is eternal joy. Thus it is said that God is infinitely happy simply and eternally to *be* (Ex. 3:14; Hilary, *Trin.*, 1.5; Tho. Aq., *ST* 1 Q26).

God has set eternity in the heart of humanity, yet it remains characteristic of the human finiteness that it "cannot find out what God has done from the beginning to the end" (Eccl. 3:11). We glimpse the eternal only in part and await the end of history in which the purposes of the eternal One are to be made fully clear: "Now we see only puzzling reflections in a mirror, but then"—that is, when the divine purpose is finally revealed at the end of history—"we shall see face to face. My knowledge now is partial; then it will be whole, like God's knowledge of me" (1 Cor. 13:12, 13; Didymus the Blind, *Montanist Oracles, On the Trin.* 103.2).

The Living God

To Be Incomparably Alive is God's Nature

The living God (*chai Elōhīm, Theo zōntos*) is the Subject of holy Scripture (1 Sam. 17:26; Ps. 42:2; Matt. 16:16; 1 Thess. 1:9; Heb. 12:22; Rev. 7:2). God's unutterable aliveness is contrasted with the immobility and impotence of "the gods." Jeremiah spoke of God (*Elōhīm*), in contrast to humanly fashioned idols, as "God in truth, a living [*chai*] God" (Jer. 10:10). Idols do not live, except in the mind's eye of mortals (Ps. 115:3–9). "The gods who did not make heaven and earth shall perish from the earth" (Jer. 10:11). In response to the incomparable aliveness of God, the psalmist exclaimed: "My whole being cries out with joy to the living God" (Ps. 84:2). Hence classical Christian teachers sought to clarify the sense in which it is confessed that God is alive and that God lives (Irenaeus, *Ag. Her.* 3.6; Cyril of Jerusalem, *Catech. Lect.* 18.29).

Life is that which differentiates a plant, animal, or human being from something that is dead—inorganic, nonliving matter (Tho. Aq., *ST* 1 Q18). God's being is intrinsically characterized by life, by being alive (Gregory of Nyssa, *Ag. Eunomius* VIII.5; Tho. Aq., *ST* 1 Q18). It cannot be properly conceived that God could die, because life is intrinsic to God, an attribute of the divine essence. Even when we despair of life (Job 9:21; 2 Cor. 1:8), God continues to give us life (Kierkegaard, *Sickness unto Death*). The life of God is the eternal, underived vitality of God's being.

It is God's very nature to be alive, so much so that God is properly known as the life of all that lives (Chrysostom, *Comm. on John* 47; Calvin, *Inst.* 2.3.20; Quenstedt, *TDP* 1: 289; Watson, *TI* 1:350). John's Gospel proclaimed that God the Father "has life-giving power in himself" (John 5:26; Novatian, *Treatise Concerning the Trin.* 14).

God's way of being alive is distinguishable from other forms of life. Plants, animals, and humans enjoy life at different scales of consciousness, movement, and self-determination. But in all plants, animals, and humans, bodily life ends in death. From the moment of conception, the processes of decay and death are at work in our bodies. Not so in God's life. God's life is eternally alive. God's life is not only without end but without beginning. For before anything was alive, God was alive (Gen. 1:1). When this world is gone, God remains alive (Luke 1:33; Heb. 7:3; Chrysostom, *Comm. on Hebrews* 12). "He is himself the universal giver of life and breath and all else" (Acts 17:25, 26; Chrysostom, *Comm. on Acts* 38). That which is alive has soul, or aliveness. Insofar as creatures are alive, they share in the life of God (Augustine, *Conf.* 10.5; Tertullian, *On the Soul*).

It is the living God to whom the worshiping community prays. God is present in unceasing spontaneity and limitless energy. The tetragrammaton (YHWH) points to God's incomparable aliveness (Origen, *OFP* 1. 3). Not only is God living, but also the source of our life—active and tireless (Isa. 40:28; Ps. 121:4). God is unfailingly alert and aware, as distinguished from "the gods," who, without life, are without consciousness or power (Hilary, *On Trin.* 8.43).

The Living God Is Eternally Active

It is an active, engaged God who is portrayed in Scripture, not quiescent, not merely letting creation be or leaving humans alone to their own devices (Irenaeus, *Ag. Her.* 3.5; Augustine, *CG* 5.11; Calvin, *Inst.* 2.3.10). The essence of God is known through God's energies and activities (Gregory of Nyssa, *Ag. Eunomius* 1. 18). God's will is manifested in God's actions (melākāh, energeia, through energies, operations, workings). History, according to the Hebraic view, is the story of the acts of God (Deut. 11:7; 1 Sam. 12:7; Ps. 150:2). God is active from the beginning to the end of time.

God is willing to allow companionate willing creatures. God's willing is eternally operative. God's power is never static, but always working, ever active, eternally in motion, never immobilized, never stalemated, never depressed (Isa. 40:1; Jer. 27:1; Tho. Aq., *ST* 1 Q3.1, 2; *SCG* 1. 13; Luther, *Comm. on Galatians*).

The Majesty of God

It is this sovereign One who deals intimately with creation, this infinite One who nurtures finitude, this immeasurable One who cares about the smallest sparrow, this eternal One who sustains time.

Relational Attributes Displaying God's Presence, Knowledge, and Power in the World

We have spoken above of primary or essential attributes. The ensuing attributes speak of God as One who freely brings the world into being and enters into a relation with the world.

We are now recounting those qualities that display God's way of relating to the world of creatures: being present to them, knowing them, and influencing them.

Since these characteristics all presuppose creatures in relation to their Creator, they are called relational attributes of God. Unlike God's eternality, these attributes cannot be conceived apart from God's relation to the world. For how could God be conceived to be omnipresent without a world to which to be present? Or omnipotent without a world through which the divine influence is everywhere felt?

No being relates to the world as God does. The unique ways God touches the world are called relational attributes (Quenstedt, *LT* 1.289; Watson, *TI* 1:365). In these relationships, God is accommodating to creatures' limits and capacities (Hilary, *On Trin.* 4.17, 6.16, 8.43; Heppe, *RD*:57; Schmid, *DT*:177).

Consensual Christian teaching typically begins by confessing these three relational attributes: God's ubiquitous *presence* in the world (omnipresence); God's complete *knowledge* of the world and time (omniscience); and God's almighty *power* (omnipotence).

God's Way of Being Near: Omnipresence

Paul preached that God is "not far from each one of us, for in him we live and move, in him we exist" (Acts 17:27–28; Augustine, *Trin.* 16). The holy God is present in all things: "'Am I a God nearby,' declares the Lord, 'and not a God far away? Can anyone hide in secret places so that I cannot see him?' declares the Lord. 'Do I not fill heaven and earth?' declares the Lord" (Jer. 23:24).

No particle is so small that God is not fully present to it. No galaxy is so vast that God does not circumscribe it. No space is without the divine presence. God is in touch with every aspect of creation. God cannot be excluded from any location or object in creation (Augustine, *Greatness of the Soul* 34; *Second Helvetic Conf.* 3; Wesley, *The Omnipresence of God*).

Every finite object exists in some place. Only God is able to *be* everywhere without being limited to some specific location.

We measure the size of finite things by how much space they occupy. God does not fit into these categories of location. God's presence is not simply in one location, as is ours, but all locations, and transcending all locations (Cyril of Jerusalem, *Catech. Lect.* 4.5). In worship we receive the memory of One who is the intimate companion of our existence but, at the same time, the intimate companion of all other beings, while transcending each and all (Athanasius, *Incarnation of the Word* 1. 8–10).

The Christian teaching of God's presence everywhere is more than an abstract idea without personal significance. It is an intimate comfort to those who pray to know of and experience the divine availability (Teresa of Avila, *Interior Castle* I). God is a very present help in time of need (Ps. 46:1; Rom. 8:39). To affirm that God is high and lifted up above creaturely reality does not imply that God is absent from creatures (Gregory of Nazianzus, *Second Theol. Orat.* 11–21; Calvin, *Inst.* 1.11.3).

The most holy One is precisely the One who is most personally near: "Thus speaks the high and exalted one, whose name is holy, who lives for ever: I dwell in a high and holy place with him who is broken and humble in spirit, to revive the spirit of the humble, to revive the courage of the broken" (Isa. 57:15; Jerome, Comm. on Is. 16.11). But being near one place does not imply that God is absent from another (Jer. 23:23). "The Lord looks out from heaven, he sees the whole race of men; he surveys from his dwelling-place all the inhabitants of the earth. It is he who fashions the hearts of all men alike, who discerns all that they do" (Ps. 33:13, 14; Tho. Aq., *ST* 1 Q8).

The *presence* of God was thought by classical exegetes to encompass the widest possible range of creaturely activity—natural, active, conscious, moral, bodily, sacramental, and sacred. Scholastic traditions distinguished modes of God's presence:

> God is *naturally* present in every aspect of the natural order, every level of causality, every fleeting moment and momentous event of natural history (Ps. 8:3; Isa. 40:12; Origen, *Ag. Celsus* 7.34; Cyril of Jerusalem, *Catech. Lect.* 4.5).

> God is *actively* present in every event of history as provident guide of human affairs (Ps. 48:7 f.; Augustine, *CG* 7.30).

> God is in a special way *attentively* present to those who call upon his name, intercede for others, who adore God, who petition, who pray earnestly for forgiveness (Matt. 18:19–20; Acts 17:27; Cyprian, *Epistles* 7).

> God is *judicially* present in moral awareness, through conscience (Ps. 48:1, 2; Athanasius, *Ag. Heathen* 41).

> God is *bodily* present in the incarnation of his Son, Jesus Christ (John 1:14; Col. 2:9; Hilary, *On Trin.* 8.24).

God is *sacramentally* present in the Eucharist, and through the means of grace in the church, the body of Christ (Eph. 2:12; John 6:56; Ambrose, *On the Mysteries* 5).

God is *sacredly* present and becomes known in special places where God chooses to meet us, places that become set apart by the faithful, remembering community (1 Cor. 11:23–29), where it may be said: "Truly the Lord is in this place" (Gen. 28:16; Gen. 23:18; Matt. 18:20; Augustine, *CG* 22.29).

In all these ways God is present to the world. God is present to creatures in more ways than creatures can recognize (Augustine, *Letters* 137.2).

God's Way of Knowing: Omniscience

Only God knows all creation omnisciently—altogether beginning to end—without limitation or condition. The psalmist praised God's wisdom as "beyond all telling" (Ps. 147:5; Ps. 94:9–11; Ps. 139) and God's understanding as immeasurable (Ps. 147:4–5; Augustine, On Psalms 90.7.1–10). God's incomparable way of knowing knows the end of things even from the beginning: "I reveal the end from the beginning, from ancient times I reveal what is to be; I say, 'My purpose shall take effect, I will accomplish all that I please.'" (Isa. 46:9, 10; Clement of Alex., *Stromata* 6.17).

Jesus taught his disciples: "Your Father knows what your needs are before you ask him" (Matt. 6:8, Anon., Incomplete Work on Matthew, Hom.13). Paul exclaimed: "O depth of wealth, wisdom, and knowledge in God! How unsearchable his judgments, how untraceable his ways! Who knows the mind of the Lord? Who has been his counselor?" (Rom. 11:33, 34). The New Testament constantly echoes the theme of the fully aware God found in the psalms and prophets: "There is nothing in creation that can hide from him; everything lies naked and exposed to the eyes of the One with whom we have to reckon" (Heb. 4:13). One who is greater than our self-condemning conscience "knows all" (1 John 3:20; Augustine, *CG* 5.9; *Enchiridion* 104).

How can we get our sluggish intellects in touch with the awesome conception that God knows all? The divine omniscience is best viewed as the infinite consciousness of God in relation to all possible objects of knowledge. God knows past, present, and future (John of Damascus, *OF* 2.10). God knows external events and inward motivations (Hilary, *On Trin.* 9.29). God does not perceive fragmentarily as humans perceive, as if from a particular nexus of time, but knows exhaustively, in eternal simultaneity (Irenaeus, *Ag. Her.* 2.26–8; Catherine of Siena, *Prayers* 7). God looks to the ends of the earth, sees the whole of the heavens (Isa. 46; Job 28), knows the secrets of the heart (Ps. 44:21). "You have traced my journey and my resting places, and are familiar with all my paths. For there is not a word on my tongue but you, Lord, know them all" (Ps. 139:3, 4). "Such knowledge is beyond my understanding, so high that I cannot reach it" (v. 6). "Darkness is not dark for you and night is luminous as day" (v. 12).

Jesus taught: the very hairs of our heads are numbered by the Father (Matt. 10:30; Chrysostom, *Hom. on Matt.*, Hom. 34.2–3), suggesting that every discrete aspect of personal existence is known to God (Justin Martyr, *First Apol.* 12). No sparrow falls without God's recognition (Matt. 10:29; Kierkegaard, *Gospel of Suffering*). God searches the hearts of all (Rom. 8:27).

We know some things, but God knows incomparably more, greater, and better (Ambrose, *To Gratian on Chr. Faith* 5.6; Augustine, *On Trin.* 15.22; *CG* 12.18; Tho. Aq., *ST* 1 Q14.13). "The eyes of the Lord are everywhere" (Prov. 15:3; Benedict of Nursia, Rule, 19), implying that God sees all simultaneously. God knows objects as distanced from one another, but not from God, for there can be no distance of any object from God (Augustine, *CG* 5.11). God's knowing is said to be (*a*) eternally actual, not merely possible; (*b*) eternally perfect, as distinguished from a knowledge that begins, increases, decreases, or ends; (*c*) complete instead of partial; and (*d*) both direct and immediate, instead of indirectly reflected or mediated (Tho. Aq., *SCG* 1. 63–71).

Pantheism has exaggerated this closeness so as to imagine that God is indistinguishable from all things; hence, the pantheistic idea of God holds that God is conscious only in and through the consciousness of finite creatures. Such knowing cannot be infinite knowing. This is why pantheism has been so often rejected by Christian teaching (Hippolytus, *Refutation of All Her.* 1. 21; Augustine, *Concerning Faith of Things Not Seen*). For in seeking to affirm that God is in all things, it forgets the biblical premise that God is prior to, above, and beyond all things.

The wisdom of God is God's incomparable ability to order all things in the light of good, to adjust causes to effects, and means to ends, so that the divine purposes are firm and never finally thwarted (Prov. 2:2; Isa. 10:13; 1 Cor. 1:21; Athanasius, *On the Incarnation* 15; Calvin, *Inst.* 1.16).

The Mystery of Divine Foreknowing

God foreknows the use of free will, yet this foreknowledge does not determine events. Rather, what God foreknows is determined by what happens, part of which is affected by free will.

God knows what will happen, but does not unilaterally determine each and every event immediately—that would dishonor human freedom and the reliability of secondary causes. God fully understands and knows all these specific secondary determining causes that are at work in the natural order, but that does not imply that merely by fiat God constantly acts so as to overrule or circumvent these causes. God's merely foreknowing these causes does not negate or undermine their causal reality (Athanasius, *On the Incarnation of the Word* 1–6; Hilary, *Trin.* 9.61–75). Hence God's foreknowledge does not imply God's omnicausality or absolute determination so as to eliminate all other creaturely wills. God knows what other wills are doing by divine permission (Justin Martyr, *First Apol.* 45–53). God's knowledge is precisely of free choice, of human and creaturely willing (Athanasius, *Four Discourses Ag. Arians* 3.30; Augustine, *CG* 5.9; Luis de Molina, *Scientia Media*, RPR:424–6).

God not only grasps and understands what actually will happen, but also what could happen under varied possible contingencies. If God's knowing is infinite, God knows even the potential effects of hypothetical but unactualized possibilities, just as well as God knows what has or will come to be. God knows what would have been had things been otherwise and had different historical decisions been made (Augustine, *On Spirit and Letter* 58; *Ag. Two Letters of Pelagians* 3.25–4.4; Calvin, *Inst.* 3.21, 22). This assumes that God knows, easily and without effort, an infinite number of alternative universes that could have been but as yet are not.

This affirmation is encompassed in the celebration of God's omniscience. God knows not only what is, but what possibly might be, yet is not, and what can be but will never be, and what might eventually be chosen but as yet remains undecided and subject to creaturely freedom. This has been called "God's knowledge of the hypothetical" or *scientia media*. It is God's knowledge of the middle or hypothetical ground between freedom and necessity, which is neither the necessary knowledge that God has of himself (*scientia necessaria*), nor the knowledge that God has of the freedom of his creatures (*scientia libera*, Tho. Aq., *ST* 1 Q14; Watson, *TI* 1: 375). Hence it is said that "God's necessary knowledge precedes every free act of the divine will; free knowledge follows the act of will" (Alsted, *Theologia Scholastica* 98, RD:79; Augustine, *On Spirit and Letter* 58).

Suppose the opposite were true, that God's knowing were almost infinite but not quite; and that God knew only what has happened and will happen, but not what might have happened. Such a "God" would hardly be omniscient. Suppose that God knew what free agents have chosen and will choose, but not what they will consider choosing but reject. This is a misleading view that would block God from awareness of the inward depths of the free subject self struggling to decide between possibilities. It fails to grasp the biblical vision of God who has "searched me and known me. You know when I sit down and when I rise up; you discern my thoughts from far away. You search out my path and my lying down, and are acquainted with all my ways. Even before a word is on my tongue, O Lord, you know it completely" (Ps. 139:1–4).

Consensual teaching has thought hard about the difficult question of how God's omniscience correlates with the contingent freedom of creatures. If God knows what I later will do, does that take away my freedom? Although it may at first seem so, the consensus of classical Christian teaching is to answer no. Human freedom remains freedom, significantly self-determining, even if divinely foreknown (John of Damascus, *OF* 4.21; Augustine, *CG* 5.9).

God's foreknowledge of events does not destroy the reality of other influences than the divine. God knows whether a marigold seed will bear a flower, but that knowledge does not override the conditions that would affect the growth of the plant. God does not arbitrarily take the place of natural forces and levels of causality that God himself has graciously provided creatures.

God foresaw that Jerusalem would fall to the Babylonians. But the faithful are not imagining that foreknowledge in itself directly or unilaterally caused the defeat without any other historical, human, or natural forces or influences at work.

The biblical principle underlying such distinctions is "God makes all His works good, but each becomes of its own choice good or evil" (John of Damascus, *OF* 4.21; Gen. 1–3). Suppose it were asserted that God's knowledge of future events completely destroys the effectiveness of the free self-determining influences that God foresees. That would result in a fatalism that undercuts human freedom. That would be tantamount to asserting that there is only one will in the universe, the will of God, and that no other wills exist. That is an extreme view, contrary to Christian teaching about creation, human freedom, self-determination, and human dignity (Luis de Molina, *Scientia Media*, RPR:424–30).

Origen's debate with Celsus was the prototype of all these arguments. It grew out of an exegetical issue: Did Judas freely commit his traitorous deed, or since it was prophesied in Scripture (Ps. 108), must God be held responsible, since God foreknew it? Celsus argued the latter. Origen argued both that Judas willed it and that God foreknew it. "Celsus imagines that an event, predicted through foreknowledge, comes to pass because it was predicted; but we do not grant this, maintaining that he who foretold it was not the cause of its happening" (*Ag. Celsus* 2.20). It is foolish to say that in whatever God foreknows there is no freedom, thought Origen, for it is precisely the acts of free will that God foreknows.

A related potential misunderstanding flows from this question: If God is unchangeable, how can God know duration or succession? The classic consensual answer: If God is infinite in knowing the world, God must be aware of duration and succession, even though not bound by them. If God did not understand duration and succession, God would understand even less about time than we do.

God does not cease being eternal in the process of knowing time. God views all times as eternal now. God thus beholds and understands the process of temporal succession. We do not know next year until next year, but God knows next year already. We learn only successively through experiencing, but God does not have to learn something God already knows. We know things in part and by pieces, but God knows things fully, all at once, while yet being aware of how temporal things slowly come to be or evolve. What we consider to be future events are to God not future but present events, so what we call divine foreknowledge is to God simply present knowledge (Tho. Aq., *SCG* 1. 70, 71; Calvin, *Inst.* 3.22). Summing up: God *conceives* all things simultaneously but *perceives* all things in terms of their duration and succession (Watson, *TI* 1:371; Pope, *Compend.* 83).

God's Way of Influencing: Omnipotence

God's influence upon the world is unlike any other mode of influence—unlimited in capacity, though spare in correction. Omnipotence may be defined as the perfect ability of God to do all things that are consistent with the divine character (Athanasius, *Ag. Heathen* 28–47; Augustine, *CG* 5.10). God can do all that God wills to do. Omnipotence points to the necessary form of power pertinent to the One worthy to be worshipped (Hilary, *On Trin.* 3.6, 9.72; Quenstedt, *LT* 1:289). God is not limited in any of the divine attributes by anything external to himself. No power in history has any other empowering source ultimately than God (Ps. 59:11–16; Origen, *Comm. on Rom.* 13.1; Calvin, *Inst.* 1.5).

"Almighty" refers to God's way of expressing His will. It is how God alone exercises influence: Everywhere and over all. This extent of the influence of God is called *omnipotence*, that is, over all things, yet over all things in such a way as to empower and enable the freedom of other things besides God. This does not imply that God wills in every instance everything that God can possibly will, for that would suggest that God is capable only of willing but not also capable of withholding influence (Clement of Alex., *Exhort. to the Heathen* 4; Tho. Aq., *ST* 1 Q25.1; *ST* 1 Q19).

The Scriptures abound in expressions of the almighty power of God. "The Lord God omnipotent reigns" (Rev. 19:6). The creeds confess: "I believe in God the Father *Almighty*" (*Der Balyzeh Papyrus*, *CC*, 19; Athanasius, *Defense of the Nicene Definition* 3; Cyril of Jerusalem, *Catech. Lect.* 6).

God's power employs natural, historical, and human means for its accomplishment, but the use of means does not imply that God is limited by the restricted means that God alone created and freely sustains (*Clementina, Recog.* 8.1–30; Gregory of Nyssa, *On "Not Three Gods"*).

God's power is most fully known through acts of self-giving love, as made known on the cross (Col. 2:14, 15). It is a power that also works through limited, but real, finite historical processes. God's power is so great that it is non-defensive and able even to allow other freedoms to challenge it without being anxious about its own security or identity (Gen. 11:1–9; Theophilus of Antioch, *To Autolycus* 1. 4; Augustine, *CG* 11.1). God is at ease with human competencies and incompetencies, free to laugh about desperate human pretensions (Ps. 2:4). The nations are, in the presence of God, less than nothing, like a drop in the bucket (Isa. 40:15).

Humans may fail to accomplish an act of willing by either failing to know what is to be done; or knowing what should be done but not willing it; or lacking the power to do what is willed. God's power lacks none of these deficiencies of will since God enjoys untrammeled awareness of what can be done. God wills that the good be done, even if beyond the range of our finite perceptions. God has the power to accomplish what God wills (Irenaeus, *Ag. Her.* 1. 22; Tertullian, *Ag. Hermogenes*, 8, 17; Tho. Aq., *SCG* 1. 72–88).

Is Anything Too Hard for the Lord?

When it was announced to Abraham that Sarah at ninety would have a son and become "the mother of nations," Abraham laughed, and Sarah laughed too (Gen. 17:15–17; 18:12). Then Yahweh said: "Is anything too hard for the Lord?" (Gen. 18:14). After the captivity of Jerusalem in the sixth century BC, most thought it utterly impossible that the course of history would reverse and their land would be returned to them. It was then that Jeremiah affirmed his confidence in God, that "There is nothing too hard for you" (Jer. 32:17). Having spoken of how hard it is for the rich to enter the kingdom of God, Jesus, when asked who could be saved, similarly affirmed the boundless power of God: "For men this is impossible; but everything is possible for God" (Matt. 19:26; Chrysostom, *Hom. on Matt.*, Hom. 63.2). Nothing that God conceives and wills to do is beyond God's ability or power to accomplish (Augustine, On the Creed, LF:563; Calvin, *Inst.* 2.7.5).

Yet God's power is sometimes alleged in wild and imprecise ways implying paradoxical riddles: Can God do that which is logically self-contradictory? Can God abolish the past? Can God make a square into a triangle? Can God make a stone larger than God can lift? (Origen, *Ag. Celsus* 5.23). Each of these familiar trip-up questions hinges on a hidden comic premise: To answer either yes or no without inquiring into the absurdity or contradiction presumed in the question is to fall into an unnecessary trap that can easily be avoided.

There is only one way of speaking properly of any restriction upon God's power that does not detract from God's almighty power. The Bible has identified it concisely: God "cannot deny himself" (2 Tim. 2:13; Augustine, *Sermons* 214.4; Tho. Aq., *ST* I–IIae Q100; Calvin, *Inst.* 3.15.2). This key biblical principle of the divine self-constraint may be expressed in various forms:

- God would not do that which is inconsistent with what God knows, or repugnant to God's goodness, or not in accord with other qualities of God's character (Chrysostom, *Comm. on Timothy* 5).

- Scripture maintains that it is "impossible for God to lie" (Heb. 6:18; Calvin, *Inst.* 1.17), for to lie would be inconsistent with God's goodness (Tho. Aq., *ST* Q25, I). God cannot deceive himself, for this would be counter to God's integrity, congruity, omniscience, and constancy.

- God cannot cease being, or even desire to cease being, because that would be inconsistent with God's very being as eternal and blessed, eternally happy in the divine enjoyment of being (Augustine, *CG* 5.10).

If God is incomparably merciful, God will not do anything that lacks mercy. God "cannot" be not good. God "cannot" be unjust (Tho. Aq., *SCG* 2.25). "Cannot" is here expressed in hypothetical quotation marks, for aside from that which is inconsistent with God's being, there is nothing that God cannot do, hence it is a kind of comic game with language even to play-like saying "God cannot." It is God's nature to act in a way that is congruent with God's essential being and character (Gregory of Nyssa, *Great Catech.*, prologue; Pearson, *Apostles' Creed* 1; Petavius, *De Deo* 5.5–11; Suarez, *Summa.* 1.5.1; Wesley, *WJW* VII:265).

Omnipotence does not include the power of God to act in ungodly ways (Tho. Aq., *ST* 1 Q25). It is only a lack of imagination that might prematurely call this a limitation on the power of God. The essential idea of omnipotence is that God has adequate ability to do whatever the being and power and knowledge and goodness of God requires. There are some things that God either could not do without denying himself, or would not do being who God is (Tho. Aq., *ST* 1 Q25; Calvin, *Inst.* 1.4.2; 1.14.3).

It is no diminution of the divine majesty to acknowledge that God "cannot" do that which by definition intrinsically cannot be done. Suppose someone asserts that God can do something that is intrinsically contradictory or absurd. That does not increase the power of God. Rather it traps the idea of God in a comic premise. Contradictions are by definition unable to be actualized (such as that A may be both A and not A), so what good does it do to elevate them to some presumed dignity by the spurious assertion that God can actualize them? (Tho. Aq., *SCG* 2.25).

Hence it is hardly an offense against the divine integrity to insist that God does not know what is intrinsically unintelligible (Alvin Plantinga, *God, Freedom, and Evil*:39–41). It is no disparagement to the divine omniscience or constancy that God knows changing contingencies as changing contingencies. Rather it would be an offense to God's knowledge to assert that God could not know contingencies, or to God's presence to assert that God could not be present in finite localities. Similarly, it is no offense to divine omnipotence that God "cannot" do that which by definition cannot be done (Anselm, *Proslog.* 7.12). The New Testament celebrates God's capacity to do *more* than we can conceive: "Now to him who is able to do immeasurably more than all we can ask or conceive" (Eph. 3:2).

God's Power Permits Other Powers to Act Through Secondary Causes

God's power is not bound always to exercise every conceivable form of power in every situation. God has also the power to withhold influence temporarily, and to allow creaturely powers to influence, and other wills to have their own effect (Tho. Aq., *ST* 1 Q25). God even allows wills contrary to the divine will to act and express influence within fleeting temporal limits. Wills that are able to stand but liable to fall are permitted to fall (Wesley, *WJW* 6:313–25; 7:335–44).

The worshiping community understands that the all-powerful God paradoxically sustains in being those creatures that oppose God's authority and goodness (Westminster *Conf.* 5,6, *CC*:200–2). When fallible wills fall, God continues to act to nurture, support, encourage, and redeem these wills, and finally to consummate his purpose by bringing good out of evil (Justin Martyr, *On the Sole Government of God*; Westminster *Conf.* 7–15; Wesley, *WJW* 10:361; 6:506–13).

Human freedom is grounded in, permitted by, and derived from the power of God. Human freedom can assert itself within ordinary causal chains against God's power, but only in limited and fragmentary ways that can never finally alter or challenge the power of God (Augustine, *CG* 11.12; Calvin, *Inst.* 1.18.1, 2).

Classical pastoral care has wisely distinguished God's *absolute* power from God's *ordered* power (that is: God's power as expressed through the orderly conditions of nature). God's absolute power, in classical theology, is without limit and can be exercised without mediating causes in the creation, as in miracle or direct agency. God's ordinate power works through the order of nature by means of secondary causes and influences (Origen, *OFP* 2.9; Watson, *TI* 1:355).

The effective power of God is exercised uniformly through the orderly operation of secondary causes in a reliable, intelligible, natural causal order (Lactantius, *On the Workmanship of God*; Tho. Aq., *SCG* 1. 70). Absolute, unmediated divine power is not the usual way we experience the power of God. Rather, it is usually expressed through mediated powers in nature and history.

God works through the order of nature without denying God's absolute power. Yet it is also within God's power to transcend the very natural law that God has freely provided. Although eighteenth-century rationalism wanted to rule out miracle, classical Christianity affirms that God is capable of transcending the very order that God has created (Augustine, *CG* 12.2;. C. S. Lewis, *Miracles*).

The Transcendent One Present in Our Midst

The unlimited presence, knowledge, and influence of God has often been summarized in a single idea: transcendence. God is the utterly transcendent One (Gregory of Nazianzus, Second *Theol. Orat.*) who is nonetheless incomparably present in our midst (Third *Theol. Orat.*; Calvin, *Inst.* 1.5.5; Wesley, *WJW* 10:361–63). Transcendence and immanence are not separable in the Hebraic faith. The very One who is beyond the finite and human is intimately manifested and warmly knowable within the human sphere.

It is a common misjudgment to take only one side of this equilibrium so as to miss the interfacing point: It is precisely the holy God who is *with* us. It is the transcendent God who is immanent, palpably indwelling in the human world (Athanasius, *Incarnation of the Word*; Tho. Aq., *God Knows Lowly Things*, *SCG* 1. 70). The Holy One (*gadosh*) of Israel is always understood to be "among you" (Isa. 12:6) as intimate partner in dialogue, "my refuge and defense" (Isa. 12:2).

The divine life defies rash comparisons. "'To whom then will you liken me, whom set up as my equal?' asks the Holy One" (Isa. 40:25; Tertullian, *Ag. Marcion*, 1.4). Yet, this One remains everywhere at home, every moment engaged, ceaselessly involved in the world. No one is a stranger to this all-present One. God shows through the events of human history the affection that the vine keeper shows toward the vineyard (Isa. 5:4).

The biblical tension between transcendence and immanence remains taut: The source of all things has the tenderness of a father (Hos. 11:1), the care of a mother (Isa. 49:15). This holy God above all has chosen to be radically empathic with human failings (John 1; Hilary, *On Trin.* 4.17; Tho. Aq., *ST* 1 Q25; Kierkegaard, *Training in Christianity*).

In speaking of God's presence, knowledge, and power in creation, we have identified *relational* divine attributes—those that emerge out of God's relation to the creation, distinguishable from divine qualities characteristic of the independent existence of God apart from creatures.

Summarizing the divine relational attributes:

- God's way of being with the world is omnipresence.

- God's way of knowing the world is omniscience.

- God's way of influencing the world is omnipotence.

3

THE CHARACTER
OF GOD

THE PERSONAL ATTRIBUTES are divine qualities, such as life, spirit, will, and freedom. God enjoys these perfectly, and communicates them to human beings in proportion to their capacity to receive them (Hilary, On *Trin.* 1.19, 4.2, VI.9; Augustine, *Trin.* 15.42; Tho. Aq., *ST* 1 Q29). Each step toward the clarification of divine attributes leads to greater personalization. With each step we move ever closer to discerning features of divine-human interaction.

God is free, living, active, spiritual, and personal, while not ceasing to be God—unsurpassably present, knowing, and influential. The consensus is searching for characterizations of God that are adequate to the divine reality attested in scripture (Tho. Aq., *ST* 1 Q6; Quenstedt, *TDP* 1:288).

To this point we have been considering only those characteristics of the divine life that are attested by Scripture (1) *as intrinsic to God alone* without reference to creatures—in that God is necessary, infinite, eternal, one, and alive—these are known as primary or *essential* attributes; and (2) as displaying God's way of being present to, knowing, and influencing the *cosmos* generally (omnipresence, omniscience, and omnipotence), known as *relational* attributes, conceivable primarily in relation to the world of creaturely beings. But in this chapter we are speaking of those attributes of the character of God that manifest qualities analogous to (3) *human* personality, freedom, and will.

The Divine Thou

God as Incomparably Personal

A personal relationship involves and requires an interactive speaking and listening relationship of free beings. Even though God's way of being a person far transcends human ways of being persons, nonetheless the divine-human encounter is portrayed in Scripture as a personal relationship of meeting, communication, becoming mutually committed, experiencing frustrations and failures, splitting up, and becoming reconciled again (Exod. 28:43; Num. 11:33; 1 Sam. 10:1–5; Pss. 4:1; 17:1; 74:1; Hos. 14:1; Irenaeus, *Ag. Her.* 2.1). All these are things that happen to persons.

Scripture portrays God as one who is self-determining, conscious, feeling, and willing. God has intricate, evolving relationships with other personal beings (Matt. 7:21; 26:39; Augustine, *Trin.* 15.42). God is known and celebrated in the life of prayer as personal, and understood by means of metaphors of human personal responsiveness (Matt. 6:10; John 6:38–40).

Persons by definition have feelings. Each one has an identifiable self, intellect, and capacity for response. God is represented in Scripture as having much of the psychological makeup of what we know as personhood: God speaks (Gen. 1:3), sees (Gen. 11:5), and hears (Ps. 94:9). By rough analogy with human feelings it is said that God can be angry (Deut. 1:37), jealous (Exod. 20:5), and compassionate (Ps. 111:4). God has intellect and emotion. No stone or abstract idea or amoeba can speak words, listen, care for others, get angry, respond to hurts. Only personal beings can experience these feelings (Origen, Homily 18.3; Tho. Aq., *ST* 1 Q29).

Although God is far more than what we can signify by our term *personal*, God is certainly not less than personal being. But what do we mean when we speak of God as "person"?

Two preliminary observations clear the way for the answer: God speaks as "I," and God has a *name*.

God Speaks as "I"

God can say "I." Whatever being can say "I" is a person. For knowing oneself or another as capable of saying "I" requires self-consciousness, intentionality, the will to communicate, and self-determination. Rocks and plants, however beautiful, cannot call themselves "I" because they lack the capacity for personal awareness. They lack words to say it. They lack the freedom to conceive it. This is why rocks and plants are so different from human beings and superpersonal intelligences (angeloi, angels) and God. All creatures share being, but all creatures do not share personhood.

A central feature of anyone who can say "I" is a memory that is sustained over varied experiences (Augustine, *Conf.* 1–3). Even with a vastly varied history of experience, the person remains an "I" throughout all those stages of development. I am different in experience from what I was as a child, but I still remain "me." I may choose one way in one moment, another later, but it is still me choosing differently. Memory helps me grasp the continuity in my choosing, and to identify what it means when I say "I." Memory binds together my awareness of my self as a history of choosing (Kierkegaard, *Either/Or* 2.2).

God is spoken of in Scripture as one who chooses, who has memory, who lives through a history of choosing, and whose character is known as One who has made certain choices. These are things that look like human personality, but God's personality is different, for God has an eternal memory of all things. God experiences all times in eternal simultaneity. God holds in unified integrity the awareness of all events. God's memory is in some ways like, but in more ways unlike, human memory.

There are times when God *seems* to have forgotten the faithful (Pss. 13:1; 44:24) and when God is earnestly asked to remember the people in their affliction (Lam. 3:19). Yet Scripture marveled that God would always remember the covenant, remaining ever faithful to it, even when the people had forgotten it (Gen. 9:15, 16; Lev. 26:42; Jer. 44:21; Gregory of Nazianzus, *Theol. Orat.* 28.28).

God Reveals His Name

God is not a nameless energy or abstract idea. Hence God is not an "it." God is inadequately described by impersonal terms such as ground of being or the Unconditioned (Tillich, *Syst. Theol.* I), external infinity (S. Alexander, Space, Time, and Deity, 2:353), Reality Idealized (E. S. Ames, Religion:153–55), the Absolute (Hegel, Phenomenology of Mind), or the Creative Event (H. N. Wieman, Source of the Common Good). For to none of these abstract descriptions is a personal name attached.

God has a name. This points to a major difference between persons and things. To Moses, God's name is revealed with clues embedded in the name itself. Calling Yahweh *by name* is something quite different than speaking abstractly of an "unmoved Mover," or trying to pray to "Reality Idealized," or petitioning to an undifferentiated "ground of being" (Aristotle, *Metaphy.*; Ames, *Religion*; Tillich, *Syst. Theol.* I), all of which duck away from naming God with a personal name. Different from these is the God of Scripture, whose name is constantly being revealed through events to persons in history. "How wrong it would be if we were to believe people's testimonies on the basis of what others say about them, yet not believe God's Word when he talks about himself" (Ambrose, On Abraham, 1.3.21).

The history of revelation is the history of the meeting of named beings, not unnameable abstractions or distilled ideas. The Pentateuch reports that as early as Cain and Abel, persons "began to invoke the Lord by name" (Gen. 4:26). Scriptural accounts constantly call God by name, and therefore assume a divine-human interpersonal relationship, a meeting between personal beings (Irenaeus, *Ag. Her.* 3.1; Tertullian, *Ag. Praxeas* 17).

Pronouncing the divine name of the incomparably holy One (Yahweh, El, Adōnaï) was regarded as a most perilous matter. "You shall not make wrong use of the name of the Lord your God; the Lord will not leave unpunished the man who misuses his name" (Exod. 20:7). Each of the various names God allows himself to be called was thought to reveal something decisive of the character of the One named. It was no small or accidental matter that God revealed the divine name as Yahweh or El or Elōhīm or El Shaddaï, for these names provided trace indications of the unique sort of person God is (Exod. 20:24; 23:21; Ezek. 43:7–8; Calvin, *Inst.* 1.10.3; 1.13.3–4).

Impersonal Terms Are Inadequate for God

Since God is a person, God cannot properly be thought of without using personal terms (Hilary, On *Trin.* 3.23; Augustine, *Conf.* 5).

This point was vigorously pursued by early Christian teachers. It became an important feature part of the careful regulation of Christian language about God. It helped to defend Christian teaching

- from pantheism, the view that God is the world (which cannot see any difference between God and the world, or between creator and creature)

- from polytheism (which abuses the analogy between human personality and divine personality by unilaterally attributing to God human limitations and faults)

- from agnosticism (which denies that anyone can know the divine person even if such a person existed)

- from atheism (which denies that any eternal personal being exists)

The fullness of personhood exists in God alone. It is not that God's personhood is derived from human understandings of personality. That would convey an inadequate reflection of the sovereign freedom which is found incomparably in God and only inadequately in ourselves (Augustine, *Trin.* 15.42; Barth, *CD* 1/1:279, 3/4:245; Oden, *KC* 4:114). Yet this is not to deny that human beings, too, have a refraction of personhood, which is not wholly dissimilar from God's personhood (Tho. Aq., *ST* 1 Q29) since humanity is created in the image of God.

God Is Spirit

That "God is Spirit" is the most direct definition of God that Jesus offered (John 4:24). Jesus was speaking to a woman of Samaria, teaching that "those who worship him must worship in spirit and in truth," correcting the idea that the worship of God is confined to particular places such as Mount Gerizim (Chrysostom, Comm. on St. John 33–34).

Pneuma (spirit), like the wind, is known only by its effects (Tertullian, *On the Soul* 11–12). God is invisible, for "No one has seen God at any time" (John 1:18; Gregory of Nazianzus, *Second Theol. Orat.*; Calvin, *Inst.* 1.13.14; 2.2.20). God as Spirit cannot be objectified in the same way that bodily and physical matter may be viewed as objects (Origen, *OFP* 1.1).

God as pure Spirit is "the Father of our spirits" (Heb. 12:9), who creates other self-determining, responsible beings, and enters into interpersonal interaction and communion with them (Augustine, *Trin.* 8.3). The ascription of spirituality to God awakens a profound rejoicing in the human spirit, along with a humble acknowledgment that the human spirit is akin to God the Spirit (Clement of Alex., *Stromata* 4.3). It is also a guard against the demeaning of humanity and the physical or temporal localization of God (Athenagoras, *A Plea for the Chr.* 15).

Intellect, affect, and volition are essential powers of personal spirit. We know this because we possess in lesser degree these competencies that God possesses in completeness (Tertullian, *On the Resurrection of the Flesh* 7, 8; Augustine, *CG* 13.24). It is due to our own individual experience of feeling that we can know that God also feels. It is from our own acts of willing that we can understand in some small measure that God has sovereign freedom.

Christian teaching does not conclude, however, that the human ability to think, feel, and will is capable of providing a fully adequate understanding of God's mind, experience, and will. Rather, our natural analogies stand constantly under the guidance and critique of Scripture, and of the ecumenical tradition's exegesis of Scripture (Tho. Aq., *ST* 1 Q13; Calvin, *Inst.* 1.13.20). Moreover, it is on the basis of God's knowing, feeling, and willing that it is possible rightly to consider and understand human knowing, feeling, and willing (Augustine, *Enchiridion* 26; Barth, *CD* 3/4; Oden, *KC* 2).

In reducing the reality of God to the finite world, pantheism regards the world as God's body indistinguishably. In doing so it has met constant resistance from classic Christian teaching. The first commandment forbids reducing God to a visible image or idol or object of the senses (Exod. 20:3). In doing so, it makes a decisive moral claim based on the divine attribute of spirituality. That God is Spirit means God is invisible and incorporeal, not a body, not reducible to matter, not an object of empirical investigation, not evident to our eyes (Tho. Aq., *ST* 1 Q3): "On the day when the Lord spoke to you out of the fire on Horeb, you saw no figure of any kind; so take good care not to fall into the degrading practice of making figures carved in relief, in the form of a man or a woman, or of any animal on the earth or bird that flies in the air, or of any reptile on the ground or fish in the waters under the earth" (Deut. 4:15–17).

The Freedom of God

God's Freedom Makes Ample Room for Human Freedom

Pivotal among personal qualities attributed to God in Scripture is will. What is God's distinctive way of being free? To speak of divine freedom is to ascribe to God in infinite degree something we know quite well—personal freedom.

We ascribe *willing* to God because we experience our own finite willing as radically dependent upon some Whence or source of prior causes, without which our willing would remain absurd and unexplainable (Hilary, *Trin.* 8.12). If there is any movement or change at all in the causal order, it must be caused. To avoid the intellectual clumsiness of an infinite regression of causes, we infer that there must be a primal source of all causes (Gregory of Nazianzus, *Second Theol. Orat.* 8; Tho. Aq., *ST* 1 Q19). If willing exists at all in creation, some source of willing beings must be posited, however named.

We ourselves experience our own self-determination as incalculably good. The proof of that is to take away freedom, and test out whether anyone likes that. Anything that is good to such an extraordinary degree we may properly ascribe in infinite proportion to God, an argument by way of heightening, the way of eminence (Augustine, *Trin.* 10.13; Tho. Aq., *ST* 1 Q96).

Humans are here swimming in a sea of which we already have knowledge— intimate, personal knowledge— namely, of ourselves, since we are to some extent free (Josh. 24:15; Phil. 2:13; Origen, *OFP* 3.1.1–12; Augustine, *CG* 5.10; Calvin, *Inst.* 2.3). No sentence could be read without assuming the power to read or not read it. That implies some capacity for self-determination (Cyril of Jerusalem, *Catech. Lect.* 4.18–21; Augustine, *On Free Choice of the Will* 2.28; Anselm, *On Freedom of Choice* 3).

We are now studying God's qualities of personhood in close conjunction with our own self-examination and with our personal self-knowledge (Augustine, *On Grace and Free Will*, 21; Calvin, *Inst.* 1.1.1, 3.2–4). For what we mean by being a person is to some large extent precisely this: a capacity to will (Ambrose, *Six Days of Creation* 6.3.10).

Discerning the Will of God

The divine will is the infinite power of God to determine God's own intentions, execute actions, and use means adequate to the ends intended (Tho. Aq., *ST* 1 Q19). God's will is the effective energy inherent in God by which God is able to do all things consistent with the divine nature (Calvin, *Inst.* 1.18.1).

The will of God is eternally directed toward the good, according to Scripture. Hence it is a will that lives in complete felicity (Augustine, *CG* 22.30). "Whatever the Lord pleases, that he does" (Ps. 135:6).

Since the One who wills is God, that will must be independent, unified, and eternal (Hilary, *Trin.* 9.26; Anselm, *Monologium* 7). The will of God is intrinsically connected with the related divine attributes of omnipresence and omniscience. The freedom of God is the sufficient reason why anything exists at all (John of Damascus, *OF* 3.14; Calvin, *Inst.* 2.3.10).

Since we have already discussed God's power, it might seem pointless to speak further of God's freedom or willing. However much interwoven, God's power and God's will may be functionally distinguished. One may have power without willing to exercise it (Tho. Aq., *ST* 1 Q25). One of the powers of will is the will not to exercise power.

The Divine Will and Other Wills

Choice is definitive of personal existence. What makes us persons is that we know ourselves to be able to act in one way rather than another.

Human freedom shares in divine freedom, yet within the limits of finitude. In Scripture both kinds of freedom are seen in close connection: "Freely you have received, freely give" (Matt. 10:8; John 8:32–36; 1 Pet. 2:16). We pray to God: "Grant me a willing spirit" (Ps. 51:12).

Scripture frequently attests to the derived character of human freedom, derived, that is, from God's own freedom (Irenaeus, *Ag. Her.* 3.17.1–2). "In Christ indeed we have been given our share in the heritage, as was decreed in his design whose purpose is everywhere at work. For it was his will that we, who were the first to set our hope on Christ, should cause his glory to be praised" (Eph. 1:11–12).

God wills to empower other wills. God "wills himself and things other than himself; himself as the end, other things as ordered to that end. It befits the divine goodness that other things should be partakers therein" (Tho. Aq., *ST* 1 Q19.2).

In this way human freedom is ordered in relation to divine freedom. We are persons because God is a person. It is from divine freedom that human freedom is derived and made understandable.

The Primordial and Consequent Will of God

Classical Christian teaching has persistently held that God's will may be viewed in two ways:

- Primordially, God wills what God wills eternally, that is, before creation,

- Consequentially, God wills what God wills in consequence of creation and in the light of the specific contingencies of creaturely beings (Ps. 143:10; Eph. 1:1–9; John of Damascus, *OF* 4.19–21; Heppe, *RD*: 90; Hodge, *Syst. Theol.*, 1: 404).

Since the divine intellect knows all things eternally, and thus antecedently to the world and time, so the divine volition wills all things *antecedently* from the viewpoint of providence. God is not without a will prior to creation. This is God's original will for the world before the fall of human freedom.

Yet as history develops after the fall and thus *consequently*, God is and remains free to express and execute the divine will within the changing conditions of fallen history (Ps. 40:8; Matt. 6:10; John 7:17; Tertullian, *On Prayer* 4.1–2; Origen, *OFP* 3.1.6–22). This occurs not merely through direct intervention, but also through the layers of divinely ordered natural causality.

God is said to will primordially or antecedently when God wills something independently of creatures, without regard to other wills or any subsequently developing contingent circumstances. For example, it is said that God antecedently wills the good (Rom. 12:2). The good that God wills consequent to contingent circumstances is also good, but good in relation to those circumstances.

God's antecedent will is sometimes called God's secretive or absolute or decreeing will. It is simple, independent, eternal, efficacious, and inseparable from God's very being (Rom. 9:18, 19; Heppe, *RD*:90). This general will predates later developing historical circumstances in which the divine good will is willed in and through contingent circumstances following the fall (Tho. Aq., *ST* 1 Q19; T. Jackson, *Works* 5:331–36).

Within the tangled conditions of history, God wills consequent to whatever changing historical circumstances prevail. As a consequence of particular contingencies occurring in the history that God creates and permits, God *consequently wills* under contingent conditions. "If we ask anything according to his will, he hears us" (1 John 5:14).

Even after human wills have done all the damage and good they can do under the divine permission of human freedom, God still rules and overrules, commands and countermands, prewills, wills, and postwills through and beyond all human willing.

God's freedom remains free to respond to what is humanly willed. The consequent will of God follows in the wake of divinely permitted human willing (Rom. 1:10; 1 Cor. 16:12). It is the will of God in response to human willing (1 John 2:17; John 7:17; Cyril of Alex. *Comm. on John* 4.5). "It is possible to will a thing to be done now, and its contrary afterwards; and yet for the will to remain permanently the same" (Tho. Aq., *ST* 1 Q19).

In this way the divine will exists in itself *prior to* the complications of fallen human history, yet the divine will also operates and functions *in response to* human fallenness. God can express the divine good will amid changing historical circumstances and contingencies, but it must be remembered that God's will remains the same, eternal covenant love, even amid intensive responsiveness to whatever human or historical misery might occur (Cyril of Jerusalem, *Catech. Lect.* 4.4, 5; Hooker, *Eccl. Polity* 1.5). Although God can will changes, God does not change the eternal divine purpose. Though God can respond to contingencies, God does not make the divine eternal will finally contingent upon the contingencies God has permitted (Tho. Aq., *ST* 1 Q86; Molina, *Scientia Media, RPR*: 425).

This is why classical Christian teachers have often distinguished between God's single, unified "necessary will" antecedent to creation, and God's "free will," freely utilizing variable means of response to the freedom of creatures (Eph. 1:1–11; Hilary, On Matt. 21.28–32; John of Damascus, *OF* 19). The terms *primordial* and *consequent will of God* may be prematurely assumed by modern readers to be the product of the recent tradition of process philosophy and theology (Whitehead, Hartshorne, Cobb, Ogden), but it is evident that Whitehead himself borrowed these concepts from classical Christian teaching (Clement of Alex., *Instr.* 1.9; Tertullian, *Ag. Marcion* 2.4–17; Tho. Aq., *ST* 1 Q19). It is a telling irony that Whitehead's followers, apparently unaware of how the classical tradition employed deliberate distinctions between the antecedent and the consequent will of God, have used the distinction as the basis of a sustained polemic *against* the very tradition of classical theism upon which their reasoning depends. Once again ancient Christian teaching has been borrowed, diminished, and fashioned into a tool by which its borrowers have then supposedly "transcended" classical Christian theism.

The Convergence of Divine and Human Willing

Human volition is and remains, however deeply corrupted, always the gift of the divine volition. God's primordial will is that humanity be saved, but on the way to the last day, many contingencies have emerged.

God does not deal with human beings as sticks. God does not throw them, like stones, in order to coerce virtuous responses. This would deny free personal responsiveness. God deals with human beings not coercively but persuasively, respecting human freedom and its ever-present correlate, human responsibility.

When we act counter to God's command, God is still able to take our idolatry and sin and make it work toward a greater good, all to God's glory. Such contingencies may be viewed as the consequent will of God, consequent to historical challenges, failures, and fallenness (Heb. 10:5–10).

Jesus poignantly exclaimed: "O Jerusalem, Jerusalem, the city that murders the prophets and stones the messengers sent to her! How often have I longed to gather your children, as a hen gathers her brood under her wings; *but you would not let me.* Look, look! there is your temple, forsaken by God." (Matt. 23:37–39, italics added). That means: God antecedently wills to save Jerusalem—and all humanity by extension of the metaphor—but Jerusalem has the power of will, divinely granted, momentarily to delay, or temporarily to "not let God complete" the antecedent divine intention except at the intolerable cost of God's having to destroy or override the gift of human freedom. Human willing is able to resist the will of God temporarily, though never ultimately (Chrysostom, *Concerning the Statues* 17; Calvin, *Inst.* 2.3).

The Divine Goodness

Three of the four sets of divine attributes have been described above:

1. The divine being (primary and essential attributes of God: Sufficiency, underived existence, unity, infinity, immeasurability, eternity, life)

2. The divine majesty (the relational attributes of God: All-present, all-knowing, almighty)

3. The divine Person (free, congruent, interactive Spirit)

We are now poised for the fourth cycle of qualities that describe God's character:

4. The divine goodness (holy, constant, compassionate)

Holiness and Love are Intrinsic to the Divine Character

Among chief moral characteristics attributed by Scripture to God are holiness, justice, righteousness, constancy, truthfulness, goodness, and love. Moral attributes are divine qualities beheld primarily in God's meeting with, fidelity to, and guidance of free human creatures who are morally accountable within human history. These are features intrinsic to the divine character as made known by Scripture in the history of salvation. Classical Christian exegetes were constrained by Scripture to acknowledge that God is incomparably holy (Ps. 105:3; Isa. 43:14, 15), good (Pss. 25:8; 86:5), merciful (Ps. 130:7; Jer. 33:11), and just (Isa. 45:21; Zeph. 3:5).

Though plants, animals, and earth are recipients of divine mercy, justice, and love, they are not held morally accountable for appropriate responses as fully as are human beings. Higher capacities for reason, language, and responsiveness are largely lacking in these creatures, in comparison with human beings (Gregory of Nyssa, *On the Making of Man* 27–30).

Some measure of honesty, justice, and love is necessary for the maintenance of human society, for child raising, and for human happiness. These moral qualities are viewed in Scripture as intrinsic to the divine being itself and most fully beheld in God alone (Hilary, *On Trin.* 6.19, 9.61, 176–7; Basil, *Hex.* 9, *Letters* 2–7).

The great variety of moral qualities attributed to God by Scripture revolves particularly around two—*holiness* and *love.* These may be said in summary form to constitute the moral character of God (Ps. 93:5; Hos. 11:1–9; John 17:11–26; Jerome, *Ag. Pelag.* 2.23).

Holiness (Hebr: *qodesh*) is the essential perfection of God that necessarily stands opposed to all idolatry and sin (Amos 4:1–3). Among attributes that link closely with holiness are righteousness, justice, moral purity, veracity, and faithfulness. That God is *love* implies that benevolent affection, good will, and empathic understanding are the defining qualities in God through which God relates compassionately to creatures (Clement of Alex., *Stromata* 4.16–18). Among attributes that Scripture most closely associates with divine love are goodness, grace, mercy, and compassion. It is only by keeping these two primary moral qualities of the divine being closely bound that we may rightly behold the character of God (Pss. 31:21–24; 146:8; John 3:16; 1 John 2:15–17; 4:7–21; Rev. 15:4; Eucharius, Exhortation to Valerian).

In Scripture we learn how God's goodness interpenetrates the variable forms of God's power (Ps. 90; Tho. Aq., *ST* 1 Q25), how God's mercy accompanies the omnipresence of God (Ps. 51), how God's compassion pervades the judgment of God (Ps. 103). But such connections seem hollow and unconvincing apart from an actual history of God's holy love that we can share. The moral characteristics of God penetrate and interfuse with the divine omnipresence, omniscience, and will. Moral requirements that responsible persons feel impinging upon them through conscience correspond in some degree to qualities that are ascribed in their unlimited degree to God (Tertullian, *An Answer to the Jews* 1,2; *Ag. Marcion* 2.12–16; Cyril of Jerusalem, *Catech. Lect.* 4.15–21; Ambrose, *Duties of Clergy* 1.24).

The Holiness of God

God Is Holy

Any sentence that contains the word "holy" shows how profoundly humans struggle with frail human language to express an insight that emerges deeply from the interior life of Christian worship. It points to a sweeping awareness of the difference that lies between God's goodness and our own. So deeply is this experienced that it seems impossible for human languages to conceptualize anything at all about God's perfect goodness, because of the blemishes we feel in our moral awareness and earth-bound finitude.

Often we do best finally to stand in awe of God and silently celebrate God's holy presence (Gregory of Nazianzus, *Second Theol. Orat.*). But because we must say something rather than nothing, and because this quality of God is so central to worship and so prevalent in Scripture, it is necessary for Christian teaching to make some attempt to express it with language if we are going to speak at all of the character of God.

To say that God is holy is nothing other than to say that God is perfect in goodness, both in God's essential nature and in every act or energy, or operation that proceeds out of that nature (Gregory of Nyssa, *Answer to Eunomius' Second Book*). If holiness is perfect goodness, it includes within it already the idea of perfect being, which Anselm defined as "that than which nothing greater can be conceived" (*Proslog.* 3,4).

Holiness implies that every excellence fitting to the Supreme Being is found in God without blemish or limit. All other excellent features of God's character such as goodness, justice, mercy, truth, and grace are unified and made mutually harmonious in infinite degree in God (Isa. 6:1–10; 43:10–17; 1 Pet. 1:12–16; Rev. 4:8; John of Damascus, *OF* 1. 14). To glimpse this divine harmony is to glimpse God's holiness (Chrysostom, Hom. on Statues 7.9).

God's holiness consummates and harmonizes all the other divine characteristics (Athanasius, *Ag. Heathen* 38–40). Holiness points especially to the undivided glory of God in all of God's diversely good qualities (Tho. Aq., *ST* 2–2 Q81). All attributes of God are indivisible, due to the unity of God, for God's being is fully present in each attribute. Hence holiness is not to be conceived as one trait among many other divine traits in such a way that these other traits may or may not include holiness. Rather, holiness summarizes, unifies, and integrates all the other incomparably good characteristics of the divine life.

The call to holy living is heard in Jesus' call to his disciples: "There must be no limit to your goodness, as your heavenly Father's goodness knows no bounds" (Matt. 5:48; 1 Pet. 1:15, 16; Clement of Alex., *Stromata* 6.12). Jesus taught his disciples to pray, "Hallowed be thy name," and thereby attributed holiness to God the Father (Matt. 6:9), a confirmation of God's holiness heard throughout the common acts of Christian worship. God is revealing his holiness to all nations through the events of history: "When they see that I reveal my holiness through you, the nations will know that I am the Lord, says the Lord God" (Ezek. 36:23; Tertullian, *Of Idolatry* 14; Wesley, *WJW* 6: 414, 526).

Character is Revealed in God's Actions and Guidance

Holiness is the fullness of moral excellence intrinsic to the divine character. God's holiness is revealed in God's character, God's actions, and God's righteous claims upon creatures (Calvin, *Inst.* 2.8.14–15; 3.12.1; Heppe, RD, 92).

God is good without defect. "Who is like you, O Lord, among the gods? Who is like you, majestic in holiness, worthy of awe and praise, who works wonders?" (Exod. 15:11). "You alone are holy" (Rev. 15:4). "God is untouched by evil" (James 1:13). The end time celebrants of the Book of Revelation are found singing: "Holy, holy, holy is God the sovereign Lord of all, who was, and is, and is to come!" (Rev. 4:8).

The divine holiness is conveyed in everything God does, the entirety of God's activity (Gregory of Nyssa, *Ag. Eunomius* 1. 17–24; Calvin, *Inst.* 2.12). All God's actions are holy, for there is no inconsistency between God's being and God's activity. God acts so as to express God's character, which summarizes and unifies all other divine excellences. The constant excellence of God's acts expresses the perfection of God's being (Tho. Aq., *SCG* 1. 40, 41). Even when God does temporarily permit that which seems harsh, there is an awareness in Scripture that discipline occurs with some purpose consistent with God's holiness (Hab. 1:13; Chrysostom, *Comm. on Job* 35). God does not forever countenance wrong-doing, and will in time overrule it and bring it to a better purpose (Augustine, *Enchiridion* 3). God's ultimate redemptive activity can be counted upon because of God's character—replete with infinite goodness. "As he who called you is holy, be holy yourselves in all your conduct" (1 Pet 15–16; Didymus the Blind, Comm. on 1 Pet.). God's holiness is finally the criterion for human moral activity, even though in our finitude perfect goodness is always inadequately expressed.

"I am the Lord your God; you shall make yourselves holy and keep yourselves holy, because I am holy" (Lev. 11:44; Leo I, Sermon 94.2). This is not to say that God simply requires what is impossible. For it is not impossible for creatures to reflect *proportionally* the goodness of God *as* their gifts and capacities allow it (Origen, *OFP* 1.3.5–7). It is in this sense that God calls men and women to be holy and provides them with the means of grace (prayer, Scripture, sacraments) in order to reflect God's holiness in partial, yet real, vital, and significant ways (Gregory of Nyssa, *Comm. on the Canticle*, sermon 5, *FGG*: 183–203).

In being called of God, Isaiah was grasped by this overwhelming sense of awe as he felt his own radical moral limitation and the moral taint pervading human culture: "Holy, holy, holy is the Lord of Hosts; the whole earth is full of his glory. . . . Woe is me! I am lost, for I am a man of unclean lips and I dwell among a people of unclean lips" (Isa. 6:3–5; Jer. 51:17, 18; Calvin, *Inst.* 1.1.3; R. Otto, *The Idea of the Holy*). God is better, holier, purer than we can imagine (Ps. 71:22, 23). Yet creatures can refract aspects of God's goodness within their finitude (Catherine of Siena, *Prayers* 3).

Refracting the Divine Holiness

God creates beings who are capable of actualizing creaturely goods, and thereby are able to reflect in some measure the incomparable glory of divine goodness. God draws the good willing of humans toward the incomparable divine goodness.

God does not coerce creatures into doing good. That would deny one of the most fundamental goods of human creatures, freedom (Irenaeus, *Ag. Her.* 4.37). Would it not take away from human freedom all the formative goods of discipline, education, and the habituation of will if God were either to coerce good or make creatures unable to do evil? Only those who despair of freedom think that God would have done better by making it such that freedom would necessarily, inevitably, and unerringly will and do the good (Origen, *OFP* 2.1, 2; Augustine, *CG* 14.11).

Insofar as idolatry and sin infest human life, God actively opposes them, and this opposition is itself an expression of God's holiness. Sin impedes the moral goodness for which God created the world. God permits sin to come into human life, but only on behalf of a greater good—namely, freedom—and God overrules sin wherever it appears to threaten God's greater purpose (Augustine, *Enchiridion* 4–9). It is in this light that Scripture speaks metaphorically of God as angry at our sins and jealous of our gods that obstruct our full reception of divine grace. God the Spirit supports and encourages our efforts to recover the capacity to better reflect God's holiness. In this sense God's anger is an unremitting expression of God's own holiness.

God is Set Apart from Sin

God's holiness includes the idea of set-apartness or separation from all that is sinful, unworthy of God, or unprepared for God's righteousness. Seen in this way, the holiness to which we are called requires disconnecting from anything that would separate anyone from God (Gregory of Nazianzus, *In Defense of His Flight to Pontus*; Teresa of Avila, *Life CWST*, 1:288).

There is profound ethical import in the teaching of God's holiness. Those who are called to holiness of heart and life are thereby called to consecrate themselves to a life of radical responsiveness to God's love and accountability to God's own justice (Mother Syncletica, 19, *SDF*: 196; Baxter, *PW* 15: 539–44; Wesley, *WJW* 7: 266).

Paul instructs the church at Corinth to "not unite yourselves with unbelievers; they are no fit mates for you. What has righteousness to do with wickedness? . . . The temple of God is what we are" (2 Cor. 6:14–16). He exhorted them: "Separate yourselves." "Touch nothing unclean" (v. 17; Chrysostom, Comm. on 2 Cor. 13.6.17). "Let us therefore cleanse ourselves from all that can defile flesh or spirit, and in the fear of God complete our consecration" (2 Cor. 7:1; Calvin, *Inst.* 14.14.21). Sinners need the cleansing of repentance and faith to come into God's presence (Chrysostom, *Baptismal Instructions* 9.21; Luther, *Ninety-five Theses* 1).

God is so utterly distant from corruption that even to enter into the presence of this One or to come into the sanctuary where this One dwells requires that the worshiper go through an act of purification or a period of penitence, centering, mortification, and discipline (Acts 21:26; James 4:8; Teresa of Avila, *Way of Perfection* 10). God is not to be treated like any worldly reality.

In this way the faithful are called through grace to be partakers of God's holiness (Heb. 12), restored to their primordial capacity to reflect, like a mirror, the radical holiness and purity of God, even though their mirroring is always imprecise (Irenaeus, *Ag. Her.* 5.16).

Righteousness Essential to God's Being

As God who is holy calls us to holiness, so does God who is just call us to justice. God who is wholly just requires reasonable justice in human relationships (Amos 5:24; Mic. 6:8; Ps. 15:1–2). Those called to the just life are to be placed beside the plumb-line of divine justice (Amos 7:7, 8).

Justice is the perpetual and constant will to render to each his or her due or right (Tho. Aq., *ST* 1 Q58.1). "These are the words of the Lord: Maintain justice, do the right; for my deliverance is close at hand, and my righteousness will show itself victorious. Happy is the man who follows these precepts" (Isa. 56:1, 2; Clement of Alex., *Stromata* 6.12; Augustine, *CG* 20.28).

That God will judge justly in the final judgment is a source of comfort to believers and a call to penitence to those who pervert justice. The good news is that God has provided the gift of Christ's righteousness to clothe us in God's own uprightness in the time of final judgment (Rom. 5:17; Chrysostom, *Comm. on Timothy* 4). The righteousness of God, therefore, consists simply in the fulfillment of God's will through our willing by the power of grace. God works in us in accord with his own good purpose (Theophilus, *To Autolycus* 3.9–12).

Righteousness in its most complete form exists *essentially* in God alone, and derivatively in creatures. "All his ways are just" (Deut. 32:4). God "does no wrong, righteous and true is He!" (Deut. 32:4). "Righteousness and justice are the foundation of his throne" (Ps. 97:1, 2; Ps. 89:14).

The righteousness of God is revealed in God's covenant love and faithfulness: "Your unfailing love, O Lord, reaches to heaven, your faithfulness to the skies. Your righteousness is like the lofty mountains, your judgments are like the great abyss" (Ps. 36:5, 6; Calvin, *Inst.* 1.17; 3.11–13).

Attesting to God's Righteousness amid Evil Days

Christian teaching seeks to speak rightly of God's justice (theos-dike, theodicy) under conditions in which it is assailed. Theodicy seeks meaningfully to set forth God's goodness and justice as seen in creation and redemption, despite apparent contradictions of them in history (Justin Martyr, *Dialogue with Trypho*, 92–94; Augustine, *Enchiridion* 3–6).

Unfair distribution of rewards and punishments are best understood in relation to the anticipated resurrection of the just and unjust, the end-time vindication of God's justice, beyond history's injustices (Tertullian, *Resurrection of the Flesh*). The best that human choosing can do is to follow God's requirement insofar as conscience, reason, law, and grace make it known. Meanwhile, lacking completeness, we still may affirm God's own righteousness as completing what is humanly incomplete, celebrating: "The Lord is our Righteousness" (Jer. 23:6; Luther, *Treatise on Good Works* 11).

God's Righteousness Expressed in Law and Gospel

God provides the law and enables it to be heard in the human heart. "The law of the Lord is perfect and revives the soul. The Lord's instruction never fails, and makes the simple wise. The precepts of the Lord are right and rejoice the heart. The commandment of the Lord shines clear and gives light to the eyes" (Ps. 19:7, 8).

Even Paul, who was so keenly aware that human sin could pervert the best of laws and the law in turn could intensify sin, nonetheless affirmed, "The law is in itself holy, the commandment is holy and just and good. Are we to say then that this good thing was the death of me? By no means" (Rom. 7:12, 13).

God's righteousness is expressed in the history of providence. God's guiding and overruling governance in history is grasped only by examining universal history. God's righteousness patiently and surely pervades the historical process, assuring its rightful outcome, yet honoring human freedom by allowing it to actualize itself under both sin and grace (Rom. 1:18–25; 3:21–28; 5:1).

Central to the account of God's righteousness made known in history is the gospel, that God's righteousness is made known in Jesus Christ and is available to all who believe (Rom. 3:22; Chrysostom, *Comm. on Rom.* 7). Paul preached that the same righteousness of God that was known by Abraham and the prophets was made known in Jesus (Rom. 1:17; 3:21; 4:3–6). Righteousness has God as its source (Phil. 3:9). It is most fully revealed in Christ's death and resurrection. Through his perfect obedience to God's will in life and death, Christ bore the curse of our alienation from God (Gal. 3:13; Chrysostom, *Comm. on Galatians* 4; Tho. Aq., *ST* 1 Q21; Wesley, *WJW* 5: 313). The sinner receives Christ's righteousness by grace through faith (2 Cor. 5:21; Eph. 2).

We feel God's judging righteousness immediately and personally in the pain of an offended conscience (Justin Martyr, *The Sole Government of God*; Calvin, *Inst.* 3.2; 3.10; 3.19 f.; Wesley, *WJW* 6:186). "Remember where you stand," warned the Epistle to the Hebrews. "You stand before Mount Zion and the city of the living God, heavenly Jerusalem, before myriads of angels, the full concourse and assembly of the first-born citizens of heaven, and God the judge of all, and the spirits of good men made perfect, and Jesus the mediator of a new covenant" (Heb. 12:18–24).

As persons who acquire habits, personality traits, and, in the long run become moral or immoral in our character, we habitually come to act in ways that make us more or less fit to receive divine blessings. As decision-makers we act concretely in good or evil works that either please or displease the holy, just, and good God (Prov. 29:26; Luke 11:483).

God is just in punishing sin, yet in Jesus God has taken our sin upon himself: "We come to you therefore as Christ's ambassadors. It is as if God were appealing to you through us: In Christ's name, we implore you, be reconciled to God! Christ was innocent of sin, and yet for our sake God made him one with the sinfulness of men, so that in him we might be made one with the goodness of God himself" (2 Cor. 5:20, 21; Cyril of Alex., Letter 41). In Christ, "God's justice has been brought to light. The Law and the prophets both bear witness to it: It is God's way of righting wrong, effective through faith in Christ for all who have such faith— all, without distinction" (Rom. 3:21). It is God's own righteousness, therefore, that has become "the remedy for the defilement of our sins, not our sins only but the sins of all the world" (1 John 2:2; Origen, *Ag. Celsus* 8.13).

The Constant Goodness of God

The Divine Reliability—Constant, Unchanging Love (Immutability)

Scripture stresses the constancy of God's purpose, based on the divine reliability— the trustworthiness of God's character. Other things "will perish, but you endure; they will all wear out like a garment, and they pass away; but you are the same, and your years have no end" (Ps. 102:26–27). Even though the people change their minds about the covenant, the Lord does not alter commitment to the covenant: "I am the Lord, unchanging" (Mal. 3:6). The psalmist marveled at the reliability of the Lord whose "plans shall stand for ever, and his counsel endure for all generations" (Ps. 33:11; Origen, *Ag. Celsus* 1. 21).

The divine constancy is celebrated in the New Testament, for whom God is the source of every good gift, "the Father of the lights of heaven. With him there is no variation, no play of passing shadows" (James 1:17; Augustine, On the Gift of Perseverance 22.62). God remains always consistent with his own nature as insurmountably good (Gregory of Nyssa, *Great Catech.* I). God's essential nature does not change from better to worse, but remains always only the best (Julia of Norwich, *Showings*, CWS:197–99). God as known in Christ is "the same yester-day, today and forever" (Heb. 13:8). Faith's confidence in the divine reliability is caricatured if stated without reference to other divine qualities—mercy, love, and justice. If pressed in isolation from God's character as responsive, empathic, and compassionate, then the assertion of the divine reliability turns easily into an abstract, speculative assertion of divine rigidity and unresponsiveness.

The celebration of divine reliability is a religious affirmation that no change can or will take place in the divine nature—that God will never cease being God, incomparably good and powerful. But that does not imply that God does not re-spond to changing human circumstances: "For, continuing unchangeable in His essence, He condescends to human affairs by the economy of His Providence" (Origen, *Ag. Celsus* 4.14).

That God can will change is essential to his sovereign freedom, but this does not imply that God changes in essential nature as good (Chrysostom, *Exhort. to Theodore* 1. 6). God is "unchangeable, yet changing all things, never new, never old, making all things new, yet bringing old age upon the proud, and they know it not; always working, ever at rest; gathering, yet needing nothing" (Augustine, *Conf.* 1.4; CG 14.10).

It is precisely because God is unchanging in the eternal character of his self-giving love that God is free in responding to changing historical circumstances, and versatile in empathy. "The unchangeable God holds an unchangeable pur-pose, but steadiness of purpose requires variety in execution" (Hall, *DT* 3:89; Whitehead, *Process and Reality*:521). Early Christian teachers held together the unchanging love of God with the responsiveness required by that unchanging love: "For abiding the same, He administers mutable things according to their nature, and His Word elects to undertake their administration" (Origen, *Ag. Cel-sus* 6.42). Here process theology has depended upon the classic Christian theism against which it has so often caricatured polemically.

The biblical narrative views God not as immobile or static, but as consistent with his own nature, congruent with the depths of his own essential goodness, stable, not woodenly predictable. If God promises forgiveness, "he is just, and may be trusted to forgive our sins" (1 John 1:9), because the character of God is dependable.

This affirmation prompted the classical exegetes to rigorously probe those Scriptures that speak of God "repenting" (*nacham*, Gen. 6:6, 7; Exod. 32:14; 1 Sam. 15:35; Jer. 26:3, 13, 19; Amos 7:3; Jon. 3:10). Does this thereby imply a fundamental change in the divine being or essence? No. The Bible represents God as responsively dealing with new human contingencies by taking ever-new initia-tives and thereby sloughing off older forms that had served their time (Tertullian, *Ag. Marcion* 2.24; John of Damascus, *OF* 1. 11, 12). But such passages never imply that something has changed in the essential being of God or that any divine at-tributes have mutated.

What may appear to be a change of God's mind may upon closer inspection be a different phase of the hidden unfolding of the provident divine plan. The execution of the divine purpose is firm precisely because it is responsive to temporal contingencies (Augustine, *CG* 22.2). The worshiping community celebrates: "From age to age everlasting thou art God" (Ps. 90:2). Creaturely purposes, actions, and intentions have beginnings, stumblings and endings, but God's character does not change. In dealing flexibly with the changing scenes of history, God remains faithful to his own constant will (Lactantius, *Div. Inst.* 4.12; Calvin, *Inst.* 2.8–10; 3.2; 3.8).

Times do change, yet God is always actively changing the times as needed according to a changeless purpose: "Blessed be God's name from age to age, for wisdom and power are his. He changes seasons and times" (Dan. 2:20–21a).

The Divine Veracity, Faithfulness, and Congruence

Closely related to this divine reliability is the scriptural witness to God's truthfulness (veracity). This implies God's faithfulness to the truth that God alone is and fully knows. God's awareness is not torn apart or internally conflicted. There is a steady congruence between who God is and what God does. God's actions and disclosures are in no way inconsistent with God's essential goodness (Chrysostom, *Comm. on John* 73; Augustine, *Of True Religion* 94–113; Calvin, *Inst.* 2.8).

By veracity we mean simply that God is true, and being true, tells the truth, and becomes revealed as truth through history. That God not only makes known the truth but *is* the truth. This is a steady theme of Scripture (John 3:33; 8:13–26; 1 Cor. 11:10; Augustine, *On Profit of Believing* 34). It is "impossible for God to lie" (Heb. 6:18). Yahweh is the "God of truth" (Ps. 31:5), whose "word is founded in truth" (Ps. 119:160).

The faithfulness of God means that God proves true to his promises by keeping them. God's faithfulness is a continuing reliable application of divine truth to changing, developing historical circumstances. Trusting God's fidelity, the faithful are kept by him "sound in spirit, soul, and body, without fault when our Lord Jesus Christ comes. He who calls you is to be trusted; he will do it" (1 Thess. 5:23, 24). For "the Lord is faithful" (2 Thess. 3:3), the incomparably "true one" (Rev. 3:7) upon whom supplicants can rely as trustworthy (Irenaeus, *Ag. Her.* 4.20.; Luther, *Preface to the Psalms*).

The church fathers were aware, long before modern psychotherapy, that one of the primary conditions of constructive psychological change is congruence, the capacity to feel one's feelings fully, to remain in touch with one's experiencing process, and to share in another's estrangement without losing one's self-identity (Ambrose, *Letters to Priests*). It is when one senses the inner congruence of another, and knows one is in the presence of another who is in touch with him- or herself, that it becomes possible to enter more fully into one's own estrangement, and become more congruent within oneself. (Centuries later Carl Rogers would define congruence as the state in which "self-experiences are accurately symbolized" ("A Theory of Therapy, Personality and Interpersonal Relationships," in *Psychology: A Study of a Science*: 206; Oden, *KC*, 2). The model of congruence is not the therapist but the incomparably congruent One, God.

The Divine Benevolence

The divine benevolence is that attribute through which God wills the happiness of creatures and desires to impart to creatures all the goodness they are capable of receiving (Tertullian, *Ag. Marcion* 2; Augustine, *Trin.* 8.4, 5; Anselm, *Proslog.*

23–25). The psalmists delighted in meditating day and night on the enduring generosity of God (Pss. 1:2; 77:12).

God is not only good in himself, but wills to communicate this goodness to creatures. Having freely offered life to creatures, God then allows life to be sustained and perpetuated, to propagate and defend itself, to further define itself adaptively, and in so doing to enable innumerable secondary values (Neh. 9:20, 21; Song of Sol. 1:15–2:6; Tho. Aq., *SCG* 1. 38). God displays the goodness intrinsic to the divine character by bestowing upon living creatures prolific capacities for enjoying creation, for receiving the goods God has created, and for creating secondary goods that both God and creatures can enjoy (Gregory of Nyssa, *Great Catech.* I; Tho. Aq., *ST* 1 Q6).

The Compassion of God

God Is Love

Nowhere is God defined more concisely than in the First Epistle of John: "God is love" (1 John 4:16; Hilary *Trin.* 9.61). The love of God is that excellent way by which God communicates himself to creatures capable in varying degrees of reflecting the divine goodness. Consequently love is of all terms the one most directly attributable to God as essential to God's very being.

God's holiness does not remain trapped within itself, but reaches out for others. When Scripture tells the story of how God reaches out, it does not merely use objective, descriptive, scientific language, but rather the warmest, most intimate, most involving, engaging, and powerfully moving metaphor in human experience: love (Clement of Rome, *Corinth.* 48–56; the terms *amor, dilectio, caritas,* in Augustine, *CG* 14.7).

God's love reveals the divine determination to hold in personal communion all creatures capable of enjoying this communion (Catherine of Genoa; *The Spiritual Dialogue*). Love is beheld in God's desire to communicate the depth of divine goodness to each and every creature and to impart appropriate goods to all creatures proportional to their capacity to receive the good (Tho. Aq., *SCG* 1. 91). All things are loved by God, but all things are not loved in the same way by God, since there are degrees of capacity, receptivity, and willingness among varied creatures to receive God's love (Tho. Aq., *ST* 1 Q20).

The primary purpose of creation is that God wishes to bestow love and teach love, so that creatures can share in the blessedness of divine life, of loving and being loved (Teresa of Avila, *Way of Perfection* 6–7). No other purpose of creation transcends this one (Basil, *Hex.* 7.5).

It is impossible to speak of Christian teaching without speaking of God's love. To make clear what God's love means is the central task of Christian preaching (Calvin, *Inst.* 2.16.1–4). The music God makes in creation is not a dirge but a love song to, for, and through creatures (Origen, *Song of Songs, Prologue*).

Agape and Eros

Love is a confluence of two seemingly paradoxical tendencies: The desire to enjoy the object of love, and the will to do good for the beloved. One impulse takes and the other gives (Ambrose, *Duties* 2.7; Luther, *Heidelberg Disputation* 28). In Greek, the passion to possess another is called eros, whereas self-giving love is called agapē. They are joined in creative tension in all human love.

Although *agapē* and *eros* seem to be opposites, they may come together and flow in balanced simultaneity and support each other's impulses. Both are expressions of the inestimably high value the heart sets upon that which is loved (Gregory of Nyssa, *On the Soul and the Resurrection*). Both involve a prizing: Love prizes the beloved so earnestly that it cannot rest without its possession (*eros*), without experiencing the completion of itself in the other. Love prizes the beloved so highly that it does not withhold any feasible gift or service (*agapē*). *Eros* yearns for the self's fulfillment through another; *agapē* yearns for the other's fulfillment even at a cost to oneself (C. S. Lewis, *The Four Loves*; Nygren, *Agapē and Eros*).

To separate *eros* and *agapē* or to oppose them or set them sharply off against each other may fail to understand how one dimension may strengthen the other. *Agapē* may give itself unstintingly for the other, while it yet longs for answering love from the beloved. John's epistle deftly captured the heart of this reciprocity: "We love because he first loved us" (1 John 4:19; Wesley, *WJW* 11: 421).

God loves creatures in the first form (*eros*) of taking delight in them, in having and beholding them, as parents enjoy children. In perfect desire God desires creatures to be what they most truly are. But this perfect enjoyment melds with the second dimension of love, *agapē*, the will to be radically for creatures even when creatures are stubbornly against themselves.

One who loves may love wrongly or unworthily. Augustine thought that the heart of the problem of sin was misguided love, which loves the lesser rather than the greater good (Augustine, *Chr. Doctrine* 1. 23–33; *On Patience* 14). The deeper that love becomes rooted in reality (i.e., the reality of divine love), the more fully is the passion for the other complemented by the self-giving spirit (Clement of Alex., *Stromata* 4.15). Ordered love first loves God, the One most lovable (Chrysostom, *Comm. on John* 78–79).

Love may remain completely unreturned without ceasing to be love. Love for one's beloved is not finally dependent upon its being reciprocated. Love that promises to be returned yet remains for a long time unreturned, or love that confronts vast obstacles is the subject of the greatest literature and drama (Abelard, *The Story of My Misfortunes*; Kierkegaard, *Stages Along Life's Way, The Works of Love*). "Even its shadows are beautiful" (Clarke, *CDG*:85). But love that becomes fulfilled is that which finds some balance of giving and receiving, of self-fulfillment and fulfillment of the other, of *eros* and *agapē*, of love received and love poured out if not now, over time, bound by fidelity, and if not in time in eternity (Ambrose, *Duties* 2.7.37). A perfect love would be that which receives to the limit whatever goods can be received from a relationship and gives without bounds whatever goods can be given (Tho. Aq., *SCG* 1. 91; Teresa of Avila, *Way of Perfection* 6). "Is there a man among you who will offer his son a stone when he asks for bread, or a snake when he asks for fish? If you, then, bad as you are, know how to give your children what is good for them, how much more will your heavenly Father give good things to those who ask him!" (Matt. 7:9–11).

We are called to love God "as ourselves" (Luke 10:27), thus assuming that we will be loving ourselves, prizing ourselves, acknowledging our own worth, and putting a high value upon our own lives (Ignatius, *Ephesians* 14; Augustine, *On Chr. Doctrine* 1.23–26; Luther, *WLS* 2:830). But to organize our lives primarily around the love of ourselves is wretched and dehumanizing, because we were intended to love a more encompassing object of love than ourselves alone (Augustine, *Of True Religion* 87).

God loves all creatures in the twofold sense that God unapologetically enjoys them for their own sake and desires their answering, enjoying love in response to eternally patient, self-sacrificial love (Augustine, *On Chr. Doctrine* 1. 22). God *feels the worth of creatures* and *longs to do them good*. Because God loves in both of these ways in full and fitting balance, we say that God is love.

The Scope of God's Love

Ultimately the cost is God's only beloved Son, Jesus Christ, the most crucial reversal in the drama of God's love. "God loved the world so much that he gave his only Son, that everyone who has faith in him may not die but have eternal life" (John 3:16). As God loves in this way, by self-sacrificial giving and serving the needy neighbor, so do we learn how to love, by loving as God loved, in whatever ways are possible for us as enabled by grace (Augustine, Hom. on the First Epis. of John 6–7; Tho. Aq., *ST* 1 Q20; Calvin, *Inst.* 2.7).

God loves sinners, because he sees in them something they may not see in themselves, namely, lovability, or at least potential lovability, and the possibility of restoration to the fullness of the divine fellowship (Augustine, *Man's Perfection in Righteousness*). "Christ died for us while we were yet sinners, and that is God's own proof of his love towards us" (Rom. 5:6–8). Those whose human love mirrors God's own holy love are much beloved of God.

The end of history is understood in the light of Jesus' resurrection, which anticipates the end and through which believers can share in the end and therefore the meaning of history. "He who dwells in love is dwelling in God, and God in him. This is for us the perfection of love, to have confidence on the day of judgment; and this we can have, because even in this world we are as he is. There is no room for fear in love; perfect love banishes fear" (1 John 4:17–18; Bede, On 1 John 4.17)

Despite all the distortions of human loving, the faithful are enabled by grace to experience perfect love in the form of hope, viewed in relation to the end time. Perfection in love is precisely to have confidence in the work that God is working in the whole of history. Perfect love lives out of a deep affinity with faith. For perfect love is none other than to have confidence in God's redemptive work. This perfect love we can have. For it is within our reach, enabled by grace, to trust in God's love (Gregory of Nyssa, *On the Soul and the Resurrection*; *On Perfection*, *FGG*:83, 84; Teresa of Avila, *The Way of Perfection* 6).

Holiness and Love United

God is holy love. Holiness and love point directly to the center of the character of God. In God's holiness all of God's moral excellences are summed up and united. In God's love, God's holiness is manifested in relation to creatures (Augustine, On Nature and Grace, 84). God loves by imparting his holy love to creatures in the fullest measure possible. The circle of this love is complete only with the answering love of the beloved, when the creature's heart and life joyfully reflect the beauty of God's holiness (Pss. 29:2; 96:9; Augustine, On Psalms 96).

Holy love is most radically beheld in God's treatment of sin, especially in the cross of Christ. This does not imply that prior to human fallenness these qualities were not already present in the divine character, but that they were fully revealed there on the cross. Holy love is attested by Scripture of God from the beginning. The "Lamb that was slain" fulfills a promise set forth "since the world was made" (Rev. 13:8), even "before the foundation of the world" (1 Pet. 1:20).

It is especially through beholding and responding to this salvation event, Jesus Christ, that Christians have come to understand the holy love of God and the relation between God's holiness and God's love. It was the *love* of God that sent God's only Son into the world (John 3:16). It was the *holiness* of God that required the satisfaction of divine justice through the sacrifice of the Son. These two themes are brought together powerfully in the first Johannine letter: "The love I speak of is not our love for God, but the love he showed to us in sending his Son as the remedy for the defilement of our sins" (1 John 4:10; Chrysostom, *Comm. on John* 27–28; Augustine, *Hom. on the First Epis. of John* 7; *Enchiridion* 32). Similarly in Paul's letters, it is precisely in God's act of *love* that God's *righteousness* and holy justice "has been brought to light" (Rom. 3:21). "It is God's way of righting wrong, effective through faith in Christ for all who have such faith—all without distinction" (v. 22; Luther, *Comm. on Galatians*, MLS:109–15).

Wherever holiness is spoken of in Scripture, love is nearby; wherever God's love is manifested, it does not cease to be holy. Neither holiness nor love alone could have sufficed for the salvation of sinners (Anselm, *Cur Deus Homo* 1). For a love that lacked holiness would hardly be just if it ignored sin, and holiness without love would hardly be able to effect the reconciliation.

God's holy love bridges the gulf. "It is precisely in this that God proves his love for us; that while we were yet sinners, Christ died for us" (Rom. 5:8). Love is the way holiness communicates itself under the conditions of sin (Clement of Alex., *Instr.* 1. 9). God's holiness detests sin; the motive of reconciliation is God's love for the sinner, which is so great that it is willing to pay the costliest price to set it aright.

The most profound New Testament moral injunctions hold together God's holiness and love precisely as they had become manifested in Christ: "Live in love as Christ loved you, and gave himself up on your behalf as an offering and sacrifice whose fragrance is pleasing to God" (Eph. 5:2; Ignatius, *Letter to Ephesians* I). The mystery and power of this fragrance is to be found precisely in the delicately balanced interface of holiness and love.

Grace and Mercy: The Forbearance and Kindness of God

The reckoning of divine attributes would be incomplete if we failed to point finally to God's grace, mercy, and forbearance. Closely intertwined, they are nonetheless distinguishable in scriptural teaching.

Grace means unmerited favor. To affirm that God is gracious is to affirm that God does not deal with creatures on the basis of their works, merit, or deserving but rather out of abundant divine compassion (Ignatius, *Magnesians* 9–10; Luther, *Comm. on Galatians*). It is through grace that God's mercy is freely given precisely to penitent sinners (Matt. 9:36). Yet this gift does not imply that recipients have no responsibilities to be accountable for it: "For it is by grace you are saved, through trusting him; it is not your own doing. It is God's gift, not a reward for work done. There is nothing for anyone to boast of. For we are God's handiwork, created in Christ Jesus to devote ourselves to the good deeds for which God has designed us" (Eph. 2:8–10; Augustine, *On Grace and free Will*).

Divine *mercy* is the disposition of God to relieve the miserable, salve the wounds of the hurt, and receive sinners, quite apart from any works or merit (Chrysostom, *Comm. Philippians* 4; Luther, *The Freedom of a Chr.*; Calvin, *Inst.* 3.2.7; 3.12.4–8). God's mercy is never disconnected from God's holiness or justice (Anselm, *Cur Deus Homo* 1. 19–2.4; Tho. Aq., *ST* 1 Q21). Even where sin gains power over the human will, God offers mercy, still seeking to restore the fallen creature to the good life. The restoration comes only through the suffering of God the Son who willingly dies for sinners (Rom. 8:1; 1 Cor. 5:11–21). Mercy is the form taken by divine love when sin has blocked off other avenues. Nowhere is God's almighty power manifested more clearly than in showing mercy to sinners. No mercy is greater than that beheld on the cross, reaching out to redeem sin.

The *forbearance* of God is seen when divine love and mercy delay or lessen retribution, making one aware that "God's kindness is meant to lead you to a change of heart" (Rom. 2:4; Calvin, *Inst.* 2.8). The psalmist prayed for the kindness of

God to be revealed: "But you, O Lord, are a compassionate and gracious God, slow to anger, abounding in love and faithfulness. Turn to me and have mercy on me; grant your strength to your servant" (Ps. 86:15, 16).

The mercy of God is patient: "With the Lord one day is like a thousand years, and a thousand years like one day. It is not that the Lord is slow in fulfilling his promise, as some suppose, but that he is very patient with you, because it is not his will for any to be lost, but for all to come to repentance" (2 Pet. 3:8, 9; 1 Pet. 3:20; Fastidius, On the Christian Life 21). The forbearance of God is "compassionate and gracious, long-suffering, ever constant and true, maintaining constancy to thousands, forgiving iniquity, rebellion, and sin, and not sweeping the guilty clean away" (Exod. 34:6, 7).

. Reprise: Having dealt with the primary attributes of God (uncreated, sufficient, necessary being, eternity, life), and the relational attributes (insurmountable influence, presence, and knowing), and the personal attributes of the divine life (spirit, will, freedom, self-determination), and the moral attributes (holy love, grace, mercy, and forbearance), there yet remains one more attribute of God that brings these all together in a blessed focus: the extraordinary notion of *divine happiness*. Only God can be happy in the way that God is happy.

The Divine Happiness

To say that God is eternally blessed means that God rejoices eternally in the outpouring of goodness, mercy, and love upon creatures, each in accordance with their ability to participate in God's being. The blessedness of God, or divine beatitude, means that God's life is full of joy, both within the Godhead and in relation to creatures. God's enjoyment of redeemed creation is compared to the joy of a bridegroom who rejoices over the bride (Isa. 62:5). God's joy is eternal joy (Calvin, *Inst.* 3.25.10–12), causing the rivers to "clap their hands"; "let the mountains sing together for joy; let them sing before the Lord" (Ps. 98:8, 9; Catherine of Genoa, Spiritual Dialogue).

The blessedness of God is enjoyed and shared by the angelic hosts and by the faithful, and for that reason they are called, by way of refraction, blessed (Augustine, *CG* 11.11, 12; Valerian, Hom. 15–16). The Lord takes delight in the celebration of the faithful (Prov. 15:8). The fitting response of the faithful to the joy of God is the life of praise.

There is no end to the life of praise, for the faithful, sharing in the eternal life of God, thereby participate in eternal life, in ceaseless divine blessedness (Catherine of Siena, *Prayers* 17). "As the abounding grace of God is shared by more and more, the greater may be the chorus of thanksgiving that ascends to the glory of God" (2 Cor. 4:15). "Through blessedness every desire is given rest, because, when blessedness is possessed, nothing else remains to be desired, since it is the ultimate end. He must, therefore, be blessed who is perfect in relation to all the things that He can desire" (Tho. Aq., *SCG* 1. 100). In this way beatitude belongs in full measure to God, and to creatures in proportion to their nearness to God (Tho. Aq., *ST* 1 Q26; Teresa of Avila, *Exclamations of the Soul to God*, *CWST* 2: 402–20). The presence of God is described by Ezekiel as an "encircling radiance," "like a rainbow in the clouds" (Ezek. 1:28).

Do scriptural expressions of God's rejection of idolatry and sin constitute an interruption of the divine happiness? Terms such as "God's anger" are based on analogies that point to God's veto on the entitlement of sin. Since the foreknowledge of God always already envisions the triumph of grace over sin, and since God is eternally aware of both fallenness and its being overcome, and since the fall provides for God a new contingency in which God's mercy and grace can once again be powerfully manifested, God rejoices also at the overcoming of sin, even while sin is amid history gradually being judged and overruled (Julia of Norwich, *Showings*, *CWS*: 263–65, 320 f.; Calvin, *Inst.* 2.10). "Where sin was thus multiplied, grace immeasurably exceeded it, in order that, as sin established its reign by way of death, so God's grace might establish its reign in righteousness, and issue in eternal life through Jesus Christ our Lord" (Rom. 5:21; Tertullian, *Ag. Marcion* 5.13, 14).

The gamut of divine attributes is therefore brought to a exhilarating culmination in Scripture's witness to the beauty of God's holiness. "Might and beauty are in his sanctuary" (Ps. 96:6).

Among all themes of Christian teaching, none is more capable of eliciting theological delight than the study of the divine perfections. It is a joyful act to study eternal joy. It is merciful that God has allowed sinners to study God's mercy. It is the delight of theological reflection to see in their proper light the unity, harmony, balance, and proportion of the characteristics of the divine life. A right understanding of this proportionality goes far to prevent misunderstandings of God. This is why the divine attributes have so often been considered an essential part of early baptismal instruction (Cyril of Jerusalem, *Catech. Lect.*; Chrysostom, *Two Instr. to Candidates for Baptism*; Augustine, *Instr. of the Uninstructed*; Luther, *Smaller Catech*; Westminster *Conf.*).

Conclusion: What Do We Mean When "We Say God"?

What follows are the key terms attributable to God as essential to God's being. Each belongs to the preliminary definition of God—preliminary, that is, to subsequent Christian instruction, and definition insofar as the reality of God yields to human language and definition. Each word in the ensuing sentence provides a glint of color within the mosaic pattern of characteristics of the divine life, which seeks to be beheld in its wholeness.

God is the source and end of all things, that than which nothing greater can be conceived; uncreated, sufficient, necessary being; infinite, unmeasurable, eternal One, Father, Son, and Spirit; all-present, all-knowing, all-powerful, and all-empowering creator, redeemer, and consummator of all things; immanent without ceasing to be transcendent, Holy One present in our midst; whose way of personal being is incomparably free, self-determining, spiritual, responsive, and self-congruent; whose activity is incomparably good, holy, righteous, just, benevolent, loving, gracious, merciful, forbearing, kind; hence eternally blessed, eternally rejoicing, whose holiness is incomparable in beauty.

The next chapter will seek to clarify whether such a reality exists.

THE REALITY
OF GOD

4

WHETHER GOD EXISTS

I T IS EVIDENT THAT GOD EXISTS as a conception in our minds. The larger question remains for Christian teaching and moral decision-making as to whether that One who exists in our minds also exists in reality.

Does a being exist whose counsel is infinitely wise, whose power surpasses all temporal powers, whose actions are such that they are worthy of being called infinitely good? (Anselm, *Monologium*; *Proslog.*; Calvin, *Inst.* 1.1.3; Descartes, *Method* 4, *Meditations* 3; Witsius, *ESS* 4: 33).

The question of the *existence of God* hinges on whether that necessary, eternal being remains merely a conceptual idea that we imaginatively *project* toward reality, as Feuerbach and Freud thought (Feuerbach, *The Essence of Christianity*, Freud, *The Future of an Illusion*; whose arguments were anticipated by Gregory of Nazianzus sixteen centuries ago, *Second Theol. Orat.* 18.15) or whether our *idea of God's being is derived from God's actual being* (also *Orat.* 30; Anselm, *Proslog.* 2–4; Descartes, *Meditations* 5). How we answer this determines all that follows in classic Christianity.

Whether the Existence of God Can Be Reasonably Argued

Unlike classical Christianity, modern theology has seldom been organized in the way followed by the classic consensus, namely, by first establishing a clear conceptual idea of God, then asking whether that One exists. Rather, modern theology has typically sought first to establish that "God" in some sense (with spare definition) exists, then secondly to append to that bare definition of God the most vital attributes of the Scripture's understanding of God—will, spirit, freedom, personhood, justice, and wisdom.

The Classic Beginning Point

Classic Christian teachers have proceeded in the opposite way by first pointing toward the divine attributes attested in Scripture and only then by dealing with arguments for God's existence.

It has long been recognized that a natural theology that frugally argues for the bare existence of the idea of God has much more modest aims than those required by Christian discipleship and pastoral care. Modern philosophical arguments typically aim at establishing that there is a First Cause or unmoved Mover or cosmic Orderer without any reference whatever to the lofty characteristics attributed to God in Scripture. It is more difficult but more meaningful to establish that God as defined in scriptual teaching exists, rather than that "a Supreme Being" or "that which is necessary" exists (Augustine, *On Trin.* 5.3; Kierkegaard, *Phil. Frag.*; Barth, *CD* 2/1).

Viewed from the ancient ecumenical consensus, this modern method is an inverted way of proceeding from almost nothing to a little less than almost nothing. It invites confusion to try first to prove God's bare existence and then wait until later to try to tag on the crucial defining qualifications that show more specifically what biblical teaching really means by "God." Only these appendages to the bare idea of God will give substance to the reality of God as known in the worshiping community.

If nothing whatever is known of the character or attributes of God, it is hardly an exercise of great meaning to prove God's existence. It is less consequential to faith that "an unmoved Mover" exists than that the caring, covenanting, living God of Abraham, Isaac and Jesus truly lives within history and acts as attested in Scripture (Hilary, *Trin.* 5.3–25; Calvin, *Inst.* 1.14.1–3). The most urgent and demanding question for Christian believers is not whether "a supreme being of some kind" exists, but rather whether this incomparably good and powerful and compassionate source and end of all things truly *is* as revealed in Scripture (Augustine, *Expos. on Psalms*, Ps. 135:5; *On the Profit of Believing*).

It is more meaningful to follow the path of early Christian teaching: first to name God rightly, accurately characterizing what scripture *means* by the sovereign caring God, and only then to ask whether that One *is* as characterized and whether that set of meanings is true to the facts of life as we know it, and can be accounted for confidently through reason and shared human experience. The search for consensuality has led me to proceed in a way that is unconventional in modern times but traditionally familiar, by first naming God rightly according to scripture, and only thereafter introducing classic ecumenical reasoning concerning the existence of God.

The New Testament and its earliest interpreters such as Clement of Rome, Ignatius of Antioch, and Polycarp of Smyrna were concerned primarily with the proclamation of the love, power, and justice of God the Father through the Son rather than with God's bare existence. The generation of writings represented by the Epistle to Diognetus, the Epistle of Barnabas, and the Didache contained only the slenderest forms of specific theistic arguments for the existence of God. In due time they were followed by cautious emerging forms of theistic reasoning in Christian apologists such as Justin Martyr, Irenaeus, Theophilus, and Clement of Alexandria.

The forthright statement of the nature and character of God indeed has genuine self-evidencing power—for how could something necessary to existence not exist? (Anselm, *Monologium* 1.1; Tho. Aq., *ST* 1 Q12). But that consensual form of reasoning must now be plausibly set forth.

The Question of God Arises Unavoidably out of Human Existence

To some the existence of God seems so obvious that it hardly can claim to be the subject of serious inquiry or doubt. Yet God's existence has in fact been doubted and debated (Tho. Aq., *ST* 1 Q1). Others who firmly believe in the existence of God have hesitated to say that it can be convincingly demonstrated or that any argument makes any difference (Augustine, *Soliloquies* 1. 6–12; John of Damascus, *OF* 1. 4, 5; Kierkegaard, *Concl. Unsci. Post.* 1. 2).

To ask whether God exists is to pose a question of fact, not merely of theory. The question is, quite simply: Is this so? To establish a fact is to show the state of things as they are. Fact is distinguished from fancy. In classic Christianity the existence of God is not merely a theory or hypothesis but a necessary axiom of rational minds.

The question is not whether we can conceptualize God, since we have already stated those conceptions in the previous chapter. Now we ask whether these scripturally attested attributes of the conceived divine reality indeed correspond with One who truly exists. This is a poignant human question, which at crisis times becomes a decisive, practical, momentous question (Irenaeus, *Ag. Her.* 2.6; Augustine, *Conf.* 7.10).

No one can decide this question for another. Everyone listening must judge for him- or herself whether this One *truly is* (Luther, *Letters of Spiritual Counsel*, LCC 18:109; Kierkegaard, *Concl. Unsci. Post.*).

Yet to decide that this One exists is not quite like deciding that anything else exists. For this decision assumes a wider implication that the decider shall order his or her life around the existence of this One, if this One exists at all. It is not merely a casual or theoretical decision that makes no necessary difference to the way one lives the rest of one's life (Luther, *Letters of Spiritual Counsel*). For if this One exists, then everything else about life must be ordered in terms of this datum. Rightly understood, it is an all-embracing, intrusive question, and for this reason many prefer to dodge it or to proceed as if it were an abstract, theoretical question.

If God exists in the way that classic Christianity teaches, God's existence implies far more than intellectual consent (Kierkegaard, *Either/Or* 2, "Ultimatum"). It implies befitting adoration, ceaseless praise of this incomparable being, active love of the most lovable of all beings, a love that manifests itself in the loving of all other beings in relation to this supreme being (Augustine, *Conf.* 7.1–3). There is an urgent, practical, consequential dimension that attaches itself to the seemingly harmless and simple question, Does God exist?

Can Faith Be Established by Argument?

Before proceeding it is useful to take seriously the curious argument that no argument can have any effect upon whether one believes God exists. Thus our first steps may seem like an unnecessary detour: We must plainly speak about the human corroborative function of reasonable argument in relation to belief. Only then will we be prepared to clarify biblical reasoning concerning the existence of God, after which we will pursue the reasons why the question cannot be evaded, and, in due course, distinguish different types of arguments.

All sincere talk of God's existence must begin with a humble acknowledgment that our terms cannot encompass the divine reality, even though they can point with reasonable confidence to the living God. The classical formula is: God can be apprehended but not comprehended (Lombard, *Sent.* 1.3; Tho. Aq., *SCG* 1.5–7; Heppe, *RD*:52). We can know *that* God truly exists without pretending to know *how* God exists, or without claiming to know all that God knows about God's existence. Only the infinite can adequately know the infinite (Gregory of Nyssa, *Ag. Eunomius* 1. 25).

The only understanding of God we have is acquired while moving "on the way" (*theologia viatorum*) toward the end, amid the pilgrimage of ambiguous human choices. At journey's end we hope for a final vision of the perfect being of the beatified (*theologia beatorum*, Calvin, *Inst.* 1.2.2; 1.5; Heppe, *RD*: 5; Schmid, *DT*: 17). Yet within the frame of this time and this world, something must be said about whether this infinite One exists. Otherwise the misleading impression may be left that Christian teaching appeals merely to mystery or obscurantism and not in any sense to the truth of good sense and the history of revelation (Basil, *Letters* 235; Augustine, *Trin.* 8.1; Tho. Aq., *SCG* 1.10–12).

The worshiping community confesses and intercedes on the basis of, not the theory of God's existence, but the experience of a multigenerational community of witnesses. The reality of God does not come into being on the basis of the cleverness of our rational arguments. "The heart has its reasons which reason does not know" (Pascal, *Pensées*, EL:277). These reasons must be transparently plausible to each individual believer, but more so they are credibly shared by an extensive community of discourse that has two thousand years of experiential evidence to offer. The cumulative confidence emerging from this historical evidence does not make rational arguments meaningless, but it does reinforce and confirm the rational arguments (Origen, *Ag. Celsus* 7.37; Tho. Aq., *SCG* 1. 7).

Whether God really exists as avowed remains a question to be assessed as other profound questions are evaluated on the basis of such knowledge of ourselves, our history, and social experience as it is possible to bring together into a plausible pattern of internally corresponding meaningfulness. It must be tested on the basis of all the known facts we can reasonably ascertain (Tho. Aq., *SCG* 1.3). It appeals, as do other inquiries, to clear perception and reasonable judgment based upon wide observation, and especially the broadest possible data base, namely, universal history, as well as upon moral, aesthetic, or intuitive arguments (Clement of Alex., *Stromata* 2.2; Tho. Aq., *SCG* 1. 3–8; *ST* 1 Q1).

Christianity shares with Judaism, Islam, and other theistic religions a belief in God's existence (John of Damascus, *OF* 1.1; Qur'an 3:3; Maimonides, *Guide to the Perplexed*; Tho. Aq., *SCG* 1.4). To discount all of these believers is to dismiss pertinent evidence from the majority of human beings who have lived and who are living. From its beginnings, wherever Christianity was preached among those who did not have a monotheistic faith in a personal God, it was necessary to explain why the existence of such a God is a pivotal axiom of Christian teaching (as in Acts 17:22–31). Whenever the gospel was proclaimed to the Gentiles, this question had to be answered: In what way might the God of Abraham, Isaac, and Jacob, the God of Jesus, correspond to Greek and Roman assumptions about whether gods exist or God exists? (1 Cor. 3:3; Rom. 9–11; Col. 1:9; Acts 24:3).

Classical Christian teaching has held that these rational arguments are confirmatory to faith. They corroborate what faith knows, rather than produce or establish faith (Anselm, *Proslog.*, preface). These are not each one independent, hermetically sealed, unchallengeable "proofs," but taken together, they confirm and validate what faith already knows of God's existence and to corroborate faith's persistently intuited conviction that God exists (Augustine, *Conf.* 3, 4). They are a form of loving God with the mind (Tho. Aq., *SCG* 1.91; *ST* 1 Q11). Yet the historic church has never taken these arguments with absolute seriousness, as if everything hinged upon the success of our arguments about God. God does not depend upon our thoughts about God (Gregory of Nazianzus, *On the Great Athanasius*; Augustine, *CG* 11.2–6; Calvin, *Inst.* 1.5, 6).

The Cumulative Weight of the Arguments

Despite limits, the classical theistic arguments for God's existence have a cumulative effect when taken seriously (Gregory of Nazianzus, *Orat.* 28.6, Second *Theol. Orat.*; F. R. Tennant, Philosophical Theol. 2.4). No single argument can be sufficient for so great a reality. Any detached argument may be found lacking in this or that way, but taken together they have been held by the consensus of faith to be sufficient to bind the inquiring, rational, self-critical mind to the sure and sufficient knowledge that this incomparable, unsurpassed, active, caring God really exists (Tho. Aq., *SCG* 50.5; Watson, TI 1:263).

Those who set forth evidence for the existence of God do not present it in the same way that one would offer evidence in a coroner's laboratory. For we are not dealing here with a manipulatable, quantifiable, inert object (Origen, *Ag. Celsus* 7.46; John of Damascus, *OF* 1.1–3), but with the living God. Whether the living God in fact has the character attested by Scripture can only be established on the basis of a wide correspondence of insights from widely different spheres of knowing—natural, moral, intuitive, logical, scientific, and religious. The conclusion that God exists as revealed is seldom firmly reached on the basis of a single syllogism of reasoning, but rather on the basis of subtly diverse insights carved out of one's own personal history, yet brought together intuitively in a vast inward yes that has rich plausibility if not certitude (Augustine, *Conf.* 8). Although this plausibility may grow slowly, in time it may come to have the character of a life-shaping conviction (Kierkegaard, *Concl. Unsci. Post.*).

Consequently, not every argument that follows will be, or should be expected to be, sufficient to all conceivable circumstances. Doubt creatively accompanies each of these arguments. Doubting the arguments is an appropriate way of seeking to ascertain how firmly they are indeed rooted in reality. A critical, probing faith is a necessary and useful stage toward an assured and confirmed faith (Job 3:1–26; Clement of Alex., *Stromata* 8.9; Luther, *Letters of Spiritual Counsel*).

The Biblical Assumption that God Exists

In the Bible, God's existence was so widely assumed that it was thought that "only a fool would say in his heart 'there is no God'" (Ps. 14:1). It does not seem to have occurred to most of the prophets and apostles that there is a compelling need formally to prove or even argue in detail for the existence of God.

Hilary argued that there is nothing so proper to God as to be (*Trin.* 1. 5). Augustine thought that God's existence was more certain than our own (*Conf.* 7.10). Scripture's first phrase, "In the beginning, God" (Gen. 1:1), unmistakably expresses this prevailing biblical assumption: It is not that we arrive at a well-argued conclusion that God is, but from the beginning God *is*, and only later may we perhaps debate, think, and argue about it (Tho. Aq., *SCG* 1. 4). Scripture does not teach that "in the beginning we have a rational capacity that enables us to generate the idea of God's existence, which in due time is able to conclude that God exists." Rather, before any human rationality or argument, there is God.

Nonetheless, rational and experiential argument has a modest but useful function in the formation of souls. Personal faith may not be borne of argument, but it may be supported and confirmed by argument (Lactantius, *Div. Inst.* 7.9; Anselm, *Proslog.* 1). The reason faith persists in looking for rational clarity and confirmation of its premises is this: Faith's premises are felt to be so valuable that they deserve the best intellectual reflection possible to confirm argumentatively what faith already knows inwardly (Augustine, *Letters* 102, 103; Tho. Aq., *SCG* 1. 10).

Why Ask?

When we fail to use our best intelligence around such pivotal questions as the existence of God, we diminish the power of faith by the dullness of our minds. We are being called to love God with our minds, testing the validity of every argument concerning God (Augustine, *Soliloquies* 1. 3; Tho. Aq., *ST* 1 Q2).

Thomas Aquinas began *Summa Theologica* by playfully testing out two erroneous views that demean all theistic reasoning: (1) Arguing the existence of God seems worthless because there can be no argument about a self-evident truth or about an undemonstrable mystery. Why waste mental energy trying to think about whether God exists, some say, if God necessarily exists? (2) If we already have a solid, sincere faith, we surely would not want to detract from piety or faith by substituting argument for it, some say. Both these assertions tend to be a lazy embarrassment to a reasoned faith, which could, if it utilized its intellectual abilities, provide plausible reasons for its faith (Tho. Aq., *ST* 1 Q2, *SCG* 1.5). When we examine the main alternatives to theistic reasoning, we find the critics of theism just as heavily laden with difficulties (Garrigou-Lagrange, *God*, I; Tillich, *Syst. Theol.*,I; Mascall, *He Who Is*: 41; Hick, *The Existence of God*: 6). Consistent skepticism argues not only that we cannot know anything about God, but that we cannot reliably know anything about anything (Hume, *Dialogues Concerning Natural Religion*:57).

Countering these cynical responses, five types of argument have been predominant in classical Christian theistic reasoning:

1. Arguments from Order and Design (Purpose or Teleological Arguments)

2. Arguments from Humanity: Mind, Human Nature, and General Consent (Innate and Anthropological Arguments)

3. Arguments from Change, Causality, Contingency, and Degrees of Being (Cosmological Arguments on how the world works)

4. Arguments from Conscience, Beauty, Pragmatic Results, and Congruity (Moral, Aesthetic, and Pragmatic Arguments)

5. Argument from the Idea of Perfect Being (Necessary Being or Ontological Argument)

We will set forth the principal forms of these arguments as they have appeared perennially in classical Christian teaching.

How to Reason from Order or Design

The argument from order or design, the most ancient, simplest, and clearest of all theistic arguments, is easiest to apply to the practice of Christian counsel and spiritual formation. Aristotle thought that it was known by Hermotimus of Clazomenae (Metaphy. 1 13, 984b). An ancient fragment of Anaxagoras stated the essential argument: "All things that were to be, all things that were but are not now, all things that are now or that shall be, Mind arranged them all" (Anaxagoras *frag.* B 12). Adapted by Augustine (*Conf.* 11.5; *Letters* 137), this argument became the fifth of Thomas's five ways, called the teleological argument because it argues toward God from purposes and ends (i.e., final causes, Tho. Aq., *ST* 1 Q2.3; *SCG* 1.13). It has two principal forms: order and design.

The Argument from Order

The premise: Order is everywhere observable. Even the doubtful or despairing can see that there is order—a useful arrangement of things in a system of nature that implies intelligence and purpose in the world. The universe is characterized by extraordinarily complex layers and modes of order. It is implausible that these could have occurred by chance (Athanasius, Ag. Heathen 38).

It remains a premise of scientific inquiry that the world is characterized by intelligibility, which itself is often called the "natural order." Even when physicists discover some irregular principle of indeterminacy, such as the Heisenberg principle, when nature at times appears unpredictable, there is, even in the principle of random indeterminacy of atomic interaction, a moving wave of meaning and order. Careful observation of plant and animal life, physical elements, centrifugal forces, and stellar movements yields that overwhelming conviction of orderliness (Gen. 1; Ps. 8; Lactantius, *Div. Inst.* 1.2; Gregory of Nyssa, *On Infants' Early Deaths*).

The heart of the argument: If there is any order at all in the world, it is necessary to hypothesize an orderer, not necessarily a divine orderer, but an orderer of some kind (Augustine, *Conf.* 11.5). There cannot be orderliness or purposiveness without a ground of order or a mind that shapes the order. Governance in the world implies some kind of governor (Plato, *Laws* 10.904; Cicero, "On the Nature of the Gods" 2,5; for a critique see Hume, *An Enquiry Concerning Human Understanding*, 11; *Dialogues*, 5; Kant, *Critique of Pure Reason*).

Formally the argument may be summarized in this way: (*a*) The visible world is a cosmos, an orderly unity whose order is constant, uniform, complex, and intrinsic to the universe itself. (*b*) Such an order cannot be explained unless it is admitted that the universe has a cause that displays intelligence capable of bringing it into being. (*c*) Therefore, such a cause of the universe exists, which is to say, God exists as the intelligent cause of the universe (Tho. Aq., *ST* 1 Q2.3).

Discordant elements cannot work harmoniously together unless by some intelligent direction (John of Damascus, *OF* 1. 3). "In the world we find that things of diverse natures come together under one order, and this is not rarely or by chance, but always or for the most part. There must therefore be some being by whose providence the world is governed. This we call God" (Tho. Aq., *SCG* 1. 13). The argument was anticipated in Scripture: "Does he that planted the ear not hear, he that moulded the eye not see?" (Ps. 94:9). "Who can look at the world and not sense there there is a God?" (Hilary, Hom. on Ps. 52.2).

The argument from order cannot be stated without implying two of the divine attributes previously discussed: the *omniscience* by which God is able fully to know the created order so as to order it, and the *omnipotent* power by which God is able to bring such an order into being. This theistic argument offers a reason to believe that the all-wise and almighty God to whom Scripture witnesses, exists in reality and not merely as a conception in our minds (Gregory of Nazianzus, *Orat.* 28.2; Calvin, *Inst.* 1.5.5; 1.14.20).

The power of the argument from order is best seen by trying to take seriously its contrary hypothesis, that there is no cause whatever of the order observed. For then one is attributing the order to chance, which still leaves the order unexplained. To say the order occurred by chance means either that we are unable to ascertain what the cause is while nonetheless affirming that some cause must exist, or that there is no cause and events occur without any reason or possible explanation (Tho. Aq., *ST* 1 Q105; Calvin, *Inst.* 1.5.11; 1.16.5). Both of these ways of viewing chance fail to account convincingly for the primary evidence—order in the world—which demands some sufficient explanation. This argument is on some occasions found useful in caring for persons trapped in syndromes of doubt or despair, to remind them that their doubt or despair exists within an intelligible order (Eccles. 2:20; 1 Cor. 1:8; Clement of Alex., *Stromata* 7.7; Luther, *Letters of Spiritual Counsel*).

The Argument from Design

The classic statement of the argument from design came from Thomas Aquinas: "We observe that things without consciousness, such as physical bodies, operate with a purpose, as appears from their co-operating invariably, or almost so, in the same way in order to obtain the best result. Clearly then they reach this end by intention and not by chance. Things lacking knowledge move toward an end only when directed by someone who knows and understands, as an arrow by an archer. There is consequently an intelligent being who directs all natural things to their ends; and this being we call God" (*ST* 1 Q2.3).

An arrow moving through the air is a metaphor of a guided, orderly trajectory of an inanimate object moving toward a predetermined end, since the arrow is guided by intelligible forces that determine its path. To have guidance, one must hypothesize a guide. The conceiving of ends, and the choosing of means appropriate for the attainment of ends, can be done only by a personal mind—an intelligent being. If purposiveness is experienced in the world, then one must hypothesize a purposing being (Ps. 8; Chrysostom, Comm. on Ps. 8; Methodius, *On Free Will*, 2).

The instinct of animals serves as an illustration of an activity toward an intelligible purpose that the animal itself has not understood or foreseen. A bird builds a nest in spring without having been taught. Under the guidance of instinct it fulfills a purpose that it has not grasped: the perpetuation of the species. Although the bird does not understand its own mating and nesting, these are not meaningless or merely shaped by chance, but filled with purpose, with complicated means that tend toward ends unknown but meaningful (Ps 104:1–14).

Similarly: If someone found a watch in a forest, one could assume that some intelligent mind had worked on it and produced it. This conclusion would be even more plausible if one discovered that its complex structure is adapted to the measurement of time (Paley, *Natural Theol.* I: 37). "I saw houses and knew that the householders were in residence. I saw the world and I understood providence. I saw a ship sink without anyone to steer it, and I noticed the pointless behavior of human beings who were not steered by God. I saw different cities and states well organized and understood that everything holds together by the ordering of God" (Ephrem, Self-examination, ESOO 1:123).

How to Reason from Human Nature: Mind, Human Nature, and General Consent

The second group of theistic arguments hinges on the analysis of human consciousness, human nature, or human social experience as the basis for the necessary conclusion that God exists. They form a bridge between the above argument from design and the moral arguments to be discussed below. All theistic arguments tend to converge in mutual complementarity—one of their most striking features (Tho. Aq., *ST* 1–2 Q109).

Accounting for the Appearance of Mind in Nature

The emergence of minds in natural history requires the hypothesis that God exists. The argument from mind differs from the arguments from order or design which use largely inanimate or animal metaphors (arrows, clocks, animal adaptation), whereas the argument from mind proceeds from the empirical observation of emerging intelligence in history and natural-historical development, especially human mind.

The pervasive presence of intelligibility in the world and in our minds requires the premise of God. This argument begins with the remarkable fact that intelligent consciousness undeniably exists in the world. Not only is the world itself intelligible, but also our minds are capable of grasping something of that intelligibility. That we live in an intelligible world is a fact that is absolutely necessary to any language or discourse whatever. The premise of intelligibility is a necessary precondition of our minds' even thinking about anything (Clement of Alex., *Stromata* 5.13; Calvin, *Inst.* 1.3). The fact that intelligence exists to apprehend that intelligibility is itself the most astonishing event of natural history's development.

At times the senses may deceive. The only way we can grasp those deceptions is on the basis of the larger assumption of the intelligibility of things and the trustworthiness of the inquiring mind in ferreting out deceptions. Human reasoning begins with a fundamental trust in its own power of reasoning. Descartes rightly reasoned that the one thing he could not possibly doubt was that he had the capacity to doubt (Descartes, *Principles of Philosophy* 1. 7). If I can doubt my own thoughts, I must be able to think, to inquire, to examine, and to criticize, and these are functions that could not work without both an intelligible world and a perceiving intelligence.

Human consciousness grows slowly, through adaptation, acculturation, socialization, and education, to understand, explore, question, and grasp the structure, order, and intelligibility of reality. Through the study of chemistry, astronomy, physics, botany, biology, and psychology, we look for reliable knowledge of ourselves and our world. We formulate reliable laws of causation based upon these observations. Then we subject these laws to reexamination, constant scrutiny, and revision. No such examination could occur without the dual premise of the intelligibility of these things and perceiving intelligence (Bonaventure, *Breviloquium;* Tho. Aq. *Comm. on Boethius 5.7*).

The scientific enterprise assumes that there is a fundamental correspondence between our minds and the intelligibility of what we can reasonably know (Kant, *Critique of Pure Reason*). Scientific inquiry appeals to commonly repeatable experiments as the basis of validating that an experience has been accurately and consensually observed (Tho. Aq., *SCG* 1.7; *ST* 1 Q1; Nicolas de Cusa, *U&R*:241). Logical inquiry appeals to reliable laws and rules of rational deduction and inferences in making conclusions. We assume that these laws observed in nature apply to all cultures. Otherwise they are considered deficient in some way and subject to further investigation and revision (Augustine, *Conf.* 4.10; *CG* 12; Hume, *Dialogues Concerning Natural Religion, Phil. Works*, 2:457).

Intelligence can think about only what is intelligible (Tho. Aq., *ST* 1 Q14.1, I). This conclusion has wide-ranging relevance for Christian teaching about God. There is only one universe. That is what uni-verse means: there is only one (*uni*) turn (*vertere*), one circle of being (Gregory of Nyssa, *Ag. Eunomius* 1.22). If there were two universes, then it would be necessary to hypothesize some relation between these universes, which itself would then be an embracing universe, of which there could be only one. It is precisely this *universe* in its totality that displays an order or intelligibility that corresponds with the order and intelligibility that we experience in our own minds (Tertullian, *Ag. Praxeas* 5.6; Tho. Aq., *SCG* 1.55; Watson, *TI* 1:271).

If a *universe* exists, and if our minds are able to grasp anything about it, both it and we must have intelligibility. If intelligibility exists at all, it must have some ground and source (C. S. Pierce, *Collected Papers* 6: 345; F. R. Tennant, *Philosophical Theol.* 2,4, 4; H. Bergson, *Creative Evolution*; Calvin, *Inst.* 1.5; 1.14).

It is implausible to hypothesize a spontaneous emergence of intelligibility for such a massive order of intelligible events and beings as the observed universe, natural history, and human history (Wm. Temple, *Nature, Man, and God*; Paley, *Natural Theol.*; S. Alexander, *Space, Time and Deity* 2: 353).

The point: The intelligibility or mind that we find everywhere in the universe could only be the result of an unsurpassably intelligent being. Reason suggests what Scripture attests: that the One revealed as all-wise reaches out to illumine the human spirit (Tho. Aq., *ST* 1 Q12). As the law of gravity exists prior to our discovering it, as the laws of motion are there prior to our moving anything, so must the larger intelligibility of the world exist prior to any intelligent awareness that we might have of it (Tho. Aq., *ST* 1 Q19).

It is useful here to note the sweeping difference between things and minds. It is misleading to think simplistically of minds as things. Whereas things are inert, minds are alive, conscious and capable of perceptions, feelings, and willing. Finite minds, of course, exist within finite bodies. The body is a thing, but as death shows, the thing a body is without mind is radically different from the thing a body is with mind. Bodies are perceived by minds, never without minds. Here reason intuits what Scripture proclaims clearly: As there cannot be any ordered body or thing without some sort of mind to order it, so there cannot be a human mind or universal history without positing a greater source, ground, and end of human intelligence. This we call God (Lactantius, *Div. Inst.* 1. 2; Watson, *TI* 1: 285). This argument is summed up in a Clementine Homily: "There is an unbegotten artificer who brought the elements together, if they were separate; or, if they were together, artistically blended them so as to generate life, and perfected from all one work. For it cannot be that a work which is completely wise can be made without a mind which is greater than it." (Ps-Clement, *Hom.* 6.25).

Inspirer of the Personal Good

Free and responsible personhood is history's highest achievement and most precious value. Accordingly, a divine person must be posited as the premise of human personhood. One cannot reasonably have human personality drop out of the blue in history without hypothesizing a divine person that elicits and awakens human personality (Justin Martyr, Second Apol. 6; John of Damascus, *OF* 1.1; Whitehead, Religion in the Making: 154; Hartshorne, PSG: 233).

This is a sub-set of the above argument on the appearance of mind in nature, but focusing on personhood rather than mind. Since we are persons and as such experience a constant struggle for values that we regard as expressive of our personal being, then we have compelling reasons to conceive of One existing who engenders in us the desire to actualize values corresponding to our personal being.

Idealism from Plato to Hegel has viewed matter as inspirited. According to Hegel, Spirit is unfolding itself reasonably in time, and Absolute Spirit is embodying itself inexorably in history (Hegel, *Phenomenology of Mind; Reason in History*; Augustine, *CG*, 12). Accordingly, everything that happens in the material world is Spirit coming into ever-new actualizations. Every time (*Zeit*) is an expression of Spirit (*Geist*). The highest form of Spirit thus far manifested in history is human personality.

Humans are not just out there alone in an autonomous struggle for the good. It does not make any sense for existence to be enmeshed in the struggle for good without being in some sense supported by a supreme being who also is aiming for the good (for further expressions of this argument, see H. N. Wieman, *The Source of Human Good*; and E. S. Brightman, *The Problem of God*).

The Argument from the Constitution of Human Nature

This argument leads us to another variation, which, though seeming to be slight, represents a deeper turn: the very thought of God in the human mind assumes and requires that God is. Stated differently, God must exist because the idea of God is an element of human nature itself. Thus the very constitution of human nature points beyond itself to its Creator (Origen, De *Princip.* 1. 1.7; Tho. Aq., *SCG* 2.4).

This is an induction from wide observation of human experience: everywhere in the history of human consciousness there is the idea of God. Again and again it reappears as if belonging to our very minds and essential nature. It is as if God is a necessary premise of ordinary human thought and experience. Scripture also attests this view. At the Areopagus in Athens, Paul argues that God who created the world and all in it created humanity so that every culture and period of history are destined in their own way "to seek God, and, it might be, touch and find him; though indeed he is not far from each one of us, for in him we live and move, in him we exist; as some of your own poets have said, 'We are his off-spring'" (Acts 17:27, 28; Chrysostom, *Comm. on Acts*, 38; Calvin, *Inst.* 1.5). The assumption that human beings cannot even be defined apart from God is integral to biblical anthropology: "On the day when God created man he made him in the likeness of God" (Gen. 5:1).

When Paul spoke of the Gentile world in Romans 1 and 2, he assumed they already had a prior elementary knowledge of God written on their hearts (Rom. 1:18): "They display the effect of the law inscribed on their hearts. Their conscience is called as a witness" (Rom. 2:15). The will deceives itself by adoring creaturely goods as greater than the Creator (Rom. 1:26, 27; Tertullian, *Chaplet* 6; Calvin, *Inst.* 1.18; 2.1). Yet repeatedly in Scripture the assumption is made that in the nature and constitution of humanity there is an awareness of One upon whom everything else depends, One to whom all creatures are finally responsible (Gen. 1:26, 27; Pss. 8, 19, 51; Rom. 1, 2; Heb. 2:6; John 1:9; Augustine, *Conf.* 13.10).

It is on this basis that some classic Christian teachers argue that the awareness of the existence of God is both innate and connate—that is, intrinsically existing in a person from birth (*in-nasci*) and coming with birth (*con-nasci*), and therefore belonging to the essential or original constitution of humanity (Tho. Aq., *ST* 1 Q75; Calvin, *Inst.* 1.15.1–4; Gerhard, *LT* 1: 250; Watson, *TI* 1: 271).

The constitution of human nature is such that it is intrinsically capable of developing an awareness of God as ordinary human self-consciousness emerges, accompanied in due time by language, moral development, socialization, memory, reason, and will (Augustine, *Conf.* 10.15; Tho. Aq., *SCG* 1.8). "There are two teachers who have been given to us from the beginning, creation and conscience, which have taught the human race without ever uttering a word" (Chrysostom, Sermons on Hannah, 1.3). God has "implanted the knowledge of his existence in everyone by nature. The creation, its preservation and its government all proclaim the majesty of the divine nature" (John of Damascus The Orthodox Faith, 1.1).

The point: If humanity has the idea of God implanted in its very nature, then some sufficient reason must be set forth to explain why. Of many possibilities, the most evident and plausible one is that God implanted it.

Argument from the General Consent of Human Cultures

Another argument, once frequently employed, then generally ignored, but now recovering some of its credibility, hinges on the general consent of human cultures to the premise that God is (*consensus gentium,* the consensus of peoples). This is another corroboratory argument that, lacking the force of a fully adequate demonstration, is best used only to support and amplify other arguments, yet it cannot be cheaply dismissed without ignoring the cumulative wisdom of human history.

The argument is strengthened by making a firm disclaimer at the outset: the claim for consensus is not the same as the claim for unanimity. No major teacher of the Christian tradition has been so careless as to suggest that every single human being in fact consciously knows or believes that God exists, even though the argument is sometimes caricatured in this way. It would be foolish to say that every single human being agrees precisely on anything at all.

Rather, it is argued that belief in God is so widespread both in primitive cultures and throughout history, and atheism so theoretical, limited, and sporadic, that it is demonstrably a human consensus, despite occasional disclaimers, that God exists (Theophilus, *To Autolycus*; Lactantius, *Div. Inst.* 1.5–6). To argue the contrary—that God does not exist—is to ignore and dismiss the historical weight of human experience. If humankind at virtually all known times and places has assumed belief in a divine order that transcends human and historical disorders, then that is a fact that cannot be completely ignored by serious investigators (Justin Martyr, *First Apol.* 2.6; Origen, *Ag. Celsus* 7.32).

While the argument from consensus should not be used in isolation from other arguments, neither should it be completely set aside. Arbitrarily or capriciously to adopt a conviction contrary to that which is most widely prevailing in human history can hardly be called scientific (Clement of Alex., *Stromata* 5.12–14). General consent implies wide human experiencing and reflection out of many different cultural assumptions in all historical periods—far more varied cultures, for example, than have affirmed modern empirical method in the last century. Whether these reasons and experiences are valid or not must not be decided in advance by arbitrarily rejecting the more durable hypothesis in favor of merely the more recent (Justin Martyr, *First Apol.* 18–24).

Even when we look at societies in which brutal attempts have been made systematically to eradicate belief in God (such as the Soviet Union, and China during the period of the Cultural Revolution), the belief continues to persist, and even to show through with special poignancy and power in those very societies, precisely amid persecution (Justin Martyr, *Dialogue with Trypho,* chap. 93; Tertullian, *The Soul's Testimony*; A. Solzhenitsyn, *The Cancer Ward; The Gulag Archipelago*). Even at the height of Maoist power, the notion of the mandate of heaven remained firmly entrenched. Atheistic systems also have profound practical analogies to belief systems, so much so that atheistic belief itself may be argued as essentially an inverted form of theistic belief (R. Niebuhr, *NDM* 1. 1–5; Herberg, "The Christian Mythology of Socialism," *FEH*: 180–90). Atheists indeed exist, but are on the whole exceptional, if all cultures and universal history are being surveyed (Origen, *Ag. Celsus* 7.37; Calvin, *Inst.* 1.3–5). There is no evidence whatever that their ranks are increasing. Whether they wish to or not, atheistic systems must struggle hard to make themselves plausible against this powerful historic and social consensus, which is their most frustrating obstacle.

The idea that there is general consent of humanity to the belief that God exists was widely held among early Christian teachers (Clement of Alex., *Stromata* 5.12–14; Theophilus, *To Autolycus, ANF* 2:85; Minucius Felix, *Octavius,* 32–33; Tertullian, *The Soul's Testimony*). This fact of wide consent is usually connected with the intuited notion that the idea of God is naturally implanted or inborn or innate in human consciousness (Justin Martyr, *First Apol.* 2; *Dialogue with Trypho,*

93; Clement of Alex., *Stromata* 5.12; Tertullian, *The Soul's Testimony* 2; Origen, *Ag. Celsus* 7.37; *OFP* 4; Lactantius, *Div. Inst.* 1.2.5; Augustine, *Conf.* 10.23).

Arguments from Change, Causality, Contingency, and Degrees of Being

Does God exist? The only answer some will consider plausible must be based upon observation of evidence gathered in the world of experience. Arguments that deliberately proceed in this way are called cosmological arguments since they are based on observed knowledge of the whole world. The four principal forms of cosmological arguments are from motion, change, contingency, and degrees of being.

Among classical exponents of these arguments is Thomas Aquinas, whose "five ways" of reasoning toward God from the world constitute the principal historical statement of the cosmological arguments. Although Thomas did not invent these arguments, he brilliantly synthesized them and organized them for future use, relying heavily upon Aristotle, Augustine, Dionysius, John of Damascus, and Maimonides. Each argument starts from a solid base in the world of experience and posits God as the source of that world as we experience it.

Any Motion Requires an Original Mover: The Argument from Change

The first of these begins with a simple, testable observation: our constant awareness of change or motion: Things are in motion. Things change. Something must have moved the motions that we see moving. Observed motion Z is moved by some motion Y, which is moved by X, which is moved by a long series of previous motions. Is it reasonable to assume that there was never any original motion that started such movement? Wherever you see a process of movement, it is more reasonable to hypothesize that movement is moved by something, for it cannot in every respect cause its own movement. Everything that changes is changed by something influencing it (Plato, Laws 10.894; Phaedrus; Aristotle, Metaphy. BWA 1, 12; David Hume, Dialogues Concerning Natural Relig., 2–4, 9; Kant, Critique of Pure Reason). "All mutables bring us back to a first immutable" (Tho. Aq., On Truth 2).

If you wish to provide an explanation of change, you have two alternatives: either you must hypothesize (*a*) an infinite regression of change with no explanation of an original mover, which is an intellectual embarrassment, an offense to reason (Gregory of Nazianzus, *Second Theol. Orat.* 6), or (*b*) you must hypothesize some unchanging ground that lies prior to all the multiple changes we experience in ordinary life (Tho. Aq., *Compend. Theol:* 9). Christian teaching has concluded: If change exists anywhere in the world, there must be some Source of change, or some Originative Change Agent (Tho. Aq., *ST* 1 Q2; *SCG* 1.44; *SCG* 3.66). That agent cannot be other than the same reality Christian worship celebrates and Scripture attests as God (Tho. Aq., *SCG* 1.13).

The Prime Mover which Aristotle and Thomas Aquinas called the unmoved Mover, or unchanging source of change, points through reason beyond reason toward the incomparable One celebrated in Christian worship as God the Creator (Tho. Aq., *Compend. Theol.*, 3; *SCG* 1. 13; *Comm. on Aristotle's Physics*, 8). This experiential argument is anticipated in Scripture: "Every house is built by someone, but he that built all things is God" (Heb. 3:4).

Effects Point to an Original Cause: The Argument from Causality

The next argument appears to be much like the previous one, but it is as different as cause is from change. The argument from cause begins similarly by looking at the effects and thinking backward to causes. "Efficient causes" are causes that have been effected by something other than themselves. The natural world is full of causes. The scientist's task is to ferret them out. Each cause itself has been effected by previous causes, which themselves are rooted in prior causes, for no effect can exist without some cause. Scientific observation hungers to find a sufficient cause for every effect. One cannot, without fundamental offense to the human intellect, assert that those causes go on and on without ending and without any sufficient causal explanation.

If every event has a cause, and the universe is a system of causes and effects, it stands to reason that there must be an underived causal agent, a necessary being that underlies and enables all these causes and effects (Tho. Aq., *ST* 1 Q2; *SCG* 1. 14). "If there were an infinite regress among efficient causes, no cause would be first" (Tho. Aq., *SCG* 1. 13). "We must, therefore, posit that there exists a first efficient cause. This is God" (*SCG* 1. 13).

Every discrete effect must have a reason for its occurrence. What we say of every discrete event, we must also say of the universe, of which no known part is exempt from the law of causation. If every event is caused, any reasonable person will wonder about what sort of cause would be adequate to this immense effect that we call the cosmos. The only cause conceivable to such a vast and incalculable effect must be an independent, sufficient mind and infinite will capable of conceiving and initiating the universe. Such a mind must be capable of knowing the entire universe that is shaped by it, and must have the will and power adequate to bringing such a vast outlay of causes into effect. *These are precisely the qualities previously described as intrinsic to the God attested by Scripture: free, personal, eternal Spirit capable of infinite power and knowledge* (Gen. 17:1; Exod. 6:3; Athanasius, *Ag. Heathen*, 34, 35). That infinitely capable mind is what Christian confession calls God. The infinitely powerful and knowing Mind, however, has a direct kinship and correspondence with our minds, and with the underlying intelligibility of the universe (Calvin, *Inst.* 1.16–18; Watson, *TI* I:275). For mind has in fact appeared in the natural history of the universe (Ps. 102:26, 27; Origen, *De Princip.* 1. 6; Calvin, *Inst.* 1.13.23).

It is very difficult even to imagine the notion of any temporal event that is without cause or totally disconnected from a causal nexus. The reason it is so difficult is quite simple: Causality is an idea that is necessary to all finite thought. It is impossible to think without positing causality (Tho. Aq., *Compend. Theol.*:68).

Suppose that no original cause of all universal effects ever existed. Suppose nothing caused the universe. That is an even less plausible hypothesis than that an intelligent Mind created these vast complexities of matter and spirit. For if nothing caused the universe, how could it exist as an effect? How could such an assertion remain consistent with everything else we know of causality and reality?

Suppose that matter never had a beginning, but always existed. Still that requires a causal explanation. For that assertion does not exempt an evolving universe from causal inquiry as to its origin. If eternal matter, whence came the matter? How did it become so elaborately organized? Even more, how can we make sense out of the astonishing fact that mind emerged within the matter? To assert that matter can spontaneously produce mind is to assert an effect greater than the cause (W. Temple, *Nature, Man and God* 8).

Argument from Contingency

The third cosmological argument is drawn from the fact of contingency. A contingent act is one that depends upon something else (Calvin, *Inst.* 1.16.8, 9). Contingency is the opposite of necessity and is only understandable in relation to necessity. The world is full of things that are dependent on other things. These things, if they are dependent, have the character of not being necessary, in the sense that they can either be or not be. They do not exist by some absolute necessity. They come and they go. To explain the existence of a contingent being, one must refer to something else upon which it depends (Tho. Aq., *SCG* 1. 15). On the other hand, a necessary being would be a being that must exist. Existing would belong to that being's very essence. The completely sufficient reason for its existence would be in itself. It would not depend upon some other being for its existence (Tho. Aq., *ST* 1 Q2.3).

The heart of this argument is that the existence of contingent beings requires that we admit the existence of some necessary being. If any contingent being whatsoever exists, then there must be some necessary being. Contingent beings evidently exist. Therefore, the unconditionally necessary being must exist as the sufficient explanation of any contingent being (Tho. Aq., *ST* 1 Q3.7; *SCG* 2.30).

The hinge point: Everything cannot be contingent. "Were this true, nothing would ever have begun, for what is does not begin to be except because of something which is, and so there would be nothing even now. This is clearly hollow. Therefore all things cannot be might-not-have-beens; among them must be a being whose existence is necessary" (Tho. Aq., *ST* 1 Q2.3). A nonexistent contingency can only be brought into existence by something upon which it is contingent, upon something that already exists. Hence reason suggests what Scripture attests, that such a necessary being exists, which the worshiping community has called God.

Degrees of Being or Grades of Perfection

Look about you in the world, and you will see different grades in being. We frequently use the words more and less. Without such comparative terms we would be hard put to say what we often want to say. This is evidence that some perception of grades of being and goodness is built into the structure of human language, regardless of what language we speak. Some acts are less noble, some more noble. There are gradations of truth, wisdom, and perception.

Where there is a more or a less, that necessarily implies an idea of the perfection of that category of being. For how could one have a more or a less without a most? It is unreasonable to talk about a scale of gradation and leave open the maximum of that scale. If one were to hypothesize that there is nothing there at the maximal level, then the scale itself would be incomplete and deficient (Tho. Aq., *SCG* 2.15; *ST* 1 Q2.3, Q44.1). If you have degrees of justice, that indirectly points toward what is absolutely or incomparably just, that reality that is to the highest possible degree just. One who recognizes relative justice at all must posit that absolutely just being in relation to which rough modes of justice are to be measured.

This is clearly seen in common language about the *good*. At one point we see something with minimal good in it, another with some good in it, and another with very great good in it. If there exists any degree of goodness, then there must exist that which is good without qualification, without which there would be no way of measuring the relative degree of goodness of things. If one can conceive at all the notion of something that is less good or slightly better, then one must hypothesize that by which "better and worse" is assessed. This is a persistent assumption of moral language. One cannot posit a good and a better without a best.

Thomas Aquinas taught that we define any degree of a genus in relation to the maximum of that genus, just "as fire, which is the maximum of heat, is the cause of all hot things. Therefore there must also be something which is to all beings the cause of their being, goodness, and every other perfection; and this we call God" (Tho. Aq., *ST* 1 Q2.3).

Similarly with *being:* If anything at all exists, then there must be to all beings something that most completely *is.* If there are degrees of being, there must be that reality that absolutely exists, without any possible diminution of being.

If there are degrees of truth, we must posit some maximum of those degrees. It is absurd to hold that there are degrees of truth but lacking any highest conceivable degree, or to avoid reference to that absolute truth in relation to which those gradients of relative truth are to be measured. Any assessment of relativity of being or goodness implies a standard in terms of which that relative being is seen as existing (Augustine, *CG* 19; *Letters* 162; John of Damascus, *OF* 1.9).

Arguments from Conscience, Beauty, Pragmatic Results, and Congruity

The Argument from Moral Awareness

Just as relative moral necessity cannot be required of the will except by that which is relatively good, so absolute moral necessity cannot be caused by any good less than the insurmountable good. A sense of absolute obligation can only come from One to whom absolute moral authority is fittingly and legitimately ascribed. It is to this transcendent ground of obligation that conscience witnesses. For conscience does not pretend to make the laws that it dictates (Clement of Alex., *Instr.* 3.1; Augustine, *Answer to Letters of Petilian* 2.85). The heart of the moral argument is this: The existence of absolute moral obligation establishes the existence of God as the cause of the moral order.

Conscience would not be able to bind our wills so radically and unconditionally if it were merely that we were binding ourselves. Just as order in the world suggests an intelligent orderer as its cause, so does moral awareness in human decision making suggest and require a sufficient source of moral consciousness and ground of moral authority in the universe (Augustine, *On the Profit of Believing* 16. 34; Kant, *Crit. Pract. Reason*; J. H. Newman, *Grammar of Assent*).

The moral argument emerges out of an irrepressible internal dialogue. There are some ways in which my freedom actualizes itself that are not adequately in touch with who I really am. I tell myself, "That is not me, or not the best me." The voice speaking is me: my conscience. There emerges a sense of serenity when I follow that conscience. I feel at one with myself. There is a sense of guilt, subjective brokenness, and self-alienation when I actualize my freedom in a way that I know is not really consistent with what I ought to be or do (Luther, *Comm. on Galatians, MLS:* 100–109; Calvin, *Inst.* 3.19.15; Wesley, *WJW* 5:135). The root word for conscience (*conscientia* or *syneidēsis*) implies knowledge of oneself, a knowledge one has with one's self, a knowledge accompanying one's own choosing and intrinsic to the process of choosing. I go about choosing; I make these choices and then I have to live with my choices.

Conscience is the knowledge I have of my own choosing. It is the way in which I compare my decisions with my truer, deeper self and with that silent measurer of my true self within myself that transcends myself (Rom. 2:15; 1 Cor. 8:7–12; 1 Tim. 1:5, 19; 4:2; Heb. 9:9; 1 Pet. 3:16; Acts 23:1). Every conscious and rational human being has that self-knowing capacity (Calvin, *Inst.* 3.2–3; Kant, *Fundamental Principles of the Metaphys. of Morals, LLA*: 11). Most of the Western intellectual tradition, including Christian theism, has argued that everyone has some form of conscience.

The Ground of Reason's Moral Claim

Kant sought to refute most of the arguments that we have previously discussed, but strictly on the basis of moral reasoning. In his view no empirical or speculative reasoning could be sufficient to establish reliable proofs of God's existence. All reason could do was correct the misunderstandings of various dubious or ambiguous arguments for God's existence (Kant, Critique of Pure Reason, "On the Impossibility of the Physico-Theological Proof"; Religion Within the Limits of Reason Alone). Instead, Kant sought to employ what he called practical reason, a form of reason that emerges out of moral consciousness, as the sole basis for arguing the existence of God (Crit. of Prac. Reason 2.2.5).

Although Kant's views are notoriously difficult to explain, his importance in modern theistic reasoning (especially liberal Protestant) is so great that he cannot be ignored. Though Kant viewed the cosmological arguments as wholly unsatisfactory, he thought they could be replaced by the reframing of the sort of moral argument that had long been a part of classic Christian theistic reasoning.

Eternity must ultimately right temporality's wrongs. Conscience, moral freedom, responsibility, and law would be absurd if there were no moral law or lawgiver. Such a lawgiver every rational being has in the impingement of conscience. Any reasonable person by self-examination can come to hear and be aware of the absolutely rational claim of the categorical imperative, which is, "Act as if the maxim of your action were to become by your will a universal law of nature" (Kant, *Fundamental Principles of Metaphy. of Morals, LLA*: 38). This moral consciousness does not accrue as a matter of gathering experience in the world, but rather is something given in and with consciousness prior to data gathering. Thus the idea of God, he argued, is a necessary postulate universally and practically required by moral reflection in any reasonable person (*Crit. Pract. Reason* 2.2.5).

Consequently we have a modern form of argument for the existence of God that is based exclusively upon a certain kind of reasoning, namely, *a priori* moral reasoning. God becomes the necessary hypothesis of the moral conscience. Kant reasoned that God is needed to bring virtue and happiness into fitting conjunction, for in this world they do not correspond. Since injustice prevails in history, there must be a transhistorical way of rectifying wrongs. One cannot have a moral order without a divinely fair mind that undergirds the rights and transcends the wrongs of history. Kant's argument is based not on revelation but, in his view, upon reason alone, and a particular type of reason—moral reasoning (Kant, *Crit. Pract. Reason* 2.2.1).

To overcome the obstacle of the non-correspondence of virtue and happiness in this life, Kant argued that reason must hypothesize three postulates: freedom, immortality, and God. We must have *freedom* if we are to sustain any idea of moral responsibility. Only if one can freely respond to a moral claim can one reasonably be addressed with, or address oneself with, a moral claim. *Immortality* is a necessary postulate because in this world happiness and virtue are not conjoined perfectly, so the reasonable person must hypothesize another world beyond this sphere that somehow will make right what is temporarily wrong in this world.

God is a necessary hypothesis of the moral consciousness because God alone can, in some final way beyond our present experience, rightly bring into harmony the disjunctive relation of virtue and happiness (*Crit. Pract. Reason* 2.2.4–6). This offered an ethical justification for religion that has come to dominate some modern Protestant traditions, particularly Protestant liberalism, which may be in large part defined as a Kantian ethic melded with selected strands of Protestant theology (A. Ritschl, *Justification and Reconciliation;* A. Harnack, *What Is Christianity?;* W. Herrmann, *Syst. Theol.*).

The Necessity of a Moral Requirer

In *A Grammar of Assent* John Henry Newman presented the moral argument to the modern mind more subtly and with a deeper acquaintance with the varied strands of ancient Christian theism. He too began with conscience: All feel responsibility. No human consciousness can fully succeed in escaping some awareness of guilt and shame. We have an inner sense of sin or moral revulsion when we do something wrong and a sense of moral justification and serenity when we do something right. This cannot be simply explained sociologically or in terms of finite parenting. The depth, extent, and power of these moral feelings require the explanation of a moral Requirer (Newman, A Grammar of Assent: 104–15; Hastings Rashdall, The Theory of Good and Evil 2.3.1; W. D. Ross, The Right and the Good).

"The wicked man runs away with no one in pursuit" (Prov. 28:1). From whom is one running away? What is one afraid of? To say merely "oneself" may not fully account for the fact that this voice within oneself, conscience, points to that which is beyond oneself (Chrysostom, Homilies on the Statues 8.3). Newman did not argue that conscience is a direct or immediate revelation of God in specific detail. Yet conscience is not something we merely give to ourselves, but is God-bestowed within every self, and constitutive of the self (Newman, *Grammar of Assent:* 112). It is not enough to say I give it to myself. Far more pertinently, I often wish I could get rid of it. I wish it would not continue to bother me. Conscience is not self-imposed, but rather is unavoidable, as if a transcendent witness within (Newman, *Grammar of Assent:* 395; W. Temple, *Nature, Man and God* 7; Wesley, *WJW* 7:132, 9:218).

Such a sense of moral responsibility cannot be explained except by supposing the existence of a superior lawgiver, a Holy One who is present and impinging upon our responsibility with the claim that we do the good we know and avoid the evil we know. Some Requirer must be implied in the subtle, inward, unavoidable requirement of conscience (Origen, *Ag. Celsus* 1. 4). In this way the will of the Creator is posited as the necessary and sufficient reason for the existence of moral obligation. Conscience is both immanent within us and transcendent beyond us. For this is the way God expresses the divine claim, at least indirectly, in the form of potential guilt, hiddenly meeting each one at the closest possible quarters—the inner precincts of each individual person's moral self-awareness (Newman, *Grammar of Assent:* 121; Kierkegaard, *Works of Love:* 136).

Evil, Conscience, and God

Moral awareness is painfully conscious that it exists in relation to that which transcends it. It desires and longs for communion and reconciliation with the One who gives moral order. It knows that it cannot be sufficiently explained in terms of environmental influences or education, although conscience is subject to further education and refinement. Rather conscience is an element essential to human consciousness, which preconditions education and socialization (Lactantius, *Div. Inst.* 6.8–10; Ambrose, *Duties* 1. 8–14; Luther, Comm. on Galatians, MLS: 118–21).

Nor can the presence of evil fundamentally undermine the moral argument, as if to say, "God could not exist in a world as bad as the one to which conscience attests." Rather, theistic exponents of the moral argument view the painful awareness of persistent evil as a powerful validation rather than a rejection of the argument, implying that "God does exist, because we are awakened to the persistence of evil through conscience in a way that points beyond the law to the lawgiver and leads to repentance, redemption, and reconciliation." (Augustine, *Enchiridion*, LCC 7: 353).

In classical Christian teaching, no evil to which conscience attests is so far distanced from the divine will that it cannot become subsequently a greater good. God permits evil to emerge out of freedom in the interest of the greater good of enhancing self-determination and personhood, and with the longer-range intent and hope of discipline and correction—all of which tends ultimately toward a more complete actualization of the divine good purpose (Calvin, *Inst.* 3.19.7).

The Argument from Beauty

Beauty gives pleasure to the senses or pleasurably exalts the mind or spirit. So universal is the capacity for beauty that this capacity is regarded as a normal faculty of human existence. The absence of any sense of beauty would be regarded as abnormal and a diminution of human dignity (Pss. 50:2; 96:6; Isa. 52:7; Methodius, *Orat.* on the Psalms). Beauty is that by reason of which we behold creaturely things as objects of admiration or ingenious inspiration or disinterested satisfaction. Something beautiful is intrinsically pleasing, and capable of pleasing most anyone who looks at it (Tho. Aq., *ST* 1–2 Q34.2; Kant, Critique of Judgment).

Beauty cannot be reduced to utility, for often we admire things whose usefulness cannot be established unless one appeals back to the primary value of beauty itself. Augustine sharply distinguished between those things to be used and those to be enjoyed. "To enjoy something is to cling to it with love for its own sake. To use something, however, is to employ it in obtaining that which you love, provided that it is worthy of love." (*On Chr. Doctrine* 1. 4). We may try to make "use" of God, as if God were a thing. Things are to be used, but God is to be enjoyed. "No one rightly uses God, for he is to be enjoyed. The last end is not a utility" (Tho. Aq., *ST* 1–2 Q16.3).

Beauty cannot be reduced to a purely inward feeling. For beauty to some degree can be shared, leading beholders to the conviction that there is something objective about beauty, that it is admirable in itself, as a sunrise would not be made less beautiful if no one were there to behold it (Clement of Alex., *Instr.* 3.1; Francis Hutcheson, *Inquiry into the Original of Our Ideas of Beauty and Virtue*; Edmund Burke, *The Sublime and the Beautiful*).

The aesthetic argument for the existence of God is the unadorned observation that if beauty exists at all in this extraordinary universe, then it must be accounted for by some sufficient cause. In view of the abundance and power of the forms of beauty in this world, no cause is sufficient short of positing a Creator who cares about creation enough to make it beautiful and recognizable as such. Where beauty is found, one must hypothesize a ground and giver of the beautiful, a source of beauty that transcends naturalistic accounts of its origin (Tho. Aq., *ST* 1 Q5).

Scripture celebrates the relation between the beauty of creation and the Creator: "The heavens tell out the glory of God, the vault of heaven reveals his handiwork. One day speaks to another, night with night shares its knowledge, and this without speech or language or sound of any voice. Their music goes out through all the earth, their words reach to the end of the world" (Ps. 19:1–4; Eusebius, Commentary on Psalms 18.5). John of Damascus commented: "'The heavens show forth the glory of God' not by speaking in voice audible to sensible ears, but by manifesting to us through their own greatness the power of the Creator, and when we remark their beauty, we give glory to their Maker as the best of all artificers" (John of Damascus, Orthodox Faith 2.6). "The world itself, by its well-ordered changes and movements, and by the fair appearance of all visible things, bears a testimony of its own, both that it has been created, and also that it could not have been created save by God, whose greatness and beauty are unutterable and invisible" (Augustine, CG 11.4). The faithful are called to beautify the house of the Lord (Ezra 7:27; Isa. 60:13) as a fitting response to the beauty of the Lord (Ps. 27:4; Song of Songs, 6:4).

If degrees of beauty exist, as our common language constantly assumes, then that which is unsurpassably beautiful, or filled with the glory of beauty, must be posited, and that we call God. It is in this sense that the psalmist sought all the days of his life to "behold the beauty of the Lord" (Ps. 27:4) and to "worship the Lord in the beauty of holiness" (Ps. 96:9), for "strength and beauty are in his sanctuary" (Ps. 96:6). "Things are beautiful," noted Thomas, "by the indwelling of God" (Tho. Aq., Expos. of Psalms 25.5).

Macrina taught that the soul that recognizes its own beauty rightly sees that beauty as a reflection of God's own beauty: "The Deity is in very substance Beautiful; and to the Deity the soul will in its state of purity have affinity" and will embrace God as like the beauty of the soul herself. Hence "the soul copies the life that is above," and "the Beautiful is necessarily lovable to those who recognize it." Although this recognition is expected finally in the resurrection, Gregory thought, it may be anticipatively experienced in the soul's ascent to God here and now. When this happens "enjoyment takes the place of desire, and the power to enjoy renders desire useless and out of date." Then the soul will "know herself accurately, what her actual nature is, and should behold the Original Beauty reflected in the mirror" (Sister Macrina, in On the Soul and The Resurrection, NPNF 2 5:449).

The Pragmatic Argument

The modern form of the pragmatic argument for the existence of God was famously stated by psychologist William James, who came to the down-to-earth conclusion that the reality of God is practically validated by the fact that believing in God makes people function better and feel better and live more productive lives. If one acts on the assumption that God exists, life works better. Those who believe in God are going to be better able to take risks, and will have better emotional health, because they trust that some intelligible power grounds both the universe and their own behavior. The premise that God exists is both psychologically healthier and sociologically more productive than its opposite. This is an argument from results, and therefore pragmatic (W. James, Essays on Faith and Morals: 115, 212, 256; C. S. Pierce, Collected Papers, 6.467).

The argument is quintessentially modern, in that it is psychological at its center, metaphysically skeptical, and avoids dealing with the truth question—attending only to results. Yet its spirit is to some degree anticipated by numerous Christian writers who have appealed to "doing" the truth as a basis for understanding it (notably Baxter, Wesley, Phoebe Palmer, and Kierkegaard), stressing the importance of praxis in the knowing of God's greatness and goodness (especially John Cassian, Ignatius Loyola, and Teresa of Avila).

Causal Law Prior to Thought

Another more subtle argument hinges on the self-evident insight that causal law exists before its discovery. The context for this argument is the scientific world where we sometimes hear the spurious assertion that the more science advances, the further the study of God must retreat. If that should be true then there would be an irreversible decline of the study of God as scientific inquiry proceeds. In this view, belief in God has been temporarily used to explain phenomena that are not as yet accounted for by scientific or causal law; as soon as scientific inquiry extends the network of causality to cover all phenomena of nature, then belief in God will have been whittled away (Feuerbach, Essence of Christianity; Marx, Humanitarianism and Liberalism; Nietzsche, The Will to Power). The following argument challenges that assumption.

The question is raised: "What are causal laws?" They are formulas that are defended by scientific inquiry. They are stated by people who are seeking to discover the way insects feed, the way the physical universe works, the structure of the atom. But all these causal laws were true and in operation before they were discovered. What existence did these causal laws have before they were formulated by us? They existed as adequately as now, but without recognition by us (Augustine, *Of True Religion* 21). The ideas are prior to our discovery (Augustine, *On Free Choice of the Will LLA*, 2.9, *On the Trin.* 14.21; Sir James Jeans, *Physics and Philosophy*; E. S. Brightman, *Moral Laws*; L. H. DeWolfe, *Theol. of Living Church*).

If laws of causality exist before they are formulated by human minds, then one must posit either a divine Mind or chance. That these laws of causality have occurred by chance or random events is far less plausible than that they correspond to a Mind that underlies all things. Such a Mind corresponds with what the worshiping community calls God (Augustine, *On Free Choice of the Will* 2.6). Mathematical studies of the probability of chance causing the emergence of life in the universe indicate that those chances are so low as to be virtually inconceivable.

The Argument from Congruity: Comprehensive Complementarity

One of the most compelling theistic arguments cannot be stated until all the above arguments have been set forth. It is the argument from congruity or comprehensive complementarity. It does not depend upon any single one of the arguments just described, but builds upon the accumulation of all of them.

The center of this argument is: *that reason which best explains the most distantly related facts is more probably true*. It is a probability hypothesis. Any postulate that gathers together a great number of disparate facts and accounts for them intelligibly and integrally is more likely true than one that accounts for fewer facts. It is argued that the hypothesis of the existence of God provides the most congruent available basis for explaining ideas otherwise regarded as absurdities. It offers purposeful integration to otherwise disparate facts of our mental, spiritual, and physical existence.

If God in fact exists, then the virtually universal belief in divine reality is vindicated. If God exists, then the intellectual hunger to ask for a first cause of causes is satisfied without the embarrassment of an infinite regress of causes or unaccounted-for motions. If God exists, then our inveterate religious nature has an object. If God exists, then the uniformity of natural law finds adequate explanation. If God exists, then human moral awareness is relieved of the charge of being an immense absurdity. There is a kind of cumulative effect from the various arguments in which one hypothesis—that God exists—solves recalcitrant problems that are far harder to solve without it (Tho. Aq., *ST* 1 Q3; W. James, *Essays on Faith and Morals*; E. L. Long, *A Survey of Christian Ethics*: 310–14 for clarification of the concept of "comprehensive complementarity").

Argument from the Idea of Perfect Being

The Idea of Perfect Being Requires Its Existence

The last argument for the existence of God is the simplest, yet hardest to grasp quickly, and impossible without meditation. In my view it is the most important argument for the existence of God, and the most beautiful. After the argument has been stated, unless it is studied carefully, the casual reader is unlikely to be even slightly impressed by it. It is so simple that its profundity escapes our notice. I have been through this argument so many times with so little effect on so many audiences that I do not expect the beholder joyfully to leap to receive it immediately, partly because of its intrinsic simplicity. But because of its exceeding weight, I will set it forth as clearly as possible. It is called the ontological argument because it hinges entirely upon rightly conceiving of God's being (Gr: ontos, being). It offers a form of reasoning that requires quiet meditation in order that in due time it may grasp one's soul. So: breathe deeply; quietly consider:

The ontological argument finds in the very idea of God the proof of God's existence. If that does not strike you as meaningful, let me express it differently: If properly thought, the very idea of God requires that the referent of that idea, God, exists. God is the only idea that refers to a reality that must exist if properly conceived.

Once more: We have an idea of an absolutely perfect being. It is possible to have that idea. The heart of this argument: *Existence is a necessary characteristic of that particular idea*, the idea of perfect being. For the idea of perfection would not be perfect if that to which it refers did not exist. *An absolutely perfect being must exist if it is to be absolutely perfect.* The fact or truth or actual reality to which that idea refers must exist, otherwise that idea is not a perfect idea.

That is it. If it went by too fast, I will take it step-by-step in its classic formulation.

That Than Which Nothing Greater Can Be Conceived Must Exist

Anselm's formulation has hardly been improved upon in eight hundred years. Anselm was asking in the *Proslogion* whether it is possible to reach the notion of the existence of God through reasoning, although he himself acknowledged the living presence of God through faith. Anselm defined God in a particular way: God is that than which nothing greater can be conceived (Anselm, *Proslog.* 2). Anyone who is going to speak with another about this argument does well to learn the phrase "that than which nothing greater can be conceived"—try it three times out loud if all else fails. Augustine had anticipated Anselm's definition in arguing that the thought of God "takes the form of an endeavor to reach the conception of a nature than which nothing more excellent or more exalted exists" (*On Chr. Doctrine* 1.6).

According to Anselm, there is no difficulty in conceiving of the *idea* of "that than which nothing greater can be conceived." The phrase means that we are speaking of perfect being, that being who is greater (in goodness, being, and power) than any other being we can conceive. Yet there are two possible ways of thinking that idea:

That Than Which Nothing Greater Can Be Conceived as:

Either A	or B
Idea in Mind Only	Idea as Existing
The idea refers to that which exists in our minds, but not in reality itself.	The idea refers to that which exists in reality, and not in our minds only.
Meditate on these two ideas	Then ask: Which idea is greater?

Ask yourself, Which idea is greater: an idea of "that than which nothing greater can be conceived" but that exists in our minds only and not in reality, *or,* the second idea, an idea of "that than which nothing greater can be conceived" that exists in reality and not just in the understanding alone?

If you say the second idea is greater, you have made an important decision, and have accepted the ontological argument. For if so, you attribute existence to that idea. You have decided that if that idea (*B*) exists in reality, it is greater than that idea (*A*) that exists only conceptually, in our minds. The lesser is lacking in only one way: its referent does not exist.

That is the crux of the argument. Most people answer with Anselm that such an idea—if in our minds only—cannot be "that than which nothing greater can be conceived" because its referent does not exist in reality. It lacks something, making it something less than "that than which nothing greater can be conceived." So the referent of the second idea must exist if that idea is to be the greater. If the second is the greater idea, as Anselm thought it must be, then the referent of that idea (real being) is implied in the idea itself.

Thus God's existence is implied in the very idea of God, properly conceived. It is necessary that God exist, because the very idea of God, properly conceived, requires God's existence. For if you opt for the first idea (conceiving of God merely as an idea in our minds, without existing), then Anselm thought that you still have not arrived at the proper conception of that than which nothing greater can be conceived. Since the first idea is a foolish idea of God, it invites fools to say, "There is no God" (Ps. 14:1), which is the biblical text for Anselm's *Proslogium* (*Proslog.* 2).

In his second, somewhat refined, statement of the argument, Anselm further argued that God "cannot be conceived not to exist. For, it is possible to conceive of a being which cannot be conceived not to exist; and this is greater than one which can be conceived not to exist. Hence, if that, than which nothing greater can be conceived, can be conceived not to exist, it is not that, than which nothing greater can be conceived" (Anselm, *Proslog.* 3). "Therefore, he who understands that God so exists, cannot conceive that he does not exist" (*Proslog.* 4). Considered hurriedly, Anselm's argument appears to be nonsensical, repetitious, and almost laughable.

Gaunilo, a monk of Marmoutiers, thought so. He countered that the idea of a perfect being does not imply its existence, for we can easily form the idea of purely imaginary beings, he said, but that does not bring them into being. We can imagine an island, or money in our pockets, but that does not mean they exist (Gaunilo, *A Reply on Behalf of the Fool*). Gaunilo's argument has been taken to be a standard, and I think inaccurate, refutation of the ontological argument.

Anselm's response to Gaunilo was far more profound: An island and money in my pocket are finite things. This argument does not apply to anything that is finite. The reason is that "that than which nothing greater can be conceived" is not and cannot be finite, since the infinite can be conceived to be greater than the finite. The only object to which this argument can be applied is "that than which nothing greater can be conceived, when conceived as existing in reality and not in our mind only." Gaunilo's objection is valid with respect to any imperfect, finite being, because in its case actual existence is not necessary to the content of the idea. But it is a flawed argument in relation to the idea of perfect being. For in this case the actual existence of the being conceived must be included in the necessary content of the idea (Anselm, *Reply to Gaunilo*, *BW*: 153; *Proslog.*, *A Reply to the Foregoing by the Author of the Book in Question*).

The more subtle (Kantian) objection to the argument is that existence is not an attribute or predicate. An idea is an idea whether it is thought to be in our heads or in reality, Kant argued. For example, if God did not exist in reality, that would not change our idea of him existing in reality (*Critique of Pure Reason* 2.3.4). But Kant's appraisal is still left with the embarrassing conclusion that having existence is no greater than not having existence.

The idea of a perfect being, Descartes thought, must have come from such a being whose actual existence is a necessary assumption of that being's perfection. (For additional statements of the ontological argument, see Leibniz, *New Essays Concerning Human Understanding* 4, 10; *Monadology* 44, 45; Spinoza, *Ethics* 1.7–11; W. Stillingfleet, *Origines Sacrae* 3.1; Charles Hartshorne, *Man's Vision of God* 10; for objections, see Tho. Aq. *ST* 1 Q2.1; Locke, *Essays Concerning Human Understanding* 4.10; Kant, *Critique of Pure Reason:*379; Edwards, *Freedom of Will*, 2.3; G. W. F. Hegel, *Lectures on the Phil. of Relig.* 3:62–67, 347).

This is in one way merely an argument, yet an argument that has penetrating power when understood. The seminal idea of the argument is found in a much earlier remark by Augustine: "God is more truly thought than He is described, and exists more truly than He is thought" (*On Trin.* 7.4; 8.3).

Even more explicitly was the argument anticipated by Hilary, in a profound reflection written during his exile in Phyrgia (356–359), commenting on the divine name, "I AM WHO I AM" (Exod. 2:14): "For no property of God which the mind can grasp is more characteristic than existence, since existence, in the absolute sense, cannot be predicated of that which shall come to an end, or of that which has had a beginning, and He who now joins continuity of being with the possession of perfect felicity could not in the past, nor can in the future, be non-existent; for whatsoever is Divine can neither be originated nor destroyed. Therefore, since God's eternity is inseparable from Himself, it was worthy of Him to reveal this one thing, that He is, as the assurance of His absolute eternity" (Hilary, *Trin.* 1. 5). Hence with remarkable prescience, long before Anselm, Hilary had pointedly concluded *(a)* that existence is intrinsic to the idea of God; *(b)* that since those things that exist normally have a beginning and end, the notion of existence is not adequate to indicate fully the eternal way in which God *is;* *(c)* that God cannot be thought not to exist; and *(d)* that the eternal way in which God exists is revealed by God already in the disclosure of God's name, "I AM WHO I AM."

Does God minus the world equal God? If one answers yes, then it must be conceded that the very idea of God is greater than the idea of the world or anything in or of the world. If that idea of such a greater-than-world being is rightly conceived, it cannot fail to have included or assumed in its definition that it exists in reality and not in our minds only. For what is greater than the world could not exist merely as an idea in our minds. The obvious evidence is that the world exists.

After many years of teaching the ontological argument in systematic theology classes, I still can seldom state it without being profoundly moved by it. I have stated it above in about a dozen ways. Those who have not "gotten it" yet might try re-reading the above several times.

Most of the arguments of this chapter have been *inductive* arguments from experience. But this last argument is essentially *deductive* and analytical in relation to a particular idea, that of perfect being. This argument is called *a priori*, i.e., prior to experience, because it is discoverable through rational reflection alone without the help of sensory input. Here we are relying exclusively upon a rational analysis of ideas, not the support of facts or the data of experience. Carelessly stated, the ontological argument seems simply to beg the question by making sure that one's conclusions are already embedded in the premises. Yet when properly formulated, it is hard to counter. That Thomas (*ST* 1 Q2.1; *SCG* 1. 10, 11) and Kant (*Critique of Pure Reason*, 2.3.4) rejected it without fully understanding it is regrettable. That Hegel (*Phenomenology of Mind*), Leibniz (*New Essays Concerning Human Understanding* 4.10), and Hartshorne (*Anselm's Discovery* and *The Divine Perfections*) have affirmed and elaborated it is to their credit.

Conclusion

We began this chapter with the question of whether the previously described idea of God is indeed true—whether this God exists. Not only reason, but Scripture, tradition, and experience have assisted in answering the question insofar as it is answerable. We have necessarily relied on rational argumentation and natural theology more here than in any other part of this book, since the question is intrinsically apologetic: Upon what reasonable grounds can God be said to exist, or even be rightly conceived not to exist?

Although the results of such an inquiry will always seem inadequate to some and remain always open to further refinement, they are not meaningless. We come away from these arguments with a cumulative pattern of reasoning that in its totality is sufficient to support the claim that God exists, and exists in the way that Christian teaching has said God exists.

In summary: *If purpose exists there must be a Purposer, if order, an Orderer. If we see design in the world, we must hypothesize a Designer of sufficient intelligence to produce an intelligible world. If mind exists in evolving history, some incomparable Mind must have enabled and created the possibility of our minds. If it is so difficult to be a human being without knowing something of God, then there must be a sufficient reason for this awareness being so persistent in human cultures and societies, even when suppressed. If such wide consent exists in history to the existence of God, that fact must be accounted for with a sufficient reason. If the idea of God is intrinsic to human consciousness, then God must exist. From the fact of change we must hypothesize a change agent. If anything moves, something must have first moved everything. There must be a being that causes all causes and that moves all movement. If contingent beings exist, there must be a necessary being. If we experience through conscience a sense of absolute moral obligation as relentlessly as we do, even against parents, against society, against superego constraints, then we must hypothesize a ground of moral obligation calling us to the highest good and possessed of weightiest moral authority. In addition to all this, the very idea of perfect being requires the existence of perfect being, otherwise that idea is less than the idea of perfect being.*

From this we conclude that God, to whose existence these arguments point, exists more fully than we who are reasoning and arguing exist (Augustine, *Conf.* 7.10) and that there is nothing so proper to God as to be (Hilary, *Trin.* 1. 5). We have ample grounds upon which to say: God exists. Reason confirms that to which Scripture attests, that God incomparably *is*.

5

WHETHER GOD
IS TRIUNE

THE IDEA THAT THE ONE GOD MEETS US in three persons is thought to be among the most mystifying of all Christian teachings. Yet we must speak of Trinity, as Augustine knew, not because we are able to fathom it, but because we cannot keep silent on a matter so central to biblical faith (Augustine, *Trin.* 1.2, 3).

The mystery of God the Father, God the Son, and God the Spirit may seem to introduce a new theme into our thinking. But we have been referring to it all along, by speaking of

- God as Father Almighty, the source of life, who makes Himself known in

- Jesus Christ by the power of

- the Spirit of God who is present throughout the historical process, working to transform it according to God's purpose.

Thus we are not veering away from previous subjects in dealing now with the triune God, but only seeking to provide increased clarity on how the living God comes to dwell with us in broken human history.

In all Christian traditions, baptism occurs in the name of the Father, Son, and Holy Spirit. Hence Christian teaching is best thought of as a commentary on baptism. It has the happy task of trying to explain what baptism in the triune name means. This is no elective, nonobligatory task, no subordinate duty that Christian theology can either choose or refuse. For God appears constantly in the New Testament as Father, Son, and Spirit. "When I say God," remarked Gregory Nazianzus, "I mean Father, Son, and Holy Ghost" (*Orat.* 33.8).

The triune confession summarizes the essentials of Christian teaching. For almost two millennia the Christian community has been using this language as a means of bringing together its most irreducible affirmations concerning God. Modern readers are urged not to reject prematurely trinitarian thinking on the wrong assumption that it amounts to worshiping three "gods"—a heresy called tritheism, consistently rejected by the classical Christian writers (Gregory of Nyssa, *On "Not Three Gods"*).

Salvation History in Triune Faith

The triune understanding of God gives us a way of looking at the meaning of God's coming into the whole of history and into human hearts—the arena of God's revelation, the subject of theology.

The simple act of baptism teaches, rehearses, and embraces the entire story of salvation. It attests to the church's attempt to view history synoptically, to grasp a unified picture of God in acts of creation, redemption, and consummation. Classical Christianity views the history of salvation as an inclusive threefold movement from beginning to end:

- It begins with an originally good creation in an undisturbed condition of human existence that plunges into the self-chosen alienation of human freedom into sin, guilt, and death.

- The pivot of history is the incarnation, ministry, death, and resurrection of Jesus Christ, God's own personal engagement in the human condition, where the Son of God speaks the Father's Word of forgiving love to human history.

- God's own Spirit is sent in order to enable faith, hope, and love in those who are willing to hear and respond to the divine Word, enabling faith to grow toward reflecting the divine goodness within human limits (Gregory of Nyssa, *On the Holy Trin.*).

Universal history is therefore a history of the activity of the triune God: (1) Given all by the Father of all, the fall of humanity from its original uprightness is (2) redeemed through God's justifying activity in the Son, and (3) our faithful response is elicited through the power of the Spirit. To say that creation as given is good, that the fall of freedom is uprighted by justification and consummated by sanctification, is therefore another way of saying that God meets us in history as Father, Son, and Spirit (Hilary, *Trin.* 7). This triune history of salvation brings together all the basic issues of Christian theology in a single wide angle frame: creation, redemption, and consummation.

This orthodox view of universal history is intimately interwoven with the triune understanding of God: God the Father is giver and ground of all things; God the Son is God Himself entering into this sphere to declare the primordial love of God and make known God's Word to us; God the Spirit empowers the fulfillment of the divine purpose in redemption (Gregory of Nyssa, *On the Baptism of Christ*).

We now exist in an ongoing historical process in which, through the gifts of the Spirit, this love is appropriated through church, sacraments, and ministry in the hope of sanctification, through which God perfects what God has created and redeemed. The Holy Spirit has been eternally present throughout the whole historical process, but is now powerfully present in the mission of enabling faith in the Son and guiding the church "into all truth" (John 16:13; Augustine, *Tractates on John* 96–100; Chrysostom, *Hom. on John* 79).

Faith's Experience of Trinitarian Reasoning

Deciding About Jesus

This summary way of thinking began very early, even while the New Testament was being written, when people began to try to make up their minds about what was happening in their encounter with Jesus of Nazareth. They recognized that in Jesus they had come to know God the Father through his Son. Jesus himself often spoke of God as Father (patēr, Mark 11:10, 25 f.; 13:32; 14:36; Matt. 6:1–32; 10:20–37; 18:10–35; 26:39–42) or familiarly as Abba ("papa," Mark 14:36). The intimate and affectionate name, Abba, echoes throughout the Pauline letters (Rom. 8:14; Gal. 4:6). At Pentecost, the disciples received the promise of the Father (Acts 1:4; 2:32).

It was not merely that Jesus was teaching about God, the Father. Rather, the church believed that God the Father was intimately and personally present in Jesus' ministry, and that Jesus himself was personally present in the life of the community as resurrected Lord. They felt the real presence of the Father with them. The Son's presence was experienced as nothing less than the Father's own living, personal presence.

The Johannine writings spoke in a voice that would affect all triune teaching: "God's only Son, he who is nearest to the Father's heart, has made him known" (John 1:18; Irenaeus, *Ag. Her.* 4.22.7; Hilary, On the Councils 36). "We know also that the Son of God has come and has given us understanding, so that we may know him who is true. And we are in him who is true—even in his Son Jesus Christ. He is the true God and eternal life" (1 John 5:20). Christ not only makes God known, but is truly God; not only reveals the truth, but is the truth; and the worshiping community understands its life to be hid "in Christ." It is this Word of God who was "with God in the beginning" and who "was God," who "came from the Father," who had "become flesh and lived for a while among us" (John 1:1–14; Irenaeus, *Ag. Her.* 3.11; Ambrose, *On the Incarnation* 6.59). In these passages, we are listening in on the earliest Christian community seeking to speak accurately of its actual experience of the real presence of God in Jesus.

This implied no disregard for the oneness of God. The earliest Christians were steeped in monotheistic faith, but they had to make sense out of this decisive event—this living presence of the risen Lord in their midst. They understood Jesus to be not part God, not merely similar to God, but in the fullest sense "true God" (John 17:3; 1 John 5:20; Rev. 3:7; Irenaeus, *Ag. Her.* 3.9; Chrysostom, *Hom. on John* 80.2). This is the reason we have triune thinking. If the first generation witnesses had not been bathed in that vital experience, we would not be talking about the Trinity today. In that sense, the core of triune teaching did not undergo a century of development before being realized, but was grasped in the first generation of witnesses.

The disciples not only experienced the presence of Father and Son but further experienced a powerful impetus of the divine Spirit that brought the Son into their hearts. They understood that this Spirit was working within their community to awaken and teach them the significance of what happened in Christ—counseling them, helping them to understand, praying with them, accompanying them. This gave them unusual courage and hope. The Holy Spirit was that living and present reality in the life of the community, distinguishable from, but not separable from, the same one God who was self-disclosed and present in Jesus (Irenaeus, *Ag. Her.* 3.17; Tertullian, *Ag. Praxeas* 1–15; Tatian, *To the Greeks* 15).

Gradually, as the Christian community moved from Jerusalem into the Greek, Syriac, and Latin environments, they struggled to articulate this experience in varied language and symbol systems. Christians today continue to be encountered by the same loving Father, risen Lord, and empowering Spirit. Christians today are relearning how to address God as Father of our Lord Jesus Christ through the guidance of the Spirit. Christians today still live out of the same remembered history of the saving deeds of God as Father, Son, and Spirit.

Unity, Equality, and Distinguishability

The nucleus of triune teaching is to learn how to affirm simultaneously three aspects: the equality and unity and distinguishability of Father, Son, and Spirit in our encounter with the one God. Physical objects have three dimensions—length, breadth, and height. They are distinguishable, but inseparable, unified in a single object, yet three-dimensional. Our experience of the physical world always has three aspects—space, time, and matter. These are unified in the being of any physical object, yet clearly distinguishable. The seeming paradox of three in one is familiar to the human experience of physical reality (Augustine, *Trin.* 8.10; Tho. Aq., *ST* 1 Q12, 13).

God has left soulprints of triunity everywhere in the created order. There are in perception (*a*) external objects encountering (*b*) the mind that is capable of (*c*) perceiving external objects. Thus in a common human function such as perception, there is a threefold unity as an act of perception which requires the mind, objects, and the act of perceiving (Augustine, *Trin.* 9.1–12). The unity of selfhood is made up of memory, understanding, and willing, showing how a personal subject-self may remain one while being threefold as memory, understanding, and will: "Whatever else can be predicated of each singly in itself, is predicated of them all together in the singular and not in the plural" (Augustine, *Trin.* 10.17–19). Love requires a lover, a beloved, and a love that unites them, in a kind of three-in-oneness, for in speaking of these three, we are speaking only of a single reality, love (Augustine, *Trin.* 8.4–10, 9.9–12). All these three-fold patterns display unity, equality, and distinguishability (Tho. Aq., *ST* 1 Q42), the crucial terms of triune teaching.

Tri-unity—Three-in-one-ness

The English word trinity from the Latin *trinitas* (*tres*, three, *unus*, one) signifies that God is three-in-one, or triune, that is, one God—Father, Son, and Holy Spirit— a teaching distinctive to Christianity. It is hardly found in philosophical theisms, and only occasionally in the history of non-Christian religions. Its key assumptions are indirectly anticipated, but not expressly taught, in prophetic Scriptures of the Old Testament.

Some will resist the notion of trinity because it is thought to be not found expressly in Scripture, but we will show that the Scriptures require the teaching of one God as Father, Son, and Spirit. These interrelated texts are found throughout the Bible, and especially in crucial summative points of biblical teaching (Augustine, *Trin.* 1.6; Calvin, *Inst.* 2.14, 15; Heppe, *RD*: 105–33). The idea of the triune God is necessary to explain some crucial texts of Scripture.

From the time of the apostolic fathers (Hippolytus, Irenaeus, and Tertullian), triune language has been definitive of orthodox Christian teaching accepted alike by Protestants, Catholics, and Eastern church communions (Council of Nicaea;

Gregory Nazianzus, *Orat.* 38.8). It provides a shorthand term used to express in a single word what Scripture teaches in many discrete passages. It is not merely a speculative or theoretical or optional teaching, but is regarded *by consensus as essential* to the Christian understanding of God (Gregory Thaumaturgus, *COC* 2: 24; Athanasian Creed; Augsburg *Conf.* I; Thirty-nine Articles). Baptism has never been administered in the name of one God and two creatures. That would have been the outcome of Arianism, so it had to be rejected as unscriptural (Athanasius, *Four Discourses Ag. Arians* 2.41; Gregory Nazianzus, *On the Great Athanasius* 13). Scripture insists that the Son and Holy Spirit are not creatures but truly God. (Hilary, *Trin.* 1.6). Scripture constrains Christian teaching to speak of Jesus as God's own Son, not a creature, and not less than God; and the Holy Spirit as God's own Spirit, not less than God, and not a creature (Calvin, *Inst.* 2.14.3–8).

The triune teaching may seem to assert a contradiction: that God is three, and that God is one. One early incomplete teaching (modalism) attempted to "resolve" this contradiction by stating that God has three distinct modes that are not simultaneous: only one of these modes is manifested at any given time. The early church vigorously opposed this premature solution on the grounds that it did not make sufficiently clear that in Scripture God does not cease being the Father when God is the Son (Dionysius, *Ag. the Sabellians*).

The obedience of the Son to the Father (John 15:10) does not imply that the Son is inferior to the Father. The Son did not become less than the Father by becoming eternally obedient to the Father's will (Phil. 2:5–11; Marius Victorinus, *Ag. Arians* 1.21–23). The Spirit serves the mission of the Son on behalf of the Father: "When he comes who is the Spirit of truth, he will guide you into all the truth; for he will not speak on his own authority, but will tell you only what he hears; and he will make known to you the things that are coming. He will glorify me" (John 16:13, 14; Didymus the Blind, *On Holy Spirit* 34–37).

If God is one indivisible unity, any distinction referred to must not divide God into two, three, or more separable parts. "God is one," proclaimed the New Testament, echoing ten centuries of Hebraic monotheism (1 Tim. 3:20). "For there is one God, and also one mediator between God and men, Christ Jesus, himself man, who sacrificed himself to win freedom for all mankind" (1 Tim. 2:5, 6; Gregory of Nazianzus, *Theol. Orat.* 4.30.14). Jesus himself clearly affirmed the Hebraic teaching of the unity of God when asked which is the first commandment: "Hear, O Israel: the Lord our God is the only Lord" (Mark 12:29). Unity is implied in the very idea of God, properly conceived (Tho. Aq., *ST* 1 Q39). There cannot be more than one necessary being (John of Damascus, *OF* 1.5). For Christian teaching does not say that they are three in the same sense that they are one, which might cause us to say foolishly, "He are one" or "they is three." God is one. Father, Son, and Spirit are three. God's unity is not a unity of separable parts but of distinguishable persons.

Scriptural Roots of Trinitarian Reasoning

Classic Consensus on the Cohesion of Old and New Testament Witness

What follows is an attempt to set forth major consensual views of the most influential classical exegetes like Athanasius, Hilary of Poitiers, Augustine, and Cyril of Alexandria, on how the one God revealed to Israel is none other than the same triune God revealed in Jesus Christ.

Their thesis: The triune teaching has become incrementally clarified as established teaching by passing through successive stages: preindications in the Old

Testament; the central disclosure of God as Father, Son, and Spirit in the New Testament; and the full development of church teaching in the Nicene definition and its subsequent interpretations.

Classic Christian interpreters agree: The first generation of witnesses have pointed to the fulfillment of the Old Testament prophesies. They could not read about the promise of God to Abraham, Moses, and Isaiah and the Psalms without noticing that these promises had been fulfilled in Jesus Christ (Athanasius, *Ag. Arians*; Aphraates, *Demonstrations*).

The Spirit of God is often mentioned throughout the Old Testament (Exod. 31:3; 35:31; 1 Sam. 16:13–23; Ps. 51:10, 11; Isa. 11:2; Gregory Nazianzus, *On Pentecost* 9). The Spirit of God is giver of life: "For the spirit of God made me, and the breath of the Almighty gave me life" (Job 33:4; Ps. 33:6). The same Spirit inspired Moses and the prophets: "Then the Lord came down in the cloud and spoke with him, and he took of the Spirit that was on him and put the Spirit on the seventy elders. When the Spirit rested on them, they prophesied" (Num. 11:24, 25; Cyril of Jerusalem, *Catech. Lect.* 16.25).

The Spirit is omnipresent: "Where can I go from your Spirit? Where can I flee from your presence?" (Ps. 139:7). Isaiah 48:16 is a principal prophetic text from which classical exegetes have argued a decisive triune intimation. The speaker is the Lord's Servant, the promised Messiah: "'Come near to me and listen to this: From the first announcement I have not spoken in secret; from the time it happens I am there.' And now the *sovereign Lord* has sent *me*, with his *Spirit*" (Isa. 48:16, italics added; Jerome, Comm. on Is. 13.16). The first person *me* has been widely thought by classical exegetes to be anticipatory of the Son, viewed as a fulfillment of prophetic promise. Already Isaiah is found speaking discretely of the Lord God by whom the Servant Messiah is sent and the Spirit with whom he is sent, thus keeping all the primary elements of triunity in place: unity, distinction, and complementary mission (Origen, *Ag. Celsus* 1.46; Augustine, *Trin*.2.5; Tho. Aq., *ST* 1 Q31).

In the first two verses of the Bible, God and the Spirit of God appear in conjunction; for it is said that "God created," and "the Spirit of God was moving over the face of the waters" (Gen. 1:1, 2; Hilary, *Trin*. 2.13–16). Where the text says: "In the beginning of creation, when God (*Elōhīm*) made heaven and earth," *Elōhīm* is *a plural noun, yet linked with a singular verb*. God and God's Spirit appear distinguishable, yet God is one (Ambrose, *Of the Holy Spirit* 2.1). When "God said, 'Let us make man in our image and likeness'" (Gen. 1:26), a startling implication emerges: The one God is speaking in the *first* person in *plural* form. Common in prophetic teaching are phrases such as: "*I* am with you, says the Lord of hosts, and my *spirit* is present among you" (Hag. 2:1–5, italics added; Cyril of Jerusalem, *Catech. Lect.* 16.25–28).

The occurrence in prophetic literature of a threefold repetition of the divine name has been viewed by classical exegetes as a precursor of triune teaching: "'Holy, holy, holy [the threefold name of the One God] is the Lord of Hosts: the whole earth is full of his glory'" (Isa. 6:2, 3; Origen, *OFP* 1.3; Ambrose, *Of the Holy Spirit* 3.16, 109–11). This threefold repetition of the divine name recurs again in the Revelation of John: "Holy, holy, holy is God the sovereign Lord of all, who *was*, and *is*, and *is to come*!" (Rev. 4:8, italics added; Athanasius, *On Luke 10:22*, sec. 6). When the one Lord appeared to Abraham by the oaks of Mamre, he was manifested in the appearance of "three men" (Gen. 18:2)—Abraham "saw three and worshipped One," commented Ambrose (*Holy Spirit* 2.Intro.4).

No single text of Scripture has been viewed as standing alone, yet many references to Fatherhood, Sonship, Word, Wisdom, and Spirit have been viewed in correlation with each other as triune allusions, as borne out in the history of triune exegesis. This exegesis has proceeded under the principle of the analogy of faith, by which one passage of Scripture is examined and understood in relation to what is known of other passages (Calvin, *Inst.* 1.6–9, 1.13.3; Baxter, *PW* 12:141–47). In this way the truth of Scripture is revealed not as separable parts, but as a whole, to be grasped integrally and intuitively by the discerning reader as a single, reliable revelation of truth.

The plural forms of speech for God are linguistic intensives, emphasizing the fullness of the divine majesty, the glory of the Lord of hosts. The plural is at times preferred even when the intent is to assert the unity of God, as in the Shema': "Hear, O Israel, the Lord is our God" (literally, "our Gods," *Elōhēnū*), "one Lord" (Deut. 6:4). "Remember your Creator in the days of your youth" (Eccles. 12:1) is literally "Remember your Creators" (*Eth-Bōrekā*). Even if these linguistic intensives do not carry the strength of a full argument, they have been viewed as a corroboratory point for the devout reading of Scripture that has become subsequently informed by fuller triune teaching (Athanasius, *Four Discourses Ag. Arians* 2.23; Hilary, *Trin.* 7.10, 12.37). At least one New Testament writer argued that Old Testament inspiration was implicitly trinitarian in intent:

> *This salvation was the theme which the prophets pondered and explored, those who prophesied about the grace of God awaiting you. They tried to find out what was the time and what the circumstances, to which the spirit of Christ in them pointed, foretelling the sufferings in store for Christ and the splendors to follow; and it was disclosed to them that the matter they treated of was not for their time but for yours. And now it has been openly announced to you through preachers who brought you the Gospel in the power of the Holy Spirit sent from heaven. These are things that angels long to see into.* (1 Pet. 1:10–12)

The Old Testament does not provide Christian teaching with a full disclosure of the triune teaching, but it does contain important preindications of it. This is what we might reasonably expect if we affirm consistently that God's will is revealed through his Word speaking through history, so that subsequent historical events are illumined by and illuminate God's self-presentation in prior events. Scripture does not treat the triune teaching as an abstract proposition of speculation, but rather reveals the unity of the diversely active God in creation, providence, redemption, and consummation.

The New Testament Unfolding of the Triune Teaching

Triune teaching is not just a belated Hellenistic invention of the post-Nicene fathers, as some modern commentators have claimed. Rather, it is from the New Testament that ancient ecumenical teaching directly derived its primary conclusions that the Father is God, that the Son is God, that the Spirit is God, and that God is One.

The surest way to establish that the Father is God, the Son is God, and the Spirit is God is by a classical fourfold exegetical exercise that shows textually how in Scripture (a) each Person (Father, Son, Spirit) is distinguishably addressed by divine *names*; (b) each is assumed to have divine *attributes*; (c) each engages in *actions* that only God can accomplish; and (d) each is thought worthy of divine *worship* (Cyril of Jerusalem, *Catech. Lect.* 7; Tho. Aq., *ST* 1 Q33; Quenstedt, *TDP* 1: 329; Watson, *TI* 1: 475; and Bavinck, *DG* 4).

The Father Is God in the New Testament

The first conclusion drawn by ecumenical exegetes is that God is called Father in Scripture. The primary textual evidence for this conclusion is as follows:

1. Jesus characteristically *called* God his "Father" (Matt. 5:45; 6:6–15; Mark 14:36). He insistently taught his disciples to call God by the name "Father." This is clear in Jesus' response to Mary: "I am now ascending to my Father and your Father, my God and your God" (John 20:17; Gregory of Nyssa, *Ag. Eunomius* 2.8). It is this Father who sends "his only Son, that everyone who has faith in him may not die but have eternal life" (John 3:16). It was precisely his persistence in speaking of God affectionately as "his own Father" that caused his detractors to become "still more determined to kill" Jesus, "because he was not only breaking the Sabbath, but *by calling God his own Father, he claimed equality with God*" (John 5:18, italics added;. Novatian, *Trin.* 21–27). Claiming equality with God was the worst offense against Jewish sensibilities to be made by Jesus. From these texts the classical exegetes had no hesitation in concluding that the Father is God (Cyril of Jerusalem, *Catech. Lect.* XI; Hilary, *Trin.* 9.61).

2. To the Father *attributes* are ascribed that could only belong to God. Among them are holiness, "Holy Father" (John 17:11); sovereignty, "Father, Lord of heaven and earth" (Matt. 11:23); eternity, "Eternal God" (Gen. 21:33; Jer. 10:10); all-powerfulness, "'Abba, Father,' he said, 'all things are possible to thee'" (Mark 14:34). One who is holy, almighty, and eternal must be nothing less than God (Cyril of Jerusalem, *Catech. Lect.* 7.1 ff; Hilary, *Trin.* 11.16; Tho. Aq., *ST* 1 Q33).

3. To the Father are ascribed *works* done by God alone as creator, redeemer, and consummator: "For us there is one God, the Father, from whom all being comes, towards whom we move" (1 Cor. 8:6). "Praise be to the God and Father of our Lord Jesus Christ, who in his great mercy gave us new birth into a living hope by the resurrection" (1 Pet. 1:3). The Father sends the Son (John 5:37; Hilary, *Trin.* 9.20). One who does the works of God must be none other than God (Athanasius, *Four Discourses Ag. Arians* 3.25).

4. On these scriptural grounds it is only appropriate that God should be *worshiped* as Father: "The time approaches, indeed it is already here, when those who are real worshippers will worship the Father in spirit and in truth. Such are the worshippers whom the Father wants" (John 4:23; Origen, *Comm. on John* 13.86–100). "If you ask the Father for anything in my name, he will give it to you" (John 16:23). One to whom worship is due must be worthy of the name God (Novatian, *Trin.* 7; Hilary, *Trin.* 6.30).

The Son Is God in the New Testament

Similarly, in classic exegesis, the Son is called by the same divine names, is ascribed divine attributes, does divine works, and therefore is worthy of divine worship. The lordship and divinity of the Son are established and set forth in the New Testament constantly by the titles given him: Word of God, who was from the beginning with God, and was God (John 1:1; Cyril of Alex., *Comm. on John* 1.2); the Son who was unhesitatingly called God (Matt. 1:23; John 20:28; Rom.

9:5; Titus 1:3; 2:13; Heb. 1:8); Lord (Matt. 12:8; Mark 2:28; Luke 6:46; John 13:13, 14; Acts 10:36; Rom. 14:9; Gal. 1:3; 2 Thess. 2:16) or with intensives such as Lord from heaven (1 Cor. 15:47), Lord of heaven and earth (Matt. 11:25), Lord of all (Acts 10:36), or Lord of lords and King of kings (Rev. 17:14; 19:16). Thomas, upon touching the resurrected Lord, exclaimed: "My Lord and my God!" (John 20:28; italics added). "We know that the Son of God has come," wrote John, and "This is the true God" (1 John 5:21, italics added; Cyril of Alex., *Comm. on John* 2.6).

"O God, thy God has set thee above thy fellows, by anointing with the oil of exultation" (Heb. 1:9). The unique phrase "O God, thy God" makes no sense without a triune premise (John of Damascus, *OF* 4.6). This Son is explicitly described as equal to God the Father (John 15:17; Gregory Nazianzus, *Orat.* 38.8; Ambrose, *Of the Chr. Faith* 3.3). He is *only Son* of the Father (John 1:14), "God's only Son" who is "nearest to the Father's heart" (John 1:18).

The frequency and intensity of these ascriptions of lordship and unique divine sonship to Jesus Christ make this one of the most distinctive and unavoidable themes of the New Testament (Gregory Nazianzus, *Fourth Theol. Orat., On the Son* 20). Those who try to interpret the New Testament without the triune premise have great difficulty making sense of many New Testament texts. Paul speaks also of Jesus as God's "own Son" (Rom. 8:32), whose name is "above every name" (Phil. 2:9; Athanasius, *Defence of the Nicene Definition* 3; Tho. Aq., *SCG* 4.11).

Second, Christ is celebrated in Scripture as having *attributes* that could be intrinsic qualities of God alone: eternal (Matt. 28:20; Heb. 1:8; 13:8; John 1:1, 14; 1 John 1:2); uncreated, underived, for the Son "has life-giving power in himself" (John 5:26), who "exists before everything" (Col. 1:17; Calvin, *Inst.* 1.13.8). Only God can be uncreated (Athanasius, *Four Discourses Ag. Arians* 1.4). He is all-knowing: "He knew men so well, all of them, that he needed no evidence from others about a man, for he himself could tell what was in a man" (John 2:25). Peter said to Christ: Lord, "you know everything" (John 21:17). The Son is remembered as foreknowing, "I saw you under the fig-tree before Philip spoke to you" (John 1:48); as "the same yesterday, today, and for ever" (Heb. 13:8); the "power of God and the wisdom of God" (1 Cor. 1:24); who will "put everything in subjection beneath his feet" (Eph. 1:22); who will transfigure our bodies "by the very power which enables him to make all things subject to himself" (Phil. 3:21). "Full authority in heaven and on earth has been committed to me" (Matt. 28:18). Only God has such power. Thus the classical exegetes concluded that, if Christ has God's attributes, then Christ is God, and the Son has been properly named as the Son of God (Athanasius, *De Synodis, Councils of Ariminum and Seleucia* 3.49–52; Cyril of Jerusalem, *Catech. Lect.* XI; Confession of Wittenberg 2).

Third, the Son of God, does *works* that are peculiar to God, and thus must be God. For who but God could create (John 1:3; Col. 1:16; Heb. 1:10); preserve and govern all things in being (John 5:17; 1 Cor. 8:6; Col. 1:17; Heb. 1:3); or oversee the expected consummation? (2 Cor. 1:2; John 5:22). Who but God can forgive sins? (Mark 2:7). Who but God can raise the dead? (John 6:39–40; 11:25; Apostolic Constitutions 5.1.7). Jesus did all these things (Gregory Nazianzus, *Orat.* 3, *On the Son*). It was the New Testament eye-witnesses first—and only therefore the later ecumenical teachers—that described Jesus as greater than Moses, greater than David, greater than Solomon, greater than John or the prophets, greater than the superpersonal intelligences that inhabit the higher regions (Matt. 3:11; 12:41 f.; Mark 12:37; Luke 11:31, 32; John 1:17; Eph. 1:21; Heb. 1:4 f.; Cyril of Jerusalem, *Catech. Lect.* 12.15). Hence the Son is God.

Fourth, only God is *worthy of worship*, for that is what it means to be God. If the Son is called God, if the Son is like God in every personal attribute or quality intrinsic to God, and if the Son of God does what God does, then the Son is worthy of worship as the only true God. This is why "the men in the boat fell at his feet, exclaiming, 'Truly you are the Son of God'" (Matt. 14:33). "To deny honor to the Son is to deny it to the Father who sent him" (John 5:23; Hilary, *Trin.* 9.23).

Father and Son remain clearly distinguishable—one is said to send, the other to be sent. One gives, the other is given. One bestows power, the other receives it (John 12:44–49; 17:18–25; John of Damascus, *OF* 3.45). Thus we cannot come away from these New Testament texts saying that God is at one time Father and at another time Son (as modalism asserts), but eternally both—distinguishable, yet equal (Hilary, *Trin.* 4,5). It is the New Testament itself and not just subsequent dogmatics that insists upon a *distinction between equal persons* in the triune God. A personal relation eternally exists between Father and Son. This is why the New Testament teaching of God is so irrevocably triune.

The Spirit Is God in the New Testament

The Holy Spirit is a speaking, encountering, interacting Person distinguishable from the Father and Son. The Spirit speaks in the first person as "I": "It was I who sent them" (Acts 10:20). It was the Holy Spirit who said, "I have called them" (Acts 13:2; Chrysostom, *Hom. on Acts*, 27). None but a person can say "I." The Holy Spirit does what only personal agents can do: the Spirit grieves (Eph. 4:3), struggles with other persons (Gen. 6:3; Isa. 63:10), provides leadership (Rom. 8:14), witnesses (1 Cor. 1:22; 5:5; Eph. 1:13, 14), and bestows gifts (Eph. 6).

Scripture views the Spirit as nothing less than God because the *names* ascribed to the Spirit are names that could only be ascribed to God: "the Spirit of God," "Spirit of the Lord," "the Holy Spirit of promise," "the Spirit of wisdom," "the Spirit of truth," and the Counselor or Comforter (Acts 1:8; John 4:24; 14:21; 15:26; Rom. 8:14; Cyril of Jerusalem, *Catech. Lect.* 16; Tho. Aq., *ST* 1 Q36). Scriptures report God as addressing hearers through "My Spirit" (Gen. 6:3; Prov. 1:23; Isa. 44:3; Ezek. 36:27; 39:29; Joel 2:28; Matt. 12:18; Acts 2:17, 18).

The Spirit is divine Counselor (Advocate, Comforter, Paraclete) whose counsel is incomparably wise (John 14:16; 15:26; 16:7). "The Counselor, the Holy Spirit, whom the Father will send in my name, he will teach you all things, and bring to your remembrance all that I have said to you" (John 14:26; Augustine, *Tractates on John* 77.2). "When the Spirit of truth comes, he will guide you into all the truth" (John 16:7–13; Hilary, *Trin.* 8.19; Calvin, *Inst.* 1.13.15). Only God could guide the believer to all truth.

Scriptures view the Spirit as God because the *attributes* of the Spirit are God's own attributes. The Spirit is eternal (Heb. 9:14), omniscient (1 Cor. 2:10–12), and all-powerful (Luke 11:20; Rom. 15:18, 19). Only the Spirit of God is able to "explore everything, even the depths of God's own nature" (1 Cor. 2:10; Cyril of Jerusalem, *Catech. Lect.* 16.1–11; Gregory Nazianzus, *Fifth Theol. Or*; Ambrose, *Of the Holy Spirit* 1.5).

The *works* done by the Spirit are God's own work. It is through the Spirit that "God has revealed to us" "things beyond our imagining" (1 Cor. 2:9–10; Clement of Alex., *Strom.* 2.7.3). It is this same Spirit of God who bears witness to the truth in Jesus Christ (Acts 5:30–32); who gives new life to believers (Titus 3:5); strengthens the faithful (1 Cor. 6:19); and gives the gifts of ministry (1 Cor. 12; Eph. 6). Only God can remit sin (John 3:5), give life (John 6:63), sanctify sinners (2 Thess. 2:13; 1 Pet. 1:2), perform miracles (Matt. 12:28; Luke 1:35), and bring life out of death (Rom. 8:11; Augustine, *Trin.* 5.8–16; Calvin, *Inst.* 1.13.14; Wesley, *On the Holy Spirit, WJW* 7:508).

The Spirit is God because the *worship* due the Spirit is a worship due to God alone (Gregory Nazianzus, *Orat.* 5.1–12; Basil, *On the Holy Spirit* 18; John of Damascus, *OF* 1.7). For "God is spirit, and those who worship him must worship in spirit and in truth" (John 4:24; Basil, *On the Holy Spirit* 26.64). Wherever persons are baptized, they are baptized in the name not only of the Father and the Son but also of the Spirit, one God (Matt. 28:19).

If these four persistent exegetical arguments are rightly conceived, it would be absurd to argue that the triune teaching is not found in the New Testament.

Trinity as Summary Digest of New Testament Teaching

There can be no triune teaching without Scripture, and there can be no adequate explanation of Scripture without the triune teaching. The Scriptures so conspicuously affirm the deity and unity of Father, Son, and Spirit that we must conclude that the Nicene fathers were right to develop the triune teaching in the way they did in their historical context. Nicaea was not an extra-biblical addition.

Here are a few core passages of Scripture in which Father, Son, and Spirit are coordinately presented—*locus classicus* texts that reveal the triune teaching in its summative sense. Only twelve are cited, but many more could be added. If we had nothing but these passages, it could be reliably established that the triune teaching was already powerfully present in New Testament teaching.

The Baptismal Formula. The apostles were commissioned by Christ to "Go forth therefore and make all nations my disciples; baptize men everywhere in the name of the Father and the Son and the Holy Spirit" (Matt. 28:19; for classical exegesis, see Hilary, *Trin.* 2.15; Basil, *Letters* 159.2; Chrysostom, *Gospel of Matthew hom. 90.2*). If there is no distinction between Father, Son, and Spirit, why the necessity of the three distinct names? If there is no equality of these persons, why are they linked together at such a crucial teaching moment in the early church? Christian baptism is administered "in the name of" not three Gods, not two creatures plus one God, not three parts of God, and not three stages of God, but one God who is eternally Father, Son, and Spirit (Gregory of Nyssa, *On "Not Three Gods"*). The history of Christian theology is best understood as an extended commentary on the baptismal formula (Gregory Nazianzus, *Ag. Eunomius* 2.1, 2; Ambrose, *On Sacr.* 1.18, 2.14–24). Its liturgical importance, its strategic location in the received canonical Gospel of Matthew as the final command of the Lord, and the fact that it has been so frequently referred to by early Christian writers make this text the centerpiece of triune teaching. It affirms the divinity, the distinctness, the equality, and the unity of the Father, Son, and Spirit. It calls for an act of adoration and profession of faith in the triune God (Cyril of Jerusalem, *Catech. Lect.* 16.4).

Jesus' Baptism. The Father, with the Spirit, blesses the Son at Jesus' baptism, according to Matthew's Gospel. When Jesus was baptized, the Holy Spirit descended upon the Son, and the Father spoke from above: "After baptism Jesus came up out of the water at once, and at that moment heaven opened; he saw the Spirit of God descending like a dove to alight upon him; and a voice from heaven was heard saying, 'This is my Son, my Beloved, on whom my favor rests'" (Matt. 3:16, 17, see also Mark 1:10–11; Luke 3:22; Augustine, *Sermon* 2.1–2). In this passage, Father, Son, and Spirit are all present in an explicit triune inauguration of the messianic ministry (Didache 7:3; Irenaeus, *Ag. Her.* 3.9; John of Damascus, *OF* 3).

Paul's Apostolic Benediction. The Pauline tradition carries many indications that the triune formula was available in oral tradition prior to Paul's writing.

Notably, Paul closed his second letter to Corinth with a threefold benediction that joined together equally and distinctly the Spirit with God and Christ: "The grace of the Lord Jesus Christ, and the love of God, and the fellowship in the Holy Spirit, be with you all" (2 Cor. 13:13). This is a solemn benediction offered up in supplication to God at a critical moment of the Epistle—its conclusion. Chrysostom shows how "all that belongs to the Trinity" is benediction (*Hom. on Cor.* 30.3): The love of God the Father which has been manifested through grace in Jesus through the power of the Holy Spirit that is blessing the church at Corinth (Gregory of Nyssa, *Ag. Eunomius* 1.16; Ambrose, *Of the Holy Spirit* 1.12.131). Paul wrote to the Corinthians: "No one can say 'Jesus is Lord!' except under the influence of the Holy Spirit. There are varieties of gifts, but the same spirit. There are varieties of service, but the same Lord. There are many forms of work, but all of them, in all men, are the work of the same God" (1 Cor. 1:4–6). It is the Spirit of God who enables the faithful to believe in the Son of God, "the same God," whom Jesus calls "Father."

The Ephesian Formula. The same triune teaching is embedded in the Ephesian formula: "Through him"—Christ Jesus—"we both alike have access to the Father in the one Spirit" (Eph. 2:18). This language suggests that there existed an oral tradition prior to the writing of this letter in which Father, Son, and Spirit, as in the baptismal formula, were frequently linked in familiar order. His prayer was that the God of our Lord Jesus Christ, The Father of glory, may give you a spirit of wisdom (Eph. 1:17; Jerome, *To the Ephesians* 1.1.15–17). The same letter calls believers to live "in the unity which the Spirit gives," since "There is one body and one Spirit, as there is also one hope held out in God's call to you; one Lord, one faith, one baptism, one God and Father of all, who is over all and through all and in all" (Eph. 4:3–6; Chrysostom, Hom. on Eph. 9.4.1–3). The letter to Ephesus teaches the oneness of God who is "Father of all," of the Lord Jesus Christ, and of the "one Spirit" that unifies the church (Hilary, *Trin.* 8.13, 11.1; Wesley, *WJW* 6:392).

Jude's Summary Call to Prayer. "Continue to pray in the power of the Holy Spirit. Keep yourselves in the love of God, and look forward to the day when our Lord Jesus Christ in his mercy will give eternal life" (Jude 20, 21; Oecumenius, Comm. on Jude 20–21). The call to prayer encompasses the love of God, the hope of Christ, and the power of the Spirit at the climactic moment of the Epistle when the writer is seeking to provide a summative statement of its instruction. Jude's letter is addressed to those "beloved in God, the Father and kept for Jesus Christ" (Jude 1), to those who were being warned against those "devoid of the Spirit" (Jude 19).

The Johannine Farewell Discourses. Nowhere is the triune teaching stated more distinctly than in John's report of Jesus' last discourse to his disciples, in which the Son promises the "Advocate, the Holy Spirit whom the Father will send in my name" (John 14:26: Didymus, *On the Holy Spirit* 30–31). The Son sends, the Spirit is sent, and the Spirit proceeds from the Father. "When your Advocate has come, whom I will send you from the Father—the Spirit of truth that issues from the Father—he will bear witness to me" (John 15:26; Tertullian, *Prescript. Ag. Her.* 28; Augustine, *Trin.* 4.20; John of Damascus, Orth Faith 1.8).

John's Prologue. The most highly developed teaching of God as Father, Son, and Spirit is in the Fourth Gospel, where all key elements come into explicit expression. The preexistence of the Son is evident: "In the beginning was the Word, and the Word was with God, and the Word was God. He was in the beginning with God. All things came into being through him, and without him not one thing came into being. What has come into being in him was life, and the life was the light of all people" (John 1:1–4; Tertullian, *Ag. Praxeas* 15; Cyril of Alex., *Comm. on John* 1.2–3). The Word is God, not less than God, God's speech to the world, God's way of letting the divine presence become known to the world. "So the Word became flesh; he came to dwell among us, and we saw his glory, such glory as befits the Father's only Son, full of grace and truth" (John 1:14; Irenaeus, *Ag. Her.* 3.10). The Father-Son unity and distinction is richly embedded in the Johannine prologue: The Word (Jesus) *is* God and is *with* God. One can be God and be with God only by being God in one sense and being with God in another sense. If Christ is God, then Christ is not less than God. If Christ is with God, then there is a distinction in the Godhead or in God's own personal being that does not change or limit the unity of God but allows for an intrapersonal dialogue within the eternal being of God (Hilary, *Trin.* 2.23–35).

The Johannine Letters. The language of John's letters is even more explicit. No one who reads 1 John: 3–5 can reasonably conclude that there is no trinitarian reference whatever in the New Testament. There we are called to "believe in the name of his Son Jesus Christ," knowing that "he abides in us, by the Spirit which he has given us." "By this you know the Spirit of God: every spirit which confesses that Jesus Christ has come in the flesh is of God, and every spirit which does not confess Jesus is not of God" (1 John 3:23–4:3; Theophylact, *Comm. on 1 John* 3:23). All essential assumptions of triune teaching appear in the passage: Jesus is the Son of God, who abides in us by the Spirit whom the Father has given us, who together constitute the revelation of the One God (1 John 5:4–10, Cyprian, *Treatises* 1.6; Augustine, *Sermons* 5.3).

The Salutation in the Revelation of John. The salutation to the churches in the Revelation of John is also a rich mine in which classical exegetes recognized the triune formula embedded: "Grace be to you and peace, from him who is and who was and who is to come," namely, the one God, Father Almighty, "from the seven spirits before his throne," that is, the seven gifts of the Holy Spirit, and "from Jesus Christ" (Rev. 1:4–5a; Andrew of Caesarea, *Comm. on Apoc.* 1.4; Tho. Aq., *ST* 1 Q39).

Philippians 2. The early Christian hymn in Philippians 2:5–11, usually thought to predate Paul, assumed that Jesus Christ is God, and with God from the beginning. This paradoxical distinction (that Jesus Christ is God and is with God from the beginning) is the invariable premise of trinitarian belief (Athanasius, *Four Discourses Ag. Arians* 1.11). "The divine nature was his from the first," who is through the Spirit confessed finally as Lord to the glory of the Father (Marius Victorinus, Epist. To Phil. 2.6–8).

Colossians 1. Here the Pauline tradition speaks integrally of the ways in which God as Father and Son acts to save the world: "He rescued us from the domain of darkness and brought us away into the kingdom of his dear Son, in whom our release is secured and our sins forgiven. He is the image of the invisible God; his is the primacy over all created things. In him everything in heaven and on earth was created" (Col. 1:13–16; Cyril of Jerusalem, *Catech. Lect.* 12.24; John of Damascus, *OF* 4.8). Through the Son the Father acts to redeem the world. So let "the word of Christ dwell in you richly," doing everything in the name of the Lord Jesus, giving thanks to God the Father through him (Col. 3:16,17; Ambrose, *Of the Holy Spirit* 3.11), expressing unity, equality, and distinction.

Salvation History Summary in Hebrews. The final triune text is the opening passage of the letter to Hebrews: "When in former times God spoke to our forefathers, he spoke in fragmentary and varied fashion through the prophets. But in this the final age he has spoken to us in the Son whom he has made heir to the whole universe, and through whom he created all orders of existence: the Son who is the effulgence of God's splendor and the stamp of God's very being, and sustains the universe by his word of power" (Heb. 1:1–4; John of Damascus, Orth. Faith 4.17; Photius, Fragments on Hebr. 1.2–3). Note the triune assumptions of the text: Christ is preexistent, one with God, the stamp of God's very being, not less than God, higher than the angels and all creaturely powers, yet distinguishable from the Father, whose coming is "attested by the Holy Spirit" (Heb. 3:7; 9:8, 14; 10:15; Athanasius, *Four Discourses Ag. Arians* 1.13; Origen, *OFP* 1.2.6).

Although triune teaching was already well formed in the oral tradition that led to the writing of the New Testament, it was not formally developed as dogma without a lengthy process of reflection, spurred by the necessity of addressing heresies. The language of Philippians 2, Colossians 1, the Fourth Gospel, and Hebrews 1 could not remain permanently unexamined. Triune teaching in the New Testament is not speaking of a few isolated texts, but of the fundament of the Gospel of John, the Johannine Epistles, and Revelation, and crucial passages in the Pauline tradition, the pastoral letters, and numerous core texts of the synoptic Gospels. Antitrinitarian views have not been able to show that these recurrent formulations are accidental, or textually spurious, or minor additions, or quirks of a single author. The conclusion: New Testament teaching of God is inevitably and necessarily a triune teaching of God.

Historical Unfolding of Triune Teaching

When Ignatius of Antioch (d. ca. 110) appealed to the Magnesians to "Study, therefore, to be established in the doctrines of the Lord and the apostles," he prayed that they proceed "in faith and love; in the Son, and in the Father, and in the Spirit," and that they be subject to the bishop "as Jesus Christ to the Father, according to the flesh, and the apostles to Christ, and to the Father, and to the Spirit" (Ignatius, Magnesians 13; Eph. 9:1; Clement of Rome, Corinth 18). The consensus did not doubt that this sort of triune language was received by Ignatius from the writings of the first generation of eyewitnesses.

The historical unfolding of the scriptural teaching of the triune God was a refinement of teachings explicit in the apostles' witness and required by consistent reflection upon their texts. The triune teaching is already deeply rooted by the time of Polycarp's prayer before his martyrdom (ca. 156): "I glorify thee, through the eternal and heavenly High Priest, Jesus Christ, thy beloved Servant, through whom be glory to thee with him and the Holy Spirit both now and unto the ages to come" (*The Martyrdom of Polycarp*).

By the time Tertullian wrote his detailed reply to Praxeas (AD 213) he was answering intricate questions on the interpretation of the triune God that were under vigorous and sophisticated debate. One must assume that there was at this time an available ecumenical oral tradition of intense familiarity with triune teaching in order for Tertullian to write to his audience in such sophisticated terms as the following: "Thus the connection of the Father in the Son, and of the Son in the Paraclete, produces three coherent Persons, who are yet distinct One from Another. These Three are one essence, not one Person, as it is said, 'I and my Father are One'" (*Ag. Praxeas* 25; *On Modesty* 21). That Tertullian himself did not invent but rather passed on this language is evident from his own testimony that "this rule of faith has come down to us from the beginning of the gospel, even before any of the heretics, much more before Praxeas" (*Ag. Praxeas* 2). It would have been impossible for Tertullian to address his audience in this way if there had not been an active and available oral tradition in which such language was understood and under sophisticated debate. Hence the triune teaching was, long before Nicaea, widely received and understood in an explicit and detailed way. It was only on the basis of intricacies of the pre-Nicene discussion that the debate that led to Nicaea may be understood. So those who imagine that triune teaching begins at Nicaea thereby show that they have not paid sufficient attention to the texts mentioned above.

Contemplation of the Triune Mystery

The problem faced by early Christian teaching was not whether Christ was God but how, within the bounds of monotheistic faith, the unity of God could be maintained while holding equally to the deity of One who is distinct from God, the Father.

In order to speak of God the Father revealed in the Son through the power of the Spirit, it is necessary to speak of trinity. But trinity is not merely a concept. One does not first define trinity conceptually and then begin worshiping the triune God. Rather it is the revealed God of Scripture who approaches in a way that elicits and requires triune teaching. Gregory Nazianzus's poem on the Trinity revealed how central was the triune understanding of God in early Christian worship:

> From the day whereon I renounced the things of the world to consecrate my soul to luminous and heavenly contemplation, when the supreme intelligence carried me hence to set me down far from all that pertains to the flesh, to hide me in the secret places of the heavenly tabernacle; from that day my eyes have been blinded by the light of the Trinity, whose brightness surpasses all that the mind can conceive; for from a throne high exalted the Trinity pours upon all, the ineffable radiance common to the Three. (Poemata de seipso I, MTEC: 44)

The contemplation of the triune mystery leads beyond language, logical categories, or concepts proper to human thought, beyond dialectic and beyond dialogue, to the Three in One, into whom the faithful are baptized. Ponder:

> No sooner do I conceive of the One than I am illumined by the Splendor of the Three; no sooner do I distinguish Them than I am carried back to the One. When I think of any One of the Three I think of Him as the Whole, and my eyes are filled, and the greater part of what I am thinking of escapes me. I cannot grasp the greatness of That One so as to attribute a greater greatness to the Rest. When I contemplate the Three together, I see but one torch, and cannot divide or measure out the Undivided Light. (Gregory Nazianzus, Orat. 40.41, On Holy Baptism)

Thought races relentlessly between ephemeral dialectical poles when we glimpse the triune mystery. But worship in ancient Christianity did not desire to lay hold of the Trinity in objective language but only to worship God in the way that Scripture enables and attests. God is neither one nor three without being three in one.

God transcends alleged monotheistic unity that remains unrevealed in history. God transcends Hellenistic polytheistic multiplicity. God transcends dualism that divides. Two is the number that divides; three is the number that transcends division (Gregory Nazianzus, Orat. 23.10). When Basil's critics complained that Christianity was submitting God to an external criterion, namely, the idea of number, Basil replied: "For we do not count by way of addition, gradually making increase from unity to multitude, and saying one, two, and three,—nor yet first, second, and third. For 'I,' God, 'am the first, and I am the last.' And up to this point we have never, even at the present time, heard of a second God. Worshipping as we do God of God, we both confess the distinction of the persons, and at the same time abide by the One" (Basil, *On the Spirit* 18.45). The number three, when applied to the deity, does not serve as a calculation or quantity but as a unifying referent in the divine unity.

The worshipper enters into the triune mystery only through that ignorance that transcends all concepts, philosophical constructs, and categories. That holy ignorance then returns again to seek language to express itself. Such a language was that of the ecumenical consensus which spoke of the consubstantiality of the Three, the unity of the one nature, and the distinction of the three persons (*hypostases*). They availed themselves of the terms *ousia* (substance) and *hypostasis* (*persona*, or person) to bespeak the mystery of three in one.

> *When I speak of God you must be illumined at once by one flash of light*
> *and by three. Three in Individualities or Hypostases, if any prefer so to call*
> *them, or persons, for we will not quarrel about names so long as the syllables*
> *amount to the same meaning; but One in respect of the Substance—that is,*
> *the Godhead. For they are divided without division, if I may so say; and they*
> *are united in division. For the Godhead is one in three, and the three are one,*
> *in whom the Godhead is, or to speak more accurately, Who are the Godhead.*
> *Excesses and defects we will omit, neither making the Unity a confusion,*
> *nor the division a separation (Gregory Nazianzus, Orat. 39.11, On the*
> *Holy Lights)*

Father, Son, and Spirit are one in every way except that of being unbegotten (with respect to the Father), of filiation (with respect to the Son), and of procession (with respect to the Spirit).

> *For the Father is without cause and unborn; for He is derived from nothing,*
> *but derives from Himself His being, nor does He derive a single quality from*
> *another. Rather He is Himself the beginning and cause of the existence of*
> *all things in a definite and natural manner. But the Son is derived from the*
> *Father after the manner of generation, and the Holy Spirit likewise is derived*
> *from the Father, yet not after the manner of generation, but after that of*
> *procession. And we have learned that there is a difference between generation*
> *and procession, but the nature of that difference we in no way understand.*
> *(John of Damascus, OF 1.8)*

If asked further to define the modes of generation and procession, Gregory the Theologian answered: "What is the procession of the Holy Spirit? Do you tell me first what is the Unbegottenness of the Father, and I will explain to you the physiology of the generation of the Son, and the procession of the Spirit, and we shall both of us be frenzy-stricken for prying into the mystery of God" (Gregory Nazianzus, *Orat.* 31.8, *On the Holy Spirit*). It is sufficient to distinguish that the Son is begotten and the Spirit proceeds from the Father, following John's Gospel, and leave speculation to the foolish, imprudent, careless and unwise.

The Triune Structure of Christian Teaching

The incarnation requires triune teaching. The Father freely determines to make himself known. The incarnate Son makes the Father known. The Spirit enables the meaning of this disclosure to be received. If there were only Father and Son, and no Spirit, there would be no consequences of the revelatory event. The Word of God to humanity would lack divine follow-up and remain a past event without effect. Suppose Jesus came and nothing else happened. Then there would be only two persons in the divine mission, and we would have a binity, not a trinity. But

Jesus' mission was in fact followed by an empowering of the Spirit, acting to fulfill and consummate this mission (Ambrose, *Of the Holy Spirit* 1.7–16). This was not just an odd erratic order into which Christian teaching accidentally fell. Rather, this triune teaching belongs intrinsically to God's personal self-disclosure, which intends to be heard and appropriated in human history.

It is not some historical fluke that the Apostles' Creed has three articles, and hence a triune structure: God the Father Almighty, God revealed in the Son, and God the Spirit currently present in the church manifesting the power of the resurrection (Interrogatory Creed of Hippolytus, *CC*: 23). Early Christian theology developed in order to explain concisely to the believer the meaning of his or her baptism. From the beginning the apostolic tradition has been baptizing in the name of the Father, the Son, and the Holy Spirit. Christian theology has always been essentially a reasoning toward, from, about, and for baptism, a summary explanation of the meaning of the baptismal celebration of entry into this community.

Note carefully the coherent logic of a traditional diagram (see figure below) found in medieval symbolism. This diagram is taken from W. J. and G. Audsley, *Handbook of Christian Symbolism* (London: Day and Son, 1865), plate 3, p. 50.

This "shield of the Holy Trinity" teaches that the Father (P = *Pater*) is not (*non est*) the Son (F = *Filius*), the Son is not the Holy Spirit (SS = *Spiritus Sanctus*), and the Holy Spirit is not the Father. The Father is distinguishable from the Son, the Son is distinguishable from the Holy Spirit; and the Holy Spirit is distinguishable from the Father. However the Father is God (*est Deus*), nothing less, and the Son is God, nothing less, and the Holy Spirit is God, nothing less, and God is essentially one (*una substantia*; Tho. Aq., *ST* 1 Q31; M. D. Wyatt, *Geometrical Mosaics of the Middle Ages*).

This picture grasps the essential logic of triune teaching that avoids tri-theism, the errant view that Christians worship three Gods. God's unity is affirmed in three persons. God is *una substantia*, one substance, which means that God remains essentially one while becoming known in *tres persona*, three persons (Augustine, *Trin.* 7.4–6). The Father is God, the Son is God, the Spirit is God.

To pray to Father, Son, and Spirit is quite different than to philosophize about ideas. That God is willing to experience concretely our human alienations, sorrows, suffering, and death is quite different from philosophical concepts of transcendence and immanence. The philosopher's ideas may interest us, but faith in the triune God requires response to the One who enters our human sphere of finitude and suffering. Rational morality and natural theology may speak of the human capacity to know and do the good, but Christian proclamation trusts and prays to the eternal One who knows what it means to be betrayed and unjustly condemned, to suffer, to be crucified, and to die.

The worshiping community enters into the life of God's fully personal presence in the world. The faithful are living in Christ, sharing in his resurrection, praying to the Father through the Son. The Spirit is eliciting and sustaining their understanding of what happened in Jesus' resurrection (Heb. 1–3; 1 Pet. 1; 1 John 4, 5).

PART III

THE WORK
OF GOD

6

GOD THE CREATOR AND CREATION

I T IS INEVITABLE THAT THE TRUTH about ultimate origins, which lies beyond direct human experience, will remain a mystery (Basil, *Hex.* I; Calvin, *Inst.* 1.14). What is known of the meaning of creation is only partially understood through reason, but known more abundantly through the Creator's personal self-disclosure through the revealed Word (Justin Martyr, First Apol. 13; Athanasius, *On the Incarnation* of the Word 2).

Christian faith in God the Creator relies primarily on Scripture's witness to divine revelation. Partial insight into the truth of revelation may also occur through scientific investigation and rational inquiry (Augustine, *Catech. Instr.* 18).

"God has placed the knowledge of himself in human hearts from the beginning. But this knowledge they unwisely invested in wood and stone and thus contaminated the truth, at least as far as they were able. Meanwhile the truth abides unchanged, having its own unchanging glory. . . . How did God reveal himself? By a voice from heaven? Not at all! God made a panoply which was able to draw them more than by a voice. He put before them the immense creation" (Chrysostom, Hom. On Rom. 3).

Creator of All Things

The universal church has always believed that the one true God made all things (Irenaeus, *Ag. Her.* 2.9.1, 2). God is ungenerate, without beginning, the original cause of the coming to be, sustenance, and destiny of all creatures (Letter to Diognetus 7.2; Tho. Aq., *ST* 1 Q44; Westminster *Conf.* 4). The making of the world by God is an indispensable clause of the creed and hence article of Christian faith (Tho. Aq., *ST* 1 Q46).

The created order was made out of nothing (*ex nihilo*), without preexisting materials (Irenaeus, *Ag. Her.* 2.10, 11; Augustine, *Conf.* 12.7; Dordrecht *Conf.* I). This counteracts the pantheistic implication that matter is eternal. It also rejects the dualistic implication of another kind of equally eternal power standing contrary to God. Humanity is not made "out of nothing" (as is God) but out of "the dust of the ground" (Gen. 2:19), just as wild animals and birds were "formed out of the ground" by God (Gen. 2:19). There is no other source of creation than the will of God (Heb. 11:3; Calvin, *Inst.* 2.2.20), which obviously loves being in preference to not being. That is clear from the evidences of creation.

The world was not created coeternal with God (Augustine, *CG* 11.4, 5; *Conf.* 11.14). The world was not put together out of pieces of God (Augustine, *Conf.* 11.5, 12.7). The creation is only of God, and only God could create the world (Shepherd of Hermas, *Mandate* 1.1). Cosmic creation is a work peculiar to God (Athanasius, *Four Discourses Ag. Arians* 2.16). Though it may unfold in an evolutionary process, the evolutionary process itself does not create itself but is created.

Time did not always exist. The world was created *with* time (Augustine, *CG* 11.6). Space and time came into being only with creation, not prior to it. There was a condition of non-being, or "time" so to speak, when time was not. Our contemplation of the creation of time and space is filled with enigma since we are creatures of time, made conscious always in time and through time. In time we meet the created order as intrinsically intelligible (Theophilus, *To Autolycus* 1.4–5; John of Damascus, *OF* 2.3), wondering from where its intelligibility derives.

Turning to God's Action—What God Does

Creation and providence are pivotal teachings of Christianity (Basel *Conf.* I) profoundly shared with Judaism and, to some degree, with other monotheistic faiths. Providence—the care of God over all things—will be discussed in the following chapter. For now the activity of God (sometimes called opera dei—the work, energy, or workings of God), as distinguished from the being of God, is now our central concern, especially as it appears in creation.

Christian teaching asks not only about who God *is*, but what God *does*—how God's power, mercy, and patience are manifested in creative, preservative, redemptive, and consummating activities (Gregory of Nyssa, *Great Catech.* 12; Calvin, *Inst.* 2.3–5). God's essence is best viewed through the outworking of God's energies, the working (*energeia*) of God in and through creatures (Chrysostom, *Concerning the Statues*, hom. 10.8, 9; Gregory of Nyssa, *On the Holy Trin.*, *Answer to Eunomius*, sec. bk.; Irenaeus, *Ag. Her.* 4.20).

Hence Christian teaching does not deal only with "God in himself" as if God could be viewed abstractly apart from God's works or cosmic activity. God is known through what God does. These works of God are stated in summary form under three great headings: *creation*, *redemption*, and *sanctification* (Luther, *Small Catech.*; Anglican Catech.), terms that summarize the whole range of activities of the triune God, and that correlate with the creedal summary.

These activities of God correspond indirectly with the work of the Father, Son, and Spirit. They find their unity in the one God, yet the effects of creation, redemption, and consummation are subjectively experienced by the faithful as gracious in different ways: (1) finite creatures learn that they are radically dependent for their existence upon Another (who wholly transcends all things, God the Father); (2) when human beings fall into sin they discover they are being helped by Another (help comes from afar, from a distant Other who comes close, the Son born of woman); and (3) when human freedom seeks to respond to the mercy and love of God it is assisted by Another (God's own Spirit). Accordingly, the one

God—Creator, Redeemer, and Sanctifier—is none other than the One God who is named in Scripture as Father, Son, and Spirit.

Already we have established *that* God *is*, and is triune. In Part Three we now seek greater clarity about *what* the triune God *does* (Lactantius, *Div. Inst.* 1.2; Chrysostom, *Concerning the Statues*, Hom. 5–7; Calvin, *Inst.* 2.3, 4; Chemnitz, *LT* 1:112). We shift our attention from God's *being* (nature, character, and existence) to God's *working*. We are turning *from* who God is *to* what God does. God originally creates and continually provides for creation.

God's First Act: Creation

The first of all God's good acts is the creation of the world. How could it be otherwise, for how can anything be good unless it exists? Chronologically and logically, creation is the proper starting point of any talk of the historical activity of God, for history begins with creation.

If Christian teaching is to speak of the God of history, there must be a stage on which history is played out. Note that there is a *redemptive* intent from the beginning in *creation*, so there is a subtle sense in which God's saving purpose—love for the world—is antecedent to God's creating action (1 Cor. 2:7; 2 Tim. 1:9; Titus 1:2; Rev. 13:8; John 1:1–20; Eph. 1:5–11; Barth, *CD* 2/2).

But there is a less subtle sense in which creation is prior to redemption, for how could one have something to redeem if that something did not exist? Our sequence is the standard order of the ecumenical teaching consensus, seen as early as Theophilus of Antioch, who having spoken of the nature and existence of God (*To Autolycus* 1), then turned immediately to discuss the works of God in creation and providence (2.1–21).

In considering creation prior to our full discussion of Christology, however, there is no hint or suggestion that creation is separable from Christ. For Pauline, Johannine, and Synoptic texts all make it clear that creation is the work of the triune God— the Father of all, the Son who is with the Father in creating, and *Creator Spiritus*, working in perfect union (Matt. 28:19; Mark 1:10–11; John 1:1–4; 1 Cor. 8:6; Col. 1:13–16; Phil.2:5–11; Heb. 1:1–4; Augustine, Sermon 232.5).

The Living God and the Gift of Life

No one can reflect upon the Creator without also reflecting upon creatures (inanimate and animate, material and spiritual) whom God thought it important enough to create (Gregory of Nyssa, *Great Catech.* 5, 6). So the Christian teaching about creation includes all creatures including ourselves. It asks why God would want creatures, especially those with potentially bad habits of human freedom. No gift we are given is more remarkable than the extraordinary gift of simply being given anything at all, the unpurchasable gift of living as free human beings.

Some complain it is unfair that living creatures were never once consulted first about whether they wanted to be alive. Consider the structural inconsistency underlying such a complaint. For one to have been consulted first about whether one wanted to live, one would have had already to *be*, that is, to have life of some kind. That would still leave unattended the question of how the one being consulted got there. The conclusion holds: Life is radically *given* to us prior to any conceivable choice of our own. No creature who has ever lived has earned it or asked for it.

The gift of *life* preconditions all other gifts. Nothing can experience, receive, or elicit any good outcome without first having been given life. Even if something "good" were to happen to a stone, it could not recognize or receive it because it is not alive (at least in any recognizable sense). The inexorable rule is this: Nothing lives without having first been *given* life. The gift is unmerited. No creature got here by choosing to be alive (Basil, *Hex.* 9; Calvin, *Inst.* 3.9.3).

The inanimate cannot choose to be animate. The nonexistent cannot choose existence. Any creature that is sufficiently alive to be aware of life has already received creation's most astonishing gift—life itself (Tho. Aq., *ST* 1 Q18; Luther, *Smaller Catech.* 1). An incalculably valuable gift calls for an unreserved, grateful, active response (Catherine of Genoa, *Spiritual Dialogue*, CWS: 132).

The Biblical Perspective on God the Creator

The creation teaching is widely diffused throughout the Scripture in the psalms, the Prophets, the synoptic Gospels and letters (Tertullian, Ag. Hermogenes 23–36; Basil, *Hex.* 2–6). Although Genesis is the most quoted and prototypical reference, the classical exegetes have often turned for wisdom about creation to other powerful scriptural affirmations of God's creating will, such as Isaiah 40, Amos 4:13, Psalms 90 and 104, Jeremiah 10, John 1, Acts 17, and Colossians 1 (Augustine, *Trin.* 16). The locus classicus texts on creation are extensive (Job 26:7–14; 38:4–11; Pss. 33:6–9; 102:25; Isa. 45:5; 45:18; Neh. 9:6; Rom. 1:20; 9:20; Heb. 1:2; 11:3; Rev. 4:11; 10:6; Chrysostom, *Hom. on Acts*, 38).

Genesis

The account in Genesis 2 and 3 is often referred to as the Yahwist account since the author's preferred name for God is Yahweh. It is more concerned with the creation of human beings, man and woman, and their dominion and destiny from the beginning, including the account of the fall and the alienation of human freedom (Tertullian, *Ag. Marcion* 2.1–17; Augustine, *CG* 13. 12).

In the Yahwist account there is from the beginning an acknowledgment of human freedom as a gift accountable to God and of human sexual differentiation as a divine gift to male and female, since God wills to bless both through these differences (Gen. 1:27). Always easily distortable, human freedom and sexuality are a crucial part of God's good creation and intention, intended for generativity, love, moral discipline, productivity, dominion, and stewardship of the earth (Chrysostom, *Hom. on Ephesians* 20).

The Genesis narratives, taken together, express much of the heart of the Jewish and Christian teaching on creation: that we are given life by one who is wise and free, who creates us for our good and whose goodness is displayed throughout the creation. There are never assumed to be two or more gods at work in creation. Under the category of true God there can be only one (Irenaeus, *Ag. Her.* 2.2.1–5; Cyril of Jerusalem, *Catech. Lect.* 6). These Yahwist motifs will be treated more fully later under the topic of human existence.

The Bible's first concern is more with the priestly account of the orderly creation of the world, light, life, and nature (Gen. 1:1–2:4a). The priestly prologue, Genesis 1:1–2:4, serves as a kind of all-embracing introduction to the history of salvation (Basil, *Hex.*, 1–2). It is the Bible's way of beginning the longest and best of all stories. It begins by constructing the stage on which covenant history is to be played. Even when the covenant is broken, God in due time heals that brokenness and calls humanity back to covenant relationship, redeeming creation after it falls. The creation narrative sets the scene and provides the context in which God's purpose is being worked out in the whole of history (Origen, *Ag. Celsus* 6.50–70).

Creation is not, according to the Hebraic tradition, primarily objective, descriptive scientific talk of how nature evolves or emerges, as if this were merely a matter of accurate observation, or as if the fate-laden historical choices of previous humans did not make much real difference to the destiny of the free creature (Chrysostom, *Concerning the Statues*, hom. 7). Rather, the scriptural witness to creation is from the first line more like a drama, the beginning of the acts of God, the first of many mighty deeds, upon which hinge both life's current meaning and the eternal destinies of participants (Ephrem, *Comm. on Gen.* 1).

The drama is all about a relationship. It is the thorny, conflicted, seductive, unpredictable unfolding epic of a covenant relationship between Yahweh and Adam, Yahweh and Abraham, Yahweh and Israel, Yahweh and humanity. The real story of creation is about the Creator-creature relationship, not about creatures as such, as if creation in itself could be considered a detached occurrence or autonomous event (Irenaeus, *Ag. Her.* 2.10.1–4).

The Bible does not rule out scientific studies or other ways of approaching the primitive history of the world. The natural emergence of the cosmic, geological, vegetative, and animal spheres can remain open for all reasonable forms of investigation. The creation narratives do not pretend to describe in empirical detail, objectively, descriptively, or non-metaphorically, the way in which the world came into being. Rather, they proclaim the awesome primordial fact that the world is radically dependent on the generosity, wisdom, and help of God, the insurmountably good and powerful One (Dionysius, *Div. Names* 8.7–9; Tho. Aq., *ST* 1 Q44–46).

The world is not God. It is as different from God as the gnat's eye from the Omniscient One. Being finite, the creation itself is not eternal. It lies within a cosmic parenthesis—between the beginning and end of all things. The whole world and everything in the world owes its being to the free, sovereign act of God (Tho. Aq., *Compend*:96). God created the world by a word. God speaks—as simple as that—and there it is.

The world is not an oozing out of some part of God—not an emanation—which would mean that the world gradually seeps or leaks out (*e*, out, *manare*, flow) of the edges of the being of God, according to the analogy of fragrance emanating from flowers. Theories of emanation have been consistently rejected by Jewish and Christian teachers because they fail to make a sharp distinction between God and the world (Hippolytus, *Refutation of All Her.* 10).

God minus the world is still God. If God should turn out to be indistinguishably merged with the world, Christian teaching would become another pantheism, which reduces God to the world. It collapses God and the world into one continuous amalgam. Only when God is unmistakably distinguishable from the world, the Uncreated from the created, can we have theism in its classic Jewish and Christian sense (Tertullian, *Ag. Hermogenes* 17–31; Tho. Aq., *ST* 1 Q45; Calovius, *SLT* 3:899).

The Days of Creation: Hexaemeron

The word *day* (*yōm*) has several levels of meaning. It is used in biblical Hebrew to mean not only a twenty-four-hour day but also a time of divine visitation or judgment, or an indefinite period of time, as in Psalms 110:5, Isaiah 2:11, 12, and Jeremiah 11:4–7; 17:16 To insist on a twenty-four-hour day as its only meaning is to intrude upon the text and to disallow the poetic, metaphorical, and symbolic speech of Scripture (Pss. 2:7; 18:18; Isa. 4:1, 2; Jer. 44:1–23). Thus when we say "day" in Hebrew we may be referring to the first period, or second period, and so on. Classical readings of Genesis 1 focused upon the first six periods as an orderly series of divine acts of (1) creating, (2) ordering (distinguishing), and (3) adorning of the world, followed by rest.

Classic consensual interpreters have written detailed expositions on the making, distinctions, and adornments enacted by God in these six days (*hexaemeron*) of divine creativity (Theophilus of Antioch, *To Autolycus* 2.11–18; Basil, *Hex.*; Chrysostom, *Hom. on Genesis*; Ambrose, *Hex.*; Augustine, *Literal Interp. of Gen.*; Dionysius, *Div. Names*; John of Damascus, *OF 2.2–3*; Bede, *Hex.*; and Tho. Aq., *ST* 1 Q66–74). Each of these six days before the day of rest is introduced by the words "And God said" (Augustine, *Literal Interp. of Gen.* 1.8). The first chapter of Genesis has produced extended theological meditations on the acts of God the creator, orderer, and beautifier, following this pattern:

The First Day. (Gen. l. 3): Light, with night following day is created (Theophilus, *To Autolycus* 2.11–13; Basil, *Hex.* 1–2), the first of three days of the work of distinction or divine differentiation of creatures (Tho. Aq., *ST* 1 Q67). It is fitting and necessary that the production of light occur on the first day, since "that without which there could not be day, must have been made on the first day" (Tho. Aq., *ST* 1 Q67). God says "Good."

The Second Day. (Gen. 1:6): The vault of heaven, waters below to form the sea and waters above to form the rain, and the firmament are created (Theophilus, *To Autolycus* 2. 14; Basil, *Hex.* 3; Tho. Aq., *ST* 1 Q68). Good.

The Third Day. (Gen 1:9–13): Seas, the lands, and plant life, yielding fresh growth and bearing seed, are all created (Basil, *Hex.* 4; Tho. Aq., *ST* 1 Q69). The precious gift of life first appeared in plants, but remained "hidden, since they lack sense and local movement," and therefore "their production is treated as a part of the earth's formation" (Tho. Aq., *ST* 1 Q70). Good.

The Fourth Day. (Gen. 1:14): Luminaries, sun, moon, stars, giving light, governing night and day (Theophilus, *To Autolycus* 2.15, 16; Basil, *Hex.* 6)—the first of three days of the work of the adornment of creation (Tho. Aq., *ST* 1 Q70). "The sun, the moon and the stars" are good, but "do not bow down to them." (Deut. 4:19). They render a threefold service to all humanity: for *light* to see by; for the changes of the *seasons*, "which prevent weariness, preserve health, and provide for the necessities of food"; and for *weather*, fair or foul, "as favorable to various occupations" (Tho. Aq., *ST* 1 Q70, italics added). It is for these varied purposes that the lights are said to "serve as signs both for festivals and for seasons and years" (Gen. 1:14b; Tertullian, *Ag. Marcion* 5.6).

The Fifth Day. (Gen 1:29): Countless living creatures of the water and creatures of the air (Theophilus, *To Autolycus* 2.16; Basil, *Hex.* 7; Tho. Aq., *ST* 1 Q71). Water is adorned with fish, and air adorned with birds. In the Genesis account we behold the creation of "different grades of life" from the life of plants, which vegetate, to the life of great and small "living creatures that live and move in the waters," to "every kind of bird." Then we come to the creation of land animals that are more complex, having the capacity for motion, as "living souls with bodies subject to them." Through this progression, "the more perfect is reached through the less perfect," (Tho. Aq., *ST* 1 Q73) in a food chain by which higher life forms feed off the lower. God thus creates an amazingly intricate and beautiful creation that is well fitted for many evidences of providential care, which all the animals illustrate. Good.

The Sixth Day. (Gen 1:24): More complexly sensate living creatures are given life: each "according to their kind: cattle, reptiles, and wild animals," and finally humanity, male and female (Theophilus, *To Autolycus* 2.17, 18; Basil, *Hex.* 9; Tho. Aq., *ST* 1 Q72). Humanity, as finitely free, is both very like and very unlike the preceding animals, since grounded in nature yet capable of freedom, self-transcendence, and consciousness, refracting the divine image. Humanity is *unlike* plants and animals, which "may be said to be produced according to their kinds, to signify their remoteness from the Divine image and likeness, whereas man is said to be made 'to the image and likeness of God.'" Yet humanity is *like* the various animals in that all receive the blessing God gives by "the power to multiply by generation." Much the same blessing of sexual generativity given to animal life is distinctly repeated in the case of humanity "to prevent anyone from saying that there was any sin whatever in the act of begetting children," (Tho. Aq., *ST* I, Q73) yet to further bond human sexual fidelity through love, so as to provide fitting care for the nurture of children. Hence human life is viewed as a paradoxical, potentially disjunctive, interfacing of nature and transcendence, of finitude and freedom, of animal-like passions and likeness to God, of sexuality and fidelity. Adam and Eve are given ordered freedom amid this complex inter-facing that the ancient Christian writers called a *compositum* of body and soul.

The Seventh Day. Divine rest. God "blessed the seventh day and made it holy, because on that day he ceased from all the work he had set himself to do" (Gen. 2:2, 3). "Nothing entirely new was afterwards made by God." The seventh day is said to be sanctified "because something is added to creatures by their multiplying and by their resting in God" (Tho. Aq., *ST* 1 Q74).

The first three periods prepare the world for the next three periods, in which living inhabitants are set in a well-prepared place and provided a rhythm of life. There are living beings for each of the four elemental regions of *air* (birds), *earth* (plants, animals, humanity), *water* (fish), and *fire* (the sun is needed for the warmth and illumination of all). The seventh day is for rejoicing over the good-ness of the former six, providing a pattern for human life—working six days and resting on the seventh.

In this way the work of God the Creator is beheld in its intrinsic moral and spiritual intelligibility as a complete act of *creation* in which heaven and earth were produced, yet without form; a work of *distinction*, in which heaven and earth were given order and beauty; and a work of *adornment* in which, just as our bodies are adorned with clothing, so God adorns the world with the production of things that live and move in heaven and on earth. All the elements for life—air, earth, fire, and water—receive their form through the divine work of making differences among creatures (Tho. Aq., *ST* 1 Q70).

Let It Be: Heaven and Earth

The Genesis narrative is written in a recurrent permissive form in six movements: "Let there be" (vv. 3, 6, 14, 15, 20, 24). The created order springs directly from the word of God, the simple divine address: "God said" (vv. 3, 6, 9, 11, 14, 20, 24, 26). It is produced, ordered and approved—all by God's speech. The command is given, and it is. God said, in effect, "I permit creation," and it was there. "There is nothing too hard for thee," declared Jeremiah (32:17). God does not have to strain to create the world.

Creation is viewed as a divine language that only God can speak (Tho. Aq., *GC*:260). It is ordered at once by the divine will and just as quickly received and ap-proved. The permission, command, production, ordering, receiving, and approval are all set forth in the brief first chapter of Genesis (Tertullian, *Ag. Praxeas* 12).

God's approbation of the goodness of creation builds majestically from good, to more complex good, to "very good" (Gen. 1:4, 10, 14, 21, 31; Basil, *Hex.* 9; Wesley, *WJW* 6:206–15). God brings forth out of nothing, according to his sovereign will, the visible universe and the invisible or spiritual sphere. Creation is entirely an act of divine freedom (Augustine, *CG* 11.24).

Scripture speaks of heaven as the abode of God. Moses prayed that God would "look down from heaven, thy holy dwelling-place" (Deut. 26:15). Jesus prayed to "Our Father in heaven" (Matt. 6:9). It is a key mark of Christian confession that God created not only the earth but also the intricate extent of the heavens (Gen. 1:1; Tertullian, *Ag. Hermogenes* 17–34) that embrace all cosmic creation transcending the earth.

The Angelic Hosts

An angel (*angelos*) is a messenger of God, a spiritual creature endowed with free will and capable of divine praise, yet unencumbered with bodily existence (Irenaeus, *Ag. Her.* 3.8; John of Damascus, 2.3; Quenstedt, *TDP* 1: Wesley, *WJW* 6: 361). Angels are incorporeal, lacking bodies (Athanasius, Four Discourses Ag. Arians 2.19; Tho. Aq., ST I Q51, I). They are not limited to the here and now (Gregory Nazianzus, *Second Orat.* on Easter, *Orat.* 45.5; Tho. Aq., *ST* 1 Q51). "An angel, then, is an intelligent essence, in perpetual motion, with free-will, incorporeal, ministering to God, having obtained by grace an immortal nature" (John of Damascus, *OF* 2.3). Since endowed with free will, angels may be tempted. Fallen angels who have disavowed their uncorrupted essence and have conspired in disobedience (Tertullian, On the Flesh of Christ 14; Augustine, *CG* 12.6; Chemnitz, LT 1: 122; Quenstedt, *TDP* 1: 443; Wesley, Of Evil Angels, *WJW* 6: 380–81) are to be discussed at the end of this study.

Jesus himself was a recipient of the ministry of angels (Matt. 4:11; Luke 22:43). A countless number of angels are said to surround the throne of God (Heb. 12:22; Rev. 5:11). Little may be said descriptively of the transcendent depiction of angels except the brightness of their countenance, a luminosity unlike any of this world (Matt. 28:2–4; Luke 2:9; Acts 1:10). "They have no need of tongue or hearing but without uttering words they communicate to each other their own thoughts and counsels. . . . It is not as they really are that they reveal themselves to the worthy men to whom God wishes them to appear, but in a changed form which the beholders are capable of seeing. . . . They behold God according to their capacity, and this is their food" (John of Damascus, *OF* 2.3).

Why are we still discussing angels in the modern world, where naturalistic assumptions seem largely to have undercut even the possibility of angels? Because our purpose is to represent accurately the classical Christian understanding of God the Creator, which virtually without exception has affirmed the spiritual world, created by God. The sacred texts tell of superpersonal intelligences— angelic hosts. The liturgy, the Scriptures, and the hymnody are filled with such images. In Scripture and most Christian history, any view of the world that lacked angels would have seemed implausible, lacking something essential to creation. The early creeds typically affirmed the gift of the heavens and the world of spirit that transcends all empirical vision, not merely the earth and physical matter, as if all that makes a difference is the world that is seen.

Christianity has passed through many worldviews. It still requires some empathic effort for the modern worldview to enter into the worldview of those who make known to us the revelation of God that both transcends and penetrates all particular worldviews. Even within the frame of contemporary scientific worldviews (and there are many, even as there are many premodern worldviews) it is hardly reasonable to rule out superpersonal intelligences in this vast cosmos that we still know so incompletely.

Covenant Creation and the Covenant People of God

God Creates the Covenant People out of Nothing

The prophets of the eighth, seventh, and sixth centuries BC grasped and developed this surprising analogy: God created the people of Israel out of nothing, just as God creates everything else. As God creates Israel as a nation "from nothing" (as later Latin writers would speak of creation *ex nihilo,* out of nothing), so does God create all things (Augustine, *Conf.* 12. 7). The people of Israel were nobody. God created them from dust. As Israel was not a people except for Yahweh, so the prophet declared that the world would be nothing except for Yahweh (Isa. 43:16–21; Jer. 31:17–25).

Hence, the creative power of God is to be found not only in the beginning but in the process of history, amid the currently unfolding human story (Augustine, *CG* 3.17–31). God not only creates Israel, but when Israel is frayed down to nothing God then wonderfully re-creates Israel (Isa. 40:1; Jer. 30:12; Dan. 3:1). Out of the awareness that Israel had been created by the divine mercy and covenant, the prophets then reflected back on the creation of all things by analogy to Israel's special creation (Augustine, *CG* 16.36–43; Calvin, *Inst.* 2.8.29; 2.10.1). Even when Israel abandoned its destiny, and covenant responsibility, God remembered, sustained, and re-created the covenant. Thus a "new covenant," a "New Jerusalem" is attested by Jeremiah and others (Jer. 31:31; Isa. 65; Irenaeus, *Ag. Her.* 4.9).

The cosmos is viewed by analogy from Israel's post-exilic historical experience. God is always doing something new in history, always creating or re-creating a new people, ever restoring that which has fallen to nothing (Athanasius, *On the Incarnation* 4–15). Through the unexpected turns of history, Yahweh is making known unchanging divine covenant love (*chesed*, Ezek. 16; Isa. 54:5; Mark 2:19; Calvin, *Inst.* 1.5.1–12; 1.17.2). The messianic expectation of God as creator of a new people is directly grounded in Israel's actual historical experience, from being no people to becoming a people, and having lost their national identity rediscovering it as secured by Yahweh (Hos. 1:8–11).

Creation is Made for Covenant

The prophets give a wrenching account of a durable relationship between the steadfast God and the wavering people of God. The relation of God and Israel mirrors the relation of God with the whole of humanity. Creation itself is seen as evidence of covenant from the beginning, but the meaning of the covenant is only gradually revealed by means of actual historical events (Augustine, *CG* 11.21; Gallic *Conf.*, art. 7–8; Westminster *Conf.* 4). The covenant intention of God is present from the beginning, but it becomes clarified and appears more palpable only slowly through a twisted history in which the covenant relationship is declared, established, tested, redeemed, and consummated. God creates the world in order to enter into a covenant relationship with the world particularly through Israel, by whom God's covenant love is mediated to the rest of the world.

Covenant is not merely an idea, but a history; it takes time—centuries, in fact—gradually to manifest itself and become experientially embraced. It is something like a friendship—it does not just momentarily happen. Can you imagine a personal relationship that appears suddenly, totally, with no possibility or need for further disclosure? Friendships are more often experienced through a history of disclosure. We discover, through knowing and dealing with some other person, whether that person is reliable or not, is caring or not. Covenant history is something like such a gradually developing relationship (Hos 1; Jer 31,

Is. 53–54). Such human relationships have to be fought for and won, defended, reworked, and tested. This is the kind of relationship that comes to exist between God and Israel, something like a rocky marriage or an important but embattled friendship. Many events are remembered and recollected to establish an awareness of God's dependability. The relationship does not simply or flatly exist, but must be hammered out through a series of hazardous and wonderful experiences (Hos. 1:1, Irenaeus, *Ag. Her.* 4.20–25).

Throughout all these experiences, God is creative, continuing to create, re-create, and sustain this covenant relationship. It is through this kind of history that the people of Israel understood themselves to be recipients of the covenant love of God, yet they understood the whole of that history to be already present in the preknowing, eternal mind of God and saturated with the corrective will of God from the very beginning (Augustine, *CG* 5.9; Tho. Aq., *GC*, p. 87).

Nehemiah grasped the correspondence of God's activity as Creator and Redeemer in these terms: "You are the Lord, you alone; you have made heaven, the heaven of heavens, with all their host, the earth and all that is on it, the seas and all that is in them. To all of them you give life, and the host of heaven worships you. You are the Lord, the God who chose Abram and brought him out of Ur of the Chaldeans and gave him the name Abraham; and you found his heart faithful before you, and made with him a covenant" (Neh. 9:6–8). The analogy: Abram (hence Israel) is called to being and faith by the One who calls all into being (Bede, On Ezra and Nehemiah 3.29).

The constancy of the laws established by God for the universe was viewed by the prophets as a sign that the covenant would endure forever. The analogy is between the natural order, which is reliable, and divine creation, which depends upon the divine faithfulness (Isa. 45; Lactantius, *Div. Inst.* 3.28; Tho. Aq., *GC*:82).

The Hebrew prophets were keenly aware of the radical difference between God and world, eternal and temporal power, Giver and gift (Pss. 113–4; Isa. 30:28). "Who has measured the waters in the hollow of his hand, or with the breadth of his hand marked off the heavens? Who has held the dust of the earth in a basket, or weighed the mountains on the scales and the hills in a balance?" (Isa. 40:12). It is the one God who creates the world, permits its freedom to fall, acts to redeem what has fallen, and brings the whole story to fitting consummation (Athanasius, *Incarnation of the Word* 20–32; Second Helvetic *Conf.* 6).

Creation Looks Toward Consummation

The Hebrew prophets envisioned a future in which the whole universe would share in the renewal of all things. History awaits "a new heaven and a new earth" (Isa. 65:17; 66:22,;. 2 Pet. 3:13; Rev. 21:1). The new heaven and the new earth are not alien to the old heaven and the old earth but a fulfillment of it (Cassiodorus, Expos. Of Ps. 148.6).

When the primordial design of God has been distorted by human sin, God continues to re-create and restore covenant relationship. Hence God's creative action is not something that exists only at the beginning of time but remains and persists here and now, to be beheld both in personal and national life (Isa. 40:26–28; Mal. 2:10).

In this way the prophetic vision of beginnings is linked firmly with an eschatological vision of endings. The prophets beheld both the beginning of history and the end of history as God's active work. They hoped for a culmination of distorted history in a way that would be consistent with the divine purpose from the beginning (Augustine, *CC* 12.21–25).

God's Wisdom in Creation

The priestly account had focused on the six days of creation followed by Sabbath rest. The Yahwist narrative (Gen. 2–3) told the drama of the creation of humanity and the original divine-human relationship broken by sin. The prophetic accounts viewed God's purpose in creation in the light of God's creative activity in ongoing covenant history.

The wisdom literature (Job, Proverbs, Ecclesiastes, and certain Psalms) provided new variations on these themes attesting God's purpose in creation. These writings shifted the focus more toward God's creative activity in nature, wisdom, and practical judgment, while sustaining all of these previous themes.

In this genre, the world becomes a spectacular object of human research, observation, and enjoyment (Ps. 104; Eccles. 1:5). The created order evokes astonishment (Ps. 19), humility (Job 38:1–42:6), and hymns of praise (Pss. 48:10; 68:32–35). Its orderliness and beauty are testimonies to the eternal wisdom of God: "When I consider your heavens, the work of your fingers, the moon and the stars, which you have set in place, what is man that you are mindful of him?" (Ps. 8:3, 4; Augustine, *On the Psalms* 8). "The heavens show forth the glory of God," while this firmament, this creaturely sphere, shows myriad evidences of God's handiwork (Ps. 19; Augustine, *On the Psalms* 19).

There are creation hymns in the Psalms that speak of the whole world as filled with the wisdom of God (Pss. 104; 136:1–9; Origen, *OFP* 2.9; Gregory Thaumaturgus, *Four Hom., Hom. One*). Creation mirrors the incalculable wisdom, power, and glory of God (Theophilus of Antioch, *To Autolycus* 2.10, 11; Origen, *OFP* 1.2.9–12; Lactantius, *Div. Inst.* 7.5–6).

Wisdom is present with God from "the beginning of his works, before all else that he made, long ago. Alone, I was fashioned in times long past, at the beginning, long before earth itself. When there was yet no ocean I was born, no springs brimming with water. Before the mountains were settled in their place, long before the hills I was born" (Prov. 8:22–25). All creation is good as given because it is imprinted with the providential image of Wisdom (Athanasius, *Four Discourses Ag. Arians* 2.78, 79; Basil, *Hex.* 9. 3–6).

This corresponds with another theme in the wisdom literature: the beauty of God, and of God's world, rightly leading to praise (Gregory Nazianzus, *Orat.* 38. 10). The earth is an appropriate object of celebration, provided we avoid idolatry (Tertullian, *On Idolatry*; Calvin, *Inst.* 1.11.12; Wesley, *WJW* 7:268). The divine majesty appears in these works (Ps. 139:14–17; Eccles. 3:11). God is a master craftsman who pours out his creative activity upon the world. The world reflects this artistry and is made radiant by a glory that points back to its Creator, mirroring the divine generosity (Basil, *Hex.*, 6; Chrysostom, *Concerning the Statues*, hom. 10. 5, 6).

The Triune Creator

The apostolic witness did not set itself over against Moses, the Prophets, or the wisdom literature in their views of creation, idolatry, covenant, and the divine handiwork. These earlier Hebraic teachings on creation became transmuted in the light of the apostles' experience of Jesus of Nazareth (Irenaeus, *Ag. Her.* 4.20; Athanasius, Four Discourses Ag. Arians 2. 19–24). The prophetic tradition of creation was reappropriated, yet reconceived through the lens of their relation with the Son, the unique Revealer of the Father's purpose in creation (Tertullian, *Ag. Marcion* 5.5; Cyril of Alex., *Treasury of Holy Trin., FEF* 3:212).

The early Christians prayed in much the same language as did Jews before them "to the sovereign Lord, maker of the heaven and earth and sea and everything in them" (Acts 4:24), but with the understanding that the creator had been revealed as the redeemer in Jesus. God created the world by direct address (2 Cor. 4:6). God called into being what did not exist (Irenaeus, *Ag. Her.* 2.10.1–4, 3.8). These were all typical phrases found in Jewish celebrations of divine creation.

Creation Seen in the Light of Redemption

In John's prologue, the world is created by the Word of God who is made flesh in Jesus. The Word of God in Jesus is coeternal with the Father. (John 1:1–17; Basil, *On the Holy Spirit* 8.21; Gregory of Nyssa, *Ag. Eunomius* 2.8–11). The Word of God is God himself, Creator of the universe. The Creator, made known personally in Jesus, comes into our history to present himself clearly to our view.

John's Gospel begins in a conscious parallel to Genesis 1: "In the beginning was the Word" (John 1:1). The evangelist could not make any more dramatic affirmation than to identify Christ with the Word present in creation, by whom the world was made. There was no better place to start in making contact with Jewish belief than to identify the Word spoken in Jesus as the same Word who is from the beginning (Col. 1; Tatian, *Orat. Ag. Greeks* 7). "The Word, then, was with God at the beginning, and through him all things came to be; no single thing was created without him" (John 1:2, 3; 1:14; Irenaeus, *Ag. Her.* 3.11, *ANF* I:426–29; Athanasius, *Four Discourses Ag. Arians* 1.11–21; Ambrose, *Of the Holy Spirit* 2.1–4; *Of the Chr. Faith,* 1.54–57).

Paul took a similar beginning point in the letter to the Romans: God's divinity and eternity are known through creation. Look at the creation carefully, and you will see some stamp, some distinct impression of the Creator's purpose. God's invisible nature is known through that which is visible (Rom. 1:20). This is the very One who is made known in Jesus: "Source, Guide, and Goal of all that is—to him be glory for ever! Amen" (Rom. 11:36; Origen, *Ag. Celsus* 6. 65; Gregory of Nyssa, *Ag. Eunomius* 2.7).

In Jesus' resurrection we meet "the God who makes the dead live and summons things that are not yet in existence as if they already were" (Rom. 4:17). Acts reports that Paul spoke to the Athenians of "The God who created the world and everything in it, and who is Lord of heaven and earth," who is "himself the universal giver of life and breath and all else. He created every race of men of one stock, to inhabit the whole earth's surface" (Acts 17:24–26).

The same One who creates, redeems. The Son is "the image of the invisible God; his is the primacy over all created things. In him everything in heaven and on earth was created, not only things visible but also the invisible orders of thrones, sovereignties, authorities, and powers: the whole universe has been created through him and for him" (Col. 1:15–17; Origen, *OFP* 2.6; Basil, *Hex.* 1.6; *On the Holy Spirit* 16). In Christ all things were created and now subsist. It is he who sustains the universe by his word of power. (Athanasius, *Defence of the Nicene Definition* 3.7). In Hebrews it was written, "By faith we perceive that the universe was fashioned by the word of God, so that the visible came forth from the invisible" (Heb. 11:3; Gregory Nazianzus, *Second Theol. Orat.* 6; *On Pentecost, Orat.* 41.14; Cyril of Jerusalem, *Catech. Lect.* 9.1, 2).

In this way the New Testament church affirmed the received Jewish tradition's celebration of God's goodness in creation and of the utter dependence of all things upon God, yet added a decisive point of interpretation: the Father's creation is seen in the light of the Son, to whom fitting response is enabled through the Spirit (Augustine, *Trin.* 3.4; 5.13–15).

The work of creation is "always applied in Scripture not partially but to the whole, entire, full, complete Godhead" (Dionysius, *Div. Names* 2: 65). "For in the [Nicene] Creed, to the Father is attributed that 'He is the Creator of all things visible and invisible'; to the Son is attributed that by Him 'all things were made'; and to the Holy Ghost is attributed that He is 'Lord and Life-Giver'"—hence, "to create is not proper to any one Person, but is common to the whole Trinity. . . . God the Father made the creature through His Word, which is His Son; and through His Love, which is the Holy Ghost," who "quickens what is created by the Father through the Son" (Tho. Aq., *ST* 1 Q45). The prophets, priests, and apocalyptic writers had been waiting for the final disclosure of meaning in history, which the apostles viewed as having occurred in Jesus life, death, and resurrection (1 Cor. 1 Augustine, *Literal Interp. of Gen.* 9.15.26, *FEF* 3: 86).

The New Creation

Christ reveals the purpose of creation. The Spirit works to create a new community of faith, hope, and love, a resurrected fellowship in fallen history. The New Testament doctrine of creation is not just about the first thing that happens in time but also about the new creation occurring in the community of faith. The new creation is happening in our hearts (Chrysostom, Fourth Instruction, 12). By analogy to the first creation, where there was once nothing, now there is new life (Clement of Alex., Who Is the Rich Man That Shall Be Saved? 12). Christ "re-formed the human race" (Irenaeus, *Ag. Her.* 4.24.1). "When anyone is united to Christ, there is a new world; the old order has gone, and a new order has already begun" (2 Cor. 5:17; Epistle of Barnabas 5). The focus is not on primal events, but on a report of the renewal of believing individuals in communities in the here and now. The analogies are spiritual gestation, embryonic formation, and the joy of birth (Recognitions of Clement 9.7; Wesley, *WJW* 5:212).

The expectation of a new creation is a motif that had already appeared powerfully in the Prophets (Isa. 65:17; 66:22; Jer. 31; Lam. 3:23). It took on deepened meaning in the New Testament view that the new creation had palpably begun in the community of Jesus Christ by the power of the Spirit. Where two or three are gathered together (Matt. 18:20), there the living Christ is in their midst and the new age begun. "Circumcision is nothing; uncircumcision is nothing; the only thing that counts is new creation!" (Gal. 6:15; Calvin, *Inst.* 2.11.11; Wesley, *WJW* 1:161).

This new creation is already begun, not only in the life of the faithful, but also extending by way of hope into the life of the world. Paul's vision of the new creation has relevance not only for human history, but for the whole cosmos: "The creation waits in eager expectation for the sons of God to be revealed. For the creation was subjected to frustration, not by its own choice, but by the will of the one who subjected it, in hope that the creation itself will be liberated from its bondage to decay and brought into the glorious freedom of the children of God. We know that the whole creation has been groaning as in the pains of childbirth right up to the present time." (Rom. 8:19–22; Methodius, *From the Discourse on the Resurrection* 2).

We get the impression of the cosmos laboring for birth on a multi-phased scale stretching into all the ages, hoping (in a way that only an entire universe might "hope") that God would fulfill the promise of cosmic redemption, and end the frustration caused by the consequences of sin, even though this mysterious struggle in which we are now engaged remains now ambiguous. Even though we may not here and now fully grasp God's will, in God's own time it will be known as reconciling all things (1 Cor. 13; 2 Cor. 5) so as to bring the whole cosmos within range of the redemptive purpose of Christ (Eph. 1). "The creation will perish in order that it may be renewed, not destroyed for-ever, so that we who are spiritually renewed may dwell in a new world, where there will be no sorrow" (Methodius, *On the Resurrection*, 1.9).

The God of Creatures

It is a primordially good world that God creates; only later is it to become distorted by the companionate finite wills that God permits. Doubtless the world has its dark corners and cruel characters. Ever present is the potential for destructiveness, loss, and distortion (Lactantius, *Div. Inst.* 7.4). But if we could see it as a whole as God sees it, we would see the cosmos as unimaginably good in its complex entirety. God pronounced it good at the outset, good in its outcome, and good in its whole (Gen. 1:4, 13; 18; Archelaus, *Disputation with Manes* 21; Ambrose, *Hexaemeron* 2.5).

Any world not created good is not God's world. Any bad world, irretrievably evil, is different from the Jewish-Christian view of God's world (Augustine, *Literal Interp. of Gen.* 9.15.26; Dionysius, *Div. Names* 4.1). Judaism and Christianity have had to fight steadily against alternative views of the world, whether pantheistic or dualistic. An evil can only emerge out of some good. Goodness is God's diminishable but not wholly defeatable work and gift (Irenaeus, *Ag. Her.* 5.16). Even those things that appear evil were created for some good purpose unforeseen by human eyes (Lactantius, *Div. Inst.* 7.4, 5).

Humanity is given dominion and stewardship over the earth. The world, according to the Genesis account, is not given purposelessly, and not given with eyes closed to its potentially harmful contingencies, and not apart from a redemptive plan in mind. The stewardship of creation was entrusted, according to Hebraic religion, to one particular part of the cosmos—humanity. "You shall have dominion" (Gen. 1:26, 28) implies that you take care of it. God entrusts the world to your care and benefit. In the guardianship of this fragile world you are called to respond fittingly to the One who gives and transcends all creaturely values (1 Pet. 4:10; Epistle of Barnabas XIX–XXI; Tertullian, *Ag. Marcion* 2.4–6). Humanity is called to order the world rightly under the permission and command of God, to make appropriate use of God-given rational capacities, strengths, imagination, and courage, and to shape the world in a fitting response to God's unpurchasable gift of life. All this is implied in the notion of stewardly dominion over all that God gives in creation (Luke 16:1–12; Origen, *Ag. Celsus* 4.73–88).

The natural order is purposefully offered as the arena in which myriad acts of human freedom may engage in making human history. Nature is to be greatly respected, nurtured, and cared for, but not worshiped. The natural ordering of the cosmos is necessary for freedom to have reliable causal chains in which freedom can test out its capacity for responsiveness to the Creator (Athanasius, *Ag. Heathen* 19–27; Basil, *Hex.* 9; Calvin, *Inst.* 1.11.1, 2.1–5).

God's Goodness Wills to Communicate Itself

Why did God create something rather than nothing? Something exists because God willed something rather than nothing. It is out of God's will to create, which comes from God's goodness and wisdom, that the world is created.

But why *this* world with personal beings in it, and not another without them? Because God willed to communicate personally with companionate beings (John of Damascus, *OF* 2.12–30; Calvin, *Inst.* 1.15.1–4). God determined to communicate the divine glory and goodness to creatures proportional to their capacity to receive (Tho. Aq., *ST* 1 Q47). "God Who is good and more than good, did not find satisfaction in self-contemplation, but in His exceeding goodness wished certain things to come into existence which would enjoy His benefits and share in His goodness" (John of Damascus, *OF* 2.2; Gregory Nazianzus, *Orat.* 38.9).

God's goodness is so good that it would be less good if God had held his goodness mutely from view and did not communicate it to human beings. God's power is so powerful that it would be less powerful if it did not make itself known in tenderness as love. God's justice is so just that it would be less just if it never risked making a historical realm in which to allow divine justice to be played out, struggled for, recognized, and wherever possible work out. God's joy is so joyful that it would be less joyful if it never had anyone or anything else with which to share its joy. So it could hardly be imaginable, assuming God's incomparable goodness, power, justice, and joy, that God would create nothing (Augustine, *Conf.* 11.1–10).

That which is good wishes voluntarily to communicate itself. It does not wish simply to withhold itself from communication—for an uncommunicated and unknown good is less good than one communicated, known, and beheld. God's love is not to be hidden as if under a bushel basket (Mt 5:4; Incomplete Work on Mt., Hom. 10; Tho. Aq., *ST* 1 Q44, 45). Consequently, that which is unsurpassably good would most certainly will to communicate itself in some way to some world. Especially this is so if the unsurpassably good being is personal, and desires to awaken in finite persons a corresponding awareness of the goodness of creation. This is a greater creation than would exist if there were nothing but rocks, illimitable space, and inert matter that could not significantly respond. The sole motive of creation is God's gracious willingness to share goodness with creatures (Augustine, Sermon on Mount 1.6.17; Salvian, *The Governance of God* 4.9–11; Clement of Alex., *Strom.* 2.21).

No particular world is necessary to God. Creation is the free act of God. There is no external compulsion or necessity upon God—nothing outside God prior to the beginning that says, "God, for some reason apart from yourself, you must create a world." "It is not therefore necessary for God to will that the world should always exist" (Tho. Aq., *ST* 1 Q48). God could have refrained altogether from creating, had it not been that God's goodness irrepressibly takes joy in being shared.

If God is to enjoy a relation with the world, then there obviously must be a world. As becoming known posits another knower, so becoming loved and enjoyed posits an accompanying lover and enjoyer (Paulus Orosius, *Seven Books Ag. the Pagans* 7, *FC* 50: 283; Raymond Lull, *The Book of the Lover*; Catherine of Genoa, *Spiritual Dialogue* I, *CWS*: 109–14; Kierkegaard, *Works of Love*). If there is to be a history of this rocky relationship in a divine-human covenant, then there must be a place, a locus, a world in which it occurs. "For He brought things into being in order that His goodness might be communicated to creatures." (Tho. Aq., *ST* 1 Q47).

The Created Good Liable to Fall

God could have freely created any world, this world or any other world, but this is the one God chose to create—not those supposedly "better" ones our minds proudly imagine we could have invented had we been in charge. God's purpose is in fact being fulfilled precisely through the struggle and destiny of this world of freedom under accountable conditions, not those fantasized others (Gregory of Nyssa, *Great Catech.* 6).

Christian creation teaching takes a middle course between (a) the radical optimism of utopians, who neglect the power of evil, and (b) the radical pessimism of the Marcionites, Gnostics, Manichaeans, and others who consider the world as *maya* or illusion, something to be escaped from as much as possible. Both modern naturalistic optimisms and modern historical pessimisms are resisted by the central Christian tradition, which celebrates a hope based upon the goodness of God in creation, linked always with a realistic awareness of human fallenness. That fallenness is not just attributable to fate, but resides precisely in human willing, corporate and personal (Cyril of Jerusalem, *Catech. Lect.* 4.18–21; R. Niebuhr, *NDM* I).

This fallen world might seem less good than those that we might in imagination abstractly conceive. But we view it with our clouded eyesight. Yet even under these very conditions of risk, it remains a remarkably good world. It unites in an astonishing finite harmony the many widely different levels of creaturely goodness. Thomas Aquinas celebrated the tremendous variety in God's design, the profusion of things in the world: "God makes creatures many and diverse, that what is lacking in one is supplied by another. Goodness in God is simple and consistent. Among creatures it is scattered and uneven. Contrast and oddness come not from chance, not from flaws in the material, not from interference with the divine plan, but from God's purpose. He wills to impart his perfection to creatures as they can stand it" (*ST* 1 Q47). Hence the whole universe participates in the divine goodness more perfectly than any single observer ever could conceive.

God does not make things badly. God is intent upon creating and sustaining a creation that is proportionally as good as sluggish matter can be. God has created a history of human freedom that is proportionally as good as distortable freedom can be, viewed in the long run of universal history, whose future only God can see. Yet all creaturely goods remain derivative and consequent goods. Some creatures, especially human beings with intelligence and self-determination, are ingeniously capable of twisting and knotting the created goodness of the world (Ambrose, *Of the Chr. Faith*, 3.20; Wesley, *Original Sin, The New Birth*).

Repeatedly the Christian tradition has had to fight the notion that the created order is created in a profoundly defective way, or that it is sinful simply by existing (Tertullian, *Ag. Marcion* 1.2–23; Athanasius, *Incarnation of the Word* 43). Sin is not caused by God, but by skewed human freedom. Sin is of our making, not God's. Creation is good. Sin is a fabrication of the freedom of creatures (Athanasius, *Ag. the Heathen* 2). Freedom is created good, even if prone to fall (Cyril of Jerusalem, *Catech. Lect.* 2.1; Augustine, *Nature of the Good*; *Ag. Manichaeans* 36, 37).

Against World-Hating

In the first two centuries AD, Christian teachers had to face Docetists, Gnostics, Manichaeans, and other dismal theorists who detested the Jewish and Christian insistence that creation is good. They thought this was a dreadful world. They could not imagine that God could have been so ill advised as to create this sordid place. They thought finitude was demeaning and matter intrinsically alienating. They concluded that such a bad world could not have been created by a good God. From its beginnings Christianity has had to deal with these world-haters who throw away so much of their free will by despairing over their God-given human condition of finite freedom.

The early Christian worshipers responded to Gnostic competitors in a traditional Hebraic way: even though the times are distorted and fallen, still it is God who made the world and wishes to restore it. Augustine battled against Manichaeans who were saying that matter is so bad that we must remove God from the embarrassment of having created this regrettable world. Augustine had to show that God creates a good world by wisdom and grace, and through the abuse of freedom it becomes distorted (Augustine, *Ag. Manichaeans*).

This Gnostic/Manichaean view has enduring political significance even today. For if the world is evil, it can be treated with contemptuous neglect. Christianity attested the value of this world to God by celebrating God's own determination to become flesh and share in human history. Christianity is the most materialistic of all religions, argued William Temple in *Nature, Man, and God*, because of the incarnation. Humankind is created as a unique interface embracing those two creaturely worlds, "a sort of connecting link between the visible and invisible natures" (John of Damascus, *OF* 1.12).

Summing up: Dualism is rejected; creation is *ex nihilo*; creation is good; the three persons of the Trinity act as one through creation, giving it, redeeming it, and bringing it to consummation.

The Happiness of God in Creating

Creaturely life is given in order that we might "glorify God, and enjoy Him forever" (Westminster Catechism I). The glory (*kabod, doxa*) of God attested by Isaiah (40:4, 5) and Ezekiel (1:29), which was manifested in salvation history and is destined to "fill the earth" (Num. 14:21, 22), was beheld by the shepherds at Christ's birth (Luke 2:9), in his earthly life (John 1:14), at the transfiguration (Mark 9:2–8; John of Damascus, *OF* 2.2) and the resurrection (John 11:24–25).

God is glorified in an extraordinary way by the creation of intelligent beings capable of praising and thereby of reflecting God's own glory in temporal, historical, physical, and moral acts (Ambrose, *On the Decease of Satyrus* 1.45, 46). God's glory is manifested in creation. That does not tarnish God's goodness, but enhances and enlarges it (Cyril of Jerusalem, *Catech. Lect.* 9).

God did not create humanity for human pride or merely to make humans egocentrically happy about themselves. That, for most of the biblical writers, is a form of pride, despair, and hence unhappiness (Arnobius, *Ag. the Heathen* 22–25; Luther, *Sermons on the Catech.*, *MLS:* 224–25). When we pursue happiness only for ourselves, we forfeit a deeper, wiser happiness (Wesley, *WJW* 6:431, 443, 7:267). The end of creation is indeed the glory of God, but this does not diminish the value of human life.

Rather, God offers us a higher happiness, ordered in relation to the proportional variety of goods more available to humans than any other creatures (*Epistle to Diognetus* 8–11). Indeed, the purpose of creation is to make us happy in that sense, to make all creaturely life blessed, and to permit happiness to abound in creation, as seen in relation to the source and ground of happiness (Catherine of Siena, *Prayers* 13; Bonaventure, *Life of St. Francis* 8, *CWS:* 250–61).

The One who in the fullest sense is happy is the eternally happy One: God. All creatures are in some way capable of sharing in that eternal happiness (Tho. Aq., *ST* 1 Q26). Thus the glory of the Creator and the happiness of creatures are inseparable. Human happiness is not an incidental part of the original purpose of God in creation, but central to it (Gregory of Nyssa, *On the Making of Man*).

The possibility of the praise of God by creation is increased greatly when beings are created who are capable of speech, memory, will, and understanding. God is glorified in an extraordinary way by intelligent creatures capable of reflecting God's own glory in an actual historical world (Lactantius, *Div. Inst.* 2.10–16).

If something is to be happy, it must first be alive (Basil, *Hex.* 7–8). God not only produces matter and the space to hold created beings and enable life, but time's duration to sustain and enable them (Pss. 27:1; 36:9; Jer. 17:13).

Time

Repeatedly, Christian teaching has sought carefully to clarify the relation of eternity and time. With the creation of the world came the beginning of time. With the world, time began. Before time existed, nothing was but God (Augustine, *CG* 11.6). "There was no time, therefore, when you had not made anything, because you made time itself" (Augustine, *Conf.* 11.13, 14).

Time and space were coordinately created together. Both are intrinsic to the created order—not uncreated, hence not God. That time is created is opposed to the idea that God inserted the world into a time that was already proceeding, or into a preexistent framework. The world and time are not coeternal with God (Augustine, *CG* 11.1–13). Christians have found it more precise to say that the world was created *with* time (*cum tempore*) than *in* time. That means that in the very act of creating the world, God created time. "Eternity is neither time nor part of time" (Gregory of Nazianzus, *Second Orat. on Easter, Orat.* 45, 4). Time was not proceeding before the creation of the world (Augustine, *Conf.* 11.13). The work of God is done in history, yet God eternally transcends history. Time is finite, measurable, divisible in parts. Eternity is infinite, unmeasurable, not divisible in parts (Augustine, *Conf.* 11.15).

While affirming the distinction between eternity and time, it is still possible to affirm that the universe is from the temporal point of view "everlasting," in the particular sense that before it no time was and at its end there will be no time. Thus creation is rightly said to be as old as time itself, yet eternity encompasses all times. Hence eternity is not chronologically "antecedent" to time, but, rather, time logically presupposes eternity. For there was no time "before" creation—the "before" implies a time, and a "time" before time is evidently self-contradictory (Augustine, *Conf.* 13.48–53).

The eternal is simultaneously present to every moment of time, including past and future time. In the light of the incarnation, the now is rightly viewed as eternity currently manifesting itself as time (Kierkegaard, *Phil. Frag.* I). God had eternity in which many different potential creations could have been conceived. Any world that God creates, however, must have a beginning (Augustine, *Tractates on John*, 1). Everything in time must have a beginning and an end; only God is without beginning and without end.

The Creator endows the world with time, the Redeemer restores time, the Spirit consummates and sanctifies time. God is the one source and end of time. God is not bound to time in the same way that creatures are. "For He is the Maker of time, and is not subject to time" (Gregory of Nazianzus, *Orat. on the Holy Lights* 12). "In Christ he chose us before the world was founded, to be dedicated, to be without blemish in his sight, to be full of love" (Eph. 1:4; Ambrose, *Of the Chr. Faith* 1.9–12).

7

GOD'S CARE FOR
THE WORLD

PROVIDENCE IS GOD'S OWN ACT by which God orders all events in creation, nature, and history, so that the ends for which God created them will be in due time realized. The final end is that all creatures will, in God's own time, manifest God's glory and reflect the divine goodness as they are capable.

John of Damascus defined providence as "the care that God takes over existing things." "Providence is the will of God through which all existing things receive their fitting issue." (*OF* 2.29).

The Meaning of Providence

Providence is the expression of the divine will, power, and goodness through which the Creator preserves creatures, cooperates with what is coming to pass through their actions, and guides creatures in their long-range purposes (Calvin, *Inst.* 1.16; *Heidelberg Catech.*, Q27; Belgic *Conf.* 13). Hence classical Christian exegetes have thought of providence in the three interrelated phases of upholding, cooperating, and guiding:

- The unceasing activity of the Creator by which, in overflowing bounty and good will, (Ps. 143:9; Matt. 5:45) God *upholds* creatures in time and space in an ordered existence (Acts 17:28; Col. 1:17; Heb. 1:3);

- God *cooperates* with natural and secondary causes to employ fit means to good ends through orderly and intelligible processes of natural causes (Prov. 8:29–31; Westminster *Conf.* 5.2); and

- God *guides* and governs all events and circumstances, even free, self-determining agents, overruling the regrettable consequences of freedom and directing everything toward its appropriate end for the glory of God (Eph. 1:9–12).

The Christian teaching of providence holds up before us the caring of God for all creatures and the ordering of the whole course of things for good beyond our brief and sporadic forms of knowing. The principal actor in the drama of providence is the triune God who, in incomparable wisdom, orders events toward those ends most appropriate to the gifts and competencies of each discrete creature. The secondary actors and supporting cast include free human beings who play against the backdrop of nature's vicissitudes and history's developing hazards (Augustine, *CG* 3.).

Providence is like prudence on a cosmic scale. Prudence is the behavior that acts circumspectly, in harmony with sound reasoning, to avoid extremes and seeks appropriate means for intended ends. God's providing may be understood by analogy to motherly or fatherly caring for the young, through foresighted choices of fitting means to reach good ends (Chrysostom, Hom. on Eph. 1.1.10; Tho. Aq., *SCG* 3.16–19; *ST* 1 Q22). Such caring requires not only formulating a plan but also acting patiently to carry out the plan over a long course of time.

The root meaning of the term *providence* is to foresee, or to provide (Greek, *pronoia*, Latin, *pro-videre*, to see ahead, to be able to anticipate). The question of providence concerns how God *thinks ahead* to care for all creatures, fitting them for contingencies, for challenges, and for potential self-actualization to the glory of God. God's providing looks ahead for needs as yet unrecognized by creatures. But more than simply foresight, providence has to do with the active, daily caring of God for the world amid its hazards (Bede, *Comm. on Acts* 17.28).

The Relevance of the Question

The teaching of providence is much closer to the daily life of the believer than at first it might seem. It is interwoven with the power and courage to live the responsible life day by day, to persevere through trying difficulties, and to celebrate divine guidance amid hostile environments (Augustine, *Serm. Mount* 1.23.78–79). It is faith in providence that enables Christians to pray that God will carry them through hazards, care for them, and be present to them amid ordinary and extraordinary human struggles. Without God's providing, the act of praying would be absurd (Augustine, *Of the Work of Monks* 31–37). The Belgic Confession of 1561 declared that: "This doctrine affords us unspeakable consolation, since we are taught thereby that nothing can befall us by chance, but by the direction of our most gracious and heavenly Father, who watches over us with a paternal care, keeping all creatures so under his power that not a hair of our head (for they are all numbered), nor a sparrow, can fall to the ground without the will of our Father, in whom we do entirely trust" (*COC* 3: 397).

Although providence is a well-known teaching, it is often misunderstood. No part of Christian teaching is more pertinent to pastoral care than the classical view of providence, which can be found all through the writings of Irenaeus, Lactantius, Augustine, and Thomas Aquinas, as well as major Protestant thinkers—Luther, Calvin, Edwards, and Wesley. Many practical questions of care of souls amid sickness, personal crisis, poverty, and death hinge on how well one understands this pivotal issue. From a right understanding of providence follows a more realistic assessment of human limitations, sin, and the meaning of suffering in relation to the goodness of God. Pastors are advised not to speak prematurely of Christian teaching on evil without first studying carefully the scriptural teaching on providence.

Three affirmations summarize the Christian teaching of providence: God is preserving the creation in being. God is cooperating to enable creatures to act. God is guiding all creatures, inorganic and organic, animal and rational creation, toward ends that exceed the understanding of those being provided for.

The Divine Economy

God cannot be seen in his essence, but his purpose can be discerned through his works (Tatian, *Address to the Greeks* 4; Theophilus, *To Autolycus* 1.5; Basil, *Letters* 234.1). Classic Christian teachers have searched the Scriptures to grasp the range, means, and ends of God's providential ordering, God's *oikonomia* (economy).

The verb *oikonomeō* means "to administer or oversee" a complex process or community (Athenagoras, *Ag. the Heathen* 43). The treasurer of an organization is one who exercises *oikonomia*, as did Judas among the disciples, and as did God in allowing Judas to do so (Chrysostom, *Hom. on John*, 65.2). To economize means to arrange and dispose according to plan, to supply the necessities of life (*Apost. Const.* 2.25.2). It implies administration through a design or plan. *Oikonomia* implies the proper regulation of a complex process, as when the body economizes the digestion of food, or as when a mother's milk is "economized" in relation to giving birth (Clement of Alex., *Instr.* 1.6). The notion of *oikonomia* entered into trinitarian language when it was said that God had economized together with his Son and Spirit fittingly to accomplish what was prepared from the beginning (*Letter to Diognetus* 9.1).

God is said to manage and "economize" not only the affairs of history but also the processes of nature, the earthly seasons, and the heavenly cycle of changes (Origen, *Ag. Celsus* 1.66–69). God ordered revelation economically by revealing himself in two covenants (Origen, *Ag. Celsus* 5.50). Justin ascribed to the divine economy the varied dispensations of grace (*Dialogue* 17). Paul's conversion was viewed as a part of the divine economy (Chrysostom, *Comm. on Ephesians* 6.12). Many wonderful events of early church history were understood to have occurred "by the economy of God" (Eusebius, *CH* 2.1.13; 5.1.32; 7.11.2). Suffering was also viewed in relation to the divine economy (Gregory Nazianzus, *On His Father's Silence, Orat.* 14.19). The angelic powers were viewed as an expression of the divine economy (Justin, *Dialogue* 85; Origen *Ag. Celsus* 5.45; Chrysostom, *Hom. on 1 Timothy*, 15).

In his summary of classic Christianity, John of Damascus concluded that "if providence is God's will, then, according to right reason, everything that has come about through providence has quite necessarily come about in the best manner and that most befitting God, so that it could not have happened in a better way" (*OF* 2.29). Since God is good, this providing, even when we fail to recognize it, is in some hidden way preparing something for human benefit.

Classic Christian Arguments on Providence

Arguments concerning providence hinged largely upon God's necessary existence, the divine attributes of wisdom, power, and justice, and the radically derived nature of creaturely existence. If God is rightly described in the classical discussion of divine attributes, then such a being could not exist without exercising providential care over a world wisely created.

This is a deductive argument that begins with the divine attributes and asks about their consistent application to the ordering of the world (Augustine, *Divine*

Prov. and the Problem of Evil 2.1–5): It is inconsistent with divine *wisdom* that God might create an immense universe and leave it ungoverned. It is unthinkable to suppose that God would purposefully bring this vast cosmos into being and then not provide for its preservation and maintenance and the fulfillment of its original purpose. It is inconsistent with the divine *omnipotence* to limit God's influence to the beginning of creation and not to its sustenance and development. It would be equally inconsistent with divine *justice* that God would create beings with moral sensitivities and conscience, only to make a travesty of such moral awareness by abandoning human development to fate, chance, or unguided self-determination. It is inconsistent with God's *holiness* that God would allow evil to triumph in history without being finally corrected by active, redemptive divine love. Thus the divine attributes that are necessary and intrinsic to God's nature logically require and imply God's free and gracious preservation and governance of the world (Cyril of Jerusalem, *Catech. Lect.* 5.4).

The *will* of God determines the end for which providential means are fashioned. God's *all-wise knowing* understands, foresees, and grasps the appropriate relation of means to ends in the right ordering of creation. God's incomparable *goodness* wills the good of creatures consonant with each creature's ability to receive and participate in the good. God's incomparable *power* ensures the execution of the intent of the divine will (Chrysostom, *Comm. on Job* 29.2).

The intelligibility and constancy of nature requires some explanation of the ground of this intelligibility and constancy. Each part functions in remarkable order and harmony with all other parts. The extraordinary complexity of nature remains in principle intelligible, even if we inaccurately grasp it. The natural order is unfailingly reliable: The seasons continue in their regularity. Plants and animals continue over aeons to adapt and propagate themselves, even when endangered by catastrophes. This immense system of natural ordering, so reliable in its movement, so varied and beautiful, proceeding from age to age without interruption, elicits in the beholding human mind the awesome and compelling conclusion that everything exists under the continuing governance of an almighty mind (Gregory of Nyssa, *Great Catech.* 10).

Inert, inanimate matter cannot spontaneously organize itself or initiate any motion, for that requires mind. The language of natural law itself suggests and requires the intelligible order and governance implied in providence (Tho. Aq., *Compend.* 130).

The course of universal history itself, when properly and thoroughly studied, yields an inexorable impression that human frailty is being guided and human societies protected from their own follies (Augustine, *CG* 5.10–26). The preservation of the church through enormous hazards and historical crises has often been held to be the supreme evidence of God's providence (Eusebius, *CH* 8).

Views Opposing Providence

The historic Christian understanding of providence must be distinguished from a whole series of imbalanced views with which Christian faith has struggled. The classical understanding of God's providence has in fact gradually become more clearly defined through a history of debate with partial and inadequate views. Eight views in particular have challenged the ancient ecumenical tradition, which has gradually become defined in these ways:

- Providence is not a *pantheism*, which confuses God and the world by absorbing God into the world.

- The providing God is quite different from the God of *deism*, which cuts God off from the world by making God the Creator of the world that God then abruptly leaves, as a watchmaker might leave a watch behind, implying a complete separation between God and the world.

- Providence is not a *dualism*, which views the world as divided into two parts under a good power and a bad power that compete for control, neither of which could be final, and therefore neither of which could be God.

- Providence is distinguished from an *indeterminism*, which holds that the world is not under any intelligible control at all.

- Providence is not a strict or unqualified *determinism*, which posits a control so absolute that it destroys human responsibility, freedom, and accountability, viewing all events only in terms of their natural causal determination.

- Providence is also sharply different from a view of God's *omnicausality* that holds that God so does everything that all other agents do nothing.

- Providence distinguishes itself from a doctrine of *chance*, which denies that the controlling power can be intelligible or personal or rational.

- Finally, providence differs from a doctrine of *fate*, which denies the benevolence or sovereign freedom of the supreme being.

Divine Preservation and Cooperation with Natural Causality

Classical Christian teachers have simplified the enormous complexity of acts of providence into a clear-cut threefold pattern of upholding, allowing, and guiding actions (or preservation, concurrence, and governance). These three kinds of providence encompass the vast range of the care that God extends over all creatures and their development.

- By God's sustaining or conserving providential activity (*conservatio*), God preserves all things in being.

- By God's cooperative providential activity (*cooperatio*), God concurs and cooperates with secondary causes in the created order, and with human free, self-determined wills, to permit and enable the events of creaturely life.

- By God's governing providential activity (*gubernatio*), God guides all things through fitting means toward ends appropriate to God's larger purpose in creation (Augustine, *CG* 12.13–15; John of Damascus, *OF* 2.44; Heppe, *RD*: 251).

What God creates, God preserves, permits, and guides.

God Preserves What God Creates

Preservation refers first to the effective action of God by which all creatures are kept in being. Preservation is the providential means by which God maintains, upholds in being, and perpetuates what has been created (Ps. 138:7; Tho. Aq., *SCG* 3.65.9). God "sustains the universe by his word of power" (Heb. 1:3).

Divine preservation encompasses both nature and history: "O Lord, you preserve both man and beast" (Ps. 36:6). The biblical focus is more often upon the fervent, personal awareness that one's own life is being daily preserved: "For your name's sake, O Lord, preserve my life" (Ps. 143:11).

If God should withdraw this preserving activity from creaturely being, there would simply be nothing there. For no creature can sustain itself in being without this divine preserving activity. "When you hide your face, they are terrified; when you take away their breath, they die and return to the dust. When you send your Spirit they are created" (Ps. 104:29, 30). In this One "we live and move and have our being" (Acts 17:28). "He exists before everything, and all things are *held together* in him" (Col. 1:17, italics added). It is as though the wisdom of God is the continuing cosmic mucilage of creation, holding the creation together (Chemnitz, *LT* 1: 125; Wesley, *Letters, To Thomas Church* 2).

Just as "the preservation of light in the air is by the continual influence of the sun" (Tho. Aq., *ST* 1 Q104), so are all things continually dependent upon God for their perpetuation. The divine preservation of the cosmos is a free act of God. As God was free to create or not to create all things, so is God free to continue or not continue all things in being. Yet God continues by grace to uphold all things by the word of his power (Heb. 1:3; Chrysostom, *Hom. on Hebrews* 2). Believers are instructed in the ways by which God sustains every living creature (Ambrose, *Expos. of Chr. Faith* 1.2–5). God maintains each creaturely being in its own unique way, with its own distinctive capacities for actualizing creaturely goods, in ways that reflect the divine wisdom even in insensate being (Calvin, *Inst.* 15.14; 1.16). God is said to be the first or primal cause preconditioning all subsequent secondary causes. In this created order myriads of secondary causes are every moment occurring, all sustained by his word of power (Heb. 1:3).

Hence in summary: the Creator is the Preserver (John of Damascus, *OF* 2.29; Tho. Aq., *ST* Q103; Gerhard, *LT* 4:83). "What is preserved depends on the preserver in such a way that it cannot exist without it. In this way the being of every creature depends on God, so that not for a moment could one subsist, but would fall into nothingness, were it not kept in being by the operation of the Divine power" (Tho. Aq., *ST* 1 Q104; Augustine, *Literal Interp. of Gen.* 4.12; Gregory, *Moralia* 16).

Based on the biblical promise that "whatever God does lasts forever" (Eccles. 3:11), Thomas argued that finally nothing God has created will be annihilated, although its form of composition may change: "If God were to annihilate anything, this would not imply an *action* on God's part," he mused, "but a mere *cessation* of His action" (Tho. Aq., *ST* 1 Q104, italics added; Hollaz, *ETA*: 421 , 442).

The Cooperation of God with Secondary Causes

Providential concurrence, or divine cooperation with secondary causes, is the second basic mode of God's caring activity discerned by classical exegetes. In both ancient and modern times, this part of Christian teaching has been crucial to the nurture of a healthy relation between Christian faith and the natural sciences.

God's concurring activity refers to that cooperation of divine power with subordinate powers and secondary causes that sustain, empower, and enable those myriads of natural causes simultaneously flowing through all times. Nature is an immense complex of multilayered causality.

Christian teaching has pursued various means of relating God's providence to natural law and causality. How is God cooperatively present and empowering in those causes? Classical exegetes taught the ever-recurring cooperation of divine power with all subordinate powers and secondary causes, according to the reliable laws of their operation, whether those laws pertain to the natural, rational, or moral sphere (Lactantius, *Div. Inst.* 3.25–30; Tho. Aq., *ST* 1 Q90; Quenstedt, *TDP* 1:431).

These laws and powers do not work miscellaneously or autonomously, as if accountable to themselves. Natural and moral law are viewed by classical exegetes as being entirely dependent upon the constant cooperation of God. This simply means that God concurs (*concursus*, runs alongside) with secondary causality (Tho. Aq. *ST* 1 Q22; *SCG* 3.94). "God's providence does not remove but posits second causes" (Wollebius, *CTC* 30, in Heppe, *RD*: 258).

The scriptural testimony upon which classical teachers based these conclusions held divine and natural causality together without denying either: "In truth all *our* works are *thy* doing, O Lord our God" (Isa. 26:12, ital. added). "You must work out your own salvation in fear and trembling; for it is God who works in you, inspiring both the will and the deed, for his own chosen purpose" (Phil. 2:13; Origen, *OFP* 3.1). God's concurrence does not do away with the efficacy of natural causes—on the contrary, it empowers and enables secondary causes.

Concurrence and Freedom

One principle is evident throughout: God accommodates the divine majesty and power to the limited capacities of creatures. God allows creaturely goods to be received and achieved through creatures in a way that, taken as a whole, magnifies and manifests the divine glory (Pss. 8:1–5; 72:19; 139:5; Calovius, *SLT* 3:1194).

Divine providence does not exclude free human agency but enables and sustains it. There are indeed limits on human freedom, but God's providence, in fact, grants and permits freedom. God by grace sustains the human nature that falls into sin. God permits sin in an otherwise good and intelligible order in order to honor human freedom, yet limits and finally overrules whatever distortions human freedom can create that might distort the outcomes of human history (Augustine, *CG* 5.9–11).

This concurrence is occurring everywhere in anything that is occurring. If something moves, it moves by divine concurrence. Anywhere any secondary cause is at work, God is at work, not absolutely or unilaterally determining that secondary cause, but cooperating so that it can work. It works, not as if autonomously on its own, but through the laws appropriate to its level of participation in being (Tho. Aq., *SCG* 46; Hollaz, *ETA*: 440).

This implies respect for human freedom and responsibility, for God does not simply *operate* our wills or directly will for us instead of allowing us to will. That would hardly be consistent with the stress in Scripture on God-given responsible freedom. If God were omnicausally and absolutely determining every event at this moment without any secondary causes, freedom would not be real, and therefore any assumption that persons are responsible for themselves would not be true. The Bible affirms in God we "live and move and have our being" (Acts 27:28). That does not mean that human choice is displaced or annihilated by the choice of God. These are misconstructions of providence found in both pantheistic and fatalistic distortions of Christian teaching (Hippolytus, *Refutation* 6; Pope, *Compend.* 1; Bavinck, *DG*, I).

Hence it is said that God's cooperative action does not unilaterally operate our wills, but cooperates with our wills so as to be present in and with our every activity. God funds and resources our free wills. These effects are not produced by God apart from natural means, or by an individually abstracted human will as if a single willing agent could be separated from its social, natural, historical context. God is the primordial causal agent that cooperates with multiple second-ary causes. Within and through the whole complex, evolving matrix of natural causality there emerges actual human free will, created good but permitted to go awry, able to stand, liable to fall (Clement of Alex., *Strom.* 2.14, 15; Wesley, *The New Birth*).

God has permitted that freedom which is capable of falling. A fine distinction must be noted here: God cooperates so as to allow the *effects* of our freedom but to not applaud its *defects*. God allows freedom to be penultimately *effective*, even permitting freedom to distort an otherwise good creation, but that does not mean that God affirms or enjoys or permanently abides the *defective* side of freedom (Augustine, *Ag. Two Letters of the Pelagians* I; Calvin, *Inst.* 3.22–24; Heppe, *RD* 9:220; Schmid, *DT* 2).

At this point Christian teachers have worked cautiously to preserve the teach-ing of the holiness of God from the charge that God directly causes evil. The *freewill defense* has become a time-tested response to the charge that God is the author of sin. Accordingly, it is not God that causes sin, but rather it is human freedom, which is a good but distortable creation of God, that elicits sin. We do the sinning ourselves; God does not do it. It is not sin with which God cooper-ates, but human freedom. God cooperates by empowering free will to act and by providing the secondary arena of natural causality in which our freedom is able to stand, though liable to fall (John of Damascus, *OF* 2.24, 25). Hence the memorable formula: *God concurs with the effect but not with the defect of our ac-tions* (Tho. Aq., *SCG* 3.77).

This useful formulation helps protect Christian teaching against the notion of absolute divine omnicausal determination, such as that found in some forms of religious piety, which asserts a consistent determination of all things by God and nothing else. Such an argument has not, on the whole, been a characteris-tic of Christian doctrines of providence, even in traditions that have strongly stressed predestination. Christian doctrines of providence have sought earnestly to preserve the dimension of the free, responsible will that falls and becomes radically self-alienated through sin (Augustine, *Spirit and Letter*, 52–58; Wesley, *WJW* 6:311).

Two opposite views lack sufficient grounding in scripture: first, that God ab-solutely determines human effects without any cooperation of human freedom, and second, that human freedom occurs without divine cooperation. The concise scriptural affirmation balances these points: "Apart from me you can do nothing" (John 15:5); that is, without the cooperative grounding of our freedom in divine providence, we could not even have in the first place the freedom that is prone to go awry (Maximus the Confessor, Four Hundred Chapters on Love 2.38–39).

One cannot even sin without providence. Sin can come into being only in an order in which its preconditions are permitted by God. God cooperates by allow-ing moral freedom and natural causality to function. Out of this matrix freedom becomes fallen and self-alienated. That God permits us freedom to fall does not imply that God directly causes the fall, or that God delights to see freedom fall-ing, or that God creates freedom already as fallen. God permits freedom to work its own blessedness or self-condemnation (Clement of Alex., *Strom.* 2.14, 15; John of Damascus, *OF* 2.25–29; 3.13).

God freely chooses to order life in such a way that human freedom may be a companion to God's freedom without denying God's almighty power or goodness. There is no need to derogate secondary causes, for it is through these natural causes that God intends to convey to humanity the full blessings of providence (Calvin, *Inst.* 1.17, 18; *Heidelberg Catech.* 104; K. Barth, *CD* 3/3; Tho. Aq., *ST* 1

Q105; J. Cocceius, *Summa Theologiae* 28.25). "Every power in any agent is from God." (Tho. Aq., *SCG* 3.67). Hence "God works in every worker" (*ST* 1 Q105).

There is clear evidence for providence in the observable fact that natural bodies are moved toward ends, even though they do not understand their end. "It is impossible for things that do not know their end to work for that end, and to reach that end in an orderly way, unless they are moved by someone possessing knowledge of the end," so wherever there is purposeful movement toward an end, the cause must lead back to God either immediately or by some form of mediation (Tho. Aq., *SCG* 3.64).

Even more remarkable is the fact that things of contrary natures merge harmoniously together in a single order. If one hears in the distance a lyre of diverse sounds playing in concord, one would easily perceive "that this lyre was not playing itself" (Athanasius, *Ag. Heathen* 38). In naturalistic reductionism there is no adequate explanation for the intricate symphony of nature. In classic Christianity, God is the "cause of the whole" (Tho. Aq., *SCG* 3). Thus Scripture ascribes to God the concurrent governance of all things (Ps. 46:8–11).

Divine Governance of the World

When Abraham's faith was tested with Isaac, "Abraham named that place Jehovah-jireh; and to this day the saying is: 'In the mountain of the Lord it was provided'" (Gen. 22:14). The name Jehovah-jireh, which means "the Lord will see and provide," embraces the central insight of God's governing providence. The end promised to Abraham was clear. Yet he was required to trust that providence would find a means. Although God's ways are past our finding out (Rom. 11:33), the trusting community nonetheless beholds clues in nature, traces in history, and luminous disclosures in Scripture of the ways God uses evil for good and turns human wrath into his praising (Ps. 70:10).

God the Spirit is at work to guide all creaturely processes providentially toward larger purposes than those known by empirical and rational means. As in discerning the pattern of a mosaic from a piece of it, even if we see only one small corner of history, we may grasp enough to trust that if we were able to see the whole of history, we would understand and enjoy the beauty of God's glory manifesting itself in all of history as in Christ (Origen, *Ag. Celsus* 2.51; Hom. on Gen. 8.10).

Saturating this whole historical process is God's own guiding, directing activity. Each of billions of events has its own tendency at any given moment. Seen in the light of the scriptural revelation of God's providential activity, all of this is moving toward a plausible, trustable end: the fulfillment of God's purpose in creation (Ambrose, *Hexaemeron* 5.19; Tho. Aq., *ST* 1 Q103).

God is constantly resisting, constraining, limiting, and working to prevent the consequences of sin from inordinately undermining God's larger purposes. God would never allow sin finally to frustrate or overcome God's good purpose in creation. Eventually it is faith's hope that, both within and beyond history, God will overrule whatever distortions, injustices, and alienations human freedom is able to create (Athenagoras, *Plea*).

This is why the community of faith has always found comfort in the teaching of God's providence. God is working in complex ways to allow the glorious and wretched story of abused freedom to play itself out so that the divine goodness may be manifested through and beyond our free activity and the struggles of other creatures. God's providential governance is especially pertinent to the guidance of fallible human intelligence and moral freedom and political imagination.

God's supervision functions without coercing or eliminating the priceless dimension of human self-determination (John of Damascus, *OF* 2.29).

Providence is the term we use to speak of that entire history stretching between creation and consummation that has its central focus in the teaching of redemption. Redemption is the provision God makes to deal with a foreseen, permitted, restrained, condemned, and vanquished evil (Calvin, *Inst.* 3.14; Pope, *Compend.* 1: 453). Sin has a long career. The divine governance of currently ambiguous moral history must be seen finally in the light of God's grace. In this way, the teaching of providence is the central bridge between creation and redemption (Jerome, *Epis. to Eph.* 1.7–10).

The Scope of Divine Governance

No creature is so great as to be beyond the need of God's care (Ps. 103). No creature is so small as to be overlooked by God's care: ravens (Ps. 147:9), sparrows (Matt. 10:29), lilies and grass (Matt. 6:28, 30), and the hairs of our heads (Matt. 10:30). God's providential sustenance embraces the physical world (Job 37:5), animal creation (Ps. 104:21), the affairs of nations (Isa. 40), and justice in societies (Job 12; Amos 5). God is responsive to prayer (Matt. 7:7). Nothing is beyond God's providence, even the superpersonal intelligences or angels that have elicited so much speculation. Our lives are begun, continued, and ended through divine providence (Ps. 145:15). Everything is encompassed by this sustaining, preserving, cooperating, guiding power of God.

The scope of providence may be envisioned as the center of four widening concentric circles, encompassing all four classes of creaturely beings and sustaining each of them in correlated yet distinguishable ways. In an ascending scale they are:

- lifeless matter (inanimate creaturely being)
- living plants (living, but immobile, vegetable beings)
- animals (living mobile beings lacking human rationality)
- humans (living, rational, accountable, self-determining moral agents)

Each sphere presupposes the sustenance of the previous spheres. In this way divine governance becomes an important meeting point for the encounter of Christian truth with the spheres of scientific and humanistic study in the university: physics, botany, zoology, and anthropology. God's governing activity is adapted to the four spheres in which it operates—physical, biological, animal, and moral (J. Cocceius, *Summa Theologiae* 28; Newman, *Idea of a University*; Rashdall, UEMA 1–2).

Plants and children are in some ways alike, but in many more ways different. One would not take care of the family cat in the same way that one would take care of the family piano, because animal creation requires a very different kind of care than does a physical object. God's governing and guiding activity operates simultaneously on all four of these levels, adapted at each level to the particular capacities of that level (*ST* 1 Q69–72).

God provides and sustains each sphere of creaturely being in accordance with its own particular conditions, needs, requirements, and nature. To imagine that God would employ the same mode of care in reference to creaturely beings so different as a rock, a tree, a bird, and a grandparent would be to mistakenly estimate God's understanding of the variety of needs, natures, and requirements of each of these creaturely spheres. Amid all the differences in these four spheres,

God works through ordinary channels of natural law, secondary causes, adaptive instincts, and various levels of creaturely freedom to enable creatures to reflect the divine glory by actualizing creaturely goods (Calvin, *Inst.* 1.14–17; 3:20).

God's Distinctive Provisions for Material Creation

Since physical matter is lifeless and can be moved only as it is moved by something else, it is reasonable to expect that physical creation will be governed by physical causality, not by ideas or persuasion. Rocks are moved by spades, not thoughts. You cannot give a stone a moral command and expect it to be obeyed, because a stone does not have rational or moral awareness. These are competencies presupposed in the moral order of responsible freedom. Lifeless matter is governed by physical laws (Jerome, On *Jeremiah the Prophet* 4.2.4–7).

It is a useful gift of the Provider that these physical forces, the study of which is called physics, are reliable, intelligible, and do not vary. We are made more thankful for this by imagining the uncertainty of a universe in which the natural order might be conceived as unreliable, or reliable only on certain Tuesdays. Only an invariable order is appropriate to inanimate material reality, which, without spirit, life, or mind, can only move when moved. It is by such laws of motion and causation that the physical world works, the stars turn in their orbits, the seasons change in their orderly way, and time moves relentlessly on (Ps. 33:6; Jer. 31:35; 33:22; Second Clement, *Recognitions* 8.40–50).

Classical Christian exegesis has interpreted the laws of nature, causation, motion, and physical order as God's own method of working in the governance of matter (Prov. 8:22–31; Tertullian, *Ag. Hermogenes* 20–32). They are not independent of God. To assert that lifeless matter is governed by natural law, but without any influence of any ordering mind or source of intelligibility, is tantamount to asserting that there is no law or governance at all in nature, that nature is adrift as a spontaneous interaction of material substances without design or intelligible order. The appearance of order in any form must posit some ordering agent as sufficient cause (Ps. 65:9–13). It is in this spirit that the psalmist poetically attributed to God the ordering of all physical causes: "He brings up the mist from the ends of the earth, he opens rifts for the rain, and brings the wind out of his storehouses" (Ps. 135:6, 7; Theophilus, *To Autolycus* 1.5, 6).

God's Distinctive Provisions for Plant Creation

Plant life is also under the divine governance, but in a different way than lifeless matter which only moves when moved. Material laws remain operative in plant life, but something is added: the laws of vegetation, reproduction, the capacity to take in sun and water and minerals and transform them into a living organism. The difference between lifeless matter and vegetative matter is enormous: it is called life, which Scripture views as breathed into matter by God (Tertullian, *Treatise on the Soul* 2; John of Damascus, *OF* 2.12). God governs organic life in a very different way than inorganic nonlife.

In terms of sheer mass, most of the universe is taken up with lifeless matter. Life is a precious rare event on the outer crust of the earth, and infinitely rare when viewed in relation to the whole known cosmic order. The conditions for supporting life anywhere in the universe are extremely rare. We know of only one planet in the universe where plant life exists (Wesley, *WJW* 2:515). This underscores the fact that when plant life occurs, it is extraordinarily precious and not to be discounted or treated as superabundant or worthless.

Plants are highly capable of adaptation to changing atmospheric, natural, and interspecies circumstances. This whole drive of life to sustain itself intergenerationally has remarkable evocative power for the ancient religious imagination, awakening praise of God's providential care for plant life (Deut. 32:1, 2; Tho Aq., *ST* 1–2 Q17.8). All this occurs by providential permission through natural adaptations within the created order. When faith beholds God's caring work in the varied spheres of mineral, vegetative, and animal life, its joy echoes in the psalm: "He veils the sky in clouds and prepares rain for the earth; he clothes the hills with grass and green plants for the use of man. He gives the cattle their food and the young ravens all that they gather" (Ps. 147:8, 9).

God's governance extends throughout the continuous generativity and adaptivity of vegetable creation (Gen. 1:11, 12). Each sphere is dependent upon the ground it is standing on. Plants root in the ground. Animals move on earth. Humans are dependent upon both. This dependence is suggested by the sequence reported in Genesis 1 of the days of creation (Basil, *Hex.* 5; Ephrem, *Comm. on Genesis* 1.22.1–2).

Note that the evolving process has higher purposes than the plant itself can conceive. The purpose of plant life is to sustain animal life, and ultimately human life and historical development, through which the divine-human covenant can be played out. God's plan does not come about without plants. Unlike rock and sand, plants respond to caring (Ps. 1:3). They wither when uncared for. God provides for plant life with more diverse competencies to enable more complex functions than mineral life (Jer. 2:22; Chrysostom, *Gospel of Matt.* 22.1–3).

Faith in providence is seen in the practice of offering thanks for food: "The eyes of all are lifted to thee in hope, and thou givest them their food when it is due; with open and bountiful hand thou givest what they desire to every living creature" (Ps. 145:15, 16; Ps. 136:25).

God's Distinctive Provisions for Animal Creation

Scripture attests to the extent of God's care over the whole of animal creation: "With open and bountiful hand thou givest what they desire to every living creature" (Ps. 145:16). As the laws of physics are not sufficient for botany, so are the laws of botany not sufficient for zoology. Animals differ from plants in that they are capable of self-movement, but also in that they have a capacity for a fuller range of sensation. Animals can agonize in misery and experience pleasure and satisfaction far more complexly and consciously than can plants. God cares for animals by providing them with sensory capacities and instincts that enable them to adapt in astonishingly varied ways to changing atmospheric conditions, physical and vegetative environments that enable self-preservation and preservation of the species (Gen. 1:20–25; Basil, *Hex.* 8). God takes joy in animal creation, even with the greatest of species, the leviathan, of whom it is said: "thou hast made thy plaything" (Ps. 104:26).

In all animal creatures, preservation of the species is a more critical priority than preservation of the individual animal. Without reproduction, a species would last only one generation, hence animal sexuality is viewed as an important part of providential ordering of animal species (Tho. Aq., *ST* 1 Q72). They are to "Be fruitful and multiply" (Gen. 1:22). Each individual animal is given powerful instincts for survival (Isa. 18:5, 6; Ezek. 19:2, 3).

The complex design and ordering of animal life is such that rational creatures have much to learn from it. "Go to the ant, you sluggard, watch her ways and get wisdom. She has no overseer, no governor or ruler; but in summer she prepares her store of food and lays in her supplies at harvest." (Prov. 6:6–8; Jerome, *Life of Malchus* 7) Jesus took from animal life the most influential of all metaphors for the Christian teaching of providence: "Look at the birds of the air; they do not sow and reap and store in barns, yet your heavenly Father feeds them" (Matt. 6:26).

The Extent of God's Provision for Human Creation

Scripture celebrates God's care over all human creation. Human life is ultimately dependent upon God who breathes life into humanity. Human creation is also dependent upon the health and conservation of plant and animal creation, which themselves are dependent upon the earth, the soil, and upon inanimate, lifeless, physical matter (Gen. 1:29–30; Ps. 104:1–35; Gregory of Nyssa, *On the Origin of Man, ACCS OT* 1:42). Yet while being dependent on mineral, vegetable, and animal orders, human creation is clearly superior to them in language, memory, imagination, and in musical, mathematical, and construction skills. The Lord endowed human beings "with strength like his own." "Discretion and tongue and eyes, ears and a mind for thinking he gave them. He filled them with knowledge and understanding, and showed them good and evil" (Sirach 17:3, 6, 7).

God's care embraces all human history and the course of all national and cultural destinies. "God reigns over the nations" (Ps. 47:7). "His sovereignty is never-ending and his rule endures through all generations" (Dan. 4:34). Under the conditions of recalcitrant sin, divine care may take the form of judgment: "He takes away their wisdom from the rulers of the nations and leaves them wandering in a pathless wilderness" (Job 12:24). But its intent is healing and corrective: "The Lord disciplines those whom he loves" (Heb. 12:6).

God's care embraces not only collectivities, but each individual personally. "In God's hand are the souls of all that live, the spirits of all humankind" (Job 12:10). God's cares for good and bad alike. The heavenly Father "makes his sun rise on good and bad alike, and sends the rain on the honest and the dishonest" (Matt. 5:45). God's care extends to every aspect of human life, "even the hairs of your head" (Matt. 10:30). It is a comfort to believers to remember God's care. "For you, O Lord, will bless the righteous; you will hedge him round with favor as with a shield" (Ps. 5:12). Divine care never ends or diminishes: "The guardian of Israel never slumbers, never sleeps" (Ps. 121:4).

From birth to death God's care extends. "My times are in your hand" (Ps. 31:15). "You know me through and through: my body is no mystery to you, how I was secretly kneaded into shape and patterned in the depths of the earth. You saw my limbs unformed in the womb, and in your book they are all recorded; day by day they were fashioned, not one of them was late in growing" (Ps. 139:14–16; Job 10:8). God foreknows all human events yet without intrusion on the integrity of human freedom (Job 14:5). Human free will has room to play in history, but it cannot overrule God's purposes: "A man's heart may be full of schemes, but the Lord's purpose will prevail" (Prov 19:22).

Sin and Evil Viewed in the Light of Providence

Divine Permission of Choices Leading to Evil Outcomes

Classical thought on providence has often argued that God's permission of evil is not inconsistent with divine goodness. Thomas Aquinas tightly summarized the reasons why providence does not altogether exclude evil:

- An unfree world where all evil is excluded would not be as good as the actual world in which freedom is permitted to fall into evil, called to struggle against evil, and offered redemption from evil. "If evil were completely excluded from things, much good would be rendered impossible. Consequently it is the concern of divine providence, not to safeguard all beings from evil, but to see to it that the evil which arises is ordained to some good" (Tho. Aq., *Compend.* 142).

• There can be no evil unless it depends upon something good (Augustine, *Enchiridion* 11). "Accordingly, although God is the universal cause of all things, He is not the cause of evil as evil. But whatever good is bound up with the evil, has God as its cause" (Tho. Aq., *Compend.* 141: 151). The freewill defense holds that evil comes from distorted freedom, not from God, whereas the will that wills good is quietly shaped already by God's goodness.

• Evil is not an effect caused by God, but a *defect* of secondary causes that are permitted by God. "Without prejudice to divine providence, evil can arise in the world because of defects in secondary causes" (Tho. Aq., *Compend.* 141). It is possible to have a defect in the secondary agent (human will) "without there being a defect in the primary agent" (divine will) (Tho. Aq., *SCG* 3.71).

• Many creaturely goods are enabled in this world that could not occur unless there were evils against which to struggle. Patience, for example, could not be nurtured in a perfect world. Thomas's example: There could not be new generation of a species unless there were also death in that species (*SCG* 3.71).

• The perfection of the universe requires some beings that are subject to defects. "If evil were completely eliminated from things, they would not be governed by divine providence in accord with their nature; and this would be a greater defect than the particular defects eradicated" (Tho. Aq., *Compend.* 142). "For example, if the inclination to generate its like were taken away from fire (from which inclination there results this particular evil which is the burning up of combustible things), there would also be taken away this particular good which is the generation of fire" (Tho. Aq., *SCG* 3.71). That fire is potentially destructive does not mean that it is of itself evil. A world without fire is doubtless a less good world than a world with the risks that fire brings.

• If all evils were removed, the good could not be known, because "the good is better known from its comparison with evil," just as "good health is best known by the sick."

• Finally, "if complete equality were present in things, there would be but one created good, which clearly disparages the perfection of the creature." It is a better ordered world when some things are better than others than if there were no grades of goodness whatever. "It does not pertain to divine goodness, entirely to exclude from things the power of falling from the good" (*SCG* 3.71). But that does not imply evil in the Originator of distortable freedom.

For all these reasons, providence does not exclude evil. Hence to the question, "If God exists, whence comes evil?" Thomas surprisingly replied: "If evil exists, God exists. For, there would be no evil if the order of good were taken away, since its privation is evil. But this order would not exist if there were no God" (*SCG* 3.71).

Why Evil?

Much of the energy of patristic reflections upon providence focused on how to correlate the claims of providence with the harsh presence of evil and suffering in this world that God has ordered. How can evil and suffering be compatible with the caring providence of an incomparably powerful and good God? Several kinds of solutions were presented:

- Sin is due to the abuse, not the use, of free will. The *abuse* of free will occurs when we put our egocentric interests above the common interest. The original goodness of freedom of the will becomes distorted when humans choose contrary to God's will as revealed in moral reasoning, law, conscience, and the gospel (Augustine, *Spirit and Letter, NPNF* 1 2:106–9).

- Although the abuse of free will was foreseen by God, it could have been prevented by God only at the price of depriving human existence of its most noble attribute, namely, free will (Tertullian, *Ag. Marcion* 2.5–7; Cyril of Alex., *Contra Julian* 9.13; Theodoret, *De prov., Orat.* 9.6).

- We learn by experience, by moving through stages of growth, and by struggling toward good through evil. It is often only when we are forced to face adversity that we learn and grow strong by meeting challenges and overcoming obstacles. So faith learns gradually to affirm that what at one point appears to be unmitigated evil or suffering may at a different point appear to serve our well-being or improvement, increasing patience and compassion (Lactantius, *On Anger of God* 13; Augustine, *Divine Prov. and the Problem of Evil* 1.6).

- The abuse of freedom points toward repentance. Penitent faith reclaims freedom of the will by grace. In this way even the abuse of freedom is a stage that may lead closer toward redemption. God permits freedom to fall in order that we may arrive at a deeper consciousness of our own finitude and our own inability to attain righteousness on our own. Hence temptation, sin, and suffering are paradoxically linked closely with providence. By our failures to follow the law we are trained to rely not upon our own righteousness, but grace (*Letter to Diognetus, ANF* 1:27, 28; Gregory I, *Morals on Job* 3.42).

- God would not permit evil at all unless He could draw good out of it (Augustine, *Enchiridion* 10–17).

In the last judgment the dilemma of evil will be resolved. On the road that leads to the last judgment the workings of providence doubtless will remain opaque to finite reasoning, hence bringing us closer to the divine mystery. Our finite minds are simply unable to conceive the wisdom of this infinite process in which we live and move. Faith in divine providence calls the believer to walk without seeing, based on what is known from God's disclosure in Christ (Chrysostom, *Concerning the Statues* 9.9; *Letters to Olympias*).

Providential Permission, Hindrance, Overruling, and Limiting

The providence of God guides human freedom in four phases: by permitting, restraining, overruling and limiting our choices.

The governance of God functions situationally in ways that bear striking resemblance to the ways good human parenting functions: by *permitting* freedom to discover its competencies and interests; by *hindering* freedom from getting itself into too much trouble; by *overruling* free self-actualization when it seriously mistakes its own best good, harms others inordinately, or seems to jeopardize the divine purpose; and by *limiting* other forces in freedom's way to prevent them from triumphing cheaply or tempting inordinately.

First, God guides us by *permitting* our freedom to play itself out in consequences, even if we become a cause of our own suffering and others' suffering. Freedom could have no meaning if it did not risk going astray. To posit a freedom that cannot possibly fail is to run away from the human freedom God gives. God graciously allows human freedom the room both to stand and to fall. Divine permission does not imply *carte blanche* to sin, but rather that God, in order to allow the larger good of enabling freedom, does not always exercise his absolute power to destroy sin.

Scripture frequently attests to the willingness of God to allow freedom even when it becomes alienated and counterproductive: "My people did not listen to my words and Israel would have none of me; so I sent them off, stubborn as they were, to follow their own devices" (Ps. 81:12; Prov. 1:31; Jer. 18:12; Origen, *OFP* 3.1). When freedom is abused, its consequences must be lived with. When Israel is stubborn can the Lord not "feed them like lambs in a broad pasture?" (Hos. 4:16).

Moral wisdom is not enhanced by rewarding irresponsibility. Paul and Barnabas at Lystra stated that divine providence has permitted "all nations to go their own way; and yet he has not left you without some clue to his nature, in the kindness he shows" (Acts 14:16, 17).

Second, God guides by *hindering*, and at times directly resisting, our ill-motivated actions. God guides not by coercing freedom directly but by putting obstacles in the way of our hurting ourselves, like the parent who builds a fence so the child will not go into the street. The child still may find a way to get into the street, but not without confronting the serious effort of the parent at placing an obstacle in harm's way. "It was I," the Lord revealed to Abraham, "who held you back from committing a sin against me" (Gen. 20:6). Satan's complaint to God in the prologue of Job asked: "Have you not hedged him round on every side with your protection?" (Job 1:10; 3:23). Israel lamented in captivity that God's ways had hedged escape so that there was no other way out than sincere repentance (Lam. 3:7). The psalmist prayed for constraint on his own freedom to harm himself: "Hold back thy servant also from sins of self-will, lest they get the better of me" (Ps. 19:13; Augustine, *Expos on Psalms, Ps.* 71).

Third, God guides us by *overruling* us when we wander completely out of line. By such active direction, egocentric sinners are saved from harm and guided toward ends beyond their competence to know (Ezek. 20:33; Mic. 4:7). "Blessed is the man whom God corrects" (Job 5:17; Clement of Rome, *Corinth*, 16). "He who refuses correction is his own worst enemy, but he who listens to reproof learns sense. The fear of the Lord is a training in wisdom" (Prov. 15:32, Prov. 15:33). Jeremiah in frustration declared: "This is the nation that did not obey the Lord its God, nor accept correction" (Jer. 7:28).

Whatever evil results from freedom abused, God can override. The sons of Jacob sold their brother Joseph into slavery. Then, as governor of Egypt, he became the means of the redemption of the whole family. Joseph mirrored God's own providence when he said to his pleading brothers: "You meant to do me harm; but God meant to bring good out of it by preserving the lives of many people, as we see today. Do not be afraid. I will provide for you and your dependents" (Gen. 50:20).

Scripture attests that God is forever working through hidden routes. Thinking about providence gradually increases faith's awareness of those circuits through which even our distortions of God's good creation become a means to receive grace. Wheel turns within wheel (Ezek. 1:16), and God turns our misdeeds into potentially redeemed relationships (Calvin, *Inst.* 3.2.26; Wesley, *WJW* 7:409).

Finally, God guides wisely by going ahead of our present freedom to prepare a new way. This is God's *prevening* work which hedges our way toward new options, opening some doors, closing others. Grace prevents freedom's way from leading to disaster, or from tempting inordinately. The care of God attested by Scripture places fitting limits upon challenges to our faith and boundaries upon what the opponents of our good can do to us. This view of providence is epitomized by Paul's consolation for the faithful enduring severe trials and afflictions: "God keeps faith, and he will not allow you to be tested above your powers, but when the test comes he will at the same time provide a way out, by enabling you to sustain it" (1 Cor. 10:13; Job 1:12; 2:6).

When faith perceives itself as being guided in these ways, it affirms its confidence that "in everything, as we know, he cooperates for good with those who love God and are called according to his purpose" (Rom. 8:28). Faith in providence places its active reliance upon the permitting, restraining, overruling, and preventing power of God's infinitely good guidance.

God's Care for the World

Abraham's faith that "God will provide" (Gen. 22:8) was manifested through severe testing. His story became the key narrative of faith in providence for classical Jewish and Christian teaching (Heb. 11:17; Irenaeus, *Ag. Her.* 4.21; Methodius, *Banquet of the Ten Virgins* 5.2; Calvin, *Inst.* 1.16.4).

Mothering metaphors were used to speak of the tenderness of God's care for the world: "As a mother comforts her son, so will I myself comfort you," wrote Isaiah (66:13). The Giver of Life who creates all things does not then just leave them alone, or gaze passively upon them, but continues to nurture and care for them, and is constantly active on behalf of them (Ps. 104; John of Damascus, *OF* 2.29).

History as Providential Narrative

The stuff of human history is woven with endless strands of rebellion. For men and women are not automatons but endowed with free will. This has been the case from the very first biblical picture of human existence, off on the wrong foot with Adam and Eve stumbling. After the fall it is an alienated will with which God has to deal, but a will that is nonetheless still given the possibility of choosing appropriate responses to the grace of God (Ephrem, *Hymns on Paradise* 1.10).

The story of the biblical witness is not an idyllic account of perfect harmony between creature and Creator, but of an ongoing struggle involving temptation, revolt, rebellion, and tragic alienation. Eden is disrupted. The revolt continues with Cain, the generation of the flood, and the tower of Babel. There is a rhythm of rebellion and judgment, of oppression and exodus, of creation and redemption, of grace and repentance, of merit and reward (Augustine, *CG* 16). All these rhythms move in an interactive way through the Yahwist and Deuteronomic histories and continue throughout the whole biblical account. As God is architect of the world and initiator of the cosmic process, so God continues to be engaged as the guide and architect of the historical process, since it encompasses free agents who are prone to go awry (Wesley, *WJW* 6:318).

Israel was the first people to write a history of providence. It is a history of God's caring for all creatures, God's dealing with all humanity, God's unremitting involvement with the world. History is viewed in terms of its purpose, moving in a linear way from an original covenant with God toward the fulfillment of that covenant in a complex historical struggle that required moral accountability at each stage by the people of Israel to God, who gave them breath and life, who offered them a national identity and existence (Justin Martyr, *Dialogue with Trypho*).

A pattern of understanding gradually emerged in Hebraic consciousness: God is leading people through a curious path that they do not always understand, yet whose end is *shālōm*—peace, blessedness, and human fulfillment. The ultimate expectation of the historical process is that through it God is accomplishing a slowly unfolding redemptive design. Human conflicts, acquisitiveness, and pride are seen as petty episodes within the larger context of that ultimate hope.

Faith in divine providence is the trust that God is silently working out the divine purpose through the historical process, even when we cannot fully recognize it, and that whatever the distortions and disruptions of history, God's purpose will be accomplished in the long run (Augustine, *CG* 22). Amid the awesome dissolution of long-standing historical structures, as beheld by Isaiah, God is working out a longer-ranged plan, through which the caring governance of God is unfolding (Isa. 40:1–11). Even when God allows emperors like Cyrus to hold for a time unparalleled power, God is only temporarily using Cyrus as an instrument of instruction for the people of Israel, and through them universal history (Isa. 44:28; 45:1; Arnobius, *Ag. Heathen*).

Similarly in Ezekiel, even the powers seemingly at enmity with God can finally do nothing other than serve God's plan (Ezek. 38). At the court of Nebuchadnezzar, Daniel grasped the astonishing vision that the hidden purpose of God was being worked out precisely through the captivity of the people (Dan. 2–3; Isa. 8:10).

The Divine Imprint on Nature and History

God works to implant in the nature of things the potentiality of their future development. The scriptural witness to providence steadily attests this: God plants seeds that grow only slowly in history. It is as if a genetic imprint goes into the structure of each element of creaturely life, so that each creature is given some limited, creaturely potential for the fulfillment of the will of the One who is the ground, artificer, and designer of those imprints through unfolding secondary causes. God undergirds the natural processes, which inconspicuously and unawarely cooperate with God (Isa. 49:19; 60:20; Matt. 13:1–38; 1 Cor. 3:1–9).

The providential care of God is already in the nature of things, in the generation of things, in the transmission of things, and in their awesome movement through history. God is present in seedtime and harvest, cold and heat, summer and winter, the clouds and the rain, the fruits of the earth—all are the gifts of the caring God (Gen. 8:22; Calvin, *Inst.* 2.11–12).

So it is with human life, human labor, and human choice, which are all given their ground and possibility by God's own sovereign freedom. It is indeed necessary for each individual human to gain and grasp freedom on his or her own. Human freedom may assert itself in skewed directions. But these can never constitute a permanent denial or undoing of divine providence. Our worst distortions of human freedom are best viewed in a larger providential frame of reference in which God continues to care for fallen, broken freedom, having mercy upon the sinner and silently governing all things (Ps. 67:4; Isa. 9:6, 7; Heb. 11:40).

Biblical teaching does not view divine providence as dependent upon our recognition of it (Isa. 14:24–32; Ps. 67:4). God remains the unconscious "desire of all nations" (Hag. 2:7) in a hidden way by implanting in all human consciousness the restless hunger for God, so that God is quietly the longing of all humanity, "the desire of all nations," not just the people of Israel or the church, although it is through the covenant people that this hope in time becomes gradually manifested in eternity (Augustine, *CG* 18.45–47).

Why Do the Righteous Suffer?

Both the reality of good and the possibility of the diminution of the good proceed from God, but in different ways. The good proceeds as a freely bestowed gift to which creatures may respond, whereas evil most often emerges as a consequence of sin, in which human beings fail to respond to the created good and to the Creator. One person's abuse of freedom may intrude on the destiny of another person. Meanwhile all goods and absences of good exist only under the protection of God's power and by the permission of God (Lam. 3:38).

"I will strengthen you though you have not known me, so that men from the rising and the setting sun may know that there is none but 1: I am the Lord, there is no other; I make the light, I create darkness, author alike of prosperity and trouble. I, the Lord, do all these things" (Isa. 45:4–7). This does not imply that God directly creates misery, but that God maintains a healing, redemptive purpose in allowing misery to follow after ill-willed deeds (Heb. 12:3–13; Origen, *OFP* 3.12; *Ag. Celsus* 4.64–70).

At times doubts appear so intractable that it would seem that this idea of God's governance is a mistake. It may feel as if God has forgotten his people, as in the captivity or the holocaust. Yet even in the hardest cases, there still remains in the heart of Israel's faith the embers of the latent hope that, nonetheless, somehow God will demonstrate his care in some new, unprecedented way so as to reveal the meaning of these obscure portions of the historical process. In some way unknown to us, it will all be made clear in the course of history. Finally at the end of history there will be resurrection. Where it appears that God has permitted not just a small mistake but a great personal tragedy (as in the case of Job or Hosea), and when it appears that irremediable errors and injustices have occurred, there ensues a weighty struggle between faith and doubt in which faith in providence is sorely tested (Job 3:1–26; Lam. 1:1–22; Mark 15:35; Gregory I, *Morals on Job* 28, 35).

This recurring, wrenching struggle has given rise to a series of standing biblical riddles concerning providence: Why do the wicked prosper? Why do the righteous suffer? Why are the sins of grandmothers apparently visited upon granddaughters? All these themes were dealt with by Jeremiah, Isaiah, Ezekiel, and, above all, Job. Job's fundamental response to his pathos-laden struggle was that he did not know the answer because God's ways were beyond his ways, God's wisdom beyond his own wisdom (Job 40:3–5; 42:1–6). But, nevertheless, even for Job, faith somehow remained sustained and unshakable, even though plagued with penultimate confusion and doubt. These remain riddles, not because of the weakness of faith, but precisely because of the tenacity of faith in providence, inasmuch as they affirm the mysterious purpose of God even amid the wretched byways and curious meanderings and sufferings and inconveniences of actual living persons (Olympiodorus, *Comm. on Job* 42:1–3).

Given the inveterate tendency of human freedom to fall, God continues to offer redemptive possibilities. If Eden is Plan A, and Eden does not work out, due to the self-determining volatility, frailty, and fallibility of human freedom, then

God has a Plan B and a Plan C, etc. All contingencies, however, are known by eternal divine wisdom from the beginning (Ephrem, *Comm. on Gen.* 2.33). The Word, the Son, has from the beginning been made ready for revelation in the fullness of time (John 1:1–14; Eph. 1:4–10). God is willing to relate responsively to the intrinsically unpredictable development of human freedom. This story finally comes to a crossroads in Jesus Christ. Jesus constitutes a *krisis* for the world in the sense that he confronts the world with that crossroad—whether to trust God's coming governance or not (Origen, *Comm. on Rom.* 5).

Since the fall, God has been overseeing a plan for the redemption of fallen freedom. The plan pivots around Christ's coming and is to be consummated in Christ's final return. Nothing will finally thwart this divine purpose (Isa. 11:1; Chrysostom, *Comm. on Dan.* 7.7).

The Care of the Father Discerned Through the Son

God's purpose in history became fully disclosed in the history of Jesus (Eph. 3:1–13). The story of Jesus' last days echoes and transmutes the frequent theme of the prophets, that even when we oppose God we can only in the long run serve his purposes. For in the story of Jesus' death on the cross, even the injustices, betrayals, and crimes done against Jesus become precisely the means by which God brings deliverance to humanity (Col. 2:14; Heb. 12:2; Ps. 76:10). What God wills for humanity is brought about even when humanity does not will the good that God wills. Nothing that we choose can put a final obstacle in the way of the accomplishment of the divine purpose (Chrysostom, *Hom. on Col.*, 6).

The teaching of providence became intensely personalized in relation to the history of Jesus. The Sermon on the Mount strikes the key note. We hear not only about the governor of nature and nations but "Our Father in heaven" (Matt. 6:9). The same fatherly one who "makes his sun rise on good and bad alike, and sends the rain on the honest and the dishonest" (Matt. 5:45) is personally present in the flesh in Jesus.

> *Therefore I bid you put away anxious thought about food and drink to keep you alive, and clothes to cover your body. Surely life is more than food, the body more than clothes. Look at the birds of the air; they do not sow and reap and store in barns, yet your heavenly Father feeds them. You are worth more than the birds! Is there a man of you who by anxious thought can add a foot to his height? And why be anxious about clothes? Consider how the lilies grow in the fields; they do not work, they do not spin; and yet, I tell you, even Solomon in all his splendor was not attired like one of these. But if that is how God clothes the grass in the fields, which is there today, and tomorrow is thrown on the stove, will he not all the more clothe you? How little faith you have! (Matt. 6:25–31)*

Jesus called his hearers to trust the Father as one who cares about "the least of these" (Matt. 25), who notices the tiniest sparrow (Luke 21:18). The guidance of God as father (Abba) became the central feature of Jesus' highly personal conception of God's preservation and governance of creatures (Cyril of Jerusalem, *Catechesis* 7.5–15).

In the end time it is hoped that whatever doubts one may have had about the curious meanderings of God's providence in history will somehow be resolved in a way fitting to God's purpose. It is hoped that question marks will be erased as the conclusion of the process is revealed. Since we are now *in* the process, it is difficult for us to know or grasp its conclusion, except as it is reflected "through a glass darkly" (1 Cor. 13:12; Chrysostom, *Hom. on Cor.* 34.2).

Even with limited vision each believer is invited to "Cast all your cares on him, for you are his charge" (1 Pet. 5:7). The Epistles of Peter dealt with the problems of suffering and discipline amid persecution. They expressed the vital hope that in the end time the purpose of God made known in Jesus will be fully revealed for all to behold (Oecumenius, Comm. on 1 Peter 5). For now the providential purpose of God is sufficiently clear in the ministry of Jesus and above all in Jesus' resurrection (Acts 17:18; Rom. 6:1–5; Phil. 3:10, 11).

At the beginning of his letter to Rome, Paul spoke of God's caring and providing activity as manifesting itself through law, conscience, and nature, so that everyone has reason enough already to know and recognize the providence of God, so much so that our repeated failures to recognize it are inexcusable (Rom. 1:20). The turning point is set forth in Romans 3:21: "But now, quite independently of law, God's justice has been brought to light. The Law and the prophets both bear witness to it: it is God's way of righting wrong, effective through faith in Christ for all who have such faith—all, without distinction" (Rom. 3:21; Augustine, *Spirit and Letter* 15.59; 44). In this light, all things are seen to work together for good to those who love God.

The Christian belief in God's providence is thus brought into its most distinctive Pauline formulation in this summary phrase: "In everything, as we know, he co-operates for good with those who love God and are called according to his purpose" (Rom. 8:28; Ambrosiaster, *Comm. on Paul's Epistles*, Rom. 8:28). Those who realize this are "those who love God" in response to God's love in Christ. They realize that there is "nothing in all creation that can separate us from the love of God in Christ Jesus our Lord" (Rom. 8:39; *Augustine on Romans* 58).

Few themes are more widely dispersed throughout the Scriptures than that of the caring of God for all creation. It appears in the Pentateuch, the Prophets, the wisdom literature, the synoptic writers, Paul, John, and the general Epistles. The biblical story concludes with an account of how those who oppose God's providence will be overthrown (Rev. 19) and the purpose of God finally, despite fierce opposition, will be consummated.

General and Special Providence

Without general providence the scope of divine care is not universal. Without special providence the act of praying is absurd (Tertullian, *On Prayer*). Classical consensual exegetes have consistently argued both for general providence and for the special competence of God to become intimately involved at any particular point in human history while still respecting the intelligible natural order (Tho. Aq., *SCG* 2).

General and special providence are complementary, and not considered contrary or antithetical (Tho. Aq., *Compend*:127). God's *general* providence works through regular and uniform natural law, not by arbitrary incursions into the natural order (Ps-Dionysius, *Extant Fragments: On the Promises 4–6; From the Books on Nature, 1–4*). General providence in human affairs is not exerted as if on utterly moldable material substance, as if without freedom or will or self-determination. For divine guidance occurs in whatever way is most fitting in the caring for free, self-determining human agency, the wills of morally accountable persons, just as parental care looks for the most fitting situational mode of guidance (Prov. 4:11; Isa. 58:11; John 16:13; Augustine, *Tractates on John* 96.4; Wesley, *WJW* 7:171).

It is a misjudgment to view God's providence toward humanity as routinely coercing free wills. God did not create human freedom to destroy it. Rather

God's own infinite Spirit groans with our spirits to draw our freedom toward the good—not to coerce but to persuade and enable our wills to do the good we can envision (Rom. 8:14–39; Cyril of Alex., *Explanation of Rom.*, Rom. 8:22).

The notion of general providence needs to be held carefully in close tension and proximity to two other scriptural teachings crucial to the discussion of human existence: First is the *solidarity* of human, social existence—for we live our lives out together as families, as nations, in larger social constructs than simple individuality. Were God's providence limited to private interiority and abstracted individuality, the divine influence would be less than that declared by Jesus and the prophets (Rom. 5:17–19; Origen, *Comm. on Rom.* 5).

Secondly, the call and need for sacrificial *self-denial* or self-surrender is often closely intertwined with the unfolding of providence. For there may be important moments in which the good of the realm can only be served when a particular individual's good is constricted, or when one may be required to suffer for others. The Christian life is characterized by denying oneself, bearing the cross, and following Jesus (Mark 8:34; Caesarius of Arles, *Sermons* 159.5). A right understanding of providence must leave room for the ironies of solidarity and self-denial, which are so boldly contrasted with the excessive individualism and narcissism so commonly assumed as normative in human consciousness (Baxter, *PW* 11:60).

Special Providence

God not only works through the general structure of natural law and historical development to promote the well-being of the whole, but also in special contexts and with particular persons who trust God, who fervently pray, who are responsive to the specific promptings of grace, and who through experience learn the sense in which all things work together for good. All things work together for good for those who love God (Rom. 8:28) in a sense that is not and cannot be perceived by those who are not responsive to divine grace in history, who have neither sought nor received any special insight into the meaning of history (Clement of Alex., *Strom.* 4.6–8; Wesley, *WJW* 6: 225, 315). Among those who know little of the grace of God, the implication is not that divine providence is absent, but that it is present with less awareness. For God's providence is not dependent upon human awareness of it (Baxter, *PW* 12:183–85).

Special providence means that God acts through particular events in exceptional ways, as in the answering of prayer, and not by general providence alone. Deism resisted the notion of special providence on the grounds that since God has created a good and intelligible system of natural order, God would not arbitrarily break that order on the whim of special or egocentric supplications. Some argued on the strength of general providence that God is powerless to intervene within the context of natural causality, and that it would be inconsistent with the divine majesty if God became enmeshed in special or petty occurrences of human history (John Toland, *Christianity Not Mysterious*; Matthew Tindal, *Christianity as Old as Creation*). Classic Christian teaching has rejected these forms of deism.

In luminous events the care and purposes of God appear to be more clearly revealed and visible to us. Through them faith is awakened to be sustained through adversity. Through a history of such events, the providing of God becomes gradually clarified as trustable. The study of providence is a study of ordinary and actual history, illumined at times by special acts of clarity where the divine purpose is plainly revealed. There are many times at which it is deeply puzzling what God might be doing within the long ranges of history. Our attentiveness is intensified at times and places in which God's will to communicate seems greatly increased.

Binding Time as the Hidden Purpose Becomes Known

Providence becomes further illuminated when viewed in the light of any human activity that shows a firmly conceived human purpose worked out over a very long period of time—earlier hidden, later revealed. A long range vocational decision that is clearly grasped inwardly by the chooser may not be understood by those looking at the decision from the outside. Many successive steps may be required to reach this long-range goal. Not only is the overall plan of a career path complex, but a person must be ready to meet unexpected contingencies. If there are significant obstacles, each must be met in relation to the overall goal. Sometimes the path may be meandering. Yet through all these fleeting events there remains a firm long-range goal, a decision that shapes everything else. It is often only at the very end of a long process that we are finally positioned to realize how the purpose was being worked out all through the times of uncertainty. Various aspects of the earlier phases may now be pieced together and made understandable through the later phases.

We bind our time to long-range objectives that shape our decision making in the present (G. Kaufman, *Syst. Theol.*:301). We limit our freedom while pursuing a long-drawn-out goal that requires discipline. But in the midst of this lengthy development, others who are not privy to the original decision may fail to grasp crucial aspects of it.

It is as if God has made far-reaching decisions or decrees about human history that we do not yet fully perceive but meet only at some particular point along the way of their fulfillment. We glimpse only some tiny part of God's larger historical purpose. God knows what is occurring through the process. We may or may not recognize the deeper intention of God. Faith in providence is trust that whatever is occurring has some meaning within God's larger purpose, even if not fully understood by egocentric human subjects (Augutine, *CG* 2).

Resurrection as the Revelation of the End of History

It is impossible for Christian believers to think about the meaning of history without thinking of the end of history. Hence the resurrection is a crucial element in the Christian teaching of providence in history.

The resurrection of Jesus was for the primitive Christian community the primary clue to the end of history. It is the key to the meaning of the whole meandering, convoluted human story. The idea of a general resurrection was widely understood in the first century as meaning the *end* of the historical process (Matt. 22:23; John 11:24). Resurrection is by definition at the end of all things, the end event. One cannot understand the meaning of history until history is over. Similarly one cannot understand the meaning of an individual's life until that life is over, for otherwise its meaning would still be subject to change.

One may not know the purpose of another's long-range commitment until the goal of that commitment is reached. That is why the apocalyptic writers focused so intently on the question of what happens at the *end* of the historical process: only then would history's meaning finally be clear (Heb. 6:8; 1 Pet. 4:7; Rev. 21:6; 22:13). The resurrected Lord appearing to his disciples signaled to them that the end had come; the final scene of history had anticipatively been revealed. They knew where history was headed, because its *end* was already being revealed.

The resurrection of Jesus constituted a powerful reversal of historical expectations. Those who met the living Lord experienced a sweeping reversal of consciousness. It was an event without precedent. It meant that even though history continues apace, those who live out of the resurrection are already sharing in the last days. By receiving and trusting in the Word spoken in the resurrection, they were in effect already participating in the end, and therefore the meaning, of the entire world-historical process (Acts 26:23; 1 Thess. 4:16; Ambrose, *On Belief in the Resurrection* 2.47–48).

In this way the meaning of history was anticipatively disclosed before the actual ending of the historical process. Resurrection is an intractably historical way of understanding, a very Jewish way of reasoning, about how God lets us know his purposes—namely, through history. The courage of the early church to face persecution and death was directly based upon their continuing experience of the presence of the resurrected Lord.

Christianity proclaims that the purpose of the otherwise obscure process of history, which involves fallen freedom, sin, evil, and frustration, is revealed in Jesus' resurrection. That is precisely the reason one can, in the New Testament sense, trust in God's providence. No event reported in the Christian teaching of providence is more crucial than resurrection (see Wolfhart Pannenberg, *Jesus, God and Man*, who has astutely clarified what the resurrection meant to the people who beheld and responded to it, and remembered it). Those who are grasped by the resurrection of Jesus are already anticipating, already living within the end of the process. That is the basis upon which trust is possible.

The resurrection teaches us that even though outcomes are not objectively known, the one who guides the outcomes is trustable. It is through the resurrection that the disciples gained the capacity for that trust. Through the resurrection the faithful have foretasted the end (1 Pet. 2:3). It is as though they have glimpsed the vision that reveals the will of God for the whole. They "have had a taste of the heavenly gift and a share in the Holy Spirit, when they have experienced the goodness of God's word and the spiritual energies of the age to come" (Heb. 6:4, 5; Ambrose, *Concerning Repentance*, 2.2.7–12).

PART IV

THE STUDY
OF GOD

T HE CLASSICAL CHRISTIAN EXEGETES did not ordinarily begin their
writings (homilies, essays, books, Scripture studies) with detailed
discussions of theological method. Nonetheless they were keenly aware of
how they were proceeding. They were more likely to plunge into the substantive
clarification of the sacred texts attesting the being and activity of God, and
only subsequently consider and examine their method of knowing. This classic
approach indicates:

- that reflection on method best occurs as a retrospection upon the actual
  practice of the study of God, rather than an arbitrary limitation upon
  practice before study has begun;

- that the study of the knowledge of God is best derived from the life-long
  practice of the Christian life rather than vice versa;

- that the living God is prior to and more crucial than our methods of
  inquiry.

Early Christian teachers first addressed the fundamental question of the *Subject* of the study of God, and only later and subordinately the questions of *method*.
Among those who proceeded conspicuously from subject to method were: Ignatius
of Antioch, Athanasius, Chrysostom, Basil, Hilary, and Ambrose. None set out

first with a deliberate account of method. It was not until Gregory of Nyssa, Augustine, and Vincent of Lérins in the late fourth and early fifth centuries that the operative method of the ecumenical theologians became increasingly clear. By the time of Gregory the Great and John of Damascus, these methods were thoroughly integrated into exegesis, preaching, and theological debate, but often referred to only obliquely.

Having already asked the foundational questions of who God is, whether God is, and whether God is triune Creator and Provider, we are now to the point of being poised to pursue six practical questions about the method of study of classic Christian teaching:

- whether the deliberate study of God is necessary to faith;

- whether the revelation of God requires written texts, traditions, reasoning, and histories of experience to enable its reception;

- whether church tradition is an authoritative source of theology;

- whether the study of God is a science;

- whether the right study of God requires a particular temperament; and

- whether the study of God can be viewed as an academic discipline that corresponds with other disciplines.

8

WHETHER GOD CAN BE STUDIED

Is the Study of God Possible?

The study of God can only be an inquiry that fallible, finite human beings undertake. God does not study theology, for God already knows his own mind with full adequacy, and without needing our words or expert phrases about him (John of Damascus, *OF* 1.1.2; Wesley, *WJW* 6:338).

Insofar as we speak any words at all about God's coming into our presence, we speak in fragile language about that knowledge we as creatures have of the infinite divine reality, however patchy that might be (Dionysius, *Div. Names* 1).

All talk of God occurs within the limits of finitude and out of a community of prayer. That community lives within an ever-flowing stream of time. It passes through many languages, national histories, and cultural memories. No human knower sees as God sees. We must employ human speech if we are to speak at all of this One about whom any speech is always inadequate, yet so important (Augustine, *On Chr. Doctrine* 1.6–13; Luther, *Bondage of the Will* 12).

Hence there is an element of comedy about any talk of God. The life of grace delights in its contradictions (Kierkegaard, *Concl. Unsci. Post.*:250–70). For we are striving with all our might to talk about that which is finally quite indescribable—indeed, ineffable! (Dionysius, *Div. Names* 1.1; John of Damascus, *OF* 1.1). Nonetheless, we keep on trying to say a little better whatever we can about this incomparable reality that we actually know and meet in our own hearts, and in the history of Jesus, and in universal history. It often seems as if it would be more conscionable to give up speaking at all. But that would require the end of discipline, of teaching, of preaching, of baptism and of all hymnody except humming.

Christian Theology Emerges out of Christian Community

The intellectual enterprise that we call Christian theology is an activity that occurs within the precincts of a worshiping community. That is precisely what distinguishes it from psychology of religion and philosophy of religion—legitimate disciplines that differ in method and subject matter from theology. Islamic theology begins within the framework of Islamic prayer, law, and community life. Jewish theology begins within a community of remembrance and expectation. So does Christian theology emerge precisely within a community whose "life lies hidden with Christ in God" (Col. 3:3; Ambrose, *Paradise* 29). When we inquire seriously into Christian teaching, we normally do so as baptized members of the body of Christ—thus as communicants, worshipers, and recipients of the gospel—or as inquirers who wish to know what the church teaches (Augustine, *Catech. Instr.* 1, 2).

God has committed his revelation to the custody of the continuing apostolic community under the guidance of the Spirit (Simplicius, *The Necessity of Guarding the Faith, Epis. to Acacius, SCD* 159). The Bible is the church's book, lodged within the church for safekeeping and to continue to inspire and instruct the faithful (Irenaeus, *Ag. Her.* 3.4). It is the church (not the university) that has for centuries kept it, translated it, studied it, meditated upon it, and repeatedly looked to it for daily guidance. The Holy Writ given to the church has spawned a lively history of religious ideas, theories, concepts, and symbols (Eusebius, *CH* 6).

The eternal truth of Christian teaching must be spoken anew within various historical circumstances. The idea of an evolution of Christian language is hardly inimical to Christian orthodoxy, but precisely in line with the intent of orthodoxy, which prays that God's Spirit will spawn ever-new communities in each new historical context, language, and symbol system, each faithful to the truth of classic Christian teaching (Augustine, *On Chr. Doctrine*, prologue 1.1). The achievement of orthodoxy was never in making all believers look exactly alike. Rather it sought to engender life in Christ in speakers of varied languages. It prayed that the good news of God's coming into human history might be rightly known by all participants in human history (Vincent of Lérins, *Comm.* 23; Newman, *Development of Chr. Doctrine*). This required learning the world's languages.

Orthodoxy

The term orthodoxy—that least modern of all words—is largely a product of the classical Christian tradition. Orthodox means "right opinion" (orthos + doxa), or "sound doctrine," especially religious teaching, and more particularly that teaching which holds closely to the Christian faith as formulated by the earliest classic Christian teachers. An opinion is orthodox if it is congruent with the apostolic faith.

In order to achieve multigenerational continuity, societies require persuasive legitimation and thoughtful tradition maintenance. Examples of secular orthodoxies that have achieved temporary continuity and still survive marginally (especially in universities) are Freudian, Marxian, and behaviorist. While these have barely survived a hundred years, classic Christianity has survived for two thousand.

Since the second century, Christianity has been called upon to answer challenges to its faith. These came from novel, experimental, and often distorted views of its own apostolic witness. It became necessary to defend Christian teaching. The faithful had to respond to toxic challenges both from within and without (Hippolytus, *Refutation of All Her.* 10). The defense of the faith to those outside the community was called apologetics (2 Tim. 2:24–26; 1 Pet. 3:15; Justin Martyr, *First Apol.* 13; Augustine, *Letters* 120). Its defense within the community was called sacred doctrine.

This has required repeated attempts to bring apostolic teaching into a consistent, balanced formulation within ever-changing cultural settings. We see this drive for balance and intellectual cohesion especially in the case of Cyril of Jerusalem's Catechetical Lectures and John of Damascus *On the Orthodox Faith*. Classic Christian teachers labored to bring into ordered unity and equilibrium all the doctrines of Christian teaching according to the consensual affirmations of the early ecumenical councils of Christian leaders and teachers (*OF* 1.1, Cyril of Jerusalem, *Procatechesis*; Rufinus, *On the Creed*; Peter Lombard, *Four Books of Sentences*).

Although the terms orthodox and catholic and ecumenical have built up modern connotations that they did not have in the first millennium, I am using these terms as they were used in the first millennium: orthodox is sound doctrine in accord with apostolic teaching, catholic is "according to the whole" [church], and ecumenical is the whole world. Classic consensual Christian teaching uses all three terms not as simply equivalents but as references to the whole church.

Postmodern Orthodoxy

In the mid-seventies when academic theology was in a wildly feral mood, I take responsibility for being the first to employ a term that at the time was puzzling to many but later widely valued as a description—an oxymoronic term—"postmodern orthodoxy." This described autobiographically what had been happening to me personally in the late sixties and early seventies. This was a decade before "post-modernity" became a headline buzzword among academics. At that time the term postmodern was largely used by a handful of architects and a few linguists. It had hardly intruded into the sanctum of theology. In the academic ethos of the seventies, any talk of "orthodoxy" was regarded as unthinkable in a self-respecting university, and especially in avant garde theological schools. This period spawned a large shelf of pseudo-lofty tomes on theological method, but very little that was solidly grounded in classic Christian teaching.

I have found no instance where the terms "postmodern" and "orthodoxy" were juxtaposed in published form before 1979 in *Agenda for Theology* where I employed it to describe a unexpected reversal in my own journey. I was trying to point to a classic consensual form of then embryonic theological reasoning that was already (against all expectations) living out of the conditions of the *collapse* of modernity (not the legitimation or triumph of modernity!—which "postmodern" later came unsuitably to signify).

Orthodoxy is post-modern if it has seriously passed through and dealt with the possibilities and limits of modern consciousness on its pilgrimage through the third millennium. This is a pilgrimage that has in fact brought about a rediscovery of the early Christian consensual tradition. Since the seventies I have been hungering and thirsting for classic consensual Christian wisdom. I have found it abundantly in the texts of classic Christian exegesis, pastoral care, liturgy, ethics, and theology. After Harper Collins published this *Agenda*, letters began pouring in to assure me that many others were going through a similar unexpected reversal from form-critical liberalism to orthodoxy, but had not yet found language for it. These voices grew into the "young fogeys" of the eighties who were at first interested especially in the comic contradictions of academic theology.

Classic Christianity views modernity from the point of view of its historical dissolution. We have already witnessed in the turn of the third millennium the further precipitous deterioration of social processes under the tutelage of autonomous individualism, narcissistic hedonism, and naturalistic reductionism. These are the key features of despairing modern consciousness. There is a growing hunger for means of social stabilization, continuity, parenting, intergenerational tradition maintenance, and freedom from the repressions of modernity. Postmodern orthodoxy is Christian teaching that, having passed through a deep engagement with the failed ideologies of modernity, has rediscovered the vitality of the ancient ecumenical Christian tradition.

The term "postmodern" later became very commonly abused in the 1990s by carrying the opposite meaning, as if modernity had transcended all continuities in history. The point: I have never used post-modern orthodoxy in any sense than its ironic-oxymoronic sense. By 1989 in *After Modernity What?*, I was preferring the term "post-critical orthodoxy" due to these abuses. In this 2009 revised edition of the earlier Systematic Theology of 1987-93, I am attempting to restate more prudently the basic intent of *Agenda for Theology* consistent with conditions that now prevail thirty years later, yet more textually grounded and sober about the urgent need for sustaining the truth of classic Christian reasoning.

Teaching the One Faith to Many Cultures

In spite of all limitations, we simply must study God, because God has touched our lives and has become our very life. There is no period of Christian history in which the attempt to study God has been completely disregarded or has entirely ceased, and no period when it has been more urgently needed than at the outset of the third millennium.

Christianity has long assumed a profound moral requirement that believers should learn to think and teach *consistently* about God, and that they should teach nothing contrary to that which has been revealed in universal history as seen by the apostolic teaching as consensually received. Out of this imperative has come the development of many variant systems of Christian teaching, intended both to teach converts and to defend against error, while holding strictly to the classic Christian consensus, variously called orthodox, catholic or ecumenical.

Systematic or basic theology is a slowly developing expansion of what Luke called "the apostles' teaching" (Acts 2:42), teaching "built upon the foundation of the apostles" (Eph 2:20; Marius Victorinus, *Epis. to Eph* 2:20). Its most primitive forms were baptismal creeds, catechetical teaching, preaching, letters, and expository and pastoral theology aimed at edification.

The New Testament assumed that there was a "unity inherent in our faith" (Eph. 4:13; Chrysostom, *Hom. on Eph*. Hom 9,10) that undergirded all the differences of perspectives and gifts that the apostolic witnesses brought to it. Each personally stamped account of the meaning of Jesus' ministry—those of John, Paul, Peter, James, Luke, Mark, and others—was marked with distinct characteristics of its author under divine inspiration. Despite differences of language, syntax, and cultural situation, however, all these apostles understood themselves to be proclaiming the same Lord, united in the same faith, and not different gospels. The earliest Christian teachers did not think that these teachings were their own personal innovations, but revelations made possible by God's grace, as Paul specifically stated: "I must make it clear to you, my friends, that the gospel you heard me preach is no human invention. I did not take it over from any man; no man taught it to me; I received it through a revelation of Jesus Christ" (Gal. 1:11, 12).

To those who asserted the body of Christ could be divided, Paul countered: "Surely Christ has not been divided among you! Was it Paul who was crucified for you? Was it in the name of Paul that you were baptized?" (1 Cor. 1:13; Tertullian, *On Baptism* 15; Chrysostom, *Hom. on 1 Cor.*, Hom. 3.5). During the earliest centuries the unity of the church was remarkably well preserved by the guidance of the Spirit even amid and through ruthless political repression, persecution, harassment, and false claims of revelation.

The Unity of the Apostolic Classic Consensus

The unity of the classic Christian consensus was textually expressed by the ecumenical councils and defined by the three creeds most widely affirmed in the Christian world:

- the Apostles' Creed, which expanded the baptismal formula;

- the Nicene Creed, which defined the triune teaching; and

- the "Athanasian" or Quiqunque Creed, which more precisely set forth the sonship of Christ.

These consensual affirmations did not arise out of speculation or philosophical debates. Rather, they emerged out of a baptizing, worshiping community that stood accountable to apostolic teaching while being repeatedly challenged by alternative false teachings. Though not a perfectly received consensus, these coherently triune and mutually confirming confessions allowed the church to proceed for the next millennium on the basis of ecumenically established definitions considered definitive for all Christian teaching of all times.

The creeds were not catholic because a majority of bishops decided they were, but because they were guided by the Spirit to express the most common conviction and experience of lay Christian believers everywhere (Vincent of Lérins, *Comm.* 27.38). Had this doctrinal defense not been undertaken, the church would later have been faced with having to struggle ever anew against non-apostolic distortions of God as revealed. These would eventually have made great differences in the practical life, organization, ethics, and teaching of the church. The church had to protect itself from becoming captivated by various philosophical, political, and religious schools (Hippolytus, *Refutation of All Her.* 10.2).

The Christian community has always been a learning and teaching community, concerned with the unity, coherence, and internal consistency of its reflection upon God's self-disclosure (Matt. 28:19, 20; John 21:15–17; Cyril of Alex., *Comm. on John,* 12.1). Jesus himself was a remarkable teacher, and the pastoral office that has patterned itself after him remains intrinsically a teaching ministry, in addition to serving in priestly and prophetic offices.

The concise account of apostolic activity found in Acts 2:42 reveals a pattern familiar to early Christian communities: "They met constantly to hear the apostles teach, and to share the common life, to break bread, and to pray." This still remains a rough sketch of the core spheres of activity of the Christian community: first, teaching, then the nurturing of community through sacramental life, and prayer. If the church's teaching is deficient, then its fellowship, sacrament, and worship are likely to suffer from that deficiency (John Cassian, *Conference* 2.15.1).

The primary mandate of the church is not to teach miscellaneous opinions about psychology, politics, or sociology that are not derived from the church's unique gift: revelation in Christ. The church has received authorization to teach nothing contrary to that which has been delivered and received consensually through the history of revelation.

Beyond that the mandate to teach is best viewed modestly. On the one hand, theology does not serve well by attempting to feed as a parasite on all the other disciplines of the university, as if it had nothing of its own to say. On the other hand, theology does even worse when it seeks to imperialize the various disciplines, imagining that it knows more about biology than biologists, and more about medicine than physicians, and more about the economy than the economists.

Revelation Requires Scripture, Tradition, Experience, and Reason

By what authority or on what ground does Christian teaching rest? How does the worshiping community know what it professes to be true?

The study of God relies constantly upon an interdependent matrix of sources on the basis of which the confessing community can articulate, make consistent, and integrate the witness to revelation. These four are *scripture, tradition, experience*, and *reason*, all of which depend upon and exist as a response to their necessary premise: revelation. All are functionally present in the most representative of classical Christian teachers, notably: Irenaeus, Chrysostom, Ambrose, Augustine, and John of Damascus.

Revelation—The Primary Premise of the Christian Study of God

Each phase of the classic fourfold approach to the study of God hinges on the unswerving central premise of revelation: that God has made himself known (Irenaeus, *Ag. Her.* 3). God has not concealed but revealed the divine will, love, and mercy through a palpable historical process. Anyone who carefully examines the course of universal history may experience the sweep of that revelation (Pss. 33:9; 40:5; 105:5; 126:2, 3; Augustine, *CG* 18; Pannenberg, *Revelation as History*).

Jewish and Christian reasoning about God characteristically looks at the whole of history, viewing history itself as the arena of God's activity and of human responses to it. This history tells a unique story that forms the memory of the worshiping community. It tells of creation, of the fall, of a flood, a covenant, an exodus, a captivity, and a crucifixion and resurrection, a Spirit-bestowed church and an expected judgment. By looking intently upon that history, any discerning mind can see that the whole fabric of events reveals the presence, reality, power, and character of God (Tertullian, *Ag. Marcion* 3; Augustine, *On Psalms* 90). The giver of history is known through history (Augustine, *CG* 16).

As new events occur in ever-emergent history, their meanings are illumined, in this community, by reflection out of that primary revelatory event and its Revealer, Jesus as the Christ. The worshiping community is constantly reflecting upon each new phase or moment of history in relation to that original event of revelation.

This mode of reasoning was familiar to the Hebraic community prior to Jesus, where past revelatory events such as exodus and captivity became the lens of understanding out of which the history of Jesus was interpreted. This is a distinctively Hebraic mode of thinking: "When your son asks you in time to come, 'What is the meaning of the precepts, statutes, and laws which the Lord our God gave you?' you shall say to him, 'We were Pharaoh's slaves in Egypt, and the Lord brought us out of Egypt with his strong hand,'" (Deut. 6:20–22; Rom. 3:21–31; Irenaeus, *Ag. Her.* 4.21). In this way the recollection of a real history is the basis of knowledge of God's revelation, which occurs in events, not by spawning ideas.

This is the central hypothesis of the Christian way of studying God: that through Christ the Revealer of God, we see into the meaning of other events from beginning to end. Jesus Christ is that single page in the novel where the clue to the whole story is found, the crucial moment in the historical process in which the part reveals the whole. Through this particular lens, we come to know the One who is unsurpassably good, the One who is the ground of our being, who gives life, in whom all things cohere (Col. 1:3–20; Tertullian, *Ag. Marcion* 5.19; Augustine, *Letters* 185.1–5). It is out of participation in that event that Christian community continues to come alive, proclaim God's word, celebrate life together, and partake of the sacramental life that brings the community again in communion with that Word (Ignatius, *To the Ephesians* 6).

Four Resources in the Study of the Revealed God

Christian Scripture, Christian tradition, Christian reasoning, and Christian experience all exist in response to God's historical revelation in Israel and Jesus Christ. This may be pictured as follows:

Sources for the Study of God

Revelations	Scripture	Tradition	Experience	Reason
Out of the **Word** *Revealed* Comes	Out of the **Word** *Written* Comes	Out of the **Word** *Remembered* Comes	Out of the **Word** *Personally* and *Socially* *Experienced* Comes	Out of the **Word** Made *Intelligible* Comes
→	→	→	→	
Knowledge	Witness	Church	Life in Christ	Theology

The sources of the study of God are in this way seen in a sequence that moves from originative event (Christ the Revealer of God the Father) as proclaimed by the community, to the record of the earliest proclamation (written word), to the traditioning—or "passing along," *paradosis*, transmission—of that word intergenerationally through time (tradition), which elicits personal and social awareness and experience of the salvation event (experience), which then becomes the basis of the reflection required to think consistently about the meaning of the salvation event (reason)—each layer depending on the previous one (Clement of Alex., *Strom.* 6.10; Augustine, Chr. Doctr. 4.21; Tho. Aq., *SCG* 1.9; Calvin, *Inst.* 1.6, 7; 3.20; Hooker, *Laws of Eccl. Polity* 3.8).

The Preached Word Precedes the Written Word

The oral tradition of apostolic preaching preceded the written tradition of New Testament Scripture. That is the proper sense in which it is rightly said that the tradition of preaching stands chronologically prior to Scripture. The unwritten oral apostolic tradition was a preached word, a teaching of the living church prior to the writing down of New Testament Scripture. Apostolic preaching itself is a product of oral tradition, taken, like a still photo of a moving picture, and frozen at one crucial point, so that the original oral witness to revelation could be transmitted to subsequent generations.

But after the first generation of witnesses, the church viewed the transmission of tradition from the vantage point that assumes Scripture as already having been written and ever thereafter funding and enabling new embodiments of the same apostolic teaching (*Conf.* of Dositheus, *CC*:485–516; *Heidelberg Catech. COC* 3; Tavard, *Holy Church, Holy Writ*).

Paul was referring to the apostolic tradition he had received and passed on when he wrote: "Stand firm, then brothers, and hold fast to the traditions which you have learned from us by word or by letter" (2 Thess. 2:15). "By word" refers to the preached word, whereas "by letter" refers to epistles and gospel narratives (Basil, *On the Spirit* 29.71). Until Mark, Paul, John, and others began to write their Gospels and letters, there existed much lively preaching and oral tradition, but as yet only minimal written tradition in addition to Hebrew scripture (Chrysostom, *Catech. Lect.* 5.12). The written apostolic tradition emerged only when the oral tradition was in danger of losing some of its immediacy and authority through the impending deaths of the eyewitnesses. The writing down of that witness made the revelation more exact and transmissible to subsequent generations through a continuous succession of ministries of preaching and teaching.

Scripture Funds Tradition, Reason, and Experience

A constant equilibrium of these four interdependent resources is required in order to receive and reflect upon revelation: Scripture, tradition, experience, and reason. All four are grounded in, responsive to, and springing out of historical revelation.

Revelation remains the precondition of all four basic sources of the study of God. Revelation is that from which the whole subject matter proceeds. There could be no Christian study of God without God's own initiative to become reliably known (Gen. 35:7; Ps. 98:2; Isa. 65:1; Rom. 1:18; 16:25, 26; Rev. 1:1, Origen, *Ag. Celsus* 3.61).

The phrase "interdependent four-sided matrix of sources" is in some traditions termed a *quadrilateral method,* referring to four bulwarks of defense of Christian teaching, which if constructed within these walls will provide the worshiping community with a secure and true apostolic identity. A more dynamic picture of these same Christian sources is that of flowing wellsprings cascading through Christian history.

Since this study lives out of the classic consensus, we will utilize the ancient ecumenical (patristic) sources more than modern sources, as we ask how revelation both empowers and requires a written word (Scripture), a remembering community (tradition), an appropriation process (experience), and internal consistency (reason).

The method we are employing here was intuitively familiar to the primitive worshiping community. It became increasingly clear to ancient ecumenical teachers during the first four centuries, but we do not find augmented explanations of it until Augustine, Vincent of Lérins, and Peter Lombard, and then much more explicitly in the Reformation and modern periods. The medieval synthesis held together revelation and reason as mediated by the conciliar tradition's interpretations of Scripture. The Reformation again asserted the written word as primary source of theology, yet strongly avowed the ancient ecumenical consensus provided that it could be shown to be consistent with canonical Scripture.

It was not until the development of eighteenth-century pietism that the personal experience of salvation again received the more explicit attention that had been paid to it in fourth-century theology (the Cappadocians, Chrysostom, and Augustine) and early monasticism (Pachomius, Basil, and John Cassian). For a functional view of this method, it is best seen as operating in the liturgies of Catholic, Orthodox, and Protestant traditions of prayer through the hours of the day, and notably in the Anglican formularies, the *Homilies*, the *Book of Common Prayer*, the Thirty-nine Articles of Religion, the works of Cranmer, Jewel, Hooker, Taylor, and Wesley, as well as in Scholastic Lutherans like Gerhard, and in Reformed teachers like A. J. Niemeyer.

Scripture: The Written Word.

Divinely inspired Scripture is the chief source and norm of Christian theology. Why is a written word required, if God is revealed in history? Because the written word preserves and triggers memory.

After the resurrection and before the writing down of the New Testament documents, many in the primitive Christian community expected the historical process to be concluded quickly (Mark 13:32–37). They assumed that an end time was eminent. But as history surprisingly continued, this community slowly began to realize that it needed to write down its message as historical experience continued to be extended for an indefinite (though limited) duration. If emerging generations were to be addressed with this invaluable message, this would require writing down the history of Jesus the Revealer, and of the first generation of witnesses to him (Luke 1:1–4; Acts 1:1–5; John 21:23–25; Chrysostom, *Hom. on John* 88.2). After the death of the original eyewitnesses, Scripture is the primary written access of believers to the history of revelation (Chrysostom, *Hom. on Acts* 1). Tradition is simply the history of the exegesis of Scripture. The process of passing along the tradition must occur ever again in each new historical circumstance (Quinisext Synod, canon 19).

The New Testament contains these writings that survived—documents that ultimately went through a complex intergenerational process of being transmitted, read in public worship, studied avidly, interpreted through preaching, analyzed, and finally in due time authorized as being ecumenically received credible witnesses to this revealing Word (Gregory of Nyssa, *Answer to Eunomius*, 2). Already the Hebrew Bible was viewed by Christians as divinely inspired Holy Writ. To these documents were added the New Testament—those narratives and letters authorized to be read aloud in Christian congregational worship all over the known world.

The New Testament became formally canonized as Holy Writ (Athanasius, *Festal Letters*). It was valued among Christians as highly as the books of law, prophets, and wisdom, which it fulfilled and explained. The New Testament included letters, instructional documents, and accounts of Jesus' ministry, written in the first century.

The prime criterion for authorization was authenticity of apostolic authorship. This canonization process was accomplished by a living, growing, human historical community, by the consenting church in ecumenical concurrence, utilizing the best historical information available to it (Tertullian, *Prescript. Ag. Her.* 15–44; *Apost. Const.*, "Eccl. Canons," 85; Councils of Alexandria, Carthage, Hippo). It took several centuries for this process of consensual formation to develop into an accepted canon of apostolic tradition. By the fourth century virtually all dioceses of Christian believers had basically agreed upon those documents that were universally accepted as apostolic tradition (Synod of Laodicea, canon LIX). Catholic, Protestant, and Orthodox traditions have all agreed on the central premise that Scripture is the primary source and guideline for Christian teaching, although differences emerged on the status of the deutro-canonical Apocrypha ("hidden" writings included in the Greek Septuagint). Both Testaments are received by the church as sacred writing (Council of Rome, *SCD* 84), as depositum of faith inspired by God the Spirit (Leo XIII, *Providentissimus Deus*, *SCD* 1951), to be

guarded and handed down by the church and interpreted in the light of the consensus of the ancient ecumenical teachers (*SCD* 786) and the sense of the church,
according to sound principles (Pius X, *Lamentabili*, *SCD* 2001).

The Bible, composed of two sets of testimonies or covenants (Old and New), is
the deposit of the sufficient and adequate witness to God's self-disclosure. Other
valued sources of the study of God—tradition, reasoning, and experience—remain
essentially dependent upon and responsive to Scripture, since they must appeal
to Scripture for the very events, interpretations, and data they are remembering,
upon which they reflect, and out of which their experience becomes transformed.
Scripture remains the central source of the memories, symbol systems, hopes,
teachings, metaphors, and paradigms by which the community originally came
into being and has continually refreshed and renewed itself (African Code, canon
24). Christianity differs from Judaism primarily in that it is not still looking for
that fundamental messianic event to disclose the meaning of history. It remembers that event as having occurred in the ministry of Jesus, whose living presence
is received and experienced in Holy Communion and the preached Word (Justin
Martyr, *Dialogue with Trypho*; R. Niebuhr, *NDM* 1.1).

Each Scripture text is best received, understood and interpreted in the light of
its relation to the Bible as a whole. All texts are open to be illuminated by both
scholarly historical inquiry and by reverential personal insight under the guidance of the Spirit (Origen, Hom. on Numbers, 27; Augustine, *The Spirit and the
Letter*).

The Spirit's witness does not completely cease with the canonization of Scripture, but continues by providing a guiding light for the benefit of consensus
formation and personal experience. New events emerge in the ongoing historical
processes that are to be understood in the light of the word made known in Scripture. Yet no fundamentally new or different knowledge is required for the saving
knowledge of God than that which is revealed in Scripture (Council of Rome, *SCD*
84: 33, 34; Westminster *Conf.* 1.1–10).

Tradition: The Word Remembered

The teaching office given to the church requires transmission of the history of the
events of God's self-disclosure to subsequent generations without distortion. This
multi-generation task of accurate transmission in all its oral and written forms
is called tradition—the passing along (*paradosis* or transmission) of apostolic
teaching from parents to children, generation to generation.

The proper use of tradition, as Jews and Christians have lived it out concretely,
is a vital social reality. Its task is to receive and transmit the history of revelation.
The task has sometimes been wrongly conceived or implemented, so as to convey
archaic traditionalism or rigid formulas or in-group biases that do not adequately
convey the vitality of the sacred writings. Tradition invites not only written and
spoken words. It wants to be danced, sung, feasted upon, and celebrated, as in a
Bar Mitzvah or wedding. Tradition is shared in a social process through seasonal
celebrations and the recollection of mighty events (Quinisext Synod 66).

Christians have a complex history of their own. In each new developing historical situation, believers have come to discover, reformulate, and restate in their
own language the unchanging revealed Word. These ever-new formulations of
each new period of the tradition's reflection about revelation continue to live out
of Scripture. Each one is new, since historical experience is ever new (Gelasius,
Decretal, *SCD* 164–166).

Fruitful experiences of previous Christian communities are awaiting fresh assim-
ilation into the apostolate by contemporary believing communities. Contemporary

believers stand, not at the beginning of history, but amid it, and not as isolated individuals but with a community of prayer and song and story that has stored a mass of data about the lively experiences of an actual risk-taking historical community (*Apost. Const., Eccl. Canons*). Only the narrowest individualism would imagine that every believer must begin from nothing, as if no others had ever had any experience of God.

Classic writers have one distinct advantage over modern sources: they have already been thoroughly tested, questioned, probed, analyzed, and utilized in different historical situations. Modern interpretation does well to build upon that extensive examination. The gospel has been expressed with greater fullness and clarity in some centuries than in others. Some brilliant insights into scriptural truth have had to await "their century" for a hearing.

Theology builds progressively upon previous generations of the study of God, using stores of wisdom both old and new (Matt. 13:52; Augustine, Sermon 74.5). Rediscovered insights into Scripture and tradition keep coming to the attention of the church at unexpected times (Cyril of Alexandria, Fragment 172, Reuss, MKGK 209). Each age has the possibility of contributing something to the storehouse for subsequent ages that will study God, yet that fact does not imply that the received faith itself is being substantively changed from generation to generation (Simplicius, *The Unchangeableness of Chr. Doctrine, SCD* 160).

The Word Experienced

The Spirit speaking through the Scripture awakens in us the awareness of God's revelation in history, allowing us to recollect and participate in attested events that bestow meaning on the whole of history. The vast range of experiences, metaphors, symbols, and recollections of a historical community become accessible to later generations. We are invited to correlate our personal experience with the social and historical continuum of the faithful (Deut. 6:20–25).

It is misleading to pit tradition against experience, since tradition is precisely the continuing memory of this vast arena of social and historical experiencing. There is a profound affinity between the community's tradition and our personal experience: one is historical-social-ecclesial and the other is personal-individuated-unique, yet both are forms of embodiment of life in Christ. What was once someone else's experience becomes a part of my own experience. Christian teaching seeks to enable this community's experience to become personally validated and authenticated as my own (Wesley, *WJW* 1: 470; 5:128; 8:1; Buber, *The Hasidic Masters*; Herberg, *Faith Enacted in History*).

If a corporately remembered experience is to become personally appropriated, it must be or become congruent with one's own concrete experience, with what one is feeling. The integration of the tradition into one's own feeling process most powerfully occurs in worship. Christian teaching does not simply reflect on corporate memory as an abstract or distant datum, but, rather, seeks to integrate social memory congruently within one's own feelings (Basil, *On the Spirit* 28).

Experience is to the individual as tradition is to the historical church. Both are enlivened by the Spirit. Experience seeks to enable the personal appropriation of God's mercy in actual, interpersonal relationships. Faith becomes personal trust appropriated in a disciplined and responsive way of life, sharing the love and mercy of God with whomever possible (Clement of Alex., *Strom.* 2.2).

Any truth that does not connect with personal experience is likely to remain opaque to the single individual, no matter how clear it may be to all others. A truth that has not become a *truth for me* (Kierkegaard, *Concl. Unsci. Post.*) is not likely to bear up through crises. The personal side of theology is effective when daily life is providing experiential evidences of the reliability of faith's witness. This does not imply, however, that personal experience may unilaterally judge and dismiss Scripture and tradition. Scripture and tradition are received, understood, and validated through personal experience, but not arbitrated or censored by it. Rather Scripture and tradition amid the living, worshiping community are the means by which and context in which one's personal experiences are evaluated (1 John 4:4; 1 Cor. 4:3, 4; James 3:1; Tertullian, *Prescript. Ag. Her.* 33; Oecumenius, *Comm. on James,* 1:19).

Reason: The Word Made Intelligible

The fourth bulwark of the quadrilateral stronghold is reason. Willingness to apply critical reasoning to all that has been asserted is required in order to avoid self-contradiction, to take appropriate account of scientific and historical knowledge, and to see the truth as a whole and not as disparate parts (Ambrose, *Duties* 1.24–28). The study of God is a cohesive, rational task of thinking out of revelation. Faith does not cease being active as it undertakes the process of rigorous thinking. One need not disavow the gifts of intellect in giving thought to their Giver (John Cassian, *Conferences*, First and Second Conferences of Abbot Moses).

Right use of reason in Catholic, Orthodox, and Protestant traditions resists the overextension of the claim of reason. Reason must not imagine itself as either omnicompetent or incompetent. The Christian tradition does not characteristically view reason as autonomous, as if completely separable from other relational, historical, and social modes of knowing the truth. Reason, rather, seeks to provide for religious discernment some appropriate tests of cogency and internal consistency (Theophilus, *To Autolycus* 1.3–2.4; Athenagoras, *Plea for Christians* 12–18). Reason explains, guards, and defends revealed truth (*Qui pluribus, SCD* 1635), and faith should not be thought of as contrary to right reason (*Syllabus of Errors, SCD* 1706).

The Christian study of God is, as Anselm taught, a faith that is seeking to understand itself (*fides quaerens intellectum*), a faith that is in search of its own intrinsic intelligibility in a way that respects mystery and knows its own limits. Christian teaching lives out of a community of faith that does not hesitate to ask serious questions about itself (Anselm, *Proslog.* 1). The knowledge we have of God is always a knowledge prone to potential distortions twisted by our own self-assertiveness, sin, evasions, and constricted vision.

We have limited competency to see even ourselves honestly, much less the whole of history. Nevertheless, the study of God proceeds with the powerful resources of Scripture as enlivened by the power of the Spirit, with candid admission of the recalcitrant egocentricity of the one seeking to know (Clement of Alex., *Strom.* 2.10–19). The study of God requires intellectual effort, historical imagination, empathic energy, and participation in a vital community of prayer (Augustine, *Answer to Skeptics*).

As the Word becomes proclaimed and heard, we appropriate it amid changing cultural experiences, reflect upon it by reason, and personally rediscover it in our own experience. The study of God best proceeds with the fitting equilibrium of these resources. The best minds of the historical Christian tradition, such as Origen, Gregory of Nazianzus, Augustine, Anselm, and Calvin, all utilized this equilibrium of sources in a functional, interdependent balance.

Creedal Tradition as an Authoritative Source for the Study of God

The Rule of Faith

The rule of faith (*regula fidei*) defines what is to be believed as necessary for salvation. The Bible contains all that is necessary to be believed, and the church is commissioned to teach nothing less than that faith revealed in Scripture (Second Helvetic *Conf.*; Tavard, *Holy Writ and Holy Church*). The creed is derived closely from the whole course and gist Scripture (Luther, *Brief Explanation*, *WML* 2). The rule of faith is summarized in the baptismal confession.

An article of faith must be based upon revelation, stated in Scripture, and ecclesiastically defined with ecumenical consent (Gallican *Conf.*, *COC* 3; Vincent of Lérins, *Comm.* 2, 20–24). Teachings that lack any of these conditions are matters of opinion left open for continued debate and speculation. The room for individual opinion among Christians is vast, provided those opinions are not repugnant to the rule of faith and charity (Chrysostom, *Hom. on 2 Tim*, 2–3).

Nothing is required of any believer other than that which is revealed by God through Scripture as necessary to salvation, as believed consensually by the Christian community as an article of faith reliably received by common ecumenical consent. The task of Christian teaching is to clarify, illuminate, cohesively interpret, and defend the convictions distinctive to Christianity that empower and enable the Christian life (Mark 7:4–9; 1 John 2:12–14).

Upholding the Earliest Apostolic Tradition.

Timothy was instructed: "Keep before you an outline of the sound teaching which you heard from me, living by the faith and love which are ours in Christ Jesus. Guard the treasure put into our charge, with the help of the Holy Spirit dwelling within us" (2 Tim. 1:13, 14). The first task of the Christian teacher is to "hold fast" the sound teaching passed on from the apostles. Timothy was not at liberty to teach his own private opinions or prejudices. Paul had provided a living model (hypotypōsis) for the Christian leader to follow (Tertullian, *On Prescript. Ag. Her.* 25).

There are strong injunctions in the New Testament itself to carefully transmit the apostolic teaching. Jesus taught the disciples that the Spirit would be given to "guide you into all the truth" (John 16:13). Paul faithfully passed on the tradition he had received, which he regarded as unalterable data: "I handed on to you the facts which had been imparted to me; that Christ died for our sins, in accordance with the scriptures" (1 Cor. 15:3). Paul regarded those in public ministry "as stewards of the secrets of God" who are "expected to show themselves trustworthy" in passing along the tradition (1 Cor. 4:1, 2). Timothy was implored to "keep safe that which has been entrusted to you. Turn a deaf ear to empty and worldly chatter, and the contradictions of the so-called 'knowledge,' for many who lay claim to it have shot far wide of the faith" (1 Tim. 6:20, 21). Along with objective accuracy, there remains a personal element in the transmission of tradition: "Stand by the truths you have learned and are assured of. Remember from whom you learned them; remember that from early childhood you have been familiar with the sacred writings which have power to make you wise and lead you to salvation through faith in Christ Jesus" (2 Tim. 3:14, 15; Gal. 1:8, 9; Clement of Alex., *Exhort. to the Heathen* IX; *Strom.* 2.11, 12; Jerome, *Letters* 52.7).

Humanly devised traditions that claimed to be divine revelation (among New Testament examples are detailed food or Sabbath prohibitions) were resisted and not confused with the divinely revealed tradition received from the apostles. "Do not let your minds be captured by hollow and delusive speculations, based on traditions of man-made teaching and centered on the elemental spirits of the universe and not on Christ" (Col. 2:8; 1 Tim. 1:4). Jesus rebuked the Pharisees because they neglected the commandment of God "in order to maintain the tradition of men" (Mark 7:8; Tertullian, *On the Soul* 1–2; *On Prescript Ag. Her.* 7). But the godly tradition concerning the memory of Jesus Christ must be maintained accurately and faithfully, since it is the living memory of God's own coming to humanity (Chrysostom, Hom. on Gal. 1.6).

The Didache enjoined readers to keep what had been received without adding or subtraction. Irenaeus (*Ag. Her.* 3.4.3) and Tertullian (*On Prescript. Ag. Her.* 29–35) thought that all heresies would be easily recognizable by their habit of making innovations upon the received the original apostolic tradition. Clement of Alexandria argued that the apostolic tradition was prior to heresy (*Strom.* 7.17). By searching the Scriptures any believer can compare later proposals for Christian understanding with the apostolic witness. Origen accepted as Christian teaching only that which had been taught by the apostles and mediated through accurate memory of tradition (*OFP* preface). Cyprian called Christ the fount of tradition (*Epis.* 73, 74). Antiquity of teaching, meaning the ancient teaching of the apostles, was one of the criteria of the Vincentian rule of faith (Lérins, *Comm.* 2–3). "The Holy Spirit was not promised to the successors of Peter that by His revelation they might make known new doctrine, but that by His assistance they might inviolably keep and faithfully expound the revelation or deposit of faith delivered through the apostles" (Vatican Council I, Constitution 1.4).

The importance of apostolic tradition is seen in a letter from Irenaeus to Florinus (in Eusebius, *CH* 5.20) in which Irenaeus remembered clearly that he had conversed personally with Polycarp, who himself had talked with the eyewitness John concerning the miracles and teachings of Jesus. Through only one intermediary, Irenaeus understood himself to be accurately and faithfully in touch with the original events of Christian revelation.

During the time in which Rome was the capital of the western world, it is not surprising that when local traditions were compared with one another and found to be somewhat different, localities would appeal to the Roman church to help them identify the truest form of the tradition. After all, people from all over the known world were meeting in Rome. Where better would there be a place to establish consensually the most authentic and consensual forms of traditioned memory? Thus the Roman memory of apostolic teaching came to have a widely respected value, along with Antioch, and Alexandria. In time the bishop of Rome came to have a widely acknowledged role as a crucial guardian of the apostolic tradition (Irenaeus, *Ag. Her.* 3.3; Tertullian, *On Prescript. Ag. Her.* 21, 32–36). The churches spread across the Roman Empire appealed to Rome to maintain tradition accurately and to guard those documents that most accurately presented the original tradition. Even the heretics appealed to the apostolic tradition for their support, only to find their views in due time rejected by the church itself on behalf of the apostolic written testimony. The position of Rome as capital of the empire made it an obvious center for Christian guardianship, along with Alexandria representing Africa and Antioch representing Asia. Even at the height of its prominence, however, Rome was never without correctives from other quarters.

The authority of any ancient Christian writer has weight only to the degree that he by general consent accurately represented the mind of the whole church. No single voice taken alone can claim to carry every nuance of the full consent of the whole church in all things. However great Augustine may have been, his views of predestination were never fully received and often modified, so those particular views can hardly be regarded as having received the consent necessary for being viewed as ancient ecumenical consensual tradition. Vincent of Lérins argued that even the church's greatest theologians may err, but these errors are in time corrected by the lack of consent (*Comm.* 10–11, 17, 28).

The strongest and surest medium of tradition is liturgy. Teaching is important, but not more so than the language of common prayer. The practices of baptism, Eucharist, Lord's Day services, and many elements of the Christian year are powerful safeguards for the retention of the teachings of the apostles. Even if preachers were known to be heretical, as long as they celebrated Holy Communion and baptism in due order, the liturgy is not invalidated, and the rite itself performs the ironic task of contradicting what has been badly taught (Augustine, *The Letters of Petilian, the Donatist* 45, 82).

By this means it is made clear that the Holy Spirit again and again turns human pride and distortion to the praise of God. The church has been guided by God's Spirit through many historical crises. New languages, concepts, and symbol systems have arisen repeatedly in the history of Christian teaching. For a time a disproportionate emphasis may have been given to one or another concept, but eventually all these concepts must stand the test of time and either be confirmed or rejected by the living ecumenical church under the guidance of the Spirit. The result is that by Scripture, creeds, transgenerational institutions, liturgy, and catechetical teaching, the Spirit continues to illuminate the mind of the church and to make the apostolic teaching recognizable.

Critical historical inquiry into Scripture and tradition is not antithetical to faith. Sound, probing criticism is constantly needed in order to discern the meaning of Scripture's testimony to the meaning of history. The Holy Spirit uses this too, to burn away the dross, to blow away the chaff. We are called by the Spirit to test all things in relation to divine inspiration: "Do not stifle inspiration, and do not despise prophetic utterance, but bring them all to the test and then keep what is good in them and avoid the bad of whatever kind" (1 Thess. 5:21; Dionysius of Alex., *Epistle 7*).

The Councils Seek Ecumenical Consent

It is in the light of this long-term sifting and discerning process that the general councils of the church must be seen and understood. The superintending church leaders (episkopoi—bishops) were authorized by their anointing and by lay consent to speak officially for the church. Their authority never functionally operated independently of either lay consent or apostolic tradition—at least not for long. Their views would not be received if they were not rooted in the ancient faith or if they are contrary to the mind of the historic church as a whole.

General councils are not infallible in themselves, but the Spirit that guides the church is fully trustable. The evidence has been repeatedly reconfirmed by general consent that the ecumenical councils have been blessed by the guidance of the Holy Spirit. The councils have sought to define questions under dispute in the light of scriptural teaching. Sometimes the general councils have failed to gain consent, as in the case of the Arian Council of Ariminum (AD 359) or the Council of Ephesus (449) that temporarily approved the Eutychian heresy, only later to be corrected by the church consensus (at Chalcedon, 451). That consent is what lets the councils know the mind of the church, and thus whether the council's decision was Spirit-led. A council's decrees must be ratified or confirmed by ecumenical consent if they are to be regarded as established. When that consent over a long period of time is given, the council becomes received as ecumenical teaching and is viewed by the whole church as rightly defining the church's teaching (Second Council of Nicaea, canon I). Conciliar decisions may remain unsettled for a very long time. Even while some questions are under suspended judgment, the church lives by Scripture, by its rule of faith and sacramental life, and by preaching.

Seven councils of the historic church are recognized as ecumenical councils, having the consent of the whole church over the largest span of time:

1. Nicaea, AD 325, defining the triune God in a way that rejected Arian claims;

2. Constantinople, AD 381, affirming Jesus' humanity against Appollinarianism and the Spirit's divinity against Macedonianism;

3. Ephesus, AD 431, affirming the unity of Christ's Person, and Mary as *theotokos*, against the Nestorians;

4. Chalcedon, AD 451, affirming the two natures of Christ against Eutychianism;

5. the Second Council of Constantinople, AD 553, against Nestorianism;

6. the Third Council of Constantinople (680–681) against Monothelitism; and

7. the Second Council of Nicaea (787) against Iconoclasm (Gregory I, *Pastoral Care*; *Epis.* 9. 105, 10.13; Tanner, *DEC* I; for definitions of rejected views see *EEC*).

The Living Tradition

The events of history make known the revelation of the will of God. This revelation is made palpable and concrete by the giving of a sacred deposit, Holy Writ, to be kept intact, neither added to nor taken away from. Paul repeatedly stressed: "If anyone, if we ourselves or an angel from heaven, should preach a gospel at variance with the gospel we preached to you, he shall be held outcast" (Gal. 1:8, 9). Jude thought it had become "urgently necessary to write at once and appeal to you to join the struggle in defense of the faith, the faith which God entrusted to his people once and for all. It is in danger from certain persons who have wormed their way in" (Jude 3, 4). From these passages it is evident that the effort at consensual definition and unified defense of the heart of faith began very early in Christian experience and did not await the second or third century (Theophylact, Comm. on Jude, 3).

This tradition was to be handed down from generation to generation. "Guard the treasure put into our charge, with the help of the Holy Spirit dwelling within us" (2 Tim. 1:14). "You heard my teaching in the presence of many witnesses; put that teaching into the charge of men you can trust, such men as will be competent to teach others" (2 Tim. 2:2). At this time there were no systematic theologies, but only highly prized apostolic texts circulating from congregation to congregation, containing accounts of the life of Jesus, a short outline of the beginning of church history immediately after the crucifixion, and a series of letters and visions written by or on behalf of primary apostolic eyewitnesses (Tertullian, *On Prescript. Ag. Her.* 36–44; John of Damascus, *Barlaam and Ioasaph* 36.335).

As these writings were read, preached, and canonized, the church has continued to live out of them, generation by generation. Among the most fundamental consensual decisions of the church is the affirmation that the Spirit will not lead the church in any direction that is contrary to the delivered written word (Basil, *On the Holy Spirit*; Pius 4, *SCD* 930; J. Meyendorff, *Living Tradition*). The church lives out of the Spirit who called forth the testimony of scriptures. Those who insist upon expounding one Scripture in such a way that it is repugnant to another Scripture have not listened sufficiently to the one Spirit attesting the one Lord through the many voices of Scripture (Thirty-nine Articles XX). Scriptural arguments for teaching and discipling are best derived from a fair and careful comparison of all relevant texts of Scripture, heard in the light of the classic consensus (Augustine, *Proceedings of Pelagius*, 14.35). In this way the Bible is received as containing everything required to believe as an article of faith. The church keeps the book, learns from the book, and seeks to assess varied interpretations of the book in terms of total witness of the book itself.

Scripture and Tradition

Persecution Required an Oral Tradition

The written word of canonical scripture is to be openly proclaimed to all, but in addition to this some of the most revered early writers (notably Basil) assumed that the church had received a reliable oral apostolic tradition guarded through centuries of persecution by forced silence permeated by mystery.

Some otherwise fair-minded historians offer only grudging attention to this hounded, threatened, molested, countercultural tradition of hagiography and martyrdom that was so persecuted and despised that it could not even write things down but had to commit them to memory.

Among numerous examples of holy unwritten tradition mentioned by Basil are triune immersion, common prayer on the first day of the week, bending knees in prayer and the sign of the cross. In these cases there is no residue in the canon of scripture of a written apostolic tradition. But that absence did not diminish their authority during the first five centuries. These practices were received consensually as unwritten traditions from the apostles shrouded in silence "out of the reach of curious meddling and inquisitive investigation. Well had they learned the lesson that the awful dignity of the mysteries is best preserved by silence. What the uninitiated are not even allowed to look at was hardly likely to be publicly paraded about in written documents" (Basil, *On the Spirit* 27.66).

By analogy, Moses did not make all parts of the tabernacle open to all. Unbelievers did not enter at all, and the faithful were admitted only to its outer precincts. The Levites alone were allowed to serve in worship offering temple sacrifices. Only one priest was allowed to enter the holy of holies, and that only once each year.

Basil applied this analogy: "If, as in a Court of Law, we were at a loss of documentary [written] evidence, but were able to bring before you a large number of [oral] witnesses, would you not give your vote for our acquittal?" On this basis Basil cherished the phrase "with the Spirit" in the doxology "as a legacy left me by my fathers"—specifically citing Irenaeus, Clement, Origen, Dionysius of Rome, Gregory Thaumaturgus, Firmilian, Eusebius, and Julius Africanus. "Thus I apprehend, the powerful influence of tradition frequently impels men to express themselves in terms contradictory to their own opinions . . . How then can I be an innovator and creator of new terms." Basil argued that memories and practices evidently familiar to those generations immediately following the apostles and "continued by long usage" should remain highly valued in Christian teaching (*On the Spirit* 3.29; Augustine, *Letters*).

Yet oral tradition, however precious, is always subject to uncertainty and speculation, as we have found in form-criticism. Thus the focus of orthodox Christian teaching remains fixed upon the written word and the early written documents interpreting that word. Meanwhile Basil still calls the worshiping community to listen attentively to those known oral and hagiographic traditions widely received as apostolic memory and practice, and not dismiss them quickly as if they had no value, as if modern readers could look only to documentary written evidences recognized under the rules of the game of reductionistic historical methods.

The Plain Sense of Scripture and Spiritual Interpretation

When conflicting interpretations of scripture arise, the classic rule of interpretation may be appealed to: "Ask your father and he will tell you, your elders, and they will explain to you" (Deut. 32:7, see also the proverb on "not removing ancient boundary stones; Prov. 22:28; Vincent of Lérins, *Commonit.* 21, 27). These boundary stones were consensually assumed to be firmly established in the early ecumenical councils and consensual exegetes, so that subsequently those who "rashly seek for novelties and expositions of another faith" were found wanting by general lay consent of "all the people" who say to these councils, "So be it, so be it [Ps. 105:48]" (Lateran Council, SCD 274).

The Synod of Dort exhorted both universities and churches "to regulate, by the Scripture, according to the analogy of faith, not only their sentiments, but also their language, and to abstain from all those phrases which exceed the limits necessary to be observed in ascertaining the genuine sense of the Holy Scriptures." As "witness and keeper of holy Writ" the church is not so unconstrained that it may "so expound one place of Scripture that it be repugnant to another" (Irish Articles, 75).

The plain sense or literal meaning of a scripture text must be sought first. But where a text has multiple meanings and layers of potential interpretation, its spiritual meaning is sought and often adequately defined by classic exegesis.

The earliest exegetes, Irenaeus, Clement, Origen, and Tertullian, while leaving room for varied interpretations of scripture, assumed a position of basic subordination of all legitimate interpretations to the rule of faith—the baptismal confession. Where one text of scripture appeared contradictory to another, they reasoned by analogy from clear passages, looking for spiritual insight consistent with the rule of faith, assuming that the Holy Spirit had veiled the outward expression for some purpose. As the person has body, soul, and spirit in union, so does the interpretation of scripture often have not only a literal and moral, but also a spiritual or anagogic or mystical meaning (Irenaeus, *Ag. Her.* 3; Clement, *Stromata*; Origen, *OFP* 4; *Ag. Celsus* 5.60; 6.7; Tertullian, *Ag. Praxeas* 18–21).

Against Proof-Texting Quotes Contrary to Their Context

Some may charge that the method of classical Christian exegesis condones noncontextual proof-texting. Classic Christian teaching allows that a canonical sacred text may be quoted in the service of preaching without exhaustive explication of its context, provided it is not quoted against its context, or used in some way contrary to that which is implied or assumed in its context. This assumes that the context is always open for further inquiry.

This distinction protects Christian teaching from being reduced simply to a detached historical exercise of investigating the contexts of the written word, a valuable activity but not identical with Christian preaching or teaching. It also protects Christian preaching from the tendency to overextend the text apart from its context uncritically, without attending to the author's intent or meaning.

The classic exegetes developed a highly refined pattern of referencing. From apostolic times the privilege to cite scriptural loci has belonged to the freedom to preach. No one can preach reliably without quoting or in some way referencing scripture. It is precisely the attempt to preach without scripture that has undermined preaching in our time. It is a modern prejudice that requires that each scripture reference be exhaustively placed in its cultural frame of reference. That prejudice becomes an excuse for controlling the text.

Ancient ecumenical orthodoxy unapologetically makes reference to texts of holy writ without the tedious necessity of detailing their context. Meanwhile there remains another legitimate arena of historical inquiry in which each of these texts may be studied in their varied contexts. The fullness of this inquiry requires more time than most have available, if they are daily involved in the real responsibilities of family and vocation. Hence God has provided an ordered sacred ministry distinguishable from and representative of the general ministry of the laity, which is being freed and supported in order to study all these matters in sufficient detail to make them clear to the whole *laos* of God. This is the very purpose for which ministers are freed from other vocational burdens: to engage in this daily study of holy writ, including its historical context, the social location of writers and speakers, the history of its transmission and interpretation, and the array of cultural differences through which the address of God the Spirit moves.

Whether the Study of God Is a Science

The Scientific Character of Christian Inquiry

Insofar as it seeks to make accurate observations, test evidence, provide fit hypotheses, arrange facts in due order, and make reliable generalizations, the study of God may be called a science. From the birth of the university, theology has been viewed as a science in the sense of a way of knowing. Historically viewed, the very word, science, is deeply interwoven with the study of God. It employs both inductive and deductive argument. It relies upon the same primary laws of thought and the same categories of reason upon which all scientific inquiry depends. A science is a branch of study concerned with the observation and classification of facts and the establishment of verifiable general laws through induction and hypothesis. Such studies are familiar to Christian teaching, so much so that their history cannot be defined apart from their use in Christian teaching.

The methods of inquiry into Christianity are held by many classical Christian writers to be a "science," according to the classical definition of *scientia* as an orderly knowing or knowledge, or a *disciplina*, as instruction or teaching or body of knowledge (Bonaventure, *Breviloquium*, prologue; Tho. Aq., *Compend.*:2, 22, 35, 36, 42). But the facts into which Christian teaching inquires are brought from an arena that is thought by some to be excluded from scientific investigation: religious consciousness, moral awareness, the life of the spirit, and the history of revelation (Hume, *Dialogues*; Kant, *Critique of Pure Reason*).

No scientific inquiry proceeds without axioms and postulates that do not admit of empirical demonstration. Geometric inquiry, for instance, depends upon the postulate of parallels, but that postulate is far from being finally demonstrable. The view that scientific inquiry is independent of all authority is itself quite distorted. Theology is that sort of science that proceeds with a specific postulate: historical revelation (Irenaeus, *Ag. Her.* 4.33.7.8), the premise that history reveals its meaning.

Theology has a definite object to investigate, namely, the understanding of God as known in the Christian community. There is no doubt that such an understanding exists, and that it is capable of being analyzed. It is a historical fact that the modern university since the thirteenth century has been spawned in large part by the inductive and deductive methods developed by Jewish, Muslim, and Christian inquiry concerning God. For centuries there has been a community that takes as a subject of scientific investigation the modes of awareness of God that recur in Christian communities: the belief in God, that God exists, that God is triune, and that God pardons sin (Schleiermacher, *The Chr. Faith*; Aulen, *The Faith of the Chr. Church*). Those who claim that such an inquiry is irrational must come up with good reasons for their claim.

No botanist claims to originate the basic order by which plant life lives. Rather, the botanist ascertains an order that is already present in the nature of the facts themselves. Similarly the theologian is not the master of the facts, but their servant. The theologian cannot construct a system of Christian teaching to suit his or her fancy, any more than the geologist can rearrange the strata of rocks according to aesthetic whim. Christian theology simply wishes to set forth that understanding of God that is known in the Christian community in a way that is fitting to its own proper order, harmonizing that wide body of facts and data so as to preserve their intrinsic relation to one another (Rufinus, *On the Creed*; Nicolas of Cusa, *Concerning Wisdom*, U&R: 101–27).

The Presentation of Evidence in the Study of God

The spirit of scientific inquiry is open-minded and unprejudiced. It does not omit relevant facts and is receptive to new evidence. This is the fundamental attitude or spirit that provides common ground for all the various sciences.

Within this common spirit there are wide differences between the methods used in various sciences. For example, insofar as psychology is a science, it gathers empirical evidence on the basis of controlled studies, but psychology has found it difficult to rule out intuitive insight and holistic reasoning. Insofar as history is a science, it bases its conclusions on historical evidence and documentary witnesses, and has the same problems with establishing textual authenticity that theology does.

The forms of evidence differ widely for physical, historical, and spiritual truth (1 Cor. 2:10–16; Clement of Alex., *Strom.* 1.6–20). Truth in the physical realm must be established by empirical data gathering and experiment, and truth in the historical realm by testimony, documentation, and correlation of evidence. Truth in the spiritual realm must be tested in a more complex way, by examination of oneself, of history, of conscience, of one's sense of rational cohesion, and of claims of divine self-disclosure. Each sphere of inquiry must submit evidence appropriate to its subject (Irenaeus, *Ag. Her.* 4.31–33; Origen, Comm. on 1 Cor. 2:10).

The forms of evidence that are presented in Christian teaching include scientific inquiry and demonstration, but they also include the kinds of evidence found in legal science, namely, the presentation of cases, circumstantial evidence, and testimony of eyewitnesses (2 Cor. 13:1; Acts 22:18). As legal inquiry proceeds from texts, testimony, and precedents, so the study of God deals with consensual precedents, with texts and testimonies of eyewitnesses to God's self-disclosure, and with consensual precedents that interpret these events (Luke 1:2; 2 Pet. 1:16).

Christian teaching characteristically appeals to many different levels of evidence—historical testimony, moral awareness, life experience, the social history of a people, and the history of revelation—in order to establish a convergence of plausibility along different and complementary lines (1 Thess. 1:10; Titus 1:13; 1 John 5:9; 3 John 12).

As logical reasoning begins from concepts and ideas and proceeds to conclusions, so does much theological reasoning proceed from idea to idea inquiring into how those ideas are related logically. Well-developed and rightly presented evidence tends to elicit in the mind a sense of conviction of truth that resembles what Christianity calls belief or faith. Judgment moves with evidence (John 5:31–36; 1 Tim. 2:6; Hilary, *Trin.*,6.27).

The reason we demand higher certainty for religious assertions than historical assertions is a telling one: They have more behavioral consequences if we accept them. When the same level of evidence exists for Caesar and Christ, the testimony concerning Caesar remains largely uncontested, whereas that of Christ is hotly contested. The reason is that inquirers know all too well that they have a stake in the result of the inquiry. The eternal destiny of the soul is alleged to be at risk. While it makes little difference to us now what Caesar said or did, it makes decisive difference whether God has become flesh and is revealed personally (Augustine, *Tractates on John* 23.3.1–2). Information about Caesar does not require me to bear a cross. Information about Jesus if rightly understood does.

At first it may seem to be a decided disadvantage to Christian teaching that it cannot establish its facts with the same objective or controlled certainty that physics and chemistry usually can. But there may be a hidden advantage to this seeming limitation. For if religious truth were capable of absolute objective certainty, then faith would become as mechanical as a math formula and as cold as a glacial ice flow. If religious conclusions had this compulsory and objective character because of the absolutely overwhelming character of objective evidence, then would there not be less room for decision and risk in faith? God would no longer be the incomprehensible, majestic One worthy of our worship and obedience, but merely a rationalized object of empirical data gathering. No longer would "the just live by faith" (Hab. 2:4; Rom. 1:17; Heb. 10:38), with all the character building this involves. Christian faith would cease to be a choice altogether (Kierkegaard, *Either/Or* 2; *Fear and Trembling*; *Concl. Unsci. Post.*:198, 226).

Whether the Study of God Requires a Special Temperament

Just as a wise judge requires a judicial temperament, or a teacher a pedagogical temperament, so does a good mentor in Christian truth require a "theological temperament." The classic Christian pastors referred frequently to certain tempers, dispositions, or habits of mind that tend to engender responsible study of God. However much modern skepticism may disparage these qualities, they remain important ideals, if not imperatives. Among these qualities are:

Humility in the Face of Truth. The lowered level of egocentricity and the humbled self-awareness that accompany sound Christian discipleship arise out of a realistic consciousness of one's actual ignorance, the limitations of one's knowledge, one's tendency to be deceived, and one's egoistic interpretation of the facts (Clement of Rome, *Corinth*, 1.13; Gregory Nazianzus, *First Theol. Orat.*). It is to the humble that God teaches "his ways" (Ps. 25:9). "Do you see that man who thinks himself so wise? There is more hope for a fool than for him" (Prov. 26:12). "Thus Scripture says, 'God opposes the arrogant and gives grace to the humble'" (James 4:6). Jesus said: "Let a man humble himself till he is like this child, and he will be the greatest in the kingdom of Heaven" (Matt. 18:4, Rufinus, *On the Creed* I; Sulpitius Severus, *Life of St. Martin*, preface).

Reverence. Awe in the presence of God is viewed as "the beginning of wisdom" (Simeon, *Hymns of Divine Love* 20; Maximus the Confessor, *Four Centuries on Charity* 4.1, 2). Those who live out of this reverence are far more likely to "grow in understanding" (Ps. 111:10; Cyprian, treatise 12.20). "The fear of the Lord is the beginning of knowledge, but fools scorn wisdom and discipline" (Prov. 1:7). When Moses beheld the bush on fire but not being burned up, he asked why. Yahweh answered: "Come no nearer; take off your sandals; the place where you are standing is holy ground" (Exod. 3:5; Ambrose, *Flight from the World* 5.25). Not everyone stands ready to come into God's presence: "Who may go up to the mountain of the Lord? And who may stand in his holy place? He who has clean hands and a pure heart, who has not set his mind on falsehood, and has not committed perjury. He shall receive a blessing from the Lord" (Ps. 24:3–5).

Patience. Patience is the habitual disposition to bear with trials and frustrations without complaint, to exercise forbearance under difficulties, to be undisturbed by obstacles, delays, and failures, and to persevere with diligence until the gridlock is broken or the predicament rightly grasped (Tertullian, *On Patience,* ANF 3:707–17). Those who would think with haste about God are apt to pass God by. Only through patience does one "acquire one's soul" (Luke 21:19; Kierkegaard, *Edifying Discourses* 2.2; 3.1).

Prayer for Divine Illumination. The thoughtful study of God begins with an attitude of openness and receptivity to God, inviting God's presence and inspiration to enable one's thoughts to be, so far as possible, fitting to the divine reality (Origen, *Letter to Gregory* 3). It continues with the supplication: "Take the veil from my eyes, that I may see the marvels that spring from thy law. I am but a stranger here on earth, do not hide thy commandments from me" (Ps. 119:18, 19; Origen, *Ag. Celsus* 4.50). James urged us to ask for wisdom: "If any of you falls short in wisdom, he should ask God for it and it will be given him, for God is a generous giver who neither refuses nor reproaches anyone. But he must ask in faith, without a doubt in his mind" (James 1:5, 6; Augustine, *On Chr. Doctrine* 4.30).

The Heartfelt Obedience that Faith Elicits. If the study of God remains unaccompanied by "the obedience of faith" (Rom. 1:26), it is likely to become undisciplined self-expression. No temperament is more crucial to the quest for Christian truth than obedience, or wholehearted responsiveness (*hypakoē*) to the divine address. Obedience implies not merely hearing the truth, but acting upon it without delay so as to embody it now in one's life (Simeon, *Hymns of Divine Love* 45; Oden, *Radical Obedience:*9–11).

Jesus said: "Why do you keep calling me 'Lord, Lord'—and never do what I tell you? Everyone who comes to me and hears what I say, and acts upon it—I will show you what he is like. He is like a man who, in building his house, dug deep and laid the foundations on rock" (Luke 6:46–48). "What of the man who hears these words of mine and does not act upon them? He is like a man who was foolish enough to build his house on sand" (Matt. 7:26). "Happy are those who hear the word of God and keep it" (Luke 11:28). "Only be sure that you act on the message and do not merely listen; for that would be to mislead yourselves. A man who listens to the message but never acts upon it is like one who looks in a mirror at the face nature gave him. He glances at himself and goes away, and at once forgets what he looked like" (James 1:22–24). Paul called for "the obedience that comes from faith" (Rom. 1:5), which through Christ's obedience leads to righteousness (Rom. 5:19; 6:16; Heb. 5:8), which in turn calls for our active responsiveness that it may become complete (2 Cor. 10:6; Ambrosiaster, *Comm. on Paul's Epistles,* Rom. 6:17).

Integrity. Classical pastoral writers viewed integrity of thought and speech as a mark of responsible Christian teaching (1 Cor. 5:8; 2 Cor. 8:8). "In your teaching, you must show integrity and high principle, and use wholesome speech to which none can take exception" (Titus 2:7, 8). Aptness to teach was thought to include one's ability when serving in public ministry to confine oneself strictly to the exposition of the truth of Scripture and its implications, suppressing to a large degree subjective opinion, supposed private revelations, unnecessary matters of controversy, and matters upon which one has no authority to speak (Quinisext Council, canon 19;. Baxter, *PW* 5:428). Integrity requires the determination to study and teach integrally the whole Word of God in fitting balance, without omission of central truths, after the pattern of Paul, who wrote: "I have kept back nothing; I have disclosed to you the whole purpose of God" (Acts 20:27; Tertullian, *On Prescript. Ag. Her.* 25–26; Wesley, *WJW* 8:283, 317).

The Willingness to Suffer for the Truth. No Christian teacher or exponent is worth listening to who is not willing to suffer if need be for the truth of what is taught (1 Pet. 4:13–5:9; *The Martyrdom of Polycarp*). The readiness to suffer for the sake of the truth is an intrinsic part of the whole fabric of Christian living, and hence teaching, and thus not an optional part of the equipping of the public teacher of Christianity (Phil. 3:10; Cyprian, *On the Lapsed*; Kierkegaard, *Attack on "Christendom"*).

Paul stated the principle clearly to Timothy: "Take your share of hardship, like a good soldier of Christ Jesus. A soldier on active service will not let himself be involved in civilian affairs" (2 Tim. 2:3, 4). Paul's teaching was personally validated by his willingness to be "exposed to hardship, even to the point of being shut up like a common criminal; but the word of God is not shut up" (2 Tim. 2:9). Those who teach faithfully of the one who was "nailed to the cross" know that some hearers will find in the truth a "stumbling-block" and "folly" (1 Cor. 1:23; Rom. 8:17, 18). Jesus did not hesitate to make it clear that his disciples must be prepared if necessary to "be handed over for punishment and execution; and men of all nations will hate you for your allegiance to me" (Matt. 24:9; Irenaeus, *Ag. Her.* 4.33.9).

Luther divulged in a comic-pathetic voice how much he owed to his enemies, for "through the raging of the devil they have so buffeted , distressed, and terrified me that they have made me a fairly good theologian, which I would not have become without them" (Luther, *WLS* 3:1358–60).

The Disciplined Mind

Christian reflection calls for many of the same intellectual abilities that are expected of the philosopher or jurist or historian (Augustine, *On Chr. Doctrine* 2.1–12): clear reasoning, right discernment of the relations between seemingly distant and varied teachings, multilayered powers of intuitive insight, sound movement from premises to conclusions, capacity for critical analysis, and the power of internally consistent reflection (Justin Martyr, *Dialogue with Trypho* 1, 2; Augustine, *Soliloquies*).

One is ill prepared who has not learned how to spot leaps in logic and spurious arguments. So varied are the questions under consideration, and so complex the evidence, that serious misjudgment at one point is likely to elicit a wave of distortions at subsequent points. A disciplined mind is ready to listen wisely, collect facts, hold many facts together in creative tension, and draw conclusions upon which the faithful can rely (Minucius Felix, *Octavius* 13–20; Augustine, *Catech. Lect.* 1.1–3).

A steady temperament is required for the right study of God: fairness of judgment, impartiality in weighing evidence, and respect for others (Augustine, *On the Profit of Believing* 14–22; Tho. Aq., *ST* 1 Q16). Without deep self-awareness, Baxter argued, studies easily become irrational and misguided (*PW* 16: 97–101).

Since Christian teaching rests upon both truth-seeking and clarity of communication, it requires qualities necessary to those disciplines: the search for an accurate text, empathic willingness to listen to ancient sources whose assumptions differ from one's own culture, and an intellectual balance that brings complex materials into meaningful focus (Clement of Alex., *Strom.* 8).

The laity pray for the gift of discernment in their mentors and teachers (Prov. 14:6; Phil. 1:10; 1 Cor. 2:14). Discernment seeks to grasp first principles and fundamental convictions that lie prior to all argument so as to precondition reasoning. The realm of inspired truth into which the student of Scripture enters is not just an account book or a machine or a math problem or a political campaign or an advertising strategy (Baxter, *PW* 2:238). Rather it is a realm that requires listening—to the Spirit witnessing inwardly within oneself, to the witness of others, and to the Source and End of all things, whose mighty deeds in history call forth the inquiry (Clement of Alex., *Exhort. to the Heathen* 9). "You shall know his power today if you will listen to his voice" (Ps. 95:7).

Viewed merely as an intriguing or fascinating subject, however, the study of God may become reduced simply to an object of aesthetic interest, so that one becomes easily tired of hearing of the infinite. The subject of God would soon become boring (Kierkegaard, *Either/Or* I, "The Rotation Method").

This is why the study of God is said to depend through grace upon certain intellectual and moral virtues for its proper accomplishment: patience, love of truth, courage to follow one's convictions, humility in the face of the facts, loyalty to the truth, and a profound sense of awe in the presence of the truth (Tho. Aq., *ST* 1–2 Q59–66). These same virtues are also required in other sciences, but in the study of God their absence is more keenly felt. The student of theology cannot claim exemption from these requisites on the grounds of special providential calling or extraordinary experience (Calvin, *Inst.* 2.8; Baxter, *PW* 5: 575–84). Rigorous study is rightly viewed as a duty for those who serve in the office of ministry, and not merely a matter of inclination (Ambrose, *Duties* 3.2, 3).

Anyone who seeks to understand the living God celebrated in Christian worship must be willing to enter into the sphere in which praise, intercession, and supplication are taken seriously. One cannot conveniently stand outside the church and expect to know what is happening inside from reading about it. If the Christian life can only be known from within, then the study of God is a subject that requires entry, engagement, and concrete participation in the worshiping community (Gregory Nazianzus, *Orat.* 2,). Just as there could be no thorough study of Verdi without ever hearing Verdi, and no profound sociology of bedouin life without ever living with bedouins, so there can be no good theology without actively and sympathetically entering into the community whose understanding one is seeking to set forth (Basil, *Concerning Baptism*; Ambrose, *On the Mysteries*).

A Habit of Mind

It is only with sustained practice that one gradually grows into having a well-furnished theological habit of mind disposed to look carefully at language about God and to use language responsibly in the light of Scripture, tradition, and good moral sense (Tho. Aq., *ST* 1–2 Q49; Baxter, *PW* 21:162). It is a habit that is willing to ask probing questions about human thoughts on God and to view those questions in the light of Scripture and tradition, correlated with personal and social experience (Augustine, *On Chr. Doctrine* 4; Calvin, *Inst.* 2.15, 16; Wesley, *WJW* 6:351). Mentors in Christian teaching may be deficient if they lack prudence, contextual wisdom, and the capacity to enter the world of moral action and practical outcomes. One who lacks a capacity for imagination, wonder, and reflection may not be suited to seek a more comprehensive view of things (Bonaventure, *The Mind's Ascent into God*). Thomas Aquinas described the study of God as a habit of mind that seeks to combine theoretical wisdom and analytical ability with practical and social wisdom.

To learn to dance one must take that first step, even if awkwardly. Good theology is more than a tome or a string of good sentences. It is a way of dancing, an embodied activity of the human spirit in a community embodying life in Christ. Learning to live in God's presence is something like learning to dance; it is not best learned merely by reading books.

As in sport one learns to play according to the rules—one does not invent new rules as the game proceeds—similarly, the study of God requires learning to think according to well-established, well-tested rules. The inquiry into method in the study of God seeks to review these elementary rules (for influential ecumenical models see Cyril of Jerusalem, *Procatechesis*; Augustine, *On Chr. Doctrine*).

The goal of the study of God is the delight of knowing God better with our minds, the pleasure of making sense, the joy of understanding and knowing the blessedness of divinity—an incomparably intriguing subject (Tho. Aq., *ST* 1–2 Q31–34; Calvin, *Inst.* 3.25.10). What other study touches everything else in touching its own distinctive subject matter?

The Hazards of Searching for God

The very greatness of the subject matter of God tends to intoxicate. Those who come under its influence may wrongly imagine that they are thereby morally above other Christians. When certain Corinthians thought they had become extraordinarily well informed, Paul wrote: "This 'knowledge' of yours is utter disaster to the weak, the brother for whom Christ died" (1 Cor. 8:11). Again: "This 'knowledge' breeds conceit; it is love that builds. If anyone fancies that he knows, he knows nothing yet, in the true sense of knowing. But if a man loves, he is acknowledged by God" (1 Cor. 8:1–3; Irenaeus, *Ag. Her.* 4.12.2; 4.33.8).

The study of God indeed enlarges our minds, provides the intellect with the loftiest themes upon which the human mind can dwell, addresses moral conscience with the veritable claim of God, and seeks to enliven the deepest religious impulses in human life. Yet it can elicit pride. At best, it brings "good tidings of great joy" (Luke 2:10), addressing every hearer, however bored, anxious, or guilty, with the blessing of God's pardon and peace. It invites people to a new life of responsible love and accountability to God for their neighbor. Yet it can become egocentrically distorted. Those who nonetheless choose to walk this path do well to remember the injunction of Moses: "For you they are no empty words; they are your very life" (Deut. 32:47).

The Study of God in General Lay Ministries and Ordained Ministries

The study of God is a habit of mind that seeks to call upon God's name appropriately, pray and praise fittingly, proclaim God's action meaningfully, and set forth courageously the ethical responsibility flowing from the gospel. As a rigorous, unified discipline of study, theology in turn is correlated with companion university disciplines that seek truth in all areas.

This raises the question of how theology is at once specially related to ordained ministries whose purpose is to enable and empower the general ministry of the laity. Not only the ordained, but laypersons in general, especially parents, are called to be teachers of faith, since Scripture and Christian teaching are rightly studied by all believers (Luther, *Comm. on Rom.* 12:7; Chemnitz, *MWS*:14; Gerhard, *De Natura Theologiae*, 4).

Yet it has long been the custom to use the term *theology* to speak of that knowledge necessary for the office of ordained ministry. In this sense theology is particularly related to a vocational practice that presupposes a particular standard of education (*paideia*) based on aptitude (*hikanotēs*, in Latin *habitus*) and certain gifts (*charismata*) engendered by the Holy Spirit (1 Cor. 12; Eph. 4:7–16). Leaders who perform pastoral service must know how to teach the faith, "rightly dividing the Word of truth" (2 Tim. 2:15) made known in Scripture, so as to lead sinners from idolatry, through doubt, to faith, hope, and love in Christ (1 Cor. 13). To do this they must become pastoral theologians—those who think deeply about the pastoral gifts and tasks as part of their responsibility for the care of others in the Christian community (Chrysostom, *On the Priesthood* 2–6).

Lay theology is that knowledge which all baptized believers are expected to have grasped, at least in an elementary fashion. Confirmation centers upon the question of developing in young people and inquirers a rudimentary awareness of the truth of the Christian faith and of the baptism in which we are baptized. Whether lay or clergy, the subject matter is precisely the same. But theology in preparation for ordained ministry pursues more deliberately, intentionally, critically and intensely the ground, roots, consequences, and practical effects of that same faith, in order vocationally to prepare the person to serve in the office of public ministry (Synod of Laodicea, canon 46; Second Council of Nicaea; Theophilus of Alex., *Prosphonesus*, canon 6).

Those who answer the call to sacred ministry must be prepared for an intensive inquiry into the living God, the Word of life, and life in the Spirit at a depth that laypersons do not ordinarily assume to be necessary for themselves (Tho. Aq., *ST Suppl.* Q34–40; Chemnitz, *MWS*:14).

Many laypersons have attained high proficiency in the study of God (Descartes, *Meditations*; Milton, *Areopagitica*; Kierkegaard, *Concl. Unsci. Post.*). There remains, however, a missional distinction, though not a difference in faith, between general ministry and ordained ministry. For the ordained minister is duly authorized and appointed to perform a representative ministry on behalf of the whole community of the baptized (Ambrose, *On the Duties of the Clergy* 1.1; Leo I, *Letters* 6, *To Anastasius*; Gregory I, *Pastoral Rule* 1). The whole body of the faithful needs leadership in order rightly to hear the preached Word, receive the sacraments, and be ready to benefit from thoughtful pastoral care (Thirty-nine Articles of Religion 23–30).

The Study of Religion and the Study of God

Since God has never left himself without witness (Acts 14:17), humanity has never been without religion in some form. The hunger for God does not fully disappear even in an atheistic society in which religion is coercively disavowed. God is nearer to human life than we can know even while we are searching for God (Acts 17:24–28) or running away from God (Jonah 1, 2).

The best Christian teaching is not contemptuous of other religions, but views each history of religious struggle as evidence of divine providence and the presence of the Holy Spirit in all human history. Christians can learn from these histories of religions powerful insights that bestow greater light upon the biblical understanding of God (Tho. Aq., *SCG* 1.20; Wesley, *WJW* 6:508; 8:203, 244, 471).

There is a creative tension between the two etymologies of the term religion. In the first, religion is an instinctive aspiration of the human mind, an inbuilt inclination to ponder or to go over and over again thought of absolute duty (*religere*), as if an absolute duty were somehow owed by all who live (Cicero, *De Natura Deorum* 2.28). In the second, religion is that which binds (*religare*) humanity to an awareness of the divine through rites, institutions, customs, and morality, in which the religious sentiment finds expression in worship, duty, and fellowship (Lactantius, *Div. Inst.* 4.28, 29).

These two views may be linked in the view that human nature tends instinctively to turn to God in prayer so persistently that this eventually becomes bound, by custom and established practice, into a religion. Religion has to do with *religio*, a reverent, dutiful turning of the spirit toward God manifested in conduct and in communities of worship (Chrysostom, *Concerning the Statues* 4.6–12). Religion refers to the means by which one's life before God becomes sustained and expressed in terms of community, ritual, institutional life, and moral responsibility (Acts 25:19; 26:5; 1 Tim. 5:4; Augustine, *CG* 10.1; Calvin, *Inst.* 1.12.1).

Christianity and the Religions

Religion is viewed in classic Christianity as a universal human phenomenon. Religion implies an institutional context, priesthood, ritual, and worship, however varied in human history. Christianity is a religion, but a religion in a special sense that it views itself as completing and fulfilling the idea of religion. A religion may be said to be "true" insofar as it leads people to the true God and to life in communion with the true God (1 John 5:20; James 1:26, 27). Christianity does not claim that no truth exists in other religions, but rather, amid all the half-truths that parade under the religions, including Christianity, the true God has become personally revealed once for all in history.

Religion addresses the interior life, the inward life of the soul, in giving thanks, confessing our human inadequacies, and seeking a comprehensive view of reality. Thus religion affects behavior in the most diffuse and fundamental ways (Tho. Aq., *SCG* 3.2.120; *Compend. Theol.*:248).

If so, what then is the relation of Christian study of God to general religious consciousness? The heart of Christian study of God concerns that knowledge of God the Father that is revealed in the Son through the Spirit (Lactantius, *Div. Inst.* 4.29). Christian Scripture and tradition view the religions in this sense as preparatory for the revelation of God the Father through the Son, the Revealer, Jesus Christ (Lactantius, *Div. Inst.* 6.10; Eusebius, *Preparation for the Gospel*).

If religions in human history all have to do with the way human beings worship and respond to God, then Christian theology seems to belong to the broader study of religion. Classical Christian teachers have often thought of Christianity under the concept of "true religion," arguing that it is the appropriate and most fitting turn of humanity toward God, namely in response to God's own turning toward humanity (Augustine, *On the Profit of Believing* 28).

How Christianity Differs from Religion

All the standard questions raised in universal religious consciousness are also raised in Christianity: Who am I? How did the world come to be? What is good or evil, right or wrong? To whom am I finally accountable? Will I live after death? How can I know the eternal One who transcends all temporal realities? Why do I suffer? These are questions that are familiar to Islam, Buddhism, Hinduism, and other world religions. Christian theology is not entering an arena of questioning that has never been entered by other religions. But the overall interpretation of the meaning of universal history that it provides comes, not from human insight or ingenuity or moral struggle or intellect, but from God's own personal coming into history. All religions contain some truth concerning God, for God has not left himself without witness. Yet Jesus' own words ring in the ears of believers: "No one comes to the Father except by me" (John 14:6; Augustine, *Christian Instruction* 1.34.38).

Christianity is sometimes termed *true religion* by the classical exegetes because it has all the requisites of true religion. If religion in its proper sense is the fitting worship of God and the disposition of the soul toward God in a manner agreeable to God, and if religion manifests itself in love for the neighbor and the embodiment of the virtuous life, then Christianity is true religion, whose object of worship is not a false god but the One who makes himself truly known as God (Augustine, *CG* 19.25; *On the Profit of Believing* 14). The classical teachers have not meant to imply thereby that any existing statement holds absolute knowledge of God (such as God has of himself), but that in the future history will prove that Jesus Christ is Lord. It is true in the form of promise, the promise of that fuller knowledge of God that the faithful are promised to have at the end time. Paul candidly admitted: "My knowledge now is partial; then it will be whole, like God's knowledge of me" (1 Cor. 13:12). Christianity is viewed as conveying God's saving work with full adequacy, so that humanity needs no further disclosure of subsequent divine revelation. Christianity is not true religion because its moral code is adequate to reflect God's righteousness, but because God's forgiveness of our moral lapses is sufficient. One hid in Christ is declared righteous before God (Rom. 3:28; 1 Cor. 2:4, 5), which means that the believer by grace is assuredly accepted in God's sight. "In him you have been brought to completion" (Col. 2:10). The sole source of true religion is not any human moral or intellectual achievement, but God's own justifying grace (Rom. 5:1–3; 6:14–18; 11:5, 6; Eph. 2:8, 9).

The incarnation is what makes Christianity distinctive in the sphere of the history of religions (Lactantius, *Div. Inst.* 4.5–12; Augustine, *CG* 10.1). Other religions have distinctive features too, but only in Christianity is the promise of God to Israel fulfilled by God's own personal coming in the flesh. Christianity differs from the religions of the world in that its understanding of God comes, not from human striving, intellect, and will, but from God's own self-disclosure in human history, through the people of Israel, which culminates and clarifies itself finally only in Jesus Christ. After Jesus, religion can never be the same (Arnobius, *Ag. Heathen* 2.70–78).

The Reasoning of Revelation

Scriptural Teaching Concerning Reason

Reason (*dialegomai, ratio*), as classical Christianity understood it, includes all the capacities of the soul to behold and receive truth (Augustine, *Letters* 137; 120.1). These include intellectual, emotive, and volitional (thinking, feeling, and willing) aspects of the self, insofar as these faculties are required to discern and interpret the truth (Augustine, *Conf.* 4.1).

The biblical writers welcomed reason that is open to the evidences of faith. Isaiah appealed to his hearers: "Come now, let us reason together" (1:18). Amos denounced idolatry and greed for its unreasonable stupidity (Amos 3:14–4:3). It is the fool, not the wise one, who says in his heart, "There is no God" (Ps. 14:1; Pss. 53:1; 92:6). Paul spoke of the Corinthian faithful as persons "of good sense"

(1 Cor. 10:15, "of discernment"). He protested against the opponents of faith as those who were unreasonable or "wrong-headed" (2 Thess. 3:2).

Biblical faith has been wrongly caricatured as contrary to reason or disinterested in rational analysis and critical judgment. This has encouraged obscurantism to parade as faith, and piety to refuse to seek any reasons for faith (Augustine, *Letters* 120). This stands contrary to the apostolic counsel that believers be prepared at the proper moment to give reasons for the hope that is in them. "Be always ready with your defense whenever you are called to account for the hope that is in you, but make that defense with modesty and respect" (1 Peter 3:15). "We must be so well instructed in the knowledge of our faith that whenever anyone asks us about it we may a be able to give them a proper answer and to do so with meekness and in the fear of God. For whoever says anything about God must do so as if God himself were present to hear him" (Didymus the Blind, Catena CEC 65).

Classical Christian exegetes sought to communicate both the importance and the limits of the faithful service of reason. They tried to avoid the rationalist exaggeration that reason is omnicompetent, thereby leaving no role for God to speak in the history of revelation (Tertullian, *Apol.* 46–47). They also resisted the opposite exaggeration, that reason is completely undone and incompetent in the presence of the mysteries of religion (Justin Martyr, *Dialogue with Trypho* 2). The emotive flow as such cannot substitute for analysis, observation, logical consistency, and historical awareness. Feelings may mislead (Amos 6:1). Faith asks for rigorous, critical reflection within the bounds of humble contrition touching everything human. Those who have been most profoundly grasped by the power of the Spirit are least satisfied with emotive expression alone. They owe it to themselves to seek whatever clarity is possible concerning the consequences of that experience (Tho. Aq., *ST* 1 Q78).

Reasoning out of a Community

The study of God is not well understood if viewed as an individualistic inquiry apart from a community that seeks to embody and celebrate it. In studying any discipline, one must enter into its language, artifacts, thought world, community life, symbols—whatever that particular discipline requires—and live with those resources for a while, taking them seriously.

Likewise, a participative element is required in Christian theology (Pss. 95:2; 34:8; Matt. 19:15–22; Acts 11:5; Teresa of Avila, *Life*; Calvin, *Inst.* 1.1–3; Bucer, *De Regno Christi* 3). Its evidences may not be completely plausible, persuasive, or even meaningful to one who has not made any participative effort, or to one who has not attentively listened to someone else who has made that effort and lived it out in his or her own daily behavior (Clare of Assisi, *Rule*; Calvin, *Inst.* 4.15). It is a psychological axiom that our behavior authenticates our belief system so radically that we trust the neighbors' actions far more than what they say they believe (James 1:23, 24; Clement, *First Epis. Corinth* 9).

Theology is a joyful intellectual task because the source of its task is the source of profoundest joy (Tho. Aq., *ST* 1–2 Q2–5). At the moment at which I feel my theological endeavors becoming tedious and dreary, I have been forgetting that the center of the adventure is the joy of God's presence—the ground of true happiness, the end of human despair. The study of God furnishes the human mind with its most sweeping intellectual challenge. It offers an unparalleled opportunity to think consistently, constructively, and fittingly about the One who gives life (Gen. 1:18–31).

Empathic Listening for Consistency

Christian theology necessarily requires the rational exercise of thinking, because it is by definition reasoned discourse about God, modestly framed in a way consonant with the immeasurability of its Subject (Gregory Nazianzus, *Orat.* 27, First *Theol. Orat.*). Seen from the viewpoint of the university, theology is a discipline. As such it requires self-critical reasoning about the word of God delivered through Scripture, liturgy, proclamation, and counsel.

Theology has long been suspected both of being too simple and far too difficult, a reputation well-earned on both counts. Much of the language of Christian confession is delivered through premodern cosmologies, prescientific views of the world. Yet the conflict of cosmologies is not as deep as the conflict between faith and unfaith in the hearer. Even when clothed in the latest language and symbols of modernity, Christianity with its "Word made flesh" cannot remain completely nonoffensive (Kierkegaard, *Training in Christianity*). Since classical Christianity is a *tradition* of exegesis, it has from the second and third centuries faced the awkwardness of having had its eternal Word spoken and echoed through various prevailing views of the world—dated understandings and misunderstandings of nature, psychology, and society that in turn differ widely from current conceptions of causality, physics, and reality.

Christianity has been faced many times before with many other "modernities." Modernizers wrongly imagined that the gulf between modern and premodern consciousness was larger than other gulfs the traditions of exegesis have managed to bridge. Our contemporary problems of cross-cultural communication do not pile higher than those faced by Athanasius, Augustine, John of Damascus, Thomas Aquinas, or Luther. Each had to struggle with making archaic language and symbol systems accessible to their own "modern" hearers of the fourth, seventh, thirteenth, or sixteenth centuries. Augustine's *City of God* was written amid the collapse of Rome. Gregory I's *Pastoral Care* was written amid continuing attacks from the barbarian tribes. The *Orthodox Faith* by John of Damascus was written amid the first waves of the Arab conquest.

A major obstacle to the modern hearing of classical Christian reasoning is an inveterate *modern chauvinism* that assumes that human consciousness today is intrinsically superior to all premodern modes of thinking—and, conversely, that all premodern thinking is assumed to be intrinsically *inferior* to modern consciousness. That premise is deeply ingrained in the insolence of modernity. In order to begin to hear the distinctive reasoning of the classical Christian consensus, that recalcitrant cultural egocentricity must be outwitted. How? The student of God must learn how to enter with historical empathy into archaic, seemingly outmoded, premodern frames of reference, accurately trying to hear what a text or a person is trying to shout as from a distant hill. The fact of distance does not mean that the message is in error.

It remains a problem of reason and will (being willing to reason, and reasonably willing) to learn how to employ *empathic imagination* to get into another frame of reference, to understand the mind of others of former times who think with different categories and out of different language frames—in this case chiefly Hebrew, Greek, and Latin but also at various periods in Aramaic, Coptic, Arabic, German, etc. Classical Christian writers have preached and taught in all these symbol systems and more. They have often transcended their own thought world and embraced other symbol systems in the service of the truth (among the best exemplars: Paul, Irenaeus, Justin Martyr, Clement of Alexandria, Augustine, Thomas Aquinas, and Raymond Lull).

In listening for the internal consistency of the deep nuances of classical Christian reasoning, we face complex problems of cross-cultural translation of meanings readily available in one period but almost inaccessible to another. An intellectual effort is required by the serious student of God's revelation who must take in a wide range of data, listen to strange voices, place text in context, and pray for the guidance of the Spirit (Augustine, *On Chr. Doctrine* 3).

Reason and Certitude

Doubt and the Hunger for Certainty

It is understandable that a finite human being, troubled with the vicissitudes of life, should hunger for certainty in knowledge, or at least for high reliability, to whatever degree is possible. But how is it possible to be sure that we know what we think we know? In certain crucial times, especially amid sorrow, illness, and death, our usual rational explanations become stretched to their limit.

As every pastor knows, these are the very times when meaning of life questions are profoundly asked. Life constantly undoes our theories of knowing (Luther, *Letters of Spiritual Counsel* 1,2; for much of what follows, I am indebted to Søren Kierkegaard, *Concl. Unsci. Post.*, and Reinhold Niebuhr, *NDM* 1–2). Classical Christian teaching speaks of a circle of knowing: through the inner assurance of the Holy Spirit and the reliability of Scripture, the divine self-disclosure is knowable.

Reason may be defined as *the capacity for internal consistency of argument based on evidence*. Both deductive and inductive processes are combined in this definition. Reason can too narrowly be defined in either an abstract, rationalistic, nonexperiential way or an excessively empirical, experiential way.

Classical Christian reasoning has not characteristically proceeded by discarding sense experience. It wants to use its deductive rational capacity, but only while utilizing to the fullest extent possible the inputs of sense experience, though admittedly there are finite limits to sense experience also. Reason depends, as Thomas Aquinas knew, upon sense perception, even though the senses may err. Thomas's arguments for the existence of God all began with sense experience, by looking around at the orderly processes of nature, causality, contingency, and language (Tho. Aq. *ST* 1 Q2).

The *experimental method* that we find in modern natural and behavioral sciences is based upon careful observation of change under controlled conditions on the basis of sense experience. Vast scientific and historical accomplishments have resulted from this experimental method. Yet this method has been alleged by some modern advocates (e.g., B. F. Skinner, Ivan Pavlov, Karl Popper, A. J. Ayer) to be the only way to know anything. There is little doubt that Christianity can make admirable use of empirical data gathering and scientific experimentation, but they are of limited value when we are talking about the central concerns of Christian teaching: the meaning of history, sin, grace, atonement, and sacramental life. The experimental method is useful when quantifiable objects are measured and changes observed, but God is not a quantifiable object. Christian teaching does not dismiss or deride experimental psychology, sociology, biology, or physics. It has learned much and can learn more from the data of the experimental sciences, natural and behavioral, and does not object to those methodologies by which quantifiable objects are being investigated (Origen, *OFP* 2.3, A. Plantiga, *Faith and Philosophy*).

The physical sciences ordinarily seek to isolate a single variable and try to account through some kind of quantifiable data-gathering process for a demonstrable change in that single variable that is repeatable and that can be experimentally reproduced and validated in a laboratory. But can one utilize that method effectively when attempting to speak significantly to the question of the meaning of suffering, the forgiveness of sin, or the overarching purpose of the historical process? The empirical method has limited usefulness in approaching poetry, literary analysis, religious experience, or love, all of which are grasped intuitively by a *Gestalt* or pattern of looking at personal knowledge that is seldom subject to exhaustive empirical analysis. Christian teaching in particular is looking for a pattern at work in all human history, to grasp the meaning of history (Augustine, *CG* 18), so empirical method can take one only part way toward this understanding.

Convergence of Plausibility

The search for comprehensive coherence is the attempt to grasp or see as most probably true that proposed solution to a problem which is on the whole supported by the greatest net weight of evidence from all quarters—deductive and inductive reasoning, logic and scientific method, historical reasoning, Scripture, and tradition. It is a centered intuitive act of drawing together of insights or data from widely varied resources and searching for their interrelated implicit meaning or convergence of plausibility (Vincent, *Commonitory*).

The knowing of God is at times something like a detective story, but one in which the answer is crying out to be revealed, the clues lying about everywhere. Some of the evidence is circumstantial, some requires careful data gathering; other steps need clear reasoning, faithfulness to credible sources, or sharp intuition. Comprehensive coherence is that kind of reasoning which says that the most adequate explanation of something is the one that brings into focus the most widely varied inputs into a single, cohesive, tentatively meaningful frame of reference. Intuitive reasoning based on facts seeks to ascertain whether the overall evidence is reasonable or not. It differs from strict laboratory or experimental conditions in its breadth, variety, and imagination. Scientific experimentation tries to bracket out these broader intuitions and insights and focus upon a single, manipulatable, objective variable. But the single-variable approach can box the inquirer into a vision that is highly constricted (Cusa, *U&R*; Reinhold Niebuhr, *NDM* 1:18–24, 104).

The study of God, ironically, is distinguished from empirical science in that it seeks to account for the greatest possible number of variables, rather than a single variable. For this unique study asks about the meaning of history. This is one way of describing the central task of theology: to give a credible account for the meaning of history, creation to consummation, viewed as God's story (Luke 1:3; 1 Chron. 11:11; 2 Chron. 13:22; Ps. 81:10). To deny a hearing to any kind of data by a prior and arbitrary limitation of method risks losing that part of the truth (Gregory I, *Dialogues*). Historically, theology has been relatively more willing to investigate speculative hypotheses, eschatology, psychological intuition, paranormal phenomena, and moral conscience than have the behavioral sciences, which have often ruled out such hypotheses.

Augustine remarked that "every good and true Christian should understand that wherever he may find truth, it is his Lord's" (*On Chr. Doctrine* 2.18). If God is the deepest truth (even though not fully fathomed), wherever the truth appears, there is some evidence of God's presence (Clement of Alex., *Strom.* 1.13).

We ourselves have not lived for more than a few decades, yet human beings have lived in cities for at least twelve thousand years. Our sufferings for one another are placed by the historical reasoning of the New Testament in the context of the "purpose of God hidden for ages" (Eph. 3:9; Jerome, *Epis. to Eph.* 2.3.8–9; Col. 1:26).

The puzzle of being a human being is the fact that we live in nature, and are restricted by nature, yet we are capable of self-transcendence, of life in the spirit. We are not explainable to ourselves merely in terms of naturalistic reductionisms, yet we are not transnatural or superpersonal angels or unembodied intelligences. Human existence is lived on the boundary between the natural and transnatural—rooted in nature and the causal order, yet with capacity for self-determination and self-transcendence (Kierkegaard, *Sickness into Death*).

This is symbolized in the Christian community by shorthand language: body and soul (*sōma* and *psychē*). The person (psychosomatically, paradoxically conceived) is wrapped in causal chains, yet exists as free: finite, yet capable of transcending finitude. Human life is "a sort of connecting link between the visible and invisible natures" (John of Damascus, *OF* 2.12).

Limits of Radical Skepticism

If all who claim to have received a revelation from God were to be viewed as equally plausible, hypertolerant fanaticism would have a field day. The easy credit would lead to bankruptcy.

Reason comes into play by sorting out the legitimacy of claims of alleged revelation in the light of all that one has already learned about God through comprehensive coherence (1 Thess. 5:21; 2 Cor. 11:1–21). Data received must often be corrected on the basis of subsequent experiences, and those experiences in turn await being corrected by later experiences, only to find that later experiences then have to be again corrected by earlier experiences, and so on (Jer. 5:3). The dilemma deepens when we ask: How can we be assured that there are not yet-to-be-discovered important data that will challenge or contradict our currently assumed reliable and constructive knowledge?

Our reasoning depends upon assumptions and postulates to which no data-gathering process can appeal, and that no data-gathering process can establish and that no reasoning process can prove without assuming these postulates precisely while the proofs are being attempted (Origen, *OFP* preface). Two examples are the intelligibility of nature and the principle of consistency. One: Any attempt to communicate through language involves the assumption that we are living in an intelligible order. Yet how can one prove that assumption? It remains an axiom, an assumption that lies quietly behind our reasoning (Augustine, *Soliloquies* 2). Two: If genuinely contradictory ideas can be true at the same time, then no argument for or against any conclusion has any force. Yet there is no way to establish that principle empirically, and no way to demonstrate it rationally without first depending on it (Anselm, *Concerning Truth* 9).

This leads us toward the temptation of complete skepticism about knowing anything at all. The ancient skeptic Carneades asserted that it is impossible to know anything about anything at all. He thought that we must base any truth on premises that we already hold, and that if we attempt to prove the premises, we can only move back toward other premises upon which we base our proof (N. MacColl, *The Greek Skeptics;* Augustine, *On the Profit of Believing*).

The pathetic-comic conclusion: The reason no philosophy has been able to teach or embrace a complete skepticism is that it is impossible to do it. *To believe that nothing can be known is to believe that even the meaning of that belief cannot be known.* If you believe that you can know nothing, you have to be skeptical also of that belief (Tho. Aq., *ST* 2–2 Q60). So even the most radical skepticism stumbles back upon internal contradiction.

Even if you should try seriously to *teach* the notion that nothing can be known, you are involved in an absurdity, because to teach it would be to assert that you know something. Skepticism is the yielding of the mind to a conviction of the impossibility of certainty, accompanied by a self-deceiving complacency about such a condition. Since skepticism *believes* that there is no truth, it must itself be classified as a *faith* in the reliability of ignorance (Pope, *Compend.* I, p. 48; DeWolfe, *TLC*, I).

This irony helps the study of God to move through and beyond the morass of skepticism: Though absolute certainty is not deductively or inductively attainable, complete skepticism is even more logically absurd, and cannot be maintained in practice. It is unreasonable to lay a radical demand upon ourselves, as we take steps toward life in God, to prove everything empirically, as some scientific and philosophical critics of religion expect. But that is no excuse for not taking as seriously as possible the breadth of the evidentiary process so as to try to bring into our consciousness as many factors as we possibly can that will appeal to a comprehensively cohesive form of reasoning and a convergence of plausibility.

The Genius of Historical Reasoning

This is why the predominant form of reasoning in classical Christianity theology has been a somewhat different form of thinking—by historical reasoning (Augustine, *Questions on Joshua* 25,26). The Old Testament view of reasoning about God is historical in scope and method. Yahweh repeatedly refers to himself in distinctively historical terms: "I am the God of Abraham, Isaac, and Jacob" (Exod. 3:15, 16; Mark 12:26) and rehearses to his people the mighty deed he has done in history (Joshua 24:2–13; Ps. 136; Eusebius, *Preparation for the Gospel*).

God meets us not just in our inner thoughts but in history, demonstrating the divine presence and power through events (Deut. 11:1–4). "The Lord is righteous in his acts; he brings justice to all who have been wronged. He taught Moses to know his way and showed the Israelites what he could do. The Lord is compassionate and gracious, long-suffering and forever constant" (Ps. 103:6–8). That the Lord is compassionate and gracious is known by recollecting God's historical activity (Irenaeus, *Ag. Her.* 5.21, 22; Cyril of Jerusalem, *Catech. Lect.* 6). The Lord is known not in "words of wisdom, but in demonstration of the Spirit and of power" (1 Cor. 2:4; Chrysostom, Hom on Cor. 6.3)

One who wishes to get in touch with God's demonstration of his justice and mercy in history must look candidly at universal history and learn to reason about all of history in unison from the vantage point of a special history— from the children of Abraham to the resurrection. To know Yahweh one must look toward the distinctive ways in which Yahweh has become self-revealed in history. The Hebraic way of reasoning is to tell a story. History telling or narrative is the distinctively Hebraic way of reasoning—a highly complex mode of social and historical reasoning (Ezra 1:1–4; Neh. 1:1–4; Amos 1:1–5).

Ordinarily the final meaning of a person's or nation's history can be assessed only at the end of the story. No one can write a definitive biography of a person until his life is over, because the life of a living person could always take a new turn, and make subsequent choices that would bear upon the meaning of the whole. The way a person faces death is a key to how he has faced life.

Suppose the meaning of human history is to become knowable only at its end, as virtually all late-Judaic apocalyptic writers assumed (the Books of Enoch, the Apocalypse of Baruch, and War of the Sons of Light against the Sons of Darkness), for *apokalypsis* refers to the final uncovering of meaning that had been hidden. Jesus was born into a community saturated with such expectations—that the end of a grossly distorted history would eventually reveal its meaning, however disastrous the present may appear (Daniel, 2 Esdrus, and the Assumption of Moses).

Suppose, however, that an event occurs in history that *reveals the meaning of the end before the end*. This is what happened in the history of Jesus—his incarnation, crucifixion, and finally resurrection—the one mighty deed of God that bestows significance upon all human deeds (Lactantius, *Div. Inst.* 4.25–30, Chrysostom, Hom. on Rom.).

Supposing that such a revealing event had occurred in history, would it not be necessary that it be followed by a remembering community, one that sought to preserve the meaning of the whole historical process revealed in that event? Would it not be understandable if a community of celebration followed that event that remembered it, shared in it, and proclaimed its meaning to all who would hear? (John 20:30–31; Origen, Fragment 106 on the Gospel of John).

Such a community has emerged in Christian history, reasoning out of this event, seeking to make it understandable in each new cultural-historical context. Through a gradual process of news reporting, preaching, scriptural interpretation, and canonization, the documents witnessing to this event became received as Holy Writ, attested by the Spirit as reliable accounts of originative event through which the meaning of history—God's Word to humanity—became known. Something like this process occurred in the historical Christian community. Each phase of history has required astute historical reasoning (Justin Martyr, *Dialogue with Trypho* 82–142). Each new situation of the church has demanded a modestly recapitulated form of historical reasoning—the recollection of revelatory events amid *each emerging* particular new historical condition. Hence, theological reasoning is historical reasoning.

What Good Purposes Does Reason Serve in the Study of God?

There are six classical indicators that show why reason is required by revelation. Reason is needed:

- to receive the truth,
- to distinguish truth from falsehood,
- to reveal reason's own limits,
- to question contradictions,
- to interpret the truth, and
- to transmit it to new generations.

To Receive Revelation. A revelation can be made only to a potentially rational being. Stones do not receive revelation. Without reason even the most obvious revelation could not be apprehended or grasped. If God wished to reveal the truth to a stone, it would first be necessary to create in a stone some capacity to understand, or the capacity to reason, in order for it to receive the revelation (Tho. Aq., *ST* 2–2 Q2). One must assume in any revelation both the capacity to apprehend truth and the active openness of the mind to the truth offered (Clement of Alex., *Strom.* 6). "For three weeks he [Paul] argued with them [the synagogue of Thessalonica] from the scriptures, explaining and proving" (Acts 17:2; Chysostom, *Hom. on Acts* 37).

To Decide Whether Revelation Has Occurred. All alleged revelations cannot be taken seriously. Some are patently spurious, fraudulent, or manipulative claims (Hippolytus, *Refutation of all Heresies*, 7; Kierkegaard, *Authority and Revelation:*

The Book on Adler). The community has to sort out which self-proclaimed revelations are true and which are not. When a murderer claims that he acted by divine revelation, faith must utilize its rational-analytical capacity to sort out what is alleged to be true through divine revelation as distinguished from that which, by a larger process of comprehensive coherence, can be consensually received and understood as truly God's own revelation (Tho. Aq., *SCG* 1.3). Reason is required in order to judge the evidences of religious claims to revelation (Clement of Alex., *Strom.* 6.7–11; Wesley, *WJW* 6: 350–61; Hodge, *Syst. Theol.* 1.3: 58, 59). The evidence must be fitting to the truth purported. Truth conveyed through history requires historical evidence plausibly set forth. Truths of nature require natural, empirical, scientific evidence. Truths of the moral sphere require moral evidence. The "things of the Spirit" (Rom. 8:5) require the self-evidencing assurance of the Spirit (The Pastor of Hermas, 2.10–11).

To Reveal Reason's Own Limits. Reason serves faith by pointing both beyond itself and to its own limits (Augustine, *Sermons on New Testament Lessons* 76). It is through reason that we may see that reason aims beyond its own natural competencies. It is reasonable that right reason know its own boundaries. Augustine wrote: "God forbid that He should hate in us that faculty by which He made us superior to all other living beings. Therefore, we must refuse to believe as not to receive or seek a reason for our belief, since we could not believe at all if we did not have rational souls. So, then, in some points that bear on the doctrine of salvation, which we are not yet able to grasp by reason—but we shall be able to sometimes— let faith precede reason, and let the heart be cleansed by faith so as to receive and bear the great light of reason; this is indeed reasonable." (*Letters* 120:1, *FC*)

To Question Contradictions. No one can reasonably be required to believe absurdities. The mind is God-given. It has a responsibility to reject falsity. If a claim of religion requires that which negates or contradicts a duly authenticated revelation of God, it is to be rejected as false religion, and inconsistent with faith's reasoning. Paul went to great lengths with the Galatians to urge consistency of teaching (Gal. 1:8). If human beings are to be held responsible for themselves before God, they must have some capacity both to know the good, and to recognize their own failure to do good. The earliest Christians were warned against naiveté: "Do not trust any and every spirit, my friends; test the spirits, to see whether they are from God, for among those who have gone out into the world there are many prophets falsely inspired" (1 John 4:1; Bede, *On 1 John*). Furthermore, a standard of judgment is given: "This is how we may recognize the Spirit of God: every spirit which acknowledges that Jesus Christ has come in the flesh is from God" (1 John 4:2; John Cassian, *Conferences* 1.20).

To Interpret and Apply Revealed Truth. Even if a community had received divinely revealed truth, and recognized it as such, it must still use practical moral reason to discover the implications of this truth in a specific historical context, expressed in its own language. Even after we have learned that God is revealed as just and requires justice, we still must ask what that justice means for us and how it is to pertain to our particular situation. This requires reason (Tho. Aq., *SCG* 3.; Wakefield, *CSCT*: 20–22). It is by reason that the believer learns to utilize analogies in the service of the truth, to make observations from nature and history, and to remove doubts by setting forth reasonable arguments. The teachings of faith are exhibited, clarified, and made rhetorically persuasive by good reasoning (Augustine, *Conf.* 11.25–31). Reason serves faith by helping to remove objections to faith (Augustine, *Letters* 102.38).

To Transmit the Meaning of Revelation. To transmit truth to another, one must employ reasoning. To communicate from one rational mind to another, one must presuppose the rational capacity of both speaker and hearer. Reason is needed if one seeks either to understand or to make understandable the truth of Christian faith. No preaching or teaching can occur without some rational capacity. By reason, faith's wisdom is correlated with the insights of philosophy, history, political ethics, psychology, and other sciences (Clement of Alex., *Strom.* 4.18).

Classic Christianity welcomes that reasoning which receives revelation, distinguishes between true and false revelation, reveals reason's own limits, questions contradictions, interprets the truth of revelation in the present, and transmits revelation to emergent historical situations.

A Balanced Reliance upon Reason

Although reason is intended to be put to these good uses, it is always prone to distortion. Since the fall of man, reason has been blind, proud, vain, tangled in self-deceit (Rom. 1:21; 1 Cor. 3:1; Gal. 4:8; Eph. 4:17, 18). Fallen reason is not able, without grace, to lift itself up to a fair recognition of the divine mysteries (Matt. 11:27; 1 Cor. 2:14–16).

Hence reason may find itself harnessed for the service of evil, as well as for good. Reason may be utilized to resist revelation, to deny faith, hope, and love (Rom. 8:6; 1 Cor. 2:11; 3:18–20; R. Niebuhr, *Moral Man and Immoral Society*). Fallen reason stands in need of repentance, cleansing, and conversion, that it too might become captive to the obedience of Christ (2 Cor. 10:4, 5).

Because of its proneness to self-deception, natural reason unaided by grace is not to be viewed at all times as an adequate rule for judging faith or revelation (Gerhard, *Loci* 2: 362). "Theology does not condemn the *use* of Reason, but its *abuse* and its affectation of directorship, or its magisterial use, as normative and decisive in divine things" (Quenstedt, in *DT*.35).

There can also be an overdependence upon speculative reasoning, or a distorted technical reason that functions without moral constraints. Hence unbalanced forms of rationalism may pervert the function of reason and thereby undermine the appropriate service of reason to the study of God. Classical Christian writers have sought to show that faith does not conflict with right reason, that there is harmony between revelation's historical way of reasoning and reason's respect for all the evidence, and that human reasoning is made more plausible and whole when the evidences of historical revelation are rightly weighed.

The orthodox Lutheran theologian Johann Gerhard wisely maintained: "Anyone who would deny those things which are visible in a greater light because he had not seen them in the smaller, would fail to appreciate the design and benefit of the smaller, so also he who denies or impugns the mysteries of faith revealed in the light of grace, on the ground that they are incongruous with Reason and the light of nature, fails, at the same time, to make a proper use of the office and benefits of Reason and the light of nature" (Gerhard, *Loci* 2: 372).

In sum, classic Christian teaching concedes to reason what is rightfully its due:

- God does not reveal himself to irrational, but rational creatures, capable of distinguishing between true and false evidence.

- Revelation does not imply faith in the absurd or impossible, or faith based on ignorance.

- Christian faith opposes anti-intellectual obscurantism as much as it does extreme skepticism.

- Faith resists both a blind fideism that believes without examining the evidence, and a defensive skepticism that believes only its doubt of the credibility of all evidence (Tho. Aq., *SCG* 1.4–7; Wesley, *WJW* 6: 350; Hodge, 1.3).

The Causes of Resistance in the Academy

It is germane to ask why there is such stiff resistance in the academy to this simple way of consensual reasoning. It is in fact difficult to find any religion texts within the prevailing university ethos today that contain frequent scripture references with accompanying consensus-bearing patristic texts. (It is a bit easier to find older traditional systematic theologies that contain frequent scripture references, but few contain any glimpse of the history of exegesis, and among Protestants almost none).

The costly division of the disciplines of theology into departments of exegesis, historical theology and systematic theology has created three competing methods that do not mix comfortably today, as they had done for centuries. Today's exegetes largely disdain systematization as a disregard of context; historians deride the pretense of unity and systematic cohesion thought to be a goal of much systematic theology; systematic theologians have increasingly ignored exegesis and historical theology. This study draws them closer together by combining high density textuality with classical order. The reason the disciplines do not mix comfortably is that each discipline is seeking to gain acceptance to some non-theological method prevailing in the secular university. Each discipline is deflected by that struggle for acceptance.

This straightforward procedure of classic Christian teaching makes the study of classic Christianity much more precise, defined, and manageable. Accordingly, reflection focuses on textual analysis of the sacred text, and the history of its consensual interpretation. That is enough because that is itself a huge task. The hard work of teaching and discipling believers is made more definite, exact, straightforward and specific. It is far less speculative than trying to adapt Christianity to some modern ideology. Better to invite theology to adapt itself directly to specific texts that have had amassed authoritative gravity for two millennia.

How Faith Reasons

The term faith (*pistis*) is utilized in the New Testament with several levels of meaning. Faith is:

- the recognition through the active life of the Spirit, of "the evidence of things not seen" (Heb. 11:1)

- an active trust or confidence, as when one asks "in faith, nothing doubting" (James 1:6)

- a belief, trust, and assurance in God's righteousness in Christ that is active by love and yields the fruit of good works

- the act of believing; for example, when one says, "I believe" (Apostles' Creed) one is saying "I have faith that . . ."

- a body of truth confessed as necessary for salvation, as in "the faith once delivered to the saints" (Jude 3), or the Christian religion for which the believer contends (1 Tim. 6:12)

- reliability, or constancy in fulfilling one's promises, as when Paul speaks of the "faithfulness of God" (Rom. 3:3)

- trust in the intelligibility of the cosmos that premises scientific inquiry (Ps. 89:1–8)

- obedience, or the obedience of faith, which stands ready to be guided by duly constituted authority (Rom. 16:26)

All these varied shades of meaning cohere, interflow, and coalesce in Christian teaching concerning faith (Ambrose, *Of the Chr. Faith*, prologue, 1.4; 2.Intro.; 2.11, 15; Augustine, *On Psalms* LI; Luther, *Freedom of a Chr.*; *TDNT*; *TDOT*). Faith includes the capacity to discern by grace the things of the Spirit, and to trust in the reliability of the divine Word (Cyril of Jerusalem, *Catech. Lect.* 5). Faith embraces the complementary meanings of the trusting frame of mind that has confidence in Another and the trustworthiness that can be relied upon (Tho. Aq., *ST* 1–2 Q1–13; Calvin, *Inst.* 3.2).

Faith does not occur without grace: "Yes, it was grace that saved you, with faith [*pisteōs*] for its instrument" (Eph. 2:8). When grace enlivens reason, reason is not subverted but empowered. Human reasoning, by grace, appropriates divine truth without ceasing to be human reasoning (Basil, *Letters, To Amphilochius*, 235–236). Since faith is the discernment of spiritual truth, faith is not separable from reasoning, rightly understood. Rather, faith is a way of reasoning out of God's self-disclosure, assisted by grace. Since faith enlarges human vision, the logic of faith is an enlarged, not a diminished, logic (Tho. Aq., *SCG* 1.1–9, I: 59–78).

The Capacity of Faith to Discern the Truth

Faith is the eye that sees what the senses cannot see, the ear that hears what the senses do not hear. One who lacks this eye and ear "refuses what belongs to the Spirit of God; it is folly to him; he cannot grasp it, because it needs to be judged in the light of the Spirit" (1 Cor. 2:14; Gregory Nazianzus, *Orat.* 28). Believing is that faculty that "makes us certain of realities we do not see" (Heb. 11:1). It enables the heart to recognize "the truth as it is in Jesus" (Eph. 4:21; Jerome, *Epis. To Eph.* 2.4.21). No other human faculty is sufficiently competent to recognize this truth. For faith is to the unseen world what the senses are to the visible world (Maximus, *Four Centuries on Charity* 3.92–99).

Faith in God is not alien to the human condition, because "the Spirit of God himself is in man, and the breath of the Almighty gives him understanding" (Job 32:8). This Spirit already at work within us discerns the truth, receives its evidence, and celebrates its veracity (Augustine, *On Trin.* 4.22–32). The coming of Jesus is like the coming of a light that is offered to "enlighten every one," even though some prefer darkness (John 1:9–12). The Revealer "knew men so well, all of them, that he needed not evidence from others about a man, for he himself could tell what was in a man" (John 2:25; Theodore of Mopsuestia, *John* 2.2.24–25). Since God empathized with our limitations, he radically adapted the evidence of revelation to the human condition, so that even amid our self-assertive deceptions we might be able to recognize the truth incarnate and the Spirit of truth (John 1:14; 16:13). One who prejudicially resists this evidence has "a distorted mind and stands self-condemned" (Titus 3:11). Such persons "defy the truth; they have lost the power to reason, and they cannot pass the tests of faith" (2 Tim. 3:8).

In this way the Scriptures viewed faith as sound reason. Hence faith and reason are deeply bound and melded together in inextricable spiritual kinship. The same Spirit who has called forth faith also awakens reason to receive "the mystery that has been kept hidden for ages and generations, but is now disclosed to the saints" (Col. 1:26). This is a mystery that sin-laden reason of itself does not fathom.

Faith calls upon reason to recognize and credit the evidences of God's self-disclosure. In this way the judgment of the mind is given the honor of examining the evidences of faith. While faith is raised up to receive and embrace revelation, reason is bowed low to behold its self-giving love. Faith does not despise reason, but presents those evidences for revelation in history that are understandable to reason (Wesley, *WJW* 6:351).

But what are these evidences that faith presents to reason? They are Scripture's recollections of the divine self-disclosure in history. Through the presentation of these evidences, the believer is taught to "be always ready with your defence [*pros apologian*, ready to provide reasons] whenever you are called to account for the hope that is in you" (1 Pet. 3:15). Luke wrote his Gospel as "a connected narrative" (*diēgēsin*) for Theophilus, "so as to give you authentic knowledge" (*epignōs*, Luke 1:4) of the coming of the Savior (Luke 2:11). So every believer, and especially everyone in public ministry, needs to be supplied with such "authentic knowledge" to provide credible reasons concerning the reliability (*asphaleian*, certainty) of that in which they have been instructed (Luke 1:4). It was just such "an outline of the sound teaching which you heard from me" (2 Tim. 1:13) that Timothy was instructed to keep before him, so that the reasons for faith might be readily available to him.

The Recognitions of Clement (mid fourth century, anon.) commended the process of asking hard questions of faith, requiring faith to reason about itself:

> Do not think that we say that these things are only to be received by faith, but also that they are to be asserted by reason. It is not safe to commit these things to bare faith without reason, since assuredly truth cannot be without reason. And therefore he who has received these things fortified by reason can never lose them; whereas he who receives them without demonstrations, by an assent to a simple statement of them, can neither keep them safely, nor is certain if they are true. . . . And therefore, according as any one is more anxious in demanding a reason, by so much will he be the firmer in preserving his faith. (Second Clement, *Recognitions* 2.69)

Christianity's Social Conception of Evidence

The classical Christian writers argued that the acceptance of legitimate and reasonable authority is itself an eminently reasonable act, for both scientific and religious knowledge. When the believer trusts the church's authority to discern and canonize Scripture, distill from it the creed, and hold to a rule of faith as a guide to scriptural truth, that is viewed as a reasonable act (Irenaeus, *Ag. Her.* 5.20.2). Cyprian observed that whoever is able to call God Father, must first call the church Mother (Epistles 70).

If reasons appear that make it clear that the church's judgment has become untrustworthy, or its consensual judgment misguided, then the believer has a duty to question that imprudent authority. Such a predisposition toward ecclesial trust does not imply an abandonment of reason; rather, it assumes that the community is merely providing the believer with evidence for consideration, reflection, and testing against related forms of knowing (Chrysostom, *Hom. on 2 Tim.* 2–3). Augustine wrote to Jerome: "If I am puzzled by anything in [Scripture] which seems to go against the truth, I do not hesitate to suppose that either the manuscript is faulty or the translator has not caught the sense of what was said, or I have failed to understand it myself" (*Letters*, 82.3).

Children conditionally accept the word of their parents and teachers who are seeking to present them with evidence about which they then can duly examine, test, and draw their own conclusions. Educators do not normally regard that act of conditional acceptance as irrational but rather as a reasonable openness to evidence under competent guidance. It is far less reasonable to suppose that the child must begin with a consistent attitude of radical distrust toward those who are seeking to permit the examination of evidence.

Similarly, the knowledge received through Scripture and church tradition remains subject to further exploration, experiential confirmation, and amendment by subsequent evidence. To depend upon Holy Writ and holy church for supplying the very evidence with which faith deals does not imply sacrifice of intellect, however, but proceeds as a reasonable act of openness to evidence.

The Capacity to Believe the Evidences of Faith

However great may be the differences between philosophy and theology, as different as are reason and revelation, these two spheres are not locked in endless opposition. One thinks in the light of natural intellect, the other in the light of God's self-disclosure in history. Viewed together, both think either toward or from the truth.

Revelation addresses a human faculty seated in the human constitution, the faculty of believing. This faculty is at work, accepting the truth on sufficient evidence, wherever human knowing occurs, and especially spiritual knowing (1 Cor. 2:11–16; Heb. 7:14–25; 11:1–6; Clement of Alex., *Strom.* 2.2.8–9). As faith receives revelation, so faith then seeks to pass on the evidences of revelation to others, utilizing reason where appropriate to state, clarify, and make plausible these evidences (Augustine, *Ag. the Epis. of Manichaeus* 1–4).

The study of God seeks to develop a disciplined reflection out of *its own unique subject matter: the reality, presence, mercy, and love of God as understood by the worshiping Christian community.* It is an orderly exposition of evidences of divine revelation on the basis of Scripture, tradition, and historical and experiential reasoning.

BOOK TWO

THE WORD OF LIFE

1

WHY CHRIST?

An Unforgettable Life

Christianity arose out of a particular human life ending in a disturbing, terrible death—then, resurrection. The meaning of Christianity is undecipherable without grasping the meaning of Christ's life and death and living presence.

"Christ is the central spot of the circle; and when viewed aright, all stories in Holy Scripture refer to Christ" (Luther, *Serm. on John 3:14*). It is from Christ that Christianity derives its name, its mission, its identity, its purpose, its very life (Acts 11:26; John 15:1–5; Augustine, *Hom. on the Epist. of John* 1).

Christian Teaching Is Personally Grounded

At the heart of Christianity is a relation to a person. It is not essentially an idea or institution. It is a personal relationship to Christ. He is the one to whom faith clings and in whom faith trusts. "Being a Christian does not mean, first and foremost, believing in a message. It means believing in a person" (Gutiérrez, *PPH*:130). Christian teaching hopes to show the way that leads to faith in this person. The Christian community emerges and lives out of personal trust in this person (Chrysostom, *Comm. on John* 57).

There is a discipline that attempts to understand this personal relation. The discipline belongs both in the academic world and the worshiping community. It studies God, hence is called theology. One of its major forms, Christian theology, studies God as known in persons who live their lives in close relation to this person.

Any who wish to reflect seriously upon Christian worship and the Christian life will want to know as much as possible about this relation. Those who are distracted from this purpose signal that they have elected not to inquire into classic Christian teaching, whose central interest is this relation. Those who remain focused on this inquiry must then try to understand why this one person is so important in this community.

Christians know God as the One revealed in Jesus. Other ideas in Christianity are measured in relation to that idea of God known in Jesus. The approach to that idea of God knowable only through the story of Jesus must begin with the study of Jesus himself.

His Unseen Influence

It is hard to think of a single person who has affected human history more profoundly than Jesus of Nazareth. This alone would make his story significant. Yet this is not the primary reason he is studied. He is not investigated as Alexander the Great or Napoleon would be—for their colossal power or dominance. His influence is not outwardly measured in terms of worldly power, but transforming power (Martyrdom of Polycarp; Athanasius, *Incarn. of the Word* 46–57; Clare of Assisi, *Testament*).

Historical study cannot ignore the history of Jesus. His footprints are all over human history, its literary, moral, and social landscape, and on every continent. Who has affected history more than he? No other individual has become such a permanent fixture of the human memory. He has been worshiped as Lord through a hundred generations.

Through the centuries Jesus has been memorialized in stone, painted on frescoes, and celebrated in song. Human history would not be our history without him. Something would be missing if historians ignored him or decided to study all figures except the one who has affected human history most. Indeed that is what makes it so puzzling when his name is purposely erased from high-school history texts.

The intellectual and moral reflection that has ensued from his life has penetrated every crevice of intellectual history, psychology, politics, and literature. One cannot understand human history without asking who Christ is and what he did and continues to do. No one is well educated who has systematically dodged the straightforward question —a question that committed Jews or Muslims may ask and study as seriously as Christians or agnostics or hedonists—Is Jesus the Christ?

The Decisive Question

Jesus turned this same question around when he asked Peter in a person to person voice: "But who do you say that I am?" Peter's confession was clear: "You are the Christ, the Son of the living God" (Mark 8:29). This declaration remains the concise pattern for subsequent Christian confession, worship, and faith (Bede, *Hom. on Gospels* 1.16–17). In saying this, Peter stood in a personal relationship with another living person, Jesus of Nazareth—not with an idea, abstract system, or institution, but an actual *you* in a real relationship.

Note that the confession was not *about* Christ, but *to* him. Peter says: "You are the Christ" to one who is alive. If Christ is not still alive, forget about Christian confession—there is no one to whom to confess.

The meaning of Jesus' life and death has never been a permanently obsolete issue to any generation since his appearance. It remains even today a matter of intense debate as to who Jesus was and what his life and death mean. Deeper even than the mystery of his historical influence is the simpler question that rings through Christian reflection: Why did God become human? (Anselm, *Cur Deus homo*).

Answering *why* is the subject of classical Christian teaching.

The Facts and Their Meaning

The bare facts of his life can be sparely stated. Date of birth: between 5 BC and AD 4. Place: Palestine. Ethnic origin: Jewish. Vocation: probably first a skilled construction artisan like his father, then a traveling preacher of the coming rule of God. Length of ministry: three Passovers (John 2:13; 6:4; 12:1). Date of death: Friday, 14 Nisan (the first month of the Jewish year), probably, by our calendar, April 7 AD 30 (or by some calculations 3 April, AD 33). Place of death: Jerusalem. Manner of death: crucifixion. Roman procurator: Pontius Pilate (AD 27–33). Roman emperor: Tiberius.

But the study of this person focuses not simply upon bare facts, but upon what his life meant—especially as it comes down finally to a single, decisive question: whether he is rightly understood as "Lord"—as the expected Messiah of Israel, Son of God—or not. There is no way to dodge this question so as to conclude that Jesus might be *partially* Lord or *to a certain degree* the Christ or *maybe* in some ways eternal Son or *perhaps* truly God. He must either be or not be the Messiah. He must either be or not be crucified and risen Lord of glory. Both women and men have given their lives to answer yes (Perpetua, *Passion of the Holy Martyrs, Perpetua and Felicitas*; Justin Martyr, *First Apology* 35).

The New Testament is bothersome because it calls upon every woman and every man within hearing distance to decide on their own about the true answer.

Person to Person: His Question to Us

Who Do You Say That I Am?

You. "Who do you say that I am?" This is the startling question that Jesus' life constantly asks. The nearer anyone comes to him, the more clearly he requires decision. It is the unavoidable issue that the observer of Jesus' life must finally struggle with. For Jesus himself presses the question and awaits an answer. To avoid that issue is to avoid him. To avoid him is to avoid Christianity altogether (Kierkegaard, *TC*: 66–71). Transformations occur when we listen. The closer we make him the object of our study, the more we become aware that he is examining us.

The evangelists' portraits of his life, offered by eyewitnesses, are poignant, simple, and stirring. He was born of a poor family, of a destiny-laden but power- less nation. The earliest traditions report that he was born in a squalid cave or stable among animals in an out-of-the-way village. He immediately became the refugee baby of a fleeing family seeking to escape a wave of killing. The town he grew up in had the reputation that "nothing good could ever come from there." He spoke a language (Aramaic) that few spoke then, and now has been virtually forgotten.

He is never said to have written anything except with his finger in the sand. He worked with his hands as a common laborer. He owned nothing of value. To the poor he brought good news of the coming governance of God. His disciples were simple folk, involved in artisan trades. They included some reprobates whose lives were reshaped by their unforgettable meeting with him. Even in the face of cynical criticism, he did not cease to dine and converse with outcasts, to mix with the lowly and disinherited. He washed the feet of his followers. He intentionally took the role of a servant. He reached out for other cultures despised by his own people. Of all the people who might have been able to grasp the fact that he was to be anointed to an incomparable mission, it turned out to be a "woman who was a sinner."

Remarkable things were reported of him. He touched lepers. He healed the blind. He raised persons from the dead. These events pointed unmistakably to the unparalleled divine breakthrough that was occurring in his people's history—the decisive turnaround in the divine-human story of conflicted love.

He heralded a new age. He called all his hearers to decide for or against God's coming reign. He himself was the sign of its coming. He called for complete accountability to God. His behavior was consistent with his teaching. He was born to an ethnic tradition widely despised and rejected; but he himself became even more despised and rejected by many of his own people.

His enemies plotted to trap him and finally came to take his life. His closest friends deserted him when his hour had come to die. He knew all along that he would be killed. Sweat poured from his face as he approached death. He was betrayed by one of his closest associates. He submitted to a scurrilous trial with false charges.

His end was terrible. His back felt the whip. He was spat upon. His head was crowned with thorns. His wrists were in chains. On his shoulders he bore a cross through the city. Spikes were driven through his hands and feet into wood. His whole body was stretched on a cross as he hung between two thieves. All the while he prayed for his tormentors, that they might be forgiven, for they knew not what they were doing. He rose from the dead.

Is There a Plausible Explanation?

This is a sketch of the Gospels' portrait of Jesus. It is this one whom the disciples experienced as alive the third day after his death. This is the unique person whose extraordinary life we now try to understand.

How is it plausible that two thousand years ago there lived a man born in poverty in a remote corner of the world, whose life was abruptly cut short in his early thirties, who traveled only in a small area, who held no public office, yet whose impact upon us appears greater than all others? How is it that one who died the death of a criminal could be worshiped as Lord by billions?

This is the surprising paradox of his earthly life, but even this is not its deepest mystery. Why are people willing to renounce all to follow him and even die in his service? How is it possible that centuries later his life would be avidly studied and worshipers would address their prayers to him? What accounts for this surprising relation he has with this community?

Classic Christian teaching answers without apology: what was said about him then is true now; he *actually was*:

Son of God,

promised Messiah,

the one Mediator between God and humanity,

truly God

truly human,

who liberated humanity from the power of sin by his death on the cross,

who rose from the dead to confirm his identity as the promised one.

That answer better explains what his life is and means than any of its alternatives. It is theoretically possible for the study of Jesus to function without that basis, but in practice it is exceptionally difficult, for one is then forced to stretch and coerce the narratives to make any sense of them at all. The New Testament documents give determined resistance to any reader who discards that hypothesis (Jesus is Lord) because they imagine that they know a better explanation of his true identity. There is no other or better way to explain this amazing life. According to Christian confession, Jesus is either Messiah or nothing at all.

The Subject

The study of Christ (Christology) is that discipline that inquires critically and systematically into this person, his relation to his Father and to us. In him the true relation between God and ourselves is alleged to be knowable.

Studying Him as One Who Is Following Him

I may be saved by grace through faith without passing an examination on Christology. But his life compels some explanation. When he tells me that my eternal destiny depends upon trusting in him, what am I to say? His life and death remain the central point of interest of Christian discipleship and education.

He is not fully studied as if only a man, though he was a man. This is a man for whom studying him means following him in his way. He cannot be studied in a book alone but on a long road.

The events surrounding this individual are alleged to stand as the supreme truth of the history of revelation. The study of Christ implies the study of the divine plan for which humanity was created. In him the purpose toward which history is moving is allegedly revealed. In Christ God actively embraces wounded humanity and enables humanity to answer to God's active embrace.

This is not a study that can be rightly undertaken by those who remain dogmatically committed to the assumption that nothing new can happen in history or that no events are knowable except those that can be validated under controlled laboratory conditions. Here the laboratory is life, human life, human history, cosmic history.

The Study Occurs in the Midst of a Worshiping Community on Pilgrimage

The meaning of Christ's life is studied within the context of a worshiping community, just as Islamic theology occurs within the community of Islam. No one can study basketball without ever attending a basketball game. The "game" in this case is a living person, Jesus Christ. If the once dead, now living Christ is regarded as now finally dead and gone, the game is not being played.

The New Testament itself frequently disavows that it contains an entirely new idea or understanding of God, for the one known in Jesus was already many times promised in history before Jesus, as seen in the Law and Prophets (Heb. 1:1–5). Yet in Jesus the reality of God is brought home and relationally received in an unparalleled way.

Our purpose is to understand and teach Jesus the Christ as he has been understood and taught by those whose lives have been most profoundly transformed by him. If we were studying Hasidic Judaism, we would hope the same of a Hasidic teacher. If we were studying Islamic Sufism, we would hope the same of a Sufist teacher. Christians also do well to study honestly the Vedas, Tao, the Mishnah, Gemara, Tosefta, or the Qur'an as carefully as they would hope others might take the New Testament. Let the evidence be fairly presented. Christian teaching does not wish to obstruct other voices from presenting competing claims or contrary evidence, but to ensure the accurate presentation of its own evidences.

Jesus' life has been at times partially, wrongly, or self-interestedly remembered. From these aberrations and digressions have flowed vexations for humanity: wars, divisions, inequities, and systemic injustices. A poorly developed, ill-formed understanding of Jesus Christ has at times blocked off the Word that he intends to speak to us. They have stunted the personal relation he offers us. Hence it is imperative to think clearly about him if we are to understand the personal relationship he offers.

The Meaning of "God" Is the Meaning Christ Has Given to the Name

The meaning of the word "God" is for Christians the meaning given the name of God by Jesus.

Many morally concerned Christians can honestly understand the church's speech about the Father and the Spirit more readily than about the incarnate Son. The classic Christian teachers respected those whose integrity requires that they raise ethical questions earnestly and historical questions rigorously (Justin Martyr, *Trypho*; Origen, *Ag. Celsus*; Augustine, *Ag. the Skeptics*). That determination made them all the more determined to communicate the meaning given to the name God by Jesus.

Note this irony, however: Those who most doubt his claims often have been already seized in awe by those claims. They would not be so earnestly inquiring and doubting if the majesty of his presence were not so real. Hence it is often said, as Jesus himself said, that earnest doubters and idolaters may be nearer to salvation than those still morally asleep. Some who have been most actively engaged in social justice and political change who deny the identity ascribed to Christ by the apostles may nonetheless remain profoundly affected by his continuing presence. Many are struggling for justice because they have first undergone the pedagogy of his meekness, peacemaking, and hope. Those who most wearily wonder about the mystery of Christ have often been deeply affected by him already, and may by study come to that self-recognition.

This principle, aptly stated by John Knox, remains applicable to a secular-weary culture that is once again actively turning toward a new encounter with Christ: "Whether we affirm or deny, the meaning of 'God' is the meaning which Christ has given to the name" (*MC*: 7). H. R. Mackintosh remarks in the same vein: "The name of God has the final meaning that Jesus gave it. . . . He is an integral constituent of what, for us, God means" (*PJC*: 290, 292). The defining meaning of God for Christians is that meaning most clearly made known in Jesus' life.

Identification with the Lowly

The incarnation is God's own act of identification with the broken, the poor, with sinful humanity. God did not enter human life as a wealthy or powerful "mover and shaker." God came in a manger, amid the life of the poor, sharing their life, identifying with the meek.

There is embedded deeply in the best of early ecumenical teaching a pungent critique of sexual inequalities and of the propensity of male users of power to abuse that power. Gregory the Theologian pointed out in the fourth century that "the majority of men are ill-disposed" to equal treatment of women, hence "*their laws are unequal* and irregular." Does a husband who is unfaithful to his wife "have no account to give? I do not accept this standard; *I do not approve this custom.*" (Gregory of Nazianzus, *Orat.* 37.6, italics added).

When political activists imagine that only they are capable of providing a critique of the dynamics of social oppression, it is fitting to note this powerful strain of early Christian social criticism. The theologies of liberation still await a greater dialogue with classic Christian teaching. Marxist critics were not the first to ask about social location of interpreters or for an economic account of injustice. These criticisms run deep within early Christian history (Oden, *The Good Works Reader*, 2007). The ethical consequences of the gospel have been often grasped by those inquiring into Jesus Christ (notably Clement of Alexandria, Chrysostom, Ambrose, Francis of Assisi, Menno Simons, Grotius, Zinzendorf, and the Blumhardts).

It is not enough to speak of God's own redemptive coming as if it lacked social consequence. These consequences have been spelled out in different cultures by Augustine, Thomas Aquinas, Calvin, Hooker, and Wesley. What that means for the increase of love and justice in society has been repeatedly addressed prior to our times, notably in such figures as W. Wilberforce, Phoebe Palmer, F. D. Maurice, J. H. Newman, and W. Rauschenbusch. None of these attempts to transform culture has a perfect score. But where does any perfect score appear within any human culture?

The temptation toward a moralized narrowing of theology into ethics seems to be an essential feature of all modern Christian thought (P.T. Forsyth, *PPJC*, 7, 9). That narrow view can be opened up by serious digging into classical Christian teachings concerning Jesus.

The plea for ethical accountability in speech about God is justified. It is a test that classical Christianity passes better than much modern Christianity (Athanasius, *Incarn. of the Word* 46–57: Augustine, *CG* 14). This moral narrowing that remains endemic to popular modern religiosity runs the risk of reducing the Word of Life to moralism (Fitzsimons Allison, *The Rise of Moralism*). Since Feuerbach and Nietzsche it has been a standard conceit of western intellectuals to suppose that a high view of the Son of God necessarily promotes a low view of moral responsibility. Those who buy into Marxist economic interpretation repeatedly sound this alarm. Such distortions are inconsistent with classical Christian teaching, where the assumption prevails that the confession of Jesus Christ as Lord has insistent moral meaning and culture-edifying implications. Christians who call for an identification with the poor do so out of a long tradition of voluntary poverty and generous giving, which follows from Christ's willingness to become poor for our sakes.

The Gospel

Jesus Himself Is the Good News

Jesus did not come just to deliver good news, but to be himself the good news. The gospel is the good news of God's own coming. Jesus is its personal embodiment. The cumulative event of the sending, coming, living, dying, and continuing life of this incomparable One is the gospel.

The gospel does not introduce an idea but a person—"we proclaim *him*!" (Col. 1:28, italics added). The "him" proclaimed is one whose life ended in such a way that everything that has occurred before and after has become decisively illumined by his epic narrative. "Him we proclaim, warning every man and teaching every man in all wisdom, that we may present every man mature in Christ" (Col. 1.28). What was written about him was not written simply as biography but as a gift and a living challenge. For biographies are written of persons who are dead, thus inactive. A biography is a written history of a person's whole *bios* ("life"). A biography of a person still alive is by definition incomplete. Rather the gospel is the account of a person who remains quite active, palpably present, whose heart still beats with our hearts, one who died who is now alive (Augustine, *CG* 13.18–24; Bonhoeffer, *Christology*).

The Gospel: A Summary of the Person and Work of Christ

Reflections on Jesus are often divided into discussions of his person and work, that is, who he was and what he did. The good news (euãggelion, gospel) unites these two: the person of the Son engaged in the work of the servant-messiah. These are united in the good news of human salvation. "Gospel" is the unique term that concisely summarizes and links the person and work of Christ. Only this person does this work, which constitutes God's good tidings to human history.

"Gospel" (*euãggelion*) is a distinctive New Testament theme, occurring over one hundred times, and embedded in Jesus' preaching from the outset. His coming was announced as "good news of great joy that will be for all the people" (Luke 2:10; Cyprian, *Treatises* 12.2.7). "I must preach the good news of the kingdom of God to the other towns also, because that is why I was sent" (Luke 4:43; Tertullian, *Ag. Marcion* 4.8). The medieval Anglo-Saxon root (*godspell*) meant "good news" or "glad tidings" (Anglicizing the Latin *bonus nuntius*). The gospel, Luther thought, is to be sung and danced (*Intro. to NT, WLS* 2:561, commenting upon David bringing the ark to the City of David, 2 Sam. 6:14; cf. Maximus of Turin, *Sermon* 42.5; Gregory I, *Morals on Job* 27.46).

The Second Helvetic Confession sparely defined the gospel as "glad and joyous news, in which, first by John the Baptist, then by Christ the Lord himself, and afterwards by the apostles and their successors, is preached to us in the world that *God has now performed what he promised* from the beginning of the world" (13, *BOC* 5.089, italics added; Ursinus, *CHC*: 101). God is now fulfilling what had been promised all along (Origen, *OFP* 4.1).

The good news of Jesus' coming was understood as fulfillment of prophetic expectation, as in Isaiah: "How beautiful on the mountains are the feet of those who bring good news, who proclaim peace, who bring good tidings, who proclaim salvation" (Isa. 52:7; Irenaeus, *Ag. Her.* 3.13; Eusebius, *Proof of the Gospel*, 3.1). In Isaiah's time the good news referred to the return of Israel from exile, yet it prefigured Jesus' proclamation of deliverance of all humanity from sin (Augustine, *CG* 18.29; Calvin, *Comm.* 3:99–101).

The Earliest Christian Preaching in Acts

The earliest interpretations of the meaning of Jesus' life are found in the oral traditions that flowed into the preaching reported in Acts (M. Hengel, *Acts and the History of Earliest Christianity*). That preaching has been concisely summarized by C. H. Dodd (*APD*:21–24) in these six points:

1. "God fulfilled what he had foretold through all the prophets, saying that his Christ would suffer" (Acts 3:18; 2:16; 3:24).

2. This has occurred through the ministry, death, and resurrection of Jesus, of Davidic descent (Acts 2:30–31), "a man accredited by God to you by miracles, wonders and signs" (Acts 2:22).

3. "God raised him from the dead" (Acts 2:24; see 3:15; 4:10), making him Lord and Christ (Acts 2:33–36), and "exalted him to his own right hand as Prince and Savior that he might give repentance and forgiveness of sins to Israel" (Acts 5:31).

4. God has given the Holy Spirit to those who obey him (Acts 5:32). "Exalted to the right hand of God, he has received from the Father the

promised Holy Spirit and has poured out what you now see and hear" (Acts 2:33).

5. Christ "must remain in heaven until the time comes for God to restore everything" (Acts 3:21; 10:42). Having suffered as Messiah and having been exalted as Messiah, he would return as Messiah to bring history to a fitting consummation. So:

6. "Repent and be baptized, every one of you, in the name of Jesus Christ for the forgiveness of your sins. And you will receive the gift of the Holy Spirit" (Acts 2:38).

These points recapitulate the core of the earliest Christian preaching. Subsequent creedal confession would generally adhere to this sequence and build upon it (J. N. D. Kelly, *Early Christian Creeds*; *SCD*; *CC*; *COC* 1).

The Pauline Kerygma

Paul's conversion is usually dated to a short time after Jesus' death. He understood himself to be passing on to others the tradition he himself had received from the risen Lord (1 Cor. 15:1–7; 16:22). Hence the earliest layer of Paul's proclamation could hardly be assumed to have undergone extensive changes, philosophical mutations, or ideological developments that would have required considerable time to emerge and become integrated into other communities.

The alternative hypothesis is implausible—that Paul might have been surreptitiously passing on to Corinth views that had only later gradually developed between AD 33 and 50, for he himself specifically notes that this is the tradition he received, transmitting to Corinth what had been transmitted to him "from the beginning straightway" ("from the outset," 1 Cor. 15:3; Chrysostom, *Hom. on First Cor.* 38). Paul specified his primary sources for the oral tradition he passed on, for he personally knew and had received "the right hand of fellowship" from "James, Peter and John, those reputed to be pillars" of the earliest Christian community (Gal. 2:8–9; Marius Victorinus, *Epist. To Gal.* 1.2.7–9), and from the risen Lord.

The gospel Paul had earlier received and subsequently passed on was carefully preserved in a Letter whose authenticity is seldom disputed: "Now, brothers, I want to remind you of the gospel I preached to you, which you received and on which you have taken your stand. By this gospel you are saved, if you hold firmly to the word I preached to you. Otherwise, you have believed in vain. For what I received I passed on to you as of first importance: that Christ died for our sins according to the Scriptures, that he was buried, that he was raised on the third day" (1 Cor. 15:1–4; Chrysostom, *Comm. on Cor.* 38.2–5).

The core of Pauline preaching was collated and summarized by C. H. Dodd:

The prophecies are fulfilled, and the new age is inaugurated by the coming of Christ.
He was born of the seed of David.
He died according to the Scriptures, to deliver us out of the present evil age.
He was buried.
He rose on the third day according to the Scriptures.
He is exalted at the right hand of God, as Son of God and Lord of quick and dead.
He will come again as Judge and Savior of men.

(*APD*:17)

The Ascription of Lordship

There is strong evidence that the earliest Christian proclamation attested Jesus as Kurios (Lord), confirming Luke's report of Peter's first sermon in Acts 2:36. In debating the scribes, Jesus made it clear that the Messiah was not merely David's son, but David's Lord, implying that he himself was this divine Lord (Mark 12:37; Augustine, *Tractates on John*, 8.9; Taylor, *NJ*:50–51; Ladd, *TNT*:167–68). If so, this earliest Christian ascription of Lordship comes from Jesus himself and not from his disciples alone. This passage undercuts the common form-critical habit of late dating, which theorizes that the ascription of deity only slowly evolved and that Lordship was only much later attributed to Jesus (Bultmann, *TNT* 1: 121–33).

The earliest Christians were rigorously monotheistic, worshiping and proclaiming the one God. It was as monotheists that they worshiped and proclaimed Jesus Christ as Lord (Ursinus, *CHC*: 202–204). Thus the kernel of triune teaching was already firmly implanted in this earliest core of Christian confession (Pearson, *EC* 1: 260–75).

Early Creedal Summaries

Second century creedal digests echoed these primitive New Testament confessions. Ignatius (ca. AD 35–107) provided this early summary of core events that were to form the second article of the Apostles' Creed on Christ: "Be deaf, therefore, whenever anyone speaks to you apart from Jesus Christ, who is of the stock of David, who is of Mary, who was truly born, ate and drank, was truly persecuted under Pontius Pilate, was truly crucified and died in the sight of beings of heaven, of earth and the underworld, who was also truly raised from the dead" (Ignatius of Antioch, *Trallians* 9:1–2).

Irenaeus (ca. AD 130–200) was firmly convinced that the following confession had been reliably received directly from the apostles themselves and had not passed through a series of dilutions resulting from its development: "The Church, though scattered through the whole world to the ends of the earth, has received from the Apostles and their disciples the faith . . . in one Christ Jesus, the Son of God, who became flesh for our salvation" (Irenaeus, *Ag. Her.* 1.10.1). These short creedal confessions were designed to be memorized verbatim at baptism, in order that believers may have "salvation written in their hearts by the Spirit without paper and ink" (Irenaeus, *Ag. Her.* 2.4.1; Cullmann, *Earliest Christian Confessions*).

Far from being appended to Scripture, the baptismal rule of faith was understood as a summary of Scripture that contained nothing other than the teaching found in the earliest eyewitnesses who penned the Scripture (Pearson, *EC* I: 383). For this reason, since it was directly quoting the apostles, the rule of faith as recalled and passed on by Tertullian was understood by the church of North Africa to be resistant to any possibility or need of change or supposed "improvement" (*irreformabilis; On the Veiling of Virgins* 1).

The *Heidelberg Catechism* followed this same pattern: "What, then, must a Christian believe? All that is promised us in the gospel, a summary of which is taught us in the articles of the Apostles' Creed, our universally acknowledged confession of faith" (II, Q22, *BOConf.* 4.022). Protestant confessions such as the Second Helvetic characteristically accepted the classical Christian teaching of ancient ecumenical formulae "summed up in the Creeds and decrees of the first four most excellent synods convened at Nicaea, Constantinople, Ephesus and Chalcedon—together with the Creed of blessed Athanasius, and all similar symbols," and "in this way we retain the Christian, orthodox and catholic faith whole and unimpaired" (Confession 11, *BOConf.* 5.078). Orthodox, Catholic, and Protestant doctrinal definitions share this common consensus. It is to these ancient ecumenical formulations and their leading expositors that classic consensual Christian teaching primarily appeals, provided that "nothing is contained in the aforesaid symbols which is not agreeable to the Word of God" (Second Helvetic Confession 11, *BOConf.* 5.079).

The Gospel of God

It is this good news that awakened the church. Since the gospel brought the church into being, the church cannot claim to be sole arbiter of the gospel, but must humbly receive it (Eph. 5:23; Col. 1:18–24; Ursinus, *CHC*:102–104). The church does not possess or own or contain the gospel. The very purpose of the church is to proclaim and make known the gospel that calls the church into being (Luther, *Serm. at Leisnig* [1523]; Melanchthon, *Loci Communes*).

Paul defined the subject of his letter to Rome as the "gospel of God" (Rom. 1:1; Origen, *Comm. on Rom.* 1.1–2). Mark entitled his narrative "the gospel of Christ" (Mark 1:1). Both thereby underscored the transcendent origin of the events surrounding Jesus of Nazareth.

The deepest need of humanity is for salvation from sin. This is the quandary to which the gospel speaks. The church that forgets the gospel of salvation is finally not the church but its echo. The church that becomes focused upon maintaining itself instead of the gospel becomes a dead branch of the living vine. The church is imperiled when it becomes intoxicated with the spirit of its particular age, committed more to serve the gods of that age than the God of all ages (Augustine, *CG* 4; Kierkegaard, *Judge for Yourselves!; Two Ages*).

Key Definitions: Person, Work, States, and Offices

Shorthand terms have often been used in the ecumenical tradition to encompass large masses of dialogue and consensual thinking into condensed formulae. In what follows I will introduce the most important of these terms pertaining to Christ, namely, those distinguishing between Christ's person, his work, his states of descent and ascent, and his offices (prophet, priest, and king). Time is saved by carefully learning and remembering these distinctions from the outset.

The Person and Work of Christ

The overall design of classical Christology is essentially simple and need not be confusing even to the novice. It hinges on a clear-cut distinction between who one is and what one does. A living person is not the same as that person's work. The work (*opus*) is done by the person (*persona*, Gk. *hupostasis*). We do not commonly say that the person's work is precisely the person, because the person precedes and transcends his work. Rather we say the person's work (acts, actions, behaviors) reveals who the person is. Hence person and work are distinguishable, but not separable.

Nothing proceeds rightly in setting forth the work of Christ unless the unique Person doing the work is first properly identified. Every person is unique. But the Person of Jesus Christ is unique in a way that is utterly distinguishable from all other unique persons, since without ceasing to be human, this person is God in the flesh.

The work done by Jesus Christ could not have been completed by any other Person than one distinctly capable of mediating the alienated relationship between deity and humanity. To reconcile that relationship, one must have personal credentials in both ordinary humanity and true divinity. The reconciler must have standing with humanity and have standing with God. One must have a particular identity, a unique personhood to do that work (Leo I, *Serm.* 27; 63).

Classic exegetes thus begin their reflection with the distinctive *identity* of Christ, or the *person* of Christ as truly human and truly God—who he is (Augustine, *Trin.* 4; Hilary, and Gregory of Nazianzus on second article of the Trinity). For no one could fully accomplish this task unless that one were truly human and truly God.

Theandric Union: The Deity of Christ Is the Premise of His Saving Activity

Quietly operating in the overall design of classic Christian teaching is the principle of economy (*oikonomia*—the arrangement, plan, order, design of the foreseeing God). The central ordering economic principle of all talk of the person of Christ is the union of his humanity and divinity, one person having two natures. This is called the *theandric* (divine-human) *premise* (or the premise of theandric union). Theandric is a contraction of two words: *theos* and *anthropos* (*theanthropos* = God-man; Augustine, *Trin.* 1.13).

The mission of divine grace is the central ordering principle of all talk of the *work* of Christ, encompassing his life, death, exaltation, and continuing presence. "The doctrine of the mediator consists of two parts: the one has respect to the *person* of the mediator; the other to his *office*" (Ursinus, *CHC*:164 italics added). An intrinsic order is here implied. One must first establish the personal identity of the Son, and only on that basis can one consider the work of the Son or the saving action of God in Jesus Christ. That is the sequence through which classic Christian teaching proceeds.

Person and work, though conceptually distinguishable, are intrinsically related, hence inseparable, always appearing together (just as *you* are presupposed in what you *do*, your acts cannot be considered apart from you). There is no mediation between God and man without this mediator who must be truly God and must be truly human.

The saving significance of his work for us is the reason why we study his person, his unique divine-human identity. Who Christ *is* is necessary to what he does. What he *does* proceeds from who he is. Melanchthon rightly understood: "Who Jesus Christ is becomes known in his saving action" (*Loci*, pref., *CR* 21:85).

The Order of Deity, Humanity and Union: The Key Issues of the Person

There is an aesthetically beautiful simplicity in the ordering of classical Christology. It examines in compact sequence three questions: the deity of the person; the humanity of the person; and the unique personal union of God and humanity in one person (Athanasius, *Four Discourses Ag. Arians* 3:26–28; Novatian, *Trin.* 9–28). The most decisive questions associated with the identity of Christ fall under one of these three:

- Is the Son truly God?

- Is the Son truly human?

- If both are answered yes, then how can these two affirmations be made to cohere?

This is the classic trajectory we will track in the ensuing chapters.

The Order of Salvation: The Basic Issues of His Work

Only when the classic exegetes had identified the Worker did they speak of the work of the Savior. The work of Christ is a phrase that sums up all the saving activity of God the Son on behalf of humanity. Whatever he has done that has saving significance is viewed all together as his saving work. Under the rubric of the work of Christ we will speak more broadly of his birth, life, and teaching, but focus primarily on his mission, death, and resurrection, as do the gospel narratives.

The study of salvation is called soteriology (*peri tes sōtērias logo*—that which concerns the Word of salvation). It studies the reconciling *work* this unique Person came to accomplish: the *redemption* of humanity. The Mediator came to mediate between God and humanity in a redemptive work that could only be accomplished by this unique Person. The study of God's saving action includes the work of redemption (the atoning death and victorious resurrection) and the receptive application of that work in the community of faith and the world. The door of entry into the study of salvation is the discussion of the estates and offices of the Redeemer.

The order of salvation (*ordo salutis*) proceeds from person to work. The work includes everything from his descent from heaven to his ascent to heaven.

The Descent and Ascent of the Son

For this Person to do this work, it was necessary that he come to humanity in a manner fitting to his theandric identity. Humbled from an exalted state, he came to share in our human sphere in life and death. Having accomplished this mission, he returned as resurrected Lord in exaltation.

The redemption envisioned by God in eternity was accomplished in time by his Son Jesus Christ. Hence the whole complex story of his coming and going may be summarized in two basic states or phases. Classic Christianity plots the entire narrative in these movements:

His Descent	His Ascent
Movement Downward	Movement Upward
The Son must come from above	He must go from the world
The Son is sent from the Father	He must return to the Father
The Son who descends	He will ascend to heaven

Classic Christianity teaches that the Son who descends must ascend. The usual way of expressing these phases doctrinally is:

Humiliation	Exaltation
From incarnation to death	From resurrection to heavenly session
katabasis (descent)	*anabasis* (ascent)

Thus it is summarily said that the Son appeared in two states ("estates" or conditions), first as lowered, then as raised.

Humiliation does not mean that God has been degraded or diminished, but rather that God the Son freely enters our human condition by becoming flesh and becoming obedient unto death and burial (Phil. 2:6–9), after which there can be no further humbling. Then he is exalted to return to the bosom of the Father (Hilary, *Trin.* 2, 22; Longenecker, *CEJC*:58–63).

The Offices of the Earthly Work as
Prophet, Priest, and King

An office is a position of trust, an assigned service or function, with specified duties and authority. The ancient Hebraic offices to which the expected One would be anointed were prophet, priest, and king. These provided a sufficient frame of reference for organizing and summarizing the whole redemptive work of Christ on earth within the bounds of his descent and ascent.

- as *prophet* he taught and proclaimed God's coming kingdom;

- as *priest* he suffered and died for humanity;

- as *king* he is exalted to receive legitimate governance of the coming reign of God.

Sequential Correlation of Estates and Offices

Note that there is a sequential correlation between the two estates and three offices: he is humbled to undertake his earthly prophetic ministry, which ends in his priestly ministry; he is exalted to complete his ministry of governance in guarding and guiding the faithful community toward the fulfillment of the promises of God. One who grasps this sentence thoroughly has already touched the vital center of the inner structure of classic reasoning about the Word of Life. We will make clear each of its elements as follows.

Surveying the Christological Landscape
in Advance

Looking ahead in overview: Even a beginner in the study of Christian teaching can distinguish between (1) the person and work of Christ, (2) the two natures of the one person in theandric union, (3) death and resurrection as key to the work of Christ, (4) the two estates, and (5) the three offices by which he accomplished his work.

These simple terms grasp the essential structure of classical Christology. Everything else falls into place in relation to this clear-cut structure. Classic Christianity seeks to make these distinctions plain and useful for baptismal instruction, discipling, and spiritual formation.

The order we are following is a composite of patterns formulated by the most deliberate systematic minds of the early periods of Christian teaching: Irenaeus, Tertullian, Gregory of Nazianzus, Cyril of Jerusalem, Hilary of Potiers, Augustine, and John of Damascus. This sequence is found in all of these figures. This sequence owes very little to any writer after the eighth century.

The same sequence is found in the structure of Thomas Aquinas' treatise on the Savior. It falls into two major divisions:

The Mystery of the Incarnation	The Mystery of Redemption
The Person of Christ	The actions and sufferings of Christ
Divine-human union (Christology, *ST* 3 Q48–51)	Birth, life, death, exaltation (Soteriology, *ST* 3 Q52–55)

Calvin's similar order (*Inst.* 2.14–17) has profoundly shaped Protestant Christology:

Two Natures United	Order of Offices	Descending and Ascending States
Shows how the two natures of Mediator unite in one Person (*Inst.* 2.14)	Prophet Priest King (*Inst.* 2.15)	Christ has fulfilled the work of Redeemer to acquire salvation for us by his birth and death through DESCENT, and through his resurrection and ascension by ASCENT (*Inst.* 2.16–17)

The Name Jesus Christ Encompasses His Person and Work

Christ (Messiah) is a title, Jesus a personal name. The unified name Jesus Christ welds together the person and office of the Savior. The inclusive name itself reveals the heart of the interfacing of the Jesus of history and the Christ celebrated by faith.

This office (Christ) cannot be viewed or understood apart from this person (Jesus). The person is never seen or attested "off duty" or as separable from the office, for Jesus is always the sent Son, the anointed One, whose work is the giving of himself, whose person is the Word made flesh, whose enacted word is his life. He cannot be reduced either to Jesus or the Christ as if divisible. The narratives of Jesus do not mention anything he *did* that could be understood as disconnected from *who he was* as Sent and Anointed One.

The teachings of Jesus are important to faith not simply because they are profound ideas, but because they are the teachings of this incomparable Mediator, Jesus Christ. There is no mention of his *teachings* whatever in the Apostles' Creed and no attempt in any of the classic confessions to set forth the teachings of Jesus as conceptually separable from his person and work. His teaching with words is made clear in his embodied Word, the embodiment and personification of his teaching in his ministry and death and resurrection.

Faith in Jesus Christ is not the acceptance of a system of teaching or doctrine, but personal trust in him based upon an encounter with this living person whose life is his word and whose word is embodied in his life. His message is proclaimed only through his action, especially in the events surrounding his death. Jesus not only *has* a word to speak for humanity but himself *is* that Word. He not only *does* good works but also *is* the inestimable good work of God on our behalf.

This is why the most basic form of Christian confession is that *Jesus Christ is Lord,* which presupposes the pivotal recognition that *Jesus is the Christ.* Nothing is more central to New Testament documents than that confession based on that recognition. This is the quintessential integrating statement of the person and work of Christ.

Yet modern criticism has despairingly sought for a century to pry Jesus loose from his identity as the Christ on the one hand (Harnack and the German liberal tradition focusing separately upon Jesus' teachings) or from any significant correlation between the remembered kerygma of the disciples with the known historical person of Jesus (Bultmann and Tillich, who had grave doubts that anything at all can be reliably known about Jesus, even though the community's memory of the kerygma might be proximately known). Both the liberal tradition and the post-liberal tradition failed to sustain the orthodox apostolic witness by disuniting the Word from the historicity of the teacher.

The Nicene Organizing Principle of the Classic-Ecumenic Study of Christ

The prevailing organizing structure for the classic sequence of Christian teaching of Christ is found in the second article of the Creed of the 150 Fathers of the Council of Constantinople (traditionally called the "Nicene Creed," but more accurately called the Nicaea-Constantinopolitan Creed of 381).

This creed may be found in virtually any prayerbook or hymnbook of the Christian tradition—Catholic, Orthodox, liberal or evangelical Protestant. It contains everything essential to this study and to Christology. Classic Christology consists in a commentary on the sequence of key biblical phrases compacted in the creed.

The three articles of the creed reveal its deliberate overarching triune structure, confessing faith in one God: God the Father, God the Son, and God the Spirit. Having already looked into the *first article on God the Father* in the first part of this study ("The Living God"), we will now treat point by point the series of topics of the *second article on God the Son*, leaving it to the end of this study to discuss the *third article on God the Spirit*. In this way it becomes clear how the whole of theology is a preparation for and confirmation of baptism.

Luther thought that "all errors, heresies, idolatries, offenses, abuses and ungodliness in the Church have arisen primarily because this [second] article, or part, of the Christian faith concerning Jesus Christ, has been either disregarded or abandoned" (Lenker ed., 24:224). "You must stay with the Person of Christ. When you have Him, you have all; but you have also lost all when you have lost Him" (Luther, *Serm. on John 6:37*).

Outline of the Central Article of the Nicene Creed

Note that the creed's second article is ordered according to the pivotal twofold division that summarizes classic Christology: the person and the work of Christ (who the Redeemer is and what the Redeemer has done to redeem humanity), conceptually distinguishable yet practically united in a single integrated gospel. In this way the creed provides the core outline of this inquiry (with key Greek and Latin terms), as follows:

PART I. Who Christ Is—Word Made Flesh

    Faith in the One Lord: Truly God, Truly Human

        Personal trust: I believe (*credo*; Gk. *pisteuomen*).

        Belief in one Lord (*in unum Dominum*; Gk. *eis ena Kurion*).

    Confession of the Name Jesus Christ

        I believe in Jesus (*Credo in . . . Jesus*).

        Jesus is the Christ (*Christum*), anointed as proclaiming prophet, self-offering priest, and messianic king.

    One Person: Deity and Humanity in Theandric Union

Only Son of God (*Filium Dei*; Gk. *ton huion tou theou ton monogenē*).

> The Son is eternally Begotten (*unigenitum*; Gk. *monogenē*, "only-begotten").

> Of the Father (*ex Patre natum*; Gk. *ton ek ton patros gennēthenta*).

> Begotten before all worlds (*ante omnia saecula*; Gk. *pro pantōn tōn aiōnōn*).

True God

> The Son is God of God (*Deum de Deo*).

> The Son is Light of Light (*Lumen de Lumine*; Gk. *phōs ek phōtos*).

The Nature of Divine Sonship

> The Son is true God of true God (*Deum verum de Deo vero*; Gk. *Theon alethinon ek Theou alēthinou*).

> The Son is begotten, not made (*genitum, non factum*; Gk. *gennēthenta, ou poiēthenta*).

> The Son is consubstantial with the Father (*consubstantialem Patri*; Gk. *homoousion tō Patri*, of the same essence as the Father).

Creator and Savior as Preexistent Word: The Preincarnational Life of the Son

> By the Son were all things made (*per quem omnia facta sunt*; Gk. *di ou ta panta egeneto*).

> The Son's mission was for us humans (*qui propter nos homines*; Gk. *ton di hēmas tous anthrōpous*).

> He came for our salvation (*et propter nostram salutem*; Gk. *kai dia tēn hēmeteran soterian*).

The Humbling of God to Servanthood

> God the Son descended to human history (*descendit*). The descent from heaven (*de coelis*) to earth.

The Incarnation: Truly Human

> For us the Son became incarnate (*incarnatus*; Gk. *sarkōthenta*).

> Was conceived by the Holy Spirit (*de Spiritu Sancto*).

> Born of the Virgin Mary (*ex Maria virgine*).

> Was made man (*homo factus est*; Gk. *enanthrōpēsanta*).

PARTS II AND III. Our Lord's Earthly Life—He Died for Our Sins

Our Lord's Earthly Life (Prophetic Office)

His Suffering and Death (Priestly Office)

> Jesus was crucified (*crucifixus*).

> For us (*pro nobis*; Gk. *huper hēmen*).

> Tried under Pontius Pilate (*sub Pontio Pilato*).

> Suffered (*passes*; Gk. *pathonta*).

> Died and was buried (*sepultus est*).

Part IV. Exalted Lord

> [He descended into the abode of the dead (*descendit in inferna* (not in the Creed of the 150 Fathers, but appearing in the creed of Rufinus, AD 390)].

> He was raised again from the dead (*resurrexit*; Gk. *anastanta*).

>> According to the Scriptures (*secundum Scripturus*).

>> On the third day (*tertia dei*).

He ascended into heaven (*ascendit in coelum*).

His Coming Kingdom (Regal Office)

He now sits at the right hand of the Father (*sedet ad dexteram Patris*).

And he shall come again (*et iterum venturus est*) to judge the quick and the dead (*COC* 2:57–58).

Why This Organizing Principle?

"Before you go forth," wrote Augustine, "fortify yourselves with your Creed," for it is composed of words received from "throughout the divine Scriptures," but which "have been assembled and unified to facilitate the memory" (Augustine, *The Creed* 1). The creed is compact, memorizable, serving the teaching function of bringing together the heart of the matter of Scripture.

Note that this organizing principle expresses both a logical and a chronological order. It is *logical* in that it proceeds from Christ's identity to his activity, from his person to his work, from his being to his doing, from *who* the Mediator is to *what* the Mediator does to benefit humanity. This Person is required for this saving act, for who else could do this work of reconciliation?

Since there can be no salvation without a Savior, there is no soteriology without Christology. For if Jesus were not truly divine Son, then his atoning action on the cross would have been insufficient—merely an example of human heroism or altruistic generosity.

The order of the creed is *chronological* because the story of salvation is a history. This is a basic premise of Hebraic religion. History (which declares God's salvation) unfolds chronologically as a linear, sequential development. Consequently the study of Christ proceeds according to the order of time (*chronos*), within which a pivotal moment occurs that divides time—appearing at the fullness of time (*kairos*).

This historical sequence could be schematized as a cycle of descent ending in death, followed by ascent ending in exaltation. The descending sequence is called the humbling (lowering, lowliness, humiliation) of God, because it takes the story of the Mediator chronologically from preexistence to death, in a descending order from the highest of the high to the lowest of the low. It reveals the lowliness of God to the greatest conceivable extent. In this study we will take that descent step by step in Parts I, II, and II ahead. Part IV must be portrayed in the reverse ascending order, since it begins in the depths and moves upward toward exaltation into the reception of the Son into the heavenly kingdom; hence it is called the exaltation of the messianic king.

In this way the twofold movement of descent and ascent, the humbling and exaltation of God the Son, provides a way of organizing exceptionally diverse materials of New Testament Scripture into a single memorable confession of faith encompassed in the Nicene Creed.

The four Parts of this study may be stated concisely:

He came.

He lived.

He died.

He rose.

The first question to be faced is: Who came?

PART I

WORD MADE FLESH

The Map of the Road Ahead

Four classic questions encompass the classic teaching the person of Christ:

1. *Quis* (who)?

2. *Quid* (what)?

3. *Quomodo* (how)?

4. *Ad quid* (why)?

Who assumed humanity in the incarnation?
What nature did the eternal Son assume?
How are deity and humanity united in one person?
Why did the Son become flesh?

Modern journalism quotes this sequence as the essence of good reporting (who, what, how, and why), unaware that it derives from classic Christian teaching, which itself sought to report the best of good news.

The answers to these four questions may be summed up in advance: *(1) the divine Logos assumed, (2) human nature, (3) so as personally to unite deity and humanity in Christ, (4) for the redemption of humanity* (Athanasius, *Incarn.* of the *Word*, 3–30; Pohle-Preuss, *DT* 4:5; Bellarmine, *De Christo* 1.1). This is a high altitude map of the spectacular territory we are now to traverse on foot, traditionally called "the Person of Christ."

2

THE BODY LANGUAGE
OF GOD

HE CORE QUESTION FOCUSES UPON the identity of Jesus. Who is this
itinerant teacher? Why is he so incongruously called "Mary's son"? There
is little doubt that such a question was beginning to be asked already
during Jesus' own lifetime. It emerged early in Jesus' ministry, continued steadily,
and remains puzzling to us today. "Who do you think you are?" (John 8:53;
Augustine, *Tractates on John* 43.14–15), they asked of him.

Such questioning was a response to the words and deeds of Jesus and not
merely made up and projected upon him decades later by ignorant and fanciful
disciples. This question always arises necessarily out of concrete meeting and
dialogue with Jesus of Nazareth.

The Deity of Christ

Who Does He Think He Is?

Four castings of the same identity question appear in Gospel reports of Jesus.
The core question was posed by extremely varied inquirers: by the religious
establishment, by civil authorities, by the general populace, and among the inner
circle of his disciples:

First, as *asked by the religious leaders*: Who can forgive sin but God alone?
When he healed a paralytic, Jesus said: "Your sins are forgiven." Some asked:
"Who is this man who speaks against God in this way. No man can forgive sins;
God alone can!" (Luke 5:21; Calvin, *Comm.* 14; Novatian, *Trin.*, FC 67:54). Later
when he pronounced as forgiven "a woman who had lived a sinful life" (Luke
7:37), "the other guests began to say among themselves, '*Who is this who even
forgives sins?*'" (Luke 7:49, italics added; Tertullian, *Ag. Marcion* 4.18).

Second, *as asked by the civil authorities*: Is he the beheaded John returning from the dead? Jesus must have made the civil authorities anxious about political succession, legitimated power, order, and authority. Herod jailed and finally beheaded John the Baptist, a relative of Jesus. The theory was being circulated that Jesus perhaps might be John returning from the dead. Herod complained: "I beheaded John. *Who, then, is this* I hear such things about?" (Luke 9:9, italics added). The question of his identity became an urgent matter for civil order and ultimately the cause of his death.

Third, a*s asked by the populace*: Who is this? Jesus' identity perplexed the general populace. This became clear at one decisive point—"When Jesus entered Jerusalem, the whole city was stirred and asked, '*Who is this?*'" (Matt. 21:11, italics added).

Fourth, a*s asked by Jesus himself to the inner circle*: But who do you say I am? A decisive moment in Jesus' ministry came when he put the question squarely to the disciples: What about each of you? "Who do *you* say I am?" (Mark 8:29; italics added).

When he told them that he would soon be betrayed, would die, and be raised again, Mark reported candidly that "they did not understand what he meant" (Mark 9:32; Luke 9:45). It was not until the resurrection that his identity was clearly revealed (Chrysostom, *Hom. on Matt.* Hom 58.1).

The Question Today

This question accompanied the footsteps of Jesus all along the way. It has hardly lost its force today. The same question surfaces for anyone who seriously reads the New Testament texts—"Who is this?" (Mark 4:41). Who can read the New Testament without wondering about this question of Jesus' identity? It cannot be taken up casually as a purely historical exercise, for to ask "Who is he?" is to ask "Who is God?" and "Who am I myself?" (Ephrem, *Three Homilies* 50).

This question remains decisive for classical Christian teaching. If it should turn out to be the case that Jesus was quite different from who he said he was, then we might as well end this book here and not bother about its remaining pages. If there is a radical gap between who he claimed to be and who he really was, then little remains of the New Testament witness except burdensome bones of religious trivia. If, on the other hand, it might be possible to demonstrate to fair-minded inquirers that the report concerning Jesus is essentially a truthful recollection, then the consequences of that must reverberate to every dimension of personal and social life (Augustine, *Sermons* 63.1–3; *CG* 16–18).

Is it possible to set forth credible evidence that Jesus is the one he is attested to be—the One and Only God become fully human, a historical individual personally uniting two distinct natures, human and divine—so that only this one could be the Expected One worthy of worship? That is the important subject of the study of the person of Christ. Other questions are tiny by comparison (Bede, *Hom. on Gospels* 16,17). If this proves right, then all else follows; if this proves wrong, then nothing else could possibly avail to make Christianity worth pursuing. If true but undemonstrable, then a heavy cloud hangs over Christian testimony.

This is in fact the decisive question that the New Testament as a whole asks every hearer. The examination of this sort of evidence will occupy us throughout this entire middle section of this study, the heart of this book. It will focus initially upon three key issues: did Christ's claims about himself correspond with the remembering church's attestation about him? Did Christ's living and dying reveal a character and behavior that corresponds with these claims? In what sense did the resurrection constitute a unique validation of these claims? The historical evidence cannot be fairly assessed without probing these three vital questions (Irenaeus, *Ag. Her.* 4.5–10; Mark 8:29; Matt. 10:32–33).

Claims Made By and About Christ

Jesus did not ask his hearers to accept his moral reflections or philosophical ideas but simply to believe in him (Hilary, *Hom.* Ps. 1.22–23). His ministry confronted every hearer with the same basic decision: are you ready to live in the presence of the coming governance of God?

He taught that trusting in him would deliver the sinner from sin. Failing to believe in him would leave the sinner so mired in sin as to miss eternal life (John 3:15–18; Cyril of Alex., *Comm. on John* 2.1).

He did not merely call for faith in the Father apart from the Son, as if distanced from himself. Rather he understood himself to be nothing less than the living embodiment of the Father's Word (John 12:44–50, 15:1–8; Ambrose, *On Chr. Faith* 5.10.19–20).

Early in his ministry, when Jesus attended the synagogue of his village of Nazareth, he reportedly read this passage from Isaiah 41:1–2, as recorded by Luke: "'The Spirit of the Lord is on me, because he has anointed me to preach good news to the poor. He has sent me to proclaim freedom for the prisoners and recovery of sight for the blind, to release the oppressed, to proclaim the year of the Lord's favor.' Then he rolled up the scroll, gave it back to the attendant and sat down. The eyes of everyone in the synagogue were fastened on him, and he began by saying to them, 'Today this scripture is fulfilled in your hearing'" (Luke 4:18–21; Tertullian, *Ag. Marcion* 4.8; *Ag. Praxeas* 11; Calvin, *Comm.* 16: 230).

The point is unmistakable: Jesus, in Luke's view, thought that Isaiah was referring to him! The climax of the episode is not Isaiah's prophecy but Jesus' response to it. All four Gospels hold that he assented to the recognition that he was the expected deliverer of Israel (Matt. 16:15–20; Mark 8:29–32, 14:62–63; Luke 9:20–22, 24:46; John 11:25–28; Cyril of Alex., *Comm. on Luke,* Hom. 49). When he preached the coming kingdom of God, he assumed that his own ministry was the inauguration of that governance. Entrance into the reign of God was thought to depend entirely upon how one answers the question—"Who is this one?" "Many prophets and kings wanted to see what you see but did not see it, and to hear what you hear but did not hear it" (Luke 10:23; Cyril of Alex., *Comm. on Luke,* Hom. 67).

The Scandal of Self-Reference

It is characteristic of great religious teachers that they are self-effacing. Jesus seems quite different. He was constantly remembered as saying outrageous things about himself, like: "I am the way and the truth and the life. No one comes to the Father except through me" (John 14:6). "Anyone who loves his father or mother more than me is not worthy of me" (Matt. 10:27). These ring with absurdity unless there is a plausible premise behind them that can help them make sense (Hilary, *Trin.* 7.33). One of the most shocking aspects of the New Testament is the frequency with which Jesus makes reference to himself, his mission, his sonship, his coming kingdom. No wonder he is regarded as delusional by some amateur psychiatrists whose naturalistic assumptions rule out taking seriously his own explanation of himself.

Compounding the irony, all of this was said by one who most earnestly *taught humility* and urged others to "become as little children." Preaching meekness, he warned his hearers against self-centeredness, and when they quarreled over who would be the greatest, he corrected them (Mark 10:35–45; Chrysostom, *On the Incomprehensible Nature of God* 8.32–33). *Either he did not follow his own teaching at all, or there must have been something utterly unique about him that enabled him to teach from a very different premise of authority than anyone else.* The most shocking hypothesis is simply to suppose that he was telling the truth about himself and that reports of him were substantially accurate. This is the faith of classic Christianity. Here is the evidence that appears repeatedly in classic sources:

He accepted the ascription of Messiah. Jesus understood himself to be the messiah of historic Jewish expectations. In doing so he transformed the very notion of messiah in accepting that designation.

The most penetrating evidence comes from the earliest written Gospel—according to Mark. Jesus understood his ministry as a sign of the end time: "The time has come." "The Kingdom of God is near. Repent and believe the good news!" (Mark 1:15; Jerome, *Comm. on the Gospels*, Catena, *CG* 1:370).

When asked by the high priest before the Sanhedrin: "Are you the Christ, the Son of the Blessed One?" Jesus broke his previous reserve and replied, "I am." "The high priest tore his clothes. 'Why do we need any more witnesses?' he asked. 'You have heard the blasphemy'" (Mark 14:61–62; Clement of Alex., *Fragments* 2).

The most remarkable part of Peter's confession, "You are the Christ" (Mark 8:29), is not so much that Peter said it but that Jesus accepted the ascription, and "warned them not to tell anyone about him" (Mark 8:30; Origen, *Comm. on Matt.* 12.10). The Jesus of Mark's Gospel was not just another prophet, such as Elijah or John, but the one to whom the prophets attested. He was less a sign pointing to the door of life than the door itself (Mark 13:4–37; John 10:7–9; Rev. 3:8; Athanasius, *Four Discourses Ag. Arians* 1.1–11). We have no earlier or more reliable evidence of Jesus' proclamation than these Markan sayings (Jerome, *Hom.* 84).

He accepted the ascription of Son of Man. There can be little doubt that he assumed the title "Son of Man" as particularly definitive of his mission. It was a recognized messianic title from Daniel 7:13, Ezekiel (2:1, 3; 3:1–10; 8:1–12), 2 Esdras 13, and the *Similitudes of Enoch*. It implied descent from above (Justin Martyr, *Dialogue with Trypho* 31–33; Gregory of Nyssa, *Ag. Eunomius* 3.4; Augustine, *Trin.* 3.18; H. E. Tödt, *The Son of Man in the Synoptic Tradition*). After the Pharisees investigated the healing of the man born blind, Jesus asked him: "'Do you believe in the Son of Man?' 'Who is he, sir?' the man asked. 'Tell me so that I may believe in him.' Jesus said, 'You have now seen him; in fact, he is the one speaking with you'" (John 9:35–37; Theodore of Mopsuestia, *Comm. on John* 4.9.34–37). Either Jesus viewed himself as the Son of Man descended of the Father, or John's account is irreparably flawed and untrustworthy.

He accepted the ascription of Son of God. Jesus understood himself to have a unique relation of Sonship to God the Father. Much of John's Gospel focuses upon the intimacy and eternality of that relationship. John remembers Jesus as saying: "I and the Father are one" (10:30; Hippolytus, *Ag. Noetus* 7.1). The text implies mutual, coeternal accountability, with Father and Son assumed to be distinguishable, one sending and one being sent (Novatian, *On Trin.* 27).

Jesus explained to Philip: "How can you say, 'Show us the Father'? Don't you believe that I am in the Father, and that the Father is in me? The words I say to you are not just my own. Rather, it is the Father, living in me, who is doing his work" (John 14:9–10; Hilary, *On. Trin.* 7.36–40).

When the seventy-two returned from their mission, Jesus, "full of joy through the Holy Spirit," Jesus said: "No one knows who the Son is except the Father, and no one knows who the Father is except the Son and those to whom the Son chooses to reveal him" (Luke 10:21–22; Chrysostom, *Hom. on Luke 7*; cf. Matt. 28:16–20; John 17:6–26; Irenaeus, *Ag. Her.* 4.6). John remembers him saying: "All things have been committed to me by my Father" (Matt. 11:27).

Defects of Alternative Explanations

From the earliest time, there have been alternative explanations about Jesus that have been tested and consensually rejected by the believing community: he was not God but was more like God than most of us (Arius); the disciples projected upon a mere man a messianic identity (Ebionites); he was demon-possessed (Jesus' Pharisaic opponents).

Did Jesus merely share with God a moral intention? This diluted view of his person, that he merely shared an ethical purpose with God, an agreement with God in moral intent, not personal union with God, is found throughout *liberal culture-Protestantism* (Ritschl, *CDJR*:385–90, 442–80). It overlooks passages attesting his sonship and coeternality and equality with the Father.

It is not likely that the unique Father-Son relationship is something that the remembering church later fantasized or manufactured and then projected back upon Jesus after the resurrection, since evidences of the intimate Father-Son relationship appear in the earliest identifiable oral sources that predate the written sources (Jeremias, *The Parables of Jesus*:70; F. Hahn, *TJC*:295–310; V. Taylor, *Mark*: 597).

Jesus was distinctly remembered much later by eyewitnesses as having aroused indignation among his adversaries precisely "because he claimed to be the Son of God" (John 19:7; Augustine, *Hom. on John,* 116). Such an impression cannot easily have been made up, since the motivation to make it up seems wholly lacking and implausible. Jesus as portrayed by John assumed that the encounter with him was indeed an encounter with God. To know him would be to know God. To love or hate him amounted to loving or hating God. Trusting Jesus was trusting God (John 8:19; 12:44–45, 14:1–9; 15:23; Chrysostom, *Hom. on John* 74).

The "I Am" Statements

At this point we are only beginning to explore the classic arguments that Jesus is God, but it is at least clear that Jesus as remembered in the earliest texts understood himself as the heavenly Son of Man of prophetic expectation, possessing a unique relation of Sonship to God the Father, and accepted the ascriptions of Lordship and Messiah, such that our relation to God hinges radically upon our response to him.

The direct question to Jesus, "Who do you think you are?" was asked by his pious opponents in a conversation that centered on the question of whether Jesus might possibly be crazy (or demon-possessed). When he answered, "I am not possessed by a demon," he then added a phrase that convinced opponents that he was indeed crazy: "If anyone keeps my word, he will never see death." At this his opponents exclaimed, "Now we know that you are demon-possessed!" They were outraged: "Are you greater than our father Abraham! He died, and so did the prophets. Who do you think you are?" (John 8:49–53). Jesus' answer astonished them: "My Father, whom you claim as your God, is the one who glorifies me." "Before Abraham was, I am!" (John 8:54, 58; Chrysostom, *Hom. on John,* 55). This caused his shocked hearers to pick up "stones to stone him," for this is what they perceived their duty to be in relation to blasphemy. Either Jesus was indeed blaspheming against the holy divine name, "I am" (= Yahweh, Exod. 3:14) or he was revealing something about his identity that stands as the central feature of the gospel (Augustine, *Tractates on John* 49.15).

John's Gospel is organized around a series of key "signs," each culminating in an "I am" (*ego eimi*) statement reminiscent of the declarations of Yahweh. When he raised a dead man he said, "*I am* the resurrection and the life" (John 11:25). In giving sight to the man born blind Jesus said, "*I am* the light of the world" (John 8:12). When he fed the five thousand, he declared, "*I am* the bread of life" (John 6:35). He later said, "*I am* the door of the sheep" (10:7) and "*I am* the good shepherd" (10:10, italics added).

These are extremely immodest statements if applied to an ordinary human subject (Apostolic Constitutions 5.1.7). Jesus did not teach as the prophets taught when they pointed beyond themselves to the source of the divine revelation. Rather he taught and spoke in the first person, as Yahweh had spoken in the form of "I am" in the Exodus account of deliverance. Luther thought that by this means Jesus deliberately used language "to stop all mouths" (*Serm. on John 8:12*, 1531). The way he taught people is a clue to the remarkable presence he commanded. "He taught as one who had authority, not as their teachers of the law" (Matt. 7:29; Chrysostom, *Hom. on Matt.* 25).

The Temple guards remarked, "No one even spoke the way this man does" (John 7:46). When he taught in the Temple courts, the religious leaders were amazed and puzzled: "How did this man get such learning without having studied," to which Jesus answered; "My teaching is not my own. It comes from him who sent me" (John 7:14–16; Augustine, *Tractates on John*, 29.3–5). Even those of remote Nazareth "were amazed at the gracious words that came from his lips. 'Isn't this Joseph's son?' they asked" (Luke 4:22).

Resurrection as Ultimate Validation

His identity was not fully grasped by the disciples until the resurrection. Thomas' recognition was particularly dramatic. Having been told by the others: "We have seen the Lord!" (John 20:25), Thomas testily replied: " 'Unless I see the nail marks in his hands and put my finger where the nails were, and put my hand into his side, I will not believe it.' A week later his disciples were in the house again, and Thomas was with them. Though the doors were locked, Jesus came and stood among them and said, 'Peace be with you!' Then he said to Thomas, 'Put your finger here; see my hands. Reach out your hand and put it into my side. Stop doubting and believe.' Thomas said to him, 'My Lord and my God!' " (John 20:25–28; John Cassian, *On the Incarnation* 6.19).

Jesus could have rejected this ascription. Rather he received it, chiding Thomas not for his adoration, but for the tardiness of his belief, delayed by the requirement of having to "see." One who could welcome such an ascription must either be God or deceiver (Chrysostom, *Hom. on John* 87; Kierkegaard, *TC*: 40–71). Such claims are not to be found merely in obscure corners of the New Testament or in minor writers. They are found widely throughout all strata of the Gospels and in all Gospels, and they recur in both the early and late epistles. The picture of Jesus that confronts us in the New Testament is too consistent to be fantasized or projected, too unrelenting to be fabricated. These are the claims that we constantly meet on whatever page we read of the New Testament. Turn to most any paragraph of the New Testament and see if you can read it without the premise that God has come in Jesus and the claim that in Jesus we are being met by nothing less than God (Augustine, *Sermon* 145A).

The resurrected Lord taught that he would return to judge the world at the end time—a prerogative belonging only to God. Matthew's report of his language is audacious: "Whoever acknowledges me before men, I will also acknowledge him before my Father in heaven. But whoever disowns me before men, I will disown him before my Father in heaven" (Matt 10:32–33; Chrysostom, *Hom. on Matt.*, Hom. 34.3).

Why Delusion Is an Implausible Charge

All this is very unusual language, especially in the monotheistic Hebraic tradition. It is unconvincing to argue that Jesus did not say these things. They are so extraordinary that it seems implausible that they would have been invented by the disciples and put in Jesus' mouth decades later. The delusion premise has a major flaw: If the reports were inaccurate, they would be challenged and easily discredited. This would require the witnesses to be quite sure they reported accurately, to avoid being discredited. The traditions reported by synoptic writers could have been contested and corrected by many living eyewitnesses during the period of oral transmission. This is why so much deliberate attention is given in the New Testament to accuracy and credibility of testimony (Luke 1:1–4; Mark 1:1; John 15:27, Acts 1:21–22; 1 John 1:1; Origen, *Hom. on Luke* 1.6; Chrysostom, *Hom. on Acts* 1).

These assertions in themselves cannot be considered reasonable arguments for the deity of Christ, but they do require some reasonable explanation, seen from within a community that cares about truth-telling in God's presence. They defy the premise that Jesus was a great teacher *even if he was not* the messianic Son he claimed to be, for if he were not the messianic Son, then he surely must have been a deluded and deceptive teacher (Justin Martyr, *Dialogue with Trypho* 32–38; Augustine, *Trin*. 3). It is a bad teacher who fails to tell the truth about himself, especially if the centerpiece of his teaching is himself, his own identity, his Sonship, and messianic mission. If he is in error about that central premise, then how could he be trusted as a teacher about anything else? Some imagine that the best way to communicate with the modern skeptical mind is to speak only of Jesus' teaching and say nothing of his embarrassing alleged identity as eternal Son. But ironically that fantasy is made unacceptable by Jesus' own teaching about himself if he is not the One he appears to be.

If he were a man claiming to be God, he would be far more than egocentric—either he must be deluded, or it must be true (Kierkegaard, *TC*: 26–39). This is an assertion of such incredible, outrageous import that it must be either radically true or radically false. The New Testament does not give the reader the option of just taking a little snippet of its testimony while leaving the scandalous center of it behind (Theodore of Mopsuestia, *Comm. on John* 6.15.27). Only if he was indeed the Christ, the God-man, can he be considered sane. We do not get the impression from any source that he was delusive in any other way. There is no supporting evidence that Jesus was in any way psychologically imbalanced, as one would expect to find in one purported to be seriously deluded (Tertullian, *Ag. Praxeas* 22–24; Stott, *BC*: 28–33). Everything else we know about Jesus leads us to believe that he was honest and not deceptive. It seems implausible that he who resisted deception so strongly in others would himself become so deceptive. Upon examining the record, some may conclude delusion, but it is far more plausible to conclude with the remembering ecumenical consensus that the delusion of Jesus' detractors was greater than any Jesus might have had about himself.

Scriptural Reasoning About Christ's Deity

The primitive Christian community had deep roots in Jewish monotheism. With such a heritage, it must have required an extraordinary motivation to confess Jesus Christ as Lord or speak of him without qualification as the one God. The motive would have had to have been powerful enough to overcome rigorous piety and religious training to the contrary.

These witnesses, however, had met him as risen Lord. Only on this eventful and experiential basis were they able to draw the conclusion that he was the heavenly Son of Man, messianic King, Son of God, and indeed truly God (Gregory of Nazianzus, *Third Orat. on the Son, Orat.* 29; *BOC*: 500, 592).

No ancient Christian creed fails to confess the deity of Christ, for that would omit the central feature of Christian confession (Athanasius, *On the Incarn.*; Augustine, *CG*). Christ is called "God" in the same sense and with the same meaning that the Old Testament applies that address to Yahweh, the one God to whom worship is owed, to whom the divine attributes rightly apply. Accordingly, Jude confessed Christ as "our only Sovereign and Lord," the same One who "delivered his people out of Egypt" (Jude 4–5; Irenaeus, *Ag. Her.* 3.6.2, 3.19).

Classic exegetes thought that no argument of itself could finally convert the heart. Rather than by argument, such a conclusion can only be a deep-seated decision of the whole heart and mind, based upon whatever evidences one may be able to bring together to achieve a reliable sense of comprehensive coherence.

Whatever hypothesis best explains the widest range of evidence is the one upon which one may best ground one's active, risk-laden trust. The classic tradition is not without careful arguments to attempt to grasp and understand what faith knows—that Christ is God (Tertullian, *Apology* 21). Here they are:

Classic Reasons That Christ Is God

There are five key arguments that flow together in classic Christian teaching to achieve this trust that Christ must be truly God.

IF—the Son is addressed in scripture by ascriptions *that could only be appropriate for God;*

if the Son possesses attributes *that only God could possess;*

if the Son does the works *that only God could have done;*

if the Son is worshiped *as God without disclaiming it; and,*

if the Son is viewed by the apostles as equal *to God;*

THEN—Question: where these five streams flow together, do they mutually compel faith to confirm that the Son indeed must be confessed as truly God?

These five arguments recur in classical exegesis of hundreds of New Testament texts.

1. Reasoning from Ascriptions. If Jesus Christ is repeatedly *called God* in Holy Writ, then Christ must either be God or the writ lacks authenticity. The Son's deity is taught because it is expressed in Scripture in "lofty utterances" such as "Only-begotten"; "the Way, the Truth, the Life, the Light"; "the Effulgence, the Impress, the Image, the Seal"; "Lord, King, He That is, The Almighty" (Gregory of Nazianzus, *Orat.* 29.17). Paul salutes the church of Corinth with the phrase: "Grace to you and peace from God our Father and the Lord Jesus Christ" (1 Cor. 1:3). "For us there is one God, the Father, from whom are all things and for whom we exist, and one Lord, Jesus Christ, through whom are all things and through who we exist" (1 Cor. 8:6; Ambose, *On the Holy Spirit* 13.132). Matthew identifies him as the same Immanuel expected by Isaiah (Matt. 7:14), "God with us" (Matt. 1:23). John calls him the only Son of God, "God the One and Only," the only one to have seen God (John 1:18). "I have come down from heaven, not to do my own will, but the will of him who sent me" (John 6:38; Augustine, *Sermon* 14A.5).

There is no accompanying recollection that Jesus protested when these terms were ascribed to him (Chrysostom, *Hom. on John* 87; Augustine, *Comm. on John*, John 20:10–29, Tractate 121). James refers to him as "Lord of glory" (2:1). The author of Revelation calls him "King of kings and Lord of lords" (19:16; Apringius of Beja, *Tractate on the Apocalypse*, 19.15–16).

2. Reasoning from the Divine Attributes. If to him were ascribed *attributes* that could only rightly be ascribed to God, and if canonical Scripture bears truthful witness, then he must be God (Hilary, *Trin.* 11; Pearson, *EC* I: 219–30). Among divine attributes repeatedly ascribed to Christ were:

> holiness ("the Holy and Righteous One," Acts 3:14)

> underived being (Col. 1:15)

> uncreated eternality (John 8:58; 17:5; "the same yesterday and today and forever," Heb. 13:8; Heb. 9:14; Hilary, *Trin.* 9.53)

> unsurpassable power (Matt. 28:20; Mark 5:11–15; John 11:38–44)

> exceptional knowledge (knowing the hearts of all, Acts 1:24; Matt. 16:21; Luke 68; 11:17; John 4:29, Hilary, *Trin.* 9.62)

> absolute veracity ("the truth," John 14:6)

> eternal love ("that surpasses knowledge," Eph. 3:19)

3. Reasoning from God's Actions. If it should be the case that Christ in fact *performed actions and operations that only God could do and acted in a way that only God could act,* by forgiving sin (Mark 2:1–12); giving life to the dead; by engendering new life in the Spirit (John 5:21); by being himself raised from the dead (Matt. 28:1–15; Luke 16:1–14; Hilary, *Trin.* III), *then he must be nothing less than true God* (Ursinus, *CHC*: 188–89). If Jesus Christ searches the hearts and reveals the thoughts of men, stills the storm, lays down his life and takes it up again, he could only be God. His works reveal who he is as eternal Son, and on this premise do "his benefits interpret His nature" (P. T. Forsyth, *PPJC*:6).

4. Reasoning from the Adoration of the Worshiping Community. If Christ was worshiped as God and *unresistingly received worship due only to God* (1 Cor. 11:24, 25; John 5:23; 14:14; Acts 7:59), *then he must either be a blasphemer or God.* There was little reserve in the adoration given him. That "Jesus is Lord" (Rom. 10:9) is the heart of the Christian confession. John's Gospel states that "He who does not honor the Son does not honor the Father, who sent him" (John 5:23; Chrysostom, *Hom. on John* 39). This is an especially powerful statement in the light of the perennial Hebraic religious antipathy against the worship of a human being. Recall Paul's refusal of idolatrous worship at Lystra (Acts 14:8–20).

5. The Son is Equal to the Father. The Son does not need to grasp at equality with God since he is always and already the eternal Son of the Father (Phil. 2:6,7). His accusers were determined to kill him because "he was even calling God his own Father, making himself equal with God" (John 5:18).

Conclusion of the classic Christian consensus: one who is addressed in Scripture by ascriptions that could only be appropriate for God, who possesses attributes that only God could possess, who does the works that only God could have done, who is worshiped as God without disclaiming it; and, who is viewed by the apostles as equal to God—such a one must be God.

The Experiential Argument: Redeemed Lives Require a Redeemer

In addition to the above scriptural and traditional arguments, the consensual exegetes frequently recall a simple but disarming argument from experience—namely, the experience of the faithful community. The disciples experienced a profound consciousness of redemption. How did that experience emerge? It is possible to reason from the influence of Jesus upon redeemed persons to the character of his person as influencing cause. He cannot be less than God himself if he influences persons as Redeemer. If such faith is allowed to search in its own way for who Christ is, the name upon which it insists is God. No name but God is sufficient. No lesser identity will satisfy (Gregory of Nazianzus, *Orat.* 29, *On the Son*; Liddon, *DL*:152).

This sort of Christology is derived from the fact that people experienced Christ as having the value of God (Ritschl, *CDJR*: 412–451). No one can reasonably predicate of a mere human being the saving efficacy that is known by the redeemed (Chrysostom, *Hom. on John* 24.2).

The argument was aptly stated by Wilhelm Herrmann: "This thought, that when the historical Christ takes such hold of us, we have to do with God Himself—this thought is certainly the most important element in the confession of the Deity of Christ. . . . In what Jesus does to us, we grasp the expression God gives us of His feeling towards us, or God Himself as a Personal Spirit working upon us. This is the form in which every man who has been reconciled to God through Christ necessarily confesses His Deity" (*Communion with God*:143; Hilary, *Trin.* 12.56).

History Itself Vindicates Christ's Deity

Gregory of Nyssa proposed this threefold demonstration from history, empirically discernible, that God became incarnate in Jesus:

1. Animal sacrifice comes to an end in Jesus—a fact of history. Before Christ came, idolatry "held sway over man's life." "But, as the apostle says, from the moment that God's saving grace appeared among men and dwelt in human nature, all this vanished into nothing, like smoke."

2. The martyrdom period was endured and the community of faith survived. In the period of persecution, the church could not have survived had the incarnation been based upon myth or misunderstanding. It is a mockery of the martyrs and failure to listen to the testimony of their lives to assume that their faith was only in a man, not God-man. No hypothesis explains the church's survival of the genocidal history of martyrdom more adequately than that God was in Christ (Gregory of Nyssa, *ARI* 18; Lactantius, *Death of the Persecutors*).

3. The historic fact of the destruction of Jerusalem signified that a new covenant had been offered to humanity, confirming Christ's deity. (Gregory of Nyssa, *ARI* 18; Eusebius, *CH* 8–10; Augustine, *CG* 18).

Others after Gregory of Nyssa would make similar historical arguments (Augustine, Salvian, Victor of Vita). Although not a line of reasoning that can stand alone apart from other inferences from holy Scripture, it serves a corroborating function in supporting the conclusion that Jesus had unparalleled effect upon the course of universal history. It is a type of argument that begins with history and shows how actual history reveals the presence and work of the living God (Mark 1:1–11; Eusebius, *Proof of the Gospel* 9.5).

Christ's Deity Is the Differential Feature of Christianity

Without the hypothesis that Jesus is God-incarnate it is hard to make sense of any part the New Testament (Calvin, *Inst.* 2.12; Wesley, *WJW* 2:352–53). These claims by Jesus and the apostles, taken together, have led Christians to conclude that the valid beginning point for understanding this particular man is plainly and simply that he is truly God while not ceasing to be truly human (Creed of Epiphanius; Council of Ephesus; Council of Chalcedon).

The deity of Christ is the differential feature of Christianity (Augustine, *Trin.*, *FC* 45:52–58). Even Hegel could discern that "the Christian religion has this characteristic: that the Person of Christ in his character of the Son of God himself partakes of the nature of God" (Hegel, "On Philosophy," *On Art, Religion and Philosophy*: 277).

A suffering messiah who is less than God may elicit our pity or admiration, but not our worship. A messiah to whom one cannot pray is not the Christ of the New Testament. If the Messiah is God's own coming, then Christ is God, according to apostolic reasoning.

Jesus is Lord: What This Means

It is an article of apostolic faith to confess "one Lord" (*Credo in unum Dominum,* Gk. *eis hena Kurion,* Creed of 150 Fathers; Apostles' Creed). What did the lordship of Christ mean?

That Jesus was confessed as "Lord" dates to the earliest known record of Christian preaching. The text that demonstrates the early date of this confession is a prayer of Paul's of unquestionable authenticity: "If any man love not the Lord Jesus Christ, let him be *anathema marana tha*" (1 Cor. 16:22a), which means: "a curse be on him. Come, O Lord!" (v. 22b). "That Paul should use an Aramaic expression in a letter to a Greek-speaking church that knew little or no Aramaic proves that the use of *Mar* (*Kurios*) for Jesus goes back to the primitive Aramaic church and was not a product of the Hellenistic community" (Ladd, *TNT*:431). Just as Jesus had been *Mar* (Lord) to the earliest Aramaic speaking Jerusalem Christians, so did he quickly become confessed as *Kurios* among the earliest Greek-speaking Christians (1 Cor. 1:2; 1 Thess. 1:1; Mark 2:28; *Didache* 10:6; Rev. 22:20; Rawlinson, *NTDC*:231–37).

The Aramaic word for Lord (*Mar*) was primitively applied to Christ in Paul's poignant, closing salutation to the Corinthians: "Come, O Lord!" (*Marana tha,* 1 Cor. 16:22). Hence Jesus was called Lord from the earliest known layers of Christian proclamation. This phrase was sufficiently available to the earliest tradition of preaching that Paul could assume that his Corinthian hearers would understand it (Rawlinson, *NTDC*:235).

The most frequent designation for Jesus in early Gentile Christianity, "Jesus is Lord" (*Kurios Iesous*), was the received confession of the Pauline tradition, with over two hundred and fifty references. "If you confess with your mouth, 'Jesus is Lord,' and believe in your heart that God raised him from the dead, you will be saved" (Rom. 10:9; 2 Tim. 2:22). "No one can say, 'Jesus is Lord,' except by the Holy Spirit" (1 Cor. 12:3; Chrysostom, *Hom. on First Cor.* 29).

To confess Jesus as Lord after his resurrection was to confess his divinity. Prior to the resurrection *Kurios* could have meant "teacher" or "master," but after the resurrection it indicated his present reign in the coming kingdom: "God has made this Jesus, whom you crucified, both Lord and Christ" (Acts 2:36; Gregory of Nyssa, *Ag. Eunomius* 5.3; cf. Phil. 2:9–11). "He really is Lord, not as having step by step attained to lordship, but as having by nature the dignity of being Lord" (Cyril of Jerusalem, *Catech. Lect.* 5.5). *Kurios* soon came to be used interchangeably with *Theos.*

In over six thousand instances in the Septuagint, *Kurios* translates the ancient Hebraic tetragrammaton *YHWH,* the name for Yahweh (Lord) in the Old Testament. *Kurios* was not a polite vocative reference to human leadership in the New Testament kerygma. That Jesus is Lord means that he is the One speaking who said: "I am who am," and "I am has sent me" (Exod. 3:14). This incomparable One (Yahweh, *Kurios, Deus*) "has nothing for an opposite." "When asked the opposite of that which 'is', we answer rightly that it is 'nothing'" (Augustine, *Faith and the Creed* 4.7).

Christ as *Kurios* is viewed as pretemporal agent of creation ("through whom all things came," 1 Cor. 8:6; Heb. 1:2–3) and posttemporal agent of consummation (1 Cor. 15:25–28). "Then the end will come, when he hands over the kingdom to God the Father after he has destroyed all dominion, authority and power" (1 Cor. 15:24; Augustine, *Eighty-Three Questions,* 69.5). It was this Lord who met Paul personally on the road to Damascus and to whom Paul ascribed worship that belongs only to God. Judgment is the consummating act of his lordship in the final day (Rom. 14:10; 2 Cor. 5:10).

The Lordship of Christ and the History of Religions

The history of religions school has focused upon the correspondence between Christianity and its background in the history of religions. These points of correspondence do not constitute the slightest scandal to classic Christianity, whose testimony has always referred unapologetically to contingent history as the arena of divine redemption. Like Judaism, Christianity has always understood itself as a history of divine-human covenant worked out through a history of salvation.

No creditable ecumenical teacher ever assumed that Christianity was separable from a history of salvation, or from a universal history in which God is never left without witness in the world (Acts 14:17), who is the light that enlightens all who come into the world (John 1:4; Isaac of Nineveh, *Ascetic Homily* 48), who is known in various and sundry ways in general human history, yet who has come to be finally known in his Son (Heb. 1; Ambrose, *On the Sacrament of the Incarnation of the Lord* 6:59).

On this premise, the dialogue with world religions has proceeded in classic Christianity. The dialogue is not best understood under the metaphor of a diplomatic negotiation of competing interests of varied cultures. Rather it must inquire into the truth of all attested revelations, including Christianity. If the revelation of which Christianity speaks is only for Christians, then there is no compelling need for dialogue. But that does not square with Scripture. The Great Commission is to go to all nations and proclaim the gospel.

Continuing dialogue with Islam, Buddhism, and Hinduism presents a vexing set of challenges to the Christian community to account for its statements about Jesus. Yet in the vital dialogue with world religions, Christians are tempted to dilute the testimony to the universal relevance of Jesus' coming and instead focus more amiably upon the moral teaching of Jesus or his extraordinary life.

It remains a pivotal Christian assertion that Christ is the truth even for those who do not recognize him as their truth (Barth, *How to Serve God in a Marxist Land*: 57–58; *CD* I/2:344). "The world was made through him, yet the world knew him not" (John 1:10; Cyril of Alex., *Comm. on John* 1.9). He is Savior of all humanity even when humanity does not acknowledge his salvation. He remains the Life of the world even if the world remains in darkness (Gutiérrez, *PPH*:12, 16).

3

DIVINE SONSHIP

The Nature of Divine Sonship

The confession that Jesus Christ is Son of God stands as a key confession of the primitive oral tradition, amplifying other concise confessions ("Jesus is the Christ," "Jesus Christ is Lord"). John's first Letter states: "If anyone acknowledges that Jesus is the Son of God, God lives in him and he in God" (1 John 4:15; Augustine, *Comm. on First Epist. of John*, Hom. 8.14). The 150 Fathers at Constantinople confessed the Son born of the Father by whom were all things made (*COC* 2: 58; 1 Cor. 8:6; *SCD* 13, 54, 86).

"Son of God" is concisely defined by the *Russian Catechism* as "the name of the second Person of the Holy Trinity in respect of his Godhead: This same Son of God was called *Jesus*, when he was conceived and born on earth as man; *Christ* is the name given him by the Prophets, while they were as yet expecting his advent upon earth" (*COC* 2:466).

The Title "Only Son": What it Means

Both the Pauline term "his own Son" (Rom. 8:3), and the Johannine term "his only Son" (John 1:18) point to the unique pretemporal relation of Son to Father. The Son is unique, one and only (*monogenēs*, "only-begotten") eternal Son, uncreated Son of God (*Filium Dei*, Creed of 150 Fathers).

This Sonship points to an eternal relationship, not to a temporal beginning point. Gregory of Nazianzus noted sharply: "Father is not a name either of an essence or of an action, most clever sirs. But it is the name of the *relation* in which the Father stands to the Son, and the Son to the Father" (*Theol. Orat.* 29.16, italics added). "One and only Son" (John 3:16, 18) indicates that Jesus is the only one of his class. The Greek term for one and only Son, *monogenēs (Latin: unigenitum)*, came to have a pivotal function in all subsequent Christian teaching.

The One Son by Nature Distinguished from the
Many Sons and Daughters by Grace

His eternal sonship is by nature, while the believer's daughterhood or sonship in him is by grace. The daughterhood and sonship in which believers participate is not independent or autonomous, but entirely dependent upon their relation to this one and only Son of the Father. The term "one and only Son" distinguished all "holy men who are called sons of God by grace" from the one and only Son who is by nature consubstantial with the Father, in whose Sonship our sonship is hidden (Russian Catech., *COC* 2:467; Augustine, *Trin.*, *FC* 45: 171–83; Chemnitz, *TNC*).

Calvin refined this distinction: "That we are sons of God is something we have not by nature but only by adoption and grace, because God gives us this status. But the Lord Jesus, who is begotten of one substance with the Father, is of one essence with the Father, and with the best of rights is called the only Son of God (Eph. 1:5; John 1:14; Heb. 1:2), since he alone is by nature his son" (Calvin, *Catech. of the Church of Geneva*; *BOC*:18–20).

God sent his Son "that we might receive the full rights of sons" and daughters (Gal. 4:5). The mission of the Son is to bring humanity into a reconciled relation to the Father (Chrysostom, *Hom. on Gal.* 4). The faithful are called "into fellowship with his Son Jesus Christ our Lord" (1 Cor. 1:9). Through faith and love believers share in the life of fellowship with "the Father and with his Son, Jesus Christ" (1 John 1:3; Augustine, *Comm. on First Epist. of John*). "Because you are sons, God sent the Spirit of his Son into our hearts, the Spirit who calls out, 'Abba, Father'" (Gal. 4:6; Marius Victorinus, *Epist. to Gal.* 2.4.3–5).

If the eternal Father had no eternal Son, it could not be said, as so often said in scripture:

- that God both sends and is sent;

- that God could be both lawgiver and obedient to law;

- that God could both make atonement and receive it;

- that God could both reject sin and offer sacrifice for sin;

- that God could at the same time govern all things, yet become freely self-emptied in serving love (Hilary, *Trin.* 9.38–42).

The Resurrection Declared What Was Prefigured
in the Annunciation and Baptism

He who in due time was declared Son of God by his resurrection had been announced as Son of God at his annunciation and anointed as Son of God at his baptism.

Paul drew from a pre-Pauline oral tradition in announcing the startling subject matter of the gospel—Christ Jesus, God's Son—"who as to his human nature was a descendent of David, and who through the Spirit of holiness was *declared with power to be the Son of God [huiou theou] by his resurrection* from the dead: Jesus Christ our Lord" (Rom. 1:1–4, italics added). In Jesus we meet a human being descended of David "as to his human nature," whose hidden identity as Son of God was finally revealed in the resurrection. The resurrection was placed first in Paul's sequence of topics, because only through that lens did the faithful rightly grasp the events that had preceded it (William of St. Thierry, *Expos. Rom.*, *CFS* 27: 21–23; Luther, *Comm. on Epist. to Rom:* 20).

Long before the resurrection, the annunciation narrative had already signaled the identity of the coming One, according to Luke. Though his divine sonship would not be widely recognized until his resurrection, from the first announcement of the coming of Jesus, the angelic visitor indicated to Mary that "the holy one to be born will be called the Son of God" (Luke 1:35), the "Son of the Most High" (Luke 1:32; Irenaeus, *Ag. Her.* 3.9.1; 3.10.1).

In the narrative of Jesus' baptism, the voice from on high declared: "You are my Son, whom I love; with whom I am well pleased" (Mark 1:11; Matt. 3:13–17; Luke 3:21–22; Lactantius, *Div. Inst.* 4.15). The Baptist also "gave this testimony" to the expected one who would "'baptize with the Holy Spirit.' I have seen and I testify that this is the Son of God" (John 1:32, 34). This did not imply an adoptionist teaching, by which it might be assumed that prior to his baptism Jesus was not the Son of God, but was at that point adopted. Rather he was named what he always was (Hilary, *Trin.* VI.23–36).

Sonship and Time

In the relation of Father and Son, no notion of time appears (Augustine, *Hom. on John*). Jesus did not become Son at a particular stage but is eternally and pretemporally the Son, whose sonship was affirmed and celebrated at his baptism. Augustine argued that since "He is the Only-begotten Son of God, the expressions 'has been' and 'will be' cannot be employed, but only the term 'is', because what 'has been' no longer exists and what 'will be' does not yet exist" (Augustine, *Faith and the Creed* 4.6).

The Son enjoyed a pretemporal relation with the Father prior to the incarnation (Rom. 8:3; John 1:1–10; 1 John 4:9–14), a relation that time-bound mortals will never adequately fathom, but to which human speech can joyfully point. The notion of "pre"-temporal is paradoxical, because it must use a temporal prefix ("pre") to point to that which transcends the temporal. Nothing exists "before" time except God.

Cyril of Jerusalem astutely noted that "He did not say: 'I and the Father *am* one,' but 'I and the Father *are* one'; that we might neither separate them nor confuse the identities of Son and Father. They are one in the dignity of the Godhead, since God begot God" (*Catech. Lect.* 11 FC 61:226, italics added). That the Son is called "Very God of very God" means "that the Son of God is called God in the same proper sense as God the Father" (*Russian Catech,* COC II: 467; Council of Nicaea, *SCD* 54).

Son of the Father, Son of Mary

The Mission of the Son

The mission of the Son is to save humanity. "The Father has sent his Son to be the Savior of the world" (1 John 4:14). "When the time had come, God sent his Son" to "redeem those under law" (Gal. 4:4, 6). This only Son of the Father became flesh, entered history, and shared our humanity (John 1:14–18).

It was this One who suffered and died: "Although he was a son, he learned obedience from what he suffered and, once made perfect, he became the source of eternal salvation for all who obey him" (Heb. 5:8–9). His way of being a son was not a pampered, favored way, but a hard, narrow way. By this same narrow way do the faithful still enter into daughterhood and sonship, learning to trust the Father through life experiences suffered.

The Son was delivered to death, bore our sins, reconciled us to the Father, and brought us life (Rom. 5:9–11, 8:32), which is lived "by faith in the Son of God" (Gal. 2:20; Chrysostom, *Hom. on Gal.* II). Salvation hinges upon the fitting answer to the simple, straightforward question: "Whose son is he" (Matt. 22:41) whose narrow path led to the cross?

Whether Jesus Viewed Himself as Son of God

Did Jesus think of himself as Son of God? When tried before the Sanhedrin, charges were made to which Jesus did not reply. Put under oath (Matt. 26:63) he was asked directly the crucial question of his identity as Son: "Are you the Christ, the Son of the Blessed One?" (Mark 14:61). To make sense of this question, a premise is required: someone—either he or another—had claimed that he was the Son of God during his lifetime (Tertullian, *Ag. Praxeas* 16–18).

Jesus' response before the Sanhedrin rulers, according to Mark, finally ended the suspense that had been in question during his entire earthly ministry: "'I am,' said Jesus. 'And you will see the Son of Man sitting at the right hand of the Mighty One and coming on the clouds of heaven'" (Mark 14:62). Note the shocking parallelism: Now I am being judged by you, but at some point you will be judged by the Son of Man who is now being judged. Only God exercises final judgment—hence the charge of blasphemy (Calvin, *Comm.* 17:255–58).

This passage reveals the intricate interweaving of the two titles "Son of Man" and "Son of God," their affinity in the minds of the proclaiming church, and their complementarity. The Son of God "has been given authority to judge because he is the Son of Man" (John 5:27; 18:31; Tertullian, *Ag. Praxeas* 23).

Harnack balked. He thought that "The sentence, 'I am the Son of God' was not inserted in the Gospel by Jesus himself," but constitutes "an addition to the Gospel." Hence in his view, "The Gospel, as Jesus proclaimed it, has to do with the Father only and not with the Son" (*What Is Christianity?*:92, 154). From Harnack's complaint has emerged a whole scholarly industry—biblical historical criticism's attempt to detach Jesus from divine sonship, a massive hundred-year enterprise that is now facing bankruptcy (Stuhlmacher, *HCTIS*:61–76; Maier, *EHCM*:12–26; Wink, *BHT*:1–15).

It is likely that the acceptance of the title "Son of God" by Jesus has its origin and explanation not in the later memory of the disciples but in Jesus himself (Matt. 11:25f., Luke 10:21f.; Guthrie, *NTT*:301–20; T. W. Manson, *Teaching of Jesus*:89–115).

The divine sonship theme appeared prominently at the five most crucial moments of Jesus' ministry: his baptism, temptation, transfiguration, crucifixion, and resurrection (Mark 1:11; 9:2–8; Matt. 3:13–17, 17:1–8; 27:40). In the temptation narrative Jesus was challenged as Son of God to perform miracles for his own benefit (Luke 4:1–13). He refused. A similar taunt was flung at his crucifixion: "Let God rescue him now if he wants him, for he said, 'I am the Son of God'" (Matt. 27:44). Whether Jesus referred to himself as Son of God remains under debate, but these passages make it clear that Jesus was perceived by rememberers (including detractors) as having received and not disavowed the title Son of God.

The Reliability of Johannine Testimony

John's Gospel requires special treatment on the theme of sonship, since it was for this very purpose that John wrote his Gospel—to make more explicit what had been implicit in the other Gospels—"that you may believe that Jesus is the Christ, the Son of God" (John 20:31: Tertullian, *Ag. Praxeas* 25).

If we were required for critical considerations to rule out John's Gospel in forming our assessment of Jesus' identity as Son of God, then the ample resources of canonical scripture would instantly become vastly skewed and off-center. Some critics have preferred to take John out of their private canon because of its presumed lateness. Hence it cannot be left to conjecture as to why classic Christian teaching regards John's Gospel as a reliable narrative:

Technical studies have shown that John's meticulous inclusion of specific topographical and factual details lends overall credibility to the Palestinian origin of his report (Cana, John 2:1–12; the discussions with Nicodemus, 3:1–21, and the Samaritan woman, 4; Bethesda, 5:2; Siloam, 9:7). John reveals careful knowledge of place names, customs, geographical sites, specific people and private relationships, and the precise movement of people from place to place that could hardly have been invented subsequently (or if invented, what could possibly be the purpose of such invention? R. D. Potter, *Texte und Untersuchungen* 73:320–37). Johannine language is closer to the Dead Sea Scrolls than the Synoptics, thus pointing to its Palestinian origin, even though the author was more likely in Ephesus when writing. The Fourth Gospel contains "evidences of a familiarity with Palestinian conditions during our Lord's life which could not have been possessed by one who had not come in personal and contemporaneous contact with them" (Hall, *DT* 6:307; W. F. Albright, in W. Davies and D. Daube, *Background of the NT and Its Eschatology*:170–71).

Although debates may continue as to the precise identity of its author, there can be little doubt, based on internal evidence, that the Fourth Gospel was written by one who had direct eyewitness contact with the events reported. If John was exceedingly careful in remembering details, but entirely inaccurate in reporting his major subject—Jesus as Son of God—that would constitute an implausible inconsistency rejected by widely respected scholars. J. B. Lightfoot, C. H. Dodd, C. K. Barrett, G. E. Ladd, R. E. Brown, David Wells, and other scholars have shown that John represents a reliable tradition of memory of Jesus. The Gospel shows how missionary teaching was occurring in settings far away from Palestine yet was grounded in the history of Jesus in Palestine (C. H. Dodd, *Historical Tradition in the Fourth Gospel*; L. Morris, *Studies in the Fourth Gospel*; A. J. B. Higgins, *The Historicity of the Fourth Gospel*; J. L. Martyn, *History and Theology in the Fourth Gospel*).

The tendency of some modern critics to discredit the Johannine testimony is unjustified. Its high level of spiritual discernment makes it improbable that it might have been a manipulative attempt on the part of a later writer to falsify the narrative or put words in the mouth of Jesus inaccurately or to serve partisan interests. Where the Fourth Gospel restates points made in the other Gospels, there is reason to believe that it does so more accurately, more precisely, or in more specific detail than the others (C. K. Barrett, *The Gospel According to St. John*; W. Sanday, *Criticism of the Fourth Gospel*). Attempts to discredit John's Gospel may be based more on ideological resistance to his high appraisal of the eternal Son than any internal or external evidence. Classical Christianity has chosen to rely on the historical trustworthiness of John as equal to that of the synoptic writers.

The sonship of Jesus to the Father is at the heart of the Johannine tradition. Jesus speaks of God as Father over a hundred times in John's Gospel. The Son's words, accordingly, are God's own words (John 8:26–28). "The Father loves the Son" in a special way and "shows him all he does" (John 5:20), "so that 'all things that the Father has' belong to the Son, not gradually accruing to him little by little, but are rather with him all together and at once" (Basil, *On the Spirit* 8.20). Even as he walked toward death, he understood himself to be specially and uniquely sent and loved by the Father (John 10:17; Pearson, *EC* I: 49–69).

His union with God was more than a diffuse sharing in God's purpose. It was such that he was uniquely God, the Son being in the Father, and the Father in the Son (10:38; 14:10–11). What the Father intended, the Son knew; and what the Son was doing, the Father knew (John 10:15; Matt. 11:27; John 10:30; Augustine, *Hom. on John, Tractate* 47–48). Yet Son and Father are distinguishable. The Father sends, the Son is sent; one commands, the other obeys (John 15:10–20; Tho. Aq., *ST* 3 Q20).

Does the Sonship Tradition Reinforce Social Inequalities?

Rich familial images pervade early Christian teaching: God as Father sends his Son for redemption. The church as mother maternally nurtures this growth. One cannot understand this paternity without this maternity: "You are beginning to hold Him as a Father when you will be born of Mother Church" (Augustine, *The Creed* 1).

Modern egalitarian complaints against Christianity, leaning toward romanticist, quasi-Marxist, proletarian, and some secular feminist ideologies, are prone to turn angry and testy, claiming that there is an overemphasis upon super-and subordination and little notion of equality in Christian Scripture and tradition. The seldom mentioned, but distinctive and beautiful, contribution of Christianity to the teaching of *equality* is found in its teaching on the *servant* of God. Equality implies servanthood (Phil. 2:6–11; Epiphanius, *Ancoratus* 28).

We find in classic exegesis a powerful statement on equality and gentleness. In triune teaching it distinctly belongs to God to be *both equal and less than himself*! "It pertains to the Godhead alone not to have an unequal Son" (Council of Toledo, *CF*:103). The internal logic of triune relations implies and requires that God the Son is by nature equal to the Father, while voluntarily becoming utterly responsible to the Father. Intrinsic equality becomes voluntary poverty and subordination. The formula is so simple in its profundity that it first appears innocuous or unreasonable.

God the Son, by being truly human without ceasing to be truly God, is both equal to the Father and less than the Father—equal by nature and less by volition to service. By this paradox, the usual logic of equality is turned upside down. In the Godhead all historical inequalities are finally transcended. Equality and servanthood thus belong together and cohere congruently. This we see reflected in the *Symbol of Faith* of the Eleventh Council of Toledo, which serves as a consensual guide to Christian reflection on equality and servanthood:

> Similarly, by the fact that He is God,
> > He is *equal* to the Father;
> by the fact that He is man,
> > He is *less* than the Father.
> Likewise, we must believe that He is both greater
> > and less than Himself:
> for in the *form of God*
> > the Son Himself is greater than Himself
> > because of the humanity which He has assumed
> > and to which the divinity is superior,
> but in the *form of the servant*
> > He is less than Himself, that is, in His humanity
> > which is recognized as inferior to the divinity.
> For, while by the flesh which He has assumed
> He is recognized not only as
> > less than the Father
> > but also as less than Himself,

according to the divinity He is co-equal with the Father;
both He and the Father are greater than man whose nature
the person of the Son alone assumed.
Likewise, to the question whether the Son might be equal to,
and less than the Holy Spirit, as we believe Him to be
   now equal to,
   now less than the Father, we answer
according to the form of God He is equal to the Father
   and to the Holy Spirit;
according to the form of the servant,
   He is less than both the Father
   and the Holy Spirit

(Eleventh Council of Toledo, *CF*:170–71; indentation and italics added)

The Preincarnational Life of the Son

Without the premise of preexistence, there can be no thought of the incarnation or Christmas. The temporal birth assumed and required a pretemporal life. The existence of the Logos necessarily preceded the incarnation. If the Savior is God, then that One must be eternal God, hence must have had some form of preincarnate being prior to the incarnation in time, just as he continues in exaltation after his incarnate life (Phil. 2:6–11; Chrysostom, *Hom. on Phil.* 7).

The Logos that is eternal by definition must exist before time. This is hardly an optional point of Christian theology. Far from being a later development shaped by Greek philosophy, the seeds of this premise were firmly embedded in the earliest Christian preaching, for how could the Son be born in time or sent from the Father on a mission to the world if the Son had no life with the Father before the nativity? There is no "before" with him. "Begotten before. Before what, since there is no before with Him? . . . Do not imagine any interval or period of eternity when the Father was and the Son was not" for the Son is "always without beginning" (Augustine, *The Creed* 3.8). "The Sources of Time are not subject to time" (Gregory of Nazianzus, *Orat.* 29.3).

What is the price of the neglect of this premise? It might seem that this might be alleged to be a later or inconsequential addition to the earliest tradition. That might be plausible if this theme were not so persistent in the earliest strains of oral tradition preceding Paul, or if it were not found in all the New Testament's major writers. Not only attested by Paul, but by Luke-Acts, Hebrews, John, James, and other New Testament writings, the eternal life of the Son of God is assumed to be antecedent to the incarnation. Lacking the premise of preexistence, the nativity narratives are rendered meaningless. If the Son came into being only at his birth, then there can be no triune God, for the Son would not be eternal, hence not God (Augustine, *Hom. on John* 6:60–72, *Tractate* 27).

If the eternal Son did not exist with the Father before his earthly ministry, then the teachings of Paul and John are drastically discredited. This is why the premise of preexistence is so insistent and pervasive in New Testament and ecumenical teaching (Pearson, *EC* I:195; Forsyth, *PPJC*:261–90). "In the past God spoke to our forefathers through the prophets," but "in these last days he has spoken to us by his Son" (Heb. 1:1–2). The Word of God is spoken through the life of the Son. These two recurrent terms—Word and Son—are principal titles ascribed to the pretemporal existence of the One who assumed flesh in Jesus. "He is called Son, because he is identical with the Father in essence," and "Word, because he is related to the Father as word to mind" (Gregory of Nazianzus, *Theol. Orat.* 30.20).

The preexistent Logos theme has set boundaries for Christian teaching. It defends against the error that Jesus was first and foremost a good teacher whose teaching and death later caused his disciples to ascribe to him attributes of divinity. The modern expression of this is the tradition from David F. Strauss to Herbert Braun that seeks to reduce all talk of transcendence to human psychological or anthropological categories. The logic of the earliest kerygma was that God has chosen to come to humanity—not humanity to God.

Preexistence in the Pauline Tradition

Preexistence is not exclusively a Johannine idea, as is evident from its recurrent treatment in Pauline Letters (1 Cor. 8:6; 2 Cor. 8:9; Eph. 1:3–14). Paul taught preexistence in conspicuous passages. The Son was "in very nature God," yet "did not consider equality with God something to be grasped" because he already shared fully in the divine life and was willing to become obedient unto death in order that the divine life be manifested to humanity in servant form (Phil. 2:5–11; Gregory of Nyssa, *Ag. Eunomius* 3.2.147). Not only is the Son "before all things," but also "in him all things hold together" (Col. 1:16; Chrysostom, *Hom. on Col.* 3). The Son who is before all things is coeternal with the Father, hence nothing less than God (Hilary, *Trin.* 12.35–43; *BOC*:577). It was through the resurrection that the primitive Christian community came to grasp and confess that the living Lord is eternal Son (Rom. 1:1–4).

"When the time had fully come, *God sent his son.*" Only one who already exists could be sent. This one was sent to be "born of a woman, born under law, that we might receive the full rights of sons. Because you are sons, God sent the Spirit of his Son into our hearts, the Spirit who calls out, 'Abba, Father'" (Gal. 4:4–5, italics added). The triune premise saturates this Pauline passage. The speech of the Father through the Son is communicated through the Spirit to enable the sonship and daughterhood of the faithful.

Allusions to the preexistence of Christ appear embedded in the earliest oral traditions antedating Paul's Letters (Phil. 2:6–11; 1 Cor. 15:47; Col. 1:17; 1 Tim. 3:16; F. Craddock, *The Pre-Existence of Christ*). They do not display any indications that they might have been appended later. They are attended with no speculative details or mythic ornamentations, but rather presented as intrinsic to the faith presumably shared by all who proclaim the gospel of God. Here form criticism may be correctly put to a service quite opposite from that assumed by many form critics, since they point toward establishing an early date for the preexistence theme (Taylor, *PC*:62–78; A. M. Hunter, *Paul and His Predecessors*:40–44; C. F. D. Moule, *Colossians and Philemon*, *CGTC*:58).

Christ as Word of God—Logos Christology

The main stem of New Testament usage of Christ as Word (Logos) comes not from Greek philosophy but from the ancient Hebraic *dabar Yahweh* ("Word of God") by which the world was made and the prophets inspired (Manson, *Studies in the Gospels and Epistles*:118). Bultmann argued for the Hellenistic origin of the Logos language of the New Testament, but the more probable roots are Semitic (Cullmann, *CNT*: 249). John 1:1–3 is best seen in recollection of Genesis 1:1 (Ephrem the Syrian, *Comm. on Tatian's Diatess.* 16.27; Augustine, *Trin.* 15.13).

John's Gospel speaks of the Logos as active agent through whom God created the world ("through whom all things were made," John 1:3). This is consistent with Paul's language, that all things come *from* God the Father *through* Christ the Son: "For us there is one God, the Father, *from* whom all things came and for whom we live; and there is but one Lord, Jesus Christ, *through* whom all things came and through whom we live" (1 Cor. 8:6, italics added; Chrysostom, *Hom. on First Cor.* 20.6; Ambrose, *On the Holy Spirit* 13.132). It is this eternal Word (*logos*) that becomes flesh (*sarx*), contrary to common Hellenistic assumptions and expectations. If the preaching of the early Christian kerygma had been seeking to accommodate to a Hellenistic audience, it would certainly not begin by saying: Logos becomes flesh. It is this enfleshed Logos, the Son, through whom God the Father is revealed (John 1:17–18; Athanasius, *Ag. Arians*, 2.18.24–36; Newman, *Ari.*: 169).

Pauline and Johannine views are far less in tension on preexistence than some have imagined. If preexistence receives intermittent but crucial reference in Paul, it receives persistent and decisive reference in John. The eternal Logos, whose glory the disciples beheld in Jesus Christ, not only appeared in time but also, according to John's Gospel, was "in the beginning." The Logos was God and was with God in the beginning (John 1:1–2), through whom "all things were made; without him nothing was made that has been made" (1:3; Didymus the Blind, *Comm. on 1 John* 1.1).

The preexistence theme is found in the Markan report of Jesus' own teaching of himself as heavenly Son of Man come down from above (Mark 5:7; 9:7–31; 13:26; 14:61–62). This is consistent with his saying in the Fourth Gospel: "Before Abraham was born, I am" (John 8:58; Gregory I, *Forty Gospel Homilies* 16). Preexistence is assumed in the prayer of Jesus who, when his "time had come," prayed: "And now, Father, glorify me in your presence with the glory I had with you before the world began" (John 17:5). The Son was glorified in the presence of the Father with a glory that was voluntarily given up in his earthly life. In humbling himself, the preexistent Logos constrained his divine glory with the Father to take on the form of a servant.

Only he existed before he was born. For the Son has two natures: "He was God before all ages; he is man in this age of ours" (Augustine, *Enchiridion* 10.35). "He was not first God without a Son [and] afterwards in time became a Father; but He has the Son eternally, having begot Him not as men beget men, but as He Himself alone knows" (Cyril of Jerusalem, *Catech.* 11). Hence the views of Paul of Samosata, Photinus, and Priscillian were rejected by orthodox exegesis insofar as they taught that the Son "did not exist before He was born" (John III, Council of Braga, *SCD* 233: 93).

The Humbling of God to Servanthood

Humiliation and Exaltation

The humbling of the Son to servanthood is a major dogmatic grouping of topics that includes all Christological issues between his incarnation and his burial. It is distinguished from the raising of the Son to governance, which includes all topics from his resurrection to final judgment (Hilary, *Trin.* 9–11). Within this broad frame, Christ's mediatorial work is seen in three offices that correlate generally with this chronological progression: prophetic teaching, priestly sacrifice, and regal governance, schematized as follows, as a map for the discussion ahead:

Stages of Descent and Ascent

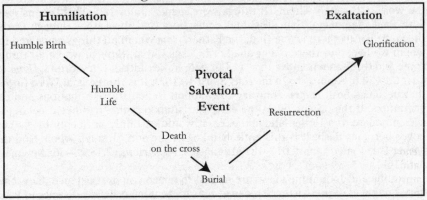

Three Messianic Offices Linked with these Stages:

Prophetic	Priestly	End-time
Teaching	Sacrifice	Governance

The prophetic office is undertaken primarily during the descent, the period of humiliation. The priestly sacrifice focuses upon the pivotal event—the death of Christ—marking the end of God's humbling and the reversal leading to exaltation. Fulfillment of the regal office is primarily associated with exaltation, ascent to the Father. The cross marks the boundary between descent and ascent of the Son. The salvation event had been prophetically promised to occur through suffering and death (Isa. 53:4–9).

Each step of Jesus' life descended toward his death, followed by his further descent into the grave. The sacrificial death of the Savior marked the clear line between the two overarching phases of the Son's ministry, in which divine powers and attributes were at first voluntarily constrained, then exercised (Chrysostom, *Hom. on Phil.* 7,8).

The *humiliation* of the eternal Son was marked by a temporary but not absolute *cessation* of the independent exercise of divine powers. This was chosen in order to show forth the voluntary acceptance of humanity, birth, finitude, suffering, and finally death and burial (Phil. 2:6–8). His *exaltation* was marked by a full *resumption* of the exercise of divine powers (Phil. 2:9–11). The Son's exaltation confirmed the hidden meaning of his humiliation (Gregory of Nazianzus, *Orat.* 87).

The Humbling of the Eternal Son Under Limits of Time

The humbling of God was not an enforced humbling, but an elected, voluntary humbling (Theodoret, *Epist. to Phil.* 2.6.7). The humiliation (tapeinōsis) was temporary, lasting from birth to death, or more precisely from the Son's first moment of conception to his last moment in the grave. The phase of exaltation begins with his resurrection and continues to the last day.

The eternal Son humbled himself first to birth, then to death, and only then was exalted to return to glory with the Father. The contrast between the two overarching phases of mediatorial ministry is based upon contrasting phrases of

Philippians 2: he "made himself nothing" (verse 7), and "Therefore God exalted him" (9). The sequence of conditions was an original glory followed by suffering servant life followed once again by glory.

The humbling motif is found in the Nicene Creed in the phrase: "He came down from heaven" (*descendit de coelis*; Creed of 150 Fathers, *COC* 2:58). The descent theme is presupposed in the titles Son of God, Son of Man, Logos, and Lord, for how could the eternal Son become incarnate as a child without "coming down"—a spatial metaphor of descent, of self-chosen lowering of power, and of taking upon himself all human limitations including death? (Origen, *Comm. on John* 20.18; *Doc. Vat. II*: 563–67).

What is meant by the phrase, he "made himself nothing" (Phil. 2:7; Gk. *heauton ekenosen*; Lat. *semet ipsum exinanivit*)? This is sometimes referred to as the renunciation (or exiniation) of the Son, whose earthly ministry was characterized by self-emptying (*kenosis*) or voluntary abnegation of the divine glory (Hilary, *Trin.* 9.48). Not until the resurrection did he resume the full exercise of divine dominion.

The Disavowal of Uninterrupted Exercise of Sovereign Powers

This voluntary renunciation consisted essentially in the disavowal or partial and temporary abdication of full and uninterrupted exercise of divine powers, while the Son accepted the incarnate life and assumed the form of a servant (Chrysostom, *Hom. on Phil.* VI; Newman, *Ari.*:163–66). It is this self-giving, serving love that Paul was commending as a primary pattern of human behavior to the Philippians.

This involved the temporary obscuring of the divine sonship to human eyes, being hidden in the flesh of humanity (Cyril of Alexandria, *Third Letter to Nestorius*). "He has hidden His majesty in humanity, does not appear with lightning, thunder, or angels, but as one born of a poor virgin and speaking with men of the forgiveness of sins" (Luther, *Serm. on John* 4, *WLS* I:154).

The metaphor of voluntary emptying should not be confused with emptiness. Embedded in the metaphor is a paradox, for when one cup is emptied into another, the other becomes full. The self-emptying of the Logos is the filling of the incarnate Son, for in emptying himself, God reveals himself as enfleshed, filling a human body with his fullness (Gregory of Elvira, *On the Faith* 88,89).

During his saving mission, the Son "through the eternal Spirit offered himself unblemished to God" (Heb. 9:14). While engaged in his earthly ministry, "God gives the Spirit without limit" to the One sent by the Father (John 3:34–35; Chrysostom, *Hom. on John* 30.2; Augustine, *Hom. on John* 14). The humbling of the Son ceased when, upon accomplishing this mission, the Holy Spirit was given to the church as the Son ascended to the Father.

The triune premise is essential for understanding of the descent and ascent motifs. It was not the Godhead that became incarnate, but one of the persons of the Godhead. The Godhead as such was not humbled or lowered, but the one person of the Son embracing two natures, wherein the human nature was humbled. Hence it is said that the subject of the humiliation is the human nature, unconfusedly united with the divine nature, which "neither died nor was crucified" (Hollaz, *ETA*: 767; Schmid, *DT*: 381).

Form of God, Form of a Servant

The locus classicus text of this teaching is Philippians 2:5–11. The context in which this pivotal passage occurs is an appeal to follow Christ's way of lowliness. Paul had just instructed the Philippians to "do nothing out of selfish ambition or vain conceit, but in humility consider others better than yourselves. Each of you should look not only to your own interests, but also to the interests of others" (Phil. 2:3–4). This way of lowliness was pioneered by Christ himself: "Let this mind be in you, which was also in Christ Jesus" (v. 5; Mark the Ascetic, *Letter to Nicolas*, Philokal. 1:155–56). What follows is quite likely an early Christian hymn or hymnic fragment, used or adapted by Paul (*ACCS* NT 8:236–254).

In the Form of God: Morphē Theou

The One who became Servant was the very One who "being in the very nature God [*morphē Theou*]" (Phil. 2:6), namely the preexistent Logos who subsisted in the form of God before the incarnation, enjoyed an existence equal to that of God (Council of Ephesus, SCD 118). The divine nature was his from the beginning.

The same theme recurs in Colossians: "There is but one Lord, Jesus Christ, through whom all things came, and through whom we live" (1 Cor. 8:6); "by him all things were created" (Col. 1:15). The premise of this language: Christ pretemporally existed in the form and glory of God. He "did not consider equality with God something to be grasped" (forcibly retained, Phil. 2:6).

By contrast, recall that Adam's disobedience had been a presumptuous grasping for equality with God. Christ did not grasp self-assertively at the divine majesty which he already possessed (Hilary, *Trin.* 12.6).

He Made Himself Nothing

He voluntarily became lowly (*heauton ekenosen*, "He emptied himself," Phil. 2:7). He did not inordinately claim the glory he rightly had. He made no display of it. The Son temporarily gave up the independent exercise of divine attributes and powers that manifested his equality with God. The text does not focus specifically upon what was emptied, but rather upon what the self-emptying called forth— the servant life. *Kenosis* did not extinguish the Logos, but the Logos became supremely self-expressed and incarnately embodied in the flesh.

Taking the Form of a Servant

In taking "the form of a servant [*morphen doulou*]" (Phil. 2:7), the contrast is sharpened between (a) the eternal One in the form of God who (b) voluntarily takes a constricted and limited temporal form as if slave. He came among us "as one who serves" (Luke 22:27), symbolized by his washing the feet of his disciples (John 13:1–20; Hilary, *Trin.* 11.13–15). Augustine warned against misreading this lowliness: "The form of a servant was so taken that the form of God was not lost, since both in the form of a servant and in the form of God He himself is the same only-begotten Son of God the Father, in the form of God equal to the Father, in the form of a servant the Mediator between God and men, the man Christ Jesus" (Augustine, *Trin.* 1.7; *Enchiridion* 8.35). A brilliant analysis of this text is found in Hilary: "The emptying of the form is not the destruction of the nature. He who empties Himself is not wanting in His own nature. He who receives remains. . . . No destruction takes place so that He ceases to exist when He empties Himself or does not exist when He receives. Hence, the emptying brings it about that the form of a slave appears, but not that the Christ who was in the form of God does not continue to be Christ, since it is only Christ who has received the form of a slave" (*On the Trinity* 9.44).

Agreeably Leo thought the lowering to be necessary to the mediatorial role: "In what way could He properly fulfill His mediation, unless He who in the form of God was equal to the Father, were a sharer of our nature also in the form of a slave; so that the one new Man might effect a renewal of the old; and the bond of death fastened on us by one man's wrong-doing might be loosened by the death of the one Man who alone owed nothing to death" (*Letters*, 124.3).

Made in Human Likeness

"Being made in human likeness" (*homoioma*, Phil. 2:7), being born, being under the law, he lived in poverty. The Son of God became that very kind of servant that corresponds with the conditions of human finitude. He lived in time and space under conditions that involved suffering, and death. It is not merely that the Son became a man. The emphasis is rather placed upon the comparison between the life of God and the life of humanity, the ordinary human life seen from the perspective of one who has descended from on high, from the most exalted state of glory. From that state he entered into the disadvantaged life of the poor, the neglected, those bound in rough circumstances, the hidden sufferers. In short, he became a slave (Phil. 2.7b; Leo I, *Epistle 28 to Flavian* 3).

The conditions common to humanity included physical development (being born and passing through stages of growth), intellectual development (learning as humans learn), and even moral development (submitting to parents and to the law), within a distinct historical context, under a particular political regime, of a particular ethnicity, and in a particular family. "His experience was that of every other man, eating, drinking, sleeping, waking, walking, standing, hungering, thirsting, shivering, sweating, fatigued, working, clothing Himself, sheltered in a house, praying—all things just as others" (Luther, in *SCF*:144).

"In him God becomes oppressed man" (Cone, *BTL*:215; Boff, *LibT.*:60–61). "Down, down, says Christ; you shall find Me in the poor; you are rising too high if you do not look for Me there" (Luther, *Serm. on Matt.* 22:34–46). Being God he was found in human form, yet analogous to a human condition of the lowliest sort imaginable—as if a slave.

He Humbled Himself and Became Obedient unto Death

Though more than human, he was willing to become the least among humanity, despised and rejected (Julia of Norwich, "The Homeliness of God," *IAIA*: 89). This humiliation extended over the whole of his earthly life.

The cross cast its shadow upon every step of his way from his baptism to his death (Barth, *CD*;4/4: 52–67). He "became obedient to death" (Phil. 2:8).

"Although he was a son, he learned obedience from what he suffered" (Heb. 5:8). In his active obedience he chose to fulfill the obligation of the law; in his passive obedience he endured the penalty of human sin. Hence through the active and passive "obedience of the one man the many will be made righteous" (Rom. 5:19).

The humbling of the Son ends in death by crucifixion, "rectifying that disobedience which had occurred by reason of a tree, through that obedience which was [wrought out] upon the tree [of the cross]" (Irenaeus, *Ag. Her.* 5.16.3). In this disgraceful way—"even death on a cross" (Phil. 2:8)—he became "a curse for us" (Gal. 3:13). Such was, in brief, the humiliating *schema* (Phil. 2:7, "way of life") accepted by the Son.

Why was this necessary to the divine plan? "He humbled himself, being made obedient even unto death, even death on a cross, so that none of us, though being able to face death without fear, might shrink from any kind of death that humans beings regard as a great disgrace" (Augustine, *On Faith and the Creed* 11). From his death we take hope. From his slavery we derive courage amid our analogous forms of limitation and suffering.

Voluntary Obedience of the Son to the Father

The notion of voluntary subordination appears in the sayings of Jesus: as enfleshed Son he wills to do nothing by himself, acknowledging that the Father is greater than he (John 5:30; 10:15, 30; 14:28; Matt. 11:27; Titus 2:13; 1 John 5:7).

To be temporarily subordinated within the conditions of time means to stand voluntarily in a lower class or order or rank. The subordination of which Paul spoke in Philippians 2:5–8 was a temporary one that ended when Jesus was exalted to the glory of the kingdom.

The peculiar heterodox view called "subordinationism" overextends this orthodox confession by arguing that the Son is not just temporally but eternally and by nature unequal to the Father (rejected by the Councils of Nicaea and Constantinople—a tendency found in Sabellianism, Arianism, and Monarchianism). Any subordinationism that fails to recognize Christ's return to equality with the Father in glory has not been ecumenically received. Instead, the temporal subordination freely chosen by the Son demonstrated his obedience to the Father in his mission to fallen human history.

The Son, Not the Godhead, Was Humbled

The triune premise must be held firmly in place for such language to make sense. It speaks not of the temporary subordination of one divine nature to another, but of the voluntary, temporary subordination of the will of the Son to the Father, of one divine person to another on behalf of his mission to bring salvation to humanity (Eleventh Council of Toledo, *CF*:170; see also *SCD* 284). It was the Son and not the Godhead that was humbled.

Amid the incarnate humbling of God, "so far as He is God, He and the Father are one; so far as He is man, the Father is greater than He," and in this paradoxical way, "He was both made less and remained equal" (Augustine, *Enchiridion* 35). In making for himself no reputation and taking the form of a servant, he did not lose or diminish the form of God (*BOC*:602–605).

This irony was given powerful ecumenical expression by the Eleventh Council of Toledo: "for in the form of God even the Son Himself is greater than Himself on account of the humanity He assumed, than which the divinity is greater; in the form, however, of a servant He is less than Himself, that is, in His humanity" (*SCD* 285; *BOC*:602–604).

The Consequent Moral Imperative for Faith: Voluntary Servanthood

At the outset of this passage Paul was calling upon the Philippians to follow Christ's example of lowliness of mind. His object is to elicit among the Philippians a similar attitude of self-submission, hoping that they would walk in humility, considering others better than themselves (Phil. 2:3)—that is what originally elicited Paul's recollection and insertion of the primitive Christic hymn received from the oral tradition. Similarly you are not to grasp at equality with your neighbor but to choose the form of a servant in all dealings (Francis of Assisi, *The Admonitions*, *CWS*: 25–29; Augustine, *Since God Has Made Everything, Why Did He Not Make Everything Equal? EDQ* 41).

The humbling of the Son is not simply a single event of the birth narrative by itself. Rather, having been born into the world, the Son grew to maturity and had to choose again and again the way of the humble One, every moment of his life, until such choosing ended in death (John of Damascus, *OF* 3.21–29). All this was done willingly for human benefit. The narrative of Jesus' earthly life reveals an ongoing ethical dimension in the humbling of God that awaits event after event to unfold in its own characteristic way of life: washing feet, reaching out for the sick and neglected, identifying with sinners, living without material comforts, dying on a cross.

His poverty consisted in the self-renunciation by which he assumed servant form—he was born in a stable, remained poor throughout his life, worked with his hands in common labor, was without a home of his own, and finally in his crucifixion was stripped of his robe and laid in the grave of another—all signs of poverty, of complete and willing lack of worldly resources. This poverty has made redeemed humanity rich by enabling persons to share in his glory by faith (Francis of Assisi, *Admonitions*, *CWS*: 32).

By his death he purchased life. By his divestiture we gain our inheritance. By his payment, we receive our passage (*viaticum*) to the eternal city (Gregory Thaumaturgus, *Four Hom.* 1; Chrysostom, *Hom. on 2 Cor.* 19; Schmid, *DT*:385). "Though he was rich, yet for your sakes, he became poor, so that you through his poverty might become rich" (2 Cor. 8:9).

Reprise: The Descending Sequence of Downward Steps of the Son's Humbling

The humbling of the eternal Son proceeded in a long sequence of ever-lowering stages culminating in death and burial. Each step is an historical event told in the Gospels as a real and true narrative of a fully human life. Taken together, key events of the humiliation of the Son reported in Scripture are pictured as this poignant sequence of ever-lowering steps:

Being in the very nature God

He does not grasp for the equality with God due him

He empties himself

He voluntarily gives up unbroken independent exercise of the divine attributes

He is conceived by the Holy Spirit

He is born of a poor virgin in a humble manger

He was born a Jew, a son of the law

He was made one gender on behalf of two, a man, born of a woman

He willingly took the form of a servant

He first became a child

He become subject to human growth and development

He was circumcised signifying subjection to law though he was Giver of the law

He was made like his brothers in every way that he might make atonement

He humbled himself

He became obedient

He became voluntarily subject to instruction by parents

He worked in economic subjection lacking property

He was a common laborer in a manual occupation

He voluntarily subjected himself to the teachers of the law

He faced all the ordinary discomforts of human finitude

He took up our human infirmities

He was despised and rejected by men

He endured the reproaches and ill-treatment by others

He was a man of sorrows, familiar with grief

He faced suffering of body, mind, and spirit

He endured political subjection to unjust political authority

He became obedient, even unto death

Even the death of the cross

He experienced the abandonment of his followers

He became a curse for us, dying "outside the camp"

He was buried in a borrowed grave

He descended into the nether world to preach to the captives

Each step descended further than the previous one. It was an ever narrowing descent from heaven to hell. In sum he as Son of God humbled himself in every conceivable way. He became obedient to reveal the true nature of humanity amid the dreadful conditions of the history of sin. In doing so he was prepared to serve as the representative of humanity in the Father's presence, presenting to God the perfect obedience due from humanity (Rom. 6:14; 13:10).

What the law was powerless to do "God did by sending his own Son in the likeness of sinful man to be a sin offering" (Rom. 8:3). "God made him who had no sin to be sin for us, so that in him we might become the righteousness of God" (2 Cor. 5:21; Gal. 3:13; 4:4–5; Augustine, *On Romans* 48).

Nowhere in nature is the heart of God so fully revealed as it is in the history of Jesus: "God's transcendent power is not so much displayed in the vastness of the heavens, or the luster of the stars, or the orderly arrangement of the universe or his perpetual oversight of it, as in his condescension to our weak nature," wrote Gregory of Nyssa. "We marvel at the way the Godhead was entwined in human nature and, while becoming man, did not cease to be God" (*ARI* 24).

The Hidden Majesty: The Obscuration of the Divine

The divine humiliation was not an impoverishment of God but an incomparable expression of the empathic descent of divine love (Calvin, *Inst.*, 2.13.3–4). God never did anything in history more revealing of the divine character than to become incarnate and die. By his coming the poor were blessed, the hungry satisfied, weeping was brought to laughter, the excluded embraced, and the reviled welcomed (Luke 6:20–23).

The earthly ministry of the Son was not first to reveal the divinity of the Son, but rather to *obscure it so that the mission might be fully accomplished through his suffering and death for all* (Hilary, *Trin.* 9.6). The divinity of the Son was eclipsed for a season only to more fully manifest its glory in due time through the resurrection of the flesh. His majesty and deity became most clear through this unique descent.

God the Son assumed human nature for the very purpose that he might experience this humiliation of his human nature on behalf of the redemption of humanity (Council of Ephesus). In this humbling, the divine nature of his person was concealed, not in the sense of being deceptively disguised, but under the assumed servant form (*morphē doulou*) it was simply unrecognizable to sons and daughters of Adam and Eve drenched in a history of sin.

The Voluntary Restraint of Independent Exercise of Divine Attributes

The nature of God did not change in the incarnation. Rather it was precisely through lowliness that the Servant-caregiver was revealed and became knowable in history. He who is the "same yesterday and today and forever" (Heb. 13:8) became formed in our likeness without ceasing to be unchanging God. His divinity was not reduced, retracted, relinquished, or suppressed, but enhanced, set forth, offered, and expressed in this particular manner: humbly enfleshed. "He withdrew His power from its normal activity, so that having been humiliated He might also appear to be made infirm by the nonuse of His power. . . . Though He retained His power, He was seen as a man, so that the power would not be manifest in Him" (Ambrose, *Comm. on Phil.* 2, in Chemnitz, *TNC*:493).

These are the elements that make the central mystery of the incarnation unfathomable to human egocentricity, yet transparent to faith. This humbling remains the central datum of Christian proclamation and experience. While lying in the cradle and dying on the cross, he did not cease to be the One in whom "all things hold together" (Col. 1:19), in whom the fullness of the Godhead was dwelling bodily (Col. 2:9).

In his temporal lowliness the Son "abstains from the full use of the divine attributes communicated in the personal union" (Jacobs, *SCF*:145). It is as if the heir of a vast estate may have a great inheritance left to him, yet in his minority he may have only that use of it that is permitted by his guardian.

Classic Christianity was careful to define that he resigned "not the possession, nor yet entirely the use, but rather the independent exercise, of the divine attributes" (Strong, *Syst. Theol.*:703). On certain occasions, on behalf of his mission, he does not abstain from full use but rather exercises divine attributes (as in miracles). He could have exercised this power that was temporarily and voluntarily surrendered: "Do you think I cannot call on my Father, and he will at once put at my disposal more than twelve legions of angels? But how then would the Scriptures be fulfilled that say it must happen in this way?" (Matt. 26:53–54; Chrysostom, *Hom. on Matt.* 84).

Gregory of Nazianzus cautiously taught with measured restraint and discrimination: "What is lofty you are to apply to the Godhead and to that nature in him which is superior to sufferings and incorporeal; but all that is lowly to the composite condition of him who for your sakes made himself of no reputation and was incarnate" (*Orat.* 19.18).

Note that the relational divine attributes of holiness, love, and justice are exercised during his earthly ministry, but those pre-relational (prior to creation) divine attributes (aseity with unlimited power, knowledge, and presence) are voluntarily restrained.

Note also the irony: The hidden majesty wills to become visible, comprehensible, and existent in time, yet in a lowly way. "Invisible in His nature, He became visible in ours; surpassing comprehension, He has wished to be comprehended; remaining prior to time, He began to exist in time. The Lord of all things hid his immeasurable majesty to take on the form of a servant" (Leo 1, *Letter to Flavian*). Kierkegaard chose a parabolic form by which to speak of this obscuration in his unforgettable parable of the king and the maiden (*Phil. Frag*:31–43).

If constantly exercised, the divine omnipotence could have exempted Jesus from suffering for our sins, but this would have run counter to the purpose of his mission. Rather, he was willing to lay down his life, reminding his hearers that "No one takes it from me, but I lay it down of my own accord. I have authority to lay it down and authority to take it up again" (John 10:18; Athanasius, *Ag. Arians* 3.29.57).

The Omniscience of the Son Voluntarily Constrained

The New Testament picture of the Omniscience of the Son is complex: in some passages he knows what is going on in the minds of others and knows future events; in other passages he expresses surprise at learning something by observation or he professes ignorance and asks questions that assume he did not know the answer (Athanasius, *Four Discourses Ag. Arians* 1.11; J. S. Lawton, *Conflict in Christology*; Taylor, *PC*:286–306). What is the difference? In one sentence he is viewed from the point of view of his deity; in another from the point of his humanity.

This troublesome point is greatly illumined by the triune premise, and confusing without it: the divine Logos eternally experiences full awareness of the cosmos, yet as incarnate Logos united to Christ's humanity he has become voluntarily subjected to human limitations, ignorance, weakness, temptation, suffering, and death. As eternal Son he is equal with God in knowing and foreknowing, but in the mystery of his humiliation he is servant, obedient, willing to be vulnerable to time and finitude. As conceived in the womb, as born of Mary, as child of Joseph, the eternal Logos constrained or temporarily abnegated the full and independent exercise of eternal foreknowing, so as to become a little child (Gregory of Nazianzus, *Fourth Theol. Orat.*). Hence the paradox: unless we become as little children (as did the eternal Son) we will not grasp the meaning of God's coming governance (John of Damascus, *OF* 3.22).

Chrysostom offered a compassionate reason why the saying that the Son "knows not the day or hour" was providentially given for the good of the disciples: to diminish anxiety, for if everyone "knew when they were to die, they would surely strive earnestly at that hour" (Chrysostom, *Hom. on St. Matt.* 77.1). "Since He was made man, He is not ashamed, because of the flesh which is ignorant, to say 'I know not,' that He may show that knowing as God, He is but ignorant according to the flesh" (Athanasius, *Four Discourses Ag. Arians* 3.43). The reason he assumed "an ignorant and servile nature," was "because man's nature . . . does not have knowledge of future events" (John of Damascus, *OF, FC* 37:324–25). Thus it is said that ignorance was assumed economically by the Lord (Athanasius, *Four Discourses Ag. Arians* 1.11, 3.28; Newman, *Athanasius* 2:161–72). So in his human nature he voluntarily chose to remain ignorant of the day on which the final judgment would occur (Matt. 24:36). "No one knows about that day or hour, not even the angels in heaven, nor the Son, but only the Father" (Mark 13:32).

When the Son of God took upon himself the weakness of humanity, he did not relinquish the strength of God.

Mild He lays His glory by,
Born that man no more may die,
Born to raise the sons of earth,
Born to give them second birth.

C. Wesley, "Hark the Herald Angels Sing"

4

THE INCARNATION

THE ETERNAL SON ASSUMED HUMAN NATURE without ceasing to be God (John 1:17; Augustine, *Hom. on John*; *BOC*: 20). The word "incarnation" (Lat. *incarnatus*; Gk. *sarkosis*) means enfleshing, or becoming flesh, the union of human nature with the divine in one person.

"The Word became flesh" (John 1:1). The term "flesh" points to our entire created nature. In the assumption of humanity "nothing was lacking that belongs to human nature" (Augustine, *Enchiridion* 10.34).

Incarnation is the necessary premise of all subsequent events of Christ's coming (Ephrem the Syrian, *Comm. on Tatian's Diatess.* 1.1; Basil, *Hom. on Christ's Ancestry* 2.6). He was sent to humanity that humanity might be drawn to God (Athanasius, *Incarntion of the Word* 54.3). The incarnation must be studied, guarded, and transmitted carefully because it is the foundation of all Christian teaching on salvation (Hilary, *Trin.* 9.55).

How Both Genders Were Honored Equally in the Incarnation

The classical exegetes reasoned that both maleness and femaleness were honored equally in the incarnation. Augustine taught that God's "temporal plan ennobled each sex, both male and female. By possessing a male nature and being born of a woman He further showed by this plan that God has concern not only for the sex He represented but also for the one through which He took upon Himself our nature" (*On Faith and the Creed* 4.9). "That dispensation has honored both sexes, at once the male and the female, and has made it plain that not only *that sex which He assumed* pertains to God's care, but also *that sex by which He did assume* this other, in that He bore [the nature of] the man [*virum gerendo*], [and] in that He was born of the woman," (4.9, italics added).

A Man Born of Woman

Mary is female, Jesus is male. The meaning: God's way of coming involves both genders in a particular way fitting to each gender. First, female, for the birthing of the God-man without human father. And equally second, male, for the mission of the anointed messianic servant, according to the Jewish expectation of a male of Davidic descent. But there could have been no birth without a mother. Hence, God "did not despise the male, for he assumed the nature of a man, nor the female, for he was born of a woman" ("*nec mares fastidivit, quia marem suscepit; nec feminam, quia de femina factus est,*" Augustine, *Letters* 3; Pohle-Preuss *DT* 5:18n). The reason the male is second in order but not in importance is that this birth was without father.

The core text of this classic feminine/masculine incarnational equilibrium is found in Paul's Letter to the Galatians: "But when the time had fully come, God sent his Son, born of a woman, born under law, to redeem those under law" (Gal. 4:4). Paul says: born of a woman, a particular woman, without male assistance, not born of woman and man (Theodoret, *Epis. To Gal.* 4.4–5). "He is human in that he was made from a woman, made under the law. The nativity of his flesh shows his human nature. The virgin birth is an indicator of his divine nature" (Leo I, *Letter 28 to Flavian* 4).

The incarnation required a birth. Giving birth cannot be done by males. There is no way physiologically. This forms a plausible hypothesis for explaining why the Savior was male: *if the mother of the Savior must necessarily be female, the Savior must be male, if both sexes are to be rightly and equitably involved in the salvation event,* according to the classical exegetes. Augustine reverses the gender preference allegation by making the female birth-enabler the primary basis upon which the incarnate Lord was more plausibly to be male, seen in the light of the ancient prophetic promise that the Messiah would be of the male line of David (Jer. 33:14–18).

God was not ashamed of female and male bodies, or of human embodiment, or of sexuality. This is a central point of incarnation teaching. Augustine must have been in a lively mood when he wrote: "Now the reason why the Holy Spirit was not born of a dove, whereas Christ was born of a woman, is this: The holy Spirit did not come to liberate doves, but to declare unto man innocence and spiritual love, which were outwardly symbolized in the form of a dove. The Lord Jesus Christ, having come to liberate human beings, including both men and women destined for salvation, was *not ashamed of the male nature, for He took it upon Himself; or of the female, for He was born of a woman*" (Augustine, *The Christian Combat* 22, italics added; see also *OTR* 14:27).

Was Made Man

Augustine gasped a "profound mystery" in the thought that "as death had befallen us through a woman, Life should be born to us through a woman. By this defeat, the Devil would be tormented over the thought of *both sexes, male and female,* because he had taken delight in the defection of them both. The freeing of both sexes would not have been so severe a penalty for the Devil, unless we were also *liberated by the agency of both sexes*" (Augustine, *The Christian Combat*, 22, italics added). It is hard to explain why this text has been largely ignored in an era in which all aspects of sexuality have been explored. The tempter was exasperated, Augustine reasoned, by the thought that both the female and male sex were being decisively used by God for human salvation. This is an inclusivist argument embedded in the heart of patristic thinking on the incarnation. Both male and female can equally relish this inspired reflection upon divine equity.

Similarly, Gregory of Nazianzus resisted the idea of making woman responsible alone for the temptation of Adam: "The Woman sinned, and so did Adam. The serpent deceived them both; and one was not found to be the stronger and the other the weaker. . . . Christ saves both by His Passion . . . let the one flesh have equal honor" (*Orat.* 37.7).

The deeper conflict being dealt with in the incarnation is not the difference between the sexes, however, but the divine-human controversy resulting from sin. The mediation of this post-Adam, post-Eve controversy required a mediator who was fully human. Julia of Norwich envisioned in Christ a humanity that both encompasses and transcends sexual differentiation: "I am, as I hope, a member of this 'man,' by the mercy of God, for the blessed comfort I saw is large enough for all of us" (*RDL* 79).

Did God show sexist bias or partiality against females or males in the birth of the incarnate Lord? Does God prefer one gender over another in becoming flesh? Is the Incarnation sexist? Not according to classic consensual teaching. A renewed emphasis is due on the virgin mother of the male messiah in Christian teaching of the incarnation that is sensitive to gender bias (Augustine, *Since God Has Made Everything, Why Did He Not Make Everything Equal?*, *EDQ* 41; Tho. Aq., *ST* 3 Q1.5–6).

The incarnation did not disregard sexuality. The Incarnate One could not be both truly human and lacking in sexuality. God did not hesitate to identify himself with the very flesh that is so profoundly associated with sexuality and so easily corrupted by sexual self-assertion (Augustine, *Trin.* 10).

Sexual Difference, Not Inequality

Gregory of Nyssa held that the incarnation required sexual difference, but not sexual inequality. "The only thing alien to the Divine is evil. Nature is not evil. . . . There is only one way for a man to enter life. . . . [Our opponents] are offended at the means of the visitation. What other method, then, of entering life do they prescribe for God? They fail to realize that the whole anatomy of the body is uniformly to be valued . . . the generative organs have the future in view, and it is by them that the succession of the race is maintained" (Gregory of Nyssa, ARI 28).

The purpose of the virgin birth was not to avoid the generative organs, but to show that the flesh of the Lord was produced "by the efficacy and power of the Holy Spirit" (Augustine, *Questions on the New Testament*, Appendix 50).

God the Son was made human (*homo factus est*; Gk. *enanthrōpēsanta*), or became incarnate (*incarnatus*; Gk. *sarkōthenta*) by the Holy Spirit (*de Spiritu Sancto*), and was born of the Virgin Mary (*ex Maria virgine*). The saving event was for us humans (*qui propter nos homines*). He became incarnate for our salvation (*propter nostram salutem*, Creed of 150 Fathers).

The Scriptural Teaching of Incarnation

Paul wrote and probably even sang of One "Who, being in very nature God," became "made in human likeness" (Phil. 2:6–7). "Though he was rich, yet for your sakes he became poor, so that you through his poverty might become rich" (1 Cor. 8:9). Paul did not invent this tradition but received it from the early Christian preaching prior to his conversion.

The Pauline tradition interpreted the incarnation in comprehensive cosmic terms: God has seen fit in the fullness of time "to bring all things in heaven and on earth together under one head, even Christ" (Eph. 1:10), in whom "all things hold together" (Col. 1:17). "For in Christ all the fullness of the Deity lives in bodily form (Col. 2:9).

The testimony of John on incarnation generally concurs with that of Paul, yet it is expressed differently. John's Gospel was primarily interested in the way in which the divine *doxa* (glory) shines through the veil of *sarx* (the flesh) and dwells in it. "The Word became flesh and made his dwelling among us" (John 1:14; Chrysostom, *Hom. on John* 12).

John's primary purpose was not to write a heroic biography of an eminent moral leader, but to reveal this pivotal truth of Jesus' distinctive personal identity: He is "from above" (John 6:33). He speaks as a preexistent Word (John 8:42). He is sent by the Father to the world (John 1:14; 5:23–38). He left the Father's presence and glory (John 6:62; 8:38) and descended from heaven into the human-historical sphere (John 3:13; 6:33). The notion that the Son was *sent* by the Father occurs forty-two times in John's Gospel (e.g., 3:17; 9:39; 10:36). Those who cannot connect with this point will have no story to hear.

The evidence of the Father's sending *is* the incarnation (Augustine, *Hom. on John* 31). The Sent One is the one and only Son of God ("unique Son," "only begotten Son," "the Only Son of the Father," John 1:14, 18; 3:16, 18; 1 John 4:9). It is this one who becomes flesh (*sarx*) (John 1:14; 19:17, 34, 37), fully human (*anthropōs*) in every way. Incarnation focuses upon the joyful mystery of the announcement that God takes on our humanity (Chrysostom, *Hom. on John*; Baxter, *PW* 21:314–18). This event is shaped by a redemptive necessity. It has a compassionate motivation with a missional purpose: to save humanity. It is accomplished by its chosen means: virginal conception.

Incarnation Defined

The incarnation is concisely defined in the Orthodox Catechism: "The Son of God took to himself human flesh without sin, and was made man, without ceasing to be God" (Russian Catechism, *COC* II: 471). The incarnation occurred not by conversion of divinity into flesh but by the assumption of humanity into God (Athanasius, *On the Incarn. of the Word* 14–15). God became flesh not by changing into another reality, but by assumption of the flesh (*assumptio carnis*). Remaining what he was, he became what he was not (Hilary, *Trin.* 3.16; Athanasius, *Four Discourses Ag. Arians* 1.35). In Gregory of Nazianzus' renowned formulation: "What He was He continued to be; what He was not He took to Himself" (*Orat.* 19.19).

God has elected to use an extraordinary form of body language to communicate to humanity. "Since human nature is essentially composite, and can neither express itself nor receive anything—cannot even think or aspire—except by use of the physical organism and of its material environment, God adapts His method to the nature which He has created, and uses what we have to use—the human body—as the instrument of His self-manifestation, of redemption, and of sanctifying grace" (Hall, *DT* 6:78; Fulgentius, *Incarn. PL* 65).

In becoming truly a man, God did not cease to be truly God. "Nor did he lose what he was, but he began to be what he was not" (Augustine, *Hom. on John*). Similarly Origen, in transmitting the tradition he received, stated that God "was made man, was made flesh, although he was God; and being made man, he still remained what he was, namely, God" (*OFP* 1, pref., 3). Classic discussions of the incarnation include Athanasius (*Incarn. of the Word*), Ambrose (*The Sacrament of the Incarn. of our Lord*), Anselm (*On the Incarn. of the Word, TIR*), Richard of St. Victor, (*Trin.*), Peter Lombard, (*De Incarnatione Verbi*), Thomas Aquinas (*ST* 3, Q1–26).

Avoiding Distortions

The Fourth Ecumenical Council (Chalcedon, AD 451) further defined incarnational teaching so as to protect it against distortions: The Son is "consubstantial with the Father [*homoousion tō patri*] according to divinity, and consubstantial with [*houoousion hemin*] us according to human nature" (Chalcedon, *SCD* 148). "Thus like us in all respects, sin only excepted. Before time began [*pro aiōnōn*] he was begotten of the Father, in respect of his deity, and now in these 'last days,' for us and on behalf of our salvation, this self same one was born of Mary the virgin, who is God-bearer [*theotokos*] in respect to his humanness [*anthrōpotēta*]" (Chalcedon, *CC:* 36).

Classic Protestant definitions of incarnation resonant closely with these ancient ecumenical definitions: "The incarnation is a divine act, by which the Son of God, in the womb of His mother, the Virgin Mary, took into the unity of His person a human nature, consubstantial with us, but without sin, and destitute of a subsistence of its own, and communicated to the same both His divine person and nature, so that Christ now subsists forever, as the God-man, in two natures, divine and human, most intimately united" (David Hollaz in Schmid, *DT:*303; Ursinus, *CHC:*196–202; Barth, *CD* 3/4, 4/2).

The Mystery of Godliness is Great

Incarnation remains a mystery even when best explained (Gregory Thaumaturgus, *Four Hom.* 3; Lactantius, *Div. Inst.* 4.8). Reverence forbids the pretense that human knowledge is competent to make a minute or exhaustive scrutiny of the empirical or physical dimensions of this mystery (Maximos, *Various Texts*, *Philokal.* 2:167–68). "How silently, how silently, the wondrous gift is given!" (Phillips Brooks, *HPEC:*68).

The New Testament writers recognized that the mystery would not be resolved by ever-deeper logical or historical analysis. "Beyond all question, the mystery of godliness is great: He appeared in a body, was vindicated by the Spirit" (1 Tim. 3:16). Augustine pointed to the outer limits of all explanation: "Let us grant that God can do something which we confess we cannot fathom. In such matters the whole explanation of the deed is in the power of the Doer" (Augustine, *Letters*, To Volusianus, 137.2.8).

It was inevitable that such a premise would generate a paradoxical tradition of poetic language: "The Teacher of children became Himself a child among children, that He might instruct the unwise. The Bread of heaven came down to earth to feed the hungry" (Cyril of Jerusalem, *Catech. Lect.* 12.2). "The Word, though remaining what It was, became what It was not" (Theophilus of Bulgaria, *Enarratio in Evangelium Ioannis* I 14).

"Reason stumbles at this article." As to *how* the incarnation occurred, Luther wrote "you are to believe, not to know and to understand, until the solution appears on the blessed Day of our redemption" (Luther, *Christmas Serm. on John 1:1–14*; Kierkegaard, *TC:*40–56). "According to our nature, then, He offered Himself that He might do a work *beyond* our nature" (Ambrose, *The Incarn. of our Lord* 6.54, ital. add.). Such statements are not nonsensical (as Tillich imagined in *ST* II:94), but an acknowledgement of the limits of language in the presence of divine mystery.

Goodness Communicates Itself

Gregory of Nyssa asked: If God had the power to save humanity by fiat, by a simple sovereign act, then "why did God take a tedious, circuitous route, submit to a bodily nature, enter life through birth, pass through the various stages of development, and finally taste death?" (*ARI* 15). Because goodness communicates itself, and the greatest good communicates itself in the greatest way (Hilary, *Trin*.1.12).

"It belongs to the essence of goodness to communicate itself to others," and particularly to those creatures most capable of responding (Tho. Aq., *ST* 3 Q1). Thus it was "most fitting that by visible things the invisible things of God should be made known" (Tho. Aq., *ST* 3 Q1.1; Rom.1:20). By this condescension God brought human history to a decisive climax and reversal (Arnobius, *Ag. Heathen* 55–65; Augustine, *Trin.*, FC 45:396–403). The incarnation was a stooping down of compassion, not a default of power (Leo I, *Tome*).

Augustine brilliantly employed the analogy of speech to set forth the unchanging integrity of God throughout the incarnation: "For just as our word in some way becomes a bodily sound by assuming that in which it may be manifested to the senses of men, so the Word of God was made flesh by assuming that in which He might also be manifested to the senses of men. And just as our word becomes a sound and is not changed into a sound, so the Word of God indeed becomes flesh, but far be it from us that it should be changed into flesh. For by assuming it, not by being consumed in it, this word of ours becomes a sound, and that Word became flesh" (Augustine, *Trin.*, FC 45:477).

God's Empathy a Wholly Voluntary Act

No more complete revelation of empathic love is possible than this: that God almighty shares our human frame, participates in our human limitations, enters into our human sphere (Tertullian, *Apology* 2; Oden, *KC* 2–3). The empathic divine Physician is willing to come into the toxic sphere of the epidemic to share personally the diseased human condition.

He "measures all by comparison with his own suffering, so that he may know our condition by his own" (Gregory of Nazianzus, *Theol. Orat.*, 30.6). They are narrow-minded who "define God's majesty from its inability to share the properties of our nature" (Gregory of Nyssa, *ARI* 27).

The enfleshing was completely voluntary and in no way coerced (Hilary, *Trin.* 11.8–9; L. Hodgson, *And Was Made Man*). The Son did not have to come to us; he chose to. The salvation event begins in an initiative taken not by "human decision or a husband's will, but born of God" (John 1:13).

None of us had the choice of whether or not to be born, with one exception— the Servant Lord, who "was not born without His will. None of us is born because he will, and none of us dies when he will: He, when He would, was born; when He would, He died: how He would, He was born of a Virgin; how He would, He died on the cross" (Augustine, *On the Creed* 8). Only the Son elected human life.

God's New Beginning

The advent of the Expected One had long been anticipated by the prophets and angelic hosts. The hope of God's own coming had been deeply but inconspicuously embedded in various prophetic witnesses (Tertullian, *Ag. Marcion* 3; Lactantius, *Div. Inst.* 4.5–19; Hilary, *Trin.* 5; Ambrose, *Cain and Abel*). Isaiah especially had foretold that a child would be born who would be called Mighty God (*el gibbor*, Isa. 9:6). The name "Immanuel" (Isa. 7:14) prefigured that it was nothing less than God who promised to come to humanity. It was a human child that was called "God with us."

The redemption for which the incarnation occurred has universal significance for the whole of human history (Hilary, *Trin.* 3.24–28). The consummation of history is anticipated in the coming of the eternal Son. "If Christ is God, as He truly is, but did not assume manhood, then we are strangers to salvation" (Cyril of Jerusalem, *Catech. Lect.*, 12.1). The end of salvation is already known in the enfleshing of the Word.

Why Did God Become Man? Cur Deus Homo?

The question around which Anselm's great book revolves is: "For what reason or necessity did God become man," when God could have restored life to the world "by a sheer act of will"? (*Cur Deus Homo, LCC* 10:101). Anselm reasoned that: "It was quite impossible for him to save man in some other way" (*LCC* 10:107), since fallen humanity needs an impeccable divine mediator who shares our human condition.

The purpose of the incarnation has been summarized in various ways by complementary scriptural texts:

> *To reveal God to humanity (John 1:18; 14:7–11).*
> *To provide a high priest interceding for us able to sympathize with human weaknesses (Heb. 4:14–16).*
> *To offer humanity a pattern of the fullness of human life (1 Pet. 2:21; 1 John 2:6).*
> *To provide a substitutionary sacrifice for the sins of all humanity (Heb. 10:1–10).*
> *To bind up the demonic powers (1 John 3:8).*

He came first to live and then to die for others (Hilary, *Trin.* 3.24; Augustine, *Trin.*, FC 45:387–403). "God the Word was made man for this reason," wrote John of Damascus, "that the very nature which had sinned, fallen, and become corrupt should conquer the tyrant who had deceived it" (*OF* 3.12). All these motifs may be taken together as having a single purpose: redemption. "The sole purpose of Christ's incarnation was our redemption" (Calvin, *Inst.* 2.12.4).

The means by which God chooses to effect the redemption of humanity is congruent with the essential nature and attributes (love, holiness, and power) of God (Augustine, *Trin.*, FC 45:145–47). "For God was pleased to have all his fullness dwell in him, and through him to reconcile to himself all things, whether things on earth or things in heaven, by making peace through his blood, shed on the cross" (Col. 1:19–20; Origen, *On Prayer* 23.2; Ephrem, *Comm. on Tatian's Diatess.* 14).

John of Damascus could be counted upon to bring these diverse motifs together in a beautiful fabric of consistent reasoning: "The Son of God became man in order that He might again grace man as He had when He made him. For He had made him to His own image, understanding and free, and to His own likeness, that is to say, as perfect in virtues as it was possible for human nature to be, for these virtues are, as it were characteristics of the divine nature—freedom from care and annoyance, integrity, goodness, wisdom, justice, freedom from all vice. Thus, He put man in communion with Himself. But, since by transgressing the commandment we obscured and canceled out the characteristics of the divine image, we were given over to evil and stripped of the divine communion. . . . But, since He had shared with us what was better and we had not kept it, He now takes His share of what is worse, of our nature I mean to say, that through Himself and in Himself He may restore what was to His image and what was to His likeness" (*OF* 4.4).

The Necessity of the Incarnation

He Came to Die

Scripture states the point starkly: he came to die (Athanasius, *Four Discourses Ag. Arians*, 3.58). The relation between his birth and death can be stated schematically:

The Mystery of the Incarnation	The Mystery of the Passion
He came	to give his life as ransom (Mark 10:45)
God sent his Son	to redeem (Gal. 4:5)
God so loved	that he gave his only Son (John 3:16)
He humbled himself	becoming obedient unto death (Phil. 3:8)
To this end I was born	Crucify! Crucify! (John 18:36; 19:6)

The reason for the incarnation is stated directly in the Letter to the Hebrews: "Since the children have flesh and blood, he too shared in their humanity so that by his death he might destroy him who holds the power of death" (Heb. 2:14; Gregory of Nazianzus, *Third Theol. Orat. on the Son* 29.20).

The Intrinsic Connection of Incarnation and Atonement

The purpose for which the Son came was clearly set forth by the Gospel writers: "the Son of Man did not come to be served, but to serve, and to give his life as a ransom for many" (Matt 20:28). "For God did not send his Son into the world to condemn the world, but to save the world through him" (John 3:17; Leo I, *Sermon* 23.4).

Anticipating the cross, Jesus said: "The hour has come for the son of Man to be glorified" (John 12:23). "It was for this very reason I came to this hour" (John 12:27). Only the incarnate Son could also be the mediator of the sacrifice essential to the atonement (Chrysostom, *Hom. on Matt.* Hom 65.7; Tho. Aq., *ST* III Q1).

Redemption could only occur through sacrifice. There could be no dying Mediator without the Mediator's birth. Hence the Son's death and birth are intrinsically connected (Chrysostom, *Hom. on Hebr.* 18.1; Chemnitz, *TNC*:220–22).

To those who wonder whether incarnation is possible, classical Christian teachers reply that without it redemption is impossible (Augustine, *Hom. on John*). "For this reason he had to be made like his brothers in every way, in order that he might become a merciful and faithful high priest in service to God, and that he might make atonement for the sins of the people. Because he himself suffered when he was tempted, he is able to help those who are being tempted" (Heb. 2:17–18; Photius, *Fragments on Epis. To Hebr.* 2.18).

Augustine's gift for epochal summary helps us grasp the intrinsic connection of the incarnate person and his mediatorial work: "Now when Adam was created, he, being a righteous man, had no need of a mediator. But when sin had placed a wide gulf between God and the human race, it was expedient that a Mediator, who alone of the human race was born, lived, and died without sin, should reconcile us to God" (*Enchiridion* 108).

Calvin stated the point with precision: "Since neither as God alone could he feel death, nor as man alone could he overcome it, he coupled human nature with divine that to atone for sin he might submit the weakness of the one to death; and that, wrestling with death by the power of the other nature, he might win victory for us." Thus he "took the person and the name of Adam in order to take Adam's place" (*Inst.* 2.12.3).

An ancient Latin Easter hymn had the wit to celebrate the irony of a happy failure (Adam's) from which redemption could arise: "*O felix culpa quae tantum ac talem meruit habere redemptorem*"—"O happy fault, which deserved to have so great and glorious a Redeemer" (Daniel, *Thesaurus Hymnologica* 1, c.:303; this theme is found in Augustine, Rupert of Deutz, *De Trinitate*, 3.20, Hugh of St. Victor, John Donne, *Selected Works* [1839], *Serm.* I). Wesley concluded: "For if Adam had not fallen Christ had not died" ("God's love for Fallen Man," *Serm.* 2, *WJWB*: 425).

Bridging the Conflict Between God's Holiness and Human Sin

To mediate is to act as a peacemaker between conflicted parties so as to effect peace (Augustine, *CG, FC* 14:99–101; Tho. Aq., *ST* 3, Q26.1). The mediator intervenes between alienated powers so that the quarrel may end.

The quarrel in this case is that between God and humanity generated by the history of sin. Christ is "the mediator between God and man, because He is God with the Father, and a man with men. A mere man could not be a mediator between God and man . . . Behold the mediator: Divinity without humanity cannot act as mediator; nor can humanity without Divinity; but the human Divinity and the Divine humanity of Christ is the sole mediator between Divinity and humanity" (Augustine, *Serm. on NT Lessons* 47). Only the incarnate Word of God allows this mediation, uniting humanity and deity in one person, bringing God to humanity, and humanity to God (Cyril of Alex., *Comm. on John* 1.9).

The mediation occurred as an event in time. There is "one mediator between God and men, the man Christ Jesus, who gave himself as a ransom for all men—the testimony given in its proper time" (1 Tim. 2:5–6). No one could overcome the divine-human estrangement unless able to so take "what was ours as to impart what was his to us, and to make what was his by nature ours by grace" (Calvin, *Inst.* 2.12.2).

"The inexpressible beauty of our redemption" was expressed by Anselm in these typic parallels:

> As death entered through one man's disobedience,
> So life is restored through one man's obedience;
> As sin came through the temptation of a woman,
> So salvation came through one born of woman;
> As the enemy conquered humanity by tasting of a tree,
> So Christ conquered the enemy by bearing suffering on a tree.

(*Cur Deus Homo, LCC* 10:104–105).

No mere mortal could save humanity while humanity itself was mired in sin: "The wounds of mankind are beyond our healing", remarked Cyril of Jerusalem. "The evil cannot be repaired by us" (*Catech. Lect.* 12). "Who could accomplish this, unless the Son of God should become also the Son of man, and thus receive to himself what belongs to us, and transfer to us that which is his" (Calvin, *Inst.* 2.12.2; Augustine, *Tractates on John* 41.5).

The Incarnation Reveals True Humanity

In becoming human, God teaches by embodiment the value of true humanity. The incarnation has far-reaching importance beyond Christology. It also teaches us about our very selves (Gregory of Nazianzus, *Fourth Theol. Orat., On the Son*; Barth, *The Humanity of God*). Hence incarnation belongs to learning about man, not about God alone. "God has now shown us the high place human nature holds in creation, for he entered into it by genuinely becoming man" (Tho. Aq., *TATT*:279). The incarnation made us partners in the divine nature (2 Pet. 1:4; Hebr. 12:10; Hilary, *Trin.* 1.18). "Know your worth, O Christian; you are made a partner of the divine nature" (Leo I, *Serm.* 21.3).

Before his conversion out of Manicheanism, Augustine had been afraid "to believe Him to be born in the flesh, lest I should be compelled to believe Him contaminated by the flesh" (*Confessions* 5.10). After his conversion to Christ, he learned that if the incarnation showed us nothing else it sufficiently revealed these "two wholesome facts"—"that true divinity cannot be polluted by flesh, and that demons are not to be considered better than ourselves because they have not flesh" (Augustine, *CG* 9.17).

"It is not for the angels to be proud of Christ's incarnation, for Christ did not assume an angelic but a human nature," Luther mused. "Therefore it would not be a surprise if the angels looked at us with envy in their eyes because we human beings, creatures far inferior to them and sinners besides, are placed above them into an honor so high and great. They worship Christ, who has become our Brother, our flesh and blood" (*Serm. on Col.* 1:18–20). God would have fallen short of his purpose if he had assumed the nature of a buffalo or rock or tree or even an angel. Rather he assumed the nature of a human being capable of communication, speech and compassion (Augustine, *Trin.* 8.10).

Jesus was not partially or occasionally human. The human nature assumed by the Logos included all that properly belongs to humanity—everything we share when we speak of ourselves as human beings—yet without defect or sin (Augustine, *Enchridion* 10.34; Benedict XIV, *Profession of Faith, SCD* 1463). The "human nature which he assumed, he did not destroy" (Augustine, *Letters* 137.3). The Logos "assumed a perfect man, soul and body and mind (spirit), and all that belongs to man, without sin" (Creed of Epiphanius, *COC* 2:36). The implication is not that a Divine person coinhabited a human body with another human person so as to be two distinct persons with one name, but rather the one name, Jesus Christ, made reference to a single person, God made flesh (Tho. Aq., *SCG* 4:64–74).

Consequent Issues of the Incarnation

The scriptural teaching that the Word became flesh required further explanation of a host of consequent dilemmas. It is useful to review some of these: Did Jesus gradually or instantly become God-man? Was the incarnation unique and unrepeatable? Did the whole of the Godhead assume flesh? Did God prefer one gender over another in the incarnation?

Did Jesus Gradually Become God?

It was a common counter-ecumenical teaching that "Christ is not God made man, but a man made God; for they [false teachers] have dared to say that it was not the pre-existing Word that became man, but that a certain man was crowned by advancement" (Cyril of Jerusalem, *Catech. Lect.* 12.3).

Christianity speaks of God becoming man, not a man becoming God. The idea is not that a particular man comes nearer and nearer to God until, being filled with increasing divine abilities or powers, gradually becomes so connected with God as to become God. Such reasoning appeared in third century adoptionism and recurred in nineteenth-century liberalism. Yet that runs directly against the intent of the language of the New Testament preexistent Logos that leaves no room for adoptionism (1 Cor. 8:6; 2 Cor. 8:9; Eph. 1:3–14; Phil. 2:5–11).

Does God Do This Often?

Augustine puzzled over this: "Why did the Lord Jesus Christ come so long after man sinned, and not in the beginning?" His measured answer: Humanity had to pass, as does youth, through its own sequence of developing stages and ages (Jerome, *Epis. To Gal.* 2.4.3). The teacher had to come in the time of humanity's readiness to learn. History was kept under the law as if under a tutor until the One would come whom the tutor served (Gal. 4:1–7; Augustine *EDQ* 44).

Further, was the incarnation unique—once for all times? If so, why did God become human only once? Or can we expect repeated incarnations? Nothing is more characteristic in the history of religions than the thought of the union of God and humanity. In some traditions this occurs by the *apotheosis* (deification) of the human who ascends to become a god and in others by the alleged descent of one or more of the gods to live with humans (but not *as human*!). Evidence for the recurrence of these notions may be found the world over in almost every known period of human history.

The Bible recognizes that such expectations had been generally present in human history. When through Paul's ministry a man crippled from birth was healed at Lystra, the crowd "shouted in the Lycaonian language, 'The gods have come down to us in human form!'" (Acts 14:11), which is why they called Paul Hermes and Barnabas Zeus. This was an impression that the apostles sought immediately to correct.

Such general expectations of apotheosis or polytheistic descent were common in New Testament times, often blended with complex thoughts of transmigration of souls and with nativistic animisms. These views differ markedly from the incarnation, which speaks of the one true God who becomes flesh and suffers and dies in history without ceasing to be God. Myths of divine-human intermixing, apotheosis, and deification of a human are all distinguished from and finally rejected by the teaching of the Word of God becoming flesh.

The once-for-all condescension of the one and only Son to assume human nature was understood to be a unique, singular, and not needing to be duplicated since the sacrifice once made does not need to be reoffered redundantly (Heb. 9:25–28; Chrysostom, *Hom. on Hebr.* 17.4–6). He is the only Mediator, not one among many (Tho. Aq., *ST* 3 Q26; Calvin, *Inst.* 3.20.19).

How Is Generation Both Eternal and Temporal?

If the nativity of the eternal Son attests a temporal birth, how can it be said that the Son was pretemporally begotten of the Father? A twofold generation is posited of the Son: an eternal generation through which Christ is Son of the Father; and a generation in time through which Christ is son of Mary, a man born of woman (Augustine, *Hom. on John*). Classical exegetes distinguished two nativities: the Son was eternal as God and temporal as man (John of Damascus, *OF* 3.7). The Second Ecumenical Council (Constantinople AD 553) firmly settled this point ecumenically on the basis of scriptural teaching by confessing "that God the Word was twice begotten, the first before all time from the Father, nontemporal and bodiless, the other in the last days when he came down from the heavens and was incarnate." (*CC*: 46).

This teaching cannot be stated more beautifully than by the ancient formularies. Language that to the doubtful may seem disingenuous to the ecumenical teachers has seemed wonderfully symmetrical, aesthetically balanced, and typologically ingenious in speaking of "two births of the one our Lord Jesus Christ Himself, one incorporeal and eternal from God the Father before all ages, the other, corporeal and in the last age, from holy Mary, ever virgin, Mother of God; and one and the same Jesus Christ our Lord and God, one in being with the Father as to His divinity, one in being with men and with His mother as to His humanity, subject to suffering in His flesh while He is impassible in His divinity, limited in His flesh while He is illimited in His spirit, at once created and untreated, earthly and heavenly, perceptible by sense and by intellect, bound by space and beyond space" (Lateran Council, AD 649; Hilary, *Trin.* 9.51–54).

Similarly at Toledo: "By the fact that He has come forth from the Father without a beginning, He is said only to be born, not to be made or predestined; but by the fact that He was born from the Virgin Mary, we must believe that He was born and made and predestined. Yet, in Him both births are wonderful, because He was begotten from the Father without a mother before all ages, and in the end of the ages He was generated from a mother without a father. He who inasmuch as He is God created Mary, inasmuch as He is man was created from Mary. He is at once the Father and the Son of His Mother Mary" (Eleventh Council of Toledo, AD 675; Gregory of Nazianzus, *Orat.* 19.19). Ponder the ironies of the schematic of the unique dual birth drawn from the Council of Toledo:

The incarnate son was paradoxically:

Father of the Mother	Son of the Mother
Without a Mother	Without a Father
Begotten from the Father	Generated from a Mother
As to divinity	As to humanity
One in being with the Father	One in being with humanity
Incorporeal birth	Corporeal birth
Born not made	Born and made
Before all ages	In the last age
Illimited in his Spirit	Limited in his flesh
Uncreated	Created
Impassible	Subject to suffering
Beyond space	Bound by space

The poetic imagination soared in the updraft of such analogies: "For, as Eve was formed from Adam without carnal conjunction, so did this one bring forth the new Adam in accordance with the law of gestation but surpassing the nature of generation. Thus, He who is without a mother begotten of a father was without a father born of a woman. And because it was of a woman it was in accordance with the law of gestation; while, because it was without father, it surpassed the nature of generation" (John of Damascus, *OF* 4.14; see Cyril of Jerusalem, *Catech. Lect.* 11).

That such masterworks of poetic imagination may seem boring to modern impatience is admitted. But they continue to claim the rapt meditative attention of anyone seeking to understand classic teaching on the incarnation.

The Enigma of Time and the Trinity

The ecumenical teachers never tired of clarifying that they spoke of an eternal begetting that never had a beginning in time. If this distinction is not grasped, the student of classic Christianity will be forever puzzled by confusions between eternal and temporal begetting.

At the Eleventh Council of Toledo the point was framed in its consensually mature form: "The Son was born, but not made, from the substance of the Father, without beginning, before all ages, for at no time did the Father exist without the Son, nor the Son without the Father. Yet the Father is not from the Son, as the Son is from the Father, because the Father was not generated by the Son but the Son by the Father. The Son, therefore, is God from the Father, and the Father is God, but not from the Son" (CF:103).

"Time does not come into the begetting of the Son from the Father. . . . For what he is now, that has he been timelessly begotten from the beginning. . . . For God was not at first childless, and then after [a] lapse of time became Father, but he had his Son from all eternity, not begetting him as men beget men, but as he alone knows who begat him true God before all ages. . . . Do not compare it with teachers 'begetting' disciples. . . . So the way in which the Father begat the Son is not attainable by human analogy. . . . It is enough for us that we should know that God has begotten one only Son" (Cyril of Jerusalem, *Catech. Lect.* 11.7–12).

"Do not imagine any space of eternity in which the Father was and the Son was not. Since when the Father was, since then the Son. And what is that 'since,' where is no beginning? Therefore ever Father without beginning, ever Son without beginning. And how, will you say, was He begotten, if he have no beginning? Of eternal, co-eternal" (Augustine, *On the Creed* 8).

Why the Son Only and Not the Whole Godhead Assumed Flesh

Incarnation teaching is closely linked with scripture-based triune teaching. The incarnation is a work of the one God, the Son being sent by the Father by the power of the Spirit (Augustine, *Trin.*, FC 5:479).

Lacking the premise of triunity, God could not at the same time be sovereign and empty himself in servanthood; nor both send and be sent; nor be both lawgiver and obedient to law; nor both offer himself as a sacrifice and receive that sacrifice (Augustine, *Trin.*, FC 45:62–63).

Only the Son, and not the whole Godhead, assumed human flesh. The Father willed the Son's coming, and the Spirit enabled the conception. The Father sent the Son on the mission to be embodied in the flesh. Only the Son assumed the body. The Spirit conceived and enabled the mission (*Leiden Synopsis* 25.6–8).

The will to redeem proceeds from the entire Trinity (Peter Lombard, *Sent.* 3.5; Gerhardt, *LT* 3, 413). The Father commissions the Son. The assumption of flesh is peculiar to the Son. The cause of conception is the Holy Spirit, while the material matrix is the womb of a lowly maiden. "To us there is one God the Father, from whom are all things, and one Lord Jesus Christ, through whom are all things, and one Holy Ghost, in whom are all things" (Gregory of Nazianzus, *Orat.* 39.12).

The error of Patripassianism insisted that it was the Father himself, not the Son incarnate, who suffered upon the cross. "If anyone says that in the passion of the cross it is God Himself who felt the pain and not the flesh and the soul which Christ, the Son of God had taken to Himself—the form of servant which He had accepted as Scripture says (Phil. 2:7)—he is mistaken" (Council of Rome, *Tome of Damasus* 382, CF:147).

It is the *logos* who was from the beginning, was with God and was God (John 1:1), was before Abraham (John 8:58), who existed in the form of God (Phil. 2:6), being of one substance (*homoousios*) with the Father, who became flesh in time (John 1:14; see Calvin, *Inst.* 2.13–14; *Leiden Synopsis* 25.10). "The Word, while being God, was made man without suffering change," but this does not imply that "the Godhead was made man"; rather it means that "the Godhead was united to humanity in one of Its Persons" (John of Damascus, *OF* 3.11; Tho. Aq., *ST*, 3, Q1). As incarnate Lord he acted in a way that only God can act: forgiving sin, giving life to the dead, revealing the secret thoughts of persons, dividing loaves and fishes, and laying down his life and taking it up again.

His Humanity

The mediator between God and humanity would have to be nothing less than God and nothing less than fully human. Any mediator that lacked either divinity or humanity could not mediate between God and man. How can someone mediate in a conflict in which the mediator has no capacity to empathize with one side or the other? Classic Christian teaching argued that his humanity was an absolute requirement of his mediatorial mission.

The key text is from the Pauline tradition: "For there is one God and one mediator between God and men, the man Christ Jesus" (1 Tim. 2:5). No mediation between God and humanity is possible if the mediator lacks any aspect of God's nature or any aspect of human nature (Tertullian, *On the Flesh of Christ* 15).

The conditions of mediation were brilliantly formulated in Hebrews: "Since the children have flesh and blood, he too *shared in their humanity* so that by his death he might destroy him who holds the power of death" (Heb. 2:14, italics added). How could one destroy the power of death without being truly God? And how could the mediator have learned obedience through suffering unless our humanity had been genuinely shared (Chrysostom, *Hom. on Heb.* 5.1)?

Hence Christ's full humanity became a fixed axiom in classic Christology: "For if Christ is God, as He truly is, but did not assume manhood, then we are strangers to salvation" (Cyril of Jerusalem, *Catech. Lect.* 12). Mediation must come through a human being (Tho. Aq., *ST* 3 Q2.5–6). By *one representative human person* (Adam) sin appeared in history. This is matched by the deepening irony that by *one representative human person* (Christ) grace appeared in history (Rom. 5:15; Cyril of Alex., *Expl. of Rom.* 5).

This could not have happened either through the agency of an angel or impersonal "Force." Since sin had been personally conceived and willed, salvation must be personally embodied and enacted. "For since death came through a man, the resurrection of the dead comes also through a man" (1 Cor. 15:21; Augustine, *Letters*, To Jerome 167.21).

The law could not do it. "What the law was powerless to do in that it was weakened by the sinful nature, God did by sending his own Son in the likeness of sinful man to be a sin offering" (Rom. 8:3). Thereafter Christianity has relied upon this parallel between the old humanity which all humans share, and the new humanity of the new man born of woman to redeem those under law (Augustine, *Augustine on Romans* 48).

"If He lacked anything as man, then He did not redeem all, and if He did not redeem all, He deceived us, since He said that He had come to save all men. But, since it is impossible for God to deceive, God did not deceive us" (Ambrose, *Letters* 48).

Thus Jesus' humanity was entirely ordinary. Jesus is pictured as a normal person in unmistakably human terms—going to weddings, visiting friends, eating and drinking, getting tired and napping. All the familiar elements of human nature are found in Jesus: body, soul, will, and spirit (Matt. 16:12, 26; 26:38; Luke 23:46). Scriptures speak of a real person having all things requisite for human existence, not an ephemeral but a real body, not an angelic but a rational human soul (*psuchē*; SCD 25, 111, 148, 216, 255, 283). Everything that we as human beings experienced in the normal course of being human, Jesus also experienced, sin excepted (Calvin, *Catech. of the Church of Geneva*; *Two Discourses on the Articles*).

Yet at the same time this human life was remarkable in the sense that it was not fallen though tempted. The narratives were aware that Jesus, recollected as being wholly without sin, exhibited and lived out precisely that kind of humanity that had been at first given to human history before our fall, to our first parents prior to their disobedience, unsullied by sin. This did not diminish but honored his humanity (Chrysostom, *Hom. on Rom.* 10; J. Knox, *The Humanity and Divinity of Christ*).

The uncorruptible divine Logos assumed our fragile, vulnerable, *created* human nature, and in doing so conquered that which stands *against our created human nature*—sin and the consequences of sin. God participated in our ambiguous, sin-drenched, human condition, yet without sin. God the Son embraced all that was common to humanity (infirmity, hunger, pain, and suffering ending in death—all that every ordinary human being experiences) after the fall, excepting sin (Ignatius, *Trallians* 9; Irenaeus, *Ag. Her.* 5.14.3). Precisely amid this assumption of the flesh, the state of integrity of original human nature was maintained (Chemnitz, *TNC*:53–54).

Like Us, Jesus Did Not Experience Everything: The Scandal of Particularity

No individual person experiences everything that all human individuals experience. To say that Jesus shared our humanity does not imply that he experienced every possible human experience—for we know that he was not an architect or thief; he was not married; he possessed no wealth. These are all human experiences that Jesus apparently did not have. But neither does any other human being experience all that is possible for all human beings, so in that sense he was more like us—by sharing in human limitation—than if he had specifically (unimaginably!) shared in every possible human experience of every time and place. He could not have lived his earthly life both in the first and fifteenth centuries in both Iceland and China—but neither could anyone else, if they were truly human, sharing in our human condition. Such a thought is absurd, and would be nothing like our own temporally placed humanity. For to be human is to be limited in time and space.

If anyone might imagine that to be representative of all humanity Jesus must have done everything possible that any human being could ever have done, that status would not be ordinary humanity. One cannot be human without being a particular human being. Jesus shared sufficiently in human experience to teach us that he is one of us (Heb. 4:15; Symeon the New Theologian, *Discourse* 2.4).

He is more like us by living in a particular time and place. He would have been less like us if he had spent his earthly ministry in all times and places. This is in part what is meant by the phrase the "scandal of particularity"—that God comes to us in a special time (when the hour had come) and a special place (the Holy Land) to a specific woman birthing a particular child, yet in a way that bestows significance upon all other times and places (Luther, *Comm. on Gal.*:353–359). What makes God's coming historical is that it is particular to a time and place

(John 16:32). What makes it revelation is that it bestows significance upon all other times and places (Mark 15:25; Apostolic Constitutions 8.34).

This is why Jesus came, like all of us, through a particular historical lineage. The Gospels sought to demonstrate this by setting down his genealogy. Luke's account demonstrates that he stood in a natural succession from David (Luke 3:23–38), and Matthew shows his lineage from Abraham (1:1–17). This (in addition to establishing Davidic descent) was the Evangelists' way of saying: we are dealing here with a human being (Ambrose, *Expos. of Luke* 3.4).

Hallowing the Human

He hallows everything human. He spoke freely of his own ordinary body and its members: head, hands, feet, blood, and bones (Matt. 26:12; Mark 14:8, 24; Luke 24:39).

Embedded in the Gospel narratives is a determined struggle against an early false teaching called Docetism (from *dokesis*, "appearance, semblance, illusion"). It supposed that since matter is intrinsically evil, Jesus Christ could not have had a human, material body, a fleshly existence; rather his body was a mere fantasy (*dokema, phantasma*; 2 John 7; Oecumenius, *Comm. on 2 John*; Calvin, *TAA*).

Oppositely, the Gospels constantly portray him as living a thoroughly human, bodily existence: he was conceived in a womb and born when a census was being taken. He had male reproductive organs, circumcised when he was an infant according to law. He grew in stature—he did not come full grown. He got hungry, thirsty, and weary (Creed of the Council of Toledo [AD 400], *SCD* 20).

He felt exhaustion, for example, when his bodily powers failed and he was unable to carry the cross. He was wounded and hurt when nailed to the cross. *The most decisive proof of his humanity is simply that he died.* There is no doubt either to the eyes of faith or to historical investigation that Jesus died. The death of Jesus unmistakably marks him as one of us (Matt. 27:50; Origen, *Comm. on Matt.* 138; Tho. Aq., *ST* 3 Q50). The well-established facts that he suffered and died were what made his messianic identity most vexing to explain to those who had been nurtured by contrary expectations.

The scandal that had to be discussed and clarified: the eternal Son suffered. "Although he was a son, he learned obedience from what he suffered" (Heb. 5:8). It was fitting that God should have made "the author of their salvation perfect through suffering" (Heb. 2:10). Why? Because only on this basis would he be "*able to help* those who are being tempted" (Heb. 2:18, italics added). Under Roman guard headed toward his execution, the fettered bishop of Antioch observed: "If the things He did were done by our Lord merely in appearance, then I am in chains merely in appearance" (Ignatius, *To the Smyrnaeans* 4).

This teaching of the suffering of the incarnate Lord is utterly distinctive of Christianity. It is hardly to be found (except prefiguratively) in Judaism and even less in Islam.

To say that the incarnate Son had a soul implies that he experienced the whole range of human emotions. Soul is that without which the body is a corpse. Soul is the animating, enlivening dimension of human existence. Jesus Christ possessed not only a human body but (like all human beings) a human soul—that liveliness without which the body is unresponsive (hence dead; Tho. Aq., *ST* 3 Q15, II; Chemnitz, *TNC*: 58–59). A good sampling of this emotive repertoire is reported in the Gospels: Mark reports that he experienced pity (1:41), anger (3:5), deep sighing (7:34), compassion (8:2), surprise (6:6), and disappointment (8:17; 9:19). Jesus is portrayed in Luke as experiencing joy (10:21), distress (22:15), and love (7:36–50). "He assumed all the natural and blameless passions of man. This is because He assumed the whole man and everything that is his," except sin, "including hunger, thirst, fatigue, pain, the tears, the destruction, the shrinking from death, the fear, the agony, from which came the sweating" (John of Damascus, *OF*, *FC* 37:323–24; Council of Toledo, *SCD* 20).

Chrysostom marveled at the canonical providence that Matthew would demonstrate Christ's sharing in our humanity in a quite different way than John: Matthew by anxiety over future torment, John by grief over history's distortions; Matthew "by the agony, the trouble, the trembling, and the sweat; but John by His sorrow. For had He not been of our nature, He would not once and again have been mastered by grief" (*Hom. on John* 63.2).

His Recapitulation of Humanity

Justin Martyr, Irenaeus, Tertullian and Athanasius all commented upon the Pauline texts implying that Jesus Christ recapitulated humanity. The kernel of this idea is that God "made known to us the mystery of his will according to his good pleasure, which he purposed in Christ, to be put into effect when the times will have reached their fulfillment—*to bring all things in heaven and on earth together under one head*, even Christ" (Eph. 1:10, italics added).

Accordingly Christ recapitulated (literally "re-headed," gathered up) all things in himself. "God recapitulated in Himself the ancient formation of man, that he might kill sin, deprive death of its power and vivify man" (Irenaeus, *Ag. Her.* 3.18.7).

Christ passed through every stage of life from birth to death in order that he might sanctify each stage. "For that which He has not assumed He has not healed; but that which is united to His Godhead is also saved. If only half Adam fell, then that which Christ assumes and saves may be half also; but if the whole of his nature fell, it must be united to the whole nature of Him that was begotten, and so be saved as a whole" (Gregory of Nazianzus, *Epist. 101*). "That which has not been assumed has not been healed. And so, He assumed the whole man, in order that He might grace the whole with salvation" (John of Damascus, *OF* 3.12).

All Humanity Honored in His Coming

Humanity is incomparably honored in the incarnation, since God assumed humanity humbling while avoiding making this an occasion for the worship of the creature. This had profound personal, experiential relevance for Augustine: "Why should there be such great glory to a human nature—and this undoubtedly an act of grace, no merit preceding it—unless it be that those who consider such a question faithfully and soberly might have here a clear manifestation of God's great and sole grace, and this in order that they might understand how they themselves are justified from their sins by the selfsame grace." (Augustine, *Enchiridion* 11.36).

The Modern Detachment of Jesus' Humanity from His God-Manhood

A major deficit of modern historicist views of Jesus is that his humanity is affirmed in such a way as to detach it constantly from the theandric person. Modern writers are prone to assume that if you have only the humanity of the historical Jesus, that is all you need and perhaps all you can ever have. The classic teaching of the union of the one and only divine-human Person is thereby cut apart and detached, and only on this misunderstood basis does it appear to be boring to those who finally come to view Jesus only as a moral hero or religious genius. Such interpreters are prone to place their faith not in the unique divine-human Person, but in his ideas or ideals and imagine that they share with him his teaching.

Such a detachment systematically ignores the central theme of the New Testament. It has to work hard to read the New Testament from these alien presuppositions. From its origins, Christianity has worshiped Jesus as the Christ, the Son of the living God, the fullness of God made manifest in history (Ambrose, *On the Holy Spirit* 3.11.85). To change this is to change Christianity so much that it becomes virtually unrecognizable.

Those who treat Jesus essentially as a moral or political guide, as a heroic fashioner of history, or as a spiritual genius cannot avoid that fact that he intends to meet them as infinitely more—as the only Son of God. Faith receives his own invitation to "come unto me" (Matt. 11:28), not fit him into our categories. "We must not force Him, so to say, to be the mere hero or genius He has no interest in being. Today as of old He hides Himself from those who would take Him by violence to make Him king" (Mackintosh, *PJC*:292;. Kierkegaard, *On Authority and Revelation*). Heroes come to accomplish their own will—Jesus came not to do his own will, but that of the heavenly Father. Geniuses are prone to be contemptuous of those in darkness. Jesus came to meet and care for those in darkness, to wash their feet, share their lives, comfort their afflictions.

5

THE MANNER OF GOD'S COMING

THE MEANS BY WHICH GOD CHOSE to come into the world would be a virginal conception and a natural birth. It had to be natural to attest his humanity. It had to be virginal to attest his divinity.

Mary is celebrated as remnant of Israel. The New Israel dawns with her radical attentiveness, receptivity, and trust in God (Gregory Thaumaturgus, *Four Hom.* I; Barth, *CD* I/2: 138). She is the daughter of Zion with whom God makes a new beginning with humanity (Isa. 1:8; Zech. 9:9; Luke 2:16–20; Bede, *Hom. on Gospels 1.7*).

The Virginal Conception

A Natural Birth of Supernatural Conception

The conception exceeded all natural causal explanations. The birth was as natural as any normal human birth.

The conception of Jesus is viewed by the ancient ecumenical consensus as the creative act of the triune God through the initiating agency of God the Spirit (Luke 2:35; John of Damascus *OF* 4.13; Tho. Aq., *ST* 3 Q31–33). In this lowly birth the Holy Spirit enabled the eternal Son to take on human nature without ceasing to be God (Augustine, *Sermon* 186.1; Tho. Aq., *ST* 3 Q20–25, 32–33). Jesus' birth was a birth in ordinary human flesh of a normal human mother who was a virgin.

The absence of an earthly natural father emphasizes that this event took place on God's own initiative. The conception was without coitus of any kind. "Without any intercourse with a man, her virgin womb was suddenly impregnated"

(Lactantius, *Div. Inst.* 4.12). The *Russian Catechism* does not miss the irony: "Why was Jesus Christ called *the seed of the woman?* Because he was born on earth *without man*" (*COC* 2:470).

The Fitness of Bodily Means

The manner of God's coming did not imply a demeaning of sexuality. Rather it constituted an exaltation and celebration of the human body as the elected means God chooses to become knowable in history—through a man born of woman. The virginal conception was not a repudiation of maleness, but a sign of the grace of God toward all humanity, male and female (Gal. 4:2; Marius Victorinus, *Epis. to Gal.* 2.4.3–5). Without male initiative a male messiah is born through the body of a woman.

Here God is confirming the holy use of two bodies as fitting instruments of revelation with both genders included: a female body giving birth to a male body for hazardous service. It is not a two-to-one vote in favor of males or females, but equally honoring both genders.

The primary intention is neither to commend sexual abstinence nor condemn sexual passion but to attest God's compassion for the fallen world and determination to save humanity from folly and sin. The fitness of these bodily means has been repeatedly affirmed by the apostolic witness and early Christian tradition (John 1:1, 17; Col. 2:9; Hilary, *Trin.* 3.16).

The Virgin Birth Confessed as a Creedal Article
of Faith and Liturgical Event

Testimony to the virginal conception is considered important enough to be numbered among the core articles of faith of the creed, the baptismal confession. The birth narrative has remained among the foremost events celebrated in the Christian year. Its advent is revered as the beginning of the liturgical year (Augustine, *Sermon* 314.1).

Even though the Apostles' Creed itself is very short, with no room for talk about such weighty matters as atonement or justification, it does include the crucial affirmation that Jesus was *conceptus de Spiritu Sancto, natus ex Maria virgine* ("conceived by the Holy Spirit, born of the Virgin Mary," *Symbolum Apostolicum*, *COC* II:45). Second century expressions of the same basic rule of faith are reported by Irenaeus and Tertullian (Rufinus, *Rule of Faith*, *COC* 2:53).

So crucial is this testimony that it is often thought that those who reject the virginal conception are likely to fail to grasp the broader significance of the incarnation and thus of the resurrection. The Reformed theologian E. W. Sartorius wrote: "Those who deny the birth of the God-man of the Virgin Mary, will always question also the pre-existence and deity of Christ in general" (*The Doctrine of Divine Love*:138; Jacobs).

The testimony to the conception has been a continuous feature of Christian proclamation since the oral traditions antedating the Gospel of Luke and of Matthew. Whatever modern critics may think, there is no doubt that the core proclamation of the church from very early times has included a witness to one "born of the virgin Mary." Surprisingly there is more information in the New Testament about the virgin birth than about the Lord's Supper.

The birth narrative has come to form an integral part of classic teaching on the identity of the Son. Liturgically the Feast of the Nativity (Christ-mass) is a focal point of the seasonal cycle of celebrations of the Christian year. If ignored or dismissed, a crucial link between Christology and liturgy is omitted (Tho. Aq.,

ST 3 Q29–30; J. G. Machen, *The Virgin Birth of Christ*; H. von Campenhausen, *The Virgin Birth in the Theology of the Ancient Church*).

It is difficult to imagine how any alternative view could provide sufficient doctrinal cohesion within the context of ecumenical exegesis of scriptural teaching. The virgin birth aids in making sense out of a wide compass of correlated doctrines: the preexistent Logos; the humanity of Christ; the deity of Christ; the personal unity of *theanthropos*; both the temptation and sinlessness of Christ; and the new birth. Hence it is thought to be an apt way of understanding the first event of the Son's earthly ministry (Calvin, *Inst.* 2.13.3; 3.20.22).

The Virgin Birth Firmly Established in Ecumenical Doctrine by Inclusion in Holy Writ

Jerome's language displayed the high regard for canonical Scripture that prevailed in ancient ecumenism: "We believe that God was born of the Virgin, because we read it" (*The Perpetual Virginity of Blessed Mary* 21). Classical exegetes assumed that the historicity of the virgin birth was firmly established quite simply by canonical authority (Ursinus, *CHC*: 205–207).

Yet the simple fact that the narrative is found in Scripture does not make it immune to historical investigation. Faith seeks to make such a historical investigation on the basis of the fullest possible assessment of evidence. Yet this must not be a limited inquiry that would arbitrarily rule out the possibility of the alleged event before one makes the investigation (Augustine, *Conf.* 17.10.16).

The birth narratives have indeed found their way into the canon. They cannot belatedly be arbitrarily weeded out of the canon on the grounds that they do not fit neatly into a naturalistic empiricist worldview (V. Taylor, *Historical Evidence for the Virgin Birth*; D. Edwards, *Virgin Birth in Faith and History*; J. Orr, *Virgin Birth of Christ*; J. G. Machen, *Virgin Birth of Christ*). If one begins by assuming dogmatically that there can be no miracle under any circumstances, hence no virgin birth can ever be plausible, then has not a determining philosophical predisposition prevailed over free inquiry into history? Is one then making a fair and open historical inquiry?

Nature is not best defended by trying to prove philosophically that God is powerless to act either within or beyond natural causes. Augustine argued that no miracle could be known without the reliability of natural law (*Trin.* 3.5–9; *CG* 10.13–32). It may be that some Christians in the first century could have accepted Jesus as Lord who had not heard of the virginal conception. But the fact that it has been considered an article of faith by the mainstream of earliest ecumenical Christianity is evident from its persistence in the baptismal and creedal traditions (Justin Martyr, *First Apol.* 33). The virgin birth remains an intensely symbolic article, yet it did not function merely as an abstract symbol in classic Christianity but purported to attest an actual event that has import for everyday living.

Pagan Piety Lacks the Historical Certainty Claimed in the Gospel Story

A fervent hope for human renewal accompanies virtually every human birth. It is not surprising that in the history of religions generally that hope would be asserted on an idealized or cosmic scale—especially amid certain periods of historical despair and awakening hope. Israel too had hopes of this sort (Isa. 7:14; 54:1; Jer. 31:1–21). Israel expected a palpable, actual, coming event in history, God's own new beginning, not a demigod or mythic idea.

In the Christian story, God is not the biological father of Jesus so as to make Jesus half God, half human. Rather Jesus is fully human, fully God. The narrative does not imply that a new Son of God is begotten who never before existed. Rather it speaks of the eternal Son of God who without any form of genital sexuality assumes human flesh in the conception and birth of this person (Prudentius, *Scenes from Sacred History* 25).

There is no clear or adequate parallel in the history of religions' myths of virgin births for what is celebrated here: that "God was manifest in the flesh" (1 Tim. 3:16) to suffer for the salvation of humanity. The Son, "who, being in very nature God" took "the very nature of a servant" (Phil. 2:6–7). Pagan pieties knew nothing of incarnate birth of God in the flesh in this lowly sense (Marius Victorinus, *Epis. to Phil.* 2.6.8).

The Gospel First Announced to the Mother of All Living

The first announcement of God's saving intention for humanity came to the first woman (Eve). The first glimpse of the gospel in Scripture is sometimes called the Protoevangelium of Genesis 3:14–19. It is the earliest anticipation of the good news of God's coming.

It was first addressed not to Adam but Eve, in a promise to the mother of all living: The Lord God "will put enmity between [the serpent] and the woman, and between your offspring and hers." From "her seed" would come the promised One who would overcome the tempter of humanity (Chrysostom, *Hom. on Gen.* 17; Heppe, *RD*:411). There is no male in "her seed" (Gen. 1:15).

The Old Testament reports miraculous births that were not virginal conceptions. Each one signals a turning point in salvation history: Sarah belatedly bore Isaac (Gen. 18), Hannah belatedly gave birth to Samuel (1 Sam. 1–3), and the wife of Zorah bore Samson (Judg. 13:2–7; Bede, *Homilies on the Gospels 2.19*). In each case the mother had been barren and had abandoned all hope of having a child. God made the impossible birth possible, elevating the lowly to put down the rich and mighty (1 Sam. 2:7–17; Luke 1:52). In each case the child played a major role in the fulfillment of divine promise.

But the virgin birth of Jesus differs from all pagan miraculous birth narratives which focus upon barrenness overcome through divinely enabled human sexual coitus and human fathering without specifically disclaiming male sexual initiative (Chrysostom, *Hom. on Hannah* 1–2). Impotence is overcome through potency—quite different from virginal conception.

The Coming of Immanuel: The Language of Virginity—Almah, Parthenos

"Virgin" (*almah*, root word: "concealment," Song of Songs 1:3; *bethulah*, root word: "separated," Judg. 21:12) in the Old Testament generally meant a woman who has not had sexual intercourse with a man, the ritual purity expected in preparation for marriage and childbearing. It may also refer to a young maiden or woman of marriageable age (*almah*, "virgin, maiden," never signifies a married woman, but always a maiden for whom virginity was presumed, Gen. 24:43). The pivotal passage in Isaiah 7:14 uses *almah* (LXX, GK. *parthenos*; Theophylact, *Expl. of Matt.*, 23). Virginity symbolized the people of Israel as betrothed to God (Isa. 62:4–5; Jer. 18:15; Ephrem, *Comm. on Is.* 62.5). Later *parthenos* would be applied metaphorically to the church (2 Cor. 11:2–3) and to the faithful (Rev. 14:4).

To clarify Jesus' messianic identity, Matthew specifically quoted Isaiah's prophecy (7:14) that "'The virgin will be with child and will give birth to a son, and they will call him Immanuel,' which means 'God with us'" (Matt. 1:23; Origen, *OFP* 4.1).

This birth was thought by Isaiah to be a "sign" (*oth*), addressed to "the house of David" (Is. 7:13), not merely for Ahaz in the singular but to "you" in the plural.

Classical exegetes followed Matthew in regarding Isaiah's prophecy as a type pointing beyond the circumstances of Ahaz to the Expected One (Irenaeus, *Ag. Her.* 3.21).

The messianic promises were widely known in popular late Judaic piety: Micah foretold that the Savior would be born in Bethlehem (Matt. 2:4–6). Malachi had prophesied that a forerunner like Elijah would prepare the way for deliverance (Mal. 3:1; 4:5; Matt. 3:10–12). Isaiah had written: "For to us a child is born, to us a son is given, and the government will be on his shoulders. And he will be called Wonderful Conselor, Mighty God, Everlasting Father, Prince of Peace. Of the increase of his government and peace there will be no end" (Isa. 9:6–7).

Gospel Witness to the Virgin Birth

Luke's Narrative of the Annunciation

The angel Gabriel came to Mary to announce that "you will be with child and give birth to a son, and you are to give him the name Jesus. He will be great and will be called the Son of the most High. The Lord God will give him the throne of his father David, and he will reign over the house of Jacob forever; his kingdom will never end" (Luke 1:31–33). "Hail Mary, full of grace, the Lord is with thee," is thus the opening moment of the salvation event as trustfully received by an attentive, grace-filled human agent (Tho. Aq., *ST* 3 Q30), the unique elect. "'How will this be,' Mary asked the angel, 'since I am a virgin?'" (Luke 1:34; note that *parthenos* here cannot be translated "young woman," for that cannot fit the context). "The angel answered, 'The Holy Spirit will come upon you, and the power of the Most High will overshadow you. So the holy One to be born will be called the Son of God.'" "For nothing is impossible with God" (Luke 1:35, 37).

Mary herself may have been one of the eyewitnesses Luke referred to as those from whom he gathered his information. Luke's prologue clearly indicated his intention to write only about that which he had "carefully investigated" concerning "everything from the beginning" of these events "just as they were handed down to us by those who from the first were eyewitnesses" (Luke 1:2; Origen, *Hom. on Luke* 1.1–6).

Matthew's Narrative of Joseph, Husband of Mary

Matthew's narrative is apparently independent of Luke's, hence corroboratory, again affirming the special conception. His genealogy ends with an atypical reference to "*Joseph, the husband of Mary*, of whom was born Jesus, who is called Christ" (1:16, italics added). It is rare in ancient literature to find a man publicly identified primarily by means of his relation to his wife. Matthew then relates how the birth came about: "Mary was pledged to be married to Joseph, but before they came together, she was found to be with child through the Holy Spirit" (1:18; Chrysostom, *Hom. on Matt.* 4.6). The angel appeared also to Joseph in a dream and explained that he had no reason to "be afraid to take Mary home as your wife, because what is conceived in her is from the Holy Spirit. She will give birth to a son, and you are to give him the name Jesus" (1:20–21), a name that held the clue from the outset to his identity—he will save (John of Damascus, *OF* 2.2; Tho. Aq., *ST* 3 Q37).

In taking special note that Joseph, following the commandment of the angel, "called his name Jesus" (Matt. 1:25), the implication was that Joseph would accept legal responsibility for Jesus. Even though Joseph "had no union with her until she gave birth to a son," precluding any notion that Jesus had an earthly father. Wherever Jesus is described as the "son of Joseph" (Luke 2:27, 33, 41, 43, 48; Matt. 13:55), the reference is to Joseph as legal not biological father, for otherwise Luke and Matthew would clearly be inconsistent with their own account (the same reasoning also applies to John 1:45; 6:42).

Mark's Son of Mary

When it is suggested that Mark does not report the birth narrative, it might also be noted that Mark does not report anything at all from the first thirty years of Jesus' life (circumcision, obedience to parents, or his growth as a lad). On closer inspection, however, Mark may not be so silent as supposed, for he pointedly refers to Jesus in an unusual reference as "son of Mary," contrary to usual Jewish custom that identified the son by relation to the father, oddly leaving Joseph's name out of the account (Mark 6:3). Hence it is possible that Mark, too, had access to the nativity narrative in some form, even if it did not fit in with the purpose of his particular task of writing.

Matthew and Luke, who probably had Mark's Gospel in hand as they wrote, both thought it useful and necessary to include a missing piece—the nativity narrative. Does this mean that the narrative is late and hence of less importance? Or does it mean that they thought the nativity narrative was in fact necessary, and that in Mark's account something important had been omitted on a point that was widely shared in the previous oral tradition? The latter seems more probable, for if they had thought otherwise, why would it even appear in their texts? More important, it is sometimes wrongly supposed that neither John nor Paul make any reference to the birth of Jesus; yet a careful examination of John 1:13, 6:42, Romans 1:2–4, and Galatians 4:4 makes it imperative that one not judge too quickly.

John's Prologue: "Not of Natural Descent"

The birth narrative was almost surely known in some form to John, whose prologue on the incarnation assumes such a strong correspondence between the believer's regeneration and the coming of God into the world.

John's prologue takes the place of the nativity narrative, focusing not upon the *mode* of God's becoming flesh but upon the *incarnation itself*, which requires some appropriate mode of entry into the world that is consistent with the pre-existent Son becoming human. In developing the theme of "Word made flesh," John writes: "Yet to all who receive him, to those who believed in his name, he gave the right to become children of God—children *born not of natural descent, nor of human decision or a husband's will*, but born of God" (John 1:12–13, italics added; Augustine, *Tractates on John* 1.15). Why is the "husband's [sexual] will" prominently inserted into the prologue? The comparison is between the eternal Son who came into the world unrecognized and the children quietly born of God who come into being through faith. If so, there is another level of this correlation: that between the Son of God born without a husband's sexual initiative and children of God born of the unseen spirit. This suggests that John likely had access to the nativity narratives and understood himself to be here complementing them, rather than challenging or ignoring them.

The question of Jesus' birth may have already been a subject of debate during Jesus' lifetime, as was suggested by the opponents of Jesus who said: "Is this not Jesus, the son of Joseph, whose father and mother we know? How can he now say, 'I came down from heaven'?" (John 6:42). This was said by his detractors who "were not as yet able to hear of his marvelous birth. And if they could not bear to hear in plain terms of his birth according to the flesh, much less could they hear of that ineffable Birth which is from above" (Chrysostom, *Hom. on John* 46.1).

Paul's Witness to the Unique Descent of Jesus: God's Sent Son Born of Woman

Paul speaks with great precision of the descent of Jesus in Romans: the gospel has to do with God's own Son, "who as to his human nature was a descendant of David, and who through the Spirit of holiness was declared with power to be the Son of God by his resurrection from the dead: Jesus Christ our Lord" (Rom. 1:2–4; Origen, *Comm. on Rom.* 1.4). Why would Paul distinguish his divine Sonship from "his human nature a descendant of David" unless he had access to some sort of genealogical or birth reports? Paul's access to the tradition of Davidic descent suggests that genealogies like those of Matthew and Luke or some similar tradition must have been available to Paul.

The passages in Galatians 4 are more intriguing and more crucial. Paul specifically quotes the virginal passage from Isaiah 54 to his congregation in Galatia. Isaiah had prophesied that a barren woman who had never born a child would burst into song and would "have no labor pains" in giving birth, for "more are the children of the desolate woman than of her who has a husband" (Gal. 4:27, quoting Isa. 54:1). In commenting on this particular passage, Paul went out of his way to make note of the crucial distinction between a "son born in the ordinary way" and "the son born by the power of the Spirit" (Gal. 4:29). He was trying to teach the Galatian church that they were the children of this free woman, "the Jerusalem that is above" who is "free" and who is "our mother," whom God had given extraordinary birth by the Spirit, not birth in "the ordinary way." These references strengthen the hypothesis that Paul may have had access to some form of the nativity narratives and was assuming that his audience was already familiar with Sarah's childbearing of Isaac, which was viewed as a prefiguring of Christ.

The crucial Pauline reference is from the same passage in Galatians: "When the time had fully come, God sent his Son, born of a woman" (4:4). Why not "man and woman"? The omission of the father in this reference makes it particularly unusual and noteworthy. The Father sends the Son by the power of the Spirit, and without mention of male sexuality woman gives birth.

The verb "born" (*genomenon*) in this passage is the same one used in Philippians 2:7: "born to be like other men." It is fitting that one equal with God should be born and become flesh in a paradoxical way—the holiest God through lowliest vessel. This is consistent with the theme of reversal common in the nativity images: no room at the inn, born of poor parents in a remote village, and the flight to Egypt.

In this way not only Luke and Matthew, but Mark, John, and Paul all attest aspects of the birth and descent of the Savior. The classic consensus is that Christ "was conceived in the immaculate womb of the Virgin, not by the will of man, nor by concupiscence, nor by the intervention of a husband, nor by pleasurable generation, but of the Holy Ghost" (John of Damascus, *OF* 3.2).

The Holy Family as Source of the Birth Narratives

Much of the extended family of Jesus appears to have been involved in the messianic event—John the Baptist, Mary, Joseph, Elizabeth, Zechariah, Simeon, Anna, the apostle John, his brothers James, Joses, Judas, and Simon, his sisters (or cousins) and uncles and aunts—all were part of a single family. Jesus' sisters are also occasionally referred to (Mark 6:3; Matt. 13:56; Origen, *Comm. on Matt.*

10.17). Mary's sister, John reports, was with her at the crucifixion (John 19:25; Ambrose, *Letter* 63.109–111). Although some of the family seemed resistant (Mark 3:21, 31; John 7:5), they later shared significantly in the mission of the church (Acts 1:14; 1 Cor. 9:5).

The presence of Jesus' mother and brothers, especially James (Acts 1:14; 15:13–21; Gal. 1:19; 2:9), in the early circle of leading rememberers makes it unlikely that legendary myths or tales about Jesus' origin would have been invented and left unchallenged by these prominent living persons during the decades following Jesus' death (Africanus, *Epis. to Aristides*; Raymond Brown, *The Birth of the Messiah*).

Only gradually, at some point subsequent to the resurrection, did the birth narratives become a normative component of the core of Christian proclamation. How could it have been otherwise? Only Mary and Joseph and perhaps a few others would have been privy to these events prior to the time when their significance would become plausible. One reason that much of the New Testament does not appear to be preoccupied with the birth narrative may have been that public teaching sought to maintain a quiet reserve about such private matters out of respect for Mary and other members of the family, perhaps in connection with the supposed "illegitimacy" question that detractors may have attempted to exploit. Already in John 8:41 the opponents of Jesus were hinting at his "illegitimacy," and that charge continued to be made by opponents of Christianity well into the second century (Brown, *Birth of the Messiah*; Augustine, *Tractates on John* 42, SCD 717f.).

Mary's Recollections

Luke in fact specifically mentions that "Mary treasured up all these things and pondered them in her heart" (Luke 2:19; cf. 2:51). This appears to present Mary as the special custodian of the mystery of Jesus' birth until the time came for a fuller proclamation. This could explain why the publicly shared tradition of the nativity was relatively slower in forming than that of the resurrection. Lateness does not imply tampering but reserve with the evidence. It was not until the later Infancy Gospel of James that a narrative would develop attempting to provide evidence for Mary's virginity.

If one takes the hypothesis that Jesus was not born of a virgin, a greater difficulty arises, namely, that an unmarried couple would be chosen to give life to the Son of God who is without sin, the One who would forgive the sins of others, who without the premise of the virgin mother would have been legally treated as an illegitimate son born out of wedlock.

The Savior Was Truly Born

Christianity is unwavering in proclaiming a Savior who was born in time. But that makes for complications in other respects, with which the classic exegetes had to deal.

The Limits of Alternatives

It is theoretically possible to conjecture that God could have entered human history in some other way than by virginal conception, but objections mount as one considers the alternatives. The formally conceivable ways of being born are reduced to only two: normally, of one male and one female parent; or virginally, of a female parent alone. There is no third for the simple reason that male sexuality cannot give birth alone.

Hence if both sexes are to be honored in the incarnation, and *if the one giving birth must be female*, then the one sex remaining—the one to be born—would have to be male. Some might argue that both the mother of God-incarnate and God-incarnate might have been female. The obvious objection: This would have been less representative of humanity than a man born of woman (Gal. 4:4). Long before modern feminism, Augustine had thought seriously about this: "Mankind's deliverance had to be evidenced among both sexes," hence if the incarnate one is male, "it reasonably followed that the deliverance of the female sex be seen by that man's birth from a woman" (Augustine, *EDQ* 11).

The virginal conception is not an embarrassed attempt to avoid sexuality. To the contrary, according to Gregory of Nyssa: "By the generative organs the immortality of the human race is preserved, and death's perpetual moves against us are, in a way rendered futile and ineffectual. By her successive generations nature is always filling up the deficiency. What unfitting notion, then, does our religion contain, if God was united with human life by the very means by which our nature wars on death" (*ARI* 28). Sexual generation is not diminished but affirmed and transmitted in the incarnation.

Without Human Father

Why without human father? Compelling reasons are offered by classic exegetes as to why Christ was born without human father:

1. The principle of economic parsimony is at work here: God only uses what is necessary and required for human salvation. God does indeed need female sexuality for the birthing of the Savior, for there can be no birth without a mother. But male sexuality did not qualify as absolutely required in the same way that a mother is required for a birth.

2. More significantly, the fatherless Messiah points beyond human fathering to the heavenly Father, who sends the eternal Son whose mission is enabled by the Spirit. In all of this there is a marked absence of the erotic assertiveness so characteristically associated with male sexuality or claims of merit to which male spirituality is prone.

3. To be qualified as mediator he must be without sin. The human nature of Christ must be set apart and preserved from defilement by sin. A divine-human mediator engendered by male genital sexuality with its prevailing tendency to focused assertiveness and propensity toward pride, lust, and idolatry would have seemed implausible to ancient minds. This does not imply that human generation as such is defiled or vicious, but that sexuality, both male and female, has become willfully distorted by the disobedience that followed the fall. A new beginning is needed for a new human history.

4. If he is to follow as the type of Melchizedek, who was without father, the Savior must be without father (Heb. 7:3).

5. Christ was one person, not two. Logically, had he been born both of the Holy Spirit and of a human father, it might be argued that he was two persons, not one. Such incipient Nestorian reasoning was circumvented altogether in the special conception (Pearson, *EC* I: 301–10; II: 203, 230).

An Actual Human Birth Points Openly to Jesus' Humanity and Historicity

It is ironic now to realize that the birth narratives probably were not first proclaimed and transmitted to underscore Jesus' divinity, but his humanity.

The primitive church was doing battle with Docetic views that doubted that the Savior could have been born at all. It is less pivotal in the narrative that Jesus was conceived without a father than that Jesus indeed had a mother and was conceived at all and born.

The struggle against Docetism shines through the primitive rule of faith recalled and passed on by Ignatius of Antioch to the Trallians, where it is affirmed that Jesus Christ "is of the stock of David, who is of Mary, who was truly born, ate and drank" (Ignatius, *Trallians* 8:1–2; *Smyrna* 1.1).

The birth narratives rejected the view that Jesus was so divine that he could not have been born at all. He was "born from her truly and properly," wrote John II, Patriarch of Constantinople, "lest one should believe that from the Virgin He took on a mere appearance of flesh or in some other way a flesh which was not real, as Eutyches irreverently declared" (*Letter to the Senate of Constantinople* [534], *CF*: 156). "He truly fed upon her milk" (Cyril of Jerusalem, *Catech. Lect.* 4.10). "He did not pass through her as the sun shines through a glass, but brought her virgin flesh and blood with Him" (Luther, *Epiphany Serm. on Matt. 2:1–12* [1538; cf. Calvin, *Inst.* 2.13.4).

The Virginal Conception Occurred by Attentive Hearing of the Word

The bodily locus of the virginal conception was not portrayed in early Christian art as the vagina, but the ear: "*The conception was by hearing,*" wrote John of Damascus (*OF* 4.14; italics added).

In early iconography the Holy Spirit is not portrayed as coming into Mary's body physiologically by sexual transmission, but spiritually by attentive hearing. The coming of the Son by an actual human birth was by "the usual orifice," the uterine birth canal; but the conception was by right hearing of the Word of God.

Accordingly, Mary remains in Christian memory the primary prototype of human readiness to receive God's coming. The gift of God's coming can only be received, it cannot be acquired on human initiative.

The Exclusion of Merit, Yet a Free Act Enabled by Grace

There is nothing that Mary does beforehand that qualifies her as worthy for this decisive role, except to trust in God's promise, as did Abraham. Protestants have laid stress upon the meaning of the virgin birth as the exclusion of all human effort, parallel to the teaching of justification by grace through faith alone without works of merit. This theme was anticipated by patristic writers, as when Hilary spoke of the incarnation as the sublime moment "when human nature without any precedent merits of good works, was joined to God the Word in the womb of the Virgin" (*Trin.* 15.26).

The virginal conception occurred entirely by consent, not coercion. The virgin Mother was receptive to the divine address. As the incarnation of the Son was voluntary, so was the virginal conception. Mary was willing to be the human bodily means by which the Word became flesh, even as the Son assumed flesh voluntarily. As the Savior's conception was voluntary but without works of merit by grace, so is the believer's new birth into the Christian life voluntary yet entirely by grace. Mary consented without impairment of the liberty that made her human. "It was only after having instructed her and persuaded her that God took her for His Mother and borrowed from her the flesh that She so greatly wished to lend Him" (Cabasilas, "Homilies Mariales Byzantines," *Patrologia orientalis* 19, 3).

The New Eve

Eve and Mary

Eve is not to be viewed alone, in isolation from Mary. Mary fulfills promises given to Eve. The "mother of all living" awaits the mother of the Savior.

The human condition has become neurotically tangled and knotted by the history of sin. "The knot of Eve's disobedience was loosed by the obedience of Mary. For what the virgin Eve had bound fast through unbelief, this did the virgin Mary set free through faith" (Irenaeus, *Ag. Her.* 3.22).

Note the parallelisms: the fall occurred by false belief; the incarnation began with true belief. "As Eve had believed the serpent, so Mary believed the angel. The delinquency which the one occasioned by believing, the other by believing effaced" (Tertullian, *On the Flesh of Christ* 17). As the destruction of the old humanity occurred through the disobedience of a virgin, so the redemption of the world occurred through the obedience of a virgin (*Doc. Vat. II*: 87–90; Heppe, *RD*, 422).

Irenaeus spoke of "the back-reference from Mary to Eve" (Irenaeus, *Ag. Her.* 3.22). This means that the faithful better understand Eve from Mary, not Mary from Eve. Those who criticize Christianity for having a sexist view of Eve's fall do well to ponder the meaning of the special role of Mary in the recovery of humanity from Eve's fall. Eve alone is an incomplete story. Mary is "the new Eve believing God's messenger with unhesitating faith" (*Lumen Gentium* 63). The narrative of Eve cannot rightly be read without Mary, as Adam's story is similarly incomplete apart from Christ.

Adam's Creation Prefigured Christ's Birth

It seems odd that some are quick to affirm that God could breathe life and created goodness generally into all humanity, yet find it difficult to affirm that God could act specially or directly to breathe life into the Savior in a way distinctly befitting his mediatorial role. How it is that some readily affirm that God created Adam, but find it wrenching to hear that God might have taken some special initiative to create the New Adam? Why is the special conception of the Savior intrinsically a less plausible miracle of creation than the creation of humanity?

Compare the Genesis narrative of the surprising creation of Adam and Eve with the Lucan-Matthean nativity narratives telling the surprising story of God's own direct and special initiative in the birth of the Savior. In both cases natural material was utilized to fulfill a preternatural purpose—the body of Adam made from mud; the body of Jesus born through an ordinary period of gestation and delivery.

Ancient exegetes marveled that the miracle of human creation prefigured the miracle of the birth of Jesus, just as the fall of Adam prefigured the restoration in Christ, and the Protoevangelium to Eve prefigured the annunciation (Rom. 5:14; 1 Cor. 15:22, 45; 1 Tim. 2:11–15; Irenaeus, *Ag. Her.* 3.19–23; Chrysostom, *Hom. on First Cor.* 39; *Hom. on Tim.* 9).

Why Two Different Routes of Davidic Descent?

Accompanying the nativity narratives are genealogies that underscore that salvation history is human history.

The genealogies are not embarrassed by the notorious sinners in the messianic line. Luther commented: "The first thing to be noted in the lineage of Christ is the fact that the Evangelist lists in it four women who are very notorious in Scripture:

Thamar, Rahab, Ruth, and Bathsheba. But nothing is said about the women of good repute: Sarah, Rebecca, Leah, and Rachel. Now Jerome and others have been concerned about the reason why this was done. I hold that the first group was mentioned because these women were sinners and that Christ also wanted to be born in that large family in which prostitutes and fornicators are found in order to indicate what a love He bore sinners" (Luther, *Serm. on Matt.* 8 September, 1522).

The main purpose of both genealogies was to establish Davidic descent, to show that Jesus fulfilled the messianic expectations of Israel (Irenaeus, *Ag. Her.* III, 16–17; Pearson, *EC* I: 313). Matthew's registry of Davidic descent moves from past to present through Joseph, son of David. Luke's registry of Davidic descent is from present to past through Heli, the father of Mary. Matthew's descent begins with Abraham and proceeds to Christ. Luke's begins with Christ and recedes back to Adam (Tertullian, *On the Flesh of Christ* 22; Origen, 1.4; *Hom.* 28 *on Luke*).

Matthew's genealogy traces Jesus' ancestry not through Mary but through Joseph, but this does not imply that Joseph was Jesus' physiological father because Matthew makes it clear that Joseph "had no union with her" (Matt. 1:25). The prevailing custom to trace lineage not through the mother but through the father's side, and without such patrilineal tracing, first-century readers might have found the genealogy puzzling and implausible. John of Damascus explained of Matthew: "One should know, however, that it was not customary for the Hebrews, nor for sacred Scripture either, to give the pedigrees of women. . . . Consequently, it was sufficient to show the descent of Joseph" (John of Damascus, *OF* 2.14; Eusebius, *CH* 1.7; Tho. Aq., *ST* 3 Q31). The "descent is reckoned by the male line," but this is only "as far as the political order is concerned," for this legal status "does not gainsay the fact that the woman's seed must share in the act of generation" (Calvin, *Inst.* 2.13.4). So Matthew recorded the Abrahamic and Davidic descent of the Messiah, and then described his birth and infancy as a fulfillment of Old Testament prophecies (Origen, *Comm. on Matt. 1:1* 18; Ambrose, *Comm. on Matt.* 1).

Matthew's genealogy follows the line of Joseph through Jesus' legal but not biological father, while Luke follows the line of Mary. Luke clarified that Jesus was not literally or biologically the son of Joseph but "was thought" to be the son of Joseph (Luke 3:23; Eusebius, *Quaestiones ad Stephanum* 2–3). According to one ancient tradition, "Herod indeed destroyed the genealogies, hoping that he would then appear as well born as anyone else. But a few careful people preserved private genealogies, either from recollections of the names or from copies; among them are those which are called *desposunoi* because they belong to the Savior's family" (*Epist. to Aristides*). In the absence of fuller information, it is extremely difficult to find a theory that fully harmonizes the genealogies, yet classic exegetes argued that they are not intrinsically contradictory (Eusebius, *Questiones ad Stephanum*). We are left to ponder:

What Child is this, who, laid to rest,
On Mary's lap is sleeping?
Whom angels greet with anthems sweet,
While shepherds watch are keeping?
This, this is Christ the King,
Whom shepherds guard and angels sing:
Haste, haste to bring Him laud,
The Babe, the Son of Mary.
Why lies He in such mean estate

Where ox and ass are feeding?
Good Christian, fear: for sinners here
The silent Word is pleading

(William C. Dix, *MH*:109)

The Mother of the Savior

The consensual teaching concerning Mary upon which Christians generally agree is the chief interest of this study. Is there an ecumenical teaching on Mary generally received by Catholics, Orthodox, and Protestants? The place to begin is with the *theotokos* doctrine largely shared by East and West.

Theotokos: An East-West Ecumenical Consensus

In ascribing to Mary the term *theotokos*, "bearer of God," there has never been intended the slightest implication that Mary gave birth to the Godhead, but only to the incarnate Son (Ecumenical Council of Ephesus; Athanasius, *Four Discourses Ag. Arians* 3.14f.; Luther; *Expos. Isaiah* 53). "We do not, however, say that the Virgin Mary gave birth to the unity of this Trinity, but only to the Son who alone assumed our nature" (Eleventh Council of Toledo; *SCD* 284).

The intent of eastern and western orthodoxy is accurately stated by John II of Constantinople (AD 533–535): Mary is "truly the one who bore God, and the Mother of God's Word, become incarnate from her" (*Epist.* 3, *SCD* 202; see also *SCD* 20, 91, 111–113). The consensus was stated with equal caution by John of Damascus: "We do not say that God was born of her in the sense that the divinity of the Word has its beginning of being from her, but in the sense that God the Word Himself . . . did in the last days come for our salvation to dwell in her womb" (*OF* 3.12; Cyril of Alexandria, *Third Letter to Nestorius*). "For the holy Virgin did not give birth to a mere man but to true God, and not to God simply, but to God made flesh" (John of Damascus, *OF* 3.12). "For, as He who was born of her is true God, so is she truly Mother of God" (John of Damascus, *OF* 3.12).

The Holy Spirit hallowed the flesh, the womb into which our Lord entered and set apart the mother for her incomparable function (Tho. Aq., *ST* 3 Q35). We are dealing with a mystery "neither grasped by reason nor illustrated by example. Were it grasped by reason, it would not be wonderful; were it illustrated by example, it would not be unique" (Eleventh Council of Toledo).

The problem many Protestants have had with the Roman Marian tradition is that it has seemed at times to have become inordinately detached from its Christological center or disconnected unproportionally as a separate subject of inquiry. Two movements have occurred simultaneously in recent years to attempt to correct this disproportion: Protestants have sought to reacquaint themselves with classical Christian reasoning about Mary; and Catholics under the guidance of the Second Vatican Council have reintegrated Marian teaching into Christology, rather than appearing to view it as relatively unconnected (*Lutherans and Catholics in Dialogue* 1–3; Outler, *A Methodist Observer at Vatican II; Doc. of Vat. II*:85–96; Evangelicals and Catholics Together; Dombes Group).

Why the Ecumenical Council of Ephesus Rejected the Nestorian Formula as Threatening the Personal Unity of Christ

The teaching of Nestorius did not receive ecumenical consent, but raised a decisive question for ecumenical teaching concerning Mary. The Nestorians were charged with asserting that there were two persons, a divine person distinguished from a human person, that this human person was conceived by the Virgin. The crisis emerged when Anastasius publicly denied to Mary the liturgically familiar title, "Mother of God" (or "bearer of God," *Theotokos*)—the implication being that she was not mother of God but only of Christ (*Christotokos*) to whom the person of the Word of God had in some way united himself. This amounted to saying that Christ is two persons, one divine and one human, not one person with two natures. It was principally to guard the teaching of the distinctive unity of the Person of Jesus Christ against Nestorianism that "Mother of God" was applied to Mary. Cyril of Alexandria and the Council of Ephesus (AD 431) cut through to the essential point, that the one born of the Virgin was Son of God at the time of his conception and birth. "She brought forth, according to the flesh, the Word of God made flesh" (Cyril of Alexandria, *Third Letter to Nestorius*).

Mary as Model of the Faithful

The virginal conception became the basis for the vast exercise of poetic and typological imagination in early Christianity. St. Methodius of Olympus, a martyr of the Diocletian persecution (d. ca. 311), early offered this poetic eulogy to the Blessed Virgin:

> Thou art the circumscription, so to speak,
> of Him who cannot be circumscribed;
> the root of the most beautiful flower;
> the mother of the Creator;
> the nurse of the Nourisher;
> the circumference of Him who embraces all things;
> the upholder of Him who upholds all things by His word;
> the gate through which God appears in the flesh;
> the tongs of that cleansing coal;
> the bosom in small of that bosom which is all-containining. . . .
> Thou hast lent to God, who stands in need of nothing,
> that flesh which He had not,
> in order that the Omnipotent might become
> that which it was his good pleasure to be. . . .
> Thou hast clad the Mighty One with that beauteous panoply
> of the body by which it has become possible
> for Him to be seen by mine eyes. . . .
> Hail! hail! mother and handmaid of God.
> Hail! hail! thou to whom the great Creditor of all
> is a debtor

(*Orat. Concerning Simeon and Anna* 10)

The Marian Tradition of the Latin West

Key affirmations of the Marian tradition in Roman Catholic teaching are the perpetual virginity of Mary, "her virginity remaining equally inviolate after the birth" (Lateran Council [AD 649], *CF* 703; see also *SCD* 256), and equally inviolate before birth, in birth (Siricius, *Epist. 9 to Anysius*, *SCD* 91; Augustine, *Concerning Faith of Things Not Seen* 5; Tho. Aq., *ST* 3 Q28.4), and "after childbirth" (Sixtus IV, *Cum Praeexcelsa* [1476], *SCD* 734). The view "that Mary seems to have brought forth many children" is rejected on the grounds that the term "brothers" (*adelphoi*) can also mean more generally "relatives" or "cousins" (Siricius, *SCD*

91; Matt. 12:46–49; 13:55; Mark 3:31–34; 6:3; John 7:3; Luke 8:19–21; Acts 1:14; M.-J. Lagrange, *Comm. on St. Mark*).

Mary's freedom from original sin was "preserved immune from all stain of original sin" (Pius IX, *Bull Ineffabilis Deus*), hence conceived immaculate (Sixtus, *SCD* 734, 735; see also *SCD* 792, 1073; Tho. Aq., *ST* 3 Q31). The Roman teaching of the virgin's bodily assumption into heaven is that Mary, "when the course of her earthly life was finished, was taken up body and soul into the glory of heaven" (Pius XII *Munificentissimus Deus*).

Vatican II summarized Roman teaching: "Because of her close and indissoluble connection with the mystery of the Incarnation and Redemption the most Blessed Virgin Mary, the Immaculate, at the end of her earthly life was assumed body and soul into heaven, and so became like her Son, who himself rose from the dead, anticipating thereby the destiny of the just. We believe that the most holy Mother of God, the new Eve, the Mother of the Church, continues in heaven her maternal role towards the members of Christ, in that she cooperates with the birth and growth of divine life in the souls of the redeemed" (Paul VI, *Doc. Vat. II*: 391).

Among Marian teachings of ancient and modern Roman Catholicism with which other believers have less difficulty in agreeing are the following: Mary is held as an example to the faithful rather for the way in which in her own particular life, she fully and responsibly accepted the will of God (Luke 1:38); because she received the word of God and acted on it; because charity and a spirit of service were the driving force of her actions; because she was the first and the most perfect of Christ's disciples. All of this has a permanent and universal exemplary value" (Paul VI). Mary is a "type of the Church, or exemplar, in the order of faith, charity and perfect union with Christ." Mary is understood "not merely as a passive instrument in the hands of God, but as freely co-operating in the salvation of mankind by her faith and obedience" (*Lumen Gentium* 56).

The Liturgical Persistence of the Nativity as Anchor of the Christian Year

The extraordinary liturgical importance of the virgin birth for the celebration of the incarnation at Christmastide makes the teaching hard to dismiss. Those who dismiss it, do so at the risk of resisting a broad church consensus that is written into the most widely shared baptismal and catechetical confessions of historic Christianity.

Many in the modern world know very little about Jesus other than the birth narratives, yet they know these by heart. Jesus' life begins with incarnation and ends with resurrection. These two events form the two key moments of the Christian year—Christmas and Easter. The virgin birth and the bodily resurrection are anchor points of the salvation event (R. E. Brown, *The Virginal Conception and the Bodily Resurrection of Jesus*). It is fitting that the salvation event begins and ends in a way fitting to the incarnate Lord. The virgin birth is the first miracle of the history of Jesus (Augustine, *CG* 18.46).

That the birth was attested in Bethlehem (literally "the house of bread," from whom comes the Bread from heaven, John 6:32–33) and of Davidic descent was from the outset viewed as fulfillment of messianic prophecy (Mic. 5:2; Matt. 2:2, 6; 1 Sam. 16:18; Luke 2:4). The angelic hosts celebrated his coming (Luke 2:10–14; Tho. Aq., *ST* 3, Q36.). The stories of Simeon and Anna in the Temple (Luke 2:22–39) and the wise men (Matt. 2:1–11; Isa. 9) indicate that he came as a light both to Jews and Gentiles—the whole world (Hag. 2:6–9; Tho. Aq., *ST* 3 Q37.3). The gifts of gold, frankincense, and myrrh were gifts befitting his hidden royal identity yet to be revealed.

Why did this teaching appear so early, and why has it been sustained so tenaciously? The incarnation was such a unique event that it was unthinkable that it could have been treated merely as a routine birth. Rather it pointed to the mystery of God's coming in our midst, in God's own way and time (Baxter, *PW* 19:70–73).

Christ's birth prepares the way for the rebirth of the believer (Peter Chrysologus, *Sermon 57*). "O holy Child of Bethlehem! Descend to us, we pray; Cast out our sin and enter in; Be born in us to-day" (Phillips Brooks, *HPEC*: 68). This is the church that, imitating his mother, daily gives birth to his members yet remains virgin (Augustine, *Enchiridion* 37–57; *BCP*, "Collect for Christmas Day").

> *Gentle Mary laid her Child*
> *Lowly in a manger*
> *There He lay, the undefiled,*
> *To the world a Stranger.*
> *Such a Babe in such a place,*
> *Can He be the Saviour?*
> *Ask the saved of all the race*
> *Who have found His favor*

(Joseph S. Cook, *MH*:107)

6

ONE PERSON—TRULY GOD, TRULY HUMAN

FOUR ELEMENTARY SCRIPTURAL TEACHINGS are essential for understanding the distinctive person of Christ:

1. Christ is truly *God*.

2. He is truly *human*.

3. He is *one* person.

4. There are in him *two* distinct natures, divine and human (*SCD* 18, 20, 33, 42, 111, 143, 148), clearly distinguishable and substantially different (*SCD* 260), yet undivided, inseparable, and unconfused (*SCD* 148, 288, 290; *BOC*:592).

Having already explored the first two points, we now turn to the last two: one person in two natures. The subject now to be addressed is among the most difficult in biblical teaching. It is intent upon showing how Jesus is truly God yet truly human as one person.

It might seem merciful to say: "Skip these pages and go on to the temptation narrative which is easily understood." But one who wishes to understand classic thinking about Christ cannot skip over the crucial explanation of how the unity of his divinity and humanity is congruently interpreted and duly qualified.

Multiplication tables must be memorized to be functionally applied. So in the study of ancient ecumenical theology, those who wish to remember these distinctions do well to memorize the classic formula-like codes showing basic consensual definitions in summary form—the decisions of the seven Ecumenical Councils.

Few code phrases have been more decisive for classic Christology than *two natures, one person* (Council of Chalcedon, *SCD* 148; *Russian Catech.*). To make this puzzling formula transparent, sensible, and useful is the purpose of this chapter.

The Personal Union: Its Scriptural Basis

Scripture Insists upon the Union of God and Man in Christ

The Savior is as simply God as if he were not man, and as plainly man as if he were not God (Athanasius, *On the Incarnation of the Word*, 1–3; Newman, *Athan.* 2:326).

First it must be established that the fully God and fully human premise is required by Scripture itself. It is not merely an appendage of tradition added to Scripture.

If this is not scriptural teaching, then this strange doctrine of "one person in two natures" cannot be classic Christian teaching. For decades it has been dismissed by critics as merely a distracting philosophical riddle.

Scripture teaches the union in the writings of Paul, John, and the Letter to the Hebrews. The purpose of Christology is rightly to reflect upon that scripture-based union so as to guard against distortions and enable its truthful proclamation (Tho. Aq., *SCG* 4:57–74, 174).

The Personal Union in Pauline Teaching

In Romans from the first sentence, Paul was speaking of Jesus Christ as a descendant of David according to his human nature (1:3) and Son of God according to the Spirit of holiness (1:4)—dual sonship that required dual natures in a single person. Paul did not hesitate to speak in the same breath of the "human ancestry of Christ, who is God over all" (Rom. 9:5).

He is crucified Lord while also being "Lord of glory" whose human body the rulers of this age have crucified (1 Cor. 2:8; Chrysostom, *Hom. on First Cor.* 7). What the law could not do, "God did by sending his own Son in the likeness of sinful flesh" (Rom. 8:3). Hence the Savior who appears within the distortions of human history is at the same time nothing less than God's own Son (Origen, *Comm. on Romans* 1.4).

The dual nature of the person of Christ is expressed throughout the New Testament Epistles, but nowhere more explicitly than in Colossians as "the image of the invisible God, the firstborn over all creation," in whom "God was pleased to have all his fullness dwell, and through him to reconcile to himself all things" (Col. 1:15–20; Cyril of Jerusalem, *Catech. Lect.* 13.33), but this could only occur "through his blood, shed on the cross" (Col. 1:20; Basil, *Hom.* 16.10, *FC* 64:26).

The same personal union is reflected in Paul's description of Christ as being in very nature God (*morphē theou*), yet with respect to his humanity "made himself nothing, taking the very nature of a servant [*morphēn doulou*], being made in human likeness" (Phil. 2:6–8). Though being in the form of God, he took the form of a Servant.

In this way he is one Mediator. The Pastoral Letters reflect the view that Christ is one person uniting two natures, for in Christ we behold "one God and one mediator between God and men, the man Christ Jesus, who gave himself as a ransom for all men" (1 Tim. 2:5), who "appeared in a body, was vindicated by the Spirit" (3:16). All these phrases of the Pauline tradition require the theandric premise. David's son is David's Lord (Rom. 1:3,4; 9:5; *Augustine on Romans* 59).

There is already embedded in the messianic prophecy of Isaiah the rudiments of the two-natures teaching: the One to come would be a truly human child born (*vere homo*), and truly divine (*vere Deus*), to be called Mighty God (Isa. 9:6). The name "Immanuel" points to this union: "The virgin will be with child and will give birth to a son, and will call him Immanuel" (Isa. 7:14; Irenaeus, *Ag. Her.* 3.21).

The Union in Hebrews

A more systematic development of Christ's two natures in one person is found in the Epistle to the Hebrews. The first chapter asserts and celebrates Christ's divinity ("his Son, whom he appointed heir of all things," Heb. 1:2; Ambrose, *On Chr. Faith* 3.11), the second chapter develops Christ's humanity ("he too shared in their humanity," Heb. 2:14), and the remaining passages set forth the mystery of the interfacing of the two natures—"the Son of God" who is able "to sympathize with our weaknesses" (Heb. 4:14–16; 3:1). This one person sent from God to humanity, is the representative of humanity and as such the high priest petitioning from man to God, who "through the eternal Spirit" offered his humanity "unblemished to God" (Heb. 9:14).

The Hypostatic Union in John

The prologue of the Gospel of John attests that the Logos, the one and only God, became flesh (John 1:1–18). The divine Logos was not diminished by the union with the flesh. To behold the Son is to behold the Father (John 14:9). The Son is given authority to bestow life (John 5:24, 40; 6:27; 10:10), to judge (5:22), to answer supplications (14:14; 15:7). Faith in the Son is the same as faith in God (John 12:44; 14:1; Chrysostom, *Hom. on John* 74.1; Augustine, *Comm. on John* 54).

The Theandric Premise Necessary for Reading the New Testament

Scriptural attestations to Jesus Christ are characterized by the constant use of both language strata—human and divine. Hardly a page of the New Testament lacks implicit reference to the Christ who is true God without ceasing to be truly human and unreservedly human without ceasing to be eternal Son.

Names and titles are ascribed to this one person that reveal or imply the union of the two natures—Jesus Christ, Son of God, Son of Man, Word become flesh, the Lamb slain for the redemption of the world. Yet in all these ascriptions, it is always assumed that we are speaking of one single person, one Mediator, one self, the one and only Son (Second Council of Constantinople, *CF*:161; Cyril of Alex., *Comm. on John* 8; Grensted, *The Person of Christ*).

If someone should imagine that Jesus Christ is two persons, one would expect him to speak of "himselves" as "we," but this never occurs. The Son is always "I," the Godhead is "we." In the Son's dialogue with the Father, there is a clear sense of "I" (Gregory of Nazianzus, *Orat.* 37.2).

The union is so permeant that readers of Scripture cannot always easily separate out what Christ says of himself *as God* and what he says of himself *as human*. When the Scripture student keeps clearly in mind that though divine this one is human and though human this one is divine, then the Scriptures make immediate sense and each narrative unfolds plausibly (Athanasius, *Four Discourses Ag. Arians* 1).

Lacking the Premise, the Texts Are Unintelligible

Distinctive qualities of both humanity and deity are ascribed to the unifying person in a such a consistent way that the text makes little sense unless one assumes that these two natures were united in a single person. He is paradoxically "before Abraham" yet "born in a manger," "suffered under Pontius Pilate" yet "the same yesterday, today, and forever."

The sentences of the New Testament constantly juxtapose the two natures in a way readers find so inescapable that to fight it is to fight the text itself. Only the theandric premise can allow these varied ascriptions in a given narrative to make sense.

Examples: The one who upholds all things by the word of his power is the same one who grows in the womb of Mary. He who knows all from the foundation of the world declares as man that he does not know the day or hour of judgment. He who created all has nowhere to lay his head. He from whose hand comes all things is the same one who agonized in the Garden. The eternal One who cannot change or suffer prays that the cup might pass from him. The eternal One who is unlimited in power suffers and dies. The one who is crucified and buried is the same one in whom the eternal life of God remains and works.

These statements are neither contradictions nor absurdities, seen in the light of the permeant logic of the divine-human personal union. Only with the two-nature/one-person hypothesis do these Scriptures make sense. Lacking this premise, the scriptural testimony will be found constantly confusing, a maze of internal contradictions. With this premise, the scriptural testimony has economy, beauty, and cohesion (Gregory of Nazianzus, *Fourth Theol. Orat. on the Son, Orat.* 30).

The Union of Two Natures in One Person

The Scriptures represent Jesus Christ as having a divine nature and a human nature in a single undivided personality (John 1:1–18; 9:48–59; Hilary, *Trin.* 8.13). The notion that two natures are united in one person is constantly assumed in the New Testament, even where it is not formally defined.

This scriptural teaching has become known in the tradition as the *personal union of the divine and human natures*, or the *hypostatic* (= *personal*) *union*, from *hypostasis*, or personal subsistences in the Godhead, as distinguished from their common essence or substance (*ousia*) as God (Council of Chalcedon, *CC*:35–36; Second Council of Constantinople, *CC*:46). Christ's personhood is as singularly unified as any one person can be, yet in a profound, mysterious union of humanness and deity (Tho. Aq., *SCG* 4:152–55, 175–82; *BOC*:47, 515).

The personal union is not a conflation or mixture of two composite things so the person could be said to be part human, part divine (Chalcedon, *CC*:36; Hooker, *Laws of Ecclesiastical Polity*, V, 51–56). Gregory's summary: "What He was He laid aside; what He was not He assumed; not that He became two, but He deigned to be One made out of the two" (Gregory of Nazianzus, *Orat.* 37.2).

Attributes Applied to One Person as Human, as Divine

In the New Testament, ascriptions are constantly applied to the one person that are taken from either or both the human nature and the divine nature. In some passages these two natures are held in tension in a single compact phrase, such as: they have "crucified the Lord of glory" (1 Cor. 2:8). It is not uncommon to hear Jesus Christ attested as truly God in one passage, truly human in another, and both in the next (John 11:1–43). The one personal subject, Jesus Christ, is consistently described as divine and human.

Hence the redeemer is called *theanthropos*, God-man, the single person being undivided. The unitive term "God-man" (or God-as-a-man) is preferred to the more general "God-in-humanity" or "godly person" because these phrases might be used equally to speak of the union of Christ with every believer, while no believer is rightly spoken of as "God-man."

The Union is Not an Oscillation

The union is not an oscillation or a pendulum. The incarnate Lord did not swing back and forth between being partly or occasionally God and partly or occasionally human (Newman, *Athanasius* 2:240–42). To allege this obscures the central paradoxical point of Christ's existence: he was always God and nothing less, expressed within the frame of time and assuming the normal structures of human consciousness.

The apostles actively proclaimed the full deity and full humanity of the Lord and left for later reflection the formal definition of their precise correlation (Hilary, *Trin.* 9). Scripture repeatedly portrays Jesus Christ as one person, a single subject self, an undivided personality in whom these two natures are inseparably united (Ursinus, *CHC*:208–12; G. Berkouwer, *The Person of Christ*).

Technical language eventually became necessary to defend against ingenious distortions of this obvious scriptural teaching. It is useful to show how this technical language still stands as a reasonable defense of scriptural teaching.

The One Person

One-dimensional phrases such as "the dying God" should be avoided or qualified because they begin by forgetting the divine-human premise. Then they collapse triunity into sonship and the deity of Christ into his humanity. Rather than the "death of God," classic exegetes spoke more precisely of the God-man "according to his humanity" who suffered and died. Yet the scriptural texts do not intend that the interpreter artificially split Christ's divine acts from his human acts, for this tends to rend the union of his person. Much current biblical criticism assumes that the humanity of Christ can be detached as an object of historical study like any other historical object to be assessed separately. This rends the personal union assumed in the texts.

All who understand the scriptural testimony to the union will be in position to see how the major ecumenical definitions sought to clarify and secure that union. All ecumenical formulations sought accountability to Scripture as expressive of the one mind of the believing church. They are best understood as attempts at consensual exegesis.

The unity of the theandric person is a simple idea, though its simplicity encases a mystery. It is the remarkable idea that one person is truly human and truly divine, uniting God and humanity in one individual. In Christ we have to do with only one person (Council of Toledo, *SCD* 20; *SCD* 42, 143, 215), in whom divinity and humanity are personally united (Council of Ephesus, *SCD* 13, 215, 288).

It is inexact to think of the Christ of Scriptures merely as godly (*theophoros*; Council of Ephesus, *SCD* 117:50), since the god-like (godly) metaphor sells short the deeper premise that the two natures are united in their personal subsistence (*hypostasis*). Hence the union is termed a hypostatic (personal) union (Third Council of Constantinople, *SCD* 289–93; see also *SCD* 13, 111, 115f., 148, 216), which began with the incarnation (Vigilius, *SCD* 204f.). No expression is more compact than that of Gregory the Theologian on this point: "He is the Way, because He leads us through Himself" (Gregory of Nazianzus, *Orat.* 30.21).

Not Two Sons

As God, the Son knew that he was human; as human, he knew that he was God, hence one Son encompassed two natures. He was not two Sons, but one uniting two. "For both are God, that which assumed, and that which was assumed; two Natures meeting in One, not two Sons (let us not give a false account of the blending)" (Gregory of Nazianzus, *Orat.* 37.2).

There are not two bodies or two souls or two conscious persons, but a single conscious person uniting the divine and human natures. It is not one or the other nature that speaks when Jesus Christ speaks, but one person bearing the congruent imprint of two natures (Second Council of Constantinople).

In the New Testament he always speaks as a single-person "I" whether in his human or divine voice, there being only one "I," not two; for if there were two "I"s, there would have been at Nazareth two persons. He unites in one person the utterly diverse characteristics needed for his mediatorial work (Ambrose, *On Chr. Faith*; 3.11; Tho. Aq., *ST* 3 Q17–19).

Classical exegetes carefully steered a middle course between two hazards: the *denial of the union* of God and humanity in Christ and the *denial of the distinguishability* of deity and humanity in Christ. It was to provide guidance for this trajectory that the ecumenical definitions developed the "one person in two natures" formula (Cyril of Alex., *Comm. on John* 8; Leo I, *Sermon* 72.1).

By uniting two-natures, the incarnate Son is *distinguished both from other human persons and from the other persons of the Trinity*: "On the one hand, He is joined to the Father and the Spirit by His divinity, while on the other He is joined by His humanity to His Mother and to all men. However, because of the fact that His natures are united, we say that He differs both from the Father and the Spirit and from His Mother and other men" (John of Damascus, *OF* 3.3).

The Divine-Human Permeation Likened to Body-Soul Interface

The unity of the human and divine natures of Christ is a mystery without adequate empirical analogy. The Colossian Letter attests "the mystery of God, namely, Christ, in whom are hidden all the treasures of wisdom and knowledge" (2:2). Yet the one analogy that ancient exegetes thought came closest to expressing the union of Christ's person is that of the psychosomatic (soul-body, freedom-nature) interface that every human being already knows (and is!).

The "Athanasian Creed" (Quicunque) summarized this analogy: "For as the reasonable soul and flesh is one man, so God and Man is one Christ" (*COC* 2). Augustine gave definitive expression to the psychosomatic analogy of divine and human natures in Christ: "There are some who request an explanation of how God is joined to man so as to become the single person of Christ, as if they themselves could explain something that happens every day, namely, how the soul is joined to the body so as to form the single person of a man. For, *as the soul makes use of the body in a single person to form a man, so God makes use of man in a single Person to form Christ. In the former person there is a mingling of soul and body; in the latter Person there is a mingling of God and man. . . .* The one process happens daily in order to beget men; the other happened once to set men free" (*Letters* 137, italics added; Chemnitz, *TNC*:95–100, 296–97). "If you inquire how the Deity is united with human nature, it is appropriate for you first to ask in what way the soul is united to the body" (Gregory of Nyssa, *ARI* 11).

No living human being can lack a body. No human being can lack a soul, for the soul is what makes the body live. The *psychē* (*anima*, soul) sees only with bodily eyes and hears only with bodily ears. Similarly Jesus Christ saw, heard, and even suffered and died as a human being. The Word dwelt in flesh, just as our souls dwell in our bodies. As the soul-body interface pervades every moment of human selfhood, so the divinity-humanity of Christ pervades every moment of his unique personhood (Hugh of St. Victor, *OSCF*: 236–39). As *psychē* transcends *soma*, as imagination soars above finitude, so does the divine nature of Christ transcend the limits of human finitude in the man Jesus.

Accordingly there is a veiled similarity (acknowledging differences) between this everyday human body/soul permeation and the unique mystery wherein God becomes human. The human *psyche* acts and suffers through the body in ways that require a body, yet always such action and suffering has an interfacing spiritual dimension that transcends the body. The human spirit (*pneuma*) is precisely characterized by that interface (Kierkegaard, *SD*:146, 147).

Every human being already knows something of the complexity and mystery of the psychosomatic interface, because each person is one. We know how subtly our bodies are affected, moment by moment, by our spirited or dispirited condition (Rom. 8:9–17; Origen, *Comm. on Rom.* 8.11). We know how deeply psychosomatic factors affect the health and malaise of the body, its immune systems, often causing allergies, ulcers, headaches, and nausea.

In human existence the bodily nature grounds the person's capacity for self-transcendence. Yet imagination and freedom transcend finitude and body. These two always exist in intense and delicate interfacing (Nemesius, *On the Nature of Man*; Niebuhr, *NDM*). The complexity and subtlety of this interface is something like that between the divine and human natures of the one person, Jesus Christ.

Grace-enabled freedom receives and owns the body willingly, as did the Son receive life willingly from the Blessed Mother, and as the Mother received with favor the Word. This is what human freedom is constantly choosing: *either* to receive joyfully *or* waste in despair over one's own living body (Kierkegaard, *Either/Or* I; *SD*; *The Concept of Anxiety*).

The "entire and singular unity of Person" was explicated by Vincent of Lérins in this ingenious way: "For the conjunction has not converted and changed the one nature into the other (which is the characteristic error of the Arians), but rather has in such wise compacted both into one, that while there always remains in Christ the singularity of one and the self-same Person, there abides eternally the characteristic property of each nature; whence it follows, that neither does God (the divine nature) ever begin to be body, nor does the body ever cease to be body. This may be illustrated in human nature: for not only in the present life, but in the future also, each individual man will consist of soul and body; nor will his body ever be converted into soul, or his soul into body" (Vincent, *Commonitory* 13).

Like all analogies, this one is best used with constraint. Any analogy loses its integrity when flattened into an equation. The body-soul analogy is not to be equated with the divine-human union because (1) soul is not uncreated—for God alone is uncreated; (2) our bodies are unlike Christ's body in that in them the Logos has not become incarnate; and (3) our bodies and souls interface in such a way that the right balance is constantly prone to being upset by the history of sin and personal sin, unlike Christ's humanity and divinity, which appear to be steadily cooperative (Tertullian, *On the Soul*; Augustine, *On Gospel of John*, *Tractate* 19.5.15). Hence the correspondence is best viewed circumspectly as an analogy and not an equation, for God is not soul and humanity is not body. Analogy differs from equation precisely in its dissimilarities.

The Limits of the Eucharistic Analogy

Similarly there is another analogy that must carefully avoid being flattened into an equation. It appeared repeatedly in classic attempts to clarify the union of two natures in Christ: the divine-human unity of Christ's person is like the divine-human action in the Eucharist.

It will suffice to quote John of Damascus, who cautiously drew the analogy in this way: "Now, bread and wine are used because God knows human weakness. . . . He does through the ordinary things of nature those things that surpass the natural order. . . . However, should you inquire as to the manner in which this is done, let it suffice for you to hear that it is done through the Holy Ghost, just as it was through the Holy Ghost that the Lord made flesh subsist for Himself and in Himself from the blessed Mother of God. And more than this we do not know, except that the word of God is true and effective and omnipotent, but the manner in which it is so is impossible to find out. What is more, it is not amiss to say this, that *just as bread by being eaten and wine and water by being drunk are naturally changed into the body of the person eating and drinking and yet do not become another body* than that which the person had before, so in the same way are the bread of the offertory and the wine and water supernaturally changed into the body and blood of Christ by the invocation and coming down of the Holy Ghost, yet they are not two bodies, but one and the same" (*OF* 4.13, italics added).

The union of the two natures of Christ is not precisely analogous to the union or *henosis* of two persons in marriage (Origen, *OFP* 2.6). For the unity of marriage leaves husband and wife "even after their union, two persons." Christ is more profoundly and intrinsically one person than two marriage partners are one person. Christ's personal union is a union that can only exist in one distinctive person in whom there is an intimate and perpetual conjunction of divine and human natures in one individual, wherein the human nature was assumed by the *logos* so as to be the *Word in person* (*enhupostatos logo*; Augustine, *Hom. on John*).

Avoiding Misunderstanding of the Personal Union of the Savior

The "two-nature, one-person" formula has remained the stabilizing center of apostolic consensus of ecumenical Christology for almost two millennia. It has repeatedly been tested by challenge. The major tendencies to heretical distortion in the two-natures union are these: it runs the risk of inordinately divinizing the human, humanizing the divine, or dualizing the one person. Keeping these factors in due balance is the challenge of classic Christian teaching of Christology.

Among the most familiar distortions of the apostolic consensus is the one that has claimed that the divine nature became entirely inactive, dormant, paralyzed, or even nonexistent during Christ's earthly ministry. There is no warrant in the text for this conclusion, for in Scripture it is precisely the Word that has become flesh to *abide* among us, not the Word that ceases to be in becoming flesh. The New Testament does not imply that the Logos in becoming flesh temporarily quit being Logos and began being merely a man. Rather "the Word became flesh and dwelt among us" (John 1:14). The central point is that God became flesh without contradiction or negation of either deity or humanity (1 Tim. 3:16; 1 John 4:2).

Another misreading holds that the union between humanity and deity in Christ was not completed in the incarnation, but was only gradually seeking to be realized (Schleiermacher, *ChrF*:377–90). Some have argued that it was only belatedly in the resurrection, not the incarnation, that the union could become realized and thus recognized as realized (Pannenberg, *JGM*; I. A. Dorner, *History of the Development of the Doctrine of the Person of Christ* I). Paul commends the mind of Christ, who "in very nature God" was found in human form as servant (Phil. 2:7). The classic consensus held that the incarnation was not incomplete, but fully manifest in the nativity.

Some versions of kenotic (divine self-emptying) theory suppose that the Trinity must have been altered in number during Jesus' earthly ministry. This was firmly countered by the Second Council of Constantinople: "For the Holy Trinity when God the Word was incarnate, was not increased by the addition of a person" (*CC*:48). God remained triune and the trinity became most profoundly expressed through the incarnation.

Popular criticisms of the personal union of Christ are often based upon some point that has been repeatedly disavowed ecumenically as a misunderstanding of it. Some criticize Chalcedon's teaching as dualistic, as a dissection of the whole, a fissure of the person (each of which the formula itself specifically rejected!). Some think it amounts to duplicity. Some view it as two abstractions instead of one reality, or two halves instead of one personal whole, wherein God now acts, and now man acts. Each of these criticisms was specifically anticipated in the precise formulation of Chalcedon, in its attempt to move cautiously between duplex personality and impersonal manhood (Leo I, *Tome*; Aldwinckle, *MTM*).

That the classic Christological formulae have undergone various reinterpretations in their long history remains a testimony to their vitality, not deadness (Mackintosh, *PJC*:300). Personal salvation, however, is not dependent upon the precise acceptance of a particular Christological formula or definition of the Person, but rather upon active faith in the Person himself.

The Personal Union Not Subject to Empirical-Rational Laboratory Dissection

Only dead things can be dissected. The worshiping community is invited to celebrate and study and revel in this living mystery, not as something fully comprehensible to objective analysis, but as a divine gift for joyful contemplation (*BOC*:489, 597, 609). Modesty of expression remains a radical intellectual requirement in the presence of this incomparable Person. This mystery was already being acknowledged in New Testament times: "Beyond all question, the mystery of godliness is great: He appeared in a body" (1 Tim. 3:16; Theodoret, *Interp. of 1 Tim.*, 3.16; Newman, *GA*).

The union of humanity and divinity in Christ is not an incidental or ancillary aspect of Christian proclamation, nor an odd accommodation to myth. Rather it is at the heart of faith, a hinge point for subsequent profound knowledge of God revealed in history and of history itself. For the Father is recognized through the Son (Matt. 11:27), the Word of Life, "that which was from the beginning, which we have heard, which we have seen with our eyes, which we have looked at and our hands have touched—this we proclaim" (1 John 1:1; Didymus the Blind, *Comm. on 1 John* 1).

The plain sense reading of the New Testament becomes increasingly problematic and confusing when any of these three errors are made: that Jesus lacks humanity, deity, or personal union. The texts will fight any reader all the way if any of these are abandoned. With such a concession, a major retrogression has occurred that finally tends to make Christology formally and logically impossible (Harvey, *HB*:275–89).

Yet it is not likely that inquirers into Christianity will ever cease raising questions about the unique theandric person attested in the New Testament. Luther commented wryly: "I know nothing about the Lord Christ that the devil has failed to attack" (*Table Talk* 1.269).

The Honest Money Changer

The experienced reader of the gospel narratives is like a skilled and honest money changer, according to Athanasius's happy analogy. He must attend carefully to the context of each scriptural passage concerning Christ, as to whether it has more particular reference to voicing his humanity, or deity, or the divine-human union.

"Expressions used about His Godhead and His becoming man are to be interpreted with discrimination and suitably to the particular context. . . . He who expounds concerning His Godhead is not ignorant of what belongs to His coming in the flesh; but discerning each as a skilled and 'approved moneychanger,' he will walk in the straight way of piety; when therefore he speaks of His weeping; he knows that the Lord, having become man, while He exhibits His human character in weeping, as God raises up Lazarus" (Athanasius, *On the Opinion of Dionysius*, 9).

The dishonest money changer constantly shortchanges either the divine or the human. The honest money changer keeps the two currencies (divinity and humanity) in fitting congruence as the worshiping community moves through narrative after narrative.

Classic exegetes recognized that language was early applied to Christ in reference to varied contexts before or after his incarnation or resurrection. The continuing problem for any reader of Paul or Mark or John is that "sometimes indeed when teaching about the supreme nature, he is completely silent about the human nature, but sometimes when treating of the human dispensation, he does not touch on the mystery of His divinity" (John IV, *Epist. to Constantius* [AD 641], *SCD* 253).

Generic Contexts for Using Language of Deity, Humanity and Union

Hence it became a constant task of Christian reflection to sort out the different classes or "generic modes" or ways of speaking of Christ's identity in the gospel stories—whether human, divine, or divine-human. By the eighth century, four standard classes had been astutely outlined by John of Damascus, the most systematic of the Eastern theologians. Accordingly, varied references are made to Christ in relation to four stages or modes, which may be characterized in outline form. Things may be said of Christ in reference to:

I. *Before* the incarnate theandric union so as to show
   Consubstantiality with the Father
   The perfection of the Person
   The mutual indwelling of the Persons in one another
   The subordination of Son to Father
   The will of the Father as fulfilled by the Son, or
   The fulfillment of prophecy, or
II. *During* the time of incarnate union so as to indicate
   The deification of the flesh, or
     By assuming the human
     By uplifting the human
   The humbling of the Word
     By lowering from glory to finitude
     By assumption of the flesh, or
     By temporarily emptying (kenosis), or
   Permeation of both deity and humanity in the union
     By uniting
     By anointing
     By an intimate conjoining

By permeating, or

By mutual indwelling, or

III. *After* the Union, so as to show the

Divine nature, or

Human nature

    Spoken of him naturally

        of his birth

        of his personal growth

        of his age

        of his finitude as hunger, thirst, weariness, fear, sleep

        of his death

    Ascribed to him fictionally "as if" human only (Luke 24:28)

    Things spoken in the matter of association and said relatively

    Things spoken by reason of distinctions in thought

    Things spoken to strengthen faith

    Things spoken with reference to his ethnic identity, or

One Person displaying both divinity and humanity, or

IV. *After the Resurrection*

As pertaining to divinity, or

As pertaining to humanity

    As actual but not according to nature (as eating after the resurrection)

    As actual and according to nature (as passing through closed doors)

    As simulated or intentionally fictional (as when he "acted as if he were going farther," Luke 24:28)

As pertaining to both natures

The options were thought to be exhaustive of the options of how the divine-human relation might appear or be presented in a given episode. A watchful interpreter will attend to which of these options would constitute the prevailing motif implied in a particular episode. Ascriptions concerning Christ are best applied in relation to the circumstance in which they occur, whether before or after the incarnation or resurrection (John of Damascus, *OF* 4.18).

This neglected ancient theandric premise awaits attentive and coherent application within current Scripture studies. Much modern critical Scripture study has limited its range to speak of only one dimension, the human nature as if able to be abstracted from the divine-human union. I hope before the end of this century some able scholar will take this brilliant analytical tool provided thirteen centuries ago by John of Damascus and apply it systematically to a consistent New Testament hermeneutic and text-based Christology.

The Logic of Intrapersonal Permeation

To permeate is to spread, to become diffused, or to penetrate (per + meare = "to pass through") something. The interpenetration of divinity and humanity of Christ in one person refers to the diffusion of each nature in the other. The Greek terms expressing this union were *koinonia* ("communication, communion") and *poieo* ("to do") or *koinopoiesis* ("communicative action" or "communication of acts").

They are referred to more commonly in the Latin as *communicatio idiomatum* ("communication of idioms or attributes," or *genus idiomaticum*, Hilary, *Trin.* 9.15–20; Tho. Aq., *ST* 3 Q16; Chemnitz, *TNC*:162–64; Barth, *CD* 4/2:73).

In seeking to set forth a plausible theory of the personal union consistent with Scripture and resistant to distortion, the classic exegetes (of East, West, and of the Protestant era), have applied a carefully devised logic of permeation that deserves to be restudied. Scholastic teachers sought to show how Christ's deity affected his humanity, what his humanity meant in relation to his deity, and how the permeation between them is communicated in the actions of the single, unified person.

The Sharing of Aspects of Each Nature with the Other

The mediatorial work required over time an ongoing interpenetration of both natures within the one person. This is what is meant by *communicatio idiomatum*— the communication of divine and human properties fully and unitively to the single person. From the unity of the person of the Mediator there follows a communication of idioms, or reciprocal ascription of properties and operations (Council of Ephesus, *SCD* 116–24; see also *SCD* 16, 201), so the properties of each nature may be predicated of the other. Calvin held to "such a connection and union of the Divinity with the humanity, that each nature retains its properties entire, and yet both together constitute one Christ" (*Inst.* 3.14.1; *BOC*: 593). The one person embraces two natures and their *idiomata*, their distinctive features or properties (from *idios*, pertaining to self, one's own, private or distinctive idioms, see Luke 9:10; 10:23).

In this way the one person may be called just as easily "Jesus" as "the Christ": "And thus, Christ—which name covers both together—is called both God and man, created and uncreated, passible and impassible. And whenever he is named Son of God and God from one of the aspects, He receives the properties of the co-existent nature, of the flesh, that is to say, and can be called passible God and crucified Lord of Glory—not as being God, but in so far as the same one is also man. When, again, He is named Man and the Son of Man, He is given the properties and splendors of the divine nature. He is called Child before the Ages and Man without beginning. . . . Such, then, is the manner of this exchange by which each nature communicates its own properties to the other" (John of Damascus, *OF* 3.4).

This permeant logic gradually entered into the life of prayer and counsel, with language such as that which Augustine suggests: "Let Christ *raise* you by that which is man, *lead* you by that which is God-man, and *guide* you through to that which is God" (*Tractates on John*, Tractate 23.6,italics added). The multilevel relation of believers to Christ is profoundly glimpsed in Christ's remarkable prayer to the Father concerning "I in them and you in me" (John 17:23; Cyril of Alex., *Comm. on John* 11.12).

Perichoresis: Where Divinity and Humanity Interpenetrate

Paul taught that "in Christ all the fullness of the Deity lives in bodily form" (Col. 2:9). The consensual exegetes interpreted this to mean that the divine nature penetrates and perfects every aspect of the human, and the human is pervaded by the divine (John of Damascus, *OF* 3.8). This was powerfully conveyed by the term *perichoresis* (Lat. *circumincession*, an embracing movement, "a proceeding around," or "walking about all sides"), literally the existence of natures in one another.

The *perichoresis* or active intermingling of the natures was that abundant interpenetration by which the divine nature of the Son pervaded inwardly the human nature so as *fully to impart* his divinity to his humanity and his God-manhood to every aspect of his action (Schmid, *DT*:306). In the Son, the deity participated in the Passion of the humanity and the humanity in the majesty of the deity without blurring or confusing either.

The Lutheran Formula of Concord summarized this patristic point for Protestants: "the entire fullness of the divinity dwells in Christ, not as in other holy men and angels, but bodily as in its own body, so that, with all its majesty, power, glory, and efficacy, it shines forth in the assumed human nature of Christ, when and as He wills, and in, with and through it, exerts its divine power, glory and efficacy, as the soul does in the body and fire in glowing iron" (*Formula of Concord, BOC*).

The picture of iron being heated was often employed: Iron being "incessantly heated"—*penetrated by fire while remaining iron* (Origen, *OFP* 3.6; Maximus, *Disputatio cum Pyrrho*). "While we speak of the cut burn and the burnt cut of the red-hot knife, we nevertheless hold the cutting to be one operation and the burning another" (John of Damascus, *OF* 3.19). In this analogy the red-hot knife is Jesus Christ—the knife his humanity, the heat his divinity—cutting and burning are distinguishable but inseparable. "For the two natures are one Christ and the one Christ is two natures" (John of Damascus, *OF* 3.19; Chemnitz, *TNC*:229–30). Yet in such an example "one must find in it that which is like and that which is unlike. For likeness in everything would be identity and not an example, which is especially true with divine things. So, in the matter of theology and the Incarnation, it is impossible to find an absolutely perfect example" (John of Damascus, *OF* 3.26).

His Human Nature Endowed with Requisite Gifts for Mission

Jesus was endowed with extraordinary gifts for his mission. These gifts were as complete as can or need be given to a human being. They were sufficient to his mission of salvation. They were given contextually as needed from the time of birth, yet these gifts had to be allowed to grow in time and emerge as competences ordinarily emerge in the development of a human person. Hence Scripture portrays Jesus paradoxically as full of grace from birth, yet also capable of growing in grace through the years (Luke 2:40, 52; Origen, *Homilies on Luke* 19–20).

Jesus taught, acted, and suffered as the Spirit guided (Acts 1:2, 10:38). "For the one whom God has sent speaks the words of God, for God gives the Spirit without limit" (John 3:34; Ammonius, *Fragments on John* 105, *JKGK* 224). While being empowered by God the Spirit, Jesus taught and acted not simply as a prophet (speaking for God), but as God (Luke 5:20–21), from whom power was perceived as streaming forth immediately from his person (Luke 6:19; Cyril of Alex., *Comm. on Luke*, Hom. 25). The Son is attested as having been unreservedly given the power of miracle, the power to know and act as God, yet this power was voluntarily constrained under the premise of a self-chosen, humble mission of servanthood. Even then, there was sufficient impartation of divine power for each stage of the fulfillment of his office of Mediator.

Who Suffers—God, Man, or God-man?

This premise of the grace of theandric union affected thinking about who suffered in the suffering of the divine-human mediator. Luther drew the distinction carefully: "If I believe that only the human nature has suffered for me, I have a Savior of little worth. . . . It is the [unique theandric] person that suffers and dies. Now the person is true God; therefore it is rightly said: 'The Son of God suffers.' For although the divinity does not suffer, yet the person which is God suffers in His humanity. . . . In His own nature, God cannot die; but now God and man are united in one person, so that the expression 'God's death' is correct, when the man dies who is one thing or one person with God" (Luther, quoted in the Formula of Concord, *BOC*: 631–32).

As human, the Savior could suffer, be powerless, and die as a human being, not in his divine nature, but through his possession of humanity. Although in his divine nature he was insensible to pain, the God-man was capable through the divine-human union to suffer pain (for discussions of passability, see Chrysostom, *Hom. on John* 60; Strong, *Syst. Theol.*:697). As mediator, he exercised divine attributes as needed, yet was self-constrained in their use due to the gradual disclosure of his mission.

Ironies abound in consequence: "Thus the Lord of Glory is even said to have been crucified, although His divine nature did not suffer; and the Son of Man is confessed to have been in heaven before His passion, as the Lord Himself has said" (John of Damascus, *OF* 3.3, John 3:13). "The same one person is at once uncreated in its divinity and created in its humanity" (John of Damascus, *OF* 4.5).

Gregory the Theologian played out this series of intriguing word pictures which are all deciphered by the premise of permeation:

> *He hungers—but He feeds thousands. . . .*
> *He is wearied, but is the Rest of them that are weary. . . .*
> *He is heavy with sleep, but walks lightly over the sea. . . .*
> *He prays, but He hears prayer.*
> *He weeps, but He causes tears to cease.*
> *He asks where Lazarus was laid, for He was Man; but He raises Lazarus, for*
>   *He was God.*
> *He is sold, and very cheap, for it is only thirty pieces of silver; but He redeems*
>   *the world. . . .*
> *As a sheep He is led to the slaughter, but He is the Shepherd of Israel, and*
>   *now of the whole world also.*
> *As a Lamb He is silent, yet He is the Word. . . .*
> *He is . . . wounded, but He heals every disease. . . .*
> *He dies, but He gives life. . . .*
> *If the one give you a starting point for your error, let the others put an end to it.*

(Gregory of Nazianzus, *Orat.* 29.20)

Orthodox Christians can affirm each of these lines without a sacrifice of intellect and in good conscience, but none can be said without the premise of "One Person, Two Natures."

Imagine a mathematician who has been struggling to understand a vast body of perplexing data. He sits facing the blurred maze of numbers and equations. Then someone hands him a simple formula that makes instant sense of the entire system of numbers. That is how the worshiping community beholds and celebrates and sings and dances the permeant logic of two-nature Christology. The logic appears constantly in the liturgy, while theological and historical reasoning tries to catch up.

Defining Personal Union

Ecumenical council definitions sought to define faith in such a way that it would not be easily distorted. Their definitions were largely elicited and required by persistent distortions that did not reflect the consensual mind of the believing church.

The Fourth Ecumenical Council (Chalcedon, AD 451, *SCD* 148) defended the scriptural teaching of the personal union of Christ by defining it as:

- unconfused (*asunkutōs*), with no mixing of the two natures, which remain distinct even while they are in communion (against the Eutychians)

- unchanged (*atreptōs*), in the sense that the deity is not transmuted into humanity, nor humanity into deity (against the Eutychians)

- indivisible (*adiairetōs*), unable to be divided—the personal union is never at any point split apart (against the Nestorians)

- inseparable (*achōristōs*), undissolved through eternity, perpetual (against the Nestorians)

Rejected Options Implied

Chalcedon was intensely economical in stating the faith in such a way that it could not be easily distorted. Among the options that were implicitly rejected were the Eutychians who tended to confuse the natures and the Nestorians who tended to divide the person (Ursinus, *CHC*:196–202). The rejected options may be summarized in this simple schema:

Heresies that reject Christ's humanity:
  Docetists (Christ as not fully in flesh)
  Apollinarians (Logos replaces human spirit)
  Eutychians (Christ as a single mixed nature)

Heresies that reject Christ's divinity:
  Eutychians (Christ not fully divine, but mixed nature)
  Ebionites (Jesus as natural son of Joseph and Mary)
  Arians (Christ as creature, not eternal)

Heresies that reject Christ's personal union:
  Nestorians (Christ as two persons)

The divine nature remains uncreated, infinite, almighty, and all-wise, while the human nature retains its own properties, namely, those characteristic of all human existence as created, finite, and subject to time and death. In this way ecumenical orthodoxy maintains Christ as truly human, truly God, one person.

To dispel distortion, the formula had to be precise: Jesus Christ "must be acknowledged in two natures, without confusion or change, without division or separation. The distinction between the natures was never abolished by their union but rather the character proper to each of the two natures was preserved as they come together in one person (*prosopon*) and one hypostasis" (Council of Chalcedon, *CF*: 154–55; A. Grillmeier, *Christ in Christian Tradition*; R. V. Sellers, *The Council of Chalcedon*).

The Ecumenical Confession of the Union

Whatever unites human beings through their participation in human nature is precisely the human nature experienced by Jesus. Whatever distinguishes one person from another also distinguished Jesus from all other human persons, for there was only one Jesus of Nazareth.

The most essential distinctions were tightly compacted in these phrases of the Quicunque Creed (AD 440), which confesses:

> Our Lord Jesus Christ the Son of God is
> both God and man;
> God of the substance of the Father, begotten before time,
> and man of the substance of his mother born in time;
> perfect God and perfect man,
> consisting of a rational soul and human body;
> equal to the Father in his divinity,
> less than the Father in his humanity;
> who, although both God and man, is not two but one Christ;
> one, however, not by the conversion of the Godhead into flesh
> but by the assumption of manhood into God.
> Wholly one, not by fusion of substance but by unity of person.
> For as the rational soul and the body are one man,
> so God and man are one Christ
>
> (TGS: 102; SCD 40)

This language has been chanted for centuries as one of the three most widely accepted confessions of the ancient church. There is not a line of this ancient creed that does not find ample confirmation in the Reformation teaching, sermons, and catechesis concerning Jesus Christ.

Protestant formularies typically followed this ancient ecumenical teaching as can be seen in the Westminster Confession: "Christ, in the work of mediation, acteth according to both natures; by each nature doing that which is proper to itself; yet by reason of the unity of the person, that which is proper to one nature is sometimes, in Scripture, attributed to the person denominated by the other nature" (Article 8, CC:205).

The saving mediatorial work "becomes impossible if one separates the two natures of Christ, as Nestorius did, or if one only ascribes to Him one divine nature, like the Monophysites, or if one curtails one part of human nature, like Apollinarius, or if one only sees in Him a single divine will and operation, like the Monothelites. 'What is not assumed cannot be deified'" (Lossky, MTEC:154). "For each of the two natures performs the functions proper to it in communion with the other; the Word does what pertains to the Word and the flesh what pertains to the flesh" (Leo I, Tome).

Divine and Human Will in the Son

The prayer of Jesus at Gethsemane shows that he had a self-determining human will which could say: "Not my will but yours be done" (Luke 22:42). Yet from that same passage it is also evident that his human will was unremittingly consecrated to follow voluntarily the divine will. "For I have come down from heaven not to do my will but to do the will of him who sent me" (John 6:38; Athanasius, Four Discourses Ag. Arians, 3.58–67).

The Savior's Human Will Obeyed His Divine Will

On this scriptural basis, it became a distinctive point of ecumenical confession that Jesus had two wills—his human will being obedient to the divine will in him—"his human will following, and not resisting or opposing, but rather subject to his divine and all-powerful will" (Third Council of Constantinople, *CC*: 51). "The two wills proper to the two natures are different, but He who wills is one" (Lossky, *MTEC*: 146; Gregory of Nazianzus, *Orat.* 30; Tho. Aq., *ST 3* Q18).

The divine will always "goes before" or "prevenes" (leads the way by grace) for the human will, so that the human will may choose freely in accord with the divine will. "And when He begged to be spared death, He did so naturally, with His divine will willing and permitting, and He was in agony and afraid. Then, when His divine will willed that His human will choose death, the passion was freely accepted. . . . And so, the Lord's soul was freely moved to will, but it freely willed those things which His divine will willed" (John of Damascus, *OF* 3.18). Jesus' will was not simply an automated or programmed response as in a mechanism or in animal instinct, but genuine human volition.

The consensus-bearing Fathers made a distinction between brute appetite and free will. It was ably summarized by the Damascene: "He willed freely with His divine and His human will, for free will is absolutely inherent in every rational nature. After all, of what good can rationality be to a nature that does not reason freely. Now, the Creator has implanted a natural appetite in *brute beasts* which constrains them to act for the preservation of their own nature. For, since they lack reason, they cannot lead; rather, they are led by their natural appetite. Whence it is that the instinct to act arises simultaneously with the appetite, for they enjoy neither the use of reason nor that of counsel or reflection or judgment. For this reason they are neither praised and deemed good for practicing virtue nor punished for doing evil. The *rational nature*, however, has its natural appetite, which becomes aroused, but is guided and controlled by the reason," and it is on this basis that "the rational nature is both praised and deemed good for practicing virtue and punished for practicing vice" (*OF* 3.18, italics added).

It is God's nature to will. It is also human nature to will. Willing, like knowing, belongs to the human condition, to ordinary human personhood. One who wills is called a person. Yet it is possible for one will to remain free while voluntarily obeying another.

"To will is inherent to all men" (John of Damascus, *OF* 3.14). How one wills particularly in a given situation depends upon judgment, not nature, and upon self-determining freedom, not external causal determinations alone.

Divine Working and Human Working in Jesus Christ

The mediatorial work of the Son required the cooperative permeation or interpenetration of the two working wills, divine and human, as seen in John's testimony: "My Father is always at his work to this very day, and I, too, am working" (John 5:17). "Whatever the Father does, the Son also does" (John 5:19; Augustine, *The Creed* 2.5). "The Father is in me, and I in the Father" (John 10:38). "For the very work the Father has given me to finish, and which I am doing, testifies that the Father has sent me" (John 5:36; Augustine, *Hom. on John* 23). "For just as the Father raises the dead and gives them life, even so the Son gives life" (John 5:21; Cyril of Alex. *Comm. on John* 2.6).

Every discrete act or work of the Mediator required this co-willing and co-working of the two natures (Chemnitz, *TNC*: 215–30). "For, since He is of one substance with God the Father, He freely wills and acts as God. And, since He is also of one substance with us, the same one freely wills and acts as man. Thus, the miracles are His, and so are the sufferings" (John of Damascus, *OF* 3.14). Just as there are two wills in Christ, we are also led by the texts to assume that there are two *actions* without division or confusion, a divine action and a human action, hence two operations (Honorius, *Two Wills and Operations*, *SCD* 251–52).

Why a Union That Included Human Nature
Was Necessary for Salvation

God did not choose to become enfleshed in a brute beast, but in human form, for animals are less capable of imaging the divine nature. If God became a frog, it would first be necessary to give the frog speech and moral awareness in order for God to become revealed to or through the frog.

But human nature, as originally given by grace, is capable of communication with God, of partaking of the divine life (Gen. 2:15–17; Gregory of Nazianzus, *Second Oration on Easter* 8; 2 Pet. 1:4). God became human, not a rock or hummingbird or spider, because humanity is already made in God's image.

Humanity is not less but more human through God's enfleshment. Yet under the conditions of the fallenness of history, the capacity of humanity to image or reflect God has become grossly distorted. This is why Christ, the perfect image of God according to which humanity was originally made, is said to have restored that lost image by assuming human nature and filling it with the divine life, enabling genuine human faith, hope, and love. Hence the incarnation is said to embody the fulfillment of humanity and to express the truly human.

There can be no mediation between God and humanity without positing a Mediator capable of empathy with ordinary humanity and of equal dignity with God (Phil. 2:6–11; Heb 2:17–18). As human, he is capable of making intercession and sacrificial offering for humanity; as divine Son his act of sacrificial offering has infinite value to the Father (Heb. 4:15).

If the one who died on the cross were only human and not Son of God, the death could not serve sufficiently as an act of atonement for the whole world. If the one who died were only God and not human, there would have been no basis for celebrating the empathy of God with humanity. Only a mediator fully divine and fully human could undergo the experience necessary to save humanity.

Conclusion: What the Work Requires,
Only This Person Bestows

Here the unifying principle of Christology reappears: What the mediatorial work requires, the mediatorial person supplies: being very God while being thoroughly human (Rom. 1:3–4), equal with God, empathic with humanity (Phil. 2:6–7)—distinguishable yet inseparable in one person—Word made flesh (John 1:14; Pope, *Compend.* 2: 110).

The theandric logic and the triune logic necessarily interface: *Christ is one person, two natures; God is three persons, one in essence.* If God were only one person, God could not send, yet be sent; be both the Giver of law and obedient to it; both offer intercession for humanity and receive the prayers of humanity; both justify and sanctify, making just and making whole.

When Christ is worshiped, he is not worshiped just as the divine nature of the eternal Son, but as incarnate (enfleshed!) Lord. John of Damascus summed up centuries of debate: "And we do not say that His body is not to be adored, because it is adored in the one Person of the Word who became Person to it. Yet we do not worship the creature, because we do not adore it as a mere body, but as being one with the divinity" (*OF* 3.8).

OUR LORD'S EARTHLY LIFE

7

THE PROCLAIMER PROCLAIMED

The Historical Jesus

As the Epistles and Gospels were being written, many remaining eyewitnesses were still alive. At the time of Paul's writing to Corinth, "most" of the "more than five hundred" witnesses to the resurrection were "still living" (1 Cor. 15:6). This must have restrained the authors from private embellishments and speculations. For if their account could have been easily dismissed by living eyewitnesses, the rest of what they said would not be taken seriously.

The early Christian teachers fused the various canonically received pictures of Jesus in a single Gestalt (Tatian, *Diatessaron*; Augustine, *The Harmony of the Gospels*). There is some evidence that an oral tradition undergirding the written texts was recognized. Origen, Athanasius, Basil, Jerome, and Augustine carried on early forms of textual and literary criticism.

The Gospel writers were not trying to write scientific biographies using modern research criteria. They were rather promising in the presence of God to tell the story accurately, "just as they were delivered to us by those who from the beginning were eyewitnesses" (Luke 1:2; Cyril of Alex., *Letter* 67.4). "The Word of God was seen and heard by the apostles. They saw the Lord, not only according to the body but also according to the Word" (Ambrose, *Expos. of Luke* 1.5).

In accurately chronicling this narrative, they were amazed at how often the actual story of Jesus' life and death was clearly fulfilling ancient Hebraic prophecy (Ammonius, *Catena of the Acts* 17.12–13). This does not imply that their views were distorted by their exhilaration over what they were reporting. Rather, by telling the story just as it happened they discovered that the promises of

Scripture were being fulfilled in Jesus' life. "What the apostles received, they passed on without change, so that the doctrine of the mysteries (the sacraments) and Christ would remain correct" (Athanasius, *Festal Letter* 2.7).

His Birth and Death Provide the Clues to the Other Events of His Life

Between Jesus' birth and death are a prolonged series of events that form the core narrative of the Gospels. Yet they are hardly mentioned in the early baptismal creeds. For example, there is no mention whatever in the baptismal confessions of the early events of his life or of his baptism, his temptation, his manner of life, or his healing, teaching, and proclaiming activity. The Apostles' Creed moves from "born of the Virgin Mary" directly to "suffered under Pontius Pilate." Why leap from Mary to Pilate?

The recollection of Jesus' earthly life was overshadowed by the interpretation of the events surrounding his death. His life was viewed by its earliest rememberers as decisively illuminated by his death and resurrection.

All candidates for baptism are expected to know the gist of the narrative told in the four Gospels. Yet in the baptismal creeds the transition from his birth to his death is abrupt, as if getting him born, buried and resurrected was the heart of the story. Why?

The apostles believed that the incarnation and resurrection held all the essential clues to the meaning of all other events of his earthly ministry. These two mysteries, the events surrounding his birth and death, are the anchor events of Christian year and of the life of Jesus. They govern the rest of the story. The interpretation of the events of Jesus' earthly ministry is fundamentally illumined by his divine sonship and resurrection.

The salvation of the faithful does not depend upon specific or detailed historical knowledge of the events of his earthly life. This is why the Apostles' Creed "passes at once in the best order from the birth of Christ to his death and resurrection" (Calvin, *Inst.* 2.16.5). The focus is upon what is necessary for salvation.

The Emergence of Distorted Modern Portraits of Jesus

Although the apostolic testimony to Jesus is clear, the overall result of modern Jesus criticism has been ambiguous.

The case today does not stand much differently a hundred years later than it did in 1906 when Albert Schweitzer dourly wrote: "There is nothing more negative than the result of the research into the life of Jesus. The Jesus of Nazareth who appeared upon the scene as the Messiah, proclaimed the morality of the kingdom of God, founded the kingdom of Heaven upon earth and died to consecrate his work never existed. He is a figure sketched by rationalism, brought to life by liberalism and clothed by modern theology with historical scholarship. This image has not been destroyed from the outside; it has collapsed internally, shaken and riven by the actual historical problems" (*The Quest of the Historical Jesus*:388; J. Peter, *Finding the Historical Jesus*). The collapse to which Schweitzer referred has once again recurred in new form in the inability of historical criticism to provide a sufficient ground for Christian preaching and worship.

It is not our purpose to provide a thorough review of the history of Jesus research, but it is necessary to set the question of the historical Jesus in the context of recent study of him. There has emerged in modern Christian history a prolific variety of differing pictures of Jesus (H. R. Niebuhr, *Christ and Culture*; Bornkamm, *JN*; H. Anderson, ed., *Jesus*). Thus it is not a meaningless detour to review how the Jesus portraiture of modern historical research emerged.

The Enlightenment Moralization of the History of Jesus

In today's culture Jesus is typically approached not as *theanthropos* or enfleshed Son of God but as a good man and reliable moral teacher. Among circles most strongly shaped by Enlightenment thinking on the basis of empirical reasoning, Christ's divinity and theandric union were of decreasing interest.

More recently the focus of modern studies of his earthly life has shifted away from the texts and toward his social location, his ideas, his political interests, teachings, pragmatic usefulness, and moral significance. The dream that has driven historians for two centuries is the thought that they might discover through historical study some real Jesus that could stand as a distinct improvement over the less palatable Christ attested in the first century language of the Scriptures. These studies do not attempt to recover the full weight of the doctrines of Trinity, preexistence, eternal sonship, and incarnation, which is where classic Christianity begins to tell the story. The tradition following German liberalism (Schleiermacher to Harnack) tended to narrow statements about Christ to inferences from the consciousness of human experience of the transition from guilt to redemption. Thus our consciousness of salvation becomes the base point, not God's saving action.

In nineteenth-century Europe, Christology became a subject that was preemptively undertaken by those pretending an objective view, who stood outside the circle of the worshiping community. With Hegel and those following immediately after him (Strauss, Feuerbach, Bauer, Biedermann, and others), there appeared an armada of modern "Christologies" determined to take charge of university studies in religion. Hegel reconceived Christ as a philosophical principle, a symbol of world process through which reason was becoming self-realized through the conflicts of history. David Friedrich Strauss presented an alleged "Jesus" without any supposed "mythical" elements. From these there followed a long string of "lives of Jesus" (Renan, Edersheim, Glover, Weiss), mostly amounting to humanistic biographies lacking almost all reference to Christ's eternal sonship, the premise so crucial to New Testament writers. Ritschl followed Kant in attaching to Jesus the idea of the perfect moral personality who founds a universal moral community to work toward the kingdom of God on earth (Ritschl, *CDJR*; Kant, *Religion with the Limits of Reason Alone*).

The Altered Face

Since the resultant "Christ" had become completely altered, their whole view of Christianity became altered, for there is no way to change the teaching concerning Jesus Christ without changing every other aspect of Christianity—its teaching of Trinity, creation, providence, human existence, salvation, ethics, the church, ministry, and sacraments. An abandonment of classic teaching concerning Jesus Christ is tantamount to the abandonment of historic Christianity.

These trends have resulted in an overriding tendency to project upon the history of Jesus a modern moral perspective alien to the texts themselves—a human striving for salvation, the desire for moral self-redemption, and the increasing politicization of theology. Feuerbach and Freud concluded that all references to God are merely projections of human needs. This fantastic procedure of reduction maintained some cache until modernity itself collapsed (as described in *After Modernity What?*).

The moralistic Christ that emerged out of the period of German liberalism has indeed been in disrepute since Schweitzer among scholarly circles but still plays sentimentally in the universities and churches of liberal Christianity. "The Christ that Harnack sees, looking back through nineteen centuries of Catholic darkness, is only the reflection of a Liberal Protestant face seen at the bottom of a deep well" (G. Tyrell, *Christianity at the Cross-Roads*).

How The Quest for Jesus' History Became Distorted

The Abandonment of the Theandric Premise

Twentieth-century liberal studies of Jesus almost entirely unburdened themselves of the very theandric premise that enables the texts to be coherently interpreted, thereby making "Christology" seem to be virtually an oxymoron. The study of the New Testament has become plagued with absurdities lacking the very premise that the text itself considers essential.

It took a long time to become fully evident that the "historical Jesus" being sought was largely a fantasy based upon philosophical biases and not upon fair or thoroughgoing historical investigation.

The "lives of Jesus" movement (from Strauss through Renan and Wrede) was in Schweitzer's view an exercise in modern literary imagination that said more about modernity than about Jesus. Renan viewed Jesus as the noblest of all men and the type of the evolution of the human race, but not God-incarnate. Schweitzer focused upon the very feature that liberal pictures of Jesus had most neglected: his imminent eschatology, especially in passages that expected immediately the apocalyptic woes of the last days; and when the end did not appear, he surrendered himself to martyrdom, unaware that he would be later called the Christ.

By the time of Bultmann, the proclamation of the early church had replaced Jesus as the object of intense study. Bultmann considered the historical criticism of the Gospels a scientific matter and the kerygma embedded in the Gospels as an existential matter for personal decision. Accordingly, faith in the kerygma is not subject to historical verification. Criticism cannot embarrass faith. There is a salvation event, but it does not include a resurrection, only a cross as an event that took place in history. The resurrection occurred to the disciples, not to Jesus. Little can be known of Jesus except that he elicited the kerygma. Preaching may still point to a bare *that* (*Dass, that* Jesus elicited the kerygma), but not to *what* he did or said. Jesus is posited as that event from which the kerygma derived its interpretation (Bultmann, *TNT* 1; *Essays Philosophical and Theological; Jesus Christ and Mythology*). "To believe in such an eviscerated *Dass* is to us certainly a crucifixion of the intellect," countered Bernhard Ramm, "for it asks us to believe in an event from which every shred of the personal must be abstracted" (*EC*:156). The historian's Pyrrhic victory over the evidence had finally been announced—their conclusion is that nothing at all is reliably knowable of Jesus.

The New Quest Followed the Old in Ruling Out the Theandric Premise

In popular academic studies of Jesus, as distinguished from the worshiping community: "Old Liberalism thought it had discovered an ethical prophet. Schweitzer discovered an apocalyptic Jesus, who he himself admits is not a help but an offense to modern man. Bultmann became skeptical of ever reconstructing the historical Jesus. The post-Bultmannians, illustrated by Bornkamm and Robinson, have found an existential Jesus who achieved authentic existence" (Ladd, *TNT*:178–79). The "historical Jesus" that has emerged has become a "fifth Gospel and the test of the other four" (H. Schlier, *Das Ende der Zeit* 3:11; Stuhlmacher, *HCTIS*: 71).

What was thought to be a clarifying simplification (the mandatory and absolute abandonment of the theandric premise) had the unintended effect of making New Testament interpretation much more strained, defensive, obtuse, and complicated.

Meanwhile the New Testament text stubbornly insists upon divine sonship, and to study the text without its essential premise is to search despairingly for an alternative to its premise. Under such circumstances, the text has only one means by which to defend itself against alien and preemptive interpreters—its own straightforward and resilient language.

Thesis: A postcritical inquiry into the life of Jesus is due. It can only be postcritical by proceeding as the texts themselves proceed—with, not without, the theandric premise. Why did it take so long for Jesus research to realize this?

The Classic Christian Theandric Starting Point

The postcritical study of the historical Jesus has not yet begun in our time, because the theandric union has not been taken seriously. Once the documents' own central premise is received as the beginning point, then the historical study of Jesus can resume.

If we take the New Testament rather than modern naturalistic reductionism as our starting point, then everywhere we turn in the texts we are being met by one who is thoroughly human who claimed to be God. Throughout the texts he is attested as Son of God, and according to Christian confession was God-incarnate. Little attempt is made in the texts to theorize about how that could or could not be. No attempt is made to protect Jesus from the charge of paradox, for he was from the outset a *skandalon*, "a stumbling block to Jews and foolishness to Gentiles" (1 Cor. 1:23; Kierkegaard, *TC*).

Two certainties are most deeply shared by all writers of the New Testament: that Jesus was fully human, and that in him God has personally appeared in our midst. Christian teaching seeks to account for that unusual confluence of testimony. The way is narrow that leads to an adequate statement of Jesus Christ, one that avoids the polar errors of diminishing either his humanity or deity.

The Ecumenical Consensus

The ancient ecumenical consensus is clear: The study of the incarnate Lord begins neither with divinity or humanity abstractly, but by meeting personally Jesus Christ, the unique theandric person, God-man, one person divine and human as attested unanimously by the eyewitness apostles.

In recent decades the teaching of evidences for the incarnation has hardly been universally accepted as a self-evident starting point for meeting Christ. Modern academic approaches prefer to begin with the man Jesus and attempt to show how deity came to be dubiously ascribed to him in one way or another. The method is called "*Christology from below*," i.e., the attempt to reach Jesus by stripping him of all reference to his deity, and by strictly applying bare historical and empiricist criteria to the incarnational mystery.

This appeared at first to be a constructive renewal of Christology, yet typically ended either by denying Christ's deity altogether or losing it in a morass of critical speculation. In the hands of reductionist critics, the classical Christian affirmation of the true humanity of *theanthropos* quickly becomes diluted into the mere humanity of an itinerant preacher. This stripping can occur by means of various methods: sociological, psychological, historical, and political.

The deeper sympathies of this study are with the classical ecumenical procedure that begins, as did John's Gospel, by speaking first to last of the embodied Word made flesh. It is possible, however, without denying that commitment, to include in the study of Christ a careful textually grounded inquiry into the history of Jesus, a history that moves inexorably toward his death. The events surrounding his death came to impinge upon the terms that his rememberers used to describe and report him. Yet such an examination is prone to forget the theandric union that alone makes the text worth reading if the text itself is telling the truth.

The Critical Inquiry Follows Only from the Scandal of the Incarnation

The witness of the apostles and ancient church teachers did not begin by simply taking for granted Jesus' full deity and full humanity. Rather they set forth a chronicle of the events of history—centering in the resurrection—that constituted their reason for receiving Jesus as God's own embodied Word. These witnesses have a historical datum to deal with: the God-man, a person who was born and died not outside, but in history.

The God-man (*theanthropos*) of the New Testament is always one person, human and divine, hence neither from below reductionistically or from above exclusively, but always an actual, historical, divine-human person.

God's saving action is not directly accessible to so-called objective historical investigation when that investigation proceeds prejudicially with criteria that rule out God, thereby ruling out the precise subject at hand of the New Testament: *theanthropos*.

Jesus as Set Forth in the Sacred Text

The classic view does not impede critical inquiry into the historical process through which Jesus was received and recognized as divine Son. The critical inquiry to which the New Testament invites all requires freedom to explore the oral and written traditions in which Jesus was received in due time as Son of God without denying the personal union of incarnate Lord. That critical freedom of inquiry is not yet guaranteed in the modern university.

When we meet the Jesus of the text, he is constantly calling us to a decision. It is a decision about who he is. Historical scholarship wants to suspend judgment while these facts are being examined. Yet the decisive question persists in the New Testament texts: Is Jesus really the expected One?

The Jesus of the texts presses us closely: you must decide, yes or no. The decisive *skandalon* of the Gospel question is: Does the evidence show that Jesus indeed is the Anointed One? Only in facing this question does the critical inquiry into Jesus begin.

Classic Christianity does not rule out the "inquiry from below." Rather it views historical inquiry itself as being questioned and transmuted by the fact of *theanthropos*. This is the decisive historical datum to be inquired into, insofar as imperfect historical inquiry can approach revelation.

For two millennia there have been those who said that the resurrection did not happen to Jesus, but only to those who remembered him, that he was later proclaimed as Messiah and much later as God by those whose faith had emerged after his death. This view has reappeared in Bultmann's writings. Others have recently argued that Jesus did not regard himself as Lord, but after his resurrection was so regarded by his disciples. Hence Christological reasoning begins with the event of Jesus' resurrection and works backward to the incarnation. Jesus' divine sonship becomes rightly identified only in the light of Jesus' resurrection. This view has been set forth powerfully by W. Pannenberg.

The apostolic texts themselves state the point differently. They attest that Jesus in his last days in Jerusalem clearly made himself known as Lord, Messiah, and Son of God. Hence the basic assumptions of Christology concerning Jesus' divine-human identity are found in Jesus' own life and proclamation, not exclusively in postresurrection insight of the disciples. This is the classical view. In this chapter, I will set forth reasons why the first view (that of Bultmann, Braun, Buri, Marxsen, and Tillich) was unable to account for the power of the early Christian witness. I will argue for the classical Christian consensus, which is shared by, among recent writers, Barth, Manson, Taylor, Ladd, Guthrie, Wells, Ramm, Fitzmeyer, and Ratzinger, and include within it certain aspects of the view of Pannenberg.

The Part Jesus Himself Played in the Formation of the Teaching of Christ

The roots of the earliest views of Jesus' identity are found in Jesus himself. He himself decisively impacted the historical transition from Jesus the proclaimer of the kingdom to Jesus the One proclaimed. After much preparation, he willingly received the ascription of the Anointed One of God, sent to inaugurate the kingdom as God's own coming to save humanity.

The teaching and transfiguration narratives indicate that he was actively preparing his disciples for the events surrounding his death which revealed his identity and destiny. Jesus' messianic identity was not determined exclusively by the disciples' postresurrection insight, but by Jesus' own leading, guiding, and teaching of the disciples about himself before and after the resurrection.

The pivotal transition is *from* Jesus' preaching *to* the church's memory. The narrative moves from his proclamation of the coming kingdom toward the major clue that he himself is the sign of its coming, and from there *to* the church's memory of Jesus viewed primarily through the lens of his death and resurrection (Cullmann, *CNT*; Longenecker, *CEJC*; Fuller, *FNTC*; J. A. T. Robinson, *Twelve NT Studies; The Human Face of God*; Marshall, *ONTC*; C. F. D. Moule, *OC*; J. Knox, *The Humanity and Divinity of Christ*; H. Conzelmann, *TNT*; V. Taylor, *The Formation of the Gospel Tradition*, Braaten, *ChrD* I; Perrin, *MPNTC*). Jesus himself played the decisive role in the transition from preacher to Preached One.

Following the Sequence of the Transition from Proclaimer to Proclaimed

Before the Resurrection

The reign of God is the central feature of Jesus' public ministry. He came preaching the kingdom. There is hardly a firmer point of consensus in modern Scripture studies.

A crucial reversal occurred in Jesus' ministry. The expected reign of God introduced God himself in personal form to the world. The kingdom that was coming is now recognized as God's own personal coming. That means the kingdom appears when God personally appears. The kingdom is inaugurated when God's own power is incomparably and personally manifested. Those who order their lives in relation to the kingdom live as open to the coming of God.

There can be no doubt that Jesus' preaching awakened and intensified the expectation of God's own imminent coming. His acts of healing and exorcism were signs of God's own coming. His parables pointed to the way God comes to humanity in his only beloved Son.

But Jesus' personal presence meant more: His proclamation of the coming reign of God required of his hearers a direct decision for or against that coming, and about himself as its evidence. He himself is the evidence.

The evidence is personal—a real person embodying the Word of God to humanity: "I am the way" (John 14:6). "He who is the way does not lead us into by-paths or trackless wastes. He who is the truth does not mock us with lies. He who is the life does not betray us into delusions which are death. He himself has chosen these winning names to indicate the methods that he has appointed for our salvation. As the way, he will guide us to the truth. As the truth, he will establish us in the life" (Hilary, *Trin.* 7.33).

A decision must be faced by each hearer. It must be made now. Why? There is no more time remaining before God's own coming. Since God's coming is now, all are called urgently to repent and trust in God's emergent rule. To delay is to say no.

After the Resurrection

After the resurrection the lens for viewing the life of Jesus was their experience of his living presence. What they remembered as having occurred before the resurrection was transmuted in a decisive way by the present risen Lord and the abundant recollections of his appearances.

The rememberers of Jesus looked back to him as the Anointed One who fulfilled the promises that God had made to Israel. They understood that the reign of God was appearing and that he was its evidence. He constituted God's own coming into history, God's own Word to humanity. The new start for humanity that the Father had begun in the Son would be finally completed by his coming again on the last day, as he had promised.

It is mistaken to imagine that the postresurrection frame distorted their perception. Rather it sharpened the acuity of their perception of earlier events. This point is pressed inordinately if it asserts that the disciples after the resurrection lost all touch with the actual historical reality of Jesus, and all they could remember was the Jesus they romanticized through the memory of the resurrection. The resurrection, indeed, transmuted their understanding of Jesus' ministry, for it declared that he was Son of God. He was "designated Son of God in power according to the Spirit to holiness by his resurrection from the dead" (Rom. 1:4; Origen, *Comm. on Rom.* 1.4). That can hardly be said to be a diminution of insight. Rather it was an eye-opener: They more crisply realized what had been happening to them all along. Shortly thereafter, after verbally proclaiming this everywhere they could, they began to write the documents we now have as our only access to these events.

The disciples did not invent this insight without Jesus (Taylor, *LMJ*). Rather Jesus nurtured and elicited this recognition in both his earthly and postresurrection ministry (Luke 9:45–47; 24:44–45; Irenaeus, *Ag. Her.* 5.1–3).

The Confession of Lordship

If I Heal, Then the Kingdom Has Come

The issue now narrows to its sharpest point: Did Jesus merely point to God's coming reign to follow, or was he in his person God's own personal coming into history? That in fact was the decision Jesus put to the disciples both before and after the resurrection.

John the Baptist had preached the imminent coming kingdom of God. Jesus, however, was not regarded merely as one who pointed to a coming kingdom, but as one who inaugurated the kingdom, who established it, the One through whom God's own coming became decisively manifested.

Jesus preached: "If I drive out demons by the finger of God, then the kingdom of God has come to you" (Luke 11:20; Cyril of Alex.; *Comm. on Luke,* Hom. 80, 81). This is widely acknowledged even by the most skeptical critics as embedded in the earliest layer of sayings of Jesus in the oral tradition.

This and similar sayings may be the core layer of the earliest ascriptions of deity to Jesus made by the disciples and received by Jesus himself. If so, the most primitive Christology is already embedded quietly in his eschatological proclamation of his own role in God's imminent coming. Accordingly, the decision one makes for or against Jesus entirely determines one's relation to God's coming (Mark 1:21–28; 8:29; Irenaeus, *Ag. Her.,* 4.6.6–7). Even critics who view ascriptions of deity to Jesus as being of a much later period nonetheless view Jesus as the one through whom the kingdom comes.

Resurrection as Evidence of Identity

What specifically happened to enable the rememberers to move from their memory of Jesus the proclaimer to the worship of Jesus as Anointed of God, Son of God, Son of Man? The short answer: resurrection. The more precise answer will await the examination ahead of biblical texts relating to events surrounding Jesus' death.

His death and resurrection stood as a demonstration—the Father's own historical way of proving—that the Son was the expected one of Israel, anointed to inaugurate God's kingdom, to bring salvation, and to offer a once-for-all priesthood of sacrifice for the sins of humanity. *The cross was viewed as a sacrifice for humanity's sin and the resurrection as a vindication of Jesus' earthly ministry and deity. The single event of cross/resurrection constituted an unprecedented victory over sin, guilt, and death and a binding up of the power of evil.*

In this way the history of Jesus and God's coming reign coalesce. The one person is both proclaimer of the kingdom and proclaimed in the kingdom. The preaching of Jesus was gradually transformed by his own risen presence into the church's preaching about Jesus.

It did not take the disciples long to learn to say, "Jesus is Lord" (Rom. 10:9; 1 Cor. 12:3; Phil. 2:11). This learning did not emerge gradually over decades through a slow hellenization process or gradual accretions of messianic insight. Rather it came abruptly for many and with great power in the immediate awareness of the risen Lord present amid the remembering community. The confession "Jesus is Lord" could easily have been made on the very day the resurrected Lord was first met, and in some it occurred earlier.

This explains why the early rememberers were found so diligently "searching the scriptures" (John 5:39)— especially the prophets and psalms, to grasp how those expectations were being fulfilled in "these last days" (Heb. 1:2). The rememberers did not search the Scriptures to concoct supposed events that occurred to Jesus. Rather the events that occurred to Jesus caused them to search the Scriptures to understand better what had actually happened to him (Chrysostom, *Hom. on John,* 40.3). They first beheld his entry into Jerusalem and only then recalled its connection with Zechariah's prophecy (9:9).

Confirming the Reliability of Apostolic Texts

The question then becomes: Can New Testament report be trusted? The solution to this puzzle has been greatly assisted by four compelling arguments that cumulatively confirm an affirmative answer: the brevity of time between the death of Jesus and the letters of Paul; the late Judaic practice of detailed memorization; and the shared community of worship and teaching that formed early and resisted amendment; and the determination of the Father to communicate his love to humanity through his Son. These are all empirically based arguments—reasoning based on evidence.

First, If the length of time between the event and its recollection is extensive, doubt increases as the opportunity for embellishment arises. One case in point deserves special note—the brevity of time between the resurrection and the beginning of apostolic testimony, especially in the case of Paul.

If Mark wrote near the destruction of Jerusalem (AD 70) then there would only be about forty years in which major mutations of the tradition could have taken place. If Paul began writing about AD 50, that time frame is reduced to twenty years. 1 Corinthians 15:1–7 identified the older apostolic tradition that Paul received, not one that he subsequently invented. That tradition apparently dates to only a few months after Jesus' death (Ramm, *EC*: 121–23).

Herbert Butterfield has argued that the essential interpretation of Jesus was largely settled within the first twenty years after Jesus' death (*Writings on Christianity and History*). If so, there is little to recommend the highly speculative theories of critics that enormous mutations of culture and consciousness had time to take place between Jesus and the memory of Jesus (see Hengel, *Between Jesus and Paul*).

Second, the Jewish pedagogy of that period stressed precise memorization of long passages of sacred writing (B. Gerhardsson, *Memory and Manuscript*). It is hard for us to imagine a culture that puts a high value upon the accurate recollection of oral traditions, since we are so heavily dependent upon written and electronic communications of all sorts (M. Wilson, "The Jewish Concept of Learning: A Christian Appreciation," *Christian Scholars' Review* 5:350–63). Our modern memories are not nearly as well developed as the functional memories of those committed to sustaining a tradition of testimony through memorization.

Third, classical Christianity proceeds with a general trust in the shared consensus of the reports about Jesus. It is based not only on the trustworthiness of a particular eyewitnesses, but on the consensus of many eyewitnesses in concert.

Fourth, and more importantly there is a crucial argument concerning providence that enters into all early Christian reasoning about the reliability of the apostolic testimony: if God determines to offer salvation to humanity in Christ, and if that offer must be transmitted through first oral and then written testimony, then it is not plausible that God would allow that testimony to be falsified. God would not come to humanity in a costly way, only to allow humanity to immediately forget, misunderstand, or distort it. God's own Spirit would not allow the church to be led drastically astray in the recollection and canonization process. That argument proceeds from the premise that the Spirit created the church.

The Risen Lord: The Authoritative Interpreter of His Own Narrative

Was it the case that a series of distinctly different or even competing views of Jesus Christ developed of early Christian preaching? Did conflicting Christologies thus emerge in the earliest Palestinian context as so often reported in contemporary theology? Were the earliest of these substantively different from later expressions of the Gentile mission? Did the focus shift from Jesus' death to his exaltation and belatedly to the message of redemption? The early apostolic consensus resisted these notions of a developing series of different Christologies on the ground that the central narrative was protected from distortion by the Holy Spirit, and that the apostles were in profound sort of agreement that only the Spirit can create (for careful arguments, see Fuller, *FNTC*; Marshall, *ONTC*; Hahn, *TJC*; Cullmann, *CNT*).

The tendency of the narratives of apostolic preaching in the New Testament letters and Acts ran directly against the hypothesis so trendy today that the basic core of Christological teaching required a long period of time for development that finally confessed Jesus as Lord. The nucleus of the preaching of the Gentile mission was already present in the Palestinian church. The preaching of Acts provides glimpses of its earliest inclination to trust the unifying power of the Holy Spirit who was the major impetus for the creation of the church. "The lordship of Christ is a case in point. It is tampering with the evidence to suggest that this was not grasped by the Palestinian church" (Guthrie, *NTT*:403; Acts. 2:36).

The texts attest that it was the resurrected Lord himself who led the church to an interpretation of his earthly ministry (Luke 24:25–27), not the other way around (Augustine, *Sermon* 236.2; Cyril of Alex., *Comm. on Luke* 24). The church was not forced by emergent cultural challenges to interpret Jesus as having been resurrected and belatedly viewed as Son of God. This is a fantastic conjecture for which no adequate evidence exists. It is a desperate hypothesis invented by desperate modern skeptics who are revulsed by the text itself. In order to defend their fantasy, they must invent even the conditions for its emergence.

It was Jesus, present through the power of the Spirit, who did the interpreting, according to the memory of the apostles. Paul wrote: "We have not received the spirit of the world but the Spirit who is from God, that we may understand what God has freely given us. This is what we speak, not in words taught us by human wisdom but in words taught by the Spirit, expressing spiritual truths in spiritual words. The man without the Spirit does not accept the things that come from the Spirit of God, for they are foolishness to him, and he cannot understand them, because they are spiritually discerned" (1 Cor. 2:12–14; Theodoret, *Comm. on 1 Cor* 178).

That Christ is now alive remains the chief premise of Christian teaching. Lacking that premise, Christianity is easily turned into tedious moral obligations, pretentious sounding historical research, unsufferably vague speculative philosophy, or desperate self-help psychology.

Can Jesus Be Explained?

The question "Can this person (Jesus Christ) be explained?" raises the larger question of whether any person can be explained. To explain (*explanare*) literally means to flatten out or make something level or plain so as to bring it down to ordinary understanding. To explain something is to classify it. No person can be explained exhaustively. One explains finally only things, not persons.

Jesus, being unique, fits even less neatly into our preset categories, since there is no class into which he can readily be placed. Theandric personal union happened only once. Christianity asks that Jesus first be met and then interpreted, not first explained and then sought.

A standard eighteenth-century Enlightenment attempt at a flat explanation of Jesus, however, remains fixed dogma in chic academic circles. The explanation runs this way: the extraordinary admiration of the disciples for their leader gradually turned into reverence, which evolved into superstition, which then projected miracles onto previously innocuous events. Such an explanation says more about the explainers than about the one being explained.

The One Lord Elicited the Unified Interpretation

The more plausible evidence indicates that the theandric person himself provided unity and interpretation to the disciples, engendering unexpected confidence and hope, knitting them into a community of proclamation that "turned the world upside down" (Acts 17:6). It was Jesus himself personally who first called forth the worshiping community, not the community that called forth the risen person. It was not the rememberers who invented the mission, but the mission who called forth the rememberers.

There are indeed differences in reports about Jesus, none reflecting doctrinal disagreement, yet their very diversity lends strength to the centered authenticity of their varied testimony. The diversity of documents and witnesses makes their underlying personal unity all the more impressive. The worshiping community has always found nourishment precisely in the variety of these testimonies—in some periods some witnesses are stressed more than others, but in time the whole canon is needed for an adequate mosaic of Christ. They portray a single God-man, not alternatives between God and man.

There are literary differences that emerge out of varied authors speaking to varied audiences, speaking within different cultural settings and employing different conceptual resources to proclaim the good news of God's coming. The differences do not arise out of opposing views of Christ's identity, but out of the variety of contexts his risen life was affecting. The references set forth in this chapter seek to show commulatively that the New Testament sources and the history of their interpretation constitute a single stream whose unity of direction is powerful enough to include, absorb, and provide corrective cohesion for numerous varieties of interpretation, as long as the theandric core is in place.

The Personal Unity of Canonical Diversity

Systematic theology is an extension of baptismal formula, creed, and catechism, which themselves are "an epitome and brief transcript of the entire Holy Scripture" (Luther, *Large Catech.*).

If classical Christology is to be challenged, it must be questioned on the basis of the texts to which it understands itself to be accountable. If scholars look at these texts and do not like what they see, if the portrait does not appeal to them, they do well to resist the temptation to "retouch it, lest they be found guilty of trying to correct the Wisdom of God by the wisdom of man" (W. M. Horton, Forward, J. W. Bowman, *The Intention of Jesus*).

The unity that coheres in Jesus himself takes complementary expressions in the New Testament. Christ is not attested with a single monotonous voice, but with a vast choir of voices in a cast of thousands. The unity of the mosaic of voices is grasped by viewing them in concert. There are villains, bums, heroes, and ordinary folk in the drama Scripture attests.

Jesus himself is the unifying personal center of cohesion of these diverse writings. The cohesion of New Testament documents is seen in the one person to whom they all refer and who elicited and made possible these diverse glimpses of that one person. That cohesion is not best grasped by juxtaposing texts merely as scholastic proof-texts, but personally—by penetrating to the singular theandric person, Jesus Christ, to whom the early kerygma, confessions, and liturgies so clearly witness.

The Academy's Prevailing Myth of the Myth About Jesus

There is a fashionable academic myth about "the myth of Jesus" which runs something like this: Jesus was an eschatological prophet who proclaimed God's coming kingdom, but did not regard himself as Messiah or Son of God. He called his hearers to decide now for or against that kingdom. After he was condemned to death and died, the belief emerged that he had arisen. Only after an extended period of oral history did the remembering community develop the idea that Jesus would return as the Messiah, Son of Man. Eventually this community came to project its eschatological expectation back upon the historical Jesus, inserting in his mouth the eschatological hopes that it had subsequently developed but now deftly had to rearrange so as to make it seem as if Jesus himself had understood himself as Messiah. Only much later did the Hellenistic idea of the God-man, the virgin birth, and incarnation emerge in the minds of the remembering church, who again misremembered Jesus according to its revised eschatological expectation.

This academic guild myth portrays Jesus as being naively used by his disciples for purposes he never intended. It has prevailed in university studies of Jesus during much of the past century. The secular press loves this myth. It is nonsense projected as if it were scientific history by revisionist historians and their sycophants.

The Implausibility of the Myth

How such a vacuous, implausible interpretation could have come to be widely accepted is itself perplexing enough. Even less plausible is the conjecture that the earliest rememberers would actually suffer martyrdom for such a tenuous cause. One wonders how those deluded believers of early centuries gained the courage to risk everything to go into an unknown world to preach and die for this message that came from an imagined revolution of a fantasized divine-human Mediator. This "critical" premise itself requires a high threshold of gullibility.

Yet it is no exaggeration to say that these views prevail in many if not most academic settings where biblical studies are fragmentarily occurring within the prevailing naturalistic assumptions of modernity. Biblical studies in the look-alike liberal seminaries doggedly echo these mythic patterns.

To anyone accustomed to allowing historical documents to speak for themselves, such an interpretation seems patently absurd. It seems to ordinary Christians more plausible to believe that God became flesh than to credit such a circuitous series of hypotheses and speculations. This in fact is why the believing church has paid so little attention to historical criticism, and why it is so seldom preached and is virtually unpreachable with a straight face (Maier, *EHCM*; G. Klein, *Bibelkritik als Predigthilfe*).

Some would prefer it not be mentioned in polite company that the older official Marxist view of Jesus corresponds almost hand in glove with this curious view: the Jesus portrayed in the New Testament is a second-century mythical projection of writers whose views can best be explained in terms of social location, economic determinism, and class conflict (Marx, "Luther as Arbiter Between Strauss and Feuerbach," *Writings of the Young Marx*; Lenin, "Socialism and Religion," see *Soviet Encyclopedia*, s.v. "Jesus").

The University Where the Myth of Tolerance is Perpetuated

The achievement of an ethic of tolerance in western culture was largely an attainment inspired and informed by classic Christian teaching. The university as a context for the relatively free market of ideas is largely an invention of patristic and medieval Christianity with beginnings in Alexandria, Paris, Oxford, Padua, and Prague, where classic Christian teaching was a strong component of the prevailing worldview. Later the Renaissance universities sought to integrate Christian learning with the wisdom of the ancients (H. Rashdall, *The Universities of Europe in the Middle Ages* I; P. Stuhlmacher, *HCTIC*). In religious toleration movements, leading roles were played by Menno Simons, John Milton, Lord Baltimore, Jeremy Taylor, Richard Baxter, Joseph Butler, and Roger Williams— all firmly grounded in Christian teachings of salvation.

Modernity has taken this toleration ethic, gradually forgetting its roots, and imagined ignorantly that it did not exist before modern times, and, under the pretense of a secularized toleration, has proceeded to rule out ancient Christian wisdom systematically from its curricula, preventing its being taught even as a hypothesis (Oden, *Requiem*). Academic Christianity has hoped that it might gain working credit with Enlightenment advocates who think of themselves as tolerationist, but who have difficulty tolerating even the most bland or preliminary inquiry into God.

The Truncated University

Meanwhile the disciplines of the modern university have become increasingly trapped in empiricist methodological reductionisms. Philosophy dutifully ceased speaking of wisdom or the meaning of history and confined its work largely to the analysis of language or logic. Psychology in the empiricist tradition has tried to reduce human behavior to discrete calculable determinants, objectifiable in terms of laboratory experimentation. In due course historical analysis was drastically infected by the empiricist passion to flatten and quantify historical data and to rule out evidence deemed unqualified under empirical assumptions.

It is in this sort of truncated university that Christian teaching has recently sought wherever possible to speak the truth about Jesus Christ. Seeking a hearing in historical circles, theology's own methods have inadvertently become correspondingly reductionistic. Biblical studies have become the slave of a particular philosophy: naturalistic empiricism. Classic Christian teaching of Christ must never again try to gain credentials in an ailing university at the cost of selling its birthright. Christ as taught by the apostles brings a view of universal history, creation to consummation, that can never be reduced to the methods of naturalistic reductionism.

Guild critics have a penchant for holding on to distortions that fit their predispositions long after the facts should have dispelled those distortions. For example, it was once thought that there was a pre-Christian "Gnostic redeemer myth", which was later adapted to the memory of Jesus' death (Bultmann, *TNT* 1). For decades it has become increasingly clear that textual fragments that point to a redeemer among Gnostic sources were derived from early Christian preaching, not vice versa. It was once held that the virgin birth narratives had numerous parallels in history of religions. Now it is clear that the New Testament nativity narratives differ markedly from the lusty mythic generativity of the Greek pantheon and that the literary roots of New Testament narratives come from the Old Testament, not Hellenistic influences. It was once widely thought that pre-Pauline Hellenistic Christian congregations infused the memory of Jesus with Hellenisms. Now it is clear that "these Hellenistic congregations were invented by German scholars in the early years of [the 20th] century" (Neill, *TGI*: 61). The most unlikely of all premises is that faith manufactures its own data.

Detached from its historic Christian moorings, secular historical biblical criticism has adapted hand in glove to the hubris of deteriorating modernity (H. Frey,

KJK). In the struggle to gain respectability for religious studies in secular universities with a long record of excluding religion in the name of toleration, there has been special pressure on biblical studies departments to dissociate from any sort of theological stigmatization and to assert inordinately the supposedly "objective and scientific" character of the discipline.

Gregory applied a bittersweet analogy to similarly distorted dialogue in his day: "For indeed a little wormwood most quickly imparts its bitterness to honey; while not even double the quantity of honey can impart its sweetness to wormwood" (Gregory of Nazianzus, *Flight to Pontus* 12).

How Advocacy Becomes Covert Within "Criticism" in Modern Portraiture of Jesus

Critics violate a primary ethical demand upon historical study when they impose upon a set of documents alien presuppositions and then borrow from the canonical prestige of the document by claiming that it corresponds with their favored predispositions. The modern attempt to study the God-man attested in the New Testament has done this repeatedly. The text has often become a mirror of ideological interest: Kant's Christ becomes a strained exposition of the categorical imperative; Hegel's Christ looks like a shadow-image of the Hegelian dialectic. Schleiermacher's Christ is a reflection of the awkward mating of pietism and romanticism; Strauss's Christ is neatly weeded of all supernatural referents. Harnack's portrait of Christ looks exactly like that of a late nineteenth-century German liberal idealist; and Tillich's Christ is a dehistorized existential idea of being that participates in estrangement without being estranged. More recent postmodern versions are extended verses of the same chorus.

Amid such reductionisms, the meaning of Christ is never entirely lost. That fortunately is not within the power of the critics. But it is repeatedly skewed, repainted, "improved," modernized, crippled, and distorted. Walter Wink rightly called to question that form of historical biblical criticism that is "not nearly so interested in being changed by his reading of the Bible, as in changing the way that the Bible was read in order to conform it to the modern spirit." Like a business experiencing bankruptcy, historical biblical criticism "still has an inventory of expensive parts, a large capital outlay, a team of trained personnel, a certain reputation," but it lacks one thing, "the ability to fulfill its purpose—effectively to produce and compete on the relevant market" (Wink, *BHT*:1, 13).

Historical biblical criticism has been allied with polemical concerns since its eighteenth-century inception as an ideological agent of "Enlightenment." It has expressed a determined interest from the beginning in discrediting not merely the authority of Scripture, but authority in general—all authority as such. Just read the biographies of Reimarus, Rousseau, Lessing, Strauss, Feuerbach, and Nietzsche (Jacques Derrida, *The Ear of the Other*).

The modern critics of Scripture are another mutation of those described by Gregory of Nazianzus. He provided a stunning social location profile of the rebellious "improvers" of religion in his time "who have endured no inconvenience for the sake of virtue, who only begin to study religion when appointed to teach it, and undertake the cleansing of others before being cleansed themselves; yesterday sacrilegious, to-day sacerdotal; yesterday excluded from the sanctuary, to-day its officiants; proficient in vice, novices in piety; the product of the favor of man, not of the grace of the Spirit; who, having run through the whole gamut of violence, at last tyrannize over even piety; who, instead of gaining credit for their office by their character, need for their character the credit of their office" (Gregory of Nazianzus, *On the Great Athanasius* 9). Such wisdom could have been written this morning.

Reversing the Hermeneutic of Suspicion:
The Social Location of Critics

The most exposed and vulnerable aspect of the academic critics of scripture is the social location of the critics themselves. It is a neglected arena of critique. While they are criticizing the social location of classic Christianity, their own social location has not been carefully enough observed and reported. The telling evidence is that they hold comfortable chairs in rutted tenure tracks, yet from that seemingly secure fortress snipe at all who differ. They plead the ethic of inclusion while they are among all the most ideologically exclusive. These writers have for fifty years focused on the analysis of the social location of the writers and interpreters of Scripture. Now they themselves are vulnerable. That kind of analysis is ripe to be turned upon the social prejudices of the "knowledge elite"—the guild of scholars asserting their interest in the privileged setting of the modern university.

This sort of analysis has often been called the "hermeneutic of suspicion"—a principle of interpretation that reduces ideas and events to their social location or placement within hidden economic interests. Studies of sacred Scripture and tradition have been filled with these socio-economic suspicions during the past half century. This analysis of suspicion now needs to be directed toward the suspicious critics. When will the hermeneutic of suspicion be candidly applied to the social location of the advocates of the hermeneutic of suspicion?

Such a critique of criticism is needed, as has occurred so many times before in church history. Examples are Tertullian against Marcionism, Athanasius against Arius, Augustine against Manicheanism, Luther against the medieval scholastics, and Wesley against antinomian forms of double predestinarianism.

It must first be shown that these modern critics have belatedly rediscovered a critique that was for centuries familiar to classic Christian teaching. This form of critical reasoning has often been used by Christian apologetics, especially in the pre-Nicene period. It may be found previously in Hippolytus, Origen, and later in Augustine, Luther, and above all Kierkegaard. Yet today it is imagined by some to be a recent invention (Fuchs, *Hermeneutik*; Ricoeur, *History and Truth*; *Interpretation Theology*; Gadamer, *Truth and Method*). Athanasius, long before Marx, argued that the gods had social utility. Chrysostom before Feuerbach realized that the gods were projections of human psychological needs (*Contra Gentes* 15–18).

The hermeneutic of suspicion has been callously applied to the history of Jesus but not to the supposed "history" of the historians. The hermeneutic of suspicion must now be fairly and prudently applied to the critical movement itself: its ideological location within Euro-American politics and economics and upward social mobility among elites. This is the most certain next phase of biblical scholarship—the criticism of criticism. My recent study of *How Africa Shaped the Christian Mind: Rediscovering the Seedbed of Western Christianity*, is an example of this sort of criticism. But why has it taken so long?

Bultmann, Käsemann, and Ebeling have argued that historical criticism stands as a bulwark against works-righteousness that destroys false guarantees for faith (*KM*; Käsemann, *ENTT*; Ebeling, *WE*). In academic practice, however, historical criticism has become for its professorial practitioners a justifying work. It masks itself as scientific and objective.

Biblical criticism "sought to free itself from the community in order to pursue its work untrammeled," and hence has become "cut off from any community for whose life its results might be significant. . . . The community of reference and accountability became, not the liberal church, but the guild of biblical scholars" who had a vested professional interest in building influence in the university, in perpetuating their schools and methods (Wink, *BHT*; cf. P. Ricoeur, *The Bible as a Document of the University*).

The empassioned secular bias of much historical biblical criticism has become fixated upon a curious game, seeking to resurrect not Jesus Christ but its own fantasized "historical Jesus" as an object of its historical curiosity, media attention, and upward social mobility. Amid this attempted burial and resurrection, the historian seeks to remain tightly in control of what is admitted as evidence and of judgments about the evidence. No one else beside this high priest may now enter this inner sanctum. "Only the historian can answer" (Bultmann, *TNT* 1:26). Only New Testament specialists, according to this bias, have any right to enter into the Christological arena (Wink, *BHT*; P. Stuhlmacher, *HCTIS*).

"Bluntly stated, biblical criticism was a certain type of evangelism seeking a certain type of conversion." It has now, like revivalism, become bankrupt, having been "married to a false objectivism, subjected to uncontrolled technologism, separated from a vital community, and has outlived its usefulness" (Wink, *BHT:14–15*). Jesus had harsh words for such obstructionists: "Woe to you experts in the law, because you have taken away the key to knowledge. You yourselves have not entered, and you have hindered those who were entering" (Luke 11:52; Maximus of Turin, *Sermon* 43.2).

The comedy of making secularized proselytism look like scientific inquiry is a little like "those persons who in the theatres perform wrestling matches in public, but not that kind of wrestling in which the victory is won according to the rules of the sport, but a kind to deceive the eyes of those who are ignorant in such matters, and to catch applause" (Gregory of Nazianzus, *Ag. Eunomians, Orat.* 27.2).

There still remain in excellent universities courageous scholars who, while sincerely affirming classical Christianity, continue to be deeply engaged in useful critical studies, though often bearing the marks of pariahs among certain self-contained critical elites (see G. Wainwright, *Doxology*; G. Lindbeck, *The Nature of Doctrine*; D. Wells, *PC*; Clark Pinnock, *The Scripture Principle*; Ramm, *EC*; Guthrie, *NTT*; Ladd, *TNT*; Marshall, *IBHJ*; Henry, *GRA* 4). They may feel as did Gregory describing his own historical situation surrounding the Second Council of Constantinople, AD 381: "that which the palmerworm left did the locust eat, and that which the locust left did the caterpillar eat; then came the cankerworm, then, what next I know not, one evil springing up after another"—all for our "testing and refining" (Gregory Nazianzus, *Orat.* 42.3).

8

THE PUBLIC MINISTRY
OF JESUS

FOLLOWING THE CHILDHOOD NARRATIVES, Jesus' public ministry began
with his baptism, immediately followed by the narrative of his temptation.
Each step of his ministry of proclamation and teaching pointed relentlessly
toward his final days in Jerusalem. There is no compelling need here to discuss
each event of Jesus' earthly ministry. Rather the focus of classic Christian
teaching is fixed on the meaning of the whole constellation of events before,
during, and after his earthly life.

Childhood Narratives: Circumcision,
Flight, Obedience, Growth

The beginning childhood narratives in the Gospels provide anticipations of the
end of his ministry, the climax of salvation history (Tertullian, *On the Flesh of
Christ* 2). They recollect Jesus' childhood from the special viewpoint of his destiny
as Mediator seen through the lens of his death and resurrection.

The Circumcision of Jesus

The initiation into the Hebrew covenant community carried with it the obligation
to follow the way of holiness, putting away sin. Jesus' circumcision prefigured his
death as a setting aside of the flesh. Circumcision signified God's covenant with
Abraham (Gen. 17:11) as "an everlasting covenant between me and you and your
descendants after you for the generations to come, to be your God and the God
of your descendants after you" (Gen. 17:7). According to his covenant promise,
Yahweh alone would be their God, whom they would serve and trust (Augustine,

CG 16.27). Circumcision is a sanctification metaphor, signifying the setting aside of something for holy use (oil, bread, wine, water, or temple—in this case the male generative organ).

Without any harm to sexual function or disdain of sexuality, the circumcision of males aimed symbolically at consecration of that organ by which life itself is reproduced, which because of its extraordinary creative power and goodness is most likely to be corrupted by idolatry and sin (Col. 2:11). Since the corrupted will presses to be expressed everywhere in human life, it is likely to impinge most significantly upon that most erotic and generative aspect of human life: sexuality.

To "circumcise the heart" is to so renew it constantly in obedience that its inveterate self-assertiveness would be curbed (Deut. 10:16) in order that all one's redeemed powers may be fully consecrated to God (Gen. 17:23; Deut. 30:6; Wesley, *WJW* 5:203–209). Circumcision anticipatively symbolized purity of heart or purification of the whole person in readiness for the feast of divine love (Jer. 9:25), pointing to a responsive willingness to hear and obey God (Jer. 6:10). "God, your God, will cut away the thick calluses on your heart and your children's hearts, freeing you to love God, your God, with your whole heart and soul, and live, really live" (Deut 30:6, Peterson tr.)

Jesus was circumcised in order to signal his active obedience to the full requirement of the law (Justin Martyr, *Dialogue with Trypho* 67). This event is celebrated in the Christian year on January 1, New Year's Day, the ancient Feast of the Circumcision, eight days after Christmas.

Old and New Covenant Circumcision

Circumcision under the conditions of the new covenant was to become an inward sign of the righteousness of faith (Rom. 4:10–12; Ambrosiaster, *Comm. on Paul*, Rom. 4.11), not an outward work of merit or an occasion for boasting. Without the obedience of faith, Paul says, circumcision becomes uncircumcision (Rom. 2:25–29; Origen, *Comm. on Rom.* 2.16–29). Insofar as it might suggest that we gain merit by works, it is to be resisted (Gal. 5:2ff.), but its true meaning and import should be recognized and respected (Col. 2:13; Isa. 52:1). Circumcision "was not given in order to produce righteousness but as a sign and seal of the righteousness which was Abraham's by faith" (Severian, *Catena, Comm. on Paul*, Rom. 4:12).

Only after Christ's death could the special meaning of his circumcision be more fully discerned. It would then be understood that the believer's circumcision is (far from an outward act) not only a spiritual act of putting off the flesh or shedding of blood for the covenant, but more so it precisely Christ's circumcision (Cyprian, *Testimonies*).

Christ was "circumcised"—his flesh set apart—in the most radical way by his death. His circumcision is reckoned or imputed to all baptized believers according to Paul: "In him you were also circumcised, in the putting off of the sinful nature, not with a circumcision done by the hands of men but with the circumcision done by Christ, having been buried with him in baptism and raised with him through your faith in the power of God, who raised him from the dead" (Col. 2:11–12; Chrysostom, *Hom. on Col.* 6; Tertullian, *On the Resurrection of the Flesh* 23).

The crucial links between circumcision under the law at the beginning of his public ministry to the end of his ministry in crucifixion-resurrection and Christian baptism are these:

In Circumcision Under the Old Covenant

The flesh is cut back	While the heart is made full
Blood is shed	Life is promised
Useless flesh separated	Spirit emboldened
The sinful nature is cut off	To become consecrated to the covenant
The libido is constrained symbolically	To prepare spiritually
The will is purified	The new will is freed
Passion is constrained	To be set apart for righteousness

So Jesus Christ was

Crucified and Buried	Raised

So in baptism the believer is

Buried with him	Raised with him
The old life put away	New life received
Sin is conquered	The way of holiness established

John of Damascus carefully explained the link between circumcision of the old and baptism of the new covenant: "For just as the circumcision does not cut off a useful member of the body, but only a useless superfluity, so by the holy baptism we are circumcised from sin, and sin clearly is, so to speak, the superfluous part of desire and not useful desire. For it is quite impossible that any one should have no desire at all nor ever experience the taste of pleasure. But the useless part of pleasure, that is to say, useless desire and pleasure, it is this that is sin from which holy baptism circumcises us" (John of Damascus, *OF* 4.25). In the circumcised heart, passion and desire remain, but they are channeled toward moral and spiritual usefulness.

Presentation at the Temple

Jesus was presented in the Temple on his fortieth day as a son of the covenant, faithfully honoring the ancient tradition of the economy of salvation (Irenaeus, *Ag. Her.* 3.10). "When the time of their purification according to the law of Moses had been completed, Joseph and Mary took him to Jerusalem to present him to the Lord (as it was written in the Law of the Lord, 'Every firstborn male is to be consecrated to the Lord')" (Luke 2:22–23; Exod. 13:2, 12). All this was done "in keeping with what is said in the Law" (Luke 2:24; Tho. Aq., *ST* 3 Q37).

The poverty into which Christ was born is revealed in that the family could not afford a lamb for offering, but only "a pair of doves" (Lev. 12:8; Origen, *Leviticus, Hom.* 8.4). "It was not enough for the teacher of perfect humility, who was equal to the Father in all things, to submit himself to the humble Virgin. He must submit himself also to the Law, that he might redeem those who were under the Law" (Bonaventure, *Tree of Life, CWS*: 131; Gal. 4:5).

In Jerusalem Simeon had long been devoutly awaiting for God's own coming (Isa. 52:9). "It had been revealed to him by the Holy Spirit that he would not die before he had seen the Lord's Christ. Moved by the Spirit, he went into the temple courts. When the parents brought in the child Jesus to do for him what the custom of the Law required, Simeon took him in his arms and praised God, saying: 'Sovereign Lord, as you have promised, you now dismiss your servant in peace. For my eyes have seen your salvation, which you have prepared in the sight of all people, a light for revelation to the Gentiles and for glory to your people Israel'" (Luke 2:26–32; Augustine, *Sermon* 277.17).

The elderly prophetess Anna, who had been worshiping in expectation "night and day, fasting and praying," met the parents and "spoke about the child to all who were looking forward to the redemption of Jerusalem" (Luke 2:38; Tertullian, *On Fasting* 8). In these events, Joseph and Mary did "everything required by the Law of the Lord," and returned to Nazareth (Luke 2:39).

The Flight to Egypt

By the holy family's flight to Egypt, the Son's life was preserved for the hour that was to come. Joseph, Mary, and Jesus are portrayed as a refugee family, escaping to Egypt to evade Herod's gruesome search.

It seems fitting that one who had no place to lay his head would be from the outset a part of a refugee family fleeing persecution under a tyrannical political power (Matt. 2:13–18; Origen *Ag. Celsus* 1.66). This, says Matthew, was to fulfill the expectation of the prophet Hosea: "Out of Egypt I called my son" (Hos. 11:1; Matt. 2:15). The displaced immigrant family withdrew to Nazareth after Herod's death (Matt. 2:19–23).

The Passover in Jerusalem and the Questioning of the Rabbis in the Temple

In Luke's account, the boy Jesus at twelve was found "sitting among teachers, listening to them and asking them questions" (Luke 2:46). He instructed the rabbis not by high-handed assertions but by tempered questionings, in a way that "stimulated them to enquire into things which so far they could not know whether they knew or not" (Origen, *Luke*, Hom. 20).

By his listening to the doctors in the Temple and asking them questions (Luke 2:41–51), the Gospel makes clear that he submitted to the rigorous conditions under which human intellect develops. That he astonished them with his understanding is evidence of his full use of intellectual competencies under the enabling of the Spirit. He was willing to undergo gradual human development so that he could share fully in all the ordinary stages of human growth (Luke 2:40; 1 Sam. 2:26). He learned obedience (Heb. 5:8). He was taught by degrees to pray, to read, to meditate on Holy Writ, and to serve as an apprentice artisan (Mark 6:13). His answer to his mother, "Why were you searching for me? . . . Didn't you know I had to be in my Father's house?" (Luke 2:49), suggests that as a youth he was already aware of his distinctive mission and unique filial relation to God (Origen, *Hom. on Luke* 19.6).

Subjection to Parents

His active obedience to law in his earthly life readied him for his passive obedience in death (Calvin, *Inst.* 2.16.5–7). Jesus is remembered as a dutiful son in relation to his parents, a fit expression of the humble human coming of God the Son in time. "Then he went down to Nazareth with them and was obedient to them" (Luke 2:51; Origen, *Hom. on Luke* 20.5). It was for our salvation that the Lord became "subject to creatures," for "he had taken upon him human nature on the condition of being subject to parents," just as the faithful are called to voluntarily take on the ordinary duties of life in service with accountability (Calvin, *Comm.* 16:172).

"Jesus grew" (Luke 2:52; Calvin, *Inst.* 4.16.18). Origen explained that Jesus did not appear as a full grown man, but even while he was "yet a child, since He 'emptied Himself,' kept advancing," for "after emptying Himself He was gradually taking again the things of which He had voluntarily emptied Himself" (*Comm. on Jer., Hom.* 1.7). "He increased in stature of soul, and His soul became great by reason of the great and mighty works which He did" (Origen, *Lev., Hom.* 12.2).

The logic of the humbling of God is characterized by paradox, surprise, and reversal: As God, the God-man does not advance but descends into ignorance and humiliation. As man, the God-man does advance in wisdom and stature to demonstrate his full participation in the human condition (Athanasius, *Four Discourses Ag. Arians* 3.42–53).

Human beings are not born virtuous. Virtues can only develop through risk-laden decision making. "The being born, you have; but also the growing, you ought to have; because no man begins with being perfect" (Augustine, *On the Creed* 8).

Jesus "grew in wisdom and stature" (Luke 2:52). If so, he must have been subject to the normal laws of psychological development, the same processes through which humans generally move to maturity. "He is said to have progressed in wisdom and age and grace, because He did increase in age and by this increase in age brought more into evidence the wisdom inherent in Him, further, because by making what is ours altogether His own, He made His own the progress of men in wisdom and grace" (John of Damascus, *OF 3.22*).

Jesus' Baptism: Its Meaning

Jesus' baptism inaugurated his ministry and began the messianic age (Matt. 3:13–4:11; Mark 1:9–13; John 1:32–34). Prophetic expectation held that the messianic event would begin with the outpouring of the Spirit (Joel 2; Augustine, *Trin.* 15.26.46). He has "all the gifts of the Spirit without interruption" (Gregory I, *Morals on Job* 2.56.90). The public designation or sealing of Jesus' messianic office occurred in his baptism with the descent of the Spirit (Tho. Aq., *ST* 3 Q39).

His baptism constituted his ordination to his public ministry, prefigured his death and the sacramental coming of the Spirit to the worshiping community succeeding him, prefiguring the rites of Christian baptism, confirmation, and holy orders. Jesus' baptism combined numerous elements of weighty prophetic-symbolic significance.

The Baptism of John

"His own baptism by John is one of the most certainly verified occurrences of his life" (Bornkamm, *JN*:54). John's ministry bridged the Old and New Testaments in two ways: by epitomizing the prophetic tradition under the old covenant and by preaching repentance looking toward the new (*Incomplete Work on Matt.*, Hom 4; Tho. Aq., *ST* 3 Q38). In receiving John's baptism, the Lord's identity began to be recognized (Chrysostom, *Hom. on John* 16).

When Jesus "came from Galilee to the Jordan to be baptized by John," John "tried to deter him, saying, 'I need to be baptized by you.'" Jesus insisted that "it is proper for us to do this to fulfill all righteousness" (Matt. 3:13–15; Augustine, *Questions* 58). The embedded irony in the narrative: John protested that Jesus

was no fit candidate for the baptism of repentance, and Jesus insisted upon identifying with sinners "to fulfill all righteousness" (Chromatius, *Tractates on Matt.*
13.2–3; Hugh of St. Victor, *OSCF* 291–93). Jesus' baptism was not to signify repentance of his own sins, but his compassionate identification with the consequences of sin in human history (Theodore of Mopsuestia, *Fragm.* 14).

Jesus was baptized in the very river by which Joshua had entered Canaan.
Christian baptism enables the crossing of another river (from sin to grace) so as to
make the transition into the reign of God's love, prefigured by the Israel's crossing into the promised land (Josh. 3:17; 4:1–24; Ps. 114:3–5; 2 Kings 5:14; Origen,
Hom. on Josh. 4.1).

The Descent of the Spirit Enabling His Ministry: The Opening of Heaven
"As he was praying, heaven was opened and the Holy Spirit descended on him in
bodily form like a dove" (Luke 3:21; Matt. 3:16). The opening of heaven signals
the coming of forgiveness of sin (Origen, *Hom. on Luke* 27.5). The divine-human
intercourse, which through sin had become constricted, was through Christ's
baptism opened (Matt. 7:7–8; 27:52; John 9:10–32).

In Jesus' baptism, the Holy Spirit descended. This anticipates what is to occur
in Christian baptism everywhere: the enabling Spirit is given to the believer. In
this way the descent of the Spirit is not for Jesus alone, but for all those whose
lives are hid in him by faith (Maximus of Turin, *Sermon* 13A.3).

The Spirit appeared in the figure of a dove to welcome humanity to the peace of
God that was already at work in Christ (Origen, *Canticles, Hom.* 2.12; Hippolytus,
Theophany 6; Calvin, *Comm.* 16: 204). "For the dove's body has no gall in it. So
after the deluge by which the iniquity of the old world was purged away, after,
so to speak, the baptism of the world, the dove as herald proclaimed to the earth
the assuagement of the wrath of heaven—sent forth from the ark and returning with an olive branch, which is a sign of peace even among the nations"
(Tertullian, *Baptism* 8; Augustine, *Questions* 43).

After Jesus' baptism, his teaching and healing ministry proceeded with the
awareness that "The Spirit of the Lord is on me, because he has anointed me
to preach good news to the poor" (Luke 4:18, quoting Isa. 61:1). "I baptize with
water," the forerunner attested, "but among you stands one you do not know. He
is the one who comes after me, the thongs of whose sandals I am not worthy to
untie." It is he "who will baptize with the Holy Spirit" (John 1:26–27, 33; Origen,
Comm. on John, 6.168–69). John testified: "I have seen and I testify that this is
the Son of God" (John 1:34; Cyril of Alex. *Comm. on John* 2.1). This recalled Isaiah's testimony to the coming time when it would be said of the anointed One:
"Here is my servant, whom I uphold, my chosen one in whom I delight; I will put
my Spirit on him and he will bring justice to the nations" (Isa. 42:1).

A voice from heaven confirmed the awesome significance of this event. As the
triune God affirmed Jesus' baptism, so Christian baptism occurs in the name of
God the Father, Son, and Spirit (Matt. 28:19; Hilary, *Trin.* 8.25). All three persons
of the Trinity are present in the Evangelists' testimony attesting and celebrating
his unique Sonship: "As soon as Jesus was baptized, he went up out of the water.
At that moment heaven was opened, and he saw the Spirit of God descending like
a dove and lighting on him. And a voice from heaven said, 'This is my Son, whom
I love; with him I am well pleased'" (Matt. 3:16–17; Mark 1:11).

These words are derived from two messianic texts: Psalm 2:7, the *coronation*
formula of the messianic King of Israel, and Isaiah 42:1, the *ordination* formula of
the Servant of the Lord (Eusebius, *Comm. on Is.* 2.22). The conflation of these two
formulae did not occur accidentally or thoughtlessly. It alluded to the fact that

the messianic King would be, far from a victorious political deliverer, a suffering servant who would die as a ransom for sinners (Augustine, *Sermon* 2.1–2).

The Spirit's Guidance in Jesus' Ministry

The baptism of Jesus not only marked him as the coming Messiah but also supplied him with gifts of the Spirit requisite to his messianic mission. In Jesus' baptism by the Holy Spirit, his human nature was being equipped with everything needed to fulfill his ministry. "Now that the full time is come for preparing to discharge the office of Redeemer, he is clothed with a new power of the Spirit, and that not so much for his own sake, as for the sake of others" in order that "believers might learn to receive" (Calvin, *Comm.* 16). Similarly in Christian baptism, believers are being equipped with gifts requisite to their vocation (Eph. 4:17–13).

In his baptism he prefigured his body, the church, which through baptism receives the Holy Spirit (Hugh of St. Victor, *OSCF*:282–89). Christ's baptism stands as the inauguration of the sacrament of baptism in which all the faithful participate, and through it are incorporated into Christ. In being baptized, Christ himself undertook and fulfilled what was later offered to all (Bonaventure, *Tree of Life*, *CWS*:133).

The sevenfold gifts of the Spirit, according to prophecy and classical exegesis, were bestowed upon Jesus at his baptism. As a shoot "from the stump of Jesse, from his roots a Branch will bear fruit. The Spirit of the Lord will rest on him— the Spirit of wisdom and of understanding, the Spirit of counsel and of power, the Spirit of knowledge and of the fear of the Lord—and he will delight in the fear of the Lord" (Isa. 11:1–2; Ambrose, *Holy Spirit* 1.16). These gifts (wisdom, understanding, counsel, fortitude, knowledge, piety, and fear of the Lord, as rendered by Bonaventure, *Tree of Life*, *CWS*:174) were soon to be distributed to the church. In due time the church received "an anointing from the Holy One" (1 John 2:20; Acts 2:1–13) to manifest Christ's gifts.

The Lowly Sign: Water

Water seeks the lowest level. Water is the sign of baptism, as wine and bread are the signs of the Eucharist. The baptism of Jesus was necessary not that Christ be purified, but that he once for all consecrate the lowly sign of baptism—water— which was to become the down-to-earth grace-laden instrument through which humanity would be redeemed (Hugh of St. Victor, *OSCF*: 301–10). "He was baptized as Man—but He remitted sins as God—not because He needed purificatory rites Himself, but that He might sanctify the element of water" (Gregory Nazianzus, *Orat.* 29.20).

In Jesus' baptism as distinguished from that of believers, the pure water symbolized not the need for his being cleansed from sin since he was without sin, but rather that which cleanses from sin. Thus Christ was not himself regenerated in the baptism by John, but submitted to identify with sinners and to offer an example of humility, just as he submitted to death not as the punishment for his own sin, but to take away the sin of the world: "For baptism found in Him nothing to wash away, as death found in Him nothing to punish. . . . Both baptism and death were submitted to by Him not through a pitiable necessity, but of His own free pity for us" (Augustine, *Enchiridion* 49).

By this revelation, the water of baptism became set aside and consecrated to a special purpose—to bring the cleansing power of the Spirit to humanity. Water, an ordinary and common element yet necessary for human life, was thereby extraordinarily blessed in baptism with symbolic excellence as a means of grace by which life would be bestowed upon humanity (Bonaventure, *Tree of Life*, *CWS*:133).

As water runs downward, not upward, so Jesus' incarnation was first to be a humbling, downward movement toward suffering and death, even as Christian baptism is a sharing in his way of lowliness, meekness, and peace. Jesus in being baptized assumed symbolically the self-effacing position of identifying with the sin of humanity, yet he did so in a way that already pointed toward the reconciliation of that sin, since he was at that moment being designated as messiah to redeem sin (Augustine, *Tractates on John* 4–6; Gregory I, *Forty Gospel Homilies* 4).

Numbered Among the Transgressors: Identification with Sinners

His baptism was a body language statement that he was willing to become fully identified with the condition of humanity suffering under the consequences of sin (Tertullian, *On Baptism* 10–13). It was for others rather than for himself that Jesus was baptized. Even at his baptism Jesus was identifying with the suffering servant of Isaiah, in that he was "numbered with the transgressors" from the outset, already on the road toward pouring "out his life unto death" and bearing "the sins of many" (Isa. 53:12; cf. Matt. 3:15; Chromatius, *Tractate on Matt.*13.2–3). Baptism, as a symbol that prefigures death, burial, and resurrection, already prefigures the end of Christ's earthly ministry.

"The general reason why Christ received baptism was, that he might render full obedience to the Father; and the special reason was, that he might consecrate baptism in his own body, that we might have it in common with him." He who "had not need of baptism" received what was "suitable to the character of a servant," "for the sake of others" (Calvin, *Comm., Harmony*, 16:202). "Baptize Me, John," wrote Hippolytus of Jesus, "that none may despise baptism" (*Theophany* 4.5).

In Jewish tradition the high priest was ritually washed before being anointed. Hence the anointing of Jesus' messianic mission was preceded by this washing— baptism. Thus the washing by John of Jesus constituted a prefigurative fulfillment of the high-priestly role he was to undertake leading to his death.

In this way, the baptism of Jesus already prefigured and anticipated the cross. Later John would write: "This is the one who came by water and blood—Jesus Christ. He did not come by water only, but by water and blood" (1 John 5:6). The water is the water of his baptism and the blood is the blood of his atonement. Water symbolized the beginning of his messianic ministry in baptism, blood the ending of that ministry in death. Jesus' messianic office, begun at his baptism, became a finished work on the cross (Oecumenius, *Comm. on 1 John* 5.6).

Jesus Neither a "Man Made God" Nor "Adopted as Messiah" at His Baptism

Christianity does not celebrate a man who became God, as if it happened "that a certain man was crowned by advancement," so that "Christ is not God made man, but a man made God" (Cyril of Jerusalem, *Catech. Lect.* 12). He did not attain divinity as if an accomplishment (Athanasius, *Four Discourses Ag. Arians* 1.37–38). "We do not say that man became God, but that God became man.

The notion that Jesus was adopted as Son at his baptism (Cerinthus, in Irenaeus, *Ag. Her.* 1.21, 1.26, 352; Hippolytus, *Ag. All Her.* 7.21) was carefully considered by ecumenical councils and rejected. "This Son of God is also Son by nature, not by adoption" (Eleventh Council of Toledo; *SCD* 143, 299, 309ff.). "He is not the supposed Son of God, but the true Son, not the adoptive Son but the real Son, for He was never estranged from the Father because of the man [human nature] which He assumed" (Council of Friuli; Methodius, *Symposium* 8.9).

Jesus did not "earn" his baptismal messianic identification by rightly developing his human soul so as to become worthy of divine adoption. The Second

Council of Constantinople specifically rejected the view that he "freed himself gradually from interior inclinations and, having improved through the progress of his works and having become irreproachable in his conduct, was baptised as a mere man in the name of the Father and of the Son and of the Holy Spirit" (*Against the Three Chapters*, CF:162). A parent cannot adopt a boy who is already his son (Tho. Aq., *ST* 3 Q23.4).

The modern form of adoptionism is reflected in the tradition following Schleiermacher, for whom Jesus' consciousness of God was such that through it we come to increased God-consciousness. According to this view, Christology begins not with the preexistent Logos, but with a present experience of the new life as immediately dependent upon Jesus' consciousness of God. By taking us up into the energies of his God-consciousness, he reconciles, saves, and brings persons into vital union with God. This view still struggles to find an accommodation with ancient ecumenical definitions.

The Temptation of Jesus

In preparation for his public ministry, Jesus underwent a rigorous period of testing or trial—the temptation in the wilderness (Ephrem, *Comm. on Tatian's Diatesseron* 4.4–5). Demonic assaults continued for forty days and nights—a period of fasting that came to prefigure the Lenten season of self-examination. "For forty days he was tempted by the devil" (Luke 4:2; cf. Matt. 4:1–11), reminiscent of Moses (Exod. 24:18; 34:28) and Elijah (1 Kings 19:8; Theodore of Mopsuestia, *Fragm.* 18; Hilary, *On Matt.* 2.1–4).

Jesus was "led by the Spirit into the desert to be tempted" (Matt. 4:1). As the Lord led the people of God under Moses into the desert for testing for forty years, so was Jesus led to be tested by Satan for forty days. In the desert he was "with the wild animals, and the angels attended him" (Mark 1:13), just as the people of God had been attended in the desert (Exod. 23:20, 23; 32:34). This trial was a part of the divine purpose—to demonstrate that the Son was unswervingly responsive to his mission (Eusebius, *Proof of the Gospel* 2: 166; Chrysostom, *Hom. on Matt.* Hom. 13.1).

Why He Was Tempted as We Are, Yet Without Sin

As his ministry proceeded relentlessly toward the cross, Jesus was frequently challenged, buffeted, and "tempted" by detractors, the scribes and lawyers (Mark 8:11; Luke 10:25–29) who sought self-incriminating statements (Mark 12:15; Luke 23:2)—a premature declaration of his messianic identity or anything to show that he was not a true teacher of Israel.

Ultimately he would be "tempted in every way just as we are"—not spared the trials of body and spirit that accompany human existence generally—yet he would remain "without sin" (Heb. 4:15). Only this hard route would demonstrate his readiness for the ministry of redemption of humanity, which included his empathic capacity to be touched with the feeling of our infirmities (Theodoret of Cyr, *Interp. of Heb.* 4).

The temptation that was unresisted by Adam and so led humanity to destruction (Gen. 3) was resisted by Christ so as to lead humanity to redemption (Augustine, *CG* 13–14; Gen. 22:1; 1 John 3:8). By thwarting Satan's deceptions, his ministry of reconciling God and humanity began (Didymus the Blind, *Comm. on 1 John*).

Necessary to Demonstrate His Full Humanity

A necessary part of Jesus' mediatorial role was that, like us, he struggled against sin and temptation. "Because he himself suffered when he was tempted, he is able to help those who are being tempted" (Heb. 2:18; Gregory Nazianzus, *Orat.* 30; Philokal. 1:119–20).

The temptation narratives assume that Jesus' temptations were real, not imagined. He entered the gravitational field of genuine temptation, but was sufficiently centered in his own filial self-identity and vocation that he never succumbed to any degree. Demonic temptations were viable appeals to his authentic freedom. His resistance was a free act of saying no on behalf of a larger yes to his vocation (Origen, *OFP*:215–18; J. Edwards, *Works* 2:227–31).

He consistently resisted the gravitational pull of temptation. Our human imaginations have become perennially distorted in excessive pride and sensuality (Baxter, *PW* 19:154–56; Newman, *PPS* 5:120–27). Jesus may be said to have been more profoundly tempted than fallen humanity, for his greater powers (voluntarily constrained) were tempted to greater potential abuse (Hilary, *On Matt.* 3.1–2).

His sinlessness did not impair the value of his moral example, nor did it diminish his capacity for sympathy with the human condition. His temptation was factual and required choice and strength to overcome. A faith that remained forever unchallenged would be a faith untested and inadequately experienced, hence unprepared for mediatorial work (Theodoret of Cyr, *Interp. of Heb.* 2; Gregory I, *Sermons, SSGF* 2:3.16).

His Temptations Had to Be Real in Order for Him to Share Our Humanity

Several perplexing questions arise directly out of the assertion of his unsullied righteousness. First, is temptation even possible where sin is never the outcome? Arguably, there could have been no genuine temptation of Jesus had he not been subject to some possibility of spiritual pride, fatigue of spirit, or inordinate desire (Photius, *Frag. On Heb.* 2.18). If he were in his human nature absolutely immune to any potential pride or sensuality, then what could the temptation have meant, and how could he then have been truly like ours, sharing in our infirmities?

Temptation was compared by ancient Christian writers to the testing of the authenticity of gold, which must pass through rigorous testing to establish its genuineness, but in a true test, *if* it is indeed gold, there is *no actual possibility* of outcome other than that it be and remain gold. It goes through the examination, a real test, but the inevitability of genuine gold passing that test is already given from the beginning. Similarly, however severely the Servant Messiah may have been tested, if he is the eternal Son, there is no viable prospect (although a theoretical possibility can be conceived) that he would ever fail the test of moral and spiritual accountability (Pss. 12:6; 66:10; Prov. 25:4; Isa. 1:25; Zech. 13:9; 1 Pet. 1:7; 4:12; Augustine, *Comm. on Psalms* 12; Calvin, *Comm.* 7:79–80). But that could not be determined by simple fiat in advance. Rather, as in the case of the quality test of a metal, the material must go through real testing in order to be fairly evaluated (Hilary of Arles, *Intro. Comm. on 1 Pet.* 4.12).

Consistently resisting temptation is a condition that can only be chosen, not externally caused since it is an act of freedom. It is an impossibility that arises from the radical clarity of his own will, which was so permanently directed toward good by the power of the Spirit that it was morally inconceivable that he should fall into sin. Further, resistance to temptation is a condition Jesus was required continuously to choose (Tho. Aq., *ST* 3 Q41). "Moralists distinguish two kinds of freedom of the will—the lower kind whereby it is free to choose evil as well as good, and the higher kind whereby, having definitely chosen good, it makes the choice of good a permanent act, and moreover, chooses between different means which are all free from evil. In this higher sense the human will of Christ was free" (Stone, *OCD*:81; Theophylact, *Comm. on 1 Pet*, 4.12).

The human fall into sin is rightly said to be "inevitable but not necessary" (Niebuhr, *NDM* 1:255–60). Yet *the Messiah's resistance to sin* may be said to be (due to his unique personal identity) *inevitable but not externally necessitated. For it is an act of freedom, but inevitable since it is the freedom of the eternal Son.* Hence the outcome of his temptation was "certain (not necessary)" (Curtis, *ChrF*:249). Newman drew the distinction precisely: he assumed a nature "of itself peccable," such that, "if it had not been His, might have sinned" (*SN*:148).

By frequent observation we associate temptation with its apparently inevitable consequence: sin. So wherever there is genuine temptation, we have come to expect that in due time there is bound to be sin somewhere along the way. The experience is all too familiar: manifold temptations finally lead at some point to a fall. But with Jesus, the case has to be stated differently: there was no external necessity that he would or would not sin, but it was morally inevitable (being who he was) that he would uprightly pass the trial of temptation, whatever it might be (Chryostom, *Hom. on Matt.* 13.1; Augustine, *CG, FC* 14:108–109).

It is not the case that only sinners are capable of being tempted. If it is asserted that temptation is real only if one does in fact sin, then that leads to an awkward conclusion—that the most compulsively addicted sinners are the profoundest experts on temptation and its best interpreters (Cyril of Alex., *Comm. on Luke,* Hom. 12). That is hardly born out by experience (Newman, *Mix.*: 97–99; Ramm, *EC*:81). It is not the case that Jezebel, Ahab, and Judas understood temptation better than Noah, David, and Job simply because they yielded to it more frequently. If the sinner yields to temptation and the saint resists temptation, that does not imply that the sinner knows the real nature of temptation but the saint does not.

The Dynamics of Seduction: When Evil Appears Good

The dynamics of seduction provide a closer view of the nature of temptation. It does not have to be sexual seduction—any form of seduction will do. The seductions most prevalent in Scripture have to do with pride, not sexuality. But since sexuality perennially is more intriguing than pride, we will take advantage of its accessibility as an example.

Seduction draws freedom into a realm in which evil appears good. Seduction's very purpose is to make evil look better than it is, even supremely good. That is precisely how it intends to "trick". It is possible for a virtuous person who in theory could be seduced to enter into the arena of seduction and feel the tentative attraction of this apparent good, yet still be able to resist. Whether the attraction becomes stronger or weaker depends entirely upon that person's free response. So in this sense it was possible for Jesus to enter into the realm of real attempts at seduction, to be truly tempted, yet not to collude in any way with the tempter.

Seduction requires collusion. It takes two wills to be seduced. Nobody simply "gets seduced" as a wholly passive matter. One will is drawn to concurrence by another, where one woos the will of another into cooperative consent (Augustine, *Retractions* 1.15.2; Hugh of St. Victor, *OSCF*:122–24; Goethe, *Faust*; Kierkegaard, *Repetition*). Seduction is not a coercion of will, but a drawing or tempting of that will (Newman, *PPS* 5:120–27). Always to succumb is not to be tempted but to be a pushover. Genuine temptation presupposes some freedom to resist it (Tho. Aq., *ST* 3 Q41). Augustine accordingly sought to discriminate between three different stages of temptation: suggestion, imagined pleasure, and consent (Augustine, *On Continence*; John of Damascus, *On the Virtues, Philokal.* 2:337ff.).

There was no collusion by Jesus with evil that seemed good. In each of the three temptations of Jesus, the tempter sought to present evil in the guise of good. The tempter is portrayed as deceiver who deliberately engages in the trick of seducing (*planaō*, 2 John 7; Titus 1:10; Rev. 12:9; 20:3–10) where the worse choice always looks better than it is. Jesus did not to any degree collude with such deception. He exercised his freedom not to collude, thereby not abusing his freedom through collusion (Clement of Alex. *Stromata*, FGNK 3:92–93).

God is not the tempter, but it is clear that God allows circumstances in which responsible creatures are tempted in order to strengthen character and moral fiber (Baxter, *PW* 19:155). As a trial of virtue, temptation becomes an occasion for spiritual growth, without which the human spirit would be less strong (Newman, *US*:142). Temptation is therefore in the long run for our good in the economy of providence, though it is not directly initiated by God (James 1:13; Cyril of Jerus., *Sermon on Paralytic* 17).

Imagine a form of so-called human freedom that could not be tempted. That would lack all the qualities necessary for the growth and strengthening of faith, hope, love, freedom, and virtue. One protected from all forms of temptation will not grow. The moral musculature when not exercised will atrophy. "He who has not been tempted knows nothing," Luther remarked. "For this reason the Psalter in all its words treats of practically nothing but temptation, tribulation, and affliction and is a book full of concern about them" (*Table Talk* 5, no. 6305). Jesus was truly tempted and capable of being tempted. This draws us closer to him as one of us (Chrysostom, *Hom. on Heb.* 5.7).

Jesus was not exempt from those interpersonal developments that accompany human existence generally. If so, Jesus' physical, psychological, and sexual development occurred as they do in normal human development. This is a deductive statement derived from classic Christian premises implicit in classic sources. Whatever may have occurred in the Savior's inner consciousness remains a matter of speculation, but it must be consistent with the assumptions that we have previously set forth as requisite to his work as reconciler between God and humanity: that he was fully human, sharing in our human frame; that he was tempted yet without sin; that he was truly the Son of God who assumed human flesh; and that the Spirit was providing him with gifts requisite to his ministry, including the gift of continence insofar as sexual self-constraint is required for the fulfillment of his particular messianic mission (Chromatius, *Tractate on Matt.* 14.5).

No Human Being Experiences Everything— A Principle Applicable to Sexuality

It is a firm principle of our humanness that we do not live in every age, do not speak every language, do not have every woman as a mother, but only one mother. That principle is applicable to the maleness of Jesus and the femaleness of Mary. The fact that Jesus' bodily life did not take all possible forms is more like our bodily life than unlike it. No one can be simultaneously both male and female, since male and female are structurally complementary (Gen. 3:16–19; Chrysostom, *Hom. on Gen.* 17.30–41).

Scripture makes it clear that Jesus experienced the usual range of physical and emotive responses and vulnerabilities common to humanity—hunger, thirst, sleep, grief, pain. "Surely he took up our infirmities" (Isa. 53:4), but that does not imply that Jesus had every single particular disease or felt every conceivable type of pain there is to feel (Gregory Thaumaturgus, *Twelve Topics on the Faith* 12). It is more rather than less like our humanity that he had specific, limited periods of grief or pain or a parching thirst at a particular time, not some abstract, general pain or thirst (John 19:28; Augustine, *Hom. on John* 219). This same must be said of his specific mode of sexuality: his, like ours, was not everything but something particular—not male *and* female, but male, not married *and* unmarried, but unmarried.

It does not count against Jesus' humanity that he did not become married or that he did not have children, unless one wishes to argue the absurd premise that all singles are less than human—an objectionable premise that Christianity rejects (Matt. 19:3–9; 1 Cor. 7; Augustine, *On Cath. and Manichean Ways of Life* 1.35.79) . Yet there is a comic justification for why chaste celibacy cannot be the ideal mode for everyone: if absolutely preferred, a completely celibate generation would be the last one.

Christianity celebrates sexuality not merely as a form of hedonistic self-expression but within a network of covenant relationships. Christianity values sexuality both in its *marital* expression of covenant fidelity and in its equally valid form of *freedom from marital commitments*. Paul was unmarried but commended marriage (1 Tim. 3:1–3; Titus 1:6). Those who absolutely "forbid people to marry" were considered "deceiving spirits" and "hypocritical liars, whose consciences have been seared as with a hot iron" (1 Tim. 4:1–3; Gregory of Nyssa, *On Virginity* 7; Jerome, *Letters* 48.2). Yet without devaluing marriage, the special value and calling of freedom from marital commitments was clearly stated by Paul: "I would like you to be free from concern," (1 Cor. 7:32). Celibacy is an act of freedom, enabling detachment from worldly entanglements and singleness of mind and heart, but this does not imply that marriage is inferior or less worthy for those called to marriage (1 Cor. 7:9, 28, 36, 38; Hugh of St. Victor, *OSCF*:325–43).

Three Archetypal Forms of Temptation of the Messianic Servant

No sooner was Jesus baptized into messianic office than he was "immediately beset by temptation" (Tertullian, *Baptism* 20). All three synoptic Gospels report that he was tempted immediately after his baptismal commissioning, signaling that his temptation was connected intrinsically with his vocation.

The three forms of temptation (Matt. 4:1–11; Mark 1:12–13; Luke 4:1–13) portray Jesus wrestling with his messianic vocation—whether to follow this calling to servant-messiahship or to interpret the messianic role in terms of

- creature comforts

- miraculous power

- conquest according to popular expectations

These three temptations are portrayed in classic exegesis as representative of human temptation generally, yet are here applied primarily to his messianic mission to reconcile humanity to God (Bede, *Hom. on the Gospels* 1.12). In all three phases, Jesus was tempted to use his extraordinary powers for ends other than those for which they were given: (1) to prove his sonship by a work of power that would guarantee creature comforts (turning stone into bread); (2) to personal abuse of spiritual power (letting the angels catch him from falling from the top of the temple); and (3) to worship rebellious and illegitimate authority for the sake of world dominion (attaining power by worshiping Satan). A daunting genre of early Christian preaching turned to these gospel texts as a summary of common human temptations—prototypically by Jesus, but symbolically by all humanity (Gregory I, *Forty Gospel Hom.* 16.2–3).

The Temptation to Channel the Vocational Role
Toward Creature Comforts

Having fasted during a forty-day period in preparation for his public ministry, Jesus was very hungry, for "it belongs to a man to suffer hunger when fasting." It was under these conditions that the tempter seized the opportunity to attack— "For as at the beginning it was by means of food that [Satan] persuaded [Adam and Eve], although not suffering hunger, to transgress God's commandments, so in the end he did not succeed in persuading Him," the New Man, though he was hungry, to turn stones into bread (Irenaeus, *Ag. Her.* 5.21). Jesus answered according to the Law: "Man does not live on bread alone" (Luke 4:4; Deut. 8:3; Origen, *Fragm. On Luke* 96).

The Temptation to Exercise Higher Powers Disobediently

Jesus was tempted to exercise deceitful wonder working as a way of validating his messianic mission. The scene is the holy place in the holy city: "Then the devil took him to the holy city and had him stand on the highest point of the temple. 'If you are the Son of God', he said, 'throw yourself down. For it is written: 'He will command his angels concerning you, and they will lift you up in their hands, so that you will not strike your foot against a stone'" (Matt. 4:5–6; cf. Mark 1:12–13; Luke 4:1–13). The tempter reinforced this temptation by quoting Holy Writ (Ps. 91:11–12), yet not quoting it accurately and leaving out a phrase not suited to his purpose. Origen noted that this showed that the devil had "read the Scriptures, not in order to be made better by the reading of holy things, but to destroy those who cling to the letter" (Origen, *Hom. on Luke* 31).

Jesus categorically resisted this temptation, answering, "Do not put the Lord your God to the test" (Luke 4:12; Deut. 6:16). It is less faith than presumption to put oneself deliberately into a situation of peril—to jump off and speed toward the ground—only for the purpose of offering the angels an occasion for stopping the descent at the last moment.

The Temptation to Idolatry, Worshiping
Illegitimate, Demonic Power

The tempter then revealed who he truly was (for "'Satan' signifies an apostate," Irenaeus, *Ag. Her.* 5.21), by showing Jesus "in an instant all the kingdoms of the world. And he said to him, 'I will give you all their authority and splendor, for it has been given to me, and I can give it to anyone I want to. So if you worship me, it will all be yours" (Luke 4:5–7; Hilary, *On Matt.* 3.4). The kingdoms shown Christ were those ruled by the tempter himself, governed by covetousness and vainglory, the means through which he reigned in the world (Origen, *Hom, on Luke* 30). Jesus answered: "Worship the Lord your God and serve him only" (Luke 4:8; cf. Deut. 6:13; 10:20; Ephrem, *Comm. on Tatian's Diatessaeron* 4.8B-C).

All three temptations presumed to offer Jesus the glory of ruling without suffering and dying. This is precisely the deception that sought to divert him from the mission on which he had been sent by the Father, the distinctive vocation of servant Messiah. The deceiver's intent was to disqualify the Savior and thereby thwart God's redemptive design (Augustine, *Comm. on Psalms* 8).

It was fitting, thought Irenaeus, that the tempter should "be bound with the same chains with which he had bound man, in order that man, being set free, might return to his Lord, leaving to him (Satan) those bonds by which he himself had been fettered, that is, sin" (Irenaeus, *Ag. Her.* 5.21). In this way the tempter was unawarely falling into his own trap (Chromatius, *Tractate on Matt.* 14.5).

The Sinlessness of Jesus: Classic Reasoning

Church teaching affirms that Christ was conceived, lived, and died without sin (Creed of Epiphanius, *SCD* 13; see also 18, 65, 148, 251). The sinlessness of Jesus is traditionally argued from two viewpoints: first, deductively from premises previously established and, second, inductively from direct testimony of friends and indirect testimony of opponents.

Deductive Reasoning

There are three common deductive arguments: First, if God does not will contrary to God's will, and if sin is to act counter to God's will, then the God-man would not sin. Since the divine will does not will against itself, and since sin is defined as willing against the divine will, the deduction is required: the eternal Son would not sin (Gregory of Nazianzus, *On the Son, Theol. Orat.* 4.30.14).

The second brings us closer to salvation history: *Only the sinlessness of the eternal Son could be the fitting moral foundation for his atoning work.* Such a deduction was early intuited as the remembering community began to reflect upon Jesus' death: "Such a high priest meets our need—one who is holy, blameless, pure, set apart from sinners, exalted above the heavens" (Heb. 7:26; Chrysostom, *Epis. to Heb.* 13.7).

The most striking deduction concerning his sinlessness is the third, based upon the extraordinary premise that he understood himself to have legitimate power to forgive sins. He was remembered as such both by friends and detractors. It is not surprising that the early rememberers would reason deductively: *Only one who was without sin could presume to forgive sin* (Heb. 8:1–13; Athanasius, *Letter 61 to Maximus*).

Inductive Arguments Based on Observation and Testimony

In addition to these deductive arguments, are there compelling evidences that lead us to conclude that he was without sin? Or were these statements about Jesus' sinlessness more likely later accretions to the memory of him, protectively attributed to him by a romanticizing church that overlooked or failed accurately to remember his sins? The latter is the common view in much contemporary New Testament criticism. However, the breadth and nature of evidence for his innocence is such that it is difficult to argue that it had no basis in Jesus' actual life. Among the classic arguments for innocence are three in particular.

Why It Is Unlikely that the Testimony to Impeccability Was Deluded

First, it is unlikely that the testimony to his blameless behavior was deluded. Deluded people may claim to be sinless, but they usually do not convince anyone beside themselves. That is why we call them deluded. But in Jesus' case, many appear to have been radically convinced—so much so that they were willing to sell all, deny themselves, bear their cross, and go abroad to proclaim this message at great risk—that Jesus was what he said he was (Incomplete Work on Matt., Hom. 29). The rememberers perceived in him no discrepancy between what he claimed and what he did.

Secondly, the fact that his claims were so all-embracing makes it even more remarkable that he was perceived as sinless. Excessive claims are more easily demolished. This fact argues that his character was congruous with his claims (Matt. 27:3, 19; Cyprian, *Treatises* 12.2.15).

Third, there is no doubt that Jesus was attested as sinless. The question remains as to whether the accounts were accurate recollections. The primary basis upon which one seeks to assess the truth of historical statements of this sort is the evidence that accumulates during one's public life. It remains an astonishing fact that the most remembered life in history was not remembered to have harmed anyone or shown any elements of moral venality or reprehensibility. Neither friends nor foes remember or report him as sinner.

The Verdict of His Enemies: The Evidence of
Those Who Crucified Him

The testimony even of his enemies favors his innocence. It is thus necessary to listen carefully to the testimony of his enemies, remembering that he was under extremely close surveillance. Recall that when Jesus was under fire from the scribes and Pharisees and finally in a formal trial for his life, many charges were hurled at him. They were constantly trying to trap him in his own words (Mark 12:13). They tailed him, watched him, surveilled him constantly, looking for some slight misstep (Mark 3:2). In a trial one would expect all pertinent charges to be declared. There were plenty of opportunities to dredge up skeletons that might have otherwise been in his closet. If it were the case that his life had been sullied by irresponsible acts, it would be likely that amid these hostile encounters some of those charges would have surfaced. If attempts were made to cover up, wouldn't the authorities have had all the resources to get to the bottom of it?

If he had been guilty of hypocrisy, he would have been an easy target for dismissal. Suppose he had been guilty of hypocrisy. Suppose he called others to justice yet was himself unjust, or called others to love yet remained unloving. Wouldn't one expect some charge of hypocrisy to surface during the heat of embittered debate? It would have been an extraordinary hypocrisy indeed if this man, who assumed the power to forgive sin, had offended in some evident way. He must have included himself in the call to tell the whole truth, and in the call to perfect love. Thus he would have been easily cast out on the charge of hypocrisy if there had been any doubt among his contemporaries about the consistency of his behavior with his teaching. Recall that the synoptic Gospels regularly report opinions of detractors, yet there is no hint of any charge of this sort. But there was in fact a telling absence of the charge of hypocrisy (Luke 23:14; Ambrose, *Expos. On Luke* 10.100–102).

On closer inspection, each supposed fault of Jesus pointed to a deeper good in his character. It is an intriguing fact that, amid all the controversy about him, Jesus was not plausibly charged with moral or character fault, except for the wholly untruthful charges of blasphemy and subversion that finally resulted in his death. He was indeed charged with gluttonous eating and drinking and mixing with sinners, with obscure forms of Sabbath breaking, and chiefly with blasphemy. Yet in each of these cases, the charge itself was a distinct badge of honor in relation to his authentic identity and messianic mission. He was a "friend of sinners," harlots, and publicans because he invited them to enter God's kingdom, not because he was being corrupted by them. He did not truly break the law by healing on the Sabbath but fulfilled it. To forgive sins was God's own prerogative, and he was blaspheming only if he was not indeed God-incarnate (Gregory Nazianzus, *On His Father's Silence*). Each alleged moral deficit was a necessary part of his teaching ministry. Some have argued that Jesus was not unambiguously good according to the reports about him, for he became angry, drove merchants away from the Temple with a whip, spoke harshly to his mother, and broke the Sabbath law. Yet in each of these cases, what seemed to be a questionable behavior was at its depth an excellent act that only appeared deficient when detached from its context (Bonhoeffer, *Christology*: 112; Aldwinckle, *MTM*:195–99).

It is instructive and even moving to listen carefully to the final verdicts of his enemies who colluded in Jesus' death.

- Judas cried out, "I have betrayed innocent blood" (Matt 27:3).

- Pilate queried, "What crime has he committed?" and protested, "I am innocent of this man's blood" (27:23–24), declaring: "I have examined him in your presence and have found no basis for your charges against him" (Luke 23:14).

- Pilate's wife said, "Don't have anything to do with that innocent man" (Matt. 27:19; Chrysostom, *Hom. on Matt.* 86.1).

- Herod cleared him of charges, as Pilate remarked, "Neither has Herod [found any basis for the charges], for he sent him back to us; as you can see, he has done nothing to deserve death" (Luke 23:15).

- The centurion at the cross declared, "Surely this was a righteous man" (Luke 23:47; Cyril of Alex., *Comm. on Luke* 153).

- Even the thief sized him up instantly, according to Luke: "this man has done nothing wrong" (Luke 13:41; Cyril of Jerusalem, *Catech. Lect.* 13).

This is an astonishing confluence of testimony even among those who had conspired in bringing his life to a bloody end.

His Character Attested by Those Who Knew Him Best

The disciples of Christ walked daily and lived closely with him under harsh circumstances. They shared a common purse, ate together, labored, risked, and traveled together for three years (Acts 1:21–22). Being a disciple was not a casual relation. The disciples must have had the opportunity to see him under all sorts of conditions, in fair and foul weather, struggling and relaxing, at weddings and upon the death of a friend. Would not it be expected that such familiarity would breed contempt? It did not happen in this case. They were leading witnesses to his perfect love and holiness.

Recall that the disciples were steeped in the Jewish tradition of the ubiquity of sin, which assumed that "there is no one who does good, not even one" (Ps. 14:3). They had to go against all that they had learned about the universality of sin to assert the faultlessness of Jesus, but they could do precisely this only if the facts of the case warranted it.

John wrote: "In him is no sin" (1 John 3:5). This is the same author who had said, "If we claim to be without sin, we deceive ourselves" (1 John 1:8; Bede, *On 1 John* 1). Viewed under the premise of his theandric God-man identity, both are true and consistent. "There are many great people in the world who are respected as if they were perfect, but none of them could take away the sins of the world because none of them could live in the world entirely free of sin" (Bede, *On 1 John* 3.5).

Calling hearers to follow in the steps of Jesus' example of sacrificial service, the First Letter of Peter declared: "He committed no sin, and no deceit was found in his mouth" (1 Pet. 2:21–22, quoting Isa. 53:9). He was compared to "a lamb without blemish or defect" (1 Pet. 1:19; Chrysostom, *Catena, CEC* 47). Only one who was "righteous" could die "for the unrighteous" (1 Pet. 3:18; cf. Heb 4:15). Paul followed the earliest oral tradition of Christian recollection of Jesus when he wrote that "God made him who had no sin to be sin for us, so that in him we might become the righteousness of God" (1 Cor. 5:21, italics added). Only one who "had no sin" could legitimately be placed in a position to "condemn sin."

What Christ Is Reported to Have Said of Himself

When a woman caught in adultery was brought him, he said, "If any one of you is without sin, let him be the first to throw a stone at her," and they "began to go away one at a time, the older ones first, until only Jesus was left" (John 8:7, 9, italics added). Jesus bluntly asked his detractors after this incident: "Can any of you prove me guilty of sin?" (John 8:46; Origen, Comm. on John 20.277–288). Note the counter-point of these two texts in the same chapter: no one in the circle of accusers was without sin. All went away in response to the question except one—Jesus. And those who had gone away were challenged to prove him guilty of sin (Origen, OFP 2.6.4).

Further, there is no evidence in the words of Jesus of any inward struggle with guilt over moral failure. Among the saints, those who have walked the furthest on the way of holiness are those likely to be most keenly aware of their own guilt. St. Teresa of Avila, for example, understood most acutely how distant she was from the full possibility of the holy life, but it was not because she was living distantly from that life but so near it (Teresa, Life, CWST 1: 179–290). Yet Jesus, whose closeness to God the Father could hardly be questioned, showed no evidences of such guilt or remorse (Origen, Comm. on John 20.277).

Hard Sayings Examined

Three perplexities remain:

1. Why did Jesus remark, "Why do you ask me about what is good?" When Jesus responded to the rich young ruler who had addressed him as "Good Teacher," his response pointedly affirmed that "No one is good—except God alone" (Mark 10:18). Was Jesus saying that he, too, was not good, or not as good as God (as the false teachers argued)? Jesus was here challenging the young man about his assumptions about what is good in order better to call him to repentance. The question, "Why do you call me good?" was a query addressed the young man, not a statement about Jesus (Hilary, On Trin. 9.2). It probed for a thoughtful and serious answer. Its teaching purpose was to confront the young man with his own predicament, not to talk about Jesus' moral virtue or status (Clement of Alex., Rich Man 8; Origen, OFP 1.13).

2. Did Jesus' participation in a sinful society make him unavoidably a sinner? If simply being born into a society already makes one a sinner, then sin finally has nothing to do with free choice. If every society is thought to be by definition equally sinful—according to some grim logic of equality—and in such a society sin is automatically and necessarily transmitted in an absolutely equal way to every person prior to any act of freedom, then it would have to be asserted that either Jesus was somehow immune to society's influences or he was sinner. Neither of these conclusions is consistent with testimony about him. The deeper answer hinges on the Spirit's constant enabling and shepherding of his freedom, providing him with requisite gifts for ministry, enabling him to resist temptation of every kind, including evil that might result from collusion with social injustices (Luke 4:18; Cyril of Alex. Comm. on Luke, Hom. 12).

3. *Does Jesus become less human by having not sinned?* If we say that
    Jesus is not fully human because he never sinned, then we have made
    a grossly un-Hebraic statement about humanity—namely, that because
    human nature is created sinful, God as Creator created sin (as opposed
    to the biblical view of God-given freedom as ever prone to the abuse of
    freedom). To require of Jesus that he take on our sinful, fallen nature in
    order to be fully human is not to make Jesus more fully human but less
    human (Creed of Epiphanius, *COC* 2:36). That oddly amounts to requiring
    that humanity *must* miss its mark (*hamartia*) if it is to be human! That is
    patently self-contradictory, hence in error (Hilary, *Trin.* 9.4,40).

The Son of Man

The early importance of the title "Son of Man" is clear from its frequency of use
in the Gospels—over fifty times excluding parallel sayings. Most occur in the
primitive strata of Gospel sources.

The Earliest Layer of Messianic Titles Highlighting
Both His Descent and Ascent

A crucial feature of the Johannine use of the "Son of Man" title was the assumption
that he who had descended from heaven would ascend once again (John 3:13;
Daniel 7:13, 14; Augustine, *Comm. on John, Tractate* 12). Jesus said to Nathanael:
"You shall see heaven open, and the angels of God ascending and descending on
the Son of Man" (John 1:51; reminiscent of Jacob's ladder), suggesting that the
Son of Man is the gate of heaven, the unique personage wherein humanity and
deity come into concourse and union.

The preexistence, descent, and ascent of the Son are encompassed in this unusual name: "No one has ever gone into heaven except the one who came from
heaven—the Son of Man" (John 3:13). "He is called Son of Man, not as having
had His generation from the earth, as each one of us, but as 'coming upon the
clouds of heaven' to judge the living and the dead" (Cyril of Jerusalem, *Catech.
Lect.* 10). The descent and ascent themes are coordinated in the Fourth Gospel:
"I came from the Father and entered the world; now I am leaving the world and
going back to the Father" (John 16:28; Augustine, *Sermon* 265B.2). In *Enoch*, the
Son of Man was a messianic title indicating a pretemporal heavenly figure who
would descend to earth, judge the nations, inaugurate the kingdom of glory, and
clothe the righteous with robes of glory, who would share in fellowship with the
Son of Man eternally (*Enoch* 46:48; 62:6–16; 69:26–29).

The title "Son of Man" is frequently reported in the Gospel narratives as being
used by Jesus himself. It is found in all Gospels repeatedly, and from Jesus'
own lips sixty-five times. "Son of Man" appears to have been utilized almost
exclusively by Jesus himself and by the earliest pre-Pauline tradition, but it does
not appear in the Letters of Paul and did not find its way into the creeds (I. H.
Marshall, ed., *New Testament Interpretation*:79). The textual evidence implies that
this was a title that Jesus himself used, not one that was later ascribed to him
by others.

The Secret Revealed

He resisted being called "Messiah" until the right time, in order to protect
against popular distortions inconsistent with his mission. By drawing on the late
prophetic term "Son of Man," Jesus was pointing obliquely to his messianic role
but transmuting it in an unusual way as descending from the Father into incarnate

mission, and ascending to heaven after his resurrection. "He called himself the Son of Man because this title made an exalted claim and yet at the same time permitted Jesus to fill the term with new meaning. This he did by coupling the role of Son of Man with that of the Suffering Servant" (Ladd, *TNT*:158). The unique sort of messiahship Jesus embodied ran against popular Jewish hopes. He would suffer and die before he would be raised again to inaugurate the reign of God.

As end-time Son of Man, Jesus would return to judge and finally to bestow the kingdom, but before his death and resurrection, he was the Son of Man living as a man among men and women and would suffer and die for others (Bede, *Hom. on Gospels* 1.17). The kingdom comes in unexpected form and works secretly, hiddenly, like yeast. The messianic secret is that the heavenly Son of Man was already unexpectedly present in human history, moving inexorably toward the hour in which all would be revealed. "If anyone is ashamed of me and my words in this adulterous and sinful generation, the Son of Man will be ashamed of him when he comes in his Father's glory with the holy angels" (Mark 8:28). The saying is valued by critics as embedded in the deepest layer of oral tradition coming from Jesus (Bornkamm, *JN*:228; Bultmann, *TNT* 1:28; H. E. Tödt, *The Son of Man in the Synoptic Tradition*:329–31). It is likely that Jesus identified his mission with that of the Son of Man, but that only became fully clear to the disciples after the resurrection.

Among Jesus' hearers, many would be familiar with the Old Testament title "Son of Man," especially that found in Daniel 7. In Daniel's vision, the Son of Man was seen "coming with the clouds of heaven. He approached the Ancient of Days and was led into his presence. He was given authority, glory and sovereign power; all peoples, nations and men of every language worshiped him. His dominion is an everlasting dominion that will not pass away, and his kingdom is one that will never be destroyed" (Dan. 7:13–14; Jerome, *Comm. on Daniel* 7.13–14). Many elements of Jesus' identity and ministry are thereby anticipated: Son of the Father, recipient of an eternal kingdom; presented before the Ancient of Days; ruler of a reign of peace that would extend to all nations, never to end. The Son of Man was expected to represent those who have remained faithful to God, who share in the kingdom of which the Son of Man will be ruler, who will stand in God's presence (Dan. 7; Irenaeus, *Ag. Her.* 3.19, 4.33; Tertullian, *On the Flesh of Christ* 15).

The Son of Man Sayings

The Gospel sayings of and about the Son of Man fall into three phases. First, to the earthly Son of Man as seen in Jesus' earthly ministry (Mark 2:12; Luke 7:34; 9:58). The Son of Man came to seek and save the lost, was conscious of his mission as messianic redeemer (Luke 19:10); came eating and drinking, calling all to repentance (Matt. 11:19); claimed and evidenced authority to forgive sin (Mark 2:10 and parallels); was Lord of Sabbath; was able to interpret scribal regulations (Mark 2:27 and parallels); yet had nowhere to lay his head (Matt. 8:20).

Second, the term referred to the suffering and dying Son of Man, to the impending death, and resurrection of the Son of Man (Mark 9:9; Luke 17:24–25; 24:7). He came not "to be served but to serve, and to give his life as a ransom for many" (Mark 10:45; Isa. 53:10–12). The Son of Man was a pretemporal heavenly being who was expected to come in poverty, humility, and vulnerability as a man for others. At Caesarea Philippi it may have been first understood that the Son of Man would be like the suffering Servant of Isaiah 53. Thereafter it was clear that the Son of Man "must suffer" (Mark 8:31); be delivered into the hands of men and the chief priests (Mark 9:31; 10:33); and be condemned to death (Matt. 20:18; Luke 18:31); remain three days in the earth (Matt. 12:40; Irenaeus, *Ag. Her.* 3.12.5), and rise again (Mark 10:33).

Finally, this unique title pointed to the end-time coming of the Son of Man in his future activity as Judge and Savior, coming in glory to inaugurate the reign of God (Mark 8:38; 13:26; Luke 12:8; Augustine, *CG, FC* 24: 33). The Son of Man will return at an unexpected hour (Luke 12:40; Matt. 24:44); and will come soon (Matt. 10:23; 16:28; Mark 9:1); will come with clouds and great glory (Mark 8:38 and 13:16 with parallels); and will sit at the right hand of power (Mark 14:62 with parallels).

It was only belatedly at his trial that his identity became fully and publicly clarified: Jesus was asked by the high priest whether he was the Messiah, Son of God. At this crucial point, Jesus stated outright what Messiah means: "'I am,' said Jesus. 'And you will see the Son of Man sitting at the right hand of the Mighty one and coming on the clouds of heaven'" (Mark 14:62). The context of the scene was that the priests were judging him. The ironic twist was that all too soon he would be judging them.

The Journey Toward Jerusalem

From Jesus' baptism with water to his baptism with blood on the cross, it was becoming increasingly clear that an unparalleled event was occurring. That evolving recognition is what the Gospel writers narrated. They described the unfolding of events that made it plausible. Each step of Christ's earthly journey pointed anticipatively toward the atoning work of his death which was confirmed through his resurrection.

Peter's Confession and the Recognition of the Messianic Servant

Jesus and his disciples had been preaching in the northern part of Israel, even as far north as the border. The preaching ministry that had begun in Galilee was soon to turn abruptly toward Jerusalem.

In preparation for that final struggle, Jesus sought to make clear to his closest disciples what was at stake in his mission (Hilary, *On Matthew* 17.1). At Caesarea Philippi he asked: "Who do you say that I am?" Peter answered boldly for the others with words that were to become the heart of the most basic Christian confession: "You are the Christ" (Mark 8:29). It was because Peter "replied for the rest of the Apostles" and ultimately for the rest of humanity, that "he is called the foundation" (Ambrose, *Incarn. of Our Lord* 4.33; Baxter, *PW* 17: 477–79).

Jesus freely welcomed this confession with a saying that would greatly affect the history of the church: "Blessed are you, Simon son of Jonah, for this was not revealed to you by man, but by my Father in heaven. And I tell you that you are Peter, and on this rock I will build my church, and the gates of Hades will not overcome it. I will give you the keys of the kingdom of heaven; whatever you bind on earth will be bound in heaven, and whatever you loose on earth will be loosed in heaven" (Matt. 16:17–19; Epiphanius the Latin, *Interpretation of the Gospels* 28).

Then Jesus "began to teach them openly that the Son of Man must suffer many things and be rejected by the elders, chief priests and teachers of the law, and that he must be killed and after three days rise again" (Mark 8:31; cf. Matt. 16:13–23; Luke 9:18–22; Tho. Aq., *ST* 3 Q46). Late Judaic expectation had not anticipated a suffering and dying messiah. It had focused upon the Davidic king who was to reign, not die (Ladd, *TNT*:330). Gradually it became clearer to some disciples, although it was still kept from general knowledge, that it is only through suffering and death that the Son of Man would fulfill his mission (Pearson, *EC* 1:157, 317; Marshall, *ONTC*: 63–97).

Those who would accompany him in this mission must be willing to follow his path of proclaiming the coming reign of God and self-giving love for others: "If anyone would come after me, he must deny himself and take up his cross and follow me. For whoever wants to save his life will lose it, but whoever loses his life for me and for the gospel will save it" (Mark 8:34–35). Willingness to suffer and if necessary die on behalf of the truth of God's coming thereafter became the distinguishing mark of discipleship (Chrysostom, *Hom. on Matt.* Hom. 55.1). Yet even this step must be rightly and carefully taken, for "the law of martyrdom alike forbids us voluntarily to go to meet it (in consideration for the persecutors, and for the weak) or to shrink from it if it comes upon us; for the former shows foolhardiness, the latter cowardice" (Gregory Nazianzus, *Orat.* 43.6). Jesus' willingness to die was neither masochistic nor neurotic. Martyrdom is neither to be sought nor avoided, but if necessary received as an implication of discipleship (Augustine *CG* 1:22–29).

How the Transfiguration Prefigured the Exaltation

Jesus' decision to go to Jerusalem to "suffer many things" was illuminated by a crucial event that prefigured his identity: the transfiguration. The transfiguration is that event on a mountain near Nazareth where Jesus was "transfigured" (*metamorphoō*), or transformed, in conversation with Moses and Elijah, and a voice from heaven affirmed his divine Sonship and the gravity of his mission (Matt. 17:1–8; Mark 9:2–8; Luke 9:28–36).

The transfiguration was a moment of extraordinary salience in previsioning this end. "After six days Jesus took Peter, James and John with him and led them up a high mountain, where they were all alone. There he was transfigured before them. His clothes became dazzling white, whiter than anyone in the world could bleach them. And there appeared before them Elijah and Moses, who were talking with Jesus" (Mark 9:2–11; Origen, *Comm. on Matt.* 12.37–39; Tertullian, *Ag. Marcion* 4.22). According to Luke's report, "They spoke about his departure"—*exodus* (death)—"which he was about to bring to fulfillment at Jerusalem" (Luke 9:31; Bonaventure, *Tree of Life*, *CWS*:135). He revealed to his closest disciples his messianic identity, the necessity of his coming death, and his resurrection according to Scripture (Chrysostom, *Hom. on Matt.* 56–58).

Divine Sonship Confirmed from on High: A Foretaste of Glory

If there existed any debate on the Gnostic fringes of the postresurrection community as to whether the transfiguration event really occurred, the Second Letter of Peter sought to conclude it. That Letter went out of its way to counter such doubts and attest the truth of the transfiguration: "We did not follow cleverly invented stories when we told you about the power and coming of our Lord Jesus Christ, but we were eyewitnesses of his majesty. For he received honor and glory from God the Father when the voice came to him from the Majestic Glory, saying, 'This is my Son, whom I love; with him I am well pleased.' We ourselves heard this voice that came from heaven when we were with him on the sacred mountain" (2 Pet. 1:16–18; Andreas, *Catena* CEC:88)—Mount Tabor (Hilary of Arles, *Comm. on 2 Peter*).

Just before the transfiguration, Jesus had said, "I tell you the truth, some who are standing here will not taste death before they see the Son of Man coming in his kingdom" (Matt. 16:28). This was said to prepare them for his imminent suffering, death and resurrection (Chrysostom, *Hom. on Matt.* 55.5, 56). The transfiguration was a preview of the kingdom, the Lord appearing in a vision of glory (Baxter, *PW* 18:462–67). On the mount of transfiguration those closest disciples who would soon taste the blood and death of persecution were allowed for a moment to taste the glory to come (Bede, *Comm.*, on Mark 8:39; Origen, *Comm. on Matt.* 12.28). "Therefore it was fitting that He should show His disciples the glory of His clarity (which is to be transfigured), to which He will configure those who are His" (Tho. Aq., *ST* 3 Q45).

The transfiguration signified in advance "the future clarity of the saints" and represented "His body's future clarity" (Tho. Aq., *ST* 3, Q45.1, 2). Clarity implied the agility, subtlety and impassibility of the glorified body (Maximos, *Four Hundred Texts, Philokal.* 2:134–35; Gregory I, *Moralia on Job* 32). "You were transfigured on the mountain, O Christ our Lord, and the glory has so caught the wonder of Your disciples, that when they see You crucified they will understand that Your Passion is voluntary, and they will proclaim to the world that You are truly the Splendor of the Father" (Hymn for the Feast of the Transfiguration, *Menologia*, Lossky, *MTEC*:149, amended).

The Anointed One

"Messiah" is among the most important of all concepts in Christian teaching. By it the person of Jesus is rightly identified in relation to his office in the history of Jewish expectation (Pearson, *EC* 1:142). The New Testament was written in order that hearers might believe "that Jesus is the Christ" (John 20:31; Irenaeus, *Ag. Her.* 3.16.5).

Messiah (Gk. *Christos*, Heb. *Mashiah*, "anointed") was the Expected One, Son of David anointed to be the deliverer of Israel (Augustine, *CG, FC* 14: 47–56). The resurrection would both confirm and clarify the messianic designation. Peter proclaimed after the resurrection: "God has made this Jesus, whom you crucified, both Lord and Christ" (Acts 2:36)—"that is, *Anointed*" (Tertullian, *Ag. Praxeas* 38; J. Knox, *Jesus: Lord and Christ*). All Christian creeds confess Jesus as *the Christ*. (*Credo . . . in unum Dominum Jesum Christum,* Creed of 150 Fathers). What does that mean?

For What Purpose Was the Messiah Anointed?

The name Christ "signifies that he is anointed by his Father to be King, Priest and Prophet. Scripture applies anointing to these three uses," attributing these three offices to Christ (Calvin, *Catech. of the Church of Geneva*). "The title 'Christ' pertains to these three offices: for we know that under the law prophets as well as priests and kings were anointed" (Calvin, *Inst.* 2.15.2).

A single title unites three offices. The systematic connection must be clearly established between the title "Christ" and the three offices. Classic Protestant teaching is best stated by the *Heidelberg Catechism:* "Why is he called Christ, that is, the Anointed One? Because he is ordained by God the Father and anointed with the Holy Spirit to be *our chief Prophet and Teacher,* fully revealing to us the secret purpose and will of God concerning our redemption; to be *our only High Priest,* having redeemed us by the one sacrifice of his body and ever interceding for us with the Father; and to be *our eternal King,* governing us by his Word and Spirit, and defending and sustaining us in the redemption he has won for us" (*Catech.* 2.Q31).

By the time of writing of the early Pauline Letters, *Christos* had become a proper name joined with the name "Jesus" for all who attested the resurrection.

The disciples were first called *Christianoi* ("Christians") in Antioch (Acts 11:26; Theophilus, *To Autolycus* 1.1, 12) where Gentile voices were predominate.

Classical exegetes insist that his identity as Anointed One comes not from human hands, but from God alone: "He is called Christ, not as having been anointed by human hands, but anointed eternally by the Father to His High-Priesthood over men" (Cyril of Jerusalem, *Catech. Lect.* 10.; Augustine, *Trin.*, FC 45:515–16).

Long before modern critics raised this issue it was being debated in early Christianity: whether Jesus disavowed a title that was later ascribed to him by others, and whether Jesus become the Christ only when called the Christ. The ecumenical consensus was summarized by John of Damascus: "We say that the Son and Word of God became Christ the instant that He came to dwell in the womb. . . . It is when the Word was made flesh that we say that He received the name of Christ Jesus" (*OF* 4.6; cf. Gregory Nazianzus, *Orat.* 30.21; Cyril of Alexandria, *To Emperor Theodosius* 28). Athanasius argued that Christ did not become so only when named by others, but was so before being thus humanly confessed (*Ag. Apollinaris* 2:1–2).

The Expected One in the Prophetic Tradition

If we had in hand only the Old Testament texts expecting the messiah and knew nothing yet of the New Testament, we would still know a great deal about the Expected One. He was to be set apart as servant of God to bring deliverance to captives (Ps. 89:3–4; Isa. 9–11; Jer. 30:8–9; Ezek. 37:21–23). Micah expected that the ruler of Israel would come from Bethlehem (Mic. 5:2). Haggai expected that One "desired of all nations" would come bringing the glory and peace of God (Hag. 2:6–7). Malachi expected a messenger who would prepare the way for the Lord, an angel of the covenant who would appear in the Temple. Isaiah prophesied of "A voice of one calling: 'In the desert prepare the way for the Lord; make straight in the wilderness a highway for our God'" (Isa. 40:3). The whole world, Jews and non-Jews, would benefit from God's own coming (Isa. 42:1–17; 49:6–13; Jer. 16:19–21; Mal. 1:11). In all these ways the prophets expressly taught of God's own future coming. The Expected One would have a distinctive kingly role in the coming reign of God (Isa. 57:9; Jer. 23:5; Hos. 3:5; Mic. 4:8–9; Zech. 9:9).

Isaiah expected a king in the line of David who would cleanse from sin, gather Israel, bring peace, and reign forever (Isa. 11), upon whom the "Spirit of the Lord will rest" (Isa. 11:2; Calvin, *Comm.* 7:370–96). Zechariah expected the messianic king to ride into Jerusalem on "a colt, the foal of a donkey" as a sign of victory, bringing salvation, peace, and the governance of God over the earth (Zech. 9:9–10; Justin Martyr, *First Apology* 35; *Dialogue with Trypho* 53). Daniel prophesied that the Anointed One would be a ruler who was expected to appear 490 years ("seventy sevens" or "seventy weeks," Dan. 9:24–25) after the rebuilding of Jerusalem (Clement of Alex., *Stromata* 1.21). Early Christian exegetes figured that Daniel's prophecy was realized during the period in which Jesus lived (Origen, *OFP* 4.1). Late Judaic messianism expected "one who will build a house for my Name, and I will establish the throne of his kingdom forever. I will be his father, and he will he my son" (2 Sam. 7:13–14; cf. Matt. 1:1; Mark 1:11; Heb 1:5). Pious Jews in Jesus' time were intensely aware of these allusions and expectations.

The messianic king was viewed in Psalm 2 under two principal metaphors: "Son" of the Father (Ps. 2:8), and "Anointed One" destined to rule nations (Ps. 2:2, 8) as king whose kingdom would be inaugurated in Jerusalem (Ps. 2:6; Acts 4:25–28; Augustine, *Expos, Ps 2*). That this Expected One would be God is clear from the name "Immanuel" (Isa. 7:11), and from other prophetic titles ascribable only to God: "Mighty God," "Everlasting Father" (Isa. 9:6). Isaiah more than any other source stressed that the Expected One would suffer for us. The innocent victim would take the place of the guilty. On him our sins would be laid. He would be wounded for our transgressions (Isa. 53).

The *Apocalypse of Baruch* and 4 Ezra gave form to intense apocalyptic expectations of messianic coming that were current in the period in which Jesus lived. They expected one who would judge the nations and inaugurate an enduring reign of peace. The *Similitudes of Enoch* spoke of a preexistent heavenly Son of Man whose mission would be to establish the reign of God, a commentary on Daniel's vision of the Son of Man (*Enoch* 48:10; 52:4). The Qumran community looked for an Anointed One, "the Messiah of Righteousness," "the Branch of David" (Dupont-Sommer, *The Essene Writings from Qumran*:314–16). Herod and the Pharisees were acutely aware of these prophecies and feared that they would have dire political consequences (Matt. 2:1–18; John 11:47–48). But Jesus taught that his messianic kingship is "not of this world" and is not to be achieved by coercion (John 18:36). When the people "intended to come and make him king by force," Jesus "withdrew again to a mountain by himself" (John 6:15; Chrysostom, *Hom. on John* 42).

The Identification of Jesus as Messiah

Jesus himself used the term "Messiah" with restraint, and for good reason. If the people had been given the signal that he was Messiah, it is quite possible that it would have been instantly misinterpreted as a signal for political rebellion or an intensification of the expectation for a worldly kingdom, which ran contrary to Jesus' mission (Augustine, *Tractates on John*, 115.2). Since the popular meaning of the term "messiah" was quite different from the actual mission of the Messiah, Jesus understandably did not make frequent public use of that term, and his messianic identity emerged only slowly and under constricted circumstances with only a few select disciples (Ambrose, *Expos. of Luke* 7.9).

When Jesus performed miracles, he often warned his hearers to keep quiet and avoid public notice. The leper was given a "strong warning: 'See that you don't tell this to anyone'" (Mark 1:43–44; Tertullian, *Ag. Marcion* 4.9). Jairus was strictly forbidden from telling others about the raising of his daughter (Mark 5:43; Jerome, *Hom. 77 on Mark*). After Peter's confession, Jesus warned the disciples "not to tell anyone about him" (Mark 8:30; cf. 9:9; Chrysostom, *Hom. on Transfiguration* 57.2).

Recent theories that Jesus altogether rejected the designation of Messiah (Bultmann, *TNT* 1:26–32) were anticipated by early critics of Christianity who did not follow the received apostolic tradition (see responses by Irenaeus, *Ag. Her.* 3.1–4 and Justin Martyr, *Dialogue with Trypho* 35–40). Jesus understood himself as Messiah, but not the political messiah of popular expectation. His messianic mission led not to a political kingdom but to a crucifixion, not to living powerfully but dying powerlessly, not to a crown of majesty but of thorns (Clement of Alex., *Instr.* 2.8).

Jesus accepted the messianic title, blessed his disciples when they recognized it, and finally under oath on trial acknowledged it. But prior to his trial, he was cautious about this disclosure because he knew how wrongly it could be perceived. After his resurrection he was proclaimed as Messiah, yet a Messiah who transformed prevailing messianic expectations by his death and resurrection (Eusebius, *PG* 1:193; Ursinus, *CHC*:171–72).

Messianic Expectation During Jesus' Ministry

Intense expectation accompanied Jesus' ministry. The first thing Andrew did after spending a day with Jesus was to "find his brother Simon and tell him,

'We have found the Messiah' (that is, the Christ)" (John 1:40–41). The next day Philip, having been called by Jesus, "found Nathanael and told him, 'We have found the one Moses wrote about in the Law, and about whom the prophets also wrote,'" whom Nathanael called "Son of God" and "King of Israel" (John 1:43–50; Chrysostom, *Hom. 20 on John*).

Jesus' final entry into Jerusalem was interpreted by many as the coming of the messianic king of prophetic expectation (John 12:13–15). In sharp contrast with the power of worldly kings, the messiah was expected to come gently with righteousness, bringing salvation (Zech. 9:9). The messianic expectations of the people overflowed in the shout: "Blessed is he who comes in the name of the Lord! Blessed is the coming kingdom of our father David" (Mark 11:9–10; cf. Ps. 118:25–26). Days later it would be evident how shallow were these expectations, when the crowd shouted once again, but for Jesus' crucifixion (Mark 15:13).

When accused before Pilate, Jesus was directly asked, "Are you the king of the Jews?" (John 18:33). He indirectly answered, "You are right in saying I am a king, and for this I came into the world, to testify to the truth" (John 18:37). In Mark's account, Jesus answered, "Yes, it is as you say" (Mark 15:2). In Matthew's account there is a fuller explanation: "'Yes, it is as you say,' Jesus replied. 'But I say to all of you: In the future you will see the Son of Man sitting at the right hand of the Mighty One and coming on the clouds of heaven'" (Matt. 26:64), which caused the high priest to charge blasphemy. Jesus' execution was due to this acknowledgment that he understood his ministry as that of the Messiah, Son of Man. The formal accusation was sedition, in relation to the alleged claim that he was a pretender to kingship and hence a threat to civil order (Mark 15:26).

Names and Titles Ascribed to the Anointed One

The Titles as a Congruent Mosaic

Central elements of Christian teaching are compacted in the several major titles repeatedly attributed to the messianic Lord. Taken together (and in most cases even taken separately) they embrace key affirmations of the Christian confession of Christ: his preexistent sonship, his humble coming in the flesh, his suffering, death, and resurrection, his prophetic, priestly, and regal ministries, his unique role as divine-human mediator and reconciler, his union with the faithful, and his future offices of judgment and consummation. Each title forms a colorful fragment in the mosaic of a larger unified vision of the saving event (Lactantius, *Div. Inst.*). Separately each is intriguing; together they are beautiful (Cyril of Alex., *Comm. on Luke,* Hom. 153).

His very name, Jesus (from Jehosua or Joshua), means Savior (Matt. 1:21). The identity of Jesus is the main subject of the New Testament. The variety of word pictures used to celebrate the mystery and glory of this identity is profuse (Ambrosiaster, *Comm. on Paul's Epistles*, Rom. 1.3).

He is the rock of our salvation, the foundation on which the church is built, chief cornerstone, the head of the body, the vine that takes leaf, bridegroom of the end-time banquet, brother of his disciples, and friend of sinners (1 Pet. 2:6; Eph. 1:22; Luke 7:34; Matt. 25:6; John 20:17). From on high, he has elected to be a servant of the lowly—suffering Servant, minister, counselor, peacemaker (Isa. 42–43; Rom. 15:8; Acts 3:26). He is the Help of the Lord, the Prince of Salvation. As Son of the Father, beloved of the Father, uniquely related to the Father, preexistent Logos (John 1:1–18), and "the radiance of God's glory and the exact representation of his being" (Heb. 1:2). He has become for us the physician of souls, the fountain of cleansing, the bread and water of sustenance, the door of access to life with God (Augustine, *Sermons* 137.3–4).

As Messiah, Jesus is the Lord's anointed agent of salvation, author of salvation (Heb. 3:2), Redeemer, Mediator (Isa. 59:20; 1 Tim. 2:5), Light of the world, the Desire of the nations, the Expected One of Israel (Isa. 17:3; Hag. 2:7). He was called "Jesus Christ the Righteous" (1 John 2:1; Bede, *On 1 John* 2), the Righteous One (Acts 3:14), Sanctifier, the Holy One (Heb. 2:11; 1 John 2:20), who presides over our justification in the court (as the "guarantee of a better covenant," Heb. 7:22), and our sanctification in the Temple (as "priest forever," Heb. 7:17). Jesus is the "author and perfecter of our faith" (Heb. 12:2), "the mediator of a new covenant" (Heb. 12:24), "the way and the truth and the life" (John 14:6), or, more simply, "the life" (John 11:25). The variety of his names and titles is stunning. For believers the joy of this variety of colors and strands is like a puzzle asking to be put together.

The respectful study of these ascriptions has served as an elementary exercise in classic Christian teaching. Cyril summarized: "The Savior comes in various forms to each man for his profit. For to those who lack joy, He becomes a Vine; to those who wish to enter in, He is a Door; for those who must offer prayer, He is a mediating High-Priest. Again, to those in sin, He becomes a Sheep to be sacrificed on their behalf. He becomes 'all things to all men' remaining in His own nature what He is. For so remaining, and possessing the truly unchangeable dignity of the Sonship, as the best of physicians and a sympathetic teacher, He *adapts Himself to our infirmity*" (Cyril of Jerusalem, *Catech. Lect.* 10; italics added)

The titles ascribed to Christ are not used because they adequately designate his reality, but because they point inadequately to him by the only means available—words:

> *Having no other words to use, we use what we have. You are called the*
> *Word, yet You are above Word; You are above Light, yet are named Light;*
> *You are called Fire not as perceptible to sense, but because You purge light*
> *and worthless matter; a Sword, because You sever the worse from the better;*
> *a Fan because You purge the threshing-floor, blowing away all that is light*
> *and windy, and laying up in the garner above all that is weighty and full; an*
> *Axe, because You cut down the worthless fig-tree, after long patience. . . .;*
> *the Door, because you bring us in; the Way, because we go straight; the*
> *Sheep, because You are the Sacrifice; the High Priest, because You offer the*
> *Body; the Son, because You are of the Father (Gregory Nazianzus, Orat. 37.4*
> *amended).*

Cyril of Jerusalem warned against diminishing the ascriptions by squeezing out of them their obvious metaphorical functions: "He is called a door. But you must not think of a wooden door. You must think of a spiritual door that reasons, and is alive, and knows all about those that enter" (*Catech. Lect.* 10.3).

The Correlation of the Ascriptions Applied to Jesus

Each title has its own history of transmission and development against the backdrop of Jewish hopes and Hellenistic assumptions. Yet in every case the history of that term was transmuted by the ministry of Jesus, so that his stamp was placed ever after upon it—for how can one now think of the term "Christ" without relating that ascription to Jesus?

One convenient way of roughly organizing the more than one hundred interconnecting titles applied to Jesus follows along lines suggested by Cullmann:

1. Titles that apply to the *pretemporal, prehistorical existence* of the Logos (Word, Son of God)

2. Titles pertaining to his *future work* in the consummation of the reign of God (Messiah, Son of Man, king)

3. Titles pertaining to his *earthly ministry* in history (Suffering Servant, prophet, priest), and

4. Titles pertaining to his *present lordship* (Lord, Savior; Cullmann, *CNT*; Hahn, *TJC*; Wells, *PC*:67).

The Filial Center of the Titles:
The Privileged Use of Abba

The intimate Sonship relation to the Father is expressed in Jesus special use of the Aramaic *Abba*, a highly personal form of address to God, in petition and intercession. Jesus himself, and not just the rememberers of Jesus, prayed and communed with his Father. This is plainly indicated by internal evidence in the synoptic Gospels. Even the Gentile congregations must have had to overcome cultural resistance in stubbornly retaining its primitive Aramaic form (*Abba*, papa, Gal. 4:6; Rom. 8:15; Augustine, *Epistle to the Gal.*, 31.4.6).

There is *"no analogy at all* in the whole of Jewish prayer for God being addressed as Abba" (Jeremias, *The Prayer of Jesus*:57). The uniqueness of Jesus' usage is due to a very good reason—the Jewish aversion to familiarity with Yahweh. Yet Jesus characteristically employed this most personal and intimate term, almost in defiance of the prevailing Jewish aversion, and did so regularly. This pattern is recalled in all four Gospels (Mark 14:36; Matt. 6:9; 11:25–26; 26:24, 39, 42; Luke 10:21; 11:2; 22:42; 23:34; John 17, passim).

Paul went out of his way to explain to his Roman readers that Christian believers can also by faith share in this intimacy, using the personal term *Abba* of God, because they now participate in a relationship with God the Father that has been made possible by Jesus, the Son. Human fatherhood is now understood by analogy to the divine Fatherhood made known through the Son (Rom. 8:15; Gal. 4:6; Mark 14:36; Irenaeus, *Ag. Her.* 5.8.1; Barth, *CD* 1/1:93–95, 279–80; 3/4: 245–46).

Matthew recalled Jesus' startling instruction that the privileged term *Abba* was more fitting for our heavenly father than even our literal earthly father: "And do not call anyone on earth 'father,' for you have one Father, and he is in heaven" (Matt. 23:9). The deeper meaning of fatherhood is best seen by reading from God's fatherhood to human fatherhood, not the other way around. One can best understand one's own father in relation to God's own providential parenting and guidance of human history, not alone in terms of an interpersonal history (Jerome, *Comm. on Matt.* 4.23.10).

9

THE WORK HE CAME
TO DO

ONLY ONE MEDIATOR CAN MAKE REAL the work of mediation between God and humanity. That one must be truly human and truly God in personal union. Only such a unique person would be able to do what is necessary for saving fallen humanity.

The *person* of Christ is the requisite premise for the *work* of Christ. The personal union of deity and humanity is the basis upon which salvation is brought to humanity. Now we turn to the *work* of Christ—the end for which the Son was sent in person. The concept of *office* draws together and seals the unity between person and work in sacred Scripture.

Offices of the Anointed One

The office (Heb. *kahan*, or ministry; Gk. *diakonia*) of Christ encompasses the three tasks to which the Christ was anointed: "He is the Christ, anointed not simply with oil, but with the Holy Ghost, to be the Highest Prophet, Priest and King, and raise us through these three offices from our fall" (*Gk. Orthodox Catech.* 28; Gregory of Nazianzus, *On the Son, Orat.* 4.30.21).

Jesus was anointed to mediate between the righteousness of God and the wretched history of sin. The office of Christ is to mediate between God and humanity—hence called the mediatorial office (Augustine, *Trin.* 4.8; Ursinus, *CHC*: 164–72). Fulfilling this reconciling mission is the declared purpose of the incarnation. The Son of God assumed human nature "that he might reconcile the Father to us and become a sacrifice" (Leo I, *Serm.* 38; Augsburg Confession, 3).

Ministries of the Mediatorial Office:
A Summary of Christ's Work

The Son of God became incarnate to do the threefold work of messianic prophet, priest, and king. His work consisted in fulfilling the expectations of the prophetic office, enacting the once for all sacrifice of the priestly office, and inaugurating the full manifestation of the kingly office. These were the three offices to which servants of God in the Old Testament were anointed (Augustine, *CG* 17).

The realization of Christ's saving work is seen in three movements: *Jesus first appears as a teacher in the prophetic office; then as high priest and lamb sacrificed in his suffering and death; and finally by his resurrection receives his kingdom and remains active in his office of reigning in his coming kingdom* (Chrysostom, *On Epis. to Heb.* 14.1–2; Calvin, *Inst.* 2.15.1).

This is the shorthand way of summarizing all essential phases of Christ's activity as Mediator. It brings together the whole range of messianic themes in Scripture. As prophet he revealed the divine will (Augustine, *CG* 17.3). As priest he made provision for the redemption of sin (Augustine, *Trin.* 4.14.1). As king he applied and completed that redemption (Newman, *SD*:52–62; Dorner, *System of Christian Doctrine* 4: 247–340). Visually the threefold office of the Mediator can be sorted out as follows:

The Work Of Christ

Prophet	Priest	King
To teach	To sacrifice	To empower
Christ preaches	Christ atones	Christ governs
Pedagogy	Expiation	Guidance and protection
Earthly ministry	Dying ministry	Glorified ministry
Messianic beginning	Messianic sacrifice	Messianic consummation
Mosaic type	Aaronic type	Davidic type
The Rabbi	The Lamb	The end-time Governor
God revealed	Humanity redeemed	Redemption applied

Jesus fulfilled and consummated these three offices as: a prophet like Moses whom God has raised up from among his own people (Acts 3:22); "a priest forever in the order of Melchizedek" (Heb. 7:17); and "King of kings" (Rev. 17:14). There is an implicit *chronology* in this sequence: in his earthly ministry Jesus first appeared as prophet, then in his suffering and death as priest, and only then in his glorification as ruler of the spiritual kingdom (Chemnitz, *TNC*:334–38; Thielicke, *The Evangelical Faith* 2: 342–421).

From his baptism to Holy Week he undertook primarily a *prophetic* office as teacher and lawgiver. During his last week of earthly ministry, Passion Week, and especially in his prayer of consecration (John 17), he assumed the high *priestly* office, and in dying offered himself as a sacrifice for the sins of the world. By his resurrection he assumed legitimate *governance* of the future of history (Rom. 1:4; Origen, *Comm. on Rom.* 1.4). The gospel narratives fill in the details of this chronology. The Letters look back upon the significance of these events.

The Three Ministries as Organizing Principle
of Christ's Mediatorial Work

The three offices of his mediatorial work are fully treated in Scripture and tradition. The division of the messianic task into these three offices was richly anticipated in the Jewish tradition and its rabbinic interpreters. It is thoroughly developed by major voices of the Christian tradition from Eusebius and Cyril of Jerusalem through Augustine and Thomas Aquinas (Augustine, *Harmony of the Gospels* 1.3; Tho. Aq., *ST* 3, Q22.1).

By the time of the Reformation it had become a central organizing structure of Protestant teaching. It reappears in both scholastic orthodox and liberal Protestant writers. Even those who object to some aspects of the classic three-office formula nonetheless make use of its categories. For it is virtually impossible to speak of the Christ of the New Testament without his teaching, sacrificial, and governance tasks.

The classical exegetes viewed Moses as the prophetic type of Christ, who appeared as the new Lawgiver, and the Fulfiller of prophecy (Cyril of Jerusalem, *Catech. Lect.* 10). They viewed the Aaronic, Levitical, and Melchizedek priesthoods as the anticipatory type of Christ, who completed and typified the priestly office (Augustine, *CG* 16.22). And they viewed David as the anticipatory type of Christ as promised messianic king, anointed receiver of the coming messianic kingdom (Augustine, *Letters* 149.2.17)

A threefold remedy was required for the recalcitrance of sin. As prophet Christ penetrated the self-deceptions of sin, effectively calling humanity to repentance; as priestly sacrifice, Christ took our sins upon himself and reconciled us to God; as legitimate recipient of final authority and power, Christ began to reorder the distorted powers at work in the world.

"Our *minds* were confused; as Teacher and Prophet, He undertook to enlighten us by His wonderful teaching. Our *hearts* were corrupt; as High Priest and Mediator, He undertook by His precious blood, to purify them. Our *wills* were held bound by the Devil; as an all-Holy King, He undertook to drive out the Devil, and release us from bondage" (Greek *Orthodox Catech.* 30, italics added).

Early Christian preaching enlarged upon all three motifs:

- Jesus was incomparably a *prophet* (Acts 7:37; Bede, *Comm. on Acts* 7.37). In his teaching office he is called rabbi, master, teacher, and shepherd.

- His prophetic work led to the *cross*, where he became the "high *priest* whom we confess" (Heb. 3:1), God's own Mercy-seat or "sacrifice of atonement" (Rom. 3:25), a living "sacrifice to God" (Eph. 5:2), the Lamb of God who takes away the sin of the world (John 1:29; Rev. 5:6; Eusebius, *Proof of the Gospels* 1.10.15–17), our advocate with the Father (1 John 2:2), "the Shepherd and Overseer" of our souls (1 Pet. 2:25).

- By his *resurrection* he was declared "*King* of kings and Lord of lords" (1 Tim. 6:15), the captain of salvation (Heb. 2:10), "Prince and Savior" who brings "forgiveness of sins to Israel" (Acts 5:31; Chrysostom, *Hom. on Acts* 13), end-time judge to whom "the Father has entrusted all judgment" (John 5:22), who came not to judge but to save the world (Augustine, *On Trin.* 1.13.29).

This threefold anointing has served countless generations as a structure for organizing and summarizing the vast range of biblical teachings of salvation.

The Oil of Anointing

Anointing was a symbol of consecration to God, especially used for an office of divine service. As water was a symbol of cleansing, blood a symbol of expiation, and light a symbol of divine illumination, so was an anointing oil the principal symbol of consecration to office (Pearson, *EC* 1:167, 178–80).

The Exodus account provided instructions for the making of "a sacred anointing oil, a fragrant blend, the work of a perfumer" (including fine spices, myrrh, cinnamon, cane, and olive oil) to anoint the Tent of Meeting, ark, and altar. "You shall consecrate them so they will be most holy, and whatever touches them will be holy" (Exod. 30:22–29).

Elijah anointed Elisha to be prophet and Hazael to be king (1 Kings 19:16). Priests were anointed both with oil (symbol of consecration) and blood (symbol of expiation, Exod. 30:30; Lev. 8:30). When David was anointed by Samuel as king, "from that day on the Spirit of the Lord came upon David in power" (1 Sam. 16:13). The people prayed for requisite gifts of the Spirit to accompany the anointing. "*Anointed* was in old times a title of *kings, high-priests, and prophets.* Why then, is Jesus, the Son of God, called The Anointed? Because to his manhood were imparted without measure all the gifts of the Holy Ghost; and so he possessed in the highest degree the *knowledge* of a prophet, the *holiness* of a high-priest, and the *power* of a king" (*Russian Catech., COC* 2: 466).

All three offices are crucial to the expectations of late Judaism immediately preceding the New Testament, when the popular hope of messianic fulfillment was intensified (Augustine, *Tractates on John* 15.25–27). The messiah was expected as a *prophet* who would come to "explain everything to us" (John 4:25), who would teach, who would "give his people the knowledge of salvation" (Luke 1:77) and "preach good news to the poor." Some expected that the return of the prophet "Elijah must come first" (Matt. 17:10), before or in connection with the appearance of the messianic king. The remnant of Israel who most fervently awaited the messiah applied *priestly* metaphors to that expectation of one who would redeem Israel "through the forgiveness of their sins" (Luke 1:77), as "Lamb of God" who would "take away the sins of the world" (John 11:27). As *king* he was expected to be "born king of the Jews" (Matt. 2:2), as seed of David, born in Bethlehem (John 7:42; Matt. 12:23).

Jesus comes to transform each of these offices decisively: He *teaches* not with mere words but as God's own personal coming as God's living Word to human history; he *intercedes* not as the Levitical high priest with animal sacrifice, but by the sacrifice of his own body; and he *governs* not as the rulers of this world but as legitimate heir of divine empowerment (Ursinus, *CHC*:170–76).

The Offices Uniquely Cohere in Jesus Christ

The three offices of the Expected One uniquely cohere in the ministry of Jesus. As the "one mediator between God and men" (1 Tim. 2:5), he is at the same time the teacher of true religion, expiator of sin, and bearer of legitimate authority to guide and judge future history (Gregory of Nyssa, *Ag. Eunomius* 2.12).

No one before Jesus had adequately united the three offices. Moses, the prototype of the prophet and lawgiver, was neither priest nor king. Aaron, the priest, was neither prophet nor king. David, the prototype of the messianic king, was not a priest. Ezekiel came close to an integral fulfillment of the offices, so he became a prototype for the coming Messiah (Ezek. 1:28; Jacob of Sarug, *On the Establishment of Creation* 1.4).

In one figure alone were all offices adequately united, sufficiently displayed, and fully consummated—Jesus Christ. In these three complementary ways, he uniquely embodied the "wisdom of God" so as to become simultaneously "our righteousness, holiness, and redemption" (1 Cor. 1:30; Ambrosiaster, *Comm. on Paul's Epis.*). Jesus is not a king without being a priestly king, for his kingship cannot be understood without his suffering, atonement, and intercession. He is not just a priest without prophetic truth, for his priesthood is made understandable by his pungent, parabolic teaching of the kingdom and call to repentance. He is indeed a king, but a caring, interceding, shepherding, priestly king who loves those he admonishes, rules, and guides. In this way all three offices cohere in one mediator. "I tell you that many prophets and kings wanted to see what you see but did not" (Luke 10:23; Cyril of Alex., *Comm. on Luke,* Hom. 67).

Wherever one of these three functions has become excessive, imbalanced, or detached from the others, there have emerged false teachers. Misjudgments have occurred because one or another office has been neglected, falsified, or exaggerated. The history of Christian teaching of the work of Christ has repeatedly had to resist such imbalances. A balanced teaching of salvation depends upon holding these three ministries in proper tension and equilibrium (Cyril of Alex, *Comm. on Luke* 1.77).

Defining the Prophetic Office: Christ as Prophet

The prophetic office of Christ refers to the work of Christ in revealing divine truth to humanity, proclaiming the divine plan of redemption, and calling all to accept the salvation offered.

The epitome of the prophet was fulfilled by means of Jesus' *words* (Matt. 7:28–29), *deeds* (John 10:25), the *example of his life* (1 Pet. 2:21–23). He willingly suffered for the truth.

Christ as Prophet

A prophet is one who speaks for God, an authoritative teacher of God's will, who serves as a channel of communication between the divine and human spheres, so as to bring to light what had remained in darkness (Is. 9:2; Origen, *Comm. on John* 13.134; Ursinus, *CHC*:172–73). By the prophet a divine message (Heb. *dabar,* "word"; Gk. *logos*) from God, an oracle of Yahweh, is communicated through a human messenger (Heb. *nabi*; Gk. *prophētēs*) or seer (Heb. *roeh).* In a wider sense, prophet signifies a teacher (Gk. *didaskalos*; Lat. *magister*).

Intrinsic to the messianic office is the work of proclamation—making public the knowledge of the events of salvation, promulgation of the saving work of God in history (Ambrose, *On Belief in the Resurrection* 2.66–75). The work of prophecy is pertinent only where revelation occurs. Prophecy is not a form of knowing that human initiative may actively seek or scheme to lay hold of. The prophetic act occurs only through the initiative and electing wisdom of God, which inspires human receptivity to the divine address. The prototype for all prophetic speech is the receptivity of the eternal Son to the will of the Father (Augustine, *CG* 18.27–35).

Jesus was received *by the people* as a prophet (Matt. 16:13–14; Mark 6:15; Luke 7:16; Lactantius, *Div. Inst., FC* 49: 261–79). Jesus made no protest when the Samaritan woman said to him, "I can see that you are a prophet" (John 4:19). Jesus was viewed *by the apostles* as a prophet. This is clear from Peter's speech to the people of Israel: "For Moses said, 'The Lord your God will raise up for you a prophet like me from among your own people; you must listen to everything he tells you'" (Acts 3:22, quoting Deut. 18:15; cf. Stephen's speech to the Sanhedrin, Acts 7:37). It was with Moses and Elijah (prophetic prototypes) that Jesus conversed in the transfiguration.

More so, the Gospel narratives report that *Jesus made reference to himself* as a prophet: "Only in his home town and in his own house is a prophet without honor" (Matt. 13:57; Mark 6:4). "I must keep going today and tomorrow and the next day—for surely no prophet can die outside Jerusalem!" (Luke 13:33; Pearson, *EC* 1:169, 366).

More Than a Prophet

Yet as fulfiller of the prophetic type, Jesus was (like John the Baptist, to whom prophecy had pointed) "more than a prophet" (Matt. 11:9), for "of none of the Prophets was it said: that 'the Word was made flesh'" (Ambrose, *Incarn. of Our Lord* 6.48; John 1:14). The human-divine Mediator was not merely God-inspired, but God-incarnate.

By contrast with the prophets, who proclaimed "Thus says Yahweh," Jesus characteristically said: "Truly I say to you" and "I am." No prophet except of a unique sort would say, "Thus I say." The prophets pointed beyond themselves to One who by his divine Sonship would bring salvation: "In the past God spoke to our forefathers through the prophets in many times and in various ways, but in these last days he has spoken to us by his Son" (Heb. 1:1–2).

Jesus not only *spoke*, but *was* the truth enfleshed, God's own Word of truth. He did not merely teach revelation by words, but was himself that revelation, a living Word, the Word of Life (1 John 1:1; 1 Pet. 1:23). "I am the way and the truth and the life. No one comes to the Father except through me. If you really knew me, you would know my Father as well" (John 14:6–7). One cannot come to faith without trusting personally in Jesus Christ or receive the good news without receiving him personally.

All the other prophets were humans speaking for God. *The Mediator was the God-man speaking for God to humanity and to God for humanity* (Leo I, *Serm.* 27). The incomparable credential of Jesus' prophetic teaching was the personal union of deity and humanity in him.

The truth to which the Spirit would guide is the truth made known personally in him. Of no other prophet could that be said. As such Jesus was prophet par excellence, the incomparable interpreter of God. "I do nothing on my own but speak just what the Father has taught me. The one who sent me is with me" (John 8:28–29).

Since he himself is the truth, only he can adequately reveal the truth. Jesus consummately possessed both the gift of prophecy and vocation of teacher. "For this reason I was born, and for this I came into the world, to testify to the truth" (John 18:37; Augustine, *Tractates on John* 115.2–4). Calvin summarized the purpose and end of Jesus' prophetic office as "an office of teaching bestowed upon the Son of God for the benefit of his own [people], and its end is that he illumine them with the true knowledge of the Father, instruct them in truth, and make them household disciples of God" (*Catech. of the Church of Geneva*).

Not to Abolish, But to Fulfill the Law

Jesus was the last prophet and the first preacher of the gospel. His ministry united law and gospel. It made clear both the inner requirement of the law, and what God has done that the law could not do to fulfill the requirement of the law for sinners (Matt. 5:17–20; Chromatius, *Tractate on Matt.* 20.1).

His teaching went to the heart of the law, its spiritual meaning and center, its radical character as divine demand (Augustine, *Our Lord's Sermon on the Mount* 2.21–25). This reinterpretation of the law occurred prototypically in the Sermon on the Mount, but more generally through his entire earthly ministry of proclamation and teaching (Baxter, *PW* 2:222–38; Wesley, *Serm.* 1, *WJWB*:466–698).

"Do not think that I have come to abolish the Law or the Prophets; I have not come to abolish them but to fulfill them. I tell you the truth, until heaven and earth disappear, not the smallest letter, not the least stroke of a pen, will by any means disappear from the Law until everything is accomplished" (Matt. 5:17; Jerome, *Comm. on Matt.* 1.5.18).

The Son was born of woman under the law, and sent to redeem those under the law (Gal. 4:4–5). His behavior so conformed to the law "that by obeying the Law He might perfect it and bring it to an end in His own self, so as to show that it was ordained to Him" (Tho. Aq., *ST* 3, Q40.4).

Paul preached that Christ is "the end of the law" (Rom. 10:4). This means that Christ is the end of our despairing effort at righteousness based upon our own merit. "For Christ means the end of the struggle for righteousness-by-the-Law for everyone who believes in him" (Rom. 10:4, Phillips). Everything previously encompassed by the divine requirement codified into law was summed up in his embodied life and finished, dying work (Matt. 3:15; Chrysostom, *Hom. on Matt.* 12.1).

He came to reinterpret the moral vitality of the law in relation to the emerging age of God's righteous love. The ethical depth of the law was sharpened, the simplicity of its demand condensed. Jesus did not abolish but illumined the moral law already written on the heart, now seen more clearly in the context of grace. The law remains as a schoolmaster leading to Christ to teach sinners their sin and as a guide in the way of holiness (Leo I, *Serm.* 46.5; Calvin, *Inst.* 2.1–4). The believer who looks "intently into the perfect law that gives freedom, and continues to do this" will be "blessed in what he does" (James 1:25).

What the law required, the Redeemer fulfilled: "For the law was given through Moses; grace and truth came through Jesus Christ" (John 1:17). His central prophetic task was to teach the good news of redemption by himself being that good news (Cyril of Alex. *Comm. on John,* 1.9). In his own synagogue he said of Isaiah 61:1–2: "Today this scripture is fulfilled in your hearing" (Luke 4:21). Then he "went throughout Galilee, teaching in their synagogues, preaching the good news of the kingdom" (Matt. 4:23).

Christ's Prophetic Work

The prophets of ancient Israel had characteristically fulfilled their office by teaching, foretelling, and healing (or some combination of these). Similarly Jesus went about doing good in all three of these forms (Matt. 5:17; 13:57; 24:8–9)—he taught the multitudes (Matt. 5–7), revealed things hidden (Matt. 24:1–51), and engaged in a ministry of healing that attested his identity as messianic king (Mark 1:30–42; Matt. 9; Luke 8:27–48).

Through his *teaching* he instructed the community of faith in all things necessary for salvation. He *foretold* the future by himself anticipating its consummation in the resurrection. Through *healing* he attested the power of the Spirit at work in his ministry (Cyril of Alex., *Comm. on Matt.* Hom. 44).

His teaching continued through his resurrection appearances (Luke 24:45; Bede, *Hom. on Gospels* 11). The preaching and teaching of the gospel continued in the acts of his apostles, who were promised to do "even greater things than these" under the power of the Spirit (John 14:12; Theodore of Heraclea, *Fragments on John,* 259).

He Went About Doing Good

Jesus' manner of life and conversation with the world were entirely congruent with the ends for which he became incarnate. These ends were to proclaim the truth by himself being the truth, to seek out the lost, free humanity from sin, and to make God's holy love known by allowing himself to be known amid the conditions of ordinary human life.

The Son's daily activity moved in a rhythm of engagement and withdrawal, rest and action, prayer and teaching (Tho. Aq., *ST* 3, Q40.1). He withdrew from intense activity for communion with the Father in prayer, yet he sat down with sinners (Matt. 9:10), for he had come purposely to meet and save them (Chrysostom, *Hom. on Matt.* Hom 30.1).

It was fitting that the Son of God should lead a life of poverty in the world, in order to show that abundant life is not dependent upon the accumulation of wealth. He became poor for our sakes that through his poverty we might be rich (2 Cor. 8:9). He had "a poor maid for His Mother, a poorer birthplace," and he voluntarily chose "all that was poor and despicable, all that was of small account and hidden from the majority, that we might recognize His Godhead to have transformed the terrestrial sphere" (Tho. Aq., *ST* 3, Q40.3; Cyril of Alexandria, *Ephesus Serm.* 3.10.9).

He had time to talk with women whose marriages were troubled (John 4:15–30) and to reach out for children (Mark 10:13–16). He provided food where there was hunger (John 6:1–15) and wine at a wedding when the supply had run out (John 2:1–11). He became a beacon of hope to lepers, the blind, epileptics, the poor and dispossessed (Prudentius, *Hymns* 9). Mark reports after the healing of a deaf mute: "People were overwhelmed with amazement. 'He has done everything well,' they said" (Mark 7:37).

He Taught with Authority

His Teaching Ministry

His teaching occurred both by precept and example. His teaching was punctuated by signs and mighty deeds that attested the special empowerment of his mission. He called all hearers to repentance as the primary requirement of participating in the coming governance of God (Bede, *Homilies on the Gospels* 1.21).

Jesus intended from the outset to initiate an ongoing community of faith that would continue to embody his ministry after his death and resurrection (Matt. 28:20; John 20:21). This community is called to share in his prophetic teaching, his priestly sacrifice, and his inauguration of the rule of God, under the empowerment of the Spirit who promises to lead the faithful into all truth (John 16:12–13; 14:26).

As he taught and preached, it became clear that he was in the process of forming a community of faith that could not be fitted neatly into the traditions and institutions of late Judaism, but would address all humanity with the personal coming of God's embodied love. He engendered a new covenant community that would reshape the people of God (Acts 2:43–47; Bede, *Comm. on Acts* 2.44).

The training of the Twelve occurred experientially by daily association with him. They listened to him teach and watched him respond to human needs and deal with adversaries. They beheld his steady compassion. They shared in his life of prayer and service, healing and witness (Luke 6:12–16; 6:28; 9:28).

His manner of teaching was simple, profound, and direct. Even the Temple guards who had been sent to arrest him reported back to their superiors: "No one ever spoke the way this man does" (John 7:46; Cyril of Alex., *Comm. on John* 5.2).

"The crowds were amazed at his teaching, because he taught as one who had authority, and not as their teachers of the law" (Matt. 7:28–29; Luke 4:32). "The Jews were amazed and asked, 'How did this man get such learning without having studied?'" (John 7:15). Nicodemus addressed him as "Rabbi" and as "a teacher who has come from God" (John 3:2). He taught in the synagogues, gathered disciples, and debated with scribes concerning Scripture, yet he was different from them in that he taught in the open fields, showed particular concern for outsiders, for women and for the poor, and profoundly identified with sinners, tax collectors, and disreputable folk (John 4:16–18; Augustine, *Comm. on John* 15.20; Bornkamm, *JN*:57).

He was acquainted with grief and knew the human heart. He deftly dealt with opponents and legalists. He grasped the essence of rabbinic teaching without being fixated upon it. He penetrated illusions without becoming trapped in them (Chrysostom, *Hom. on John* 32.2). He employed symbolic and demonstrative teaching when useful, yet he also taught directly. Even if these dialogues may have been refracted through the memories of the redactors, readers of the Gospels get a sharp picture of Jesus as an apt and ready raconteur.

His Teaching Adapted to Hearers

In Jesus we have a teacher who "has taught neither too much nor too little. He has taught me to know God the Father, has revealed Himself to me, and has also acquainted me with the Holy Spirit. He has also instructed me how to live and how to die and has told me what to hope for. What more do I want?" (Luther, *LW* 22:255–56).

His sayings are memorable for their compact pungency. This helped to ensure their authenticity in the transmission of the oral tradition.

He adapted his teaching to the capacities of those he taught. He did not teach them all at once but proceeded gradually and in awareness of hearer's limitations. "I have much more to say to you, more than you can now bear. But when he, the Spirit of truth, comes, he will guide you into all truth" (John 16:12–13). John concluded his Gospel with the comment that "the whole world would not have room for the books that would be written" if everything Jesus did or taught "were written down" (John 21:25).

He used ordinary things to attest God's coming: the surprising growth of mustard seed (Mark 4:30–32); the woman who joyfully recovered a lost coin (Luke 15:8–10); the father who joyfully received back a lost son (Luke 15:11–32); a forgiven debtor who throws in prison one who owes him a pittance (Matt. 18). He spoke in common terms of moneylenders (Luke 7:41–43); rich fools (Luke 12:16–21); the sower and soils (Mark 4:3–8, 14–20); tenants (Matt. 21:33–44), new wine in old wineskins (Luke 5:37–38); and wedding banquets (Matt. 22:2–14). He taught by parables both to penetrate to ordinary people and to protect the truth from distortion by detractors. The parables often pointed toward the resurrection: "Though I have been speaking figuratively, a time is coming when I will no longer use this kind of language but will tell you plainly about my Father. In that day you will ask in my name" (John 16:26).

It is ironic that St. Thomas, who wrote so comprehensively, would be the one to state this argument: Since the most excellent teaching cannot be expressed in writing but only in life, Christ did not directly commit his teaching to writing, so that it could be above all imprinted on the hearts of hearers (Matt. 7:29; Tho. Aq., *ST* 3 Q42.1).

This is why Christ's teaching had to be written in the experience of believers: in order that you may "show that you are a letter from Christ, the result of our ministry, written not with ink but with the Spirit of the living God, not on tablets of stone but on tablets of human hearts" (2 Cor. 3:3; Ambrose, *Paradise*, 8.39).

Why His Teaching Was Addressed to the Jews First, Then to the Gentiles

It was fitting that Christ was sent first to the lost sheep of the house of Israel (Matt. 15:24). His preaching was directed first to Israel, to demonstrate that the promises of God to Israel were being fulfilled in him. He proceeded in right order by making known God's own coming first to the Jews, then to be "transmitted through them to the Gentiles" (Tho. Aq., *ST* 3, Q42.1). Isaiah had prophesied that "They will proclaim my glory among the nations" (66:19). It was fitting that the news of God's coming should reach the world by means of the people God chose (Theodoret, *Comm. on Is.* 20.66.19).

Paul explained: "Christ has become a servant of the Jews on behalf of God's truth, to confirm the promises made to the patriarchs so that the Gentiles may glorify God for his mercy" (Rom. 15:8–9). Jesus' mission at first focused upon Israel, as "servant to the circumcised" (Rom. 15:8). Jesus spent most of his teaching ministry "in the area of Zebulun and Naphtali" (Matt. 4:13) as prophesied by Isaiah (9:1–2). From that remote spot "the people living in darkness have seen a great light" (Matt. 4:16). The light came from unimportant Galilee.

Shortly before his death, when certain Gentiles wished to see Jesus, he said: "I tell you the truth, unless a kernel of wheat falls to the ground and dies, it remains only a single seed. But if it dies, it produces many seeds" (John 12:24). "He called Himself the grain of wheat that must be mortified," noted Augustine, in order that it might be "multiplied by the faith of the nations" (Augustine, *Comm. on John*, Tractate 51.9).

Signs, Wonders, and Demonstrations of Power and Deity

Jesus' proclamation was attended by "miraculous powers" (Matt. 13:54, 58) and "miraculous signs and wonders" (John 4:48). Jesus' mighty works were remembered and interpreted in relation to his resurrection as signs of the new age, the coming kingdom. These demonstrations resist all those powers that resist God's coming: guilt, sickness, death, self-deception, and the demonic grip that sin has on human behavior (Eusebius, *PG* 1:124; Chrysostom, *Hom. on John*, 35.3).

His miracles were regarded as signs of the prophetic office, as seen in the comment of Nicodemus: "Rabbi, we know you are a teacher who has come from God. For no one could perform the miraculous signs you are doing if God were not with him" (John 3:2).

Healing, Nature, and Resurrection Miracles

Miracles reported of him (many more perhaps being unreported) fall into three types:

Healing Miracles

healing the sick

the blind (Matt. 9:27–31; Mark 8:22–26; John 9:1–7)

the lame (Luke 13:11–13)

the deaf and mute (Mark 7:31–37)

lepers (Mark 1:40–42; Luke 17:11–19)

paralysis (Luke 5:18–25)

bleeding (Mark 5:25–29)

Nature Miracles

showing command over the forces of nature

feeding the five thousand (Mark 6:35–44) and four thousand (Mark 8:1–9)

quieting the storm (Mark 4:37–41)

walking on water (Mark 6:48–51)

the catch of fish (John 2:1–11, 21:1–11)

Life Giving Miracles

raising the dead

Jairus' daughter (Mark 5:22–24)

the widow's son at Nain (Luke 7:11–15)

Lazarus (John 11:1–44)

Jesus did not perform miracles without purpose. Each one responded to some special need or served some special purpose in pointing to the coming reign of God. He did not draw attention to himself as a worker of miracles. Rather each miracle was a specific response to a personal form of suffering. He often commanded that those healed should not speak of it to others, lest false expectations be increased (Mark 1:44; 3:11; Matt. 12:15–21; 14:13–16). He did not encourage others to interpret his mission essentially as one of signs and wonders, but rather hoped that the signs would lead to faith (John 4:48; Chrysostom, *Hom. on John*, 35.2–3).

At first it might seem unfitting for Christ to perform miracles, since he himself had said, "A wicked and adulterous generation looks for a miraculous sign" (Matt. 16:4). He admonished those who, unless they saw miraculous signs and wonders, would "never believe" (John 4:48). Yet it was fitting that Christ did perform miracles that "we may believe that what he says is from God, just as when a man is the bearer of letters sealed with the king's ring" (Tho. Aq., *ST* 3, Q43.1). For this reason he said: "But if I do it, even though you do not believe me, believe the miracles, that you may know and understand that the Father is in me, and I in the Father" (John 10:38).

Jesus' ministry was summarized by Matthew: "Jesus went throughout Galilee, teaching in their synagogues, preaching the good news of the kingdom, and healing every disease and sickness among the people. News about him spread all over Syria, and people brought to him all who were ill with various diseases, those suffering severe pain, the demon-possessed, those having seizures, and the paralyzed, and he healed them" (Matt. 4:23–24). These were victims of the "strong man" (the demonic enemy), whom a stronger One was binding up (Mark 3:27). The miracles confirm the power of God's own coming (Chrysostom, *Hom. on Matt.* 14.3).

Signs of God's Coming

The miracles were viewed as signs (*sēmeia*) of God's coming and of his saving mission, as wonders (*terata*), and as demonstrations of power (*dunameis*). They were means by which his teaching and identity were presented and interpreted (*Incomplete Work on Matt.*, Hom. 8; Brown, *The Gospel According to John*; *TDNT* 7:200–68). Peter proclaimed: "Jesus of Nazareth was a man accredited by God to you by miracles, wonders and signs, which God did among you through him, as you yourselves know" (Acts 2:22; Bede, *Comm. on Acts* 2.22). The miracles were a palpable demonstration that he was of God: "Nobody has ever heard of opening the eyes of a man born blind. If this man were not from God, he could do nothing" (John 9:32–33; Hilary *Trin.* 3).

God's personal coming was itself the miracle of miracles, especially his birth and resurrection—the beginning and ending of his earthly ministry. Among all the miracles, the incarnation and resurrection continue to have unique status in the liturgical year, the cycle of seasonal celebrations of Jesus' ministry. "When we look at the two limits of our human life, we observe the nature of our beginning and our end. Man begins his existence in weakness and similarly ends his life through weakness. But in God's case, the birth did not have its origin in weakness, neither did the death end in weakness. For sensual pleasure did not precede the birth and corruption did not follow the death" (Gregory of Nyssa, *ARI*:289).

If one begins with the fixed idea that a miracle cannot under any circumstances occur, then it cannot by its very nature be authentically reported. If so, all talk of miracle and all paranormal phenomenon must be *prima facie* removed in advance from any inquiry.

Contemporary physical science is less prone to make such sweeping preemptive judgments. The nineteenth-century controversy over the possibility of miracles was largely an unedifying circular verbal quarrel about how language is to be used. If miracle is defined as suspension of natural law, then it could be asserted that such a suspension is impossible and miracles could be ruled out on the grounds that they have no analogy in normal human experience.

What Is Natural to God May Seem Unnatural
to Nature Alone

Rather, the biblical texts themselves are not concerned with whether natural law can be suspended, but with a simple observed, empirical, attested series of events: Jesus healed the sick (Luke 6:17–19; Ambrose, *Expos. of Luke* 5.46). There is less resistance to the study of miracles now than a century ago. There is more serious inquiry into miracles since they were rashly rejected by rigid empiricists. Why? In part because the theoretical physicists have continued to probe further into their own vulnerable paradigms and because quantum physics and parapsychological, psychokinetic, and telepathic studies have provided tentative premises that challenge less flexible conceptions of physical causation.

Classic Christianity teaches that events regarded as unnatural to human view may be entirely natural to God. Incarnation and resurrection were not against nature, but merely consistent with God's nature (Luke 2:1–20; Cyril of Alex. *Comm. on Luke,* Hom. 1). In both cases the natural forces were not blocked or stultified. The child grew; the body died. But the coming of God to human history stamped these birth and death events with a distinctive imprint. How else could God have come and gone? God came and left in a fitting way that both transcended and used natural human capacities, but that in no way denied or subverted natural human capacities (Lactantius, *Div. Inst.,* FC 49:280–84).

What is natural to God is unnatural to alienated human nature. Nothing is more natural to God than to be raised from the dead should God come to earth and die. Nothing is more natural to God than to be born in an extraordinary way, should God become enfleshed.

If interpreters later conclude that from their point of view these acts were deemed supernatural (above nature) or preternatural (beyond nature, inexplicable in terms of the common order of nature), they mean that they transcend ordinarily perceived natural human abilities, but not that they were unnatural to Christ or impossible for God (Luke 1:37; Chrysostom, *Hom. on Matthew,* Hom. 54.7). The miracles were as natural for the Son as creating was for the Father. Hence to describe them as irrationally supernatural is to select a dubious, limited, human vantage point from which to view them.

Christ as True Priest

This classic consensual view of Christ as prophet, teacher, and miracle worker provides the proper basis upon which we can now turn to his priestly office. In his *prophetic* activity, the *priestly*-sacrificial work of Christ had already been anticipated, but was not actively commenced until the last week of his suffering and death. Only after his resurrection would it become clear that his role as messianic *king* was intricately woven with his suffering death. These three offices penetrate each other: the prophetic ministry pointed toward his coming priestly ministry, which in turn made possible his ministry of governance.

Christ's *priestly* ministry focused primarily upon a single event: his self-giving death as a sacrifice for sin. Why does Christ suffer? Luther answered: "To carry out His office as Priest; and He intends not only to pray for sinners but also to sacrifice His body and life on the altar of the cross" (*Lenten Sermon, Luke* 23:26–31).

The Work of a Priest—Sacrifice, Intercession, Blessing

The priestly office of the Son functions in three ways: (1) he makes perfect satisfaction to God the Father through his suffering and death on the cross; (2) he intercedes with the Father for the contrite in heart, in order to (3) bring the blessing of redemption to humanity.

Christ's ministry was anticipated by the Old Testament sacrificial system in which the priest was commissioned to *offer sacrifice, make intercession, and bless the people.* Hence the priestly office may be summarized as that of making atonement, intercession, and benediction (Heb. 8:1–13; Chrysostom, On *Epis. To Heb.* 14.2; Ursinus, *CHC:*174–75). Christ's work reappropriated the threefold function of the high priest in Jewish tradition: to present annually the atoning sacrifice for the whole congregation; to intercede for the faithful; and to bless the people (Lev. 4:16–18; Council of Ephesus; Augustine, *CG*, *FC* 24:36–39).

Protestants may be surprised that Luther expressed such a high view of priestly action: "The priest comes forward to take all the shortcoming of the people upon himself as if they were his very own and pleads with God on their behalf. From God he receives the word with which he is to comfort and help everybody. The name 'priest' is therefore, still more lovely and consoling than the names 'father' and 'mother'; nay, this name brings us all the others. For by the fact the Christ is Priest He turns God into our Father" (Luther, *Comm. on Gen. 14:17–24*; Schmid, *DT:* 346). The Reformed divines concurred with Luther: "Christ's office as a priest is that according to which Christ, the only mediator . . . by His most exact fulfillment of the law and the sacrifice of His body, satisfied, on our behalf, the injured divine justice, and offers to God the most effectual prayers for our salvation" (Hollaz, *ETA:*731). "The priestly office is to provide full satisfaction in our place before God, and to intercede for us" (Wollebius, *CTC:*17).

The priestly work embraces the past, present, and future of sin: The Son voluntarily undertook the mission received from the Father by *offering himself* as a sacrificial Lamb to *atone* for the sin of the world, dying for all once for all (as a finished work spoken in *past* tense). He now *intercedes* in the presence of God for the reconciliation of penitents (in the *present* tense). He *blesses* human history by redeeming it and promises the final blessing of eternal life and the fulfillment of the reign of God (to be consummated in the *future* tense).

His cross is his finished priestly work, his heavenly intercession his present priestly work, and his blessing will ultimately consummate his future priestly work (Wollebius, *CTC* 17, *RDB:*98–110; Pearson, *EC* 1:367).

The priestly work is therefore already accomplished on the cross, yet still being executed through Christ's intercession with the Father and blessing through the Spirit. While satisfaction is a finished work on the cross, intercession and blessing are continuing activities in the divine presence and amid the blessed community (Gregory Nazianzus, *Orat.* 30; *BOC:*259–60, 414–17).

First Phase of Christ's Priestly Work: Sacrifice

The Necessity of Sacrifice: Cross as Altar

"Priest" and "sacrifice" are intrinsically interrelated terms in the Jewish and Christian traditions. It is the priest who makes sacrifice on behalf of another. It is Christ who as high priest makes a unique sacrifice on the cross for the sins of humanity (Heb. 17:11–28; Theodoret, *Dialogue*, 2; Ambrose, *Flight from the World*, *FC* 65:290–96).

"The separating medium is sin, the reconciling Mediator is the Lord," Augustine wrote. "To take then away the separating wall, which is sin, that Mediator has come, and the priest has Himself become the sacrifice" (*Hom. on John* 41.5). In Christ "the same one was to be both priest and sacrifice," wrote Calvin. "Christ plays the priestly role, not only to render the Father favorable and propitious toward us by an eternal law of reconciliation, but also to receive us as his companions" (*Inst.* 2.15.6; see also Tho. Aq., *ST* 3, Q22.3).

Christ was stretched out on the cross as if he were a victim on an altar. "Therefore in the cross on which Christ has suffered we should see nothing but an altar on which Christ sacrifices His life and discharges His priestly office also by praying that we may be rid of sins and freed from eternal death" (Luther, *Serm. on Matt.* 27:33–56).

Through his satisfaction, Christ made a once-for-all offering of himself. It is on the basis of this self-offering that he intercedes for us and continues to advocate the cause of sinners in the Father's presence. This intercession leads to that ultimate benediction, which is to be consummated finally in the blessing of his return (Newman, *PPS* 2:42; 6:241–42; *SN*:304; Baxter, *PW* 7:205–208).

By this satisfaction, he paid the price or ransom for the sins of the world. Through intercession he enables the faithful to obtain the gifts of the Spirit so that God's uprighting action may be effectively applied to them (Gregory of Nazianzus, *Theological Orat.* 4.20; Pearson, *EC* 1:173–78). Sacrifice belongs essentially to the humble *descent* of the Redeemer, while intercession belongs more explicitly to his *ascent* to glory. The crucial themes of descent and ascent pivot on the priestly sacrificial act—the cross (Basil of Seleucia, *Easter Hom. JF* B:46).

The Temple

The principal scene of the high-priestly function in Judaism is the Temple, the holy place where the greatness of God is present and revealed. Since this scene fuels the Christian teaching of salvation, it is essential that the believer understand the altar, the tabernacle, and the high priestly activity, and how they were transmitted from Judaism to Christianity.

At the inner core of the Temple stood the altar. The antiquity of this sacrificial function is already implied in the Genesis report that "Noah built an altar to the Lord and, taking some of all the clean animals and clean birds, he sacrificed burnt offerings on it" (Gen. 8:20; Ephrem, *Comm. on Gen.* 6.13.2).

The architecture of the Temple set up intentional barriers to secular functions. The external portion contained the court where the covenant people entered and assembled. A laver (a place of cleansing) stood at the entrance, and there was an altar of burnt offering. Only priests were admitted into the central portion, the Sanctuary—set aside for holy things. On the table of unleavened bread were placed twelve loaves, renewed every Sabbath. The light of the Spirit beamed forth from seven lamps on a golden candlestick. The air was filled with the odor of incense emitting from an altar of incense (Deut. 30:34; Luke 1:10–11; Bede, *On the Tabernacle* 3.12).

In the inner core of the temple was the Most Holy Place into which only the high priest entered once a year, the sacred space of the ark of covenant. The glory of God rested upon the kapporeth or mercy-seat, which covered the record of transgression from God's eyes. "There, above the cover between the two cherubim that are over the ark of the Testimony, I will meet with you" (Exod. 25:18, 22; Isaac of Nineveh, *Discourse* 22; Pope, *Compend.* 2:245). Such an environment was presupposed in the early church's reference to the body of Christ as a temple.

In Christianity, the dying, rising, incarnate Son himself is viewed as temple: "Destroy this temple; and I will raise it again in three days" (John 2:19; Lactantius, *Div. Inst.* 4.18, 25). His human nature, which is our own nature, became the holy place in which "The Word became flesh and made his dwelling among us. We have seen his glory, the glory of the One and Only, who came from the Father" (John 1:14). Hence it may now be said that "the tabernacle of God is with men" (Rev. 21:3). "Jesus Christ has come in the flesh" (1 John 4:2). "A new and living way" has been opened for us "through the curtain, that is, his body, and since we have a great priest over the house of God, let us draw near to God with a sincere heart in full assurance of faith, having our hearts sprinkled to cleanse us from a guilty conscience and having our bodies washed with pure water" (Heb. 10:20–22; Gregory of Nyssa, *Life of Moses*, 2.174).

The body of Christ, from another viewpoint, is the church, the community of those whose lives are hid in Christ. Christ is the church's glory, so much so that Paul could write: "For we are the temple of the living God" (2 Cor. 6:16). Similarly First Peter addressed the church: "You also, like living stones, are being built into a spiritual house to be a holy priesthood, offering spiritual sacrifices acceptable to God through Jesus Christ" (1 Pet. 2:5; Didymus the Blind, *Comm. on 1 Peter*, 2.4).

Second Phase of Christ's Priestly Work: Intercession

The essence of the Mediator's intercession is: "I pray for them" (John 17:9). His sacrifice is the objective basis upon which his advocacy before the Father occurs. Thus "if anybody does sin, we have one who speaks to the Father in our defense— Jesus Christ, the Righteous One. He is the atoning sacrifice for our sins" (1 John 2:2; Bede, *On 1 John* 2.2).

Jesus' Ministry of Intercession

Christ's eternal intercession is something that only the eternal Son can do. The principal feature of the picture of Christ "in session" (that is, "sitting at the right hand of God") is his intercessory ministry for humanity in the presence of the Father (Calvin, *On Reform*, SW:143–44; Wollebius, *CTC* 18). "He prays for us, as our Priest; He prays in us, as our Head; He is prayed to by us as our God" (Augustine, *Comm. on Ps. 85*; Schmid, *DT.* 368). "He entered the Most Holy Place once for all by his own blood, having obtained eternal redemption" (Heb. 9:12). In him we have an Advocate, an intercessor who speaks to the Father on our behalf (1 John 2:1). He is qualified to intercede for us because he is "touched with the feeling of our infirmities" (Heb. 4:15; Symeon the New Theologian, *Discourse* 2.4). He bears in heaven the marks of the wounds he received from us (Ambrose, *Comm. on Luke* 10).

The intercession for the faithful in which Christ was once engaged on earth (John 17) continues until the last day in the heavenly sphere. "In him and through faith in him we may approach God with freedom and confidence" (Eph. 3:12). Christ is "a priest forever" (Heb. 5:6; Oecumenius, *Fragments on Heb.* 5.6).

The Faithful Pray in Christ's Name

He offers the prayers of the faithful to the Father. This is why Christians call upon the Father in the name of Christ. "My Father will give you whatever you ask in my name" (John 16:23–26; Origen, *On Prayer*, 15.2). Christ mediates and enables the appropriation of his merit to the faithful (Cyril of Alex., *Comm. on John* 11.2; Chemnitz, *TNC*:411–14).

The effect of his intercession is to increase faith's joy, trust, and capacity for devotion. "Let us then approach the throne of grace with confidence, so that we may receive mercy and find grace to help us in our time of need" (Heb. 4:16). "Therefore he is able to save completely those who come to God through him, because he always lives to intercede for them" (Heb. 7:25). For this intercession Christ entered not "a man-made sanctuary," but "he entered heaven itself, now to appear for us in God's presence" (Heb. 9:24; Photius, *Fragments on Heb.* 9:24–25).

Christ intercedes not only for those most responsive to grace, but for sinners, following the pattern of the suffering Servant who "made intercession for the transgressors" (Isa. 53:12). Christ's intercession is for all sincere penitents (typified by the unmeritorious thief in Luke 23:34). Christ intercedes for all humanity. Those who have chosen not to believe have voluntarily elected not to enjoy the effect of his intercession (Augustine, *Sermon* 285.2; Cyril of Jerusalem, *Catech. Lect.* 13.30; Quenstedt, *TDP* 3:257).

Christ intercedes especially for the church, for "those you have given me" (John 17:9, 24). He intercedes not only for the immature in faith that they may be brought fully to repentance and faith (Luke 13:8), but also for believers that they may be kept ever more deeply rooted in faith (John 17:8–11; Cyril of Alex., *Comm. on John* 11.8). He intercedes for those in union with the community of faith (John 17:21) and in union with Christ himself (John 17:13–18), that they might be made holy (John 17:19). Likewise the Christian community is called to intercede for all sorts and conditions of humanity: "I urge, then, that requests, prayers, intercession and thanksgiving be made for everyone" (1 Tim. 2:1).

Believers become intercessors by virtue of their participation in Christ. Christ's intercession enables, engenders, and makes acceptable the worship of the people of God who "are being built into a spiritual house to be a holy priesthood, offering spiritual sacrifices acceptable to God through Jesus Christ" (1 Pet. 2:5). Hence the whole people of God and not clergy alone are called "a chosen people, a royal priesthood, a holy nation, a people belonging to God" (1 Pet. 2:9; Leo I, *Sermons* 4).

The Empathic Intercession of God: The Son in Heaven, The Spirit in the Heart

This intercession occurs by the triune power of the sending of the Father, the obedience of the Son, and intercession of the Son by the power of the Spirit. Not only does God the Son make intercession for us but so does the Spirit: "We do not know what we ought to pray for, but the Spirit himself intercedes for us with groans that words cannot express. And he who searches our hearts knows the mind of the Spirit, because the Spirit intercedes for the saints in accordance with God's will" (Rom. 8:26–27). Father, Son, and Spirit join in intercession for fallen humanity: the Father hears, the Son advocates our cause, and the Spirit prompts our hearts to speak rightly (Augustine, *On Romans*, 54).

The intercession of Christ and the Spirit are complementary—the Spirit in our hearts and the ascended Son in the presence of the Father. Hence it is said that there are two intercessors, one eternally in the temple of the celestial city and the other temporally in the temple of our hearts, both agreeing, both groaning for our redemption, both enabling communion with the Father. By the work of Son and Spirit we have an introduction, access, a right of humble approach to the Father: "For through him we both have access to the Father by one Spirit" (Eph. 2:18; Marius Victorinus, *Epis. to Eph.* 1.2.18).

The empathy of the triune God is manifested in the joint intercession of Son and Spirit to the Father. It is as if God feels with us precisely and accurately in our struggle. This is a distinctive aspect of Christian teaching not duplicated in the history of religions. God is with us precisely amid our temptations, intimately experiencing with us our special personal difficulties, and imparting strength for good choice. God the Spirit is privy to the secrets of our hearts. God the Son knows what it means to be tempted and to suffer. The point is succinctly stated in Hebrews: "Because he himself suffered when he was tempted, he is able to help those who are being tempted" (Heb. 2:18; Chrysostom, *Epis to Heb.* 5.2–7).

Third Phase of Christ's Priestly Work: Blessing

Blessedness flows from God's own sacrifice and intercession. The blessing of God in Christ is the sum of all that is being obtained through his sacrificial act.

God's Benediction

Benediction attests divine acceptance of the reconciling act. In the Jewish tradition the signaling of this blessing was a crucial priestly act (Ambrose, *Jacob*, *FC* 65:151–69). It is to this end that priests of the Torah were called and appointed: "God has chosen them to minister and to pronounce blessings in the name of the Lord" (Deut. 21:5;).

While it is God who blesses the people in benediction, it is the people who bless and praise God in acts of adoration and doxology. The *presbuteroi* (elders, priests) act on behalf of the mediator between sinners and God.

When Moses and Aaron came out of the Tent of Meeting, "they blessed the people; and the glory of the Lord appeared to all the people" (Lev. 9:24). Through Moses the Lord gave Aaron instruction on the appropriate form of blessing: "This is how you are to bless the Israelites. Say to them: 'The Lord bless you and keep you; the Lord make his face shine upon you and be gracious to you; the Lord turn his face toward you and give you peace'" (Num. 6:22–26). Classic Christian interpreters cannot but view this threefold blessing in relation to the triune premise: the Lord as providential keeper of all by the Father, the Lord as the grace and mercy known to sinners through the Son, and the Lord as the peacemaking gift of the Spirit (Paterius, *Expos of the Old and New Testament*, Leviticus 5; Ambrose, *Of the Holy Spirit*; Barth, *CD* 3/2:580–82).

The Blessing of Christ

Christ has "blessed us in the heavenly realms with every spiritual blessing" (Eph. 1:3). Apostolic benedictions (such as those found in 1 Cor. 1:3 and 2 Cor. 3:14) are offered on the basis of Christ's sacrifice and continuing intercession. Christ's blessing is imparted through the Holy Spirit, through whom all benefits of the Son's coming are aptly applied (Theodoret, *Comm. on 1 Cor.* 166). Hence in summary: "The Blessing of the Gospel is obtained by Jesus the Priest, announced by Jesus the Prophet, and imparted by Jesus the King through the Mediatorial Spirit of the new economy of grace" (Pope, *Compend.* 2:244).

The aim of the priestly work of Christ is to deliver to humanity his "very great and precious promises, so that through them you may participate in the divine nature" (2 Pet. 1:4); and so "through him to reconcile to himself all things, whether things on earth or things in heaven, by making peace through his blood, shed on the cross" (Col. 1:19).

Christ's as Priest in the Order of Melchizedek

Yahweh set aside Levi as a priestly tribe and Aaron as a priestly family out of which the high priest (whose type Jesus Christ would fulfill) was chosen.

But Christ's priesthood was not understood solely in the tradition of Aaron or Levi. Even more distinctively it was seen "in the order of Melchizedek" (Ps. 110:4; Heb 7:3). This was shorthand language used by the Letter to Hebrews to show that Jesus' unique ministry is holy and spotless, not one made by a priesthood tainted by self-interest; that it is eternal in the heavens and not merely one that occurs in time and on earth; that it is a once-for-all offering, not requiring seasonal repetition; that it is a regal priesthood, for Melchizedek ("King of righteousness") was both king and priest, of unknown genealogy, hence anticipatory of the eternal sonship of Christ, who was, like Melchizedek, "the king of peace"; that it was Melchizedek who offered bread and wine (Gen. 14:18) prefiguring the Supper of the Lord; and finally that it was Melchizedek who blessed and received tithes from Abraham, who was ancestor to both Aaron and Levi, thus indicating that his priesthood is older and greater than the Levitical. By this astonishing co-alescence of vectors Melchizedek was understood as the "first priest of all priests of the most high God" (Theophilus, *To Autolycus* 31). This signaled that Christ transcended usual Jewish expectations about a regularized line of succession in priesthood, for his priestly offering, like Melchizedek's, was without immedi-ate predecessors, directly from God (Ephrem the Syrian, *Comm. on Heb.* 7.3; Severian of Gabala, *Fragments on Epist. To Heb.* 7.3; Tho. Aq., *ST* 3, Q22.6; Heppe, *RD*:458).

PART III

HE DIED FOR OUR SINS

THE PRIMITIVE CHRISTIAN CONFESSION received by Paul was "that Christ died for our sins according to the Scriptures, that he was buried, that he was raised on the third day" (1 Cor. 15:3–4; Chrysostom, *Hom. on Cor.*, 38.2–3).

That Christ died "for our sins" is an article of faith confessed in every creed and taught in every catechism. There can be no adequate recollection of Jesus without confessing the meaning of his suffering and death (Augustine, *CG* 13,17).

10

THE DEATH OF JESUS

J ESUS' DEATH HAS NEVER BEEN CONSIDERED an optional part of the story. It was the very purpose for which the Word was made flesh—that he might "suffer death, so that by the grace of God he might taste death for everyone" (Heb. 2:9). It was not an easy death. Intrinsic to the meaning of his death was his suffering for others.

He Suffered

Jesus absorbed the full force of human anger and drew it into the sphere of divine love. The sufferings of his whole life, particularly those of his last days, embraced the full range of human misery—physical and emotive, personal and interpersonal, inward and outward (Chrysostom, *Hom. on Matt.* 55; Catherine of Siena, *Prayer*:170–9). In Judas's betrayal, Peter's denial, the Sanhedrin's trial, the mockery of soldiers and insults by onlookers, the suffering he endured involved the full extent of human rejection, hatred, abuse, deception, and vindictiveness.

The Road to Golgotha

The Gospel narratives have been described as a Passion story with an introduction. The space Mark gives to the Passion is about three-fifths of the total, Matthew two-fifths, and Luke at least a third (Chrysostom, *Hom. on Matt.* 54–90; Augustine, *Serm. on NT Lessons* 46). John's Gospel is divided into two approximately equal halves: the signs of God's coming and the end of his coming (or Book of the Signs and Book of the Passion; Chrysostom, *Hom. on John*, Hom. 23, 24). The Passion story narrates the suffering death, *passionem, pascho*, of Christ (Acts 1:3).

One of the main reasons why the Gospels were written down at all was to provide some explanation of how it could possibly be that Jesus is both messianic Son *and* that he suffered and died. These colliding assertions created a dilemma of implausibility that required evidence and explanation (Calvin, *Comm., Harmony* 16:299–304; Guthrie, *NTT*:21–37).

In retrospect, every event prior to Jesus' death pointed inexorably toward his death as a date to be kept, a target to be reached, an hour that was coming (John 1:39; 2:4; 11:9; 16:4; Augustine, *Tractates on John* 94.1–2; John Knox, *The Death of Christ*). In considering whether to go to the Feast of Tabernacles, Jesus remarked to his relatives: "I am not yet going up to this Feast, because for me the right time has not yet come" (John 7:6–8; Tertullian, *Flesh of Christ*, 7). His decision to go to Jerusalem was irreversibly laden with the prospect of death (Augustine, *Tractates on John* 28.5–7).

He Must Suffer

Jesus' suffering was considered a necessary and intrinsic part of his messianic ministry. "The Son of man must suffer" and "be killed" (Mark 8:31). There was no alternative. Repeatedly Jesus had tried to draw his disciples closer to the truth of this paradox. The enigma was not just that the Messiah was coming, but that he must suffer and die (Cyril of Alex., *Comm. on Luke,* Hom. 50).

It is unlikely that this was a saying later attributed to Jesus by the remembering church. The hellenizing church did not characteristically use or easily find useful to their proclamation the "Son of Man" title—other titles were more easily adaptable to their purposes. There was no previous or prevailing analogy in Judaism of the merging of the Son of Man with the suffering Servant theme.

Jesus was mindful of the poignant Old Testament metaphors of vicarious atonement (Mark 10:45; 14:24; Isa. 53; Exod. 32:30–32). He was aware that these Scriptures were pointing toward him and being fulfilled in him.

Finally with the cross in view he would declare: "Father, the hour has come" (John 17:1). As he entered Jerusalem for his last tumultuous days, he stated that "it was for this very reason I came to this hour" (John 12:27; Chrysostom, *Hom. on John* 67.1). When Peter tried to defend him, Jesus said, "Put your sword away! Shall I not drink the cup the Father has given me?" (John 18:11).

The Passion Story Narrates the Humbling of the Son Even to Death

Jesus' Passion is the narrative of what he suffered on our behalf. This is distinguished from his action—what he did on our behalf.

The root of passion is suffering (*pascho*, "to suffer," Latin *passus, passionem*). In its narrower definition, Jesus' Passion focused intensively upon *a single week* of his life—his last struggle ending on a cross. The events of that week clarified his messianic identity and saving work (Lactantius, *Div. Inst.*, FC 49:284–315; Augustine, *Tractates on John* 104.2).

In its broader definition, Jesus' Passion included all the afflictions he suffered during *his whole incarnate life*—including his temptation, his being despised and rejected, reproached and plotted against (Matt. 12:24; John 7:1; 8:6; 9:16), and his suffering of physical pain, hunger, fatigue, and poverty (Augustine, *Sermon* 87.1; *CG*, FC 24:130–37, 160–71). That he must endure hostile opposition was symbolized from the outset in Matthew's narrative of Herod's massacre of innocents at Bethlehem. That he would have nowhere to lay his head was foreshadowed early by the flight of his family to Egypt (Matt. 2:13–18; Origen, *Ag. Celsus* 1.66; Peter Chrysologus, *Sermons* 150.9–11).

He suffered like others suffer, but his suffering was interpreted as differing from others' in that through it the innocent Son bore "the sin of the world" (John 1:29). Others suffer through an ambiguous mixture of human guilt and innocence. He suffered innocently, without the slightest admixture of guilt (Origen, *Comm. on John* 6.204–6; Pearson, *EC* 1:316–32).

His Descent to Death

His entire earthly ministry was concisely summarized by Paul: he "humbled himself and became obedient unto death" (Phil. 2:8). The full extent of his humiliation was seen in his unjustified execution and innocent death. There human hatred did all the damage it could do to the Only Son of God (Leo I, *Sermon* 55.4; Newman, *PPS* 6:73–76).

The descent of the Son in his earthly ministry takes us from his birth to the travail of his life, and directly to his death and burial, and his descent into the abode of the dead. The descent into the nether world paradoxically combined his deepest abasement with his victory over sin and death. In a similar way, the incarnation had combined the glory of the divine condescension of the Son with the abasement of his lowly birth—in poverty, under the law, with no room in the inn.

Throughout his suffering he identified with sinners. "God made him who had no sin to be sin for us, so that in him we might become the righteousness of God" (2 Cor. 5:21; Eusebius, *Proof of the Gospel* 4.17). This is the vocation that he assumed and accepted at his baptism, the vocation that continued until he uttered, "It is finished" (John 19:30; Hilary, *Trin.*, 10.11). The same lowliness that was to be finally manifested on the cross had been already anticipated in Jesus' *baptism*, by which he chose to be "numbered with the transgressors" (Isa. 53:11).

Just before the Passover feast, knowing that his time had come and that he was soon to be betrayed, he "wrapped a towel around his waist;" "poured water into a basin and began to wash his disciples' feet, drying them with the towel that was wrapped around him" (John 13:4–5; Theophilus, *Sermon on the Mystical Supper*). By this means he showed his willingness to stoop and serve. He taught and enacted the way of lowly service. "Do you understand what I have done for you?" "Now that I, your Lord and Teacher, have washed your feet, you also should wash one another's feet" (John 13:12–14; Augustine, *Tractates on John* 58.4–5).

Jesus' Suffering Prophetically Foretold

Although his sacrificial death had been anticipated in prophecy, it required the actual event of dying before it would be adequately understood.

His triumphal entry into Zion was prophesied by Zechariah: "See, your king comes to you, righteous and having salvation, gentle and riding on a donkey, on a colt, the foal of a donkey;" who will "proclaim peace to the nations" (Zech. 9:9–10). Jesus' entry into Jerusalem was remembered as fulfilling this prophecy (Clement of Alex., *Instr.* 1.5.15).

Jesus predicted that "one of you will betray me—one who is eating with me" (Mark 14:18). This recollects Psalm 41:9. The "thirty pieces of silver" fulfilled Zechariah 11:12. Similarly: "They gave me vinegar for my thirst" (Ps. 69:21). "All who see me mock me; they hurl insults, shaking their heads" (Ps. 22:7). Isaiah had prophesied of one who would be "pierced for our transgressions," "crushed for our iniquities" (Isa. 53:5). John explained the importance of these events for salvation history: "This happened so that the words Jesus had spoken indicating the kind of death he was going to die would be fulfilled" (John 18:32; Augustine, *Tractates on John* 114.5).

His Suffering Was Real, Voluntary, Innocent, and Purposeful

Four assumptions underlie Christ's suffering: he suffered truly, voluntarily, innocently, and meaningfully by divine permission. To understand Jesus' death, all four points must be held closely together.

His sufferings were *real*, not imagined. He was indeed "a man of sorrows, and familiar with suffering" (Isa. 53:4). If this suffering and death had been a fantasy, there could be no satisfaction for sin. He actually suffered "a real suffering and death" (*Russian Catech.*, *COC* 2:475; Council of Constantinople II, *SCD* 222). If he did not truly suffer, remarked Irenaeus, he has "misled us, by exhorting us to endure what He did not endure Himself" (*Ag. Her.*, 3. 18.6, 7).

His suffering was *voluntarily* accepted by the Son on behalf of all humanity. "He said, 'Here I am, I have come to do your will,' And by that will, we have been made holy through the sacrifice of the body of Jesus Christ once for all" (Heb. 10:9–10; Cyril of Jerusalem, *Catech. Lect.* 13.6). He was not externally compelled to be baptized with the baptism of sinners, to set his face steadfastly toward Jerusalem or go to Gethsemane, or drink the cup of suffering. Rather he received and drank that cup not because he liked to suffer—the very thought caused him to sweat profusely—but rather because it was an intrinsic part of the purpose of his mission to humanity (Chrysostom, *Epis. to Heb.* 18, 19l; Catherine of Siena, *Pray.*:17–18).

Without the premise of *innocence* he could not have served adequately as unblemished Lamb (Heb. 7:26; Rev. 15:1–8; Apringius of Beja, *Tractate on the Apocalypse* 19.6–9).

These sufferings occurred *meaningfully*, and by the Father's permission. They were allowed to happen according to a hidden divine purpose and permission, not by fate, chance, or absurd accident; they have meaning in relation to the history of salvation. "This man was handed over to you by God's set purpose and foreknowledge" (Acts 2:23; Arator, On the Acts of the Apostles 1).

The Last Meal

Jesus celebrated his last meal with his disciples in intense expectation of the coming reign of God, aware that he would soon leave them. "I will not drink again of the fruit of the vine until that day when I drink it anew in the kingdom of God" (Mark 14:25). This meal took place near the time of the festival in which a Passover lamb was sacrificed in remembrance of the liberation of the people of Israel from Egypt (John of Damascus, *OF* 4.13). "Jesus gives himself, in the form of bread and wine, as one given over to death" (Bornkamm, *JN*:161).

Mark 14:24 reports that Jesus said to his disciples at their last supper: "This is my blood of the covenant which is poured out for many." Matthew 26:28 adds: "for the forgiveness of sins." Paul's version states: "'This cup is the new covenant in my blood; do this whenever you drink it, in remembrance of me.' For whenever you eat this bread and drink this cup, you proclaim the Lord's death until he comes" (1 Cor. 11:25–26; Cyril of Alex. *Letters* 17.12).

Facing Death

The events surrounding Jesus' death were not done in a corner. They occurred under governmental authority, with the knowledge of the highest religious leaders, in a capital city, as the result of a formal trial ending in a torturous public death. These events became common knowledge in the Roman world (*Scots Confession* 9, *BOConf* 3.09; Hengel, *Crucifixion*: 2–21).

Powerful forces colluded in ending Jesus' life. The priestly establishment sought Jesus' life because he had challenged their authority. The scribes and Pharisees resisted Jesus because he opposed their rigid and pretentious interpretation of the law. The political establishment wanted tranquility, which they saw him upsetting. The Sanhedrin sought to end Jesus' life because his popularity had made him dangerous to them and threatened their leadership roles.

John's Gospel gives us a realistic glimpse into the cynical and hysterical political reasoning of his opponents: "Then the chief priests and the Pharisees called a meeting of the Sanhedrin. 'What are we accomplishing?' they asked. 'Here is this man performing many miraculous signs. If we let him go on like this, everyone will believe in him, and then the Romans will come and take away both our place and our nation.' Then one of them, named Caiaphas, who was high priest that year, spoke up, 'You know nothing at all! You do not realize that it is better for you that one man die for the people than that the whole nation perish.'" "So from that day on they plotted to take his life" (John 11:47–50, 53). Thus "Jesus no longer moved about publicly among the Jews. Instead he withdrew into a region near the desert, to a village called Ephraim" (John 11:54).

Long before his entry into Jerusalem, Jesus had recognized that there was a definite plot against his life (Matt. 12:50; 26:38; Mark 12:33; Luke 22:44). Jesus expected a sudden and violent end that would bring grief to his companions. This seems clear from his pointed reference to the messianic bridegroom, that "the time will come when the bridegroom will be taken from them, and on that day they will fast" (Mark 2:20). Recalling Zechariah 13:7, he told his disciples at the Last Supper: "'You will all fall away,' Jesus told them, 'for it is written: "I will strike the shepherd, and the sheep will be scattered"'" (Mark 14:27).

Jesus could see his death coming. "I have a baptism to undergo, and how distressed I am until it is completed!" (Luke 12:50; Tertullian, *On Baptism* 16; *Of Bodily Patience* 13). The events were concisely recounted. They moved relentlessly to an irreversible climax—from Gethsemane to trial to cross. There is profound human tension in the narrative of Gethsemane: "Now my heart is troubled, and what shall I say? Father, save me from this hour? No, it was for this very reason I came to this hour" (John 12:27–28).

The Garden Arrest

All synoptic Gospels report Jesus' agony in the Garden of Gethsemane, where he prayed that his Father would "take this cup from me" (Mark 14:36; cf. Luke 22:42; Matt. 26:39).

"This cup" was a metaphor of punishment, of divine retribution for sin (V. Taylor, *Mark*:54; Mark 14:26–42; Calvin, *Inst.* 2.16). Sweat poured from his face like "drops of blood falling to the ground" (Luke 22:44; Bonaventure, *Tree of Life*, CWS:141–42). Matthew reported Jesus' poignant words at Gethsemane, reaching out for human companionship: "My soul is overwhelmed with sorrow to the point of death. Stay here and keep watch with me" (Matt. 26:38; Newman, *Mix.*:324–40). Yet he was in effect deserted by his disciples who were overcome with sleep.

He was betrayed and gave himself up voluntarily (Gregory Nazianzus, *On the Theophany*). He "did not defend himself, but stood to submit to judgment" (Calvin, *Inst.* 2.16.5; Matt. 27:12–14). He was surrounded by soldiers and bound with chains. When the betrayer came with "men of blood" (Ps. 54:24) "by night with torches, lanterns and weapons to seek his life," he "offered himself to them;" healing instantly the ear of the servant cut off by his disciple, "and he restrained the zeal of his defender who wanted to injure the attackers" (Bonaventure, *Tree of Life*, CWS:142–43).

His Public Condemnation Under Pontius Pilate

Why do the creeds insist as an article of faith that he was tried under Pontius Pilate ("sub Pontio Pilato"; Creed of 150 Fathers)? This locates the salvation event as a datable event of history. Christianity, like Judaism, is a historical religion. The redemption of the world is an event located in ordinary human history (Russian Catech.), specifically "under Pontius Pilate," pointing to the historical concreteness of this event attested by eyewitnesses (Apostles' Creed, *SCD* 2; Council of Constantinople 2, *SCD* 222; *SCD* 20, 86, 255). Christian salvation teaching differs radically from pagan deliverance myths in that its salvation event is the only one with a historical date (Mark 15:1–15; Ursinus, *CHC*: 217–19).

Nisan was the first month of the ancient Jewish year when the festival of Passover was celebrated. It was on the fourteenth day of Nisan that "Christ our Passover lamb, has been sacrificed" (1 Cor. 5:7; John 18:28), that "Christ died for our sins according to the Scriptures, that he was buried" (1 Cor. 15:3). Jesus died as "lamb of God" (John 1:29, 36) on the day when the Passover lambs were sacrificed (Chrysostom, *Hom. on John* 83.3). As the birth of the Savior was an actual event that occurred on a particular day in history (Clement of Alex., *Stromata* 1.21) so was his death (Origen, *Ag. Celsus*) datable with reasonable accuracy (Eusebius, *CH* 1.9–2.7).

It is an act of confession that this event occurred "under Pontius Pilate." The reason why is stated in the Reformed Confessions: "That we may know his death to be connected with his condemnation. . . . He died so that the penalty owed by us might be discharged, and he might exempt us from it. But since we all, because we are sinners, were offensive to the judgment of God, in order to stand in our stead, he desired to be arraigned before an earthly judge, and to be condemned by his mouth, so that we might be acquitted before the heavenly tribunal of God." (*Scots Confession* 9, *BOConf.* 3.09; Calvin, *Inst.* 2.16). It was crucial that his death be public, not natural, and innocent at the hands of others (Athanasius, *Incarn. of the Word* 21–25).

It was Pilate who held civil jurisdiction over the execution of Jesus as a seditious zealot, yielding to pressure from the Sanhedrin, even if he may have thought that Jesus was innocent. Ironically, Pilate both bore "testimony to his innocence" and at the same time formally condemned him. Both acts were "by the same judge to make it plain that he suffered as our surety the judgment which we deserved" (Calvin, *Catech. of the Church of Geneva*, LCC 22:98; *Inst.* 2.16.5). To be "acquitted by the same lips that condemned him" (Calvin, *Inst.* 2.16.5; Matt. 27:23; John 18:38) brings to mind the vicarious metaphor of the Psalms that the servant of God *repaid* what he did *not steal* (Ps. 69:4; Tertullian, *An Answer to the Jews* 10).

In John's account, when Pilate quipped, "You are a king," Jesus answered: "You are right in saying I am a king. In fact, for this reason I was born, and for this I came into the world," and for the same reason he was crucified: "to testify to the truth" (John 18:37; Augustine, *Tractates on John*, 115.4)

Although the official charge was sedition, the central event of the trial was "Jesus' own confession before the high priest that he is the Messiah, a confession made openly for the first time" (Bornkamm, *JN*:163). Jesus was condemned on the charge of blasphemy by the Sanhedrin for his claim to be the heavenly Son of Man and for his offending statement that those who now were judging him would soon be subject to judgment from the Son of Man (Mark 14:62). Athanasius employed the simile of the adroit wrestler to show his readiness to meet the challenges in whatever form they come.

Jesus was clothed in a mocking robe of purple (John 19:1–4) and ridiculed as King of the Jews while being struck and spat upon. Victims were routinely tortured by whipping. It is likely that Jesus' blood flowed freely from this scourging, hence he became too weak to carry his cross all the way to Golgotha (cf. Isa. 53:7). "As they led him away, they seized Simon from Cyrene, who was on his way in from the country, and put the cross on him and made him carry it behind Jesus" (Luke 23:26). Simon, from Cyrenaica in North Africa (Libya), a passerby, likely a Passover pilgrim (his sons Alexander and Rufus may have been known to Mark and Paul, Mark 15:21; Rom. 16:13), was "compelled to carry his cross" (Matt. 27:32; Cyril of Alex., *Fragment* 306).

Crucified, Dead, and Buried

Why Crucifixion?

Jesus did not choose his manner of death. The death that was chosen by others was intended to disgrace him maximally, yet it preserved his body undivided and proved the ultimate trophy in the struggle against the power of death (Deut. 21:22–23; Athanasius, *Incarn. of the Word* 21–24).

Early Christian art has portrayed every misery of body and soul being encompassed: his wrists bound in chains; his face spat upon; the flesh of his back lashed and left bleeding from a Roman whip; his heart exhausted; his torso wrenched by the cross; his eyes beholding the grief of his mother; hearing the hateful rejection of the crowd that earlier had adored him. On his head was placed a crown of thorns (Catherine of Genoa, *Spiritual Dialogue*, *CWS*:108).

He was put to death by a most horrible means (Gal. 3:13; Athanasius, *Incarn. of the Word* 24–25; Chrysostom, *Hom. on Gal.* 3.13). His whole body, "already a mass of wounds," was "stretched and tortured on the cross" (Quenstedt, *TDP*:66; Jacobs, *SCF*:148; Prudentius, *Poems* 2:*FC* 2); his limbs almost torn apart by his own weight; his hands and feet nailed to wood; his lungs gasping for air. His side was gashed with a spear. One of the most excruciating forms of suffering in crucifixion was extreme thirst. When Jesus, parched with thirst, craved for relief, he was offered only strongly spiced wine mixed with gall which he refused (Matt. 27:34; Chromatius, *Tractate on Matt.* 19.1–7), as he was willing to be fully conscious until his death.

Death by crucifixion usually took two days. Its length and horror were precisely what commended it as a public political punishment. In Jesus' case it was a matter of hours. The cause of death was blood loss, shock, exposure, and dehydration. Legs were sometimes broken with hammers to induce death if the process took too long—Jesus died before this was required. He suffered "the most extreme form of death in order that His martyrs would fear no kind of death" (Augustine, *The Creed* 3.9; *EDQ* 25).

There is in the Gospel narratives no sentimental idealization of the cross, as later developed. Their focus was upon its saving significance and worth (Ambrosiaster, *Epis. to Gal.* 3.13.1–2). Paul wrote defiantly: "May I never boast except in the cross of our Lord Jesus Christ, through which the world has been crucified to me, and I to the world" (Gal. 6:14). Luther stressed the personal importance of the cross for believers: "I believe that He bore His cross and passion for my sins and the sin of all believers and thereby has consecrated all sufferings and every cross and made them not only harmless, but salutary and highly meritorious" (*Brief Explanation*, *WML* 2:370).

He Took Our Curse upon Himself

"Is there something more in his being crucified than if he had died some other death?" asks the *Heidelberg Catechism*. Answer: "Yes, for by this I am assured that he took on himself the curse which lay upon me, because the death of the cross was cursed of God" (Q. 39). "He hung upon the tree to take our curse upon himself; and by this we are absolved from it" (Calvin, *Catech. of the Church of Geneva*; Gal. 3:10). Hanging on a tree was purposefully intended to expose the corpse to ultimate disgrace (Deut. 21:22–23).

"A form of death had to be chosen in which he might free us both by transferring our condemnation to himself and by taking our guilt upon himself. If he had been murdered by thieves or slain in an insurrection by a raging mob, in such a death there would have been no evidence of satisfaction," but by his arraignment as a criminal we know that as one innocent he voluntarily "took the role of a guilty man" (Calvin, *Inst.* 2.16.5).

That he hung between thieves fulfilled the prophecy that "he was numbered with the transgressors. For he bore the sin of many, and made intercession for the transgressors" (Isa. 53:12; Mark 15:28; Calvin, *Comm.* 8: 130). Even on the cross he continued his ministry of pardon and reconciliation (Gregory of Nazianzus, *On Holy Easter*, Orat. 45.24).

The Cross

The sign on the cross read: "Jesus of Nazareth, the King of the Jews" (John 19:19). The religious authorities protested, but Pilate insisted. Pilate's inscription was viewed by the church as an ironic declaration of Jesus' true identity (Origen, *Comm. on Matt.*130).

"These three languages were conspicuous in that place beyond all others: the Hebrew because of the Jews who gloried in the law of God; the Greek, because of the wise people among the Gentiles; and the Latin, because of the Romans who at that very time were exercising sovereign power of many, in fact, over almost all countries" (Augustine, *Tractates on John* 117.4)

The classic exegetes stood amazed at the ironic depths of the layers of the narrative (Leo I, *Sermon* 55.1). Those who most radically symbolized the sin of the world through their very act of absurd rejection played bit parts in the story of the salvation of humanity.

The very rabble who were rejecting his testimony were at the same time paradoxically offering up the victim who would redeem. While they cried "Crucify," he prayed "Forgive" (Augustine, *Sermon* 382.2). He who knew what was in the human heart prayed for his persecutors: "Father, forgive them, for they do not know what they are doing" (Luke 23:34; Pope, *Compend.* 2:162).

Christianity transformed the symbolic significance of crucifixion. Until the day of Jesus' death, it had been a demeaning symbol of political repression. Its distinctive shape—"the four arms converge in the middle"—became a symbol of "the one who binds all things to himself and makes them one," wrote Gregory of Nyssa. "Through him the things above are united with those below, and the things at one extremity with those at the other. In consequence it was right that we should not be brought to a knowledge of the Godhead by hearing alone; but that sight too should be our teacher" (*ARI* 32). The cross teaches those "rooted and established in love" "to grasp how wide and long and high and deep is the love of Christ" (Eph. 3:18). "Make this sign as you eat and drink, when you sit down, when you go to bed, when you get up again, while you are talking, while you are walking; in brief, at your every undertaking" (Cyril of Jerusalem, *Catech. Lect.* 4.14).

"He came Himself to bear the curse laid upon us. How else could He have 'become a curse,' unless He received the death set for a curse? and that is the Cross," Athanasius reasoned. "It is only on the cross that a man dies with his hands spread out" to encompass humanity (Athanasius, *Incarn. of the Word* 24)!

His Cry on the Cross

The pathos of his human suffering was poignantly expressed in his cry: "My God, my God, why have you forsaken me?" (Mark 15:34; Matt. 27:46, quoting Ps. 22:1).

He did not cease quoting Scripture even on the cross (Jerome, *Comm. on Matt.* 4.27.46). "At the height of his agony he did not cease to call God his God" (Wollebius, *CTC* 18). He did this "that they might see that to his last breath he honors God as his Father," said Chrysostom. It is less a cry of abandonment or despair than of "bearing witness to the sacred text" (Chrysostom, *Hom. on Matt.* Hom. 88.1).

This memorable phrase was committed to memory by the Evangelists in its original Aramaic, *"Eloi, Eloi, lama sabachthani?"* They were speaking to gentile audiences. This is a clear indication that it belonged to the earliest tradition and had been often repeated in the earliest Christian preaching—otherwise it would not have been remembered by Greek speakers in Aramaic terms.

The paradox is that the dying by which he totally identified with sinful humanity left him totally isolated from those with whom he was identified. It was a lonely death, with jeers from the soldiers, rejection from the crowd, the priestly caste pretending righteousness, and the political order washing its hands. Even one of the criminals hanging near him "railed at him" (Luke 23:39). On the cross he was "forsaken" as if being the remnant of Israel. His mother was nearby, feeling his forsakenness. But was he forsaken by his heavenly Father, as the verse seems to imply? "For it was the height of his abandonment when they crucified him," wrote Origen, yet "you will be able to understand the saying . . . when you compare the glory Christ had in the presence of the Father with the contempt he sustained on the cross, for his throne was 'like the sun in the presence of God'" (*Commentary on Matt.* 135, quoting Ps.89:36–37).

His Sonship Uninterrupted Through Struggle and Temptation: My God

His apparent abandonment was essential to his learning of obedience. Maximos the Confessor wrote that it is only when God apparently abandons us that he saves us, as in Jesus' death and in the testing of Job and Joseph. Abandonment "made Job a pillar of courage and Joseph a pillar of self-restraint" (*Four Hundred Texts on Love,* Philokal. 2:112).

But his cry from the cross did not imply a literal or ultimate abandonment of the Son by the Father. It is not "as if, when Jesus was fixed upon the wood of the cross, the Omnipotence of the Father's Deity had gone away from Him; seeing that God's and Man's Nature were so completely joined in Him that the union could not be destroyed by punishment nor by death" (Leo I, *Serm.* 68.1). "It was not he who was forsaken either by the Father or by his own Godhead," wrote Gregory Nazianzus. "But, as I said, he was in his own person representing us. For we were the forsaken and despised before" but now by his representative act saved (*Orat.* 30.5).

His cry on the cross did not come from "a despair contrary to faith." Rather it shows that "this Mediator has experienced our weaknesses the better to comfort us in our miseries" (Calvin, *Inst.* 2.16.11–12).

The Psalm quoted (22:1) is a messianic reference. It helped the readers of Matthew and Mark—who were well acquainted with the messianic aspect of the Psalms—make the crucial connection: Jesus is the Expected One of Israel. The same Psalm 22 also includes reference to the messianic Son's hands and feet being pierced: "They have pierced my hands and my feet. I can count all my bones; people stare and gloat over me. They divide my garments among them and cast lots for my clothing" (Ps. 22:16–18).

In hearing his cry on the cross, no believer is in a position to object that his own hour of darkness is darker than the dark hour of God the incarnate Son. In whatever anguish, however vile, the believer thus can recall that he is crying out in companionship with One who also experienced utter human abandonment and who continued nonetheless to pray to the heavenly Father.

These are words of suffering and struggle, but "not the words of a desperate spirit; so also the voice of faith rings at the same time in this utterance, while he called God his God and perseveres in prayer" (Irenaeus, *Ag. Her.* 1. 8.1). The evidence for this is that even at the height of his agonies he did not cease to call the Father "*my* God." His suffering was mitigated by his uninterupted sonship to the Father, affirming even then "*my* God" (Wollebius, *CTC* 18; Calvin, *Inst.* 2.16.12).

His Death

A Real Death—Without Death He is Not Fully Human

Jesus died in six hours. The spear in his side was a test to see if he was dead. The water mingling with Jesus' blood was a "Sign to all attesting eyes, of the finished sacrifice" (Venantius Fortunatus, paraphrased by Richard Mant, *HPEC*:131; on the miracle of blood and water from his side, see J.H. Newman, *Mir.*:356–58).

His death, like the death of any human being, required and involved the dissolution of the natural union between his soul and body. It did not, however, imply the dissolution of the union between the divine nature and the human nature that were united in him (Tho. Aq., *ST* 3 Q50–51). "Thou, of life the Author, death didst undergo" (Venantius Fortunatus, *HPEC*:156; *SCD* 16; see also *SCD* 3–42, 286, 344, 422).

Early critics of Christianity complained that Christ "ought never to have experienced death." Gregory of Nyssa ingeniously observed a deeper logic of divine empathy, that "the birth makes the death necessary. He who had once decided to share our humanity had to experience all that belongs to our nature, how human life is encompassed within two limits, and if he had passed through one and not touched the other, he would only have half fulfilled his purpose, having failed to reach the other limit proper to our nature" (*ARI* 32).

Death as Victory

His death is portrayed in the Gospels as a struggle with the demonic powers, not simply with physical suffering or social rejection. Hence his death, as wretched as it was, was at the same time grasped as an incomparable victory, not simply over suffering, but through suffering over evil (Doc. Vat. II:15–17). By means of his death the ruler of this world was being "driven out" (John 12:31) and "now stands condemned" (John 16:11).

Isaac Watts wrote in 1707 the words now sung by Christians around the world:

When I survey the wondrous cross
On which the Prince of glory died,
My richest gain I count but loss,
And pour contempt on all my pride.
Forbid it, Lord, that I should boast,
Save in the cross of Christ, my God:
All the vain things that charm me most,
I sacrifice them to his blood.
See, from his head, his hands, his feet
Sorrow and love flow mingled down!
Did e'er such love and sorrow meet?
Or thorns compose so rich a crown?

Were the whole realm of nature mine,
That were an offering far too small;
Love so amazing, so divine,
Demands my soul, my life, my all

(*HPEC*:136–37)

"It Is Finished"

His life had come to an end, but more so, the purpose and mission for which he had come had been completed and the prophetic expectations looking toward him had been fulfilled and accomplished (Cyril of Jerusalem, *Catech. Lect.* 13.32; Ursinus, *CHC*: 220–22). "By the departing word 'It is finished,' Christ indicates that all scripture is fulfilled. He says in effect: World and devil have done as much to Me as they were able to do, and I have suffered as much as was necessary for the salvation of men." So "no one need argue that something still remains to be fulfilled" (Luther, *Serm. on John* 19:30).

His saving work was complete. The ransom for sin had been paid. The penalty for sin had been endured. The full fury of human hostility toward God had been spent. The divine-human conflict was at end. Redemption was sufficiently and perfectly accomplished (Augustine, *Tractates on John* 119).

No testimony to the finished work of Christ surpasses that of Gregory the Theologian: "Many indeed are the miracles of that time: God crucified; the sun darkened and again rekindled . . . the veil rent; the Blood and Water shed from His Side; the one as from a man, the other as above man; the rocks rent for the Rock's sake; the dead raised for a pledge of the final Resurrection of all men; the Signs at the Sepulchre and after the Sepulchre, which none can worthily celebrate; and yet none of these equal to the Miracle of my salvation. A few drops of Blood recreate the whole world, and become to all men what churning (rennet) is to milk, drawing us together and compressing us into unity" (Gregory Nazianzus, *Orat.* 45.29; from the Greek *rinnen*, to run, to flow).

Darkness spread over the country at the hour of his death. "When the sun saw its master being dishonored, it shuddered and ceased to shine" (Cyril of Jerusalem, *Catech. Lect.* 4.10). The curtain of the Temple that veils the Holy of Holies was torn asunder (Mark 15:38).

Steps away from the very place where Jesus died, the bishop Cyril of Jerusalem taught his catechumens in 351 AD: "This Golgotha, sacred above all such places, bears witness by its very look. The most holy Sepulchre bears witness, and the stone that lies there to this day. The sun now shining bears witness, that failed during the hour of his saving passion. (Cyril of Jerusalem, *Catech. Lect.* 10.19).

The Letter to Hebrews compared his death to a sacrificial offering: "But when this priest had offered for all time one sacrifice for sins, he sat down at the right hand of God. Since that time he waits for his enemies to be made his footstool because by one sacrifice he has made perfect forever those who are being made holy" (Heb. 10:12–13; Theodoret, *Interp. of Heb.* 10; *SCD* 938).

Over a millennium passed before Luther's echo would be heard: "The Person is eternal and infinite, and even one little drop of His blood would have been enough to save the entire world" (Luther, *Comm. on Isa. 53:5*).

He Was Buried

The Faithful Are Willing to be Buried With Him in His Death

It is not a minor point that the baptismal confession insists that Christ was buried (*sepultus est*; Gk. *taphenta*, Creed of 150 Fathers; Ancient Western Form of the Apostolic Creed, *SCD* 2–4).

The *Heidelberg Catechism* asks: "Why was he 'buried'?" and answers plainly: "To confirm the fact that he was really dead" (Q 41).

The ancient Christian writers held to this precise distinction: the Lord's body experienced genuine death and destruction (*phthora*) in the sense of death as separation of soul from body, but not corruption (*diaphthora*) in the lengthy or extensive decaying sense of the "dissolution of the body and its reduction to the elements of which it was composed" (John of Damascus, *OF 3*.28). This was required in order to fulfill prophecy.

It was fitting that Christ was buried in order that he might undergo full solidarity with the finite human condition, and offer us the hope of one day rising through and with him (Tho. Aq., *ST* 3 Q51; Pearson, *EC* 1:372–74). "He was buried that he might witness that our sins were buried" (Wollebius, *CTC* 18)! "For you died, and your life is now hidden with Christ in God. When Christ, who is your life, appears, then you also will appear with him in glory" (Col. 3:3–4; Augustine, *Tractates on John*, 65.1).

Baptism means just this: dead to sin, buried with Christ, and raised with him to new life. "We were therefore buried with him through baptism into death in order that, just as Christ was raised from the dead through the glory of the Father, we too may live a new life. If we have been united with him in his death, we will certainly also be united with him in his resurrection. For we know that our old self was crucified with him so that the body of sin might be rendered powerless, that we should no longer be slaves to sin—because anyone who has died has been freed from sin" (Rom. 6:4–7).

Did God Suffer and Die? The Question of the Death of God

Even in early centuries the foes of Christianity were saying: "If God cannot die and Christ is said to have died, Christ cannot be God because God cannot be understood to have died." Novatian answered that "what is God in Christ did not die, but what is Man in Him did die" (*Trin.* 25). It was the incarnate Son and not the Father who suffered death upon the cross and became a true sacrifice (Clement of Rome, *SCD* 42; Council of Ephesus, *SCD* 122).

Leo explained: "As was fitting to heal our wounds, one and the same 'mediator between God and men, the man Christ Jesus' could die in one nature and not in the other. The true God, therefore, was born with the complete and perfect nature of a true man; he is complete in his nature and complete in ours" (*Letter to Flavian*, quoting 1 Tim. 2:5).

"For he still pleads even now as man for my salvation. He continues to wear the body which he assumed, until he makes me divine by the power of his incarnation; although he is no longer known after the flesh—the same as ours, except for sin" (Gregory of Nazianzus, *Theol. Orat.* 4.30.14).

The Son "died according to the assumption of our nature, and did not die according to the substance of eternal life. . . . He himself, by a kind of new operation, though dead, opened the tombs of the dead, and indeed his body lay in the tomb, yet He himself was free among the dead" (Ambrose, *Incarn. of Our Lord* 5.37).

It was only on the basis of the triune premise that classic Christian exegetes could find a sound approach consistent with the rest of Scripture's witness: "Christ, while being two natures, suffered in His passible nature and in it was crucified, for it was in the flesh that He hung on the cross, and not in the divinity. Should they say, while inquiring of us: Did two natures die? We shall reply: No, indeed. Therefore, two natures were not crucified either, but the Christ was begotten, that is to say, the Divine Word was incarnate and begotten in the flesh, and He was crucified in the flesh, suffered in the flesh, and died in the flesh, while His divinity remained unaffected" (John of Damascus, *OF* 4.8).

Thus Luther was unwilling to disallow entirely the cautious use of the phrase "the death of God"—rightly understood in this sense: "For God in His own nature cannot die; but now, since God and man are united in one Person, the death of the man with whom God is one Thing or Person is justly called the death of God" (Luther, *On the Councils and Churches*, WLS 1:198; cf. *WML* 5:223). "For though suffering, dying, rising are attributes of the human nature alone, yet since Christ is the Son both of God and of Mary in one indivisible Person with two distinct natures, we correctly say of the entire Person: God is crucified for us, God shed His blood for us; God died for us and rose from the dead, not God apart from manhood but the God who has united Himself into one Person with human nature" (Luther, *Serm. on Col. 1:18–20*; Ursinus, *CHC*:214–16).

Cross as Curse, Altar as Reversal

The wood of the tree became a rich metaphor encompassing both cross and altar: "He himself bore our sins in his body on the tree, so that we might die to sins and live for righteousness; by his wounds you have been healed" (1 Pet. 2:24).

The reversal is startling: the wood of the cross became the wood of the altar. Note the terrible irony: the cross was to this incomparable high priest his very altar. On this wood he was slain, and from it he was raised again (Heb. 11:19; Augustine, *CG* 16.32; Pope, *Compend.* 2:162). Hence "we have an altar" distinguishable from that of the Levitical priesthood (Heb. 13:10). "The cross was the altar on which He, consumed by the fire of the boundless love which burned in His heart, presented the living and holy sacrifice of His body and blood to the Father" (Luther, *Eight Serm. on Psalm 110*).

The cross is at the same time a curse suffered by Jesus and a redemption from the curse we experience when we try to save ourselves under the ever-extending demands of the law. "Christ redeemed us from the curse of the law by becoming a curse for us, for it is written: 'Cursed is everyone who is hung on a tree'" (Gal. 3:13, quoting Deut. 21:23; cf. Rom. 8:3–4). Paul's unusual way of putting this anomaly is: He who knew no sin was "made sin that in him we might become the righteousness of God" (2 Cor. 5:21; Ambrose, *Sacrament of the Incarnation* 6.60). "Hence faith apprehends an acquittal in the condemnation of Christ, a blessing in his curse" whose "blood served, not only as a satisfaction, but also as a laver to wash away our corruption" (Calvin, *Inst.*, 2.16.6).

Hence we "fix our eyes on Jesus" who "for the joy set before him endured the cross, scorning its shame, and sat down at the right hand of the throne of God" (Heb. 12:2). He took away the curse of the law, "nailing it to the cross. And having disarmed the powers and authorities, he made a public spectacle of them, triumphing over them by the cross" (Col. 2:14–15; Chrysostom, *Baptismal Instructions* 3.21).

11

IN OUR PLACE

THE CROSS HAD TO BE CARRIED and endured before it could be preached. Jesus came to be the sacrifice, not clarify the concept of sacrifice. He did not come to teach about the cross, but to be nailed to it. He came that there might be a gospel to preach.

Christianity proclaims not merely that Christ died, but that his death had significance for the otherwise apparently absurd course of human history. The Christian teaching of the cross asks what his death meant, what effect it had, how it worked for us and our salvation. This subject matter is called atonement.

The Atonement Embodied in One Person

Sin dug a gulf in a relationship. The cross bridged it. Sin resulted in estrangement. The cross reconciled it. Sin made war. The cross made peace. Sin broke fellowship. The cross repaired and restored it (2 Cor. 5:18–21; Hilary, *Trin.* 8.51).

A Death, Not a Concept

To atone is to reconcile a broken relationship on behalf of another. Atonement is viewed in Christianity not as a conceptual problem for human speculation, but an actual event in the history of divine-human covenant. The Christian teaching of atonement is not just about the general idea of dying for others, but about an actual, terrible, sacrificial death. It happened to a man from Nazareth on a particular hill on a particular day (Augustine, *Harmony of the Gospels* 3.14–23).

The significance of that death is not merely an expression of human violence and hatred, or of Jesus' moral courage. It accomplished an incomparable work of divine mercy for humanity.

The word the cross speaks is not a word we say to ourselves. It is a word that God speaks to us through an inescapably concrete, irreversible, disturbing event.

The heart of its meaning is confessed in the creed: he died *for us* (*pro nobis, huper hemon*; Creed of 150 Fathers). "He died" is a fact. "For us" is the meaning of that fact.

Mapping the Trajectory of the Study of the Cross

The teaching of salvation began by inquiring into the unique identity of the Savior. That identity could not be adequately clarified without setting forth major events of his earthly ministry, all of which foreshadowed his last days and finally came to focus intensely upon the events surrounding his death (Chrysostom, *Hom. on Rom.* 11; Ambrose, *Letter* 16). While the inquiry into the person of Christ focuses upon the personal union of deity and humanity, the work of Christ focuses upon what this incomparable person did. In sum, he served as a ransom for the sins of humanity (Mark 10:45; Gregory of Nazianzus, *Theol. Orat.* 4.20).

The pivotal principle that integrates the study of Christ is: *what the work of salvation required, the person of the Mediator supplied.* This is the economy of salvation.

Salvation requires a Savior. This unique work can only be done by this unique person. This salvation can only be accomplished by this Savior—not just anyone dying on any cross. This principle holds together the varied parts of this study. Its key question: What did the Savior (*soter*) do to bring about salvation (*soteria*)?

Admittedly it is more important to the believer to know *that* he is saved by the cross than precisely *how.* Yet the recipient of saving grace is at some point compelled to ask how and why, to whatever degree it is possible (Ambrose, *Of Christian Faith* 2.11). We will follow the centrist classic Christian consensus on the meaning of Jesus' death. It was thought through thoroughly over the earliest centuries of Christian study of Scripture.

The Crossroad of Christian Reflection

No Cross, No Christianity

To preach is to announce the cross. To worship is to come to the cross. To believe is to trust in the One crucified (Rom. 5:6–11; Origen, *Comm. on Rom.* 5.6; Cyril of Alex, *Expl. of Rom.* 6.5).

It is impossible to imagine Christianity without a cross. Christian worship is spatially ordered around it. The history of Western art and architecture holds the cross before us constantly. In death the graves of Christians are marked by a cross (Cyril of Jerusalem, *Catech. Lect.* 13.33).

A flood of impressions and images collide and meld in the portrayal of the rugged power and meaning of the cross. In a burst of ecstasy, many of these are amassed in a single passage by John of Damascus. In Jesus death,

> death has been brought low, the sin of our first parent destroyed, hell
> plundered, resurrection bestowed, the power given us to scorn the things of
> this world and even death itself, the road back to the former blessedness made
> smooth, the gates of paradise opened, our nature seated at the right hand of
> God, and we made children and heirs of God. By the cross all things have
> been set aright. . . . It is a raising up for those who lie fallen, a support for
> those who stand, a staff for the infirm, a crook for the shepherded, a guide for
> the wandering, a perfecting of the advanced, salvation for soul and body, an
> averter of all evils, a cause of all good things, a destruction of sin, a plant of
> resurrection, and a tree of eternal life (John of Damascus, OF 4.11).

All these are implied in the death of Christ. But how do such diverse pictures cohere? The point of cohesion is the divine-human reconciliation. It happened on the cross, where "all things are reconciled" (Col. 1.20).

The Crimson Thread of Scripture: The Atoning Death

The reconciliation of God and humanity is among the most basic themes of Scripture. It is the scarlet thread running throughout the whole of Scripture (Clement of Rome, *Corinth* 12). So central is this theme that it is no exaggeration to say that the events surrounding the cross constitute the central interest of New Testament proclamation (Chysostom, *Hom. on Col.* 3; F. Turretin, *On the Atonement of Christ*; Berkouwer, *The Work of Christ*). Christ's death makes our salvation possible. Hence the cross is called the procuring cause of salvation.

At the heart of the divine-human reconciliation is Christ's death (Rom. 5:10; Phil. 2:8; Heb. 2:9–14), which means the cross (Eph. 2:16; Col. 1:20), which means the giving of the lifeblood of Christ (Matt. 26:28; Mark 14:24; Eph. 1:7; 2:13; Col. 1:14; Heb. 9:12, 15; 1 John 1:7). Christ's atoning work is grounded in the Father's love (John 3:16). It manifests God's righteousness (Rom. 3:25; 2 Cor. 5:21). It forms the basis of our reconciliation with God and neighbor (Rom. 5:11; 2 Cor. 5:18–19; Chrysostom, *Hom. on Cor.* 11.5).

"For God was pleased to have all his fullness dwell in him, and through him to reconcile to himself all things, whether things on earth or things in heaven, by making peace through his blood, shed on the cross" (Col. 1:19–20; Cyril of Jerusalem, *Catech. Lect.* 13.33). On this basis it is possible to speak summarily of the whole work of Christ simply as a "ministry of reconciliation" (2 Cor. 5:18) or peacemaking (Rom. 10:15; Eph. 2:14–17; Chrysostom, *Hom. on Eph.* 5.2.13; Clare of Assisi, *Letter to Ermentrude*, CWS:107–108; Deotis Roberts, *Liberation and Reconciliation: A Black Theology*).

The Divine Plan Leads to the Cross

The cross occurred by divine ordering and foreknowing. According to the eternal wisdom of God's *oikonomia* (arrangement or plan), which the Father had ordained, God the Son would come to save humanity from sin by means of his sacrificial death (Eph. 1:1–10; Marius Victorinus, *Epis. to Eph.* 1.1.9; Pearson, *EC* 1: 612–13).

The *plan of salvation* is familiar to believers, and can be simply summarized in traditional language: "The eternal Son of God took what is ours into personal union with what was His, and completed His human equipment as our Redeemer by a life of painful and exemplary obedience to the Father's will. Thus equipped, He redeemed mankind by His death and resurrection, and was thereby consecrated for a heavenly priesthood, in which He has become the Author of salvation. This salvation is accomplished through His mystical body, to which His Holy Spirit has imparted life, and in which He operates so as to enable men to work out their salvation" (Hall, *DT* 7:112–13; Eph. 1; Rom. 5; 2 Cor. 5).

The triune God arranged this great plan or economy (*oikonomia)* for our restoration through which the Father would be rightly brought near (propitiated) to sinners, the Son himself being the means of this reconciliation, and the Holy Spirit would enkindle the heart to receive this good news (Leo I, *Serm.* 77.2). Lacking the cross, the pivotal event of the entire narrative would be missing.

The Cross Uniquely Joins Holiness and Love

The heart of atonement teaching is: Christ suffered in our place to satisfy the requirement of the holiness of God, so as to remove the obstacle to the pardon and reconciliation of the guilty. What the holiness of God required, the love of God provided in the cross.

The Holiness and Love of God Are Intrinsically Related by Being Personally Embodied

God is holy. God's holiness constrains, orders, and conditions God's love. God's love infuses, empowers, constrains, and complements God's holiness.

God would not be as holy as God is without being incomparably loving. God would not be as loving as God is without being incomparably holy. God's holiness without God's love would be unbearable. God's love without God's holiness would be unjust. God's wisdom found a way to bring them congruently together. It involved a cross (John 3:15–18; Gregory of Nazianzus, *Poem* 2; Hilary, *Trin.* 6.40; Watson, *TI* 2, 19, 20, 25; Miley, *Syst. Theol.* 2:65–239; N. Burwash, *Manual of Christian Theology* 2:147–90).

The Discord Between Holiness and Evil

The holy God rigorously opposes evil. Whatever is freely chosen by responsible moral agents, yet causes unnecessary harm, God resists. The resistance comes from the author of human freedom through conscience.

Conscience is given universally to humanity to attest to the "ought" in all that is. Conscience witnesses within us, however imperfectly, of God's own revulsion at moral evil (Rom. 2:15; 2 Cor. 1:12).

God has created a universe governed by moral law in which the consequences of sin are guilt, loss, pain, and death. These consequences always occur in specific interpersonal communities where each person's decisions impact others (1 Cor. 8:7–12; Chrysostom, *Hom. on Cor.* 20.8–10).

The consequences of righteousness are freedom, happiness, well-being, and life. Sin tends inexorably to result in suffering, though often indirectly, intergenerationally, obliquely, ricocheting socially, and lacking in full awareness of its causes. Righteousness tends in the long run toward happiness. Human happiness consists in refracting God's holy love within the limits of human finitude (1 Tim. 6:11; Ambrose, *Duties*, 1.36.185; Tho. Aq., *ST* 1 Q26; Wesley, *WJW* 6:431, 443). This refraction has become radically distorted by the history of sin (R. Niebuhr, *NDM* 1; Gustavo Gutiérrez, *A Theology of Liberation*:265–76).

The Radical Seriousness of Sin

The holiness of God required a penalty for sin, just as promised, otherwise there would be no way to count on the moral reliability of God's word. Lacking penalty for sin, the moral order is jeopardized. There is no approach to the mystery of the cross without this premise. The just God does not lightly say to humanity: "when you eat of it you will surely die" (Gen. 2:17), only to set aside the penalty after the transgression (Pope, *Compend.* 2:253–316).

A massive disruption has occurred with the history of sin. It is not merely that unholy humanity can no longer find its way back to God, but more profoundly that the Holy One is offended and estranged by the outrageous injustices of willed human sin (Rom. 2:1–16, 3:9–20; Origen, *Comm. on Rom.* 2, 3).

The Gospel breaks through the impasse. The good news is that God through Christ has done what the law could not do: sent his Son as an offering for sin. Christ expiated sin by his own sacrificial death. The Lord laid upon him the iniquity of us all (Isa. 53:6). This is the life-giving way that the incomparably wise, holy and loving God chose to deal with the death-laden estrangement caused by sin (1 John 2:2; Tho. Aq., *ST* 3 Q46–51).

How God's Incomparable Love Answers the Requirement
of God's Incomparable Holiness in a Sinful World

God's holiness made a penalty for sin necessary. God's love endured that penalty for the transgressor and made payment of the penalty viable.

It is God's holiness that manifests God's love on the cross. It is God's love that sustains and embodies God's holiness on the cross. There the holiness of the love of God is once for all clarified, and the love of the holy God is fully embodied (Chrysostom, *Hom. on Rom.*, Hom. 9).

It is only in the cross that Christianity finds the proper balance of God's holiness and love. There holiness opposes sin. There God's love provides a ransom for the history of sin (Baxter, *PW* 15:218–19; Aulen, *FCC*:102–30).

Love was the divine motive; holiness the divine requirement. "God demonstrates his own love for us in this: While we were still sinners, Christ died for us" (Rom. 5:8). This love was so great that God "did not spare his own Son, but gave him up for us all" (Rom. 8:32; Ambrosiaster, *Comm. on Paul's Epis*, Rom. 8:31–32).

The Imbalance Caused by Neglect of Either
God's Holiness or Love

Suppose a plan of salvation in which God's holiness would be stressed but God's love neglected. If God's holiness should remain unmitigated by God's love, the supposed "salvation" could easily turn into a distorted picture of God as angry avenger who unmercifully permits the slaying of his own Son to even the score for the divine honor. Anselm's view is sometimes perceived (unfairly I think) as tending in the direction of this excess.

The seemingly conflicting divine attributes are brought into proper equilibrium in the mission of the Son. "In the love of the Triune God is found its source, in the justice of the Triune God its necessity, and in the wisdom of the Triune God its method" (Tillett, *PS*:100). It is finally on the cross that "Love and faithfulness meet together; righteousness and peace kiss each other. Faithfulness springs forth from the earth, and righteousness looks down from heaven" (Ps. 85:10–11; cf. Francis of Assisi, *Letters*, *CWS*:53–57, 68–71).

The Lord says: "Be holy, for I am holy" (Lev. 11:44). Leo the Great explained: That means "choose me and keep away from what displeases me. *Do what I love*; *love what I do*. If what I order seems difficult, come back to me who ordered it, so that from where the command was given help might be offered. I who furnish the desire will not refuse support" (Leo I, *Sermon* 94.2, italics added).

The Reversal: God's Own Sacrifice

Atonement is defined as the satisfaction made for sin by the death of Christ that makes possible the salvation of humanity (1 John 2:2; Rom. 3:25; Baxter, *PW* 6:511–18). The Hebrew root words that convey the atoning deed (*kaphar, kippurim*) carried nuances of "purge, cleanse, expiate, purify, cross out, cover, spread over, or forgive." These words ordinarily denote the satisfaction made for sin by sacrificial offerings. One atones by providing a fitting expiation for an injury or offense (Bede, *On 1 John* 2.2).

Human Propitiatory Acts Saturate the History of Religions

Much of the history of religions is intensely concerned with expiation. The history of religions amply demonstrates that human beings from time immemorial have been aware of their guilt. Conscience sees to that, with as much variability as persistence.

Expiatory acts sought to remove this guilt through conciliatory actions offered to God. The expiations so commonly found in the history of religions focus upon the restoration of the damaged divine-human relationship by means of propitiatory actions initiated by penitents. Classic Christianity shows that God himself has made the reconciliation by sending his Son (Cyprian, *Epist.* 51).

The Reversal of All Expiatory Initiatives in the Cross

In Christianity it is not humans who come to God with a compensatory gift, but rather God who comes to humanity in self-giving in order to overcome the divine-human alienation. This is a very different idea of satisfaction than is common in the history of religions (1 John 2:1–17; Origen, *OFP* 2.7.4).

It is not that human beings conciliate God, but that "God was reconciling the world to himself in Christ" (2 Cor. 5:19). God does not passively wait to be reconciled but actively goes out and humbly suffers for sinners to reconcile them. God does not wait for humanity to approach but approaches humanity (Ambrose, *On the Sacrament of the Incarnation* 6.59). The saving event is not about God receiving our gifts, but God giving his own Gift, his Son, in order to offer us the benefit of salvation (Augustine, *CG* 22.22). The Word tabernacled in our nature (Theodore of Mopsuestia, *Comm. on John* 1.1.14). Our humanity is enriched by his coming to dwell with us (Cyril of Alex., *Comm. on John* 1.9).

In Christianity It Is God Who Sacrifices, Not Humanity

The particular sacrifice of which Christianity speaks involves a once-for-all reversal: Sacrifice does not focus primarily upon our giving God what God would not have without us, but upon our becoming totally receptive to the radical divine gift (Oecumenius, *Comm. on 1 John* 2:1–17), which implies a radical human task: being for others as God is for us (Maximos, *Philokal.* 2:245–49). Viewed schematically:

The Reversal

Preparation for the gospel	The gospel
History of religions	The reversal of religions
Humanity approaches God	God approaches humanity
Humans suffer for God	God suffers for humanity
God receives human gifts	God gives God's own self
Sinners attempt conciliation	God reconciles sinners

This is why Christian worship and ethics focus so intently upon gratitude. The beginning point is thankful acceptance of the divine gift. Worship centers on thanksgiving (*eucharistia*). Counter to ordinary human expectations, the Christian life consists in taking the risk of allowing ourselves to be endowed with gifts from God.

The Finished Work: Reconciliation

The atonement is a finished work. This means that in the cross the saving act has decisively occurred (John 19:30). It is a work that is objectively done and complete, a once-for-all accomplished redemption. It does not require some further sacrificial work on the part of the crucified Lord.

Reconciliation as an Objective Event

Reconciliation is not merely an attitudinal change on our part to welcome God back into congenial human company. Rather the cross is the central event of salvation history that has once for all changed the divine-human relationship. In it an unmerited divine gift is actually offered. "While we were still sinners, Christ died for us"; for "when we were God's enemies, we were reconciled to him through the death of his Son" (Rom. 5:8–10; Origen, *Comm. on Rom.* 5.6).

The means by which the sin/death syndrome is broken is Christ's atoning death and resurrection. The end result and purpose of its having been broken is reconciliation with God. Both of these meanings inhere in the old English term "at-one-ment:" "God was reconciling the world to himself in Christ, not counting men's sins against them" (2 Cor. 5:19). The means is Christ, the end is not counting sins (Ambrosiaster, *Comm. on Paul's Epis.* 2 Cor. 5).

Justification pronounces a word of acquittal from guilt to the offender. Reconciliation is the restoration of the justified to communion with God (Rom. 5:1–11; Chrysostom, *Hom. on Rom.* 9).

The Call for Human Responsiveness

Divine-human reconciliation is meant to be subjectively received by its beneficiaries. Though from God's side atonement is a finished act, from our side communion with God cannot be said to have come full circle until those beloved of God receive the reconciling event already accomplished, and thus become reconciled to God (Rom. 5:10) God makes his appeal through us. "Be reconciled to God" (2 Cor. 5:20; Chrysostom, *Hom. on Cor.* 11.5).

For this cause, Paul pleads with the Corinthians: "We implore you on Christ's behalf: Be reconciled to God" (2 Cor. 5:21). The reception requires a behavioral reversal. "As God's fellow workers we urge you not to receive God's grace in vain" (2 Cor. 6:1). This is not an offer for us to reconcile ourselves to God, but simply to receive God's reconciling act. Until that occurs through repentance and faith, the sinner remains behaviorally unreconciled to God, even though God offers it already as a gift (Augustine, *Enchiridion* 18–20). Though the divine-human reconciliation is an objective, finished act, yet at the same time the indicative implies an imperative (Rom. 12:1–8; Origen, *Comm. on Rom.* 12). This gift implies a task (Leo I, *Serm.* 77). The Holy Spirit works to apply this finished gift to believers. This is the subject of sanctification to be treated later.

Classic exegetes concluded that Jesus' atoning death was *necessary,* there being no salvation except through the meritorious death of Christ. It is both unlimited and conditional: it is *unlimited in extent* since it avails for all sinners and for all sin. It is *conditional* in its application, since it is efficacious only for the penitent and believing sinner. "The universality of the atonement is of God; its limitation is of man" (Tillett, *PS*:110).

The atoning work may be viewed from different vantage points: first as a doctrine of *God's* own righteousness; second as an act of reconciliation between

God and humanity; third, as the full and finished redemption of humanity. Each constitutes a different angle of vision upon a single event: the cross (Origen, *Comm. on Rom.* 5).

From the viewpoint of God's *righteousness*, atonement is the revelation of the justice of God. It is God's own surprising and radical way of making things right, namely, through the cross. From the perspective of *reconciliation* the cross is the peacemaking event in the divine-human relationship. From the third perspective of *redemption*, atonement is the resulting liberation from bondage to sin (Rom. 3:22–24; Ambrosiaster, *Comm. on Paul's Epis. Rom.* 3.24).

Four Biblical Word Pictures of Atonement

Four familiar word pictures help us in understanding God's atoning action: the loss of a family member, the sacrifice offered at the Temple, the liberation of slaves through ransom, and fair procedures in a just courtroom.

The *family* metaphor speaks of a generous father who is willing to give his only son for the deliverance of the whole family—in this case the human family.

The most important sphere from which atonement metaphors were derived is the context of *Temple* sacrifice, referring to a priestly mediation through which God and humanity are reconciled through a sin offering for transgressors as a propitiation of violated divine holiness.

The *diplomatic* metaphor speaks of a ransom being paid, a price of exchange made for those imprisoned and completely unable to help themselves.

The *court* metaphor speaks of a bar of fair judgment under the law that has imposed a fair penalty due to disobedience of law, yet a substitute penalty has been offered by an advocate or friend of the court.

These four metaphorical spheres intensely mesh, combine, and interlace:

In the *family* (*patria,* Eph. 3:15) of God, the Son (*huios,* John 1:18; 3:16) is sent to save the whole human family. Christ is the Son whom the Father gives for the benefit of all. "When the time had fully come, God sent forth his Son, born of woman, born under the law, to redeem those who were under the law, so that we might receive adoption as sons" (Gal. 4:4–5; Ambrose, *On the Chr. Faith* 1.14)

In the holy *temple* (*hieron,* 1 Cor. 3:16; 2 Cor. 6:16) the sacrificial death of the Savior readies the sinner for meeting with God. Christ is our priest (*hiereus,* Heb. 7) in the temple, himself serving as the only sacrifice that God accepts, since it comes on God's own terms.

In the *court* or judgment seat (*bema,* 2 Cor. 5:10) of righteousness, Christ's perfect obedience to law discharges the duty owed to the court and fully pays the debt (Acts 13:38). Christ is our advocate (*parakletos,* 1 John 2:1) in court, by doing what the law demands (his active obedience) and paying the penalty for us (his passive obedience through his death).

In the *diplomatic* arena, those who are enslaved by an alien power are liberated through the suffering and death of another. Christ is liberator of those sold into a dark hell-hole of bondage (Gal. 4:4.22–30).

In the family, love is the central motif. In the temple, holiness is required.

In the court, righteousness or justice is required. In ransoming slaves, what is most needed is a sufficient ransom payment.

The interweaving logic of these four word-pictures will help resolve confusions and problems of atonement texts:

1. In this reconciliation, the Son was sent on a hazardous mission for others. The whole of his life is an act of obedience to the Father. "This is how God showed his love among us: He sent his one and only Son into the

world that we might live through him" (1 John 4:9–10), in a mission that required his death to bring the family back together.

2. In this atoning act, the divine-human conflict is reconciled by a once for all temple sacrifice. "He did not enter by means of the blood of goats and calves; but he entered the Most Holy Place once for all by his own blood, having obtained eternal redemption" (Heb. 9:12; Ephrem, *Comm. on Heb.* 9.11).

3. In this reconciliation, prisoners are liberated. "You were bought at a price" (1 Cor. 6:20; Augustine, *Sermon* 231.2) through the death of one who came to "give his life as a ransom for many" (Mark 10:45).

4. In this reconciliation, the law is obeyed and fulfilled. If one asks how Christ overcame the divine-human alienation, the general answer must be: by his obedience. "For just as through the disobedience of the one man the many were made sinners, so also through the obedience of one man the many will be made righteous" (Rom. 5:19; Origen, *Comm. on Rom.* 5; Pope, *Compend.* 2:253–316).

Christ's Obedience: Active and Passive

The uniting principle of his life work is: through his work his identity is revealed. His work is active in his life and passive in his death. What Christ did and suffered gradually becomes the revelation of who Christ is as eternal Son. His identity is freely made known not through deductive reasoning but through the events of his acting and suffering.

What He Did Distinguished from What He Suffered

The means by which Christ rendered satisfaction was twofold: his active obedience to the law and his obedient suffering unto death (*Book of Concord*: 541). Christ's obedience is often analyzed in terms of his active obedience by which he fulfilled and obeyed the law through his life, and his passive obedience by which he passively endured suffering unto death (Calvin, *Inst.* 2.16).

Jesus' obedience countermands and amends Adam's disobedience. "For just as through the disobedience of the one man the many were made sinners, so also through the obedience of the one man the many will be made righteous" (Rom. 5:19). It is a single obedience, with both passive and active phases, by which "we have been both set free from punishment because he passively bore punishment for us, and given the privilege of eternal life, because he actively fulfilled the law for us" (Wollebius, *CTC* 18).

Luther summarized: "In a twofold manner Christ put Himself under the Law. First, He put Himself *under the works of the Law.* He was circumcised, presented, and purified in the temple. He became subject to father and mother, and the like; yet He was not obliged to do this, for He was Lord of all laws. But He did so willingly, not fearing or seeking anything for Himself in it," Luther wrote in order to sum up his active obedience. And, "In the second place, He also put himself under the penalty and punishment of the Law willingly" (Luther, *Serm. on Gal. 4:1–7, italics added*), fulfilling his passive obedience through his death.

In Life and in Death

His obedience is "not only in suffering and dying, but also that he in our stead was voluntarily subject to the Law." His obedience is imputed [i.e., reckoned vicariously] to us for righteousness, so that, on account of this complete obedience, which, by deed and by suffering, in life and in death, He rendered to His heavenly Father for us, God forgives our sins" (Formula of Concord, *Sol. Dec.* 3, 14).

Viewed schematically, Christ's substitutionary act involved a twofold obedience:

Christ's Obedience

Active	Passive
a vicarious obedience	a vicarious punishment
his life under the law	his death on the cross
for righteousness	for sin
fulfilling the righteousness required of humanity	enduring the punishment deserved by humanity

Those who take time to ponder this graphic will save time later in grasping the dynamics of the atonement.

By His Active Obedience (His Life) He Fulfilled the Law for Us

By his active obedience, Christ enacted and embodied the righteousness required for eternal life. He was "born under law, to redeem those under law" (Gal. 4:4; 1 Cor. 1:30). He came not "to abolish the Law or the Prophets," "but to fulfill them" (Matt. 5:17).

According to God's reckoning, the faithful are viewed as if Christ's righteousness had become theirs (Gal. 4:4–5; Rom. 5:8; 8:3; 10:4; Matt. 5:17). He fulfilled the law for us, so that the righteousness demanded by the law and rendered by Christ might become ours through faith. On this basis, "Christ is the end of the law so that there may be righteousness for everyone who believes" (Rom. 10:4). The faithful person is "found in him, not having a righteousness of my own" (Phil. 3:9; Augustine, *On Grace and Free Will* 26).

Sinners would not have been ready to come before the holy God had not some fitting way been found by which it could truthfully be said that sinners had satisfied the requirement of the law—a seemingly impossible requirement. Christ provided this way by fulfilling the law in our place, in order that sinners who repent and receive by faith this vicarious fulfillment of the law might be accounted righteous before God (Schmid: *DT* 352; Menno Simons, *True Christian Faith, CWMS*:341).

By Passive Obedience (His Death) He Paid the Penalty for Others

The quintessential act of atonement was Jesus' obedience unto death, the sacrifice of his life in utter, unreserved obedience. Uniting the themes of obedience and sacrifice, the Letter to Hebrews states: "We have been made holy through the sacrifice of the body of Jesus Christ once for all" (Heb. 10:10, commenting upon Psalm 40:6–8).

Passive obedience means Christ's willingness to suffer and die. He bore the guilt of others and paid their penalties. By his suffering and death, Christ removed the discord between God and humanity (Augustine, *Enchiridion* 41). By this means he rendered a satisfaction fully sufficient for and available to all who have faith. Merit sufficient to salvation flowed from the satisfaction rendered (Anselm, *Cur Deus Homo* 1.19–2.6).

He learned obedience through the things that he suffered (Heb. 5:8). It is ironic that God "should make the author of their salvation perfect through suffering" (Heb. 2:10; Chrysostom, *Hom. on Heb.* 4.4). The risen Christ chided the travelers on the road to Emmaus: "How foolish you are, and how slow of heart to believe all that the prophets have spoken! Did not the Christ have to suffer these things and then enter his glory?" (Luke 24:26; Cyril of Alex., *Comm. on Luke* 24).

As his passive obedience was necessary for the expiation of sin, his active obedience was necessary for the guidance of faith toward life eternal (Baxter, *PW* 21:337–41; Brandenburg-Nürnberg Articles of 1533). One without the other would be lacking either in pardon or righteousness. "Thus he honors obedience by his action, and proves it experimentally by his Passion" (Gregory Nazianzus, 30.6). These two modes of obedience must be held closely together—"What He did for us, what He suffered on account of us" (Augustine, *The Creed* 3.6).

The Cross as Sacrifice

Christ "gave himself up for us, a fragrant offering and sacrifice to God" (Eph. 5:2; Chrysostom, *Hom. on Eph.* 17.4.32–5.2). The death of Christ was a true sacrifice in the ancient Hebraic sense. Sacrifice formed the core of Levitical worship and ritual. In ancient Jewish tradition, the sacrificial destruction or transformation ordinarily occurred by the death of a living animal or sometimes by the burning of foods or pouring out of fluids. By sacrificing some valued creature for one's sins and offering it up unreservedly to God, the supplicant acknowledged God's rightful lordship over his own life, which was symbolically being offered up and destroyed (Ps. 27:6; Phil. 4:18; Pohle-Preuss, *DT* 5:113).

Sacrifices ritually acknowledged the holiness and sovereignty of God and sought to draw offenders nearer to God's holiness, however keenly aware of sin they were. A sacrifice is defined in scholastic theology as "the external offering up of a visible gift, which is destroyed, or at least submitted to an appropriate transformation, by a lawful minister in recognition of the sovereignty of God" in order to conciliate God's holy rejection of sin (Pohle-Preuss, *DT* 5:111; Tho. Aq., *ST* 1–3 Q85.2).

Biblical Motifs of Sacrifice

The sacrifices of the Old Testament formed an anticipatory type of the self-offering Christ was to make. The sacrifices of Abel and Abraham were key Old Testament types that were reinterpreted in the New Testament.

The practice of sacrifice dates back to earliest human narratives—of Abel, who "kept flocks," who "brought fat portions from some of the firstborn of his flock. The Lord looked with favor on Abel and his offering" (Gen. 4:2–5; Ambrose, *The Prayer of Job and David*; Augustine, *CG* 15.15–17).

Abel's Costly Sacrifice

The apostles preached that it was "by faith" that Abel offered this blood sacrifice. It was distinguished from the disapproved plant offerings of Cain. The sacrifice of Abel had powerful significance for early Christian belief, for "by faith he still speaks, even though he is dead" (Heb. 11:4).

Why was Abel's offering "better" than Cain's (Heb. 11:4)? Because it occurred *by faith* in God's promise, however dimly its fulfillment was perceived. It contained an implicit acknowledgment of sin and an anticipatory faith in a coming sacrifice more fitting. And it was a costly act, as was Christ's. For the offering of this sacrifice was the indirect cause of Abel's own death at the hands of his brother. The New Testament did not miss this striking reversal: *through Abel's offering he himself was made a sacrifice* (Ephrem, *Comm. on Heb.* 11.4).

The Offering of Isaac (Gen. 22)

The ram offered by Abraham was the prototypical vicarious offering through which another was spared—that of the only beloved son (Isaac) through whom the divine promise was to be fulfilled (Ambrose, *Isaac, FC* 65:10–12). The life of the ram in the thicket would be offered for the life of another. The Epistle to the Hebrews comments on its weighty significance as a figurative resurrection: "By faith Abraham, when God tested him, offered Isaac as a sacrifice. He who had received the promises was about to sacrifice his one and only son, even though God had said to him, 'It is through Isaac that your offspring will be reckoned.' Abraham reasoned that God could raise the dead, and figuratively speaking he did receive Isaac back from death" (Heb. 11:17–19).

The dilemma was that the very one through whom humanity was promised to be blessed (Isaac as the one and only bearer of Abraham's seed and promise) was according to God's command to be sacrificed. It took unreserved faith in God for Abraham to proceed to Mount Moriah (Augustine, *CG* 16.24; Kierkegaard, *Fear and Trembling*:27–37). This faith prefigured the resurrection faith in the sacrifice of the one and only Son. The word rendered "figuratively" (Heb. 11:19) is *parabole*, a parable or figure or type. Abraham believed God could raise the dead (Ephrem, *Comm. on Heb.* 11.17). Abraham's willingness to offer his only son and the salvation of his son were viewed parabolically as anticipatory of the Father-Son relation in the cross and resurrection of Jesus ("Hence he did get him back, by what was a parable of the resurrection" Heb. 11:19, Moffatt tr.).

The Levitical System of Sacrifices Prescribed Under Mosaic Law

In the Old Testament, sacrifice was regarded as mercifully instituted by God as an expression of covenant, enabling the wayward people to draw near to God (Lev. 17:11). It was not merely a rational invention of human ingenuity or social identification. Rather, the sacrificial system was a divinely provided means of enabling the approach of sinners to God.

The blood of sacrifice symbolized both the life and the death of the victim. It usually involved the violent death of a victim sacrificed in order to make the approach of reconciliation. It offered a covering over of sin and thus the removing of defilement.

The Passover Lamb

The blood of the Passover lamb was given for others and put on the doorframes of the houses of the Israelites. "The blood will be a sign for you on the houses where you are; and when I see the blood, I will pass over you" (Exod. 12:13). Hence the life of the people was preserved by the death of the victim. "And when your children ask you, 'What does this ceremony mean to you?' then tell them, 'It is the Passover sacrifice to the Lord, who passed over the houses of the Israelites in Egypt and spared our homes when he struck down the Egyptians'" (Exod. 12:26–27). The blood of the lamb was the life of Israel (Chrysostom, *Hom. on John* 17; Augustine, *Comm. on John* 55).

John the Baptist said of Jesus: "Look, the Lamb of God, who takes away the sin of the world!" (John 1:29), pointing toward a sacrificial victim whose self-offering would be in the place of another (Augustine, *Sermon* 19.3). Luther's language concerning Christ as lamb is particularly vivid: "He permits Himself, as the Pascal Lamb, to be killed and roasted on the tree of the cross that He may sprinkle us with His blood and that the angel of death, who had received power over us because of sin, should pass us by and do us no harm. Thus Paul well says: 'Christ, our Passover, is sacrificed for us'" (Luther, *Serm. on John* 19:25–37, quoting 1 Cor. 5:7). "Worthy is the Lamb, who was slain, to receive power," sang the angelic hosts of the book of Revelation, "ten thousand times ten thousand," encircling the heavenly throne (Rev. 5:11–12).

No Remission Without Shedding of Blood

Blood was symbolic of the offerer's own soul or life. Blood symbolized the dedication of a life wherein the one who offered life substituted for the indebted life of another (Augustine, *EDQ* 49).

Wherever there is blood, there is life. Life is in blood. Yet blood means more than simply physical life. It means life poured out sacrificially for others (Clement of Alex., *Instructor* 1.6). It is not the blood itself that makes atonement, but the life or animate creation or soul in the blood that is offered as a prayer for atonement (John 6:52–59; Augustine, *Tractate on John* 26.17–18).

The sacrificed victim implies not merely a death, but a death that enables life. Hence the sacrifice is not meaningless. The offering of blood was viewed as the offering and enabling of life, not death. This connection was clearly set forth in Levitical law: "For the life of the creature is in the blood, and I have given it to you to make atonement for yourselves on the altar" (Lev. 17:11; 16:9, 20–22; Isa. 53:4–10). The atoning lifeblood of the victim covers the guilt of the penitent.

The original meaning of holocaust (*holos*, "whole," and *kaustos*, "burnt") is a sacrifice wholly consumed by fire, a complete offering, unreservedly dedicated (Mark 12:33; Hilary, *Trin.* 9.24). The offerer could not actually surrender his own human life—Yahweh abhorred both suicide and human sacrifice. Hence the supplicant offered up his own life symbolically by presenting in place of his life some valued, unblemished creature. The supplicant was implicitly confessing that he was unable to stand in the presence of the Holy One as sinner—so radically that he deserved to die.

No Jew, however negligent, could have failed to grasp the central point that "without the shedding of blood there is no forgiveness" (Heb. 9:22). The offerer of sacrifice, by the laying on of hands, designated the animal to be *for him* (or for the covenant people) a means of atonement, thanksgiving, or petition. The imposition of hands on the head of the victim symbolized that the sins of the people were being heaped upon it (Lev. 4:13–20). The atoning virtue, or power to cover sins, was assumed to reside in the shed blood (Chrysostom, *Hom. on Heb.* 16.3–4).

Vicarious Sacrifice in the Temple as Preparation for the Gospel

Essentially the sacrifice was a human gift to God, presented by those aware of their sins and hoping that the severity of divine holiness might be turned to clemency. In this sense sacrifice was something like a protective covering enshrouding the sinner in the presence of God. The idea of covering is the root idea of the Hebrew *kaphar*, "to make atonement" (Exod. 29:36–37; Num. 5:8; Leo I, *Sermon* 59.5).

Through the death of animal brute creatures who were not culpable, rational creatures who were culpable were saved from death. The death of the victim was vicarious, in the place of the people, and expiatory, ceremonially removing their

sins as an obstacle to the divine-human relationship so as to bring God nearer
(hence it was called propitiatory). The virtue of the sacrifice was not determined by
cost or economic value, but by the inward sincerity of the contrition that accompanied it. "A broken and a contrite heart, O God, you will not despise" (Ps. 51:17).

The prophets protested the abuses of this sacrificial system without rejecting
the system itself. They were concerned that too often it tended to neglect justice
to the needy and mercy to the poor (Amos 5:21ff.; Isa. 1:11; Mic. 6:7; Jer. 7:22).
They repeatedly rejected the presumption that the clemency of God could be
bought or traded. The Temple sacrifice system would continue in later Judaism
until the destruction of the Temple in AD 70, when it came to an abrupt end and
Judaism became transmuted in the Diaspora.

The classic Christian exegetes drew this overarching conclusion: through this
sacrificial system, the people of Israel were being prepared for the incomparable
act of sacrifice that was to come in Jesus Christ (Arnobius, *Ag. the Heathen* 7).
They sensed that "The law is only a shadow of the good things that are coming"
(Heb. 10:1).

The Sacrificial Offering of Christ

God the Son offers himself "as a sacrifice of atonement" in order "to demonstrate
his justice" (Rom 3:25), so as to be both "just and the one who justifies those who
have faith in Jesus" (Rom. 3:26).

Only the One Mediator Could Suffice

No blood less than that of the incarnate Son of God would have been sufficient
to enable a declaration that the sins of all humanity have been forgiven (Gregory
Nazianzus, *Second Orat. on Easter*). No one except the God-man could be at once
just and Justifier (Rom. 3:26; 1 Tim. 2:5–6).

The law in itself did not accomplish the deliverance of humanity from sin
(Rom. 8:3). Only by identifying with the sinner, by becoming an offering for sin,
did the Son deliver from sin. "And so he condemned sin in sinful man, in order
that the righteous requirements of the law might be fully met in us" (Rom. 8:4;
Cyril of Alex., *Expl. of Rom.* 8.4).

Both Priest and Sacrifice Once for All

To whom did Christ offer this sacrifice? "God was reconciling the world to
himself in Christ, not counting men's sins against them" (2 Cor. 5:19; Augustine,
Enchiridion 13.41). It was God who was both offering reconciliation and receiving
the reconciled.

Augustine parsed the perplexing distinction in this precise way: "The man
Christ Jesus, though *in the form of God* He received sacrifice together with the
Father with whom He is one God, yet *in the form of a servant*, He chose rather to
be than to *receive* a sacrifice, that not even by this instance any one might have
occasion to suppose that sacrifice should be rendered to any creature. Thus He is
both the *Priest* who offers and the *Sacrifice* offered" (Augustine, *CG* 10.20, italics
added; *On the Trinity*, 4.14.1[19]).

It became a key point of classic atonement teaching that Christ is both priest
and sacrifice: "Priest and victim, then, are one" (Ambrose, *On the Christian Faith*
3.11). "For us he became to thee both Victor and Victim; and Victor because
he was the Victim: For us, he was to thee both Priest and Sacrifice, and Priest
because he was the Sacrifice" (Augustine, *Confessions* 10, 43). He is "both the offerer and the offering" (Augustine, *Trin.* 3.14).

The sacrifice of the incarnate Lord on the cross was a once for all occurrence, never needing to be repeated. "Unlike the other high priests, he does not need to offer sacrifices day after day, first for his own sins, and then for the sins of the people. He sacrificed for their sins once for all when he offered himself" (Heb. 7:27). This conclusive act of self-offering is contrasted with the repetition of the Aaronic priestly rituals (Heb. 8:3; 9:26; 10:12; Gregory Nazianzus, *On the Theophany*). Through his death sin is removed, and the approach of humanity to God made possible. Christ "has appeared once for all at the end of the ages to do away with sin by the sacrifice of himself" (Heb. 9:26). Christ as representative Mediator "sacrificed once to take away the sins of many people; and he will appear a second time, not to bear sin, but to bring salvation to those who are waiting for him" (Heb. 9:27–28).

Christ Our Eucharist

When he took the cup at the first Lord's Supper, he said to his disciples: "This is my blood of the covenant. . . . I will not drink again of the fruit of the vine until that day when I drink it anew in the kingdom of God" (Mark 14:24–25). This signaled that his death decisively marked the coming of the kingdom of God.

Jesus' death becomes our once for all Passover lamb. Jesus died during the time that the pascal lambs were being slain. Paul had received the Jerusalem kerygma that had already made the decisive connection between Jesus' death and the lambs sacrificed for the Passover feast. He delivered to his hearers "as of first importance" the gospel he had received: "that Christ died for our sins" (1 Cor. 15:3–4; Gregory Nazianzus, *Second Orat. on Easter*). He understood Christ as "our Passover lamb" who "has been sacrificed" (1 Cor. 5:7). In the words of institution for the Lord's Supper as reported by Paul—"This cup is the new covenant in my blood" (1 Cor. 11:25)—Christ's lifeblood sealed the new covenant, as sacrifice had sealed the old covenant.

The Supper remains a perpetual reminder of the Son's own self-offering on our behalf (Jeremias, *Eucharistic Words of Jesus*:150–53). It celebrates both Christ's death and coming again: "For whenever you eat this bread and drink this cup, you proclaim the Lord's death until he comes" (1 Cor. 11:26; Ambrose, *Sacra.* 4.6.29).

The Eucharist celebrates Christ's effectual and acceptable sacrifice to God. The assumption is that the once-for-all sacrifice of the cross is the energizing grace of every Eucharist, there being in reality only one sacrifice, the cross (*Apostolic Constitutions* 2.7–8). The liturgy points in the indicative case to the reality that the finished sacrifice of Jesus is complete and sufficient for all. The indicative implies this imperative: in the lives of believers this grace is still in the process of being given and looks toward being made complete in glory: "By one sacrifice he has made perfect forever those who are being made holy" (Heb. 10:14).

The Unique Conditions Required for the Salvation of Humanity

Why Vicarious Atonement Was Both Necessary and Sufficient

That which is necessary for salvation must exist as its indispensable condition. Christ's atoning death is considered an essential requisite to the salvation of humanity.

That the cross is *sufficient* for salvation means that Christ's death has provided *all* that is needful for redemption from sin. The cross is considered both necessary and sufficient for salvation.

How did the ecumenical consensus establish that the sacrifice of Christ was both necessary and sufficient?

A Moral Necessity, Not Externally Necessitated

In speaking of the necessity of the cross, there is no intended implication that God is under an external necessity to resolve the dilemma caused by the history of sin. The moral necessity of atonement is an implication of God's moral will. It is necessitated only by the sovereign freedom of the holy God to love rightly.

The cross presupposes a chronic history of sin. The cross is the remedy for this vast human malady. The need for the cross is circumvented only if it is fantasized that no such malady exists, and that there is after all no controversy between God's holiness and human sin.

Atonement is intrinsically connected with the premise that all humanity is trapped in the death grip of otherwise irreversible syndromes of sin. These syndromes manifest symptoms of the desperate condition of human freedom: anxiety toward the future, guilt toward the past, and boredom in the present. These are intensified by idolatry that makes that anxiety, guilt, and boredom harder to bear and easier to transmit (Oden, SA, parts 1–3). These universal ailments make atonement necessary.

Why Couldn't God Have Found a Better Way to Save from Sin?

It is zealous exaggeration to say that God could not have redeemed humanity in any other way than Christ's crucifixion (Luke 1:37; Tho. Aq., ST 3 Q46.2). But it is difficult to imagine any alternative way of salvation that more fully satisfies the rigorous requirements set by the confluence of God's holiness, justice, and love amid the wretched conditions requiring reparation for the history of sin (Anselm, Cur Deus Homo 12–14). There was no easy or cost-free way for one man to become a substitute for the whole history of sin.

God does not characteristically waste precious resources. Had there been a less costly way to reconcile sinners that could have avoided the death of his beloved Son, that way would have been chosen (Athanasius, Incarn. of the Word 1–5). But given the chronic history of sin, it was necessary that Christ be "born under law, to redeem those under law" (Gal. 4:4–5).

The Apostles do not permit the hubris of our second-guessing God's justice. God's motives are by definition good exceeding all human wisdoms. The way God found was the best way, given the facts of human alienation.

The Cross Was Consistent with God's Goodness and Human Freedom

But why this particularly harsh, narrow, difficult way of salvation. Why an ugly cross and not another, milder, easier way?

If God were merely saving rocks or plants, the plan would have been different—for they do not have freedom to respond and resist. The plan of salvation had to be worthy of the *character of the holy and loving God* and fitting to the *conditions of human freedom* so radically fallen into distortion and self-alienation.

The plan had to be consistent with the extraordinary gifts the Creator had already bestowed upon humanity: reason, imagination, language, the capacity for justice and love, and self-determining intelligence. Any design short of all these conditions would have displayed less than the incomparable wisdom of God and would have been inconsistent with all that is known of the divine character (Baxter, PW 9:35; 20, pref.).

The way of salvation had to be also consistent with the original purpose of God in creation. God could have created or not created human beings, but he in fact decided to create. God could have created companionate rational creatures with vastly different native capacities and powers but did not. Given the assumption that human beings had already vastly skewed the original purpose of their creation, God's plan of redemption had to be consistent with the nature and destiny of human creation (Origen, *OFP* 2.9; Tho. Aq., *ST* 1 Q47).

One option was thereby crossed off the list of possibilities—annihilation. It would have been less fitting if God had simply started over by obliterating or demolishing the whole botched history of human freedom. But it was more fitting and more consistent with the character of God that God should carry on through with the original divine plan, overcoming the fallenness of free accountable beings (Gregory Nazianzus, *Orat.* 38).

Fallen Human Freedom to Be Redeemed, Not Merely Inorganic Matter, Plants, or Beasts

It is more complex to redeem fallen human freedom than inorganic or organic matter. The plan of salvation had to pertain to the specific conditions of historically-chosen, self-alienated human freedom, not simply the less complicated situation of inorganic objects or plant or animal life.

The natural law suited to *lifeless matter* (under orderly natural causation) assumes that there is no capacity for response or subtle communication in mere air, or earth or fire or water. The conditions of renewal of inorganic life would be different from the botanic laws pertinent for *plant life,* which assume capacities (for life, growth, and reproduction) in plants that rocks do not have (although plants must live in the same orderly world with rocks, air, and water). The zoological laws pertinent for *animal life* assume capacities (mobility) that are not present in plants (although the laws pertinent to plant life also largely pertain to animal life, for animals must live in the same world with plants on whom their lives depend).

The moral laws that pertain to *human life* assume capacities (language, reason, imagination, conscience) that have shaped the history of fallen freedom. These capacities are not so fully present in animals or inorganic matter (Gen. 1:24–27; Basil, *Hexaemeron*, 9.2–3).

This means that the problem of sin cannot be prematurely or blithely solved by having prideful human beings pretend to instruct and demand of God to flatly or absolutely decree salvation apart from any interaction between grace and freedom. A theology of absolute divine decrees that neglects human freedom might seem a simpler conceptual idea. It might appear to be more consistent. But it is lacking in the interactive complexity of the grace-freedom interface that is constantly assumed in Scripture (Gregory of Nyssa, *Origin of Man*).

Rejected Options

Therefore three options have been consistently rejected in the attempt of classic Christianity to make sense out of the biblical wisdom that leads to the cross: The first is to avoid divine coercion. The God who created freedom would not act simply by fiat. If human freedom is to be honored and transformed, it cannot merely be coerced by decree but rather must be reshaped by persuasion and drawn by a convincing demonstration of unconditional love.

Secondly, there must be no idea of pardon without repentance or reparation. The idea that God could have pardoned without exacting any measures to repair the damage done by human freedom is morally insufficient and inconsistent with divine holiness.

Third, the prospect of no redemption at all is theoretically conceivable, but hardly consistent with the incomparable love of God attested in Scripture. The notion that God might simply have left humanity forever mired in its own fallen history might be arguable on the grounds of God's absolute holiness, but it fails to recognize the depths of divine compassion for the lost. If humanity had remained forever lost in sin, then the very purpose for which humanity had been created would have been absurdly brought to nothing (Augustine, *Grace and Free Will*; Epis. 167.19; *Grace and Orig. Sin*, 1.18–21).

Penalty as a Consequence of Law

To the above constraints must be joined another pivotal moral consideration.

The Moral Necessity of Penalty

Only the fair and rightful execution of penalty guarantees the continuity and intelligibility of a reliable moral order. God does not forgive without atonement or expiation for past guilt. To do this would be to treat God's own moral order flippantly. This is why atonement was necessary.

It was necessary that the penalty be applied if violated, for to establish a just penalty for a violation of law and then to permit the violation to pass with impunity is to mock justice. Pardon without atonement nullifies justice (Ursinus, *CHC*: 220–21). Absolute impunity mocks fairness. A law without penalty is morally unserious, even dangerous. Withhold from your child all negative feedback and see what happens (Heb. 1:8; Oecumenius, *Fragments on Heb.* 12.9). That takes uncommonly optimistic assumptions about humanity to assume that all negative reinforcement can be taken away without human harm. Suppose a legislature passed a law against theft with a specific reasonable penalty yet the executive refused ever to enforce the law and no penalty was ever administered. Would that not have the effect of making void the law, making it a mere matter of words, thereby risking the increase of theft? Suppose God had ordered the moral universe in this way—issuing commands or requirements with penalties that were never administered—would not that end in a morally ruinous situation repugnant to moral order and law? (Anselm, *CDH*; Grotius, *DCF*).

The Command: The Soul that Sins Shall Die

Recall the original command of God to the first human partners: "When you eat of it [the tree of the knowledge of good and evil] you will surely die" (Gen. 2:17; Chrysostom, *Hom. on Gen.* 14). In Ezekiel the same formula appears slightly reworded: "The soul who sins is the one who will die" (Ezek. 18:4, 20; Origen, *OFP* 2.9). Paul rejoins: "For the wages of sin is death" (Rom. 6:23).

The *Heidelberg Catechism* summarizes the valid options: "God wills that his righteousness be satisfied; therefore, payment in full must be made to his righteousness, either by ourselves or by another. Can we make this payment ourselves? By no means. On the contrary, we increase our debt each day" (2, Q 12–13).

Repentance Without Grace is Fruitless

Throughout the history of covenant, God has promised mercy to those who are sincerely penitent. Yet divine mercy is not premised merely upon human repentance as such, but rather upon atoning sacrifice accompanied by repentance and good willing, as attested in both Testaments (Augustine, *Conf.* 4.16).

"Repentance does not of itself heal this breach; nor is true repentance naturally possible for sinners, because of the blinding, hardening and weakening effect of sin upon our minds, hearts and wills" (Hall, *DT* 7:132). Sinful men and women, unable to save themselves or pay this moral indebtedness, are left in their natural condition in effect "without hope and without God in the world" (Eph. 2:12; Jerome, *Epis. to Eph.* 1.2.12).

This is why atonement was required, and why it was necessary that the Son of Man come "to seek and to save what was lost" (Luke 19:10).

Whether Christ's Sacrifice Was Voluntary

Despite normal human resistances to death, the Gethsemene narrative indicates that the Son voluntarily laid down his life (Augustine, *Trin.*, FC 45:150–52), willingly submitting his will to the Father's will in order to show the extent and depth of God's love for humanity. "I lay down my life—only to take it up again. No one takes it from me, but I lay it down of my own accord" (John 10:17–18).

The animal victim, on the other hand, had no choice, being under the power of the one making the sacrifice. The Epistle to the Hebrews contrasts the moral efficacy of Christ's sacrifice with the morally problematic nature of animal sacrifice. "He did not enter by means of the blood of goats and calves; but he entered the Most Holy Place once for all by his own blood, having obtained eternal redemption" (Heb. 9:12). "How much more, then will the blood of Christ, who through the eternal Spirit offered himself unblemished to God, cleanse our consciences from acts that lead to death, so that we may serve the living God" (Heb. 9:14; Chrysostom, *Hom. on Heb.* 15.5).

It would be unjust if the innocent one were compelled involuntarily to suffer for what the guilty had done voluntarily. But this reasoning does not apply if the innocent one has *voluntarily* consented and benevolently willed to suffer out of the compassionate motive of love toward sinners (John 10:17–18; Gal. 2:20; Eph. 5:2; Heb 9:14; 10:7–9).

The voluntary submission is a crucial factor in distinguishing Christ's death from suicide. Christ did not kill himself as do those who commit suicide (as if death were preferred to life). He willingly exposed himself to death only when that became the necessary implication of the way he lived his life in mission (Augustine, *CG* 1.17–27).

Christ Died for Our Sins

Jesus' Death Was Vicariously Offered in Place of Sinners'

Isaiah's vision of the suffering Servant of the Lord formed the prophetic prototype of vicarious suffering. The exchange theme is portrayed with no less than eleven different metaphors of substitution in one chapter (53):

"Surely he took up our infirmities" (v. 4)

"He carried our sorrows" (v. 4)

"But he was pierced for our transgressions" (v. 5)

"He was crushed for our iniquities" (v. 5)

"The punishment that brought us peace was upon him" (v. 5)

"By his wounds we are healed" (v. 5)

"The Lord has laid on him the iniquity of us all" (v. 6)

"He was led like a lamb to the slaughter" (v. 7)

"For the transgression of my people he was stricken" (v. 8)

"The Lord makes his life a guilt offering" (v. 10)

"He will bear their iniquities" (v. 12).

He was "delivered over to death for our sins and was raised to life for our justification" (Rom. 4:25); the good shepherd "lays down his life for the sheep" (John 10:11). Christ was punished for what sinners should have suffered. Though sinless, he died the sinner's death. Substitutionary penal theories of the atonement are based upon those clear passages of the New Testament featuring the exchange metaphor (Romans 3:21–26; Galatians 3:13; and 2 Corinthians 5:21).

Luther employed a wedding metaphor to speak of substitution: "For it behooves Him, if He is a bridegroom, to take upon Himself the things which are His bride's, and to bestow upon her the things that are His. For if He gives her His body and His very self, how shall He not give her all that is His? And if He takes the body of the bride, how shall He not take all that is hers? . . . He by the wedding-ring of faith shares in the sins, death and pains of hell which are His bride's, nay, makes them His own, and acts as if they were His own, and as if He Himself had sinned" (Luther, *Christian Liberty*, WML 2:320).

Substitution: The Exchange Metaphor

Substitution occurs when one takes the place of another. Christ took the place of sinners, suffering the penalty of sin that was due them (Matt. 20:28; 2 Cor. 5:21; Gal. 2:20; 1 Pet. 3:18).

The language is specific: Christ died not only *for me* (vicariously) but *in my stead*, in place of me (as a substitute for me, or as a substitutionary sacrifice). Only because he took my place, I shall not die. Because he died in my place, I now live and may live eternally through him (Chrysostom, *Hom. on Gal.* 2.20–21).

The crucial substitutionary terms are *huper*, which means "for" or "on behalf of" another, "on account of," "for the advantage of" another, or "for the benefit of," and *anti*, which means "in place of" or "instead of" another, a preposition of price, transaction, or exchange.

He "gave himself up for us as a fragrant offering and sacrifice to God" (Eph. 5:2; Barth, *CD* 4/4: 158; Baxter, *PW* 12:204–206). The exchange metaphor appears frequently in the earliest tradition: "O the sweet exchange, O the inscrutable creation, O the unexpected benefits that the wickedness of many should be concealed in the one righteous, and the righteousness of the one should make righteous many wicked" (*Letter to Diognetus* 9). The substitution theme echoes down the centuries all the way to the hymns of nineteenth century evangelical revival.

"God demonstrates his own love for us in this: While we were still sinners, Christ died for us" (Rom. 5:7–8). The vicarious act did not depend upon any merit in the offending party. The full weight of human sin is therefore transferred to and deposited on the crucified One. In Luther's muscular terms: "We are called Christians because we may look at the Christ and say: Dear Lord, You took all my sins upon Yourself. You became Martin, Peter, and Paul, and thus You crushed and destroyed my sin. There (on the cross) I must and will seek my sin. You have directed me to find it there. On Good Friday I still clearly see my sin, but on the Day of Easter no sin is any longer to be seen" (*Easter Serm.* 1530).

The believer participates in Jesus' death, that being dead to sin, he may have newness of life (Rom. 6:1–11; Gal. 2:20). "He died for us" that "we may live together with him" (1 Thess. 5:10). He did what we could not do for ourselves.

Since he has freely given his life for us, we can freely receive our lives from God (Calvin, *Inst.* 2.17.4). He died for all "that those who live should no longer live for themselves, but for him who died for them and was raised again" (2 Cor. 5:15).

One Died for All, Therefore All Have Died

The indicative that Christ died for sin, was cursed for us, and bore our iniquities, implies an imperative, that we die to sin. On the cross and in the history of the saints and martyrs, love is known by its willingness to die for others: "This is how we know what love is: Jesus Christ laid down his life for us" (1 John 3:16). Therefore "we ought to lay down our lives for our brothers," being willing to give up what we have for those in need (1 John 3:16–17). Those who live in Christ are called to live for others.

As Adam represented all the human family in its previous history, Christ represented the whole of humanity in its future history under the new covenant. "We are convinced that one died for all, and therefore all died" (2 Cor. 5:14; Augustine, *Ag. Julian* 6.15.48; Ursinus, *CHC*:221–25).

There is a special sense in which the death of Christ implies the symbolic death of all humanity before God—namely, the end of their judgment for sin. The consequence of the death of Christ belongs to them all, just as if each person had already died for his or her own sins (1 Tim. 2:6), except that another has performed the substitution for all. All are heirs, as if offered a title claim by virtue of his representative death for them (Rom. 5:12–21; Irenaeus, *Ag. Her.* 3.22.3). But sadly, not all receive this great gift.

Athanasius reasoned that just as a whole city is secured from banditry by the presence of a single just and powerful ruler, so the presence of the Word in human history checks "the whole conspiracy of the enemy" against humanity, and puts away death (*Incarn. of the Word* 8–9).

If one asks for evidence of the efficacy of his death, wrote Athanasius, just look at the course of history since his death. There one will find empirical evidence in the courage of the martyrs. This is most notable in the case of women martyrs, who "scoff at death, jesting at death and saying what has been written of old: 'O death, where is thy victory? O grave, where is thy sting?'" (Athanasius, *Incarn. of the Word* 27).

All humanity has been affected. "As there never was, is or will be any man whose nature was not assumed by our Lord Jesus Christ, so there never was, is or will be any man for whom He has not suffered; though not all are redeemed by the mystery of His passion" (Council of Quiersy, 853, *SCD* 319).

A Ransom for Slaves

The atoning significance of Jesus' death was best summarized by Jesus himself: The Son of Man came "to give his life as a ransom for many" (Mark 10:45). A ransom (*lutron*) was a price paid to redeem prisoners from servitude. "There is one God and one mediator between God and men, the man Christ Jesus, who gave himself as a ransom for all" (*antilutron huper pantōn*, 1 Tim. 2:6). *Antilutron* is a substitutionary ransom—something happened to Christ, which, as a result of his action, need not happen to sinners. "Christ ransomed us from the curse pronounced in the Law, by taking the curse on himself for us" (Gal. 3:13; Chrysostom, *Hom. on Gal.* 3.13).

Luther thought that "redemption was not possible without a ransom of such incalculable worth as to atone for sin, to assume the guilt, pay the price of wrath and thus abolish sin. This no creature was able to do. There was no remedy except for God's only Son to step into our distress and himself become man"

(*Epist. Serm., 24th Sunday After Trinity*, 43, 44, *SML* 8:376). The term *redemption* refers to the payment of a price by which one becomes freed. From this it came to be used as a synonym for deliverance or liberation (Luke 12:28; Rom. 8:23; Eph. 4:30).

Made to Be Sin for Us—Treated As If a Sinner

The substitution did not make Christ a sinner but caused him to be viewed and dealt with as such. Christ was willing to be regarded as a sinner for our sakes. If the Son was to reconcile with the Father those who had been cursed by sin, he had to become a "curse for us." It is not that he was a curse, but that "for my sake He was called a curse," wrote Gregory Nazianzus (*Orat.* 30.5).

This is why Christ was treated *as if* a sinner. He was numbered with the transgressors: "God made him who had no sin to be sin for us" (2 Cor. 5:21). The meaning of this perplexing phrase is that God made him who was sinless to become a sacrifice for sin (Eleventh Council of Toledo, *SCD* 286). "So, was the Lord turned into sin? Not so, but, since He assumed our sins, He is called sin (Ambrose, *Incarn. of Our Lord* 6.60).

God came personally to condemn sin in the flesh. "For what the law was powerless to do in that it was weakened by the sinful nature, God did by sending his own Son in the likeness of sinful man to be a sin offering. And so he condemned sin in sinful man, in order that the righteous requirements of the law might be fully met in us, who do not live according to the sinful nature but according to the Spirit" (Rom. 8:3, 4; *Augustine on Romans*, 48; *CG* 10.22).

Few points of ecumenical teaching have received such wide consensus as the premise that Christ's death was a sacrifice for the sin of others. For ecumenical discussions of Christ as sacrifice, see Athanasius (*On the Incarn. of the Word* 20); Gregory Nazianzus (*Orat.* 30); Gregory of Nyssa (*ARI* 23); Basil (*Hom. on Ps.* 48:3–4); Cyril of Jerusalem (*Catech. Lect.* 13.33); Cyril of Alexandria (*Ag. Nestorius* 3.2); Leo I (*Serm.* 44.3; 58.3); Augustine (*Trin.* 13.15; *Confessions* 10.69; *Serm.* 115.4–5); Gregory I (*Moralia* 17.46); and John of Damascus (*OF* 3.27). God "did not spare his own Son, but gave him up for us all" (Rom. 8:32; 5:6; Matt. 26:28; Jerome, *Comm. on Matt.* 4.26.29)

Penal Substitution as Sufficient Vicarious Satisfaction

A vicarious satisfaction requires a surrogate or substituted bondsman, by which someone else is substituted in the place of the debtor, and a payment of penalty, whereby the debtor may be declared free (*BOC*: 205, 292). Penal substitution is comparable to an attorney in a murder trial willing to become a substitute for you, taking your penalty upon himself, ready to die for you. Penal substitution is a much more radical form of identification than verbal counsel or advocacy. It means taking the penalty for another. The mediatorial work could not take effect unless the Son actually bore the penalty for those he was sent to redeem.

God-incarnate renders full satisfaction for the entire enormity of the history of human sin. Christ's satisfaction, being infinite (Council of Quiersy, *SCD* 319), was abundantly sufficient (Fifth Lateran Council, *SCD* 740). The sufficiency of the sacrifice is attested in eucharistic prayer: "Thou, of thy tender mercy, didst give thine only Son Jesus Christ to suffer death upon the cross for our redemption; who made there (by his one oblation of himself once offered) a full, perfect, and sufficient sacrifice, oblation, and satisfaction, for the sins of the whole world" (*BCP*).

What Could Qualify as an Adequate Substitution
for Humanity's Sin?

No finite creature can render adequate satisfaction for grievous sin against infinite majesty. Infinite satisfaction is rendered only by one infinite in majesty, hence no human other than God-incarnate (Calvin, *Inst.* 2.17).

In classic Christian reasoning, four conditions have qualified Christ as the uniquely sufficient sacrificial victim:

his sinlessness, that the sacrifice might be spotless and undefiled;

his humanity, that he shared fully our human condition;

his deity as only beloved Son, that he might merit ransom for all;

his federal headship of humanity and identification with sinners, that he might be a fitting substitute for all.

Only one who fulfilled all these conditions could be offered up for the sins of all human history. Only this one could be a ransom "for all" (1 Tim. 2:6).

The classical exegetes argued that it was not the intensity or precisely equivalent extent of his suffering and dying, but the dignity of his person that made his suffering sufficient for all (Gregory of Nyssa, *ARI* 17–28). His sufferings were finite, but his sacrifice had infinite value due to his Sonship (Athanasius, *Four Discourses Ag. Arians* 2.14–18).

His Death Is Sufficient Sacrifice for the
Whole History of Sin

It is not the atonement that is limited, but our receptivity to it. Our unwillingness to allow the Spirit to apply it to us is the limiting factor.

The atonement is addressed to all humanity, intended for all, sufficient for all, yet it is effectively received by those who respond to it in faith (Hilary of Arles, *Introductory Comm. on 1 John*; Wollebius, *CTC* 18). "For the grace of God that brings salvation has appeared to all men" (Titus 2:11).

Even though only some are consciously receptive to this salvation, it nonetheless is given on the cross for all and sufficient for all. Scriptures that assume universal sufficiency are John 1:29; 3:16; 6:51; 12:47; and 1 John 2:2; 2 Cor. 5:14–15; Heb. 2:9; 6:4–6; 1 Cor. 8:11; 2 Pet. 2:1; 3:9. But the universal sufficiency of saving grace does not intrude on human freedom to coerce a response. God primordially willed the salvation of all. The reason that some who have heard it do not share in his grace must be found in their own self-determining will (Cyril of Alex., *Comm. on John,* 4.2).

Sufficient for All, Effective Through Faith

As to sufficiency, the cross is for all—for the world. As to efficacy, the cross becomes effective for some—for those who share in it by faith. From this derives the distinction of *universal sufficiency* and *conditional efficacy*: as to sufficiency it is universal; as to efficacy it is limited to those who accept God's offer of salvation through Christ. "For his part, he offered himself as a sacrifice strictly for all, and obtained for all grace and salvation; but this benefits only those of us who, for their parts, of their own free will, have fellowship in his sufferings, being made conformable unto his death . . . through a lively and hearty faith, through the Sacraments . . . and, lastly, through the crucifixion of our flesh with its affections and lusts" (Russian Catechism, *COC* 2:476).

It is by faith that one becomes a conscious partaker in the atoning deed (Hilary of Arles, *Intro. Comm. on 1 Pet.*, 4.1–19; Clement of Alex., *Strom.*). There is "no other sacrifice for sin" required or sufficient (*Scots Confession* 10, *BOC* 3.09). In the *Thirty-nine Articles* the sacrificial death of Christ is defined as the "perfect redemption, propitiation, and satisfaction for all the sins of the whole world, both original and actual" (Thirty-nine Articles, *Article* 31).

The atonement encompasses all sins whatever, original as well as actual, past and future, great or small, in time or eternity (Titus 2:14; 1 John 1:7; 2:2; Heb. 1:3). It further embraces all the penalties of sins (Gal. 3:13; Rom. 5:8–9; Heb. 2:14–15). The satisfaction is rendered, quite simply, for the sin of the world (John 1:20). To say "For all" means that the atonement is antecedently willed for all; yet respecting and not coercing human freedom it means that Christ represents all who freely come to God by him. The propitiation given for all becomes effectively accepted only when the penitent responds in faith (Gal. 3:26).

Paul does not speak of an effective reconciliation without faith, but that "God presented him as a sacrifice of atonement, through faith in his blood" (Rom. 3:25; Ambrosiaster, *Comm. on Paul*, Rom. 3.25). The atoning work is done and completed quite independently of our acceptance of it but calls for our acceptance of it (Barth, *CD* 4/3: 517ff.). It is not as though we must add something to Christ's sacrifice to make it sufficient, but that it is received for what it is when we have faith in it.

A Time of Forbearance to Allow for Repentance

Christ's atoning death provided for a delay in the end time execution of the sentence against sin, a time in which God's kindness is intended to lead to repentance (Rom. 2:4; 2 Pet. 3:9), a time characterized by the continuing grace of God in the common life and God's continued guidance of history (Clement of Rome, *Corinth* 7).

Since repentance can occur only to the living, this forbearance is limited in duration. "In the past God overlooked such ignorance, but now he commands all people everywhere to repent. For he has set a day when he will judge the world with justice by the man he has appointed" (Acts 17:30–31). The urgency of preaching hinges on the limited time of repentance. No hearer has unlimited time to decide, nor can history guarantee continuance without end (Chrysostom, *Hom. on Acts*, Hom. 38).

The patriarchs were saved by faith in the promise of God's coming. They trusted in God's mercy even when they could not see the further working out of salvation history. Of them Jesus said that "many will come from the east and the west, and will take their places at the feast with Abraham, Isaac and Jacob in the kingdom of heaven" (Matt. 8:11).

Some have held that neonates and retarded innocents will be saved by this atonement insofar as they are judged to be incapable of refusing it and that those who do not know right from wrong cannot be said to have consented to the Adamic history of distortion (Hugh of St. Victor, *OSCF*, 2.17). Reformed theology has generally held that elect children will be saved "by Christ through the Spirit, who worketh when, and where, and how he pleaseth" (Westminster Confession 10). The details are left to the mystery of God.

Vicarious Expiation and Propitiation

Christ is a propitiatory covering, sacrifice, or atonement for our sin effective through faith (Rom. 3:25; 1 John 2:2; 4:10; Heb. 2:17). This means that the death of Christ is the sacrificial means by which God is brought nearer or rendered propitious to one having that trust in God's promises by which God becomes favorably disposed to sinners (Augustine, *Spirit and Letter* 44).

To expiate is to make satisfaction. Christ is said to be the living expiation or "the atoning sacrifice for our sins" (1 John 2:2), enabling God and humanity to draw nearer or be made propitious or favorable. Propitiation has a different root, deriving from *prope*, "near." That is propitious which brings God nearer. Propitiation is an act that enables sinners to approach God's holiness (*BOC*:118, 191). Propitiation (*hilasmos, hilasterion*) is the means by which another is rendered propitious or favorable to one's cause or willing to listen to one's plea (1 John 4:10; Origen, *Comm. on Rom.* 3.25–26). That is propitious which renders one favorably disposed toward another who has been previously alienated.

The focus of expiation is upon the removal of obstacles to the relationship. The focus of propitiation is slightly different: upon the welcoming attitude of the Holy One for whom these obstacles are removed (Eleventh Council of Toledo, *SCD* 286; *BOC*:253, 259).

Through the cross, God is brought near and conciliated, made propitious, or favorable to our hearing and plea. Those who have been without hope in the world have been "brought near through the blood of Christ" (Eph. 2:13). It is Christ's work both to expiate sin and to enable God to draw nearer to sinners (Ambrosiaster, *Epis. To Eph.* 2.13). He became like us in every way except sin "in order that he might become a merciful and faithful high priest in service to God, and that he might make atonement for the sins of the people" (Heb. 2:17).

Note the context in which the idea of propitiation characteristically occurs: it is only after having been found guilty, having been sentenced by the judge, and bound over to the court for execution of sentence, that there is any need or opportunity to ask for clemency. In such cases the prisoner is better off if the aggrieved judge is rendered propitious or is disposed to show favor (Chrysostom, *Hom. on Heb.*, Hom. 5).

The Wrath of God Conciliated

The wrath of God is a recurrent phrase that indicates the continuing revulsion of the holiness of God against sin. The holy God cannot abide injustice, pride, deception, and willful diminution of the good (Tertullian, *Ag. Marcion* 5.13). God's righteous wrath is directed against sin (John 3:36; Rom. 1:18; 5:9; Col. 3:6; Ambrosiaster, *Comm. on Paul's Epis.*, Rom. 1.18; 5.9).

What happened in Christ was an act of substitution by which God demonstrated that his wrath had been turned aside. This enabled an entirely new relationship with humanity, not yielding to sin, but binding it up so as to make a new start (Marius Victorinus, *Epis. To Eph.* 1.2.1–15).

This is quite different from the prevailing forms of conciliatory rituals in the history of religions, where supplicants offer sacrifices to try to change a god's attitude from wrath to friendship (Arnobius, *Ag. the Heathen* 7). Oppositely, here it is God who is taking the initiative to change the broken relationship with humanity. The picture of a human being placating an angry deity is not characteristic of New Testament teaching. More characteristic is the picture of God's quiet, costly approach to alienated humanity to overcome sin through sacrificial suffering (Jerome, *Letter to Pammachius*, 27; *Liturgy of St. James*).

Victory by Justice, Not Power

The way of salvation had to be consistent with the wisdom, majesty, and holiness of God. The cross constituted this "victory" (*nike*, 1 Cor. 15:54–57, 1 John 5:4).

But this forces the extraordinary question as to how the cross could under any circumstances be considered a victory.

Gregory Nazianzus knew that "the method of our new creation" must be one that would honor freedom without reinforcing pride. "All violent remedies were disapproved as not likely to persuade us, and as quite possibly tending to add to the plague through our chronic pride; but God disposed things to our restoration by a gentle and kindly method of cure," just as a sapling must be slowly bent (*Orat.* 45.12).

The Cross Demonstrates God's Matchless Way of Absorbing Violence

In no other way could we have learned, wrote Irenaeus, of God's way of redeeming humanity from sin and evil than by the death of the mediator on the cross. In a single packed sentence (among the most influential in early Christian teaching of salvation), Irenaeus distinguished between the violence of the Deceiver and the nonviolence of the Redeemer: "Since the apostasy tyrannized over us unjustly, and though we were by nature the property of the omnipotent God, alienated us contrary to nature, rendering us its own disciples, the Word of God, powerful in all things, and not defective with regard to His own justice, did righteously turn against the apostasy, and redeem from it His own property, *not by violent means* (as the Deceiver had obtained dominion over us at the beginning, when he insatiably snatched away what was not his own), *but by means of persuasion,* as befits a God of counsel, who does not use violent means to obtain what He desires; so that neither should justice be infringed upon, nor the ancient handiwork of God go to destruction" (*Ag. Her.* 5.1.1, italics and parentheses added; D. Browning, *Atonement and Psychotherapy*).

Augustine argued that there was no other more suitable way of freeing humanity from sin than incarnation and atonement. Other means were not lacking to God, but no other means were more fitting to God (*Trin.* 13.10; 13.15.19).

The Deceiver Caught by His Own Deceit

Demonic power is trapped by its own lust for power. Since the devil had become "a lover of power," wrote Augustine, "it pleased God that for the sake of rescuing men from the power of the devil, the devil should be overcome not by power but by justice" (*Trin.* 13.13).

On the cross, Christ held back what was possible to him (conquering by power), in order that He might first do what was fitting (conquering by powerlessness). "Hence it was necessary that He should be both man and God. For unless He had been man, He could not have been slain; unless He had been God, men would not have believed that He would not do what He could, but that He could not do what He would" (Augustine, *Trin.* 30.14; *CG* 20.7).

Viewed schematically the opposing ways demonstrated in the atonement are:

The Way of the Deceiver	The Way of the Son
Snatching power	Persuading freedom
Through the fall	Through the cross
Unjust means of bondage	Just means of redemption
By absolute violence	By absolute powerlessness

Redemption could only occur through an actual history that exhibited God's wisdom through the way of the Son (Gregory of Nyssa, *ARI* 20).

Gregory of Nyssa observed that "the sick do not dictate to their physicians the measures for recovery" (*Great Catech.* 17). He provided an influential explanation of the atonement, grounded in the premise that all the divine attributes must be seen in their intrinsic interconnectedness. The divine goodness pitied human fallenness. The divine omniscience knew the best means of rectifying it. Those means had to be completely just. "His *goodness* is evident in his choosing to save one who was lost. His *wisdom and justice* are to be seen in the way he saved us. His *power* is clear in this: that he came in the likeness of man" (Gregory of Nyssa, *ARI* 24, italics added).

The Irony of Defeated Demonic Deception

What method could be rightly chosen, given the severe obstacles? The Enemy, who held humanity in bondage, suffered from an intense desire to rule. It was by Satan's own inordinate pride and desire rather than God's sheer coercive power that the means of redemption were determined.

The most famous metaphor was provided by Gregory of Nyssa. It may seem grotesque, but it carried the point through with force: "The Deity was hidden under the veil of our nature that so, as with ravenous fish the hook of the Deity might be gulped down along with the bait of flesh; and thus, life being introduced into the house of death, and light shining in darkness, that which is diametrically opposed to life and light might vanish" (*Great Catech.* 24). *Satan would not have been transfixed upon the hook of deity had it not been for Satan's inordinate desire to corrupt all flesh.*

On these grounds, Gregory argued that God's atoning action was not primarily an act of deception, but an act of justice, by bringing wisdom, righteousness, and love together in an unprecedented way. Justice means rendering to each his or her due, and "due recompense" was rendered to the Deceiver. In this case "the deceiver reaps the harvest of the seeds he sowed with his own free will (Gregory of Nyssa, *ARI* 26). Christ "shared in their humanity so that by his death he might destroy him who holds the power of death—that is, the devil—and free those who all their lives were held in slavery by their fear of death" (Heb. 2:14–15).

The Value of Christ's Death for Us

Objections to Classic Atonement Teaching

Standard objections to classic Christian reasoning about the cross are:

1. that God is unjust to punish his beloved Son for the sins of another; or

2. that it is an immoral arrangement by which one receives benefit from another's suffering without moral effort or discipline; or

3. that God is cruel to punish sin if sin is inevitable.

These chief objections have tended either to misplace the human problem (the depth of the predicament of sin), or the gracious character of God (his willingness to forgive), or the imperative that is embedded in the indicative of God's merciful action (how grace requires free response).

The ironic question arose very early in the second century as to whom, if a ransom metaphor is employed, would the ransom be paid? Some argued that the devil had temporarily acquired a right over the souls of free beings who had fallen into demonic syndromes not unwillingly but of their own choice. Hence it was asked whether, when God freed the captives, would it not be just and reasonable that such a temporary right be paid off? Out of the ongoing struggle to answer these three objections, several prototypical theories of atonement have developed and contended for consensual legitimacy in Christian history.

Reconciling the Theories of Reconciliation

The purpose of theories of atonement is to set forth rightly the connection between the death of Christ and the salvation of humanity. All major theories attempt this. The essential points of the atonement were all securely embedded in Scripture texts, which were scrupulously studied, quoted, and interpreted by patristic and Reformation writers.

Through this lengthy history, four essential types of atonement exegesis have persistently waxed and waned through the traditions of interpretation. These four traditions are not pure or exclusive types but amalgamations of overlapping biblical themes that tend to cohere and repeat in a series of interpreters. The four are the *exemplary, governor, exchange,* and *victor* motifs. They are best viewed as complementary tendencies rather than as cohesive schools of thought represented by a single theorist. All four are to be found in classical Christian writings. Various features of all four have been voiced by the most authoritative and representative classical consensual interpreters. Each approach stresses a constellation of related texts.

The Exemplary or Moral Influence Motif

Moral Aspects of Atonement in Classical Christianity

Several aspects of the example theory are well integrated into classical Christian teaching. The death of Christ is viewed in the New Testament as a demonstration of the love of God, which seeks to elicit responses of love from humanity. "For Christ's love compels us, because we are convinced that one died for all, and therefore all died. And he died for all, that those who live should no longer live for themselves but for him who died for them and was raised again" (2 Cor. 5:14–15).

Thus as a complement to vicarious, substitutionary, and victorious motifs, Christ's death also exercises a moral influence upon believing humanity. "Be imitators of God, therefore, as dearly loved children and live a life of love, just as Christ loved us and gave himself up for us as a fragrant offering and sacrifice to God" (Eph. 5:1–2; Chrysostom, *Hom. on Eph.* 18).

As Christ became obedient unto death for others, so the faithful are called to "Have this mind among yourselves, which you have in Christ Jesus, who though he was in the form of God, did not count equality with God a thing to be grasped, but emptied himself, taking the form of a servant" and "became obedient to death—even death on a cross!" (Phil. 2:5–8). The cross is commended as a pattern of mind to have "among yourselves." "Christ suffered for you, leaving you an example" (1 Pet. 2:21; Augustine, *Sermons* 284.6).

Nowhere is the deep nature and malignity of sin more truly revealed than in the cross. Also revealed there is the pattern of righteousness—the sinless life given for others—which the Christian is enabled to follow by grace. The cross reveals the love of God for sinners and makes a challenging appeal for a loving response, eliciting repentance for sin (Ignatius, *Eph.* 1). These aspects of the exemplary theory of atonement are thoroughly integrated into the most consensual, classical views of the cross (Augustine, *Trin.* 1.6–13; Thomas à Kempis, *Imitation of Christ*; Isaac Watts, "When I Survey the Wondrous Cross," *HPEC*:136). "To those who are rescued from the prisoners' yoke, Redemption further procures the power of following the way of the cross by imitation" (Leo I, *Serm.* 72.1). In the best consensual expressions of this motif, the cross is not reduced to moral example, but has exemplary power.

The Cross in the Pelagian-Abelardian-Socinian Tradition

The tradition of Abelard and Socinus, anticipated by Pelagius, is not a consensual tradition, but a distortion that reappears in heavier or lighter tones periodically. Without denying objective aspects of the atonement altogether, this tradition has overstressed the subjective appropriation of the cross, holding that the central intent of the death of Christ was to serve as supreme example of divine love eliciting and enabling a loving human response, so as to draw humanity toward the love of the Father (J. S. Lidgett, *The Spiritual Principles of the Atonement*: 460–61). The moral responsibility of man is encouraged by the example of Jesus' death as a martyr. By his death he confirmed the sincerity of his teaching.

Abelard taught that the principal value of Christ's death was its exemplary effect through the responses of love that the cross elicits. Christ's death was significant because it was thought to move the beholder to repentance and faith (Abelard, *Epitome of Christian Theology; Comm. on Rom.*). The Council of Sens (1141) rejected Abelard's tendency to give attention largely to its subjective appropriation while neglecting the objective change in the divine-human relationship (*SCD* 150–51; Bernard of Clairvaux, *On the Errors of Abelard*, 22).

Similar but more radically nonconsensual was Socinus, who viewed Christ as a prophet and teacher who saved his pupils by instruction from evil defined as ignorance and blessed them with the benefits of knowledge. His death was viewed as a final act of moral heroism, a unique example of suffering patience, eliciting repentance and faith (F. Socinus, *Praelectiones Theologicae*, xv–xxix; Mozley, *Atonement*:147–51; Stevens, *CDS*:157–61).

The Power of His God-Consciousness
Demonstrated on the Cross

According to Friedrich Schleiermacher, the father of liberal theology, Christ's perfect God-consciousness is the basis for the divine-human reconciliation. Deeply compassionate for humanity, Christ identified with the lowly and exposed himself to the suffering that comes from sin, and this happened most impressively upon the cross. As faith was elicited from others who beheld this self-giving, they were drawn into the circle of influence of his God-consciousness, sharing in his sense of sonship, relieved of the sense of God's anger, aware of God's good will (*ChrF*:100–104; Sheldon, *EC*:389). His redemptive activity consists in the moral influence he has on believers, whom he raises up into the power of his God-consciousness (*ChrF*:425). Avoiding expiatory language and resisting the premise of divine wrath toward sin, the pivotal event of Schleiermacher's atonement was "His sympathy with sin, which was strong enough to stimulate a redemptive activity sufficient for the assumption of all men into His vital fellowship" (ChrF: 462). Seeking to free atonement theory from objectivism, he overstressed the subjective side, tending "to make our poor experience the measure of what God is" (Cave, *DWC*:227).

Similar in tone is the Congregationalist theologian Horace Bushnell, who argued that Christ's death was offered not for the purpose of satisfying divine justice, but to reveal God's love. His moral influence elicits repentance. The value of Christ's death for us lies in the influence that death exerts on human persons and through them upon the fabric of human society and history. Christ's life, teaching, works, and death serve the purpose of influencing the moral quality of life of persons and societies (Bushnell, *The Vicarious Sacrifice*; Schleiermacher, *ChrF*; Ritschl, *CDJR*; B. Jowett, *Comm. on Epist. of St. Paul*, 2d ed., 1859; Hastings Rashdall, *The Idea of Atonement*). Many more recent attempts to "reform" the doctrine of atonement by rejecting the classic consensual language of vicarious sacrifice are tired repetitions of the tradition of Schleiermacher, Bushnell, and Ritschl parading in new clothes.

Classic Objections to the Exemplary Concentration

Though the ethical emphasis has at times been somewhat neglected and has repeatedly required some form of recovery, it is prone to being overstated. Several perennial objections have been raised.

This approach to atonement tends to view the death of Christ as little more than the death of a noble martyr. What redeems is finally his human example of faithfulness to duty, eliciting moral responses. "To be sure, the example is precious but far too high for us; we cannot follow," wrote Luther. "It is as if I were to come to some river bank where roads and highways end. I see nothing but water before me and am unable to get across. . . . There it would not help me if someone were to point out to me the goal which I must attain" (*Expos. of St. John* 14:6).

Humanity does not need merely to be instructed by example but by an actual historical event of redemption from sin acceptable to God. According to classic Christianity, we are not only ignorant but corrupt; not merely finite but sinners; not merely those who feel guilty but who are guilty. Christ's death means more than mere instruction. It involves the good news that the prisoner is released and can go home free since another has paid his penalty, dying in his place. "Those err who hold that Christ is a Legislator who forms moral habits and, as a sort of Socrates, proposes perfect examples of moral conduct. For although Christ does indeed give direction to actions, He first prepares and renews a man within and thereupon controls also the body, the hands and feet. For works follow faith just as the shadow follows the body" (Luther, *Lectures on Isaiah*, 52:7).

The exemplary view does not say enough about who the teacher was. In the New Testament the efficacy of his work depends upon the theandric identity of his person. Classical Christianity affirms that Jesus engaged in prophetic teaching, but the crucial premise of this teaching is that he was "a teacher come from God" (John 3:2; John 12:44–5; Cyril of Alex. *Comm. on John*, 8). He taught them not as the scribes, but as one having authority in his own person (Mark 1:22; Strong, *Syst. Theol.*:728–40; Hodge, *Syst. Theol.* 2:566–73; Hall, *DT* 7:33–34).

Exemplary theory has too optimistically assumed that the will is not radically bound by sin and that no punishment for sin is required. The theory is based upon a weakened, diluted conception of the nature of sin. The exemplary view of atonement is likely to go hand in glove with optimistic Pelagian anthropology.

More seriously, the exemplary view misses the point that finally it is not humanity only that needs to be reconciled, but primarily the holiness of God. The only necessity for reconciliation it discovers is found in the moral nature of humanity, the will to follow a good example. It fails to grasp why the righteousness of God necessarily requires punishment of sin.

The Orderly Governance Motif

The Grotian View of Atonement

Arminian Dutch jurist Hugo Grotius sought to show that Christ's death paid the penalties due for our sins without demeaning divine righteousness. The death of Christ demonstrates the lengths to which God will go to uphold the moral order of the universe.

This theory focused not upon the substitutionary satisfaction offered to God, but on the moral necessities intrinsic to God's government of the universe, for God's government cannot be maintained if sin is not punished. Pardoned offenders must be reminded of the high value God places upon the law and the high price of violating it. The necessity for atonement lies in a governmental necessity of God to punish sin or provide a substitute for such punishment compatible with God's righteous governance. If God had simply forgiven humanity by fiat without the cross, that would not have had moral efficacy for humanity.

God is moved to make humanity happy and blessed and chooses this as his best means. While Grotius is its chief representative (*On the Truth of the Christian Religion; DCF; LWHG*), this view is also found in Joseph Bellamy, Samuel Hopkins, R. W. Dale, Thomas Ralston and John Miley.

Imputation Diluted or Disputed

Later advocates of this approach have often resisted the biblical teaching of imputation. This view has little regard for those texts of Scripture that show that our sins were directly imputed (*logizomai*, accounted, reckoned) to Christ or that the righteousness of God was unilaterally imputed without further requirement upon unmeriting believers. The moral governance advocates objected to an uncritical view of absolute substitution of merit for demerit that might neglect human moral responsiveness (*Denny, Studies in Theology*:74–99; Miley, *Syst. Theol.* 1:441–530).

The emphasis here is upon God's compassion, not penal substitution. Since God is love, it is sometimes held that there is no need for his "wrath" to be propitiated. Sin is viewed as a challenge to the human moral order, as a hurdle to be overcome morally, rather than primarily as an outrage against God's holiness. The strength of this view is its sturdy resistance to unethical neglect of the moral order. The weakness is its neglect of scriptural teaching on sacrifice and the priestly office of the Mediator.

The crucial texts challenging this view are found in Romans 4 (see *ACCS* NT 6:105–121); 2 Corinthians 5:19 ("not counting their sins against them"; Ambrosiaster, *Comm. on Paul's Epis.* 2 Cor. 5:19); Luke 22:37 ("For I tell you that this scripture must be fulfilled in me, 'and he was reckoned among the transgressors'"; Cyril of Alexandria, *Comm. on Luke,* Hom. 145); and Gal. 3:13 ("taking the curse on himself for us"; Chrysostom, *Hom. on Gal.* 3.13).

Exaggerated expressions of this view do not adequately account for these scriptural passages that view the cross as propitiating God himself, as the revelation of God's righteousness, and as an execution of the penalty of law. Critics argue that this view does not adequately account for the fact that God has already actually and objectively purged sin in the cross, and failing to see the cross as the finished work of salvation. It is prone to add repentance as a necessary human good work to God's own saving work (Hodge, *Syst. Theol.* 2:578–81; Strong, *Syst. Theol.*:740–41). There is a tendency to represent repentance itself as the atoning act.

The Exchange or Satisfaction Motif

Since the exchange motif appears frequently in Scripture and the classic consensual teachers, it was thoroughly commented upon before Anselm in the twelfth century. But Anselm has become the principal voice in the Latin West to give it stark clarity and definition. His inquiry began by asking why God became human. The answer must lie in the necessity of the incarnation to solve the dispute between God and humanity.

The Offense Is Against God's Holiness

Anselm emphasized the need for making reparation to God for sin, especially by use of analogies from the medieval penitential system to the idea of satisfaction in describing the Godward effect of Christ's death.

Sin is no minor offense, for God had firmly declared that the sinner must die. The penalty must be executed. God would be less than holy if sin were permitted to go unpunished. It is in keeping with God's justice that sin not be cheaply remitted, but must be punished, or some satisfaction offered. Since sin is infinitely offensive against divine holiness, the agent of satisfaction for sin must be infinitely holy. Either satisfaction or punishment was required by God's very nature.

The necessity for the punishment of sin lies the nature of God's justice. It is not simply a residue of the moral nature of humanity.

No finite being could make a sufficient satisfaction. Only one mediator who is both truly God and truly human could, by taking the place of sinners, make a complete satisfaction to divine justice. In this way the death of Christ becomes understood as a debt sufficiently paid to the Father. The death of Christ is the equivalent of all the demands of retributive justice against all for whom Christ died (Anselm, *CDH*).

Rather than rely upon Anselm alone to express this view, it is better to rely upon the patristic sources upon which he himself relied: Athanasius, Gregory of Nyssa, Gregory of Nazianzus, Augustine, and Cyril of Alexandria, as shown above.

Protestant Developments in Substitutionary Atonement Teaching

The Reformed tradition has shared much of the Anselmic language and assumptions, focusing upon the themes of penal substitution and the sacrificial efficacy of the cross. Christ takes our place. Calvin argued that Christ "took upon himself and suffered the punishment that, from God's righteous judgment threatened all sinners; that he purged with his blood those evils which had rendered sinners hateful to God; that by this expiation he made satisfaction and sacrifice duly to God the Father; that as intercessor he has appeased God's wrath; that on this foundation rests the peace of God with men" (Calvin, *Inst.* 22.16.2).

The core of the substitutionary view of atonement is concisely expressed in the Westminster Confession: "The Lord Jesus, by his perfect obedience and sacrifice of himself, which he through the eternal Spirit once offered up unto God, hath fully satisfied the justice of his Father, and purchased not only reconciliation, but an everlasting inheritance in the kingdom of heaven, for all those whom the Father hath given unto him."

Some forms of the exchange motif disproportionally focus upon medieval commercial analogies (ransom, payment, debt) to the neglect of other moral, social, and familial analogies. In some of its expressions, this view may fail to emphasize adequately the active obedience of Christ in his entire life under the law and focuses primarily upon the passive obedience of Christ in his suffering and death. Some expressions tend to exalt God's majesty or honor above God's holiness or love. Critics argue that the New Testament rather views the death of Christ not as a substituted penalty, but a substitute for a penalty (Raymond, *Syst. Theol.* 2: 257).

The Victor or Dramatic Motif

This view stresses those biblical texts that speak of reconciliation under metaphors of victory over demonic powers (Mark 3:27; Irenaeus, *Ag. Her.* 5.21.3). The predicament is that sinners have chosen (through a long post-Adamic collective history) to belong to the demonic order because of their sin. The Son pays the price of their redemption from bondage. In his resurrection he broke the power of demonic sin, guilt, and death, leaving Satan broken, though continuing to rage in history. Where sin and death had reigned, righteousness and life now reign. The atonement is constituted by the fact that Christ has broken the power of evil (Augustine, *Trin.* 13.15).

The keynote of the cross is victory, Christ's victory over the powers of sin, guilt, pride, inordinate sensuality (the flesh), the devil, wrath, and death (1 Cor. 15:54–57, 1 John 5:4). He took away the curse of the law, "nailing it to the cross. And having disarmed the powers and authorities, he made a public spectacle of them, triumphing over them by the cross" (Col. 2:14–15). The victory has cosmic significance (Col. 1:15–23; Aulen, *CV*:120–31; Rom. 8:18–21).

The Johannine tradition provides prime textual ground for this view, wherein "the whole world" as fallen is assumed to be "under the control of the evil one" (1 John 5:19); "The reason the Son of God appeared was to destroy the devil's work" (1 John 3:8; Didymus the Blind, *Comm. on 1 John*); "Now the prince of this world will be driven out" (John 12:31). When the prince of the world is bound, all that he held in captivity is released" (Leo I, *Serm.* 22.4).

This view, prominent among early Christian writers, was to some degree displaced by Anselm, then returned to centrality with Luther and Protestantism, and is well expressed in Luther's "Ein feste Burg":

And though this world, with devils filled,
Should threaten to undo us,
We will not fear, for God hath willed
His truth to triumph through us;
The Prince of Darkness grim,
We tremble not for him;
His rage we can endure,
For lo, his doom is sure;
One little word shall fell him

(*MH* 1964, 20)

Gustaf Aulen's influential account of this view downplays the substitution and satisfaction motifs in Scripture (Gal. 1:4; 1 Cor. 15:3; 2 Cor. 5:21); is selective in his use of sources; "establishes his point only by ignoring other facets of their accounts"; focuses inordinately upon the conflict within God; and "gives little notice to what it [salvation] cost God" (McDonald, *ADC*:263–65).

Comparison and Integration of the
Complementary Tendencies

The differences between these four motifs correspond generally to what is perceived to be the deepest predicament of humanity—ignorance, misery, sin, or the bound will.

Ignorance	Misery	Sin	Bound Will
Then the atonement is likely to be viewed as:			
Moral illumination and influence	Inauguration of a reign of happiness	Salvation by Christ in our place	Redemption from curse of sin
The corresponding social predicament is viewed as:			
Lack of education	Poverty or neurosis	Willful rebellion	Demonic captivity
The predicament of the psychosomatic interface centers more particularly, in each case, upon the:			
Ignorant mind	Sensate experience	Lost soul	Bound will
These theories of atonement have been principally formed in these four related, complementary traditions:			
Pelagian-Abelardian	Grotian-Arminian	Augustinian-Anselmian	Irenaean-Cappadocian
Symbolic focus becomes trained upon:			
Moral example	Executive clemency	Sacrifice	Victory
Each is ordinarily called by its key phrase:			
Moral influence	Rectoral governance	Substitution	Christus Victor
Sometimes expressed by the summary term:			
Marturial	Rectoral	Commercial	Dramatic
The prevailing tendency is:			
Experiential-subjectivist	Legal-administrative	Penal-substitutional	Ransom-doxological
Each has a special locus of influence within Protestantism without denying the others:			
Liberal	Arminian	Calvinist	Lutheran
Key advocates of each tradition in the modern period are:			
Schleiermacher	Miley	Hodge	Aulen

Ignorance	Misery	Sin	Bound Will
Each motif gives resistance to some theme regarded as potentially excessive:			
Resists original sin	Resists imputation	Resists works-righteousness	Resists commercial metaphors
The potential problematic issue latent in the theory:			
Pelagian optimism	Legalistic synergism	Predestinarian decrees	Antinomianism
Thematic focus:			
The subject self	Moral reliability	Exchange	Conflict
Primary setting:			
Intrapsychic awareness	Public order	Transactional exchange	Demonic conflict overcome
Recent inheritors include:			
Unitarianism	Liberation theology	Neo-evangelical theology	Neoclassical orthodoxy

This graphic provides more detail than some non-professionals will desire, but it will help lay persons understand where to go for more information about each of these options.

The satisfaction and victory themes come closer to being consensual approaches (in the tradition of Irenaeus, the Cappadocians, Augustine, Anselm, and Calvin) than the others. All four need some corrective voices from the others to form an adequate teaching. They are best viewed as complementary. The scriptural and classic ecumenical teaching of atonement requires a good balance of the moral nature of man, moral government of God, the substitution of Christ for us in our place, and the consequent victory of Christ over demonic powers (J. K. Mozley, *The Doctrine of Atonement*; R. S. Franks, *The History of the Doctrine of the Work of Christ*; L. W. Grensted, *A Short History of the Doctrine of the Atonement*; L. Morris, *The Atonement of the Death of Christ*). To miss the profound complementarity of these approaches is to miss their power to change behavior. All are in Scripture for a good reason.

The Meaning of Daily Suffering in the Light of the Cross

Anyone who understands that God suffers for humanity has come close to the heart of Christianity. The story of Jesus is essentially that of God suffering for us (Cyril of Alex, *Comm. on Luke* 24:25–27).

Classic Christian teaching speaks of *daily* suffering to underscore that suffering is endemic to the human situation. Suffering invariably accompanies freedom, for freedom is perennially prone to anxiety, guilt, and boredom (Kierkegaard, *The Concept of Anxiety*; Niebuhr, *NDM* 1; Oden, *SA* 1–3). Suffering doggedly tracks the heels of human freedom. The suffering of Christ for us is primarily directed to that suffering that results from sin, from which every human suffers daily.

Gospel as Theodicy

The recollection of Christ's suffering is itself an act by which faith participates in God's own humbling (Peter of Damascus, *Treasury, Philokal.* I, 234–39). A high Christology is the key to a deep-going theodicy.

Theodicy is the attempt to speak rightly of God's justice (*theos-dikē*) under conditions of suffering and evil. Theodicy is an intellectual discipline that seeks to clarify the hidden aspect of God's goodness despite apparent contradictions of that goodness in history. Its task is to vindicate the divine attributes of omnipotence, love, justice, and holiness in relation to the continuing existence of evil in history (Augustine, *EDQ* 21).

Just being a human being is enough to qualify anyone to ask the question: "Why do I suffer?" Human existence seems to make it inevitable (Gregory I, *Morals on Job* 13.28–37).

If this profound problem finds a place anywhere in the university curriculum, it falls in the lap of theology. But fewer universities than ever have curricula in theology, and when they do, they often want it taught as if it were psychology or politics. Though theodicy is treated sporadically in literature and philosophy, it is not widely treated in psychology or sociology or even biblical exegesis. Universities do not appoint professors of theodicy, yet everyone suffers. The meaning of suffering was a central concern of the ancient Christian writers (Polycarp, Irenaeus, Athanasius, Chrysostom, Augustine, Gregory I). Without seeking it, they all had their share of suffering.

The Inherent Difficulty of the Question

No theological question is more difficult or recurrent than why bad things happen to good people. But there is one even deeper perplexity for Christians—why the absolutely just One has suffered so absolutely.

Regardless of what theory one may have of suffering, the theory never ends the suffering. The best theorists continue to suffer and even to inflict suffering upon others by means of their theories. Yet caring persons cannot simply reply with silence to the exasperating fact of suffering. In order not to say nothing, we must say something (Job 17:14; Gregory I, *Morals on Job* 27.59–60).

For classic Christian teaching, the wisest theodicy flows out of a deep reflection upon the cross (Bede, *On 1 Pet.* 2:19–20). There the profound problem of human suffering becomes transmuted by the even deeper mystery of God's suffering for humanity (Ambrosiaster, *Comm. on Paul*, 2 Cor. 1.5–7). As a problem in the sequence of classic Christian teaching, theodicy belongs just after atonement, hence we focus on it at this point.

There can be little persuasive talk of the goodness and power of God if the evil of the world is never in any way decisively overcome, sooner or later. The alleged almightiness of God would be thrown into question if evil were never conceivably overcome. For how could one think of God either as incomparably good or mighty if evil were more or equally powerful?

Those who cannot provide inquirers with some plausible understanding of suffering and evil in relation to God's saving activity are ill-prepared to minister to them. It is just at this point that clarity about the cross becomes a pastoral necessity (Augustine, *CG* 1.10; for a summary of classic views, see Oden, "A Theodicy for Pastoral Practice," *Pastoral Theology*:223–48).

The gospel of salvation is intricately connected with the interweaving problems of evil and suffering. If there were no problem of evil, there would be no felt or experienced need for the gospel of salvation. The gospel is good news precisely about evil's defeat (Chrysostom, *Catena*, 1 John 3:8, *CEC*:123).

Doctrines of Evil Correlated with Teachings of Salvation

There are several (at least eight) main views of salvation that have offered alternative explanations of that pivotal form of evil that defines and shapes other evils. Christianity has interacted with all these views. Summarily, these may be schematized in this way:

The Prime Evil Viewed As	The Sphere of its Evidences	Its Prototype	Salvation Found in
1. The tyranny of passion	The cosmos	Stoic compliance	Reason
2. The inability to enjoy	The passions	Epicureanism pleasure	Hedonic enjoyment
3. Death	The intrinsic vulnerability of life	Hellenism	Immortality
4. Pain	The feelings	Buddhism	Nirvana
5. Ignorance	The intellect	Platonism	Philosophy
6. Property	Class alienation	Marxism	Revolution
7. Emotive Repression	Neurosis	Freudianism	Psycho-analysis
8. Sin	The will	Classic Christianity	The Cross

It cannot be our purpose here to review comparative views of evil in various developing historic periods or cultures, however important that subject may be. But it is our purpose to show that Christian theodicy exists in the context of the all-too-familiar human problem of suffering—a problem dealt with in all classic Christian traditions—and that the cross of Christ stands as the decisive event illuminating Christian theodicy. In what follows we explore the fourth column above, since this study focuses on classic Christianity.

Christianity: The Evil of the Bound Will Makes Other Evils Evil

Christianity views the pivotal evil that shapes and penetrates all other evils to be the evil of the will, especially as manifested in transgenerational sin. Christ offers forgiveness of sin as a binding up of the evil that creates and elicits other evils.

The good news of God's atoning work on the cross assumes that the radical evil in the world is not finally death, pain, ignorance, class conflict, or libido repression, but sin. The deepest root of evil lies in freedom, in the distortions of moral self-determination.

Suffering: Surveying the Human Predicament

It may seem absurd that so much of human history and acculturation have so often been formed around the seemingly odd premise that suffering is a punishment.

But that correlation appears virtually everywhere in the history of human experience, and especially in morality and religion. The logic is unsparing: if we receive the due reward of our deeds, and if we suffer, the thought suggests itself that we suffer because of our evil deeds.

The Common Experience of Suffering for Others:
The Social Nature of Suffering

The deeper level of the perplexity of suffering is not when people suffer for their own sins—that has a ring of justice. It is rather when they suffer for the sins of others—that seems unjust.

Your neighbor may have to suffer innocently for something you have done (even inadvertently). Who does not know how it feels to suffer from something someone else has done? Sad but true, there appears to be universally experienced a profoundly vicarious aspect to human suffering. It is as if all humanity had become mixed in a transgenerational stew where one person's willed evil causes others to suffer. No one comes out unhurt. One generation hurts another. One member of a family system hurts another.

The premise of individualism does not help toward a solution of an enigma that is intrinsically social: there is an inexorable, ever-changing *relational inter-weaving* of human beings in covenant histories: the histories of tribes, cultures, languages, associations, and nations.

It is odd that the most profound forms of human intimacy are revealed in suffering. We are cursed by others, yet no one discerns exactly from whose voice the curse came. We are blessed by others, yet often these blessings seem to come from nowhere.

The Consequences of Sin Are Socially Transmitted
in Subsequent History

Why has it recurred so convincingly within so many cultures that human beings are cursed and punished by their own or other's bad choices, which Jews and Christians call "sin"? The consequences of sin, like all self-determined historical acts, become locked into causal chains. These consequences cannot be simply stopped. It does no good to say: "Stop the world, I want to get off." To pretend that the consequences of sin could be suddenly halted would be to suspend the present natural order of cause and effect, where one person's bad choice causes another to suffer. To change that would require the redesigning of the world totally, and no one is up to that.

This is why Irenaeus, Athanasius, and Augustine argued that evil is not substantially or originally existent in our created nature, but that it has emerged out of an unnecessitated history, a result of human freedom—self-chosen and abused. Its history is basically self-determined by will, not necessitated. That is not our created nature, but our fallen nature. It has a history—everything east of Eden. If so, the view that evil is natural to humanity needs correction, as does the mistaken view that evil is as old as God (Athanasius, *Contra Gentis* 2–7, Augustine, *Questions*).

Consequent Innocent Suffering

Sufferings for the most part appear to be the inevitable consequences of the corporate sins of humanity working intergenerationally to affect persons mostly but not wholly innocent of their own original acts of wrongdoing. Each individual then places his or her own distinctive stamp upon the history of sin. My flawed choices are added to a history of flawed choices. When we make wrong uses of good creaturely gifts (like sex and power and wealth and influence), when we choose the lesser good above the greater, it is often the case that others who did not make our choices have to suffer the consequences of our bad choices.

These causal chains flow like all natural ordering flows, from person to person, mother to daughter, family to family, neighbor to neighbor, seller to buyer, nation to nation (Jer. 31:29–30). What we sow will somehow be reaped, if not by us, by others who may suffer from our choices. Our choices propel unwelcome and unintended reverberations into others' futures.

That all sin stands under the penalty of death is proven by this empirical fact: There has never yet been a sinner who has not in time died.

In the late Judaic apocalyptic tradition, grossly unfair distributions of rewards and punishments were viewed as proof of the anticipated end of history, the final resurrection of the just and unjust. Jesus' resurrection meant the beginning of that end time. We leap ahead of our story by referring to the resurrection, but only a little, since it comes immediately after the cross, our current subject. The resurrection would provide a way by which the faithful may come to participate already in the end time, when all wrongs shall be righted (Jerome, *Epis. to Eph.* 1.2.1–9).

Much of the Old Testament viewed prosperity as a sign of God's favor, and adversity as an indication of divine displeasure over sin. But such a view was inadequate to explain innocent suffering, such as that of Job. Finally lacking a formal solution to his urgent queries, Job submitted himself to the infinite majesty of God, confessing that "no plan of yours can be thwarted"; "Surely I spoke of things I did not understand, things too wonderful for me to know" (Job 42:3; Olympiodorus, *Comm. on Job* 42.1–4). In this way the evil of suffering led to the good of repentance. "When I tried to understand all this, it was oppressive to me—till I entered the sanctuary of God. Then I understood their final destiny. Surely you place them on slippery ground" (Ps. 73:4–18).

How Does Christ's Death Impinge upon Human Suffering?

Christ's Death Negated Neither Our Freedom Nor Natural Causality

Christ's death did not change the way the world is put together as a natural order of cause and effect. Causality was not banished and the chance that I might harm you was not taken away. That would have paid too high a price for freedom from sin, namely freedom from freedom, a parade of automatons, causal chains without self-determination in a nonhistory lacking freedom (Augustine, *Freedom of the Will* 3.3.8).

Christ's death does not reduce the freedom that risks causing evil and suffering. Rather Christ's death is proclaimed as the birth of a new freedom amid the complexities of causal chains (Augustine, *Conf.* 2.4–8).

This can be celebrated without attempting to pronounce in detail upon the eternal destiny of each individual. We do well to trust God to care rightly for those who have not heard adequately of divine mercy. The promise is that "He is the atoning sacrifice for our sins, and not only for ours but also for the sins of the whole world" (1 John 2:2).

God Personally Knows the Suffering from Which We Are Saved

But what is meant by punishment for sin? Above all, God knows. For God has felt the full brunt of human violence (Leo I, *Serm.* 58; Catherine of Genoa, *CSW*: 72–

85). Christians know that this has happened as an actual event in human history. God knows fully what we know partially—that sin cannot finally endure in God's world, that it must be atoned for, paid for, and has been transcended and bound up by God's love (Bede, *Hom. on Gospels* 11.9; H. W. Robinson, *Suffering Human and Divine*). The cross is the actual event in which that ransom or payment was made once for all. From the moment of Christ's last earthly breath, the world is redeemed from sin and reconciled to God, and the divine-human account is paid up—a reality in which faith may share.

This does not imply that everyone necessarily wills to share in the freedom Christ offers: "If any soul were finally and forever to put aside Him Who has vicariously borne the punishment of sin, it must bear its own punishment, for it places itself under those conditions which brought from Christ's lips the cry 'Forsaken.' . . . The alternative is this: to meet the future alone, because *forsaken*, or to be saved in Him Who was 'forsaken'" (C. C. Hall, *Does God Send Trouble?*:540).

The Absurdity of Continued Bondage

How is it possible that one might now continue to remain in bondage to sin, Paul asked in Romans, chapter 6? If actually freed by God from sin, how could one absurdly continue to believe that God is now punishing us for sins already atoned for? To say that is to disbelieve that God has effectively taken punishment for our sins.

The cross has become for Christians a mirror through which humanity may behold both its own sin and God's willingness to share the suffering that sin creates. Through the cross, suffering is, first of all, faced and borne and, secondly, transcended by the awareness that God confronted, bore, and transcended it. This is Christian theodicy. It is called the good news.

The Mystery of Human Suffering Viewed in the Light of the Cross

The faithful stand in the lively awareness that each of us was there—at the cross. All humanity was there. All sins were representatively being atoned and reconciled. "Were you there when they crucified my Lord?" the black evangelical tradition asks. Each one must finally answer yes or no.

Of the boy who is the main character in the novel *Bevis*, Richard Jefferies writes: "The crucifixion hurt his feelings very much: the cruel nails, the unfeeling spear: he looked at the picture a long time, and then turned over the page saying, 'If God had been there He would not have let them do it.'" But the whole point of the cross, as J. S. Whale points out, is that God was there! For it was God who was *on* the cross (*PT*: 45)!

Evil Does Not Disappear

There is never an adequate theoretical answer to the riddle of suffering because actual suffering wishes most to be solved in practice not in theory. But the cross points to an event in relation to which suffering is transformed from absurdity to renewed meaning.

Even then, suffering remains a continuing mystery even to the faithful, as it did to Job. Paul's thorn does not go away. The daughters of Eve labor with pain. Rachel weeps. Mary wept.

Christianity does not promise an end of pain, but a word that God shares it with us.

Why the Cross Remains a Meaningful Disgrace

Yet the cross remains repulsive. We turn our eyes away from a public execution. How could it have happened that Christianity could be such an aesthetic and beautiful religion and have such an ugly central symbol?

The answer is that only there do we most fully discover how far God has gone to reach out for us. Before beholding the cross, we were unaware that God was searching for us, reading our hearts, seeking us out, desiring to atone for our sins, ready for reconciliation. The cross is evidence that God the Son comes far out to look for us and is willing to suffer for us so as to reconcile us to the Father (Rom. 5:10; 2 Cor. 5:18–19; Tertullian, *On Patience* 12).

The cross hardly looks like a place where evil is being overcome. Rather it appears to be history's most massive example of injustice. This is one aspect of the cross that is unavoidable: the brutality of sin. This world is just such a place where such things can and do happen. The innocent do suffer. This we learn from the cross, where the most undeserved suffering and the most deserving goodness meet with devastating irony.

The cross reveals the meaning of history, specially at those points in history where it least appears as though God is truly righteous or where it appears that God may be indifferent to human suffering. The meaning: God suffers for sinners, wiping away their sin.

One of the most amazing facts about the New Testament is that it was written under conditions of radical social dislocation, oppression, injustice, war, written by people who were suffering from torture and persecution, and written to people whose lives were constantly endangered because of their faith and made more complicated because of their baptism. Yet no book is so filled with hope and joy and mutual support and encouragement. It is virtually free from the bitterness that so prevails in human life. Whatever they had to suffer, they suffered in the awareness of their sharing in the dying and rising Word of life.

The Christian life is a continuing spiritual warfare whose crucial victory is already known and experienced, but whose ancillary battles continue in human history until the last day.

The warfare is deep in the human spirit, appearing in the subtle forms of pride, seduction, greed, and envy. This is not something that can be done away with by means of another march on the capitol, a more searching docudrama, stalwart investigative reporting, a revolution, or a committee for neighborhood improvement, however important those might be. "For our struggle is not against flesh and blood, but against the rulers, against the authorities, against the powers of this dark world and against the spiritual forces of evil in the heavenly realms. Therefore put on the full armor of God" so that "you may be able to stand your ground," with the belt of truth, the breastplate of righteousness, the shield of faith, the helmet of salvation, with prayer, with feet prepared for running, and with "the sword of the Spirit, which is the word of God" (Eph. 6:12–18; Jerome, *Epis. To Eph.* 3.6.11–13).

Whom the Lord Loves, He Disciplines

It is because parents love children that they discipline them. Lacking discipline they would be unprepared for the world ahead. Caring parents at times must punish children out of love and not as an end in itself, as an occasional and incomplete, but necessary corrective means (Heb. 12:7–10; Chrysostom, *Hom. on Heb.* 29.2).

In the Christian tradition suffering is indeed sometimes viewed as educative, sometimes as a trial of faith, sometimes as a purifying agent or means by which God's righteousness is vindicated. The context for learning about punishment for sins is not in a law book but a cross, where God is known as willing to bear our punishment (Oecumenius, *Fragments on Epis. To Heb.* 12.9).

The Mystery Unfolds

The Christian way is narrow. It says, "Take up your cross." "Share in his death and resurrection."

Gnosticism was an early competitor of Christianity that appeared to offer simpler nostrums—an instant means of escape from evil, a quick key to the secrets of the cosmos. "Mystery" for such religions meant something to be understood by a knowledge elite. Once understood, it would no longer be a mystery.

The mystery of the cross for Christian believers is quite the opposite: the more one knows of it the further out it extends as a mystery. The mystery of holy, sacrificial love is to be beheld, savored, and embraced—not resolved. "How great is the love the Father has lavished on us, that we should be called children of God!" (1 John 3:1).

Christianity ironically intensifies the problems of evil and suffering when viewed as philosophical problems to be intellectually resolved. For Christians proclaim that God is all-powerful and all-good, and more so that this is no where more evident than on the cross! Suffering is not for Christians merely a conceptual problem to be solved, but rather a personal challenge to be met (Chrysostom, *Hom. on Heb.* 30.1).

There is never a neat or satisfactory conceptual answer for the father whose only son is brutally, senselessly killed. But Christianity points to an actual event in which the eternal Father lost his only Son in a brutal, violent death.

God's Suffering With and For Us

This is Christ's way of transforming the dilemma of theodicy. Instead of solving the riddle of suffering conceptually, Christianity speaks of God's actual suffering with us and for us. It is a narrative of an event that occurred in history.

This removes from our suffering our tendency to despair over its meaninglessness. "We have this treasure in jars of clay to show that this all-surpassing power is from God and not from us. We are hard pressed on every side, but not crushed; perplexed, but not in despair; persecuted, but not abandoned; struck down, but not destroyed. We always carry around in our body the death of Jesus, so that the life of Jesus may also be revealed in our body. For we who are alive are always being given over to death for Jesus' sake, so that his life may be revealed in our mortal body" (2 Cor. 4:7–11; Origen, *On Prayer*, 29, 30).

The most profound Christian theodicy does not reason deductively but tells the story of God's suffering for us. No argument can convince the sufferer (1 Pet. 2:21; Andreas, *Catena CEC*:57–58). Only the actual history of God's own coming to suffering humanity could make a difference.

God's way of coming to humanity is almost entirely unexpected, except for prophetic utterances. It is a foolish method—the cross. Christianity alone among world religions speaks of God on a cross.

Christianity is the religion of the cross. The cross is Christianity's most accurate visual summary.

PART IV

EXALTED

LORD

THE EMMAUS DISCIPLES were discouraged as they left Jerusalem after the crucifixion. "We had hoped that he was the one who was going to redeem Israel" (Luke 24:21).

When the risen Christ met them on the road at Emmaus, he chided them as "foolish" and "slow of heart to believe" (Luke 24:25). He reminded them of the necessity of the crucifixion, that the Christ would suffer. When the women at the empty tomb "did not find his body, they came back saying that they had even seen a vision of angels who said he was alive," yet they could hardly believe it (Luke 24:22–24).

It was only after the resurrection that he could fully proceed to teach: "And beginning with Moses and all the Prophets, he explained to them what was said in all the Scriptures concerning himself" (Luke 24:27; Augustine, *Sermon* 235.1–2).

The doctrine of Christ's exaltation (*hupsosis*, Acts 2:33; 5:31; *huperupsosis*, Phil. 2:9; *doxasis*, John 17:5; *stephanosis*, Heb. 2:9) reflects on the biblical testimony to *the full resumption of the exercise of the divine powers that had been voluntarily constrained* during the descent from incarnation to crucifixion.

12

CHRISTUS VICTOR

WITH THE CRUCIFIXION AN OLD ERA ENDS. With the resurrection of Jesus a new era begins. He who died rose. He who rose ascended. He who ascended promises to return.

The Exaltation of Christ

The Resumption of Power

Having laid aside the infirmities of the flesh through his death, the resurrected Son received and resumed the full exercise of the divine glory which had been voluntarily yielded in the humiliation.

After the descent, the servant form is transmuted into triumph. All limitations are withdrawn from full communication of divine attributes to the human nature of Christ. The uninterrupted exercise of the divine glory is resumed. The full power of administering the kingdom is taken up again. The exalted Christ is now free to exercise the full spiritual authority that rightly belongs to the theandric union.

"Being therefore exalted at the right hand of God" (Acts 2:33) is explained by Theodoret: "When he says 'by the right hand of God' he plainly reveals the ineffable economy of the mystery that the right hand of God, which created all things, which is the Lord by whom all things were made and without whom nothing consists of things that were made, through the union lifted up to its own exaltation the manhood united to it" (Dialogue 2).

Four Phases of the Ascent: From Grave to Glory

Traditionally understood, the exaltation of Christ encompasses four teachings confessed in the Creed of Rufinus and early baptismal summaries: descent to the nether world, resurrection, ascension, and session at the right hand of God. All four clauses appear in some texts of the Apostles' Creed. These clauses appear in numerous early creeds: the rule of faith of Tertullian (ca. AD 200, *Ag. Praxeas 2, CC*:22), the Interrogatory Creed of Hippolytus (ca. 215), and an African Variant (ca. 400, *CC*:22–24). (The return of the Lord will be discussed in a future chapter.)

The exaltation began at the nadir of descent—in the grave. It then became publicly manifested in the resurrection. In the ascension, its cosmic setting moved from earth to heaven. The exaltation is thereafter consummated in the heavenly session of the Son seated with the Father in heaven. Schematically expressed:

Stages of the Exaltation

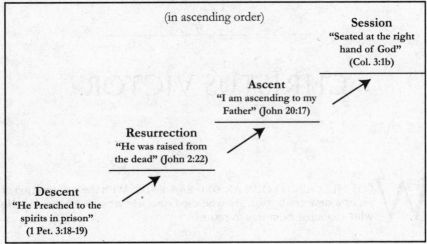

(in ascending order)

Session
"Seated at the right
hand of God"
(Col. 3:1b)

Ascent
"I am ascending to my
Father" (John 20:17)

Resurrection
"He was raised from
the dead" (John 2:22)

Descent
"He Preached to the
spirits in prison"
(1 Pet. 3:18-19)

All stages of this sequence are integrally expressed in a single passage of the First Letter of Peter: "For Christ died for our sins once for all, the righteous for the unrighteous, to bring you to God. He was put to death in the body but made alive by the Spirit, through whom also he went and *preached to the spirits in prison*," whose death enabled a baptism to new life that "saves you by the *resurrection* of Jesus Christ, who has *gone into heaven* and *is at God's right hand*" (1 Pet. 18–22, italics added).

This sequence is condensed into the concise fourfold confession of the ancient creed: "He descended into hell, on the third day rose again from the dead, ascended to heaven, sits at the right hand of God the Father almighty" (*CC*:24).

Rightly viewed, all four steps belong together as a single reversal called exaltation—a cohesive classical Christian teaching of an unified article of faith (Acts 5:31; Wollebius, *CTC* 18, *RDB*:110–15; *Leiden Synopsis* 28; Pope, *Compend.* 2:167; Strong, *Syst. Theol.* 706; Barth, *CD* 4/2:132). The single purpose of Christ's resurrection, ascension, and intercession, according to the ancient account of Irenaeus (AD 180), is "to comprehend all things under one head [*anakephalaiosasthai*], and to raise up all flesh of all mankind" (*Ag. Her.* 1.10.1). Thus the doctrine of exaltation is a key Christian doctrine, and a central feature of the ancient confessions of faith.

The sequence is aptly summarized in Philippians, chapter 2: "He humbled himself by becoming obedient to the point of death" (v. 8). "Therefore God has highly exalted him" (v. 9). The bestowal of Lordship is proclaimed: "And gave him the name that is above every name" (Phil. 2:9). The homage of universal acknowledgment is promised: "That at the name of Jesus every knee should bow, in heaven and on earth and under the earth, and every tongue confess that Jesus Christ is Lord, to the glory of God the Father" (Phil. 2:9–10).

What the Son did not self-assertively gain by "grasping" or "snatching" equality with God, he received upon completion of his mission by the gift of the Father (Augustine, *EDQ* 50).

Cyril of Jerusalem drew together the teaching of the exaltation for young Christians: The Son descended into the nether world where he conquered death; rose again from the dead, whereby his messianic vocation was confirmed; ascended into heaven, whereby he returned to glory; and now sits at the right hand of the Father where he receives power and governance, glory and dominion from the Father in the kingdom of grace, power, and glory. (*Catech. Lect.* 14; Tho. Aq., *ST* 3 Q56–59; Schmid, *DT*:379–81).

His death having culminated his *descent* (from preexistent glory through incarnation to birth, ministry, death and burial, and descent), his resurrection began his *ascent* (from the empty tomb, resurrected, ascended to heaven, to intercede and sit at the right hand of God). The moment of reversal from descent to ascent is celebrated in one of the two most important events of the Christian year: Easter Sunday, comparable in importance with the celebration of the Incarnation at Christmas.

Christ Is Alive

The exalted Lord lives now. He lives personally and not merely as a concept or symbol. He lives actually, not solely in the memories of his disciples (Chrysostom, *Hom. on Phil.* 8.2.5–11). He lives not only in earthly history but in that eternal life that transcends history, to which he ascends. He lives not in latent power or mere potentiality, but rather in full possession of blessedness and power. All this is meant by exaltation (Irenaeus, *Ag. Her.* 3.12.2).

"It was not the Word of God who needed or received exaltation. For the Word was in the beginning exalted with the Father. It was the Son of Man who was exalted from lowliness. This exaltation occurred when he had glorified God in his death" (Origen, *Comm. on John* 32.25).

The Participation of the Faithful in the Exaltation

The support, sustenance, and completion of the mission of the gospel depends upon the continuing real presence of the living Lord. Without ascension and session, the incarnate mission would be incomplete.

The exaltation is a regenerative process that occurs not only to Christ, but to the faithful in Christ: "God raised us up with Christ and seated us with him in the heavenly realms in Christ Jesus, in order that in the coming ages he might show the incomparable riches of his grace" (Eph. 2:6–7; Jerome, *Epis. to Eph.* 1.2.7). If Christ were a dead body, unraised and unascended, only inorganic matter resolved into its constituents, there could be no continuing his mission. But his body is alive.

Chrysostom rejected the false teaching "that his glory consists entirely in his being worshiped by us. The implication is that he would not be glorious until he received our worship. Is this all his glory means? Those who think this way are far from the greatness of God" (*Hom on Phil.* 8.2.9).

The events of Christ's descent, resurrection, ascension, and session are understood by classic Christian teaching as actual, palpable events in history. Yet they are also events in which believers continue to participate by grace in four ways:

- By his *descent* he is known to be fully empathic with our human condition in death. His descent enables us to share in his victory over the demonic powers and to face our own sin.

- His *resurrection* enables the faithful to rise from the death of sin to new life in Christ.

- With his *ascension* the believer is brought into the presence of the heavenly Father.

- His *session* allows us access to the heavenly Father, and his *intercession* is for our sanctification (Cyril of Jerusalem, *Catech. Lect.* 14; Tho. Aq., *ST* 3 Q52–59).

In these ways his exaltation has personal, behavioral, and redemptive consequence for the life of the believer. It reveals the pattern of the Spirit's work to enable the believer to die to sin, rise by grace, walk in the way of holiness, and prepare for eternal life (Athanasius, *Ag. the Arians* 1.41).

Union with the Living Christ

Redemption occurs not through assent to doctrine but through union with the living Christ by faith. This life could not occur with a dead Christ. The engendering power of Christianity could not be proclaimed if Christianity spoke only of a person who was but no longer is. If he ceased to be alive, he could not have an effect on our present life with God (Rom. 6; 1 Cor. 15; Marius Victorinus *Epis. to Phil.* 2:5).

Believers are joined to the Lord in a spiritual union and fellowship with each other that is sustained by their relation to this living Person. The continuing life of Christ includes our life in Christ. In this union Christ shares empathetically in our struggle even now, and we share in the fullness of his life with God the Father (Cyril of Jerusalem, *Catech. Lect.* 21).

There is hardly a point in Christian teaching at which we seem to be further distanced from modern consciousness than the exaltation of Jesus. When we look toward him with jaded modern eyes, we tend to reduce him to something manageable. So modernity struggles to identify experientially how his consciousness has affected our modern forms of consciousness (Schleiermacher, *ChrF*:417–21). The only conception of a living Christ that is allowable under the constraints of modern naturalism is that his influence lives in the memory and actions of others, analogous to the way heroes exert continuing influence. But the worshiping community celebrates that he acts upon us as one who himself is personally alive. The missing element in such an analysis is his own continuing personal life.

The ancient ecumenical testimony is that Jesus now lives so as to engender life in us. His living presence is the real energy and force and power of historic Christianity and present Christian life. Detached from the living Christ, the branch withers, the flower fades.

The classic Christian study of salvation is essentially a study of what the redemptive event of his dying and rising means for us. Failing to grasp the pivotal significance of this salvation event is to fail to grasp the Word of God. This is why Christian teaching has focused so intently upon these last events of Jesus' earthly ministry.

The Living Word Is the Life of the World

The exaltation concerns the giving of life and recovery of life when it appears to have been defeated by death. He put death to death (Ephanius, *Ancoratus* 92).

To Jesus the attribute of "life" has been unconditionally ascribed in Scripture (John 5:26; 11:25; 14:6; 1 John 5:20). "In him was life, and that life was the light of men" (John 1:4; Chrysostom, *Hom. on John* V).

Jesus is called "the Life," "our life," "the Prince of life," "Word of life" (1 John 1:1, 2; Acts 3:15; John 11:25; 2 Cor. 4:12). "It was his task to swallow up death. Who but the Life could do this?" (Calvin, *Inst.* 2.12.2). "God has given us eternal life, and this life is in his Son. He who has the Son has life; he who does not have the Son of God does not have life" (1 John 5:11–12; Oecumenius, *Comm. on 1 John* 5).

Jesus' words bring life (John 5:24; 6:68; 8:51) because they are God's own words (John 3:34; 14:10) embodied in human form. "The words that I have spoken to you are spirit and they are life" (John 6:63; Cyril of Alex., *Comm. on John* 11.9). The early preaching of Acts spoke of Jesus as "author of life" (Acts 3:15), who "gives all men life" (Acts 17:25). It was the "full message of this new life" that the apostles were called to proclaim (Acts 5:20).

The Crucified Lord Gives Life to the World

Among prerogatives that belong only to God is the ability to give life, to be the source of all that lives. As God the Son, he is called the "way of life" (John 14:6; Didache 1; Teaching of the Twelve Apostles 1–2). "For as the Father raises the dead and gives them life, even so the Son gives life to whom he is pleased to give it" (John 5:21). The Son who has died has power to offer life to the world (Cyril of Alex., *Comm. on John* 5:21). In the same way that God the Father has life in himself, so does the Son have life in himself (John 5:26;). Those who participate in the life of the Son of God are enabled to receive eternally the life that comes from God (John 3:35; 6:47; 10:10).

To posit speech without a speaker is absurd. The speaker's word becomes audible only when there is a will of the speaker to communicate. The address of the Father is heard through the body language of the Son. Christ is "living Word" whose glory we have beheld (John 1:14; Ephrem, *Comm. on Tatian's Diatesseron* 14.5; Lucian of Antioch, *Rule of Faith*).

He gives life to the world by the power of his life (Heb. 7:16, John 6:33). He came "that they may have life" (John 10:10). "For God so loved the world that he gave his one and only Son, that whoever believes in him shall not perish but have eternal life" (John 3:16).

He offers to all who would receive the "right to eat from the tree of life" (Rev. 2:7), to drink "from the spring of the water of life" (Rev 21:6), and to have their names "written in the book of life" (Rev. 20:15; Augustine, *CG* 20.15). He offers the "crown of life" (Rev. 2:10). Life is offered to the world by means of repentance, faith, and baptism (Acts 11:18; John 11:25ff.; Rom. 6).

As a vine sustains branches, Christ provides life to those who live in union with him (John 15:1–8). He is like a shepherd who not only preserves the life of the flock but announces, "I give them life" (John 10:28), and who lays down his life for them (1 John 3:16), giving "his life as a ransom for many" (Matt. 20:28). "Just as the living Father sent me and I live because of the Father, so the one who feeds on me will live because of me. This is the bread that came down from heaven" (John 6:57). It is by faith active in love that "we have passed from death to life" (1 John 3:14).

The Father's mission to bring life to the world required the death of the Son: "I tell you the truth, unless a kernel of wheat falls to the ground and dies, it remains only a single seed. But if it dies, it produces many seeds. The man who loves his life will lose it, while the man who hates his life in this world will keep it for eternal life" (John 12:23–25).

The crucified Son's mission of offering life to the world has a weird beginning episode: the descent into the nether world.

Descent into the Nether World

Between the articles of the creed on our Lord's death and his resurrection stands the confession that he descended into the abode of the dead, hades, the unseen world. "The gospel was preached even to those who are now dead" (*nekrois euēngelisthē*, 1 Pet. 4:6).

Both the Hebrew *sheol* and Greek *hades* refer to the nether world, the shadowy realm of the dead, "the place or the state of souls departed" (Isaac Barrow, *On the Creed, Serm.* 28). The place of descent is not specified as *gehenna* (the place of punishment), but *hades* (the abode of the departed). Into this place of the dead the soul of the Lord entered while his body remained entombed.

The biblical references to the descent, in addition to Psalm 16:10, may be largely grouped into Pauline texts (Eph. 4:8–10; Rom. 10:7; Col. 2:14–15), Petrine texts (1 Pet. 3:18–20; 4:4–6), and Lucan texts (Luke 23:43; 2:30–31; Acts 13:37).

The *Russian Catechism* defines *hades* simply as "a place *void of light*," "the state of those spirits which are separated by sin from the sight of God's countenance, and from the light and blessedness which it confers" (*COC* 2:477; Jude 6).

No article of the creed is more encumbered with ambiguities than the descent into the nether world.

Dating Its Inclusion in the Creed

Although the descent into hades appears in numerous ancient creeds after AD 390, it does not appear directly in earliest kerygmatic or baptismal summaries. It was not mentioned in Marcellus's text of the Old Roman Symbol, but this cannot be taken as an argument from silence to mean that it was not known or confessed earlier than it has left a written record of evidence. By the time of Rufinus (the Aquileian form of the creed, about AD 390–400), it was found in the creed that Rufinus regarded as the one traditionally committed to memory in North Italy, and that had a long history of recollection before that time.

The descent into the abode of the dead appeared in the Athanasian Creed (Quicunque; *SCD* 40), and in the received Western text of the Apostles' Creed of Caesarius of Arles (Received Text T, Western Form of the Apostolic Creed, *SCD* 6). Though it was not specifically mentioned in the creeds of the councils of Nicaea, Constantinople, or Toledo, it was assumed, confessed and affirmed by these major pre-Nicene writers: Polycarp, Justin Martyr, Origen, Hermas, Irenaeus, Cyprian, Tertullian, Hippolytus, and Clement of Alexandria. It was assumed by the most influential post-Nicene consensus-expressing ecumenical teachers of both East and West (Athanasius, *Four Discourses Ag. Arians*; Augustine, *Letters*, 164, *To Evodius*), and by leading Protestants (Luther, *Brief Explanation*; Calvin, *Inst.* 2.16.8–11; Baxter, *PW* 21:77–78).

Many scriptural passages relating to this article are obscure and difficult to interpret. One might be tempted to ignore the article altogether, were it not for its persistence in the received creedal and dogmatic traditions of both east and west.

Status of the Article in the Creedal Tradition

Three major reasons are cited for resisting the descent as an essential article of faith: it is made up of a composite of ambiguous biblical texts; it assumes and reinforces an outmoded cosmology; and it did not regularly appear in the written creeds until the fourth century.

Although these reservations should cause us to be cautious in statements on the descent, the consensual view generally has remained that the confession has sufficient biblical grounding. It has survived in liturgical and creedal statements in widely dispersed traditions for over fifteen centuries. Roman Catholics, Lutherans, Anglicans, Greek Orthodox, and many Protestants declare regularly in worship as an article of the creed: "he descended into hell."

Though this phrase "did not become customary in the churches at once, but gradually," and though interpretations vary, Calvin set the precedent for the Reformed tradition by teaching that "if it is left out, much of the benefit of Christ's death will be lost," hence "in setting forth a summary of doctrine a place must be given to it" (Calvin, *Inst.* 2.16.8).

Why the Article Touches Modern Consciousness

While modern journalists might imagine that they invented the theme of the death of God, classical Christian exegetes have been investigating this theme since the second century, hence long before Nietzsche. Though it seems counterintuitive, this phrase comes closer than many other articles of the creed to touching secularizing consciousness in a deep and vulnerable way.

The disciples on the road to Emmaus were aware of the utter death of their hopes. So are those who have shared the élan of modernity often painfully aware of the death of the best human idealisms and aspirations.

Good Friday is the time of the cross of God the Son. Holy Saturday is the traditional time of recollection of the death of God incarnate (viewed as the human flesh of the God-man). It is that uncanny moment in the Christian year when God appears to be simply silent, absent, and hidden from view—dead—in another abode (that of the dead). The liturgy of Holy Saturday recollects this shocking descent of the divine Son. God's Son is dead. But this does not exhaust the meaning of the descent into hell.

Since so much of modern life is so much like what the Bible describes as hell, modernity finds it thought-provoking to hear of God entering hell on behalf of the gospel. But apostolic teaching has been pondering these themes since the epistles of Peter and Paul and the gospel of Luke.

Theories of Descent: A Healthy Variety of Traditional Interpretations

The ambiguities and complexities of these texts have invited a broad variety of interpretations. Irenaeus argued that "the Lord observed the law of the dead, that He might become the first begotten from the dead, and tarried until the third day 'in the lower parts of the earth'" (*Ag. Her.* 5.31.1). Clement of Alexandria proposed that Christ preached the gospel in hell to bring salvation to awaiting believers (*Stromata* 6.6).

Tertullian wrote that Christ remained "in Hades in the form and condition of a dead man; nor did He ascend into the heights of heaven before descending into the lower parts of the earth, that He might there make the patriarchs and prophets partakers of Himself" (*On the Soul* 55). Chrysostom argued that the descent referred to Christ's power to work miracles and to hold sway over the demonic powers (*Hom. on Matt.* 57; *Hom. on Second Cor.* 25).

The descent has been variously interpreted by Reformed scholastics as the *last phase of Christ's humiliation* or by Lutheran scholastics as the *first phase of*

Christ's exaltation (cf. 1 Pet. 3:18, 19; Acts 2:27). Luther stressed the existential power of the confession. He argued that the descent referred primarily to the victory of Christ over the demonic powers: "I believe that He descended into hell to overthrow and take captive the devil and all his power, guile and wickedness, for me and for all who believe in Him, so that henceforth the devil cannot harm me; and that He has redeemed me from the pains of hell, and made them harmless" (Luther, *Brief Explanation*, *WML* 2:371). Calvin believed that its chief reference was to the radical extent of Christ's suffering (*Inst.* 2.16.9–12). Bucer and Beza taught that it simply meant that Christ was buried. Sohnius argued that the descent referred to the entire state of humiliation of the eternal Son from incarnation to burial (*De Verbo Dei*).

The Final Phase of the Humbling of God: The Abode of the Grave

These varied views of the descent may be broadly categorized into four major types of emphasis. The first is that the confession simply meant that Jesus died and descended into the grave (the burial motif). The second view alleges that the descent points to Christ's empathic suffering and participation in the depths of human alienation (the humiliation motif). The third points to Christ's victory over the demonic powers (the exaltation motif). The fourth option is that Christ descended to preach in the abode of the dead (the kerygmatic motif).

All four express, either separately or together, the premise of *reversal*, that this inconspicuous article of the creed constitutes a decisive pivot in the logic of descent and ascent: it is the final phase of the humiliation and the beginning phase of the exaltation. Some combination of these four types may emerge in future generations of orthodox exegesis as a refined, received consensus. A closer look at these four motifs:

Sheol *as Simply Death*

The first, most straightforward of these views holds that Jesus' entry into *sheol* simply meant nothing more or less than he died like any other human being. This anti-Docetic emphasis stressed the truth that Jesus entered as fully into human experience in death as he did in life. Hence it was to be expected that his soul would go where all human souls go after death: to the resting place of the dead (Bucer, *Enarrationes in Evangelia*: 511–512, 792; Pearson, *EC* 1:382). "Even Christ's soul had to descend into Hades, because his whole divine-human person was punished with real death in order that sin might be atoned for and the covenant of grace consummated" (Heppe, *RD*: 491).

Calvin astutely pointed to the limitation of this interpretation: it implied a "useless repetition" in the creed whose very purpose is to note "the chief points of our faith" in "the fewest possible words." If descent simply means burial, it is unlikely that the same idea would be repeated in such a compact summary (*Inst.* 2.16.8).

The Empathic Suffering Motif: Assurance of Accompaniment Through Alienation

Secondly, the Reformed tradition held that the descent into hell more specifically meant that Christ empathized in an unparalleled way with the depths of human pain, suffering, and alienation. Accordingly, the descent was not a part of Christ's triumph, but constituted the last phase of Christ's humiliation, the humbling of God in suffering, absolute limitation, and in entire obedience, the final stage of the humble condescension of the Son (Ursinus, *CHC*; Schmid, *DT*). There was no depth of human alienation with which our Lord was unacquainted (Calvin, *Inst.* 2.16.8–11).

In this way the descent became an experiential component of the doctrine of assurance. "Why 'descended into hell'?" The *Heidelberg Catechism* teaches the seeker to answer in a highly personal way: "That in my severest tribulations I may be assured that Christ my Lord has redeemed me from hellish anxieties and torment" (Q 44). Where the Lord has been, I may go without terror.

A variant of this view holds that what is finally signified by hell can be experientially grasped by thinking of that depth of loneliness which no word or touch of love can penetrate. Suppose one were to find oneself in such a state of abandonment, a place where no other voice or touch could reach. That would be the sort of total unresponsiveness, abandonment, and aloneness that is symbolized by *sheol*. It was into such a state of total physical unresponsiveness that Jesus entered when he died and descended to *sheol*. Hence Christ shared the abyss of whatever abandonment humanity is capable (Ratzinger [Benedict XVI], *IC*:226–29).

Descent as Victory over Sin and Death

Third, in his descent, Christ conquered the demonic powers, destroyed the power of hell, and seized from the Enemy all authority. This exaltation motif is found especially among those who stressed victory over demonic powers in their teaching of atonement (notably Irenaeus, Gregory of Nyssa, and Luther).

According to this view, Christ did not descend into hades to suffer for us either with or under the demonic powers, for his sacrificial work had already been finished on the cross (John 19:20). His purpose rather was to triumph over the demons, as celebrated in the Apocalypse: "I am the Living One; I was dead, and behold I am alive for ever and ever! And I hold the keys of death and Hades" (Rev. 1:18).

The Letter to Hebrews points toward the view that Christ was in hell destroying the demonic powers on behalf of imprisoned humanity: He fully "shared in their humanity so that by his death he might destroy him who holds the power of death—that is, the devil—and free those who all their lives were held in slavery by their fear of death. For surely it was not angels he helps, but Abraham's descendants" (Heb. 2:14–16). Christ's descent into the abode of the dead was purposefully to declare the binding up of the demonic powers and free the faithful of Abraham from their slavery and likewise all whose lives are possessed by fear of death. Christ "disarmed the powers and authorities" (Col. 2:14–15). The purpose of the descent was not to redo the work done on the cross, but to *announce to the depths of cosmic creation the binding up of the demonic powers*.

The visual expression of this victory motif in the history of art has been Christ breaking down the gates of hell: "He broke down the gate and 'iron bars' of hell, setting at liberty all the righteous who were held fast through original sin" (Augustine, *Serm. on the Passion* 160; Tho. Aq., *ST* 3 Q52.5).

The victory motif was celebrated by Bonaventure with poetic intensity: Christ "tore the prey away from him, broke down the gates of hell and bound the serpent. *Disarming the Principalities and Powers, he led them away boldly, displaying them openly in triumph in himself* (Col. 2:15). Then the *Leviathan was led about with a hook*" (*Tree of Life, CWS*:159; Job 40:25).

The startling Gospel references to the saints in the tombs who were raised with Jesus (Matt. 27:51–53; John 5:25–29) lend supportive evidence for this view. They were viewed as living evidence of Christ's liberating visitation of the abode of the dead.

The Preaching of Christ in the Nether World

The fourth thematic focus speaks of the preaching of Christ in the nether world. Not only did he visit; he preached. The confession made provision for salvation for those already dead by preaching to them judgment and gospel. It was thought that the worthy dead would thereby have an opportunity to hear the preaching of Christ (Irenaeus, *Ag. Her.* 5.31). "He showed forth His power on earth by living and dying, so also He might manifest it in hell, by visiting it and enlightening it" (Tho. Aq., *ST* 3, Q52.1).

The First Letter of Peter is the focal text for this view: "For this is the reason the gospel was preached even to those who are now dead, so that they might be judged according to men in regard to the body, but live according to God in regard to the spirit" (1 Pet. 4:6).

The perplexing sequence suggested in 1 Peter 3:18–20 has prompted some to argue that the descent occurred not before but *after* the resurrection and that it attests Christ's victory over the powers of evil. Note the sequence: "For Christ died for sins once for all, the righteous for the unrighteous, to bring you to God. He was put to death in the body but *made alive by the Spirit through whom also he went and preached* to the spirits in prison" (1 Pet. 3:18–19, italics added; cf. Augustine, *Letters,* 164, *To Evodius*).

This key passage contains a metaphor (spirits in prison), a time frame (long ago), and an illustration (Noah): "He went and preached to *the spirits in prison who disobeyed long ago* when God waited patiently in the days of Noah while the ark was being built. In it only a few people, eight in all, were saved through water, and this water symbolizes baptism that now saves you also" (1 Pet. 3:19–21, italics added; Luther, *Serm. on First Peter,* LW 30:112–15; *Torgau Serm.*).

This further prompts the question: to whom might Christ have been preaching? Competing ancient interpretations of the phrase "the spirits in prison" have arisen. Some have argued that Christ was preaching only to those who had ridiculed Noah as a preacher of righteousness. "The spirits shut up in prison are the unbelievers who lived in the time of Noah, whose spirits or souls were shut up in the darkness of ignorance as in a prison; Christ preached to them, not in the flesh, for he was not yet incarnate, but in the spirit, that is, in his divine nature" (Augustine, *Letters,* 164, *To Evodius*).

Others say Christ was preaching more generically *to the captives* of various times. The Damascene summarized patristic teaching on the descent: "The deified soul went down into hell so that, just as the Sun of Justice rose upon those on earth, so also might the light shine upon them under the earth who were sitting in darkness and the shadow of death; so that, just as He had brought the good news of peace to those on earth, so also might He bring that of deliverance to captives and that of sight to the blind. And to them that believed He became a cause of eternal salvation. . . . And thus, having loosed them that had been bound for ages, He came back again from the dead and made the resurrection possible for us" (John of Damascus, *OF* 3.29).

Other early exegetes concluded that Christ was preaching *to the ancient patriarchs and prophets* who believed in the Messiah. Christ "descended into the inner parts of the earth, so that there he might make the patriarchs and prophets sharers of himself" (Tertullian, *Apology* 47; *On the Soul* 55; cf. Justin Martyr, *Dialogue with Trypho* 138, 139; Irenaeus, *Ag. Her.* 5.31; Eusebius, *CH* 1.13).

Some say Christ simply preached *to the dead.* They were presumably captive in the absolute limitation of death. Others say that Christ preached to those who were *symbolically dead* amid the disbelief by which they were drowned in the flood, which could have been avoided by faith. Either Christ had already given them fair warning through the preaching of Noah, or Christ was returning to them to proclaim the victory of the resurrection and to declare judgment. To whomever he preached, Cyril of Jerusalem noted that his preaching had effect: "though his descent was alone, his ascent was with a numerous company" (*Catech. Lect.* 14).

The Eastern tradition combines two motives to explain the meaning of his descent into the abode of the dead: (1) to "preach his victory over death," and (2) "deliver the souls which with faith awaited his coming" (*Russian Catechism*, COC 2:478). His body must have descended to the grave, but did his soul separate from his body to descend into the abode of the dead? The Greek Catechism answers: "While His body lay dead in the tomb, His deified soul descended into Hell, and carried to the souls which, since time began, had lain bound there, the good news of reconciliation" (*Gk. Orthodox Catech.* 37). This view is accompanied by the caveat that we should not "trouble ourselves with sublime and acute thoughts as to how this occurred" (Jacobs, *SCF*:150).

The Earliest Pauline and Lucan Texts of the Descent

In making the point that each believer has grace as Christ has apportioned, the Letter to Ephesians quotes Psalm 68:18 that "When he ascended on high, he led captives in his train and gave gifts to men" (Eph. 4:7–8). This is followed by this rhetorical question: "What does 'he ascended' mean except that he also descended to the lower, earthly regions?" (Eph. 4:9). This suggests that the descent into hades narrative was available in the pre-Pauline oral tradition, and that it had as its purpose the giving of gifts, endowing those in the unseen world with gracious abilities (J. B. Lightfoot, *St. Ignatius* 2:131–33). Others argue that "the lower, earthly regions" does not refer to the nether world, but simply to the earth.

Paul joined the descent and the ascent themes together in Romans 10:6–7, where he admonished his hearers that it not be asked who will go into the abyss to bring up Christ from the dead: "But the righteousness based on faith says, Do not say in your heart, 'Who will ascend into heaven?' (that is, to bring Christ down) or 'Who will descend into the abyss?' (that is, to bring Christ up from the dead)." No one needs to do again what Christ already has done either in his descent or ascent, but all are called to participate by faith in what Christ has done. Origen comments: "We are not to think that Christ is in heaven in such a way as to be absent from the depths . . . These things are not limited to a particular place but are present everywhere, nor can they be called up from the lower depths, but they can be grasped only by the mind and the intellect" (*Comm. Romans*, CER 4:202).

Luke-Acts provided much of the textuary for various interpretations concerning the article on the descent. One textual reference used in Acts by both Paul and Peter was the allusion to Psalm 16:10 as applied to Christ, "you will not abandon me to the grave, nor will you let your Holy One see decay" (Ps. 16:10).

Preaching at Pisidian Antioch, Paul is reported by Luke to have made a special point of preaching that "the one whom God raised from the dead did not see decay" (Acts 13:37), fulfilling the promise of Psalm 16:10. In reference to Christ's resurrection, Peter declared that David had been promised that God "would place one of his descendants on his throne. Seeing what was ahead, he spoke of the resurrection of the Christ, that he was not abandoned to the grave, nor did his body see decay" (Acts 2:30–31).

Also in Luke, Jesus promised the penitent thief that he would be *with him that very day* in Paradise (Luke 23:43). This suggested to some classic exegetes that the soul of Jesus immediately after his crucifixion descended to that condition in which all the dead reside (Gregory Nazianzus, *Orat.* 29, *On the Son* 20; Wesley, *NUNT*:294). Paul thought that we are closer to God in paradise ("the eternal house in heaven") than in our earthly, bodily existence (2 Cor. 5:6–9).

Conclusion

Noting all the difficulties of these passages, it may be concluded that there is scriptural grounding for the belief that Christ descended into the abode of the dead, but hardly for speculation in detail upon precisely how or why this descent occurred—otherwise such knowledge would have been revealed in the scriptures. "How Christ descended and when, this the Scriptures have not specially revealed to us" (John Parsimonius, in Schmid, *DT*:399). Hence these questions may be left open for further inquiry within the worshiping community to whom the sacred text has been committed.

The Formula of Concord rightly warned against excessive speculation: Since this article "can be comprehended neither by our senses nor reason, but is to be received by faith alone, we unanimously advise that there be no controversy concerning this matter, but that we teach this article with the greatest simplicity . . . satisfied to know that Christ has descended to those in hell, that He has destroyed hell for all believers" (*Formula of Concord* 9).

13

THE RISEN LORD

THE CREED CONFESSES THAT JESUS was resurrected on the third day (Ancient Western Form of the Apostolic Creed, *SCD* 2). The truth about Jesus was not finally revealed until his resurrection. The resurrection was the seal and confirmation of Christ's saving activity on the cross. Christ Jesus was "declared with power to be the Son of God by his resurrection from the dead" (Rom. 1:4; John of Damascus, *OF* 4.18).

The redemptive value of his death for others was made effective by his resurrection. The resurrection is that mystery by which the value of his death for others is realized (Origen, *Comm. on Rom.* 1.4). Resurrection is the necessary complement and sequel to the incarnation.

The Lord Is Risen Indeed

The best human intelligence could not have predicted this reversal. The signs that pointed toward it were disbelieved. What looked like the collapse of God's mission turned out to be its most signal victory. God's saving event stood contrary to all normal human expectations.

The resurrection threw instant light upon all that had preceded it. Every aspect of his teaching that had earlier seemed to be a "hard saying" (John 6:60) was now seen in the light of his resurrection as a sign of hope (Chrysostom, *Hom. on John* 47.2–3; 87.1).

Modern chauvinism assumes the inferiority of premodern insight. When modern chauvinism looks at the resurrection, it can see little but irrationality and myth. When classical Christianity looks at the resurrection, it beholds clarity, revelation, plausibility, and evidence of the highest order (Theodore of Mopsuestia, *Comm. on John* 7.20.17). Peter and John inferred "his resurrection from the bundle of linen clothes, and from that time on they believed that he had burst the bonds of death" (Cyril of Alex., *Comm. on John* 12.20.9)

Resurrection Defined

Jesus' resurrection is that event in which the Messiah was raised from the dead, his body brought to life to demonstrate to the disciples the completed work of redemption (Augustine, *CG, FC* 24:68–71, 423–32).

The root meaning of resurrection (*anastasis; exanastasis*; verbs: *anístēmi, egeirō;* Lat. *resurrexist*, Creed of 150 Fathers) is simply to raise or arise from the dead. Resurrection is God's own way of demonstrating the defeat of death. God brought forth his body reunited with his soul and so appeared before the disciples risen from the tomb (Hilary, *Trin.* 9.9–18, *SCD* 422). "Thanks to his resurrection—his death manifested its power and efficacy to us" (Calvin, *Inst.* 2.16.13).

Resurrection is not merely an optional addendum or incidental epilogue to the gospel. It is intrinsic to the gospel, crowning the narrative, and validating the earthly ministry of Jesus. The reasons why resurrection is necessary to Christian teaching are drawn together by Thomas Aquinas: because justice required that the humbled be exalted (Luke 1:52); because faith in his divinity is thereby kindled (2 Cor. 13:4); because it gives believers hope that they too will rise again (1 Cor. 15:12); because by it we too may die to sin and walk in newness of life (Rom. 6:4); and because only by the resurrection is God's saving work on the cross confirmed (*ST* 3, Q53.1).

A Temporal Event Reveals the Hidden Meaning of Universal History

Christians understand the cross-resurrection event to be the most illuminating event in salvation history. The despair of all past history is reversed by it. The hope of all future history is set in motion by it. It is of all events the most edifying disclosure of God's plan of salvation. To understand the resurrection is to understand the meaning of history from its end (Augustine, *Sermon* 229M.1; Gregory I, *Forty Gospel Homilies* 24).

"The Lord has risen indeed" (Luke 24:34) has thereafter been the hallmark of Christian testimony. The appearances of the risen Lord occurred at particular places and times, beginning from a stone sepulchre near Golgotha (John 19:41) and continuing for forty days. Yet they had universal historical significance (Lactantius, *Div. Inst., FC* 49:297–99; Chrysostom, *Hom. on John* 87.1–2).

The Raising of Humanity

By rising from the grave the Lord raised up a new human nature and honored humanity in an unparalleled way (Rom. 5:15–19; Acts 2:24; 1 Cor. 15:20–23). By the resurrection, the drama of God's coming was brought to an astounding climax and resolution: God became human that humanity might share in the life of God. That did not imply that we cease being creatures or lose our humanity in God, but that we in faith become partakers of or members of Christ's own resurrected body. His resurrection makes possible the intended and fitting consummation of our humanity (Irenaeus, *Ag. Her.* 3.19.1; 5.16.2; 5.21.1; Athanasius, *On the Incarn.*, 54; John of Damascus, *OF* 3.17).

The witnesses were numerous, competent, and willing to suffer for their testimony. The testimony of the apostles was accompanied by God's own testimony: "This salvation, which was first announced by the Lord, was confirmed to us by those who heard him. God also testified to it by signs, wonders and various miracles, and gifts of the Holy Spirit" (Acts 2:3–4).

It was Jesus himself who proved he was alive by showing up. "After his suffering, he *showed* himself to these men and gave many convincing *proofs* that he was

alive. He appeared to them over a period of forty days and spoke about the kingdom of God" (Acts 1:3, italics added). The resurrection is an event that explains
why the good news was proclaimed, why the gospel story was told (Chrysostom,
Hom. on Acts, 1). It was not that the gospel story "solved" the enigma of the resurrection or fathomed its mystery. The Spirit continues to bear inward witness
to the truth of this saving event in our hearts (Rom. 8:9–17; Origen, *Comm. on
Rom.* 8.16).

Sabbath observance for Christians is on resurrection day (Sunday) as a continuing testimony of the church to the centrality of the resurrection. The resurrection is not celebrated on Easter alone but every Lord's Day. "The first day of
the week" was not celebrated in Jewish tradition until the Gospel was proclaimed
(Matt. 28:1; Mark 16:2, 9; Luke 24:1; John 20:1, 9; Acts 20:7; 1 Cor. 16:2).

His Death and Resurrection Inseparable as a
Single, Integral Salvation Event

It is best to think of Christ's death and resurrection as a single event or complex
of events, rather than two separable events. For "He was delivered over to death
for our sins and was raised to life for our justification" (Rom. 4:25).

The cross "contains in itself the mystery of Easter" (Leo I, *Serm.* 71.1). "Christ
underwent suffering for our sins in order to pay our debt and so that his resurrection might prefigure the general resurrection of us all" (Theodoret, *Interp. of
Rom.* 4.25). Cyril of Jerusalem understood that one sees Jesus' death most clearly
through the lens of the resurrection: "I confess the Cross, because I know of the
Resurrection" (*Catech. Lect.* 13).

Similarly Calvin: "So then, let us remember that whenever mention is made of
his death alone, we are to understand at the same time what belongs to his resurrection. Also, the same synecdoche applies to the word 'resurrection': whenever
it is mentioned separately from death, we are to understand it as including what
has to do especially with his death" (*Inst.* 2.16.13).

The Hope of Resurrection

Beliefs prior to Jesus about the general resurrection shaped the New Testament
interpretation of Jesus' resurrection.

History as Revelation

To understand why the resurrection is so decisive for Christianity, it is necessary
to consider whether there is meaning in the whole narrative of universal history.
Put in a late Judaic frame of reference: The resurrection is best understandable
as a historical event in the context of apocalyptic hopes.

Universal history is the most comprehensive horizon of the human imagination. The revelation of God cannot be grasped apart from the end of universal
history. If God is revealed in history, history as God's address cannot be finally
revealed until it is over. Universal history, if its meaning could be grasped, would
necessarily constitute the decisive revelation of God.

The intellectual burden of Christian teaching has always been to inquire rigorously into the meaning of universal history. The creeds of the churches have
sought to interpret the whole of history from beginning to end, not merely a part
of history. The meaning of universal history is the proper subject matter of theology. What the resurrection is all about is disclosing the meaning of universal
history.

Final Revelation Is Knowable Only at History's End

If the whole of history is revelation, then revelation is complete only at the end of history, for it is only on the last day that one may hear the completed story of "what history says" or grasp the resolution or conclusion to which history has come.

History could come to an end at any moment. At no point in history is there a certain guarantee that it will continue. Whatever its duration, *it is only from the end of history that its final meaning can be discerned.*

Julia of Norwich grasped the decisive analogy: "We can never fully know ourselves until the last moment" (*Aphorisms, IAIA*:191). As a person's life is only interpretable when one's last responsible decision is made, so is the life of history only interpretable on its last day.

Since the course of future history could always reverse our theories about it, the meaning of universal history remains a puzzle until the last day. It is precisely to this dilemma that the hope of final resurrection speaks.

Resurrection in the Light of Apocalyptic Expectation of the End

The apocalyptic movements of late Judaism were keenly aware of the incompleteness of history. They understood how limited human vision of history is. They looked toward completeness, toward final resolution of the injustices of history. The meaning of history was not to be derived from past or present history, but only from the last day of history.

They sought to reflect anticipatively and imaginatively upon the end, for only then would the meaning of history be apparent or even possible to grasp. Hence the whole of history is not interpretable from any of its parts, which could be reversed on the last day. History is interpretable only from its final day. Upon that day apocalyptic writings are precisely fixed (Rev. 22:6–13; Oecumenius, *Comm. on the Apocalypse* 22.10–19).

Apocalyptic writers were among the first to unveil the idea of universal history by focusing in an unprecedented way upon the end of history. Until apocalyptic thought, there could be, strictly speaking, no cohesive or integral idea of universal history, because the end was missing. Subsequent philosophies of history have been decisively shaped by these writers. Those in the early Christian tradition who especially shaped western views of universal history are Hippolytus, Irenaeus, Arnobius, Lactantius, Eusebius, and above all Augustine.

End-Time Expectation Saturated the Environment in Which the New Testament Was Written

For apocalyptic writings in the intertestamental period, the resurrection is the key for grasping the meaning of the whole of history (Pannenberg, *TKG*:51ff.). Jesus' resurrection does not make sufficient sense if artificially abstracted from this actual history of expectation.

Many first-century documents attest intense expectation that the general resurrection (and hence the end of history) was imminent. This is seen in the Qumran scrolls and late Judaic apocalyptic writings. A quarter century after Jesus' death, Paul was still expecting that the general resurrection (the end of history) would occur soon (1 Thess. 4:13–18; 1 Cor. 15:51; Theodoret, *Interp. of 1 Thess.* 5.3; Ambrose, *On Belief in the Resurrection* 2.92–3).

The unitive grasp of the whole of history (including its end) has been truncated in modern (especially existentialist) reading of history. For those in the twentieth century who become fixated primarily upon here-and-now decisions instead of objective history, the meaning of universal history tends to become collapsed into our present experience. In psychological and existentialist interpretations, the revealing whole of history is lost. What remains are our introversions. The study of Christ needs to transcend a subjectivist existentialist exegesis that collapses history into introverted inwardness or subjective decision (Bultmann). On the other hand, it cannot take flight into an entirely suprahistorical view that sees salvation history as existing over and above universal history. Both tendencies resist revelation as universal history and have been rightly resisted in our time by Pannenberg (*Revelation as History*), as they were previously resisted by Irenaeus (*Ag. Her.*), Lactantius (*Div. Inst.*), and Augustine (*CG*). "All theological questions and answers are meaningful only within the framework of the history which God has with humanity and through humanity with his whole creation—the history moving toward a future still hidden from the world but already revealed in Jesus Christ" (Pannenberg, *BQT* I, 15).

How Jesus Transformed the End-Time Expectation

Jesus' Ministry Constantly Pointed to Its End

During his entire earthly ministry, Jesus' identity (according to his own testimony) awaited future confirmation. It was a story in anticipation of a hidden conclusion. He did not play into the hands of those who sought to force him into an instant identification. He often taught that the confirmation of his ministry would be clearly and certainly revealed in future events.

When the Pharisees demanded a sign from heaven, Jesus resisted their demand, not because there was no way to legitimize his claims, but because the time for their confirmation was not yet (Mark 8:11–12; Matt. 12:38–42; 16:1–4; Luke 11:16, 32). At that stage Jesus merely pointed to his deeds as preliminary verification of his claim to authority (in his response to John's disciples, Matt. 11:5–6, and in Luke 11:20). But the final confirmation, he said, would have to await the resurrection and the coming judgment of the Son of Man.

The apocalyptic understanding of history was radically transformed by the history of Jesus, especially through his own bodily resurrection (John 20:19–22). Until then, he was willing to reveal only that the future of God is at hand and that he himself was the sign of its imminent coming.

What the Resurrection Meant to Jesus' Contemporaries

Resurrection is the word God speaks from the end of history. First-century Jews knew that resurrection meant the end of history.

The general resurrection event was a way of speaking about the universal awakening at the end of time of those who sleep in the grave (Dan. 12:2–3; 1 Thess. 4:13–16; Baruch 30:1; 4 Ezra). Resurrection was the event of the consummation of history. It was an action that only God had power to take.

Universal resurrection is the event that occurs at the end of history. Resurrection *is* the end of history. Thus *if resurrection takes place in our midst, then we are already at the end.*

The testimony to the resurrection cannot be discounted as unreliable history, for it is clear that witnesses to it were radically transformed by what they saw. It requires some empathic effort for modern persons to understand what an actual resurrection would have instantly and self-evidently meant to Jesus' contemporaries.

The key: *The resurrection would have meant that the end time had begun.* Only the reader who has grasped this is ready to move on. If its plausibility remains unclear, ponder the preceding arguments of this page.

Jesus' Resurrection in the Light
of Apocalyptic Hopes

Jesus shared with apocalyptic hopes the intense focus upon the end. Jesus came proclaiming a particular understanding of the end—namely, that it is immediately at hand and already being anticipated in his own ministry of healing and proclamation. When he rose from the dead, he confirmed what had been anticipated in his proclamation (Bede, *Hom. on the Gospels* 11).

In Jesus the End Is Now

Jesus' earthly ministry is an anticipation of the end time, an expectation or anticipative act of receiving (prolepsis) or preparation for receiving the end time (hence it is called a proleptic consciousness). Everything is in readiness for the end.

In him *the end event is already being anticipatively experienced* in the present. The end occurs in a sense "ahead of time" as a "*foretaste* of the age to come," as if the end were already flowing freely into the present. The end was not only conceptualized in advance but it was in effect beginning to "happen in advance" (i.e., proleptically).

Whether hearers would participate in God's saving event therefore depended upon what they decided about Jesus and whether they participated by grace through faith in his life, death, and resurrection.

In Lazarus "we see in a single instance what is to be understood more generally of all in the future" (Maximinus, *Sermon* 14.3). The same voice that called Lazarus will call us at the resurrection (John 11:3; Gregory of Nyssa, *On the Making of Man* 25.11).

The Risen Lord Meant the End, the Final Revelation

In Jesus' resurrection the disciples understood themselves to be hearing the final word that history was to speak. After that everything else was to be seen in relation to that. To anyone who earnestly shared the hope in the general resurrection, the resurrection of Jesus would have revealed the meaning of universal history. It glimpsed and foretold the end of history. The meaning of the whole was made known through the lens of this one end-time event (Pannenberg, *JGM*: 53–88).

The moment the disciples were met by the risen Jesus, they understood that they were already standing at the beginning of the end time, the last days, the general resurrection. In an instant it became clear to them that the end had indeed appeared and begun and that Jesus was "the firstfruits of those who have fallen asleep" (1 Cor. 15:20). Jesus' resurrection was at once recognized as the firstfruits of general resurrection (1 Cor. 15:20; Col. 1:18). Jesus was regarded as the first born from the dead, the one through whom the believing community learned to look for the final coming of the kingdom of God, and the fulfillment of the apocalyptic hope (Cyril of Alex., *Letters* 17).

This recognition was not a matter of gradual or lengthy development. *The kernel of the confession of the Lordship of Jesus Christ was fully formed in the single instant of meeting the risen Lord* (Athanasius, *Letter* 59.10) Having already undergone extensive anticipatory development, it did not need to undergo other further developments in order to be understood (Gregory I, *Forty Gospel Hom.* 26). Thereafter the faithful lived in communities that confessed to "know Christ and the power of his resurrection and the fellowship of sharing in his sufferings, becoming like him in his death, and so, somehow, to attain to the resurrection from the dead" (Phil. 3:10; Gregory Nazianzus, *Orat.* I).

Lacking Resurrection, Faith in Vain

Either the resurrection was an event in history or the whole of Christianity is pathetic (1 Cor. 15:17). So central was the resurrection in defining the meaning of history that Paul wrote: "If Christ has not been raised, our preaching is useless and so is your faith" (1 Cor. 15:14). The gospel depended upon an event—resurrection—to validate the ministry of the person—Jesus as the Christ. "If Christ has not been raised, your faith is futile; you are still in your sins" (v. 17). The reduction of Christianity to humanistic hope is rejected in the strongest terms: "If only for this life we have hope in Christ, we are to be pitied more than all men" (v. 19; Cyril of Jerus., *Catechet. Lect.* 13).

Resurrection as a Distinct Event in Human History

On historical evidence, Pannenberg backs into this same conclusion but ever so cautiously: "only if one examines it [the Christian proclamation] in the light of the eschatological hope for a resurrection from the dead, then that which is so designated is a historical event, even if we do not know anything more particular about it" (Pannenberg, *JGM*:98). Those who first attested the resurrection did not have to use such guarded language, but they did not live in our era, saturated as it is with reductionist empiricism.

Due to this matrix of historical expectation, resurrection did not mean simply a resuscitation of an individual corpse. A resuscitation such as that of Lazarus could (like Jesus' resurrection) point toward the end, but it was not the end, for Lazarus had no signs of being called to messianic sonship. He lacked theandric identity.

Jesus' resurrection is a more intricately layered event, framed by prophetic expectation. When a dead body appears to be resuscitated, there is a temporary revitalization of a single individual from the dead. Yet no one would imagine that Lazarus would be freed from the destiny of dying in the future.

In Jesus' resurrection, there is a major difference—the resurrected one lives on. The same body is transformed into a glorified body for which there is no future death—imperishable (1 Cor. 15:35–56). The general resurrection was expected as a universal historical event, not something that happens only to one or a few resuscitated individuals who were themselves again bound to die.

Jesus' Resurrection Confirms His Identity as Anointed Son of Man

Any Jew learned in scripture who beheld the crucified and resurrected Jesus could have made the connection: in the risen Jesus, God was confirming that Jesus really was who he was suspected of being—Son of Man, sent of God, Anointed One. The claims that before the resurrection seemed blasphemous to Jewish ears now seemed to be confirmed in God's own uniquely eventful way.

Before the resurrection there had been an ongoing debate as to whether Jesus was regarded as Son of Man or regarded himself as such. But there can be little doubt that immediately after the resurrection he was viewed as Son of Man, an identity confirmed by his own appearing. After the resurrection the conclusion was unavoidable: we have met on earth the expected Son of Man who will come again to consummate history in a fitting way (Leo I, *Tome* 5).

"Jesus' unity with God was not yet established by the claim implied in his pre-Easter appearance, but only by his resurrection from the dead" (Pannenberg, *JGM*:53). Newman had similarly argued that there is no reason for supposing that prior to his resurrection the disciples adequately grasped that He was God in our human nature (*SD*:138–41).

By This Sign the Final Revelation Made Known

If true, the resurrection would have meant to beholders that God is finally revealed in his chosen Son. The promised kingdom is already appearing! It is a reliable tenet of Hebraic historical logic that if the Messiah is risen, then God is unsurpassably revealed, for only at the end of history is the meaning of history knowable.

The end of history is in a sense already present in Jesus' rising from the dead. The general resurrection is foretasted in Jesus' resurrection. In this way, *Jesus' divinity is implied from his resurrection* (Rom. 1:4; Ambrosiaster, *Comm. on Paul*, Rom. 1.4). If risen, then Son of Man, Son of God.

All who shared the expectation of a general resurrection felt themselves grasped by the end time in the living presence of the risen Jesus. They acquired an incredibly confident and otherwise implausibly courageous attitude toward history, suffering, and life's ambiguities. Why was the New Testament community so confident about the historical process? Because in Jesus' resurrection, the end was already beheld. The resurrection is thus the clue to the whole of history, through which God is finally made known (Pannenberg, *JGM*; Oden, *This We Believe*).

His Messianic Authority Made Clear—The Atoning Value of His Death Was Confirmed

Jesus had explained "plainly" to his disciples in advance that "the Son of Man must suffer many things and be rejected by the elders, chief priests and teachers of the law, and that he must be killed and after three days rise again" (Mark 8:31).

Through the resurrection it was made clear that his sacrificial offering of himself for others had been accepted. His atonement for humanity was received of God, and thus humanity raised up, made new, brought near to God (Cyril of Jerusalem, *Catech. Lect.* 14).

Christ became exalted as messianic king through the resurrection. From the tomb he arose to give his disciples the Great Commission wherein the legitimate authority of the risen Lord became explicit: "All authority in heaven and on earth has been given to me. Therefore go . . ." (Matt. 28:18).

Peter proclaimed that the risen Christ had "commanded us to preach to the people and to testify that he is the one whom God appointed as judge of the living and the dead. All the prophets testify about him that everyone who believes in him receives forgiveness of sins through his name" (Acts 10:40–43).

The resurrection was the first evidence of the ascent of the humbled Son. While no one could see his descent into the abode of the dead, the resurrection was beheld. Descent and resurrection are correlated as victory hidden and victory revealed. His life and death embodied the full measure of obedience to the Father (actively through his life, passively through his death). Thereafter history would be divided into promise and fulfillment of the Christ, the old and new law, the prophetic anticipation and the messianic fulfillment of divine promise.

It was a resurrection of the body. The bodily resurrection was consistent with the bodily incarnation, demonstrating that the creator God is vindicated in and through material creation (Origen, *Dialogue with Heraclides*, LCC 2:440–41). Resurrection is not counter to the purpose and order of creation, but God's way of redeeming humanity by remaking fleshly creation (Isa. 26:19; Rom. 1:4). Cosmic history is being brought toward a redemption that involves the whole of creation and not merely human history (Rom. 8:19–23).

On the Third Day

He rose on the third day (tertia dei; Creed of 150 Fathers). Like "suffered under Pontius Pilate," this phrase of the creed reminds us that the redemption of the world was a datable event, an occurrence in history, not an abstract idea.

In Jewish calculation, each day in which he was dead, whether part or whole, is counted as a day, hence he died and was buried on Good Friday (the fourteenth of Nisan), remained in the tomb on Holy Saturday (pascal Sabbath, second day), and arose on Easter morning (the sixteenth of Nisan, third day). It was customary to count each new day as beginning at sunset. Thus Christ was in the sepulchre during part of two days, and the full day between (Augustine, *Trin.* 4, FC 45: 157).

Three days of burial, no less, no more, were required to establish the fact of his death. Athanasius set forth reasons why the resurrection could not reasonably have been sooner or later than the third day. If earlier, his death would have been denied. If only two days, "the glory of his incorruption would have been obscure." It had best not be later because the witnesses to his death would disperse and the identity of his body might be placed in question (*Incarn. of the Word*, 26).

The Sign of Jonah

The eighth-century BC prophet Hosea had used the third day time frame for the healing of Israel: "on the third day he will restore us, that we may live in his presence" (Hos. 6:2; cf. 1 Sam. 30:12; 2 Kings 20:5, 8; Lev. 7:17–18). The risen Christ himself "opened their minds so they could understand the Scriptures. He told them, 'This is what is written: The Christ will suffer and rise from the dead on the third day'" (Luke 24:45–46).

The third day was linked liturgically with the wave offering, when "on the day after the Sabbath" the Levitical priest was instructed to "wave the sheaf before the Lord" (each person having brought the priest "a sheaf of the first grain you harvest"); for "On the day you wave the sheaf, you must sacrifice as a burnt offering to the Lord a lamb" (Lev. 23:9–12). The sheaves were waved as a sign to the people that the sacrifice had been offered and accepted. Similarly it occurred in the case of the resurrection, that God's own sign of acceptance (analogous to sheaf-waving) occurred on the day after the Sabbath, namely Easter Sunday (Pope, *Compend.* 2:169ff.).

The chief prefigurative type that entered into the memory of the proclaiming church was Jonah. Jesus had said that no sign would be given to his "wicked and adulterous generation" "except the sign of the prophet Jonah. For as Jonah was three days and three nights in the belly of a huge fish, so the Son of Man will be three days and three nights in the heart of the earth" (Matt. 12:39–40). Jesus' death and resurrection was like Jonah's entombment in and disgorgement from the great fish (Ambrose, *Flight from the World*, FC 65:296–97).

Raised by Whose Power? The Triune Premise

The resurrection was the act of the triune God—not only of the Father, but also of Son and Spirit. Since God is three in one, it is fitting to teach that "God raised him from the dead" (Col. 2:12; cf. 1 Cor. 15:4; Acts 2:24; 13:30), raised by the glory of the Father, by the Son's own will, through the Spirit.

Paul taught that Christ was "raised from the dead through the glory of the *Father*" (Rom. 6:4, ital. add.). God the Father, who gives "the Spirit of wisdom," "raised him from the dead" (Eph. 1:20).

It is not inconsistent, according to the triune premise, to affirm that Jesus rose by his own power. For the *Son*, being God, had power to raise himself. Christ explicitly stated of himself that he had authority to lay down his life and "authority to take it up again" (John 10:18). This implied a voluntary act of surrendering his life in death, and an equally voluntary act of resuming his life (Eleventh Council of Toledo, *SCD* 286). When his detractors demanded that he prove his authority to them, Jesus answered in a way that assumed that he himself was the agent of raising in the resurrection: "Destroy this temple, and I will raise it again in three days" (John 3:19).

The *Spirit* is equally active as an agent of the resurrection, as Paul writes: "And if the Spirit of him who raised Jesus from the dead is living in you, he who raised Christ from the dead will also give life to your mortal bodies through his Spirit, who lives in you" (Rom. 8:11). It was "through the Spirit of holiness" that Christ Jesus "was declared with power to be the Son of God by his resurrection from the dead" (Rom. 1:4).

This distinction is useful: *when the resurrection is viewed as the vindication of Jesus' own divine power, it is viewed as the act of the Son. When the resurrection is viewed as the confirmation by the Father of the Son's life and death, it is viewed as the work of the Father. The triune premise is embedded in Jesus saying: "Whatever the Father does the Son also does"* (John 5:19; Chrysostom, *Hom. on John* 38).

Can it be rightly said that the Son brought back to the triune God an enriched Trinity, enhanced by his human experience? Has he who was sent from heaven by the Father into the hazard of history brought out of history a new experience to the deity? It is not fitting to say that God learned something from incarnation or crucifixion, due to the premise of foreknowledge, since the all-wise God foreknew all that was to be known about the unfolding historical events that the disciples witnessed. Being eternal, God lives in eternal simultaneity with all events past and future. Yet since God and humanity are one in Jesus Christ, the costly, hard won experiences of being human. though foreknown from eternity, are received into the eternal memory of the Godhead. Assuming the permeant logic of the theandric union, there is now a person in the Trinity in whom human experience has become indissolubly united in and with the eternal God: "The heart of man and the heart of God beat in the risen Lord" (Mackintosh, *PJC*: 371).

Resurrection: An Event Without Analogy

Of everyone else it is understandable that healthy skepticism might assume the high improbability of resurrection from the dead. But in Jesus' case, we are not talking of the usual human situation, for he is the unique theandric surprise unexpectedly embodied in time who breaks through our native skepticism.

The more one learns about Jesus, the more the presumption reasonably shifts in favor of his resurrection—precisely due to who he is. The church was attesting not the resurrection of just anyone, but of the one mediator: Jesus Christ. It is only because of who he was—his identity as Son of God—that he had the power to raise himself up, a deductive argument based upon the premise of theandric union.

The Raising of Enoch, Elijah, and Lazarus
Distinguished from Jesus'

In neither Enoch nor Elijah do we have the crucial premises of theandric union and messianic vocation that apply to Jesus. Nor is there an attested direct ascent into heaven. Different distinctions applied to Enoch and Elijah: "Recall that Henoch [Enoch] was translated; but Jesus ascended," and "Elia [Elijah] ascended as into heaven, but Jesus, into heaven" (Cyril of Jerusalem, *Catech. Lect.* 14; Gen. 5:24; 2 Kings 2:11).

In three miracles in the Gospels Jesus is reported as raising others from the dead: the son of the widow of Nain (Luke 7:11–18), the daughter of Jairus (Matt. 9:18–26; Mark 5:22–24, 35–43; Luke 8:40–56), and Lazarus (John 11:43). All point anticipatively toward the coming unparalleled resurrection of Jesus the Son of God.

Yet all three of these events are quite unlike the resurrection of Jesus in that those raised *all died again!* (Tho. Aq., *ST* 3, Q.53.3). The primary occurrence attested in these narratives is that Christ speaks and the dead hear as if they could hear his voice from the abode of the dead. This suggests that somehow the dead in the tombs were able or made able to hear and obey him.

Only by Jesus may it be claimed: "I have authority to lay [my life] down and to take it up again" (John 10:18). This is what most sharply distinguishes Jesus' resurrection from all others. Others have been raised by a power not their own. Jesus was raised by his own power, God's own power. This is why his resurrection is without analogy.

The Untombed at Jesus' Death

It is in this light that Matthew's startling account of the moment of Jesus' death must be understood: "The tombs broke open and the bodies of many holy people who had died were raised to life. They came out of the tombs, and after Jesus' resurrection they went into the holy city and appeared to many people" (Matt. 27:52–53).

This text does not imply that they rose before Jesus' resurrection, assuming that he was "the firstfruits of those who have fallen asleep" (1 Cor. 15:20). Nor does the passage imply that these believers either continued thereafter to live immortally on earth or ascended into heaven, but rather that "they rose to die again" (Tho. Aq., *ST* 3, Q53.3; following Augustine, *Letters*, 164, *To Evodius*). While all of these who rose again from the dead anticipated and prefigured (or, in the case of Tabitha, attested the power of) Jesus' resurrection, none was of the same genre as the bodily resurrection of Jesus on earth and in heaven.

The Same Body

The same body Jesus received from Mary was raised, glorified, and transformed. "He showed us the conditions of our resurrection in His own flesh, by restoring in His Resurrection the same body which He had from us" (Novatian, *Trin.* 10, Ursinus, *CHC*:234–39). The Council of Constantinople (AD 543) rejected the Origenist tradition's hypothesis of the ethereal nature and sphericity of the risen body. The glorified state was a real reunion of Christ's soul with his same body.

At a very early date Ignatius had grasped a pivotal dialectic: "Son of Mary and Son of God" was "first able to suffer" as crucified, "and then unable to suffer" as exalted (Ignatius of Antioch, *Eph. 3*). "The body was made impassible, which it had been possible to crucify" (Leo I, *Serm.* 71). Yet there were not two bodies (one crucified, another resurrected), but one.

It was fitting that the risen Christ reassume the same wounded body so as to retain its wounds: to confirm the disciples in their faith in the resurrection; in order rightly to intercede for humanity so as to show the Father what had been suffered for humanity; to demonstrate that it was the same body that had been crucified that was glorified; and to be able to exhibit on the last day the justice of judgment upon the disbelieving and mercy for the redeemed, "as an everlasting trophy of His victory" (Tho. Aq., *ST* 3, Q54.4; Augustine, *CG* 22).

The showing of marks or signs (*tekuria*) on his hands and feet, eating, and drinking with his disciples pointed to the mystery of his risen body: He was the same, yet glorified, "of the same nature but of different glory" (Tho. Aq., *ST* 3, Q55.6). "Look at my hands and my feet. It is I myself! Touch me and see; a ghost does not have flesh and bones, as you see I have" (Luke 24:39). He was seen "by us who ate and drank with him after he rose from the dead" (Acts 10:41).

Only the permeant logic of theandric union could have enabled the kind of reasoning we find embedded in the dialectical language of Ambrose: "For the same one suffered and did not suffer; died and did not die; was buried and was not buried; rose again and did not rise again; for the body proper took on life again; for what fell, this rose again; what did not fall, did not rise again. He rose again, therefore, according to the flesh, which, having died, rose again. He did not rise again according to the Word, which had not been destroyed on earth, but remained always with God" (Ambrose, *Incarn. of Our Lord* 5.36).

Characteristics of the Risen Body: The Same Body Glorified

After the forty days of resurrection appearances and the ascension, the Lord's body passed into its glorified state. "What that state is we know only so far as may be learned from what the Apostle teaches from the nature of the bodies with which believers are to be invested after the resurrection" (Hodge, *Syst. Theol.* 2:628). The resurrected life of the believer is like Christ's glorified body (Phil. 3:21).

Nonetheless, his same risen body was also described as a transformed body, a "glorious body" (Phil. 3:21), a body fit for eternity, a body that could move through doors and walls at any time and appear and disappear; and even those who knew him well did not always recognize him quickly (Luke 24:15–16, 31). Christ caused "immortality to be given to the flesh through resurrection" (Marius Victorinus, *Epis. to Phil.* 3.21).

The resurrection body had direct continuity with the body that had died, but it now appeared in a changed state of glory. It was not merely flesh and blood physically resuscitated, but a glorified body (Origen, *OFP*:252–54). He was capable of appearing and disappearing, of moving from one state to the other while sustaining the identity with the earthly body, and vanishing instantly (Luke 24:31, 36). He truly ate, yet without need (Leo IX, *Symbol of Faith*, *SCD* 344; see also *SCD* 422; Bede, *Comm. on Luke* 24:41; Tho. Aq., *ST* 3, Q55.6). It was to the mystery of this spiritual body that the resurrection narratives pointed when they spoke of Christ entering a room through closed doors (John 20:19) or vanishing (Luke 24:31) or suddenly appearing (Mark 16:12; 1 Cor. 15:51–52).

Is the Resurrection Evidence Sufficient?

Is the empty tomb a psychological rationalization or fantasy of the rememberers, hence not "open to empirical verification" (Tillich, *Syst. Theol.* 2:127, 155–58)? To answer this question, the evidence needs to be fairly presented, as it might be in a fair trial under unprejudiced conditions.

He Appeared to Many

Do the texts support the opinion that the beholder must have first had faith before they saw the risen Lord? No. Thomas had to be convinced visibly by the evidence prior to his confession. The resurrected body of Jesus was seen by those who had not yet come to faith. The despairing Emmaus travelers first saw him and then spoke with him before they recognized him and only then believed (Luke 24:13–32). He was perceived but not personally recognized by the travelers until he was made known in the breaking of bread (for "they were kept from recognizing him," Luke 24:16). He was mistaken for the gardener until he called Mary by name (John 20:15).

All four Gospels report numerous appearances of the risen Lord. He was seen by Mary Magdalene (Matt. 28:1; Mark 16:9; John 20:11–18); the women return-ing from the tomb (Matt. 28:8–10); Peter (1 Cor. 15:5; Luke 24:34); the Emmaus travelers (Mark 16:12, 13; Luke 24:33–35); the disciples, excepting Thomas, as-sembled in Jerusalem (Luke 24:36–43), and including Thomas on the next Sun-day night (Mark 16:14; John 20:26–29); seven disciples (including Peter, Thomas, Nathanael, James, and John) beside the Sea of Galilee (John 21:1–24); "more than five hundred of the brothers at the same time, most of whom are still living" (1 Cor. 15:6); James (1 Cor. 15:7); and all those who witnessed the ascension (Matt. 28:18–20; Mark 16:19; Acts 1:3–12). Paul added to his list: "and last of all he appeared to me also" as to one "untimely born" (1 Cor. 15:8; Cyril of Jerusa-lem, *Catech. Lect.* 14). Acts reported that these appearances spanned forty days (1:3). There may have been other appearances unrecorded.

Luther summarized the types of testimony: "The resurrection of the Lord Christ is made certain (1) by the testimony of His adversaries, (2) by the testi-mony of His friends, (3) by the testimony of the Lord Himself, and (4) by the tes-timony of dear prophets and of Holy Scripture" (Luther, *WLS* 1:181). What follows seeks to assess this evidence fairly.

The Earliest Evidence: The Tomb Was Empty

On Easter morning, women visited the sepulchre where he had been laid. They were astonished to find his body not there. The first layer of evidence is simply an empty tomb.

Shortly thereafter the apostles were actively proclaiming that Jesus had risen. It is hardly convincing that they could have gotten by with inventing this story if it could have been easily squelched by producing the body. But no one could produce the body.

However, there are three standard objections that must be countered.

His Death Could Not Be Made Up

First could it be that Jesus did not actually die on the cross? Perhaps he only fainted? (a theory proposed early by the Gnostics and later by Thomas Huxley, *Christianity and Agnosticism*:76–80).

This hypothesis was carefully examined and found deficient by classic schol-ars on five different grounds: (1) The evidence of his death seemed sufficient to his enemies and to civil officials. The centurion who supervised the crucifixion assured Pilate that Jesus was dead, in effect officially verifying the death (Mark 15:44–45; Ambrose, *Prayer of Job and David* 1.5.13). (2) The text states plainly the reason the soldiers did not break Jesus' legs: They "found that he was already dead" (John 19:33; Augustine, *Tractates on John* 120.1). (3) Joseph of Arimathea "asked Pilate for the body" (John 19:38). "With Pilate's permission, he came and took the body away" (John 19:38; Augustine, *Trin.* 4.13). He was accompanied by Nicodemus. If he were still alive, no one would have described him as "the body." (4) It is clear from John 19:35 that "John was present at these events" as an eyewitness (Theodore of Mopsuestia, *Comm. on John* 19.35). (5) Jesus' body had gone through a complex burial process: "Taking Jesus' body, the two of them wrapped it, with the spices, in strips of linen" in accordance with "Jewish burial custom," and there was "in the garden a new tomb" in which Jesus was laid (John 19:40–42; Chrysostom, *Hom. on John* 85.4).

Hence it is implausible to imagine that between Friday and Sunday Jesus was not dead. Surely his heartbeat or breath would have been noticed by those attending his wrapping. It is implausible that he could have survived being wrapped in linen and then had strength to remove the boulder that had been set to seal the tomb precisely to prevent any loose talk about a possible resurrection, or that he could have done all this and still not disturbed the Roman guard.

The Location Could Not Have Been Mistaken

Second standard objection: Suppose the women were looking in the wrong place. Two of the women (Mary Magdalene and Mary the mother of Jesus) had seen where Jesus was laid (Mark 15:47; Luke 23:55) and witnessed the burial, since the eyewitness states in explicit detail their exact location: they were "sitting there opposite the tomb" (Matt. 27:61; Chrysostom, *Hom. on Matt.* Hom. 88.2–3; Simpson, *RMT*:45–46; K. Lake, *Historical Evidence for the Resurrection*:246–53). It is far-fetched that the women who prepared his body for burial would have forgotten where their Lord was buried.

The Body Could Not Have Been Stolen

Third, perhaps the body was stolen. Could someone have removed the body? It is unlikely that the disciples would or could have covertly removed the body, because a specific plan had been initiated by Pilate to prevent just that (Chrysostom, *Hom. on Matt.*, Hom. 89.1; Simpson, *RMT*:40–43). The chief priests and Pharisees told Pilate: "We remember that while he was still alive that deceiver said, 'After three days I will rise again.' So give the order for the tomb to be made secure until the third day. Otherwise, his disciples may come and steal the body and tell the people that he has been raised from the dead."

Pilate ordered his guards to "'make the tomb as secure as you know how.' So they went and made the tomb secure by putting a seal on the stone and posting the guard" (Matt. 27:62–66). "Because the tomb was sealed, there was no deceitfulness at work" (Chrysostom, *Hom. on Matt.* Hom. 89.1). "How could they [the disciples] have burst through the circle of defenders? It would have taken many hands to remove such a great stone that sealed the tomb" (Chrysostom, *Gospel of Matt.* Hom 90.1).

There may have been an unsuccessful conspiracy to bribe the guards, according to Matthew. The chief priests and elders devised a plan to give "the soldiers a large sum of money, telling them, 'You are to say, "His disciples came during the night and stole him away while we were asleep"—a story which has been "widely circulated among the Jews to this very day" (Matt. 28:12–15). Augustine joked at the thinness of the evidence for such a story. Are you going to "bring forward as witnesses men who were sleeping? Truly, it is you who have fallen asleep, you who have failed in examining such things. If they were sleeping, what could they have seen? If they saw nothing, how are they witnesses?" (*Expos. on Ps. 64* 13).

It is implausible that thieves could have deceived the guards, moved the huge boulder, and *taken the body but left the graveclothes*—what possible motive could be conceived for that? Alternative explanations strain credulity (Chrysostom, *Hom. on Matt.* Hom. 90.1; Daniel Whitby, in *Angl.*:270).

If the authorities themselves had removed the body, then they would have had at their disposal the ample means of silencing the earliest proclaimers of resurrection. Or if the civil or religious authorities had it in their power to disprove the resurrection, the integrity of the earliest witnesses could have been quickly refuted.

But it was not within their power to disprove the resurrection because they did not have a body. The authorities would have had sufficient motive to squash the resurrection report, but only if they had a body—but they did not. Hence the tomb was empty. Their very silence gives weight and plausibility to the kerygma. "We know that his resurrection was confirmed by the testimony of his enemies" (Scots Confession 10).

All these skeptical theories have serious difficulties. Classical exegetes thought that no hypothesis is more plausible than the straightforward narrative we have, told by persons who hardly can be charged with either psychosis or insincerity. Their testimony was simple: God raised Jesus up to authenticate his messianic mission, to prove his divine sonship.

Finally historical judgment must fall on one side or the other: either the remembering community brought to life the deceptive story of a risen Christ or a living risen Christ brought to life the remembering community. There is no middle way.

The Graveclothes Were Left Collapsed and Undisturbed

Careful unpacking of the evidence presented by John 20:1–9 yields a remarkable conclusion: Jesus' body was not there, but the graveclothes were there precisely in the place and in the exact form in which he had been lain. The account bears peculiar marks of a direct eyewitness account in its precision and detail. John reached the tomb first and looked in, but Peter entered it first. John entered the tomb and saw something that immediately convinced him that Jesus had risen (Eusebius, *To Marinus*, Supplement, 2–3).

The account is precise: he "went inside. He saw and believed" (John 20:8). But exactly what evidence did he see that elicited instant belief? Not just the absence of the body, but the *particular way the graveclothes were lying*, precisely as they would have been as if on the body but now collapsed without the body and left in an undisturbed condition. Joseph and Nicodemus had wound the linen around the body, inserting spices in the folds, and used a separate linen for the head (John 20:40; Chrysostom, *Hom. on John*, 85.4).

The resurrected body in some way moved through the graveclothes leaving them limp. How do we know this? There was a space between the head napkin and the body clothes. "He saw the strips of linen lying there, as well as the burial cloth that had been around Jesus' head. The cloth was folded up by itself, *separate from the linen*" (John 20:6–7, italics added; cf. Cyril of Jerusalem, *Catech. Lect* 14)! This is what they report as having objectively seen that elicited belief instantly. The linens had not been disturbed by anyone and lay limply like a discarded cocoon (Leo, *Serm.* 71.3; Stott, *BC*:53). His glorified body had passed through them (H. Latham, *The Risen Master*, 1–3) without disturbing them. It is astonishing that we have such a precise description of such a crucial moment by an eyewitness that has survived twenty centuries. "The linen clothes also, which enveloped Him and which He left behind when He rose" were early regarded as silent "witnesses." Three centuries later, Cyril of Jerusalem was confident that the specific location of this sepulchre had been correctly remembered and identified, "the spot itself, still to be seen" (namely, the site of the Church of the Holy Sepulchre, the very place where Cyril was offering his catechetical lectures, *Catech. Lect.* 14).

Eusebius reasoned: "The cloths lying within seem to me at once to furnish also a proof that the body had not been taken away by people, as Mary supposed. For no one taking away the body would leave the linens, nor would the thief ever have stayed until he had undone the linens and so be caught. . . . For God, who transforms the bodies of our humiliation so as to be conformed to the body of

Christ's glory, changed the body as an organ of the power that dwelt in it, changing it into something more divine. But he left the linen cloths as superfluous and foreign to the nature of the body" (*To Marinus*, Suppl. 2).

True or False Testimony?

Could the testimony be based on an invention or hallucination? If the testimony had been sporadic or dubious, these reports might be easier to dismiss. But one must search for some explanation of the extensive testimonies to Jesus' resurrection.

Three hypotheses seem to exhaust the possibilities: they were either inventions, hallucinatory projections, or true. The first is sometimes called the fraud theory, and the second the projection theory. These challenges have been carefully examined and answered by the classic exegetes.

If one believes from the outset that there cannot under any circumstances be a third alternative (that he truly rose), then one must scramble hard for some way to support one of the other two hypotheses. If the examination rules out from the beginning the possibility that any resurrection can ever occur in any sense, then the examiner is no longer looking at historical evidence concerning the resurrection—there is no need of that—but rather imposing a predisposing philosophical bias upon historical investigation.

The Invention Theory Is Implausible

The problem with the hypothesis of invention is that the narratives are exceedingly graphic and enriched by the specific features of an eyewitness. They show every evidence of being the testimony of people who were there and candidly reporting exactly what they saw (Augustine, *Harmony of the Gospels* 3.24). The narratives of the discovery of the empty tomb seem to be too particularized to be fabricated, too molded by specific detail to have been invented.

If the Easter narratives were invented, we would say that they were not very good inventions. If someone had wanted to contrive a resurrection story, would it sound like the meeting on the Emmaus road? If one were inventing the story, one might at least have played down the resistance and anxieties of the disciples. The Gnostic noncanonical narratives of the resurrection indeed do display many such embellishments, but they do not have the plausibility and concreteness of the New Testament narratives.

The Projection Claim Generates Serious Objections

A hallucination is the supposed perception of an object that does not exist. Did all these above-named (more than five hundred) eyewitnesses see a risen Christ that was not there? The problem with the hypothesis of hallucination or projection is that it requires two elements missing in the Gospel narratives: intensified wish projection and memory-eliciting occasions.

The core of the projection theory is found in Hegel, anticipating Freudian views of wish projection: "The need for religion finds its satisfaction in the risen Jesus" (Hegel, *The Spirit of Christianity*, OCETW:292). The projection theory requires that there be a strong disposition on the part of the rememberers in a particular, predisposing direction.

The texts indicate the opposite tendency, "because their hearts were not disposed so as to accept readily the faith in the Resurrection. Then He says Himself [Luke 24:25]: O foolish and slow of heart to believe; and [Mark 16:14]: He upbraided them with their incredulity" (Tho. Aq., *ST* 3, Q55.6). The evidence against projection is compelling (Augustine, *Sermon* 236).

(1) No sequel to death was expected. The body was received by grieving friends and bound in linen. There seems to be no doubt that Jesus was dead and buried. The tomb was sealed. Burial rites began Friday and were still continuing on Sunday ("the day after the Sabbath") when the women came to the sepulchre. If large numbers of disciples had been expecting some sequel, there surely would have been some indication that they were eagerly awaiting it. Why bind the body in graveclothes if a resurrection was expected? Why seal the tomb? Rather, they came to the tomb expecting to proceed with the burial (Cyril of Alex., *Comm. on Luke,* Hom.153). They did not come expecting to find the tomb empty. If they had been expecting the resurrection, they surely would not have done as the text of Mark indicates: "Trembling and bewildered, the women went out and fled from the tomb. They said nothing to anyone, because they were afraid" (Mark 16:8).

(2) The disciples were hard to convince. When the appearances were first reported, the disciples had an exceptionally hard time convincing anyone that they were true: "They did not believe it" (Mark 16:11). Luke's account stated the point more strongly: "But they did not believe the women, because their words seemed to them like nonsense" (Luke 24:11). To the skeptical disciples, who had ordinary expectations, the words of the women seemed like nonsense. This skepticism stands against the projection theory. Subsequently when "Jesus himself stood among them and said to them, 'Peace be with you,'" "they were startled and frightened" (Luke 24:36). Jesus "rebuked them for their lack of faith and their *stubborn refusal to believe* those who had seen him after he had arisen" (Mark 16:14, italics added). That hardly sounds like the disciples were predisposed to expect a resurrection so intensely that they fabricated it from whole cloth (Ambrose, *Expos. Of Luke* 10.179).

Thomas even more stubbornly refused to credit the reports—"Unless I see the nail marks in his hands and put my finger where the nails were, and put my hand into his side, I will not believe it" (John 20:25)! Far from being portrayed as intensely expecting the resurrection, the disciples were portrayed as stubbornly resistant, cautious, and skeptical. Jesus indicated their resistance when he described them as "slow of heart to believe" (Luke 24:25; Augustine, *Sermon* 352.4).

John's Gospel specifically notes that at the time Peter and "the other disciple" (John himself) reached the empty tomb to inspect it, "They *still* did not understand from Scripture that Jesus had to rise from the dead" (John 20:9, italics added). Thus they were no frame of mind that corresponds to a projection.

(3) The hallucinatory hypothesis also requires another element distinctly missing in the narratives: a memory-eliciting occasion. The hallucinatory argument might have been strengthened if any of these appearances had happened in a sacred location where it might have been plausible that the hallucination would have been elicited or the subconscious hope activated. But the random and miscellaneous circumstances under which Jesus appeared to the numerous people were the most ordinary of circumstances—not special places with hallowed memories to be reawakened: some were walking on a road away from Jerusalem at a spot not even clearly identifiable today. Some were out fishing on the Sea of Tiberias; others were on a mountain in Galilee; others were at some nondescript point between the Garden and the city of Jerusalem.

The range of moods in which the disciples were found by the risen Lord were extremely varied: grief (Mary Magdalene), skepticism (Thomas), fear (the women), remorse (Peter). Some appearances were to persons alone, others to small groups, others to large groups. There is no pattern in the situations of the appearances and no plausible psychosocial evidence on which to base a theory of hallucinatory projection. So the hallucinatory hypothesis must itself press and stretch the evidence in order to pretend plausibility.

Deciding Fairly About the Evidence: Why the Account Is True

The only remaining option is that the account is true. According to Thomas Aquinas' analysis, Jesus sufficiently manifested the truth of his resurrection by showing that he had (1) a physical body after death (he is remembered as eating); (2) an emotive life capable of interpersonal relationships (by greeting and talking with others); (3) an intellectual life (by dialogue and discoursing on Scripture); and (4) the divine nature (by working the miracle of the draft of fishes, and by ascending).

Each of these four testimonies or proofs "was sufficient to its own class," so as to maintain a correspondence between the testimony of human observers and testimony of Scriptures (Tho. Aq., *ST* 3, Q55.6). Daniel Whitby concluded: "'Tis equally incredible that they [the disciples] should deceive or be deceived" (*Angl.*:271).

Something Must Have Changed Their Lives

The radically changed behavior of the disciples after the resurrection is the most obvious evidence of the resurrection. They do not intend or propose that we look at their behavior—all they want us to do is look at the evidence on which they base their testimony. But their behavior itself becomes a compelling argument for the authenticity of their testimony.

Their lives were completely reversed by the resurrection. They were changed persons after the resurrection. This is evident in their actions. They had left the burial scene with a deep sense of loss, facing the collapse of what they had hoped would be the decisive event in Israel's history. Suddenly these same persons we see portrayed in Acts as willing to "risk their lives for the name of our Lord Jesus Christ" (Acts 15:26), who were proceeding to "turn the world upside down" to attest the living Lord (Acts 17:6). Their behavioral change was instantaneous, radical, and enduring. Some cause must be posited to account for such a sweeping change.

Two Cases in Point—Peter and James

What caused Peter's change? During the trial Peter had denied that he had ever known Jesus—three times! Peter and the other disciples had anxiously met "together, with the doors locked for fear of the Jews" (John 20:19). Within days after the resurrection he was preaching with such extraordinary power that "three thousand people were added to their number that day" and baptized (Acts 2:41). What had changed him? "He spoke of the resurrection of the Christ, that he was not abandoned to the grave, nor did his body see decay. God has raised this Jesus to life, and we are all witnesses of the fact" (Acts 2:31–32). Soon he was calling all hearers to repentance, healing the lame, challenging the Sanhedrin, and suffering persecution on behalf of this testimony. What had happened? It is not just that something had happened, but that everything had changed. It is unconvincing to imagine that a falsification or mistaken perception could have elicited this change.

What caused James's change? He was one of the relatives of the Lord who had resisted him, who "did not believe in him" (John 7:5). But after the resurrection, James became a major figure among those attesting the resurrection. Paul specifically noted that "he appeared to James" at some later point after he had appeared to the five hundred (1 Cor. 15:7).

The primary evidence for the resurrection today remains: changed lives, walking testimonies, people willing to proclaim the good news the world over. "It is prodigious to think that a poor ignorant young man, of meanest birth and breeding of a most hateful nation, and hated by that nation to the death, because pretending that He was a prophet sent from God, and after this His death, only avouched to be so by twelve fishermen, pretending with loud boasts of miracles, false as God is true, to testify His Resurrection through a greater falsehood, and promising to all that would believe it nothing besides this power of working miracles but death and miseries at present, which their experience proved to be true; I say, it is prodigious to think that He and His disciples should with no other charms work such a lasting faith in all the wisest part of men, that neither time nor vice, though most concerned to do so, should ever be able to deface it" (Daniel Whitby, *Angl.*:272).

After Jesus' resurrection, many religious leaders desired to stamp out any sign of the preaching of his resurrection. But the wise rabbi Gamaliel urged caution in applying this test: "Let them go! For if their purpose or activity is of human origin, it will fail. But if it is from God, you will not be able to stop these men; you will only find yourselves fighting against God" (Acts 5:38–39). Gamaliel "all but preached the gospel" (Chrysostom, *Hom. on Acts*, 14).

The Nature of Resurrection Evidence

The most indisputable evidence for the resurrection is the continuing existence of the Christian community itself. Some hypothesis is necessary to make plausible the transformation of the disciples from grieving followers of a crucified messiah to those whose resurrection preaching changed the course of world history. That change could not have happened, according to the church's testimony, without the risen Lord. There would have been no community to remember the cross had there not been those whose lives were transformed by their actual meeting with the risen Lord (Chrysostom, *Hom. on Acts*, 1).

It is only a living Christ, thought Athanasius, who could be empowering the witness of martyrs who do not flinch from torture. The demonstration of his resurrection lies in factually embodied evidence—that of persons whose lives have been decisively changed by the One who is alive. One dead gradually ceases to influence. Christ's death increased his influence. The works of costly witness and service are not "of one dead, but of one that lives" (Athanasius, *Incarn. of the Word* 30).

Attested as a Fact

Jesus' resurrection is not considered myth or symbol in the New Testament documents but simply a fact attested by credible witnesses: "God has raised this Jesus to life, and we are all witnesses of the fact" (Acts 2:32; Cyril of Jerus., *Catech. Lect.*, 13).

The church did not receive its life from a moral teacher whose body was decomposing in the grave, but from one whose incomparable power made him known as risen Lord. The conclusion that the resurrection actually occurred as an event in history, not merely as a figment of imagination, is integral to the gospel (Chrysostom, *Hom. on Cor.* 39.3–4).

There is no evidence that the resurrection narratives were contrived and foisted upon the remembering community some months or years after Jesus' death. The resurrection testimony could not have exercised the power that it did in the lives of the apostles if it were not rooted in an actual occurrence immediately attested (Ambrose, *On His Brother Satyrus* 2.103). Its truth value for its attestors depended entirely upon its authenticity as historical occurrence.

Differences in Detail of Resurrection Reports Enrich Their Authenticity

Those who were reporting the resurrection were reporting an event for which they had no adequate language. Of such an event it is not to be expected that the reports will display absolute coherence in every detail. That seldom occurs even in a court of law where testimony is strictly controlled.

Whether there were one or two angels (Mark 16:5; Luke 24:4) or whether the resurrection appearances were all in Jerusalem (Mark) or Galilee (Luke) or in both places (Matthew and John) remains a matter of textual analysis that takes into account the sources and context of the writers.

There was no fixation upon neatly harmonizing the chronologies. This reveals the confidence of the attestors in the authenticity of the accounts. Differences of detail were due to the fact that each Evangelist was selecting from numerous testimonies, traditions, and recollections available to him. The alleged inconsistencies are due to our historical ignorance or lack of attentiveness to the texts (Augustine, *Harmony of the Gospels*).

Many witnesses were still alive at the time Paul wrote to Corinth. They were available to correct statements made about these appearances.

Witness to the Resurrection a Criterion of Apostolicity

When it became necessary to choose someone to replace Judas among the Twelve after his apostasy, the stated criterion was that he must be an eyewitness who has "been with us the whole time," "beginning from John's baptism to the time when Jesus was taken up from us. For one of these must become a witness with us of his resurrection" (Acts 1:21–22). Matthias was chosen.

On a special basis Paul was regarded as an apostle, for "Last of all, as to one untimely born, he appeared also to me" (1 Cor. 15:8). Thus Paul also was considered a witness to the resurrected Lord (Chrysostom, *Hom. on Cor.* 38.5–7).

The Willingness to Die a Premise of Testimony to the Resurrection

Witness to this event necessarily called for the witnesses' readiness to die for this truth. Lacking historical credibility, it would hardly be a truth to die for. Those willing to attest the resurrection in fact did so at the risk of their lives. This makes it more than casual testimony.

Cyril of Jerusalem wrote: "Twelve disciples were witnesses of his resurrection, and the measure of their witness is not their winning speech, but their striving for the truth of the resurrection unto torture and to death" (*Catech. Lect.* 4.12). Their witness to his resurrection made them more alive than ever, despite the risks. "Paul, this athlete of Christ, who was anointed by Christ . . . was nailed to the cross, and through him made glorious" (Augustine, *CG* 14.9).

Resurrection No Less Possible Than Creation

Is it more difficult to believe that God can create renewed life out of death than out of nothing? When compared to the miracle of creation, resurrection does not look so implausible. "If any one is in Christ, he is a new creation "(2 Cor. 5:11–15; Chrysostom, *Fourth Instruction* 12–16, ACW 31:71–72).

Both creation and resurrection are finally a matter of God speaking a word: "If you ask reason to explain this, you will never believe it. But then God will prove His divine power and majesty. Thus He did when He created heaven and earth out of nothing. He spoke only one word, and immediately they stood there. So it will be at the time of the resurrection" (Luther, *Serm. on the Death of Elector Frederick*).

Naturalistic reasoning puts up stiff resistance to the entire idea of resurrection. Understandably so, for "no article so contradicts experience as this one does. For our eyes see that all the world is swept away by death. . . . Therefore it is necessary for every Christian to have before him the testimony of the Holy Scripture concerning the resurrection" (Luther, *Serm. on John* 20:1). The textual evidence is of utmost value to the worshiping community, and not to be easily dismissed (Eusebius, *To Marinus*, 2–3).

Modesty in Evidentiary Presentation

It is too much to ask of any historical event that it be historically validated according to the analogy of laboratory experiment. Historical argument generally proceeds without the types of verification required in natural science and would be hampered by them.

The resurrection was a unique event without analogy in human experience. There was no other instance with which the witnesses could compare it. "Therefore the generalizations and rules of historical inquiry cannot, when exclusively employed, enable us either to demonstrate its reality or to overthrow its credibility" (Hall, *DT* 7:170).

This is why a general principle of modesty and toleration is fitting to this subject. There remains an element of mystery in all historical events, and not only those attesting divine revelation. Trustworthy historical inquiry does not claim omnicompetence.

It is demeaning to the resurrection narratives to treat them as if they are merely objective reporting. Hegel's admonition, though overstated, should be carefully weighed: "To consider the resurrection of Jesus as an event is to adopt the outlook of the historian, and this has nothing to do with religion. Belief or disbelief in the resurrection as a mere fact deprived of its religious interest is a matter for the intellect whose occupation (the fixation of objectivity) is just the death of religion, and to have recourse to the intellect means to abstract from religion. But, of course, the intellect seems to have a right to discuss the matter" (*OCETW*:292).

Gregory Nazianzus plunged deeper. He thought that the limits of historical argument would be inevitably met in the mystery of the empty tomb, so that God's strength would be made perfect through our weakness: "For when we leave off believing and protect ourselves by mere strength of argument, and destroy the claim which the Spirit has upon our faith by questionings, and then our argument is not strong enough for the importance of the subject (and this must necessarily be the case, since it is put in motion by an organ of so little power as is our mind), what is the result? The weakness of the argument appears to belong to the mystery" (*Orat.* 29.21). If one appeared to present an airtight case of evidence for resurrection, so that the argument appears stronger than the event it attests, then the human ability to present evidence towers over the event itself. That would detract from the mystery to which the intrinsically limited evidence seeks to point (Kierkegaard, *TC*, 2).

No Event of Jesus' Life Musters More Evidence
Than His Resurrection

No aspect of Jesus' ministry was more minutely recorded than his resurrection. Due to the pivotal importance of his resurrection, the evidence for it appears to have been assiduously collected, transmitted, and embedded in the essential proclamation of salvation attested by the earliest Christian communities. The Gospel narratives seem to be saying to us that if we cannot credit the last validating episode of his life, we are not likely to grasp anything else said about him (Augustine, *CG* 22.12–22).

The Gospels set forth the multiple layers of resurrection evidences. To refuse to consider the evidence is not only biased historical inquiry, it amounts to a fundamental philosophical decision about what is knowable. "The decision to accept Jesus as Lord cannot be made without historical evidence—yes, historical—about Jesus. If it were a decision without any historical evidence it would not be about Jesus (a historical person) but only about an ideology or an ideal" (C. F. D. Moule, *The Phenomenon of the NT*:78).

The resurrection provided evidence to the disciples that Jesus is the Christ (Tertullian, *Ag. Marcion* 5.9–10). A major reason for writing the Gospels was to summon up this evidence (John 20:31; Hilary, *Trin.*, 6.41–42) and communicate it accurately. The gospel Paul proclaimed far and wide was summarized simply as "the good news about Jesus and the resurrection" (Acts 17:19). The faithful thought that those who rejected the resurrection were thereby rejecting the whole revelation of the Son of God (Tertullian, *On the Resurrection of the Flesh*), who "enlightened our faith with proofs," (Bonaventure *Tree of Life*, *CWS*:16).

Resurrection: The Proof of Lordship

What the Resurrection Demonstrates

The resurrection was viewed in the New Testatment as evidentiary demonstration of Jesus' messianic identity. This notion of proof comes directly from Jesus himself. Jesus clearly indicated that he would rise from the dead within three days. Luke, who said that he had "carefully investigated everything from the beginning," and who reported things "just as they were handed down to us by those who from the first were eyewitnesses" (Luke 1:2–3), insisted that "After his suffering, he showed himself to these men and *gave many convincing proofs* that he was alive. (Acts 1:3, italics added; Chrysostom, *Hom. on Acts*, 1).

The disclosure of Christ's deity was to come not by rational argument alone but by historical argument of events which would stand as *tekmērion* ("infallible proofs"), "an evident sign affording positive proof." Jesus' resurrection was *the* decisive event that proved the truth already attested in Scripture (Chrysostom, *Hom. on Acts*, 1; Tho. Aq., *ST* 3, Q55.6).

The first Christian confession was the simple, straightforward acknowledgment: "Jesus is Lord." Such a statement could never have been plausibly made if it lacked the evidences for the resurrection.

That Jesus is Lord meant that he now lives, despite his death, as the living God. The Gospels were written to proclaim the kingdom of God known through the resurrection, not to satisfy the picayune or ideological interests of social history or literary criticism centuries later.

His birth and death were natural in the sense that he really was born and really died in a way familiar to ordinary human existence. Yet his conception and resurrection were preternatural (transcending empirical explanation) in the sense that he was both conceived and resurrected in a way without any analogy in ordinary human experience. There is strong congruity in both respects between the nativity and resurrection accounts. If he were indeed the unique eternal Son of the annunciation, it is only natural to expect that he would leave the world in a unique way fitting to his appearing (Gregory of Nyssa, *On the Christian Mode of Life*, FC 58:141–2).

The Earliest Testimony: 1 Corinthians 15:3–7

Suppose it could be demonstrated that we have in hand a source exceptionally close to the resurrection event itself. Would that not mute the argument that the resurrection has its source in a much later remembering church rather than an event that had just occurred on the first Easter? We do have such an account. The most primitive written source attesting the resurrection is Paul's Letter to Corinth. There are several reasons why this source is of very early date.

Paul was by his own attestation using language that had been directly passed on to him from eyewitnesses. "For what I received I passed on to you" (1 Cor. 15:3). By reliable evidence, Paul was converted about AD 33 or shortly thereafter. Hence we have an account of what the church already considered to be an established tradition only a few months after the event itself (Chrysostom, *Hom. on Cor.*, 38.2).

The fact that the early church accepted Paul's testimony as a beholder of a resurrection appearance—probably within months after the other disciples—also attests to the exceptionally early date of this tradition: "and last of all he appeared to me also, as to one abnormally born" (1 Cor. 15:8; Theodoret, *Comm. on 1 Cor.*, 266).

Ironically, the probable reason why the attestations of women were not in Paul's account of 1 Corinthians 15 is that Paul was here attempting to provide an account that would be acceptable under the specific conditions of a court of law of his time. Since women were not admitted as official witnesses in a court of law, the appearances to women were not mentioned. Paul's omission thereby indicates that he had deliberately shortened his list to provide the most officially acceptable evidence available. This does not mean that the women's testimony was questionable or that Paul had discounted it, but that it did not have sufficient standing in formal court testimony. But it did not escape the notice of the classic exegetes that it was to women that Christ appeared first (Ambrose, *Expos. Of Luke* 10.144–6). Women were "first to see and proclaim the adorable mystery of the Resurrection; thus womankind has procured absolution from ignominy, and removal of the curse" (Tho. Aq., *ST* 3, Q55.1).

Why were women, not men, the first beholders? "Because the women whose love for our Lord was more persistent," Thomas reasoned, "did not depart" after the others had withdrawn from the sepulchre—hence "were the first to see Him rising in glory" (Tho. Aq., *ST* 3 Q55.1; cf. Phoebe Palmer, *The Promise of the Father*; Elisabeth Schüssler-Fiorenza, *In Memory of Her*).

The Modern Mythographers: Rewriting the Texts to Fit with Reductive Naturalism

Is the Resurrection Merely the Rise of Faith?

If one begins by entirely eliminating the possibility of resurrection, then the worshiping community's reflection upon the revelation of God is effectively immobilized. This has in fact happened in the tradition from David Friedrich Strauss to Bultmann. Bultmann concluded that "The resurrection itself is not an event of past history." "The real Easter faith is faith in the word of preaching. If the event of Easter Day is in any sense an historical event additional to the event of the cross, it is nothing else than the rise of faith in the risen Lord (*New Testament and Mythology*, KM:42).

Tillich also specifically denied that the resurrection of Jesus had "the character of a revived (and transmuted) body"—rather it was thought to have had the character of only a diffuse "spiritual presence," not a body (*Syst. Theol.* 2:157). The only "event" he can identify is that which occurs in the minds of the disciples when they connected Jesus with the reality of the New Being, and it is that "event" that became "interpreted through the symbol 'Resurrection.'" (*Syst. Theol.* 2:157). Bultman and Tillich, under the spell of existential analysis, desperately attempting to accommodate to modern consciousness, do not take the evidence seriously; rather in fact they interdict all evidence, because they have already decided in advance that it is not credible evidence. This is why they find the New Testament so hard to read and so belabored in its interpretation.

A prevailing assumption of much modern historical interpretation is that nothing preternatural can happen or ever has. Almost anything can be alleged as a historical event except an event that alleges a divine cause. Yet the Bible constantly alleges God as causal factor in events. Hence the conflict continues between modern historicism and the Bible.

In the parable of the poor man, Lazarus, Jesus pictured him as saying to Abraham: "If someone from the dead goes to them"—those who find their righteousness in the law—"they will repent." Abraham answered: "If they do not listen to Moses and the Prophets, they will not be convinced even if someone rises from the dead" (Luke 16:30–31). Here is an anticipation that some would not be prepared to listen to any evidence of God's coming—*even the evidence of one risen from the dead!* (Jerome, *On Lazarus and Dives* 86).

The Reductionist Bias

The kind of evidentiary presentation that is so painstakingly displayed in the New Testament is peremptorily ruled out in advance on the basis of a rigid philosophical commitment to naturalistic reductionism. This preempting takes place largely in the modern university and only occasionally in the clergy—seldom in the worshiping congregation or even in the general modern populace.

If one begins by first deciding that no resurrection can ever occur and that no evidence could ever convince anyone that a resurrection had happened or ever could, then there is little sense in trying to convince such a person of this resurrection. One had best seek to show such a person that such a premise amounts to a predecided bias, a prejudgment based on philosophical grounds prior to the presentation of evidence. Much of the effort of New Testament studies of the last century has proceeded under just this bias and with this handicap. No amount of evidence for an event will persuade one who remains doggedly committed to a philosophical predisposition that has already in advance precluded the possibility of that event's occurrence.

The challenge then becomes to explain the New Testament without the resurrection or to assert reasons for a plausible belief in resurrection yet without a resurrection. For over a hundred years, this line of reasoning has been applied to the debunking of the bodily resurrection by means of alleged criticism and psychological analysis.

If one depends exclusively upon a historical method that starts with a postulate that begs the question by assuming that an alleged event cannot happen, then that method has ceased to study history and has begun to assert untested axiomatic philosophical predispositions (1 Tim. 4:1; Ambrose, *Of Christian Faith*, 2.15.133–5).

Modern skepticism approaches the resurrection narratives with a predisposition to disbelief, sometimes with absolutely fixed determination not to hear the evidence, not unlike the Athenians who first heard of the resurrection from Paul: "When they heard about the resurrection of the dead, some of them sneered" (Acts 17:32). Luther found the same response in his time: "Moreover, to this day there are many who laugh all the more at this article, consider it a fable, and do so publicly, the greater their mind and learning are" (Luther, *Bondage of the Will*).

No Historical Event Can Be Duplicated or Seen by All, Each Only Attested by Some

The natural sciences cannot, without overleaping their method, put the resurrection (or any historical event) under duplicable conditions, for history is not reduplicable. That is where history differs from science. Good natural science is aware of its own limits and does not transgress them. When the natural sciences claim that nothing can be observed or be said to exist except that which comes within empirical observation, "they venture into an extra-scientific field and indulge in an a priori dogmatism for which their specialized methods of inquiry afford no basis" (Hall, *DT* 7:166).

Jesus appeared to numerous witnesses (Acts 10:40–41). But why not to everyone, instead of some? The resurrection in this sense is more rather than less like other historical events—seen only by some (Tho. Aq., *ST* 3, Q55.1). What other historical event was ever seen by all?

Peter preached that "God raised him from the dead on the third day and caused him to be seen. He was not seen by all the people, but by witnesses whom God had already chosen—by us who ate and drank with him after he rose from the dead" (Acts 10:40–41; Severus of Antioch, *Catena on Acts* 10.42). That this event was attested only by some, not all, humanity qualifies rather than disqualifies it as a historical event, for ironically an event alleged to be seen by all could hardly have been an event in ordinary history. When the decisive event comes, it comes quietly, personally, in low key, and like ordinary events it happens in the presence of some and not others.

"The man without the Spirit does not accept the things that come from the Spirit of God, for they are foolishness to him, and he cannot understand them, because they are spiritually discerned" (1 Cor. 2:14). For the apostles, this spiritual discernment depended heavily upon accurate evidence (Chrysostom, *Hom. on Cor.*, 7.9–11).

The Believers' Participation in Christ's Resurrection

The resurrection forms the basis for the believer's hope amid death. By sharing in Christ's resurrection by faith, the believer is delivered from the power of death.

Four benefits to believers accrue from the resurrection: "For by it (1) *righteousness* is obtained for us (Rom. 4:24); (2) it is a *sure pledge* of our future immortality (1 Cor. 15); and (3) even now by its virtue we are raised to *newness of life*, that we may (4) *obey God's will* by pure and holy living (Rom. 6:4)" (Calvin, *Catech. of the Church of Geneva*, italics and numbers added; cf. Augustine, *Trin.*, *FC* 45:382–87).

Luther wrote of the believer's new life quickened with him: "I believe that He rose on the third day from the dead, to give me and to all who believe in Him a new life; and that He has thereby quickened us with Him, in grace and in the Spirit, that we may sin no more, but serve Him alone in every grace and virtue" (*Brief Explanation*, *WML* 2:370).

14

ASCENSION AND SESSION

T HE ASCENSION CANNOT BE RELEGATED to an incidental or minor
episode in Christian memory. It is recalled in all four Gospels, again in the
Acts, in Paul, First Peter, and Revelation. None of the ancient creeds or
baptismal formulae neglect the specific confession that he ascended into heaven
(ascendit in coelum; Creed of 150 Fathers; SCD 2–4, 13, 20, 54, 86, 255).

His body rose from the finite world of space, time, and matter into the heavenly
sphere to enter into the presence of the Father as intercessor for the faithful
(1 Pet. 3:18–22; Heb. 1:3; 4:14; 9:24; Rev. 12:5; 19:11)

The Ascended Lord

Having engaged in ordinary human history, he rose through the clouds to transcend
all earthly categories and historical realities (Bede, *Hom. on Gospels* 11.15). His
ascent to heaven did not imply merely a disappearance to sheer invisibility but
rather was attested as a lifting up to a lofty destination—with the Father in heaven.
Luke summarized the time frame of Jesus' earthly ministry as "the whole time the
Lord Jesus went in and out among us, beginning from John's baptism to the time
when Jesus was taken up from us" (Acts 1:21–22).

The cross completes the time of humiliation. The ascension hastens the time
of exaltation. Ascension marked a decisive transition. It showed that the period of Christ's resurrected bodily appearances had come to an end and that he
had returned exalted to the Father to intercede, establish, and consummate his
divine governance. His earthly mission is complete, his heavenly ministry begun
(Athanasius, *Incarn. of the Word* 26–30; J. G. Davies, *He Ascended into Heaven*).

The Promise of the Father

Jesus asked his disciples not to leave Jerusalem but to "wait for the gift my Father
promised, which you have heard me speak about. For John baptized with water,

but in a few days you will be baptized with the Holy Spirit" (Acts 1:4–5; Hilary, *Trin.* 8.30).

During the forty-day interval between the first Easter and the ascension (Acts 1:3) the disciples were gradually weaned away from dependence upon his visible presence and prepared for his exaltation to the Father by ascension. During this interval "he continued to teach them the mysteries of the kingdom of God" (*Russian Catech.*, *COC* 2:479; Ursinus, *CHC*:244). He "opened to them all things which were about to happen," to ready them for yet unfolding history (Lactantius, *Div. Inst.* 4.21).

At their last meeting the disciples asked him, " 'Lord, are you at this time going to restore the kingdom to Israel?' He said to them: 'It is not for you to know the times or dates the Father has set by his own authority. But you will receive power when the Holy Spirit comes on you'" (Acts 1:6–8; Ephrem, *Comm. on Tatian's Diatesseron,* Acts 1.7).

The Son Must Be Lifted Up

His ascent to heaven had been foreshadowed in his resurrection appearance to Mary Magdelene at the garden tomb when he said: "Do not hold on to me, for I have not yet returned to the Father. Go instead to my brothers and tell them, 'I am returning to my Father and your Father, to my God and your God'" (John 20:17; Theodore of Mopsuestia, *Comm. on John* 7.20.17). "After he had destroyed his enemies through his passion, the Lord, who is mighty in battle and strong, required a purification that could be given to him by his Father alone. And this is why he forbids Mary to touch him" (Origen, *Comm. on John* 6.287).

The earliest written testimony to the ascension is found in Paul, for whom the ascension implied the filling of the whole universe with the reconciling love of God: "He who descended is the very one who ascended higher than all the heavens, in order to fill the whole universe" (Eph. 4:10; cf. Eph. 1:20; Rom. 10:6–7; Jerome, *Epis. to Eph.* 2.4.10). The earliest Christian kerygma received by Paul taught that he became "obedient to the point of death, even death on a cross. Therefore God has highly exalted him" (Phil. 2:8,9).

Similar echoes of the earliest preaching are also found in John: "No one has ever gone into heaven except the one who came from heaven—the Son of Man. Just as Moses lifted up the snake in the desert, so *the Son of Man must be lifted up,* that everyone who believes in him may have eternal life" (John 3:13, italics added; John 6:62; Hilary, *Trin.* 10.54). In Mark's account the ascension is not explicitly narrated but foretold in the saying that the Son of Man will sit "at the right hand of the Mighty One" (Mark 14:62).

Luke's account of the ascension is succinct: "When he had led them out to the vicinity of Bethany, he lifted up his hands and blessed them. While he was blessing them, he left them and was taken up into heaven. Then they worshiped him and returned to Jerusalem with great joy. And they stayed continually at the temple, praising God" (Luke 24:50–53; Bede, *Hom. on Gospels* 11.15). "Christ is no sooner crucified than he begins to be worshiped" (Cyril of Jerusalem, *Catech. Lect.* 4.12).

"It was the Son of Man who was exalted from lowliness. This exaltation occurred when he had glorified God in his death" (Origen, *Comm. on John* 32.25). "The text says *he humbled himself* with reference to the assumption of the flesh. So too it says *he exalted him* with reference to the flesh" (Athanasius *Ag. Arians* 1.41). In the incarnation and ascension "the Word did not depart from the Father. He both came to us, and did not forsake the Father. . . . What was lifted up into heaven, if not what had been taken from earth?" (Augustine, *Sermon* 242.6).

The Same Body

The body that rose and ascended is not a different body than was crucified and rose: "On the third day he arose from the dead, with the same body in which he suffered, with which also he ascended into heaven, and there sitteth" (Westminster Confession 8). He ascended to the seat of heaven, the session of the judge, the throne of God, to be seated at the right hand of the Father in the flesh (Innocent III, *SCD* 422; see also *SCD* 73, 462, 709), being lifted up "on the fortieth day after the resurrection with the flesh in which He arose and with His soul ascended" (Council of Lyons, *SCD* 462; see also *SCD* 344, 429, 709).

Luke's account of the ascension portrays the Son returning to God, taking into God's presence the evidence of atonement—his own body! He ascended "so that, seated at the right hand of Majesty, he might show to the glorious face of his Father the scars of the wounds which he suffered for us" (Bonaventure, *Tree of Life*, *CWS*:162).

It could not be an ephemeral pseudo-body that Jesus took into the presence of God as evidence of atonement: "He suffered a true passion in the flesh, died His own true bodily death, rose again by a true resurrection of His flesh and the true resumption of His body by His soul. He ate and drank in His risen flesh, and then ascended to heaven and is seated at the right hand of the Father. In the same flesh He will come to judge the living and the dead" (Innocent III, *CF*:175; Tho. Aq., *ST* 3, Q59). He remained truly human in his ascension (Gregory Nazianzus, *On Pentecost*).

His ascended body was fitting to his theandric nature: "He ascended, not leaving behind on the earth as a useless piece of clothing His human nature; but carrying it inseparable from Himself and incorruptible and endowed with such nobility as was to be expected from human nature united with the divine one" (*Gk. Orthodox Catech.* 39). The Son who is worshipped with the Father and Spirit is at once truly human and truly God in his ascended body: "His flesh is not adorable, in so far as it is created. When, however, it has been united with God the Word, it is adorable" (John of Damascus, *OF* 4.3). Christian worship does not adore the flesh of Christ as if separable from his theandric identity.

The Benefits of Christ's Ascension

The event of ascension has decisive ethical and behavioral consequences. Those who are raised with Christ are instructed to "set your hearts on things above, where Christ is seated at the right hand of God" (Col. 3:1).

The way to the ascension of the faithful is revealed by Christ's ascension. The way is made by his going to prepare a place for us (John 14:2; Cyril of Alex., *Comm. on John* 9). "I believe that He ascended," Luther wrote. "Therefore, He can help me and all believers in all our necessities against all our adversaries and enemies" (*Brief Explanation*, *WML* 2:371).

The *Heidelberg Catechism* emphasizes the benefits received from Christ's ascension: "First, that he is our Advocate in the presence of his Father in heaven. Second, that we have our flesh in heaven as a sure pledge that he, as the Head, will also take us, his members, up to himself. Third, that he sends us his Spirit as a counterpledge by whose power we seek what is above, where Christ is, sitting at the right hand of God, and not things that are on earth" (Q 49; cf. Pearson, *EC* 1:459).

By ascending, he did not abandon his disciples (Leo I, *Serm.* 74), but rather increased their faith in that which is unseen and gave them hope of following him. Thus the withdrawal of his bodily presence "was more profitable for us than His bodily presence would have been" (Tho. Aq., *ST* 3, Q57.1). "For at his departure He had endowed them with power and strength" (Lactantius, *Div. Inst.* 4.21). "Christ left us in such a way that his presence might be more useful to us." In ascending he did not "cease to be present with believers still on their earthly pilgrimage, but to rule heaven and earth with a more immediate power" (Calvin, *Inst.* 2.16.13). "Do not think that because He is absent in the flesh He is therefore absent in the spirit; He is here in the midst of us, listening to what is said of Him, seeing our thoughts, searching our hearts and souls; He is ready even now to present all of you, as you come forward for Baptism in the Holy Spirit, to the Father" (Cyril of Jerusalem, *Catech. Lect.* 14).

In the ascension our common humanity is honored incomparably. In witnessing the ascension, the disciples "were not only afflicted with sadness but also were filled with 'great joy' when the Lord went into the heights of heaven. It was certainly a great and indescribable source of joy when, in the sight of the heavenly multitudes, the nature of our human race ascended over the dignity of all heavenly creatures. It passed the angelic orders and was raised beyond the heights of archangels. In its ascension, our human race did not stop at another height until the same nature was received at the seat of the eternal Father. Our human nature, united with the divinity of the Son, was on the throne of his glory. The ascension of Christ is our elevation" (Leo I, *Sermon* 73.3–4).

To Heaven

The ascension begins in the thick of human history and ends in the abode of blessed spirits (John 14:2). It begins in time-space reality and ends in eternity. It begins in the presence of the disciples and ends in the presence of the Father. The scene shifts from earth to heaven (Cyril of Alex., *Comm. on John* 9).

The key destination image is that of the throne of God (Isa. 66:1). Heaven receives the risen Lord as a kingdom would receive a beloved Son returning from a long and hazardous journey. The return of the Lord is to the Father's house (John 14:2), the celestial city (Heb. 12:22), the transcendent Jerusalem (Gal. 4:26), the abode of angels (Matt. 6:9–10), the place not made with hands (Heb. 9:24), paradise (Luke 23:43).

Heaven is the abode of God. It exists beyond space and time. The ascended Lord has gone to prepare a place for believers (John 14:2). Augustine advised that "it is sheer curiosity and a waste of time to inquire as to the 'where' and 'how' of the Lord's body in heaven; we have only to believe" (*Faith and the Creed* 6.13). Peter's earliest known preaching stated: "He must remain in heaven until the time comes for God to restore everything, as he promised long ago through his holy prophets" (Acts 3:20–21; Origen, *Ag. Celsus*, 8.22). Now it is sufficient to know that "God has highly exalted him" (Phil. 2:9).

Skeptics have imagined for decades that they have entirely done away with all "three-storey worlds" and "above" and "below" language by consigning such language to outdated mythology. Yet it is doubtful that the language of descent and ascent in the New Testament ever really intended such a flat, non-metaphorical, literal three-story picture, even in the first century, either for descent into the nether world or ascent to heaven (see Augustine, "Is There an 'Above' and a 'Below' in the Universe?" *EDQ*, 29). In the most important text of Christ's abasement, his cry from the cross, there is no literal thought of directionality. The cry comes from "out of the depths" and is addressed to the Father who transcends all finite points in time and space. The heavens into which Christ ascended are not to be thought of as existing within time-space categories as a palpable temporal place, but as the ethereal sphere in which the

God of glory is eternally manifested (Augustine, *Trin.*, *FC* 45:23–24, 438–46). Paul was not pointing in a specific direction when he preached that God had "raised him from the dead and seated him at his right hand in the heavenly realms, far above all rule and authority, power and dominion, and every title that can be given, not only in the present age but also in the one to come. And God placed all things under his feet and appointed him to be head over everything for the church, which is his body, the fullness of him who fills everything in every way" (Eph. 1:20–23).

Ascent of the Son, Descent of the Spirit

He withdrew visibly in order that he might send the Holy Spirit (John 16:7). The sending of the Spirit could not be fully manifested until the Son had ascended, for in the triune economy, Pentecost would not come until after ascension (Tho. Aq., *ST* 3, Q57.6).

"I am going to him who sent me" (John 16:5) in order to intercede with the Father on behalf of sinners. "'Where I am going you cannot follow me now, but later on.' This was undoubtedly because they were not yet able to understand, not yet able to imitate the mystery of his passion and death. Yet they truly recognized the majesty of his ascension as soon as they saw it" (Bede, *Hom. on Gospels* 2.11)

"When he ascended up to heaven, they questioned him not in words but followed with their eyes . . . Their human affections were saddened by the loss of their visible object. But he knew that it would be for their good because that inward sight that the Holy Spirit would use to console them was the better sight" (Augustine, *Tractates on John* 94.3–4).

Jesus made it clear that the Spirit would be given only when he was glorified (John 7:39). Logically, it was fitting that his sacrifice be presented to the Father before the Spirit was sent forth to empower the mission. Before his departure, Jesus had stated: "It is for your good that I am going away. Unless I go away, the Counselor will not come to you; but if I go, I will send him to you" (John 16:7). "It was necessary therefore that the form of the servant should be removed from their eyes" (Augustine, *Trin.* 1.9).

This is why the descent of the Spirit is located in right order at this point in the story of salvation. Following the incarnation the sequence is the ministry of Jesus *on earth*, then after the resurrection the ascent *in heaven*, the session at the right hand of God in heaven, including Christ's intercession and cosmic reign, looking toward his coming again (Gaudentius, *Sermons* 14; Baxter, *PW* 19:81–83). The biblical narrative dictates the logic of this way of unfolding conceptually the order of salvation, and this has been a consistent order for two thousand years. To reverse it in any way would be to do violence to the text.

The Spirit's Descent Prophesied and Fulfilled

The psalmist had anticipated the gift of the Spirit following a victorious ascension of the Savior: "When you ascended on high, you led captives in your train; you received gifts from men, even from the rebellious—that you, O Lord God, might dwell there" (Ps. 68:18). It is this psalm to which the Ephesian letter refers in its interpretation of the ascension: "When he ascended on high, he led captives in his train and gave gifts to men" (Eph. 4:8; Jerome, *Epis. to Eph.* 2.4.8).

Luke's account of the descent of the Spirit is dramatic: "When the day of Pentecost came, they were all together in one place. Suddenly a sound like the blowing of a violent wind came from heaven and filled the whole house where they were sitting. They saw what seemed to be tongues of fire that separated and came to rest on each of them. All of them were filled with the Holy Spirit and began to speak in other tongues as the Spirit enabled them" (Acts 2:1–4). After the Resurrection, with the sending of the Holy Spirit, the gift of tongues was granted—"that they may serve the Lord with one accord" (Cyril of Jerusalem, *Catech. Lect.* 13; Zeph. 3:10).

Peter interpreted Pentecost in this way: "God has raised this Jesus to life, and we are all witnesses of the fact. Exalted to the right hand of God, he has received from the Father the promised Holy Spirit and has poured out what you now see and hear" (Acts 2:32–33). The gift of the Holy Spirit at Pentecost confirmed the truth of the ascension and began the new era of the Spirit.

"A Gentile *mission* seems to have arisen for the first time as a result of the conviction that the resurrected Jesus had now already been exalted to Lordship in heaven and consequently the news of his Lordship is to be carried to all nations" (Pannenberg, *JGM*:71). The mission, however, did not arise from human conviction, but from the resurrection event that called forth that conviction.

Seated at the Right Hand of the Father

He sits at the right hand of the Father (*sedet ad desteram Patrus*; Creed of 150 Fathers). To sit on the right hand of the Father means to participate fully in God's majesty imparted through the exaltation (Matt. 24:30; 25:31; Luke 22:69; Heb. 1:3; Augustine, *On the Creed* 11). Christ governs in the kingdom of power, grace, and glory, reigns eternally, has dominion over all things (Calvin, *Catech. of the Church of Geneva*; Ursinus, *CHC*:254–57).

The Name Above Every Name

Sitting is a judicial metaphor, for "it is the judge's place to sit" (Gregory I, *Hom. 29 on the Ascension*). "Sitting denotes either abiding, or royal or judiciary dignity. Hence, to sit on the right hand of the Father is nothing else than to share in the glory of the Godhead with the Father, and to possess beatitude and judiciary power" (Tho. Aq., *ST* 3, Q58.2).

It is this glory of which Jesus prayed when he said: 'And now, Father, glorify me in your presence with the glory I had with you before the world began" (John 17:5). It is of this power that Peter preached when he said: "God has made this Jesus, whom you crucified, both Lord and Christ" (Acts 2:36). This is the vision that comforted Stephen in his death—he saw the Son of Man on the right hand of God (Acts 7:56; Calvin, *Inst.* 2.16.15).

"We do not hold that the right hand of the Father is an actual place. For how could He that is uncircumscribed have a right hand limited by place?" (John of Damascus, *OF* 4.2). Neither "right hand" nor "sit" is reduced to a literal spatial act in ecumenical teaching. Rather it is taken by common sense as a metaphor (John of Damascus, *OF* 4.2). "Your arm is endued with power, your hand is strong, your right hand exalted" (Ps. 89:13). "Your right hand, O Lord, was majestic in power. Your right hand, O Lord, shattered the enemy" (Exod. 15:6). "The expression 'at the right hand' must therefore be understood in this sense: to exist in a state of perfect blessedness, where there is justice and peace and joy" (Augustine, *Faith and the Creed* 7.14; Tho. Aq., *ST* 3, Q58.2).

Jesus is given that name above every name, that at his name every knee should bow and every tongue confess that he is Lord (Phil. 2:6–11). "In heaven Christ gloriously fulfills his intended offices of prophet, priest, and king (Calvin, *Inst.* 2.16.15).

Why the Heavenly Intercession?

The principal feature of the heavenly session of Christ is that he enters into an intercessory ministry for humanity in the presence of the Father, pleading humanity's case before the Father (Hilary, *Hom. on Psalms* 53:4). In him "we have one who speaks to the Father in our defense" (1 John 2:1).

His intercession with the Father must be made by one who was tempted yet without sin, who suffered for sinners. Only one who has known empathically what it means to suffer in the world can make this intercession rightly (Heb. 2:14–16). The intercession occurs in heaven (Heb. 6:13–20) as "a hope that enters into the inner shrine behind the curtain" (Heb. 6:19; Theodoret, *Interp. of Heb.* 6).

Christ intercedes for the penitent faithful on earth, and continues forever (Heb. 9:11–28) transcending time. "When this priest had offered for all time one sacrifice for sins, he sat down at the right hand of God. Since that time he waits for his enemies to be made his footstool, because by one sacrifice he has made perfect forever those who are being made holy" (Heb. 10:12–14). "The work of mediation between God and man depended on the entrance into heaven of the mediator, as the intercessory nature of the Jewish high priest depended on his gaining access to the holy of holies" (Guthrie, *NTT*:399).

The faithful take comfort in this eternal access to the Father, that their prayers may be heard, that they will be kept from evil (John 17:15), knowing that Christ's sacrifice is sufficient (Heb. 9:23–24), and that where Christ is they may be also so that they too may behold God's glory (John 17:24). We are commanded and permitted to offer our prayers in his name (John 14:13, 14). The essential pattern of Christ's intercessory ministry is already anticipated in the high-priestly prayer of John 17 (Augustine, *Tractates on John* 111.2; Pearson, *EC* 1:451). Jesus prayed that the faithful "may be with me where I am" (John 17:24; Cyril of Alex., *Comm. on John* 11.12).

Christ's teaching office continues through the contemporary body of Christ, the church, whom he promised to be with "always, to the very end of the age" (Matt. 28:20), to whom the deposit of faith is entrusted (Jerome, *Comm. on Matt.* 4.28.18–20). Armed with the apostles' teaching, the church is being prepared for unexpected challenges yet to unfold. No error is completely novel or surprising to those thoroughly instructed by the apostolic witness and ecumenical teaching. No distortion is so great that it cannot be corrected "with antidotes from her spiritual pharmacopoeia" (Pohle-Preuss, *DT* 5:148).

How the Order of Salvation Summarizes the Gospel Narrative

The story of salvation has many twists and turns, but the heart of the story line is concisely stated by the great Lutheran teacher, Chemnitz: "For in incarnation there occurred a personal union of the Godhead of the Logos with assumed humanity, in which the whole fullness of the Godhead dwelt personally from the first moment of conception. But by reason of self-renunciation, its employment and manifestation were for a time postponed, and, as it were, suspended, so that it did not exercise itself through the assumed humanity immediately and always. Moreover, by the ascension, infirmities being laid aside and self-renunciation removed, He left the mode of life according to the conditions of this world, and departed from the world. Moreover, by sitting at the Right Hand of God, He entered upon the full and public employment and display of the power, virtue, and glory of the Godhead" (*TNC*, 32; cf. Pearson, *EC* 1:463–66). If any part of this gospel narrative is mislaid, its full power is not felt.

Calvin suitably summarized the work of Christ in heavenly session with the Father: "He therefore sits on high, transfusing us with his power, that he may quicken us to spiritual life, sanctify us by his Spirit, adorn his church with diverse gifts of his grace, keep it safe from all harm by his protection, restrain the raging enemies of his cross and of our salvation by the strength of his hand, and finally hold all power in heaven and on earth" (*Inst.* 2.16.16). Thus the work of Christ does not end on the cross, but the benefits gained on the cross are advocated in heaven.

Christ the King

Although legitimate authority was pretemporally given to the Son, he did not exercise that authority directly during his humiliation but awaited its proper reception at the conclusion of his earthly ministry.

His Death the Premise of His Kingship

The rightful authority of Christ is based on his sacrificial death. This kingship is assigned to Christ by virtue of his sacrifice.

The Lordship of Christ is his rightful governance over the future fulfillment and application of the redemption made possible through his suffering (Creed of Epiphanius, *SCD* 13).

Christ entered into messianic kingship through the unexpected route of suffering, cross, death, and burial. The risen Lord taught his disciples on the Emmaus road: "Did not the Christ have to suffer these things and then enter his glory?" (Luke 24:26). It was only through his Passion and death that he entered into the exercise of all power in heaven and earth (Matt. 28:18).

Legitimate governance was conferred in his resurrection and ascension. Upon this basis he sent forth his apostles to declare the emergent reign of God and call all to enter it freely. "For Christ did not enter a man-made sanctuary that was only a copy of the true one; he entered heaven itself, now to appear for us in God's presence" (Heb. 9:24). In this way Christ's spiritual kingship came closely bound with his priestly task (Chrysostom, *Epis. to Heb.* 16.8–17.5).

In the spiritual community he brought forth, Christ does what governors and rulers do: He governs and defends. The Latin terms are *gubernatio*—"governance, rulership, guidance," and *defensio*—"protecting, guarding from harm." This governance occurs without coercion, for he rules by his Word and guards by his Spirit. Through this guiding and guarding activity, Christ orders, directs, and preserves the church (Lactantius, *Div. Inst.*, FC 49:298–300; Bucer, *De Regno Christi*, LCC 19:177). "Such is the nature of his rule, that he shares with us all that he has received from the Father. Now he arms and equips us with his power, adorns us with his beauty and magnificence, enriches us with his wealth" (Calvin, *Inst.* 2.15.4).

Exalted Lord as King

While his prophetic and priestly offices were expressions of his descent to engage in the humble work of serving, his ruling office was precisely to be exalted and glorified in resurrection, ascension, and session (Gregory Nazianzus, *Orat.* 30). The office of governance requires infinite wisdom and care in the right use of power in the ordering, judging, legislating, and guiding of the community of faith.

A king is a sovereign invested with supreme authority, "that he may rule over a certain people, according to just laws, that he may have power to reward the good and punish the evil, and that he may defend his subjects" (Baxter, *PW* 2:207–209). "The King of Kings is Christ, who was immediately ordained of God, that he might govern, by his word and Spirit, the church which he purchased with his own blood, and defend her against all her enemies" (Ursinus, *CHC*:176).

"His Prophetic Offices lasted for three years; for during three years our Lord traveled throughout Palestine teaching His unique truths like the Prophets of old. His Priestly Office lasted during the three days of His Passion, when He offered Himself as a victim for the redemption of the world. But His Royal Office does not know eclipse, and will continue forever and ever" (*Gk. Orthodox Catech.* 39).

His Kingdom Not of This World

His kingdom is not like kingdoms that are ruled by force (Augustine, *CG, FC* 24:63–66). This kingdom is governed by the Spirit, by self-giving love (Calvin, *Inst.* 2.15.3–4).

The kingdom of God is therefore hidden within us and does not come by force or external observation or power (Luke 17:20–21). It consists in "righteousness, peace, and joy in the Holy Spirit" (Rom. 14:17), gifts conferred by his governance (Calvin, *Inst.* 2.14.4). The kingdom is present now by faith (Clement of Alex., *Comm. on Luke*, Hom. 117).

In the presence of Pilate he said: "My kingdom is not of this world. If it were, my servants would fight to prevent my arrest by the Jews. But now my kingdom is from another place" (John 18:36). Pilate, confused, retorted: "You are a king, then!" Jesus: "You are right in saying I am a king. In fact, for this reason I was born, and for this I came into the world, to testify to the truth" (John 18:37). This decisive exchange established four key points of Christian teaching: He is indeed a king. He is not a worldly king. His kingdom is spiritual. His mission was to attest that coming, spiritual kingdom (Eusebius, *To Stephanus* 15.4; Augustine, *Tractates on John* 115.3–4).

The Mediator never staked out a claim for economic advantage. He lived in such abject poverty that he had "no place to lay his head" (Luke 9:58). He did not disavow the right to acquire possessions, and in fact he possessed such simple things as his own sandals and clothing. But his intent was never to gain worldly power or temporal ascendancy.

This kingdom "is not divided by the number of those who reign; nor lessened by being shared, nor disturbed by its magnitude, nor disordered by its inequality of ranks, nor circumscribed by space, nor changed by motion, nor measured by time" (Bonaventure, *Tree of Life*, CWS:169). Being a spiritual kingdom, this kingdom does not decay as do earthly kingdoms.

Jesus' Distinctive Embodiment of the Royal Office

Jesus began his public ministry by proclaiming the reign of God at hand. Yet it was not until the very end of his ministry in the events surrounding his death that he received that kingdom and undertook its governance.

Through his death he redeemed humanity from bondage to sin. As he approached the cross, he prepared himself for the struggle toward the promised victory: "Now is the time for judgment on this world; now the prince of this world will be driven out" (John 12:31; Theodore of Mopsuestia, *Comm. on John, Fragment* 109.12.31). It was indeed by spiritual force that the demonic powers had to be cast out (Mark 3:27). This occurred ironically by their own force being spent on the death of the Son (Gregory of Nyssa, *ARI* 20–24).

His resurrection and ascension signaled to the disciples that the reign of God had begun and that Jesus had decisively received the hidden kingdom now being openly revealed. The messianic kingship established through his exaltation is an eternal kingdom that will endure forever (Heb. 10:12). Yet this kingship will pass through a series of phases before its consummation.

His ascension and session points to his formal possession of his royal throne and authority. As judge he will reappear in the final days to judge the living and the dead. The faithful expect "the appearing of our Lord Jesus Christ, which God will bring about in his own time—God, the blessed and only Ruler, and King of kings and Lord of lords" (1 Tim. 6:14–15; Augustine, *Trin.*, *FC* 45:38–49).

The Kingdom of Power, Grace, and Glory

His dominion is called the kingdom of power in reference to the world, the kingdom of grace in reference to the church, and the kingdom of glory in reference to the future life. This sequence is useful in showing that the governance of Christ pertains to the whole of history: to the past and present world, the present church, and the future of history (Schmid, *DT*:370–72).

The kingdom of power exists amid the dying world in which Christ reigns quietly amid and beyond human cultures and dominions. The kingdom of grace in history is representatively present in the covenant faithful. The kingdom of glory is by anticipation present in history and fully imparted beyond history.

The Kingdom of Power

The kingdom of power is that sovereignty through which Christ exercises sustaining governance over the world, disposes all things in heaven and earth, for the preservation, calling, and salvation of his people. All things are sustained by the word of his power. His dominion extends over all (Pss. 2:9; 8:6; 110:2; 1 Cor. 15:25–27; Eph. 1:20–21; Heb. 2:8).

The coming Christ already has jurisdiction over the world's future destiny. The providential governance of the world is in Christ's hands, all things being inconspicuously ordered for the guidance and protection of the emerging new humanity which Christ is calling and gathering. God rules over the demonic powers whose exercise of evil power is permitted only for a time (Origen, *OFP*, 242–50).

In the letter to the Ephesians, the Apostle gives thanks for the new relation with the passing world that is made known in the resurrection and ascension. When Christ was raised from the dead, God seated him at his right hand in the heavenly places, "far above all rule and power and dominion, and above every name that is named, not only in this age but also in the one to come. And he put all things under his feet" (Eph. 1:20–22a). "Truly this is an awesome reality—that the whole of creation should finally bow before a man in whom God the Word dwells" (Chrysostom, *Hom. on Eph.* 3.1.22).

It is Christ's death for all that confirms his right to rule over all. Only one who dies for all has a right to rule over all. Only God the Son could die efficaciously for all (Athanasius, *Four Discourses Ag. Arians* 2.14).

The Kingdom of Grace

The kingdom of grace is that sovereignty through which the Son bestows spiritual blessings in this life through word and sacrament. He awakens, calls, empowers, and preserves the church.

The subjects of the dominion of grace are believers united to Christ through word and sacrament. The dominion of grace is the church, which Christ enables, furnishes, equips with gifts requisite to mission, and defends against ever-incipient temptation and apostasy (Matt. 25:34; 28:20; John 3:5; 17:17, 24; Titus 3:5).

The realm in which this kingdom is present is the inner life in the Spirit. It is not a physical or economic sphere subject to empirical identification or material measurement. "For the kingdom of God is not a matter of eating and drinking, but of righteousness, peace and joy in the Holy Spirit" (Rom. 14:17). It is ruled by the Spirit under the new covenant in which God has promised: "I will put my laws in their minds and write them on their hearts" (Heb. 8:1; cf. Jer. 31:33).

The kingdom of grace is governed by preaching the gospel, teaching the covenant community the truth, continuing the restraint of sin by law, providing what is necessary for salvation, pardoning the penitent, justifying by grace, converting through repentance and faith, and sanctifying through the Spirit.

The kingdom of grace is simultaneously a kingdom *of heaven* (because Christ intercedes in heaven) and a kingdom already being received here *on earth* (because Christ enables citizens of this kingdom to enjoy the fruits of his guidance and protection already in present history). Jesus taught his disciples to pray: "Your kingdom come, your will be done on earth as it is in heaven" (Matt. 6:10; Chrysostom, *Hom. on Matt.* 19). And yet the kingdom is not to be simply equated with the visible church, which within history remains plagued by weeds among the wheat, and blemished by tainted admixtures.

Christ's kingly rule is manifested among those who live in union with him, though the church in history includes both wheat and thorns (Matt. 13:25–40). The kingdom is already begun, yet awaiting its consummation; in time, yet eternal. Citizens of this kingdom exist paradoxically in two cities, the world and the church, earth and heaven, present conflicts of power and future righteousness (Augustine, *CG* 15.1–9).

"The immeasurable greatness of his power" is being manifested already *"in us who believe,* according to the working of his great might which he accomplished in Christ when he raised him from the dead and made him sit at his right hand" (Eph. 1:19–21, italics added; Jerome, *Epis. To Eph.* 1.1.21).

The Kingdom of Glory

In eternity, the kingdom of Christ is changed from glory to glory, from grace within history to completion beyond history, in a kingdom of peace and righteousness without end (Luke 1:33). "But each in its own turn: Christ, the firstfruits; then, when he comes, those who belong to him. Then the end will come, when he hands over the kingdom to God the Father after he has destroyed all dominion, authority and power" (1 Cor. 15:23–24).

The *kingdom of glory* is that future fulfillment of the messianic mission through which the wrongs of history will be righted. It is portrayed as a blessed governance by the exalted Savior of the faithful in eternity. "Father, I want those you have given me to be with me where I am, and to see my glory, the glory you have given me because you loved me before the creation of the world" (John 17:24).

A creative form of recycling and demolition accompanies the completion of history, namely, the destruction of all obstacles to the reign of grace and righteousness. The church is being made holy, cleansed "by the washing of water through the word," that it might be presented "to himself as a radiant church, without stain or wrinkle, or any other blemish, but holy and blameless," in the same way that husbands and wives may love each other purely and without defilement by other loves (Eph. 5:25–29).

Christ's governance extends to the church in particular and to the world in general, and all that is preserved through grace until the consummation of history. Within history Christ's kingdom is in but not of the world, hidden in a world sustained by divine providence. "In putting everything under him, God left nothing that is not subject to him. Yet at present we do not see everything subject to him. But we see Jesus" (Heb. 2:8–9; Severian of Gabala, *Fragm. On Heb.* 2.5–9).

Even amid this present distorted world, Jesus Christ is Lord and King, and even when we cannot see his kingdom reigning, we can still behold his glory and participate in the promise of his kingdom, quietly growing like a tiny mustard seed or yeast in bread.

Evil is permitted, but only for a time. Even during this limited time, it is curbed and restrained by grace. Evil will finally be overcome in the last days. Meanwhile, "We know that in everything God works for good with those who love him, who are called according to his purpose" (Rom. 8:28). "If someone asks for something which will not contribute to his good, he will not get it, because it is not good for him to get it" (Theodoret, *Interp. of Rom.* 8.28)

The Expectation of Christ's Return

With the coming of the Son thoroughly attested, his Second Coming is expected. The present age begins with the ascension and ends with the Parousia ("return, coming again"). This present age is the age of the risen and ascended Lord, awaiting the returning Lord. It is an article of baptismal faith that he shall come again (Creed of 150 Fathers).

Luke's account deliberately connected Christ's ascension with Christ's return: "This same Jesus, who has been taken from you into heaven, will come back in the same way you have seen him go into heaven" (Acts 1:9–11). Similarly John: "If I go and prepare a place for you, I will come back and take you to be with me that you also may be where I am" (John 14:3).

The reign will continue until all enemies are overcome, including sin, guilt, and death (1 Cor. 15:20–28; Rom. 8:9–11). Finally it shall be said that: "The kingdom of the world has become the kingdom of our Lord and of his Christ, and he will reign for ever and ever" (Rev. 11:15).

Bede summed up the hope of his future return: "He will come to judge in the same form and substance of a body in which he had come to be judged [by Pilate]. To him God truly gave, and did not take away, an immortal nature. His eternal and divine glory which once was manifested to three of his disciples on a mountain, will be seen by all the saints" (*Comm. on Acts* 1.11).

Cyril ended his *Catechetical Lecture* on the exalted Lord with this prayer: "May [God] raise you up together with Him from your dead sins to His heavenly gift, and deem you worthy to 'be caught up in clouds to meet the Lord in the air,' in His good time; and until that time of His glorious second coming arrives, may He write all your names in the book of the living, and after writing them, never blot them out" (Lecture 14).

The messianic reign of the promised Davidic heir had thereby begun. The blessings of the messianic age were already beginning to be experienced. They await a future consummation in the return of the messianic king. The New Testament ends on a note of expectancy with Christ's own benediction and promise: "'Yes, I am coming soon.' Amen. Come, Lord Jesus" (Rev. 22:20–21).

This concludes the basic review of classic consensual Christian teaching on major points of doctrine concerning Jesus Christ the Son of God.

A Modest Proposal for Christological Reform

Conscience constrains me to make a humble and direct appeal to academic colleagues who seek to teach truthfully about Jesus Christ. What follows is especially directed to those who approach the study of Jesus from a historical perspective. Permit me to make this challenge on behalf of the integrity of historical inquiry.

The Theandric Person as History

Historical inquiry into Jesus has not yet rigorously begun in our time. It will not begin until the premise of theandric union—truly God, truly human—is entertained as a serious hypothesis by historians.

The incarnate Son is always greater than our methods of investigating him. The living Lord breaks through the very historical limitations to which he voluntarily submitted. This is why historical inquiry is always to some degree puzzled by Jesus, for he is intrinsically puzzling to reductionist inquiry.

The notion that novelty is proof of error—so prevalent in early Christianity—has been reversed in modern times by the conviction that novelty is proof of truth. This is often linked with the judgment that all premodern reflection is prone to error precisely because of its antiquity.

The Value of Historical Method

The study of Jesus cannot rightly proceed without historical inquiry, since he lived in history. Nowhere is the case better stated than by Francis Hall: "The historical method is indispensable for adequate study of our Lord's human life, and the remedy for its misuse is its abundant proper use" (*DT* 6:316; cf. Baxter, *PW* 13:408–14).

Christian teaching has at times been tardy in grasping the decisive importance of careful, honest historical inquiry. This may be because these methods were developed out of an ethos of rationalist polemic against orthodoxy, and indeed much of the result has been cynical and destructive. Yet however distorted in practice by reductive philosophical predispositions, the historical method itself is of great value in the study of Jesus Christ. Hence it is unwise to reject prematurely historical method in defense of faith, even where historical method has been grossly abused. Historical method has an enduring role in the inquiry into Jesus.

Historical method must be better protected from abuse and extended to include forms of inquiry able to take seriously the assumptions of classic Christian teaching. The postcritical study of Christ need not imply a disavowal of historical critical study. It commends a form of historical inquiry that transcends fatuous secularizations and naturalisms—one that listens to all, not selected bits of filtered evidence.

Faith and History

The deepest faith does not impatiently try to turn historical scholarship into piety. Yet there is no need for piety to be overwhelmed or intimidated by the pretenses of modern historical research, whose methods have often been counter-productive, imperialistic, and distorted by unexamined philosophical predispositions.

One who is tone deaf cannot be a music critic. An adequate account of Jesus is not likely to be given by one who begins by assuming that God cannot become flesh or save humanity from sin.

Accurate historical inquiry is presupposed in the study of holy writ. Historical inquiry seeks to state straightforwardly what transpired and what was said in what context with what nuances of meaning. There is need for humility about the tendency of criticism to exaggerate its own competencies (F. Hahn, "Probleme historischer Kritik," *Zeitschrift für die Neutestamentliche Wissenschaft* 63:1–17).

The history of Jesus is the point of constant reference for the Christian teaching of salvation, for Christianity is not merely about the *idea* of deliverance, but of *a person* through whom this deliverance appears. "He who says, 'Jesus' says also 'history'" (Neill, *TGI*:71). The good news is about an actual event in history.

The history of Jesus is from first to last the history of the unique *theandric* person. Those to whom that term is not already thoroughly familiar have not been reading this book.

Historical inquiry into Jesus will not resume until that premise is grasped. To attempt a history of Jesus without the theandric premise is like attempting sculpture without stone or mathematics without numbers.

The history of Jesus must be studied in the same arena in which any past event is studied: by historical methods. Yet this is a history that challenges and tests ordinary methods of investigation.

However important, historical research cannot yield saving faith. One does not necessarily come closer to faith by piling up historical evidence, though there is no faith without evidence. While history cannot establish or prove faith, the study of history is nonetheless an essential companion to the study of faith, insofar as faith attests revelation in history, and asks for historical evidences for its judgments about history. The risen Christ is not made nervous by unprejudiced historical inquiries into his earthly ministry. The gospel insists upon the presentation of evidence.

Historicist Demands on the Study of Jesus

By "historicism" I mean the bias that turns historical study into an inquiry controlled by the historian rather than by the events being studied. When the study of history becomes an ideology or a bias toward a certain kind of knowing known only to an elite circle of researchers, it becomes historicism.

Nineteenth-century Jesus research ended with the self-congratulatory conceit that modern Christianity had come to know Jesus "as no other age" so as to advance constructive thought far above and beyond all previous world views (Fairbairn, *PCMT*:20; pref., viii). This conceit still plagues the study of Jesus in the twenty-first century.

The twentieth century, which began with Schweitzer's devastating critique of biased modern assumptions about Jesus, ended with the slow death of wearisome radical critical exegesis. More and more layers of fact have been uncovered about a less and less well-defined messianic figure who has become further and further distanced by the very methods that were presumed to be bringing him nearer.

The waning momentum of modernity still wishes to reduce the Christ event to historical determinants, explaining the theandric mystery in terms of the gradual historical development of antecedent ideas or themes in the history of religions.

Since Jesus comes to us as a concrete historical person, he must be studied historically, but he breaks through our finite assumptions about what is possible amid a history characterized by self-deception. The incarnation is a historical event, but a unique and unparalleled historical event that marks the pivotal point of history and furnishes the key to understanding all other developments in history.

Can History Contain a Revelation?

Lessing despaired that "accidental truths of history can never become the proof of necessary truths of reason" ("On the Proof of the Spirit and of Power," Lessing's *Theological Writings*:53). He wondered if any eternal truth could ever be contained in fragile, passing, fleeting, unsubstantial historical events.

It was in response to this that Kierkegaard wrote *Philosophical Fragments*, seeking to show that a historical point of departure—namely, the incarnation—is possible for eternal happiness. No modern philosophical interpreter has been a more steady or reliable companion to this writer than Kierkegaard. It is doubtful that a Kierkegaardian Christology has ever been written. If this study does not suffice, at least it celebrates much of the core of Kierkegaard's intent (as expressed in *Philosophical Fragments, Concluding Unscientific Postscript, Training in Christianity, Christian Discourses,* and *The Point of View of My Work as an Author*), yet I am aware that with him the pendulum did swing too far in a subjectivist direction.

There is a profound moral requirement upon faith that it speak historical truth and not lie or dissemble about facts. This is a commitment that requires daily renewal. Even though this commitment has sometimes plunged faith into either empiricist or rationalistic excesses, the respect for evidence remains an important means by which the Holy Spirit protects the worshiping community from petty innovations and erroneous teachings.

The history of Jesus has benefited from a long history of criticism. That history reverberates with high decibels in heavy metal tones in our time. Despite all its artillery, reductionist debates have never succeeded in peeling the onion to nothing, nor could they ever. Any salvation that can be destroyed by historical criticism is not the salvation the New Testament attests. After all these critical inquiries, Jesus continues to meet people of today personally on his own terms. He was never the product of a series of redactive errors, ideological distortions, or literary deceptions.

Prominent biblical critics have imagined that they have found legitimate ways of circumventing the theandric offense. Echoing the tradition that followed Hegel, they pretend to treat the question of Christ exclusively as a critique of the ideas of those who remembered Jesus, hence as having little to do with the person himself. But the living person keeps on intruding on the historical reverie.

H. R. Mackintosh described the prevailing dilemma of biblical studies accurately almost a century ago: "There has never been a Christianity in the world which did not worship Christ the Lord as personally identical with Jesus of Nazareth. A criticism, therefore, which after repudiating His exaltation, strives to disinter the real Jesus from the mounds of untrustworthy legend, is reduced for lack of matter to constructions of a subjective and imaginary character. These constructions proceed on lines which almost by definition make valid results impossible; for, resting as they do in partially naturalistic assumptions, they are led to argue, first, that no transcendent Person such as the Christ of faith could possibly exist, and secondly, that even if He did, it is inconceivable that a subsequent age should be credibly informed of His reality" (*PJC*:318). This is the road that is finally coming to an end.

These attempts have failed finally to come to terms with the single most elementary affirmation of the New Testament proclamation, that Jesus *is* Lord (as distinguished from the view that Jesus is merely *proclaimed* as the Christ, or that Jesus *became* the Christ through a remembering process, or that the Christ is reducible to a modern rendering of the *moral teaching or influence* of Jesus).

Paul taught that Jesus had been declared the Christ not by his followers but by God through his resurrection (Rom. 1:4). That is a startling fact far greater in significance than that there may be stages of development leading to that declaration. An event must not be confused with its historical development.

The Life of Jesus Is That of the Incarnate Lord

The account of Jesus' earthly ministry cannot be told as if it were purely a heavenly or transhistorical event, for it is the story of a human being. Nor can it be told as if it were merely the story of a human being, for it is the account of God's own coming. His life story is a thoroughly human story, but at the same time the story of God's coming.

How are we to proceed to account for this particular life? Certainly by making full use of historical inquiry. But not by preemptively weeding out all reference to the divine initiative and thereby destroying the central datum to be investigated.

Historical judgment is not abandoned when the apostolic teaching is understood as having been itself raised up by the risen Lord. The apostles remembered better than they understood. We are able to know him now because they knew him and reported him with sufficient adequacy—sufficient for human salvation.

The burden of classic Christian teaching is to show through argument and evidence that Christ was who he said he was. If he was indeed God incarnate, then an inquiry into Christ that accidentally missed that fact would be inadequate.

The truth of his life—that he was God incarnate—was not fully realized by his closest disciples during his earthly life. It was only adequately realized after his resurrection. Once grasped, it became the fulcrum of apostolic teaching.

The events of his life were events of the God-man. Apart from this fact, these narratives remain enigmatic and baffling. Any attempt to account for his life without accounting for this fact is, according to apostolic testimony, pitiable and untrue.

Logos became *sarx*, flesh, historical person. The uncreated One assumed the life of a creature. God entered history and became a single individual in it. If so, the meaning of history is to be found not in ideas, not in the history of earthly power, but in a man born of woman, a particular man as Son of God, Son of God as a particular man. Let this theandric premise be taken seriously and the study of the historical Jesus can once again be resumed.

BOOK THREE

LIFE IN THE SPIRIT

S OME OF THE MOST INTRIGUING QUESTIONS of classic Christian teaching lie straight ahead. The topic now is the work of the Holy Spirit in the renewal of persons in community. I will be as brief as the subject allows. The intent is not to include anything the historic church does not consider consensually essential.

Introducing the Study of the Spirit

The Father and Son are giving the church an incomparable gift: the outpouring of God's own Spirit. "God does not give a Gift inferior to Himself" (Augustine, *Faith and the Creed* 9.19). The Son promised that the Spirit would follow his ministry on earth. Incomparable blessings would ensue with the ministry of the Spirit. Having once been given the gift of the Spirit at Pentecost, the believing community has never been left without this Comforter (John 14:18; Chrysostom, *Hom. on John* 75).

The Spirit leads the faithful into all truth by pointing constantly toward the truth embodied in Jesus (John 16:13; Ignatius, *Eph.* 9). In any glimpse the human mind may have of God's revelation, the way has always already been prepared by God's own Spirit (Matt. 3:3). "Pave within you the way" (Chromatius, *Tractate on Matt.* 8.1). "Remove the stones from the road" (Is. 40.4).

The study of the Spirit is called pneumatology (from the Greek word, *pneuma*, spirit). It is the systematic analysis and interpretation of the texts of scripture and consensual tradition that deal with the regenerating and consummating work of the Holy Spirit (*hagion pneuma;* Ephrem, *Comm. on Heb.* 6.6).

The Neglect of the Teaching of the Holy Spirit

The modern tendency is to depersonalize the Spirit, to treat God the Spirit as reducible to a general idea of spirituality. This stands in contrast to the biblical view of God's own intensely personal meeting with ordinary living persons dwelling in regular houses and cities in everyday history. This is always a meeting that requires decision. Thus this meeting exercises that capacity unique to humans as distinguished from animal creation: deliberate and reasoned willing, always occurring in a specific Now—a given context.

It is a scandal to modern critical scholarship that standard exegetical and theological discussions of the Holy Spirit have given little attention to the great early treatises on the Holy Spirit by Didymus, Basil, Gregory of Nyssa, Gregory Nazianzus, and Ambrose. It remains a mixed blessing that modern charismatic and Pentecostal voices have so stressed special aspects of the work of the Spirit that some other Protestant voices have tended to back away completely from all teaching concerning the Spirit. The texts of scripture, however, leave no doubt in our minds of the importance of teaching of and by the Spirit (Basil, *On the Holy Spirit* 9.22–23).

"The subject of the Holy Spirit presents a special difficulty," wrote Gregory of Nazianzus, because by the time we get to it in the long sequence of teaching topics, we are already "worn out by the multitude of questions." So we become like those who have "lost their appetite, who having taken a dislike to some particular kind of food, shrink from all food; so we in like manner have an aversion from all discussion" (*Orat.* 31, *Of the Holy Spirit*).

The work of the Spirit has been far less studied and consensually defined than the work of the Son. When Paul asked his hearers at Ephesus, "Did you receive the Holy Spirit when you believed?" they answered, "No, we have not even heard that there is a Holy Spirit" (Acts 19:2). Even now many think it possible to teach the gospel of Jesus without any thought of the work of the Spirit (Ammonius, in Cramer, *Catena on Acts* 19.5).

From God "For Us" to God "In Us"

The final third of *Classic Christianity* focuses upon Life in the Spirit. It asks how the work of God in creation and redemption is being brought to consummation by the Holy Spirit. This renewal is occurring inwardly in persons and socially in communities (Origen, *OFP* 1.3.2). It promises ultimately to encompass the whole of nature and cosmic history.

We stand at a crucial pivot of Christian teaching, shifting the focus from the work of the Son to the work of the Spirit in the church in applying the benefits of the work of the Son.

In the previous pages we have spoken of God *for* us. Now we speak more deliberately of God working *in* us. We speak not of events addressing us as it were from the outside of our experience (*extra nos,* outside us) but more deliberately of active inward processes and events by which persons in community are convicted, transformed, regenerated, justified, and brought into union with Christ, one by one (Heb. 3:14; 1 Pet. 5:1). This is God's work within humanity (*intra nos,* in us) viewed individually and socially. "Just as God stepped out of his nature to become a partaker of our humanity, so we are called to step out of our nature to become partakers of his divinity" (Hilary of Arles, *Intro. Comm. on 2 Pet.* 1.4).

The forgiveness of God the Son, having been once for all offered on the cross, must be ever again received in each new moment in time. At each stage we are being freshly enabled to receive it. In Christ we learn what God has already done on our behalf. By the Spirit we are being enabled to *reshape our doing* in response to what God has done, to reform our loves in relation to God's incomparable love.

"I appeal to you therefore, brethren, by the mercies of God, to present your bodies as a living sacrifice" (Rom. 12:1). "The difference between asking and appealing is that we ask about unimportant matters but appeal about important one. . . . Our bodies are sacrifices because the flesh is put to death. They are living sacrifices, because the Spirit has given them life" (Luculentius, *Commentary 3 on Rom.* 12.1).

With this pivot, our own decisions and actions now become a crucial part of the salvation story—the history of the body of Christ. God not only forgives sin through the Son but through the Spirit works to actually overturn the power of sin in our actual daily interpersonal behavior and life in community.

The Lord and Giver of Life

The Spirit is "Lord and Giver of Life" (Nicene-Constantinopolitan Creed, 1 Cor. 15:45). "The Spirit gives life" (John 6:63; 2 Cor. 3:6; Ambrose, *Of the Holy Spirit* 1.15). "God our life is the life of all" (Hildegard of Bingen, *Symphonia*:143).

The new life involves entry into a family (Rom. 8:12–17; Gal. 4:6) in relation to an incomparably caring parent (*Abba*, "Papa"). The Spirit bears witness within our spirits that we are children of this *Abba* in this family (Origen, *Comm. on Rom.* 8.16).

Flesh (*sarx*) refers not merely to the physical body but to the whole person under the power of sin who becomes acclimated under the power of sin to pursue works of the flesh (Gal. 5:19–21). All who faithfully receive the Spirit are born anew, given a new spiritual beginning and called to grow toward good health in grace (John 3:1–8; Justin Martyr, *First Apol.* 61). The new person in Christ is born of the Spirit to faith active in love (Rom. 8:1–7). It is lived out in freedom for the neighbor, freeing persons to fulfill their original human purpose whatever the historical conditions, to enjoy all things in God, to receive life day by day from the eternal Giver (Gal. 5; Calvin, *Inst.* 3.10; 3.23.12).

The Third Article of the Creed: I Believe in the Holy Spirit

All ancient baptismal confessions and classic creeds confess in this or similar language: I believe in the Holy Spirit (pneuma hagion; Lat: Spiritum Sanctum; Der-Balyzeh Papyrus; Roman Symbol, Psalter of Rufinus). "We believe in one Holy Spirit the Paraclete" (Eastern Form of the Apostles' Creed, Cyril of Jerusalem, *Catecheses*, 9). This article of baptismal faith became expanded through a history of exposition and controversy into the doctrine of the Holy Spirit.

In learning by heart the Creed of Epiphanius (first reported as a long-received written tradition in AD c. 374), the one to be baptized rehearsed twelve clauses that summarily set forth the work of the Spirit:

> *We believe in the Holy Spirit who*
> *spoke in the law,*
> *and taught by the prophets,*
> *and descended to the Jordan,*
> *spoke by the Apostles,*
> *and lives in the saints;*
> *thus we believe in him: that he is the Holy Spirit,*
> *the Spirit of God,*
> *the perfect Spirit,*
> *the Spirit Paraclete,*
> *uncreated,*
> *proceeding from the Father* [ek tou Patros ekporeuomenon]
> *and receiving of the Son* [ek tou huiou lambanomenon], *in whom we believe.*
> (*SCD* 13)

The primitive rule of faith as recorded by Irenaeus about 190 AD shows the prominent role of the Holy Spirit recognized by the early Christian community. Salvation history is placed within the context of the work of the triune God. It is the Spirit who bears testimony in the present age to the Father and the Son. The confessing community believes "in the Holy Spirit, who proclaimed through the prophets the dispensations of God, and the advents, and the birth from a virgin, and the passion, and the resurrection from the dead, and the ascension into heaven" (Irenaeus, *Ag. Her.* 1.9.1)

The earliest Christian teachers understood that this rule of faith had been passed along by apostolic testimony in an unbroken line from Jesus to the present. According to Tertullian, God "sent from the Father the Holy Spirit the Paraclete, the sanctifier of the faith of those who believe in the Father and the Son and the Holy Spirit. That *this Rule has come down from the beginning of the Gospel*, even before all former heretics, not to speak of Praxeas of yesterday, will be proved as well by the comparative lateness of all heretics as by the very novelty of Praxeas of yesterday" (*Ag. Praxeas* 2, italics added).

The Second Ecumenical Council (Constantinople I) would settle the question of the deity of the Spirit as firmly as Nicaea had defined the deity of Christ and triunity of God in the Nicene-Constantinopolitan Creed (381). It set forth an ecumenically received summary definition of the person and work of God the Spirit in these terms: "We believe in the one God . . . And in the Holy Spirit, the Lord and life-giver, Who proceeds from the Father, Who is worshiped and glorified together with the Father and Son, Who spoke through the prophets" (Creed of the 150 Fathers, *SCD* 86).

The Personal Pronoun: If Not "It," Is the Spirit "He" or "She"?

We acknowledge the prevailing form of address to the Holy Spirit as "He" in the English-speaking Christian tradition. Yet it is still useful to ask whether it is appropriate within the bounds of classic Christian assumptions to address the Spirit in the feminine gender.

The issue is only partly decided on grammatical grounds: *Ruach* in Hebrew is feminine. *Pneuma* in Greek is a neuter, yet even when the neuter is used, masculine pronouns may accompany it. Even in the New Revised Standard Version, whose mandate specified that "masculine-oriented language should be eliminated as far as this can be done without altering passages that reflect the historical situation of ancient patriarchal culture," crucial passages could not be rendered in the neuter: "When the Spirit of truth comes, he will guide you into all the truth; for he will not speak on his own, but will speak whatever he hears, and he will declare to you the things that are to come" (John 16:13). God is named as *Abba* (Father); the messianic Son (*ben, huios*) stands in the male line of David; the Spirit is *ruach* or *pneuma* (feminine or neuter).

Gregory of Nazianzus was amused by any who would insistently hold "God to be a male" which he regarded as a misplaced analogy. You cannot conclude that God, because Father, is therefore male. Nor can you conclude that "Deity is feminine from the gender of the word, and the Spirit neuter," since the designation "has nothing to do with generation. But if you would be silly enough to say, with the old myths and fables, that God begat the Son by a marriage with His own Will, we should be introduced to the Hermaphrodite god of Marcion and Valentinus who imagined these newfangled Aeons" (*Orat.* 31.7, *On the Holy Spirit*).

God has become revealed in scripture largely but not exclusively in masculine terms such as king, lord, husband, judge, master, and father. Not exclusively, however, because the work of the Spirit is at times compared to mothering and nurturing actions: "As a mother comforts her child, so will I comfort you" (Isa. 66:13). Here God the Spirit is not named Mother but compared to a mother (R. Frye, *Language for God and Feminist Language*:17–22).

Elizabeth Achtemeier has persuasively shown that the prophets did not suffer from a failure of imagination to grasp God as female, for they were surrounded by cultures dominated by feminine deities, but they chose not to use feminine language "because they knew and had ample evidence from the religions surrounding them that the female language for the deity results in a basic distortion of the nature of God and of his relation to his creation" (in D. Miller, ed., *The Hermeneutical Quest*:109)—namely, the deification of nature, pantheism, and immanental religion. "When you have a Goddess as the creator, it's her own body that is the universe. She is identical with the universe" (J. Campbell, *The Power of Myth*:167).

Grammatical heroics that attempt a complete withdrawal from masculine language are often rhetorically awkward, especially where nouns are repeated to avoid whatever gender pronoun might be regarded as offensive. Similar absurdities arise where verbs are preferred that require no object, where the odd repetition of the word "God" is used as a substitute for "he," and direct address is shifted to "you." The enthusiast is sorely tempted to rewrite scripture to gain a hearing with a particular audience.

But no one prays to an "it," even if steeped in modernity. Liturgical "reforms" that systematically expunge the name Father from all acts of Christian worship are unacceptable to most worshiping communities. The reason is deeper than egalitarian motivations, for Jesus repeatedly called God Father (*Abba*). This became a defining feature of his teaching (Mark 14:36; Rom. 8:15; Augustine, *Epis. to Gal.* 31.1.4.6).

It is God the Spirit who teaches us to cry out "*Abba*" (Rom. 8:16; Ambrosiaster, Epis. to Gal. 2.4.7). If Christian worshipers are reluctant to address God by the name Jesus specifically taught them to speak, they hardly can be said to have learned how to pray. "We are bound to be baptized in the terms we have received and to profess belief in the terms in which we have been baptized" (Basil, in Torrance, *The Trinitarian Faith*:193; *Incomplete Work on Matthew*, Hom. 35).

Both Genders Honored by God

Neither male nor female language adequately grasps the fullness of the divine reality (Gregory Nazianzus, *Orat.* 27; John of Damascus, *OF* 1.4–8). Classic consensual Christianity maintains faithfulness to the historic language of the church but, in doing so, seeks fairness in contemporary cultural conflict.

If both sexes are to be honored in the incarnation, and if the one giving birth must be female, then the one born would in fairness be male (Augustine, *EDQ* 11). This is the decisive line of reasoning as we have seen in the Incarnation: *If the mother of the Savior must of necessity be female, since only females are mothers, the Savior would as a consequence have to be male if both sexes are to be significantly involved in the salvation event.*

The only alternative would be to have a female mother of the Savior and a female Savior. For an androgynous or hermaphroditic Savior would fail to share in the specific nature of our sexual human condition. The female birth-enabler is an intrinsic part of the divine economy in the coming of the Messiah as prophesied in the male line of David. Augustine summed up that God "was not ashamed of the male nature, for He took it upon Himself; or of the female, for He was born of a woman." Hence we are "liberated by the agency of both sexes" (*The Christian Combat* 22).

But where does this leave the language of God the Spirit? To denude language of all gender reference is quixotic and disrespectful of human sexuality. This alternative reveals a narrow ideological bias reflecting an antihistorical frame of mind. It is also a denial of our very created nature as engendered beings.

No woman or man I know wishes to be called an "it." If so, how can one be satisfied with "it" language addressed to God? The scandal of particularity remains. God meets us in specific times and places amid people with specific names and genders and of particular parents of a particular race and culture.

To back away wholly from gender reference is to stand offended at the gospel of a man born of woman (Marius Victorinus, *Epis. to Gal.*, 2.4.3–4), and of the Spirit who transcends the gender differences between *ruach* and *pneuma*.

The Shortfall of Language in the Study of the Spirit

The Spirit's own guidance is needed in the study of the Spirit, "not that we may speak what is worthy of God, for this is impossible" but that we may not fail to speak altogether; hence it belongs to "grace itself to grant both to us to speak without deficiency and to you [the disciple] to hear with discretion" (Cyril of Jerusalem, *Catech. Lect.* 16.1).

Speech about the incarnate Lord is speech about one who is revealed in the flesh as a man born of woman. But speech about the Holy Spirit is speech about one who desires to work quietly, who remains unpretentiously concealed, hidden in the silent depths of the heart and the quiet hedgings of history.

The incarnate Lord was seen; the Word of Life "handled," "touched," personally addressed (1 John 1:1, 2). When the Spirit moves, however, the mover is silent and invisible (Basil, *On the Spirit 9*). What is most important in this inquiry is often least quantifiable and least empirically observable, though the consequences and effects of the Spirit may be visible (Augustine, *Sermons* 7.4).

The Appeal to Mystery

The Spirit is intrinsically a mystery, like the currents of air and clouds whose movements are too complex and hidden to predict (John 3:8; Ambrose, *On Chr. Faith* 2.6.47). It is easy to know that the wind is moving, but difficult to predict precisely from where to where, even on a vast scale with the best measuring devices. The fact that we cannot see the wind does not mean that it does not exist (Chrysostom, *Hom. on John* 26.1–2). However evident may be the work of the Spirit to the heart, it is not visible to the eye or audible to the ear or tangible to the touch (Augustine, *Tractates on John* 12.5).

The work of the Spirit everywhere leaves traces of the divine presence. These are best expressed not in flat empirical descriptions but in powerful touches, signs, and symbols as indirect and hidden as the work itself. Key metaphors in scripture are: breath, dove, fire, oil.

Some teachings are universally known to faith but consensually regarded as finally remaining mysterious and unexplained. Among these are the eternal generation of the Son, the procession of the Spirit, the dynamics of grace and human freedom, and the triune God. "We say, three persons, not in order to express it, but in order not to be silent" (Augustine, *Trin.* 5.9). Though it may seem "undignified to give any answer at all to the statements that are foolish," the mute alternative is more dangerous "lest through our silence error may prevail" (Gregory of Nyssa, *On the Holy Spirit NPNF 2 5:315*).

No rational thought exceeds the deeper rationality of the triune God, since "God who creates is Himself the highest of the objects of thought, both for those who think, and that which is thought of" (Gregory Nazianzus, *Orat.* 21.1).

The Limits of Scientific Inquiry into God the Spirit

To the skeptical gaze of naturalistic reductionism, there seems to be little evidence of these silent footprints of the Spirit—hardly a trace, hardly an aroma. Tenderly God touches, breathes upon human history. What is revealed of the Spirit is more whispered than spoken (Job 26:13–14; John 3:8; Chrysostom, *Hom. on John* 26). The Spirit withholds disclosure from the objectivizing gaze of the scientist who wishes chiefly to measure, graph, control, and submit reports.

This does not mean that insight into the Spirit's revelation in history is impossible, but rather that it must listen attentively to its subject's voice (1 Kings 19:12). "The Spirit is breath. The wind sings in the trees. I would like, then, to be an Aeolian harp and let the breath of God make the strings vibrate and sing. Let me stretch and tune the strings—that will be the austere task of research. And let the Spirit make them sing a clear and tuneful song of prayer and life!" (Congar, *IBHS* 1.10).

The teacher of orthodoxy must be "not, like our modern wise men, yielding to the spirit of the age, nor defending our faith by indefinite and sophistical language, as if they had no fixity of faith" (Gregory Nazianzus, *Orat.* 18.16).

Why the Spirit Remains Inaccessible to Objective Investigation

The ancient church teachers thought that there must be some hidden purpose in the fact that God has constrained empirical inquiry into the Spirit, and thus withheld from the faithful vast ranges of pertinent information concerning the work of the Spirit (Gregory Nazianzus, *Orat.* 31.5; Cyril of Jerusalem, *Catech. Lect.* 16.23).

Yet they remained convinced, along with Paul, that all will ultimately be revealed (1 Cor. 13:12, 13). The providential purpose of the hiddenness of the Spirit is to awaken and engender that trust which walks by faith, not sight (2 Cor. 5:7; Fulgentius, *To Monimus* 1.11.5).

No subject of Christian teaching is more prone to fanaticism and novelty and subjectivism than the Holy Spirit. This is why Scripture guides subjective experience at every step along this long road. Each individual's personal experience is prone to self-deception and interest-laden distortions (Jer. 14:13–14; R. Niebuhr, *NDM* 1; H. R. Niebuhr, *RMWC*).

In no other precinct of Christian teaching are we more prone to make confident appeals to personal experience, yet these appeals do not guarantee that our feelings will be grounded in the apostolic testimony. The work of the Spirit deserves especially careful attention precisely because it is so prone to manipulation and ideological abuse (Acts 8:19; Cyril of Jerusalem, *Catech. Lect* 16.10).

On Not Being Wise Above Scripture

In listening to the Spirit the consensual tradition has sought not to be wise above Scripture. The faithful are not called to try to exceed the ways in which God's own Spirit has become self-attested through holy writ (1 Cor. 1:18–31). "It is not our duty to indulge in conjecture" (Irenaeus, *Ag. Her.* 2.28.6).

In receiving the Spirit we have "not received the spirit of the world but the Spirit who is from God, that we may understand what God has freely given us. This is what we speak, not in words taught us by human wisdom but in words taught by the Spirit, expressing spiritual truths in spiritual words" (1 Cor. 2:12, 13; Chrysostom, *Hom. on 1 Cor.* 7.7).

Faith "sees *something* of that which it does *not see entire*, nor is it permitted to *ignore* what it is *not allowed to comprehend*" (Hugh of St. Victor, *SCF*:53, italics added). Christian teaching does well to speak modestly of the Spirit as the Spirit has become self-revealed in the history attested by scripture (Cyril of Jerusalem, *Catech. Lect.* 16.2; 17.2).

The Way Ahead

Grasping the Cohesive Movement of Christian Teaching: Spirit, Church, Consummation

The classic tradition has reasoned by means of an orderly progression of interconnected topics from the study of the Spirit (pneumatology) to salvation (soteriology) and moving from there directly into the church (ecclesiology), leading toward the end of history (eschatology). These are the key stops on the theological map of the way ahead.

Here is the essential movement. The reality of the church emerges out of the saving action of God in Christ through the Spirit; the church is the providential means and sphere through which persons are enabled to participate in eternal life. The birth of the church of Jesus Christ is engendered by the regenerating power of the Spirit. The nurture of the church occurs by grace through Word and Sacraments. The present church shares in the communion of saints in time and eternity. In this way, the flowing sequence of classic Christian teaching draws all post-Ascension topics of theology into coherent order (John of Damascus, *OF* 3.1, 6, 19).

These topics are inseparably integrated. "Where the Spirit of God is, there is the Church and every kind of grace" (Irenaeus, *Ag. Her.* 3.24). To elect to live without the grace offered in the church is like a neonate refusing nourishment from a mother's breast.

In systematic study we proceed not chronologically but economically, methodically, and according to the logic of Christian memory. We are listening for consensual, ecumenical voices; not in order of their historical sequence, but by means of their reasonable unfolding and tested organization of Christian teaching.

At key turning points along the way of consistent Christian teaching we regularly check and reset our bearings, seeking a sense of right location and due organization of topics. At this point we are seeking to understand the classic Christian teaching of the Holy Spirit and church within the whole scope of Christian historical reasoning (Chrysostom, *Hom. on John* 73).

The two-thousand-year-old order of early baptismal confession firmly sets the sequence of topics. It moves obviously from *Spiritum Sanctum* through *ecclesiam* toward the *vitam venturi seculi* ("life of the world to come," *COC* 2:59). As early as Irenaeus, Cyril of Jerusalem, and Hilary, the topics of salvation, grace, and the church were being located within the "third article" of the creed, the sequence of teachings on the work of the Spirit (Irenaeus, *Ag. Her.*; Cyril, *Catech. Lect.*; Hilary, *Trin.*). We follow the steps of patristic and centrist Catholic and Protestant teaching, as we see it unfolding in Augustine, Thomas Aquinas, Peter Lombard, and Calvin. There we find the discussion of church and the human future located in a clearly conceived sequence following the doctrines of the Spirit, repentance, faith, and justification. (Augustine, *Enchiridion*; Calv. *Inst.* 3–4; Zwingli, *True and False Religion, WZ* 3:176; Calv. *Inst.* 4.14). Persons come to faith only from within a community created by the Spirit, not in a vacuum. The Spirit is the life of the community—uniting God with humanity and the faithful with each other. The newborn believer cannot lisp God as *Abba (pater)* without *ekklēsia* as mother (*mater,* Cyprian, *Letters* 39).

The Spirit's Presence as Datum of History

It is a matter of historical record that the church has come into being. It is impossible to study human history of the last two millennia and ignore entirely the community of called-out people (*ekklēsia*) created by the Spirit. That would just be bad history. The Spirit is active in history wherever sent by the Father as the Gift that the Son is making to call forth the faithful. The Son explicitly promised that the Spirit will abide until the Son returns (John 14:15–24; 16:5–15).

The central motif of the work of the Spirit is attesting and bringing into lively historical embodiment the work of the Son (Luke 24:44–49; John 15:26; Acts 1:4–8). This does not imply a unilateral divine accomplishment by absolute fiat, for the Spirit works patiently through human wills, engaged lives, concrete actions, and the foolishness of preaching (1 Cor. 1:18–31). While the finished sacrifice of the cross is a once-for-all event, the Spirit-enabled reception of the Word occurs again and again. This awakening takes place in extremely diverse times and places until the Lord's return (John 20:22; Acts 19:2; Chrysostom, *Hom. on John* 86).

Macaulay was awed by the durable continuity of the apostolic tradition: "No other institution is left standing which carries the mind back to the times when the smoke of sacrifice rose from the Pantheon, and when came leopards and tigers bounded in the Flavian amphitheater." The most grandiose royal dynasties are but of yesterday compared with the apostolic tradition. The great monarchies of France and Germany are of recent origin—monarchies now gone, while the ancient ecumenical councils still speak with full vitality. The church saw "the commencement of all the governments and of all the ecclesiastical establishments that now exist in the world; and we feel no assurance that she is not destined to see the end of them all. She was great and respected before the Saxon had set foot in Britain, before the Frank had passed the Rhine, when Grecian eloquence still flourished at Antioch, when idols were still worshipped in the temple of Mecca" (Macaulay, "Essay on L. von Ranke's History").

PART I

THE PERSON OF
THE HOLY SPIRIT

1

THE PERSON OF
THE HOLY SPIRIT

MAIN AFFIRMATIONS IN CLASSIC CONSENSUAL Christian teaching of
the Holy Spirit are:

The Spirit indwells in the hearts of the faithful

to attest God the Father as known through God the Son

to draw together the called-out people for celebration and proclamation

to reveal the truth to those yielded to the Spirit's promptings

to equip for service

to seal the promise of things to come

to elicit faith, hope, and love

ultimately to heal the history of sin.

The last third of classic Christian teaching seeks to understand what the Spirit
does to accomplish this work (Ambrose, *Of the Holy Spirit*, 1.9.107; Cyril of Alex.,
Thesaurus, LCF:266; John of Damascus, *OF* 3.1).

The Deity of the Holy Spirit

Attributes of God the Holy Spirit

Who is the Holy Spirit so often spoken of in Scripture?

*Certain characteristics are ascribed to the Holy Spirit that could only belong to
God*: omniscience (Isa. 40:13; 1 Cor. 2:10–12), omnipresence (Ps. 139:7–10), omnipotence (Job 33:4; Ps. 104:30; Rom. 15:18, 19), eternality (Heb. 9:14).

Scripture attests the Holy Spirit as eternal (Heb. 9:14), life giving (Rom. 8:2), one (Eph. 4:4), of one essence with God, "the Lord, who is the Spirit" (2 Cor. 3:18; Basil, On the Spirit 1.9–12; Calvin, Inst. 1.13.14–15). Hence the Holy Spirit is rightly called God (Acts 5:3, 4) and worshiped as true God.

The names of the Spirit in Scripture point to the character of the Spirit (1 Cor. 2:11–14; 2 Cor. 3:17, 18; cf. Matt. 12:28, Luke 11:20). The works of the Spirit are those only the true God could do. By the Spirit the demonic powers are overcome (Matt. 12:28), sinners enter the kingdom of God (John 3:5), the Son is raised from the dead (Rom. 8:11). The Spirit who raises from the dead and has life within himself must be God (Theodore of Mopsuestia, Pauline Comm. Gk. Ch.; 2 Cor. 3.17; Theodoret of Cyr, Com. on Cor. 178).

God is called the Spirit because the Spirit is as invisible as breath or wind (pneuma, John 3:8). This One is called "Holy Spirit" because incomparably holy (Rom. 1:4); and called "the Spirit of God" (Gen. 1:2; Matt. 3:16) because through his work the truth is revealed; and called "the Spirit of Christ" (Rom. 8:9; 1 Pet. 1:11) because he is sent by the Son to empower the Son's mission to the world (Ursinus, CHC:271).

These names designate and point to and confirm the deity of the Spirit, who is nothing less than "the Spirit of the Lord" (Luke 4:18; Acts 5:9), "the Spirit of him who raised Jesus from the dead" (Rom. 8:11), "the Spirit of the living God" (2 Cor. 3:3).

God the Spirit is celebrated as the author of revelation, bestower of truth (John 14:17), "the Spirit of wisdom and understanding, the Spirit of counsel and of power, the Spirit of knowledge and of the fear of the Lord" (Isa. 11:2; cf. Exod. 28:3; Eph. 1:1 7), who empowers grace and enables supplication (Zech. 12:10; Heb. 10:29).

The Worship of God the Spirit

The Spirit is called Lord (1 Cor. 12:4–6) because the Spirit is entitled to the same worship rightly offered up to the Father and the Son (Basil, On the Spirit, 8.44–21.52). The Spirit's name is placed on equal terms with the Lord in the apostolic benediction (2 Cor. 13:14). The Spirit's equality with Father and Son is clear from the great commission (Matt. 28:19), an equality that does not imply that the Spirit is indistinguishable from the Father and Son (Athanasius, LCHS 4.3–4; Gregory of Nyssa, On the Holy Spirit).

Since the Holy Spirit is God, it is fitting to Christianity to worship God the Spirit. The Holy Spirit is praised in Christian worship as One who brings to fulfillment "all other things, but Himself lacks nothing; living not as needing restoration, but as Supplier of life; not growing by additions, but straightway full, the self-established, omnipresent, source of sanctification" (Basil, On the Holy Spirit, 1.9).

Daily prayer in the Orthodox tradition begins with this act of praise to the Holy Spirit: "O Heavenly King, the Comforter, the Spirit of Truth, who art everywhere and fillest all things, Treasury of blessings and Giver of Life, Come and abide in us, and cleanse us from every impurity, and save our souls, O Good One" (Manual of Eastern Orth. Prayers 2). This provides a daily summary recollection of the entire doctrine of the Spirit.

The Personal Uniqueness of the Holy Spirit

Gregory Nazianzus brilliantly recapitulated the key biblical ascriptions to the Holy Spirit.

God the Spirit has always existed, and exists, and always will exist,

who neither had a beginning, nor will have an end . . .

ever being partaken, but not partaking;

perfecting, not being perfected;

sanctifying, not being sanctified;

deifying, not being deified . . .

Life and Lifegiver;

Light and Lightgiver;

absolute Good,

and Spring of Goodness . . .

by Whom the Father is known and the Son is glorified. . . .

Why make a long discourse of it?

All that the Father has the Son has also except the being Unbegotten;

All that the Son has the Spirit has also except the Generation (*Orat.* 41.9).

The mission of the one Spirit is indicated by varied names and offices ascribed in scripture. As compassionate Lord, the Spirit is Comforter (John 14:16), as reclaimer, the Spirit of adoption (Rom. 8:15), as regenerator, the Spirit of Life (Rom. 8:2), as life giver, the Spirit who awakens faith (2 Cor. 4:13), as merciful One, the Spirit of Grace (Heb. 10:29), as teacher, the Spirit of Truth (John 14:17), as counselor, the Spirit of Wisdom (Eph. 1:17), as sanctifier, the Spirit of holiness (Rom. 1:14; Cyril of Jerusalem, *Catech Lect.* 15.5; Calvin, *Inst.* 3.1.3).

Jesus himself chose the silent simile of the "Holy Breath" of the word of the Lord to designate the Comforter who would follow him (John 20:22). "Christ breathed the Spirit in a corporeal fashion and thus showed that as from the mouth of a man comes the corporeal breath, so from the divine substance in a way that befits it comes the breath that proceeds from it" (Cyril of Alexandria, *Comm. on John* 14.16, tractate 9, cf. *Letters* 55.40–43).

The One God in Person to Person Meeting

The Spirit is none other than the One God, who has met Israel as Yahweh, the God of Israel, God of Hosts, Spirit of Yahweh (Num. 11:29; Judg. 3:10; Ps. 139:7; Isa. 61:1). It is not "allowable to suppose that there are many Holy Spirits who come into being by, as it were, a daily production" (Ambrose, *Of the Holy Spirit* 2.6.52; cf. Athanasius, LCHS 3.2–4).

Since the Spirit manifests the love of the Father for the Son, and of the Son for the Father, the Spirit is their common gift (Peter Lombard, *Sent.* 1.17.6). "For he is called properly what they are called in common, because the Father is a spirit and the Son is a spirit, and the Father is holy and the Son is holy. In order that the communion between them might be signified by a name which is appropriate to both, the Holy Spirit is called the gift of both" (Augustine, *Trin.* 5.11).

As God tabernacled with humanity in the flesh through the Son, so does God dwell within the human heart through the Spirit. The disciples are regarded as "a holy temple in the Lord": "And in him you too are being built together to become a dwelling in which God lives by his Spirit" (Eph. 2:22; Marius Victorinus, *Epis. to Eph.* 1.2.21–22).

The Inward Theater

The theater in which God has chosen to meet rational creatures quietly is the inward realm of conscience, moral reasoning, prayer, and study, especially study of the revealed Word. The world-historical setting in which this encounter takes place is cosmic history seen through the eyes of prophecy, covenant history, universal history, the law and the gospel (Rom. 1:20; Basil, *Hex.* 1.6).

The Spirit is God's own quiet coming to execute the Father's plan in due time, to attest the Son's saving work, to enlighten, counsel, and strengthen redeemed life until the Son's return (2 Cor. 1:3–4; Ambrose, *Paradise* 8.38; *Holy Spirit* 3.3).

There is nothing too subtle or dense for the Spirit to penetrate or too sinful for the Spirit to cleanse or too weary for the Spirit to refresh or too dead for the Spirit to breathe life into again. The Spirit strives with us, prays for us, groans with us (Rom. 8:18–27; Augustine, *Hom. on 1 John* 8).

New life in the Spirit is offered through the proclaimed and written Word and enacted in the Sacraments by grace. As the Word is made flesh in the Son, so the body of Christ is being enfleshed in a real but imperfect measure in the church through the person and work of the Spirit (Augustine, *On Nature and Grace* 38.45).

The Personal Nearness of the Holy Spirit Within the Human Heart

The Spirit searches our hearts (1 Cor. 2:10–11), teaching human persons individually and within communities of worship (Rom. 8:12–27).

The Omnipresence of the One Spirit

The omnipresence of God the Spirit is celebrated in Psalm 139: "Where can I go from your Spirit? Where can I flee from your presence? If I go up to the heavens, you are there; if I make my bed in the depths, you are there" (Ps. 139:7, 8).

There is no place where God's Spirit is not. There is no time when God's Spirit was not. "It is the nature of the Holy Spirit to be both over all and in all," both transcendent and working immanently in human hearts (Ambrose, *Of the Holy Spirit* 3.19.150). Omnipresence is contrasted with pantheism, since even within all the closeness of personal engagement, God the Spirit remains the holy God, not reducible to worldly description.

In "coming" to one place the Spirit does not "leave" another. God the Spirit can "descend," "indwell," and "fill" without changing place or emptying. Such statements are grounded in the premises of omnipresence and eternality—attributes ascribed properly only to God. "The Spirit is not, then, sent as it were from a place, nor does He proceed as from a place." We are left with the impression that the Spirit is *coming down* to us, while in truth our minds by grace are being enabled to *ascend* to the Spirit (Ambrose, *Of the Holy Spirit* 1.9.119–21). "Spirit cannot be cabined or confined," since the Spirit is "omnipresent in space and time, and under all conditions present in its fulness" (Hilary, *Trin.* 2.31; cf. Athanasius, *LCHS* 1:26).

God's Spirit and the Human Spirit

God the Spirit breathes life into the souls of human persons (Tertullian, *Apology* 48). Since God is addressed as Thou, not it, those who image or mirror God (all human beings) are rightly addressed as you, not it (M. Buber, *I and Thou*; Brunner, *The Divine Human Encounter*). While human beings have spirit, God is Spirit (Brunner, *Dogm.* 2:63).

The *Spirit* of God is not separable from God, even as your own spirit is not separable from you. Nothing less than God is meeting us when God's Spirit is present (2 Chron. 5–7; John 1:32–33; Augustine, *Tractates on John* 5.1–2). God's own Spirit is shared effortlessly with other spirits without ceasing to be entire, as a "sunbeam whose kindly light falls on him who enjoys it as though it showed for him alone, yet illumines land and sea and mingles with the air" (Basil, *On the Holy Spirit* 1.9).

It was the Hebrew word for breath (*ruach*) that became translated into Latin as *anima* and Greek as *psuche* (animated life or animal soul). All who are alive breathe. Breath is an indicator of aliveness. *Nephesh* (soul, life, blood soul) names the power of life, pointing also to the root metaphor of breathing in Hebrew. When the Psalmist sings: "Into your hands I commit my spirit" (Ps. 31:5), my *ruach*, my distinctively personal living aspect, he is referring to the center of personal selfhood, of feeling, awareness, and willing activity.

It is ironic that a word so connected with life should come to have overriding nuances of death in the history of English translations of *pneuma*. Ghost is Old English for the common word for breath or spirit. The word for spirit in many European languages translates the Hebrew *ruach* and the Greek *pneuma*. *Geist* is the Teutonic word for Spirit, from which our Old English form Ghost is derived. Older English translations speak of the Holy Ghost, an archaic way of speaking of the Holy Spirit. As the Incarnation speaks of God's embodiment, so the Holy Spirit speaks of God's invisible life that is more like wind than flesh or organic cells, more like breathing than something that can be objectively weighed or easily measured in a laboratory (Theodore of Mopsuestia, *Comm. on John* 2.3.7–8). The Spirit blows "where it chooses" (John 3:7; Ambrose, *On Chr. Faith* 2.6.47).

In scripture "every thing which has not a solid body is in a general way called spirit." Both angelic and demonic powers in this sense are referred to as spirit. The human person constantly participates in the unseen world of spirit. God the Holy Spirit differs from all these created forms of spirit, being God who "beholds the beginning of the world, and knows the end" (Cyril of Jerusalem, *Catech. Lect.* 16.15).

Personal Language Is Fitting to the Personal Nature of the Holy Spirit

The Spirit is addressed as a person, less "it" than "Thou." Not impersonal but personal pronouns are regularly used to refer to the Spirit in scripture: "I will send him to you" (John 16:7; Didymus, *On the Holy Spirit* 34.36). "Him to you" is person to person, not it to it (Cyril of Jerusalem, *Comm. on John* 10.2).

If the Holy Spirit were not so uniquely a personal "Thou," it would be possible to address him as an abstract concept. But in Scripture he always meets us as a person—free and communicative, capable of love and judgment (Matt. 28:19; Acts 28:25). This is why personal language is not optional but required in praying to the Holy Spirit.

This personalization is reflected in the language of the council at Jerusalem when the Apostles spontaneously declared, "It seemed good to the Holy Ghost and to us" (Acts 15:28) that a particular action was to be taken, as if to say that Peter and James and John and others were there, and the Holy Spirit was also there in the conversation, personally sharing with them, dwelling with them as incomparable partner in their effort (Calvin, *Comm.* 19:77–80).

The *proprium* of a person is what is "one's own." It is that in any personality which differentiates it from other personalities. The *proprium* of the Holy Spirit is that in God the Spirit which differentiates him from the Father and the Son without denying the unity of the one God. When we look to Scripture for those characteristics that are continually attributed to the divine person of the Holy Spirit in terms especially fitting to his personal activity, we find language like that found in the *Heidelberg Catechism*: "Thus it is said that [the Holy Spirit] teaches, comforts and guides us in all truth, that he distributes gifts as he will; that he calls and sends apostles" (Ursinus, *CHC*:272).

The Spirit Acts Personally

The apostolic testimony applied intensely personal analogies to the Holy Spirit: guiding (Rom. 8:14), convicting (John 16:8), interceding (Rom. 8:26), calling (Acts 13:2), commissioning (Acts 20:28). God the Spirit is attested as acting in infinite measure like the way the best persons we know act.

Like a person, the Spirit can be resisted (Acts 7:51), avoided (Augustine, *Tractates on John* 94, 95), or responsively answered (Acts 10:19–21). Only a person can be vexed (Isa. 63:10) or grieve (Eph. 4:30). Only one with intelligence and the capacity for communication can speak from heart to heart. These are qualities of personhood. Only a person can teach, talk, reveal his will to other persons, become angry (Isa. 63:10).

As persons speak and communicate of a hidden inner life, so does Scripture speak of a hiddenness of the Holy Spirit. Yet the Spirit speaks (Mark 13:11; Acts 8:29; 21:11; 1 Tim. 4:1; Rev. 2:7) to disclose his will and listen responsively to creatures. Only a person can be lied to—no one can lie to a stone or vegetable since there is no responsiveness there. Ananias was in trouble not for lying to Peter but for lying to the Holy Spirit. Those who lie to the Holy Spirit, lie to God (Acts 5:3–9). Lying to God is much more consequential than lying to man (Basil, *On the Spirit* 16.37).

The Spirit is found actively directing the mission of the apostolate. The Spirit set aside Paul and Barnabas for their specific work (Acts 13:2), selected overseers for the flock (Acts 20:28; Ambrose, *Of the Holy Spirit* 2.13.145), bore witness (Acts 5:32; Rom. 8:16), distributed gifts freely as he chose (1 Cor. 12:11). These functions imply intelligence, will, feeling, purpose—all characteristic of personhood, which God possesses in incomparable measure (2 Cor. 12:8, 11). "The Israelites could not look steadily at the face [*prosōpon*] of Moses because of its glory." If so, "will not the ministry of the Spirit be even more glorious?" (2 Cor. 3:7, 8; Chysostom, *Hom. on Cor.* 7.1).

The Christian community confesses its belief not merely *about* but *in* God the Spirit. "Belief in" is directed to a person; "belief about" is directed to ideas or things (Gregory Nazianzus, *Orat.* 31.6).

Meeting God Personally

Unless we pretend that God is less a person than we ourselves, God the Spirit who speaks to us must be addressed personally. As it is through our own personal spirit that we breathe out words, so God the Spirit is known as a person is experienced, as "endowed with free volition, and energy . . . as the companion of the Word and the revealer of His energy," wrote John of Damascus (*OF* 1.7).

The modern depersonalization of God the Spirit occurred during the last two centuries, especially under the sway of philosophical idealism: Hegel reduced the Spirit to a logic of history. Tillich reduced the Spirit to an existential category of being itself. Process theology reduced the Spirit to creative energy. Much liberation theology reduced the Spirit to political praxis. Each reduction is tempted by unconstrained application of an impersonal analogy to the person of the Spirit (*Shepherd of Hermas* 2.3). The apostolic witness resisted such reductions.

Since the word *person* has been ecumenically "sanctioned by the usage of more than 1,500 years, and there is no other word which would really be better, more generally understandable and less exposed to misconception," Christian teaching continues to speak of God the Spirit as person (Rahner, *TI* 4:101–2). Without personal language, God the Spirit soon becomes reduced to a symbolic generalized "dimension of depth" (Tillich, *ST* 1:113)—an impersonal spatial metaphor. A person is not "a dimension".

Baptism is offered *in the name of the Holy Spirit*, as well as Father and Son. One cannot baptize in the name of an abstract quality, or an attribute, but only in the name of a living, authorizing person. To baptize in the name of the Father and Son and "the conceptual attribute of spirituality" would be a curious and inconsistent abuse of language. So the Spirit is a divine person and not merely spirituality as a concept applied to divinity (Ambrose, *Of the Holy Spirit* 1.13). "There are three in God to whom we can say 'You'" (Lonergan, in Fortman, *AHS*:162).

Sin Against the Spirit

We sin against the Spirit either by "grieving the Spirit," or by "blaspheming the Spirit," a distinction that must be neither overstated nor neglected.

Grieving the Spirit

The Spirit may be resisted (Acts 7:51). The convicting counsel of the Spirit may be quenched, choked, and virtually driven back by our resistances (1 Thess. 5:19; Athanasius, *Festal Letters*, 4.4). An endeavor may be begun in the Spirit that is later threatened with apostasy or defection (1 Tim. 1:19; Basil, *On the Spirit* 30.77).

There is not one single way of grieving the Spirit, but many. The Spirit may be ignored or refused, having been once loved and accepted, as the Galatians had turned from grace back to law (Gal. 3:2, 3; Augustine, *Epis. to Gal.* 19.3.1).

When the covenant people rebel against Yahweh through their neglect, egoism, and faithlessness, rejecting the offer of God's tender mercies, they grieved the Holy Spirit (Isa. 63:10). Paul implored his hearers to "not grieve the Holy Spirit" (Eph. 4:30; Ambrosiaster, *Epis. to Eph.* 4.30). One may grieve the Spirit, however, without blaspheming the Spirit.

Blaspheming the Holy Spirit

In Levitical law, blasphemy implied an explicit abuse and rejection of the divine name, hence of the divine reality. Jesus amazed his hearers when he said, "Every sin and blasphemy will be forgiven men, but the blasphemy against the Spirit will not be forgiven. Anyone who speaks a word against the *Son* of Man *will* be forgiven, but anyone who speaks against the Holy *Spirit* will *not* be forgiven, either in this age or in the age to come" (Matt. 12:31, 32, italics added; cf. Mark 3:27, 28; Luke 10:12; Nicetas of Remesiana, *The Power of the Holy Spirit, FC* 7:37).

This was said in specific response to "teachers of the law who came down from Jerusalem" to trap him, who predictably concluded, "He is possessed by Beelzebub!" (Mark 3:22; cf. Matt. 12:24).

The blasphemy referred to is that of directly ascribing to the power of evil the coming of God into history through the Son and the Spirit (Mark 3:28, 29, and parallels). This sin instantly places the self beyond the range of forgiveness, because every step toward repentance and faith is enabled by the Holy Spirit (Gregory of Nyssa, *On the Holy Spirit*). To blaspheme the Holy Spirit is gravely to misunderstand oneself in God's presence (Athanasius, *Ag. Arians*).

Whether Any Sin is Unpardonable

Paul's life offers ample evidence that blasphemy as such is forgivable (1 Tim. 1:13), since Paul himself blasphemed the church in his acts of persecution, and was forgiven.

Blasphemy against the Spirit, however, is not unforgivable in the sense that God is powerless or unwilling to forgive, but in the sense that the sinner is militantly unwilling to receive forgiveness. It is not that the sin is unpardonable because the atoning work of the Son is not sufficient for that sin. Rather the work of the Son is sufficient to salvation, but if that work is willfully demeaned, blocked, and detested by those for whom it would otherwise be entirely sufficient (Heb. 6:4–6), this sin is said to be unforgivable because as long as we are so deluded that we cannot repent, we have chosen not to be forgiven, having voluntarily closed off the possibility of being forgiven by closing ourselves to the Spirit. Those guilty of such sin are in the nature of the case unable to receive forgiveness (Cyprian, *Letters*, FC 51:46–49, 287–91; Thomas Aquinas, *ST* 2-2, Q14).

For those who obstinately turn away from the help of the Spirit, there is nothing more left. There is no further help to be given beyond the help God offers for salvation. It is possible for persons to pass beyond that limit and become so hardened against God's saving action that no further recourse is left to be opened. Those who absolutely turn away from life in the Spirit are left by their own choice "without hope and without God in the world" (Eph. 2:12). One who persists in the so-called Macedonian heresy (irreversibly asserting that the Spirit is not God) will be found "unpardonable because it cuts him off from Him by Whom he could confess: nor will he ever attain to healing pardon who has no Advocate" (Leo I, *Sermons* 75). Meanwhile God is never defeated by our blasphemies, only we (Calvin, *Inst.* 3.3.21–24).

The Person of the Holy Spirit in Triune Teaching

Redemption From the Father, Through the Son, By the Spirit

God the Father engenders the plan of salvation, offering to send the Son by the power of the Spirit. God the Son embodies and executes the atoning, redemptive plan to save humanity. God the Spirit applies the benefits of redemption under conditions of continuing historical development to empower the actual salvation of the faithful.

The three parts of this large work reflect the structure of classic Christian teaching as it is based upon on the triune life: *The living God* offers life. *The Word of life* takes responsibility for redeeming human life when fallen. *Life in the Spirit* brings to consummation the new life.

The power to bring all things into being proceeds from the Father. The power to repair and redeem the brokenness of all things belongs to the Son. The power to consummate and realize God's saving work belongs to the Spirit.

This is not a tritheism that posits three Gods, for in all these powers the faithful speak strictly of the one and only almighty God. "With the Holy Ghost through One Son, we preach one God" (Cyril of Jerusalem, *Catech. Lect.* 16.4). Abraham "saw Three and worshipped One" (Ambrose, *Of the Holy Spirit* 2.intro.4).

Inseparable, Distinguishable, Coeternal

Only within the triune premise can the seeming inconsistencies, vexations, errors and perplexities of biblical testimony be resolved. Whatever is said of God is rightly said of Son and Spirit. "Anyone who has seen me has seen the Father" who sends "the Spirit of truth" (John 14:9, 16; Nicetas of Remesiana, *Power of the Holy Spirit*, 7; Calvin, *Inst.* 1.9.3).

The Spirit enables that access to the Father which is merited by the Son: "For through him [Christ] we both have access to the Father by one Spirit" (Eph. 2:18). When Irenaeus writes: "Through the Spirit we rise to the Son; through the Son we rise to the Father" (*Ag. Her.* 5.36.2), he has this definite sequence in mind. We are resurrected to new life through the power of the Spirit to share in the life of the Son, who intercedes for us before the Father as those who share in his body (Origen, *OFP* 1.3.5).

The integrated language of Father, Son, and Spirit is not an invention of later post-apostolic teaching, but embedded so deeply in apostolic testimony itself as to be inseparable from it (Heb. 9:13–14). God the Spirit proceeds from (*ek*) the Father through (*dia, per*) the Son, as coessential (*homoousios*), coeternal, and co-equal with God the Father and God the Son (Tertullian, *Ag. Praxeas* 4; Gregory Nazianzus, *Orat.* 31.4; Basil, *On the Holy Spirit* 1.3).

The consensus-making process summarized generations of biblical study of the internal logic of triune teaching: "the Father from no one, the Son from the Father alone, and the Holy Spirit equally from both; and without beginning, always, and without end; the Father generating, the Son being born, the Holy Spirit proceeding; consubstantial, co-equal, co-omnipotent and co-eternal; one origin of all things" (Fourth Lateran Council, *TGS*:122–23). These are not empty phrases, but in each case condensed from scripture study and generations of liturgical history (Rufinus, *Comm. on Apostles' Creed* 35).

The Spirit Proceeding

The Holy Spirit is "uncreated, proceeding from the Father, and receiving from the Son" (Creed of Epiphanius). The relation of Father and Spirit is described not as generation, as in the case of the Son, but as a sending-forth (*pempō*, John 14:26; Basil, *On the Holy Spirit* 9.22–23) and a procession (*ekporeuomai*, John 15:26; Gregory of Nazianzus, *On the Holy Spirit*, *Orat.* 5[31].8–10). Basil drew from Paul the summary formula: "From the Father through the Son" (*Ag. Eunomians* 3.6).

The procession of the Holy Spirit from the Father and the Son was defined in the West at the Third Synod of Toledo (AD 589), adding "proceeding from the Father *and the Son*" (*Filioque*) to the Nicene Creed, an addition never accepted by the East. The Western tradition thus confessed a dual procession, wherein the "Spirit proceeds eternally from the Father and the Son, yet not as from two origins, but as from one origin, not by two breathings but by a single breathing" (Council of Lyons II, *SCD* 460). This became the chief theological cause of division in the history of the church of East and West, still a neuralgic point but in process of being mediated through irenic historical study.

Protestant formularies generally reflect the Western tradition, as do the Anglican articles: "The Holy Ghost, proceeding from the Father and the Son, is of one substance, majesty, and glory, with the Father and the Son, very and eternal God" (Thirty-nine Articles, 5). The Eastern tradition considered the *Filioque* as tending toward a Sabellian subordination and depersonalization of the Spirit (John 15:26; Photius, *On the Holy Ghost*; Synods of 869, 879; Lossky, *MTEC*).

The Unity of God in Salvation Teaching

The Father is moved with love toward fallen humanity to send the Son. The Son assumed human nature, suffered, died, and was resurrected to redeem humanity.

The Holy Spirit empowers recipients of this good news to appropriate and apply it. The biblical underpinning of this teaching is the Petrine salutation to God's scattered elect, who have been "chosen according to the foreknowledge of God the Father, through the sanctifying power of the Spirit, for obedience to Jesus Christ and sprinkling by his blood" (1 Pet. 1:2).

The whole range of God's triune activity thus works toward salvation: "The Father loves those who have fallen, the Son redeems those who have been loved, and the Holy Ghost calls and teaches those who have been redeemed" (Quenstedt, *TDP* 1). This deliberate sequence proceeds *from* the benevolence of God the Father toward humanity, *through* the atoning death of the Son in offering redemption, and *toward* the grace of the Spirit in applying redemption.

The same unified triune reasoning was expressed by the medieval Scholastics in terms of the integral interlinking of the various causes of salvation—the *original* cause of salvation as the love of God the Father, the *meritorious* cause of justification as the sacrifice of the Son, the *efficient* or effective cause of actually received salvation as the power of the Spirit eliciting by grace the response of the free will of the redeemed sinner (Thomas Aquinas, *ST* 2–1 Q112).

It is therefore fitting to ascribe creation primarily but not exclusively to the Father through the Son (Gen. 1–3; John 1), justification primarily but not exclusively to the Son through the Spirit (John 3:17; Gal. 4:4, 5), and sanctification primarily but not exclusively to the Spirit (2 Thess. 2:13; Titus 3:3). "Those operations in which eternal determination and origination are prominent are ascribed to the Father, those in which mediation and agency appear are referred to the Son, and those of efficiency, quickening and perfecting are attributed to the Spirit" (Hall, *DT* 8:7; cf. Owen, *Works* 3:9–17). The primary premise of any such reflection is that the *one* God is present in all triune acts and outworkings (Athanasius, *LCHS* 4.5).

The Role of the Spirit in Triune Relationship

The persons of the Trinity are defined essentially by their relations to each other, not by their separate characteristics as if imagined independent from the whole. If each person is "a subsisting *relation*," the Trinity is relational by definition (Tho. Aq, *ST* 1, Q29.4, italics added). "No one is his own spirit, no more than he is his own father or his own son," even as "no one is sent of himself" (Ursinus, *CHC*:272).

The Spirit is especially beheld in the relation of love between Father and Son, the "bond of love" between Father and Son (Augustine, *Trin.* 15.17–20). The Spirit is the inwardly enlivening principle of union, hiddenly uniting soul and body, inwardly uniting Christ and the church, unobtrusively uniting the church itself (Richard of St. Victor, *Trin.* 3.11).

As human personhood exists essentially as a *relation* between memory, intelligence, and will, so does the triune God exist as a relation of the Father as divine mind and memory, the Son as his expressed knowledge or Word, and the Spirit as the willing bond of love between Father and Son (Augustine, *Trin.* 14.15–15.28). In this way the image of God in humanity is revealed in the traces of the Trinity (*vestigia Trinitatis*) in the human capacity to remember, understand, and love. Augustine's triune analogies of mind, knowledge, and love (*mens, notitia, amor*) and memory, intelligence, and will (*memoria, intellectus, voluntas*) frequently reappeared in medieval discussions of the Trinity (Alexander of Hales, *Summa Universae Theologiae* 1, Q46; Tho. Aq., *ST* 1, Q27.4; Alan of Lille, *De Arte* 1, sent. 25), which later would come to form the "very rhythm of reality in the Hegelian Idealism of the 19th century" (Heron, *HS*:92).

The Relation of the Spirit to the Father and Son

The entire work of grace is ordered and directed by the one triune God who draws closer as the Spirit works through varied administrations and gifts. "The same God works all of them in all" (1 Cor. 12:6). The distinctions between the three persons of the one triune God are constantly reflected in texts of scripture.

Wherever the one God, Father, Son, and Spirit, is working so as to *generate or bring forth*, that work proceeds from the Father. Wherever the one God, Father, Son, and Spirit, works to *manifest his will and speak his Word*, that work is said to be more properly the work of the Son. Wherever the one God, Father, Son, and Spirit, works to realize, accomplish, and consummate what God has *begun and continued*, that action is more properly ascribed in Scripture as the movement of the Spirit (Gregory Nazianzus, *Orat.*, 30, 31).

If sent by the Father (John 14:26), the Spirit must be in some sense distinguishable from the Father. If "another Paraclete" (John 14:16) is sent in the name of the Son (John 14:26), the Spirit must be distinct from the Son.

Ambrose concluded: "So, then, the Father is holy, the Son is holy, and the Spirit is holy, but they are not three Holies. . . . Cherubim and Seraphim with unwearied voices praise Him and say: 'Holy, Holy, Holy, is the Lord God of Sabaoth.' They say it, not once, lest you should believe that there is but one; not twice, lest you should exclude the Spirit; they say not holies [in the plural], lest you should imagine that there is plurality, but they repeat thrice and say the same word, that even in a hymn you may understand the distinction of Persons in the Trinity, and the oneness of the Godhead" (*Of the Holy Spirit* 3.16.109–110).

Radiant Refraction of the Three-in-One Light

Paul concludes a major part of Romans with a hymn that recalls that judgments of God are unsearchable, and his paths are "beyond tracing out." (Rom. 11:33). He then closes the section with an oft-quoted summary benediction in three phrases: "For *from* [ek] him and *through* [di] him and *to* [eis] him are all things. To him be the glory forever! Amen" (Rom. 11:36, italics added). "Paul is referring to the Trinity when he says this" (Augustine, *Faith and the Creed* 16). Ambrose had written: "'From him' means the beginning and origin of the substance of the universe, i.e. by his will and power. . . . 'Through him' means continuation of the universe; 'unto him' means its end" (*Six Days of Creation* 5.19). The triune God is "from, through, and to" all things.

Origen explained: "Paul indicates the mystery of the Trinity. For when he says from you and through him and to him, this corresponds to the one God and Father, *from* whom are all things, and our one Lord Jesus Christ, *through* whom are all things. Likewise he says that all things are revealed *by* the Spirit of God, thus indicating that the providence of the Trinity is present in everything" (*Comm. on Rom.*, 11.36).

God is the One God *from* whom all things come to be. God is the One God *through* whom all things are put rightly in order and when awry brought to a coherence consistent with the divine purpose. God is the One God *into* whom all things are coming to their fitting conclusion or perfection.

We are seeking here to locate the Holy Spirit within triune logic: God the Spirit is the same God we know in creation and redemption, willing what the Father wills, sent on behalf of the Son, uttering inner testimony to the work of the triune God in creation, redemption, and consummation.

"The Father creates all things *through* the Word, *in* the Spirit" (Athanasius, *LCHS* 3.4). It is in the person of the Spirit that we meet the One who brings to fulfillment that holy love which has been abundantly poured forth from the Father and offered through the Son (John 1:1–7; 1 Cor. 8:6).

In expressing this mystery, the ecumenical tradition could not help but resort to poetic utterance: We proclaim "concisely and simply the doctrine of God the Trinity, comprehending out of Light (the Father), Light (the Son), in Light (the Holy Ghost) . . . Was and Was and Was, but Was One Thing, Light thrice repeated; but One Light. . . . In Thy Light shall we see Light" (Gregory Nazianzus, *Orat.* 31.3).

Language reaches for metaphor when pointing to personal mystery: "While there is one Person of the Sent, another of the Sender, and another of the Promiser, both the Unity and the Trinity are at the same time revealed to us." "The mercy of the Trinity divided for itself the work of our restoration in such a way that the Father should be propitiated, the Son should propitiate, and the Holy Spirit enkindle" (Leo I, *Sermons* 77). "The sphere of the Father's election, the Son's redemption, and the Spirit's sanctification is one and the same" (Helvetic Consensus). "None precedes the other in eternity, nor surpasses the other in power" (*Baltimore Catechism*).

Correcting Typical Doctrinal Offenses Against the Holy Spirit

Scripture warned of offenses against the Holy Spirit. The ecumenical councils had to deal with these offenses—among them were especially these:

The heresy of *simony* succumbed to the temptation to *use the Spirit instrumentally to make money,* after the pattern of Simon the sorcerer, who tried to purchase the incomparable Gift of God with money (Acts 8:18, 19), who wanted power "that he might sell to others that which could not be sold, and which he did not himself possess" (Cyril of Jerusalem, *Catech. Lect.* 16.10). Gregory I warned that one who is "promoted to any sacred order for a price, being already corrupted in the very root of his advancement, is the more ready to sell to others what he has bought" (*Letters* 53).

Modalism tended to reduce God the Spirit to our act of naming God in a particular mode (Sabellius, Paul of Samosata, Praxeas, Noetus). The heart of this misconception was that the Spirit is a part or role played by God. This was sometimes expressed in the view that there are three distinct separable chronological modes or conceptions of God: creation, redemption, sanctification—"one of them infinite both in essence and power, and the second in power but not in essence, and the third circumscribed in both" (Gregory Nazianzus, *Orat.* 31.5), thus making doubtful the eternality of the three persons.

Advocates of *Montanism* thought that *the Paraclete was speaking directly through themselves,* yet in such a way as to reach idiosyncratic conclusions that could not be received by the whole church (Hippolytus, *Refutation of All Heresies,* v. 12). They taught that the Spirit in the last days had come upon postapostolic prophets like Montanus and his followers, Priscilla and Maximilla, who were inordinately self-assured that the Paraclete was delivering new revelations through them and that additional revelations beyond apostolic testimony were needed for faith (Athanasius, *De Synodis*). Montanus "dared to say that he was himself the Holy Ghost,—he, miserable man," who crazily named the tiny hamlet of Pepuza in Phrygia "Jerusalem," yet continued calling himself by the shared name "Christian" (Cyril of Jerusalem, *Catech. Lect.* 16.8).

Marcionism argued that *the Old Testament was not inspired by the Holy Spirit,* but only selected parts of the New. This is why the creeds found it necessary to counter that the Spirit "spake by the prophets" (Creed of the 150 Fathers).

A more widespread heresy was that of the Tropici or Metaphoricals, and the Semi-Arian Macedonians, who taught that *the Spirit was created by the Son, hence less than God,* analogous to the Arian view that the Son is less than the eternal God (Athanasius, *LCHS* 1.21, 30). The Macedonian heresy, also called the Pneumatomachi party (exterminators of the spirit), ascribed equality to the Father and the Son, but thought the Spirit of lower rank (Council of Constantinople I, Canon 1; Leo I, *Sermons* 75). The Tropici, intensely preoccupied with typological or figurative language of the scripture, maintained that Spirit is a creature (as Arianism had said of the Son), perhaps an angel of the highest rank. Ecumenical teaching countered that the Holy Spirit is not an angel as if "sent forth to minister," but rather the true God who sends and is himself sent without ceasing to be God, and able to search the deep things of God (Cyril of Jerusalem, *Catech. Lect.* 16.23; 1 Cor. 2:10, 11). Athanasius set forth classic arguments for the consubstantiality of the Spirit with the Father and the Son, showing that the Spirit is indeed to be worshiped as God (*LCHS* 1.20–27; 3:1–6; Chrysostom, *Baptismal Instructions*).

Tritheism misunderstands the Father, Son, and Spirit as if they were separate and distinct Gods, denying the unity of substance of the three divine persons, thereby separating the Holy Spirit from the intimacy of the Trinity (Gregory Nazianzus, *Orat.* 31 *On The Holy Spirit*).

These were among the major heretical diversions from the orthodox doctrine of the person of the Spirit in early Christian teaching. They were remembered as heresies, meaning simply: "teachings *other than*" those of the apostles. Major doctrinal defenses of the deity of the Holy Spirit were set forth in the fourth century by Basil, Gregory of Nyssa, Didymus, Cyril of Jerusalem, Ambrose, and Augustine, providing a thorough consensual defense of scriptural teaching against these errors.

2

THE WORK OF THE SPIRIT

T HE SPIRIT IS AT WORK WHERE NEW LIFE in Christ is being drawn forth, the truth of the Son attested, and the community of faith enlivened.

God has chosen humanity to be the special object of divine grace, the unique vessel through which the divine glory is to be revealed. According to the Nicene-Constantinopolitan Creed, it is *for us* humans and our salvation that God came. The salvation event occurred "for us men" [i.e., *propter nos homines,* for humanity, *anthrōpous*] (Creed of 150 Fathers; Cyril of Alexandria, *Letters* 55).

What moved God to act on behalf of the salvation of humanity? God's own good pleasure (Eph. 1:5, 9; Phil. 2:13) in saving sinners by grace. God was not bound to save some or all by a higher will imposed by some external necessity. Saving grace springs from God's freedom to love. Peace on earth is offered to those "on whom his favor rests" (Luke 2:14). The work of grace is a central feature of the doctrine of the Holy Spirit (Marius Victorinus, *Epis. to Eph.* 1.1.8).

The Spirit's Preparatory Work

The Christian teaching of salvation deals first with the general features of the Spirit's administration of redemptive grace, followed by the specific teachings of call, repentance, justification by grace through faith, regeneration, adoption, sanctification, and union with Christ.

The Economy of Redemption

The economy of the Holy Spirit in the administration of the work of redemption begins even before the incarnation. Administration is what the Spirit does to prepare for and make effective the benefits of Christ. "Surely you have heard about the administration [*oikonomian,* stewardship, dispensation] of God's grace that was given to me for you" (Eph. 3:2; Chrysostom, *Hom. on Eph.* 6.3.2).

Both *economy* and *administration* may seem like modern terms. We may be surprised to discover that they have gone through almost two thousand years of liturgical usage before entering modern times. They refer to a central aspect of the classic Christian teaching of the Holy Spirit. Tertullian wrote: "What then, is the Paraclete's administrative office but this: the direction of discipline, the revelation of the Scriptures, the re-formation of the intellect. . . . First comes the grain, and from the grain arises the shoot, and from the shoot struggles out the shrub: thereafter boughs and leaves gather strength, and the whole that we call a tree expands: then follows the swelling of the germen, and from the germen bursts the flower, and from the flower the fruit opens: that fruit itself, rude for a while, and unshapely, little by little, keeping the straight course of its development, is trained to the mellowness of its flavor" (Tertullian, *On the Veiling of Virgins*).

The scriptures reveal an economy of redemption—the overall ordering of God's saving activity toward humanity. Through this broad-ranging design, God has "made known to us the mystery of his will according to his good pleasure, which he purposed in Christ, to be put into effect [*oikonomian*] when the times will have reached their fulfillment—to bring all things in heaven and on earth together under one head" (Eph. 1:9, 10).

It is crucial to grasp what such an economy requires, and in what sense God eternally grasps and foreknows the entire plan, yet by foreknowing does not unilaterally decree the plan so as to make human responsiveness irrelevant (Eph. 1:3–23). Only God knows how it can be that the plan is characterized by contingency, yet finally certain in its outcome, while specific outworkings remain obscure to finite human knowing (Augustine, *CG* 5.9–1; Nicetas of Remesiana, *Power of the Holy Spirit*, FC 7:32).

This economy or plan of salvation requires an envisioned *end* or purpose for history, appropriate *means* fitting to that end, and the effective *application* of these means to accomplish this purpose. To make all these work together is to economize them, or administer them as an ordered arrangement, an *oikonomia*, a vision of the whole and how each part works within it to order and provide for the divine-human covenant relation from beginning to end (Col. 1:25; Tertullian, *Ag. Praxeas* 2). "Before the law, before the very constituting of the world, God had formed this economy for the whole universe" (Chrysostom, *Interp. of Col.* 1:26)

The Spirit's Economy Makes Salvation Ultimately Sure Through Grace

In this economy God the Spirit did not merely render salvation hypothetically possible while leaving the outcome entirely dependent upon whether other finite wills might or might not respond to grace. The salvation of which the Bible speaks is by faith known to be ultimately secured and made certain by God's own determination, even though at present it is still penultimately being worked out.

There is little ambiguity in the ultimate promise: "I give them eternal life and they shall never perish; no one can snatch them out of my hand" (John 10:27–28; Theodore of Mopsuestia, *Comm. on John* 4.10.28–29), though many hazards remain yet ahead before the full accomplishment of God's saving purpose on the last day. On the rock of Peter's confession ("You are the Christ") the community of faith is being built so securely that "the gates of hell cannot prevail" against it (Matt. 16:18). Although essentially accomplished already in Jesus Christ, its historical outworking is still in process. Meanwhile the faithful are assured by the Spirit that what has begun in Jesus Christ will be consummated in future history in a fitting way.

To speak of the saving work of the Spirit, it is necessary first to speak of the eternal purpose of God as that purpose has become manifested through finite and contingent historic events. The eternally envisioned divine purpose has gradually unfolded through a series of historical developments or economies or providences, which from the postresurrection viewpoint may be seen as times of preparation. Through providence, God coordinates the divine purposes with human freedom so as to govern fallen aspects of history without coercing the liberty of creatures (Cyril of Alex., *Comm. on Luke,* Hom. 90).

The Redemptive Purpose Pervades the Economy of Salvation

Christ came to fulfill in time the eternal intention of the divine will. When the Son came into the world, he said to the Father, "I have come to do your will" (Heb. 10:9). The intent to reconcile whatever might fall was present in the triune God prior to creation. The Son could therefore be aptly described as "the Lamb that was slain from the creation of the world" (Rev. 13:8). Salvation is being enabled through the Spirit according to the eternal counsel of God's pretemporal will (Eph. 1:11; Chrysostom, *Hom. on Eph.* 2.1.11–14).

An integral vision of history is assumed in the New Testament connecting creation, redemption, and consummation (Rom. 5). This eternal foreknowing did not woodenly imply that all companionate wills are reduced to nothing by the divine will (Chrysostom, *Hom. on Eph.* 1.5). That God permits other finite wills to exercise choice is evident from their actual creation.

Redemptive love is thus the primordial purpose and motivation preceding creation. Its manifestation is the reason God creates (Irenaeus, *Ag. Her.,* 3.18).

What God Purposes from Eternity the Spirit Enables Through Time

The Spirit's mission is to bring about and complete God's purposes within fragile human histories. The being of God the Spirit is eternal. The Spirit's work in nature and history occurs in time.

The eternal being of the Spirit is the premise of the temporal work of the Spirit. It is the nature of the Holy Spirit to accomplish God's purpose, to make it happen.

What God does is formed by who God is and what God wills. It is not as though God first does something and then that is subsequently called God's will. God *is* Spirit eternally prior to any consequent activity as Spirit.

Classical Christianity posits love and intercommunion within the triune God prior to creation. "Let *us* make humankind in *our* image" (Gen. 1:26, italics added; Chrysostom, Hom. *on Gen.* 8.8). Father, Son, and Spirit are communicating with each other before creation. "A stream is one until it falls over the precipice and divides into many drops. So is the life of God one and undivided while hidden within Himself; but when it is poured out into created things its colors stand revealed" (Kuyper, *WHS*:14, 15). The Spirit reveals and weaves together the textures and colors and contours of God's purpose in history.

The Work of the Spirit in Creation and Providence

The work of the Spirit is celebrated in liturgy as manifested throughout all creation, not stingily, but abundantly through every phase of cosmic and human history. The work of the Spirit does not begin belatedly with Pentecost, but is found profusely in all creation and its continuing providences, and throughout the entire history of salvation, which in due time comes to fulfillment in the incarnation and the Spirit's enabling of the body of Christ, whose purpose is yet to be finally consummated in the general resurrection.

The Spirit illumines reason, enables political order, and restrains the capacity for humanity to destroy itself. These are among the "general operations" of the Spirit which are conjointly being enabled by the Spirit in full concurrence with the Father and the Son: offering of life, supporting of life newly given, nurturing continuing life, strengthening life nurtured, and guiding life strengthened. This applies to all forms of life, whether plant, animal, or human. In these ways scripture celebrates God's Spirit in creating (Gen. 1:2; Ps. 104:30; Job 33:4), redeeming (Isa. 44:3, 23), and offering gifts to all creatures (Gen. 2:7; 41:38; Exod. 28:3; 31:3) according to their ability to receive.

The Spirit Provides

The Spirit of God moved to bring order from chaos, elegance from emptiness, making beautiful in its own way each creature touched, garnishing the heavens. "There can be nothing which the Holy Spirit can be said not to have made" (Ambrose, *Of the Holy Spirit* 1.5.37). "By his breath [*ruach*] the skies became fair," exclaimed Job, acknowledging that "these are but the outer fringe of his works," which only bespeak "the whisper we hear of him" in his full glory (Job 26:13–14). The finite mind is unable to grasp in how many ways the Spirit provides. "Who has understood the mind of the Lord, or instructed him as his counselor?" (Isa. 40:12, 13).

The Spirit works through providence to sustain all that is created (Ps. 104:10–14, 30; Chrysostom, *Hom. on Cor.* 8.3). The Spirit filled Bezalel and the craftsmen as they worked on the temple (Exod. 31:3; 35:31). Even the sins of the fallen, for which God is not responsible, are in time made serviceable to the whole (Origen, *Ag. Celsus* 4.54, 70; *Comm. on Numbers*, Hom. 14.2).

Only One who is "God of the spirits of all flesh" (Num. 16:22) could pour out his Spirit "on all flesh" (Acts 2:17; Bede, *Comm. on Acts* 2.17). Only this One could unify all diverse human purposes (Job 32:8), inspiring not only the civil lawgivers and sages but also the poets, and above all the prophets (Num. 1:7, 25, 26; 2 Sam. 23:2; 1 Kings 22:24; Ezek. 2:2; 11:5; Dan. 4:8, 11; Mic. 3:8), commissioning magistrates, judges, kings, and prophets, restraining evil, and enabling good. The Spirit works in universal human history, striving with persons (Gen. 6:3), witnessing to all of God's own coming (John 15:26, 27), convicting of sin (Acts 2:36), attesting God's righteousness, making sure the promises of God (Acts 2:32, 33). Cyril of Jerusalsm taught his young seekers that it is by God's own Spirit that "Othniel judged; Gideon waxed strong; Jephtha conquered; Deborah, a woman, waged war; and Samson, so long as he did righteously and grieved Him not, wrought deeds above man's power" (Cyril, *Catech. Lect.* 16.28).

The Spirit inspires human insight in literature, the arts, the sciences, philosophy, poetry, and political life. Renaissance art at times portrayed Socrates as teaching on the porch of the temple (Justin Martyr, *Address to the Greeks* 20–33). Justin was convinced that Plato knew of the Holy Spirit (*Exhortation to the Greeks* 32–38). There is no work or thought or achievement in human history that is deprived of the Spirit's gifts (Jer. 31:35; Ps. 136:25; 2 Cor. 3:3–11; John 3:34; Wisd. 7:17–20). The Spirit is present in preparing all humanity for God's own coming in the Son.

The Spirit Gives Life

Merely to be alive is to be endowed with life by the Spirit of God. To imagine the withdrawal of the Spirit is to think of death. "The Spirit of God has made me;

the breath of the Almighty gives me life" (Job 33:4). If God would withdraw "his spirit [*ruach*] and breath [*neshamah*], all mankind would perish" (Job 34:14, 15). "When you take away their breath [*ruach*], they die and return to the dust" (Ps. 104:29; cf. Gen. 2:7; Ezek. 37:9). "The Spirit which speaks and sends is a living Spirit" (Cyril of Jerusalem, *Catech. Lect.* 17.28), though death is a necessary boundary of all finite life under the conditions of sin. The Spirit is bestowing life (Theodore of Mopsuestia, *Comm. on John*, 7.20.22). Creatures are receiving life.

The Spirit is preparing the conditions for bringing contrite sinners into communion with God. Only through free, conscious beings is this communion possible. How else could the vast, silent, otherwise unperceiving creation respond to God in conscious, knowing companionship and relationship (Gen. 2:7; Gregory of Nyssa, *On the Creation of Man* 28.1–29.1). Though God may be glorified by the huge speechless cosmic and natural creation, the scriptures speak more clearly of the delight that comes to God from conscious, rational, free creatures who love God in and through all creation (Basil, *Exegetic Homilies on Ps.* 19.8).

The hard question turns upon how erring children of the divine Father might be made able to glorify the incomparably holy God. The plan of the triune God for redemption is accomplished only when God's own Spirit dwells in the fallen human heart so as to refashion it (Jer. 31:31–34; Chrysostom, On *Epis. to Heb.* 16.1).

The Spirit quickens the life of faith, seals the promise in baptism, sustains the new life in prayer, and reveals glimpses of "what is yet to come" (John 16:13; Didymus the Blind, *On the Holy Spirit* 38).

The Spirit Redeems

The primordial work of God in creation provides the pattern of the work of God in regeneration or re-creation of fallen freedom dead in sin (Eph. 2:1–10; Athanasius, *LCHS* 1.9). As the heavens were made by the breath of the Lord (Ps. 33:6), so the fallen creature is remade by God's Word through the Spirit as if breathing new life into sinners.

The Spirit accompanies the Word as breath conveys speech (John 20, 22; Cyril of Alex., *Comm. on John* 9.1; Gregory of Nyssa, *The Great Catechism* 2, 3). "The same Spirit who in the beginning moved upon the waters has in the dispensation of grace given us the holy Scripture, the Person of Christ, and the Christian Church" (Kuyper, *WHS*:25; Athanasius, *Discourses Ag. Arians*, 1.12.50; *LCHS* 1.19–22).

Through the Spirit the almighty God directly touches, meets, and indwells within the human spirit (Theodore of Mopsuestia, *Comm. on John* 6.14.15–17). God the Spirit sustains the soul through the hazards of moral struggle. God's Spirit works to draw human freedom without coercion back to its original purpose of refracting the goodness of God. Whether the freedom of the creature chooses to remain alienated from God or to be free for God, the Spirit continues to work within the inner sphere of personal freedom to glorify God in whatever ways possible by drawing freedom quietly toward its true ground (Augustine, *Confessions*, 1–4). God is at work in the soul from the beginning of its creation to its final restoration.

When the Lord "gave his life for our life," he poured "out the Spirit of the Father to unite us and reconcile God and man, bringing God down to man through the Spirit, and raising man to God through his incarnation," "attaining his purpose not by force . . . but by way of persuasion" (Irenaeus, *Ag. Her.* 5.1.1–2).

God Spoke By the Prophets Through the Spirit

The covenant community that appears in the Old Testament as seed of Abraham reappears in the New Testament as *ekklēsia* (Irenaeus, *Ag. Her.* 4.5). From the remnant of Israel there comes the promise of the new Israel. The chosen seed bears fruit for all humanity (Bede, *Comm. on Acts* 3:25).

Seen in terms of the continuous history of covenant, there is only one called out people of God, made one by the One who called them out of nothing (Hosea 2:23; Ambrose, *Of Holy Spirit* 2.10). Yet this one people has journeyed through many stages of historical development (Theodoret, *Interp. of Heb. 1*). Amid astonishing varieties of complex history, there remains a distinct thread of continuity in the economy of salvation history (Irenaeus, *Ag. Her.* 4.33.7).

The intent of prophecy is clearly set forth in John's Gospel: "I have told you now before it happens, so that when it does happen you will believe" (John 14:29; cf. 13:19). These Old Testament anticipations must not be forgotten but by the power of the Spirit. They are savored and remembered in Christian teaching (Isa. 41:23; 42:9; 43:19; Heb. 11:3–38).

In the creed the church confesses that God the Spirit "spoke through the prophets" (Heb. 1:1; 1 Cor. 12:8–10; Creed of the 150 Fathers; Cyril of Jerusalem, *SCD* 9). "*By your Spirit you admonished them through your prophets*" (Neh. 9:30, italics added; Theophilus, *To Autolycus* 2.9). Joel specifically told of a future time when the Spirit would be poured out upon all flesh (Joel 2:28, 29). Peter preached that Joel's prophecy (2:30, 31) had been explicitly fulfilled at Pentecost (Acts 2:14–21; Chrysostom, *Hom. on Acts* 5; Kuyper, *WHS*:112–16).

God has never left himself without witness in the world. The world has never been without some anticipatory form of the calling and ingathering of the people of God (Acts 14:17; Chrysostom, *Hom. on Acts* 31). Before the incarnation this covenant people was being gathered in the form of expectation; after the incarnation in the form of fulfillment (Hippolytus, *On the Consummation of the Word*).

Prior to the incarnation, the Spirit was omnipresently working in and beyond Israel to call forth the community of faith in the form of hope (Heb. 11:4–22). After the incarnation, the Spirit was omnipresently working in and beyond Israel to call forth the community of faith in the form of fulfillment, indwelling within that community to enable each member of the community to be united with the living risen Lord (Col. 3:16; 1 John 4:12–16).

The Spirit Calls Forth a Continuous History of Covenant

The Hebraic idea of the called people of God (*qahal*) is that of a people brought by Yahweh into covenant, elected not for superiority but for service (Exod. 19:3–6; Deut. 7:6; 1 Sam. 12:22; Ps. 135:4; Rom. 1:6; Eph. 1:4, 5; 1 Pet. 2:9). Paul wrote that his forefathers were "all baptized into Moses in the cloud and the sea" (1 Cor. 10:2). He was seeing the exodus from the viewpoint of the resurrection. He was describing an imitative anticipation of the future, an exhibition of things expected (Heb. 11:2,3; Cyril of Jerusalem, *Catech. Lect.* 5.1–3). Thus the manna was regarded by the consensual exegetes as "a type of the living bread," the exodus a type of baptism (Basil, *On the Holy Spirit* 1.14; Gregory of Nyssa, *The Life of Moses*, *CWS*:38–41).

Before the Son, the Spirit came to humanity in the form of figurative types and shadows of that which was to come. Upon the coming of the Son as light of the world, all previous shadows of revelation were bathed in pure light (1 John 1:4–9; Kuyper, *WHS*:53).

Those earlier anticipations (temple sacrifice, feast days, the codification of Levitical law, the ordering of priesthood) continued to have transmuted relevance to the new people of God, viewed in the light of the resurrection (Heb. 7:1–23). After the resurrection, the searching of scripture focused on the spiritual exercise of seeking to understand the anticipations of God's own coming in salvation history and universal history (Heb. 10:1–5; Origen, *OFP* 4.2.4).

The work of God the Spirit prior to the incarnation had an anticipatory meaning for those who experienced it and an interpretive meaning for those who remembered these anticipations from the viewpoint of their fulfillment in the resurrection (John 14:26; Augustine, *Tractates on John* 77.2). In due time each of these preliminary meanings would be seen from the vantage point of their fulfillment and completion in Christ.

The Continuity of Old and New

The history of the people of Israel has become Christianity's own history, without which the story of God's coming in Jesus would be vacuous and ephemeral. Marcion's attempt to "tear away" the Old from the New Testament (Cyril of Jerusalem, *Catech. Lect.* 1) and to dismiss the old covenant as if irrelevant to the new was considered dangerous (Irenaeus, *Ag. Her.* 4.7; Tertullian, *Ag. Marcion*).

The Spirit "used this gentle treatment, fitted for our needs, gradually accustoming us to see first the shadows of objects, and to look at the sun in water, to save us from dashing against the spectacle of pure unadulterated light, and being blinded. Just so the Law, having a shadow of things to come . . . [became the] means to train the eyes of the heart" (Basil, *On the Holy Spirit* I.14).

The Spirit has always been calling forth faith. In that sense, "the one, holy universal church" has sought to call and enfold believers from the time of Abel onward (Gregory I, *Hom. on Ezek.* I.8.28; 2.3.17). Even though the covenant community has always been mixed with hypocrites while in history (Hilary, *On Matthew*, 2.4; Melanchthon, *Corpus Reformatorum* 12.481–483; 21.834), in various times and places throughout history there have been anticipations of the called out community of covenant enabled through the Spirit.

As the called out community prior to the incarnation shared in God's coming salvation by way of hope in God's promise, so does the called out community after the incarnation share in God's accomplished salvation in the form of Spirit-led recollection, testimony, remembrance, and celebration of God's own coming, which is even yet awaiting God's coming again (John 14:26; Basil, *On Holy Spirit* 9.22; Eusebius, *Proof of the Gospel*).

This new called out people began to exist when after the ascension the Head of the body, sitting at the right hand of the Father, was ready to form the body through the indwelling Spirit. "God placed all things under his feet and appointed him to be head over everything for the church, which is his body, the fullness of him who fills everything in every way" (Eph. 1:22, 23).

The Pivot of History

All this happened within weeks after the death of Jesus. This intense series of events is the pivot of covenant history, the inauguration of the new aeon. This vast body of scriptural testimony becomes blended in the single proclamation of God's salvation (*yeshuah, soteria*) of humanity, the history of the divine-human covenant (Isa. 51:6–8; Luke 19:9; Acts 16:17; Rom. 1:16; 1 Pet. 1:9).

Christ, having died for our sins, was buried, descended, raised, ascended to the right hand of the Father in heavenly intercession. The new covenant was ratified, the great commission given, and all this was immediately followed by:

The outpouring of the Spirit at Pentecost

The calling out of the new people of God

The forming of the body of Christ

The introduction of the new law of love

The apostles were sent to preach the gospel to the whole world

To understand this sequence is to think in an orderly way about the coming and indwelling of the Holy Spirit. To draw near to this matrix of events invites reflection upon key symbols and signs by which it has been conveyed and remembered.

Types and Symbols of the Holy Spirit in Scripture

Symbols of the promise of the coming of the Holy Spirit that recur in the Hebrew Bible include wind, fire, water, dove, and the oil of anointing. These figures of speech all dramatically coalesce in the event of Pentecost: "Suddenly a sound like the blowing of a violent wind came from heaven and filled the whole house where they were sitting," and "all of them were filled with the Holy Spirit," who appeared to them as flaming tongues parting asunder so as to settle upon each one of them (Acts 2:2–4); they received the promised "baptism with the Spirit and with fire" (Matt. 3:11), after which they preached the baptism of repentance (Acts 13:24), and received the anointing of the Spirit that was promised to be poured out in the last days (Acts 2:17, 33; Titus 3:5, 6).

The Spirit as Invisible Wind

The breeze is not discernible to the visual sense, though one can feel it on one's skin. The breath of God is like wind (Athanasius, *LCHS* 1.7–8; Clement of Alex. *Comm. on John* 9.1).

The Spirit of God is that invisible enabling agent by which God's power is manifested while remaining unseen. *Ruach* is the outbreathing, the proceeding, the imperceptible going forth of the life of God (Athanasius, *LCHS* 1.15–19; *Ag. Arians* 1.12.50). Jesus compared the Spirit to the wind that moves where it wills (Ambrose, *Chr. Faith* 2.6.47). One cannot ever account precisely from where it comes or goes or why. Similarly we are born of God from above by the Spirit (John 3:8).

No words can be said without wind moving through the flexing chambers of our voices. As we use invisible wind to speak words and convey meanings, so God's unseen Spirit is moving by silent means to convey God's revelation (John 20;22; Augustine, *Trin.* 15.26.46).

Spirit as Cleansing Water

The Spirit is typified by water, a symbol for cleansing, reviving, and refreshing, without which life does not long continue (Cyril of Jerusalem, *Catech. Lect.* 16.12; Hildegard of Bingen, *Symphonia*:141). Water is "a perfect, gladsome, simple material substance, pure in itself" that "supplied a worthy vehicle to God" (Tertullian, *On Baptism* 3). As the Son, the living water, cleanses the faithful from all unrighteousness (1 John 1:9), so is cleansing from sin enabled by the Spirit, who like a deep source of spring water renews the believer steadily (John 4:14; Athanasius, *Defense of Dionysius*; Cyril of Alex., *Comm. on John* 2.4).

Water as a symbol or type of the Spirit becomes most explicit in John's Gospel, where during the first seven days of the Feast of Tabernacles, the people brought water from the Pool of Siloam to the altar. Then on the eighth day, "the last and greatest day of the feast, Jesus stood and said in a loud voice, 'If anyone is thirsty, let him come to me and drink. Whoever believes in me, as the Scripture has said, streams of living water will flow from within him.' By this he meant the Spirit, whom those who believed in him were later to receive. Up to that time the Spirit had not been given, since Jesus had not yet been glorified" (John 7:37, 38; Ambrose, *Of Holy Spirit* 3.20.153–156; Chrysostom, *Hom. on John* 51). The Spirit, like water, is life-nurturing, revitalizing (*Apostolic Constitutions* 7.1.43; Athanasius, *LCHS* 1.19).

Spirit as Fire Burning away Dross

Divine revelation was often experienced as accompanied by light, fire, radiance, or brightness—Moses' burning bush, Elijah on Mount Carmel, Paul on the road to Damascus, and John on Patmos all attest the presence of light or fire in divine disclosure (1 Kings 18:38; Rev. 22:5; Athanasius, *Defence of the Nicene Definition*).

Fire symbolized both the coming of God's grace toward those who were responsive and the rejection of sin by the holiness of God (Exod. 3:2; 14:20; 24:17), whose anger against sin is like a consuming fire (Heb. 12:29). Fire both "improves good deeds like gold, and consumes sins like stubble" (Ambrose, *Of the Holy Spirit* 1.14.169). By fire the dross is burned away and the pure element conserved (Chrysostom, *Hom. on John* 32.1).

As fire warms, so does the Spirit. As fire ignites, so is human speech and action ignited by the Spirit (Cyprian, *Treatises 12*). Jeremiah wrote of Yahweh's address, "I will make my words in your mouth a fire, and these people the wood it consumes" (Jer. 5:14). When Jeremiah tried to keep quiet about the word he heard from the Lord, he found that "his word is in my heart like a fire, a fire shut up in my bones" (Jer. 20:9).

Zealous service of the Spirit is likened to fire, where love is flaming into human warmth and fervent prayer (Ambrose, *Duties* 3.18). The Spirit desires to kindle this fire with all speed, "for He longs for speed in doing us good"; hence the Spirit "moves with speed like the speed of light" (Gregory Nazianzus, *Orat.* 40.36–37; Athanasius, *LCHS* I.19).

Spirit as Dove

At Jesus' baptism the Spirit descended upon him in the form of a dove. The dove is without guile, lacking any form of deception (Matt. 3:16; Mark 1:10; Luke 3:22; John 1:32; Augustine, *Christian Combat*, 22.24). The dove descended from heaven to earth, resting upon the anointed One (Gregory of Nyssa, *FGG*:189, 284). John the Baptist had testified, " 'The man on whom you see the Spirit come down and remain is he who will baptize with the Holy Spirit.' I have seen and I testify that this is the Son of God" (John 3:33, 34; Ambrose, *Sacr.* 1.6).

The dove that returned to the ark with an olive leaf furnished Noah the proof that God's judgment of humanity was ending and that the renewal of humanity was occurring (Gregory Thaumaturgus, *Fourth Hom., On Holy Theophany*). The dove was a figure or type of the Spirit suggesting peace, gentleness, grace, beauty, and guilelessness (Cyprian, *On the Unity of the Church*; *Letters*; Tertullian, *On Baptism* 8; *Ag. Valentinians*, 3).

Anointing with Oil as a Biblical Symbol of the Spirit

The figure of anointing embraced metaphors of consecrating, setting apart, giving gifts and blessings, and making fit for service. Anointing is an expression of the Spirit's comforting presence, seal, blessing, and commissioning.

Prophets were anointed that God's own Spirit might address the people directly (1 Kings 19:16). Priests were anointed that the Spirit might minister to the people through worship and sacrifice (Lev. 8:12). Civil servants were anointed that the Spirit might rightly govern the people and judge justly (1 Sam. 15:1, 17; Gregory I, *Pas. Care* 2.6).

Oil [*shemen*, Gk: *elaion*] was considered useful not only as a source of nutrition (Rev. 6:6) but also as a medicine (Mark 6:13; James 5:14). Oil also had sacrificial and ceremonial functions (Ambrose, *Letters* 52). Oil was used in the setting apart of holy places, offices, and duties (Exod. 40:9–16; Lev. 8). Oil was employed for many uses in healing, illuminating, comforting, commissioning, and anointing (Num. 4:9, 6:15; Matt. 25:3–8; Methodius, *Banquet of the Ten Virgins*, 6.4). Similarly, God the Spirit works by healing, illuminating, comforting, commissioning, and anointing (*Apostolic Constitutions* 7.4.42; cf. Calvin, 4.19).

As oil was used to light up the tabernacle (Exod. 25:6), the faithful are called to walk according to the light provided by the Spirit. The lamp of the Word that guides our path through the dark is kept burning by the Spirit (Ps. 119:105; Chrysostom, *Baptismal Instructions*).

Christ was anointed with oil as a symbol of the healing, guiding, consecrating Spirit. Cyril taught his seekers that similarly "you were anointed with ointment, having been made partakers and fellows of Christ" in baptism. This is not plain ointment, he explained, any more than eucharistic bread is merely bread after the invocation, for then it becomes Christ's gift that by the Spirit is being "made fit to impart His Divine Nature. This ointment is symbolically applied to your forehead and your other senses; and while your body is anointed with the visible ointment, your soul is sanctified by the Holy and Life-giving Spirit" (Cyril of Jerusalem, *Catech. Lect.* 21.2). In this way chrismation, or anointing with oil, accompanied baptism in ancient Christian liturgical practice.

As oil makes one's face shine, so does the Spirit make the believer radiant with the "oil of joy" (Ps. 45:7). When David was anointed, the "Spirit of the Lord came mightily upon David from that day forward" (1 Sam. 16:13; Cassiodorus, *Expos. Of Ps.* Preface, 1). Samson was filled with enormous strength when the Spirit came upon him (Judg. 14:19). God's *ruach* came upon Gideon, Jephthah, and Saul amid combat (Judg. 5:34; 11:29; 1 Sam. 11:6). As the Spirit empowered Joseph's administrative skill (Gen. 41:38, 39), so the Spirit enabled the skill of artisans to enhance the beauty of the temple (Exod. 31:2–4; 1 Kings 7:14), and so blessed Aaron's garments of consecration (Exod. 28:3). The Spirit was in Joshua in leading Israel to the promised land (Num. 27:18), in Gideon's stunning triumph (Judg. 6:34) and in enabling Ezekiel to speak to a rebellious nation (Ezek. 2:2, 3).

The prophets foresaw that the Spirit would inaugurate the messianic kingdom (Isa. 32:15; 44:3; 59:21; Zech. 12:10), which would extend even to the Gentiles (Isa. 60:3–11; Acts 2:16, 17). The turn of history finally came when John the Baptist announced that one would come after him baptizing with the Holy Spirit and with fire (Luke 3:16; Chrysostom, *Baptismal Instructions* 11:13).

Baptism as Anointing

The relation of bathing and anointing is seen early in the Mosaic covenant where Aaron was first bathed in water and then anointed.

Oil was applied in a special sequence in ceremonial cleansing first to the ear that one would be ready to hear, then to the thumb of the right hand that it might become an instrument of righteousness, then to the great toe of the right foot that one might walk in the way of holiness. The remainder was poured on the head so the whole soul might be consecrated to God in an act of overflowing grace (Lev. 8:12; Cyril of Jerus., *Catech. Lect.* 3.6).

This Levitical use of oil became the pattern for rites of healing through the Spirit and for final passage (*viaticum*). In the early church those baptized were anointed on the forehead (Exod. 28:38), that they with unveiled face might reflect as a mirror the glory of God. Once having received this anointing, this chrism, believers were ready to be named by Christian names and called into the Christian life, having received new birth into a new family.

Anointing Spirit, Anointed Son

The community prays that the Spirit will be the active agent in the rite of anointing by oil (Lev. 8; 1 Sam. 16; Athanasius, *LCHS* 1.22–4). Aaron became the model of one who being first anointed was then called to anoint others, a pattern that was followed by the high priest anointing priests and the apostles anointing the apostolate (Exod. 40; 1 John 2:27).

The archetype of the anointed One (*Mashiach, Christos*) is the Son of whom it would be said that "the Spirit of the Lord is on me, because he has anointed me to preach good news to the poor" (Luke 4:18; cf. Isa. 61:1, 2). Peter vividly remembered "how God anointed Jesus of Nazareth with the Holy Spirit and power" (Acts 10:38; Bede, *Comm. on Acts* 10.38).

All these images complement each other in speaking of the varied ministries of the Holy Spirit. All major aspects of the work of the Spirit in the New Testament are anticipated in Old Testament types. The believer is clothed with power, born from above, anointed, and set apart for service by the work of the Spirit (Cyril of Jerusalem, *Catech. Lect.* 17.12). "Thus with divine accuracy did even the types anticipate the two-fold provision for the Christian life, cleansing by the blood and hallowing by the oil—justification in Christ, sanctification in the Spirit" (A. J. Gordon, *MS*:95). So in Christian worship, our adoption into the family of God is offered liturgically as a gift of grace in baptism.

The Work of the Spirit in the Present Age

The Present Age

The present age is the age of the Spirit, to whom has been committed the work of applying the redemption of the Son to the lives of persons by calling, justifying, and sanctifying them. The new age or dispensation of the Spirit is given to comfort and guide the witnessing community following Christ's ascension. The present age is now continuing in our present history, and at some point it will be completed with the return of the Son (Jerome, *Epis. to Eph.* 2.3.20–21).

The subject matter of this ecumenical teaching is very different from comparative or developmental accounts of the varieties of Christian teaching. My passion is the search for ecumenical general lay consent in the reception of consensually received texts that reflect the one mind of the believing church. That is all I am trying to do. It is an exercise in discernment using classic texts as our guide. Given the limits of this study, we leave many ancillary questions of development to historians, except as those varieties of developments can be shown to be consensually received within classic Christian teaching over two millennia. It is this pattern of wholeness that we now seek to identify as it pertains to the work the Spirit has been doing since Jesus came.

The simplicity of scripture has always been a stumbling block to those who view themselves as wise above scripture. "Those things which appear humble are considered senile, foolish, and common. So they regard nothing as true except that which is pleasant to the ear; nothing as credible except that which can excite pleasure. No one estimates a subject by its truth but by its embellishment" (Lactantius, *DI* 5.1). So today has scripture study stumbled over the simplicity of the gospel and found offense in its clarity. Scripture remains its own best interpreter, by means of the analogy of faith applied by comparing text with text under the guidance of the Spirit (Tertullian, *Ag. Praxeas* 17–21). Christian truth is best defended in its plain sense (1 Cor. 1:18–21; 3:18–23; Tertullian, *Ag. Valentinians* 3; Ambrosiaster, *Comm. on Paul*, Eph. 1.20).

The Spirit Enables the Mission of the Son

Every gift requisite to the Son's mission is provided by the Spirit. "Jesus, full of the Holy Spirit, returned from the Jordan and was led by the Spirit" (Luke 4:1). It was "the Son, who as to his human nature was a descendant of David," who was "through the Spirit of holiness," according to Paul, "declared with power to be the Son of God by his resurrection from the dead" (Rom. 1:4). To the Son "whom God has sent," the Father has given "the Spirit without limit" (John 3:34). The living body of Christ today shares in these gifts, which are distributed at God's good pleasure.

The Spirit works to enable the faithful to hear and respond to Christ's living personal presence. The Spirit makes effectual the work of the Son in ways beyond our knowing, at a depth that cannot be uttered (Rom. 8:26; *Augustine on Romans* 54). This occurs not merely with words but with a demonstration of the Spirit and power (1 Cor. 2:4; Origen, *OFP* 4.1.17; Calvin *Inst.* 3.1.1; 4.14–19).

The Administration of Redemption in the World

The Spirit comes to guide the faithful into all truth, put doubt to flight, magnify the power of God, remember accurately the events of the Son's coming, provide for its accurate transmission, and assure the faithful of their adoption as sons and daughters in the family of God. The Spirit is given as a seal or stamp that God places upon his own, an earnest or pledge of what is to come in the final consummation (Chrysostom, *Hom. on Eph.* 2.1.11–14; Jerome, *Epis. to Eph.* 1.1:14).

The present age extends from Pentecost to Parousia, wherein the Spirit is working to awaken and sustain the continuing body of Christ, to restore humanity as a whole. We now experience the age between the first and second advent of Christ. The work of the Spirit will be crowned by the return of the Son and the judgment of history.

The notion of a *new age* (a new creation, Gal. 6:15; new covenant, 2 Cor. 3:6; new life, Rom. 6:4; a new and living way, Heb. 10:20) is recurrent in the New Testament. This makes ironic the fact that the term *new age* has been so long commandeered by faddists that it is already feeling old. It is precisely amid declining modernity that "New Age" has come to mean the old paganism. But that irony gives no sufficient reason why Christian orthodoxy should abandon a term long offered by apostolic teaching. The apostolic language is better defended against distortion than abandoned.

The Personal Direction of the Spirit

As the apostles were under the personal direction of the Son during his earthly ministry, so after the resurrection the apostolic tradition is under the Spirit (Acts 8:25–40; 10:19; 11:12). In baptism the whole person is drenched with the love of God. So in the coming of the Spirit the whole of history is being met with the revelation of that love (Chrysostom, *Hom. on Acts* 22).

The Spirit is given in the place of Christ's bodily presence. Before the pivot of covenant history, the Spirit was not yet unreservedly self-offered as indwelling. Afterward, when the risen Lord ascended, he promised that the Spirit would come as helper and abiding companion of the people of God, and that the Spirit would accompany the witnessing community until he personally returned (Gregory of Nazianzus, *On Pentecost*, Orat. 41.11).

The Spirit reproves and challenges the faithful to accountability to the holy God, and comforts the faithful in their sin. "His coming is gentle; the perception of Him is fragrant, his burden most light," Cyril taught. "He comes to save, and to heal, to teach, to admonish, to strengthen, to exhort, to enlighten" (Cyril of Jerusalem, *Catech. Lect.* 16.16).

The Spirit Allows Due Time for Conveying the Word to the World

The present age is the age of Gentile inclusion, not Gentile hegemony or superiority, but inclusion in the salvation history into which Israel has been covenanted from the time of Abraham. The present age is providentially being allowed time for the gathering-scattering community to attest God's saving action through the Son and the Spirit (Bede, *Comm. on Acts*, 19.4–5). In the time remaining in world history, God intends to restore whatever might have fallen through sin so as to apply the work of the Son fittingly to all who have ears to hear, eyes to see.

Prior to his ascension, even Jesus did not actively extend his mission beyond Israel, for he explicitly said at this preresurrection stage, "I was sent only to the lost sheep of Israel" (Matt. 15:24). After his ascension, however, a new age had begun. The disciples were commanded to go into all the world and preach the gospel to every creature until Christ's return. The penitent Gentiles were privileged to enter into the sphere of divine reconciliation just as much as the penitent Jews. Paul reminded Gentile hearers that "formerly" (before the present age of the gospel) "at that time you were separate from Christ, excluded from citizenship in Israel and foreigners to the covenants of the promise, without hope and without God in the world. But now in Christ Jesus you who once were far away have been brought near through the blood of Christ" (Eph. 2:12, 13; Ambrosiaster, *Epis. to Eph.* 2.13–14).

The entire present age from Pentecost to Parousia is an age of testimony, proclamation, self-giving witness (*marturia*), so as to fulfill Israel's calling to become a blessing for all humanity, so that "all people on earth will be blessed through you" (Gen. 12:3). "When the Counselor comes, whom I will send to you from the Father, the Spirit of truth who goes out from the Father, he will testify about me. And *you also must testify*" (John 15:26, 27a, italics added; Ambrose, *Of Holy Spirit* 1.1.25).

Because Judaism was provincially grounded, focused as it was upon the promised land and the temple in Jerusalem, as the children of Abraham, it could not be the vocation of Judaism in its Levitic form to expand and serve and transmute the whole of humanity. From Judaism by grace has come something other than Judaism—a people with a universal mission, capable of being adapted within all races, all cultures, all particular histories, all stages of human development, all worldviews.

If the decisive spatial category of Judaism was "the land," for Christianity it was "the world" (Justin Martyr, *Dialogue with Trypho*). The ministry of the Spirit that was revealed through law and prophets was anticipatory of the wider and more inclusive indwelling of the Spirit following the work of the Son on the cross (Cyril of Alex., *Comm. on John* 10.2).

By means of the Eucharist, the Son and Spirit found fit means for remission of human sin and sanctification of persons. In Christian preaching Christ's sacrifice for sin was applied to all who would repent and believe. This new wine must be poured into new wineskins (Mark 2:22). "No one sews a patch of unshrunk cloth on an old garment. If he does, the new piece will pull away from the old, making the tear worse" (Mark 2:21; Chrysostom, *Concerning the Spirit*, Hom. 16.9). The old sacrificial system that had been maintained in temple Judaism was not adequate to universal human needs. As the Son had a time of earthly ministry that he came to fulfill, and having finished has returned to the Father, so does the Spirit have a time of ministry on earth, which begins with a particular event, Pentecost, and continues until the general resurrection. As the earthly history of the Son is open to historical inquiry, so is the history of the Holy Spirit (Eusebius, *Proof of the Gospel*; *CH*; John of Damascus, *OF* 3.19).

Evil in the Present Age

The present age is being ultimately shaped and constrained by the power of the Spirit while at the same time it penultimately struggles with the continuing remnants of the power of evil. The "present evil age" from which Christ came to rescue humanity will remain an age of human fallenness until the end of history.

The reason: the consequences of sin do not end with the sinful act. These consequences continue until the final days, though the ultimate defeat of evil has already occurred on the cross and been declared already defunct by the resurrection. This victory has already begun in human hearts (Eph. 5:13–16; 6:12–16; 2 Tim. 3:12, 13; Marius Victorinus, *Epis. to Eph.* 2.5.13).

Believers expect to be engaged in a continuing struggle with the world, the flesh, and the devil, to test and strengthen their faith (Gal. 5.13–18; Augustine, *On Nature and Grace* 61). They are called to "put on the full armor of God so that you can take your stand against the devil's schemes. For our struggle is not against flesh and blood, but against the rulers, against the authorities, against the powers of this dark world and against the spiritual forces of evil in the heavenly realms" (Eph. 6:10–12; Jerome, *Epis. to Eph.* 3.6.11).

The Spirit's Work in Applying the Work of the Son

The Spirit works as personal agent of the mission of the Son to reveal the Son and bring his redemptive work to consummation (Hilary, *Trin.* 8.19).

The Spirit Remembers the Son with Complete Reliability

The Spirit is sent by the Father in the name of the Son: "But the Counselor, the Holy Spirit, whom the Father will send in my name, will teach you all things and will remind you of everything I have said to you" (John 14:26; cf. 1 John 2:27; Gaudentius of Brescia, *Sermon* 14). From this text derive classic interpretations of the inspiration of scripture (Chrysostom, *Hom. on John*, Hom. 23). It is primarily by this canonically received holy writ that the Spirit teaches "all things"—all that is necessary for salvation, brought to accurate and sufficient remembrance.

The Spirit assists our recollection of the history of salvation, both by inspiring a written record of it and making certain that record is sufficiently reliable to be an adequate memory of the salvation event (Augustine, *Hom. on John,* 104). Beyond the text itself, the Spirit works internally toward helping the believer to discern the meaning of the prophetic and apostolic witness, to compare scripture with scripture, and to prompt reason to reflect consistently on their testimony to God's revelation (Origen, *Hom. on Jer.* Hom. 21.2; 39).

Theories of inspiration of scripture go amiss when they attempt to locate the authority of scripture autonomously in the text itself or the writer while neglecting to pray for the Spirit who inspires, transmits, and rightly recalls the text. The inspiration of scripture is essentially a doctrine of the work of the Holy Spirit, and only secondarily therefore a doctrine of independent authority or textual transmission or scientific verification (2 Tim. 3:16; Chrysostom, *Hom. on 2 Tim.* 5; Calvin, *Inst.* 3.2).

The apostolic witnesses were specifically instructed when facing persecution: "Just say whatever is given you at the time, for it is not you speaking, but the Holy Spirit" (Mark 13:11; Cyril of Jerusalem, *Catech. Lect.* 16.21). This is not an alternative revelation different from that declared in Jesus that the Spirit is bringing, but rather the ever-fuller clarification of the revelation Jesus brought from the Father (Gregory of Nazianzus, *Orat.* 31). The Spirit does not speak independently of the triune God as if the Spirit possessed an autonomous authority apart from the Father and Son. The Spirit recalls the plain truth of what happened in Jesus, causing it to be rightly remembered by those who pray for grace (Gregory I, *Forty Gospel Hom.*, 30).

As the Son attests the Father, so the Spirit attests the Son (John 15:26; Gregory of Nazianzus, *On Holy Spirit, Orat.* 5[31].8–10). "For he who does not believe the Spirit does not believe in the Son, and he who has not believed in the Son does not believe in the Father . . . for it is impossible to worship the Son save by the Holy Spirit; impossible to call upon the Father save by the Spirit of adoption" (Basil, *On the Spirit* 1.11).

It is precisely what the Son conveys from the Father that the Spirit truthfully conveys from the Son to the believer's heart. The Son promised that "when he, the Spirit of truth, comes, he will guide you into all truth. He will not speak on his own; he will speak only what he hears, and he will tell you what is yet to come. He will bring glory to me by taking from what is mine and making it known to you" (John 16:13, 14; Chrysostom, *Hom. on John* 78.2).

The Spirit elicits not only accurate memory of salvation but freely willed confession of Christ: "Therefore I tell you that no one who is speaking by the Spirit of God says, 'Jesus be cursed,' and no one can say, 'Jesus is Lord,' except by the Holy Spirit" (1 Cor. 12:3; cf. Ambrose, *Of the Holy Spirit* 3.22.167).

The Son Intercedes Through the Spirit for the Life of the World

The Son tasted death for all humanity (Heb. 2:9). Before the Comforter came to dwell in the present age, however, it was necessary that the Son first appear before the heavenly Father to attest the sacrifice he offered for humanity's sin as sufficient for their salvation. Entering in the Father's presence as humanity's advocate, mediator, priest, and brother, the ascended Son sat at the Father's right hand, where he was restored to the position of equality he had enjoyed before the humbling descent of the incarnation. The artistic imagination of Renaissance Christianity soared dramatically in portraying this reconciling event of the Son showing his wounded hands and feet to the Father as the basis of his intercession: "Father, I want those that you have given me to be with me where I am" (John 17:24; Origen, *OFP* 3.6.1–3; Cyprian, *On Morality* 7.22).

The Son's ascension to the Father signified a refilling with that majesty of which he had been emptied. It was expedient that the Son go away, for only if he went to intercede with the Father could he send the Spirit to comfort the body of believers (Cyril of Alex., *Comm. on John* 11.9).

The Son's acceptance by the Father was thus the basis of the Spirit's pledge or seal of our acceptance by the Father. When Jesus was accepted by the Father, those whose lives are hid in him through the Spirit were also accepted by the Father (Eph. 1:7). God's acceptance of penitent sinners is thus settled once for all on the cross. What remains is for each hearer to make a full personal response to the Spirit's witness (Justin Martyr, *Dialogue with Trypho* 110).

The Spirit Applies the Benefits of the Son's Death to Believers

The Sons' heavenly intercession is presupposed in the holy table which is set for the Eucharist. "Without the expiatory work of Christ for us, the sanctifying work of the Spirit in us were impossible; and on the other hand, without the work of the Spirit within us, the work of Christ for us were without avail. . . . The fact that the Comforter is here is proof that the Advocate is there in the presence of the Father" (Gordon, *MS*:38).

Peter preached: "God has raised this Jesus to life, and we are all witnesses of the fact. Exalted to the right hand of God, he has received from the Father the promised Holy Spirit and has poured out what you now see and hear" (Acts 2:32, 33). Pentecost was the clear signal that redemption had been accomplished by the Son and was now being administered by the Spirit (Proclus, *Orat.* 16).

There is an intrinsic connection between Jesus' proclamation of the expected divine governance and the actual divine governance that has in fact come in the indwelling of the Spirit: "Luke makes it plain that the intention of the clause 'Thy kingdom come' is to implore the aid of the Holy Spirit. For in his gospel, in the place of 'Thy kingdom come,' he says 'Let the Holy Spirit come upon us and purify us,' " (Gregory of Nyssa, *The Lord's Prayer* 3, *LCF*:149).

The Triune Work Economized

This cohesive economy unfolds in the long history of revelation: The law is given, with its ordering of sacrifice, to bring the people of God under its tutelage. Christ comes to culminate all sacrifice on the cross so as to do for us what the law could not do. The Spirit communicates and applies to humanity the finished work of the cross (Rom. 8:1–4; Augustine, *Spirit and Letter*; John of Damascus, *OF* 3.1).

The Anglican Catechism viewed the saving work of the one God as the work of the Father in creation; the work of the Son in reconciliation; and the work of the Spirit in sanctification (*BCP*; cf. *Councils of Ariminum and Seleucia* 23). The Spirit "is given to those who believe," concluded the Council of Antioch, having come to the faithful for their "comfort, and sanctification, and initiation." It was the Son who died for us and rose again, not the Spirit. The Spirit did not perform any high priestly function, as did the Lamb of God. The work of the Spirit in us is distinct from that of the Son for us. For "the Holy Spirit could not be crucified, Who had not flesh and bones, but the Son of God was crucified, Who took flesh and bones" (Ambrose, *Of the Holy Spirit* 1.9.107). The Spirit is remembered in scripture as "proceeding [*ektoreuomenon*] from the Father and receiving [*laubanomenon*] from the Son" (Epiphanius, *Creed*, Second Formula).

Similar summaries recur in Protestant teaching: "As the Father revealed himself through the Son, so the Son by the Holy Spirit now reveals himself through the church; as Christ was the image of the invisible God, so the church is appointed to be the image of the invisible Christ; and his members, when they are glorified with him, shall be the express image of his person" (Gordon, *MS*:32).

"As Christ is represented as the ambassador of the Father, so the Holy Spirit is represented as the ambassador of the Son, coming vested with his authority, as the interpreter and executor of his will" (A. Clarke, *CT*:157).

The Spirit must penetrate our motives, the hidden springs of our thought, the nuances of character, the dynamics of will. Yet this inwardness is not lacking in social consequence: "Souls in which the Spirit dwells, illuminated by the Spirit, themselves become spiritual, and send forth their grace to others," Basil observed, and in this social process "the weak are held by the hand, and those who are advancing are brought to perfection" (*On the Spirit* 1.9).

Birth, Nurture, and Growth Through the Spirit

The Spirit in the present age is giving *birth* to the called out community, quickening its life, adding to its common life by converting persons one by one (Chrysostom, *Hom. on John* 24.2–3). As Christ has life in himself, so does the Spirit as Life Giver breathe life into the worshiping community.

The church is not only engendered, but also *nurtured* by the Spirit, its walk daily illumined by the Spirit through the written and preached Word attesting the revealed Word. The believing church is protected from utter failure by the Spirit, who has promised not to abandon the church, though the church may temporarily fall into error (Matt. 28:20; Chrysostom, *Hom. on Matt.* Hom. 90.2).

The Spirit continues to work to consecrate, *sanctify*, and perfect the church, setting it apart from the world for its special mission and ministry within the world, abiding in this community the sins of Churchmen, indeed, "reduce these benefits, but the Spirit continues to retain sinners within the Church, in order that He may make the grace of repentance available to them" (Hall, *DT* 8:22, 23).

The Spirit Creates Redeeming Communities

At Pentecost the Spirit who is eternally present to all humanity was poured out in an exceptional indwelling among the apostles. After Pentecost the Spirit was found constantly to be forming actual living communities of grace and testimony. All those united to Christ by faith are united with the called out community by the Spirit (Cyprian, *The Unity of the Catholic Church, LCC* 5:124–42).

The Holy Spirit after the incarnation was not creating an atomized conglomerate of isolated regenerated persons but rather a community, a family of the regenerated, an ordered household, an organic body. *Ekklēsia* is called to be a bonded, caring community, a *koinonia*, a new social creation of grace, the resurrection of the people of God raised up in the light of God's own coming, a peculiar people (Eph. 1:10; 2:13; Ambrosiaster, *Epis. to Eph.* 1–2; Kuyper, *WHS*:119, 120).

The Spirit works in the church to form the *ekklēsia* (1 Cor. 12:13), to dwell in the body of believers (2 Cor. 6:16), to build up the community of faith (Acts 2:47; Eph. 2:21, 22; 1 Pet. 2:5, 6), to elicit true worship (Phil. 3:3, John 4:24; Athanasius, *LCHS* 1.32–33; Goodwin, *Works* 6:13–39). The Spirit empowers the church's witness (Acts 1:8). The Spirit calls living persons to specific vocational tasks (Acts 13:2), unifying diverse gifts in the one body of Christ (Phil. 2:2–4).

The Son placed under the governance of the Spirit not merely redeemed individuals one by one but also the redeemed community as a whole. The Spirit works in the community to offer new life, birthing, regenerating (John 3:3; Titus 3:5), baptizing believers into the body (1 Cor. 12:13), indwelling in their hearts (1 Cor. 3:16), freeing from guilt, sin, and death (Rom. 7:9–8:2), strengthening the inner life amid hardships and challenges (Eph. 3:16–19), bearing witness to their daughterhood and sonship with the Father (Rom. 8:16), sealing believers until the day of redemption (Eph. 4:30), bearing fruits of faith active in love (Gal. 5:19–23; Rom. 14:17; 15:13), guiding into all truth (John 16:13), directing the life of prayer (Rom. 8:26, 27; 1 Cor. 14:15; Eph. 6:18; Jude 20), bringing into accurate recollection the words of Christ (John 14:26), enabling fitting proclamation of the good news of God's own coming (Acts 1:8; 1 Cor. 2:1–5), revealing the deep things of God through spiritual discernment. For " 'No eye has seen, no ear has heard, no mind conceived what God has prepared for those who love him'—but God has revealed it to us by his Spirit" (1 Cor. 2:9; Chrysostom, *Epis. to Cor.* 7.4–7).

The Spirit is attested in healings, exorcisms, tongues (Acts 2:4–6; 10:46), proclamation (4:8, 31), power (6:10), prophecy (11:28; 21:4, 11), martyrdom (7:55), counsel (8:29; 10:19), mission (13:4), hedgings of the way (16:6, 7), warnings (20:23), and in the authorization of overseers to watch over the flock (20:28; Philoxenus of Mabbug, *On the Indwelling of the Holy Spirit*).

Even when we are unable to pray, "the Spirit helps us in our weakness. We do not know what we ought to pray for, but the Spirit himself intercedes for us with groans that words cannot express. And he who searches our hearts knows the mind of the Spirit, because the Spirit intercedes for the saints in accordance with God's will" (Rom. 8:26, 27). No one is so devoid of grace that he cannot pray for grace (*Augustine on Romans* 54).

The Personal Indwelling of the Spirit

The Spirit's presence in the church was understood as God's own real presence, promised to abide till the end of history, making the Son's presence real, making the Father's love known. "He is called Comforter, because He comforts and encourages," and "makes intercession," prompting supplicants to turn away from temptation (Cyril of Jerusalem, *Catech. Lect.* 16.19, 20).

The central role of the Spirit in the economy of salvation would not be fully manifested until the act of atonement was complete on the cross and confirmed in the resurrection. Only then was the time fulfilled for the Spirit's outpouring on the day of Pentecost. Then the coming fire that had been anticipated in the Shekinah (the ancient symbol of the glory of the presence of God with humanity) became poured out in tongues of fire, attesting the resurrection in all human languages (Acts 2:8).

The Counselor

The Personal Naming of the Spirit

Parakletos is one called to another's side to take his or her part, as a friend, a counselor, always lending aid, a partaker in another's cause (John 16:7; cf. 1 John 2:1). *Parakletos* is more than a descriptive noun. It is the personal name chosen by the Son by which the faithful were privileged to address God's own Spirit in the present age (Hilary, *Trin.* 8.19–27). Variously translated as Comforter, Advocate, Helper, Counselor, or Guide, the literal meaning of *parakaleo* is to call to one's aid (Nicetas of Remesiana, *Power of the Holy Spirit*, FC 7:36).

The fuller implication of this name would be revealed only through a history of the Spirit's activity. *Parakletos* is the One called to breathe life into the community of faith, who is sent personally to fill the void that otherwise would have been left by Christ's departure (Origen, *OFP*:116–19). "Unless I go away, the Counselor will not come to you, but if I go, I will send him to you" (John 16:7; Augustine, *On Trin.*, 1.9).

The Spirit had been present in history prior to the Messianic event, cooperat-ing with the Father and the Son in the plan of salvation, but after the Messianic event, the Spirit became the principal advocate to speak of and for the Son, to enliven and dwell in the body of Christ, to make his atoning work effective in history (Tertullian, *Ag. Praxeas* 27–30). As the Messiah is the personal Word of redemption, the Spirit is the personal administrator and executor of the redeem-ing Word.

Why Another Helper?

The Son had promised to send "another Helper to be with you forever" (John 14:16). The Paraclete is both sent by the Son (John 14:26) and the coming of the Son in a new form. "I will not leave you as orphans; I will come to you" (John 14:18; Augustine, *Tractates on John* 75.1).

As long as Christ was on earth, he was the comforter, guide, and guardian of the disciples. After his ascension he promised to give them "*another* Counselor." Why "*another*" if the first was sufficient? Gregory Nazianzus answered: "That you might acknowledge His coequality. For this word Another marks an Alter Ego, a name of equal Lordship, not of inequality" (Gregory Nazianzus, *Orat.* 41.12). In this way *Parakletos* became a name applied by apostolic rememberers first to the Son and then to the Spirit (Ambrose, *Of the Holy Spirit* 1.13.157).

While the *ascended Son* continues in heavenly intercession as an advocate to "speak to the Father in our defense" (1 John 2:1; Origen, *Principles*, 2.7), the *descending Spirit* is here to counsel the world of *sin*, of the *righteousness* of the Son who intercedes with the Father, and of future *judgment* of the idolatries of this world (John 16:8–11; Augustine, *Ag. Two Letters of the Pelagians* 3.4; *Sermon* 144.6). By the Son's death "the inheritance becomes available, and when he had ascended into heaven he sent down the Holy Spirit to distribute the estate among those who were joint heirs with him" (A. J. Gordon, *MS*:49–50).

The Personal Coming of the Spirit

Through the Son human history was brought into concrete meeting with the incarnate God, who felt our human infirmities, afflictions, and death. Through the Spirit, this encounter comes to even closer quarters by indwelling in our hearts and attesting the work of the Son in our hearts (Origen, *Comm. on Rom.* 8:16; Barth, *CD* 2/2, 344).

As a person enfleshed in history, Jesus could only be one place at one time. As present in the Spirit, the Son could be present to the church in all places and times. In his flesh he dwelt with humanity for a particular time. By his Spirit he came to dwell with humanity for all times (Augustine, *Question* 59.4; 61.4). By the Spirit the triune God would become accessible to all, thus nearer to the far-flung body of believers than had he remained on the earth endlessly.

The resurrected Lord had instructed the disciples that after the resurrection, "repentance and forgiveness of sins will be preached in his name to all nations, beginning at Jerusalem. You are witnesses of these things. I am going to send you what the Father has promised, but stay in the city until you have been clothed with power from on high" (Luke 24:47–49; Bede, *Hom. on Gospels* 11.15).

Pentecost: The Outpouring of the Holy Spirit

After Passover and the Feast of the Unleavened Bread in the Jewish calendar came the Feast of the Firstfruits (a liturgical foreshadowing of the resurrection; Lev. 23:17–20; Rom. 8:23; 1 Cor. 15:20–23; Cyril of Alex., *Letter* 50.14). Fifty days after firstfruits, two loaves of bread were offered, the yeast of which prefigured the formation of the church on the day of Pentecost (Lev. 23:15–21; Leo I, *Sermon* 75; Bede, *Hom. on Gospels* 2.17).

The key text of Levitical instruction for Pentecost was, "From the day after the Sabbath, the day you brought the sheaf of the wave offering, count off seven full weeks. Count off fifty days up to the day after the seventh Sabbath, and then present an offering of new grain in the Lord" (Lev. 23:15, 16). Thus Passover was followed fifty days later by *pentecostē*, the Greek term for "fifty days." It was celebrated "a week of weeks" after Firstfruits (Exod. 23:16; Bede, *Comm. on Acts* 2.1; Tho. Aq., *ST* 1–2 Q102.5, I), which presented the firstfruits of harvest, the Hebraic type of the firstfruits of the ingathering of the reign of God.

Tarrying in Jerusalem for a Week of Weeks

While tarrying in Jerusalem, the disciples were not yet authorized to set out on their mission to the world, until the Spirit had come to indwell with them to empower their testimony. The descent of the Spirit was the signal that the atoning work had been fully accepted by the Father, and that the Son was reigning with the Father in heaven (Matt. 3:16, 17; Origen, *Hom. on Lev.* 7.4; Calvin, *Comm.* 16:202–6).

The Lord had instructed the disciples to wait in Jerusalem for the Spirit. This was an auspicious moment for a new beginning in the history of salvation. The feast of Pentecost had gathered large numbers of people to Jerusalem only a short time after Jesus' death and resurrection (Acts 2:1; Chrysostom, *Hom. on Acts*, 4; Calvin, *Comm.* 8:73–74). They had come from remote parts of the known world. It was to this gathering that the Spirit came and was poured out with such power.

The Christian Pentecost referred backward to the Levitical Feast of Weeks and forward to the celestial banquet in the general resurrection. The disciples did not wait an indefinite period for the descent of the Spirit, but precisely fifty liturgically prescribed days after the resurrection (Augustine, *On Spirit and Letter* 16.28). Leo I states the reason why: "For as of old, when the Hebrew nation were released from the Egyptians, on the fiftieth day after the sacrificing of the lamb the Law was given on Mount Sinai, so after the suffering of Christ, where the true Lamb of God was slain, on the fiftieth day from His Resurrection, the Holy Ghost came down upon the Apostles and the multitude of believers" (Leo I, *Sermons* 75).

In this way Pentecost is "the sequel and completion of the Paschal feast" (Leo I, *Letters* 15). "Pentecost is a reminder of the resurrection expected in the age to come," for eternity is symbolized by seven times seven, and as a circle that begins again on the same point that it ends (Basil, *On the Spirit*, NPNF 2 8:42).

The Spirit No Longer a Transient Visitor

At Pentecost the *ekklēsia* became indwelt as temple of God, a renewed holy temple for intercession, prophecy, celebration of the sacraments, and praise (Jude 20). The one Holy Spirit who before had sporadically called, anointed, and visited chosen vessels, at last came to dwell in and with the faithful community, and in the form of hope with the whole of humanity (Heb. 8:10; John 14:15–19; Gaudentius, *Sermon* 14).

At Pentecost the Holy Spirit "descended into the temple of his apostles, which he has prepared for himself, as a shower of sanctification, appearing no more as a transient visitor, but as a perpetual Comforter and as an eternal inhabitant" (Augustine, in A. J. Gordon, *MS*:26; *Tractates on John* 94). *God the Spirit is taking up residence in the* ekklēsia *at the precise point in history when God the Son ascends to intercede with the Father.* This indwelling was promised to continue until the end of time. The One who is taking up residence with the church is named by the Son: "the Holy *Spirit*, whom the *Father* will send in *my* name" (John 14:25, italics added). Note that within this single text, the triune teaching is already fully in place (Ambrose, *Of the Holy Spirit* 1.13.134).

The Son uses plural pronouns to underscore the triunity of the indwelling: "If anyone loves me he will obey my teaching. My Father will love him, and we will come to him and *make our home* [*monēn*] with him" (John 14:23, italics added; Gregory I, *Forty Gospel Hom.* 30.2). Father, Son, and Spirit are all taking up abode in the faithful through the indwelling Spirit (Leo I, *Sermon* 76).

Before and After Pentecost—The Quickening Sequence of Events

Christ had prayed that the Spirit would be a continuing, abiding, indwelling presence with his own beloved people (John 14:16–17). After repeated promises of the coming of the Spirit (John 14:17, 26; 15:26; 16:7, 13), Jesus breathed the Spirit upon his disciples after his resurrection, saying: "Receive the Holy Spirit" (John 20:22; Chrysostom, *Hom. on John* 86.3). The Spirit was poured in fullness on the whole gathered community at Pentecost (Acts 2:17; Bede, *Comm. on Acts* 2.17).

From this poured a steady succession of remarkable disclosures. The Spirit again came through the laying on of hands of Peter and John in Samaria (Acts 8:14–17) and again fell on Gentile believers in the house of Cornelius: "While Peter was still speaking these words, the Holy Spirit came on all who heard the message. The circumcised believers who had come with Peter were astonished that the gift of the Holy Spirit had been poured out even on the Gentiles. For they heard them speaking in tongues and praising God" (Acts 10:44–46; Chrysostom, *Hom. on Acts* 24). When Paul baptized the Ephesians "the Holy Spirit came on them, and they spoke in tongues and prophesied" (Acts 19:6).

After Pentecost, "They devoted themselves to the apostles' teaching and to the fellowship, to the breaking of bread and to prayer" (Acts 2:42). "And the Lord added to their number daily those who were being saved" (Acts 2:47). After Pentecost the gifts (*charismata*) were diversely distributed by the Spirit to the whole church. Those who had been timid, quarrelsome, and confused before receiving the Spirit, went out illumined, united, courageous, and determined (Hilary, *Trin.* 13.31–35).

After Pentecost it becomes clearer that the Spirit is essential to every moment and each specific phase of the manifestation of God's salvation to and for humanity. The wide range of the Spirit's work was aptly summarized by the Augsburg Confession as ruling, comforting, enlivening, and protecting (Augsburg Conf, art. 3).

The Early and Latter Rain

Rain had long been a symbol of the refreshing, life-giving outpouring of the Spirit (Ps. 72:6, 7). "I will send rain on your land in its season, both autumn and spring rains, so that you may gather in your grain, new wine and oil" (Deut. 11:13, 14).

The comparison of the Spirit's coming with rain was easily grasped by all who knew the two rainy seasons of Palestine, early and late, the first rain at the time of planting when the seeds were just sown in fallow ground, and the latter rain when the grain was ripening for harvest. Similarly it was promised to occur in the economy of salvation that the Comforter would come both early and late, and with special power and efficacy at the latter time. The Spirit was working both in planting and harvest (Joel 2:23).

One tradition of exegesis has viewed the early rain as prophetic expectation and the latter rain as prophetic fulfillment. Another tradition viewed the early rain as Pentecost and the latter rain as the outpouring of the Spirit in the end time. In either case the Spirit comes both early and late, preveniently and consummately.

In the Paraclete, God the Spirit comes silently, as gentle rain, invisibly within the ambiguous conditions of human history. In the Parousia, the Son returns gloriously and openly under decisive conditions of the final judgment of history. The Comforter is promised to indwell from Pentecost to Parousia to work as "Guardian and Sanctifier of the Church, the Ruler of souls, the Pilot of the tempest-tossed, leading wanderers to the light" (Cyril of Jerusalem, *Catech. Lect.* 17.13).

This ordered sequence of the divine economy helps the worshiping community to grasp the import of one of the most astonishing statements of Jesus: "I tell you the truth, anyone who has faith in me will do what I have been doing. He [*Parakletos*] will do even greater things than these, because I am going to the Father" (John 14:12). "For it is a mightier thing for a shadow, than for a hem of a garment, to possess the power of healing" (Augustine, *Tractates on John* 71.3). As executor and fulfiller of Christ's mission the Spirit contextually teaches and applies the truth concretely (Augustine, *Comm. on John* 72–73).

The Tongues at Pentecost and After

The Spirit "came in the form of Tongues because of His close relation to the Word" (Gregory Nazianzus, *Orat.* 41.11). A word in the mind requires a tongue to be spoken. Thoughts without tongues remain unknown. With the distribution of fiery tongues, the Spirit came not in the form of occasional energy, but fully indwelling, coming as God "associating with us, and dwelling in us. For it was fitting that as the Son had lived with us in bodily form—so the Spirit too should appear in bodily form; and that after Christ had returned to His own place, He should have come down to us—Coming because He is the Lord; Sent because He is not a rival God" (Gregory Nazianzus, *Orat.* 41.11).

The Church's First Miracle: Tongues at Pentecost

Those who received the Spirit at Pentecost spoke in the languages of many nations. What happened was not that the visitors in Jerusalem all talked nonsense without understanding each other. Nor did they all speak the same language. Rather, the Jews gathering from diaspora spoke numerous Gentile languages as an anticipatory indication that the Spirit was intending to make the gospel known to all nations.

The national cultures named among those present at Pentecost (Galileans, Parthians, Medes, Elamites, Mesopotamians, Judeans, Cappadocians, persons from Pontus, Asia, Phrygia, Pamphylia, Egypt, Libya, and Crete) symbolically spanned all known countries in every direction from Jerusalem (Cyril of Jerusalem, *Catech. Lect.* 17.16). They were devout Jews dwelling in Jerusalem temporarily, symbolically representing "every nation under heaven" (Acts 2:5; Chrysostom, *Hom. on Acts*, Hom. 4).

Luke reports: "All of them were filled with the Holy Spirit and began to speak in other tongues as the Spirit enabled them" (Acts 2:4). Upon the outpouring of the Spirit, "each one was hearing them speak in his own language" (Acts 2:6). Presumably the sounds the apostles would have previously been hearing at the Feast of Weeks would have been unfamiliar to their own native language. Apart from the outpouring of the Spirit, these would be without understanding. But with the Spirit they were hearing and understanding (Bede, *Comm. on Acts* 2.13).

The Galileans were speaking but they were astounded and asked "How is it that we hear each of us in his own native language?" (2:8; Arator, *On the Acts*, 1). "We hear them telling in our own tongues the mighty works of God" (2:11). Many present at Pentecost attested hearing God the Spirit speak to them in their own indigenous languages. To the Greeks, the Gospel was proclaimed in Greek, to Romans in Latin, to local inhabitants in Aramaic (Acts 2:5–12). The miracle of Pentecost was that they understood each other in their various languages either by a miracle of hearing or a miracle of speaking (Gregory Nazianzus, *Orat.* 41.15).

The International Implication of the Mission of the Holy Spirit

An awesome consequence is implied: Since Pentecost the Word spoken in Christ is being empowered by the Spirit to be spoken everywhere in each one's own heart language. It thenceforth becomes imperative for the remembering, proclaiming community to attest God's own coming in all languages. The Spirit was actively promising to help facilitate this difficult process (Basil, *On the Spirit* 1.27; Congar, *IBHS* 2:145).

A stunning international implication arises out of Acts 2: The Spirit intends to assist the proclamation of the Gospel in all languages (Augustine, *Tractates on John* 6.3). Startling parallels still exist between what liturgical traditions call Epiphany, Pentecostals call *glossolalia*, and social liberationists call inclusiveness. However disparate are these three symbol systems, all coalesce in the core idea of the mission of the Word to the world through the Spirit.

None of the languages mentioned in Acts 2 were "unknown tongues." Someone knew how to speak each one of those languages. The purpose of this cross-cultural, international gift was to enable the mission of the Son to be realized through the mission of the Spirit, through clear communication of the gospel to the whole world, with its many languages. Each person was hearing the speech of the apostolate "in his own native language," whether "Parthians, Medes, Elamites" (Acts 2:8). The reference was not limited to ecstatic utterance without translatable meaning. There is an enormous difference between disconnected speech patterns that have no meaning and the gift of hearing the gospel clearly in one's own native tongue that was reported at Pentecost. The Aramaic of the disciples of Galilee was assisted by the Spirit so that Jerusalem visitors of all languages began immediately to understand it (Chrysostom, *Hom. on Acts* 4).

The disciples had no time or opportunity or learning to acquire immediately the capacity to speak in all these languages. The Holy Spirit demonstrated the divine intent to communicate to all in the church's first miracle (Bede, *Comm. on Acts* 2.37). Three thousand were saved (Acts 2:37–41).

The Spirit soon after taught Peter in the presence of Cornelius to remember "what the Lord had said, John baptized with water, but you will be baptized with the Holy Spirit" (Acts 11:15, 16). The implication was not that baptism must be inevitably connected with ecstatic utterance, but that the special ministry of the Spirit was present to point the emergent church toward the Gentile world, the world of many tongues, to proclaim the gospel to all nations in all languages (Cyril of Jerusalem, *Catech. Lect.* 17.14).

The Road to Everywhere

The early church quickly went from Jerusalem to the cosmopolitan centers of trade, at major crossroads of humanity, from Jerusalem and Antioch to Alexandria, Ephesus, Athens, and Rome, to attest this incomparable truth now revealed. The time from Jerusalem to other Mediterranean capitals was not overwhelming—a few days sea journey.

The church is from the outset composed of many persons speaking different languages. It became an important task for the church to learn quickly to speak and translate into many different languages, otherwise the speech of others would simply sound like gibberish. "The Holy Spirit taught them many languages at once, languages which in all their life they never knew," in sharp contrast with their previous unlearned condition (Cyril of Jerusalem, *Catech. Lect*. 17.16).

At Pentecost "the languages peculiar to each nation became common property in the mouth of the church. And therefore from that day the trumpet of the Gospel-preaching has sounded loud; from that day the showers of gracious gifts, the rivers of blessings, have watered every desert" (Leo I, *Sermons* 75).

Cyril of Jerusalem was aware that the first Pentecost had taken place only a short walk from the very spot where he was teaching his catechumens (the Church of the Holy Sepulchre). He reminded them that it is not only "in our time have multitudes of strangers first begun to assemble here from all quarters, but they have done so since that time" (Cyril of Jerusalem, *Catech. Lect*. 17.18), i.e., since Pentecost. Cyril as bishop was thoroughly familiar with local Jerusalem tradition and memory in the fourth century. He is attesting a steady continuum of world pilgrims to Jerusalem prior to the fourth century. For this reason, not a frivolous one, Jerusalem is called "mother of cities," for from there the good news would go out to the whole world (Cyril of Jerusalem, *Catech. Lect*. 18.34).

Beyond Babel: The Renewal of Broken Human Speech

The classic Christian exegetes loved to contrast Babel and Pentecost (Origen, *On Genesis* 1; Cyril of Jerusalem, *Catech. Lect*. 17.16–17; Gregory Nazianzus, *Orat*. 41.16; Chrysostom, *Homily 2 on Pentecost* 2). As the idolatry of Babel had resulted in the breaking down of international communication through divine judgment on sin, now the grace of God was reaching out to all nations in the midst of their egocentric incapacity to communicate (Chrysostom, *Demons Do Not Govern the World*; Cassiodorus, *Expos. On Ps*. 80.6).

The Spirit of God speaks all languages (Augustine, *Sermons* 267, 268, 269; Chrysostom, *Homily 35 on First Corinthians*), hence "supersedes the divisiveness of Babel" (*Vat. II, Mis. 4*). Pentecost was an international event signaling that God's peace was not limited exclusively to the Jews but that God was pouring out his own Spirit upon all flesh, as long ago promised (Joel 2:28).

Classic exegetes viewed the fall of language as an expression of the fall of humanity (Gen. 11:5–9; Ps. 55:9–11; James 3:5–8; Chrysostom, *Hom. on Gen*. 30). If one thinks of what the world might have been like if wholly unstained by sin, language would attest truth. Under the prevailing conditions of the history of sin, however, language became Babel— deceptive and untruthful. When the heart is self-deceived, language cannot bring truth to accurate expression (Augustine, *Tractates on John* 74.2; Calvin, *Comm*. 1:320–39).

Pentecost is an anticipation of the end time when all human speech will finally be redeemed and brought back to unblemished truth in the celestial community. In the midst of the babbling of the nations of the world, divided and conquered by sin, the Holy Spirit at Pentecost comes to unite all humanity by making all human languages congruent with God's address (Ephrem, *Hymns of Paradise* 11.14; Calvin, *Comm*. 18:77; Kuyper, *WHS*:136–38).

One may think without a tongue but not speak. *Logos* (word, thought) is attested only by means of *glōssa* (tongue). The tongue gives the mind a means of expression. Without a tongue one cannot speak one's mind. The coming renewal of broken human language is a dramatic expression of the Spirit's overarching mission of human renewal (Phil. 2:11; Rev. 5:9–13; Augustine, *Narration on Psalm 54* 11; Sermon 271; Gregory I, *Hom. on the Gospels*, 2, 30, 4).

Tongues and Interpretation: Pentecost and Corinth Contrasted

The risen Lord had indicated to the disciples in the Markan epilogue that they would "speak in new tongues" (Mark 16:17), in varied languages. Among the gifts of the Spirit in Paul's view was the gift of "speaking in different kinds of tongues" *(heterō gene glossōn)*, accompanied by a complementary gift of "the interpretation of tongues" (1 Cor. 12:10; Ambosiaser, *Comm on Paul's Epis.*, 1 Cor. 12.10). "These gifts were given to women as well as men" (Theodoret, *Comm. on 1 Cor.* 245). This need not be limited to ecstatic utterance of unknown languages but may also refer to proclaiming the gospel in other known human languages. After Pentecost these utterances were understood only by some, perhaps only a few, and needed *hermēneia*, "interpretation," a process that itself was a gift of the Spirit (1 Cor. 12:10).

The miracle of Pentecost pointed the way toward the laborious and practical task ahead for the church: to learn the world's languages. Paul placed strong emphasis upon the translation of tongues so that prophetic utterances could be rightly understood. Contemporary worldwide print, broadcast, preaching, and discipling ministries are among the Spirit-enabled modern forms of speaking in the varied tongues of humanity (Paterius, *Expos. Deut.* 2).

Paul did not hesitate to remind his hearers that he had spoken "in tongues more than all of you" (1 Cor. 14:18). He then qualified this by warning that "in the church I would rather speak five intelligible words to instruct others than ten thousand in a tongue" (1 Cor. 14:19). Shortly thereafter Paul would warn the great international Christian community at Corinth of abuses of this gift: "If anyone speaks in a tongue, two—or at the most three—should speak, one at a time and someone must interpret. If there is no interpreter, the speaker should keep quiet in the church and speak to himself and God" (1 Cor. 14:27, 28). Isaiah had earlier warned against "spiritists, who whisper and mutter" (Isa. 8:19). The Spirit wishes to communicate accurately God's merciful will to save. "Tongues, then, are a sign, not for believers but for unbelievers" (1 Cor. 14:22). "Tongues are a sign to unbelievers not for their instruction, as prophecy is for both believers and unbelievers, but to astonish them" (Chrysostom, *Hom. on Cor.* 36.2).

With Jerusalem's tongues of Pentecost, the Spirit was offering gifts that granted understanding, resolved confusions, and reordered lives. With Corinth's tongues, the pattern at times reverted to sounding more like Babel; tongues became a serious pastoral problem for Paul, who admonished that "everything should be done in a fitting and orderly way" (1 Cor. 14:40). "If we take a closer look at the origin of sin, I think that it is nothing else than the inordinate love by a rational creature of the things set in order by God" (Fulgentius, *To Monimus* 1.20.2).

Paul did not forbid the Corinthians to speak in tongues but reminded them that there are greater gifts, the more excellent way of faith, hope, and love (1 Cor. 12:31; 13:13; Theodoret, *Comm. on Cor.* 255). If one speaks in tongues without love it sounds merely like "a resounding gong or a clanging cymbal" (1 Cor. 13:1).

The Spirit freely and sovereignly bestows gifts of the Spirit. If so, it is hardly fitting for recipients to set their hearts upon receiving particular special gifts. Rather, they do well to receive gratefully whatever the Spirit offers (1 Cor. 12:11). We are taught to be willing to be filled with the Holy Spirit with the gifts God chooses to distribute (Eph. 5:18), not to seek to acquire particular gifts or control the allocation (Origen, *OFP* 1.3; Cyril of Jerusalem, *Catech. Lect.* 14.12).

The Continuing Need for Discernment: Testing the Spirits

The apostles were aware that false claims would be made concerning the Spirit: "The Spirit clearly says that in later times some will abandon the faith and follow deceiving spirits and things taught by demons" (1 Tim. 4:1). We are specifically warned not to "believe every spirit, but test the spirits to see whether they are from God, because many false prophets have gone out into the world. This is how you can recognize the Spirit of God: Every spirit that acknowledges that Jesus Christ has come in the flesh is from God, but every spirit that does not acknowledge Jesus is not from God" (1 John 4:1–3; Didymus the Blind, *Catena, CEC* 129). The faithful are instructed to test the spirits by assessing any atypical claims in relation to the whole connected history of God's self-disclosure.

The revealed Word of God as consensually and canonically received by this resilient transgenerational community through twenty centuries thus becomes the trustworthy standard by which diverse spirits can be tested. Anyone may make a reasonable test of the claims of the competing "spirits" to see if they are of God by examining whether they are consistent with what is historically and reliably known of the revealed God. God the Spirit is always meeting us in what appear to us to be new ways, yet always in continuity with the ways in which the triune God has already become self-revealed in the histories of Israel, Jesus, and the church, and the world (Origen, *OFP* 3.6.6; Vincent of Lérins, *Commonitory*, 2).

The Spirit assists in this discernment, bringing the gifts in time toward consensual reception. "God is not the author of confusion, but of peace" (1 Cor. 14:33). "We are witnesses of these things, and so is the Holy Spirit, whom God has given to those who obey" (Acts 5:32).

Holy Spirit and Holy Writ

"All Scripture is God-breathed [*theopnuestos*) and is useful for teaching, rebuking, correcting and training in righteousness, so that the man of God may be thoroughly equipped for every good work" (2 Tim. 3:16, 17; Theophilus, *To Autolycus* 2.22.9; 3.11–14; Irenaeus, *Ag. Her.* 2.16.2, 9). Scripture is breathed out by God, the product of God's Word or speech, as breathing is intrinsically connected with human speech (Ambrose, *Of the Holy Spirit* 3.14.112). Although "inspiration of scripture" is commonly used to describe this doctrine, *theopneustos* focuses upon the simple metaphor of spiration (the breathing) of God's own life into the written word (*Regulations of Horiesios* 52).

God's Own Word Breathed Into the Written Word

The Paraclete is the Spirit of truth, who brings Christ's words to reliable remembrance and bears witness to him (John 14:16, 26; 15:26). God the Spirit has shepherded the recollection of the revelation that is faithfully remembered in canonical scripture. The list or canon of scriptural texts was repeatedly received consensually as the Spirit's own address, who bestowed upon the writers the gift of rightly remembering the events through which God became revealed (Athanasius, *Festal Letters* 39; Third Council of Carthage, *SCD* 92).

In their original form and language, prior to any possibility of copyist errors or glossings, the canonical scriptures, according to ecumenical teaching, constituted the address of God to humanity enabled by the Holy Spirit working through attentive, reliable attestors. The believing church ecumenically consents to the premise that the Spirit has so reliably protected this recollection and transmission of scripture that no truth essential to salvation has been lost. The account of God's saving action toward humanity is in this way available to be read wherever canonical scripture is rightly recalled, translated, understood, and reappropriated. "When we do understand it, we are right. But when we are wrong because we haven't understood it, we leave it in the right. When we have gone wrong, we don't make out Scripture to be wrong, but it continues to stand up straight and right, so that we may return to it for correction" (Augustine, *Sermons* 23.3). This is not a recent idea spawned by fundamentalists, but what orthodox Christians have always believed. "The soul watered by sacred Scripture grows hearty and bears fruit in due season. This is the orthodox faith" (John of Damascus, *Orth. Faith* 4.17).

The New Testament repeatedly acknowledges God's Spirit as author of Hebrew scripture. Jesus regarded Psalm 110 as written by David but given by the Spirit (Matt. 22:43). Peter assumed that Psalm 2 had been spoken "by the Holy Spirit through the mouth of our father David" (Acts 4:25; cf. 1:16).

Paul told the Jewish leaders of Rome that "the Holy Spirit spoke the truth to your forefathers Isaiah the prophet" (Acts 28:25, 26; Isa. 6:9, 10). When the author of Hebrews quoted Psalm 95:7–11, he did not hesitate to say, "So, as the Holy Spirit says" (Heb. 3:7; cf. 10:15, 16).

The Authorship of God the Spirit Through Idiosyncratic Human Writers

The theandric analogy as set forth above (on the Person of Christ) was cautiously applied by classic exegetes to thinking about the address of scripture. Jesus Christ is truly human and truly God. So also the address of God the Spirit in scripture is truly human—in the sense that it is "fleshed out" in human language, in a historical setting by actual persons living finite lives—without ceasing to be truly God's own Word that abides forever (Rom. 1:3, 4; 8:3; 2 Cor. 2:8; Phil. 2:2–8).

God the Spirit is viewed by the consensual tradition as author of scripture (Origen, *Ag. Celsus* 5:60; Basil, *Hom. on Ps. 1*). The authors wrote or spoke as moved by God's own Spirit. Their consciousness, peculiarities of language, personalities, and psychological makeup became fittingly adapted instruments of the divine address (Chrysostom, *Hom. on 2 Tim.* 8–9; Calvin, *Inst.* 4.8.5–9).

The Spirit found their particular psyches, their intelligence, their readiness, their social location, their historical placement, useful to the divine plan and purpose, and spoke through them to and for all. It is the personal particularity that made the most difference in telling the story, since each hearer is unique. That their idiosyncrasies appear in holy writ is a testimony to the humanity of God. Each one's personal human existence is unique and characteristic of that person; this is especially so in respect to speech.

Nor does this necessarily imply that the writers themselves always understood fully the import of their own writings. Daniel specifically articulated this ambiguity when he, "exhausted" and "ill," wrote of his vision as recorded in scripture: "I was appalled by the vision; it was beyond understanding" (Dan. 8:27). It was while Balaam was intending to curse Israel that he was inadvertently led by the Spirit to offer Israel a beautiful blessing (Num. 22–24). Even Balaam's ass became a useful means for the divine address (Num. 22:28; Origen, *Hom. on Luke* 14.9).

Prophecy was not understood by ancient ecumenical exegesis as a product of the human imagination, but of human agency being gloriously transfigured by God's own Spirit, wherein human egocentricity did not interrupt or distort what God sought to communicate. "For prophecy never had its origin in the will of man, but men spoke from God as they were carried along by the Holy Spirit" (2 Pet. 1:21; Andreas, *Catena, CEC* 89).

Theophilus proposed a classic early form of the doctrine of God-breathed scripture: "Men of God carrying in them a holy spirit and becoming prophets, being inspired and made wise by God, became God-taught," being deemed worthy to become "instruments of God, and contain the wisdom that is from Him," attested accurately what God had been doing before their own time, in their own time, and would yet do in the future (Theophilus, *To Autolycus* 2.9).

Church Doctrine Judged by Scripture

The apostles repeatedly appealed to Christ's own precise words as having binding authority (1 Thess. 4:15; Gal. 6:2; 1 Cor. 7:10–25; Acts 20:35). Unless they made disclaimers, they often assumed that their readers would regard their own utterances as having similar binding authority insofar as they were consistent with those of the crucified Lord of glory (2 Thess. 2:15; 2 Cor. 2:9; 7:15; cf. Barnabas 9.9; Ignatius, *Philadelphians* 7.1).

Amid controversy, the precise words of Christ as apostolically attested were the final court of appeal. "Unless I find it in the originals in the gospel, I do not believe, and when I said to them, 'It is written,' they answered me, 'That settles it'" (Ignatius of Antioch, *Philadelphians* 8.2; cf. *Smyrnaeans* 7.2).

Already by the time of the writing of Second Peter, the letters of Paul were being read, along with the Hebrew Bible, as comparable with "the other scriptures" (*loitas graphas*, 2 Pet. 3:16). The Gospels and epistles were regularly read in services of worship (1 Thess. 5:7; Col. 4:16; James 1:1; 1 Pet. 1:1; Clement of Rome, *Corinth* 47.1; Justin Martyr, *Apology* I.67; Irenaeus, *Ag. Her.* 2.27.2; Muratorian Canon). Clement of Rome considered the communications he had exchanged with the church at Corinth as having been "written through the Holy Spirit" (Clement, *Corinth* 63; Tertullian, *Prescription Ag. Her.* 36).

Prior to the formal firming up of the apostolic canon, other writings besides the New Testament were also being read and highly esteemed, especially Hermas, Barnabas, Didache, Clement of Rome, which were at times read in public along with the others (Hermas, *Vis.* 2.4.3; Dionysius of Corinth and Hegesippus as reported in Eusebius, *CH* 4.23.11). After formal canonization (Council of Carthage 3, *SCD* 92), these other writings, though revered, were not considered first-generation apostolic testimony.

Though no consistent theory of inspiration of scripture was ecumenically received, certain metaphors recur in the earliest apologetics. Athenagoras spoke of the prophets as elevated to a state of ecstasy wherein the Holy Spirit breathed upon them like a musician might play a flute (*A Plea for the Christians* 7–9).

The Conveyance of the Written Word Through Generations of Cultures Is Spirit Guided

Augustine acknowledged that the writers brought to bear their own memory and imagination and will in the report of revelatory events, yet the Holy Spirit elicited these recollections so as to ensure the accuracy of their reporting, transcription, and reception. He made detailed inquiry into seeming inconsistencies and discrepancies of the Gospel narratives (*Harmony of the Gospels*).

The commonly received assumption was that the Spirit so guided the writers that without circumventing their own human willing, knowing, language, personal temperaments, or any other distinctly personal factors, God's own Word was recalled and transmitted with complete adequacy and sufficiency (Jerome, *Letters* 52.7).

The same Spirit who calls forth the canon of sacred scripture protects it from distortion and illumines our minds in the reading of it (Origen, *Principles*, preface). The Spirit gives special gifts to human authorship to guarantee an adequate and sufficiently reliable conveyance of the divine address (John 16:14; Chrysostom, *Hom. on John* 78).

Called Out People Under the Norm of Canon

The church from its beginnings has been shaped by a received tradition of holy writ in the Torah and prophets and wisdom literature. Then, as the New Testament became consensually received by the church, the worshiping community understood itself to stand under the norm of the apostolic proclamation, for apostolicity was the chief criterion of the New Testament canon.

Reliable Christian proclamation in each generation must be shaped in correspondence with the testimony of the written Word of Old and New Testaments (Decree of Damasus, Roman Synod, AD 382, *SCD* 84). The definition of the commonly received canon is an act in which the church places itself freely and unreservedly under the authority of the apostolic testimony (Tertullian, *Prescription Ag. Her.* 19–21). "Suppose there arise a dispute relative to some important question among us, should we not have recourse to the most ancient churches with which the apostles held constant intercourse, and learn from them what is certain and clear on the question at issue?" (Irenaeus, *Ag. Her.* 3.4.1).

Protestants often argue that "the church did not produce the Scriptures; but the Scriptures gave birth to the church" (Ursinus, *CHC*:290). The exception that validates this rule is the fact that in the first generation of witnesses it was the oral preaching of the witnesses that preceded the written word they preserved.

Thus classic Orthodox, Catholic, and Anglican writers are equally correct to argue (in a way that long predates form-criticism by centuries) that the remembering church by the power of the Spirit gave birth to scripture in its first generation. The first generation church delivered the scriptures so that the scriptures would deliver subsequent generations to the church.

Why Historical Revelation Requires a Written Word

If revelation occurs in history, then it must be remembered, otherwise it is a fleeting event perhaps forgotten. If it is to be remembered accurately, it requires written texts (Chrysostom, *Hom. on John* 88.2). If the written texts are able to be twisted, they must be protected from exploitation by those who do not grasp their meaning.

Christianity proclaims a Savior who meets us personally. The saving act of God is an event that occurred through the life and death of Jesus in history. Hence the recollection of the salvation event always has the character of historical and personal recollection. This constant historical reference of faith runs counter to a rationalism that seeks to formulate unhistorical ideas, or a mysticism that wishes to merge self in God (Origen, *OFP*:29, 116), both of which seek timeless truth, not the truth that is personally made known in time through a personal history.

The reason the worshiping community reveres the canonical list of received scriptures today is the same reason they were specified in the early centuries: to preserve accurately the apostolic memory through changing historical circumstances. If revelation occurs in history and calls for continued recollection amid subsequent histories, it cannot proceed safely to transmit this memory without a written word. Those most eager to revise and rewrite the scripture are often those who have undisguised ideological interests that seek to override the primitive testimony to the truth (Gregory of Nyssa, *Ag. Eunom.* 3.7.1).

It was precisely while explaining why he was "*writing* these things to you" that the author of the First Letter of John, resisting Gnostic views that the apostolic teaching needed to be supplemented with a higher form of knowing, said: "The anointing you [already] received from him [the Holy One] remains in you, and you do not need anyone [else] to teach you. But as his anointing teaches you about all things and as that anointing is real, not counterfeit—just as it has taught you, remain in him" (1 John 2:20, 26–27). John is not rejecting all human teachers, but is opposing those who would expect new revelations that pretend to surmount the anointing, recollecting, and teaching ministry of the Holy Spirit in passing along the remembered and written apostolic witness.

The classic evidences by which the written word is recognized as God's own address are

- the power of the word to change lives

- the incomparable once-for-all events to which it testifies

- the truthfulness and moral excellence of its teaching

- its "mighty effect" upon hearts

This is seen in the fact that "twelve Apostles, taken from among poor and unlearned people, of the lowest class, by this doctrine overcame and subdued to Christ the mighty, the wise, and the rich" (*Longer Catech.* Eastern Orthodox Church, *COC* 2:454, 455; cf. J. Wesley, *A Clear and Concise Demonstration of the Divine Inspiration of the Holy Scriptures*).

The Spirit Works Through the Word in the Heart to Persuade

The Spirit both inspires the scripture and convinces the hearer of its truth. The power by which the Word becomes hearable is itself the same power that breathed forth the scriptural testimony (Calvin, *Inst.* 1.9.2; 2.15.2). "The Spirit is the uniter of inner and outer, past and present, written Word and faith's hearing, Christ and ourselves" (Heron, *HS*:106).

If the scriptures were wholly unambiguous and always plain, then Peter would not have written that some of Paul's letters contain some things hard to understand. If always obvious, there would have been no need to follow the Lord's command to search the scriptures (*Conf.* of Dositheus 18).

The Personal Hearing of the Written Word

The Spirit works inwardly in the heart to elicit repentance, and to offer the gifts of faith, hope, and love. This is a work that transcends the bare text, the objective argument, or logical reasoning. The gospel speaks a personal word about the incarnate Person who has sent the Person of the Spirit to illumine its implication inwardly. In this way the Spirit works to bring the saving grace of the triune God to realization by eliciting full response to the unalloyed message of salvation, the whole counsel of God.

Two steps are implied: the Holy Spirit works in the administration of redemption first to speak *to* the human spirit through scripture and preaching, and then to work *within* the human spirit to elicit repentance and faith (Augustine, *Tractates on John* 77).

Spirit thus works both *externally* in bearing the objective testimony of scripture and preaching and *inwardly* within the hearts of the resistant as well as the faithful. It is through the work of the Spirit that humanity has come to hear of the work of the Son.

The Author of the divine address helps the hearer to understand the address itself. The Spirit assists hearers to "understand what God has freely given us" (1 Cor. 2:12; Ambrosiaster, *Comm. on Paul's Epis*, 1 Cor. 2:12). Unless the Spirit is active to penetrate our self-deceptions, how could we, trapped in a history of finely tuned deception, recognize this address? The Spirit works preveniently to make the mind proximately receptive, to enable openness to the divine address, and to prepare the believer to be unafraid to receive the truth (John of Damascus, *OF* 4.17).

This reception occurs by the internal testimony of the Holy Spirit (*testimonium internum spiritus sancti*), for only God the Spirit can authenticate the Father's own address to the hearer (Calvin, *Inst.* 1.7.4). Scripture conveys the living Word of God to us only as the Spirit makes us able to hear (Augustine, *Spirit and Letter* 28–45). "For the word of God is living and active. Sharper than any double-edged sword, it penetrates even to dividing soul and spirit, joints and marrow; it judges the thoughts and attitudes of the heart" (Heb. 4:12; Symeon the New Theologian, *Discourse* 3.6).

Now we see as if dimly through a mirror. The Holy Spirit works to make the image clearer. Ultimately we will come closer to a more perfect knowledge (1 Cor. 13). Meanwhile, in the growing experience of the worshiping community, "the words of the Lord are flawless, like silver refined in a furnace of clay, purified seven times" (Ps. 12:6).

Gregory offered a memorable picture of the master biblical teacher in his fond description of Athanasius: "From meditating on every book of the Old and New Testament with a depth such as none else has applied even to one of them, he grew rich in contemplation, rich in splendor of life, combining them in a wonderful way by that golden bond which few can weave; using life as the guide of contemplation, contemplation as the seal of life" (Gregory Nazianzus, *Orat.* 21.6).

The Personal Nature of the Word Revealed Through the Spirit

The recollection of the saving action of God in Christ could not be carelessly passed along like other memories. It dealt with God's own self-communication through a living person to a living person. Nothing happens in Christianity unless the Son meets persons inwardly through the Spirit.

The Spirit works by writing the image of Christ upon the hearts of the faithful. Your life is like a letter to each emerging neighbor: "You are a letter from Christ, the result of our ministry, written not with ink but with the Spirit of the living God, not on tablets of stone but on tablets of human hearts" (2 Cor. 3:2, 3; Ambrose, *Paradise* 8.39).

Wherever this word of scripture is read attentively, it transforms human lives, affects human societies, changes political structures, redeems human fallenness. When Paul left the elders of Ephesus, he committed them "to God and to the word of his grace, which can build you up and give you an inheritance among all those who are sanctified" (Acts 21:32).

It is the Spirit and not our cleverness that ensures that the writing and transmission of the apostolic witnesses are sufficiently accurate to deliver the testimony of salvation to subsequent generations. Hence the next generation already has in hand a written testimony to which preaching becomes accountable: an account of the history of salvation sufficient to depend upon, not merely hearsay tales or abstract theories, but historical reports of eyewitnesses.

The omnipotent God is not lacking in ability to deliver his Word to humanity accurately through the writers of scripture "without waiving their human intelligence, their individuality, their literary style, their personal feelings, or any other human factor" (Walvoord, *HS*:60). Conviction is not the result of our skill but the Spirit's work. "For though we live in the world, we do not wage war as the world does. The weapons we fight with are not the weapons of the world. On the contrary, they have divine power to demolish strongholds. We demolish arguments and every pretension that sets itself up against the knowledge of God, and we take captive every thought to make it obedient to Christ" (2 Cor. 10:4, 5; Chrysostom, *Hom on Cor.* 21.3).

The Spirit in Preaching and Sacrament

The Spirit works in preaching, seeking to elicit through speech an accurate attestation to the salvation event, and in the hearers a sufficiently accurate reception. Both the written and preached word are addressed to the unconverted to awaken their desire for the truth, and to the faithful to bring them into closer personal union with the truth (Calvin, *Inst.* 3.1–2; Barth, *CD* 1/1:51).

Luther rightly resisted the individualistic notion of a direct, unmediated operation of the Spirit, as if apart from written word, sacrament, and community. As the Son comes in the flesh within the historical continuum of a particular people, so does the Spirit meet us in community through bodily signs, water, poured-out wine, the heard words of preaching, and the written word. The Spirit "has determined to give the inward part to no man except through the outward part" (Luther, *EA* 21.208, 212). "And so Paul preached the Word outwardly to Lydia, a purple-seller among the Philippians; but the Lord inwardly opened the woman's heart" (Second Helvetic Confession, *CC*:134; cf. Acts. 16:14). The Spirit's illumination occurs "with and through the word" (Schmaldcald Articles, cf. Luther, *EA* 14.188).

Through Word and Sacrament the Spirit comes to us and operates within our hearts (*intus operans*, Luther, *EA* 29.108; 9.210) to apply the chief miracle that Christ operates upon the soul—the giving of life. When the word of God goes out in preaching, it does not come back empty (Luther; *EA* 29.208). In doing so, the Spirit does not enlarge or add to the apostolic testimony, but brings home that word to the individual contextually (Athanasius, *Ag. Arians*).

The Spirit assists the community of faith in accurately remembering, rightly interpreting, and practically applying the scripture (John 14:26; 1 Cor. 2:13; 2 Tim. 1:5). This is why the clearest and surest expositions of the scripture are to be found in the community of faith guided by the Spirit and not among individualistic interpreters (Irenaeus, *Ag. Her.* 5.26; Vincent of Lérins, *Commonitory*, 1).

PART II

SALVATION

S ALVATION REFERS TO THE ACTION OF GOD in delivering humanity. It is the divine work of rescuing fallen creatures (1 Cor. 1:21; Titus 3:5).

In the salvation of humanity, God offers the recovery of what had been lost in the fall of humanity from sin, despair, and death. What was lost is the original capability of men and women to reflect the image of God through humble trust in God's gift and command.

By descending to humanity, God has accomplished what human effort could not do. Those willing to hear are being saved *from* sin, saved *for* new life and union with the Son through the Spirit (Acts 16:30–31; Rom. 5:9, 10; Eph. 2:5–8; Chrysostom, *Hom. on Acts*, Hom. 36).

3

THE WAY OF
REPENTANCE

The Terms of Salvation

The terms of salvation are conditions under which God's saving action may be received—repentance and faith. They are the simple terms of the earliest Christian preaching: repent and believe.

John the Baptist preached, "Repent, for the kingdom of heaven is near" (Matt. 3:2). Jesus' public ministry began with the call to "repent and believe the good news" (Mark 1:15). When the disciples were sent to proclaim the coming kingdom, they preached repentance (Luke 24:47). Peter's first sermon and subsequent apostolic testimony consistently called first for repentance (Acts 2:38; cf. 3:19; 26:17, 18; Cyril of Jerusalem, *Catech. Lect.* 2; Melanchthon, *Loci:*140).

The Purpose of Preaching

To make the call to repentance and faith plausible is the task of Christian preaching. When neglected, every other aspect of the mission of the church stands imperiled. Preaching that lacks the courage to call hearers to repent is tedious and timid. Theology that lacks the capacity for admonition smells of hypocrisy (Cyril of Alex., *Comm. on Luke* 6.42; Ambrose, *Letters* 46).

The purpose of preaching is to draw the hearer toward saving faith in God. That faith can only begin with repentance. It is in the repentance of one sinner that heaven rejoices (Luke 15:10; 13:5). This is not a narrow or dated subject.

There reigns in the broken human heart a feeling of discord, a lack of congruence between what is and what ought to be (Augustine, *Conf.* 5). Christian preaching does not sidestep this feeling of incongruence but faces it openly. The crushed heart must be relieved by confession of sin (James 5:16). The longing for peace, the earnest desire for truth, the penetration of self-deceptions, the hunger for freedom from a life of sin is the direct concern of Christian testimony (Cyprian, *Treatise* 10). Every resource of language is employed to make the requirement of God as clear as possible and the eventful love of God palpable and real (2 Cor. 5:20; Augustine, *Chr. Doctrine* 4; W. B. Pope, *Compend.* 2:367–76).

What Is Meant by Being "Saved"?

To be saved is to be delivered from bondage, brought into freedom, rescued from death, given a new lease on life. That which is reclaimed by God's saving action is human life as intended to be—abundant life, eternal life, life in the Spirit (John 5, 6; Rom. 8:1–10; 1 John 5).

The technical term *soteriology* combines the Greek *sōtēria* (salvation) with *logos* (word or reasoning). It refers to a discipline of study that inquires into God's saving action. The term *conversion* refers to the whole process of behavioral reversal in all its components, with special focus upon its decisive earliest stage. *Conversion* and *salvation* are in English closely linked terms. Yet they come from different Latin root words: *convertere* (to turn around, turning toward) and *salvare* (to securely save), from *salvus* (safe, unhurt, sound, healthy).

The Hebrew and Greek words for salvation (*yeshuah, teshuah, sōtēria*) convey a complex matrix of meanings: deliverance, rescue, safety, preservation, soundness, restoration, and healing (Pss. 3:8; 51:12; Isa. 51:5–8; Eph. 1:13; 2 Tim. 2:10; Basil, *Hom. on Psalm* 61.2). The term *salvation* is best not employed in a strictly individualistic sense. In scripture it embraces the whole history of God's saving activity and the history of human reception of it. The shorthand conventional question, "Are you saved?" may intend to be an intense personalizing of the question of salvation, yet it may inadvertently neglect the broader scope of salvation history (Luke 1:69; Rom. 13:11; 1 Pet. 1:3–9; Bede, *On 1 Peter* 1,10–12; Bede, *Hom. on Gospels* 2.20).

The salvation of which Christianity speaks distinguishes it from other worldviews. No other religious tradition speaks of salvation by a messianic, theandric mediator who died on a cross to save sinners, then rose bodily to intercede for them. In receiving this salvation, humanity is offered an undeserved gift that cannot be earned, purchased, or morally merited. The way of salvation is narrow. The paths are wide and many that lead to ruin (Matt. 7:14; Chrysostom, *Hom. on Matt.*, Hom. 23.5,6).

The Premise of Lostness

Regrettably the term salvation has been cheapened by an extensive history of misuse. To understand what it means to be saved, you must first understand what it means to be lost (*appolu*, Matt. 18:1; Tertullian, *On Chastity* 7–9). Those who have not yet grasped any real sense in which they are truly lost are not yet ready to hear about being saved (Luke 15:24,32; Augustine, *Expos. of Luke* 7.213–215).

The metaphor of lostness comes from Jesus himself, who spoke of the lost son, the lost sheep, the lost coin (Luke 15). His parables set forth the power of being found, saved from lostness. A faraway pigsty was not where the prodigal son truly belonged. Only when he returned home to the father was he saved. The lost sheep were saved not because they found their own way back but because the shepherd went out and diligently searched for them (Luke 15:3,4).

If humanity had never fallen into sin, there would be no need of a Savior. Only the sick need a physician (Mark 2:17; Augustine, *Letter 157 to Hilarius*). But since human freedom has fallen, and humanity lives out of an actual history of sin, a saving act is required.

Fallen humanity has a Savior (the Son) and an Enabler (the Spirit) to make it possible that the Savior may be personally received. The Son offers the atoning deed, and the Spirit makes way inwardly for the wholehearted reception of the Son (Bede, *On 1 John* 4:13–14; Augustine, *Hom. on Epist. of John* 8). That is what the story of salvation is all about.

The Terms of Salvation

The characteristic order of the call to salvation in apostolic teaching is as follows:

Repent

Believe

Be baptized for the remission of sins

Receive the gift of the Holy Spirit

The salvation prepared for the world can only be inwardly appropriated when one repents, trusts in God's pardoning grace, and follows the narrow way. The concern of the study of salvation is the clarification of the steps along this way, the obstacles associated with these steps, and the grace that enables each step (Acts 2.4; Augustine, *On Original Sin* 2.24.28; Calvin, *Inst.* 2.6.1, Pope, *Compend.* 2: 55; A. A. Hodge, *OOT*:338). This call is addressed to every individual able and willing to hear.

"In order that this treasure might not be buried but put to use and enjoyed, God has caused the Word to be published and proclaimed, in which he has given the Holy Spirit to offer and apply to us this treasure of salvation," wrote Luther. "Neither you nor I could ever know anything of Christ, or believe in him and take him as our Lord unless these were first offered to us and bestowed on our hearts through the preaching of the Gospel by the Holy Spirit" (*Large Catechism*, Third Article).

The Study of Salvation

Salvation as a Unifying Theme of Scripture

Salvation teaching may be broadly summarized as follows: In the justifying work of the Son, the obstacles to divine-human reconciliation are overcome. In the Spirit's regeneration of new life, grace to live by faith is actually being imparted and received (Luke 3:6; Ambrosiaster, *Comm. on Paul*, 2 Cor. 5.2).

In the term *salvation*, the New Testament refers to the totality of this event in all its component aspects and to the consequences emerging out of Jesus' person and work and to God's sending of the Spirit to create the new Israel to proclaim this salvation worldwide (Acts 16:17).

Salvation is one of the most comprehensive terms of Christian teaching, gathering into a single word-picture a broad range of key points crucial to the Christian life: redemption, reconciliation, atonement, propitiation, predestination, calling, covenant, grace, conviction, repentance, forgiveness, justification, adoption, faith, conversion, regeneration, sanctification, and perseverance (Is. 12:2, *yeshuah*; Titus 2:11; Cyril of Alex., *On the Unity of Christ*; Leo I, *Sermon* 58.4, *sōtēria*).

Those who might be tempted to strike *salvation* from the Christian vocabulary in order to curb abuses of the way it has been sometimes taught must begin searching anew for terms of proximately analogous meaning—*liberation, ego strength, freedom, revolution, the overcoming of estrangement.* None of these are precise equivalents, though each may enrich the vocabulary of salvation. It is difficult even to say what Christianity is without using the term *salvation* (*sōtēria*) and its cognates (save, *yasha, sōzō,* Savior, *sōtēr;* Calvin, *Inst.* 3.14–18). Though the English noun *salvation* may have numerous nonreligious uses (save, preserve, rescue, restore), these tend to be derived by analogy from its protracted centuries of religious uses (*TDNT; OED*).

Soteriology is a bridge discipline between the study of the Son and of the Spirit, between justification and sanctification, between God for us and God in us. The work of the Son inquires into those texts that tell the story of what God has done *for* us. The work of the Spirit inquires into those texts that show what God is doing *in* us—how the eternal purpose of God is being inwardly appropriated through a succession of events—creation, fall, call, exile, redemption—grounded in the history of Israel, fulfilled in Christ, shared in by the church, and brought finally to full consummation in and beyond history (Cyril of Jerusalem, *Catech. Lect.* 15.2–3).

*Soteri*ology (Savior study, inquiry into salvation) is not finally reducible to an *anthropo*logy that studies only the humanity rescued by God's action. Anthropological reductionism (as seen in L. Feuerbach, S. Freud, F. Buri, H. Braun) assumes that theology is anthropology writ large, nothing more. All talk of God's action finally amounts merely to references to human action in this view (Feuerbach, *The Essence of Christianity,* 2). This leaves soteriology bereft of a subject (*soter*).

The Spirit's Work in Applying God's Saving Action

The Father fulfilled his saving purpose by sending his only Son to save sinners, to inaugurate the reign of God through his birth, life, teaching, ministry, death, resurrection, ascension, and heavenly intercession. The events of Jesus' last days of earthly ministry constituted the accomplished salvation event (Hilary, *Trin.,* 6.41–42).

The *application* of the work of the Son is accomplished through the Spirit. The Son by sheer grace merits our salvation. The Spirit applies the redeeming work to our temporal lives. What is accomplished for us in Christ remains to be embodied in us through the Spirit (Rom. 8:9–17; Polycarp, *Epis. to Phil.* 2; Gal. 3:1–5).

The special mission of the Spirit is to make real the fruits and benefits of Christ in believers. God the Son has already done the saving mediatorial work. God the Spirit is now enabling that saving work to be appropriated in human community. Salvation is brought to full effect "not by might nor by power, but by my Spirit, says the Lord Almighty" (Zech. 4:6). It is the Spirit's work fittingly to mature and complete the process of salvation, to bring to serviceable application and reception the work of the Son on the cross for our justification (Gal. 5:16–26; Marius Victorinus, *Epis. to Gal.* 2.5.16).

The Elements of Personal Salvation Teaching

The Spirit works to restrain, convict, regenerate, indwell, baptize, seal, and fill (Owen, *Works,* 4, 8). The study of salvation seeks to grasp the sequence of these outworkings as received by consensual exegetes. The work of the Spirit in administering personal redemption is seen in a sequence of stages. The sequence is as follows:

- The restraint of sin, by which the Spirit provides time for repentance

- The conviction of sin, by which Spirit awakens the sinner to the awareness of sin

- Repentance, by which the Spirit leads the penitent to godly sorrow for sin, reform of behavior, reparation for harm done to others, revulsion against sin, and confession of sin

- Faith, by which the Spirit enables one to place personal trust in the Savior

- Regeneration, by which the Spirit quickens life spiritually so as to begin a new life born of God, adoption into the family of God

- The indwelling of the Spirit, by which the Spirit comes to reside in the heart of the believer

- Baptism of the Spirit, by which the new person becomes dead to the old way and alive to the new

- The sealing of the Holy Spirit, by which the Spirit confirms the living Word in the heart

- Assurance, by which the Holy Spirit witnesses inwardly to the spirit of the believer that he or she is a son or daughter of God, pardoned and adopted, enabling a firm conviction that the believer is reconciled to God

- The filling of the believer by the Holy Spirit, by which the Spirit comes more and more fully to express the way of holiness in the life of the believer

- Sanctification, by which the Spirit works to bring the regenerate spirit into full participation in the life of God through union with Christ

The Overarching Order of Salvation

There is a progression, Ambrose taught, in the story of salvation. The Spirit moves "from the grace of giving life to that of sanctification, to translate us from earth to heaven, from wretchedness to glory, from slavery to a kingdom" (*Of the Holy Spirit* 1.11.122).

The phases of the ministry of the Spirit were astutely summarized by Basil: "Through the Holy Spirit comes our restoration to paradise, our ascension into the kingdom of heaven, our return to the adoption of sons, our liberty to call God our Father, our being made partakers of the grace of Christ, our being called children of light, our sharing in eternal glory, and, in a word, our being brought into a state of all 'fullness of blessing' " (*On the Holy Spirit* 15.36).

Gradually these points came under more deliberate discussion in the Reformation, arranged as an order of salvation (*ordo salutis*). Anglican, Lutheran and Reformed versions of this sequence are similar: the faithful "through Grace obey the calling; they be justified freely; they be made sons of God by adoption; they be made like the image of his only begotten Son Jesus Christ; they walk religiously in good works, and at length, by God's mercy, they attain to everlasting felicity" (Anglican, Thirty-nine Articles, 17). "The Holy Spirit has called me through the Gospel, enlightened me with his gifts, and sanctified and preserved me in the true faith, just as he calls, gathers, enlightens, and sanctifies the whole Christian church on earth and preserves it in union with Jesus Christ in the one true faith" (Luther, *Small Catech.*, creed, art. 3). "The office of the Holy Spirit may be said to embrace the following: to instruct, to regenerate, to unite to Christ and God, to rule, to comfort and strengthen us" (Ursinus, *CHC*:277).

Each stage is premised upon God's justifying grace in Jesus Christ. Through these ministries the Spirit wishes to draw and persuade, not force, the human will; to convince, not coerce, in order to enable the deepest possible experience of God's saving action. God is not willing that any should perish but that all should willingly come to repentance (2 Pet. 3:9). The sinner is not compelled to come to grace but offered grace as a gift to be received (Augustine, *On Nature and Grace* 81–84).

The Greek verb *to save* (*sōzō*) may be used either in a punctiliar or durative sense, as a point in time, or as duration in time, or as a series of overlapping processes, or as a continuous process with distinguishable components (*TDNT, sōzō*; Erickson, *CT* 3:889).

Past, Present, and Future Salvation

Jesus promised that the kingdom would come gradually: "first the stalk, then the head, then the full kernel in the head" (Mark 4:28; Tertullian, *On Veiling of Virg.* 1). The converting-saving grace of God is often found to work especially in crisis moments of personal reversal, which are then followed by a continuing work of grace that develops over time. God's saving activity occurs in history. Hence salvation is being received through a linear progression of historic saving events.

There are three tenses in the vocabulary of salvation: We have been saved from the penalty sin for our justification. We are being saved from the power of sin for our sanctification. We will be saved from the remnants of sin for God's glorification. Salvation includes the whole range of the divine activity on behalf of humanity in past, present, and future history (Calvin, *Inst.* 3.4.17–18; 4.17).

In the *past* tense, salvation is not merely an abstract idea but an actual series of historical events, reliably remembered and abundantly attested. If salvation were merely an idea in our minds and never an event in history, it is doubtful that it would be significant enough to become a subject of study. Hence, to understand the salvation of humanity, we must think eventfully and historically of what God is doing in the real world.

Thus the worshiping community speaks first in the *past* tense of God's saving activity as having already pardoned sinners, cleansed the penitent from reproach, justified them by grace, and freed them for a life of accountable love. Salvation in this sense has already occurred, and is understood as a finished work in Christ on the cross (Eph. 2:1–10; John 19:30; Leo I, *Sermon* 55.4).

Second, the worshiping community is also aware that God the Spirit is acting in the *present* to bind up the demonic powers, to forgive sin, now to raise the dead, and wash from corruption (Rom. 6; Gal. 2:20). When Paul spoke of believers being "sealed for the day of redemption" (Eph. 4:30), he was looking toward a coming consummation of a redemption that was already being experienced in the present in an anticipative way, grounded in a past event of redemption, the cross. "For he has rescued us from the dominion of darkness and brought us into the kingdom of the Son he loves, in whom we have redemption, the forgiveness of sins" (Col. 1:14).

Finally, in the *future* tense, the *ekklēsia* is looking toward a consummation of God's saving activity at the end of history. God's design to save humanity includes all time, not just part of history. The fulfillment of God's purpose in creation is awaiting a final consummation in the end of days (1 Pet. 1:3–5; 1 John 3:1–3).

In some key salvation texts all three tenses interfuse: "For the grace of God *has appeared* [past tense], bringing salvation to all, training us to renounce impiety and worldly passions, and in the *present* age to live lives that are self-controlled, upright, and godly, while we *wait for* the blessed [future] hope" (Titus 2:11, 12, italics added; Luther, *LW* 29:64–67). Paul wrote to the Philippians that he was confident that God "who began a good work in you will carry it on to completion until the day of Christ Jesus" (Phil. 1:6; Augustine, *On Grace and Free Will* 32). For the apostle, the tenses flow together when those who already "have the first fruits of the Spirit" wait eagerly for their adoption as sons and daughters, for "the redemption of their bodies," while the whole of creation still is groaning for redemption (Rom. 8:23). All that needs to be done from God's side for divine-human reconciliation has already occurred on the cross, awaiting our responsive action, to be fittingly brought to consummation by the work of the Spirit.

This deliverance has come to a vast cloud of individual believers amid and through their own specific developing personal histories. Each autobiography could be told as a personal narrative. This focus on personal testimony became the hallmark of conversion accounts throughout Orthodox (Thecla, Antony, Nicholas, Mena), Catholic (Augustine, *Conf.*; Teresa of Avila, *Life*; Thérèse of Lisieux, *Story of a Soul*) and Protestant traditions (J. Edwards, *Faithful Narrative*; Wesley, *Journals*; Phoebe Palmer, *The Way of Holiness*).

The Narrow Way of Repentance

Repentance remains a crucial Christian doctrine "to be preached by every minister" (Westminster Confession, 15). From the outset it has been regarded among "the elementary teachings about Christ" (Heb. 6:1) which are presupposed in the maturity that follows in faith (Severian of Gabala, *Fragments on Heb.* 6.1–2; Origen, *OFP* 4.1.7).

The narrow way to salvation must begin with repentance: "Godly sorrow brings repentance that leads to salvation" (2 Cor. 7:10). Narrow is the way that leads to life (Matt. 7:14; Clement of Rome, *Corinth* 7:1–8.5; Kierkegaard, *Christian Discourses*).

True contrition cannot be feigned. Nor can it lack the intent to forsake sin altogether.

Defining Repentance

Though the English word *repentance* carries the nuance of sorrow for what one has done, it does not as adequately imply reformation of character as does the Greek. Hence it is a less powerful term than *metanoia*, which implies a fundamental behavioral reversal (Matt. 3:8; Acts 26:20; Heb. 6:1, 6; Tertullian, *On Repentance*; Calvin, *Inst.* 3.3.5). *Metanoia* denotes a sweeping change of mind and heart followed by a behavioral reformation of a sinful life, a sorrowing for sin so as to forsake sin altogether. Repentance is a "coming to oneself" (Luke 15:10), a voluntary change of mind, heart, and will of the sinner in turning away from sin (Peter Chrysologus, *Sermon* 1).

Genuine repentance occurs only when one earnestly calls to mind one's own misdeeds so as to elicit profound sorrow for sin so as to renounce and forsake sin (Fletcher, *Works* 3;112–31). Repentance assumes a full commitment of heart and mind to the mortification of those sins that so easily beset us, and to the Spirit's vivification of a new life (Calvin, *Inst.* 3.3.8). Lacking deep hunger for a fundamental change of life, mind, heart, self-understanding, and behavior, a surface repentance only becomes a new temptation to hypocrisy.

Repentance is incomplete or insincere if it does not resolve to lead a new life (2 Cor. 7:10). It seeks a true and accurate recollection of misdeeds without false humility (Heb. 13:18). It does not suggest loss of appropriate self-esteem but rather requires a higher valuing of oneself by becoming radically honest before God so as to put one's feet on the way to recovery. It does not imply a diminishing of personal identity but an honoring and clarifying of one's personal identity through candid self-confrontation (Ephrem, *Comm. on Heb.* 13.17; *Nisibene Hymns*).

The Spirit has come to dwell in the faithful to comfort, guide, witness, and to bring all our redeemed powers to maturity in all spiritual graces (Cyril of Jerusalem, *Catech. Lect.* 2–5). Repentance is the first step.

Mind, Heart, and Will Join in Repentance

Repentance requires a decisive reversal of the previous sin-laden course of mind, heart, and will.

The reversal does not occur without first a *change of mind*, a revised conception of oneself, utilizing one's own best moral reasoning to recognize the intolerable cost of sin (Augustine, *Conf.* 1.18). But where the reversal touches only the mind but not the heart and will, the despair of sin deepens.

Repentance requires a *change of heart*, a deep sorrowing for sin, aware that sin, whether personal or social, is in actual fact sin against God who gives humans freedom (Ps. 51:4). Far more than a mode of analytical reasoning, repentance is a deeply felt remorse and emotively experienced regret over wrongs done voluntarily against others, offending one's own integrity and dignity and finally offending God (Theodore of Heraclea, *Fragments on Isaiah*, 57.15).

True penitence is a grieving over one's alienated self and broken relationships, a loathing of sin and godly sorrow for irresponsibility, a heavy feeling of condemnation that intends to have a constructive effect by changing character and habit (Origen, *Comm. on Rom.* 7.25; Second Clement 9.8). "'Make for yourselves a new heart and a new spirit' that you may become a subject of joy for the citizens of heaven" (Cyril of Jerusalem, *Catech. Lect.* 1.1).

Repentance requires a *change of will*, a redirected disposition to seek a new life of forgiveness and grateful responsibility. This reversal is not fully accounted for as an act of knowing or feeling. It is a grace-enabled act of volition, a determination to turn the whole self around (Chrysostom, *Hom on Rom.* 7.18; 8.9–11).

The change of mind and heart makes way for a volitional change of behavior reaching habitually into the depths of moral character. The inward feeling of remorse moves toward outward acts of turning away from the life of sin (Apostolic Constitutions 2.22–24).

The deeper purpose of the Spirit's work in and through conscience is not merely to accuse or excuse behavior by attesting moral wrong or right within, but positively to bring the human spirit back into an originally congruent relation of trust in God by leading through repentance to faith (Rom. 2:15; 1 Cor. 8:7–12; *Bede on 1 Pet.* 3.16, 21).

Repentance requires moral courage enabled by prevening grace to penetrate self-deceptions and attend realistically to the claims of conscience (Ambrose, *Expos. Of Luke* 7.213–214; H. R. Niebuhr, "On Faith in God," *RMWC*). Penitential reasoning focuses explicitly upon the sinner's actual condition in relation to the holiness of God (Chrysostom, *Baptismal Instructions*, ACW 31:126–27). Anyone who compares God's incomparable holiness, justice, and love with one's own personal behavioral choices becomes ill at ease.

Repentance Takes Place in the Presence of God: Psalm 51

Psalm 51 is traditionally understood as a penitential prayer after David had committed adultery with Bathsheba, put to death her husband Uziah, and had then been confronted with the gravity of his sin by the prophet Nathan. He prayed for mercy: "According to your great compassion, blot out my transgressions. Wash away all my iniquity and cleanse me from my sin" (Ps. 51:1, 2). Past sin tracks present awareness. Unrepented, sin only intensifies the syndrome of guilty recollection: "For I know my transgressions, and my sin is always before me." (Ps. 51:3).

Only one thing is needful: "Surely you desire truth in the inner parts; you teach me wisdom in the inmost place" (Ps. 51:6). "Cleanse me with hyssop, and I will be clean; wash me, and I will be whiter than snow" (v. 7). "Hide your face from my sins and blot out all my iniquity. Create in me a pure heart, O God, and renew a steadfast spirit within me" (Ps. 51:9, 10). Grieving over his sin, David implored: "Restore to me the joy of your salvation and grant me a willing spirit, to sustain me" (Ps. 51:12, 13; Luther, *LW* 12:382–84). The Davidic model of penitence is a drama enacted in the presence of God in the quiet inner depths of conscience (Chrysostom, *Epis. to Heb.* 9.8–9).

Sin, whether against neighbor or commonweal, finally must be understood in God's presence. "Against you, you only, have I sinned and done what is evil in your sight" (Ps. 51:4). Why is one guilty before God because of a wrong done to another human being? Because God has given the freedom that someone has abused. It is finally to God that abused freedom experiences itself as responsible (Calvin, *Comm.* 5:281–99; S. Kierkegaard, *Stages on Life's Way*).

How quietly does conscience point transcendently to God as source of moral accountability. Conscience functions not only in relation to society or neighbor or oneself but ultimately in relation to the Giver of life (Jer. 3:11–13; Rom. 2:15). In the theater of repentance there may be many who have been hurt, but there is finally only One hearer in the audience that counts. For there is only One who can finally right the wrongs: the eternal One who grants human freedom and calls it to accountability.

A Clean Sweep Is Required

The call to repentance expects a clean sweep: "Turn away from all your offenses; then sin will not be your downfall. Rid yourselves of all the offenses you have committed, and get a new heart and a new spirit. Why will you die, O house of Israel? For I take no pleasure in the death of anyone, declares the Sovereign Lord. Repent and live!" (Ezek. 18:30–32; Tertullian, *On Repentance* 4; Jerome, *Comm. on Ezek.* 6.18.31).

John the Baptist's call to repentance stood in this prophetic-penitential tradition, intensified by messianic expectation. John called for the baptism of repentance and demanded evidences of authentic conversion, fruits fitting to a life of decisive reversal (Matt. 3:9–10; Hilary, *On Matt.* 2.3). His preaching pointed toward a coming forgiveness of sins (Mark 1:4; Luke 3:3). He set the stage for Jesus' preaching of repentance, which is bound intrinsically with the gospel call (Justin Martyr, *Dialogue with Trypho*, 50, 51).

Scripture abounds in narratives of deep-seated repentance (Ps. 119:58–60; Ezek. 36:31; Isa. 57:15; 66:2), earnest prayers of contrition (Ps. 130:1–4; Dan. 9:4–7; Ezra 9:5, 6), and typic accounts of decisive reversal (the prodigal, Luke 15:17–21; the publican, Luke 18:13, 14; Saul of Tarsus, Acts 9:5–11).

The grace of repentance awakens the earnest desire for salvation from sin (Ambrose, *Jacob and the Happy Life*). It acknowledges the radical need of the alienated for a new birth to a new life.

Evangelical Repentance

Evangelical repentance is that repentance required by the gospel. It is a godly sorrow awakened in the heart by the Holy Spirit by which the sinner becomes intensely aware of sin as an offense to divine holiness and loathes sin's power (Ps. 51:1–12). The person becomes profoundly attentive to the burden and skewed power of his own freedom. He turns away from sin in grief over the misdeeds done, and toward God seeking pardon (Chrysostom, *Baptismal Instructions, ACW* 31:50–53).

The sequence of this reversal typically moves from conviction of sin to godly sorrow to heartfelt contrition (*paenitere ex animo*) to resolution to forsake all sin, then to confession (to God and to offended persons), and moral reformation, including amendment of life and acts of reparation (*Homily Ascribed to Clement* 13.11; 8.3, 4; Irish Articles 38). There is a tide of intrapsychic reasoning that flows in this progression. Convicting grace elicits a sense of anguish about the power and cost of sin, which requires self-examination, followed by an act of contrition and confession of sin, requiring a decision to renounce all sin, out of which comes a reformation of moral behavior, accompanied by a growing recognition of the offer of grace in the gospel (Tertullian, *On Repentance* 9–12; Tho. Aq., *ST* supp., Q1).

Chrysostom noted five milestones on the way of repentance: openly declaring one's sins, forgiving the sins of others indebted to us, diligent prayer, acts of loving-kindness, and unfeigned humility (*Resisting the Temptations of the Devil*).

The Second Helvetic Confession further refined this progression: "By repentance we understand (1) the recovery of a right mind in sinful man awakened by the Word of the Gospel and the Holy Spirit, and received by true faith, by which the sinner immediately acknowledges his innate corruption and all his sins accused by the Word of God; and (2) grieves for them from his heart, and not only bewails and frankly confesses them before God with a feeling of shame, but also abominates them and (3) now zealously considers the amendment of his ways and constantly strives for innocence and virtue in which conscientiously to exercise himself all the rest of his life" (Art. 14, *BOC* 5.093). Each of these three phases of repentance may be considered separately as distinguishable issues of salvation teaching: conviction, contrition, and reformation.

All aspects of this interrelated sequence are viewed together as a single, whole act of reversal. In one who feels conviction without any act of contrition, repentance remains stillborn. If one seeks to reform moral behavior without profoundly sorrowing over sins or confessing them to God (*homologeō, confessio*), then repentance has not fully matured. If I confess my sins but engage in no acts of reparation or no attempt to right the wrongs done, then repentance is not bearing sufficient moral fruit (Cyril of Jerusalem, *Catech. Lect.* 2; Rabanas Maurus, *De institutione clericorum* 2.30; Baptists' *Abstract of Principles* 9).

Conviction of Sin

Conviction is that intense personal awareness that my own life is imprisoned in sin (Rom. 7:23; Gal. 3:23; Augustine, *Tractates on John* 41.10–11; Barth, *CD* I/2:768). In order to repent of my sins I must first be enabled to recognize the power and destructiveness of sin in my most inward self. I must feel the moral bruises sin has left. This recognition is no easy matter, since willed sin develops elaborate resistances to beholding its own dynamics (Pastor of Hermas, *Similitude* 5; Menninger, *Whatever Became of Sin?*).

To be convicted is to discover personally that I am rightly under the condemnation of my own conscience and, through conscience, God's own holy life. Under conviction, "the whole heart is afflicted. From the sole of your foot to the top of your head there is no soundness" (Isa. 1:5, 6). Under conviction I am aware of the syndromes of my own anxiety, guilt, and boredom. My human condition is described by the apostle as if "sold as a slave to sin" (Rom. 7:14, Origen, *Comm. on Rom.* 7.15).

Such an intense sense of conviction came upon Isaiah that he cried out: " 'Woe to me!' I cried. 'I am ruined! For I am a man of unclean lips, and I live among a people of unclean lips, and my eyes have seen the King, the Lord Almighty.' " Yet it was just under such heavy conviction that—"Then one of the seraphs flew to me with a live coal in his hand, which he had taken with tongs from the altar. With it he touched my mouth and said, 'See, this has touched your lips; your guilt is taken away and your sin atoned for.' " (Isa. 6:5–7, cf. Dan. 4:32–36; Sahdona, Book of Perfection 5–9; Tertullian, *On Repentance* 12).

Peter boldly confronted his hearers with their acquiescence to the crucifixion: "God has made this Jesus, whom you crucified, both Lord and Christ." Their conviction was immediate: "When the people heard this, they were *cut to the heart.*" They "said to Peter and the other apostles, 'Brothers, *what shall we do*?' Peter replied, 'Repent and be baptized, every one of you, in the name of Jesus Christ for the forgiveness of your sins. And you will receive the gift of the Holy Spirit' " (Acts 2:36–38, italics added; Ambrose, *Of the Holy Spirit* 1.12.127).

It is the Spirit who convicts, and it is the Spirit who prepares the time and conditions of conviction. Often this time occurs under conditions of true worship, guided by ministries ordained of the Spirit who attest the revealed Word, placed in the frame of reference of the sacramental life quickened by the Spirit. It may be triggered unexpectedly "from out of the depths" (Ps. 130:1). In the grip of the grace of repentance, "No one has anything of his own except falsehood and sin" (Augustine, *On the Gospel of St. John* 5.1).

Such an overwhelming conviction stunned Paul as he journeyed to Damascus to persecute Christians and "take them as prisoners to Jerusalem." "A light from heaven flashed around him. He fell to the ground and heard a voice say to him, 'Saul, Saul, why do you persecute me?' 'Who are you, Lord?' Saul asked. 'I am Jesus, whom you are persecuting,' he replied." When he got up from the ground and opened his eyes, "he could see nothing. So they led him by the hand into Damascus. For three days he was blind, and did not eat or drink anything" (Acts 9:3–9; Bede, *Comm. on Acts* 9.6–9). Later when he recalled his previous resistance, he exclaimed, "What a wretched man I am! Who will rescue me from this body of death?" The answer was at hand: "Thanks be to God" that "there is now no condemnation for those who are in Christ Jesus" (Rom. 7:24, 25; 8:1; Origen, *Comm. on Rom.* 8.1–3).

The Spirit Penetrates Resistances

The Spirit penetrates self-deceptions, evasions, and defensive ploys. The Spirit works to change the lowered awareness of sin into heightened awareness, making the unrighteous hungry for righteousness, as if already facing final judgment (Second Clement, 16–20). The Spirit raises consciousness of sin—an archetypal form of "consciousness-raising." The context: Before God.

This judging activity is most poignantly seen in relation to the cross. There all humanity stands justly under the sentence of death and ready for execution, were it not for the Advocate Son who takes upon himself the penalty (1 Pet. 2:22–24; Basil, *On Baptism* 1.3). In this way "the sinner is placed on the other side of his own execution. Though alive and uninjured, the believing sinner may look back upon his own execution as accomplished" (Chafer, *ST* 6:98; cf. Rom. 8:1; 2 Cor. 5:14).

The Spirit does not coerce conviction but quietly persuades and draws out responsive cooperation in human wills (Pope, *Compend.* 2:361–76). The silent inward work occurs "Not by might nor by power, but by my Spirit" (Zech. 4:6). "For it is God who works in you to will and to act according to his good purpose"; hence you are to "continue to work out your salvation with fear and trembling" (Phil. 2:12, 13; Augustine, *On Grace and Free Will* 21). God who made you without you and atoned for you without you seeks to transform you only with your free consent (Eph. 2:8–10; Chrysostom, *Hom. on Phil.* 8; Augustine, *On Grace and Free Will* 31–37).

The paradox of conviction is this: Those who most truly repent are those most keenly aware of their dependence on the Spirit, knowing that if the Spirit had not drawn them toward the mercy of God, they would never have reversed course on their own. "No one can come to me unless the Father who sent me draws him" (John 6:44; Augustine, *Tractates on John* 26.4–6).

The heat of conviction does not always lead to repentance. Felix visibly trembled when Paul "discoursed on righteousness, self-control and the judgment to come." But he did not move to reverse his behavior. He evaded and temporized: "That's enough for now! You may leave. When I find it convenient, I will send for you" (Acts 24:25). The convenient time may never return.

"So far from co-operating with the Spirit in the new creation, the natural man presents every *resistance* and *opposition* to it. There is not only a passive *aversion* but an active *resistance* to the work" (Winslow, *WHS*:58–59, italics added; cf. Menno Simons, *Foundation of Chr. Doctrine*, *SWMS*:161).

Refusing Cheap Grace

Spiritual directors of classic pastoral care have counseled penitents to meditate upon the goodness of God in preparation for the most searching forms of self-examination, contrition, and moral redirection (Tertullian, *On Repentance*, 9, 10). Self-examination takes the risk of probing hidden faults, not as a masochistic exercise but realistically, to behold their tenacity and power, the complexity of secret sin, their layers of distorted perception.

Godly repentance refuses to be comforted until the work of conviction is thoroughly done. It is a radical act of self-examination reaching into every chamber of the house of willed experience (John Cassian, *Conferences, On Mortification*; Bonhoeffer, *Cost of Discipleship*). The possibility of repentance is precluded until one comes to take full responsibility for one's own choices (Kierkegaard, *Either/Or* 2).

Repentance includes both contrition and reformation—not only a genuine sorrow for sin, but also a desire to make reparation for sin to counteract the consequences of our previous decisions so as to show forth fruits fitting to repentance (Luke 19:8; Cyprian, *The Lapsed*; Maximus of Turin, *Sermons* 95–96).

True repentance is never easy, for "the god of this age has blinded the minds of unbelievers, so that they cannot see the light of the gospel" (2 Cor. 4:4; Ambrosiaster, *Comm. on Paul's Epis.* 2 Cor. 4.4). "Sinful volitions make sinful acts; sinful acts often repeated make sinful habits; sinful habits long continued in make sinful character; and sinful character at length determines and fixes unalterably the sinner's destiny" (Tillett, *PS*:143).

The Spirit works both through judging sins and through promising forgiveness to the truly penitent. The Spirit awakens in consciousness the knowledge of offenses against the law and makes plausible the pardon of the gospel. The law teaches us to recognize our sin and our need of grace, while the gospel shows us how God has come to humanity to provide mercy for our sins (Jerome, *Epis. to Gal.* 2. 15–16; *Augustine on Romans* 3–5; Luther, *The Freedom of a Christian*).

The sick must take seriously their illness before they feel the urgent need of a physician. The Spirit works through the law to accomplish this recognition. By the law comes increased awareness of sin (Rom. 3:20). It is the schoolmaster who brings us gradually to grace in Christ (Gal. 3:24). We would not have known sin clearly except in the light of the law (Rom. 7:7). It is like a mirror into which we look to see our true condition revealed (James 1:22–25; Oecumenius, *Comm. on James* 1.23–4). The faithful keep the law because they have been redeemed, not in order to be redeemed.

Contrition

Contrition is brokenness of heart, awareness of radical moral poverty in God's presence, the crushed spirit. The contrite heart prays for the gift of clear discernment of one's sins, seeking to penetrate and clearly expose self-deceptions and the innumerable ways that sin seeks to cover its tracks with pretended righteousness (Isa. 57:15; Mark 13:5, 6; Heb. 3:13; Theodoret, *Comm. on Is.* 18.57.15).

The essential prayer of the penitent is "God be merciful to me a sinner" (Luke 18:13). Anyone can pray the sinner's prayer except one who imagines that such a prayer does not apply to oneself. But no one can repent without the grace-enabled gift of penitence, and for that the sinner earnestly prays (Mark 2:17; Augustine, *Letter 145 to Anastasius*).

It is doubly ironic that only sinners can repent. If repentance is a condition of saving faith, then salvation is offered to sinners only. "For I have not come to call the righteous, but sinners" (Jerome, *Comm. on Matt.* 9:13). "The Lord is close to the brokenhearted and saves those who are crushed in spirit" (Ps. 32:18). The penitent are never to be denied mercy (Cyprian, *On the Lapsed*).

Salvation draws near to those who most deeply experience the hazardous vulnerability of standing in God's presence. Salvation remains furthest from those who imagine sin a small matter easily dealt with, or repentance a quick fix.

The Evasions of False Repentance

True repentance requires the abandonment of the life of sin (Clement of Alex., *Who Is the Rich Man That Shall Be Saved?* 39). It leads to the reshaping of behavior (Calvin, *Inst.* 3.4). It cannot be a hedged bet that tries to both repent and cling to sin (Kierkegaard, *Either/Or*; *Attack Upon 'Christendom'*).

Repentance is liable to being misunderstood. It can be misread as a human accomplishment by which one seems to make oneself worthy of grace. It can be mistaken as an intellectual change of mind without a change of will or heart, as if repentance were essentially the acceptance of the idea of sin, rather than that one is personally a sinner oneself. It can be misconstrued as a wrenching emotional experience involving grief over sin and catharsis, yet without moral reformation or fundamental spiritual redirection.

These misconceptions lead to false repentance (Calvin, *Inst.* 3.3.24). Each rationalization is corrected by Scripture and the good counsel of faithful believers. False repentance may become implanted in a Pelagian optimism that views the will as so capable of turning itself around that the grace of repentance becomes virtually unnecessary. False repentance may retreat into a quietism that does not regard repentance as an active change but as a unilateral divine gift that may only be passively waited for. False repentance may fizzle with a phony enthusiasm that reduces repentance to an emotion, substituting the passion of remorse for grace-enabled godly sorrow. False repentance may harden into a Pharisaic legalism that turns the grace of repentance into a new law (Tertullian, *On Repentance*; cf. Tillett, *PS*:155–74).

The Blessings of True Repentance

Jesus' teaching of the beatitudes in the Sermon on the Mount reveals the essence of true repentance: Poverty of spirit recognizes how lacking is our righteousness and how great the need for God's righteousness. Those who mourn their offenses, sorrowing over sins voluntarily committed and omitted, are made happy by God's forgiveness. The meek are willing early to surrender their own pride to God's saving purpose and accept the tendered offer of God's mercy. Those who hunger and thirst for righteousness, earnestly desiring to receive the bread and water of life, will be filled (Matt. 5:3–6; Chromatius, *Tractate on Matt.* 17.3–5).

With true repentance the love of sin is already beginning to die in one's heart. It may not be fully conquered, but the power of sin has been delivered a crippling, deathly blow, even while sin struggles to remain (Rom. 7). In real repentance the heart is broken twice: first *for* its own sin, and then broken *from* sin (Weaver, *CT*:151).

Joy in the Reversal of Sin

Rightly understood, repentance is a source of joy in the freed, renewed life (Luke 15:7, 10). At length Luther confessed to his spiritual mentor, Staupitz, that the very word that had once been so terrible—repentance—had become the most fragrant of words (*WLM* 1:40).

The special joy of repentance is that no matter how far one may have fallen, the way always remains open to receive God's forgiveness (Kierkegaard, *Christian Discourses*). "Though your sins are like scarlet, they shall be as white as snow" (Isa. 1:18; Augustine, *On Grace and Free Will* 6).

The moment our hearts acknowledge our guilt, we find to our surprise that God is greater than our hearts. "We set our hearts at rest in his presence whenever our hearts condemn us. For God is greater than our hearts, and he knows everything" (1 John 3:19, 20). "This means that God's power is greater than the conscience which belongs to the soul, because God's love knows everything" (Clement of Alex, *Stromata*, in Zahn 3:92).

Only when the sickness worsens sufficiently to drive one to the physician does healing draw near. The most that conscience can do toward salvation is reveal moral inadequacy, leading to despair, pointing beyond itself to convicting grace (Chysostom, *Hom. on Rom.* 7.3.22–25).

Worldly Sorrow, Godly Sorrow

Worldly sorrow is idolatrous regret that does not understand how profoundly sin offends God, whose holiness requires the renunciation of known sin (Chrysostom, *Baptismal Instructions*). Worldly sorrow ironically may bind one more closely into the syndromes of guilt by engendering the pretense that some fundamental change is taking place when it is not decisive but merely conceptual (Kierkegaard, *Repetition*; *E/O* 2). Worldly sorrow, however, may be used by the Spirit to increase the desire to escape the consequences of sin (Jer. 31:12; 2 Cor. 7:7).

Godly sorrow feels revulsion in the presence of sin, not merely fear of the consequences of sin. It takes ownership of personal guilt, holds the whole desperate human situation up before God, and feels the radical brokenness of the best human intentions. In godly sorrow, we "bewail our manifold sins and wickedness" (*BCP*), trembling before the holiness of God. "The sacrifices of God are a broken spirit; a broken and contrite heart, O God, you will not despise" (Ps. 51:17).

Paul had hoped that grief over sin would have its intended effect by leading to repentance: "Even if I caused you sorrow by my letter, I do not regret it. Though

I did regret it—I see my letter hurt you, but only for a little while—yet now I am happy, not because you were made sorry, but because your sorrow led you to repentance. For you became sorrowful as God intended and so were not harmed in any way by us." (2 Cor. 7:8, 9). He then stated this crucial maxim: "Godly sorrow brings repentance that leads to salvation and leaves no regret, but worldly sorrow brings death" (2 Cor. 7:10). A godly sorrow seeks to deal with the cause of guilt. Paul knew that godly sorrow would elicit a health-giving series of reversals: the earnest desire to do good, eagerness to clear one's conscience, indignation over sin, alarm over judgment, longing for reconciliation, zealous concern, readiness to see justice done, (2 Cor. 7:11; Augustine, *Sermons*, Easter Season 254.2–4).

Has modern man lost the capacity for godly sorrow? Indeed, repentance may be that act that runs most directly counter to prevailing modern assumptions— progress in history, the essential goodness of humanity, the social determination of murder, rape, and plunder. Taking personal responsibility for sin is the heart of evangelical repentance. Sin is not caused by parents or siblings or bad teachers or heredity or physiological temperament or the stars, but finally by one's own freedom that has entered decisively into self-determined collusion with wickedness, determining oneself toward bondage to dysfunctional habituation or demeaned character. Modernity has not lost the capacity for godly sorrow, but the assumptions of modernity have made ever more difficult the repentance that has always been hard.

The Resolution to Forsake All Sin

Repentance is an act aimed at the root of sin. This is powerfully indicated by the metaphor of John the Baptist: "The ax is already at the root of the trees" (Matt. 3:10; Chromatius, *Tractate on Matt.*, 11.1). One does not repent by trimming leaves one at a time, or even by cutting off an entire branch. The whole life of sin must go, must be renounced altogether, and definitely (Ambrose, *On the Mysteries* 1–3). Essential to godly sorrow is an overarching decision to renounce a corrupted life altogether and forsake all sin.

"The Lord detests the sacrifice of the wicked" (Prov. 15:8) insofar as they remain wicked precisely amid the hypocrisy of appearing to repent (Barth, *CD* 1/2:768; 4/2:557). The psalmist knew that "if I had cherished sin in my heart, the Lord would not have listened" (Ps. 66:18).

The revulsion is not toward sin in general or in the abstract, but to one's own actual besetting sins. My sin is loathed as my own, made by me, offending the One who granted me the very freedom that has gone awry. "The memory of them is grievous," states the prayer of confession (*BCP*). Actual sin is always at some level a voluntary, collusive transgression of a known moral requirement. Hence genuine conviction is directed not merely toward neurosis or imaginary sin but toward actually willed sin (John 8:6b–11; Augustine, *Sermon* 16A.5; J. Wesley, *WJWB*, *Sermons*, 3:204).

One is not saved in one's sin, but from one's sin. When genuine repentance puts on Christ, it makes "no provision for the flesh" (Rom. 13:14).

Behavioral Amendment, Reparation, and Reformation

Genuine repentance calls for fitting acts of proportional restitution, the restoration of whatever has been wrongly acquired, in which practical amends are made for injustices inflicted upon others insofar as that is reasonably possible (Cyprian, *Letters*, 51:46–55, 146; Augustine, *Sermon* 389.6). God "requires him to make restitution to the person injured if it lie in the compass of his power . . . No man should expect mercy at the hand of God who, having wronged his neighbor, refuses, when he has it in his power, to make restitution" (A. Clarke, *CT*: 124).

Reparation seeks to repair, so far as feasible, whatever has been wrongly done or previously injurious (Maximus of Turin, *Sermons* 95–96). If one has defrauded or harmed or offended or stolen, one must make fair restoration for the injury. Zacchaeus had spent his life cheating others. Called to repentance by the servant Messiah, he "stood up and said to the Lord, 'Look Lord! Here and now I give half of my possessions to the poor, and if I have cheated anybody out of anything, I will pay back four times the amount.' Jesus said to him, 'Today salvation has come to this house' " (Luke 19:5–9). Since reparation was immediate and generous, Zacchaeus became a prototype of earnest repentance (Tertullian, *Ag. Marcion* 4.37).

It may seem impossible to make up for wrongs done to others, but this must nonetheless be contextually attempted. Such acts of reparation are not repentance *per se*, but fruits of repentance (Matt. 3:8). Repentance itself is not primarily a self-initiated work but an act of receiving the grace of penitence, a receptive act that readies the self to receive the grace of pardon (Chromatius, *Tractate on Matt.* 9.1).

Whether Repentance Must Recur Daily

Repentance continues daily in the life of the faithful, sustained by Word and Sacrament. We are canonically baptized only once for the whole of our life, but every day we are washed in prayer (Augustine, *On the Creed* 1:7, 15), for every day we pray the Lord's Prayer asking not to be led toward temptation but to be delivered from evil.

In baptism we first come to participate in the body of Christ, and to share in the life that corresponds with Christ who "died for all, that those who live should no longer live for themselves but for him" (2 Cor. 5:15; Basil, *The Morals* 22). In him "you were washed, you were sanctified, you were justified in the name of the lord Jesus Christ and by the Spirit of our God" (1 Cor. 6:11; Ambrosiaster, *Comm. on Paul's Epis.*, 1 Cor. 6.11).

Falling away from the first baptismal repentance was regarded as such a serious matter that the letter to the Hebrews wonders if any recovery would be possible: "It is impossible for those who have once been enlightened, who have tasted the heavenly gift, who have shared in the Holy Spirit, who have tasted the goodness of the word of God and the powers of the coming age, if they fall away, to be brought back by repentance" (Heb. 6:4–6). Here the author seems to be arguing that one's faith must either grow or die (Heb. 6:7–8; Ambrose, *Concerning Repentance* 2.2.7–12; Calvin, *Comm.* 22:135–44). Yet scripture elsewhere makes it very clear that repentance remains a recurring act within the Christian life. Faith requires a continuing self-denial, confession, reparation, and ongoing penitence (Rev. 2:5, 16; 3:3, 19; Origen, *Comm. on John*, 28.54–56).

There remains a dual danger of making confession either needlessly hard or all too easy. The former was an exaggeration of the church under conditions of persecution in the third century, when only one act of postbaptismal repentance was permitted, as when Tertullian wrote that God "has stationed in the vestibule a second penitence to open to them that knock; but only once, because it is for the second time; it can never open again, because the last time it opened in vain" (Tertullian, *On Repentance* 7).

The consensual tradition is more fitly expressed by Leo I: "The manifold mercy of God so assists men when they fall, that not only by the grace of baptism, but also by the remedy of penitence is the hope of eternal life revived, in order that they who have violated the gifts of the second birth, condemning themselves by their own judgment, may attain to remission" (*Letters* 108).

The renewing of repentance remains a continuing necessity, so long as sin remains in believers (*Homily Ascribed to Clement*, 7). The first of Luther's Ninety-five Theses proposes that the whole life of believers is a life of repentance.

Paul directed his exhortations to repentance to the whole Christian community (Origen, *Epis. to Rom.* 12.1–2; Eph. 4:23 24). Repentance is pertinent to the ongoing Christian life inasmuch as sin stubbornly remains in the life of the regenerate. Continuing repentance is enabled by grace (*Heid. Catech.*, 88–90).

Classic Christian exegetes distinguished three types of repentance: repentance for sins committed *before* baptism that call for the decisive once for all repentance of baptismal faith. But then there is a continuing repentance *after* baptism for the marginal or lighter daily sins, requiring daily repentance as the medicine of forgiveness. Then there is a solemn third public form of repentance after baptism in the more serious sense of penitents (*poenitentes*) in the church who are struggling with *grave* sins (Augustine, *Conf.* 10; Ambrose, *Concerning Repentance* 2.2.7–12).

A deathbed repentance is always possible, as the thief on the cross suggests, but hazardous insofar as it tends to encourage the temptation to license: that one may sin now, for there will always be time to repent. But there will not always be time. As long as one lives there is always time to repent, but if one's life is cut short unexpectedly or abruptlly, precisely then there remains no time (Matt. 6:19–24; Luke 12:16–21). Delay is not recommended "because we cannot place limits to God's mercy nor fix times for Him with whom conversion suffers no delay." Yet to persons *in extremis* the prayer for forgiveness "must not be refused even when it can be asked for only by signs" (Leo I, *Letters* 108; Chrysostom, *Baptismal Instructions*, ACW 31:132–35).

Whether It May Be Said that God Repents

At times scripture speaks of Almighty God as so moved with compassion as to relent from a former judgment, or to "repent" (*nacham*, to pity, to be comforted, eased) from a previous resolve (Ps. 106:45; Jer. 18:8–10), when upon hearing their earnest prayers Yahweh does not execute a threatened judgment. In the story of Noah, "The Lord saw how great man's wickedness on the earth had become, and that every inclination of the thoughts of his heart was only evil all the time. The Lord was *grieved* [repented himself, KJV] that he had made man on the earth, and his heart was filled with pain" (Gen. 6:5, 6, italics added; Salvian the Presbyter, *Governance of God*, FC 3:41).

These passages do not imply that God did wrong or that God's character became altered, but that God freely responds to human alienation in ways that correspond to changed circumstances, reconsidering accordingly (Ezek. 18:24–32). When we say, "Now the sun is shining," and "Now it is not shining," we do not mean that the sun changes, but that our perception of it changes (Athanasius, *Defence of the Nicene Definition* 5). Similarly, what seem to be changes in God are contingencies of human history to which God is compassionately responsive.

Conversion

To convert (*epistrephō*, Lat. *convertere*) is to turn around, to pivot, to change from one life direction to another (Acts 3:19). Conversion is a reversal of disposition. Conversion requires two moves: a turning away from sin (repentance) and a turning to Christ (faith)—two phases of a single act of turning (Calvin, *Inst.* 3.3).

Repentance is a principle part, but not the whole, of conversion. Conversion is a part, but not the whole, of the doctrine of reconciliation (Watson, *TI* 2.19). To convert is to change one's life direction from unfaith to faith.

If repentance is a revulsion against the dying life of slavery to sin, regeneration is a new birth, in which new spiritual life is imparted. Conversion traces this trajectory of the reversal from repentance to regeneration.

To be born again, one must repent. Repentance is retrospective, regeneration prospective. Repentance looks back in regret and remorse toward sin. Regeneration looks forward to a new life that has emerged out of a new birth of faith (Fletcher, *Works* 3:112–31). The process considered together is conversion.

Do not make something simple artificially complicated. Calling a little child to stand among his disciples, Jesus said, "Unless you change [*straphō*, be converted] and become like little children, you will never enter the kingdom of heaven" (Matt. 18:3). "The Lord teaches that we cannot enter the kingdom of heaven unless we revert to the nature of children, that is, we must recall as if in the simplicity of children the vices of the body and mind" (Hilary, *On Matt.* 18.1). The child in their midst was compared by Origen to "the Holy Spirit, who humbled himself. He was called by the Savior and set in the middle of the disciples of Jesus" (Origen, *Comm. on Matt.* 18.3). To be converted, ask the Holy Spirit who does the converting to be in the middle of the worshiping community.

The Grace of Conversion Works by the Spirit's Persuasion

The hidden spring of this entire reversal of mind, heart, and will is the love of God. This turning of mind, heart, and will is awakened in persons through the power of the Holy Spirit. The Spirit does not coerce or overleap or overpower human self-determination, but persuades, coaxes, challenges, pries loose, and invites freedom (Augustine, *Sermon* 71.19).

If it were strictly a matter of the Spirit coercing the human will, then there could be no call to any duty of repentance, as there is in scripture: "Repent, then, and turn to God, so that your sins may be wiped out, that times of refreshing may come from the Lord" (Acts 3:19). Such an appeal assumes that the hearer may or may not decide to repent.

Enabled by grace, freedom is called to examine itself, its deceptions and evasions. God will not do the repenting for us. Throughout the whole sequence of developing penitential consciousness, grace awakens voluntary repentance. Contrition is never self-initiated, but responsive to God's gift, so as to require a definite task. Only on this cooperative basis can repentance be viewed simultaneously as a gift of God (Acts 5:31; 11:18) and a command to the human will (Mark 5:12; Luke 13:3; Acts 8:22; 17:30; Calvin, *Inst.* 3.3).

Theophilus of Antioch spoke plainly to Autolycus of his own conversion: "Do not be skeptical, but believe. I myself used to be an unbeliever, but now I have taken these things into consideration and have changed my mind. I met with the sacred Scriptures of the holy prophets, who by the Spirit of God foretold things which have already happened, and in the same order. They have also foretold things which are happening right now, again in the right order, and they have foretold things which are still to come, once more in the order of their future occurrence. Having considered the fulfillment of prophecies already accomplished, I became a believer, and I urge you to do the same. . . .You asked me to show you my God, and here he is" (*To Autolycus*, 1.14). "Whoever pays attention to [the Scriptures] will find God in them" (Tertullian, *Apol.* 18–20).

Repentance and Faith as Coordinate Teachings

Faith is the only condition of conversion, yet true faith is preceded by repentance and evidenced by acts of love. Repentance in itself does not atone, but begins to open the recipient to the benefits of Christ's atonement.

Repentance is a *turning away from sin*, while faith is a *turning toward grace*. Together they constitute a single decisive turning (Gregory of Nyssa, *FGG*:219–220). As godly sorrow for sin, repentance precedes and makes way for faith. Because sin remains in believers, the act of penitence must be daily renewed (Calvin, *Inst.* 3.3.5, 6). In this sense repentance does not precede but follows after the earliest steps of faith (Van Oosterzee, *CD*:648).

Some anticipatory faith in God's mercy is presupposed in taking the first steps in repentance, for "without faith it is impossible to please God, because anyone who comes to him must believe that he exists and that he rewards those who earnestly seek him" (Heb. 11:6; Chrysostom, *Epis. to Heb.* 22.5–7). In this way repentance and faith are so inextricably joined together in scripture that it is impossible to assign to one or the other a temporal or logical priority (Melanchthon, *Loci, LCC* 19:88).

Confession of Sin

Confession is used in two complementary ways in the New Testament: as the confession of sin and the confession of Christ. "If we confess our sins, he is faithful and just and will forgive us our sins and purify us from all unrighteousness" (1 John 1:9; Oecumenius, *Comm. on 1 John* 1.9). "If anyone acknowledges that Jesus is the Son of God, God lives in him and he in God" (1 John 4:15). One who has not confessed sin is hardly prepared to confess Christ (Clement of Rome, *Corinth* 51, 52).

Confession of sin is personal acknowledgment of one's own violation of moral law before God (Cyprian, *The Lapsed*; C. Hodge, *The Way of Life*:240–85; Tillett, *PS*:199–210). Although confession to the offended neighbor is significant and should not be neglected, the act of confession of sin is not addressed primarily to oneself or to society or to one's neighbor or confessor-counselor, but is finally made in the presence of God (Calvin, *Inst.* 3.3–4). Since it is with God-given freedom that one sins, it is necessarily the living God with whom the confessing believer finally has to deal (Clarke, *CT*:479–85). The tax collector in Jesus' parable "stood at a distance. He would not even look up to heaven, but beat his breast, and said, 'God, have mercy on me, a sinner' " (Luke 18:13; Ephrem, *Comm. on Tatian's Diatesseron* 16.16).

Without confession of sin (*exomologesis*), the power of sin continues to mount (Tertullian, *On Repentance* 10–11; Mark the Ascetic, *Letter to Nicolas, Philokalia* 1:149). "If we claim to be without sin, we deceive ourselves and the truth is not in us. If we confess our sins, he is faithful and just and will forgive us our sins, and purify us from all unrighteousness. If we claim we have not sinned, we make him out to be a liar and his word has no place in our lives" (1 John 1:8–10; Bede, *On 1 John* 1.9). One who "conceals his sins" cannot expect to grow spiritually, "but whoever confesses and renounces them finds mercy" (Prov. 28:13).

Before confession of sin, the psalmist experienced the heavy weight of guilt: "When I kept silent, my bones wasted away through my groaning all day long. For day and night your hand was heavy upon me; my strength was sapped as in the heat of the summer" (Ps. 32:3, 4). Grace came in the convicting form of heaviness, draining that strength that would resist a healing transformation (cf. Pss. 38:4; 69:20; Prov. 25:20; 1 Pet. 1:6). "Then I acknowledged my sin to you and did not cover up my iniquity. I said, 'I will confess my transgressions to the Lord.'"(Ps. 32:5) What the sinner had attempted to cover up now becomes covered by divine forgiveness: "Blessed is he whose transgressions are forgiven, whose sins are covered. Blessed is the man whose sin the Lord does not count against him and in whose spirit is no deceit" (Ps. 32:1, 2).

The relief and joy experienced in confession is viewed as an unburdening of conscience, a cleansing from the stain of guilt (John Cassian, *On the Holy Fathers of Sketis, Philokalia* 1:103, 140; Peter of Damaskos, *Treasury, Philokalia* 2:199–200). It is like a cleansing bath for the soul (Chrysostom, *Baptismal Instructions,* 31:135–39).

To be genuine, confession must be sincere, personal, definite, and unconditional, not ambivalent or blurred or halting. It must not secretly cling to sin. The line between repentance and faith is firmly drawn in the Westminster Confession: "As there is no sin so small but it deserves damnation, so there is no sin so great that it can bring damnation upon those who truly repent. Men ought not to content themselves with a general repentance" (Westminster *Conf.*, 15).

Confession: Private and Public

Confession may occur in the presence of a trusted Christian brother or sister or pastor. But confession is primarily to God, even when it seeks to communicate its transcendent significance with another person. "For that confession is sufficient, which is first offered to God, then also to a priest who serves as an intercessor" (Leo I, *SCD* 145). Thus it is commended that each one find another, whether clerical or lay, whose life is shaped by the Spirit, through whom the soul may be unburdened and hear the forgiving word (Luther, *Lectures on Gen.* 31–37, *LW* 6:297–98).

Whether "private or public," to one or many, whether "to those that are offended" (Westminster *Conf.* 15), confession is ultimately offered in the presence of God, the true physician of souls, even if penultimately to another human being (Origen, *Hom. on Ps. 36,* Hom. 1.5).

Private offenses are dealt with according to the scriptural instructions of Matthew 18:15–17 and James 5:19, 20. Public offenses are dealt with according to the guidelines found in 1 Corinthians 5:3–5; 1 Thessalonians 5:14; and 2 Thessalonians 3:6.

A balanced statement was set forth by the Second Helvetic Confession: "But we believe that this sincere confession which is made to God alone, either privately between God and the sinner, or publicly in the Church where the general confession of sin is said, is sufficient. . . . Therefore it is necessary that we confess our sins to God our Father, and be reconciled with our neighbor if we have offended him. Concerning this kind of confession, the Apostle James says: 'Confess your sins to one another' [James 5:16]. If, however, anyone is overwhelmed by the burden of his sins and by perplexing temptations, and will seek counsel, instruction and comfort privately, either from a minister of the Church, or from any other brother who is instructed in God's law, we do not disapprove; just as we also fully approve of that general and public confession of sins which is usually said in Church" (chap. 14, *BOC* 5.095; cf. Tho. Aq., *ST* supp., Q6).

By confession "genuine self-knowledge is increased, Christian humility grows, bad habits are corrected, spiritual neglect and tepidity are countered, the conscience is purified, the will strengthened, a salutary self-control is attained and grace is increased" (Pius XII, *Mystici Corporis* 86). The spiritual adviser is urged to "be discreet and cautious, so that he may pour wine and oil into the wounds of the injured person like a skilled physician, diligently inquiring into the circumstances both of the sinner and of the sin, so that he may wisely understand what advice he should give him and what remedy he should apply" (Fourth Lateran Council, *CC*:59).

Confession of Christ From the Heart Through the Mouth

Repentance calls for not only a change of the mind (*conversio mentis*) and a confession from the mouth (*confessio oris*) but also a corrective work of the hands to redo what sin has undone (*vindicta peccati*).

Paul taught that "if you *confess* with your mouth, 'Jesus is Lord,' and *believe* in your heart that God raised him from the dead, you will be saved. For it is with your *heart* that you believe and are justified, and it is with your *mouth* that you confess and are saved" (Rom. 10:9–11, italics added; Augustine, *Sermons for the Recent Converts* 214.1).

To confess Christ with the heart is to acknowledge him as he is, as Lord, Son of God, servant Messiah, Savior of humanity. Confessing with the mouth requires breathing to be heard. Speech cannot sound without breath. Breath symbolizes the empowering Spirit. Confessing requires breathing, articulating in words and sentences to fellow human beings penitent words fitting to the occasion. Especially it must be spoken where necessary among the enemies of Christ, precisely where it brings reproach and danger (Polycarp, *Martyrdom*; Hodge, *The Way of Life*:259; Tillett, *PS*: 198).

The good confession requires that believers speak openly as Christ's ambassadors under his Lordship even when speech puts them at hazard. If under safe circumstances one publicly confesses Christ yet fails to confess Christ at a risk-laden moment when confession is required in order to maintain and demonstrate faith, then one has not rightly confessed (Barth, *CD* 3/4:87; D. Bonhoeffer, *Cost of Discipleship*). One who insists upon confessing Christ purely inwardly and silently as an individual alone has not yet learned what it means to confess with one's mouth (Rom. 10:10; Ambrose, *Concerning Repentance* 7–9). Yet under persecution, even silence may become a powerful confession of Christ (Ignatius, *Eph*. 15).

Liturgically viewed, Eucharistic absolution realizes and completes confession of sin, joining it with confession of Christ. Having confessed their sin and Christ's righteousness, the faithful are prepared to "receive absolution or forgiveness from the confessor as from God himself" (Luther, *Small Catechism*, *CC*:121).

Confession and Character

Jesus taught plainly, "Whoever acknowledges me before men, I will also acknowledge from before my Father in heaven. But whoever disowns me before men, I will disown from before my Father in heaven" (Matt. 10:32, 33; Incomplete Work on Matt. Hom. 25).

It is hardly possible to conceive of a saving faith that fails to confess Christ openly. "If we deny him, he also will deny us" (2 Tim. 2:12; Aphrahat, *Select Demonstrations* 6.1).

In cultures where the confession of Christ is viewed as treason or blasphemy or idolatry or insurrection (as under Stalinist or Maoist repression), the confessing act becomes most compelling and powerful. Yet even in predominately Christian cultures (Christendom, so-called), confession is hardly a routine matter and requires courage (S. Kierkegaard, *Attack upon "Christendom"*; Barth, *CD* 3/4:52).

Where a painful break with an entire culture is required, where confession is costly, confessing Christ is accompanied by a special grace by which the faithful are comforted and enabled to be clear about their confession (Cyril of Alex.,

Comm. on John 2.1). To confess Christ may require a severe break with the world, its support structures, police security operations, and idolatries (Origen, *Exhort. to Martyrdom*, 30–43; *Hom. on Jer.* 4; Clement of Alex., *Strom.* 4.14; Ambrose, *On the Mysteries*). Faith has often flourished under such conditions. So it is today that Christianity flourishes in China and Africa, while languishing in tepid parts of the Christian west.

Moral cowardice detracts from the credibility of faith, however well trained doctrinally. Nothing betrays weak faith more than lack of courage. One whose faith has not been tested by confession has not ventured deeply into faith (Cyprian, *Letters*, *FC* 51: 94–103). Peter lacked courage at the crucifixion but was given the grace of boldness thereafter in the presence of the rulers of Israel (Acts 4:13; Bede, *Comm. on Acts* 4.13).

Martyr (*martus*, witness) referred in the first instance to the apostles as witnesses to Christ's life and resurrection. Amid persecution, *martus* became reserved for those who had suffered for the faith, and especially those who had died for the faith (Cyprian, *Letters*, 51:24–28, 49–70). The baptism of blood was viewed as equivalent of the grace of baptism where normal baptism had been unreceived. The anniversary of the death of a martyr was considered a heavenly birthday (*natalis*), and an annual celebration at his or her tomb was a familiar part of early church practice of prayer, as early as the second century (*Martyrdom of Polycarp* 18; Tertullian, *ANF* 8:693–96; Anon., *Acts and Martyrdom of St. Matthew*, *ANF* 8:530).

4

JUSTIFICATION BY GRACE THROUGH FAITH

Justification by Grace

Justification is essential to peace of conscience and reconciliation with God. No evangelical teaching is more crucial. The Christian life hinges upon its careful understanding (Calvin, *Inst.* 3.11). Rightly received, it vitalizes and consecrates all the energies of the redeemed community. It has been known to elicit courageous responses in those from whom such responses might otherwise have been least expected.

Justification Defined

Justification is the declaration of God that a person, however sinful, who trusts in Christ's atoning work is treated or accounted as righteous (Theodoret of Cyr, *FEF* 3:248–9; Barth, *CD* 2/2:125). This is not a legal fiction but a merciful divine action historically offered on the cross.

Justification makes known the reversal of God's judgment against the sinner. The sinner is declared to be no longer exposed to the penalty of the law, which is ultimately spiritual death, but restored to divine favor (Tho. Aq., *ST* 2-1 Q113; Strong, *ST*:471–83, 849). Justification is an act of God's free grace through which the sinner is absolved from guilt and accepted as righteous on account of the Son's atoning work (Luther, *The Freedom of a Christian*, *MLS*:55–68.

Justification in its biblical sense does not imply that immediately one is behaviorally or in practice ethically made righteous. Rather it means to declare or deem upright so as to acquit from guilt and punitive liability (*dikaiōsis*, *TDNT* loc. cit.; Calvin, *Inst.* 3.11–14). It refers to an actual declaration made by means of a historical event through which one is accredited right before the law and Lawgiver.

Justification does not result from higher commitment to greater ideals or better performance of the demands of the law. It is solely due to a verdict rendered that reveals God's new relation to the sinner whose life becomes hidden in Christ (Chrysostom, *Hom. on Rom.* 10).

Justification is a term that derives from the legal sphere; hence it is called a *forensic* teaching based on a judicial metaphor. Accordingly, one is justified who is made upright with the Lawgiver (*Apology of the Augsburg Conf.* 4).

The Decisive Baseline of Evangelical Teaching

Luther wrote in the Smalcald Articles, "Nothing in this article can be given up or compromised. . . . On this article rests all that we teach. . . . Therefore we must be quite certain and have no doubts about it. Otherwise all is lost" (Smalcald, 2.1, *BOC*:292).

Justification is not the summit but the ground of the Christian life, not the end but the beginning of the journey of evangelical faith. So pivotal is it to Christian preaching that if it is unbalanced in any way, reverberations are felt in the whole edifice of faith. Many pitfalls must be avoided in preaching this word and offering this teaching wisely. Put summarily: Justification's nature is pardon, its condition is faith, its ground is the righteousness of God, and its fruits are good works (J. Wesley, *WJW* 5:55, 56).

The Augsburg Confession defined justification normatively for Protestant teaching: "We cannot obtain forgiveness of sin and righteousness before God by our own merits, works, or satisfactions. But we receive forgiveness of sin and become righteous before God by grace, for Christ's sake, through faith, when we believe that Christ suffered for us and that for his sake our sin is forgiven, and righteousness and eternal life are given to us. For God will regard and reckon this faith as righteousness, as Paul says in Romans 3:21–26 and 4:5" (*CC*:69).

The Limits of Justification Under Law

Righteousness (Hebr: *tsedaqa*; Gk: *dikaiosune*) points to a right relationship with God (1 Kings 8:32). The righteous one (*tsaddiq*) stands in a right relation with God, restraining the tendency toward evil (*yetzer hara*) and following the divine leading toward good (*yetzer hatob*) through Torah and almsgiving (Exod. 23:7; Deut. 25:1; Melanchthon, *Loci*, 19).

Justification may either be viewed under the old covenant as justification by just deeds or under the new as justification by grace through faith in Christ (Justin Martyr, *Dialogue with Trypho* 90–95). One may be considered upright under the exacting criteria of the law or under the grace of the gospel (Ps. 119; Gal. 3). "The former is the method of justifying man [as] perfect; but the latter, of justifying man [as] a sinner and corrupt" by "the righteousness of another, even of Christ our Surety, imputed by grace to him that believes in the Gospel" (Helvetic Consensus Formula, *CC*:320). The choice: stand in right relation with God either by attempting perfectly right deeds or by faith in the One who once for all embodies the righteous life.

As to the righteousness of the law, Scripture teaches that "if we are careful to obey all this law before the Lord our God, as he has commanded us, that will be our righteousness" (Deut. 6:25). Note, however, that under the exact definition of justification by just deeds, no sin can be overlooked. Under law, Yahweh does not justify the sinner, only the just: "I will not acquit the guilty" (Exod. 23:7). The just judge is required by justice to justify the righteous and condemn the wicked (Deut. 25:1). Conscience does not reassure the sinner.

Both Testaments warn against imagining that anyone can actually fulfill the law completely apart from grace (Rom. 1:18–2:29; Gal. 2:16; Jerome, *Epis. to Gal.* 1.2.16–16; Luther, *Two Kinds of Righteousness*; Calvin, *Inst.* 3.11). "There is no one who does not sin" (2 Chron. 6:36). The New Testament echoes: "There is no one who does good, not even one" (Rom. 3:12; Pss. 14:1–3; 53:1–3; Origen, *Comm. on Rom.* 3.12). "For it is not those who hear the law who are righteous in God's sight, but it is those who obey the law who will be declared righteous" (Rom. 2:13; Ambrosiaster, *Comm. on Paul*, Rom. 2.13).

Standing perfectly upright before the law is conceivable as a concept, but amid the history of fallen freedom extremely unlikely. The more honestly we stand before God, the clearer it is that "all have sinned" (Rom. 3:23; Irenaeus, *Ag. Her.* 4.27.2). The only basis upon which one may stand in right relation with God in terms of the law is absolute rectitude, complete innocence. A charge can be erased under law only if one is not guilty. The entire history of sin awaits the sentence of the final judge (Rom. 3:19–23; Origen, *Comm. on Rom.* 3.19).

Justification Under Grace

An entirely different premise for approaching justification is made possible by the gospel. Justification is not made complete "according to what we deserve, but simply given as a free gift" (Leo I, *Sermons* 49).

In the unhappy path of the history of sin, good news has come: one may come into a right relation with God by being "justified freely by his grace" (Rom. 3:24: Chrysostom, *Hom. on Rom.* 7; Calvin, *Catech. of Church of Geneva*).

Old Testament Anticipations of Uprighting by Grace

Throughout history, even as early as Abel, some have come to know that one may stand upright before God by grace through faith, for "by faith he [Abel] was commended as a righteous man" (Heb. 11:4; Ephrem, *Comm. on Heb.* 11.4). So also did Noah become "heir of the righteousness that comes by faith" (Heb. 11:7; Chrysostom, *On Epis. to Heb.* 22.7). Later Abraham would become the chief prototype: "By faith Abraham, when called to go to a place he would later receive as his inheritance, obeyed and went, even though he did not know where he was going" (Heb. 11:8; Augustine, *CG* 16.28). His faith "was credited to him as righteousness" (Gen. 15:6; Rom. 4:3; Calvin, *Inst.* 3.11). Habakkuk grasped the heart of the matter, that "the righteous will live by his faith" (Hab. 2:4).

Isaiah anticipated the justification that would come through the suffering of the messianic Servant who would "make his life a guilt offering," who "after the suffering of his soul," would "justify many," and "bear their iniquities" (Isa. 53:10, 11; Procopius of Gaza, *Comm. on Is.* 53.12) This expected one appeared in Jesus.

The Coming Kingdom Where Righteousness Reigns

Jesus announced the coming righteousness of God. He himself was the sign of its coming. Those who enter his kingdom, where God's own righteousness personally comes and reigns, participate in a righteousness that exceeds that of the scribes and Pharisees (Matt. 5:20; Chromatius, *Tractate on Matt.* 20.3.1–2).

Even the obnoxious tax-collector who was grieving over his sins would "go home justified" (Luke 18:14). Those who pretend to merit righteousness are not ready for this kingdom (Luke 10:29; 16:15; Cyril of Alex., *Comm. on Luke* Hom.

110). The righteous on the last day will be found to be those who constantly offer acts of compassion to those in need, yet in doing so are unaware that their kindness has been shown to the unrecognized Son of God (Matt. 25:37, 46; Incomplete Work on Matt., Hom. 54).

Why Self-Justification Makes God's Justification Hard to Hear

It is a characteristic feature of modern consciousness that persons assume that they must be justified by their own individual works. Culture-bound, stereotyped sex-role assumptions play heavily into modern forms of works-righteousness. Men commonly justify their existence by their physical ability or athletic prowess or production or wealth; women commonly justify their existence by their beauty or nurturance.

The message of justification is difficult to accept because it seems too good to be true. It says, Stop trying to justify yourself. You do not need to. There is no way to buy or deserve God's love or acceptance. You are already being offered God's love on the cross, without passing any tests.

The word of the cross is not, I will love you *if* you jump this hoop, but "while we were yet helpless, at the right time, Christ died for the ungodly" (Rom. 5:6–8; Ambrosiaster, *Comm. on Paul*, Rom. 5.7). God who penetrates all subterfuges knows already our failures and loves us anyway, just as we are. Luther grasped with deep personal conviction Paul's preaching that on the basis of the works of the law, the holy God would not let sin go unpunished; yet on the basis of the gospel God is merciful precisely toward penitent sinners (Luther, *Lectures on Romans*).

Even though justification is a highly focused interest of the Pauline letters, it is found widely throughout Scripture. For a fuller account of the early church fathers' writings on justification teaching, consult my recent study, *The Justification Reader*, where the patristic references are more fully examined. Paul's view must be understood in relation to Mosaic law, the psalms, prophets, and the proclamation of Jesus on righteousness (Irenaeus, *Ag. Her.* 4.34.2).

Righteousness Revealed

Romans 3:22–26 summarized Paul's justification teaching: "This righteousness from God comes through faith in Jesus Christ to all who believe. There is no difference, for all have sinned and fall short of the glory of God, and are justified freely by his grace through the redemption that came by Christ Jesus. God presented him as a sacrifice of atonement, through faith in his blood. He did this to demonstrate his justice, because in his forbearance he had left the sins committed beforehand unpunished—he did it to demonstrate his justice at the present time, so as to be just and the one who justifies those who have faith in Jesus" (Rom. 3:22–26; Clement of Alex., *Instructor* 1.8–10; Augustine, *Spirit and Letter* 44; Luther, *LW* 33: 263–65; Calvin, *Comm.* 19:134–47).

The righteousness of God is now fully made known. "For in the gospel a righteousness from God is revealed, a righteousness that is by faith from first to last, just as it is written: 'The righteous will live by faith' " (Rom. 1:17; Gennadius, *Pauline Comm. From the Greek Church*, Rom. 1.17).

The Courtroom Metaphor

The core of the idea of being judged upright has its setting in the courtroom. God's justifying action is analogous to a judicial act by which God declares the sinner free from guilt and acquitted. God forgives the penitent believer and, based on this pardon, declares that person right before the final Judge. God acquits the ungodly who believe in Christ and declares them just. Condemned before, they are now acquitted and accepted personally into the presence of God (Augustine, *Spirit and Letter* 18.11).

In this court, God is judge whose judgments are right and sure (Gen. 18:25). The origin of all right law is the eternally righteous One whose righteousness exceeds all that humans call right. What God requires of us is *trust* that God is acting in an incomparably just way. In his just law the faithful "delight" and "meditate day and night" (Ps. 1:2).

In the announcement of this good news, all the elements of the courtroom situation are presupposed. The judge is God: "You have come to God, the judge of all" (Heb. 12:23). The defendant is everyone who has become tragically enmeshed in the history of sin. "The whole world" is being "held accountable to God" (Rom. 3:19) in this court. "Everyone who sins breaks the law" (1 John 3:4; Theophylact, *Comm. on 1 John* 3.4). "Your accuser is Moses" (John 5:45)—this means we hold our behavior up in comparison to the just law delivered from Yahweh to the covenant people through Moses.

The internal witness is conscience, the moral testimony of the heart. Everyone possesses the capacity for moral reasoning, since "the requirements of the law are written on their [the Gentiles'] hearts . . . their consciences also bearing witness, and their thoughts now accusing, now even defending them" (Rom. 2:15; Ambrosiaster, *Comm. on Paul*, Rom. 2.15).

In this court an indictment is being read according to "the written code, with its regulations" (Col. 2:14) which puts all our behaviors in a bad light. A sentence is being delivered: "Indeed, in our hearts we felt the sentence of death" (2 Cor. 1:9; Chrysostom, *Hom. on 2 Cor.* 2.2–4). The defendant is as good as dead: "As for you, you were dead in your transgressions and sins" (Eph. 2:1; Jerome, *Epis. to Eph.* 1.2.1).

The Advocate

There is, however, in this courtroom an incomparably well-prepared Advocate— our attorney: "We have one who speaks to the Father in our defense—Jesus Christ, the Righteous One" (1 John 2:1; Augustine, *Sermon* 213.5). A satisfaction is offered, substituting another's suffering of the penalty for sinners: "He is the atoning sacrifice for our sins" (1 John 2:2; Gregory of Nazianzus, *Orat.* 30.14). The sacrifice of one is accepted for many: "Through the obedience of the one man the many will be made righteous" (Rom. 5:19; Origen, *Comm. on Rom.* 5.19). On this basis the judge reverses the judgment, grants a full acquittal, and justifies the accused: "Therefore, there is now no condemnation for those who are in Christ Jesus" (Rom. 8:1).

Christ came to obey the law on our behalf. He became "sin for us," representing us in a substitutionary sense, that we might share in his righteousness. "God made him who had no sin to be sin for us, so that in him we might become the righteousness of God" (2 Cor. 5:21; Cyril of Alex., *Letter* 41.10). Our righteousness does not imply perfectly just ethical behavior, but a receiving of Christ's decisive act of becoming "sin for us," (Chrysostom, *Hom. on 2 Cor.* 11).

The Aquittal

In a civil court, there are three different moments at which the accused may be justified: upon arraignment, by sufficiently answering a specific accusation showing oneself by the facts to be not guilty; after arraignment, by demonstrating that regardless of what one may be accused of, however damaging the evidence, the law itself protects one from penalty, hence one is justified; and after a trial in which one is already found guilty, yet by executive clemency the penalty is remitted on the principle of pardon.

It is in this third and most sweeping sense that the New Testament most often employs the idea of justification. For all are guilty as charged of sin (before and after arraignment); hence there is no other ground left except clemency or pardon. Such clemency implies not an abrogation of the law, but an exercise of judicial discretion. The judge has some room for acting with clemency without cheapening the law. The law is being personally applied to a particular case by a particular judge as a decision rightly made which will have the effect of reestablishing and magnifying the law (Eusebius, *Proof of the Gospel* 4.17; Tho. Aq., *ST* 2–2, Q157).

The salvation event is like a sweeping act of acquittal. The defendant is instantly relieved of all charges. It is that act by which a judge officially declares one to stand upright in the presence of the judge.

When justification is applied to God's act toward the penitent whose life is hid in Christ, it becomes understood as full pardon from all guilt and a new reckoning of the sinner as righteous (*Epistle to Diognetus* 9). Pardon is not offered to declare sinners behaviorally perfect in every respect, but to remove their liability to punishment.

Justification is the acceptance of the sinner, united in Christ by faith, precisely while it remains clear that he or she *has done wrong*. It is precisely while the conscience-stricken sinner is disclaiming his innocence and openly declaring his guilt that acquittal is announced. If such a condemned person is to be delivered from guilt, it must be by a just cancellation of the charge or blotting out from the record any charge against him. Gospel justification views the convicted offender as pardoned in a way that transcends the connection between a behavior and its penal consequence (*Apology of the Augsburg Conf., BOC*:100). Pardon reverses the sentence of condemnation (Rom. 8:1; Chrysostom, *Hom. on 2 Cor.* 5.21).

Those justified are not condemned; those not justified are condemned. There is no middle way (Matt. 12:37). Clemency is the judge's prerogative. Viewed under the law the sinner is justly condemned. Under the gospel the sinner is justified. The Advocate has taken the sinner's place. "It is God who justifies. Who he that condemns?" (Rom. 8:33b, 34a; Ambrosiaster, *Comm. on Paul*, Rom. 8.33). If God "shall say that you are a sinner, say you: 'Lord, I interpose the death of our Lord Jesus Christ between my sins and you'" (Anselm, *Consolatio*, PL 158.687).

This is why the good news of God's justifying grace can be offered to sinners only. Those who assume they are not sinners have already assumed that they do not need it.

The concluding act of the justification drama occurs on the last day of human history, in Hebrew Scripture. It is called resurrection day. The same word for justification that is used in courts of law (Isa. 5:23; Deut. 25:1) is also used of God's judgment in the last day (Matt. 12:37; Rom. 2:13, 16).

Judgment on the last day is a prominent theme in Jesus' preaching. "But I tell you that men will have to give account on the day of judgment for every careless word they have spoken. For by your words you will be acquitted, and by your words you will be condemned" (Matt. 12:36, 37). This future justifying act of God is already seen in the light of the cross and is now looking toward its endtime completion: "Since we have now been justified by his blood, how much more shall we be saved from God's wrath through him!" (Rom. 5:9). Justification is a presently experienced reality, assuming union with Christ by faith, anticipating the final day of judgment (Basil, *Concerning Baptism* 1.2).

The verdict of this final-day court has already been announced, though history continues. Justification is an end-time event in which the believer stands already in an anticipatory sense. Those united to Christ are justified from all guilt— past, present, and future. God's final justifying action awaits the end of history, though the verdict is already known. Those who die clothed in the righteousness of Christ will not be condemned in final judgment, but justified.

Christ Our Righteousness

The notion that one's sins are unconditionally covered by another's righteousness may invite license. The idea that Christ is our righteousness is distortable in an antinomian, self-assertive direction. It is indeed through faith that Christ's righteousness is accounted to us (Rom. 3:24, 25), but it is misleading to conclude from this that personal qualities of Christ's actual obedience are being directly or immediately imparted (given) or infused (poured in) to the believer without faith that freely becomes active in love (Clement of Alex., *Stromata* 2.6). The faith that saves is faith that so trusts in Christ that it works actively in love (Calvin, *Inst.* 3.16–18).

The triune premise allows and requires the affirmation that the Son justifies by the Spirit according to the will of the Father. "It is God who justifies" (Rom. 8:33), for it is God the Father who sent the Son and "presented him as a sacrifice of atonement, through faith in his blood" (Rom. 3:25; 8:30–32; Gal. 3:8).

The moral quandary of justification teaching lies in pondering the reality that the sinner can be viewed by God "as if" righteous precisely while in moral performance always remaining to some extent lacking in righteousness. Justification does not mean that the sinner immediately possesses, by virtue of Christ's justifying grace, a just disposition or holy moral character, but rather that one is freed from the obligation to suffer the penalty of law, treated as if one had fulfilled the law by virtue of Christ's fulfillment of the law on one's behalf. Our righteousness is not attained by the direct ethical infusion or literal transfer of Christ's behavior to our behavior, but rather by a lifelong, active appropriation through faith of God's pardoning grace (Augustine, *Spirit and Letter* 5.3; Calvin, *Inst.* 3.4.5, 12). New life in Christ is enabled by grace to grow gradually toward behavioral conformity with the requirement of God. Even if this conformity is incomplete in this life, it lives in hope of its being completed by grace in the final judgment. "When he appears, we shall be like him" (1 John 3:2; Augustine, *Trin.* 15.16.26).

While the verdict of justification is accomplished once for all on the cross, its implications are unfolding within finite historical circumstances. This is clear from Paul's language: "We, who with unveiled faces all reflect the Lord's glory, *are being transformed into his likeness* with ever-increasing glory, which comes from the Lord, who is the Spirit" (2 Cor. 3:18, italics added; Gregory of Nyssa, *On Perfection, FC* 58:122). The faithful are described as if looking in a mirror in which they are being transformed into the image of God, "changed from one form into another, and we pass from an obscure form to a bright form, for though obscure, yet it is the image of God" (Augustine, *Trin.* 15.8.14).

Clothed in Christ's Righteousness

The prophet Zechariah had a vision that early church exegetes viewed as anticipatory of the coming of Christ: "Joshua was dressed in filthy clothes as he stood before the angel. The angel said to those who were standing before him,

'Take off his filthy clothes.' Then he said to Joshua, 'See, I have taken away your sin, and I will put rich garments on you' " (Zech. 3:4; Lactantius, *Epitome of Divine Institutes* 4.14). This prophetic figure of speech was taken by classic Christian teachers to be an anticipatory reference to repentance and restoration to favor that only became fully received on the cross (Chrysostom, *Baptismal Instructions*, ACW 31:135–39).

This clothing metaphor (Isa. 61:10; 2 Cor. 5:1–21; 1 Pet. 5:5; Rev. 4:4; 7:9) augments the courtroom metaphor. To declare sinners upright before God is to deal with them as if they were clothed in Christ's goodness, accepting them as if they were perfect doers of the law, absolved from guilt, released from debt, discharged from any penalty due, despite all past misbehavior (Cyprian, *Letters*, FC 51:272; Oecumenius, *Comm. on Apocalypse* 7.9–17).

The benefits of Christ's obedience (active and passive) are accounted or reckoned to the believer. This does not imply that the believer actually and immediately lives with perfect uprightness or acts precisely as Christ acted. The proportional participation of the believer in deeds that reflect the goodness of Christ requires a further work of the Spirit in fully applying the benefits of justification to the sinner. This is the subject of sanctification, to be discussed later. Justification remains a declarative act of God external to human willing, as distinguished from sanctification, which is an efficacious act of God the Spirit within the sinner's will, to change that will (Calvin, *Inst.* 3.16; J. Wesley, *WJM* VI:65–77; Hodge, *ST* 3:213–30; Strong, *ST:*849).

Though forgiven sins cease to exist in God's eyes, their consequences persist in the history of sin. Just because I repent of my sin does not mean that the hurt I caused another is suddenly no longer felt or other consequences obliterated. That is why reparation is such an important part of the moral follow-through for forgiveness.

But from God's eyes, the sin is forever blotted out, removed, crossed off the list of indebtedness (Isa. 1:18; Mic. 7:18–19). "I, even I, am he who blots out your transgressions, for my own sake, and remembers your sins no more" (Isa. 43:25; Ambrose, *Of Holy Spirit* 3.10.61). "As far as the east is from the west, so far has he removed our transgressions from us" (Ps. 103:12). On this basis the psalmist could meaningfully pray, "Blot out my transgressions. Wash away all my iniquity, and cleanse me from my sin" (Ps. 51:1, 2). "Repent, then," Peter preached, "and turn to God, so that your sins may be wiped out" (Acts 3:19).

God's justifying action on the cross calls for a continuing reception of grace by which sin is gradually uprooted. It is precisely justifying grace, the once offered "blood of Christ," that seeks continually to cleanse us "from all sin" (1 John 1:7), having "freed us from our sins by his blood" (Rev. 1:5; Hilary of Arles, *Intro. Comm. on 1 John* 1.7).

What Causes Justification?

The several levels of the cause of justification have been at various times conceived in this way:

- *Grace* as *originating* cause, source, and fountain of justification. By grace alone the plan of redemption is foreknown and executed: The Father's offer of mercy is by grace; Christ's atoning work for us is by grace; the Spirit's work in us is by grace. If the opening, emerging, maturing, and completing movements of repentance, faith, and obedience all occur by grace, then it is exclusively by grace that one is saved through faith.

- The *love* of God the Father for fallen humanity is designated as the *procuring* cause—the reason why the plan of salvation was at first ordered and initiated. This is sometimes described as the moving cause, the grace and love of the Father that those who have faith should be redeemed (John 4:16; Rom. 5:8; Col. 2:16).

- The *atoning value or merit of Christ on the cross* is sometimes said to be the *meritorious* cause of justification (Rom. 5:19; 2 Cor. 5:19–21; Heb. 10:10–14), the sole reason why sinners are regarded as justified.

- The grace of *repentance* is sometimes said to be the *preparatory* cause of justification, awakened and elicited by prevening grace.

- God's own *Spirit* is the *efficient* cause, the working agent who applies the justifying action of the Son to responding hearts, regenerating, enabling faith and obedience (Rom. 8:30–33; Eph. 1:13, 14).

- *Baptism* is liturgically designated as the *instrumental* cause by which this justifying faith is received and life in the Spirit is born anew (Col. 2:12; Titus 3:5; John 3:5). The grace of baptism is the means provided by which this justifying grace is initiated and declared as beginning, as if it were with a new birth.

- The *receiving* cause (sometimes called the conditional cause in the subject self) is saving *faith* as enabled by grace (Rom. 3:26–4:25; Gal. 3:8, 9). Faith is the hand by which the faithful receive the proffered blessing to make it their own, and in this sense its sole condition (Luther, *LW* 31:346–49; Merrill, *ACE*:104).

- The *formal* cause is the *justice of God*, as adapted to the human condition, which wills to make creatures also upright (Hall, *DT* 8:263).

- The *glory* of God is the *final* cause (Tho. Aq., *ST*; Gamertsfelder, *ST*:499).

These levels of causality are combined or rearranged by various traditions. What is consensually confirmed is that the central nexus of justification is saving faith, the grace-enabled human responsiveness by which sinners receive the justifying grace of Christ and become united with him (Second Helvetic *Conf.*, 15; *Westminster Catech.*, *CC*:207).

The Blessings of Justification

In daily experience we are met with perplexing questions of why good people suffer. Life does not long permit an evasion of this query: Why does God allow sin in a good world—especially sin that causes suffering to innocent parties? The only creature who can fall into sin is one with some measure of rational freedom. Only a primordially good freedom can fall into sin. In the goodness of creation, God wants to give us that freedom. Evil could be completely prevented only by absolutely preventing the goodness of freedom, or protecting freedom from all possibility of being distorted or falling. But that would be inconsistent with God's original purpose in offering humanity genuine freedom (*LG*, 279–315; John of Damascus, *OF* 2.24, 25).

Classic pastoral reasoning about suffering returns often to the well of justification teaching, where the whole question of theodicy is itself transformed. At the cross it becomes no longer a question of why God permits sin and evil. Rather, more radically, God takes fallen freedom and blots out its transgressions, and thus gives freedom a new start. In this way the good news of justifying grace responds profoundly to the perennial quandary of why human suffering is permitted in God's world (Luther, *Sermons on St. John, LW* 23:81; Barth, *CD* 2/3:292).

Justification teaching takes the dilemma of evil in a new direction surprising to philosophical reasoning. *It frames the question of evil from the cross.* There God's beloved Son suffers to upright historical wrongs. Pardon does not end suffering, but cleans the slate for freedom to begin anew. Fallen freedom cannot redeem itself. God acts justly and as justifier of fallen freedom (Rom. 3:26; Clement of Alex., *Instructor* 1.8; Calvin, *Comm.* 20:139–46). In this way God's justifying action becomes "more pleasing to God and more valuable for human salvation than ever Adam's sin was harmful" (Julia of Norwich, *RDL*:125, 127).

Why a Comforting Doctrine

The psalmist pronounced one blessed "whose transgressions are forgiven, whose sins are covered. Blessed is the man whose sin the Lord does not count against him and in whose spirit is no deceit" (Ps. 32:1; Callistus, *Epistle* 2).

If it were possible for one to provide complete restitution for all those wrongs one has done to others, then one might imagine that the grace of justification and forgiveness might be considered less necessary. But the problem remains: one cannot go back and undo all that one has wrongly or harmfully done. No restitution can ever be adequate. We have all caused harm for which we can never make full restitution. This is why we stand in such dire need of divine pardon (Tho. Aq., *ST* 2–2, Q62; E. Lewis, *Great Christian Teachings*:41).

The Anglican Articles of Religion underscore the comfort and benefit of God's justifying action: "We are accounted righteous before God, only for the merit of our Lord and Savior Jesus Christ by faith, and not for our own works or deservings; wherefore, that we are justified by faith only is a most wholesome doctrine, and very full of comfort" (Thirty-nine Articles, 11; cf. *Heid. Catech.* 1).

With typical vivacity, Luther wrote, "As often as you insist that I am a sinner, just so often do you call me to remember the benefit of Christ my Redeemer, upon whose shoulders, and not upon mine, lie all my sins . . . So, when you say that I am a sinner, you do not terrify, but comfort me immeasurably" (Luther, *Comm. on Galatians*:21–22).

Forgiving, Pardoning, Reckoning, and Reconciling

These images interfuse and mesh together in the scriptural teaching of justifying grace:

> the offender is forgiven

> the accused is pardoned

> the offense is remitted

> the lost child welcomed home.

In these ways, justifying grace reveals a subtle cohesion of divine attributes. The single turn from repentance to faith is variably symbolized as

> an act of forgiveness that encourages

> an acquittal that remits

> a new mode of accounting that crosses out the penalty

> a divine-human reconciliation that embraces the lost.

The word-picture of forgiveness (such as that of the father to the prodigal son) belongs more specifically to the family metaphor, while the act of pardon belongs more to the courtroom metaphor. The judge can pardon but not forgive. The loving parent can forgive where such forgiveness would he inappropriate in a courtroom. Though distinguishable, they are complementary. In the New Testament these two metaphors are intensely conflated: it is through divine forgiveness that an acquittal is offered. It is not that those free from condemnation are then forgiven—that would reverse the order. Rather those forgiven are thereby freed from condemnation (John 3:16; Rom. 4:5; 5:1, 16; Gal. 2:16; Chrysostom, *Hom. on Gal.*; Ambrosiaster, *Comm. on Paul*, Rom. 5.1).

These are two different angles of vision upon the same event: The forgiveness of sins and the declaration of the sinner as pardoned. One who is justified is declared just or upright on the basis of the pardon through which guilt is remitted. To receive a "*pardon* is, in the exercise of sovereign prerogative, to waive the execution of the penal sanctions of the law; to *justify* is to declare that the demands of the law are satisfied, not waived. Pardon is a sovereign act; justification is a judicial act" (C. Hodge, *The Way of Life*:154, italics added).

Only mercy and justice in unison can justify. Justification is that key moment in the history of salvation in which the righteousness of God is declared in relation to the history of sin, yet without offense to the justice of God (Calvin, *Inst.* 3.11–15; Pope, *Compend.* 2:253–316). Only the truly human, truly divine mediator could justly pardon without demeaning justice. Only the crucified Lord could at the same time remain "just" and "forgive us our sins" (1 John 1:9; Rom. 3:26.; Origen, *Comm. on Rom.* 3.24–26). Grace reigns through merciful righteousness, not mercy alone.

I cannot force my way from conviction to pardon. Pardon is exclusively an act of grace offered and revealed by the incomparable One who pardons. It is not merely willed from within myself. No matter how much I may look for humanistic comparisons to divine mercy, my word of pardon to myself is always finally hollow and insufficient. Admittedly, there may indeed be times when I need to permit myself to forgive myself or to be forgiven by another. But it is finally by Another that one is forgiven, not by oneself. Hence pardon is intrinsically interpersonal (Ps. 25:11; Isa. 40:1, 2).

Nature does not pardon. Reason can only analyze the need for pardon, as it does in effective psychotherapy. Through reason we may learn that God is just, but it is hardly a reasonable deduction that God would justify sinners precisely while they were yet ungodly (Rom. 5:8; Ambrosiaster, *Comm. on Paul*, Rom. 5.7). Conscience is the last of all human faculties to pardon sin. Its main constructive function in the presence of sin is to accuse.

Christians learn of pardon through searching scripture, coming to the Lord's table to receive Holy Communion, and hearing the inner testimony of the Spirit attest scripture as true. "If you, O Lord, kept a record of sins, O Lord, who could stand? But with you there is forgiveness" (Ps. 130:3, 4).

The relation of atonement and pardon is among the great mysteries of faith, as are the triunity of God, the incarnation, and the resurrection. All theories pale in relation to the experienced fact that pardon is best known in the Christian community at the Lord's Table and in the hearing of the Word (Luke 24:35; Luther, *Large Catech.* 5; Thirty-nine Articles, 19). Faith simply receives this revelation gratefully, rejoicing in the gift rather than pretending to penetrate this mystery with infinite curiosity (Ambrose, *The Mysteries*, FC 44:6).

Forgiveness as Gift

The central feature of forgiveness is its radical gift character. Forgiveness can only occur when freely given away (Anglo-Saxon: *for-*, away, and *giefan*, to give; Gr. *aphesis*, a letting go). Anyone who forgives another by whom he has been harmed is engaging in a gracious act.

Forgiveness is a costly gift, since the one forgiving cancels the debt and forfeits that which is due, taking responsibility for any liability or deficit (Origen, *Comm. on Rom.* 5.7–8; Calvin, *Inst.* 3.18–20; 4.1). God's forgiveness of our sins involves and requires God's taking our sins upon himself. He took the penalty for us. He bore them on the cross (Justin Martyr, *Dialogue with Trypho* 13; *Augustine On Romans* 32).

Where forgiveness pervades a relationship, it is no longer dominated by aggressive charges, counterclaims, and legalistic attempts to recover damages. Justification is a gift of God to which the human recipient has no inherent right or claim (Eph. 1:6, 7; 2:7, 8; Rom. 4:4; John 3:16; Titus 2:11). If divine forgiveness had been humanly merited, there would have been nothing to forgive. Merit would have replaced the need for forgiveness (Chrysostom, *Hom. on Eph* 2.8; Second Council of Orange, SCD 176).

The Lord's Prayer makes it clear that we are bound to share with others the forgiveness we have received from God (Mt 6:9–15; Tertullian, *On Prayer* 7; Cyprian, *Treatises, On the Lord's Prayer* 27). The two dimensions of the prayer are always together: God is forgiving us while we in turn are forgiving others (Luke 11:4). Jesus held the connection rigorously: "if you do not forgive men their sins, your Father will not forgive your sins" (Matt. 6:15; Augustine, *Sermon on the Mount* 2.11.39).

The New Accounting

Imputed Righteousness

To impute (*logizomai*) is to credit as a virtue to another or to charge as a fault to another. The New Testament makes frequent use of the bookkeeping analogy: imputing or crediting to another's account. God's grace ascribes to our account what we do not deserve.

The language of imputation has entered conspicuously into justification teaching as seen in Paul's crucial phrase "faith is credited [*logizetai*] as righteousness" (Rom. 4:5). Our debts are charged to Christ's account (Chrysostom, *Hom. on Rom.* 8). Christ's obedience is offered for our deficient account (*Augustine on Romans* 22; Calvin, *Inst.* 2.16.6; 17.4, 5). "Faith may be said to be imputed to us for righteousness, as it is the sole condition of our acceptance" (Wesley, *NUNT* at Rom. 4:9; Watson, *TI* 2:587).

The imputation metaphors are found throughout classic Christian teaching: Adam's sin has been reckoned to flow into the history of all humanity, so Adam's debt is "charged to our account." Oppositely, our sin has been reckoned to Christ. Christ paid the penalty for sin, becoming a curse for us. Our own sins are mercifully not being counted against those who trust Christ righteousness (Rom. 4:22–24; 2 Cor. 5:19), which is reckoned to the believer (Ambrosister, *Comm. on Paul.* Rom. 4.22; Calvin, *Inst.* 3.11–15).

Justification teaching employs a twofold reversal in the bookkeeping metaphor. It indicates both the discharging (nonimputation) from sin and the crediting (imputation) of Christ's righteousness (Clement of Alex., *Stromata* 5.5; Calvin, *Inst.*

4.16–17). Debt is discharged; substitutionary payment is credited. The *Epistle to Diognetus* called this "the sweet exchange" (9, *ECW*:180).

Sin is not charged against the believing sinner, for "God was reconciling the world to himself in Christ, *not counting* men's sins against them" (2 Cor. 5:19; Ambrosiaster, *Comm. on Paul*, 2 Cor. 5.19). Christ's righteousness is accredited to the believing sinner, who is "found in him, not having a righteousness of my own that comes from the law, but that which is through faith in Christ—the *righteousness that comes from God and is by faith*" (Phil. 3:9, italics added; Theodoret, *Epis. to Phil*. 3.9–10).

The believer is treated as actually righteous in relation to God. This is why my ethical deeds are not the basis for gaining standing in God's presence. Only in the cross of the Lord of glory is that possible, where sin is forgiven without offending God's own righteousness (Anselm, *CDH*; Calvin, *Inst*. 3.11.21–23).

But how can God remain holy if sin is easily dismissed? That is just the point: it is not easily dismissed. It required a cross, a death, a burial. The cross is an event in history, a sacrificial offering substituting Christ's goodness for our sin. The burden of our sin is transferred directly from our shoulders to Christ's cross (Rom. 3:21–15; 2 Cor. 5:21). On the cross there occurred a salvation event which constituted "a transfer from the Law to the Gospel, from the Synagogue to the Church, from many sacrifices to one Victim" (Leo I, Sermon 68.3).

The Link Between Imputing and Imparting

Preaching applies the forensic language of imputation to constitute a formal, juridical declaration of God's act for us as God's righteousness imputed to us (Rom. 4:5). It does not thereby imply that this forensic act nullifies any need for ongoing growth in our behavioral improvement. Paul's own language forbids this. Paul never suggested that we are saved *in* our sins but *despite* our sins and *from* our sins (Rom. 5–6; Chrysostom, *Hom. on Rom.*, Hom. 10). Christ's righteousness does not exempt believers from responsibility to reflect that righteousness in their behavior (Rom. 5:17–21; 8:5–13). The declaration intends to change human behavior toward conforming to the image of God (Calvin, *Inst*. 3.11–12).

God deals with the baptized faithful as though they were upright since they have come by faith to share in Christ's righteousness, even if they are not yet fully responsive in behavior to God's holy love. God "calls things that are not as though they were" (Rom. 4:17; Origen, *Comm. on Rom*. 4.14–17). Similarly the infant is valued by the parent not only in the form of actual behavior but also in the form of potentiality, even when the maturity is not yet actual but present already in primitive form. "We are valued in the light of what by the grace of Christ we have begun to become," wrote Francis Hall. God regards us not as we are but as we shall in the future be. Those who fail to grow toward righteousness will cease to be accounted righteous. "Justification means our being accounted righteous, rather than our being made so." In Paul's letters faithful baptism assumes that we are truly and willingly beginning to be made righteous. It "implies a real inception of this making by an imparting to us of regenerating and sanctifying grace" (Hall, *DT* 8:261–63) so as to enable us to grow up in righteousness, "speaking the truth in love" (Eph. 4:15; Theodoret, *Epis.to Eph*. 4.15; Augustine, *Comm. on John*, 26.1).

Similarly the word picture of "remitting" points to that act by which debt or guilt or penalty is set aside (literally, sent back; Lat. *remittere*). To remit is to cancel a debt or refrain from enforcing a requirement. The remission of sin is not simply the superficial covering over of immorality, for an immoral life as such cannot be imputed for righteousness if it remains forever collusive with willed sin. So justifying faith must point ahead toward a responsive life of growing upright actions and habituation that makes for righteousness, even though these do not merit God's pardon—for that has already been merited by the cross (Matt. 7:16–25; Rom. 10:10; 12:1–5; Ambrosiaster, *Comm. on Rom.* 4.5–7).

The faith that uprights the sinner looks toward a moral response to grace that becomes fruitful in good deeds (Eph. 2:8; 6:23; Heb. 12:2). The faith that precedes good works will in due course bear the fruit of good works (John 6:44; Acts 18:27; Rom. 12:3). It is hardly genuine faith if it lacks the disposition to love (Clement of Rome, *Corinth.* 50.5).

The Antinomian Temptation

The claim that grace not only pronounces, but anticipatively makes us righteous (Merrill, *ACE*:229) may inadvertently tempt believers to treat grace cheaply (Bonhoeffer, *The Cost of Discipleship*; Cyprian, *Treatise* 11). The tendency to view sin as only superficially "covered over" by the merits of Christ or by an external imputation of the righteousness of Christ may run an antinomian risk. If so, it becomes necessary to point out that God's righteousness is truly imparted on the cross and sins actually blotted out precisely in order that the justified person may become uprighted in behavioral responses (Luther, *Good Works*, *WML* 1:105–196).

Justifying faith is at once a faith in Christ that is imputed to us for righteousness and a faith in Christ that seeks to impart and draw forth righteousness (Augustine, *Spirit and Letter* 18.31; 26.45; *Grace and Free Will* 6.13). According to the *Heidelberg Catechism*, God "graciously imparts to me the righteousness of Christ" (Q56).

Reconciliation to the Family of God

The prodigal was not merely pardoned, but to his astonishment received back into the family with full rights of sonship (Luke 15:22–31): belonging, accountability, legacy. Remission of sin is followed by the reconciling embrace of the Father. Justification is not merely a cold announcement of nonliability but a warm welcome from the waiting Father (Ambrose, *Expos. On Luke*, 7.229–230; Melanchthon, *Loci*, 71, 106–8).

Restoration to divine favor is called reconciliation (*katallagē*), where alienated covenant partners are brought back together into their original pacific relation. Whereas the cool, distant language of the courtroom speaks of justification, the warm and intimate family metaphor speaks of gracious adoption into the family of God (2 Cor. 5:18–20; Hilary, *Trin.*, 8.51).

By means of the family metaphor, justification takes on a much more personal and interpersonal meaning. Here one meets not a judge but a parent, not a piece of paper but an embrace, not a release from charges but an empowering, enabling, supporting family, not a verdict but a homecoming. The new focus is not upon the removal of the charge of sin, but upon an inheritance.

Justification implies that the war between sinners and God is over, that we approach the holy God freely, assured of our participation in the family of God and its inheritance of salvation. "Therefore, since we have been justified through faith, we have peace with God through our Lord Jesus Christ, through whom we have gained access by faith into this grace in which we now stand" (Rom. 5:1, 2; Chrysostom, *Hom. on Rom.* 9).

Faith in Christ

The benefits of Christ's atoning work are applied by the Spirit and appropriated by the believer through faith. "For it is by grace you have been saved, through faith—and this is not from yourselves, it is the gift of God—not by works, so that no one can boast" (Eph. 2:8, 9; Fulgentius, *On the Incarnation* 1). It is this faith that God declares as righteousness (Rom. 3:1–4:21; Augsburg *Conf.*, art. 4). Without faith the gift of pardon is given but unreceived.

Faith is the reception of grace. The familiar phrase "justification by faith" may become misleading insofar as it suggests that our faith rather than God's grace saves (Calvin, *Inst.* 3.11–12). *The faithful are justified by grace, not by their own faith* (Melanchthon, *Loci*:89).

As repentance turns away from the past, the old Adam, the failed era of despairing freedom, so faith turns toward God's future, the new Adam, the emerging era of redeemed freedom amid the governance of God made known in Christ (Rom. 5:12–17; Eusebius, *Proof of the Gospel* 7.1). As repentance grieves over its failure to be accountable to the law, faith rejoices over God's becoming accountable for us in the gospel (Ambrose, *On Repentance* 2.9). The turn away from wrongdoing is at the same time a turn toward faith. The turnaround is conversion.

There is an inner correlation between the major phases of the order of salvation, whose topics include call, repentance, justification, faith, regeneration, adoption, sanctification, and union with Christ. To lack any of these motifs would leave something omitted in the teaching of salvation. Though distinguishable, they cannot artificially be separated and are united in the one Spirit (Augustine, *Trin.*, FC 45:251–52; 374–76).

The Knowledge of Faith that Comes Only from Choosing Faith

In apostolic teaching, faith is utterly simple and direct in its radical decisiveness. Christian teaching does well to convey that profound simplicity undisguised (Cyprian, *Treatise* 12). Salvation hinges upon grace-enabled faith, not the absolute clarity of faith's attempts to define itself. "God was pleased through the foolishness of what was preached to save those who believe" (1 Cor. 1:21; Ambrosiaster, *Comm. on Paul*, 1 Cor. 1.21).

The believer cannot find out whether God's will is trustworthy until he chooses actively to rely upon it. This surprisingly pragmatic principle of practical ethics was taught by Jesus himself: "If anyone *chooses* to do God's will, *he will find out*" (John 7:17, italics added). The implication: Only one who is willing to risk following the Lord by doing what he says will then learn his teaching (Chrysostom, *Hom. on John* 49; Augustine, *on John*, 29.6).

Active, choosing, risk-taking reliance upon God is the premise of understanding whether Jesus is the Expected One (Calvin, *Inst.* 1.14). Without choosing to follow, without committing oneself to do God's will, one is not likely to be sufficiently ready for saving grace to be rightly received and understood (Wesley, *WJWB* 1.7). In the classic Christian inquiry into faith the first thing to do is to pray for the grace to inquire rightly into faith (Augustine, *Confessions*, 1.1).

Faith Defined as Personal Trust

Faith (*pistis*) is the means by which salvation is appropriated through personal trust in the Son as Savior (Ambrosiaster, *Comm. on Paul*, Rom. 3.21–22).

Saving faith is *personal trust*—trust in a person, Jesus Christ, the one mediator between God and humanity. The Greek terms for *faith* (*pistis, pisteuō*) imply reliance upon and trust in another who has been proven trustworthy.

Faith is less *about* Christ than *in* Christ. "Everyone who believes *in him* receives forgiveness" (Acts 10:43, italics added). The jailer at Philippi was told by

Paul, "Believe in the Lord Jesus, and you will be saved" (Acts 16:31; Didymus the Blind, *Catena on Acts* 10.43, Cramer 3:189).

This personal trust is grounded in the conviction of the credibility of the apostolic testimony as witnessed by the Spirit (1 John 5:9, 10; Luther, *SML* 7:231). Faith in God implies that God's declarations and disclosures about and of himself in the history of Jesus are reliable and sufficient for faith (Bede, *On 1 John* 5.9–10; Calvin, *Inst.* 2.6).

To trust a person is a more decisive, risk-laden act than to trust empirical evidence. We say that one believes in a fact when one is assured of its truth, but one believes in another *person* only when sufficiently assured of that person's trustworthiness. Faith as personal trust is implied even in the etymology of the Hebrew verb *'aman* (to believe), to remain steadfast, to stay, to make the heart firm (Ps. 31:23; Neh. 7:2; Dan. 6:23–24; Aphrahat, *Demonstrations* 21.18).

Such faith is accompanied inwardly by the Spirit's assurance and outwardly by works of love in relation to the neighbor. Faith is the primary condition set forth in scripture for receiving justification (Ambrosiaster, *Comm. on Paul*, Rom. 3.25–6; Hodge, *OOT*:465–81; Strong, *ST*:465; Clarke, *OCT*:401–5).

Faith's Evidences

The most direct definition of faith in the New Testament requires careful examination: "Now faith is being sure of what we hope for and certain of what we do not see" (Heb. 11:1; Cyril of Jerusalem, *Catech. Lect.* 1–2). Faith is confidence in and assurance of the truth of what we hope for, and the evidence or conviction (*elenchos*) of that which cannot be seen (Clement of Alex., *Stromata* 2.2.8–9; Luther, *Lectures on Hebrews*, *LW* 29:229).

Faith attests to the reality of things we cannot fully see. In doing so it draws us toward greater certainty of what lies beyond empirical sight. Faith entails laying hold of that which cannot be attained by sense perception or logic alone (Chrysostom, *Hom. on Heb.* 22). Accordingly, faith is the joyful, consenting affirmation of mind, heart, and will to the truth of what is not empirically seen: God's self-disclosure. If revelation is the window to grace, faith is the eye that beholds grace.

The consensually received testimony of prophets, martyrs, saints, inspired writers, and revered exegetes is viewed as primary evidence of truth in the Christian community. Faith is different from conjecture, supposition, fantasy, imagination, or premature assumption. It is based upon the evidences of faith— revelation in history (John of Damascus, *OF* 3.9).

To believe without evidence is gullibility. Faith is not gullibility, because it does not believe without some forms of evidence. The task of reason is to assess the quality of evidence.

Faith reaches for evidences beyond empirical data, seeking evidences of God's promise. Hebrews 11 provides a long list of such evidences. This sort of evidentiary search is in part historical, and to that extent must be approached in the way that historical evidence is appropriately established. Yet the best historians are those most aware of the limits of historical method. The evidences of faith are also moral, hence the inquiry proceeds by moral reasoning that breaks through the rules of empirical evidence. The evidences of faith are distinctively spiritual, requiring sight into reliable testimony that corresponds with faith's underpinning, grace (Theodoret, *Interp. of Heb.* 11; Calvin, *Inst.* 3.2).

Faith is distinguished from sight, on the one hand, and doubt, on the other. Though we "live by faith, not by sight" (2 Cor. 5:7; Augustine, *Letter to Honoratus* 140.9; *To Proba* 130), faith is not a spiritual blindness but a spiritual seeing (John 6:40; Augustine, *Sermon* 14A.5).

Even though specific operations and outcomes of God's promise may remain partially obscure, faith relies on the trustworthiness of what is already clearly known of God. This is based firmly on historical and personal evidence.

It is in this sense that the letter to Hebrews celebrated the faith of Abel, Enoch, Noah, Abraham, and Moses: "All these people were still living by faith when they died. *They did not receive the things promised; they only saw them and welcomed them from a distance*" (Heb. 11:13, italics added; Chrysostom, *Epis. to Heb.* 23, 24).

The Power to Believe

Faith is the only condition required for a reconciled relation to the Giver of Life. Without faith no one would be prepared to receive God's saving gifts. Nothing will substitute. Faith is the primary condition for the reception of every subsequent stage of God's saving activity (Chrysostom, *Hom. on Rom.* 7; Luther, *Freedom of a Christian*, MLS:56–61). At no point is it possible to say that having discussed faith, we can now turn to other theological subjects so as to leave faith behind (Calvin, *Inst.* 3.2). The necessity of faith had long before been grasped clearly in the Hebrew Bible. Habakkuk understood that "the righteous will live by his faith" (Hab. 2:4).

Faith could not be viewed by Christian teaching as a duty if it is impossible. Wherever a duty is seriously required, the power to perform that duty must be reasonably implied (Kant, *Prolegomena to the Metaphysics of Morals*). If a commandment is intrinsically impossible, it cannot be morally necessary.

The power to believe is supplied not by the fallen nature, not by the self-alienated will acting autonomously, but by grace enabling a restored freedom. Were it not prepared and enabled by grace, there could be no meaningful call to faith or guilt due to unbelief (Aphrahat, *Demonstrations, On Faith*). Though faith is not the first movement of salvation, since justifying faith is preceded by preparing grace, it is the beginning and necessary foundation of that life which is being justified (Council of Orange II, *SCD* 178).

Without Faith It Is Impossible to Please God

If trusting God's Word is the absolute and irreplaceable condition of entering into the realm of God's governance, then the opposite holds: lack of faith is viewed in the New Testament as the decisive rejection of God's veracity: "Whoever does not believe stands condemned already" (John 3:18; Chrysostom, *Hom. on John* 28).

By refusing to trust and receive God's revealed mercy on the cross, we place a huge obstacle in the way of our justification. By rejecting God's free gift, we voluntarily leave ourselves alienated from God. Every human action lacking trust in God, however well intended, is fundamentally misguided. It is "off the mark" (*hamartia*, sin; Rom. 7:14; Origen, *Comm. on Rom.* 7.14–15). For what could be more unsatisfactory to God than to doubt the truth of God's costly self-disclosure? Thus the absence of faith is viewed in the New Testament as a rejection of God's truth.

Any human obsession is flawed that comes out of the self-righteous presumption that human goodness can proceed without trust in the One who gives life. The consequent language seems harsh to modern hearers: "Without faith it is impossible to please God, because anyone who comes to him must believe that he *exists* and that he *rewards* those who earnestly seek him" (Heb. 11:6 italics added; Rufinus, *Comm. on Apostles' Creed* 3). Yet this very text then goes on to show that those who have not yet heard of Jesus Christ can be drawn toward God by hope, by an implicit, anticipatory faith in God's future coming (Clement of Alex., *Stromata*, 2.2.8–9; Calvin, *Comm.* 22:270–82). These hearts are known only to God, who sees clearly the future consequences of our present motives.

It is difficult to see how someone could even approach God without believing that God exists and that he rewards those who seek him. These two premises may be anticipatively believed by animists, Hindus, and Muslims without their ever hearing of the history of Jesus, as was the case with Abel (Heb. 11:4; Chrysostom, *Epis. to Heb.* 21.5–22.4). Without belief in the reality and justice of God, one can hardly further come near the mercy of God.

The word picture of seed was used by Jesus dramatically to attest the power of faith: "If you have faith as small as a mustard seed, you can say to this mountain, 'Move from here to there' and it will move. Nothing will be impossible for you" (Matt. 17:20; Origen, *Comm. on Matt.* 13.7). What does seed have that makes it analogous to the kingdom of God? Readiness to receive the conditions of growth (Calvin, *Comm.* 16:326). The gospel is "the power of God for the salvation of everyone who believes" (Rom. 1:16; Ambrosiaster, *Comm. on Paul*, Rom. 1.16). The greatness of God's power manifests itself in bringing life from death (1 John 4:7–21). Preaching does not proceed "with wise and persuasive words, but with a demonstration of the Spirit's power, so that your faith might not rest on men's wisdom, but on God's power" (1 Cor. 2:5; Chrysostom, *Hom. on 2 Cor.* 6.3).

The Study of Faith

The ancient Christian writers found it useful to make careful distinctions in claims relating to justifying faith: They distinguished immature from mature faith active in love. (1) They spoke of the difference between the faith that is believed and faith as actively believing. (2) Faith as a specific here and now act must be distinguished from faith as habit of the good life. (3) They knew the difference between implicit and explicit faith. (4) They were clearly aware of the difference between human faith or general trusting in something (including historical faith and intellectual assent) as distinguished from divine faith made possible by grace. The academic study of beliefs (discursive faith) must be distinguished from the direct act of faith.

These distinctions have been found useful in the attempt over centuries to define the relation between Christian faith and the general concepts and phenomena of faith in the history of religions (Eusebius, *Preparation of the Gospel*; Calvin, *SW*:274; 381–84; Heppe, *RD*:526–36). Defining these distinctions is our next task. It is something like memorizing multiplication tables in order to increase efficiency in practically using numbers. It is an elementary discipline that has proven useful over many generations.

Faith as Believing and as Believed

First, the distinction between believing and what is believed. The faith that is believed is the apostolic testimony, the consensually received objective truth of the Christian faith (in Latin: *fides quae creditur*). It is in this sense that Jude urged his hearers to "contend for the faith that was once for all entrusted to the saints" (Jude 3).

It is useful to keep in mind how *the faith that is believed* differs from the personal *act of believing*, or faith that actively believes (*fides qua creditur*, faith as experientially trusting in another). To grasp the faith that is believed by another is different from believing it yourself. Both active personal believing and the more passive study of the beliefs of others are concerns of the believing community. Faith is both believed and believes. Faith can believe because it has heard of the faith that is believed (Jude 3; Oecumenius, *Comm. on Jude* 3; Irenaeus, *Fragments* 36).

Faith as Act and Habit

Second, I may engage in a particular act of faith without having established faith as a matter of habitual action or character.

The life of faith that is commended in the New Testament is not simply a single fleeting act, but rather an entire way of life, a way of walking by trusting in God continually, by repeatedly layered actions that reinforce habituation (Gal. 5:25; 1 John 1:6, 7; Bede, *On 1 John* 1.7–8).

Yet this way of walking consists of specific steps of faith, particular acts of believing, while acknowledging that faith intends to become a habitual action of the character of the faithful.

Faith as Explicit and Implicit

Third, the ancient patriarchs and prophets had implicit faith in Christ and were drawn to God without explicit faith in the orthodox language of the Trinity and prior to the Incarnation. They had faith without the rite of baptism, but anticipated baptism with male circumcision as an act of initiation. They believed in the heart by way of desire in a way that anticipated explicit faith even when the object of belief was not yet available to them in the present (Cyril of Jerusalem, *Catech. Lect.* 5.5; Tho. Aq, *ST* 2–2, Q2.7.3). Those who lived before Christ or who have not explicitly heard the good news may share in an implicit faith in the promise of God's coming without grasping particulars of historical revelation. Such faith is efficacious, or "counted for righteousness," as in the case of Abraham (Rom. 4:5; Origen, *Comm. on Rom.* 4.1–8; Heb. 11:8–19).

This distinction was refined by the Reformers: Explicit faith (*fides explicita*) is an express belief in the truth of revelation in Jesus Christ, while *fides implicita* is a virtual belief, when one implicitly affirms by way of anticipation what the apostolic teaching would later teach, even if one may not fully understand it (Luther, *On the Creed, Commandments and Lord's Prayer*, Calvin, *Inst.* 3.2.3)

When the believer seeks and wills and intends to affirm from the heart whatever it is that God has revealed as consensually received by the faithful community, that is an act of implicit faith that trusts the consensus being nurtured by the Spirit even when that faith does not adequately grasp it, while hoping to lay hold of it ever better (Vincent of Lérins, *Comm.*; Beveridge, *On the Consent of the Church*, CVL:141–53).

A similar distinction is that between an unformed or *inchoate faith* and *mature faith* which is saving faith active in love (Calvin, *SW*:381–84; *Inst.* 3.2.10). The faculty of faith that is inchoately present in every human spirit is gradually, in God's own time, being awakened by God's own Spirit. "Faculties of the human body, if denied their exercise, will lie dormant. The eye without light, natural or artificial, cannot fulfill its office; the ear will be ignorant of its functions unless some voice or sound be heard; the nostrils unconscious of their purpose unless some scent be breathed. Not that the faculty will be absent, but that there will be no experience of its existence. So, too, the soul of man, unless through faith it has appropriated the gift of the Spirit, will have the innate faculty of apprehending God, but be destitute of the light of knowledge" (Hilary, *Trin.* 2.35).

Saving Faith Distinguished from Generic Human Forms of Faith

Fourth, faith as trust is familiar to human experience of all cultures and not an exclusive possession of Christianity. Children have faith in their parents, quite apart from any deliberate thought of divine revelation. A wife trusts her husband as he proves trustworthy. A voter may have faith in a political party. Such is called *human faith* to distinguish it from that faith in Christ that is enabled by saving grace, which is termed *saving faith* (*fides salvifica*), or in some traditions divine faith.

Such a general faith knows what it knows without the empirical evidence ordinarily expected of knowledge of the material, physical world. This is a common human capacity. No culture is without it (Luther, *Large Catechism* 1; cf. M. Eliade; W. H. Smith; H. Kraemer).

Such general human faith necessarily involves the whole person: knowing, feeling, and willing. Hence saving faith does not require a new faculty of the self. Rather, God's preparing grace works within human knowing, feeling, and willing to move the self toward that saving faith that knows, feels, and wills in relation to God's own personal coming.

God has not left himself without witness in the world (Acts 14:17). Faith in God is experienced in an anticipatory sense in the worship that devout persons of all times have sought to offer to God, who has become known in creation and providence and general revelation in anticipation of God's particular self-disclosure to Israel and through Christ.

The faith of non-Israelites appeared to be a special concern of Jesus: "Other sheep I have, which are not of this fold" (John 10:16; Augustine, *Sermon* 138.5). Commenting upon the faith of the Roman Centurion, Jesus said, "I tell you the truth, I have not found anyone in Israel with such great faith. I say to you that many will come from the east and the west, and will take their places at the feast with Abraham, Isaac and Jacob in the kingdom of heaven" (Matt. 8:10, 11; Irenaeus, *Ag. Her.* 4.58. 10; Augustine, *Sermon* 62.2).

Classic Christian teaching distinguishes saving faith from this generic capacity for faith. Saving faith is unconditional reliance on Christ for salvation, an act of personal trust in the divine-human Mediator (Chrysostom, *Hom. on John*, 27,28; Clarke, *CT*:479–85; Watson, *TI* 2:23). Generic faith can become attached to any object. Saving faith is faith in Christ, renouncing all gods but the living God, disavowing all Lords but the crucified-resurrected Lord, willing to take up one's cross and follow (Pope, *Compend.* 2:376–90).

When faith is temporarily taken out of its own realm of active trust in God and subjected to rational analysis and reflection, in the way that any other subject can be investigated, it is termed *discursive faith*, or faith as a subject of intelligent discourse. Faith in this sense is sometimes distinguished from a *direct faith* that actively trusts. It is direct faith that is being investigated, but in the process of investigation it may temporarily become discursive faith.

Faith in the general sense is a premise of all human knowing, all empirical inquiry, all deductive reasoning (Clement of Alex., *Stromata* 2.4), since no one can make an objective scientific investigation without assuming the intelligibility of the natural order, an axiom that itself cannot be empirically proven (Tho. Aq., *ST* 2–2, Q9). Hence *credo ut intelligam* (whereby one believes in order to know) is a scientific axiom. "For a farmer does not plow a furrow in the earth without faith, nor a merchant entrust his life to a bit of wood on the raging high seas. Neither are marriages contracted nor anything else in life done without faith" (John of Damascus, *OF* 4. 11).

Saving Faith and Historical Faith

Fifth, saving faith in Christ is distinguished from historical faith (*fides historica*), that faith which is convinced by historical evidence that an event occurred. One may believe on the basis of historical testimony that Christ in fact died on the cross, and yet not believe that his death was a ransom for one's own sin. Saving faith "is not merely a knowledge of historical events, but is a confidence in God" (Augsburg *Conf.*, 20).

Faith as personal trust is not sufficiently understood as a matter of historical research into the events reported in scripture, yet faith willingly hears and weighs the evidences of God's self-disclosure. The seeker cannot affirm that Christ died for him without first understanding that Christ died. Establishing that fact is a matter of historical evidence. Hence some historical knowledge or confidence in the reporting of the history of Jesus is vital to saving faith, though such "historical faith" (*fides historica*) cannot in itself have saving effect or substitute for justifying faith.

Faith does not conclude that historical evidence is unimportant: "We did not follow cleverly invented stories when we told you about the power and coming of our Lord Jesus Christ, but we were eyewitnesses of his majesty" (2 Pet. 1:16; cf. 1 John 1:1). The proper rules of truth-telling eyewitnesses were assumed, as confirmed in the case of the Transfiguration: "We ourselves heard this voice that came from heaven when we were with him on the sacred mountain" (2 Pet. 1:18; Andreas, *Catena on 2 Pet.*, Cramer, *CEC* 88).

Having distinguished six ways of differentiating saving faith from other uses of the term faith, we turn to three elements of saving faith.

Elements of Saving Faith: Assent, Trust, and Decision

The faith that saves embraces in a balanced way the assent of the mind, the trust of the heart, and the decision of the will.

These elements draw the whole person into the life of saving faith: a fully convinced affirmation of the truth of God's self-disclosure; a basic reversal of emotive energies so that all loves are transformed in relation to the love of God; and a voluntary surrender of the will to God's will.

Thus the sustained life of faith embraces and transforms the whole person as knowing, feeling, and willing (Augustine, *Trinity*, 9–10). "Faith is the assent of the mind, the consent of the will and the choice of trust of the heart" (J. M. Shaw, *Christian Doctrine*:235). The Westminster Confession describes these three as the "principal acts of saving faith" (Art. 14): accepting, receiving and resting in Christ alone.

The Assent of the Mind

The Greek word *pistis* means at one level simply belief in the truth. It is that persuasion by which something is received as true. Thus one crucial element of Christian faith is the conviction that what is believed (God's word addressed on the cross and validated by the resurrection) is true and worthy of confidence (Heb. 6:18; Augustine, *On the Profit of Believing* 34). "We have this as a sure and steadfast anchor of the soul" (Heb. 6:19; Chrysostom, *Epis. to Heb.* 11.3).

Faith cannot proceed confidently without the conviction that the history of divine self-disclosure is reliable and reported with sufficient reliability to be believed with the whole mind, heart and will (Tho. Aq., *ST* 2-2, Q8). Saving faith does not function optimally either without or against reason, though it reaches beyond reason. No one is redeemed by a truth asserted which is not true.

Reliable, accredited eyewitnesses attest the truth, and it is on this basis that faith becomes plausible and possible (John 20:31; Hilary, *Trin.*, 6.41). The New Testament itself was intensely concerned to establish the authenticity of its witnesses to the events of revelation, as in John's explicit report of the breaking of

Jesus' legs in the crucifixion shows: "The man who saw it has given testimony, and his testimony is true. He knows that he tells the truth, and he testifies so that you also may believe" (John 19:35; Theodore of Mopsuestia, *Comm. on John* 7.19.35).

Faith embraces an intellectual aspect—recognition of the truth of God's self-disclosure. If faith is at one level a kind of knowing, then it must be known and taught in the same way that other forms of knowing are known and taught: through accurate data gathering and presentation, logical organization and deduction, and critical rational analysis (Origen, *OFP* 1; J. Wesley, *WJW* 7:1–45; Pannenberg, *RAH*).

Jesus urged a critical habit of mind: "If I am not doing the works of my Father, then do not believe me; but if I do them, even though you do not believe me, believe the works, that you may know and understand that the Father is in me" (John 10:37; Athanasius, *On the Incarnation* 18.1–3; Augustine, *Tractates on John*, 48). Personal trust is strengthened, not watered down, by the rigor of fair intellectual inquiry.

Intellectual assent is not the whole of faith, but remains one of its elementary aspects. Historical knowledge rightly should enhance and clarify faith, which is and remains essentially the gift of God, yet it may also thwart the growth of faith when operating out of ideological premises alien to faith (Clement of Alex., *Stromata* 5.1; Irenaeus, *Ag. Her.* 1).

John's Gospel was written for this specific purpose: "that you may believe *that* Jesus is the Christ, the Son of God, and that by believing *you may have life in his name*" (John 20:31, italics added). The belief is primarily *in* Jesus personally, but this presupposes *that* sufficient evidence is being set forth to make its plausibility obvious (Augustine, *Enchiridion*, 7–9; *Conf.* 6.5). When adequate evidence is laid out, it is expected that by grace one is being made able to believe, or at least pray for grace to believe. "Faith comes from hearing the message, and the message is heard through the word of Christ" (Rom. 10:17; John of Damascus, *OF* 4.10).

Saving faith is distinguished from the convergence of probabilities, from purely private experience, and from a direct infusion of knowledge from God (*SCD* 1242, 2025). It is the act of the will by which one yields freely to the persuasive power of God's revelation) (*SCD 1637*, 1791). Melanchthon summed up this point: "Faith signifies *assent* to the promise of God (which is in the *intellect*), and with this assent is necessarily connected *confidence* (which is the will), willing and accepting the promised reconciliation" (*CR 21*.790; *SHD* 2:361). Lacking personal trust, bare intellectual assent is hardly sufficient for salvation. "You believe that there is one God. Good! Even the demons believe that—and shudder" (James 2:19; Augustine, *Tractates* 22.72; *FC* 79:203). Such belief is not likely to survive skeptical inquiry, much less risk-taking discipleship, even unto death.

Trust of the Heart

Job's expression of deep trust in God points to the radical character of risk in faith: "Though he slay me, yet will I trust in him" (Job 13:15; Ephrem, *Comm. on Job* 13.15).

Beyond intellectual assent, personal trust embraces a centered emotive movement, a concentrated passionate leap of the whole person toward the mercy of God (Kierkegaard, *CUP*:90–97; *TC*:26–39). Faith requires the assent of the whole heart, the confident affirmation of the whole person, not of the mind only.

In trusting God from the heart, faith abandons all competing idolatrous sources of reliance. Faith excludes all other claims of gods that pretend to bestow the final meaning upon life. Faith cleaves only to One worthy of absolute trust, the triune God.

"Justifying faith implies, not only a Divine evidence or conviction that God was in Christ reconciling the world unto Himself, but a sure trust and confidence that Christ died for *my* sins, that He loved me and gave Himself for me" (Wesley, *WJW* 5:53–64). The receiver in faith's receptivity and actor in faith's activity is not separable from the person's mind, or sensory apparatus, or will. Rather faith is an act whose locus is precisely the unifying center of the human person. This is what is signified by the metaphor of the heart. "For it is with your heart that you believe and are justified" (Rom. 10:10; Augustine, *The Christian Life* 13).

Amid persecution the creed risked saying, "I believe." That required an utterance from the heart. The whole person—not just the mind or affections—is saying, "I believe." No human act more completely engages and embraces the whole person than the act of believing (Clement of Rome, *Corinth* 22–39). This act of the heart is the faith by which salvation is received (Calvin, *Inst.* 1.14; 3.2; J. Edwards, *Religious Affections*, *WJE* 1:236).

Decision of the Will

Closure of the struggle of faith comes in the decision of the will. Faith is a radical willing by which the person decisively renounces other gods. Faith is finally an unfettered kind of willing: a personal will to trust the will of God.

This volitional element of faith is not merely a momentary surrender to God, but a determination to walk daily trusting in God, responsible to the divine requirement. Grace awakens a distinctive type of volition that is willing to forgo other forms of trust in favor of personal trust in the Source and End of all finite values (Chrysostom, *None Can Harm*; H. R. Niebuhr, "On Faith in God," *RMWC*). In the no said to lesser values is a yes to the source of all creaturely values. A new will is born—the will to trust God above all else, abandoning all competing idolatries, excluding all other claims of gods that pretend to bestow the final meaning upon life, cleaving only to One worthy of absolute trust.

Faith surrenders the whole mind and heart and soul to God (Clement of Rome, *Corinth.* 10.1, 11), receiving and appropriating Christ's justifying action and freely sharing in Christ's obedience unto death as the source of pardon and renewal (Luther, *LW* 41:110–13; Calvin, *Inst.* 3.2; 3.11).

Faith in Christ is therefore a decision. "I stand at the door and knock. If anyone hears my voice and opens the door, I will come in and eat with him, and he with me" (Rev. 3:20; Jerome, *Hom. on Ps.* 9.75; *FC* 48:67). The choice is ours. "To all who received him, to those who believed in his name, he gave the right to become children of God" (John 1:12). Faith answers yes to the invitation to "come to me" (Matt. 11:28), to drink from "a spring of water welling up to eternal life" (John 4:14), responding to his call to "trust in God, trust also in me" (John 14:1; Augustine, *Tractates on John* 67.1–2).

Trust may become a habit of will enabled by continuing grace. The will rests in God as its chief present good and its future hope of good.

Jesus demanded of the rich young ruler that he sell all (Mark 10:21; Augustine, *Letters*, 157 To Hilarius). Those who wish first to bury their dead or bid farewell to their loved ones have not yet understood the radical nature of the impending reign of God (Luke 9:57–62; Origen, *AEG* 3:256). The lordship of Christ comes before one's father, daughter, mother, brother, sister, wife, family members, property, or even life itself (Matt. 10:34–39; Luke 14:26).

The Gift of Faith

Faith is of God precisely while being fully willed by human will. The convergence is powerfully expressed in the prayer "Lord, I believe, help thou mine unbelief"

(Mark 9:24; Augustine, *Sermons on NT Lessons* 65). Augustine reasoned: "Now if faith is simply of free will, and is not given by God, why do we pray for those who will not believe? This it would be absolutely useless to do, unless we believe, with perfect propriety, that Almighty God is able to turn to believe wills that are perverse and opposed to faith" (*On Grace and Free Will*, 14:29).

The New Nature

The birth of faith is accompanied by the birth of a new spiritual nature that is revulsed by sin and cannot ever again be content to live under its tyranny. With God's own Spirit aiding in the battle against temptation, even if the conflict of spirit and flesh persists, the new spiritual life is confident of finally overcoming (2 Cor. 5:6–10; 1 John 2:28; Andreas, *Catena on 1 John* 2:28, *CEC* 120).

The old sin nature has been crucified with Christ (Gal. 2:20). The power of evil is broken in the life of all who receive and trust in the atoning work of the cross, whose faith becomes active in love.

The regenerate are called to "Be self-controlled and alert. Your enemy the devil prowls around like a roaring lion looking for someone to devour. Resist him, standing firm in the faith" (1 Pet. 5:8, 9a; Bede, *On 1 Pet.*). The adversary continues to test the faithful, as Jesus remarked to Peter: "Simon, Simon, Satan has asked to sift you as wheat. But I have prayed for you, Simon, that your faith may not fail" (Luke 22:31, 32).

The full armor of God allows the believer to "stand against the devil's schemes. For our struggle is not against flesh and blood, but against the rulers, against the authorities, against the powers of this dark world and against the spiritual forces of evil in the heavenly realms" (Eph. 6:11, 12). The faithful are enabled to "Resist the devil, and he will flee from you. Come near to God and he will come near to you" (James 4:7–8; Andreas, *Catena*, *CEC* 30).

To trust in the Son is to trust in the Father by the Spirit. Paul was "sent not from men nor by man, but by Jesus Christ and God the Father, who raised him from the dead" (Gal. 1:1). "God will credit righteousness" to those "who believe in him who raised Jesus our Lord from the dead" (Rom. 4:24).

Faith trusts in "the living God" who has "appeared in a body," and now is being "vindicated by the Spirit" (1 Tim. 3:15, 16; Gregory of Nyssa, *Ag. Eunomius* 5.3). In attaching faith to the eternal Son, one attaches faith to the triune God. Hence Christian teaching speaks personally of the object of saving faith as Jesus Christ. Faith trusts in the person of Christ as truly God, truly human, mediator between God and humanity. "Salvation is found in no one else, for there is no other name under heaven given to men by which we must be saved" (Acts 4:12). To those who hesitated to personally trust in him, he retorted, "You do not know me or my Father," for, "If you knew me, you would know my Father also" (John 8:19; Origen, *AEG* 3:268–72). Some will still "demand miraculous signs," and others "look for wisdom, but we preach Christ crucified" (1 Cor. 1:23; Ambrosiaster, *Comm. on Paul*, 1 Cor. 1.22–23).

In personally trusting in Christ, faith at the same time trusts in the testimony to the work of Christ—his incarnate coming, his obedience to law, his proclamation and teaching, his life and ministry, his death and resurrection and promised coming again.

Grace Enables Faith

The close relation of faith and grace is explicitly set forth in Paul's summary formula: "By grace you have been saved, through faith" (Eph. 2:8; Ambrose, *On Sacraments* 5.4.19). Hence faith is simultaneously a gift of God and a free human act. God works in us that we may have a good will, and with us when we have a good will (Augustine, *On Nature and Grace*, 81–85). Since "it is God who works in you," you are asked to "continue to work out your salvation" (Phil. 2:12, 13). Faith does not forget to act, nor does it act by itself. It acts in constant free response to God's action (Augustine, *On Grace and Free Will* 21).

Faith's sufficiency is from God, yet so as to enable freedom, action, trust. "This righteousness from God comes through faith in Jesus Christ to all who believe." All who have sinned "are justified freely by his grace through the redemption that came by Christ Jesus" (Rom. 3:22–24; Tertullian, *Ag. Marcion* 5.13).

God does not believe for us, but enables our believing, just as God does not walk for us, eat for us, or see for us. As we may refuse to walk, eat, or see, so we may refuse to believe. But when we believe, it is truly our own action, yet always enabled by grace, exercising the gracious ability God has given us to trust in the eventful Word spoken in Jesus Christ (John of Damascus, *OF* 4.10).

One cannot posit faith without a believer any more than one can posit thought without a thinker. "For as a writing-reed or a dart has need of one to use it, so grace also has need of believing minds. . . . It is God's to grant grace, but yours to receive and guard" (Cyril of Jerusalem, *Catech. Lect.* 1.3). "Therefore, the promise comes by faith, so that it may be by grace" (Rom. 4:16; Prosper of Aquitaine, *Call of All Nations* 1.24).

Benefits of Salvation

The benefits of salvation are summarized as justification (receiving the pardon of God canceling our sin), regeneration (receiving new life in the Spirit and participation in the family of God), and sanctification (receiving the growth-enabling, completing, maturing, perfecting grace of God that leads toward holiness of heart and life).

Each tends increasingly toward the experiential actualization of life in Christ, toward concrete participation in the body of Christ. These benefits were economically expressed in the letter to Titus in this way: "He saved us through the washing of rebirth and renewal by the Holy Spirit, whom he poured out on us generously through Jesus Christ our Savior, so that, having been justified by his grace, we might become heirs having the hope of eternal life" (Titus 3:5; Augustine, *Sermons* 213.8).

Faith Working Through Love

How Faith Works and Works Believe

Faith is the sole condition of salvation. No merit is needed on our part, since the merit offered on the cross is sufficient. One is justified by faith alone, yet faith is not alone but accompanied by the Spirit's fruits of good works (Leo I, *Sermons* 90). Faith is "the alone instrument of justification; yet it is not alone in the person justified, but is ever accompanied with all other saving graces, and is no dead faith, but worketh by love" (Westminster *Conf.* 11; cf. Augustine, *Faith and Works* 16.27).

Faith is known by its works as a tree is known by its fruit (Luther, *The Freedom of a Christian*, MLS:71–80). As the tree lives out of the interconnected difference between its fruits and its roots, so the Christian life lives out of the interconnected difference between faith and works (Calvin, *Inst.* 2.2).

Faith Elicits Good Works, Not Merit

Faith bears fruit through responsive love toward the next one we see. "For in Christ Jesus neither circumcision nor uncircumcision has any value. The only thing that counts is faith expressing itself through love" (Gal. 5:6; Marius Victorinus, *Epis. to Gal.* 2.5.6).

"Faith receives, love gives" (Luther, *WA* 8.355). "Faith brings man to God; love brings God to men. Through faith man allows God to do him good; through love God does good to men." The Christian is therefore through faith a free lord subject to none and through love a ministering servant responsive to all (Luther, *Freedom of the Christian, MLS*:79–81). Faith is the foundation of the Christian life of love (Tho. Aq., *ST* 2–2, Q4). "Faith remains the doer and love remains the deed" (Luther, in *SHD* 2:275).

"Faith is the beginning, love the end. And these two in union are divine. All other things relating to a holy life are consequences of these" (Ignatius, *Eph.* 14.1). Other virtues are daughters of faith (Shepherd of Hermas 3.8.3, 4; 5.2.3). Faith and love are the whole sum of the Christian life (Ignatius, *Smyrna* 6.1).

The faith by which one lives in union with Christ is vitally active. It walks. Unattended by good works, it proves to be not a living but a dead faith. "As the body without the spirit is dead, so faith without deeds is dead" (James 2:26; Didymus the Blind, *Comm. on James* 2.26).

"But someone will say, 'You have faith; I have deeds.' Show me your faith without deeds, and I will show you my faith by what I do" (James 2:18). It is a "dead faith" that fails to lead to the obedience of faith, the life of works of love, for it lacks our appropriation of Christ's reconciling ministry. This is why "faith without deeds is useless" (James 2:20). "Faith by itself, if it is not accompanied by action, is dead" (James 2:17; Leo I, *Sermons* 10.3).

To Faith Are Added Hope and Love

Genuine faith is always found in the company of hope and love (1 Cor. 13:13). As the receptive act of responding to promised grace, faith is intrinsically connected with hope (Heb. 11:1; Barnabas 1.4–6; 4.8). As the active process of sharing grace, faith is intrinsically related to love toward the neighbor (Barnabas 2.2; 11.8–11). Faith, the "mother of us all," is characteristically "accompanied by hope, and led by love" (Polycarp, *Phil.* 3).

Hope is that excellent habit of the heart by which one securely trusts that God will be faithful to his promise and will provide the faithful with fit means to receive it. The ground of hope is the confidence that God will provide means to save. The apostle prayed, "May the God of hope fill you with all joy and peace as you trust in him, so that you may overflow with hope by the power of the Holy Spirit" (Rom. 15:13; Origen, *Comm. on Rom.* 15.13). In this way hope becomes "an anchor for the soul, firm and secure" (Heb. 6:19).

"To faith, therefore, must be added hope, and to hope, love" (Augustine, *Sermons* 16.6; cf. Gregory I, *Hom. on the Gospel* 29). Faith works precisely through love (Gal. 5:6). "Faith working by love, not faith without love, is the means and condition of man's justification before God" (Fourteen Theses, Old Catholic Union Conference, *CC* 2:546). When Paul wrote that one is "justified without the works of the law," he did not mean that faith is sufficient precisely when it "leads a bad life and has no good deeds to allege. It is impossible that such a character should be deemed a 'vessel of election' " (Augustine, *Grace and Free Will* 7.18).

Love delights in the good of the beloved (Hilary, *On Matt.* 4.27). "If a stranger fall at your feet, homeless and a foreigner, welcome Him who for your sake was a stranger, and that among His own" (Gregory Nazianzus, *Orat.* 40.31). "Not everyone who says to me, 'Lord, Lord,' will enter the kingdom of heaven, but only he who does the will of my Father who is in heaven" (Matt. 7:21; Chrysostom, *Hom. on Matt.* Hom. 24.1). "If I have a faith that can move mountains, but have not love, I am nothing" (1 Cor. 13:2).

Meanwhile, the arrogant idea of "works of supererogation" (presuming to do more than God requires) is strongly rejected (Thirty-nine Articles, 14). Christ taught, "So you also, when you have done everything you were told to do, should say, 'We are unworthy servants' " (Luke 17:10).

Faith Alone

As the embryo has no part whatever in its conception, so the recipient of saving grace makes no self-initiated contribution whatever to justifying grace. Those who are dead in sin have no part, no voice, no thought, no will whatever in the awakening moment of their regeneration. We are not justified by our loving or cleaving but only by divine grace to which faith responds in the trust that loves (Eph. 2:1–10).

When Christians speak of "faith alone," using the "exclusive particles"— "without works," "without law"—this is done in order to exclude any hint that we may be justified by our own works or actions, intentions or deeds. These precise exclusions do not intend to deny that good works follow faith as its expected fruits (Bede, *On Epis. Of James* 2.14–26; Calvin, *Inst.* 3.11–17). They seek to exclude all human boasting, all self-righteousness. The intent is "that neither renewal, sanctification, virtues, nor other good works are our righteousness before God, nor are they to be made and posited to be a part or a cause of our justification, nor under any kind of pretense, title, or name are they to be mingled with the article of justification as pertinent or necessary to it. The righteousness of faith consists solely in the forgiveness of sins by sheer grace, entirely for the sake of Christ's merit" (Formula of Concord).

Only is an excluding term. What does it exclude, when we say "faith alone" or "faith only"? Only surely does not exclude grace or the cross or obedience. For faith lives its very life out of grace through the cross that elicits obedience (Creed of Dositheus, 13). "Faith alone" rightly understood means that nothing else is required as a subjective condition than faith as the full reception of justification. God the Son offers sufficient sacrifice on the cross, faith accepts and trusts it, and the outcome is justification by grace through faith (Thirty-nine Articles of Religion, 11). The reason these explicit disclaimers have seemed so necessary is that some have set forth a skewed teaching in which good works appeared to be requisite to faith or a teaching of justification conditioned upon works of satisfaction (Augustine, *Spirit and Letter* 50–60, Sermon 151).

Melanchthon wisely distinguished that only faith justifies, but faith is not alone (*Sola fides justificat, sed fides non est sola*). Faith can never be "alone" in the sense of being without grace or without works of love. Against the thesis that works are necessary to salvation, the Formula of Concord concluded that good works voluntarily performed are commanded and commended, and that faith brings with it good works (art. 4; cf. Luther, *Instructions for Visitors*).

The Augsburg Confession taught that "faith is bound to bring forth good fruits, and that it is necessary to do good works commanded by God, because of God's will, but not that we should rely on those works to merit justification before God" (art. 6). Faith does not justify because it works, for that would shift the justifier from God to human faith (Calvin, *Inst.* 3.11–14). "We confess him by our works" (*2 Clement* 4.3). Good works make evident the sincerity of faith (Matt. 5:14–16; Rom. 2:22–24; 12:1, 2; Titus 2:14; James 1:25; Valerian of Cimiez, *Sermons* 7.5).

The Faithful Are Not Justified "On Account of" Their Faith

It is misleading to suggest that we are justified on account of our faith. Rather we are justified through faith, in the sense that faith is the only means by which Christ's work is rightly received. Faith does not in and of itself justify. No one is saved on account of *(propter)* faith, but by *(per)* faith. It is not bare faith of itself that saves, but Christ who saves through faith. The saving efficacy lies not in the response—not in the disconnected act of faith itself—but in the One to whom faith responds (Chemnitz, *TNC*:411–20, 450–51).

It is not our faith that is accepted by God, but Christ's work. It is Christ's work on our behalf that faith receives and trusts, and thereby is reconciled to God. Faith is rendered possible by grace—it is not that faith renders grace possible (Chrysostom, *Hom on Phil.*, 12.3.7–9; Calvin, *Inst.* 3.14–17). It is not as working but as trusting that sinners enter into union with Christ by faith and receive pardon. Faith does not *in itself justify* in the sense that it would brashly assume itself to be the source of righteousness. Oppositely, faith is a renunciation of all claims of righteousness, trusting in Christ's righteousness (Rom. 4; Phil. 3:9).

This teaching was prototypically defined in the Reformed tradition by the Westminster divines that God justifies "not by imputing faith itself, the act of believing, or any other evangelical obedience to them, as their righteousness; but by imputing the obedience and satisfaction of Christ unto them, they receiving and resting on him and his righteousness by faith; which faith they have not of themselves, it is the gift of God" (Westminster *Conf.*, 11; Athanasius, *Resurrection Letters*, 5).

The Increase of Faith: Degrees of Faith

That there are degrees of faith is evident from Jesus' distinction between those of "little faith" (Matt. 6:30) and those of "great faith" (Matt. 8:10; Archelaus, *Disputation with Manes* 42).

Faith may increase. Its intellectual vitality may deepen, its emotive and volitional strength grow. "Your faith is growing more and more, and the love every one of you has for each other is increasing" (2 Thess. 1:3). The disciples pled with the Lord, "Increase our faith!" (Luke 17:5). To increase faith is to strengthen it by the Holy Spirit (Cyril of Alex., *Comm. on Luke,* Hom. 113–116). Faith may grow in love, peace, hope, and joy. "Our hope is that, as your faith continues to grow, our area of activity among you will greatly expand" (2 Cor. 10:15; Chrysostom, *The Paralytic*).

Jesus spoke of those who may have "believed for a while, but in the time of testing they fall away" (Luke 8:13; Augustine, *Trin.*, *FC* 45:372). Timothy was instructed to "hold on to faith," aware that some had entirely "shipwrecked their faith" (1 Tim. 1:19; Basil, *On the Spirit* 30.77). Paul specifically named two shipwrecks—Hymenaeus and Alexander—and elsewhere we learn of others (Demas, Philetus). Even "if you think you are standing firm," Paul warned the Corinthian believers, "be careful that you don't fall!" (1 Cor. 10:12). Some may "fall away," having "tasted the heavenly gift," having once "shared in the Holy Spirit, who have tasted the goodness of the word of God and the powers of the coming age" (Heb. 6:4, 5).

Humanity cannot undo what God has done on the cross. One or another may fail to accept it, but that does not silence the Word finally spoken there or negate the act accomplished for all. Those who live in Christ are promised sufficient grace to carry them to completion of God's intention (Phil. 3:12–14; Chrysostom, *Hom. on Phil.* 12. 3.12). The parable of the unmerciful servant tells this story exactly of one who having received pardon forfeited it (Matt. 18).

Weak faith and strong faith share in all that Christ is, and hence equally justify. Yet faith may be more or less effective in bearing fruits and become more or less active in love. Though faith may increase, the efficacy of justifying faith is not proportional to its degree. For in justifying faith, all effectiveness is derived not from faith as such but from that which calls faith forth, namely, grace.

While there may be degrees of faith, justification stands firm as a once for all declaratory act of God that offers new birth. The justifying declaration is not itself something that grows and develops. It occurs, like the bang of the judge's gavel, as a once for all act of a court. It is received, like birth, in a moment, however long its period of gestation may have been. Classic exegetes concluded that weak or immature faith justifies (as in the case of the thief on the cross, Luke 23:43) as wonderfully as strong faith (Origen, *IOEP* 2:160; Calvin, *Comm.* 17:311). Both those who arrived at the vineyard early and those who arrived late are equally justified by the Lord's merit (Matt. 20:1–16; Augustine, *Sermons on New Testament Lessons*, 37).

Weak faith may lack sufficient experience with overcoming temptation to have grown in firm assurance of salvation. That may come with strength only through time and development, as with the exercise of a muscle. But the merit of Christ is equally effective whether faith is weak or strong. The strength of faith does not increase the merit of Christ. The weakness of faith does not diminish the merit of Christ (Luke 23:43; 17:5; 2 Cor. 10:15; 2 Thess. 1:3; Augustine, *Sermons on New Testament Lessons* 17).

Meanwhile Christians daily pray, "Forgive us our debts, as we also have forgiven our debtors, and lead us not into temptation" (Matt. 6:12, 13). Paradoxically those most keenly rooted in faith are those most likely to recognize their own sin most clearly.

Justification and Sanctification

The great privilege of those born of God is to be free from guilt, free from condemnation, dead to sin (J. Wesley, *WJW* 5:223–33). If it occurs subsequently that through infirmities we find the old syndromes reemerging, this reminds us that the carnal nature has not been wholly destroyed, but providentially is permitted to remain as a part of continued growth in faith, which grows only by being challenged. Though sin may remain in believers, it does not reign in those who have received justifying grace (Origen, *Comm. on Rom.* 6.12; J. Wesley, *WJW* 5:144–46). Where pardon is effectively reigning, sin is not reigning (Rom. 5:20–6:12; Augustine, *Comm. Serm. Mount* 1.22.77).

Justifying grace offers the faithful a new and reconciled relation to the incomparably holy God, while sanctifying grace works to make that relation real in actual behavior. By justifying grace the new birth begins. By sanctifying grace the neonate is nurtured and enabled to grow.

Justification is an objective act of God, a declaration of acquittal. As such, it is addressed to humanity once for all in Jesus Christ, waiting to be received by faith. Sanctification, the Spirit's work to apply the work of Christ to the heart and life of the believer, is an experiential process beginning with a new birth (by justifying grace) and continuing with growth (through sanctifying grace) toward maturation (through completing grace). Sanctifying grace elicits gradual growth in believers, who may increase or decline in strength of faith. Justifying grace is always the same—simple and declarative, instantaneously addressed to all humanity in the cross, whether the faith receiving it is weak or strong (Rom. 3–12; Pope, *Compend.* 3:28–36; Hodge, *ST:*213–30).

Since justification is a declaration on our behalf, it changes our standing before God. It has effectively occurred already in Jesus Christ on the cross. Yet each one who lives in time requires some time to grow more fully aware of it (Hilary of Arles, *Intro. Comm. on 1 Pet.* 2.2). Life in Christ does not come full grown, but grows as all life grows (2 Thess. 1:3). It is the work of the Spirit to enable this growth in the soul's own time.

Whether Good Works on Earth Are Honored in Heaven

The active life of doing good works is the implied outcome of one's continuing by grace to be accounted righteous (James 2:14–26). Where faith lapses entirely and its working in love dies, God does not continue to account our former faith to us for righteousness as if faith were still alive. The subjective continuity of our being accounted righteous is thus contingent upon faith that bears fruits worthy of repentance (Matt. 7:16–20; Chrysostom, *Hom. on Matt.* 42). A total absence of good works would indicate the lack of the justifying faith that works through love. Lacking any good works, the resulting life can hardly be called justified or faithful or accounted righteous (Leo I, *Sermons* 11.1; J. Wesley, *WJW* 5:447–67).

Each of the beatitudes is accompanied by a promised reward. The merciful are promised to receive mercy. The pure in heart will see God. The meek will inherit the earth. They sing, "Rejoice and be glad, because great is your reward in heaven" (Matt. 5:12; Incomplete Work on Matt. Hom. 9; Calvin, *Inst.* 3.17, 18). In this way those good works enabled by grace and grounded in responsive faith will be brought to fruition in the heavenly reward merited solely by Christ's obedience (Rev. 2:10; James 1:12; cf. Augustine, *Letters, to Sixtus* 194.20 Ambrose, *Duties of the Clergy* 1.15, 57).

The leading exponent of salvation by grace through faith, Paul, is also the preeminent teacher of heavenly reward for good works grounded in faith: "Each will be rewarded according to his own labor" (1 Cor. 3:8). "God 'will give to each person according to what he has done.' To those who by persistence in doing good seek glory, honor and immortality, he will give eternal life" (Rom. 2:6; quoting Ps. 62:12).

Timothy was taught realistically to expect that in this life "everyone who wants to live a godly life in Christ Jesus will be persecuted" (2 Tim. 3:12). Both Jesus and Paul repeatedly employed the metaphor of reward of future blessedness for faith working through love (Matt. 5:12; 6:1–6; 25:34–40; 1 Cor. 3:8; Col. 2:18). Good works engender in the faithful a character that corresponds with God's own holiness and love, making them more fit to receive God's gifts and share in God's kingdom as heirs of God's family (Hermas, *Mand.* 5.1.3; 10.3.2).

Those who have limited ability or opportunity yet cooperate fully with the grace they are given are fully rewarded, whether weak or strong, mentally handicapped or geniuses. The criterion of heavenly reward is not a quantitative form of justice, but an equity that God is wise enough to render proportionally (Photius, *Fragm. On Heb.* 6.7; Tho. Aq., *ST* suppl., Q96). Trust him: "God is not unjust; he will not forget your work" (Heb. 6:10; Chrysostom, On *Epis. to Heb.* 10.5).

There remains an enormous disparity between our best temporal works and the eternal reward God promises to give us. Though eternal life is indeed a reward, it is such only as a gift. "It is a reward because our works make us fit to receive it; but it is not wages, because it exceeds the intrinsic earning value of our works" (Hall, *DT* 8:274; cf. Tho. Aq, *ST* 1–2, Q114.3).

The New Birth

The Spirit Offers New Life to Sinners

Regeneration is the work of the Spirit by which new life in Christ is imparted to one dead in sin. It implies a change in the inward person by which a disposition to the holy life is originated, and in which that life begins. It is the act of God by which the governing disposition of the person begins to be responsive to the reconciling God (Formula of Concord 3–6).

Anyone who draws near the matchless event of a live human birth feels directly the unique value of human life. The pastor who visits a mother who has just given birth may on the same day visit a family that has lost a loved one in death. Nothing is more awe inspiring than to be present in the midst of the coming or passing of life—birth or death.

The doctrine of regeneration is that part of the teaching of salvation that focuses upon the new birth of life that is given even when we are dead in our sins. New birth follows from trusting in grace. The Christian teaching of new birth proposes to establish its proper definition, authorship, means, and effects.

"Peter uses the words *regeneration* and *restitution* to signify the introduction of birth after the destruction of the first generation of mankind. For how could that not have been destroyed, seeing that it is corrupt, in order to make room for the incorruptible which is coming and which will remain forever? For there is a first birth, in the descent of Adam, which is mortal and therefore corruptible, but there is also a later birth which comes from the Spirit and the ever-living Word of God" (Didymus the Blind, *Comm. on 1 Pet.* 1.23).

Defining Regeneration

The term that denotes the teaching of the new birth is regeneration. It comes from the Greek word for rebirth (Matt. 19:28; John 3:3; 1 Pet. 1.23)—which means literally to "be generated again" or to be "born once more." A new beginning is offered by the Spirit. Those who have been spiritually dead are rescued from the dominion of sin and enabled with right affections to love God and keep God's commandments (Didymus the Blind, *Comm. on 1 Pet.* 1.23; Goodwin, *Works* 1:167–87; Wakefield, *CT* 2:425). It is a spiritual remaking, a re-creation by which the sinner becomes child of God.

Though the new birth reverberates throughout behavior and the emotive life, it is not finally reducible to a psychological change or a moral turning or an external profession of religion or the mere observance of forms, rules, or duties of religion or a human remedy for human failures (Bede, *On 1 Pet.* 1.23).

New birth is the decisive work of God in the economy of salvation whereby spiritual life in Christ is imparted by the Holy Spirit (Chrysostom, *Baptismal Instructions ACW* 31:135–39). It is the birth of personal union with the living Christ. It is a renewal of life in the Spirit lost in the fall. It is characterized by a radical reversal of the direction of the will. The selfless love of God begins to take the place of the godless love of self (Augustine, *Conf.*, 4). At every phase it is the work of grace eliciting free human responsiveness.

The new birth has often been viewed as a defining doctrine of *modern* evangelical Christians which speaks often of being "born again." But even more it is a basic teaching of *ancient* ecumenical Christianity. As such, it is a teaching shared by Christian believers of all times and places (Ussher, *Brief Declaration of the Universality of the Church, Works* 2:493–97).

How the Verdict of Justification Differs from the New Birth

In justification a new relation with God is declared. In regeneration, new life is given that bestows and embodies that new relationship. Justification refers to a change in one's standing before God; regeneration, to a new beginning of a life that manifests that new standing.

Justification is God's act, a declaratory act that comes to the sinner from without. Regeneration begins a new life in which that relationship is actually manifested within the believer's thoughts, words, and actions. Justification is what God the Son does for us, distinguished from what the Spirit begins to do in us through regeneration and continues through sanctification and union with Christ (J. Wesley, *WJW* 5:506–13).

The behavioral righteousness of the believer is evidence of new spiritual birth, for "everyone who does what is right has been born of him" (1 John 2:29). But behavioral righteousness is not a precondition of new birth, for no one is born due to meriting it (Isho'dad of Merv, *Comm. 1 John* 2:29; Calvin, *Inst.* 3.11; 4.15–16). Through regeneration the Spirit comes alive in us to begin to break the dominion of sin, to enable us to walk in the way of holiness (Goodwin, *Works* 1:151–78).

New birth is not a teaching detachable from justifying grace. Rather it is the act of the Spirit by which one is enabled to enter into this new life of grace-enabled justifying faith. It occurs the moment faith is given and received. What immediately follows upon the act of faith is variously described as pardon, new birth, and adoption into the family of God (Athanasius, *On the Incarnation* of the Word 14.1–2; Pope, *Compend.* 3:5; Beyschlag, *NTT* 2: 453; C. Hodge, *The Way of Life*:286).

Justification pardons guilt; regeneration renews our broken spirit and fallen moral nature. A justification without a new birth would be like an act of pardon with nothing following it—no new life, no freedom, no responsiveness. To imagine one justified and not at the same time regenerated would be to imagine one whose past sin is pardoned but who is not alive. The agent of justification is the Son; of regeneration, the Spirit (Basil, *On the Spirit*; Owen, *Works* 3:207; Strong, *ST*:471). We are justified in a courtroom. We are regenerated in a family.

Justification refers to "that great work which God does for us, in forgiving our sins." Regeneration refers to "the great work which God does in us, in renewing our fallen nature." Justification is a change in the relation of God and humanity (hence a relational change), whereas new birth is the beginning of a behavioral (hence a visible or "real") change that actively manifests the change of relationship (J. Wesley, *WJW* 5:212).

These two strands do not compete but complement. Those justified are thereby declared sons and daughters of God, born of Spirit into the family of God. Justification and regeneration teachings are intrinsically related: "To those who believed in his name, he gave the *right* to become *children* of God" (John 1:12; Calvin, *Inst.* 3.3, 4.17.8).

Biblical Word Pictures: Receiving New Life in the Spirit

New life in Christ is described as a new birth (John 3:3–7; James 1:18; 1 Pet. 1:23) whereby a new nature is being given to the new creation in Christ (2 Cor. 5:17; 2 Pet. 1:4; Chrysostom, *Hom. on John* 24.2).

A series of parallel terms recur in scripture to describe this singular new birth: born anew (John 3:7); born of God (John 1:13); born of the Spirit (John 3:5); renewed by the Holy Spirit (Titus 3:5); resurrected (Phil. 3:10); passing from death to life (Eph. 1:1, 10); new creation (Gal. 6:15); a new person, renewed in spirit (Eph. 4:23–24); renewing of our minds (Rom. 12:2); renewal in knowledge in the image of the Creator (Col. 3:10); spiritual quickening of life where before there was not life (1 Pet. 3:18; Gregory of Nazianzus, *On the Holy Spirit*, Orat. 5.28)

These terms do not point to sequential stages of regeneration but to the single pivotal act of God's renewing of the human spirit in Christ, "as though He were creating us again" (*Letter of Barnabas* 6:11). The classic Christian exegetes expressed this teaching by examining this cluster of biblical word pictures.

The Unmerited Gift

This birth occurs through God's own initiative: "For you have been born again, not of perishable seed, but of imperishable, through the living and enduring word of God" (1 Pet. 1:23). As with the genesis of all creation, the new birth of the redeemed spirit occurs simply by God speaking a word to bring life out of nothingness (Theodore of Mopsuestia, *Comm. on John* 2.3.4–5).

Before there can be a regenerated freedom, there must be a regenerative event (Justin Martyr, *First Apol.* 61; Calvin, *Inst.* 3.19). As by physical birth one comes to life by entering into a wholly new environment, so by unmerited spiritual birth one is enabled to breathe in the new atmosphere of grace.

No one chooses to be born. One can only receive, not seize, life. No one can give birth to oneself. No one has ever claimed or demanded or even hoped to be born. Conception is a wholly receptive act of being quickened by another. So in the new birth do we wholly receive new life from God the Spirit (John 1:13; 3:1–8; 1 John 5:1–18). No one who is in fact dead has any power whatever to make an attempt first to seek to qualify for life and then ask to be born. Only upon being born may questions and hopes be conceived. Only after birth may one then begin to deal with the options and descriptions and prospects of life (Chrysostom, *Hom. on John* 24.3).

As the living of life follows birth, so does the renewed life follow regenerating grace (1 John 3:9–10; Augustine, *Hom. on Epist. of John* 5). Regeneration is intrinsically experiential, in the same way that birth is experienced: with a beginning point in time.

The Circumcision of the Heart

The promise was made to the covenant people that, when they take possession of the land of promise, "the Lord your God will circumcise your hearts and the hearts of your descendants, so that you may love him with all your heart and with all your soul, and life" (Deut. 30:6; Col. 2:11). The circumcised heart is set apart, consecrated wholly to God (Rom. 2:29; Chrysostom, *Hom. on Col.* 6.2.11).

The rite of circumcision in Israel and of baptism in the New Israel were both rites of entry into the covenant community. They were liturgically correlated with a spiritual circumcision (a setting apart of life lived toward God) and a spiritual baptism (a life of penitence and faith that shares daily in Christ's death and resurrection; Chrysostom, *Baptismal Instructions*, 31:134–38). "In him you were also circumcised, in the putting off of the sinful nature, not with a circumcision done by the hands of men but with the circumcision done by Christ, having been buried with him in baptism and raised with him through your faith in the power of God, who raised him from the dead" (Col. 2:11, 12; Theodore of Mopsuestia, *Comm. on Col.* 2.12).

The agent of the old circumcision is a knife, cutting away inconsequential tissue. The agent of circumcision of the heart is God the Spirit who enables unimportant things not essential to generativity to be set aside on behalf of a newly generated life.

The New Creation

As the Father creates creaturely life out of nothing, so the Spirit, enabling the mission of the Son, quickens spiritual life *ex nihilo*. "For God, who said, 'Let light shine out of darkness,' made his light shine in our hearts" (2 Cor. 4:6; cf. Acts 26:18). "For you were once darkness, but now you are light in the Lord. Live as children of light" (Eph. 5:8; Jerome, *Epis. to Eph.* 3.5.8).

The spiritual breath or life of God is being imparted to one who lacks life just as abruptly and completely as the breath of natural life was imparted to the first humans in the first creation.

Grounded in this analogy, Paul taught, "Therefore, if anyone is in Christ, he is a new creation; the old has gone, the new has come! All this is from God" (2 Cor.

5:17, 18; cf. Gal. 6:15). "For we are God's workmanship, created in Christ Jesus to do good works" (Eph. 2:10; Cyril of Alex, *Doctrinal Questions and Answers* 2, *Select Letters*:188). The evidence of this radical change is a life of love: "We know that we have passed from death to life, because we love" (1 John 3:14; Augustine, *Hom. on Epist. of John* V).

As with creation, God has "called you out of darkness into his wonderful light" (1 Pet. 2:9). The believer now belongs to a new creation that embraces all members of the body of which Christ is the head, all of whom, having been born anew, now live in Christ, having been "brought from death into life" (Rom. 6:13; Jerome, *Epis. to Eph.* 1.2.1).

As the incarnate Son was conceived by the Holy Spirit yet born in a natural way from the womb of a human mother, so each child of God must be begotten of the Holy Spirit in a birth that occurs precisely with and through a human body, a human soul, a human memory, intelligence, and will. As birth begins a process that continues in growth, so does it occur that the new birth of justification continues in a process of sanctification (John 3:5, 6; Augustine, *Sermon* 71.19; Calvin, *Inst.* 3.1.4; 3.21.7).

Gracious Freedom

The New Will: An Enabling of Freedom Through Grace

As the Incarnate Lord did not appear without a human body and nature that became united personally to his divine nature, so in the work of grace in the new birth of sinners, divine and human agencies work together, with human willing cooperating responsively with divine willing. As the interpenetrating relation of divinity and humanity in Christ remains a mystery, so does the birth of faith remain a mystery.

Though birth is an absolute gift, this does not imply that one being born of God is completely lacking in responsiveness to the gift. For in receiving new life from God, one is by repentance and faith willingly consenting to have the Spirit work to change one's ruling disposition (Ambrose, *Of Holy Spirit* 3.10, 64).

The human will is not a machine mechanistically driven by the Spirit, but rather a renewed personal will that can receive a new spring of action. The efficiency of the Spirit's work does not run contrary to the activity of the human will, but enabling it. Regeneration is neither a divine work without human agency, nor human work apart from God, but a work of God performed precisely under realistic conditions of human willing (Augustine, *On Forgiveness of Sins and Baptism.* 2.8; Barth, *CD*, 2/2:772).

New Birth as Resurrection

The faithful are called to live as if raised from the dead (Col. 2:12; 3:1–2), "to put on the new self, created to be like God in true righteousness and holiness" (Eph. 4:24). Those pardoned by justifying grace are "quickened together with Him and raised into newness of life" (Col. 2:13; Ambrose, *Concerning Repentance* 2.2.9). The moral quickening of believers occurs through participating in Christ's resurrection (Rom. 8:29, 30; Gal. 2:19, 20). The faithful are buried with him through baptism "in order that, just as Christ was raised from the dead through the glory of the Father, we too may live a new life" (Rom. 6:4; Athanasius, *Resurrection Letters* 5.86–92).

"In his great mercy he has given us new birth into a living hope through the resurrection of Jesus Christ from the dead, and into an inheritance that can never perish, spoil or fade" (1 Pet. 1:3, 4). If God has "made us alive with Christ even when we were dead in transgressions" (Eph. 2:1, 5), then boasting is excluded: "What do you have that you did not receive? And if you did receive it, why do you boast?" (1 Cor. 4:7). "Apart from me you can do nothing" (John 15:5). "No one can come to me unless the Father who sent me draws him" (John 6:44; Ambrose, *On Chr. Faith* 2.12.104).

Receiving a New Heart

In new birth the stony heart is remade into a "heart of flesh," as promised by Ezekiel: "I will give them an undivided heart and put a new spirit in them; I will remove from them their heart of stone and give them a heart of flesh" (Ezek. 11:19; Origen, *OFP* 3.1.7; cf. Jer. 31:31–34; Zech. 7:5; Rom. 2:5; Wesley, *NUOT*:2209).

Precisely how eternal life is imparted is not subject to empirical investigation. God the Spirit is not an object. No visible causality can be observed or tracked. But the experiential outcome can be tested and attested: new life in the Spirit.

Those born from above are continually receiving the very breath of life in the Spirit (John 3:16; 10:10; 14:6). "The Spirit is life" (Rom. 8:6). One born of God in faith "has crossed over from death to life" (John 5:24), for "the gift of God is eternal life" (Rom. 6:23). Where the Spirit is, there is eternal life" (Ambrose, *Of the Holy Spirit* 2.3.27). The time has now come when "the dead will hear the voice of the Son of God, and those who hear will live" (John 5:25; Apost. Constitutions 5.1.7).

New Birth as Liberation

This new life is understood as liberation from bondage: "You have been set free from sin and have become servants of righteousness" (Rom. 6:18). It is the truth incarnate that has "set you free" (John 8:32). If "it is for freedom that Christ has set us free," then "Stand free and do not let yourselves be burdened again by a yoke of slavery" (Gal. 5:1; Augustine, *Tractates on John* 40.9). "Now that you have been set free from sin and have become obedient to God, the benefit you reap leads to holiness" (Rom. 6:22; Augustine, *Sermon* 84[134].2; Henry, *CWB* 6:406).

Those whose bondage to sin is now broken may exercise a new freedom to "pursue righteousness, godliness, faith, love, endurance and gentleness" (1 Tim. 6:11). "Sin shall not be your master, because you are not under law, but under grace" (Rom. 6:14; Ambrosiaster, *Comm. on Paul.* Rom 6.14).

New Birth as Setting One's Feet upon the Way of Holiness

Regeneration is the beginning of a radical reversal in moral character from the inordinate love of creaturely goods to walking in the way of holiness (Calvin, *Inst.* 2.3.6). One who is being delivered from bondage to sin is being empowered by the Spirit to begin a new walk, a continuing life in Christ, both in inward disposition and outward action (J. Wesley, *NB*; Watson, *TI* 2:24). In the regenerated life the Holy Spirit works economically, first to change the inner disposition of the soul, then to change the outward behavior.

One who persists in deliberately flouting known requirements of God cannot at the same time be one born of God (Baxter, *PW* 6:530–36). The key biblical texts do not allow easy evasion: "No one who is born of God will continue to sin, because God's seed remains in him; he cannot go on sinning, because he has been born of God" (1 John 3:9; Maximus the Confessor, *Catena, CEC*:125

The struggle to keep oneself free from the entanglements of sin is aided constantly by grace: "We know that anyone born of God does not continue to sin; the one who is born of God keeps him safe, and the evil one cannot harm him" (1 John 5:18; Augustine, *Hom. on Epist. of John* V). This does not imply that one having been born into the family of God cannot fall into sin, or act as if belonging to another family. For the same letter states to the faithful that if, apart from grace, "we claim to be without sin, we deceive ourselves and the truth is not in us" (1 John 1:8; Didymus the Blind, *Comm. on 1 John*.5.15).

"Count yourselves dead to sin but alive to God in Christ Jesus. Therefore do not let sin reign in your mortal body" (Rom. 6:11, 12). You are to "offer yourselves to God, as those who have been brought from death to life" (Rom. 6:13; Origen, *Comm. on Rom.* 6.11; cf. Rom. 12:1). The new life is intended to be continually lived, not to wither and die immediately after the birth has occurred. The Spirit "who began a good work in you will carry it on to completion until the day of Christ Jesus" (Phil. 1:6; Augustine, *On Grace and Free Will* 32; Calvin, *Inst.* 3.18.1).

Word and Spirit in the Regenerate Life

Within the economy of the triune God, the work of calling, forming, preserving, and ordering the kingdom of Christ is committed to the Holy Spirit. It is a work of the Spirit to impart life—first in its original creation, and then when fallen into sin and death, to impart life anew (Owen, *Works* 3:105–52).

The Active Agent in Spiritual Rebirth

Throughout Scripture, giving life is a work of God's own Spirit (James 1:17–18; Augustine, *On Gift of Perseverance* 22.62). The acting power or agent in regeneration is the exemplary Bestower of life (*zōopoion*, Nicene Creed)—God the Spirit (John 3:3–7; Titus 3:5).

The Spirit attests Christ's work within the heart, enabling the grace necessary for repentance, faith, and new birth (Augustine, *On the Grace of Christ* 1.50–51). Through this work of the Spirit, the renewed individual is translated from the dying sphere (realm, kingdom, reign) of existence to the living: "For he has rescued us from the dominion of darkness and brought us into the kingdom of the Son he loves, in whom we have redemption, the forgiveness of sins" (Col. 1:13).

"Regeneration is the work of the Holy Spirit," wrote Ambrose "and the Spirit is the Author of that new man." The benefits of regeneration "cannot remain when its Author is shut out. The Author is not without the gift, nor the gift without the Author. If you claim the grace, believe the power; if you reject the power, do not ask for the grace. He who has denied the Spirit has at the same time denied the gift" (*Of the Holy Spirit* 2.7.64–66). "God sent the Spirit of his Son into our hearts, the Spirit who calls out 'Abba, Father' " (Gal. 4:6).

Faculties Transformed, Not Replaced

This does not imply that in new birth the Spirit works wholly without the human will or affections. For the Spirit's distinct purpose is to transform the will and affections. The Spirit works in and through the motivations, feelings, and behavior. Human faculties are not weakened or circumvented but given a new spring of action (Augustine, *The Spirit and the Letter* 5, 6, 52–54). Rebirth does not impart new human faculties, but enlivens those that had withered amid the history of sin.

Due to that toxic history, humanity is in far worse shape than a stone or lump of clay which lack will. Sinners willfully resist their salvation. The potter can mold the clay, but what if the "clay" has a determined will not to be molded? God does not force godliness or regenerating grace upon human beings, for if forced it could be neither truly godly nor truly just. God draws persons gently toward salvation by calling, illuminating, convicting, and enabling faith wherever there is an opening amid human resistances (John Climacus, *The Ladder of Divine Ascent*, step 4, sec. 121). It is no simple work for the Spirit to create a pure heart and steadfast spirit, considering human recalcitrance (Ps. 51:10).

These resistances continue to war against the Spirit even after one is born of God. "For the sinful nature desires what is contrary to the Spirit" (Gal. 5:17). Even if "in my inner being I delight in God's law," nonetheless: "I see another law at work in the members of my body, waging war against the law of my mind and making me a prisoner of the law of sin at work within my members" (Rom. 7:22, 23; Augustine, *Ag. Julian*, 2.9.32).

The Gospel Preached and Heard Through the Spirit

New birth comes through hearing the gospel. "He chose to give us birth through the word of truth" (James 1:18; cf. Col. 3:10).

The Spirit works immediately in the heart and mediately through the word addressed in scripture, prayer, and sacraments. The whole of Hebrew scripture—law and prophets—forms the backdrop for hearing the life-eliciting gospel, for "through the law we become conscious of sin" (Rom. 3:20). It is through preaching that the faithful are personally born into the Christian community (Augustine, *on Romans* 3–18).

Enabling the hearing of the word written and word preached, the Spirit draws persons toward union with Christ through the preached word, repentance, faith, conversion, and perseverance (Rom. 10:17; 1 Cor. 1:21; 1 Pet. 1:23; Formula of Concord, epitome 2–3). The word is "the sword of the Spirit" (Eph. 6:17) that cuts through human self-deceptions.

Turning Away from Idolatry, the Temple is Rebuilt

Those born anew cast aside the idols of the old way of life. They worship the true God revealed in the new man Christ. The old Adamic aeon remains inveterately idolatrous, wishing both to have gods and to be god. Whether one has worshiped wealth, power, prestige, status, sex, or education, these passing gods are to be put away as gods, however valuable they may remain as creaturely goods (Ezek. 6:1–10; Cyprian, *Treatises* 6).

The human condition is such that it is bound to orient itself toward some center of value—that value that appears to make other values valuable (Luther, *BOC*: 365; H. R. Niebuhr, *RMWC*). Before the history of sin, God was trusted as that center. Afterward, humanity became seduced by alternative claims to absolute goodness. Eating of the forbidden fruit, they thought they would become as gods themselves (Chrysostom, *Hom. on Genesis* 16, 17).

But the very temple that had become ruined by sin is now being repaired and restored, the flame rekindled, the altar rebuilt (1 Pet. 2:4–8), where the beauty of the Lord is beheld and inquired into night and day (Pss. 1:2; 29:2). No temple is fit for the indwelling of the Spirit except that set apart by God through the atoning work of the Son: the heart of the believer, humbled and contrite, yielded to the Spirit, which has become "the temple of the living God" (2 Cor. 6:16) where God rules and refashions the human spirit back into its original capacity to reflect the divine goodness (Chrysostom, *Hom. on 2 Cor.* 13).

The Lost Condition: Missing the Mark

Those who assume they have power within themselves to repent and make themselves acceptable to God are least likely to experience spiritual birth from above (Luke 4:23; 5:31). Spiritual birth is necessary because the human will has fallen into a condition of recalcitrant moral darkness and corruption. Under the conditions of the history of sin, the sinner is lacking moral compass, as in a fog, resulting from a self-deceiving will. "For what I do is not the good I want to do; no, the evil I do not want to do—this I keep on doing" (Rom. 7:19; Ambrosiaster, *Comm. on Paul*, Rom. 7.19).

When the rudder of the soul is disabled, it leads persistently to "missing the mark." This lost condition, however, is more accurately described as being glad to miss the mark, to love darkness rather than light, to love the creature more than the Creator (John 1:10; Rom. 1:18–32). The only light one may glimpse amid such a stormy sea is a lightning flash of judgment, not the healing light of day. There is no port for the storm, no compass for the vessel. Without a new pilot coming aboard to repair the rudder and redirect the ship to the port, disaster appears inevitable (1 Tim. 1:19; Hippolytus, *Christ and Antichrist* 59; Athanasius, *Ag. Heathen* 3). Such is the "lost" moral state prior to regeneration.

Regenerating grace illumines this vast moral darkness, renovates the moral will, empowers the will to do the good, takes away the love of sin and the despair over sin's seeming permanence. Trust in idols is displaced by trust in the mercy of God. The cacophony of idolatrous loves is refashioned into a symphony of creaturely values loved in relation to the love of God (Augustine, *Conf.* 4.10).

This basic reversal gives footing for one actually to begin the challenging task of removing and transmuting the state of corruption, reshaping it toward greater purity of heart and will. The regenerate life grows in attentiveness to God, maturing in the life now given, actually walking the way of holiness (Ambrose, *Of Christian Faith*; Calvin, *Inst.* 3.3).

The Beginning of a Fundamental Change of Disposition

New life begins the moment the fundamental direction of one's disposition is toward God. There must be a time before and after that moment. The time before is described in the New Testament as death, darkness, and sin; the time after as life, light, and resurrection.

The essential direction of one's disposition is either for or against the saving work of grace. "He who is not with me is against me, and he who does not gather with me scatters" (Matt. 12:30; Chromatius, *Tractate on Matt.* 50.2). There is no state of neutrality to which one can finally retreat (Origen, *Comm. on Matt.* 17.14; Kierkegaard, *Either/Or* 2).

Cyprian's personal report of his own transformed experience is typical of early testimonies to new birth: "In my despair of better things I indulged my sins as if now proper and belonging to me. But afterwards, when the stain of my past life has been washed away by the aid of the water of regeneration, a light from above poured itself upon my chastened and pure heart; afterwards when I had drunk of the Spirit from heaven, a second birth restored me into a new man; immediately in a marvelous manner doubtful matters clarified themselves, the closed opened, the shadowy shone with light, what seemed impossible was able to be accomplished" (Cyprian, *To Donatus*, 4).

Regenerating and Sanctifying Grace

Hence this distinction: regenerating grace enables life; sanctifying grace enables maturity and growth. Regeneration is sanctification at its earliest stage of being awakened, vitalized, readied to grow. Wherever persons are born from above, sanctifying grace has already begun to work. They are new creatures, born of Cod, washed, and already beginning to be sanctified in the Spirit (2 Cor. 5:17–21; Eph.

4:22–26). Regeneration is imparted as the earliest beginnings of a lengthening life of holy love that reflects God's eternal love.

The attempt to set forth the relation between regeneration and sanctification may err in one of two directions: *Either* it may underestimate the power of grace to overcome sin in this life, which implies overestimation of the power of sin to resist grace. In doing so, it may despairingly assume that God is not capable or desirous of cleansing fully from all sin. *Or* it may unrealistically assume that the regenerate no longer has any ongoing battle with sin. But experience will soon show the believer that an extended struggle with sin continues after baptism and regeneration (Calvin, *Inst.* 3.3; Thirty-nine Articles, 16).

The change brought about by the Spirit is an all-embracing reversal in which the dominion of sin is truly broken, though its consequences continue. Though remaining in believers, sin does not reign, and can no longer find a secure foothold (Baxter, *PW* 7:20, 21; J. Wesley, *WJW* 6:65).

The Mystery of the Spirit

Why does the Spirit vivify some and not others? Move later rather than sooner? Inquiry into the antecedents of new birth raises perplexing questions of election, calling, God's foreknowing of our call, and foreordaining of the economy of salvation. The answers remain shrouded in the mystery of the Spirit's movement. In observed fact, some resist, others come alive. It is presumptuous to assume that human insight can identify precisely how, when, or why the Spirit works to bring life (Gregory Nazianzus, *Orat.* 31).

Scripture repeatedly counsels the faithful not to inquire too anxiously into such enigmatic questions, but rather simply to trust God's design (James 1:18; Eph. 1:4–11; Rom. 8:28; Matt. 22:1–14; Gregory I, *Forty Gospel Hom.* 38.5–7). Classic exegetes took comfort and delight in the magnificent thought that Another is wiser than themselves. Faith is relieved that its own vast range of ignorance is complemented by the incomparable divine knowing (Dionysius the Areopagite, *Mystical Theology,* 2, 3).

The underlying conviction is that God has reasons that reason does not know. They go deeper than the facile modern assumption that all ought equally to be saved regardless of their willing (Augustine, *On Nature and Grace* 1–4; Calvin, *Inst.* 3.11–24). "As you do not know the path of the wind, or how the body is formed in a mother's womb, so you cannot understand the work of God, the Maker of all things" (Eccles. 11:5). "The wind blows wherever it pleases. You hear its sound, but you cannot tell where it comes from or where it is going. So it is with everyone born of the Spirit" (John 3:7, 8; Ignatius, *Philadelphians* 7). The work of the Spirit cannot be reduced to visibly caused chains or duplicatable descriptions.

Necessity of the New Birth

Each particular new life in Christ must have a beginning. Nothing grows without being given life to grow. By analogy, the individual Christian life must have a beginning: new birth. New life in Christ is the indispensable presupposition of growth in the Christian life (Goodwin, *Works* 1:73).

Is new birth necessary to the Christian life? Jesus said, "I tell you the truth, no one can see the kingdom of God unless he is born again" (John 3:3). "You must be born again," he told Nicodemus (John 3:7; Chrysostom, *Hom. on John,* 24). A history mired in sin cannot produce holiness. A new beginning must be made, but cannot be made out of a thoroughly corrupted history. "Do people pick grapes from thornbushes, or figs from thistles? Likewise every good tree bears good fruit, but a bad tree bears bad fruit" (Matt. 7:17, 18). Those dead in sin need a new birth precisely because they are "dead" (Eph. 2:1; Marius Victorinus, *Epis. to Eph.* 1.2.1–2).

No one is prepared to come eternally into God's presence whose transgressions have not been pardoned, or continue unabated having been pardoned. Grace calls and enables human behavior to reflect God's own holiness. So long as sin remains in control of the will and nested in the human spirit, there can be no fitting readiness for God. The inmost dispositions must be converted. Idolatries must be cast out. "Therefore, get rid of all moral filth and the evil that is so prevalent and humbly accept the word planted in you, which can save you" (James 1:21; Bede, *Concerning Epis. of James*, 1.21).

5

BAPTISM OF THE SPIRIT

The Spirit's Indwelling

The Spirit comes to abide in the faithful—to dwell (*oikeō*) in the community of those newly born of Spirit (Origen, *Comm. on Rom.* 8.9). This indwelling gift is given to all who repent and believe (John 16:12–13; Chrysostom, *Hom. on Acts*, 24; Augustine, *Tractates on John* 96.4). The Spirit is acting to distribute gifts, baptize, and seal his promise to redeem to the uttermost (Bede, *On 1 John* 4:13; Ambrose, *Of the Holy Spirit* 3.11–14).

The Holy Spirit Abides in All Who Believe

God gives the Spirit "to those who obey him" (Acts 5:32), who respond trustingly to the truth that Jesus is Lord. The Spirit is offered and given in and with personal trust in the Son, at the moment of believing response (Chrysostom, *Hom. on Eph.* 1:13; Bede, *Comm. on Acts* 10:44). When Paul asks, "Did you receive the Spirit by observing the law, or by believing what you heard?" (Gal. 3:2), the assumption is that the Spirit comes with and through responsive faith, the sole condition for making his abode in us (Rom. 8:9).

Justifying grace makes way for the personal indwelling of the Holy Spirit in the resurrected life of the faithful. "He who raised Christ from the dead will also give life to your mortal bodies through his Spirit, who lives in you" (Rom. 8:11; Theodoret, *Interp. of Rom.* 8.10–11; Tho. Aq., *ST* 1–2, Q69, 70). This personal indwelling is a community-eliciting, unifying event: "For we were all baptized by one Spirit into one body—whether Jews or Greeks, slave or free—and we were all given the one Spirit to drink" (1 Cor. 12:13; Ambrose, *Holy Spirit* 1.3.45).

Faith receives the indwelling Spirit. Precisely in the act of trusting reliance, the Spirit indwells. The only pertinent human response to saving grace is believing. Every believing, baptized Christian has begun to receive the Holy Spirit

(*Longer Catech.*, Eastern Orthodox Church, 249; Titus 3:4–6; Luke 11:13). Though the Spirit's indwelling is not reducible to the baptism, sealing, and filling of the Spirit, none of these is detachable from new birth through the Spirit and baptism in the Spirit. "Whoever has been baptized anywhere in the name of Christ, at once obtains the grace of Christ" (Firmilianus, Letter 75, to Cyprian, *SCD* 47).

Once Poured Out, the Spirit Remains to Dwell

The Spirit remains in those who have received the grace of baptism, who remain indelibly known of God. It is clearly promised that "the anointing you received from him remains in you" (1 John 2:27; Bede, *On 1 John* 2:27; Augustine, *Hom. on Epist. of John* 4).

When we were baptized in faith. God the Spirit "anointed us, set his seal of ownership on us, and put his Spirit in our hearts as a deposit, guaranteeing what is to come" (2 Cor. 1:21, 22). Having given this seal, God does not later callously withhold or cancel it. "But you know him, for he lives with you and will be in you. I will not leave you as orphans" (John 14:17, 18; Augustine, *Tractates on John* 75.1).

The Counselor has been given "to be with you forever" (John 14:16; Chrysostom, *Hom. on John* 73, 74). Just as natural birth occurs only once and is followed by a continued living, growing, walking, so does baptism intend to impart a new life which lives and grows on. The Spirit empowers the Christian life with the ever-new daily filling and indwelling of the Spirit (Rom. 8:9–11).

Jesus said, "'Whoever believes in me, as the Scripture has said, streams of living water will flow from within him.' By this he meant the Spirit" (John 7:38). "Just as when a sunbeam falls on bright and transparent bodies, they themselves become brilliant too, and shed forth a fresh brightness from themselves, so souls wherein the Spirit dwells, illuminated by the Spirit, themselves become spiritual and send forth their grace to others" (Basil, *On the Holy Spirit* 9:22).

The love of God, having begun in faithful baptism, flows abundantly from the believer's heart, proceeding from the Spirit given to dwell within all who believe (Rom. 5:1–5; 8:9–11). The faithful are those who have received "not the spirit of the world, but the Spirit who is from God that we may understand what God has freely given us" (1 Cor. 2:12), who are "controlled not by the sinful nature but by the Spirit, if the Spirit of God lives in you" (Rom. 8:9a; Origen, *Comm. on Rom.* 8.9). The new life received by faith is precisely life in the Spirit.

The Spirit Continues to Abide in Struggling Believers

The church at Corinth was a gross mixture of the carnal and spiritual, yet Paul says the Spirit was in all of them (1 Cor. 6:19). The Spirit continues to dwell even among believers who backslide and fall.

The New Testament does not speak conditionally so as to imply that *if* you sin you will lose the Spirit; rather it says: Live an upright life *because* the Spirit is dwelling within you. The Spirit is viewed constantly in the New Testament as an ever-offered gift, not a reward for having faith or good works. When obdurately resisted, the Spirit grieves (Chrysostom, *Hom. on Eph.* 14.4:30).

The absence of the fruits of the Spirit indicates that one has not yet rightly or adequately received God's saving grace (Rom. 8:9b). That the wicked have not freely received the Spirit is evident from their lack of good behavioral fruits (Oecumenius, *Comm. on Jude* 19).

You Are God's Temple

Before the incarnation, the Spirit was attested as occasionally endowing persons for specific tasks (Judg. 14:6; 1 Chron. 12:18; 1 Sam. 10:10; 16:13). Beyond these occasions, the Spirit is found abiding in certain believers such as Joseph (Gen. 41:38), Joshua (Num. 27:18), and Daniel (Dan. 4:8; 5:11–14; cf. Exod. 31:2; Theodoret, *Comm. on Dan.* 5.12).

After the resurrection, however, the Spirit is attested as dwelling continuously in the body of Christ. "Don't you know that you yourselves are God's temple and that God's Spirit lives in you?" (1 Cor. 3:16; Ambrosiaster, *Comm. on Paul,* 1 Cor. 3:16–17). "God's temple is sacred, and you are that temple" (1 Cor. 3:17; cf. 1 Cor. 6:19; 2 Tim. 1:14).

"Let us therefore do all things as those who have Him dwelling in us, that we may be His temples, and He may be in us as God" (Ignatius, *Eph.* 15.3; cf. *Philadelphians* 7.2; *Magnesians* 14). "Blessed, then are you who are God-bearers, spirit-bearers, temple-bearers, bearers of holiness" (Ignatius, *Eph.* 9.2).

Filled with the Spirit

The Spirit is being given to the believing community during the present age between ascension and Parousia. The Spirit could not have been given to indwell with the new humanity before Christ had ascended (John 16:22; Chrysostom, *Hom. on John* 79.1).

In this new age, every believer is offered the continuing privilege of living under the empowerment of the Spirit (Luke 24:49; Acts 10:38; Rom. 15:13, 19). The faithful are praying to be *filled* with the Spirit (*plēroō,* Acts 4:8, 31; 13:9; Chrysostom, *Hom. on Acts* 11.4.31). The Spirit's indwelling as such is not the subject of moral exhortation but prayerful petition. Indwelling is simply received as a gift. The imperative is to be fully receptive to the offered indwelling of the Spirit (Eph. 5:18b–20). "Only then does the Spirit come to settle within our hearts, only when nothing is there to prevent it," when the house is swept clean for him (Chrysostom, *Hom. on Eph.* 19.5.19–20).

Baptism by the Washing of Water and Spirit

It is not baptism of itself that saves, but God through grace who enables repentance and faith, of which baptism is the primary *mustērion, sacramentum,* sacramental act, sign, and evidence of new birth.

Baptism and New Birth: How the Birth of New Life Presupposes Death of the Old

Without a rebirth of the affections from which actions spring, there is no realistic reason to expect that anyone would manifest a life of faith or renounce idolatry or follow the way of holiness or accept God's saving grace. Insofar as created goods are loved and idolized more than God, and persons remain bound to the sin that inordinately loves and idolizes creatures, no new life in the Spirit will emerge out of the history of sin (John 3:4–7; 1 Pet. 1:23; Theodore of Mopsuestia, *Comm. on John* 2.3.7–8).

The sacramental expression of new birth is baptism: "We were therefore buried with him through baptism into death" (Rom. 6:4). "Before beginning the second [regenerated life], it is necessary to put an end to the first" through repentance, which is "a kind of halt." "It seemed necessary for death to come as mediator between the [old and new life], ending all that goes before, and beginning all that comes after" (Basil, *On the Spirit* 1.15). "You were taught, with regard to your former way of life, to put off your old self, which is being corrupted by its deceitful desires; to be made new in the attitude of your minds; and to put on the new self, created to be like God in true righteousness and holiness" (Eph. 4:23,

24; cf. 2 Cor. 5:17). "When your mind is detoxified and expels confusions, the spirit of your mind renews you by taking up its dwelling within you" (Origen, *Epis. to Eph.* 4.23).

The apostolic preaching held repentance and baptism closely together: "Repent and be baptized, every one of you" (Acts 2:38; Chrysostom, *Hom. on Acts* 7.2.38). In instructing Nicodemus on the new birth, Jesus said, "No one can enter the kingdom of God unless he is born of water and the Spirit" (John 3:5; Augustine, *Comm. on John*, Tractate 11, 12). Regeneration and baptism are viewed as two aspects of a single process of receiving new life: "My baptism was the beginning of life, and that day of regeneration the first of days" (Basil, *On the Spirit* 1.10). Those who have been instructed and make the good confession "go down into the water bewailing our sins and uncleanness, and come up from it having fruit in our hearts, having reverence and hope in Jesus in our spirits" (*Letter of Barnabas* 11.1). The heart thereafter is a dwelling of God the Spirit (8.15). Christ makes the church holy by "cleansing her by the washing with water through the word" (Eph. 5:26; Ambrose, *Of the Spirit* 1.6).

Distinguishing Baptism and Regeneration

Baptism intends to "destroy of the body of sin, that it may never bear fruit unto death . . . [while] living unto the Spirit and having the fruit of holiness. The water receiving the body as in a tomb figures death, while the Spirit pours in the quickening power, renewing our souls from the deadness of sin unto their original life. This is what it is to be born again of water and of the Spirit, the being made dead being effected in the water, while our life is wrought in us through the Spirit" (Basil, *On the Spirit* 1.15).

Though not separable, baptism and regeneration are distinguishable points of Christian teaching. An oversimplified identification of baptism and new birth, sometimes called baptismal regeneration, is made debatable by scriptural instances of persons being regenerated who were not baptized (the thief, Luke 23:42, 43; Leo I, *Sermon* 53.1.2; cf. Cornelius, Bede, *Comm. on Acts* 10:44, 48) and of persons who were baptized but apparently unregenerated (Simon Magus, Acts 8:13–23; Ananias and Sapphira, Acts 5:1–11).

Hence, baptism is obligatory for all who would enter the new covenant community in the same sense that circumcision was viewed as obligatory in the old covenant. But baptism, especially when outwardly viewed as a merely formal but spiritually eviscerated public rite, in itself is not represented as the objective instrument or direct efficient cause of regeneration. The new person in Christ is never "born of water" alone but also of the Spirit which is symbolized by the cleansing water (John 3:5). Given the mixed reality of the church as a body including both wheat and weeds, as Jesus warned, there may be many who appear to have been duly baptized with water and yet not sufficiently with the life-giving Spirit (J. Wesley, *WJW* 6:65–77; S. Kierkegaard, *Attack upon "Christendom"*).

The First Letter of Peter aptly compared those "saved through water" in Noah's ark to the water of baptism: "this water symbolizes baptism that now saves you also—not the removal of dirt from the body but the pledge of a good conscience toward God. It saves you by the resurrection of Jesus Christ" (1 Pet. 3:20, 21; Cyprian, *Letters* 74.11).

The Washing of Rebirth

Rebirth is constantly understood in relation to the conjoined metaphors of washing and outpouring, both images involving life-giving and cleansing water: "He saved us through the washing of rebirth and renewal by the Holy Spirit, whom he poured out on us generously through Jesus Christ our Savior, so that having been justified by his grace, we might become heirs having the hope of eternal life" (Titus 3:5-7). "You will be without any sin at all as you come up from that bath" (Augustine, *Sermon* 213.8).

This "washing of regeneration" occurs at the laver (basin or bath) of the sanctuary (Chrysostom, *Hom. on Titus 5; Baptismal Instructions*, ACW 31:224). The laver was set at the entrance of Israel's tent of meeting—a visible sign of entrance into the life of the covenant community (Exod. 40:7, 11, 30; 38:8, 39; 1 Kings 7:30, 38). Priests ritually cleansed their hands and feet before entering the holy place. Similarly, the "washing of rebirth" refers not to an external rite alone, but to the spiritual and moral turning and transformation to which baptism itself points (Acts 22:16; John 3:5; 1 Cor. 4:15; Hilary, *Trin.* 9.9).

Chrysostom taught his catechumens that the washing of new birth (Titus 3:5) "does not simply take away our sins, nor simply cleanse us from our faults, but [does] so as if we were born again. For it creates and fashions us anew, not forming us again out of earth, but creating us out of another element, namely, of the nature of water," which constantly seeks the lowest plane, following the humbling love of the servant Messiah (Chrysostom, *Baptismal Instructions* 1.3.17).

The Grace of Baptism

Pardon begins "from that hour to renew you, pouring into you his grace and Holy Spirit, who begins to crucify the nature and sin" (Luther, *WA* 2:728; Calvin, *Inst.* 4.15.1-3). Once given, baptism assures the believer of the continuing readiness of God to forgive sin (Gregory Nazianzus, *Orat.* 40). The spiritual birth that begins with baptism continues throughout the remaining life. It pronounces a credible and resilient sentence of death upon the sin of the fallen natural man (Augsburg *Conf.* 9). Though sin remains in the baptized, it is in principle shattered, and in this lies the consolation of baptism, that God has bound himself no longer to impute sin to the baptized faithful (Luther, *Sermon on the Holy Sacrament of Baptism*). The Christian life is described by Luther as daily renewal of one's baptism. The sinner may every day once again return to his baptism for comfort, for it has been given as a durable sign that God is gracious to sinners (Luther, *Large Catech.*; Calvin, *Inst.* 4.15.3-6).

Baptism is more than a sign that the believer has faith, as if faith were primary and the grace of God's renewing gift wholly secondary. Baptism is more than a public act of confession or a public testimony to one's faith (Ambrose, *Of Holy Spirit* 3.10; Thirty-nine Articles, 26). Yet baptism of itself is no substitute for active faith or faith becoming active in love (J. Wesley, *WJW* 6:65). As penitent, trusting acceptance of grace, faith is assumed to be a vital condition of baptism, which in the case of infant baptism is grounded in the premise that grace is being received anticipatively through the faith of caring parents and persons within the covenant community (Chrysostom, *Hom. on Col.* 6).

Baptism is at once both the rite of the offering of grace and the rite of the faithful reception of grace's self-offering. The sealing of that gift is the Spirit's assurance or pledge of eternal life (2 Cor. 1:22; Eph. 1:13). Yet this gift is not unilaterally coercive of the will. It can only be freely received. Even those who may "think they are standing firm" are cautioned to "be careful that you don't fall!" (1 Cor. 10:12; Chrysostom, *Hom. on 1 Cor.* 23.5 at 10.12).

Once received, baptism can be denied or neglected but not deleted or erased. No one baptized ever became unbaptized. There is no corresponding rite for taking away baptism, not even excommunication, which bars participation in the Eucharist. Hence: "Those who, having been baptized, later become atheists and then later return to the faith of the church do not need to be rebaptized. One may forget or deface one's baptism, but one cannot erase its mark as God's own gift, blessed and ordered and embraced by God (Augustine, *Hom. on 2 Cor.* 3; *SCD* 411).

Baptism is the nursery of the church by which persons enter the covenant community. This is why public confession of faith is so intrinsically connected with baptism, and why the creedal formulations grew directly out of the rite of baptism. This is why catechesis emerged in the context of baptism. "Baptized into union with him, you have all put on Christ as a garment" (Gal. 3:27; Cyprian, *Letter* 74.5.3; Calvin, *Inst.* 4.15–16).

For Whom Is the Grace of Baptism Given?

The question of whether infants of faithful families are capable of an anticipatory form of faith that awaits their confirmation is a much-debated sore point. We are well advised not to set premature limits upon what God the Spirit may or may not be able to do in bringing life to fallen human history.

Most agree that God the Spirit works within the lives of infants in a different way than adults. Whether consciously in adults through justifying grace or preliminarily in infants through preparatory grace, faith in itself can never become a meritorious cause or ground, but always remains the ordered way of receiving grace. Regardless of how the debates about the proper time of baptism may proceed, the question of God's power to work in infants hinges less on neonate capacity or activity than the divine will electing and desire to call and shape human life rightly from the beginning.

Faith whether implicitly or primitively in children or more maturely in adults is essentially the readiness to receive God's Spirit. Whatever anticipatory faith might be thought possible for infants, it amounts essentially to a disposition toward God that is ready to hear more and ready to believe God's promises, even as did Abraham when he "obeyed and went, even though he did not know where he was going" (Gen. 11:8).

Preparatory Grace Among Children

From scripture it is evident that God the Spirit may work in extraordinary ways not only in the neonate but even before birth: The word of the Lord came to Jeremiah, saying, "Before I formed you in the womb I knew you, before you were born I set you apart" (Jer. 1:5; cf. Gal. 1:15; Luke 1:41; Ephrem, *Comm. on Tatian's Diatesseron* 1.30). When Jeremiah protested, "I do not know how to speak; I am only a child," Yahweh replied, "Do not say, 'I am only a child' " (Jer. 1:6, 7; Isa. 46:3; 49:1; Jer. 25:15–26). That infants can trust God is clear from the Psalms: "You made me trust in you even at my mother's breast. From birth I was cast upon you; from my mother's womb you have been my God" (Ps. 22:9, 10; cf. Pss. 71:6; 139:13–16).

God the Spirit may work in nascent life "so efficacious that they can receive the grace of God and the forgiveness of sins" (Chemnitz, in Jacobs, *SCF*:237). Luther argued that God in some manner endows with faith infants brought for baptism on account of the believing presentation of them and the prayer offered on their behalf by their believing parents (Luther; *Catech.* 494; Augsburg *Apology*, 9).

When Jesus "called a little child and had him stand among them," he said: "Unless you change and become like little children, you will never enter the kingdom of heaven. Therefore, whoever humbles himself like this child is the greatest in the kingdom of heaven. And whoever welcomes a little child like this in my name welcomes me. But if anyone causes one of these little ones *who believe in me* to sin, it would be better for him to have a large millstone hung around his neck and to be drowned in the depths of the sea" (Matt. 18:2–60, italics added). Even the little child here appears capable of some sort of anticipatory belief in God's coming. Such "little children" carried in the arms of their parents were called to come to God the Son: "Let the little children come to me, and do not hinder them, for the kingdom of God belongs to such as these" (Mark 10:13, 14; Cyprian, *Letters*, 58). Children born into families of earnest believers may be already in an anticipatory way "in covenant with God; have the seal thereof upon them, viz., Baptism; and so if not regenerate, yet are in a more hopeful way of attaining regenerating grace," standing under the care of the church and the believing family, and are thus subject to guidance and admonition as need shall require (Cambridge Platform 16.7).

Prevenient grace leads toward justifying grace. No one is saved by prevenient preparatory grace as such, but only by faith in God's justifying verdict on the cross. Hence preparatory grace points toward and readies the soul for justification, but does not substitute for justification. The baptism of one unready for informed consent looks toward confirmation, an act of consent confirming the path preparatory grace has taken.

The New Affections of the Heart

New birth is followed by a life of reborn affections. Jeremiah prophesied, "I will give them a heart to know me, that I am the Lord. They will be my people, and I will be their God, for they will return to me with all their heart" (Jer. 24:7; cf. 31:33). The movement is from the center of the reclaimed self to the circumference of human society.

One who ascends the hill of the Lord must have "clean hands and a pure heart, who does not lift up his soul to an idol" (Ps. 24:4). Throughout scripture both sin and holiness are rooted in the heart as their center and source rather than primarily in external actions (Tho. Aq., *ST* 2–2, Q2). The first commandment for the Christian life remains to love God "with all your heart" (Matt. 22:37; cf. Matt. 5:8; Rom. 10:10). It is through a change of heart that a dispositional reversal occurs. Through repentance and faith God's love flows through human hearts: "Love comes from God. Everyone who loves has been born of God, and knows God" (1 John 4:6, 7; Augustine, *Sermons* 260C.1).

The new life bears fruit: "the fruit of the Spirit is love, joy, peace, patience, kindness, goodness, faithfulness, gentleness and self-control" (Gal. 5:22). These fruits are possible because "Those who belong to Christ Jesus have crucified the sinful nature, with its passions and desires. Since we live by the Spirit, let us keep in step with the Spirit" (Gal. 5:24, 25; Chrysostom, *Hom. on Gal.* 5.25).

Partaking of God's Own Nature Elicits New Affections

By grace we may come to "participate in the divine nature and escape the corruption in the world caused by evil desires" (2 Pet. 1:4; Ambrose, *Letters to Priests* 49). "The end of the Gospel is to render us eventually conformable to God" (Calvin, *Comm.* 22:371). In being born anew we pass from death to life (John 5:24), become new creatures (2 Cor 5:17), turn from darkness to light (1 Pet. 2:9), from hostility to love (Col. 1:21).

In this way the image of God is being renewed in humanity (Col. 3:10; Augustine, *On Trin.* 14.16.22). Regeneration is "a work of the triune God, which the Holy Ghost accomplishes in us by raising us up from the death of sin and making us *partakers of the Divine nature and life*" (*Catechism of the Evangelical Association*, Q 295, italics added). It is "a change of heart, wrought by the Holy Spirit, who quickeneth the dead in trespasses and sins, enlightening their minds spiritually and savingly to understand the Word of God, and renewing their whole nature, so that they love and practice holiness" (Baptist Abstract of Principles 7). By the new birth the faithful become "partakers of the divine nature and a holy disposition is given, leading to the love and practice of righteousness" (Baptist *Conf.*, *SBC*, 1925). "Mercy wishes you to be merciful, righteousness to be righteous, that the Creator may be seen in His creature, and the image of God may be reflected in the mirror of the human heart" (Leo I, *Sermons* 95).

The Spirit transforms broken human life: "He takes possession of a shepherd, makes him a Psalmist, subduing evil spirits by his song, and proclaims him King; if he possess a goatherd and scraper of sycamore fruit, He makes him a Prophet. . . . If He takes possession of Fishermen, He makes them catch the whole world in the nets of Christ, taking them up in the meshes of the Word. Look at Peter and Andrew and the Sons of Thunder, thundering the things of the Spirit. If of Publicans, He makes gain of them for discipleship, and makes them merchants of souls" (Gregory Nazianzus, *Orat.* 41.14).

Water and Spirit Baptism

The gospel narratives link closely the baptism of Jesus with the descent of the Holy Spirit, accompanied by the heavenly confirmation of his eternal Sonship (Luke 3:21, 22). The baptism of Jesus looks toward a future filled with the Spirit. "I baptize you with water for repentance," John told his followers, "but after me will come one who is more powerful than I" who will "baptize you with the Holy Spirit and with fire" (Matt. 3:11). "God takes evil from us in two ways—by Spirit and by fire" (Origen, *Hom. on Ezekiel* 2.13). The clay of human nature is being refashioned.

It is the water and fire of baptism that reshape and make durable the clay of humanity. This was summed up in a memorable figure by Chrysostom: "He took dust from the earth and made the man; He formed him. The devil came, and perverted him. Then the Lord came, took him again, and remolded, and recast him in baptism, and He suffered not his body to be of clay, but made it of a harder ware. He subjected the soft clay to the fire of the Holy Spirit. . . . He was baptized with water that he might be remodelled, with fire that he might be hardened" (Chrysostom, *Eutropius, NPNF 1* 9:250).

Water symbolizes lowliness and adaptability, conformity to the gravity of grace, as Cyril taught his catechumens: "By water all things subsist. . . . It comes down in one form, but works in many forms. For one fountain waters the whole of *Paradise*. One and the same rain comes down upon all the world. Yet it becomes white in the lily, and red in the rose, and purple in the violets and hyacinths . . . the rain does not change itself and come down first as one thing, then as another, but *adapting itself to the constitution of each thing* which receives it, it becomes to each what is suitable" (Cyril of Jerusalem, *Catech. Lect.* 16.12).

The Spirit's Ministry Is to Baptize

One of the defining ministries of God the Spirit is to baptize the faithful into the body of Christ (Gregory of Nyssa, *The Great Catech.* 32–40). This ministry was prophesied and anticipated by John the Baptist (Matt. 3:11 and parallels) but was not instituted as indwelling until after Christ's resurrection on the day of Pentecost (Acts 1:5), which Peter called "the beginning" (*archē*, Acts 11:15; Barth, *CD* 4/4:44) of the Spirit's descent upon and indwelling within the community of faith.

The purpose of baptism is to join believers to the body of Christ through the Spirit. "There can be no baptism without the Spirit" (Ambrose, *Of the Holy Spirit* 2.2.21). By this baptism, the Spirit joins each member to Christ's body, dying with his death and rising with his life (Rom. 6:1–10; Col. 1:12; Leo I, *Sermons* 57.5.1–2). "We are buried in the element of water that we may rise again renewed by the Spirit. For in the water is the representation of death, in the Spirit is the pledge of life, that the body of sin may die through the water, which encloses the body as it were in a kind of tomb. . . . The water, then, is a witness of burial, the blood is a witness of death, the Spirit is a witness of life" (Ambrose, *Of the Holy Spirit* 1,6.76).

Water is a fit figure of baptism by the Spirit because it is extremely permeable "on account of the subtilty of its substance." Water is that lowly element of creation that best suggests the complete readiness of creation to receive the Spirit. Water humbly and readily cooperates with the Spirit to impart to creatures the power of grace. The waters of baptism in this way "imbibe the power of sanctifying" (Tertullian, *On Baptism* 4). The grace of baptism persists unimpeded until we reject it by sinning. and even then the grace of penitence is ever ready to enable us to reappropriate our baptism (Augustine, *Letters*, 18).

Unity in the Spirit Through Baptism

The Spirit intends to unite the body of Christ through the one baptism: "For we were all baptized by one Spirit into one body" (1 Cor. 12:13). This text assumes that baptism by the Spirit is coextensive with salvation and is offered to all who believe. Paul was addressing a community of faith at Corinth troubled by various heresies and lack of discipline. Yet all were reminded of their being baptized by one Spirit into one body (Ambrose, *Duties* 1.33). "There is one body and one Spirit—just as you were called to one hope when you were called—one Lord, one faith, one baptism" (Eph. 4:4, 5). The unity of the gifts of the varied members of the body is assured by the Spirit. All believers are baptized by the Spirit into one body, fitly joined together (Eph. 4:16; Chrysostom, *Hom. on Eph.* 11.4.15–16).

The same baptism is variously described as baptism *in* or *of*, or *with*, or *by* the Spirit. In Matthew 3:11, Mark 1:8, Luke 3:16, and John 1:33, the reference is to *Christ baptizing persons into the Spirit* (baptism in the Spirit). "For in one Spirit we were all baptized into one body—Jews or Greeks, slaves or free—and all were made to drink of one Spirit" (1. Cor. 12:13; Clement of Alex., *Instr.* 1.5.31).

Baptism in the Spirit (*baptizein en pneumati)* was prophesied by John, first fulfilled at Pentecost, and administered and attested by the apostles as baptism *with or by* the Spirit.

There is only one baptism (Eph. 4:5). The New Testament understands baptism of and by the Spirit as the privilege of all who have faith, all Christians, all who belong to the body of Christ. "You are all sons of God through faith in Christ Jesus, for all of you who were baptized have clothed yourselves with Christ" (Gal. 3:26, 27; Chrysostom, *Hom. on Gal.* 3).

The Spirit is called "the Gift, because it is given to us in return for nothing on our part; Grace, because it is conferred even on debtors; Baptism, because sin is buried with it in the water; Unction, as Priestly and Royal, for such were they who were anointed; Illumination, because of its splendor; Clothing, because it hides our shame; the Laver, because it washes us; the Seal, because it preserves us, and is moreover the indication of Dominion" (Gregory Nazianzus, *Orat.* 40.4). Received in many forms, the indwelling Spirit remains one single gift.

Receiving and Believing

When Paul asked the disciples at Ephesus, "Did you receive the Holy Spirit *when you believed*?" (Acts 19:2, italics added), they answered, "No, we have not even heard that there is a Holy Spirit," having received only the baptism of John. This was not yet an adequate Christian faith and baptism. When Paul offered them Christian baptism, the "Holy Spirit came on them, and they spoke in tongues and prophesied" (Acts 19:6). This suggests that to be a disciple of John the Baptist was itself an anticipatory act pointing toward completion in the work of the Son and the Spirit. Where there are those who remain in Christian communities who have heard of Jesus Christ without having been endued with the power of the Holy Spirit, the Spirit nonetheless continues to work to elicit a Spirit-filled faith (Acts 19:1–10; Ammonius, *Catena on Acts* 19.5, in Cramer 3:313–41; Cor. 2:4, 5).

Through baptism the faithful participate in the body of Christ, living in union with Christ's risen life. They become one with Christ's righteousness, his dying and being raised, and his glory to come (Cyril of Jerusalem, *Catech. Lect.* 3.12). The water used in baptism is the outward means of grace by which the outpouring of the Spirit is made visible, the inward grace outwardly signified as a type of death and resurrection (Hugh of St. Victor, *SCF*:282–304). Paul explained: "We were therefore buried with him through baptism into death in order that, just as Christ was raised from the dead through the glory of the Father, we too may live a new life" (Rom. 6:4).

The Sealing of the Spirit

Like baptism in the Spirit, the pledge of the Spirit is offered to all believers. The believer is sealed by the Spirit at the time of repentance and faith. Despite misdeeds, those who continue steadfast in faith remain sealed to the day of redemption (Eph. 4:30; Jerome, *Epis. to Eph.* 2.4.30), assuming they "stand firm" (2 Cor. 1:21, 22). It is the very presence of the Spirit in the daily life of the believer that constitutes the seal (Ambrose, *Of the Holy Spirit* 1.79).

John said that on Jesus, the Lamb of God, "the Father has placed his seal of approval" (John 6:27). Paul added: "And you also were included in Christ when you heard the word of truth, the gospel of your salvation. Having believed, you were marked in him with a seal [*sphragizō*], the promised Holy Spirit, who is a deposit [*arrabon*] guaranteeing our inheritance until the redemption of those who are God's possession" (Eph. 1:13, 14; Didymus, *On the Holy Spirit* 20).

The Pledge of Inheritance

The sealing metaphor indicates a pledge or an earnest of an inheritance (*arrabon tes klēronomias*, Irenaeus, *Ag. Her.* 5.8). Sealing conveys guardianship, responsibility, and security (Chrysostom, *Hom. on Eph.* 15, 16; Calvin, *Inst.* 3.24). The seal promises that which will be brought to completion on a specified day— in this case, the last day. One seals one's agreements and promises with a stamp or wax seal that shows that the transaction (in this case, atoning grace received by faith) has been completed and confirmed. Once stamped or marked, it is not reversible. A seal implies an authorized securing and attesting of true ownership (Cyril of Jerusalem, *Catech. Lect.* 17.35).

All of God's promises are yes in Christ, who "anointed us, set his seal of ownership on us, and put his Spirit in our hearts as a deposit, guaranteeing what is to come" (2 Cor. 1:21, 22; Ambrose, *Sacraments* 6.2.5–6). The faithful are invited to count themselves as reconciled to God, whose signature is upon them awaiting the last day. God places this stamp upon those who trust his Word. Think of the believer as enclosed in grace, as a document is placed in a sealed, wax-imprinted envelope. The Spirit is agent of this sealing (Cyril of Jerusalem, *Catech.* 17.32; Ambrose, *Sacraments* 7).

Sealing is closely tied with the teaching of the assurance of salvation. The believer is thereby made certain of God's promise. He is kept till the day of redemption (Calvin, *Inst.* 3.2.12, 4.14.17–18). "God implants himself in the interior of that soul" in such a way that one need not "doubt that God has been in her and she has been in God" (Teresa of Avila, *Interior Castle*, mansion 5, 1).

Chrism

Anointing with oil symbolizes and prefigures this promise. Anointing is a work of the indwelling Spirit that seals the believer to eternal life.

References to the anointing of the Spirit (Luke 4:18; Acts 4:27; 10:38; 2 Cor. 1:21; 1 John 2:20, 27; Origen, *Hom. on Luke* 32.4–5) may be understood metaphorically as the indwelling and sealing of the Spirit (Chrysostom, *Baptismal Instructions ACW* 31:224–28). "The Spirit is the unction [ointment] and seal with which the Word anoints and seals all" that has been promised. The seal bears the image of Christ, "who seals, and those who are sealed partake of it, being conformed to it" (Athanasius, *LCHS* 1.23:124). "We are sealed by the Holy Spirit with the image and similitude of the Father's face, that is, of the Son" (Cyril of Alexandria, *Trin.*, 5; *Comm. on Luke,* Hom. 12).

Chrism (from *chriō*, anoint) is a mixture of olive oil and unguent or balsam used liturgically for the anointing or setting aside or sanctification of a person to a task. The richness of the oil and the fragrance of the balsam symbolized the fullness and beauty of the gift of the Spirit (Cyril of Jerusalem, *Catech. Lect.* 21). The rite of confirmation became the sacrament of the chrism wherein those baptized symbolically received the Holy Spirit, enacted in a prayer for grace (Chrysostom, *Baptismal Instructions, ACW* 31:169).

Chrismation appears as a rite linked to baptism as early as the time of Tertullian (*Of Baptism* 6) and Cyprian (*Epist.* 69, 70). After the font, writes Tertullian, the baptized were "anointed with a blessed unction—(a practice derived) from the old discipline." This is why Aaron was anticipatively called " 'Christ [anointed],' from the 'chrism,' which is 'the unction' " (Tertullian, *On Baptism* 7). As Jesus was anointed to preach (Luke 4:18), anointed "with the Holy Spirit and power" (Acts 10:38), so he anoints us, setting his seal of protection upon us (1 Cor. 1:21; Proclus, *Hom.* 2). As baptism and confirmation became distinguishable rites, confirmation became a decisive moment of ratification of baptismal vows preparatory to communion upon the age of accountability, ordinarily by laying on of hands of the *episkopos* (Anon., *Treatise on Rebaptism* 1–5).

Preventing the Falling Away from One's Baptism

As circumcision occurs only once, so does baptism. As circumcision brings persons initially into the covenant community, so does baptism. The circumcised Jew or the baptized Christian may later fall away from the original intention of the rite: inclusion in the covenant community. That does not invalidate the rite, but exposes its neglect (Eph. 2:11–16; Jerome, *Epis. to Eph.* 1.2.12; Luther, *Large Catech.* 6, BOC 4:436).

Faithful assent is constitutive for baptism. We were "baptized in the name of the Father and of the Son and of the Holy Ghost: first comes the confession [of the rule of faith], introducing us to salvation," then "baptism follows, setting the seal upon our assent." (Basil, *On the Spirit* 1.12).

Reaffirmation or confirmation of one's baptism assumes that one intentionally is confirming the grace of the Spirit received in baptism. But even then one may still ever again fall away from one's intention in confirmation. Thus the sacrament of the Lord's Supper offers the grace of forgiveness to all penitents (Hugh of St. Victor, *SCF*:304; Luther, *Large Catech.* 5).

There is an implicit moral requirement to walk in the way of holiness that accompanies the sealing of the Spirit: "Do not grieve the Holy Spirit of God, with whom you were sealed for the day of redemption. Get rid of all bitterness, rage and anger, brawling and slander, along with every form of malice. Be kind and compassionate to one another, forgiving each other, just as in Christ God forgave you" (Eph. 4:30–32; Chrysostom, *Hom. on Eph.* 15,16). Those who persist in sin thereby indicate their self-chosen absence from the body of Christ (Augustine, *Hom. on Epist. of John* 4, 5).

As the rite of ordination does not take place over years of time but on a particular hour of a particular day in time, so does baptism. Yet the ministry to which one is ordained can only take place gradually in unfolding time (Gregory Nazianzus, *Orat.* 2; Gregory I, *Pastoral Care ACW* 11:25). Similarly with the sealing of the Spirit, sanctifying grace begins at a particular point to work toward habit-formed refractions of the holiness of God (Ambrose, *Duties NPNF* 2 10:41). As holy orders are considered indelible for those effectually called to sacred ministry, so was the seal of baptism viewed as indelible to all called to faith, even if abused or neglected (Augustine, *Hom. on Epist. of John* 4; *SCD* 411).

The grace offered by the Spirit in baptism provides not only a momentary remission of sins, but the continuing offer of sanctifying grace that matures with good works (Luther, *Large Catech.*:436). Luther concisely defined the gifts of the baptismal sealing: "It effects forgiveness of sins, delivers from death and the devil, and grants eternal salvation to all who believe" (*Small Catech.* 4.2 cf. *Letter of Barnabas* 11).

The Gifts of the Spirit

Charisma is the gift of some God-given ability to render a service empowered by grace. The Pauline teaching of spiritual gifts is concentrated primarily in Romans 12, 1 Corinthians 12 and Ephesians 4 (compare these Pauline lists with 1 Pet. 4:10).

Distributed for the Body

These gifts (*charismata*) are given by the risen Lord to build up his body (Eph. 4:11) and administered by the Spirit, who knows in advance what gift best fits each believer for service (1 Cor. 12). A natural talent is a superior ability that emerges through genetic tendencies or environment or technical competencies. But a spiritual *charisma* is a gift of divine grace that is evidenced by some ability that benefits the body of Christ (Rom. 12:6; Chrysostom, *Hom. on Rom.* 21).

Spiritual gifts are not given to individuals as such, but to individuals on behalf of the whole body, the community of faith. They are not for self-congratulation but for upbuilding the body (Eph. 4:12, 16, 29). When a symphonic conductor selects violinists for a rigorous season of repertoire, he does not do so in order to advance their careers but to ensure that the music they share will be rightly balanced and harmonized. Similarly, when the Spirit distributes gifts to the body of Christ, it is not for personal self-advancement but for the health and upbuilding of the body (Chrysostom; *Hom. on Eph.* 10, 11). As one does not light a fire to warm the stove but to warm the room, quipped Kuyper, so the Spirit does not distribute gifts to enhance individuals but the community on behalf of the world's redemption (*WHS*:182).

Gifts of the Spirit are distributed not by human preference or private choice but as the sovereign act of God the Spirit (1 Cor. 12:12, 28; Cyril of Jerusalem, *Catech. Lect.* 14.12). The responsibility of the recipient is to receive the gift proffered so as to develop and exercise it to the fullest (Chrysostom, *Hom. on 1 Cor.* 29, 30).

No member of the body is wholly lacking in gifts and tasks of ministry: "Each member is the church in the world, endowed by the Spirit with some gift of ministry and is responsible for the integrity of his witness in his own particular situation" (United Presbyterian Confession of 1967). The *charismata* of the primitive church were continued and bestowed upon the whole laity, some becoming adapted and reshaped into gifts peculiar to sacred ministry, commissioned to guard the apostolic teaching and given grace to interpret it faithfully (Irenaeus, *Ag. Her.* 4.26.5–7).

God has organically joined the members of the body so that "its parts should have equal concern for each other. If one part suffers, every part suffers with it; if one part is honored, every part rejoices with it" (1 Cor. 12:25, 26; Augustine, *Letters* 99). Hence members are to bear one another's burdens as if they were their own (Gal. 6:2).

The Distribution of Varied Gifts

As no believer is lacking in all gifts (1 Cor. 12:7; 1 Pet. 4:10), so no one possesses all. Each depends upon the gifts of other members of the body to complete what is lacking in his or her own gift (Basil, *Long Rules*, 7; Chrysostom, *Hom. on 1 Cor.* 29, 30). Uniformity is not the way the Spirit works, but rather through variability, imagination, responsiveness, and exquisite diversity. At a given time, some of these gifts may be more urgently needed in the mission of the Son than others, but in due time all gifts are needed (1 Cor. 12:4–10; Ambrose, *Letter to His Sister* 62).

God's gifts continue to be given even to those unaware of them. They are given in ways proportionally adapted to finite capacities. Among early recipients of the gifts of the Spirit were Philip, who is first found distributing relief to the poor (Acts 6:2–5; Arator, *on the Acts* 1) and later witnessing to the Samaritans (8:5), and Stephen, who engaged in acts of mercy and later became the first disciple to give his life for Christ (Acts 7; Augustine, *Sermon* 214.8).

All are asked to show mercy, but to some are given special gifts of hospitality or benevolence. To the whole laity is given the task of witness and exhortation (Acts 1:8; Heb. 10:25), but some are given gifts and called more particularly to be evangelists and exhorters. Though the command to serve one another is given to the whole church (Gal. 5:13), the gift of serving is given to responsive individuals within particular circumstances (Bede, *Comm. on Acts* 6.1). Whatever one's gift, it is to be developed, nurtured, and extended by the unique cooperative efforts of the individual responding to grace.

Sexuality and the Diversity of Gifts

Both marriage and singleness are viewed as spiritual gifts relating to sexuality, each one "has his own gift from God, one has this gift, another has that" (1 Cor. 7:7). To singleness is given the gift of freedom from entangling commitments in order to have the opportunity to serve the Lord more freely (1 Cor. 7:32).

To marriage is given the gift of generativity, masculinity and femininity, bonding, and commitment to family to enable and nurture life (1 Cor. 7:29, 33; Ambrosiaster, *Comm. on Paul*, 1 Cor. 7.32–36). Though different, each gift has its own challenges and requirements. Both marriage and singleness are needed within the larger plan of redemption to redeem the time (Chrysostom, *Hom. on 1 Cor.* 19; Calvin, *Comm.* 20:251–71).

The gracious complementarity of the gift of sexual difference was early recognized as "a great proof of providence." It was theologically significant that "males and females equally have teats, but only those of the female are filled with milk," and in the organs of generativity, the male "differs from the female only in that part of his body in which is the power of injecting seed" (Second Clement, *Recognitions* 8.32). The male, who has no power to receive seed and enable growth, complements the female, who by physical design has no power to inject seed. Sexuality therefore becomes prototypical of all the gifts of grace.

Complementarity of Spiritual Gifts

Several varied lists of gifts of the Spirit are found in the New Testament. Among those conspicuously listed are apostleship, wherein one is sent on the mission of the Son by the Spirit (Eph. 4:11); prophecy, wherein one speaks the Word of the Lord (1 Cor. 14:1); evangelization, wherein one proclaims good news to all (Eph. 4:11; Acts 21:8); pastoring or shepherding the flock of God (Eph. 4:11); teaching the truth (Rom. 12:7); confession (1 John 4:2), and exhortation (Rom. 12:8); healing (1 Cor. 12:9, 28, 30) and miracles (1 Cor. 12:28); ecstatic utterance, speaking in other languages, and the interpretation of other tongues (Acts 2:4, 8; 1 Cor. 12:10); discernment (1 Cor. 12:10); serving (Rom. 12:7); and administry or governance (*kubernēsis*), which seeks to enable the work of ministry of others (1 Cor. 12:28; cf. Rom. 12:8; Theonas of Alexandria, *Epist. to Lucianus* 4).

Also described among the spiritual gifts are *faith* (1 Cor. 12:9), *encouragement* (Rom. 12:8), the ability to *distinguish* true and false revelation (1 Cor. 12:10), the showing of *mercy* and generosity (Rom. 12:8), diligent leadership, wisdom, and knowledge (Rom. 12:8; 1 Cor. 12:28). Above all there is the summative gift of *love*, which shows forth God's own superabundant benevolence and mercy (Rom. 12:9,10; 1 Cor. 13:1–13; Cyprian, *The Good of Patience* 15).

This astonishing variety of gifts each complement the other to build up the whole body. Apostolicity is a foundational gift, upon which other gifts are dependent, since no testimony is available to us except through the apostolate (1 Cor. 12:28; Eph. 4:11). Prophecy, in the sense both of proclamation and of discerning the will of God, is a gift given to both men and women (Acts 21:9; 11:27, 28; 1 Cor. 14; Joel 2). The gifts of miracle and healing (1 Cor. 12:9, 28, 30) were exercised by the early believers on certain occasions as by Paul at Ephesus (Acts 19:11, 12), yet not given in the cases of Timothy or Trophimus or Epaphroditus (1 Tim. 5:23; 2 Tim. 4:20; Phil. 2:27) or in the case of Paul's own thorn in the flesh (2 Cor. 12:8, 9). The giving of gifts occurs by God's sovereign choice. One's calling to be an evangelist or pastor (Eph. 4:11) or servant or teacher (Rom. 12:7; 1 Cor. 12:28; Eph. 4:11, 12) is authenticated and enabled by spiritual gifts commensurable with those tasks (Chrysostom, *Hom. on Eph.* 11).

Lists of Charismata

It is useful to visualize the varied lists of gifts of the Spirit in terms of three broad functions of the church: witness, community, and service.

Gifts of the Spirit

	Witness	Community	Service
	Marturia	Koinonia	Diakonia
Rom. 12:6–8	prophecy teaching	exhortation liberality	service giving aid acts of mercy
1 Cor. 12:4–11	wisdom knowledge faith prophecy tongues	discernment interpretation edification	healing miracles
1 Cor. 13	faith	hope	love
Eph. 4:11	apostles prophets evangelists teachers	pastors	
1 Pet. 4:11	speaking		serving

Such New Testament lists were not seeking to exhaust all possible gifts, or present the gifts of the Spirit in systematic sequence. Rather, they are suggestive of the incalculable diversity of gifts that are bestowed upon the one body for the upbuilding of the whole as the Spirit sees fit (Chrysostom, *Hom. on 1 Cor.* Hom. 19).

Order and Proportionality in Distribution

The gifts of the Spirit allow faith to be sustained through the hazards of time in ways that cannot be assured by human planning. The gifts of the Spirit enable a new ordering of life, reordering the failed ways of the history of sin (2 Tim. 1:6; James 1:17).

In distributing gifts, the foreknowing God "beholds the temper of each" and works proportionally in each recipient. The Spirit works both in those times and places we can see and those we cannot see; among those peoples for whom we have a name, and among those "for whom we have no names" (Cyril of Jerusalem, *Catech. Lect.* 16.22). To unknown people in Africa and Asia the Spirit works. To some are given the power of taming "hostile spirits," to others the gift of chastity, to others the gift of caring for the poor.

The Spirit does not wastefully squander the *charismata*. The principle of parsimony is evident in the distribution of gifts of the Spirit.

The seeming inequalities of gifts only appear unjust when viewed individualistically from the viewpoint of human interests, self-expression, and pride. Seen in relation to the wholeness of the body of Christ, what at first might seem to be inequality displays a profound equity wherein all members are equitably needed within the whole body (Hilary, *Trin.* 2.35; Ambrose, *The Holy Spirit* 11.71; Calvin, *Comm.* 20:251–71).

The diversity of gifts does not mean that they are unequally valued by God, though one may function more pertinently than another in a given moment. The working body needs teeth, but that does not imply that the teeth need to be biting all the time. That the body needs eyes does not imply that one must never close them. Each gift is needed, but not compulsively at all times (*Didache* 11, *ECW*: 233). "For in Christ all the fullness of the Deity lives in bodily form, and you have been given fullness in Christ" (Col. 2:9). "In him you too are being built together to become a dwelling in which God lives by his Spirit" (Eph. 2:22; Marius Victorinus, *Epis. to Eph.* 1.2.20–22).

Discerning and Testing the Gifts

The discernment of the Spirit is itself a gift of the Spirit (1 Cor. 2:14; Chrysostom, *Hom. on 1 Cor.*, Hom. 7.7). "There is a diversity of Gifts, which stands in need of yet another Gift to discern" (Gregory Nazianzus, *Orat.* 41.16). Since gifts are constantly given anew, they may be at times opaque and hard to discern; the Spirit always works ahead of our discernment.

Paul warned, "Do not put out the Spirit's fire; do not treat prophecies with contempt. Test everything" (1 Thess. 5:19–21). The gifts of the Spirit are tested primarily by the criterion of whether they further manifest the mission of the Son (1 Cor. 12:1–3; Theodoret, *Comm. on 1 Cor.*, 242).

Other Gifts

Exegetes continue to debate whether the special gifts of healing, exorcism, and glossolalia are normative for all times or reserved for apostolic or very special times. Whereas all believers are baptized (1 Cor. 12:13), not all speak in tongues (1 Cor. 14:1–12; Chrysostom, *Hom. on 1 Cor 12*, 32.4; 35.1–3).

Glossolalia, or speaking in tongues, and interpretation of tongues are gifts of the Spirit (1 Cor. 12:10). Like all good gifts, these may be used wrongly. Early in the apostolic tradition we find constraints being placed upon the healthy practice of these special gifts: no one was to speak unless the message could be interpreted, and intelligible prophecy was to be preferred (1 Cor. 14). It was precisely while regulating, but not forbidding, speaking in tongues, that Paul states that "everything should be done in a fitting and orderly way" (1 Cor. 14:40; Basil, *Long Rules* 24). Fittingness and order are proper duties of self-governance. In the reordering shaped by grace, sufficient room must be left for Christian liberty, freedom of conscience, and the gifts of the Spirit.

Luke reported that "God did extraordinary miracles through Paul, so that even handkerchiefs and aprons that had touched him were taken to the sick and their illnesses were cured" (Acts 19:12; Chrysostom, *Catena on Acts* 19.11–12, Cramer CEC 3:316). This is reminiscent of an earlier report that by touching the bones of Elisha a dead man was raised to life (1 Kings 13:21). Such ideas inevitably would lead to abuses, which would in due time prompt the reformers to reject the teaching "that the souls of the dead have influence on the living," and the practice of "praying to the souls of the saints and the hope that power or holiness may come from the dead (from their graves, from their clothes, their bones, mementos, relics)" (Batak Confession, 16; cf. Calvin, *Inst.* 3.5.6, 7).

Gifts, Fruits, and Virtues

Classic exegetes were intrigued by the thought that seven summative gifts of the confirming Spirit to the church had been prophetically anticipated by Isaiah:

wisdom, understanding, counsel, fortitude, knowledge, piety, and reverence for God. "The Spirit of the Lord will rest on him—the Spirit of wisdom and of understanding, the Spirit of counsel and of power, the Spirit of knowledge and of the fear of the Lord—and he will delight in the fear of the Lord" (Isa. 11:2, 3a; whether this enumerates six or seven gifts, the intent is to convey the fullness of the Spirit's gifts). Four are said to reclaim and perfect the intellect: wisdom and understanding pertain to the discernment of truth and its value (1 Cor. 1:24; Ps. 31:8); counsel (Isa. 9:6, lxx) and knowledge prudentially and rightly apply the truth to moral circumstances. The other three (variously translated) are said to reclaim and perfect the will: Power or fortitude or courageous strength for spiritual struggle (1 Cor. 1:24), godliness or reverent piety or delight in truth (John 14:6), and holy fear of God, or the consecrated desire to please God (Ps. 110:10; Decree of Damasus, *SCD* 83).

The sevenfold gifts of the Spirit were from early times closely connected with confirmation or reaffirmation of baptismal vows. These gifts of the Spirit offered grace to walk the way of holiness (Augustine, *Comm. on Ps.* 150; Tho. Aq., *ST 1–2* Q68; Calvin, *Comm.* 7:374–75). By these gifts the Spirit imparts to the soul the readiness to respond to grace in all that pertains to salvation. The gifts of the Spirit make the faithful ready to discern and do the will of God, following the promptings of the Spirit whatever the context (1 Cor. 1:7). Grace awakens and enlivens quiescent spiritual capacities of persons and helps them work out their salvation without displacing grace or exempting the will from disciplined effort (Ambrose, *Duties NPNF* 2 10:50).

Fruit of the Spirit

The fruit of the Spirit is summarized by Paul: "But the fruit of the Spirit is love, joy, peace, patience [forbearance, long-suffering], kindness, goodness, faithfulness, gentleness [meekness, mildness], and self-control [modesty, continence]. Against such there is no law. Those who belong to Christ Jesus have crucified the sinful nature with its passions and desires. Since we live by the Spirit, let us keep in step with the Spirit" (Gal. 5:22–25).

All these behavioral responses are made easy, light, and joyful by the power of the Spirit, from whom these fruits spring (Chrysostom, *Hom. on Gal.* 5). The transformation enabled by the Spirit is like an organism: whole and uniting its parts.

As dead leaves fall from a tree in the winter, so the old fallen leaves (works of the flesh) gradually settle to the ground: adultery, fornication, hatred, strife, idolatry, envy, murder, drunkenness (Gal. 5:19–21; Fulgentius, *On the Remission of Sins* 1.15.3). As new growth rises, there awakens the bud, then the fruits of Christian freedom, enabling faith to become active in works of love (Clement of Alex., *Stromata*, 4.8).

Cardinal Virtues Enlivened by Grace:
Faith, Hope, and Love

Sanctifying grace confers and enables many forms of behavioral excellence (*arete* or virtue). Faith, hope, and love are chief among them. They are offered and enabled by sanctifying grace and conferred by the means of grace (Chrysostom, *Hom. on 1 Cor.* 33, 34). They begin to grow in the justified sinner in the new birth and gradually mature through the day by day reception of sanctifying grace.

The character that is formed out of sacrificial suffering produces hope, and "hope does not disappoint us, because God has poured out his love into our hearts by the Holy Spirit, whom he has given us" (Rom. 5:5). Paul summarized these gifts in a way that has subsequently imprinted all Christian moral teaching: "And now these three remain: faith, hope and love. But the greatest of these is love. Follow the way of love and eagerly desire spiritual gifts" (1 Cor. 13:12–14:1; Cyprian, *Treatise, Unity of the Catholic Church* 14).

Centuries of consensual exegesis is brought to focus by Thomas: "There are three theological virtues,—faith, by which we know God; hope, by which we trust to obtain Him; and charity, by which we love Him" (Tho. Aq., *Quaestiones Disputatae de Virtutibus in Communi*, 12; Pohle, *DT* 6:365). The grace offered in baptism is the beginning of faith, hope, and love in the Christian community. These virtues transmute natural moral virtues and enable them to grow in reference to final judgment and eternal blessedness.

Cardinal Moral Virtues

In advancing faith, hope, and love, common grace also confers and enables the growth of moral virtues, which have often been summarized as four cardinal types, following a Platonic-Aristotelian tradition long esteemed by Christian exegetes: prudence, justice, fortitude, and temperance (Tho. Aq. *ST* 1–2 Q63.3). These are textually set forth in Wisdom 8:7: "And if a man love justice, her labors have great virtues; for she teachs temperance, and prudence, and justice, and fortitude." Prudence seeks to perfect the intellect in forming judgments, justice shapes the will in guarding human rights, fortitude disposes the will under threat, and temperance inclines the appetites in the ordering of the passions. This language became implanted in the catechisms: "Prudence disposes us in all circumstances to form right judgments about what we must do or not do. Justice disposes us to give everyone what belongs to him. Fortitude disposes us to do what is good in spite of any difficulty. Temperance disposes us to control our desires and use rightly the things which please our senses" (*Baltimore Catech.*). These four excellent types of moral behavior are to some extent able to be nurtured by natural, rational, and moral means, though always assisted by common and preparatory grace. They are called cardinal virtues because they are like key compass points.

The nurture of moral virtues (meaning excellent moral habits of behavior) is vital to Christian discipleship. Among these are: "Filial piety and patriotism, which dispose us to honor, love, and respect our parents and our country. Obedience, which disposes us to do the will of our superiors. Veracity, which disposes us to tell the truth. Liberality, which disposes us rightly to use worldly goods. Patience, which disposes us to bear up under trials and difficulties. Humility, which disposes us to acknowledge our limitations. Chastity, or purity, which disposes us to be pure in soul and body," and more generally religion, which is "the highest moral virtue since it disposes us to offer to God the worship that is due Him" (*Baltimore Catech.*: 100–101).

Adoption into the Family of God

When the child of a stranger is received into an enduring bond in a family so as to convey to that child all the rights and benefits that belong to the natural children and heirs, that is called adoption. Christianly understood, adoption is that act of God by which we as strangers are received into God's family, conveying to us all the privileges of sonship and daughterhood (Ambrose, *Letter* 50). Hence adoption is a more interpersonal and encompassing metaphor than a court verdict or the canceling of a debt, since it expresses the bonding of the stranger into a new relationship of covenant and undeserved inheritance (Gal. 4:4, 5; Eph. 2:12–19; Marius Victorinus, *Epis. to Gal.* 2.4.3–6).

The intent of consensual teaching of sonship has been not to exclude but include daughterhood by generic reference within the notion of *huios* (descendant, offspring, son). Inheritance is the assured possession of all who believe (Chrysostom, *Hom. on Rom.* 14).

In the creation of humanity, God breathed into Adam and Eve his own life, after God's own likeness and image, making them children of God. They were placed in the Garden with the promise of inheritance of life, conditioned upon their obedience. It is this inheritance that was lost in the fall (Gen. 3:1–24). But this image of God, the original condition of sonship and daughterhood, lost by sin, is being restored in regeneration and adoption (Hilary, *Trin.* 6.18–25). To those who believe, he gives the renewed right of inheritance in the family of God, which John's Gospel calls "the right to become children of God" (John 1:13; Cyril of Alex., *Comm. on John* 1.9). "If any one is formed in Christ, he is formed into a child of God" (Cyril of Alexandria, *Orat. on Isa.* 2.4).

The Unity of Justifying, Regenerating, and Adopting Grace

By justification the believer is pardoned for offenses against the Father. By regeneration one is given new life in the Spirit. By adoption one is permitted to reenter the Father's family.

Justification removes obstacles between God and the sinner. Regeneration by giving new life breaks the dominion of sin and reorders the direction of the heart toward the love of God. Only on this basis may adoptive grace then make the new creature a son or daughter, a member of God's family, prepared to receive the promised inheritance (Luther, *Comm. on Romans*).

Those justified become heirs (Titus 3:7). By adoption, they are "no longer foreigners and aliens, but fellow citizens with God's people and members of God's household" (Eph. 2:19; Marius Victorinus, *Epis. to Eph.* 1.2.19). "*Justification* removes our *guilt*, which is a barrier in the way of our admission into God's family; *regeneration* changes our *hearts*, imparting a fitness for the family, and *adoption* actually *receives* us therein" (Weaver, *CT*:176, italics added). "Justification consists in the pardon of the guilty, regeneration in the moral renovation of the unholy, and adoption in the gracious reception of those who are alienated from God and disinherited" (Wakefield, *CT* 2:434).

The New Testament constantly interweaves these three dimensions of salvation teaching. One who is uprighted by grace is born anew into a present resurrected life and an incomparable future family inheritance. "In his great mercy he has given us new birth into a living hope through the resurrection of Jesus Christ from the dead, and into an inheritance that can never perish, spoil or fade" (1 Pet. 1:3, 4; Didymus the Blind, *Comm. on 1 Pet.* 1.4).

No one is justified without also being given new life in the Spirit and being adopted into the family of God (Calvin, *Inst.* 3.2, 3.20). Each implies the other. Adoption is not artificially separable from rebirth, but another way of viewing the same work of grace.

It is grace alone that unifies the three dimensions: *Convicting grace* reveals to the sinner the depths of the human predicament, leading to repentance. *Justifying grace* pardons sin and invites trusting faith in the forgiving God. *Regenerating grace* redirects our dominant affections from the godless love of self to the selfless love of God. *Adopting grace* welcomes the prodigal back into the family of God (Westminster *Conf.* 12).

Throughout this renewal, the Spirit witnesses within our spirits that we are children of God, assured of the undeserved inheritance of salvation (Calvin, *Reply to Sadolet*; J. Wesley, *WJW* 5:111–44). The order of salvation moves steadily from the teaching of repentance, faith, justification, regeneration, and the indwelling Spirit toward adoption, assurance, and union with Christ (R. Watson, *TI* 2:24; Raymond, *ST* 2:361–72). This is the stream of reasoning in classic Christian salvation teaching. It is an orderly sequence held together by the unity of divine grace.

Adoption Defined

Adoption (*huiothesia*) is that work of the Spirit by which we are received into the family of God and readied for eternal inheritance (Rom. 8:15–21; Origen, *Comm. on Rom.* 8.15; Chrysostom, *Hom. on Rom.* 14). Adoption suggests legal means by which a child not of the family can be taken into the family with full rights and privileges of that relationship. Such a person is ceremonially and legally born into a new life so as to enter fully into a new family.

The Westminster Confession concisely summarized for many Protestants the benefits of those who receive the "grace of adoption." They:

> *enjoy the liberties and privileges of the children of God;*
> *have his name put upon them;*
> *receive the Spirit of adoption;*
> *have access to the throne of grace with boldness;*
> *are enabled to cry, Abba, Father;*
> *are pitied, protected, provided for,*
> *are chastened by him as by a father;*
> *yet never cast off, but sealed to the day of redemption,*
> *and inherit the promises, as heirs of everlasting salvation.*

(Westminster *Conf.* 12)

By adoption, the Father reinstates into his family as sons and daughters—hence heirs—those who, disinherited by sin, had become aliens and outcasts (Tho. Aq., *ST* 2:2047, 2263). "Now if we are children, then we are heirs—heirs of God and co-heirs with Christ" (Rom. 8:17; Ambrosiaster, *Comm. on Paul*, Rom. 8.15–17). Adoption teaching shows how a fitting means has been provided by which a stranger to the covenant (sinner, idolater, Gentile), by choice alienated from the family of God may be brought back into the family with full privileges of communion with the Father (Gal. 4:5; Rom. 8:15; Eph. 1:8).

Rebirth and adoption are complementary, not opposing word-pictures: By rebirth one is born anew into the family. By adoption one is claimed for the family by fond choice. Both have the same effect so far as inheritance is concerned. Either by birth or adoption one may belong to a family. Those adopted are given the same full rights that natural sons and daughters enjoy in approaching a loving father with their needs and hopes (John 3:3; Rom. 8:15).

In the same passage in which Paul declared that "in Christ" there is neither "male nor female" (Gal. 3:28), he elaborated: "But when the time had fully come, God sent his Son, born of a woman, born under law, to redeem those under law, that we might receive the full rights of sons [offspring, *huiothesian*]. Because you are sons, God sent the Spirit of his Son into our hearts, the Spirit who calls out, 'Abba, Father.' So you are no longer a slave, but a son; and since you are a son, God has made you also an heir" (Gal. 4:4–7). Thus the context makes it necessary that "son" be understood as generic so as to include female and male (Gal. 3:28; 4:31), "born not according to nature but according to grace" (Theodoret, *Epis. to Gal.* 4.28).

The adopting father need not be the physical father. The child need not be heir by right but by choice and grace of the parent. The adoption occurs by mutual consent. Upon adoption all affection and love due to one's own child would be due to this child (Gal. 4:7; Rom. 8:17; Ambrosiaster, *Epis. to Gal.* 4.7; Calvin, *Inst.* 3.2). "We are not sons by creation, but by the 'new creation.' We become sons not by the natural birth, but by the Spiritual birth; not by generation, but by regeneration; not by being born, but by being born again—'born from above'—'born of the Spirit'—'born of God.' This is the adoption. It has redemption beneath it, and divine life in it" (Merrill, *ACE*:148; John 1:13; Augustine, *Tractates on John* 2).

The Loss of Entitlement Restored by Grace

The pivotal premise of adoption is that sinners have lost all right to be viewed as children of God. The prodigals have run away to a far country. Their inheritance has already been irrecoverably forfeited. Even the image of God in humanity has become defaced and marred by sin (Calvin, *Inst.* 1.15). From the viewpoint of their original family rights, they are self-defined aliens, rebels, without title, having lost all rights of daughterhood and sonship. Even a king's son by rebelling against the king would lose the right of inheritance and be viewed as outlaw. Sonship implies moral responsibilities attached to being in the covenant relation of son (Ambrose, *Expos. Of Luke* 7.227; Calvin, *Inst.* 3.2.11, 3.15–17).

The delinquency of the son or daughter does not imply that the Father has ceased to love (Luke 15; Athanasius, *Festal Letter* 7). The Father continues to seek the lost, awaiting their return, ready to forgive. Until the prodigal "comes to his senses" and turns back toward home, there is no way to proceed toward reconciliation. Even then, in Jesus' parable, the son humbly confesses, "I am no longer worthy to be called your son; make me like one of your hired men" (Luke 15:17, 19; Peter Chrysologus, *Sermons* 3–5). The penitent prodigal is not left in doubt as to whether he is accepted by the Father, whose joy is communicated to him in the feast of the fatted calf.

The Great Privilege: To Become a Child of God

Apart from adoption, the one who is determined to be a slave of sin has been blocked from the family of God. "Everyone who sins is a slave to sin. Now a slave has no permanent place in the family" (John 8:35). Whatever rights as children they might have had at the outset of human history have been long since collectively forfeited to the power of sin.

The grace of adoption bridges the chasm between the history of sin and the holy God, making daughterhood-sonship once again plausible without demeaning the holiness of God. This is not a natural right, but a gift of grace. They once again become daughters and sons of God by being born anew from above by faith (John 3:3; Gal. 3:26).

To be a child of God is to be given grace to refract once again in time and space the holiness and goodness of the Father. That is the primary meaning of the phrase "created in the image of God"—able to mirror the goodness of God. Insofar as the sinner is unable to mirror the holy love of God, a major spiritual renovation is required. Those dead in sins must be raised to new life. The dead do not raise themselves (Rom. 7:7–25). So we are heirs only as joint heirs in union with the Son. "He who has the Son has life; he who does not have the Son of God does not have life" (1 John 5:12; Bede, *On 1 John* 5.11.12; Calvin, *Comm.* 22:261–64).

Discipline as Evidence of Inclusion into the Family

In the new family under the governance of *Abba*, children have the distinct advantage of the caring discipline of a loving Parent. The purpose of discipline is correction and growth toward fuller responsible freedom, holy life, and happiness (Tertullian, *Of Patience* 11).

The key passage for this teaching is Hebrews 12, where we are reminded of "the exhortation that addresses you as children—'My child, do not regard lightly the discipline of the Lord, or lose heart when you are punished by him; for the lord disciplines those whom he loves and chastises every child whom he accepts.' Endure trials for the sake of discipline. God is treating you as children; For what child is there whom a parent does not discipline? If you do not have that discipline in which all children share, then you are illegitimate and not his children. Moreover, we had human parents to discipline us, and we respected them. Should we not be even more willing to be subject to the Father of spirits and life? For they disciplined us for a short time as seemed best to them, but he disciplines us for our good, in order that we may share his holiness. Now, discipline always seems painful rather than pleasant at the time, but later it yields the peaceful fruit of righteousness to those who have been trained by it" (Heb. 12:5–11; Chrysostom, *On Epis. to Heb.* 29.2; cf. Ps. 94:12; Prov. 3:11, 12).

The surest proof of inclusion in the family is the evidence of discipline. Those who are undisciplined have not yet fully and freely joined the family. They cling to their own righteousness, resist the call to repent, and no longer benefit from the discipline always found in a loving, caring family. But under the disciplined life of faith, "How great is the love the Father has lavished on us, that we should be called children of God! And that is what we are!" (1 John 3:1; Bede, *On 1 John* 3.1). It is the disciplining Father who is preparing believers to "share in the inheritance" (Col. 1:12).

Adoption into the family does not imply a relaxation of all requirements or claims. Ironically the presence of spiritual struggle is itself evidence of adoption (Baxter, *PW* 21:219–31). After the Lord "takes possession of the heart," one begins to resist what he once loved, and to love what he once resisted. "Thence comes that continual battle which is between flesh and the Spirit in God's children, while the flesh and the natural man, being corrupt, lust for things pleasant and delightful to themselves, and are envious in adversity and proud in prosperity, and every moment prone and ready to offend the majesty of God. But the Spirit of God bears witness to our spirit that we are the sons of God" (Scots Confession, 13).

The Modern Dilution

Modern secular piety claims on the simple grounds of creation a natural relation with God unimpeded by sin. All privileges and immunities of unhampered goodness are imagined to be equally distributed as if without reference to any actual history of sin.

The secular imagination posits that if I am basically good and getting ever better, and my self-interested passions are reliable guides, if there might be a divine Giver or source, such would not reject me for any conceivable reason. Such is the diluted modern version of the teaching of adoption by nature, not grace. The resulting fantasy is a God who can't say no, who draws persons who never lack good intentions toward a Christ without a cross.

Conscience amid modernity has become so seared that we imagine we are welcomed by God while we are doing precisely what God disapproves, and remain determined to continue (Amos 5:23; Apostolic Const. 6.5.12).

Christian teaching assumes the opposite: that the history we share with the first humans has come to a disastrous end—our own sin, tempted in all things. God as caring *Abba*, a central teaching of classical Christianity, has been diluted by a thinner modern version that denies the history of corrupted freedom and, in the interest of tolerance, romanticizes human innate goodness. This view promotes a distorted vision of the family of God, as if human creation had never actually fallen, so as to remove any need for rebirth from above. Though modernity clings desperately to the belief that we are by nature children of God, classic Christianity remembers how deeply we are "by nature children of wrath" (Eph. 2:3; Augustine, *On Marriage and Concupiscence* 2.20). "By nature" implies choice (Gregory of Nyssa, *Ag. Eunomius* 3.1.116). It is only by the grace of adoption that we become children of God "through faith." Adoption into the family of God implies turning completely away from the way that leads to death.

Assurance of Salvation Through the Witness of the Spirit

Someone could own a gold mine and be wholly unaware of it. The issue at stake in the teaching of assurance is how I come to know I am included in the inheritance of the family of God. Grace provides whatever is needed to make the recognition of grace plausible (Ursinus, *CHC*:323–24). The Spirit is working to find a way to overcome our resistances, even though this takes time, and may have to be discovered through hard challenges (Calvin, *Inst.* 3.2, 3.8.8, 3.20; J. Wesley, *WJW* 1:77).

Assurance Defined

Assurance is that part of Christian teaching that asks how personal salvation is made credible, plausible, and knowable to the believer. Faith promises to bring to the faithful a blessed assurance of adoption into the family of God (Origen, *Comm. on Rom.* 8.12–17; Baxter, *PW* 9:53–59).

Scripture promises that this assurance is given by the direct witness of the Holy Spirit (Rom. 8:15, 16; Ambrosiaster, *Comm. on Paul*, Rom. 8.11–17). As the Father grants pardon, as the Son offers himself as a pardoning sacrifice, so the Spirit completes and consummates the mission of the Son by raising up new life. The Spirit not only adopts the believer into the family of God, but also imparts to the responsive believer the growing awareness of this reconciled relationship (Calvin, *Comm.* 19:289–303). Wherever these testimonies and convictions are being clearly received and plausibly appropriated, there the grace of assurance is being awakened and applied by the Spirit (Chrysostom, *Baptismal Instructions ACW* 31:107–9).

The idea of assurance appears repeatedly in the New Testament: "Let us draw near to God with a sincere heart in full assurance [*plērophoria*] of faith" (Heb. 10:22; Cyril of Jerusalem, *Catech. Lect.* 3.4). "We want each of you to show this same diligence to the very end, in order to make your hope sure" (Heb. 6:11; Chrysostom, *On Epis. Heb.* 10.5).

Adoption and Assurance

Adoption and assurance are so closely joined as to be virtually a single teaching: "Because you are sons, God sent the Spirit of his Son into our hearts, the Spirit who calls out, 'Abba, Father.' So you are no longer a slave, but a son; and since you are a son, God has made you also an heir" (Gal. 4:6, 7; Marius Victorinus, *Epis. to Gal.* 2.4.5–6). By adoption we enter the family of God; by assurance we understand that this has indeed happened and is reliably knowable (Calvin, *Inst.* 1.17.7, 8; 3.24).

The Spirit bears witness within, and assurance is what we experience as a result. It is by the power of the Spirit that we learn to say "Father" (Ambrosiaster, *Epis. to Gal.* 4.5–7). In the adoption of believers into God's family, it is God's own

Spirit who witnesses jointly with our spirit that we are sons and daughters of God. Our cry, "Abba," is prompted by the Spirit's testimony within, so that we are assured that our filial confidence is no delusion (J. Wesley, *WJW* 5:132–44).

It is not an accident that grace offers assurance. Rather it is a property of grace itself to offer testimony of its own veracity (Jerome, *Epis. to Eph.* 2.4–10). Grace is characterized by giving. The Holy Spirit is prototypically a free gift (*charis*). That is what God the Spirit does: give (Heb. 2:4; Chrysostom, *Epis. to Heb.* 3.8,9).

Conjoint Testimony of Scripture and Experience

The witness of our own spirits corroborates the inner testimony of the Holy Spirit. It is testimony of a growing good conscience toward God. Even if it is not completely grown, one experiences good conscience as growing. This experiential testimony emerges directly out of reflection upon what we feel strengthening in our souls as a result of justifying grace. It is a conclusion drawn conjointly from scriptural testimony and a conscience void of offense (J. Wesley, *WJW* 5:111–144).

Wherever the fruits of the Spirit are being borne in experience, one is led naturally to resolve: Therefore I am a child of God. "The testimony of the Spirit is an inward impression of the soul, whereby the Spirit of God directly witnesses to my spirit that I am a child of God; that Jesus Christ hath loved me, and given himself for me; and that all my sins are blotted out, and I, even I, am reconciled to God. . . . Thus 'the testimony of our own spirit' is, with the most intimate conviction, manifested to our hearts, in such a manner as, beyond all reasonable doubt, to evince the reality of our sonship" (J. Wesley, *WJW* 5:111–134).

The believer's spirit bears testimony, responsive to and alongside that of the Holy Spirit, that one is adopted into the family of God. The function of conscience (*suneidēsis*) is to bear witness to God's requirement, "accusing or else excusing" actions (Origen, *Comm. on Rom.* 2.15). Paul was required to speak hard truth. He remained confident that his conscience was bearing witness to confirm truth even against our resistances (Rom. 9:1). To the Corinthians he wrote, "Our conscience testifies that we have conducted ourselves in the world, and especially in our relations with you, in holiness and sincerity that are from God. We have done so not according to worldly wisdom but according to God's grace" (2 Cor. 1:12, 13; Ambrosiaster, *Comm. on Paul*, 2 Cor. 1.12).

The same Spirit who convinces the sinner of sin convinces the faithful of pardon. The same One who pardons assures of pardon. At the point of conviction, one may be less aware of good conscience than of sin. Yet in due time the confirmation of good conscience is drawn toward belief (1 Pet. 3:16–21; Hilary of Arles, *Intro. Comm. on 1 Pet.* 3.16).

Whether Temptations Continue Following Assurance

The teaching of adoption does not deny that the faithful are permitted to go through periods of temptation and doubt and may temporarily experience the eclipse of God. Amid such trials, no prayer is more rightly conceived than "Lord, I believe; help thou mine unbelief" (Mark 9:24)—the experience of "faith, yet not full faith" (Augustine, *Sermons on New Testament Lessons* 65).

The Westminster Confession understood providential trials in this way: "True believers may have the assurance of their salvation [in] divers ways shaken, diminished, and intermitted; as, by negligence in preserving of it; by falling into some special sin, which woundeth the conscience, and grieveth the Spirit; by some sudden or vehement temptation; by God's withdrawing the light of his countenance, and suffering even such as fear him to walk in darkness and to have no light; yet are they never utterly destitute of that seed of God, and life of faith, that love of Christ and the brethren, that sincerity of heart and conscience of duty, out of which, by the operation of the Spirit, this assurance may in due time be revived, and by which, in the mean time, they are supported from utter despair" (Westminster *Conf.* 18).

The requirement is clear: "If you confess with your mouth, 'Jesus is Lord,' and believe in your heart that God raised him from the dead, you will be saved" (Rom. 10:9; Augustine, *Ag. Lying* 6.13). No further evidence or stipulation or condition is needed or required. Paul wrote that "our Gospel came to you not simply with words, but also with power [*dunamei*] with the Holy Spirit and with deep conviction" (1 Thess. 1:5; Gregory of Nyssa, *On the Christian Mode of Life,* FC 58:129).

The very process of hungering and thirsting for righteousness itself is evidence of the emerging governance of the Spirit. The testimony of conscience against a misdeed is precisely evidence of the empowering work of the Spirit. For God is greater than our self-condemnation. It is best not to impose one person's experience normatively upon another, as if assurance must be the same for each. It is different in every individual precisely because each person is an individual (Gregory Nazianzus, *Theol. Orat.* 2.28–33).

Penitential self-examination does better to focus not merely upon the psychological dynamics of doubt and ambivalence, but more so upon the vitality of union with Christ: "Examine yourselves to see whether you are in the faith; test yourselves. Do you not realize that Christ Jesus is in you—unless, of course, you fail the test?" (2 Cor. 13:5).

The Spirit offers grace to penitents and does not permit the faithful to be tempted more than they are able to bear (1 Cor. 10:13; *SCD* 804, 806). "The ability to bear [temptations] comes from God's grace, which we obtain by asking for it" (Chrysostom, *Hom. on Cor* 24.1). God does not abandon the justified, unless irreversibly abandoned by them. That abandonment would be foreseeable by the foresight of God.

The inner witness of the Spirit of God validating the salvation event is available to all believers: "Anyone who believes in the Son of God has this testimony in his heart" (1 John 5:10). It seems implausible that with all this testimony, the earnestly seeking believer would still remain completely unillumined or unaware or unsure of its import (Baxter, *PW* 20:151–54). Only by walking on this risk-laden path will the believer "find out whether my teaching comes from God" (John 7:17). "You will fully know that 'my doctrine' comes from God the Father when you choose to follow his will rather than your own" (Cyril of Alex, *Comm. on John* 4.5).

A scriptural prototype of the experience of assurance is the man born blind whose sight Jesus restored, who did not pretend to explain how the change had occurred but was grasped by a single experiential fact: "Whether he is a sinner or not, I don't know. One thing I do know. I was blind but now I see!" (John 9:25).

Paul did not hesitate to appeal to the experience of his hearers: "Have your great experiences been in vain?" (Gal. 3:4). "They had *experienced* the presence of God amidst their persecutions" (Calvin, *Comm.* 21:82, italics added). "If so, what they have suffered will not be without meaning" (Marius Victorinus, *Epis. to Gal.* 1.3.4).

Experiencing Faith, Hope, and Love Amid Trials

Wherever faith is found trusting in God through human suffering, the Spirit's work is being confirmed experientially (Athanasius, *Resurrection Letters* 8). "If we ask according to his will, he hears us, and if he hears us in everything that we ask of him, we know that we are praying according to his will" (Oecumenius, Comm. *on 1 John* 5.15).

Wherever *hope* is buoyant, the Spirit's work is being confirmed in time. "For in this hope we were saved" (Rom. 8:24), a hope that "does not disappoint" (Rom. 5:5; cf. Rom. 15:13; 1 John 3:3; Heb. 6:18, 19).

Wherever faith is becoming active in *love*, the Spirit's work is being confirmed interpersonally. A form of knowing emerges directly out of this active loving: "We know that we have passed from death to life, because we love" (1 John 3:14; Didymus the Blind, *Comm. on 1 John* 3.14). "We know that we have come to know him *if we obey* his commands" (1 John 2:3, italics added; Calvin, *Inst.* 2.16.5–7).

When self-examination reveals only poverty of spirit, it is time to ponder this irony of scriptural wisdom: "This then is how we know that we belong to the truth, and how we set our hearts at rest in his presence whenever our hearts condemn us. For God is greater than our hearts, and he knows everything" (1 John 3:19, 20; Kierkegaard, *CDisc*:297–303). "If our heart does not condemn us, then we have confidence toward God, not in the sight of other people but where God alone can see it—in our hearts" (Bede, *On 1 John* 3.21). "If we practice what we preach, we shall persuade our heart, that is to say our consciences, that we are on the right track. For then God will bear witness that we have listened to what he says" (Oecumenius, *Comm. on 1 John* 3.20).

The Cry: Abba!

A confluence of supporting testimony flows toward this assurance: the Spirit speaking through scripture, preaching, and sacrament; the direct and efficacious presence of the Spirit witnessing in the heart; the indirect testimony of conscience; and the visible fruits of faith. Each of these edifies and builds toward a palpable sense of assurance of salvation. "We know that we live in him and he is in us, because he has given us of his Spirit."(1 John 4:13). "Examine your own heart and you will know whether or not God has given his Spirit to you, for if you are full of love, you have the Spirit of God" (Bede, *On 1 John* 4.13).

When the cry "Abba, Father" emerges spontaneously from the depths, then one can be assured that grace is working. It is ironic that the pivotal testimony assuring us of our restored relation to God is itself a simple *cry:* "Father"!

The key text that sets forth the Christian teaching of assurance is Romans 8: "Those who are led by the Spirit of God are sons of God. For you did not receive a spirit that makes you a slave again to fear, but you receive the Spirit of sonship. And by him we cry, 'Abba, Father.' The Spirit himself testifies with our spirit that we are God's children" (Rom. 8:15, 16; Ambrosiaster, *Comm. on Rom.* 8.15). We learn this by these two corroboratory witnesses: God's Spirit and our own spirit together bearing the same testimony (*summartureō*).

The Certitude of Hope

The faithful are relieved of unnecessary anxiety by asking whether they indeed are persevering in doing good, whether they love to pray, whether they are patient in suffering, and whether they attend upon the ordinances of God faithfully (Thomas à Kempis, *Imitation of Christ* 3.54; Tho. Aq., *ST* 2-2, Q112.5).

It may become a pressing personal issue as to whether grace, once received, is able to be lost. The consensual tradition on the whole has answered that our awareness of saving grace can be temporarily lost, though grace from God's side never quits. When Paul wrote that he was disciplining his body "so that after I have preached to others, I myself will not be disqualified for the prize" (1 Cor. 9:27), he was assuming that such a disqualification is possible for one already in the race. When he admonished the Philippians to "work out your salvation with fear and trembling, for it is God who works in you to will and to act according to the good purpose" (Phil. 2:12, 13), he assumed not only that God is working but that our responsive coworking is called upon to bring faith into behavioral embodiment (Augustine, *Grace and Free Will* 21). "I worked harder than all of them—yet not I, but the grace of God that was with me" (1 Cor. 15:10).

The Grace of Proximate Incertitude

When Gregory I was asked by an elderly woman whether she could be absolutely certain of her election, he wisely replied, "You ask me something which is both useless and difficult; difficult, because I am unworthy to receive a revelation; useless, because it is better that you be uncertain with regard to your sins, lest in your last hour you should be unable to repent" (Epist. 7.25).

Chrysostom knew long before Freud the capacity in the heart for self-deception: for "many of our own works are hidden from us" (*Hom. on 1 Cor. 2*). Paul wrote: "I am convinced that neither death nor life, neither angels nor demons, neither the present nor the future, nor any powers, neither height nor depth, nor anything else in all creation, will be able to separate us from the love of God" (Rom. 8:38, 39). How could inward certainty exceed this description?

If coarsely objectified as a flat object of empirical inquiry, the address of the Spirit becomes suddenly elusive, self-effacing, touching our lives only to conceal that touch in mystery. Though one may be grasped immediately by the indwelling Spirit, the forms of empirical certainty that are available to us remain those of finite creatures. It is a certainty of hope not sight, based upon faith, not possession (2 Cor. 5:7; Augustine, *Letters*, To Proba 130; Calvin, *Comm.* 20:221–22).

Prayer and Regenerating Grace

In addition to baptism and Eucharist, all of the ordinary means of grace are provided to nurture new life in God. In common worship we hear the Word read and preached. The scriptures are able to make us wise unto salvation (2 Tim. 3:15). "For you have been born again, not of perishable seed, but of imperishable, through the living and enduring word of God" (1 Pet. 1:23).

Those who seek a new birth of freedom are specifically instructed to pray for it. The Spirit promises to help those who seek help (Matt. 7:7–8; Augustine, *Sermon on the Mount* 2.21.71–72). It hardly seems plausible that God would encourage us to pray, only to disappoint and reject us when we do earnestly pray that his will be done in us.

The psalmist's petition is prototypical: "Create in me a pure heart, O God, and renew a steadfast spirit within me. Do not cast me from your presence or take your Holy Spirit from me. Restore me to the joy of your salvation, and grant me a willing spirit, to sustain me" (Ps. 51:10–12; Augustine, *Comm. on Ps.* 51).

6

UNION WITH CHRIST AND SANCTIFICATION

THE LIFE OF THE BELIEVER is united with Christ's life. Christ is in the believer no less than the believer is in Christ. "On that day you will realize that I am in my Father, and you are in me, and I am in you" (John 14:20; Hilary, *Trin.* 8.15).

"If the Spirit of him who raised Jesus from the dead dwells in you, he who raised Christ Jesus from the dead will also give life to your mortal bodies through the Spirit who dwells in you" (Rom. 8:11; Chrysostom, *Hom. on Rom.* 13). Sin does not have dominion in this regenerate person, who is "not under law, but under grace" where sin no longer reigns unchecked (Rom. 6:14). By faith, the believer participates in the Son's life with the Father, being justified by his free gift (Hilary, *Trin.* 9.55).

Union with Christ

The sinner does not deserve eternal life, but receives it through faith in Christ. Christ does not deserve death, but offers death through obedience on the cross for the sinner (Chrysostom, *Baptismal Instructions* 3.21).

In this way, Christ lives in the faithful, who are treated as if righteous, clothed in Christ's righteousness, adopted as children of the family of God (Didymus the Blind, *Comm. on 2 Cor.* 5.3; Calvin, *TAA*:134–35).

In response to justifying grace, the sinner is restored to that communion with God which once characterized the original human condition before the fall when man and woman were "naked and not ashamed" (Gen. 2:25; Chrysostom, *Baptismal Instruction* 11.28).

Human consciousness still possesses its own characteristic faculties, features, and individuality, yet is being penetrated by the life of Christ (Augustine, *On the Spirit and the Letter* 38). The believer shares in that new humanity of which Christ is the head, the body of Christ.

Peter, Paul, and John all preached and taught of this union. The letter of Peter described this communion as a partaking in God's nature (2 Pet. 1:4). Paul stressed union with Christ's death and resurrection (Rom. 6). John highlighted the union with the Incarnate Son (John 6:53–57; Cyril of Alex., *Meditation on the Mystical Supper* 10). In each case the apostles were speaking of an incomparable unity that the believer experiences with God the Father through the Son: "Our fellowship is with the Father and with his son, Jesus Christ" (1 John 1:3; Andreas, *Catena*, Cramer, *CEC*:107).

Life In Christ

In this intimate communion, Christ is said to be *in* the believer and the believer *in Christ*. "Therefore, there is now no condemnation for those who are *in* Christ Jesus" (Rom. 8:1, italics added). "Abide in me, and I *in you*" (John 15:4, italics added; *Tractates on John* 81.1). To be "in Christ" means to "have Christ in us."

To be in Christ means that the believer participates in his death and resurrection: "I have been crucified with Christ and I no longer live, but Christ lives in me. The life I live in the body, I live by faith in the Son of God" (Gal. 2:20; Marius Victorinus, *Epis. to Gal.* 1.2.19).

This indwelling fellowship has potent consequences. It implies a death to sin: "Those who belong to Christ Jesus have crucified the sinful nature with its passions and desires" (Gal. 5:24; Basil, *On Baptism* 1.15). They have renounced anything that would that keep them turned away from God: "May I never boast except in the cross of our Lord Jesus Christ, through which the world has been crucified to me, and I to the world" (Gal. 6:14). "Therefore, if anyone is in Christ, he is a new creation; the old has gone, the new has come!" (2 Cor. 5:17; Augustine, *Enchiridion* 9.31; Calvin, *Inst.* 3.11.10; 4.15.6).

Union with Christ is offered to those in whom the Spirit comes to dwell. "Your body is a temple of the Holy Spirit within you" (1 Cor. 6:19; Chrysostom, *Hom. on Cor.*, 18.3). One who unites himself with the Lord is one with him in spirit. Paul's desire was simply to "be found in him" (Phil. 3:9).

The Indwelling Spirit of the Triune God

The Spirit carries on Christ's work, calling, gathering, transforming persons into likeness to Christ, communicating to them the benefits of redemption (Irenaeus, *Ag. Her.* 5.8). Where the Spirit resides, Christ resides (Rom. 8:9–11). Christian experience daily attests the gracious presence of one God in three persons. "We know that we live in him and he in us, because he has given us of his Spirit. And we have seen and testify that the Father has sent his Son to be the Savior of the world. If anyone acknowledges that Jesus is the Son of God, God lives in him and he in God" (1 John 4:13–15; Oecumenius, *Comm. on 1 John* 4).

The principal mark of the indwelling Spirit of God is responsive love: "If anyone loves me he will obey my teaching. My Father will love him, and *we* [Father and Son] will come to him and *make our home* with him" (John 14:23, italics added; Ambrose, *Letter 49 to Horontianus*). God is taking up abode in the faithful through the indwelling Spirit (Gregory Nazianzus, *Orat.* 30).

The church prays to the Father through the Spirit for the indwelling of Christ: "I pray that out of his glorious riches he may strengthen you with power through his Spirit in your inner being, so that Christ may dwell in your hearts through faith. And I pray that you, being rooted and established in love, may have power, together with all the saints, to grasp how wide and long and high and deep is the love of Christ, and to know this love that surpasses knowledge—that you may be filled to the measure of all the fullness of God" (Eph. 3:16–19; Gregory of Nyssa, *On the Three Days*).

Partaking of the Divine Nature

Life in union with Christ is like communion with the risen Lord. Faith celebrates that union through the sacraments: partaking, eating, and drinking of him who was made known to the Emmaus disciples in the breaking of bread (Luke 24:35).

As Christ partakes of the Father, so the believer partakes of Christ (John 17:11–13; Hilary, *Trin.* 10.42). This occurs archetypically at the Lord's table: "Is not the cup of thanksgiving for which we give thanks a participation in the blood of Christ? And is not the bread that we break a participation in the body of Christ? Because there is one loaf, we, who are many, are one body, for we all partake of the one loaf" (1 Cor. 10:16, 17; Augustine, *CG* 21.25; Irenaeus, *Ag. Her.* 5.2). Jesus said: "Whoever eats my flesh and drinks my blood remains in me, and I in him. Just as the living Father sent me and I live because of the Father, so the one who feeds on me will live because of me. This is the bread that came down from heaven" (John 6:56–58; Cyril of Alex., *Meditation on Mystical Supper* 10).

Believers live in Christ in all they do. They die with him, are raised with him, dwell with him eternally, and he with them. They share his righteousness, become sons through his Sonship, heirs through his inheritance, pardoned through his sacrifice (Hippolytus, *Holy Theophany* 8; Calvin, *Inst.* 3.11, 4.17).

Theosis: In What Sense Does Sanctifying Grace Enable the Soul to Partake of the Divine Nature?

Through Christ's life, death and resurrection, "he has given us his very great and precious promises, so that through them you may *participate in the divine nature*"—share the life of God in Christ through the Spirit—"and escape the corruption in the world" (2 Pet. 1:4, italics added; Tertullian, *Ag. Marcion* 2.26–27; Hippolytus, *Refutation of all Her.* 10.29).

Those who are regenerated share in the nature of the spiritual progenitor. "No one who is born of God will continue to sin, because God's seed remains in him; he cannot go on sinning, because he has been born of God" (1 John 3:9; Didymus the Blind, *Comm. on 1 John* 3.9). "So then, just as you received Christ Jesus as Lord, continue to live in him, rooted and built up in him" (Col. 2:7).

Athanasius stated the union in this crucial expression: "He was made man that we might be made God [*theopoiēthōmen*]" (*Incarnation of the Word* 54). He was "first God and then man, in order that He might allow us to share in his deity" (Athanasius, *LCHS, To Serapion* 1.24; cf. *Defence of the Nicene Council* 14; Irenaeus, *Ag. Her.* 4.38; Origen, *Ag. Celsus* 3.28), bringing us into union with himself (Gregory of Nyssa, *Ag. Eunomius*; Augustine, *Enchiridion* 37). To receive sinners and empower them to "be made like to God" is the consummating work of the Spirit (Basil, *On the Spirit* 9.23; cf. Ps. 82:6). "The Holy Spirit works in us in his own way, truly sanctifying us and joining us to himself; and by this coalescence and union of ourselves with him he makes us sharers in the divine nature, beautifying human nature with the splendor of the divinity" (Cyril of Alexandria,

Thesaurus 34; cf. *Letters* 1). God "inserts his own sanctity into us" (Cyril of Alexandria, *Comm. on John* 10, intro.).

God offers himself to the creature in such an intimate way that the creature is awakened and transfigured by divine grace (John of Damascus, *OF* 2.12). "Now we are children of God, and what we will be has not yet been made known. But we know that when he appears, we shall be like him" (1 John 3:2; Augustine, *On Trin.* 15.16.26).

How Our Lives Enter into Spiritual Union with Christ

Union with Christ is not adequately viewed as a solidarity of workers in a common task or of business partners in a coalition of interests or of the union of mind between teacher and student. Nor does Christ dwell in us in the way that a parent influences a child or a therapist is close to a client. Rather, the union is conceived more intimately as expressed in organic analogies: as cellular members of a living, functioning body, as living branches of a living vine. As one "feeds and cares for" one's body, so "Christ does for the church—for we are members of his body" (Eph. 5:29, 30; Augustine, *Tractate on John* 9.10). Consequently, union with Christ is by definition a living union (Gal. 2:20), not a conflation of inert separable objects as if the pieces of a puzzle were being put together. Mechanistic analogies fall short of describing organisms.

As seeds are buried and await new life and growth, so in union with Christ we are buried and arise with him. In *dying* to sin, the believer dies with Christ, entering daily into the full consecration that is willing to participate bodily in God's suffering through service (Ignatius, *Romans* 7–8). Union with Christ is a participation in the resurrection. Through dying to sin, one is found to be *living anew, resurrected* in Christ (Ambrose, *Paradise* 29; Calvin, *Inst.* 4.15–17). The life of faith is *hidden* in Christ, as if the body were buried. "For you died, and your life is now hidden with Christ in God. When Christ, who is your life, appears, then you also will appear with him in glory" (Col. 3:3, 4; Athanasius, *Festal Letters* 7.3).

Union of the believer with Christ is a *spiritual* union whose enlivening energy comes from God the Spirit. The Father who raised the Son "will also give life to your mortal bodies through his Spirit, who lives in you" (Rom. 8:11; Origen, *Comm. on Rom.* 8.11).

If Christ is in you, "your spirit is alive because of righteousness" (Rom. 8:10). As the Son has life by partaking of the Father, so the faithful have life by partaking of the Son (John 6:53–57; 1 Cor. 10:16, 17). Without loss of individuality, the spirit of the person is enlivened by the Spirit of Christ, so that "he who unites himself with the Lord is one with him in spirit" (1 Cor. 6:17; Origen, *OFP* 2.9.3).

So close is this union that Luther would "say with confidence: 'I am [one with] Christ,' i.e., Christ's righteousness, victory, life, etc., are mine; and Christ, in turn, says, 'I am that sinner,' i.e., his sins, death, etc., are mine, because he adheres to me, and I to him; for by faith we are joined into one body and one bone" in an "inherence, which is by faith, and whereby Christ and I are made as it were one body in spirit" (Luther, *Comm. on Gal.*:171). The righteousness conveyed in this union is the believer's by grace through faith, but not by nature or achievement. In this way we are made partakers of its benefits (1 Cor. 11:23–26; Ambrose, *Sacraments*, 4.5.21–23; Bunyan, *Works* 1:302–12). "You are what you have received" (Augustine, *Easter Sunday Homily* 227).

The Beginning of a Beautiful Friendship

Grace has the effect of making the soul beautiful, as if a sculpture was being shaped by the divine artisan (Tho. Aq., *ST* 2-2, Q145). The image of the triune

God is being once again imprinted upon the soul, where Christ is being formed in human history (Gal. 4:19; Rom. 8:29; 1 Cor. 3:16).

The same grace has the effect of drawing human persons into *friendship* with God, wherein the righteous "become the friends of God" (Wisdom 7:14), who said: "I have called you friends" (John 15:15; Irenaeus, *Ag. Her.* 4.13.4). In love as friendship (*philia*) there is conscious mutual benevolence and affection between persons (Augustine, *Comm. on John*, 85; cf. Aristotle, *Nichomachean Ethics* 8; Tho. Aq., *Comm. on Four Books of Sentences* 3.27, Q2.1.1).

"By the Holy Spirit we are established as friends of God." That which is "specially proper to the friendship" is "to take delight in a friend's presence." For "one reveals his secrets to a friend by reason of their unity in affection, but the same unity requires that what he has, he has in common with the friend" (Tho. Aq., *SCG* 4.21; cf. Augustine, *CG* 19.8). Marriage is the most intense and enduring form of friendship (Chrysostom, *Hom. on Eph.* 20), hence a fit analogy of the union of Christ with the church.

In Union with Christ, All Believers Are United with Each Other

The union each member shares with the head, unites each one to all members of the body (1 Cor. 12:12–30; Ambrose, *Of Holy Spirit* 1.3.45). The unity of Christ is already given in Christ, yet it is always being proximately actualized as a task by the community of faith in diaspora around the world.

In Christ we are one. Our task is to embody that oneness. Already we possess unity in Christ. The indicative reality of radical unity becomes an imperative task calling for our active embodiment. God's gift becomes our task. Union is fully and freely given to us in Christ, if only partially and inadequately received in faith (1 Cor. 2:12; Chrysostom, *Hom. on Paul*, 1 Cor. 2.12, 7.7).

Though believers are many, faith makes them one (Augustine, *The Creed* 2.4). In faith the "multitude of believers were of one heart and one soul" (Acts 4:32). From Christ all spiritual blessings come. In Christ they cohere. Toward him they finally are drawn (Chrysostom, *Hom. on Eph.* 1).

Sanctification

Jesus prayed for his disciples, "Sanctify them by the truth; your word is truth" (John 17:17; Gregory of Nyssa, *Trin.*, *NPNF* 2 5:328). Paul called those who heard the gospel to "offer your bodies as living sacrifices, holy and pleasing to God— this is your spiritual act of worship" (Rom. 12:1). The subject of sanctifying grace that we have been discussing above (*theosis*, union with Christ) is commonly called *sanctification*.

Sanctifying grace is the culminating phase of the Christian teaching of salvation (soteriology). The holy life is a crucial theme of teaching on the Christian life. It is integral to the life of prayer, familiar to all who worship, and a central feature for all who receive basic pre-baptismal instruction (*Early Liturgies, ANF* 7:547).

The vision of perfect love and sustained faithful responsiveness to grace is not merely an individualistic vision but a life shared in a community (Cyril of Jerusalem, *Catech. Lect.*, 4.16). It is by means of sanctifying grace that the moral disposition is being effectively transformed.

Sanctifing grace is given in order that the believer may spontaneously and habitually love good and resist evil (Basil, *On the Holy Spirit* 9.22–23). God the Spirit is enabling the human self to will the proportionally greater good

(Augustine, *Enchiridion*; 3). That embodiment occurs within a supportive community, a *communio sanctorum* (Calvin, *Inst.* 4.1, 4.10–12).

In order that this doctrine may be taught rightly in our time, sanctifying grace must be restudied in the light of Scripture and consensual exegesis. When we study sanctifying grace as a church doctrine, we soon learn that it is a mystery pointing beyond itself to the wholeness of the Spirit's own quiet, inconspicuous mystery in our midst (Cyril of Jerusalem, *Catech. Lect.* 16).

Modernity has secularized the Christian teaching of sanctification, naturalizing and reducing it to a vision of the betterment of human life or moral improvement or political achievement or upward social mobility. This has led to serious misjudgments about salvation and sanctification, resulting in a loss of resolve and vitality of these important teachings. They have been caricatured as judgmental, perfectionistic, and out of date. Biblical sanctification themes have been trimmed down and squeezed into fashionable metaphors of psychological growth or stress reduction or creative management or *Realpolitik* or social change or moral development. My purpose is to allow the classic consensual teaching of the holy life to be stated in its own powerful terms.

Toward a Classic Ecumenical Statement of Sanctification Teaching

I intend to state only those points on which Christians of widely different viewpoints have generally concurred regarding the aim of the Christian life.

Centuries of debate have burdened the presumed agenda with persistent exaggerations and distortions of the teaching of the holy life. Protestants have sometimes spoken too abruptly of faith as if without works of love. Popular pietism has spoken of emotive faith as if without intellect. Popular Catholicism has sometimes portrayed works as meritorious apart from the good news of unmerited justifying grace.

This reappraisal of sanctification teaching emerges out of a broad tradition shared by Baptists and Catholics. I hope it will be examined fairly by Calvinists, Arminians, Lutherans, Social Liberals, and Charismatics. I hope they will see that their own teaching is being affirmed and the mind of the believing church is being accurately represented. I intend to allay quickly the worries of Reformed critics who might assume that I might be pressing for a particular view of sanctification, perhaps an Eastern Orthodox or Wesleyan-Arminian view, so as to ignore the profound views of sanctification in the Augustinian-Lutheran-Reformed tradition. That would misread my intentions. Hence I will be quoting frequently in this chapter from Augustinian, Lutheran and Reformed sources on sanctification, which I believe to be substantially consistent with the line of argument that thus far developed from the ancient-ecumenical consensus.

What Is Sanctifying Grace?

The Westminster Catechism provided a prototoype definition of sanctification as "the work of God's free grace, whereby we are renewed in the whole man after the image of God, and are enabled more and more to die unto sin and live unto righteousness."

The influential American Calvinist theologian Charles Hodge (*ST* 3:213), stated well the shared common points of the Reformed teaching of the distinction between justification and sanctification in a way that Reformed teachings would on the whole agree (and upon which the ancient patristic consensus would concur, cf. Oden, *The Justification Reader*):

Justification	Sanctification
What Christ has done for us	What the Spirit does in us
A completed, transient act	A progressive, continuing work
A forensic declaration	An effect of continuing grace
Enabling a changed relation	Enabling a change of character between sinner and the holy God

Sanctification "consists in the gradual triumph of the new nature implanted in regeneration over the evil that still remains after the heart is renewed" (Hodge, *ST* 3:224). During the entire time that sanctifying grace is continuing to work—throughout life—the believer is daily called upon to confess, repent, and pray for forgiveness.

The new birth begins a life that grows in responsiveness to unmerited grace and presses on in the way of holiness. The fullness of sanctifying grace is not necessarily received immediately at the beginning of conversion but grows through an extended developmental process (Bonaventure, *The Soul's Journey into God*, *CWS*:59).

The key text is Philippians 3: "Not that I have already obtained all this, or have already been made perfect, but I press on to take hold of [*katalabō*, capture, appropriate] that for which Christ Jesus took hold of me. Brothers, I do not consider myself yet to have taken hold of it. But one thing I do: Forgetting what is behind and straining toward what is ahead, I press on toward the goal to win the prize for which God has called me heavenward in Christ Jesus. All of us who are mature should take such a view of things. And if on some point you think differently, that too God will make clear to you. Only let us live up to what we have already attained" (Phil. 3:12–16; Marius Victorinus, *Epis. to Phil.* 3.12–15).

It belongs to God's saving economy (*oikonomia*, plan of salvation, arrangement, order) that the faithful shall be made holy by the indwelling Spirit. This occurs precisely within the limits of finitude. For "from the beginning God chose you to be saved through the sanctifying work of the Spirit and through belief in the truth" (2 Thess. 2:13; Cyril of Jerusalem, *Catech. Lect.* 5.12).

Sexual accountability is not an ancillary aspect of this process. In the tradition of Paul it is a key case in point for understanding the good life in God: "It is God's will that you should be sanctified: that you should avoid sexual immorality, that each of you should learn to control his own body in a way that is holy and honorable" (1 Thess. 4:3, 4; Chrysostom, *Hom. on Thess.* 4).

The way of life to be put aside is that of the old self "corrupted by its deceitful desires" (Eph. 4:22), falsehood, stealing, seething anger, and unwholesome talk (Ambrosiaster, *Epis. to Eph.* 4:25–29). "Get rid of all bitterness, rage, and anger, brawling and slander, along with every form of malice" (4:31), sexual immorality, greediness, obscenity, idolatry, deception (Eph. 5:3–6; Chrysostom, *Hom. on Eph.* 13,14).

"Setting Apart" Under Law and Gospel

To sanctify something is to set it apart for holy use, to separate it out from the profane world for sacred employment. To sanctify (Heb. *qadesh*, *hagiazō*, set apart, to separate) means to consecrate for holy purpose, to make holy in the proximate sense that finite creatures may maximally participate in God's holiness (Chrysostom, *Hom. on Gal.* 3.27).

Under Hebraic law, persons and things were set apart, separated, and offered to God for holy purpose. The temple, the tithe, the seventh day, the priesthood, and the vessels for holy use are Hebraic examples of such a setting apart (Gen. 2:3; Exod. 30). The furniture and utensils of the temple and priestly vestments were sanctified or set aside, consecrated wholly to that special service.

The law applying to the temple was fulfilled in the sacrifice of Christ. So the earlier forms of consecration were transmuted. They now point to the new creation enabled by a new birth. They seek to manifest the steady and growing conformity of the whole person to the will and image of God (Gregory of Nyssa, *FGG*:81–84).

Holy Living as Gift and Task

God's sanctifying work in us is not reducible to our work of moral exercises. No one is sanctified by his or her own will or ego strength or moral power, but only by grace—by God's unmerited gift. Though sanctification elicits and requires discipline, it is not limited to acts of discipline. It is from beginning to end a work of God's free and sovereign grace (Ambrosiaster, *Epis. to Eph.* 2.4–10).

The dead cannot voluntarily decide to rise. However much moral initiative I may apply, I cannot while spiritually dead in sin raise myself up to new life. The soul that is spiritually dead is unable of itself to make the slightest move toward God. The holy life is lived as if from the grave, from which the sinner hears the voice of redeeming grace, and is raised by its power (Luke 7:22; 1 Cor. 15; Cyril of Alex., *Comm. on Luke*, Hom. 37).

As in the case of justifying grace, sanctifying grace is God's own work, not our work, not our merit added to Christ's merit. Just as no one can boast for being born, no one upon receiving sanctifying grace can make a claim of merit upon one's growth process (Gal. 6:14). In the presence of God's own holiness, our sin, like Isaiah's, reaches for a "live coal from the altar to sanctify our lips" (Kuyper, *WHS*:441).

Paul prayed for the church at Thessalonica, "May God himself, the God of peace, sanctify you through and through" (1 Thess. 5:23—entirely, wholly; Gregory of Nyssa, *On Perfection* 205). The church proclaims, admonishes, and teaches this wholesome doctrine " that we may present everyone mature [*teleion*, complete, perfect] in Christ" (Col. 1:28).

Though sin remaining after baptism is encumbering, we are called to "make every effort to live in peace with all men and to be holy; without holiness no one will see the Lord. See to it that no one misses the grace of God and that no bitter root grows up to cause trouble" (Heb. 12:14; Jerome, *Letters* 66,8). "Sanctification does not exclude all cooperation," but calls for "unremitting and strenuous exertion" (Hodge, *ST* 3:226).

The Hope and Limits of Sanctification Teaching

The gracious purpose of God in creation is being revealed in the actual universal history of humanity. This purpose is redemption, which is being carried forward ultimately to a fitting consummation. God would not write a drama without a fitting ending, even if that ending is not yet grasped but only glimpsed.

The believer remains an active self-determining agent in human history, past, present, and future, hence ever tempted to fall from grace. The holy God does not abide sin in his temple. "I am the Lord your God; consecrate yourselves and be holy, because I am holy" (Lev. 11:44). "But just as he who called you is holy, so be holy in all you do; for it is written: 'Be holy, because I am holy' " (1 Pet. 1:15, 16; Barth, *CD* 2/2:515). The believer becomes the temple of God.

God requires holiness, but more so provides the means of receiving it: "Since God, who called us to salvation by the gospel, is holy, those who obey his calling must also become holy in all their thoughts and behavior, especially since he who calls us to this also provides the necessary sanctification himself" (Didymus the Blind, *Comm. on 1 Pet.* 1.15).

The holiness required is simple. It is that we faithfully receive the gift of atoning grace day by day. Christ died to deliver sinners from sin, not only from the guilt of sin but also the power of sin. The cross does not address humanity simply in theory as a formal juridical verdict of pardon, but intends to reshape each hearer actually and behaviorally toward walking in the way of sacrificial love.

We are not being asked to be wise above what is written, but to be made wise by what is clearly written. The more perfect knowledge of that which is seen as if through a glass darkly may be left to that future illumination when we will "know fully, even as . . . fully known" (1 Cor. 13:12; Clement of Alex., *Stromata* 1.94). "The secret things belong to the Lord our God, but the things revealed belong to us and to our children forever, that we may follow all the words of this law" (Deut. 29:29). "The highest righteousness of man is this—whatever virtue he may be able to acquire, not to think it is his own, but the gift of God. He then who is born of God does not sin, so long as the seed of God remains in him" (Jerome, *Ag. Pelagians, NPNF* 2 6:454).

The Surprising Breadth of the Consensus

Evangelicals and Catholics may be closer on sanctification than either party is quite ready to acknowledge. This is made clearer by examining how far the evangelical confessions reflect this patristic consensus. The New Hampshire Confession, for example, defined sanctification as "the process by which, according to the will of God, we are made partakers of his holiness." It confessed that "it is a progressive work; that it is begun in regeneration; and that it is carried on in the hearts of believers by the presence and power of the Holy Spirit, the Sealer and Comforter, in the continual use of the appointed means, especially the Word of God, self-examination, self-denial, watchfulness and prayer" (*CC*:337).

God does not command what is impossible (Hermas, *Mand.* 12.3). "Sanctification is the process by which the regenerate gradually attain to moral and spiritual perfection through the presence and power of the Holy Spirit dwelling in their hearts. It continues throughout the earthly life, and is accomplished by the use of all the ordinary means of grace, and particularly by the Word of God" (So. Baptist Convention of 1925). This language is drawn from the early ecumenical consensus on how the Spirit draws humanity toward life in God.

The Lausanne Faith and Order Conference defined sanctification as "the work of God, whereby through the Holy Spirit He continually renews us and the whole Church, delivering as from the power of sin, giving us increase in holiness, and transforming us into the likeness of His Son through participation in His death and in His risen life."

Called to Holiness

Without Spot or Blemish

Christ was anointed to be set apart sacrificially for our sakes, that we might be totally set apart for him: "For them I sanctify myself, that they too may be truly sanctified" (John 17:19; Ambrose, *The Christian Faith* 2.9.77–78). Christ "gave himself for us to redeem us from all wickedness and to purify for himself a people that are his very own," in a unique way that makes us "eager to do what is good" (Tit. 2:14; Chrysostom, *Hom. on Gal.* 2.20).

Like an incomparably loving bridegroom, "Christ loved the church and gave himself up for her to make her holy, cleansing her by the washing with water through the word and to present her to himself as a radiant church, without stain or wrinkle or any other blemish, but holy and blameless" (Eph. 5:25–27). "We refer this to the endurance of the husband, which entails his giving himself for the wife and bearing and suffering all that is hers, even sharing in all that she endures, she is being cleansed with water and the Word—that is, she is being purified in the Lord's sight when he renders her pure and by his endurance makes her ready to be sanctified by washing and the Word" (Marius Victorinus, *Epis. to Eph.* 2.5.25–26).

The covenant people of God are being enabled by grace to live the holy life, hence called to holiness. The Father chose us in the Son "before the creation of the world to be holy and blameless in his sight. In love he predestined us to be adopted as his sons through Jesus Christ" (Eph. 1:4, 5).

Walking Worthy of Our Calling

The walk of the new life is one of mercy, tranquillity, holiness, love, self-giving, righteousness (Eph. 4:20–5:2), being filled with the Spirit, giving thanks always (5:18–21).

It is a way of life that reshapes all human actions and relations—between husbands and wives, parents and children, and all those one meets daily in the domestic and economic orders (Eph. 5:22–6:9). The first half of the letter to Ephesus set forth the vocation of the called-out community. The last half (beginning "Therefore," Eph. 4:1) describes the conduct or walk of the community through time. It demonstrates the steady link between calling and community, gift and task, teaching and practice.

To walk worthy of their calling, the faithful are to walk in unity shaped by love: "Be completely humble and gentle; be patient, bearing with one another in love. Make every effort to keep the unity of the Spirit through the bond of peace. There is one body and one Spirit" (Eph. 4:2–4). The oneness of Christ's body is animated by one Spirit, "one Lord, one faith, one baptism; one God and Father of all" (Eph. 4:5, 6), yet within this unity there are diverse gifts of the Spirit (Eph. 4:7–16). The purpose of these gifts is "to prepare God's people for works of service, so that the body of Christ may be built up until we all reach unity in the faith and in the knowledge of the Son of God and become mature, attaining the whole measure of the fullness of Christ" (Eph. 4:12, 13; Theodoret, *Epis. to Eph.* 4.13).

The English word *saint* derives from the Latin *sanctus*—holy, consecrated. A saint (*hagios*) is one set apart whom God's grace is making holy, who in eternity will share fully in God's holiness, and in whose life is already recognizable some fruits of a holy, charitable, merciful, humble life (Eph. 1:18; 3:8, 18). Note that the same term is applied to those who are justified and newly born in faith (1 Cor. 1:2), being separated from sin and consecrated to God's service. Every member of the body, no matter at what stage of maturity, is called to be holy even as God is holy.

Maturing Grace Grows Out of Justifying Grace

Justifying grace offers the sinner a righteousness not his own. Sanctifying grace enables a freely willed righteousness that emerges cooperatively by grace-enabled freedom responding to God the Spirit. Justifying grace erases guilt through forgiveness. Sanctifying grace uproots the behavioral causes of guilt through the reshaping of human choices.

Justifying grace is a *finished* work of the Son on the cross. Out of this flows a *continuing* and current work of the Spirit in our hearts and social processes. In sanctifying grace, God's Spirit works precisely within and around us, seeking and enabling our cooperative response, calling upon all our redeemed powers to be applied to working out our salvation while God is working in us to will and to do according to his good pleasure (Phil. 2:12, 13; Augustine, *On Grace and Free Will* 21; J. Wesley, *WJW* 6:506–13).

The paired Augustinian terms *preparing grace* (or *prevenient*) and *justifying grace* encompass both the period of preparation that leads up to saving faith in the cross, and saving faith itself. "Conversion" points to that decisive moment in which the sinner becomes fully receptive to atoning grace on the cross and receives it as applied to him- or herself. At that point the sinner begins, by repentance and faith through God's pardon, to be cleansed from sin.

Justifying grace opens the door and makes way for the sanctifying grace that would draw the faithful toward ever fuller responsiveness. The grace of justification is joined and imparted freely through an extended process by the grace of sanctification (Augustine, *On the Perfection of Human Righteousness, 2.1ff.*).

Classic Christianity rejects "any view of justification which divorces it from our sanctifying union with Christ and our increasing conformity to his image through prayer, repentance, cross-bearing, and life in the Spirit" (Gospel of Jesus Christ, Affirmations and Denials 15). Calvin argued that justification and sanctification cannot be separated (*Inst.* 3.11.10). "Although we may distinguish them, Christ contains both of them inseparably in himself" (*Inst.* 3.16.1). Wesley similarly granted that the term *sanctified* was "continually applied by St. Paul to all that were *justified*," and that "by this term alone, he rarely, if ever, means saved from all sin," and that "it behooves us to speak in public almost continually of the state of justification," adding that we must also learn to speak "more rarely, in full and explicit terms, concerning entire sanctification" (*Larger Minutes, CC*:382, italics added). This level of consensus on sanctification teaching is grounded in the consensus of classic Christian exegetes on scriptural teaching.

Though uprighting and maturing grace work in varied ways, grace always flows from the single source—God the Father as incarnate Word working through the power of the Spirit. There is only one grace—God's own. To say that God's grace works simultaneously through justification by the Son and sanctification through the Spirit does not divide grace into two parts (the ancient error of modalism). While justifying grace works primarily *for* the sinner, and sanctifying grace works *in* the penitent faithful, both work together as the gift of one eternal Giver.

Grace and Character Formation

Sustaining the Gracious Life

The Christian life is a continuing and growing exercise in the reception of justifying grace. The will may move increasingly toward a sustained condition of receiving grace. What may have been a transient awareness at the first moment of receiving justifying grace gradually may become a more enduring and constant condition, a more permanent state of free consent sustained by sanctifying grace through Word and Sacrament. It is this habit-shaping grace that is sometimes called sanctifying grace (Tho. Aq., *ST* 1–2, Q49–52).

Sanctifying grace is viewed by medieval Christian teaching as working to elicit sustained and stable patterns of responsiveness. These are encouraged sacramentally by prayer and Eucharist in ways that tend to reflect the divine sonship (Tho. Aq., *ST* 1–2, Q49–62). This firmness is enabled by the Spirit through Word and Sacrament, and cannot be acquired simply or naturally by natural moral self-determination (Suarez, *De Gratia*, 4.2). Grace can only become a pattern of moral character if it has first become actually and effectually offered by God and received in human willing. Actual grace is a divine gift that enables persons to perform acts beyond their natural powers.

Scripture describes sustaining grace through metaphors such as seed abiding in the person (1 John 3:9; Didymus the Blind, *Comm. on 1 John*), a new birth by which the Spirit comes to dwell in the soul (John 14:23). In this way personal behavior can be compared to a treasure hidden in earthen vessels (2 Cor. 5:7), and a temple of the Holy Spirit (Ambrosiaster, *Comm. on Paul*, 1 Cor. 3:16; Calvin, *Inst.* 1.13.15; Goodwin, *Works* 6:459–70; Luther, *Treatise on Good*, WML 1:189–90).

In all these classic Christian traditions, sanctifying grace thus works negatively by purging idolatries and inordinate desires and positively by engendering virtues and dispositions that reflect God's own goodness and enable the soul to please and enjoy God.

The Grace of Baptism, Confirmation, and Holy Communion

By a growing union with Christ the behavioral disposition of the believer is strengthened in grace to become cleansed from negative misdeeds and positively drawn to virtue and to a steady disposition to do that which is pleasing to God (Hilary, *Trin.* 8.7–12). In this way grace elicits both a distancing from sin and a deepening union with God (Ambrose, *Duties*, NPNF 2 10:43). By an ongoing process of grace-enabled consecration the believer becomes further set apart for service.

The sacramental prototype of *consecration* is the believer's reception of the grace of *baptism*, by which the believer is incorporated into the body of Christ, made a member of the family of God by adoption into sonship or daughterhood. The baptismal gift is ratified by the gift of the Holy Spirit in confirmation and the growth of Christian affections, whereby the believer is equipped with those gifts requisite to proceed on the journey toward the celestial city. "God can work in our acts without our help. But when we will the deed, he cooperates with us" (Augustine, *On Grace and Free Will* 32).

The grace offered in baptism is confirmed, accepted, and ratified in *confirmation*. By this grace, the soul is indelibly imprinted with the seal of the Spirit. Those who are thus baptized and who have confirmed their baptism by being equipped with gifts of the Spirit are called in the New Testament the elect, or the saints (those set-apart) of God, implying not merely that they are called to the way of holiness, but that they are already in some measure walking in the way of holiness and growing in that way, being equipped and endowed with the gifts necessary to walk in that way (1 Cor. 6:11; 1 Thess. 5:23; Ambrose, *Concerning Repentance* 2.2.9).

The sacramental prototype of growing *union* with Christ is Holy *Communion*, by which believers are daily fed and nourished in life in Christ and sustained as members of the family of God and heirs of life eternal. The eucharistic gift feeds and sustains believers on the hazardous way through temptation and trials (Cyril of Jerusalem, *Catech. Lect.* 22). By means of the grace of these sacraments and the living Word that they make visible, the believer is enabled to cooperate with grace in doing good works fit for repentance, each motive and step of which is enabled by faith through grace (Luther, *Treatise on Good Works*).

Birth and Growth

Growth in Grace

Wheat and tares grow together (Matt. 13:30). Frequently imperfections remain mixed with even the best qualities of the most faithful.

It is characteristic of the Holy Spirit to work personally and uniquely in each recipient to do what is proportionally and contextually required and salutary to draw that person closer to God. If this were not so, then there would be nothing for personal freedom to do after receiving God's pardon, no works of love in response to grace, only quiet receptive passivity that does not cooperate or cowork. Growth in grace does not occur through quiescent inactivism or simply doing nothing (James 2:26; SCD 1221–28; J. Wesley, *JWO*:353–76).

Simplistic egalitarian criteria, whether bureaucratic, legalistic, or impulsive, are insufficient to grasp the contextuality of the work of grace. The Spirit wishes to save each person, the whole person, to the uttermost, to show a way through every trial, and to bring the faithful to final blessedness (Col. 3:1–17; Eph. 4:15–5:20; Augustine, *Conf.* 7).

It is in this personal sense that the apostles spoke of receptivity to grace increasing. Believers "grow in the grace and knowledge of our Lord" (2 Pet. 3:18; Chrysostom, *Hom. on 2 Thess.* 2). Paul preached that the Spirit who supplies grace will "increase your store of seed and will enlarge the harvest of your righteousness" (2 Cor. 9:10).

Growth in grace occurs by personal receptivity to the gifts of the Spirit. The gifts of the Spirit are given that "the body of Christ may be *built up* until we all reach unity in the faith and in the knowledge of the Son of God and *become mature* [teleion], attaining the whole measure of the fullness of Christ" (Eph. 4:12, 13, italics added; Ambrosiaster, *Epis. to Eph.* 4.13). The apostle promised that "God is able to make all grace abound to you, so that in all things at all times, having all that you need, you will abound in every good work" (2 Cor. 9:8; Chrysostom, *Hom. on 2 Cor., Hom.* 19).

"The progressive aspect of sanctification is that process of growth in Christian maturity, Christlikeness, and practical godliness which results from walking obediently in the Light (1 John 1:7), from spiritual nurture and discipline (Rom. 12:2; 2 Cor. 3:17–18), and from repeated infillings of the Holy Spirit and His continuing ministry in the cleansed and yielded believer (Acts 4:31; Eph. 3:19, 5:18; Rom. 8:26)" (OMS International Statement of Faith, 8; Ambrosiaster, *Epis. to Eph.* 3.19.1–4).

The Neonate Analogy: New Birth and Growth

The newborn baby is perfectly complete as an infant human being, yet incomplete and immature from a developmental point of view. The infant must grow and develop in body, soul, moral judgment, and spirit in order to become more fully matured as a human being (Marius Victorinus, *Epis.to Eph.* 1.3.20–21).

The perfection of the seed is different from the perfection of the flower, yet both are capable of change, growth, maturation, and progress (Matt. 13:31; Hilary, *On Matt.* 13.4; 1 Cor. 3:6). Immaturity, in this way, is far from being inconsistent with perfection, as the language is normally used, for "A child may be immature as to stage of growth, but at the same time be perfectly healthy.

Growth of the body requires time and development, while health is an immediate state of the body which determines its present enjoyment and growth. Likewise in the spiritual realm, a newborn saint may have the fullness of the Spirit, while being nevertheless quite immature, and in contrast a mature saint may lack the fullness of the Spirit. . . . What physical health is to the growth of the physical body, the fullness of the Spirit is to spiritual growth" (Walvoord, *HS*:191; Jerome, *Comm. on Matt.* 2.13.31).

The finished work of Christ's earthly ministry occurred on the cross. But the finishing work of the Spirit in the believer is currently at work in all seeking to live by faith (2 Pet. 3:18; Calvin, *Inst.* 3.19–20). Though regeneration quickens life, it does not ordinarily "effect the immediate and entire deliverance of the soul from all sin. A man raised from the dead may be and long continue to be, in a very feeble, diseased, and suffering state" (Hodge, *ST* 3:220). After the sinner is brought to new life, the needed repair process may be extensive.

How Sanctifying Grace Is Received

Grace works in time, like leaven (Matt. 13:33; Hilary, *On Matt.* 13.5). It calls for a continual dying to sin, so "put to death, therefore, whatever belongs to your earthly nature: sexual immorality, impurity, lust, evil desires and greed, which is idolatry" (Col. 3:5; Augustine, *Sermons* 350A.4).

Living faith is like a long-distance race not completed in an instant but only by continued running—more a marathon than a sprint. Bodily growing does not occur instantly like a verdict, but continuously and actively (Acts 20:24; 2 Tim. 4:7; Heb. 6:1; 12:1; Ambrose, *Duties*, 1.15.5 8).

Though a process of growth is required for every believer, there still may be moments when such spurts of growth in grace are possible. It is rash to rule out the possibility that the Holy Spirit may flood the soul with sufficient grace that the trajectory of continued walking in the way of holiness is firmly set (Photius, *Fragments on Heb.* 6.1–3; Bonaventure, *The Soul's Journey into God* 7; Fletcher, *Checks*, 7; P. Palmer, *PPSW*:185–208).

Justifying faith may be in intention or purpose victorious over sin yet not have rooted sin out altogether. The testimony of conversions prevents us from assuming that there are no remarkable instances of instantaneous transformation. But the more typical work of grace appears to be gradual, maturing like an organism grows (Chrysostom, *Hom. on Matt.* Hom. 44.4–5; John Cassian, *Conferences* 14; J. Wesley, *WJW* 6:77–99).

Those who have most powerfully experienced justifying grace often find that the roots of pride and idolatry and anger have not been destroyed instantly. Thus they are being called to continue to struggle with the vestiges of sin, even though they have experienced a complete pardon of their sins. The remnants of sin may continue to plague the believer after truly receiving justifying grace (Augustine, *On Perfection in Human Righteousness*, 19; Goodwin, *Works* 6:88–95; cf. J. Wesley, *WJW* 5:144–70).

The New Birth Looks Toward the Holy Life

Whether new birth is instantaneous or gradual depends upon the point of view from which spiritual rebirth is seen. Viewed providentially, developmentally, and synoptically from the vantage point of the entire work of the Spirit in preparing, convicting, calling, enabling faith, and sanctifying, the whole process is seen as a gradual unfolding of the divine plan of salvation.

Viewed inwardly from the vantage point of one being born, there must be posited some distinct beginning of this life. Anything that happens in the human story has a beginning in time. In this sense new birth is by definition instantaneous.

The picture of a live birth would be imprecise if birth itself was thought to occur gradually over years of time. Pregnancy occurs over time, but live birth itself is an event that occurs in a particular hour. No mother or child could endure nine months of being born, but that time of pregnancy is normal. This is why the language of conversion so often focuses on a particular instant of transformation or recognition or a distinct moment of an unparalleled new beginning. No one has literally two or more different physical birthdays.

This means that on some particular day or period of the spiritual life of the penitent, he or she *begins to trust* God's grace by faith (Basil, *On the Spirit* 15.35; Wesley, *WJW* 6:65). To begin to trust does not imply a perfect trust, but a beginning trust, which may rightly be called the regenerating grace of God the Spirit. Whether measured in minutes, hours, or days, it has some sort of beginning in time which is more like a birth than a pregnancy.

There may indeed be a gradual growth of the renewed soul, but in order to grow the soul must first be born. As life's ending at death is punctilial (ending at some *punctum*, point), so is life's beginning at birth. As living beings "die in an instant" (Job 34:20), so are they born in an instant. When Jesus said to the thief on the cross, "Today you will be with me in paradise" (Luke 23:43), God's pardoning and regenerating action began occurring in the condemned man at that particular moment (Augustine, *Sermons on NT Lessons* 17.7).

One reborn of God is not thereby immediately mature. Birth does not prevent but invites and enables the process of growth. One reborn of God is a budding saint made ready to receive a gradual process of growth toward ever fuller receptivity to the Spirit (Rev. 22:11). In new birth life is imparted yet not fully developed (Merrill, *ACE*:187). The new life in Christ is then constantly being renewed. "You have taken off your old self with its practices and have put on the new self, which is being renewed in knowledge in the image of its Creator" (Col. 3:10).

Yielding to the Spirit's Guidance

When the Old Sin Nature Remains Alive in New Believers

The new birth does not entirely destroy the old nature, the flesh, the old Adam. The old orientation to the flesh comes under the influence of the Spirit, but has not been eliminated altogether (Rom. 7:21–23; Augustine, *on Romans* 45–46).

If all possibility of temptation were eliminated, there would be no need for growth in grace, or testing, or confession, or prayer. But such is not the life in the Spirit. Flesh continues after justification to war against spirit. Previously the flesh had almost complete sway. Now the flesh is by faith's intention crucified with Christ, but this does not always imply that the way of the flesh has in every sense been utterly removed. For flesh continues to lust against spirit (Gal. 5:17; Chrysostom, *Baptismal Instructions* 3).

The adversary of the old dead life has "gone out of you, being chased by baptism. But he will not easily submit to the expulsion. . . . If he finds in you a place, swept and garnished indeed, but empty and idle, equally ready to take in this or that which shall first occupy it, he makes a leap into it, he takes up his abode there with a larger train" (Gregory of Nazianzus, *Orat* 40.35). The orientation to the flesh (*sarx*) must die daily (Rom. 8:1–11). Participation in Christ's death and resurrection is an event that will be chosen and rechosen day by day (Ambrosiaster, *Comm. on Paul*, Rom. 8.10).

Even then the new self is being called to live as if the old self were in fact truly dead (Col. 3:10; Eph. 4:24). You are to "count yourselves dead to sin and alive to God in Christ Jesus. Therefore do not let sin reign in your mortal body so that you obey its evil desires. Do not offer the parts of your body to sin, as instruments of wickedness, but rather offer yourselves to God, as those who have been brought from death to life" (Rom. 6:11–13; Irenaeus, *Ag. Her.* 5.14.1; Origen, *Comm. on Rom.* 6.12). Jesus assumed that the will is free to follow when he said, "If anyone would come after me, he must deny himself and take up his cross and follow me" (Luke 9:23; Calvin, *Inst.* 3.3).

Meanwhile believers continue to struggle with sin: "Although the saints are spiritually minded, they are still carnal in the corruptible body which remains a weight upon the soul. They will, however, be spiritual also in body when the body sown animal with rise spiritual. . . .Thus I came to understand this matter as did Hilary, Gregory, Ambrose, and other holy and renowned teachers of the church, who saw that the apostle, by his own words, fought strenuously the same battle against carnal concupiscences" (Augustine, *Ag. Julian* 70). Note here how Augustine is adjusting his thinking to the *consensus fidelium* of classic Christian teaching in a way that would gratify Vincent of Lérins.

Yielding and Filling: Mortification and Vivification

Faith requires a daily attitude of being yielded—a full readiness to respond to the promptings of grace by the Spirit. By this daily yielding, one is enabled to become more fully conformed to God's will "that we may share in his holiness" (Heb. 12:10).

One may grow in yieldedness to grace by daily surrender and obedience. "Therefore, brothers, we have an obligation—but it is not to the sinful nature, to live according to it. For if you live according to the sinful nature, you will die; but if by the Spirit you put to death the misdeeds of the body, you will live, because those who are led by the Spirit of God are sons of God" (Rom. 8:12–14; Irenaeus, *Ag. Her.* 5.10.2).

Under the tyranny of sin we were previously committing our bodies daily to a kind of "slavery to impurity and every kind of wickedness." Now that grace has come in Jesus Christ we are free to commit our bodies totally "to righteousness leading to holiness" (Rom. 6:19; Origen, *Hom. on Gen.* 3.6).

The Christian life requires simple surrender of the will to God on a continuing basis (Matt. 6:10). In proportion as God's will is done in one's life, one is walking in the way of holiness. In proportion as one is able honestly to say, "Nevertheless not my will but thy will be done" (Luke 22:42), just in that degree is one receptively cooperating with maturing grace (John Cassian, *Conferences* 14–15). The disciples at Pentecost were fully yielded. So was Peter before the Sanhedrin (Acts 4:8; Chrysostom, *Hom. on Acts* 10), and the worshiping community when they prayed (Acts 4:31). The martyr Stephen was fully yielded to the Spirit as he faced death (Acts 7:55; Augustine, *Sermon* 214.8), as were the apostles Paul (Acts 9:17) and Barnabas (Acts 11:25; *The Martyrdom of Polycarp*).

The Way of the Servant

Consensual Christian teaching did not uniformly affirm only passive or restricted roles for women. It sought a moral language shaped by the reciprocity implicit in the creation of women and men (Chrysostom, *Hom. on Eph.*; cf. David Ford, *Mysogynist or Advocate: Chrysostom on Women*, diss.). But this did not mean that all subordination metaphors must be abandoned, for it is none other than God the

Son who has taken on the ultimate subordinate role and called men and women to follow this serving model in relating to each other as male, each serving and caring for the partner on behalf of the offspring.

Christ chose voluntary poverty as the narrow way. So he became poor for our sakes that we might become rich in spirit. He chose subordination, humility, and yieldedness as the way. He became lowly for our sakes that we might become exalted in spirit (Chrysostom, *Hom. on Phil.* 7).

Be Filled with the Spirit

The faithful are called to "be filled with the Spirit" (Eph. 5:18; Ambrosiaster, *Epis. to Eph.* 5.18–19). To be filled with the Spirit (Luke 1:15, 41, 67; Acts 13:9, 52) means to submit completely to the indwelling Spirit in order that God's own work may be accomplished (Augustine, *On the Spirit and the Letter* 7.12; Calvin, *Comm.* 18:561).

Immediately after his baptism Jesus was "full of the Holy Spirit, returned from the Jordan, and was led by the Spirit in the desert" (Luke 4:1; Ephrem, *Comm. on Tatian's Diatesseron* 4.4–5). This filling was attested in the lives of the Baptist, Elizabeth, Zacharias, and the blessed Virgin (Luke 1). After the descent of the Spirit at Pentecost upon the disciples, "All of them were filled with the Holy Spirit" (Acts 2:4; Hilary, *Trin.* 8.30). When Peter preached he was "filled with the Holy Spirit" (Acts 4:8). Those chosen to be deacons were "known to be full of the Spirit and of wisdom" (Acts 6:3).

The evidences of being filled with the Spirit are the works of faith active in love. Though the sealing and indwelling of the Spirit are given to all baptized believers, those completely yielded to God and separated for responsive service are said to be filled with the Spirit and "with the fruits of righteousness" (Phil. 1:11; Chrysostom, *Hom. on Phil.* 3.1.11). They "make music" in their hearts to the Lord, "always giving thanks to God the Father for everything" (Eph. 5:20; Jerome, *Epis. to Eph.* 3.5.19), ready always to "submit to one another out of reverence for Christ" (5. 21). The contrast is that between being drunkenly controlled by spiritous liquors and being fittingly empowered by the Spirit of God so that music pours out of one's heart in praise.

Believers who are yielded to the Spirit will be empowered in their meekness. Fruits will be born from this empowerment. Believers can walk the narrow way without committing known sin as long as they remain yielded to the Spirit. "Man is a vessel destined to receive God, a vessel which must be enlarged in proportion as it is filled and filled in proportion as it is enlarged" (F. L. Godet, *Commentary*, John, in Gordon, MS:91).

Perfecting Grace and the Fullness of Salvation

The Perfect Sacrifice

The Lord by his "one sacrifice" has "made perfect [*teteleioken*] forever those who are being made holy [*hagiazomenous*]" (Heb. 10:14). This is a past act completed on the cross, but one in which believers already now participate.

The perfect work of Christ for the believer (sometimes called positional sanctification) offers itself for the maturing of those being made holy. "Jesus also suffered outside the city gate to make the people *holy* through his own blood. Let us, then, go to him outside the camp, bearing the disgrace he bore" (Heb. 13:12, 13, italics added). The completeness we already experience in union with Christ is distinguishable from but related to a growing process of maturing in the believer.

"Perseverance must finish its work so that you may be mature and whole [*teleioi kai holoklēroi*], not lacking anything" (James 1:4). "Patience builds character, so that someone who possesses it cannot be overcome but is shown to be perfect. For this reason believers are tested in order to improve their patience, so that by it their faith may be seen to be perfect" (Bede, *Concerning the Epis. of James* 1.4).

Paul's "message of wisdom" to be spoken "among the mature [*teleiois*]" is "a wisdom that has been hidden and that God destined for our glory before time began" (1 Cor. 2:6, 7). What is "destined" is not our response but God's grace in the Son before time. Personally responsive maturation moves toward a goal that Paul assumed when he chided the Galatians: "Are you so foolish? After beginning with the Spirit, are you now trying to attain your goal by human effort?" (Gal. 3:3). He exhorted the faithful to "stop thinking like children," and "be adults" (1 Cor. 14:20), as those "who are mature [*teleioi*]" (Phil. 3:15). Even to the irrascible Corinthians he wrote: "What we pray for is your improvement [*katartizesthe*]" (2 Cor. 13:9; Ambrosiaster, *Comm. on Paul*, 2 Cor. 13.5–11).

Of the various Hebrew words sometimes translated "perfect," or "blameless" (*shalem, tamim*), it is usually contextually clear that the individuals referred to are not wholly without sin (Hezekiah, 2 Kings 20:3; David, Pss. 37:37; 101:2). When the Old Testament spoke of the upright man such as Noah or Job as "perfect" (*tamin*, whole, complete, Gen. 6:9; Job 1:1, 8), this did not imply absolute moral sinlessness but complete sincerity of trust in God. They will be found in the heavenly city as "the spirits of righteous men made perfect" (Heb. 12:23; Basil, *Hom. on Ps.* 18.4 (Ps. 45); Calvin, *Comm.* 22:334).

Israel was commanded under the law to be "blameless before the Lord your God" (Deut. 18:13). Under the gospel this command was fulfilled on the cross by the obedience of the Son, in whom faith may fully trust.

Optimal Faith

Those in whom grace is working optimally are those presently living toward the end for which God made them, who are cooperating maximally with grace (Jerome, *Ag. Pelagians NPNF* 2 6:454). Those who are thoroughly cleansed from sin by faith and wholly consecrated to God have that mind in them that was also in Christ Jesus (Phil. 2:5). They are "filled with the fruit of righteousness that comes through Jesus Christ" (Phil. 1:11). They give thanks in all things (1 Thess. 5:16–18), praying without ceasing. They do not choose to set that which is wicked before their eyes (Ps. 101:3). Their passions and bodily appetites are put to the use for which they were intended (1 Cor. 9:24–27; Augustine, *To Simplician* 10). God reigns without a rival in them.

Classic Lutheran consensual teaching as found in the Augsburg Confession defines Christian perfection in this way: "For this is Christian perfection; honestly to fear God and at the same time to have great faith and to trust that for Christ's sake we have a gracious God; to ask of God, and assuredly to expect from him, help in all things which are to be borne in connection with our callings; meanwhile to be diligent in the performance of good works for others and to attend to our calling. True perfection and true service of God consist of these things" (Article 27, *Book of Concord*).

Full Responsiveness Not Intrinsically Impossible

The full powers of the regenerated life are being released. There is no fated or absolute necessity that they remain forever bound by the power of sin. God the Spirit is contextually offering grace sufficient to meet each and every successive temptation or challenge (John Cassian, *Conferences* 3). There is nothing intrinsically impossible about aiming toward "loving God with all our heart, mind, soul, and strength," wherein "all the thoughts, words, and actions are governed by pure love" (J. Wesley, *WJW* 11:366).

Through many centuries the consummating purpose of grace has been often defended against skeptical detractors (Council of Constance, *SCD* 600–604; Alexander IV, *SCD* 458). It is not arbitrarily impossible to continue increasing or growing in grace, or to persist in deepening and enriching the life of virtue in response to grace (Council of Vienne, *SCD* 471; *Trent* IV, *SCD* 802).

The body is not an absolute obstacle to the reception of sanctifying grace, but rather a means for its reception. The body, with all its passions, concupiscence, energies, libido, powers, and members, is to be taken captive to Christ and sanctified as a temple of the Spirit (Rom. 6:13; 1 Cor. 6:19, 20; 11; Heb. 10:22). There is no arbitrary limit to what the Spirit can do with a consecrated human life who cooperates steadily with grace (2 Cor. 4:10; Chrysostom, *Epis. to Cor.* 13.2; Palmer, *PPSW*:165–85). Every aspect of life is awaiting to be taken captive to Christ (Finney, *Sermons* 4.18; Mahan, *Christian Perfection*).

The Language of Perfecting Grace: Biblical Terms for Complete and Fitting

Of the thirteen Greek words sometimes translated "perfect," two in particular are pertinent to these questions. The verb *katartizō* suggests completeness, or fittingness in all details, as if something is rightly adjusted and completely fitted to its purpose (2 Cor. 13:9; 1 Thess. 3:10). The Spirit is giving gifts "for the perfecting [*katartismon*] of the saints" (Eph. 4:12), abundantly equipping and preparing God's people for works of service (John 10:10; Ambrosiaster, *Epis. to Eph.* 4.12.6; Fletcher, *Checks Ag. Antinomianism* 7; A. Clarke, *Christian Theology* 12).

The verb *teleioō* suggests completing, attaining, ending, perfecting, bringing something to its proper goal (1 Cor. 2:6; Eph. 4:13; Phil. 3:15). *Teleioō* may mean to mature, to fulfill, to make full, or to come to a fitting conclusion. Such maturing is frequently sought and commended in this life by New Testament writers. The faithful are called to grow toward maturity through patience (James 1:4) and love (1 John 4:17, 18), in knowledge of the will of God (Col. 4:12) and in holiness (2 Cor. 7:1; Cyprian, *Treatise* 9). Love "binds everything together in perfect harmony" (Col. 3:14; Chrysostom, *Hom. on Col.* 8).

The teachings of maturing grace, holiness, sanctification, and perfect love are not merely permitted but specifically defined and commended by scripture. To assume that the attempt at complete responsiveness to grace necessarily leads to pride and presumption is to misunderstand their scriptural intent. Though what follows cannot be portrayed as unchallenged consensual teaching, it is a preponderant view awaiting fuller refinement. The original Hebrew and Greek terms used in scripture to describe the fullness of salvation (*shalem, tamim, teleiosis, katartisis*) are, when appropriately grasped, well designed to serve Christian teaching.

A fine balance of tolerance and rigor is called for at this juncture. Where Catholic teaching tends to stress the sin removed by baptism, and Reformation teaching tends to emphasize the sin remaining after baptism, the excesses of either view needs the corrective of the other.

Sustained Faithful Responsiveness to Grace

There is an operating distinction in the biblical teaching of sanctification between positional sanctification in Christ (1 Cor. 1:30) and experimental (or progressive or experiential) sanctification in relation to the believer's yieldedness to Christ

(Eph. 5:26, 27; 1 Thess. 5:23; 1 Peter 3:18); and both of these are distinguishable from celestial or final sanctification in glory (1 John 3:2; Rom. 8:29).

Consistent with the ancient ecumenical tradition, the Reformed tradition has wisely taught that "(1) all believers are *positionally* sanctified in Christ 'once for all' at the moment they are saved. This sanctification is as perfect as He is perfect. (2) All believers are *being* sanctified by the power of God through the Word, and this sanctification is as perfect as the believer is perfect. So, also, (3) all believers *will be* sanctified and perfected in glory into the very image of the Son of God" (Chafer, *ST* 1: 285).

Viewed schematically:

Sanctification Tenses

Three Overlapping Phases of Sanctifying Grace

Positional	Experiential	Final
Past Tense	Present Tense	Future Tense
Perfect Sacrifice on the Cross	Behavioral Participation in Christ in Preparation for:	Celestial Glory

Positional Completeness in Christ

Paul addressed all believers at Corinth in the positional sense as 'saints', as "those sanctified in Christ Jesus and called to be holy" (1 Cor. 1:2, 30; 6:11). Yet the Corinthian letters were written to correct abuses of those who were still experimentally and progressively maturing in Christ by an extended process by which we "reflect the Lord's glory," being "transformed into his likeness with ever-increasing glory" (2 Cor. 3:18; Gregory of Nazianzus, *Theol. Orat.* 5.26; cf. John 17:17; Eph. 5:26), which seeks to "grow in the grace and knowledge of our Lord and Savior" (2 Pet. 3:18). This process looks toward fitting future consummation, or final sanctification (1 Thess. 5:23).

"Why did Paul write 'to those called to be saints' as well as to those who are already 'sanctified' and in the church? Surely this means that the letter is addressed not only to those who are already cleansed from their sins but also to those who still await cleansing, though they are among those whom God has called" (Origen, *Comm. on 1 Cor.* 1.1.7)

Sanctification (*hagiasmos*) is used in the New Testament to point both to the continuing development of the Christian life and to its fulfillment. The community of faithful baptized believers, however unfinished or incomplete in faith, is referred to as "saints" or "sanctified" (Acts 9:13; Rom. 1:7; 2 Cor. 1:1; Eph. 1:1; Col. 1:2). Hence this is called in Reformed teaching *positional* sanctification. In this sense all who share life in Christ by faith, even weak faith, are being sanctified by the power of the Spirit (1 Cor. 1:2; Phil. 1:1). For faith requires and implies that one is consecrating one's whole self to God and turning away from all that would detract from reconciliation with God.

Growth in Maturity in Christ

Experiential sanctification is an ongoing process of daily rededication, reconsecration, mortification, and vivification of the whole person to God. It calls for believers to live out their baptism in time so as to allow new challenges and circumstances to draw them further on toward the fuller reception of grace and the deepening of purity of heart (1 Thess. 5:23; Heb. 12:14; Philoxenus of Mabbug, *Memra on the Indwelling of the Holy Spirit*, Brock:118).

This continuing, yielding consecration is not separable from the initial acts of repentance and faith. Rather it is that same repentance and faith that is growing and developing under conditions of temptation and day by day hearing of the Word. It is a continuing unfolding of what was implied in the initial act of consecration (Calvin, *Inst.* 3.3). Sanctification in this sense is "the continued transformation of moral and spiritual character so that the life of the believer actually comes to mirror the standing which he or she already has in God's sight" (Erickson, *CT* 3: 875).

Final Sanctification in Christ

Paul prayed that God may "strengthen your hearts so that you will be blameless and holy in the presence of our God and Father when our Lord Jesus comes" (1 Thess. 3:13; Augustine, *Grace and Free Will* 38). The sanctification ultimately hoped for is that by which the God of peace sanctifies "you through and through," by which "your whole spirit, soul and body be kept blameless at the coming of our Lord Jesus Christ" (1 Thess. 5:23; Ambrose, *Cain and Abel* 2.6).

Exegetes differ as to whether this final sanctification may occur in this life or only at death or at the time of the general resurrection. Consensual exegesis points in this direction: it is not common, though possible, for persons to respond continuously and fully to sanctifying grace in this life (Gregory of Nyssa, *Moses*; Bonaventure, *The Soul's Journey into God*, CWS:110–16).

The doctrine of sanctification is not primarily a teaching about the human capacity as such, but about the sufficiency of God the Spirit to transform all human capacities. It is less about human ability than the Spirit's ability to reshape human capacities (Barth, *CD* 4/2:495; Outler, *TWS*:3). "In the future life we shall attain perfection. But in the present life we need all the help we can get from the apostles, the prophets, and our teachers" (Theodoret, *Epis. to Eph.* 4.13).

The Holiness of Mature Believers Distinguished from God, Angels, and Adam

If redeemed humanity is made capable by grace of full maturity in Christ, how is this maturity distinguished from (1) that perfection that only God knows, and (2) from the angelic and (3) the Adamic state?

First, the best conceivable forms of human responsiveness fail to compare with the utter holiness of God. It is useful to recall the distinction between antecedent and consequent (or absolute and ordinary) power in God: Considered antecedently, nothing is beyond God's power, because it is God's. Absolute power can extend itself in any way without limitation, since unmitigated power can work without mitigation. The sovereign power of God has chosen to create proximate, temporal companionate wills that may in self-determination stand temporarily over against God's power (Origen, *OFP* 2.9; Oden, *The Transforming Power of Grace*, 3–5).

As prevenient, providential, common grace works through secondary causes, so does sanctifying grace work through and before and above and beyond other creaturely causes, and not merely unilaterally but cooperatively. It is a category mistake to assume that grace can be reduced to simple, unilateral divine causality, without positing other layers of cooperating causality. Though it is God who gives growth, it is Paul who plants and Apollos who waters (1 Cor. 3:5–9).

Second, the incorporeal angelic beings who are assumed in scripture to be capable of serving God exceed human capabilities enormously. For all human capabilities exist within a fallen history of sin and under conditions of corporeality. Of whatever level of maturity or radical responsiveness humans may be capable, it must be distinguished from angelic perfection, which does not labor under the bodily constraints of time and space with which human virtue must contend (Tho. Aq., *ST* 1–1, Q50–74).

Third, whatever full responsiveness is now enabled by grace must be further distinguished from that originally possessed by Adam and Eve, because an intervening history of sin has drastically limited the choices available within fallen human history to choices between tainted values, goods, and eventualities, not the untainted or unimpaired actions of Eden. The unimpeded love promised to sinners must function within the capacities given by grace to human beings within the contexts of fallen history (Ambrose, *Letters to Priests* 49; Augustine, *Patience* 17; Reinhold Niebuhr, *NDM*, 1,2).

Classic Consensual Teaching on Perfecting Grace

Some uncritically define perfection as a simple state of freedom from sin attainable in earthly life. They do not qualify how freedom from sin differs from finitude or ignorance or error or infirmity. If so, the doctrine of full responsiveness to grace becomes a straw man waiting to be knocked down. Several issues have in fact been thoughtfully resolved by ecumenical consent in setting forth the biblical teaching of Christian maturity and perfecting grace. To these we turn.

Classic Christian reasoning is subtle and requires patience. To neglect any of the following eight maxims is to invite confusion. Rightly acknowledged, they strengthen the plausibility of the classic consensual view of the fullness of grace in sanctification.

Human Infirmities Amplify the Perfections of Grace

First, the moral unlikelihood of extended sinlessness is in large part a due to human finitude, as distinguished from sin. It is not due to the deficiency of grace. Sin occurs within finitude, but is chosen. Finitude is different—we do not choose it; we are it.

The very conditions of the human soul-body composite make optimal outcomes unlikely. The human condition is exceedingly vulnerable due to its very nature as finite freedom. Freedom is nested within finitude.

Classic Christian teaching has been acutely aware of the causes of human infirmity: "The infirmity of human nature flows from four separate and distinct sources: (1) concupiscence (*fomes peccati*); (2) imperfection of the ethical judgment (*imperfectio iudicii*); (3) inconstancy of the will (*inconstantia voluntatis*); and (4) the weariness caused by continued resistance to temptation" (Pohle, *DT* 7:120). God's grace is sensitive to the differences between the causes of infirmity. At each level of causality we reason differently about the relation of grace and freedom.

When all these forms of human infirmity conspire to limit human willing and acting, it seems plausible to speak in a virtual sense of a prevailing tendency to sin (*necessitas antecedens peccandi*), not as if the will were fated to fall, but in the awareness that it is highly unlikely that the will might continue interminably without special grace to resist an endless series of temptations (Origen, *Comm. on Rom.* 3.9–19; S. Kierkegaard, *The Concept of Anxiety*).

The human proneness to sin does not destroy free will or the moral culpability of sin, nor does it imply that what God has commanded is formally impossible. Yet it does make free will vulnerable, and sin virtually inevitable (Ambrosiaster, *Comm. on Paul*, Rom. 3:9–20). This is why a static form of perfection is practically unattainable over a long period of time without the assistance of special grace (Tho. Aq., *ST* 2-2, Q184).

There is a fine but conceptually plausible line between the tragic tendencies of human infirmity and voluntary transgressions of known law (Clement of Alex., *Stromata*, 2.14–16). One is tripped up by finite circumstances, the other is willed. Hence Reinhold Niebuhr was intuitively correct to insist that sin is "inevitable but not necessary" (*NDM* 1:255). Whatever can stumble will find a way of stumbling, given time for the exercise of vulnerable freedom (Tho. Aq., *ST* 1-2, Q109).

We do not decide how we are to be tempted, only how we are to respond to temptation. A person may be able to resist successfully a thousand temptations in succession while a hidden one is silently taking over at a lower level of awareness (Augustine, *Letters* 181.8).

Whatever level of sustained faithful responsiveness is made possible by grace, this does not imply that every small sin is overcome or that anyone becomes irreversibly impeccable (Council of Mileum II, *SCD* 107; Council of Vienne, *SCD* 471). For human freedom remains free within finitude. If it were the case that a person does not sin because he cannot sin, then "free will is destroyed" (Augustine, *On Nature and Grace*, 28; Jerome, *Ag. the Pelagians*).

Sustained Faithful Responsiveness to Grace
Does Not Imply Freedom from Error

Second, unimpeded responsiveness to grace does not imply the infallibility of freedom or freedom from error. As long as perception has its housing in the fragile body, one is liable to inaccurate perceptions that lead to errors of judgment, and deceptive appearances that tend toward erroneous conclusions. These conditions, being characteristic of human existence generally, remain characteristic also of those walking the way of holiness (Ambrosiaster, *Comm. on Paul*, Rom. 7.18; Owen, *Works*, 3;468–538).

Freedom is easily thrown into disequilibrium by "fears occasioned by surprise, unpleasant dreams, wandering thoughts in prayer, times when there is no joy, a sense of inefficiency in Christian labor, and strong temptations," but these are "by no means inconsistent with perfect love" (Binney, *TCI*:132). One may be entirely consecrated to God and still remain subject to the infirmities and defects that inevitably accompany finite human existence. Even amid such defects of perception, these are not charged to conscience or accounted as sin as long as the heart remains pure, the will is yielded, and the intention is shaped wholly by love of God and neighbor, inasmuch as "love is the fulfillment of the law" (Rom. 13:10; Clement of Alex., *Stromata* 4.6; Caesarius of Arles, *Sermon* 137.1).

The faithful may be misled by clouded memories or limited imaginations to form inaccurate impressions and hold distorted opinions. "This is a natural consequence of the soul's dwelling in flesh and blood. But a man may be filled with pure love, and yet be subject to ignorance and mistake" (Field, *HCT*:228). Even where information is wrongly processed, the heart may remain pure, and every act may spring from love. Such finitude is not properly viewed as sin, if sin is willful disobedience to recognizable moral truth. The Manichaeanism that asserts that finitude is sin has long been consensually regarded as a heresy (Augustine, *Reply to Faustus the Manichaean* 14.11). Walking steadily in the way of holiness does not imply that one may know with certitude that one will persevere (Chrysostom, *Epis. to Heb.* 21.1; Trent, 6.802–6).

Sustained Faithful Responsiveness to Grace
Does Not Imply Sinless Perfection

Third, the Council of Vienne, AD 1311–12, specifically rejected the doctrine of static sinless perfection, "that man in the present life can acquire so great and such a degree of perfection that he will be rendered inwardly sinless, and that he will not be able to advance farther in grace" (*SCD* 471).

The wholesome love sought and attested is not a perfection that would pretend to eliminate unconscious sin, but rather a pure heart of faith active in love that is presently overcoming all habitual sin (Fletcher, *Last Check to Antinomianism* 1). "Among holy men it is impossible not to fall into those small lapses which occur because of something said, some thought, some surreptitious act. These sins are quite different from those which are called mortal, but they are not without blame or reproach" (John Cassian, *Conference* 11.9)

Sustained Faithful Responsiveness to Grace
Does Not Imply Antinomian License

Fourth, grace as radical gift does not succumb to antinomian license which would ignore the command of God and slacken human effort to reflect the holiness of God under the flag of Christian liberty (Luther, *Treatise on Good Works*, *WML* 1:196–99).

The challenging task of growing in grace is not furthered by imagining that human beings in their sin are made acceptable to God by some sort of instant holiness. Christianity seeks to show that the making holy of the human person is God's own work, yet accomplished in such a way as not to disavow human accountability and responsiveness (Augustine, *On Nature and Grace*, 61).

The long walk on the way toward perfect love does not imply that one is no longer required to keep the commandments (*SCD* 804), or no longer to seek virtue or love one's neighbor (*SCD* 476). Nor does sustained faithful responsiveness to grace imply an immobile state, or death of the senses (*SCD* 501,1221). Optimal responsiveness is "always wrought in the soul by faith, by a simple act of faith," which, due to sufficient grace, is not in any situation intrinsically impossible (Field, *HCT*:240; P. Palmer, *Faith and Its Effects*).

Sustained Faithful Responsiveness to Grace Does Not Imply
the Overcoming of Involuntary Transgressions

Fifth, the life of perfect love commended in the New Testament is not a perfection according to an absolute moral law, but according to the remedial economy enabled by the cross, in which the heart, having been cleansed, fulfills the law by faith active in love (Rom. 4; 5; 13:8–10; Caesarius of Arles, *Sermon* 137.1). The pivotal obstacle overcome by God's saving action is voluntary sin of every kind, not the infirmities of finitude (Augustine, *On True Religion* 87; *On Nature and Grace*, 1–4).

The psalmist distinguished between willed sin and hidden sins that are not consciously willed. The Psalmist prayed: "Forgive my hidden faults. Keep your servant *also* from willful sins; may they not rule over me. Then will I be blameless" (Ps. 19:12, 13, italics added; cf. Ps. 119:133). One may be filled with the love of God and still remain liable to involuntary or unconscious temptations (J. Wesley, *PACP*:67). No *theosis* is posited by orthodoxy that ends finitude. There is no resurrection of the body that does away with the body altogether. Classic exegetes are divided as to how deeply involuntary responses are rightly to be called sin, but united in the assumption of the sufficiency of grace.

Sustained Faithful Responsiveness Does Not
Imply an Eradication of the Sin Nature

Sixth, John's letter specifically warned against the claim that sin is permanently eradicated upon belief in Christ (1 John 1:8). Yet in the next verse the letter enjoined believers to confess their sins that they may be purified "from all unrighteousness" (1 John 1:9; Bede, *On 1 John* 1.8–9).

This does not amount to a claim that the old sin nature is eradicated by faith, or that one is permanently made not able to sin. Rather, because of the work of the Son and the Spirit one is being given power in specific contexts step-by-step not to sin. The struggle against temptation continues, but is being constantly guided and hedged in by sufficient grace (Augustine, *Ag. Two Letters of the Pelagians* 4. 24–31).

If the complete eradication of all possibility of sin were God's way of dealing with our fallen nature, then there would be little point in talking further about discipline or facing temptation. Rather, both Paul and John teach that the sin nature continues after faith begins, yet the indwelling Spirit empowers the new person of faith sufficiently in each circumstance.

Sustained Faithful Responsiveness to Grace Does
Not Imply Freedom from Temptation

Seventh, the world, the flesh, and the adversary are not eradicated in this present age, though their power is being overthrown. The world continues, temptation continues, the flesh exerts its power, the devil rails, but amid these trials the Spirit works to enable fully adequate responses in each circumstance and growth toward an ever-larger pattern of full responsiveness (1 John 3:1–10; Chafer, *ST* 6:268–70).

Steady reception of sanctifying grace does not imply absolute freedom from temptation. Adam while innocent was tempted. Even Jesus who knew no sin was tempted in every way that characterizes human existence generally. To be tempted is not to succumb. To be tempted is human and belongs to self-determining creaturely existence. To succumb is sin and belongs to fallen existence. Those whose feet are set on the path to full salvation do not become free from temptation, though they grow in their ability to overcome it (*SCD* 1001–80). There is no point at which they can make no further progress in grace (Council of Vienne, *SCD* 471). With each new challenge to the will, there comes a new choice, which itself may strengthen or weaken the habits of holy accountability.

Sustained Faithful Responsiveness to Grace
Offers No Grounds for Boasting

Finally, no *tsaddiq* (just person, made upright, *dikaios*) will ever be heard boasting of his or her sanctification. No one who is struggling seriously against pride will be found referring to him- or herself as holy or completely matured in Christ (Jerome, *Ag. Pelagians* 3.14). Yet paradoxically, the very one who least claims maturity may be optimally gaining ever-greater maturation and fullness of growth in the Spirit (Mt. 28:41–44; *Incomplete Work on Matt.* Hom. 54). It is the habit of the saints to be aware that the closer they walked the way of Christ, the more were they aware of their own distance from the purity of Christ. As their vision became clearer, they could see their own imperfections more clearly (Calvin, *Inst.* 4.13; Teresa of Avila,

Life; Thérèse of Lisieux, *Story of a Soul*). However far along the road one may be, it is always premature to "boast about tomorrow, for you do not know what a day may bring forth" (Prov. 27:1; Babai, *Letter to Cyriacus* 4). For "our life here below has many turnings, and the body of our humiliation is ever rising, falling and changing" (Gregory Nazianzus, *Orat.* 16.3).

Each of these qualifiers, if clearly and plausibly stated, strengthens the case for a sober view, based on classic consensual sources, of what has variously been called perfect love or Christian perfection, or what we have called here sustained responsiveness to grace.

How Debates on the Holy Life Have Been Resolved by Ecumenical Consent

The Lord's Prayer Assumes that Sin Will Continue in Believers

The Second Council of Mileum (AD 416; *SCD* 108) rejected the view that the petition to forgive us our trespasses, when pronounced by saintly persons, was pronounced merely in token of humility, but not truthfully. The PanAfrican Council of Carthage (AD 418) rejected the Pelagian view that the Lord's Prayer petition, "Forgive us our trespasses" (Matt. 6:12; Enchiridion Symbolorum, 221–230), does not need to be said by the saints.

Sins of surprise, errors of judgment, and moral misperceptions are not consciously chosen, hence not always counted as negligence. "Who can say, 'I have kept my heart pure; I am clean and without sin'?" (Prov. 20:9; Gregory of Nyssa, *On the Lord's Prayer* 5).

There are no Eucharistic liturgies of classical Christianity that fail to offer pardon for genuine penitents. This does not place the way of holiness out of reach for believers, but puts believers constantly on the path of daily confession and renewal (Mt. 6:12; Cyprian, *The Gospel of Matthew*, Homily 19.5).

A Momentary Gift of Grace, Having Been Received, May Be Lost Through Disbelief

The consummating grace that is received by faith can be lost by unfaith. "If a man, being regenerate and justified, relapses of his own will into an evil life, assuredly he cannot say: 'I have not received,' because of his own free choice of evil he has lost the grace of God that he has received" (Augustine, *On Admonition and Grace* 6.9).

If it were considered impossible to fall from a single instant of perfecting grace, there would be no need for repentance of believers, hence no need for Eucharist, no need for preaching, and no need for discipline. Even if full receptivity to grace is possible in any given moment, that does not imply that it will be extended inevitably or durably. For "if a righteous man turns from his righteousness and commits sin and does the same detestable things the wicked man does, will he live?" This will jeopardize "the righteous things he has done," lacking justifying faith (Ezek. 18:24). "So, if you think you are standing firm, be careful that you don't fall!" (1 Cor. 10:12; Chrysostom, *Hom. on 1 Cor.* 23.5).

The way of holiness is being actualized in that degree to which it is daily sustaining trust in God's righteousness. Those justified still may have sin remaining in them, even if it is not reigning (Calvin, *Inst.* 3.3.11; J. Wesley, *WJW* 5:156–71).

In What Sense Are Believers Called to "Be Perfect"?

Abraham was commanded by Yahweh to "walk before me and be blameless" (Gen. 17:1; Ambrose, *On Abraham* 2.10.76). "It is God's will that you should be sanctified" (1 Thess. 4:3). The letter to the Hebrews called persons to "go on to maturity" (Heb. 6:1).

The best we can do is not ever as good as the best God has done already for us. "The difference between God's righteousness and ours is the difference between the face of a man and its image in a mirror. There is a certain resemblance, but the two substances are completely different" (Bede, *On 1 John* 3.7)

Scripture calls the faithful to become mature and complete in the likeness of God—"Be perfect, therefore, as your heavenly Father is perfect" (Matt. 5:48 Hilary, *On Matt.* 4.27). The meaning is this: "*You must be perfect in the perfection of grace*, just as *your Father is perfect in the perfection that is his by nature*, each in his own way. For between creator and creature there can be noted no similarity so great that a greater dissimilarity cannot be seen between them" (Fourth Lateran Council 2, italics added).

To this end Christ gave his life to redeem us and the Holy Spirit came to sanctify us. The behavioral realization of perfect love is the end toward which justifying grace points (Tertullian, *Ag. Marcion* 1.24–29). "Be imitators of God, therefore, as dearly loved children and live a life of love, just as Christ loved us" (Eph. 5:1, 2; Polycarp, *Philippians*).

Justified Sinners May Truthfully Refract God's Own Righteousness

Christ's righteousness was indeed substituted for our unrighteousness, not so as to imply no further accountability or responsiveness on our part, but rather that our freedom might be awakened, that we might "put off the old nature with its practices and put on the new nature, which is being renewed in knowledge after the image of the creator" (Col. 3:10; Gregory of Nyssa, *On the Making of Man* 30.33–34; Calvin, *Inst.* 4.17–19). The fulfillment of the law, impossible on the basis of the law alone, now becomes possible on the basis of grace, which works to elevate and transform human behavior. Moral accountability and perfect love are progressively awakened by sanctifying grace working through Word and Sacrament (Gregory of Nyssa, *FGG*:81–84).

The light of the sun is refracted on the surface of water even while the water is changing and moving. So may human freedom modestly but truly refract certain aspects of the reality of God: justice, love, understanding, knowledge, and foresight. God calls us to be holy as God is holy in proportion as finite creatures may contextually refract God's own holiness (Matt. 5:48; Origen, *OFP* 2.7.2; 4.1.37). God calls the faithful not to sin, but if any do sin, they have an advocate with the Father (1 John 2:1; Gregory of Nazianzus, *Theol. Orat.* 30.14). God's saving plan intends that sin be displaced by righteousness of character among all who are to share God's own life eternally.

There Is a Perfection that Admits of Continual Increase

Does growth in perfect love admit of continual increase? However love may be optimally enabled by grace at any moment, it is always capable of being further perfected by a love that may be empowered in some subsequent moment in a way that is heretofore unimaginable. In this sense it is argued that there is no perfection that does not admit of continual increase (Eph. 4:15, 16; Phil. 3:13–17;

Heb. 6:1; 1 Pet. 2:2–5; 2 Pet. 3:18; Gregory of Nyssa, *On Perfection*; J. Wesley, *WJW* 11:366).

What the faithful "reckon as perfect today" may be more adequately grasped tomorrow as they discern their own more refined intentions. Thus "By this gradual advance never being static," they are "able to teach us that what we supposed in our human way to be perfect still remains in some ways imperfect. The only perfection is the true righteousness of God" (Jerome, *Dialogue Ag. the Pelagians* 1.15). "All of us who are running the race perfectly should be aware that we are not yet perfect. The hope is that we may receive perfection in the place to which we are now running perfectly" (Augustine, *On the Perfection of Human Righteousness* 19).

Optimal Response Varies with Stage of Development

This question was thoroughly explored by the great ecumenical doctors of the church: Gregory the Great, Gregory Nazianzus, and Basil: The athletic prowess of the child is not that of the young adult. To walk the way of holiness in full accountability is to walk each step with purity of heart unmixed by sullied motives, to love God without alloy. What that means at each step must be understood in relation to the capacity of the soul at that specific step (Gregory I, *Pastoral Care* 3.1).

As misperceptions and defects are gradually overcome, as capacities increase, as the soul grows, as the mind becomes enriched with wisdom, so will moral requirements be sharpened and intensified. At any age, sufficient grace is being offered for fully adequate responsiveness to whatever emerges within the finite limits of the situation (Gregory Nazianzus, *Orat.* 2.28–33).

Our best human abilities are developed "in accordance with the gradual progress of our education, while being brought to perfection in our training for godliness, we were first taught elementary and easier lessons suited to our intelligence, while the Dispenser of our lots was ever leading us up, by gradually accustoming us, like eyes brought up in the dark, to the great light of truth. For he spares our weakness" (Basil, *On the Spirit* 1.14).

Before these classic teachers, Irenaeus and Tertullian were already casting the drama of human development on a world-historical stage featuring the coming of the Son as the decisive event: Christ "sanctified each stage of life" by making possible at that stage "a likeness to himself," which would in due course pass "through every stage of life. He was made an infant for infants, sanctifying infancy; a child among children, sanctifying childhood, and setting an example of filial affection, of righteousness and obedience; a young man among young men, becoming an example to them, and sanctifying them to the Lord. So also he was a grown man among the older men, that he might be a perfect teacher for all" (Irenaeus, *Ag. Her.* 2.22.4).

"The Lord has sent the Paraclete for this very purpose, that discipline might progressively be guided, ordered, and brought to perfection by his representative, the Holy Spirit. . . . The province of the Holy Spirit is just this; the guidance of discipline, the interpretation of Scripture, the reformation of the intellect, the advance toward better things. All things have their proper time and await their due season. . . . So righteousness was at first rudimentary, when nature feared God; then by means of the Law and the Prophets it progressed to infancy; thereafter through the Gospel it reached the fervor of adolescence; and now through the Paraclete it is being established in maturity" (Tertullian, *On the Veiling* 1).

Life in Christ amid the Tension of Flesh and Spirit

The Paradoxical Uprightness of the Saints

Jerome was quick to catch the irony of the Christian struggle: "We are then righteous when we confess that we are sinners" (Jerome, *Ag. Pelagians NPNF* 2 6:454). "Even the holiest men, while in this life, have only a small beginning of this obedience; yet so that with earnest purpose they begin to live, not only according to some, but according to all the commandments of God" (*Heid. Catech.* Q114).

Leo I the Great stated this point most durably for the ecumenical tradition: As our finite freedom "always has the possibility of falling back, so has it the possibility of advancing. And this is *the true justness of the perfect, that they should never assume themselves to be perfect . . .* because none of us, dearly beloved, is so perfect and holy as not to be able to be more perfect" (Leo I, *Sermons* 40, italics added). "Although Divine Grace gives daily victory to His saints, yet He does not remove the occasion for struggling," in order "that something should remain for our ever-changing nature to win, lest it should boast itself on the ending of the battle" (Leo I, *Sermons* 78). "For human nature has this flaw in itself, not planted there by the Creator but contracted by the transgressor, and transmitted to his posterity. . . . And in this strife such perfect victory is not [so] easily obtained that even those habits which must be broken off do not still encumber us, and those vices which must be slain do not wound" (Leo I, *Sermons* 90). "There are no works of power, dearly beloved, without the trials of temptations, there is no faith without proof, no contest without foe, no victory without conflict," even as "the Lord allowed Himself to be tempted by the tempter, that we might be taught by His example as well as fortified by His aid" (Leo I, *Sermons* 39).

Daily Combat

Meanwhile, the ancient adversary does not cease to "masquerade as an angel of light" and "his servants as servants of righteousness" (2 Cor. 11:14, 15). "He knows whom to ply with the zest of greed, whom to assail with the allurements of the belly, before whom to set the attractions of self-indulgence, in whom to instill the poison of jealousy; he knows whom to overwhelm with grief, whom to cheat with joy, whom to surprise with fear, whom to bewilder with wonderment; there is no one whose habits he does not sift, whose cares he does not winnow, whose affections he does not pry into" (Leo I, *Sermons* 28).

The way is not easy. "The path of virtue lies hid. . . . A great work and toil it is then to keep our wayward heart from all sin, and with the numberless allurements of pleasure to ensnare it on all sides. . . . Who 'touches pitch, and is not defiled thereby?' Who is not weakened by the flesh? Who is not begrimed by the dust? Who, lastly, is of such purity as not to be polluted by those things without which one cannot live?" (Leo I, *Sermons* 49). "The vice of pride is a near neighbor to good deeds, and arrogance ever lies in wait hard by virtue" (Leo I, *Sermons* 42).

Do not close your eyes to Satan's devices (2 Cor. 2:11), one of which is to nurture the illusion that the walk of faith is easy and broad, not narrow. "For the sinful nature desires what is contrary to the Spirit, and the Spirit what is contrary to the sinful nature. They are in conflict with each other, so that you do not do what you want. But if you are led by the Spirit, you are not under law" (Gal. 5:17, 18; Augustine, *On Continence* 18). This daily combat of the sinful nature with the Spirit begins with regeneration and continues until death (Clementina, *Recog.* 8–11).

It is wiser that the Spirit works gradually to disclose the full range of sin. The self is not suddenly flooded and washed away by sin, but sin is revealed to the self gently and gradually (Thérèse of Lisieux, *Autobiography of a Soul*). Faith does not despair over the residues of the depths of evil in one's heart. For that discovery itself is powerful evidence that the Spirit is presently working (Winslow, *WHS*:122). It is a gradual process by which one is more fully enabled to pray, "Search me, O God, and know my heart, test me and know my anxious thoughts. See if there is any offensive way in me, and lead me in the way everlasting" (Ps. 139:23, 24).

Theodicy and Growth in Grace

In order to grow, God's people are "tested in the furnace of affliction" (Isa. 48:10). "God uses even evil for a good purpose, and in a wonderful way turns perversity to good account" (Abelard, *TGS*: 117). Only after his abandonment could Joseph say to his brothers, "You intended to harm me, but God intended it for good" (Gen. 50:20; Chrysostom, *Hom. on Gen.* 67.19).

Any challenge may work toward one's salvation (Ps. 139:67–68). Any affliction may increase the depth of the work of sanctifying grace (Lam. 3:7, 9).

The Spirit's coming is "like a refiner's fire" (Mal. 3:3). "Dear friends, do not be surprised at the painful trial you are suffering, as though something strange were happening to you. But rejoice that you participate in the sufferings of Christ, so that you may be overjoyed when his glory is revealed" (1 Pet. 4:12, 13). Satan rages where the righteous continue faithful through adversity (Chrysostom, *Hom. on the Statues*). Tertullian set forth compelling evidence that the church grows precisely under persecution (*Apology* 50).

The classic Christian view of human nature is characterized by both realism and hope. Exaggerated perfectionism tends to make God's sanctifying grace into a human work of ascetic self-preoccupation. When this is fused with an exaggerated expectation that one must easily rise above infirmities and errors of perception or judgment, it may become compulsive and neurotic (Luther, *Ag. the Heavenly Prophets*; Calvin, *TAA*; Wesley, *Letters, To William Law*).

Whether Sanctification Takes Place Only in the Next Life

Christian traditions differ not so much on whether sanctification is possible, but whether it may occur before death. Some in the Reformed tradition have argued that death itself is a sanctifying transition for the elect, readying them for the holiness of God (Augustine, *Ten Homilies on 1 John*, 9.2; Calvin, *Inst.* 3.3–11; Barth, *CD* 4/2:590). Others argue, "We should expect to be saved from all sin before the article of death" (Wesley, *Larger Minutes*, June 17, 1746), and that it is an offense to the sovereignty of God to assert that God the Spirit is impotent to save persons wholly from their sins while soul and body are united. Whatever these differences, there is relatively greater consensus that the holy life is commanded under the law and enabled under the gospel (Luke 1:74, 75; Titus 2:12; 1 John 4:17).

Is one made perfect only at death? Must sanctification await death for its completion? Though it is possible for the Spirit to enable holiness as an instantaneous work of grace, it is more often a gradual work of grace that becomes fully matured only when, upon facing death, the faithful may receive death in the form of trust in God (Tertullian, *On the Soul* 50–58). Though one dies only once, one may face death many times so as to require readiness for death. It is well to remember that it is not death as such that cleanses from sin, but the atoning work of Christ (1 John 1:7; Rev. 1:5; Bede, *On 1 John* 1.7).

Examining Arguments on the Intrinsic Unattainability of Perfect Love

Sustained faithful responsiveness to grace is safeguarded by consensual exegesis on the grounds that God would not command what is impossible, that God would not promise what is intrinsically unattainable, that it remains a duty to pray for holiness, that there are attested examples in scripture of unreserved responsiveness to grace, and that texts that seem to argue absolute unattainability are explainable on different grounds.

God Does Not Command What Is Intrinsically Impossible

There is little doubt that a mature, complete, continuing response to grace is enjoined repeatedly in scripture (Exod. 19:6; John 5:14; 2 Cor. 7:1; 13:1; Heb. 6:1; 12:14; 1 Pet. 1:15–16). God would not require holiness in this life (Deut. 6:5; Luke 10:27; Rom. 6:11) if it were intrinsically impossible.

If the way of holiness were intrinsically unattainable, noted Jerome, how could it be meaningfully or reasonably commanded? Would it not make God out to be more foolish than we are to assume that the holy God would command that which is impossible to be obeyed, or that God has placed a self-determining creature under requirement but incidentally given the creature no power or means to perform what is required? "God has given possible commands, for otherwise He would Himself be the author of injustice, were He to demand the doing of what cannot possibly be done" (Jerome, *Ag. Pelagians NPNF* 2 6:452–459).

God Does Not Promise What Is Intrinsically Unattainable

A complete and mature life of loving holiness is clearly promised in scripture (Deut. 30:6; Ps. 119:1–3; Isa. 1:18; Jer. 33:8; Ezek. 36:25; Matt. 5:6; 1 Thess. 5:23, 24; Heb. 7:25; 1 John 1:7, 9; Cyril of Jerusalem, *Catech. Lect.* 15.19–21). God would not promise the fullness of salvation and unblemished holiness if intrinsically unattainable. If intrinsically unattainable, must not one conclude that God's promise would be a deception, absurdly bound to fail? The very object of preaching is complete responsiveness to grace (Col. 1:28; Eph. 4:11–13). "You must receive the gift, not of a mere covering of your sins, but of a taking them clean away" (Gregory Nazianzus, *Orat.* 40.32).

Repeatedly scripture points to the way of holiness and perfect love as the very object of covenant history and the practical end of Christ's work (Luke 1:74–75). "If we love one another, God abides in us and his love is perfected in us" (1 John 3:8; cf. Eph. 5:25–27; Titus 2:14). Would it not then be contemptuous to assume its unattainability, so as to demean the cross of Christ by making it fruitless (Origen, *Hom. on Numbers,* 26)? Rather, the Spirit is given to make attainable our actual "return to the adoption of sons, our liberty to call God our Father, our being made partakers of the grace of Christ, our being called children of light, our sharing in eternal glory, and in a word, our being brought into a state of all 'fulness of blessing' " (Basil, *On the Spirit* 115; cf. Rom. 15:29).

The Spirit would not lead the Apostles to *pray* for holiness in this life if it were intrinsically unattainable. The apostles repeatedly prayed for the full and complete life of holiness and perfect love (John 17:20–23; 2 Cor. 13:9–11; Eph. 3:14–21; Col. 4:12; Heb. 13:20, 21; 1 Pet. 5:10). If intrinsically unattainable, the implication could be drawn that the apostles were deluded in this expectation, or misguided by the Spirit in prayer (Origen, *On Prayer;* Cypriain, *The Lord's Prayer* 30).

There Are Examples of Saintliness in This Life

Some skeptics of the efficiency of perfecting grace are willing to concede that believers are commanded to be holy as God is holy, and provided with the means of sufficient grace to become holy, and promised holiness ultimately in eternal blessedness, and called to pray for holiness, yet they do not see anywhere any loving examples of holiness. Agreeing that God promises to make the faithful holy, they argue that this occurs not in this life, but only at its end or after this life.

The Westminster Confession defined the purpose of the church as "the gathering and *perfecting of the saints in this life*" (25.3, italics added). Wesley, who argued for the attainability of sustained faithful response to grace, pointedly remarked that if he knew any who were perfected in love he would not name them because the skeptics, like Herod searching for the child, would instantly pounce upon them looking for something amiss (*WJW* 11: 366; 5:202–12).

God would not have provided in scripture numerous *examples* of complete consecration and radical holiness in this life if it were for all others intrinsically unattainable. Among many examples of holy living in this life who were remembered in the sacred tradition are:

Enoch (Gen. 5:18–24; Heb. 11:5)

Noah (Gen. 6:9; Ezek. 14:14, 20)

Job (Job 1:8)

Barnabas (Acts 11:24), and

The apostles who labored among the Thessalonians (1 Thess. 2:10).

Clement of Alexandria set forth biblical examples of women of unfettered, mature faith, such as Judith, Esther, Susanna, and Sarah. He also added a remarkable list of pagan women of ancient literature whom he thought had shown forth anticipatory elements of the life of perfect love—Lysidica, Leaena of Attica, Theano the Pythagorean, the daughters of Diodorus, Arete of Cyrene, and Aspasia of Miletus (*Stromata*, 4.19).

If even a single instance is found in scripture of one who is living "blameless" or "free from sin" or "perfect," its attainability is formally established. Others who appear to have walked in the way of holiness are found in Luke 1:6; 1 Corinthians 2:6; Philippians 3:15; Hebrews 12:23. There are other passages in which the teaching of full salvation is clearly implied in the text (Rom. 14:6–8; Gal. 2:20; Eph. 3:16–19; 4:12–16, 22–24; Col. 1:28; Titus 2:14; Heb. 12:14; 1 John 3:3, 9; 4:17; 5:18).

The Case for Unattainability

Certain texts appear to support the argument that there is no full redemption from sin in this life and that it is impossible to live without sin: "There is not a righteous man on earth who does what is right and never sins" (Eccles. 7:20; cf. 1 Kings 8:46; 2 Chron. 6:36; Gregory I, *Forty Gospel Homilies* 39). "How then can a man be righteous before God?" (Job 25:4; Calvin, *Inst.* 2.7.5; 4.1.20).

These passages assert the virtual inevitability, but not the absolute necessity, of sin—a major difference. They do not deny the power of grace to overcome sin. They do not necessarily or specifically argue that no one can under any circumstances ever live without falling into sin even while being fully receptive to grace.

One text that appears to argue for practical unattainability is 1 John 1:8–10: "If we claim to be without sin, we deceive ourselves, and the truth is not in us. . . . If we claim we have not sinned, we make him out to be a liar and his word has no place in our lives." Yet the context of this text strongly requires the teaching of purification from all unrighteousness: for "the blood of Jesus, the Son, *purifies us from all sin*." The evident meaning is that Christ cleanses us from all sin, so that no one can now say, I have no need of Christ and no sin that needs to be cleansed. If we say that we have never sinned, hence do not need Christ's atoning work, we deceive ourselves. But "If we confess our sins, he is faithful and just and will forgive us our sins *and purify us from all unrighteousness*" (1 John 1:7–9, italics added).

Luther argued that evangelical perfection is not to be thought of as a completed attainment so as to require no more repentance, but as a continual striving (*EA* 14.25). Yet who more than Luther spoke of the kingdom of God as the dominion Christ exercises in begetting faith and life through the word, and granting full forgiveness of sins (*EA* 14.181)? "The kingdom of God is nothing else than to be pious, orderly, pure, kind, gentle, benevolent and full of all virtue and graces; also, that God have his being within us and that he alone be, live, and reign in us. This we should first of all and most earnestly desire" (Luther, *WA* 2.98).

The Appeal to Blamelessness

Paul called God as his witness that he and his fellow ministers had remained "holy, righteous and blameless" (1 Thess. 2:10), toiling day and night "like a father with his children" (2:11; Clement of Alex., *Instr.* 1.5.19). He did not hesitate to remind his hearers that he had not wavered in faith even amid suffering (2 Tim. 1:12), was fully ready for his eternal inheritance (Col. 1:12, 13), having "kept the faith" (2 Tim. 4:6–8; Basil, *Hom.* 22), and was ready to submit to God's will, "content whatever the circumstances" (Phil. 4:12), able to "do everything through him who gives me strength" (v. 13; Chrysostom, *Hom. on Phil.* 16.4.10–14). Paul was described by Luke as fully willing to discharge the duties of his calling whatever the hardship (Acts 20:20–26). If this is not walking blameless in the way of holiness, what could these attestations mean?

How then could Paul also consistently say, "There is no one righteous, not even one," "There is no one who does good, not even one"? The answer lies in the very point of this passage, which concluded, "Therefore no one will be declared righteous in his sight *by observing the law;* rather through the law we become conscious of sin" (Rom. 3:10b, 12b, 20). This point is then followed by the new alternative offered in Christ: "*But now* a righteousness from God, apart from law, *has been* made known" (Rom. 3:21, italics added; Chrysostom, *Hom. on Rom.* 7).

In another passage it appears that Paul did not regard his own life as fully matured in Christ, as suggested in his letter to Philippians: "Not that I have already obtained all this, or have already been made perfect, but I press on toward the goal to win the prize for which God has called me heavenward in Christ Jesus" (Phil. 3:12–14; Ambrosiaster, *Epis. to Phil.* 3.12.1). Yet one must read further in the same passage to see that the same perfection that he had not attained in the heavenly sense was the final reward toward which he was already in process of racing. He then called upon all who, like himself, were "perfect," in the sense of being cleansed from reigning sin, to be "like-minded" in pressing toward the final goal (cf. 1 Cor. 2:6; Chrysostom, *Hom. on Phil.* 11, 12): "All of us who are mature [Gk. *teleioi;* KJV, perfect] should take such a view of things" (Phil. 3:15). When Paul stated he has not yet obtained the perfect prize in the heavenly sense, he appears to be saying: I am not among the babes in Christ. I have matured. But please do not think of me as having already been perfected in love as it will appear on the last day, for in that sense I have not attained, and seek that perfection above, and strive headlong to ready myself for it. Jerome interpreted Paul's intent in this way: He was "like an archer [who] aimed his arrows at the mark set up [more expressively called *skopos* in Greek], lest the shaft, turning to one side or the other, might show the unskillfulness of the archer . . . so that what today he thought perfect, while he was stretching forward to better things and things in front, tomorrow proves to have been imperfect. And thus at every step, never standing still, but always running, he shows that to be imperfect which we men thought perfect, and teaches that our only perfection is that which is measured by the excellence of God" (Jerome, *Ag. Pelagians NPNF* 2 6:455).

An impressive list of classic exegetes held that Paul in Romans 7 was not referring to his present bondage to sin but to his former "old" self now being transcended by grace. This was argued by Irenaeus, Origen, Tertullian, Basil, Theodoret, Chrysostom, Jerome, Ambrose, Cyril of Jerusalem, Macarius, Theophylact, and at times though not always by Augustine (cf. Jeremy Taylor, *Sermon on Rom. 7:19, TPW*; Field, *HCT*:238). Later Augustinians, Lutherans, and Calvinists have more often argued that Paul was describing his own continuing struggling self in Romans 7.

Warning Not to Attribute Incommunicable
Divine Attributes to Finite Creatures

At this point we are cautioned by classic texts not to fall into an idolatrous or pantheistic pattern of merging of creature and Creator (John XXII, *Propositions Ag. Eckhart* 10; Innocent XI, *Errors of Michael de Molinos, SCD* 1225). The point is clarified by distinguishing incommunicable from communicable divine attributes.

Some attributes of God, such as aseity (uncreated being), completely transcend any possibility of being directly communicated to finite creatures. This is why they are called incommunicable attributes, as when God is addressed as "infinite in being and perfection, a most pure spirit, invisible" (Westminster Confession 2). There is no possibility of the finite creature being made infinite or self-existent. In this way, human participation in God is limited by the intrinsic difference between God and humanity.

But other divine attributes can be proximately refracted in human willing and action, for God is "most loving, gracious, merciful, long-suffering, abundant in goodness and truth" (Westminster Confession). God's mercy and love can be refracted in human mercy and love. Communicable attributes of the infinitely just and wise One may be communicated through those who are just and wise. This is why they are called communicable attributes. Restored human nature, like unfallen human nature, possesses a capacity for mature responsiveness to God unlike that of any other creature (Clement of Alex., *Stromata* 6.12).

Though these divine attributes are communicable, they never are communicated to creatures in the fullness in which they exist in God, but only proportionally in relation to the limited capacities of creatures. Creatures are always changing, progressing and regressing in virtue, whereas God's excellence is such that God is always infinitely good and just, eternally merciful and wise. The excellence of which humans are made capable by grace is perfect and complete in its own way, but this way is far short of the distinctive way in which God alone is eternally perfect (Tho. Aq., *ST* 2–2, Q24.7; Suarez, *De Gratia, Opera* 9.6, 11). To be always without sin is a characteristic of the Divine power only. When the excellences of faith are compared to the excellences of God they fall short. But there are those such as "Job, and Zacharias, and Elizabeth, [who] were called righteous, in respect of that righteousness which might some day turn to unrighteousness, and not in respect of that which is incapable of change" (Jerome, *Ag. Pelagians NPNF* 2 6:452).

The regenerate are both *like* God for having the firstfruits of the Spirit and receiving divine gifts, yet *unlike* God for having the remnants of concupiscence lodged in the flesh (Augustine, *On Forgiveness of Sins and Baptism* 8–12). We have been made sons and daughters of God, but "this is a *grace* of adopting, not the *nature* of the progenitor. The Son of God alone is God" (Augustine, *Comm. on Ps.* 50:2, italics added).

Salvation Viewed from the Vantage Point of Its Effects

Jesus is not a myth whose appropriation is achieved by an imaginative act of recollection. The risen Lord is and remains a living person contemporary with every living human being. He invites each one he meets to receive the good news of God's own coming (Matt. 24:25–27; Augustine, *Sermon* 236.2; Kierkegaard, *PF*: 22; *TC* 2).

The Mediator represents God in the presence of humanity, and humanity in the presence of God, uniting in his person that which had become separated through the history of sin. No other human being has had this distinctive mediatorial and personal significance for all others. Jesus confronts each human being with a decision about whether this gift has saving significance or not (Mark 1:15, 8:34–38; Caesarius of Arles, *Sermons* 159.4–5).

The Effects of Sanctifying Grace

The gospel promises a new heart, a new soul, a new life, out of which sinful actions are becoming less frequent and good actions more habituated. "I will give you a new heart and put a new spirit in you; I will remove from you your heart of stone and give you a heart of flesh. And I will put my Spirit in you and move you to follow my decrees" (Ezek. 36:26–28; Sahdona, *Perfection* 53).

The consequences of sanctifying grace are: grace acts to make the people of God holy and pleasing to God (Heb. 12:28; John 14:23), to adopt the faithful into the family of God (1 John 3:1), to treat their bodies as a temple of the Holy Spirit (1 Cor. 6:19, 20), and to show the way to eternal blessedness (Rom. 8:14–17; Hilary, *Trin.*, 8.27; *Baltimore Catechism*).

Redemption

Redemption is what happens to restored humanity as a result of the atonement (Origen, *Comm. on Rom.* 3.24; Athanasius, *Ag. Arians NPNF* 2 4:330–336). Redemption is the state of having been bought back from fallenness (Baxter, *PW* 8:118–27). Redemption is the effect of God's saving action. Redemption (*lutrosis, apolutrosis*) is an overarching way of describing in a single word the liberation of a captive, release from slavery or death by payment of a ransom (Origen, *Hom. on Luke* 10.2).

The essential metaphor is that of "buying back" to free from imprisonment (Luke 1:68; 2:38; Rom. 3:24; 1 Cor. 1:30). A price (Greek: *time*) of ransom (*lutron*) is included in this purchase (*agorazein, agorazo, exagorazo*, to buy), which eventuates in a release (*luein*) of the prisoner. The whole drama is viewed as a rescue (*ruesthai*).

Paul joined the three complex metaphors of justification, sacrifice, and redemption in the single sentence that the faithful are "*justified* freely by his grace through the *redemption* that came by Christ Jesus. God presented him as a *sacrifice* of atonement, through faith in his blood" (Rom. 3:24, 25, italics added; Ambrosiaster, *Comm. on Paul*, Rom. 3.25). The modern view that redemption simply means political or economic liberation, omitting the decisive element of substitutionary sacrifice for another under divine-human covenant, is a diluted secular interpretation.

The Glory of God Manifested as Holy Love

Through the work of the Son and the Spirit, the name, attributes, and governing ways of God are rightly and gloriously manifested by these means: The triune name is proclaimed throughout the world; the holiness and love of God are at long last understood in their intimate interrelationship; and the divine ordering and governance of the world are fittingly vindicated, having been severely challenged and contested within the history of sin.

The triune name could not be spoken until after the finished work of Christ and the outpouring of the Spirit. The triune work could be only vaguely glimpsed and intimated but not rightly grasped and named until the Son's resurrection and the Spirit's indwelling (Hilary, *Trin.* I.13–14).

The history of salvation had long awaited this moment: In the Son's resurrection and the Spirit's indwelling, the Son was glorified in the Father, and the Father was glorified in the Son, which could occur only when "the hour" had come (John 17:1; Theodore of Mopsuestia, *Comm. on John* 6.17.1; Chrysostom, *Hom. on John* 80).

The disciples were immediately charged to "go and make disciples of all nations, baptizing them in the name of the Father and of the Son and of the Holy Spirit" (Matt. 28:19; Jerome, *Comm. on Matt.* 4.28.18–20). Through God's actions God's essence is becoming revealed. If so, God's name may now be rightly called and known and celebrated as Father, Son, and Spirit. On the day of Pentecost, the Spirit would empower the mission to make known the good news of the Father's sending of the Son through the power of the Spirit (Basil, *On the Spirit* 1.16).

Jesus rose from the dead with a glorified body that included this spiritual community of those who live in him. It is a body to be finally manifested in the final day, when all who believe in him shall be "conformed to the body of his glory" (Phil. 3:20; Tertullian, *On the Resurrection* 45–47).

It is now feasible to see the divine attributes in the light of resurrection and Pentecost. The deep interfusing of the two major moral attributes—holiness and love—are seen as an event in Christ's atoning death and the indwelling of the Spirit. Nowhere do we learn more about the attributes of God than at the cross.

Holiness and love in God are uniquely understood as interrelated on the cross. The love of God was never fully grasped in nature as such or even in the history of providence, although God's just and intelligent ordering may indeed be glimpsed there. It was not until the finished work of the Son on the cross and the outpouring of the Spirit that the simple statement "God is love" (1 John 4:8) could be fully and rightly understood. "Love is so much the gift of God that it is called God" (Augustine, *Letters* 186). "This is how God showed his love among us: He sent his one and only Son into the world that we might live through him. This is love: not that we loved God, but that he loved us and sent his Son as an atoning sacrifice for our sins" (1 John 4:9, 10). "Christ proved his love for us by dying for us" (Bede, *On 1 John* 4.9).

Without God's holiness the cross was unnecessary. Without God's love the cross was impossible. The holiness of God opposes sin and requires punishment for sin. On the cross the divine righteousness that requires the punishment of sin and the mercy that provides the resolution of the debt are found to be dwelling in the divine nature (Pope, *Compend.* 2:278). On the cross love reconciles, unites, and reigns through the sacrifice of the Son in a way fitting to God's holiness.

The purpose of redemption is to bring together the holiness and love of God. This harmonization could not have occurred by expressing either the holiness of God's requirement alone, or the love of God for sinners in a way inconsistent with God's holiness. The cross provided the way to understand both together. The Spirit now empowers the faithful to walk in that way. The holiness and love of God have been satisfied by this reconciliation. This is why it can be said that God was glorified on the cross (1 Cor. 2:8; Augustine, *The Ascension* 263).

The Spirit's Reconciling Ministry

Reconciliation refers to the new divine-human relationship resulting from redemption and glorification (Chrysostom, *Hom. on Cor.* 11.4; Baxter, *PW* 8:113–17; Pope, *Compend.* 2:275, 276). The scene of the reconciliation is the relation between God and humanity.

Reconciliation (*katallage*) means that the favor of God has been restored to sinners who repent and trust in the efficacy of the death of Christ for humanity (Rom. 5:11; 11:15; 2 Cor. 5:18, 19). The enmity caused by sin has been removed with Christ's death and the Spirit's descent. The indicative of the cross calls imperatively for a change in the human heart from enmity to friendship, from alienation to daughterhood and sonship.

Reconciliation is the work of the Son through the Spirit, having restored fellowship and communication between God and humanity (Athanasius, *On the Incarnation of the Word;* Augustine, *Enchiridion* 13.41; Calvin, *Inst.* 3.2.2, 29; Barth, *CD* 4/2).

In this reconciliation, two sides of the relationship are significantly changed: God welcomes humanity, and humanity is called to accept God's welcome. God has mercifully set aside the long-standing quarrel with humanity due to sin. Human beings are invited to receive God's mercy and enter into a new relationship with the forgiving God (Luke 15:20). "For God was pleased to have all his fullness dwell in him to reconcile to himself all things," a reconciliation that occurred "by making peace through his blood, shed on the cross" (Col. 1:20; Chrysostom, *Hom. on Col.* 3).

It is not that humanity is reconciling itself to God, but that God is reconciling himself to humanity. For it is God who was doing the reconciling of "the world to himself in Christ" (2 Cor. 5:19). "All this is from God, who reconciled us to himself through Christ" (2 Cor. 5:18). In an objective sense, we are being reconciled in an act that truly involves us.

The believer does not by dint of human courage navigate the stormy gulf of the divine-human controversy. God overcame that barrier on the cross. It is not that we have diminished our sins to a level of divine acceptability, but that God in Christ was "not counting men's sins against them" (2 Cor. 5:19; Chrysostom, *Hom. on 2 Cor.* 11).

God's action for us must he answered by an act on our side. God's freedom for us invites a new human freedom to rise out of the history of our own sin. Grace does not degrade human freedom but lifts it to a new dignity. Salvation is not purchasable by human effort but received as purchased already by God, to be accepted by human gratitude (Col. 1:20–27). "By his death" he "presents you holy, blameless and irreproachable before him, provided you continue in the faith" (Col. 1:22; Augustine, *On Perfection in Human Righteousness* 9.20).

Cosmic Reconciliation

God's reconciling work not only has relevance for human history, but its echoes are felt throughout the spheres of cosmic nature, the angelic hosts, and the entire eschatological audience to the drama of human history. Through Christ it pleased God to "reconcile to himself all things, whether things on earth or things in heaven, by making peace through his blood, shed on the cross" (Col. 1:20; Basil, *Homilies* 16.10, *FC* 46:267).

The cross visually portrays God's arms stretched out in sacrificial suffering for the whole of nature and history, one arm embracing all past and the other embracing all future cosmic events, reaching once for all from the beginning to the end of time (Athanasius, *Incarn. of the Word* 24–25; Gregory of Nyssa, *Address of Religious Instruction* 32).

The feast is set on the table. The hungry are invited to eat and be filled. No one lacks for an invitation. The prison doors are thrown open—the imprisoned are invited to live in freedom, not licentiously as they please, but free to live precisely as those whose lives had been bought with a price. The fountain of cleansing is open to all nations and peoples. All are invited to plunge in to be cleansed of sin and rise renewed. The bridge has been built between God and humanity over the gulf of sin. Pilgrims are invited to cross over to the city not made with hands.

PART III

THE CHURCH

WHAT IS THE CHURCH? The question silently presupposes the existence of the church that asks the question.

At the core of its earliest baptismal confessions, the community has typically included some form of the solemn declaration: "I [we] believe in the holy, catholic church."

From the outset, therefore, the doctrine of the church thus has the extraordinary status of being "an article of faith," which means that it belongs among the core teachings received at baptism. The reasons why it is so esteemed are examined in chapters 7 and 8.

7

THE COMMUNITY OF CELEBRATION

THE CHURCH'S LIFE IS SHAPED BY devotion to "the apostles' teaching and to the fellowship, to the breaking of bread and to prayer" (Acts 2:42; Chrysostom, *Hom. on Acts* 7).

All essential elements of the church are embedded in this classic text. It is a fourfold précis of the church's:

- apostolic doctrine

- community life

- sacramental communion

- common worship

This is what the church does. This is what happens in this community. The church *is* known by noting carefully what the church *does*.

Complementary Ways of Looking at the Church

In one of the earliest summaries of Christian teaching, Rufinus explained, "We do not say, 'We believe in the holy Church,' but 'We believe the holy Church,'" in the sense of trusting the mother of faith, "not as God, but as the Church gathered together to God" (Rufinus, *Comm. on Apostles' Creed* 36). When the faithful confess, "I believe in the holy catholic church," the intent is not to displace faith in God with faith in the church. To believe in the church is to live out of the conviction that grace abides in her, teaches and governs her common life, and flows from God to all the faithful (*Longer Catech.* of the Eastern Orthodox Church, 253).

Complementary classical definitions of the church stressed different angles of perception of the church's essential center—whether it is the church as company of the elect (*coetus electorum*), or as body of Christ (*corpus Christi*), and as communion of saints (*communio sanctorum*).

Elect People, Body of Christ, Communion of Saints

These three perceptions stand together in close affinity analogous to triune reasoning:

- the One whose electing love *calls* the living community one by one into being is God the *Father*

- the One *embodied* in the church is God the *Son* as head of the body

- the One who brings together the *community* of life in the spirit is God the *Spirit*

Ancient consensual exegetes affirmed all three models in their integral relation. They saw their unity in the triune teaching. Their correlation is worth pondering.

These three traditions of reflection of the church emphasize either new life, reliable truth or visible community. One vision of the church may have an astute grasp of the church as the place where new life is coming into being. A second tradition may underscore the church as the place where authoritative teaching of reliable truth is being passed on to the next generation. The third may view the church essentially as a serving, reconciling visible community manifesting the love of God in the world.

These three motifs are best viewed in Scripture and classic Christian teaching as intimately connected together. When separated, they lose equilibrium and vitality and cease being mutually corrective.

Classic reasoning on the church looks for wholeness in fitting these complementary themes together. When in certain periods of history one motif has become so dominant that others tend to be misplaced or skewed, the vitality of the church is diminished. That decline is subject to historical analysis, though that is not my present task. Here is how the imbalances have come to occur:

Those who focus too exclusively on individual conversion may tend to neglect nurture in the community. Those who have an introverted focus upon sustaining a sacramentally mediated apostolic tradition may inadvertently neglect either urgent serving ministries or evangelical preaching and conversion. Those who focus upon the serving nature of the community in response to the needs of the world may tend to forget the ground of their authority or apostolic teaching.

Emil Brunner aptly summarized the linkage: "Each of the three definitions of the Ekklesia shows us a special aspect of its basis: the transcendent (*electio*), the historical-objective (*corpus Christi*), and the spiritual-subjective (*sanctorum communio*). Each of them taken by itself would necessarily lead to a one-sided conception: either to an abstract spiritual intellectualism (the number of the predestined, *numerus praedestinatorum*), or to a sacramental hierarchism (the Body of Christ, *corpus Christi*), or to an emotional and pietistic individualism (the communion of the faithful, *communio fidelium*). Only in their unity do they reproduce the reality of the Ekklesia" (Brunner, *Dogm.* 3:27).

Strengths and Limits of Evangelical, Orthodox, and Activist Visions of the Church

The vitality of the one church may be variously viewed from the viewpoint of personal conversion, or sacramental order, or change-agent communities seeking structural transformation of the orders of the family, the market, and the state.

These types have recurred in church history. Today we call them by terms familiar to contemporary church life. Yet the same Spirit of the triune God offers these variable gifts that need each other for completion.

Much evangelical teaching stresses personal holiness. Orthodoxy stresses the church's historic apostolicity and continuity. The activists stress moral service to the world, and the search for practical inclusiveness. In this way the ancient definitions of the church correlate with these three prevailing complementary forms of church life. Evangelicals may have trouble empathizing with Orthodoxy. Both of these interpret the heart of the church with a different vocabulary than social gospel and liberal visions of the church that focus more upon social change and service. Pietism may forget that the church is an inclusive community. Orthodoxy may tend to forget that the Holy Spirit is calling forth new forms of mission and distinctive forms of witness in ever-new cultural situations. Activists may forget that the church is where people are being reborn to from above.

It is not surprising that each one of these perspectives is prone to value and assess the church from the particular viewpoint of their own special (family-social-national-ethnic) history within it. We are prone to think egocentrically about alternative visions of the church that arise out of different social locations and histories. When exaggerated, such varieties have presented a challenge to classic consensual exegesis from the outset. Classic Christianity shows their linkage.

This can be visualized in the following graphic which portrays a gestalt of features clustering around these three types of reasoning. Each modern believer is likely to have emerged out of one or another column, or combination of them, and thus may tend toward forgetfulness of the excellent values in another arena:

Patterns of Recollection In the Church

Coetus Electorum	Corpus Christi	Communio Sanctorum
Focus of Common Life		
Conversion	Sacramental life	Social action
Discipline of regenerate life	Unity of apostolic teaching	Relevant service in the world
Religion of the heart	Religion of the book	Religion of the people
Typical Historical Expressions		
Evangelical	Liturgical	Liberal
Revivalism	Eastern, Roman Anglican traditions	"Mainline" Protestantism
Pietism	Catholic orthodoxy	Political theology

Key Values and Achievements		
Vitality	Authority	Solidarity
Inner life	Correct doctrine	Social change
Teaching Concentration		
New birth	Authoritative doctrine and catechetics	Reconciling base communities
The individual	The eternal	The social
Personal Regeneration	Apostolic authority	Social transformation
Church and Society Correlation		
Christ against culture	Christ of or above culture	Christ transforming culture
Heterodox Tendency		
Gnosticism	Neoplatonic idealism	Pelagian pragmatism
Focus of Human Predicament		
Sin	Heresy	Injustice
Key Mark		
Holiness	Apostolicity	Unity

These are not to be viewed as mutually exclusive types, but as intersecting vectors. They offer a frame of reference for speaking of varied ways the Holy Spirit has worked for centuries in forming the worldwide church in various cultures. For evangelicals, the Spirit works in the church to inspire scripture, quicken the Word in our hearts, bear witness to our spirits that we are children of God (2 Tim. 3:10; Rom. 8:15–17; Origen, *Comm. on Rom.* 8.16). For Catholics and Orthodox, the Spirit guides to all truth, assists in prayer, calls forth the sacramental life, intercedes with groanings that cannot be uttered (John 16:13; Rom. 8:26, 27; Augustine, *Ag. Manicheans,* 1.22.34). For social liberals, the Spirit works through the church to comfort those in trouble, bind up the brokenhearted, proclaim liberation for captives (Isa. 61:1; John 16:26; Rom. 8:22–25; Didymus the Blind, *Pauline Comm.,* 2 Cor. 1.3).

Each tradition when isolated does well to recognize in the other something essential to its own truth and authenticity. Each needs admonition from its matching partners to more fully embody the work of the Spirit.

Biblical Teaching on the Church (*Ekklēsia, Qahal*)

The discipline that studies the church is ecclesiology. The English word *ecclesiology* is derived from the Greek words *ek* (out or from) and *kaleō,* to call. This Greek word entered into the New Testament from the Septuagint, where it was used to translate the Hebrew *qahal*—assembly, congregation, those called out, gathered, congregated (Ex. 12:6). *Ekklēsia* (1 Thes. 1:1) translated *qahal* (called of the Lord) into Greek. The apostles used the word to refer to the act of assembling or the assemblage of persons brought together by God's own calling for the purpose of hearing the gospel and sitting at table with the living Lord. *Qahal* can refer to the whole congregation of Israel, whether or not in actual assembly. The assembly in post-exilic Judaism was called out of the world to make due sacrifices follow an ordered calendar of seasonal celebration, engage in ceremonies and ordinances, and teach the faithful the history of revelation. All these functions continued, though in transmuted forms, under the New Testament *ekklēsia*.

There is one noteworthy difference between *qahal* and *ekklēsia:* the *qahal* was, strictly speaking, a calling forth of the circumcised, hence of males primarily, while the *ekklēsia* always included women, men, and children. The Hebrew *'edah* (assembly, company, congregation, ceremonial community as a whole) is usually translated into Greek as *sunagōgē* (from *sun*, together; *ago*, to bring), a term occasionally applied to early Christian assemblies (James 2:2; 2 Thess. 2:1; Heb. 10:25). The church continues as *ekklēsia* because it is called forth, gathered by the call of God as "the assembly of the first-born who are enrolled in heaven" (Heb. 12:23; Deut. 4:10), assembling persons together before the Lord (Lev. 8:3), "the church established by Christ in every part of the world" (Eusebius, *Proof of the Gospel* 6.24).

My Church: Jesus' Use of Ekklēsia

In Matthew's Gospel, Jesus did not hesitate to describe the *ekklēsia* as "my church" in a highly personal sense— Jesus' own assembly, his own called out people, and himself personally as their cohesion. Jesus said, "You are Peter, and on this *rock* I will build *my church* [*oikodomēsō mou tēn ekklēsian*], and the gates of Hades will not overcome it. I will give you the keys of the kingdom of heaven" (Matt. 16:18, italics added; Theodore of Mopsuestia, *Fragment*, Reuss, *MKGK*:129). Lutheran Orthodox theologian David Hollaz commented, "The meaning is, 'Thou art Peter, a man made of rock, standing upon thy confession just as upon a rock, or most firm *petra*, and upon this rock will I build my church, so that it may be made of rock, immovable and impregnable' " (*ETA*: 1295; Schmid, *DT*:586; Epiphanius the Latin, *Interp. Of the Gospels* 28).

The personal phrase "*my* church" indicates that Jesus, according to Matthew, deliberately intended to form a continuing community of prayer, preaching, and discipline. He called and trained his disciples, and promised the coming of the Holy Spirit to guide them after his ascension.

Jesus viewed this assembly as a fitting context for the disciplining of the community. If an offender "refuses to listen" to those offering corroborated testimony of a misspent life or wrong teaching or disruption of the community, then "tell it to the church" (*ekklēsia*, Matt. 18:17) whose discipline has the power of binding and loosing on earth with eternal effect in heaven (v. 18; Augustine, *Sermon* 82.1). This community is an indestructible communion of persons who are being upbuilt by their union with their incarnate Servant Lord, a communion of which Peter and the apostolic company were the first guardians, to whom were given the tasks of proclamation of the Word, celebration of the sacraments, and disciplining of the faithful for eternal accountability (Cyprian, *Treatises* 1; Tho. Aq., *ST* suppl., Q18–23).

The Spirit is building this community "on the foundation of the apostles and prophets, with Christ Jesus himself as the chief cornerstone" (Eph. 2:20). Jesus founded the church by personally calling and gathering the apostolate around himself, training, disciplining, and commissioning them to the ministry of proclamation and sacrament, expressly stating his irreversible intention to upbuild an ongoing community that would be commissioned with power and authorized to baptize, preach, discipline, and celebrate the paschal meal with the risen Lord. Jesus regarded this *ekklēsia* as sharing in the historical unfolding of the kingdom of God. It was to be a continuing community in which he himself would continue to be a present participant (Matt. 26:26; 28:20; 1 Cor. 11:24, 24; Chrysostom, *Hom. on Matt.* Hom. 90.2).

The Renewed Israel in Continuity with the Ancient Covenant Community

The new Israel, the Christian community, is steeped in continuity with the people of Israel, yet in it we behold all things being made new (2 Cor. 5:17). The new was born of the old. "Therefore every teacher of the law who has been instructed about the kingdom of heaven is like the owner of a house who brings out of his storeroom new treasures as well as old" (Matt. 13:52; Cyril of Jerusalem, *Catech. Lect.* 18.24, 25; Augustine, *Sermon* 74.5).

At first the new community seemed to be like a sect within Judaism. There was no overt break with temple and synagogue. The gradual weaning of the church from its Jewish matrix would take many decades. It would await the fall of Jerusalem and its dreadful diaspora before the new Israel would come to full self-identity and separate existence. Only then would the elder serve the younger (Gen. 25:21–34; 48:14–21; *Epist. Barnabas* 13; 9.6; 10.9; Caesarius of Arles, *Sermon* 86.4) and the new treasure heighten the beauty of the old.

In calling forth the *ekklēsia*, Jesus did not act against but within Judaic history. It was not as if cleaning the slate of history, but as breathing new life into the ancient covenant community destined since Abraham to redeem history, of which he himself was its essential remnant. He was deliberately reconstituting the people of God into an *ekklēsia* for all people, not for one particular land or cultural identity only (*Epist. Barnabas* 4.8). He sent the Spirit to nurture and discipline them for their eternal destiny, to guide the pilgrim church to the holy city (John 16:13; Hilary, *Trin.* 2.55–57).

The Renewed Israel

The Jewish war of AD 66–70 ended in the destruction of the temple of Jerusalem, after which time temple taxes went to the pagan temple of Jupiter Capitolinus. The temple cults ended. No more sacrifices were offered. With the destruction of Jerusalem, the center of gravity shifted in Judaism from Jerusalem to diaspora, and in Christianity from Jerusalem to Antioch, Alexandria, and Rome (Irenaeus, *Ag. Her.* 4.4.1).

After AD 70 the history of Christianity was largely a history of the *ekklēsia* beyond Judaism. Under imperial Roman rule, "Jews and (circumcised) Jewish Christians were forbidden to enter the town and its environs, and circumcision was forbidden, under pain of death. Much later, from the third century, Jewish pilgrims were allowed to visit the west wall of the temple (the Wailing Wall) once a year" (Küng, *TC*:113). Most efforts by Christians to convert Jews ceased, and by the second century the daily rabbinic prayer, *Schmone 'Esre*, included a curse upon "heretics and Nazarenes." The church viewed itself as the renewing of Israel, the new people of God (Rom. 9:6; Ambrosiaster, *Comm. on Paul*, Rom. 11:1, 2; Heb. 13:12; 1 Pet. 2:9, 10; Rev. 21:3). Christians recalled that "the sound form of our faith is from Abraham, and our repentance is from Nineveh and the house of Rahab, and ours are the expectations of the Prophets" (Ephrem, *Hymns*).

Gentile hostility toward Jews anteceded Christianity. Similar attacks were made on Christians in the first three centuries. The Hebrew Bible was constantly studied by the early church, read consistently through the lens of its fulfillment in the resurrection (G. Dix, *Jew and Greek*).

The church had been prefigured in the Old Testament, from Abel's sacrifice onward. A new form of the covenant community was being brought into life through which all peoples would be blessed (Jer. 31:31–34; Acts 2:36; 13:32, 33; Eph. 3:6; Ephrem, *Comm. on Heb.* 11.4).

The new covenant community extended the call to the children of Abraham, and became Abraham's heir and seed (Rom. 4:12–16; 9:6–13; Gal. 4:20; 6:16). These Gentile strains have been grafted onto the old olive tree, Israel. "The marriage of Moses to an Ethiopian woman whom he made a woman of Israel prefigured the grafting of the wild olive on to the true olive to share in its fruitfulness" so that the black "Ethiopian bride signifies the church of the Gentiles" (Irenaeus, *Ag. Her.* 4.20.12; Num. 12:1; Rom. 11:17; Origen, *Song of Songs* 2).

All the nations from north, south, east, and west will sit at table *with* Abraham, Isaac, and Jacob in the coming reign of God (Matt. 8:11, 12; Luke 13:28, 29). "The shepherds came from nearby to see, and the magi came from far away to worship" (Augustine, *Sermon* 203.3). The distinction between Jew and Gentile, which in late Judaism had become primarily a historical-racial-ethnic difference, now is transmuted into a distinction between responsiveness and apathy in relation to God's own personal coming (Acts 2:14–39). The distinction between circumcised and uncircumcised now becomes transmuted into a very different distinction between baptized and unbaptized (Gen. 17:12; Rom. 6; 1 Cor. 7:19). God does not renege on his promises to Israel (Rom. 11:29). Israel will finally be regathered and reformed prior to the final transmutations of history (Rom. 9–11; Isa. 1:9; 8:14; 10:22, 23), according to classical Christian exegesis. The church "draws sustenance from the root of that good olive tree onto which have been grafted the wild olive branches of the Gentiles [cf. Rom. 11:17–24]. Indeed the Church believes that by His cross, Christ, our Peace, reconciled Jew and Gentile, making them both one in Himself " *(Doc. Vat. II on Non-Christian Religions* 4:664; cf. Eph. 2:14–16). The election of the Gentile faithful, as of the Jews, is an act of divine mercy, not human merit, and a calling to service, not privilege. "If some of the branches have been broken off, and you, though a wild olive shoot, have been grafted in among the others and now share in the nourishing sap from the olive root, do not boast over those branches. If you do, consider this: You do not support the root, but the root supports you" (Rom. 11:17, 18). The Jews remain most dear to God, "for God's gifts and his call are irrevocable" (Rom. 11:29; Theodoret, *Interp. of Rom.* 11.29).

The Called Community

The "called out" community is not called forth by human initiative or voluntary agreement or a coalition of interests. It is God the Son who calls to discipleship. It is God the Spirit who draws the disciple toward the holy life.

Klēsis *and* Ekklēsia

If the church is by definition a gathering of those called, the notions of calling and church (*klēsis* and *ekklēsia*) are intimately intertwined. The *ekklēsia* gathers together those effectually *called*. "For the promise is to you and to your children and to all that are far off, every one whom the Lord our God calls to him" (Acts 2:39). The church does not denote all humanity but those "called out" for life in the Spirit. *Ekklēsia* as the called together community depends entirely upon *klēsis* (calling). Those who share in this community are the *ek-klētoi*, those summoned together by the gospel, called out by the proclamation (*kerygma*). The terms used to describe this community are the church of God (*ekklēsia tou theou*), people of

God (*laos tou theou*), and church of Christ (*ekklēsia tou Christou*; 1 Cor. 1:2; 11:22; Gal. 1:13; Heb. 11:25; Rom. 16:16).

Common worship expresses this calling and makes it concrete: "You are not to withdraw into yourselves and live in solitude, as though God had already pronounced you holy. Come and take your full share in the meetings, and in deliberating for the common good. Scripture says, 'Woe betide those who are wise in their own eyes' " (*Epist. Barnabas* 4.10; Isa. 5:21; Gregory the Great, *Forty Gospel Hom.* 4).

Ekklēsia refers both to the act of congregating and to the community as a congregation. This community becomes *ekklēsia* by the repeated fact of its being summoned by the gospel, called to assemble to praise God. The church is precisely this coming together in response to God's own coming. We do well not to abandon the community in which we received the regenerating word and power, the mother of faith (Tertullian, *To the Martyrs*, FC 40:17; Gal. 4:26; Calvin, *Inst.* 4.1.4). In order to distinguish the holy assembly of Christian believers from other assemblies, it was called the *ekklēsian tou theou* (the church of God; Acts 20:28; 1 Cor. 1:2; Gal. 1:13). In time *ekklēsia* came to be applied to the place where these meetings were held. The Anglo-Saxon root word for *church* (Scots *Kirk*, German *Kirche*, Old Saxon *circe*, Swedish *Kyrke*, Slav *carkov*) stems from the Greek word *kuriakos*, belonging to the Lord, or the Lord's house.

Defining the Church

The Christian church is the community through whom the Holy Spirit administers redemption and distributes gifts, the means in and by which God makes the reconciling work of the Son vitally present to humanity. The church is the extension of the work of the Incarnate Lord as prophet, priest, and king. The church is called from the world to celebrate God's own coming, and called to return to the world to proclaim the kingdom of God.

The prototype Protestant definition of the *ekklēsia* was set forth at Augsburg: "The Church is the congregation of saints [*congregatio sanctorum*], in which the Gospel is rightly taught and the Sacraments are rightly administered" (Augsburg *Conf.*, art. 7). The congregation of saints have fellowship with each other and with "the Holy Spirit who renews, sanctifies, and governs their hearts" (Augsburg *Apology* 163). The church is a spiritual people "regenerated by the Holy Ghost" (Augsburg *Apology* 164), who "hear the voice of their Shepherd" and receive the promise of the Spirit (Schmalkald Articles).

From these definitions, later Protestants (Anglicans, Reformed, Baptists, and charismatics) have taken major cues. However varied may be Protestant expressions of the church, these classic consensual affirmations of the core of Reformation teaching on the church have remained largely intact in Protestant confessional traditions. As head, Christ infuses his disposition, temper, and will into the community. Those who stress new birth are more likely to define the church as "the whole company of regenerate persons in all times and again, in heaven and on earth . . . that redeemed humanity in which God in Christ exercises actual spiritual dominion" (Strong, *ST*:887; John 3:3–5).

The Company of Those Called

The church is a "company of the faithful, called and gathered out of the world" who "by faith are partakers of all those good graces which are freely offered through Christ" (Second Helvetic *Conf.*). The Cambridge Platform defined the church as "the whole company of those that are elected, redeemed, and in time effectually called from the state of sin and death unto a state of Grace, and salvation in Jesus Christ" (*CC*:387). *Coetus electorum* (the company of the elect) has its origin in the eternal will of God, the primordial intent and decree of God to redeem sin and call forth a redeemed community. The company is described by Paul as "the household of God, which is the church of the living God, the pillar and bulwark of the truth" (1 Tim. 3:15). It is God's own appointed means of upholding Christian truth in the world.

Orthodoxy builds on this premise, defining the church as "that holy foundation made by the Incarnate Word of God for the salvation and sanctification of men, bearing His own authority and authentication, constituted of men having one faith and sharing in the same sacraments, who . . . trace their beginning through unbroken succession to the Apostles and through them to our Lord" (Androutsos, *Dogm.*:262).

As Christ is God personally with us, so is the church Christ personally with us, teaching his truth and transmitting his grace. "The Church of Christ is not an institution; she is a new life with Christ and in Christ, directed by the Holy Spirit. The light of the Resurrection of Christ shines on the Church, which is filled with the joy of the Resurrection, of triumph over death. The risen Lord lives with us, and our life in the Church is a life of mystery in Christ" (S. Bulgakov, *Orthodoxy*). "Wherever Jesus Christ is, there is the Catholic Church" (Ignatius of Antioch, *To Smyrna* 8).

The church is the personal communion of those who have communion with the living Christ. The church is "at once the realization of God's gracious purposes in creation and redemption, and the continuous organ of God's grace in Christ by the Holy Spirit, who is its pervading life, and who is constantly hallowing all its parts" (Lausanne Faith and Order Conference, *CC*:571).

From the perspective of the sacramental life, the church consists of all who have been faithfully baptized, who thereby have made and confirmed a profession of faith in Christ from the heart—an audible, visible act in time and space (Chrysostom, *Baptismal Instructions*). "The Church is the congregation of all baptized persons united in the same true faith, the same sacrifice, and the same sacraments" of which baptism is the initial rite wherein one "becomes a member of the Church on receiving this sacrament. To remain a real member of the Church after baptism a person must profess the one true faith" (*Baltimore Catechism*:102).

The Love of Christ for His Church

The *ekklēsia* is unutterably loved, valued, prized by Christ, who offered his life for her. The bridegroom was willing to die for the bride, to ready her for the end-time wedding by cleansing her with baptism, washing away every hurt, so that she will be comforted, and without blemish, holy, completely ready for the final marriage feast celebrating the reconciliation of God and humanity (Rev. 19:7). "Christ loved the church and gave himself up for her to make her holy, cleansing her by the washing with water through the word, and to present her to himself as a radiant church, without stain or wrinkle or any other blemish, but holy and blameless" (Eph. 5:25–27; Chrysostom, *Hom. on Eph.* 20.5.25).

The magnitude of the love of Christ for the church is celebrated through a flood of linked metaphors, summed up by Chrysostom:

> *He espoused her as a wife,*
> *He loves her as a daughter,*
> *He provides for her as a handmaid,*
> *He guards her as a virgin,*

He fences round her like a garden
And cherishes her like a member:
as a head He provides for her,
as a root he causes her to grow,
as a shepherd He feeds her,
as a bridegroom He weds her,
as a propitiation He pardons her,
as a sheep He is sacrificed. . . .
Many are the meanings in order that we may enjoy a part
if it be but a small part of the divine economy of grace.

(Chrysostom, *Eutropius, NPNF* 1 9:262)

Bath and Meal

In acts of mercy to the homeless, the poor, and the alienated, the serving church offers simple acts of cleansing and feeding. Nothing is more prized to the hungry and homeless than a bath and a meal. Nothing is more characteristic of the church's essential identity and self-offering than bathing and feeding.

Entering the Community of Faith
Through Cleansing Repentance

The bathing and feeding images were foreshadowed by the exodus, when our forefathers "all passed through the sea. They were all baptized into Moses in the cloud and in the sea. They ate the same spiritual food and drank the same spiritual drink, for they drank from the spiritual rock that accompanied them, and that rock was Christ" (1 Cor. 10:1–4; Chrysostom, *Hom. on 1 Cor.* 23).

The fulfillment of this exodus prototype "appears in Christ our Lord, baptized in water at the Jordan, and then baptized in the Holy Ghost, which 'descended from heaven like a dove and abode upon him.' Then it recurred again in the waiting disciples who besides the baptism of water which had doubtless already been received, now were baptized 'in the Holy Ghost and in fire' " (Gordon, MS:65).

The continuing work of the Spirit is to vivify the body of Christ by maintaining its connection with the risen Head (Basil, *On the Spirit* 1.12–15). By being baptized in the triune name, and thus in the name of Jesus (Acts 2:38; 8:16; 10:48), one comes under the lordship and care of Jesus, one belongs to the crucified and risen Lord, sharing in his life, death, and resurrection (Gal. 3:26–4:7; Augustine, *Epis. to Gal.* 30.4.4, 5).

"I baptize you with water for repentance," John the Baptist preached. "But after me will come one who is more powerful than I, whose sandals I am not fit to carry. He will baptize you with the Holy Spirit and with fire" (Matt. 3:11; Chromatius, *Tractate on Matt.* 11.4). The Son did indeed baptize the *ekklēsia* with the Spirit, bathed, cleansed, and immersed the church in the life of the Spirit.

Baptism with fire refers anticipatively to the final judgment in which the dross of sin is being completely burned away from the fallen creation (Hippolytus, *Holy Theophany*). The conditions of entrance into the community were straightforward: repent, believe, be baptized, and you will receive the gift of the Holy Spirit (Acts 2:38; Chrysostom, *Hom. on Acts*, Hom. 7).

Those faithfully baptized belong to this one body: "The body is a unity, though it is made up of many parts, and though all its parts are many, they form one body. So it is with Christ. For we were all baptized by one Spirit into one body—whether Jews or Greeks, slave or free—and we were all given the one Spirit to drink" (1 Cor. 12:12, 13). The baptism once given at Pentecost would continue to be given from Pentecost to Parousia for the whole body. United in Christ, the church has "one Lord, one faith, one baptism" (Eph. 4:5; Ambrose, *On the Sacraments* 2.1.2).

Baptism reenacts and participates in Jesus' death and resurrection. Paul preached that "all of us who were baptized into Christ Jesus were baptized into his death," and that "we were therefore buried with him through baptism into death in order that, just as Christ was raised from the dead through the glory of the Father, we too may live a new life" (Rom. 6:3, 4). Just as in the physical body some cellular tissue sloughs off each day while new tissue is being normally generated, so in the historic church and the individual Christian life there is some non-tragic dimension of dying daily, sharing daily in Christ's passion and mission, willing to suffer for the sins of the world, looking forward to sharing in final resurrection.

The anointing of the head of the body (the messiah) symbolized the anointing of the whole body (the *ekklēsia*). This was symbolized in classic exegesis by the recollection that at Aaron's consecration the anointing oil poured on the head and beard also ran down profusely upon his body and his priestly robe. When the faithful live together in unity, "It is like precious oil poured on the head, running down on the beard, running down on Aaron's beard, down upon the collar of his robes" (Ps. 133:2), so that not only the head but the whole ongoing historical body dwells together in unity, profusely anointed by the Spirit (Augustine, *Hom. on Psalms*, Ps. 133).

Jesus' Last Meal and the Founding of the Church

Jesus' last meal can be called the founding assembly of the *ekklēsia*, a founding whose full significance was grasped only later, after Pentecost. Jesus' farewell meal was intentionally instituted to be repeatedly commemorated by his disciples until his return. It was to become the central liturgical event of the continuing life of the church, uniting all who believe in him (*Liturgy of St. James; ANF* 7:544).

On the night before he was betrayed, Jesus met with his disciples for the paschal meal that commemorated the exodus of the people of Israel from Egypt and the institution of the covenant at Sinai. Taking the cup, he said, "I will not drink again of the fruit of the vine until the kingdom of God comes." Taking the bread, he said, "This is my body given for you; do this in remembrance of me." He said, "This cup is the new covenant in my blood, which is poured out for you" (Luke 22:17–20; Cyril of Alex., *Comm. on Luke,* Hom. 142).

Jesus was aware that his death was bringing prophetic messianic expectation to a fulfillment. It would constitute the institution of a new covenant. In offering food and drink to his disciples, he was offering himself unconditionally to them in a way that would become the incomparable event of the following day—the cross (Athanasius, *Resurrection Letters* 4). At this table they became one body with him. Years later Paul recalled and passed on this awareness of unity with the living Lord: "We who are many, are one body, for we all partake of the one loaf" (1 Cor. 10:17).

Received from the Lord

Paul explicitly stated that the tradition of the Supper came from the Lord himself: "For I received from the Lord what I also passed on to you" (1 Cor. 11:23). This meal has variously been called the supper of the Lord (1 Cor. 11:20) or the "breaking of bread" (Acts 2:42, 46; 20:7, 11), or *eucharistia* (thanksgiving), or in the Latin West *missa* (mass, sending, dismissal, blessing).

The original sequence of liturgical actions instituted are simple, and still prevail throughout consensual Christianity: taking bread, breaking it, giving thanks, declaring, "This is my body, which is for you," and after the supper blessing the cup, saying, "This is the new covenant in my blood; do this, whenever you drink it, in remembrance of me" (1 Cor. 11:23–25). The time frame for communing with the Lord in this way is the time between his ascension and return. During this time the Lord will not be visibly present with his disciples but will remain spiritually present to them in this lively way (Chrysostom, *Hom. on 1 Cor.* 27.5).

This simple meal became the basis for the continuing memory of the *ekklēsia* of the Lord (*Liturgy of Mark*). The community would continue its celebration until his return. They were called to proclaim the good news to all. Each meeting of the disciples would be accompanied by the expectant hope echoing from the Aramaic tradition throughout the apostolic testimony: "*Marana tha*" ("Come, O Lord," 1 Cor. 16:22; Rev. 22:20; Chrysostom, *Hom. on Cor.*, Hom. 44; Andrew of Caesarea, *Comm. on Apoc.* 22.20–21).

What took place at that meal had epochal significance for salvation history. What had begun as a Jewish paschal meal commemorating the exodus from Egypt and the establishment of the covenant at Sinai ended by celebrating a new exodus from the Egypt of sin and the establishment of a new testament in the blood of the Son soon to be shed (Ignatius, *Philadelphians* 4). As the old covenant had been sealed with sacrificial blood, so was the new covenant to be sealed with Jesus' own blood (Justin Martyr, *First Apology* 65–66). As the paschal meal was a sign of departure from Egypt, so was the eucharistic meal a sign of a new departure, a spiritual exodus, liberation from bondage to sin. The *ekklēsia* on earth continues to be a community called to journey toward a promised land, seeking that which is above.

The Primitive Layers of Eucharistic Communion

Some recent critics hold, contrary to church tradition, that Jesus had no intention whatever of founding a continuing community since he expected the end time soon and in one isolated passage described himself as sent only to the lost ones of the house of Israel (Matt. 10:8). But the classical ecumenical exegetes appealed to apostolic witnesses to establish the fact that Jesus himself clearly intended to teach disciples, institute sacraments, and engage in a mission beyond the Jews to all nations (Jerome, *Comm. on Matt.* 1.10.5–6; Gregory the Great, *Forty Gospel Hom.* 4.1–2). They rejected Gnostic sources that focused on Jesus' sayings rather than reporting the historic events that demonstrated what he did for us.

In the most primitive layers of memory we can already identify the essential nucleus from which later formal definitions (episcopacy, triune teaching, and theandric Christology) developed. Like an embryo growing, the church did not come into existence without a historical struggle and gradual development, just as the body of the Lord did not form in the womb of the Virgin without gradual growth through stages. Nothing that happens in a community shaped by the incarnation would or could happen nonhistorically, abstractly, arbitrarily, or lacking continuity with antecedents (Acts 20:17–38; Basil, *Letters* 242–244).

Form-critics are prone to speculate on a complex multi-generational process of hellenizing developments before the distinct formation of the church. This tends to ignore the evidence of just how early the Jerusalem church developed some of its most essential features: synagogue-like worship, eldership, preaching, service to the needy, baptism, and Eucharist. All were received directly from Judaism and transmitted immediately in their basic form within the first two decades of Christianity, grounded in verbatim teaching specifically "remembering the words the Lord Jesus himself said" (Acts 20:35; B. Gerhardsson, *Memory and Manuscript*).

The Polarities of the Body of Christ

Christianity has never been merely a matter of isolated individuals being converted and voluntarily joining together to constitute autonomous, voluntary organizations of believers. Rather the body of Christ is called out by the Spirit, by divine address, from the world from the outset as a corporate, social reality. The church is from the outset defined as a single living organism, a unified interdependent growing organic body with every member depending upon the community of faith made alive by the Son through the Spirit (1 John 1:1–7; Bede, *On 1 John* 1.7).

Christ called into being a living human community to herald the coming kingdom of God. He came to inaugurate the kingdom of God through a continuing transgenerational human community. Persons are not saved in isolation but within a fellowship knit together by its common bond of union with Christ (Col. 2:2, 19; Calvin, *Inst.* 3.25, 4.16). God's plan includes and requires interpersonal testimony, interpersonal meeting, prayer, worship, hymnody, and one-on-one passing on of the tradition of apostolic testimony.

Individual conversion enlivens this community. But each individual remains incomplete without a community of worship. In this community the Head of the church is becoming embodied by taking form in the church. Those who say "Where the church is, there is Christ," join with those who say "Where believing Christians are, there is the church." Each polarity of the ecumenical tradition (liturgical versus practical, hierarchical versus lay-oriented, catholic versus evangelical) needs the corrective of the other. This tension and potential paradox is built into the nature of the church as the body of Christ continuing within ordinary history (Bede, *On 1 John* 3.24).

The deeper and related paradox is that the Son is truly human and truly God. When the church is most fully being itself, the church is participating in the humanity of the Son through love and the holiness of God through prayer.

Christ affectionately offers and imparts to and provides for the church all that it needs to live and grow. The church responds affectionately by offering to Christ its praise, worship, and thanksgiving. The church is impossible to understand or explain or account for without Jesus himself, without his initiative, his direct willing and enabling and sustaining of it (Eph. 1:22; Col. 1:18; Augustine, *On Genesis Ag. Manichaeans* 2.24.57). Hence the forms of ministry of the *ekklēsia* are from above, divinely instituted, grace-enabled, responsive to the divine initiative, yet at the same time intertwined with historical reality. The holiness of the church is always in a close quarters struggle with the actual scandals of particularity: class structure, gender, race, nation, economic interest, and historical situation.

The Spirit Builds Up the Community

Pentecost was not an event in which the Spirit was poured out upon wholly separable isolated individuals. Rather it was a community already gathered for a liturgical event in whom the Spirit came to dwell. A community was created by the Spirit in which the embodiment of Christ's mission continued corporately after his ascension, as a household, a family, a *koinonia*.

Whether viewed locally or generally, the church is a fellowship, a shared social process involving primary engagement of persons in the family of God. This runs against the mechanistic premise that the church is essentially an impersonal, imposed organization of offices and officers. It is a primary community of believing persons called together by the Spirit.

No one can simply become a Christian by oneself, or worship for a lifetime wholly by oneself, or be converted by oneself, or preach to oneself, or serve only oneself, or even read the scripture without relying upon the community that has protected it, copied it, transmitted it through time. That is not historic Christianity (D. Bonhoeffer, *Sanctorum Communio;* A. Dulles, *A Church to Believe In*). That would be like pretending that the pancreas gland could be taken out of the body and do a fine piece of work all by itself.

Believers are not called out separately to live out a merely individuated relation to God but are called together and bound together as a people. The *ekklēsia* exists as an assembly, as "a company of Saints by calling, united into one body by a holy covenant for the public worship of God and the mutual edification one of another in the Fellowship of the Lord Jesus" (Cambridge Platform, *CC*:388).

The Nurture of Transgenerational Community

Jesus anticipated that the continuing body of witness and worship that would follow him would need some organization, leadership, order, historical identity, and sociological structure. He did not, however, try to shape that structure in detail, but left much to the historical awareness and situational conscience of believers to make judgments as the Spirit was leading them, taking times and circumstances into account.

These earliest forms of Christian community and worship and proclamation shaped by the apostles are important guidelines even today. Yet they need not in every culture-specific details be regarded as woodenly binding on every period of the church's life (Thirty-nine Articles, 34).

As the new community created by Jesus was graciously personalized for the specific conditions that prevail in actual history, with all their social-historical specificity, so is the *ekklēsia* today called to be empathically responsive to specific cultural features. Then as now the church is not a fantastic philosophical idea that is beyond all reasonable possibility of actualization in history. It stands in rich, empathic continuity with each different human culture it meets, and only on this premise does it stand also in judgment of and in service to each distinctive human culture (Acts 10, 17:16–33; Chrysostom, *Catena*, Cramer, *CEC*, Acts 17.23).

The Christian community followed yet transformed familiar Jewish patterns of community nurture. Jesus himself continued to use external religious rites and institutions of worship and redemption as means of upbuilding the community. The emerging institution reflected the new situation of the history of redemption that would prevail after his resurrection. The promised coming of the Holy Spirit would empower and make effective the embodiment of the new institution.

When Paul instructed the Corinthian church on such culture-specific matters as sexual difference, as illustrated by longer hair among women than men, he stated, "If anyone wants to be contentious about this, we have no other practice—nor do the churches of God" (1 Cor. 11:16; Chrysostom, *Hom. on Cor.* 26.5). This seems to assume that common customs had already come to have a certain level of recognized legitimacy in the churches, to which the churches had clearly assented. These customs, even if not revealed by God, still are best taken seriously (1 Cor. 7:17).

The Living Body of Christ as a Community of Persons

The sociality of Christianity does not override the fact that each person must decide for himself or herself whether God's Word is trustworthy. As no one can be born for another, so one cannot be baptized for another. Each individual believer is born anew from above, not en masse, but as an individual, yet this does not occur apart from a community of preaching and discipling and sacrament. Individual faith is unimaginable without a community of witness and support.

A test case is Paul's understanding of sexual complementarity in the instance of the unfaithful spouse: "For the unbelieving husband has been sanctified through his wife, and the unbelieving wife has been sanctified through her believing husband" (1 Cor. 7:14). Life before God does not stand in abstract isolation. Even when individual unbelief is recalcitrant, when seen within the social organism of family and sexual bonding, grace remains quietly at work seeking to redeem persons in and through durable covenants, not merely individualistically and alone (Chrysostom, *Hom. on 1 Cor.* 19).

The Church Is Local and Universal

The church is local in its universality, and universal in its locality. This means that wherever the church exists locally, it bears witness to the whole church. And wherever the church is said to exist universally, it is known to be such in its local manifestations.

Ekklēsia denotes both the church as a whole and the local assembly of the whole church. A local or individual church is a company of those who are united in any given place in faith in Jesus Christ for worship, proclamation, and service in Christ. *Ekklēsia* could be applied to a gathering in a particular household, as was said of Priscilla and Aquila, greeting "the church that meets at their house" (Rom. 16:5; Chrysostom, *Hom. on Rom.* 31) or in the home of Philemon and Apphia (Philem. 2; cf. Col. 4:15). The same word was used to refer to Christian assemblies in various cities such as the church of Antioch or Jerusalem or Caesarea (Acts 14:27; 15:30; 18:22; 1 Cor. 5:4; 1 Thess. 5:27) or the churches in a given area such as Asia (Rev. 1:4). Paul specifically praised the persecuted churches in Thessalonica for becoming "imitators of God's churches in Judea" (1 Thess. 2:14; Origen, *Comm. on Matt.* 10.18).

Ekklēsia may also refer to the whole company of believers of all places (1 Cor. 10:32; Col. 1:18). It was not deemed inconsistent to view the *ekklēsia* with a highly local focus as a congregation of the faithful united with the faithful everywhere, and then in the next moment to view it from within an eternal frame of reference as the *communio sanctorum* of all times and places who share the faith of each local congregation and embrace every distinct local expression of this unity and catholicity (1 Cor. 1:2; 4:17; 16:19; Col. 1:2, 24).

The Whole Is In the Part

The local, visible *ekklēsia* is the whole (holy, catholic, apostolic) church expressed locally in a particular time and space. It is less analogous to a piece of territory in a land than a member of an organic body.

The congregation does not merely belong to the church catholic, it *is* the church catholic celebrating the good news in some specific location. The whole church is being convened and called to being in that location. The whole church is therefore thought to be present locally, as in the case of "the church of God in Corinth" (1 Cor. 1:2). That means: those of the whole company of the called out people who are meeting at Corinth. Each person is baptized into the whole church, not a piece of it.

This is why the notion of an Asian church or a proletarian church or a black church or a white church is tempted to be ethnocentrically misleading, though as a sociological description it may be useful. The church is by definition one

(Eph. 2:11–21; 4:1–16; Chrysostom, *Hom. on Eph.* 5). The church is not made universal by adding up all the local churches and getting the sum. For the whole glorified *communio sanctorum* is already there expressing itself locally by responding in faith to the call of the gospel.

Personally Lived Epistles

Christianity is not merely a set of buildings or documents but living persons spanning nations, cultures, and vast epochs of history. The apostolic tradition is guarded not as if it were an archival vault of written confessions but by breathing persons in whom faith actually lives, who nurture communities who nurture faith. Each one is like a living document, letters of Christ to humanity (2 Cor. 3:2, 3; Chrysostom, *Hom. on Cor.* 6.1–2).

Jesus, who was never reported as having written anything except in sand, did not focus on leaving behind him a set of documents so much as a living community of persons. Each of them remembered him as having met them personally. In and through that community of persons he continues to work as a present partner with their work. To belong to that community means to live life in Christ, to belong to his body, to be enlivened by his life.

The Leitourgia of the Church

The gathered community is called together to praise God for the salvation of humanity (Heb. 10:25). The work of the gathered people focuses on "the offering of gifts and the conduct of public services" (*leitourgia*, work of the people, *laos* plus *ergia*, Clement of Rome, *Corinth.* 40).

When the early Christian community gathered, they prayed (1 Cor. 14:14–16). They were "filled with the Spirit, addressing one another in psalms, hymns, and spiritual songs, singing and making melody to the Lord" with all their heart (Eph. 5:19; Jerome, *Epis. to Eph.* 3.5.19–20; Col. 3:16). They came together to hear the word of God "read aloud" from scripture (Rev. 1:2). But the reading requires an act of understanding: "The reading does not accomplish the obedience of the commandments, nor does the hearing display the completion of an accomplished deed." Rather, that alone is aimed at in the reading of the sacred text "when you perform with understanding what you read and what you hear" (Apringius of Beja, *Tractate on the Apoc.* 1.3). The readings included both the Old Testament canon and writings that were later to be New Testament canon (1 Thess. 5:27; Col. 4:16).

The assumption of the gathering was that the risen Christ himself was present in their midst, attested by preaching (Matt. 28:20; Jerome, *Comm. on Matt.* 4.28.18–20). "On the first day of the week we came together to break bread. Paul spoke to the people, and because he intended to leave the next day, kept on talking until midnight" (Acts 20:7; Chrysostom, *Hom. on Acts* 43). These gatherings were intended to illuminate the understanding, not merely to intensify ecstatic utterance (1 Cor. 14:19–36).

Worship is not finally a matter of serving or satisfying human feelings, but of serving and rightly glorifying God through song, proclamation, teaching, and acts of mercy. Almsgiving was always regularly received in the church for the care of the poor: "On the first day of the week, each one of you should set aside a sum of money in keeping with his income" (1 Cor. 16:2; Chrysostom, *Hom. on Cor.* 43.2). In the Eucharist one receives the grace of and remembers the meaning of the final meal Christ ate with his disciples, praying, "Remember, O Lord, your Church, save it from every evil, and perfect it in your love. Gather it together from the four winds and lead it sanctified into your kingdom you have prepared for it" (*Didache* 10:5).

Every act of worship in which the Son is rightly adored points to the glorification of the Father by the Son through the Spirit (Phil. 2:10, 11; Rev. 5:13, 14). Petition is addressed to God the Father in the name of the Son by the power of the Spirit (2 Cor. 13:13; Jude 20, 21). The *ekklēsia* is called to render adoration and worship to God the Father on the basis of his revelation in God the Son by the power of God the Spirit (Luke 24:52; Acts 1:24; 7:59; Rom. 10:13; 2 Tim. 4:18; Bede, *On 2 Peter* 3:18).

A consequent issue emerges: What is the relation between—

The Living Church and the Coming Reign of God

The reign of God is present wherever God's will is done. There God rules (John Cassian, *Conference* 1.13). The church is the arena in which the coming kingdom is being proclaimed and actively expected. The church is the place in the world where the coming kingdom is already beginning to happen (Cyril of Alex., *Comm. on Luke,* Hom. 117).

The kingdom is not reducible to the church. The church as it now appears is not without qualification the kingdom of God. The church is an expression of the governance of God, attesting God's already begun and coming reign. The church stands as witness to the kingdom. The church is a living organic community in which the kingdom is already coming to be. What began in Christ's ministry continues in time through the church.

The church is subject to the infirmities and temptations that accompany all finite existence. Yet it resists those impediments that appear as obstacles to the coming kingdom. The Spirit is given to cleanse these corruptions and guide the gathered community toward the fullness of truth (Acts 2:40; Titus 1:15).

The kingdom is the actualization of that for which the church hopes. The church seeks to embody the sphere of the kingdom in real-time human history (Acts 13:15). The church is of exceptional value, so "Take heed of yourselves and to all the flock, in which the Holy Spirit has made you overseers, to care for the church of God which he obtained with the blood of his own Son" (Acts 20:28; Chrysostom, *Hom. on Acts* 44).

Some are said to be "not far" from the kingdom (Mark 12:32–34), while others remain far from it, and others live already in it and it within them. Jesus prayed, "Thy Kingdom come, thy will be done on earth, as it is in heaven" (Matt. 6:10; Luke 11:2). The church is the historical means by which the reign of God is being taught, proclaimed, and mediated to humanity. As the Father has sent the Son into the world, so the Son sends the church into the world by the power of the Spirit (John 20:21; Gregory the Great, *Forty Gospel Hom.* 26). Bringing the community of faith to life is the work of the Spirit (Rom. 8:1–11).

The kingdom is not of this world (John 18:36; Chrysostom, *Hom. on John,* 84). Its transmission occurs by testimony and reasonable persuasion rather than deceit or coercion (Luke 19:37, 38; Matt. 16:15–17; 28:18; Calvin, *Inst.* 4.10, 16–17). Merely to adapt the church to the culture is not enough, for the church stands under the command "Do not conform any longer to the pattern of this world, but be transformed by the renewing of your mind" (Rom. 12:2; Origen, *Comm. on Rom.* 12.2).

The Spirit enables the responsiveness of each member of the organism, just as the life of the body enlivens every member and cell of the body. The Spirit awakens and effects in the church's life all that belongs to her unity, witness, and service (1 Cor. 2:4, 5). "It does not belittle the gospel to say that it was preached without wisdom . . . The Spirit does not enter an unclean soul, nor can he ever be overcome, however much clever speech is used to attack him" (Chrysostom, *Hom. on Cor.* 3).

It is the Son by the Spirit who out of joy has come to serve, protect, and embrace the beloved bride (Rev. 21:2, 9, 22:17).

It is a measure of the Father's love that the eternal Son gave himself up for her, his life for her life (Gal. 2:20; Titus 2:14). "Christ lives in the one who is delivered from death by faith" (Ambrosiaster, *Epis. to Gal.* 2.20).

The *ekklēsia* is not diminished when addressed as "she," nor is the Son more because addressed as "he." Nor is the Spirit less or more by being addressed conventionally in one language in the feminine and another in the neuter (Ps. 51:11; Mark 1:10; John 4:24; 16:13–15; Rom. 8:9). God wills to be addressed personally, but not as an "it," a thing. God transcends gender. The church as body of Christ transcends gender.

Biblical Models of the Church

The classic form of study of the ekklēsia proceeds by inquiry into recurring biblical metaphors and images used from the outset to speak of the church (see Hooker, *LEP*; Minear, *ICNT*; Dulles, *MC*).

The triune premise is deeply embedded in these New Testament pictures and expressions about the church as bride, ship, household, flock, edifice, body, temple of the Holy Spirit, piloted ship, people of God (A. Wainwright, *Trinity in the NT*; Erickson, *CT* 3). Six of these prototype images predominantly recur in scripture:

The Church as Beloved Bride

The relation of Christ and the church is prefigurative of the redeemed union of man and woman (2 Cor. 11; Eph. 5:21–33; Rev. 19:7–9). The metaphor had a long typological history, from Hosea (1–3), through Ezekiel (6, 23), Isaiah (54:4–8), Psalms (64), and the Song of Songs, before it was transmuted in the New Testament by Pauline and Johannine teaching.

The relation of God and people is viewed metaphorically in scripture as a marriage bond existing between a beloved husband and wife, often focused as an expected celestial marriage celebration (Methodius, *The Banquet of the Ten Virgins* 8; Council of Vienne, *DS* 901). The church is viewed as a bride adorned for her husband (Rev. 21:1–4; Second Helvetic *Conf.*), whose blemishes are erased by his love. The espousal of the bride begins at Pentecost. The wedding will be consummated in the presence of the celestial hosts (Irenaeus, *Ag. Her.* 5.25).

The Church as Flock

The *ekklēsia* is portrayed as the flock of Christ (Isa. 40:11; John 10:27, 28; Acts 20:28, 29; 1 Pet. 5:2). Of this flock Christ himself is caring shepherd (Isa. 40:11; Ezek. 34:11f.), willing to give his life for the sheep (John 10:11–15; Clement of Rome, *Corinth.* 16.1). The church is a sheepfold whose door is Christ (John 10:1–10).

The Church as Household of Faith

The family of God is compared to a household of God in the Spirit (Eph. 2:19; Marius Victorinus, *Epis. to Eph.* 1.2.19), or household of faith. In its early decades the *ekklēsia* had no buildings of its own. It met in homes (1 Cor. 16:19; Col. 4:15). The community sometimes gathered in the context of their secular responsibilities, such as those in "Caesar's household" (Phil. 4:22). The *ekklēsia* is here being compared to a large household (*oikos*) with a complex economy and many interfacing relationships (Gal. 6:10; Eph. 2:19; 3:14, 15). Complementary gifts are required to make the economy work, distributed by a wisdom higher than our own. In this household, every member, every believer, has a calling, a niche, a place of service. No one does everything. The order required for a well-functioning economy or household is not an end in itself, but a means to peace, love, relative justice, and concord—values best attained when each member of the household is functioning optimally in behalf of the whole, not self-assertively in behalf of individual interest alone (Eph. 2:19–22).

The Church as Edifice of God

The church is "a spiritual house" (*oikos pneumatikos*, 1 Pet 2:5) of living stones resting on Christ the chief cornerstone. The church as temple of God (1 Cor. 3:16, 17) is the building of God (1 Cor. 3:9) for the people called of God (Rom. 1:6, 7). Jesus compared himself to the stone that the builders rejected but that was being made into the chief cornerstone (Matt. 21:42; cf. Acts 4:11; 1 Pet. 2:7; Ps. 117:22). This edifice is called the house of God (1 Tim. 3:15), in which the family of God dwells; the dwelling place of God with humanity (Rev. 21:3).

The Church as Temple of the Spirit

The church is represented organically as body of Christ and liturgically ritually doxologically as temple of God. As body the church acts as instrument of Christ's will, mission, and work within the world. As temple the church is the place where the active presence of God is celebrated, where all in its precincts consent to become the sphere of Christ's habitation. "For we are the temple of the living God" (2 Cor. 6:16; Ambrosiaster, *Comm. on Paul*, 2 Cor. 6.16). "In him the whole building is joined together and rises to become a holy temple in the Lord. And in him you too are being built together to become a dwelling in which God lives by his Spirit" (Eph. 2:21, 22; Epist. of Barnabas 16).

The Church as Safe Ship on Dangerous Waters

The church is like a ship risking the oceanic hazards of history (Apost. Const. 2.7). The called community is frequently compared to a ship under hazardous conditions of sail, requiring astute leadership, with the risk of shipwreck always present (John 21:1–6; Acts 27; 1 Tim. 1:19). Hippolytus compared the church to a ship in which Christ is the pilot, the rudder, the two testaments of law and gospel; the anchor, the teachings of Christ; the ladder, the ascent to heaven (*On Christ and Antichrist* 59). This imagery leads to calling the part of the church where the people worship the nave (*navis*, ship), picturing the basilica as ark of salvation and Christ as navigator.

The Church as People of God

When Yahweh chose Israel, he did not covenant with an already existing national entity, but created a people from nothing, brought them up virtually from being nobodies. "Once you were no people but now you are God's people" (1 Pet. 2:10; Bede, *On 1 Pet.* 2.10). He first called Abraham, then the seed of Abraham—Isaac, and Jacob and all the sons and daughters of Israel. The original covenant people of God foreshadowed and prepared the way for the renewed covenant people of God (Irenaeus, *Ag. Her.* 4.36; 4.2, 15; Justin Martyr, *Dialogue with Trypho* 123.6).

In the New Testament the people of God came to refer not only to the seed of Abraham but more so to a postresurrection community whose proclamation would address all nations, all cultures (1 Pet. 2:10; Clement of Rome, *Corinth.* 30.1; 59.4). The people of God prior to the incarnation were a special people, the people of

Israel, the seed of Abraham (Calvin, *Inst.* 1.11.7, 2.10.10). The renewed people of God after the resurrection were not a specific race or tribe or ethnic identity, but a missionally reconstituted people who would be found reaching out for all peoples, all nations, the Gentiles (Tertullian, *Ag. Marcion* 1.21; *Apology* 21).

The Church as Body of Christ

The *ekklēsia* is the place where Christ is becoming embodied in continuing human history. As Christ's physical body was an instrument of redemption, so Christ's church continues to be awakened as a means of the Spirit's redeeming work (Cyril of Alexandria, *Letters* 45). "Now you are the body of Christ, and each one of you is a part of it" (1 Cor. 12:27; Severian of Gabala, *Pauline Comm. on 1 Cor.* 12.27).

The body of Christ remains a more concise definition of the church than any other descriptive phrase. The body is an organism. This reflects the larger organic logic of Christian incarnational teaching.

The Organic Logic of Christian Community: The Vine

The pivotal metaphors for the *ekklēsia* are biological (life), not intellectual (thought) or legal (law) or ethical (duty). The worshiping community speaks constantly of abundant life in Christ, not first of all about correct ideas about life, or emotive feelings or activities, or laws, to preserve life, but rather of the way to receive new life and live it fully.

The most trustworthy Christian teachers are those who live the Christian life. There can be no Christian duty or action or idea rightly conceived apart from Christian life.

Organic (life-giving, life-nurturing) images abound in the apostolic testimony to the gathered community. The *ekklēsia* is likened to living organisms: a family, a body, a growing plant. It is like a farm to be cultivated, the tillage of God, planted by the divine husbandman (Matt. 21:33–43; Chrysostom, *Hom. on Matt.*, Hom. 68.1). From the true vine, Christ, the branches are all abundantly supplied with nourishment and strength to bear fruit (John 15:1–11). Mechanical metaphors fall short. They lack only one thing: life (*nephesh, zōē, psuchē*).

The church is like a living vine sending forth fresh shoots, putting down roots, reaching for sunlight, hungering for righteousness, thirsting for refreshment, being fed from above. To share as a branch of this vine is to share in God's own life. "Apart from me, you can do nothing" (John 15:5; Maximus the Confessor, *The Four Hundred Chapters on Love* 2.38–39). The metaphor is simple, yet like any living organism, filled with complexity, growth, risk, and the mystery of the union of life with physical being (Chrysostom, *Hom. on John FC* 41:315).

The leaves of the vine are nourished by the roots to which they are organically connected. Each branch is joined to the others in the one rooted vine (Ps. 80; Hos. 10:1; John 15:1–11; Col. 2:19). Every part of the organism is seen as related to the whole (Jerome, *Ag. Pelagians* 3.9). For "in him all things hold together, and he is the head of the body, the church" (Col. 1:18; Eph. 5:19, 20). The whole body receives life from its relation to its Head, by whom it is governed and from whom it receives the cohesion necessary for growth (Boniface VIII, *SCD* 468).

Jesus' simile of the vine and branches corresponds closely to the intent of Paul's teaching on the living body of the living Christ. To the Romans, Paul wrote, "Just as each of us has one body with many members, and these members do not all have the same function, so in Christ we who are many form one body, and each member belongs to all the others. We have different gifts, according to the grace given to us" (Rom. 12:4–6; Origen, *Comm. on Rom.* 12.4).

The Members of a Living Organism
Have Their Life Together

The church is inadequately defined as a voluntary association of believers. This would be tantamount to saying that the members of my body individually elected to come together to create me. Rather, believers emerge only as members of the body, viewed as an organism, with Christ himself the living center, whose members are expressions of his living body, each one being formed and imprinted by his person (Chrysostom, *Baptismal Instruction, NPNF* 1 9:159–171).

The relationship between believers, who are being sustained and presently exist in this organic union, is a far deeper and more profound relation than that which exists in a voluntary association based upon political or economic interests. As the human body is not formed by the haphazard collection of parts but by organic growth of the coalescence of structurally united members into a single organism, so does the church emerge in time.

As the defining characteristics of each cell is contained in the DNA of that species, so are the defining characteristics of each member of the body of Christ contained in the pattern of Christ's life.

The organic metaphor is entirely different from contractual metaphors, such as those dating from Rousseau and the social contract theorists. When a vine comes into being, the branches do not bargain for their separable interests or discuss with the roots and trunk whether they might join together in a vine, as if they had separate identity before their contract. Rather, they grow from the embryo as an organism.

The church is a different kind of society, more like a family than a debating society or business agreement. I do not enter into my family by my own initiative but by being born into it and by growing in it. The believer is born into the church by repentance, faith, baptism, and Eucharist (John 1:13; 3:1–8; 1 John 5:1–7; Augustine, *Sermons* 5.3).

The church exists because God wills it to be so, not because persons first contractually or voluntarily agree that they desire to become a redemptive community. "You did not choose me, but I chose you and appointed you to go and bear fruit—fruit that will last" (John 15:16; Augustine, *Tractates on John* 86.2).

The members did not create the body, for they are the body. No human body was ever created by its diverse members (arms, legs, etc.). The members are formed only in the body. Even when a particular member fails or malfunctions or is cut off, the organism may continue (John 15:4–6). One cannot bring into being God's *ekklēsia* without God's own *klēsis* (a call by the unique One who calls) and the Spirit enabling the calling to be heard. The church is not of human devising. It does not belong to us. This family does not exist because people adopt each other but because they are adopted by the mercy of God into the family of God (Rom. 8:23; Eph. 1:5; Marius Victorinus, *Ag. Arians* 1.2).

Covenant Baptism into the Family of God

It is very difficult to dissolve a family even by unanimous mutual agreement. Genetically the child will always remain a member of the parent's family. So it is with the baptized in the family of God. What one becomes by baptism one never ceases to be, even when that baptism is to some degree forgotten or ignored (Ambrose, *On the Mysteries, NPNF* 2 10:317–325; Augustine, *On Baptism NPNF*

1 4:411). For the family of God continues to pray for the return of the prodigal even when far away.

The church is founded upon a covenant, but covenant is misunderstood if viewed as strictly analogous to bilateral transactions or agreements based on mutual benefit. Rather the covenant is that relationship which God has initiated with humanity and fulfilled in Christ. The covenant, having not been initiated by humanity, cannot be unilaterally negated by humanity. Even when the covenant people forget the covenant, God remembers it and remains faithful to it (Hos. 11:8–11; Ambrose, *On Repentance* 1–5).

Christ is the head of the body of which the faithful congregations and believers are members. God has appointed Christ "to be head over everything for the church, which is his body, the fullness of him who fills everything in a new way" (Eph. 1:22, 23). Baptism begins that relationship and Eucharist sustains it. Paul taught the *ekklēsia* at Colossae that they had "been given fullness in Christ, who is the head over every power and authority" (Col. 2:10).

The Living Body

The personal metaphor of the body of Christ is not adequately expressed by edifice metaphors such as temple, household, and building. The metaphor of a living organism is more subtle, unpredictable, and vulnerable, precisely because it is alive. The "life principle of this body is the Holy Spirit, though it can equally well be described as love, since the Holy Spirit is love personified" (Augustine, Sermon 341; cf. *Sermons* 276.4; 268.2).

The body simile views the church as a living organism, a human body with lungs, circulatory system, synapses, life and breath, metabolism, all connected intricately together by a neural system and a brain that give the body direction, intentionality, will, self-determination (Lactantius, *The Workmanship of God*, 7). The church is a living body, not a corpse, not a bronze statue, not a dead form lacking organic vitality. Hugh found "Nothing dead in the body, nothing alive outside the body" (Hugh of St. Victor, SCF:254).

This is why the metaphor of the church as a building had to be stretched so as to become a "living building" with "living stones" (Eph. 2:19–22; 1 Pet. 2:4, 5; Hermas, *Vis.* 3). The church is founded upon a rock, but that rock is the living Christ confessed by breathing, living, risking, trusting human beings addressed by grace (Tertullian; *Modesty* 21). This building has life within it. It is growing, and its parts are being knit together as a living organism (Aphrahat, *Demonstrations, On Faith*, NPNF 2 13:345–348).

The living body is organically ordered through growth in time. The initiative for ecclesial order does not come first from the congregation itself autonomously, but organically from the grace of Christ forming the body (Gal. 4:19). This is spiritual formation. The local church can only come into being where Christ is being formed, hence where faith is being received, embodied, and practiced. Because the living church is related organically to the living Christ, it is indeed a visible society requiring organization as an inevitable expression of its life.

The Incarnate Logic of the Church's Life:
The Union of the Body of Christ

The church is united without denying diversity, and diverse so as to express its unity—one without ceasing to be many, and many without ceasing to be one. For the church is the body of Christ, one body with two natures, divine and human, as in the incarnation there is one person with two natures. As Christ inhabits this temple, so he transcends it. The church as body of Christ has two natures, even as the Son is truly divine and truly human, eternal and temporal, in one body (Gregory of Nazianzus, *Orat.* 37.2).

The biblical way of pointing to the intimacy of this union between Christ and his church is the mystery of the union between the two natures of Christ: God and humanity in *theandric union*, a key phrase from all we have discussed above. Christ is in the church giving it life in the same way that God is in the incarnate Lord, giving life to his human body (Phil. 2:6–8; John of Damascus, *OF* 3.3). All this occurs by the enlivening power of the Spirit. As the human body of Christ grew in grace and favor with God, so the church is being called to grow in grace (Luke 5:52; Eph. 2:21). As Christ is one, so is his body (1 Cor. 12:12).

As God "willed to make use of our nature" in the incarnation, so did God resolve to impart grace to humanity "through a visible Church that would be formed by the union of men, and thus through that Church every man would perform a work of collaboration with Him in dispensing the graces of Redemption" (*Mystici Corporis* 13). Believers of all generations have pondered gratefully this mystery. By analogy the church is a mystical extension of the incarnation and the glorified body of Christ.

The church *is* Christ continuing to live, continuing to reform its branches so that they can reach for the light. The life that flows through the church comes to expression in an organization, an ordered structure of growth. The church has her very life in Christ, yet that life, like the messianic Servant's, is lived out in mission within the limitations of the world (Gregory of Nazianzus, *Orat.* 29.20).

The Spirit Enlivens the Church

The Spirit indwells within the body, enlivening, leading, teaching, nurturing, and protecting the body, praying with the body (Rom. 8:22–27; Col. 1:18; Chrysostom, *Hom. on Rom.* 14). Christ's life in the ecclesial body is compared with the life-giving function that the soul fulfills for the human body (Leo XIII, *Divinum illud munus, DS* 3328). "What the soul [the living feature] is in our body, the Holy Spirit is in the body of Christ, which is the church" (Augustine, *Sermon* 267.4.4). As soul is united to body in fleeting time, so is the eternal Spirit united with the church in developing history.

As the soul enlivens the body, so the Spirit enlivens the church. This is why there is a sense of personal presence pervading the vitality of this worshiping community, constantly beheld through her actions, liturgy, seasons, and celebrations (Athanasius, *Resurrection Letters*). Baptism is a personal act of identifying with the death and resurrection of Another. Eucharist is a personal act of receiving the bread of life with other living persons as an act of participation in the Son.

Without ceasing to be the activity of human beings, the church is enlivened by and is the activity of God. This relation is not rightly understood from pantheistic premises by which God would be regarded as identical with the body or social or natural process, but from the premise that the uncreated One is prior to all creation (Eph. 2:8–15; Jerome, *Epis. to Eph* 1.2.10).

The Incarnational Life Comes Alive in the Worshiping Community

The *ekklēsia* is in this symbolic sense an extension and perpetuation of the incarnation. Analogous to Christ, the church is truly of God while not ceasing to be truly human (Col. 1:18; 2:9; Cyril of Alex., *Letters* 17.9). "The Church is

Christ manifest in the flesh, as Jesus of Nazareth was God manifest in the flesh" (W. Robinson, *BDC*:101; cf. Origen, *Ag. Celsus* 6.48).

The church lives and is sent, as the God-man lived and was sent into the time-space sphere of finitude (John 20:21). The word of the incarnate Lord is not dependent upon particular historical or cultural conditions, yet he comes precisely within the curious particularities of those conditions (Phil. 2:5–11).

As the preexistent Word becomes fully human in a particular person without ceasing to be God, so the *ekklēsia* in a particular time and place becomes fully engaged in historical, physical, and sociological existence without ceasing to be divinely empowered, instituted, and sent. In this way the Son incorporates human beings into his own mission on behalf of the love of the Father. He allows human wills to become partakers of the divine nature through the Spirit (2 Pet. 1:4). The Apostle is measuring "the nature of God not by the laws of our own nature" but by God's own "testimony concerning himself" (Hilary, *Trin.* 1.18).

Receiving Life in Christ

The goal of this study is not to dissect language about an abundant life but to receive life, to live life. It is awkward for a dissecting analysis to speak of living union with Christ through the Spirit without tending to destroy what it is trying to describe.

Dissection is necessary if we are to learn the anatomy of something physically inert. But paradoxically life itself cannot be dissected without first ending life. In the dissecting laboratory, one takes organs apart one at a time, detaches, examines, diagrams, describes them each singly and apart, but only if the organism is dead. No living organism can be alive while dissected. Dissection requires and presupposes death. Hence there is an intrinsic tension between the objective analysis of salvation and the living of it.

The unifying motif of classic Christianity is *life with God*: the living God, the Word of life, life in the Spirit. Divine life flows from union with Christ, who dwells in the faithful through the Spirit. "He who has the Son has life" (1 John 5:12). "I am come that they may have life, and have it to the full" (John 10:10). "The words I have spoken to you are spirit, and they are life" (John 6:63). Those who have not yet beheld the incomparable gift of life and the cost of freedom have not yet begun to reflect on God (Gregory of Nazianzus, *Orat.* 18).

God's Delight in Embodiment

As God has condescended to make use of the human body for the redemption of the world in the incarnation, so God makes use of human wills and bodies and institutions and intentions in the organic life of the church as body of Christ (Augustine, *Reply to Faustus* 21.7–9).

Human freedom is not ignored or circumvented in this embodiment but celebrated and transformed. The life of the body comes from the life-Giver, the Spirit, enabling life under the rule and governance of the Head (Col. 2:9–10). Those who demean the body demean its Giver (Chrysostom, *Hom. on the Statues*, *NPNF* 1 9:412–418).

God delights in the embodied church. Classic church teaching is not body-hating. It is body-affirming. As the Son is embodied and cares for his body and is concerned when his body is endangered, so is the church whose life becomes embodied through the Spirit (Matt. 26:39–42; 1 Tim. 6:20). She cares for her body and is fittingly concerned when her body is endangered (Athanasius, *Defence of His Flight*; Cyril of Alexandria, *Letters* 45.7).

Outward and Visible Means of Inward
and Spiritual Grace

Consistent with this pattern of the incarnation is the premise that the church receives her identity by outward and visible means—sacramentally. As God by becoming incarnate has not sullied the divine nature, so the church of God does not sully her character as holy by engaging in a mission within the world to draw humanity to God and by using visible means to accomplish this mission, such as water and bread (John 12:32). Once all humanity had been alienated. "Now he has reconciled you by Christ's physical body through death, to present you holy in his sight" (Col. 1:22; Jerome, *Letter to Pamachius* 27).

It is the Word who becomes flesh (John 1:14), not flesh first that later becomes Word. The priority always lies with the divine initiative, not with human responsiveness (John of Damascus, *OF* 3.18). The Son descends from heaven; he is not adopted by elevation from earth (*Eleventh Council of Toledo*). The prevenience (preceding power) of grace antecedes all human responsiveness. The human action in engaging in the mission of the church is responsive to the divine action in calling forth the church. The continued existence of the church is taken as historical confirmation of the divinity of Christ (Origen, *Ag. Celsus* 3.30–37; Eusebius, *Proof of the Gospels*, 1).

The church lives and works daily in the very sphere in which Christ lived and worked: human history, fleshly existence, finitude, suffering and death (John 1:14; 21:27). In Christ, God accommodates revelation to our human condition. Similarly in the church the living Christ is becoming embodied precisely amid the limitations of existence in time and space. This is the Way of the incarnate Lord—descent to finitude without ceasing to be Lord (Phil. 2). It therefore is the way of the church—engagement within the life of the world without ceasing to be God's own (Rom. 12). Acts reports that on the day of Pentecost three thousand souls were added—but added *to whom*? Not the visible community alone, but also "to the Lord" (Acts 2:41; 2:27; 5:14; 11:24)! Believers were being effectively united to the Lord through the Spirit, incorporated into the body of the Head.

8

MARKS OF THE CHURCH

Word, Sacrament, and Discipline

What the Whole Church Does Truly

Numerous attempts have been made to account for the essential features of the church. Language varies in different cultures and traditions, though often in complementary ways, but Word, Sacrament, and Discipline appear in virtually all scripture-based descriptions. Some focus relatively more upon apostolic succession of the historic episcopacy, while others focus upon some particular form of church governance (congregational, presbyterial, or episcopal) as essential and necessary to a true church; others hold that a particular liturgy or confession marks the difference between true and false bodies of worship and confession, but never absent wholly are Word, Sacrament, and Discipline.

Among scripture scholars of the ancient tradition the attributes of unity, holiness, indefectibility, universality, imperishability (Heppe, *RD*, p. 662) have commonly been considered reliable marks of the church. "Gravina found six, Pazmany seven, Suárez eight, Bellarmine fifteen, Bozi a hundred" marks of the church (Küng, *TC*:266; cf.; Barth, *CD* 4/1; Brunner, *Dogm.* 3:117ff.; Schmaus, *Dogma* 4:81 ff.). Seven signs of the church were noted by Luther in his essay On the Councils and Churches: preaching the Word, baptism, Supper, the power of the keys [forgiveness], the ministry, prayer, and suffering under persecution (*On the Councils and Church* 2, *WML* 4:270–287). The most widely received, traditional, consensual Protestant definition (Second Helvetic *Conf.*, *CC*:146; Calvin, *Inst.* 4.1.7–12; 4.12–14) is Word, Sacrament, and Discipline.

In Protestant confessions these three cohere: "The true and essential and visible marks of this pure Church are the pure preaching and reception of the word, sealed through the lawful use of the sacraments and maintained by the use of the keys or ecclesiastical discipline, according to Christ's institution" (*Leiden Synopsis* 40.45). While this summary confession is commonly found among Protestants, each of its features is also present in the patristic and medieval traditions. Hence it is not to be set over against or contrary to the most common consensual confession of the church as one, holy, catholic, and apostolic.

The First Premise of the Living Church:
True Preaching of the Word

The most crucial sign of the church in the Protestant tradition is the pure preaching of God's Word, a right "profession of the true, pure, and rightly understood doctrine of the law and the gospel" (Ursinus, *Comm. on Heid. Catech.* 289).

The church is speaking truly when its proclamation is in harmony with apostolic teaching (Clement of Alex., *Stromata* 7.17). Where the old, true doctrine of the gospel is preached and the Apostles' Creed confessed, there is the communion of saints (Luther, *Sermons on the Catechism*).

"The Word is the appointed means by which God's grace is made known to men, calling them to repentance, assuring them of forgiveness, drawing them to obedience and building them up in the fellowship of faith and love" (Lausanne Conference on Faith and Order). Wherever the church is alive, these seeds of the gospel are being planted.

If preachers withhold from lay people the riches of the gospel, they expose the hollowness of their calling to preach. If there is a substantial failure to hold duly ordained representative teachers accountable to canonical scripture, the reality of the church is called into question. If those authorized to teach Christian doctrine publicly cherish heterodox opinion so as to lead astray the whole laity, who have a right to hear the gospel, the church is to that extent misplacing its identity as church.

Second Premise of the Living Church:
Due Administration of Sacraments

A second attribute or note or visible sign by which one may discern whether a community of faith is truly a church, is that the church is present where the use of the sacraments is in accordance with their institution by the Lord.

Jesus himself commanded his disciples to "do this in remembrance of me" (Luke 22:19). Christ gave himself up for the church "to make her holy, cleansing her by the washing with water through the word" (Eph. 5:26). Because intentionally authorized and commanded by the Lord, there can be no church without a fitting sacramental life. From the outset, those who have confessed Jesus as the Christ and "who accepted his message *were baptized*" and were immediately found devoting themselves to "the apostles' teaching and to the fellowship, *the breaking of bread* and to prayer" (Acts 2:41, 42, italics added). Where no one is baptized, there is no church (Cyprian, *Epistles* 72). Where the Eucharistic meal is not celebrated, the laity are not being nurtured as the body of Christ.

Third Premise of the Living Church:
Disciplined Christian Life

The active practice of disciplined Christian life is a reliable sign that the church is alive. True love is not license. Love without discipline is cheap. Where few evidences of Christian love are beheld, there are few evidences of the reality of the church. It is love that gently disciplines.

"The exercise of church discipline to combat sin" remains today a "sign of the true church," which includes "the pastoral care of the members of the Church; the preserving of the pure doctrine through the exercise of spiritual discipline and the opposing of false doctrines; the doing of works of mercy (*diakonia*)" (Batak *Conf.* 9, *CC*). This criterion is variously defined as the life of obedience, or good order, or prudent exercise of ecclesiastical discipline, or zeal for good works, or pastoral guidance under the ministry of the Word (Calvin, *Inst.* 4.12; Melanchthon 12.599–602; Ursinus, *Comm. on Heid. Catech.*:288–89).

How Far Do These Indicators Warrant the Reality of the Church?

Even where errors are perpetrated by the church as manifested in one or another locale, still if word, sacrament, and discipline are reasonably upheld intact, the true foundation, Jesus Christ, has been preserved. Despite blemishes and temporary departures from accountability to scripture, a church may remain fundamentally grounded confessionally and liturgically in Jesus Christ, living in Christ, and embodying his own life (Matt. 16:18; 1 Pet. 1:24, 25; *Conf.* of Dositheus 10–12, *CC*).

Where corruptions have not become profoundly subversive of the very foundations of the faith, it may yet be said that the preaching of the Word has been reasonably retained. The rule of thumb: "The more purely the Word of God is preached in a Church, and the nearer the preaching and doctrine comes to the norm of Holy Scripture, the purer will be the Church; the further it recedes from the rule of the Word, the more impure and corrupt will be the Church. Nevertheless it does not cease to be a Church because of some corruption, since God always begets and preserves for Himself a holy seed and spiritual sons, even when the public ministry of the visible Church has been corrupted" (Gerhard, in Jacobs, *SCF*:384, Irish Articles 69).

Though many errors pervaded the Corinthian and Galatian churches (1 Cor. 15:12; Gal. 4:21), they remained churches because they had not been utterly corrupted but only sporadically or selectively so, and had not obstinately defended these errors. Hope remained that whatever deficits were appearing, they could be restored (Thirty-nine Articles, 6, 34). Even the corrupted church can pray for the Holy Spirit to purify its motives.

The believer need not break away from a communion because it appears to lack some particular ancillary teaching or departs from received liturgical practice in some incidental way. Where there is a good faith effort to maintain purity of doctrinal standards for preaching, lawful sacramental life, and discipline in earnest, one may conscientiously embrace a church even if blemished (Calvin, *Inst.* 4.1.12). If a church wholly lacks preaching of the Word, a healthy sacramental life, and church discipline, this signals the need for reform more than simple abandonment.

Absolute purity is not expected in a church that has both wheat and tares until the end of time. Donatist and puritanical demands for ecclesial perfection may themselves be evidence of a harsh and partisan spirit inconsistent with the unity of the church. We are called to embrace the visible church that reasonably expresses these signs. To turn our backs on such a church just because it is offending temporarily is hazardous to the faith that must look to the body of Christ to be nurtured. For the community, not the autonomous individual, is mother of faith (Jerome, *Epis. to Eph.* 4.4; Calvin, *Inst.* 4.1.4), birthing and nurturing faith.

Four Evidences of the Reality and
Wholeness of the Church

By what forms of evidence is the church able to be clearly recognized as truly the church?

The most common classic answer has four elements found together in a single phrase of the Nicene-Constantinopolitan Creed: "We believe in one, holy, catholic and apostolic church" (First Council of Constantinople, 381). This classic confession is found in the most ancient ecumenical tradition most widely received by worldwide Christianity of all periods. These four terms are confessed in the diverse languages of the world in common worship.

First, the church must be *one* because it is unified by one faith in one God revealed in the one crucified and risen Lord. Second, the church is being made *holy* by participating by faith in the perfect holiness of the Son through the power of the Spirit. Third, the church is universal or general or *catholic* because it offers the whole counsel of God to the whole world. Fourth, the church is *apostolic* because it is sent into the world even as the Son was sent. Where these marks are present, the church is alive.

By her unity the church gives expression in time to the oneness of Christ's body so as to unite in hope all humanity to God's reconciling activity. By her holiness the church refracts the holiness of God amid the fallen world. Through her catholicity the church reaches out to all the world with the whole truth of the Word. From her apostolicity the church grounds herself in the accurate recollection of the events of God's own coming.

The unity of the church is not reduced to a voluntary act of uniting by the members of Christ's body, but rather it is a unity that lives out of the calling of the one Lord. The holiness of the church is not found in the moral purity of her members alone, but in the Holy Spirit who calls the *ekklēsia* and sets it apart for service. The catholicity of the church is confirmed by the universal consent given by the people of God to the good news of God's coming. The apostolicity of the church is not self-sending but being shaped by the Spirit's own sending. To say the church is one, holy, catholic, and apostolic is to confess the Holy Spirit as the one who unites, cleanses, and sends the church to the whole world.

The one condition necessary to the existence of the church is the presence of Christ. "For no one can lay any foundation other than the one already laid, which is Jesus Christ" (1 Cor. 3:11; Ambrosiaster, *Comm. on Paul*, 1 Cor. 3.11). It was only when Peter confessed, "You are the Christ," that Christ said, "On this rock I will build my church" (Matt. 16:15, 18). The cornerstone of the church is faith's confession that Jesus is the Christ.

A Stable Fourfold Criterion

Under centuries of guidance from the scripture, believers have inquired into the concise and proper statement of the attributes and criteria of the church, asking: Are there some signs (*sēmeion*, *signa*, criteria) or marks (*stigma*), or characteristics (*proprietates*), or notes (*notae*) or predicates that signal clearly where the *ekklēsia* is to be reliably found?

The right to the name "church" is conditioned upon fulfilling criteria that belong to the church. That right does not belong to the makers of dictionaries or faddists or jurists. It is reserved for the whole Christian *laos* speaking with universal consent. It has been textually defined for almost two millennia.

Not every group or assembly that tests itself under these criteria has a legitimate right to the name. Assertions are able to be tested to distinguish between authentic and counterfeit, between orthodox and heterodox, true and false Christianity.

The classic, consensual answer is that the church is recognizable by means of specific distinguishing marks that clearly differentiate it from all other social processes and human communities (Council of Constantinople 2, 213–27; Fourth Lateran Council, 430–31).

The formula: Because Christ is one, the church seeks to embody that oneness. Because Christ is holy, the church seeks to reflect that holiness. Because Christ's love is whole and addressed to all, the church's address is whole and for all. Because Christ was sent to the whole world, the church is sent to proclaim the eyewitness news of the apostles to all people.

Marks of the Living Church

The three premises stated above undergird the four classic marks of the church in the creed. These four marks or evidences of the church are traditionally ordered and defined in this fourfold pattern by the Nicene Creed, here listed in English, Greek, and Latin:

Marks of the Church

The Church is:

One	Holy	Catholic	Apostolic
mian	*hagian*	*katholiken*	*apostoliken*
Unam	*Sanctam*	*Catholicam*	*Apostolicam*

The church is one, finding its oneness in Christ. The church is holy, set apart from the world to mediate life to the world and bring forth the fruits of the Spirit amid the life of the world. The church is catholic in that it is whole, for all, and embracing all times and places. The church is apostolic in that it is grounded in the testimony of the first witnesses to Jesus' life and resurrection, and depends upon and continues their ministry.

This formulation has stood as the durable framework upon which classic exegetes have most concisely confessed in baptism the features or qualities that are essential to the church (*Longer Catech.*, Eastern Orthodox Church, 67). "By the marks of the Church we mean certain clear signs by which all men can recognize it as the true Church founded by Jesus Christ" (*Baltimore Catechism* 12.3154). These marks are spiritually discerned, hence not easily accessible to scientific laboratory examination or wooden empirical verification. If any one becomes permanently obscured, that is an indication that the church needs to be reformed—which means once again formed by Christ's own life (Calvin, *Inst.* 4.1). It is first necessary to grasp what the church means when it confesses its unity.

The First Mark: The Church Is One

Among the earliest eucharistic prayers, the unity of the church is compared to the bread of life broken for the world: "Even as this broken bread was scattered over the hills, and was gathered together and became one, so let Thy Church be gathered together from the ends of the earth into Thy kingdom" (*Teaching of the*

Twelve Apostles 9; cf. Cyprian; *Epistles* 62.13). The unity of the church is not for the faithful to create but receive.

Christ founded only one church (John 10:16; 21:15; Heb. 3:6; 10:21; Eph. 5:27; Rom. 12:4, 5; Augustine, *Sermon* 46.30). In ascribing unity to the church, we mean that all the members of the church constitute one body, having one head, one origin, one faith, one baptism. They are united by their bond to the one living Lord (Eph. 4:2–15; 1 Cor. 1:10; Gal. 1:6–8; Irenaeus, *Ag. Her.* 1.10.2; Jerome, *Epis. to Eph.* 4.4).

The church is construed to be *one* in the precise sense that "it is gathered by one Lord, through one Baptism, into one mystical body, under one Head, governed by one Spirit, bound together in the unity of a common faith, hope, and love" (Gerhard, Schmid, *DT:* 588). "All the regenerate children of God have an inner union and communion with one another through their common faith in Christ" (Jacobs, *SCF*:374). "This unity does not consist in the agreement of our minds or the consent of our wills. It is founded in Jesus Christ Himself" (Lausanne Conference on Faith and Order). This unity is not understood apart from the unity of the triune God:

Irenaeus wrote: "The church has received this preaching and this faith even though it is scattered throughout the world, and carefully preserves it intact, as if it were living in a single house. The church believes these doctrines as if it had only one soul and one heart, and it proclaims them and hands them on in perfect harmony, as if it spoke with only one voice. The languages of the world may be dissimilar, but the message of the tradition is one and the same. Just as the sun is the same wherever it shines, so is the preaching of the truth the same everywhere in the world, enlightening everyone who wants to come to a knowledge of the truth. No church leader, however gifted he may be, will teach anything different from this" (*Against Heresies*, 1.10.1–3).

The Unity of the Trinity as the Exemplary
Unity of the Body of Christ

In the light of Triune teaching, the church's unity looks toward the unity of redeemed humanity. The logic is precise: As the soul of a person has only one body, so the Spirit dwells cohesively in the one body of Christ. As the head can have only one body, so the church must be one.

The unity of the church "finds its highest exemplar and source in the unity of the Persons of the Trinity" (*Decree on Ecumenism* 2). Jesus prayed that they, the faithful, "may be one as we are one" (John 17:11). From apostolic times the church has been viewed as "a people made one with the unity of the Father, the Son and the Holy Spirit" (Cyprian, *Treatises* 9.23; Augustine, *Sermons* 33, 71, 20).

The unity of the triune God signals and anticipates the unity of the called out community. The unity of the church foreshadows the unity of humanity. Though it does not actually include all humanity, and at times appears to be a negligibly small player in history, the church is "an instrument for the redemption of all, and is sent forth into the whole world as the light of the world and the salt of the earth" (*Doc. Vat. II, Ch.* 9; Matt. 5:13–16).

A single body cannot be "separated by a division of its structure, nor torn into pieces, with its entrails wrenched asunder by laceration. Whatever has proceeded from the womb cannot live and breathe in its detached condition, but loses the substance of health" (Cyprian, *Treatises, 1, Unity of the Church*).

As the bridegroom has only one spouse, so must all who are united with Christ be one with him. As more than two bodies complicate physical generation, so would two or more spouses confound the purity of love (*Decree on Ecumenism* 8).

The Call to Unity Already Established Within Judaism

In the religion of Israel prior to the Babylonian captivity, there was only one temple. The unity of the people was symbolized by this oneness. The high priest was the visible symbol of unity of the covenant community under the one Lord (Lactantius, *DI* 4.25).

After the captivity the synagogues were built, and there were many local places of worship, yet the temple remained in Jerusalem (Ephrem, *Comm. on Heb.* 7.3). Thereafter the unity of the people was sustained genealogically, and by a unified canon that received general consent.

It was not until the destruction of the temple in AD 70 that a crisis arose in the unity of the Jewish people in diaspora. Yet even then, Jerusalem remained the symbolic center of unity, even if not a political reality. Thus in focusing on the unity of the church, the teachings of Jesus and Paul and John were sustaining a pattern well established in the old covenant.

That They May All Be One

Jesus intended that the church be one, since he prayed explicitly for its oneness— "that all of them may be one, Father, just as you are in me and I am in you. May they also be in us so that the world may believe that you have sent me. I have given them the glory that you gave me, that they may be one as we are one: I in them and you in me. May they be brought to complete unity to let the world know that you sent me and love them even as you have loved me" (John 17:21–23; Ambrose, *Chr. Faith* 4.3.36–38; Hilary, *Trin.* 6.38–41; 8.5).

The principle texts on unity of the church are from Paul: "Make every effort to keep the unity of the Spirit through the bond of peace. There is one body and one Spirit—just as you were called to one hope when you were called—one Lord, one faith, one baptism; one God and Father of all" (Eph. 4:3, 4; Ambrose, *Sacr.* 2.4.5–6). "From him the whole body, joined and held together by every supporting ligament, grows and builds itself up in love, as each part does its work" (Eph. 4:16; Chrysostom, *Hom. on Eph.* 11.4.15–16). Paul was not calling for individualistic conversions, but for building up the whole church everywhere, viewing each local congregation as intrinsically united with the living Lord with special deference and care for the embattled mother church in Jerusalem (Rom. 15:31; 1 Cor. 16:1–3; Chrysostom, *Hom. on Cor.* 43.1–4).

The unity of scattered congregations is formed by the one risen Lord. They experience their kinship whether in Africa or Asia, with the confessions and practices of the earliest churches at Jerusalem, Antioch, Rome, and Alexandria. This affinity was evidenced by their beloved organic connection with each other, marked by intercommunion and mutual recognition of sacred texts and apostolic teachers. For "in Christ we who are many form one body, and each member belongs to all the others" (Rom. 12:5; Leo, *Letter* 14). The one church is more than the many churches added up (Chrysostom, *Hom. on Eph.* 11; Clement of Rome, *Corinth* 37). All the faithful are "no longer strangers," but living under one Lord as "fellow citizens with the saints" (Eph. 2:19; Marius Victorinus, *Epis. to Eph.* 1.2.19).

The Struggle of the Church Within Present Time

Because God preserves the gathered people through great spans of time, and because persons live and die, some who belong to the church are alive, others have passed away, and others are yet unborn. It is from this structural condition of the church's temporal existence that it becomes necessary and useful to distinguish between the present and promised church. This struggle has been called the church in combat or church militant, which assumes not a military but a spiritual struggle (Chrysostom, *Baptismal Instructions* 3; Calvin, *Inst.* 3.3–2). The living regenerate church remains in constant conflict with the world, the flesh, and the devil (Rom. 7:23; Gal. 5:17; 1 John 5:4; Andreas, Catena, *CEC* 3, James 1.4). Each believer struggles daily against the powers of evil (Eph. 6:10; 1 Pet. 5:8, 9; Augustine, *Ag. Julian* 2.9.32). This ongoing adversity is intended to strengthen the believers' will and faith commitment.

The church of the celestial city is composed of victors in this worldly battle who have passed beyond all earthly conflicts, who having been faithful here have received a crown of life (Rev. 2:10). It includes persons of all nations, tribes, peoples, tongues who live now in ceaseless praise of God (Primasius, *Comm. on Apoc.* 7:9). Hence it is called the church *triumphant* (Calvin, *Inst.* 2.16.16). An excessive focus on the future as reality is called "triumphalism," which is prone to transfer the final victory into some form of present power configuration or political triumph.

The whole church embraces not only a sociological structure now visible in the world, but also those who have died in Christ and those yet to believe and to be yet united in him. The same single body that struggles against the principalities and powers today, and that expects even more severe challenges in the future, is in faith already victorious by virtue of its being presently united with its head in the heavenly city, anticipating that completed joy in the Lord wherein all the faithful shall praise God together at the end of days (Ambrosiaster, *Comm. on Paul*, 1 Cor. 15.54–58).

The community of faith that within history struggles in combat with the remaining outrages of the history of sin has an exalted future of promise: to share in Christ's righteousness, to enter into fellowship with the Father by union with the Son through the power of the Spirit (1 Tim. 6:12; Basil, *Letters* 46). "All saints have fellowship in true, essential unity: as many as cling to Christ with one faith, one love; under whatsoever prelates they live; however the latter may ambitiously contend or dissent or err, even though they be false teachers; in whatever localities in space; separated by whatever intervals of years; and this is the *communio*, of which we speak in the Creed" (Johannes Wessel, in *SHD* 2:212).

Grace works to transform sinners as entirely as the conditions of finite freedom will permit. Grace seeks so to infuse sinners with God's own redeeming power that they are being here and now readied for sharing in God's own life eternally. The community of faith is portrayed as already being presented as a bride to Christ, loved by him, arrayed in fine linen (Rev. 19:7, 8), without spot or wrinkle or blemish (Eph. 5:27; Chrysostom, *Hom. on Eph.* 20.5.27), joint heir of his suffering and glory (Rom. 8:17; Theodoret, *Interp. Of Rom.* 8.17).

Unity in Diversity

During much of its first millennium, the worldwide church was far more recognizably one in teaching, worship, polity, and disciplinary practice than today. This does not deny that there were varied cultures and assertive parties within the ecumenical whole from the outset, but the general lay consent to the ecumenical council definitions was remarkably wide-ranging from the third century to 1054, when East and West split apart, leaving tensions that have remained for almost a thousand years. A half millennium later Protestantism would fragment the church into many parts.

If the first millennium ended with the church split in two, the second millennium is ending with the church split into thousands of pieces, autonomously governed, even competing, loving divisiveness. The third millennium faces the task of once again practically embodying the unity that we already have been offered as a gift in Christ. In its outward forms in specific times and places, living in particular cultures, the church always appears sociologically and linguistically as diverse, yet remains one in its essential unity when viewed in Christ, united in its head, unified by one spirit (Eph. 4:4), in the unity of one faith (Eph. 4:5), which expresses itself in the unity of love (Basil, *Letters* 92). "In the body it is the living spirit that holds all members together, even when they are far apart. So it is here. The purpose for which the Spirit was given was to bring into unity all who remain separated by different ethnic and cultural divisions: young and old, rich and poor, women and men" (Chrysostom, *Hom. on Eph.* 9.4.1–3).

The Ecumenical Spirit

Ecumenical Temptations

The idolatrous overvaluation of unity results in uniformity, a tyrannizing excess of superficially imposed unity. The undervaluation or neglect of unity is divisiveness and egocentricity, imagining that one's own individualistic opinion is more important or more clearly ordained of God than the received consensual apostolic tradition (1 Cor. 1:10–17; Origen, *Comm. on 1 Cor.* 1.4).

The Spirit sustains the unity of the church by seeking and praying for reconciliation whenever centrifugal Forces become intense (Eph. 2:14; Cornelius I, *SCD* 44; Didymus the Blind, *On the Holy Spirit* 20). "Since the Church has received this preaching and this faith, as we have said, although she is scattered through the whole world, she preserves it carefully, as one household: and the whole Church alike believes in these things, as having one soul and heart, and in unison preaching these beliefs, and teaches and hands them on as having one mouth. For though there are many different languages in the world, still the meaning of the tradition is one and the same. And there are not different beliefs or traditions in the churches established in Germany, or in Spain, or among the Celts, or in the East, or in Egypt or Libya" (Irenaeus, *Ag. Her.* 1.10.1–2).

Few movements in Protestant history have been more divisive than modern ecumenism. Hence modern ecumenical movements are themselves called to repentance on behalf of the unity of the church. Those of us who have lived our lives as Christians in church bodies ambiguously associated with the World Council of Churches have seen enough to be wary of any proposed union that would tend to obstruct or diminish the vitality of the church's mission or exchange it for a mess of political pottage.

The existence of denominational structures is not in itself something to be lamented altogether or regarded as outside the bounds of providence or incapable of redemption. For the denominations emerged in order better to manifest the marks of the church, especially holiness and apostolic accountability. There always remains some possibility of reform of semi-apostate churches. It is better to seek reform within than simply abandon those church bodies to rampant secularization.

On the cross the Lord has "purchased men for God from every tribe and language and people and nation" (Rev. 5:9; Andrew of Caesarea, *Comm. on the Apoc.* 9–11). The church is called to dwell patiently in all cultures and generations of time, yet united in one eternal Head animating the body and making it one (Eph. 4:4–6; 1 Cor. 3:10, 11; *Longer Catech.*, Eastern Orthodox Church, 259).

Fairly Applying the Tests of the Church: The
Proximate Truth of Particular Church Bodies

Christians of one regional or historical family of churches are ill-advised to fixate upon the wrongs or evils or misjudgments of another family or branch of Christianity, or to ignore the defects of their own church tradition.

Differing church bodies are one insofar as the Word is preached purely and the sacraments rightly administered so as to elicit a disciplined community of faith. They are apostolic insofar as they hold the same apostolic teaching that has united Christians to Christ from all times and places. They are proximately catholic insofar as they seek to make their contribution to the whole body of Christ without maliciously impugning the character of other confessional bodies. "All particular churches have a claim to be regarded as Christian so long as they have not lost, but still exercise, the essential characteristics or signs of the Church—Word and Sacrament" (Dorner, *SCDoc.* 4:371). Wherever Christ is believed and followed and worshiped, the *ekklēsia* exists.

Believers with different histories do well to avoid inflammatory stereotypes and prejudicial statements that do not fairly represent the condition of other Christians and make further dialogue even more difficult than it has already been made by the history of division (Augustin Bea, *The Unity of Christians*). Yet within the ecumenical spirit there remains the dangers of false irenicism and indifferentism (J. Wesley, *WJW* 5:492–504).

Meanwhile it remains fitting that Christians join in prayer with other Christians separated from them by institutional divisions, to petition for the grace of unity, and to express the ties that bind each one to Christ. "For where two or three come together in my name, there am I with them" (Matt. 18:20; Cyril of Alex., *Fragment* 215, *Reuss*, MKGK:224). The hope is by recovery of ancient ecumenical consensus, the areas of agreement in modern ecumenical practice may deepen.

Unity Celebrates Difference

Real differences existed within the early church that were often related to differences in the immensely varied cultural contexts to which the gospel was being addressed. Some of the earliest Christians rooted in synagogue worship were more reluctant to give up Jewish ceremonies such as circumcision. Hellenizing Christians spoke a different language than that familiar in the Jerusalem church. A distinction emerged early between the churches of Macedonia and the churches of Asia, from the time of Paul's second missionary journey. There were distinctions between the wealthy of port cities and the poor of Jerusalem that the one church sought to overcome. Even in the New Testament there were divisions in the church (Gal. 1:6–9; 1 John 2:18, 19), which the apostles deplored (1 Cor. 1:11–22).

These differences did not lead to despair, but to the affirmation of cultural variety, which may be seen from another viewpoint as an expression of the true humanity and catholicity of the body of Christ. If the church failed to address these cultural differences, its worldwide mission would have been to that degree defaulted. The church expresses its oneness precisely through variety and flexibility. "For thus it pleases God to use the dissensions that arise in the church, to the glory of his name, to the setting forth of the truth" (Second Helvetic *Conf.*).

The Lord warned against pouring old wine into new wineskins (Mark 2:22; Tertullian, *On Prayer* 1). Yet he did not hesitate to set in motion new institutional structures and social constructs. Out of his mission *has* come a profusion of orders, movements, missions, and labors. By means of these varieties, spiritual formation has been deepened, missionary activity extended, and attention given to aspects of apostolic testimony previously neglected.

In Nonessentials, Liberty

The faithful are directed to keep the bond of peace with all who love the Lord, however different they may be from our own perceptions and preferences. The maxim remains valid: In essentials unity, in nonessentials liberty, in all things charity.

Sectarianism and syncretism are opposite temptations of the church in the world. One produces disunity. The other dilution. Sectarianism places undue stress upon distinctive features of a given church tradition, so as to lead to pride and self-congratulation. Syncretism, on the other pole, that is willing to do almost anything to gain a semblance of external unity, is susceptible to mating with any ideological partner around, even at the cost of loss of centered orthodoxy.

The New Testament does not offer a static view of the church but a moving series of glimpses of the living church in differing situations. "The church travels as a pilgrim cleansed by faith and baptism" (Bede, *Comm. on Acts.* 10.16). The centeredness of its witness must be grasped through the diversity of its witnesses.

The church guards the full deposit of faith once for all delivered to the apostles (Jude 3; Hilary of Arles, *Intro. Comm. on Jude* 3). It is not as if the church of the New Testament required some subsequent generations of Christian testimony to complete what was incomplete in it. The task today is not simply to copy those apostolic models woodenly but to pray for the same Spirit to form the church today who formed those models of *ekklēsia* in apostolic times.

Catholicity Welcomes Cultural Varieties
of Church Practice

There are many classic Christian teachers, notably Clement of Alexandria, Eusebius, Vincent of Lérins, Cassiodorus, Thomas Aquinas, Nicolas of Cusa, Hooker, and Baxter, who have noticed a profound ecumenical truth revealed in the study of differing and even conflicting confessional traditions.

To some it may seem disingenuous that consensual ecumenical patience in the service of the whole church seeks to affirm and discover proximate truth even in traditions of church teaching that appear to conflict with each other. Irenic Christian teaching is seeking the scriptural and historic ground of general lay consent wherever it can be honestly identified. This is not accomplished by ignoring or disavowing particular church traditions, but rather by affirming their richness and vitality, provided they do not forget apostolic teaching (2. Tim. 2:8; Augustine, *Sermons* 234.3).

Persons of good will are to be found in all church traditions, even those that have had noticeable elements of heretical teaching. It is not surprising that a variegated Christendom over two millennia would develop varied (and even on some points conflicting) confessions, creeds, catechisms, and symbols of faith, as they seek to express the leading truths of those various traditions, national churches, cultures of Christian faith, and confessional bodies, insofar as they do not offend against ancient apostolic teaching.

This variety may be indirectly and ironically a cultural-historical expression of the catholicity of the church. What Christians of varied centuries hold in common (such as the written canon, Apostles' Creed, baptism, and Eucharist) are much more crucial to historic Christianity than the points upon which they differ.

Confessions or standards of doctrine serve several purposes. They guide church members in attesting the central truth of scripture. They serve as an authoritative standard to which appeal is made during times of controversy. They may serve not only as a functional constitution for a particular ethnic or national community but also as a kind of banner or flag or symbolic declaration to the world of the ecclesial community's identity. They regulate those responsible for the teaching office of the church, especially those whose ordination calls them to accountability in preaching and instructing confirmands. They unite a diverse church body in a common doctrinal purpose, distinguishing it from the world and from all counterfeits. They defend against abuses such as the misuse of church property by those who do not share the views of the traditioning body. For all these reasons, the confessions of varied national and denominational church bodies continue to fulfill certain meaningful roles, and should not be considered always as counterecumenical or intrinsically alien to the unity of the church. But in all forms of tolerance for differences, the apostolic witness must not be ignored or diluted through schism or heresy.

Reasonably Resisting Both Schism and Heresy

Schism is a rupture of the unity of the church destroying the peace of the church and vexing the love that rightly should prevail in the body of Christ (Cyprian, *Treatises* 10). Schism means dissension, division, partisanship (John 7:43; 9:16; 10:19; 1 Cor. 1:10; 11:18; 12:25). "If division in the body is to be avoided, greater attention must be given to the lesser parts, so that they will not be harmed or feel excluded" (Chrysostom, *Hom. on Cor.* 32.3). Schism (*schisma*) implies the partisan following of a special interest or party (Chrysostom, *Hom. on Cor.* 27.3).

The schismatic spirit may attach itself either to a defensive establishment mentality or to a chronically belligerent mentality. "Schism may be the sin of the community left as well as of the community leaving" (Pope, *Compend.* 3:274). "In some real way" the separated brothers and sisters remain "joined with us in the Holy Spirit, for to them also he gives his gifts and graces and is thereby operative among them with his sanctifying power" (*Doc. Vat. II, Ch.* 15).

Hairesis means a self-chosen view, as distinct from the traditionally received apostolic teaching (Tertullian, *Prescription Ag. Her.*). Heresy is a self-willed choice of individual interpretation as opposed to consensually received scriptural teaching (1 Cor. 1:10). Heresy is the "obstinate advocacy and propagation of error directly attacking the foundations of the faith indicating "an arbitrary or self-determined choice separating one from the unity of the Church" (Jacobs, *SCF*:411). The heresies cannot prevent God's work: "Now that they are outside, they do us more good, not by teaching the truth, for they do not know it, but by provoking carnal Christians to seek the truth and spiritual Christians to expound it" (Augustine, *On True Religion* 7.15).

Wherever a heresy has led to a breach of unity of the body, it is called schism, meaning either strife within the community or more particularly separation from it (*Ag. Her.* 3.3.1; 4.23.8; 26.2, Tertullian, *Prescription Ag. Her.* 32). Within the context of Judaism the *hairesis* (Heb. *min*) referred to a sect or party, and was applied by varied audiences to Pharisees, Sadducees, Nazarenes, and to the early church (Acts 5:17; 15:5; 24:5, 14; 26:5; 28:22).

Those who presume to retain the name *Christian* yet reject the ancient ecumenical faith can hardly remain growing parts of the living Vine. Both *schisma* and *hairesis* require continuing intelligent admonition and patient efforts at reconciliation (Cyprian, *On the Unity of the Catholic Church*).

The Second Mark: The Church Is Holy

The fullest disclosure of divine holiness is beheld on the cross. God does not evidence holiness by utterly separating from the history of sin, but by engaging and transforming it. "He performs a proper function of the physician's office, being in the company of those in need to be healed" (Cyril of Alex., *Comm. on Luke* 21–22; Luke 5:32).

It is an article of faith found in the most ancient forms of the baptismal creed that confesses: "I believe in the *hagian ekklēsian*" (holy church, Marcellus of Ancyra, *COC* 2:48; *SCD* 1, 2). *Credo in sanctam ecclesiam* implies that I believe that the church is by grace made capable of reflecting the divine holiness. The church does not possess holiness independently, but by participating in God's holiness (Bede, *Hom. on the Gospels* 1.21).

It is only through the route of the worshiping community that the faithful believe in the church: The primitive African and Gallican Baptismal Creeds avoided any misunderstanding by confessing *credo per sanctam ecclesiam*—"I believe *through* the holy church" (Loofs, *Symbolik*:12, 13).

The Church's Participation in God's Holiness

As body of Christ, the church is called to holiness. Yet its holiness is enmeshed in continuing human imperfection and finitude until the end of history. The church is holy while not ceasing to be subject to the infirmities of the flesh that accompany all historical existence (Chrysostom, *Hom. on Eph.* 20).

The church washes the world's pollutants, as Christ washes the church by grace in baptism: Christ "loved the church and gave himself up for her to make her holy, cleansing her by the washing with water through the word, and to present her to himself as a radiant church, without stain or wrinkle or any other blemish, but holy and blameless" (Eph. 5:25, 26; Augustine, *On Marriage and Concupiscence* 1.38). This cleansing is still taking place, still in the process of being fashioned and elicited (Bede, *On 1 John* 1.9; Calvin, *Inst.* 4.1.17–22).

The holiness of the church is best expressed in the imperfect or unfinished tense—that God is now sanctifying the church: "You also, like living stones, *are being built* into a spiritual house to be a holy priesthood" (1 Pet. 2:4, italics added; Bede, *Hom. on the Gospels* 2.24), destined to be "a holy nation, a people belonging to God" (1 Pet. 2:9). The church is being made holy, having been called forth by the Son, now within history being sanctified by the Spirit (*Eastern Orthodox Catechism* 192).

The church is holy because her Lord is holy (1 Cor. 1:30). She participates in her Lord's righteousness (Ambrose, *Holy Spirit* 3.4.26). Her task is to fashion her members after her Lord (Ignatius, *To Smyrna*; Irenaeus, *Ag. Her.* 3.24; Cyprian, *On the Unity of the Church* 6; Augustine, Sermon 214). The church is holy because she is sanctified by Christ through his passion, teaching, prayer, and sacraments (*Longer Catech.*, Eastern Orthodox Church, 267).

Classic Protestant confessions resonated with these patristic ecumenical motifs: "The Church is said to be holy, from 1 Cor. 14:33; Rev. 11:2; because Christ its Head is holy, Heb. 7:26, who makes the Church partaker of His holiness, John 17:19; because it is called by a holy calling and separated from the world, 2 Tim. 1:9; because the Word of God, committed to it, is holy, Rom. 3:2; because the Holy Ghost in this assembly sanctifies believers by applying to them, through faith, Christ's holiness . . . awakening in them the desire of perfect holiness" (Gerhard, LT 40.36). Similarly, Ursinus said the church "is called holy because it is sanctified of God by the blood and Spirit of Christ, that it may be conformable to him, not in perfection, but by the imputation of Christ's righteousness, or obedience; and by having the principle of holiness; because the Holy Spirit renews and delivers the church from the dregs of sins by degrees, in order that all who belong to it may commence and practice all the parts of obedience" (Ursinus, *Comm. Heid. Catech.*).

The Sanctity to Which the Believing Community Is Called

Hagios (Heb. *qadosh*, Lat. *sancta*), holy, is applied to the church as a corporate body and to individual believers whose lives, set apart for service in the world, are unreservedly consecrated to God for the salvation of the world.

In this new creation of the Spirit those who are called (*kletoi*) from the unregenerate world are gathered into the church (*ekklēsia*) to be regenerated for service in and witness to the world (Athanasius, *Resurrection Letters* 7).

Jesus called his disciples "out of the world" (John 17:6) precisely while viewing them as "still in the world" (v. 11) but not "of the world" (v. 14). He specifically prayed that the Father might not "take them out of the world" but "protect them from the evil one" (v. 15), for "I have sent them into the world" (v. 18; Augustine, *Tractates on John* 108.4).

The purpose of the church is to gather out of the world a people of God whose lives are hid in Christ, who "gave himself for us to redeem us from all wickedness and to purify for himself a people that are his very own, eager to do what is good" (Titus 2:14). The *ekklēsia*, being "called out," is required to be separate and distinct from whatever is alien to God, precisely while working to save it. The notion of holiness includes both these implications: consecrated to God and set apart from the world while reaching out for the world in its alienation.

Imprinted with Christ's Sanctity

As "holiness unto the lord" was stamped on the bells of the horses and cooking pots in ancient Israel (Ephrem, *Comm. on Zech.* 14.20), so this holiness is stamped on every button or sandal, every discrete action and aspect of the church (Athanasius, *Resurrection Letters* 11). A kind of sanctity is imputed to the church by the atoning deed of the Son on the cross.

Paul addressed his first letter to Corinth "to those sanctified in Christ Jesus and *called to be holy* [*kletoi hagioi*], together with *all those everywhere who call* on the name of our Lord" (1 Cor. 1:2, italics added; Origen, *Comm. on Cor.* 1.1.7). Those who having been cleansed through baptism in Christ are now called practically to walk in the way of holiness, along with others everywhere who pray and hear the Word, however imperfectly (Rom. 12:1; 1 Pet. 1:13–24; Andreas, Catena, Cramer, *CEC* 46).

This juridical, positional holiness in the body of Christ is constantly seeking to manifest itself in a practicing, living community of word and sacrament (1 Pet. 2:1–3; Augustine, *Admonition and Grace* 7.16). There is no fooling the Lord, for "the Lord knows those who are his," yet this makes it ever more imperative that "everyone who confesses the name of the Lord must run away from wickedness" (2 Tim. 2:19; Athanasius, *Festal Letters* 9). This is the twofold watchword that Paul left with Timothy in his last letter, as if carved in indelible letters on the foundation stone of the church.

The New Testament writings often were addressed "to the saints" (2 Cor. 1:1; Eph. 1:1), or to those "called to be saints" (Rom. 1.7; 1 Cor. 1:2), Among these were many whose unholiness was being admonished, resisted, forgiven, and transformed. John's Revelation warned the *ekklēsia* at Ephesus to "remember the height from which you have fallen!" Lacking repentance, the Lord will come "and remove your lamp stand from its place" (Rev. 2:5; Oecumenius, *Comm. on Apoc.* 2.1–7). Yet the continuing misdeeds, latent apostasies, and proximate fallenness of the Ephesian and Corinthian churches did not imply that they had lost entirely all aspects of the holiness that is received in Christ.

No classic Christian writer stated this more winsomely than Chrysostom: "He who loves does not investigate character: love does not regard uncomeliness. Love is called love because it often has special capacity for affection for one who is unlovely. This is Christ's love. He saw us who are unlovely (for who in his right mind would call us beautiful?), and he loved us, and his love makes us young" (Chrysostom, *Eutropius*, 2.15; cf. S. Kierkegaard, *Works of Love*:153–71). The bride in this wedding is being made beautiful by her relation with her spouse, who elicits beauty from her eyes.

Signs of Emergent Holiness

Indicators of holiness in the church are often imperfect and embryonic. Signs of an imperfectly emergent holiness may appear in one who is as yet still noticeably lacking in behavioral righteousness (Augustine, Sermon 174.5).

The church on behalf of its holiness does not say to this person: Please come back when you are fully holy and then you will be baptized and invited to the Lord's table. Rather, the church on behalf of its holiness must draw as near to this person as possible so as to bring God's goodness to sinners, and sinners to God's goodness at each step along the way. This is seen in Jesus' own attitude toward notorious but penitent sinners, whom he held to be closer to the kingdom than those who feign righteousness (Matt. 21:31, 32; Chrysostom, *Hom. on Matt.* Hom. 67.3).

Caregiving pastors have often recognized how difficult it is to honor the church's imputed sanctity in Christ without unnecessarily driving out those who are truly seeking to embody it while doing so imperfectly (Gregory the Great, *Pastoral Care* 2.7–10). At the same time persons are being made holy by penitent baptism and regular communion and faith in justifying grace, even while they are being tempted by disbelief or lack of charity (Chrysostom, *Hom. on Phil.* 2.1.6).

The Incarnational Paradox Is Embedded in the Church's Unique Sanctity

The deeper irony is that the signs of sin that attach to the church are indirect evidences of its holiness. It could not be a holy church if it had clean hands, as if separated from its mission and task of saving sinners (John 4:9; Ephrem, *Comm. on Tatian's Diatesseron,* Mark 7:29). The very purpose of the church is the transformation of sinners; hence the paradoxical proximity of sin to the church (*Conf.* of Dositheus 11).

The distinctive mission of discipling is to bring sinners to the way of holiness. This requires that the church should love at close quarters the sinners it is calling to refract the redeemed life (Matt. 9.11; Jerome, *Comm. on Matt.* 1.9.13). The church appearing to have no sin within its boundaries is likely to be a church that has forsaken its mission (Augustine, *On Continence* 25). Since the Christian community remains salt, light, and leaven within the world, it cannot remove itself wholly from the world without removing itself from its arena of apostolic mission. It purifies and cleanses its life only by a constant rhythm of distance and closeness to the world, gathering for worship and scattering for vocation (Matt. 5:13–16; John 16:17–33).

As in triage, those most desperately wounded are first cared for. The church has repeatedly found in the most notorious sinners its most brilliant and winning advocates (from Mary Magdalene and Paul to Saint Francis and John Newton). The skid row missions have nurtured many saints, who would not have been blessed had the church abandoned the skid rows (Mark 2:17; Augustine, Letter 145 to Anastasius; Palmer, *PPSW*:222–30).

Ironic Evidences of the Church's Holiness

The chief proof of the church's holiness, ironically, is that it is found among sinners, redeeming, reaching out, healing, and sanctifying. It is "as the cockle and darnel and chaff are found among the wheat, and as wens and swellings are in a perfect body, when they are rather diseases and deformities than true members of the body. Therefore the Church is very well compared to a drag-net which draws up fishes of all sorts; and to a field, wherein is found both darnel and good corn" (Second Helvetic *Conf.*; Matt. 13:26; Chromatius, *Tractate on Matt.* 51.1.1–2).

Distasteful fish are inevitably caught in the dragnet of general proclamation and mass evangelization, which catches all kinds (Matt. 13:47–50; Gregory the Great, *Forty Gospel Hom.* 11.4). The final sorting out will occur only on the last day (Matt. 13:49; 3:12). Like the ark, the church contains all kinds of creatures in its precincts, clean and unclean (Gen. 6:19; Tertullian, *On Idolatry* 24).

Tares remain among the grains of wheat until the end of time. "Let both grow together until the harvest" (Matt. 13:30; Origen, *Hom. on Josh.* 21.1). Till then, let God judge.

If the church's task is to encourage holiness at close quarters, it cannot militate against her character as holy that she has hypocrites and false members in her precincts. Insofar as the church retains unworthy members, it prays for their amendment (Origen, *Comm. on Matt.* 10.12). It is hazardous to the wheat when the farmer tries absolutely to remove every tare, once rooted. "The tares are to be tolerated either when they cannot be distinguished or cannot be removed without injury to the wheat," as any gardener knows (Banks, *MCD*: 287).

That sinners especially resort to the church in times of dire need is an empirical evidence of the church's proximate holiness (Gregory I, *Hom. on. Ezek.* 2.4.16, 17; Chrysostom, *Hom. on the Statues, NPNF* 1 9:364). It is an ironic turn of logic that the very "efforts of others to prove that the Church is not holy show that they acknowledge holiness as a mark of truth" (*Baltimore Catechism*:120). The evidence that sinners may in God's time become saints is an ironic demonstration of the effectiveness of the means of grace provided the church.

Callistus of Rome (217–222) set forth a penitential rule of great significance to the subsequent practice of repentance (*SCD* 42). It concluded that because the Lord takes "no pleasure in the death of the wicked, but rather that they turn from their ways and live" (Ezek. 33:11), and because it is not for us to judge others (Rom. 14:4), contrite penitents like the prodigal are to be readmitted to the Lord's Table (Luke 15; Ephrem, *Hymns on Paradise* 14.7). After Callistus, the church was no less a community of set-apart people, but more clearly the community of the forgiven and forgiving people of God.

How the Church Is Being Made Holy

The consensual view upholds four reasons why, through its calling, destiny, patience, and repentance, the church is being made holy.

First, the church is being made holy through its calling. The church is holy because its calling is holy. On this premise Paul viewed the baptized as saints or the elect as positionally justified in Christ by faith precisely while rebuking, instructing, and admonishing them ethically (Ambrosiaster, *Comm. on Paul*, Rom. 3:21–31).

Each baptized member shares by the verdict of grace on the cross in the holiness of the body of Christ by faith, even if in particular ways remaining proximately immature, unfinished, unholy. The holiness of the Lord shines and radiates precisely through the sins of believers (Hall, *DT* 8:189–92). It is precisely through our human weakness that God's strength is made perfect (1 Cor. 1:25–27; 2 Cor. 12:7–10; Cyprian, *Mortality* 12).

The justification of sinners does not imply the justification of sin. Faith in the holiness of the church does not imply that the church can rest easy in its shortcomings (2 Cor. 10:13–18; J. Wesley, *Earnest Appeal*, *WJW* 8:1–45). The church is called to sanctity, and is being made holy through this calling. Every believer is called to aim by clear and distinct resolve at daily walking in the way of holiness. The call to holiness is addressed to each believer. No one has rightly heard the call to active faith who has not at the same time heard the call to holy living (Jerome, *Epis. to Eph.* 3.5.1; Calvin, *Inst.* 3.16–21; Hall, *DT* 8:197).

Second, the church is being made holy through its expected consummation and destiny. Despite historic uncertainties, the future glory of the church is made certain by the sovereign will of God from eternity (Ambrosiaster, *Epis. to Eph.* 1.4). God intends and decrees to have an unblemished celebrant assembly in eternity. Against this church the gates of hell shall not prevail (Matt. 16:18). Eschatologically viewed, she is a "Holy City, the new Jerusalem, coming down out of heaven from God, prepared as a bride beautifully dressed for her husband" (Rev. 21:2; Ambrose, *On the Mysteries* 7).

Third, the church is being made holy through patience. The church is being made holy by waiting upon God's holiness to elicit proximate human holiness, waiting upon God's timing to allow the seeds of holiness to grow in time.

This is why a key evidence of the holiness of the church is patience (Rom. 5:3, 4; 15:4, 5; Origen, *Comm. on Rom.* 9.22). The *ekklēsia* is called to let patience have her perfect work (James 1:4; Oecumenius, *Comm. on James* 1.4), to run with patience the race that is set (Heb. 12:1; Theodoret, *Interp. Of Heb.* 12.1), and in patience to possess her soul (Luke 21:19).

Fourth, the church is being made holy through repentance. This form of holiness paradoxically emerges precisely in the process of recognizing its own unholiness (Luke 18:10–13; Augustine, Sermon 351.1; Cyril of Alex. *Comm. on Luke,* Hom. 120).

The repentance leading to faith in the Word is a defining act of this community. A principal characteristic of this set-apart community when it is most truly being itself is its readiness to recognize the sin of her own members (Matt. 9:13; Origen, *Ag. Celsus* 3.59). No time is exempt from being the "time for judgment to begin with the family of God" (1 Pet. 4:17; Bede, *On 1 Pet.* 4.17).

Continuing Ambiguities of the Holiness of the Church

There are few sins in the world that are not also found among the baptized. No church has yet become purified from lust, nationalism, envy, pride, or racism, and the list could go on. The Bible does not characteristically try to dissemble the sins of the people of God, either publicly or before God. Rather the church is precisely the place where believers are to be brought to the specific awareness of the depths of their own shortcomings in order to receive convicting and forgiving grace (Amos 5:21–27; Jer. 7; Isa. 6:1–8; 1 Cor. 1:10–13; Gal. 2:11–14; Phil. 1:15–17; Cassiodorus, *Expos. Of Ps.* 5.17). The temple is no place for the pretense of righteousness.

Among the persistent issues dealt with in classical Christian teaching on the church's holiness, these six are most recurrent, here treated only briefly:

- whether sinners are embraced by the inclusive ascription in the holiness of the church

- whether the true church is unambiguously identified only at the end of history

- whether good people exist outside the church;

- whether the holy sacraments are invalidated by the ministry of unholy leaders

- whether excommunication is a meaningful expression of the holiness of the church

- whether outside the church there is no salvation

Concerning the Impenitent Who Appear Ambiguously to Belong to the Church

The first of these six issues: Whether the church is restricted to only those who are fully responding to sanctifying grace; or does it include all sinners who seek repentance and faith; or all the baptized regardless of their repentance?

It is clear from Jesus' teaching of the wide net that unbelievers are likely to be mixed with believers in this fellowship of Word and sacrament (Matt. 13:47; Gregory the Great, *Forty Gospel Homilies*, 11.4; *Augsburg Apology* 6, 7; Westminster *Conf.* 25). They do not yet organically and truly belong to the church insofar as they lack faith, but they are outwardly attached to it as dead leaves to a living vine or a parasite to an animal (Cyril of Alex., *Fragment 171*, Reuss, *MKGK*:208–09; Schmid, *DT*:596–99).

The church in a visible sense includes all those baptized. The church in the spiritual sense consists in those who respond in faith active in love to the grace given in baptism (Rom. 5:6; Marius Victorinus, *Epis. to Gal.* 2.5.6; Neve, *Luth. Sym*:187). Implanted within and clinging to the community of those whose faith is active in love are seekers and catechumens who are learning, those whose baptism is as yet unconfirmed, and others who share to some degree in the intention of the church and receive its sacraments and hear its Word, but whose faith is in varied ways immature or defective, needing further growth (Chrysostom, *Hom. on Gal.*, 5.6–7; Calvin, *Inst.* 4.2).

Paul acknowledged "with tears" that "many live as enemies of the cross of Christ" who remain within the *ekklēsia* (Phil. 3:18; Ambrosiaster, *Epis. to Phil.* 3.19). These are distinguished from those whose "citizenship is in heaven" (3:20; Marius Victorinus, *Epis. to Phil.* 3.19). The account of Ananias and Sapphira indicates that from the outset the corrupted have been mixed with believers (Acts 5:1–11; Bede, *Comm. on Acts* 5.5).

The heart of this problem is: How far may it be meaningfully said that impenitent sinners "belong" to God's holy church? This is the issue that confronted the persecuted church: How are those who have lapsed into idolatry to be dealt with?

Classic exegetes have freely employed a rhetorical device called inclusive ascription or generic attribution (technically: synecdoche) in their reasoning. This is a figure of speech by which the whole of a thing is spoken of as a part, or a part for the whole, such as bread for food, or the army for a soldier. You are now reading a book, even though in reality you are now only reading one sentence of a book, yet in reading this one sentence you are indeed reading this book.

Similarly we speak of the church as holy, yet by generic ascription including sinners for whom the whole church is praying that they come to repentance and faith. The church is made up of the faithful who are born anew of the Spirit, which by generic attribution embraces those who are planted and growing together with them in a visible body (Matt. 13:26–40; Irenaeus, *Ag. Her.* 4.66.1–2; Calvin, *Inst.* 4.1).

It should not surprise any realistic observer that some outwardly have all the appearances of belonging to the church, being baptized, professing Christianity, frequently using the means of grace, yet may not be in the presence of God true believers whose hearts are being regenerated by grace. But they are by a diffuse or generic reference still called the church. That is ascribed to the entire assembly which belongs properly to only a part of it yet in the form of hope may belong to the whole of it. Those lacking regeneration and the fruits of holiness may be members by association or outward profession or baptism, even while they lack the evidences of faith (*Augsburg Apology*, DT:591).

Fallen members of the mixed body (*corpus mixtum*) cannot be said in the strict sense, but only by generic attribution, to be included in the one, holy, catholic, and apostolic church. It is sadly possible that apostasy may predominate in some parts of the church that is otherwise called holy. What remains undefiled about the true church is its pure Word and Sacraments duly administered (Thirty Nine Articles; Ursinus, *Comm. Heid. Catech.*:288–89).

The church in history is always engaged in a struggle between flesh and spirit, always in transit from sin to grace, always expressing its holiness as a community of sinners being redeemed, and its catholicity as a particular community in time and place pointing beyond itself to the coming celestial city (Gal. 5; Matt. 13:24–43).

Is the True Church Knowable Only at the End of History?

The second question: Is the true church able to be unambiguously identified only at the end of history?

In winter, living and dead trees appear to be alike. So in the church in time, the distinction remains unclear between just and unjust, to be revealed at the end of time (Matt. 13:47; Hermas, *Sim.* 3.2, 3). Only in the future judgment, when the unjust are cast out, will the difference be revealed (*Sim.* 4.2).

The church consists of those who are on the way toward being made holy by grace. The church as we behold it in history is until the harvest of history a *corpus mixtum* composed of all that are called and baptized, including hypocrites and unbelievers mingled with believers. Yet it is the believers who live out their baptism who most truly and properly constitute the church (Belgic *Conf.* 27–30).

The difference between wheat and tares is not finally seen until both lie on the threshing floor. Meanwhile there is a difference between those who belong to the family and those who temporarily inhabit the house (Augustine, *On Baptism* 5.21).

It is folly to withdraw from the church because it lacks the full evidence of holiness in particular places or persons or situations. To withdraw from the preaching of the Word and the means of grace in common prayer and sacrament is to cut oneself off from the very vine from which nourishment comes (John 15:1–8; Augustine, *Tractates on John* 81.4).

It is equally futile to attempt to exclude all sinners from the church. This typically results in self-righteousness pretending to be grace. Legalistic culture-bound standards of conduct and biases may parade as faultless measures of holiness. These legalisms in time mock true faith and may elicit defiant reactions against excessive puritanism (*Augsburg Apology* 4).

Gregory the Great stated this irony deftly, "Good things are so to be preached that ill things be not assisted sideways. The highest good is so to be praised that the lowest be not despaired of" (*Book of Pastoral Rule*, NPNF 2 12:69).

Obstinate sinners who remain within the outward body will ultimately be cut off by their own obstinacy (*Longer Catech.*, Eastern Orthodox Church, 269). Not all who are now nominally found to be associated with the visible church on earth will enter the holy city. "Not everyone who says to me, 'Lord, Lord,' will enter the kingdom" (Matt. 7:21; Chrysostom, *Hom. on Matt.* Hom. 24.1). "If anyone does not remain in me, he is like a branch that is thrown away and withers" (John 15:6; Chrysostom, *Hom. on John* 76).

Do Civic Virtues Exist Outside the Church?

Third, is it a scandal to faith that civic virtues exist outside the church? The most common answer in consensual exegesis: God has not reserved all human virtues exclusively for those who have explicit faith in his coming. Some repulsed by formal religion are deeply attentive to the poor, at times more steadily than pious church members. They may not share in God's family, but they themselves raise caring families, remain faithful marriage partners, live tranquil and benign lives, do little harm. Some tell the truth who would not go near a church. Some who think of the church as hypocritical have high integrity themselves. Does this do discredit to the church? No. It reinforces the church's confidence in common grace, reason, and conscience.

The *ekklēsia* is not called to despise or demean these people, but to praise God for the presence of the Spirit in their lives, going before them with common grace and grace preparatory to repentance, supplying them with sufficient, actual grace, eliciting in them their cooperation with God's requirements for the good life (Augustine, *Sermons* 214.11, 38). The church prays for them, for their full responsiveness, rejoicing in the presence of grace in the human community generally in all history and nature. The church celebrates general providence, conscience, reason, kindness, and law wherever these civic and moral virtues flower.

Are the Holy Sacraments Invalidated by the Ministry of Unholy Leaders?

The fourth ambiguity: Are the holy sacraments invalidated by the ministry of unholy leaders? The classic consensus: Since the sacraments are God's gift, the tarnished moral character of the person administering them cannot detract from the value of the gift offered, for "he gives not what is his own, but God's" (Augustine, *Answer to Letters of Petilian* 2.30.69). The Donatist notion that the blemished cannot communicate the means of grace had finally to be disavowed (Augsburg Confession, art. 3, 8; Anglican Thirty-nine Articles, 27).

The means of grace do not cease being efficacious just because they are at times administered by neurotic characters. Jesus commended obedience to the teaching office of the very teachers of the law whom he opposed: "Obey them and do everything they tell you, but do not follow their example" (Matt. 23:2, 3; Incomplete Work on Matt. 3; cf. Calvin, *Inst.* 4.10.26).

The church is holy not because of the presumed holiness of its clergy, but because its laity receives in faith the pure Word and Sacrament according to the apostolic faith. Word and sacraments are made effective by the presence of Christ and are "effectual to the godly, although they be administered by ungodly ministers" (Second Helvetic *Conf.*, CC:160).

Who Is Rightly Prepared to Commune at the Lord's Table?

Fifth: The celebration of the Lord's farewell meal is intended for those who, having been baptized into the community of faith, are thus deliberately seeking the regenerate life and praying for sanctifying grace. Only the penitent are ready for the Lord's Table. Only the baptized faithful, who having fallen, have again received the grace of contrition, are ready to share in the Eucharist. This classic teaching does not imply absolute moral perfection as requisite to the Lord's Table (Formula of Concord, art. 3, 7).

If the intent of the Eucharistic invitation is to be fulfilled, there must be some Spirit-enabled self-examination and discernment of the Lord's body and blood. "The man without the Spirit does not accept the things that come from the Spirit of God, for they are foolishness to him, and he cannot understand them, because they are spiritually discerned" (1 Cor. 2:14; Chrysostom, *Hom. on Cor.* 7.8–11). Those who have a disorderly walk are to be gently admonished to pray for further grace (2 Thess. 3:6–15; Basil, *Long Rules* Q42).

One who is sowing seeds of discontent and creating division among the body is hardly ready for the unifying sacrament of the one body (Rom. 16:17; Chrysostom, *Hom. on Rom.* 32). Divisive persons should be twice admonished, and, "After that have nothing to do with him" (Titus 3:10; Athanasius, *Letter to Adelphus* 60.2). "The wisest and most faithful application of the best tests will never secure an absolutely pure Church, but that is no argument against the use of tests. Rather it is an argument in their favor. If strictness often fails, laxity must be still worse" (Banks, *MCD*:289).

Excesses tend to recur in opposite pairs: a formal religion that loses charisma, or charismatic gifts that misplace decency and order; intellectualism at the cost of passion, or enthusiasm to the neglect of reflection; idealism at the cost of realistic prudence, or prudential realism at the cost of the loss of vision; individual, privatized religion at the cost of community, or social religion at the cost of individual accountability. In each case the best guide to the recovery of equilibrium is found in the incarnate Lord, as truly God and truly human, wherein the finite becomes the vehicle of the infinite and the earthly vessel bearer of the heavenly treasure (Rom. 9:21–23; 2 Cor. 4:7; Origen, *OFP* 4.1).

Whether "Outside the Church There Is No Salvation"

Sixth, assuming that the grace that saves is grace given only through faith in the Son of God, the question persists: Is this saving grace received outside the church? The more familiar statement of the question is: How far is it to be insisted that "outside the church there is no salvation?"

This question assumes a distinction between the grace that goes before (preparatory grace) salvation and the grace that saves (saving grace). There is finally no salvation apart from faithful response to God's own coming in the flesh, in history, in his Son, which is declared through preaching or anticipatively received in the form of hope among those without opportunity to hear (Heb. 11:4–10; Origen, *Comm. on Rom.* 10.10–15).

In this sense the classic tradition of consensual exegesis confirmed Cyprian's dictum "There is no salvation outside the church" (*extra ecclesiam nulla salus,* Letters 73:21, 51:282; 25:49–51, 63–65; cf. Augustine, *Letters* 141.5; Luther, *EA* 10.162, 444; 48.218; Calvin, *Inst.* 4.1.4, *Geneva Catechism*, Q104–5). Yet the hoping and believing community is wide enough to embrace both Noah and the thief. It is over-reading Cyprian to conclude that all are damned who remain unbaptized, for that would damn Abraham into whose bosom the faithful are being drawn (Luke 16:22–23). As true Vine the Lord says to the branches, "If a man remains in me and I in him, he will bear much fruit; apart from me you can do nothing" (John 15:6; Augustine, *Tractates on John* 81.2–3).

As no child is born without a mother, it is difficult to imagine how faith could be given birth apart from the matrix of a hoping, believing, attesting community.

For who can hear without a preacher (Rom. 10:14)? The petitions of the faithful are offered "where two or three come together in my name" (Matt. 18:20; Peter Chrysologus, Sermon 132.4–5).

To separate from the church is to separate from the head of the church. To leave the ark of Noah during the flood is to go under. To be without the plank of the church amid the stormy history of sin is hazardous to the soul (Second Helvetic *Conf.*, CC:147).

Mitigating Reflections

The Westminster Confession cautiously stated that there is no ordinary possibility of salvation outside the church (25.2), leaving extraordinary means to God. The indeterminate possibility of salvation outside the church rests on four mitigating grounds, each of which has been weighed in classic Christianity:

1. The honoring of one's parents, which itself is a divine command (Exod. 20:12; Ambrose, *The Patriarchs* 1.1), may make it more understandable that a believer of another religion should earnestly follow parental guidance, assuming that the truth of God's own incarnate coming has not yet been plausibly set forth or made reasonably hearable.

2. Those who have had no opportunity even to hear or barely approach the revealed truth cannot he made responsible for fully responding to the truth, though they must respond to whatever truth they know (Rom. 10:14; Augustine, *Letters* 157; 199.48).

3. When the truth is ineffectively presented, it may be that the reason and conscience of the hearer sincerely and rightly resist the apparent inconsistencies or seeming injustices that accompany the presentation of the truth. Here reason and conscience must be respected by faith, which must itself undertake clearer proclamation (Rom. 1:20; 3:21; Chrysostom, *Hom. on Rom.* 3).

4. God is not bound to the ordinary means of grace appointed to the Christian community. It is rash to assume that there cannot be other extraordinary acts of grace or any other means by which the Spirit can address the conscience and the heart. When it is stated that outside the church there is no salvation, the assumption prevails that we are speaking of the whole *qahal*, the called people of God, which includes those who have a sincere anticipatory intent to trust God's promises (as in the case of Abel and Abraham; Heb. 11:4–22; Chrysostom, *Hom. on Heb.* 25), who would have trusted further had they had sufficient opportunity. "All just men from the time of Adam, 'from Abel, the just one, to the last of the elect,' will be gathered" (*Doc. Vat II, Ch.* 2).

"The answer of the question must be left in the hands of Him 'who desireth not the death of a sinner' but wills 'that all men be saved' " (Merrill, *ACE*:240; 1 Tim. 2:4). "For we know that God had some friends in the world that were not of the commonwealth of Israel" (Second Helvetic *Conf.*, CC:147).

The Church's Intercession for the Salvation of Humanity

The intercession of the whole church for the whole of humanity has always been a crucial act of Christian prayer. It is a commended act of piety to pray for the salvation of all, even though the scriptures hold that some by their recalcitrance will not open themselves to the saving grace offered to all.

Nonetheless Jesus said, "I have other sheep that are not of this fold; I must bring them also, and they will heed my voice. So there shall be one flock, one shepherd" (John 10:16; Augustine, Sermon 138.5).

"Those who are outside the Church through no fault of their own are not culpable in the sight of God because of their invincible ignorance. Persons who make use of the graces God gives them, even though they are not members of the true Church, actually have the desire to become members inasmuch as they wish to use all the means ordained by God for their salvation" (*Baltimore Catechism*:130–31).

It is not beyond the sovereign will of God to be extraordinarily merciful to those who remain outside the pale of baptism but nonetheless make full use of the common grace God gives them providentially. To pretend to limit God's mercy or freedom is rash.

The faithful martyrs who died without opportunity for baptism were viewed as having been in intent baptized (as a matter of principle, *de jure*), as are those who have a declared intention to be baptized even though the actual event has not yet occurred in fact (*de facto*). The former is sometimes called the baptism of *blood*, and the latter baptism of *desire*.

Following Hebrews 11, classic exegetes have speculated on a possibility of a mode of sharing in the faith of the church by "desire," as distinguished from "actually" (Tho. Aq., *ST* 1–2, Q4). This teaching of an implicit intent toward baptism makes it possible for the faithful to pray for grace that the beloved one may be saved without baptism, but only on the proviso that one is ignorant of the necessity of baptism, and would have been baptized had one understood its necessity.

Warnings Against the Spirit of Indifference

Remembering the above qualifiers, the church remains the bodily instrument and context in which Christ's saving work is remembered, celebrated, interpreted, and applied to human life. Though the Spirit is not bound by the confines of the *ekklēsia*, the Spirit chooses to work through Word and Sacrament to call the community to the Lord (*Augsburg Apology*:168).

The spirit of indifference imagines that it makes no difference what people believe as long as they hope or intend to lead a good life. The weak in faith are right to pray for divine mercy, but not to assume that such prayer will override God's righteousness. It is hazardous to make the optimistic assumption that, despite dire warnings and invitations to repentance, surely God would not carry out the promised vindication of justice.

The oxymoron of absolute relativism errs by *attaching the same value to the teaching of falsehood as to the teaching of the truth.* The sad irony of egalitarian ideology is that the virtue of equality has led to indifference to the truth. The permission to believe or do anything becomes a new dogmatism. All who desire saving grace must avail themselves insofar as possible of the means of grace. This ordinarily means placing themselves within the orbit of the believing community.

The Visibility of the Church

It is consistent with the plan of salvation that a visible community should arise as a result of God's saving work, a community of persons who acknowledge Christ as Lord and Head, who are united by their union with Christ through the Spirit (Acts 2:37–47; Calvin, *Inst.* 4.1.7–9).

The body of Christ of which Paul speaks is a visible community, not an ethereal, utopia to be found only in the imagination. "We teach that this church actually exists" (*Augsburg Apology, BOC*:171). It is into a visible body that men, women, and children visibly enter by a visible rite of faithful baptism (Bede, *Comm. on Acts* 2.38–47). They taste and eat the Bread of Life, and hear an audible word.

As the incarnate Lord came visibly amid human society, so does the body and bride of Christ express herself visibly amid human societies, ministering with tangible signs of grace and ordered in a visible fellowship that stands in succession to the apostles. As Christ has two natures, divine and human, so does the church offer divine gifts with human hands and speak the divine Word through human sentences (Leo, *Symbol of Faith, SCD* 344).

The company of the redeemed is "invisible, in respect of their relation wherein they stand to Christ," and "visible in respect of the profession of their faith, in their persons, and in particular churches" (Cambridge Platform, *CC*:387; Calvin, *Inst.* 4.1). Thus the church in classic Reformed teaching is "called *visible*, not only because the men as men are visible, but because outwardly they profess Gospel truth and celebrate the sacraments according to the lawful use for which they were instituted by God. It ought to be called *invisible* because of the Spirit and true faith, which reside in the mind alone, which no man can see, which God alone knows" (Braun, *DF* 2.4.24, 22, 7 in *RD*:668, italics added).

The Visible Elements in the Rites of Baptism and Eucharist

The visibility of the church is made clear in the visible rites of baptism with water and Eucharist with bread and wine. Just as the gospel is audibly heard through the preaching of the Word, so is life in Christ sustained by the visible bread and wine of the Eucharist. The community's discipline can only occur within a time and space sphere that can be seen and heard (Oecumenius, *Fragments on Heb.* 12.1–12), manifested through the flesh (Heb. 12:22–24; Chrysostom, *On Epis. to Heb.* 32.2–1).

Considered outwardly, those lacking faith and love may remain baptized members of the church insofar as they too enunciate her prayers and say her confession and partake of her sacraments. Meanwhile their own recalcitrance ultimately tends to blemish the very ethos in which they are outwardly beheld. Anyone can pretend to worship. Verbally saying the Creed does not imply that one is affirming it from the heart. These word-sayers are not in the fullest sense members, though they may be viewed outwardly as simulated members through their unreceived and now almost forgotten baptism. The church prays for their renovation (Augustine, *Trin.* 14.1.1).

Catholic, Orthodox, and most classic Protestant teachers stress the visible act of baptism as primary indicator of membership. Some subsequent Protestant teachings place greater stress upon effectual calling, faith, regeneration, piety, reception of the gifts of the Spirit, and holy living as evidences of membership (*RD*:665–66).

The Christian life is hid in Christ. Our poor eyes cannot adequately see the line that divides true and false believers holding the same communion cup, eating the same loaf. What the empirical sociologist has eyes to see is only the visible. What only God has eyes to see adequately is the invisible (2 Tim. 2:19; Wollebius, *CTC*:111). What communicants see imperfectly, God sees perfectly (Heb. 12:22–25; Ambrose, *Flight From the World* 5.31).

The kingdom is not of this world (John 18:36) and does not come with observation (Luke 17:20; John Cassian, *Conference* 1.13). The life of faith remains hidden in Christ (Col. 3:3; Ambrose, *Paradise* 29). Its sphere is neither empirical nor measurable nor political nor economic nor physical as such, but embodied spirit, glorified body, enfleshed word (Augustine, *Tractates on John* 65.1).

Order as an Expression of the Church's Visibility

Even within the earliest Christian congregations, there were extensive evidences of considerable organization: elections, stated leaders, defined leadership roles, lines of authority, stated times of meeting, gentle admonition for the negligent (1 Cor. 5:13; 1 Tim. 1:20), funding and support systems, letters of recommendation, procedural norms and rules (1 Cor. 7:17; Acts 15:28), rites and ceremonies, a known membership (1 Cor. 5:12), and qualifications for membership (Acts 1:23–26; 2:41, 42, 47; 18:27; Rom. 15:26; 1 Cor. 5:4–13; 16:1, 2; 2 Cor. 3:1; 11:16; Phil. 1:1; 2:30; Col. 2:5).

All this appears to have developed within the period of Paul's and Luke's ministry, before the destruction of Jerusalem, and the rudiments of it were already in place in the Jerusalem church before Paul's conversion. For Paul did not enter the church without being baptized (Chrysostom, *Hom. on Acts* 20.9.18). It was a definable organization that Paul was persecuting (Acts 9:2; Cassiodorus, *Expos. On Ps.* 53.9). Simple individual conversion was not sufficient. Cornelius and his companions had received the Holy Spirit but were called to be baptized into the community of faith (Acts 10:48; Bede, *Comm. on Acts* 10.48).

Before Pentecost Jesus' followers were generally called disciples. After Pentecost they are more characteristically called "the assembly of God," "the fellowship of saints," "the brethren," or "the churches," indicating a palpable organization and emerging structure. They gathered on the first day of the week to break bread and hear scripture expounded (Acts 20:7; Chrysostom, *Hom. on Acts* 43); widows were enrolled (1 Tim. 5:9); all things were to be done decently and in order (1 Cor. 14:40); collections were gathered for the saints of Jerusalem (Rom. 15:26); members were cautioned against "neglecting to meet together" (Heb. 10:25).

This evidence resists theories of a purely spontaneous church, as if lacking governance or ordered organization. It resists individualistic theories of Christianity as primarily individual piety or prayer completely detached from community. The modern fantasy that autonomous individuals on their own initiative formed themselves into churches as voluntary organizations runs directly counter to the historical witness of the church to its identity as formed by Christ as his living body (Eph. 4; Minear, *ICNT*; Montague, *HS*; Heron, *HS*).

Lacking visibility the church could not have founded schools, hospitals, orphanages, hospices. Nor could it hallow marriages, hold common worship, or administer sacraments. The faithful cannot look with indifference upon the institutional, visible body that has delivered them the message of the gospel, baptized, instructed, and supplied them every means of grace (Heb. 10–12–35; Chrysostom, *Hom. on Heb.* 19.4–5; *Augsburg Apology, BOC*:171–77; Schultze, *CD&ST*:187; Matt. 18:20; 1 Cor. 5:4). Any view of the church that tends to fixate upon invisibility risks becoming as unhistorical and nonincarnational as Docetism.

The church is not simply the name we give to atomized, separated, scattered, elect individuals who love the Lord, for as such they are not an organic, living community or body, as assumed in the New Testament. A community known only to God and lacking the elements of an organized society could hardly be the church to which Paul wrote (1 Cor. 12:12; Cyprian, *Treatises, 1, On the Unity of the Church*, 5). The church in which the Word is heard and Sacraments administered is visible as a local assembly gathered in a particular locale and as a worldwide community scattered amid the nations, bearing testimony and exercising various gifts (Ursinus, *Comm. on Heid. Catech.*, p. 287; *Leiden Synopsis* 40.33).

The Sign of Contradiction: In the World For the World

The Christian life is lived in but not of the world (John 17:14–19; Augustine, *Tractates on John* 108.1). It is not conformed to the world but is being transformed within it by the renewing of minds in Christ (Origen, *Comm. on Rom.* 12.1–2). The Christian is already a citizen of a celestial city precisely while living amid earthly history. That God is holy does not imply that God is unrelated to the world, but related to the world by judging and redeeming it.

The church exists as a sign of contradiction within the world, "a stone that will make men stumble" (1 Pet. 2:8). The premises of the kingdom of God contradict and oppose the kingdoms of this world. Those who follow the holy One of God (Mark 1:24; John 6:69) are prepared to suffer with their Lord and if necessary be sacrificed as he was (Cyprian, *Treatises* 11; Athanasius, *Resurrection Letters* 10). They expect to bear the cross daily in their own time and place, deny themselves, and follow the crucified Lord of glory (1 Cor. 2:7,8; Chrysostom, *Hom. on Cor.* 7.1; Calvin, *Inst.* 3.7).

"God sent the Son into the world, not to condemn the world, but to save the world through him" (John 3:17; Isaac of Nineveh, *Ascetical Homily* 74). However acquainted the church is with the world in its own time, the church remains "like a stranger in a foreign land," as it "presses forward amid the persecutions of the world and the consolations of God" (Augustine, *CG* 18.51; Tavard, *The Pilgrim Church*). However contrasted with the world, the church seeks to be for the world in a deeper way than the world can imagine being for itself.

Only by speaking the language of its own period can the church declare the perennial gospel addressed to all times and places. The church is called to discern the signs of its own times, attentive to whatever is occurring in its own special period of history, viewed from within the context of the anticipated meaning of universal history. The Barmen Declaration makes clear that the gospel is not a matter of looking to the signs of the times to determine the Christian proclamation. "We repudiate the false teaching that the church can turn over the form of her message and ordinances at will or according to some dominant ideological and political convictions" (Barmen Declaration, *CC*:521).

The church does not expect that it will always suitably embody the body of Christ or invariably attest the pure Word or unerringly walk in the way of holiness. But it does hope for a final plenary cleansing at the end of history to ready it for eternal presence with the Lord who calls it even now to be holy and without blemish (Eph. 5:27).

The church does not forever turn inward as a gathered community, but also faces outward to penetrate the vocational spheres. Its members earn honest bread in the world through fitting means. The neighbor is duly served amid the varied vocations. God is duly served through service to the neighbor. The poor are the church's only possessions (Ambrose, *Letters*, NPNF 2 10:419, 436).

Where brokenness is found in the world, the church mends; where hunger, it feeds; where suffering, it assuages. Some sins are economically intertwined, politically complicated, and cannot be simply mended by individual acts of mercy. They may require the magistracy or official persons or complex organizations to be attentive to their vocation and find better ways to act justly and love mercy. The people of God are called to do whatever is at hand to do, act with all their might, and hear the neighbor's cry and answer it, loving the ones they see (Eccles. 9:10; Luke 10:33–35; S. Kierkegaard, *Works of Love*).

The Third Mark: Catholicity

The church is constituted *kath'olou*—according to its wholeness—or as we say in English, *catholic*. The church is called catholic because she is not bound to a particular place or time, but inclusive of all believers. The one church that lives in Christ has the characteristic of being one throughout the whole earth. "That which concerns the whole" is the root meaning of catholic.

But the word means much more: That church is catholic which professes the whole faith that the whole body of Christian believers has in all its times and places professed (Vincent of Lérins, *Comm.* 2.6). The underlying conviction is that wherever belief in the triune God emerges throughout the known world among the various nations, races, languages, nationalities, classes, and cultures, in all sorts of political systems, economic orders, and social situations, there is the one body of Christ. The church by definition is *kath'olou* in this sense (*Martyrdom of Polycarp, ANF* 1:39–42; Irenaeus, *Ag. Her.* 3.4; Androutsos, *Dogm.*:280).

Wholeness of Consent, Doctrine, and Outreach

The term church catholic (*katholikēn ekklēsian*) appears early in Christian testimony, as in the writings of Ignatius about AD 110: wherever Christ is, there is the *katholikēn ekklēsia*n (Smyrna 8.2; Martyrdom of Polycarp 8.1), the church universal, which has Christ as its center and the apostles as its teachers (Ignatius, *Philadelphians* 5.1).

In the rule of faith, as typified by the Apostles' and Nicene-Constantinopolitan Creeds, catholicity is confessed as a defining mark of the church (Pearson, *EC*:145–50; Journet, *CWI*:526; Hall, *DT* 8:199). This is a reliable test: if the church should bar from its doors some particular nation or race or gender or culture, one would then know instantly that it is not constituted *kath'olou*.

The rule by which catholicity has been most commonly judged since the fifth century is the Vincentian canon: That is catholic which has been believed by all Christian believers in varied cultures, places, and times from the outset of apostolic testimony. "Every care must be taken that we may hold fast to that which has been believed everywhere, always, and by all. For this is, then, truly and properly Catholic. . . . This general rule will be correctly applied if we pursue universality, antiquity, and agreement" (Vincent of Lérins, *Commonitory*, 2.1).

By the criterion of *universality*, we confess that faith to be true which is confessed by the whole church throughout the whole world. By the criterion of *antiquity*, we follow the ancient definitions of the apostles as faithfully delivered by their successors through consensually received interpreters (Nicetas of Remesiana, *Explanation of the Creed, FC* 7:50). By the criterion of *consensual agreement*, we adopt the definitions received by general lay consent in ecumenical council (Vincent of Lérins, *Commonitory*, 2.1). "If error is the falsification of truth, then it is evident that truth must have come first. . . . Marcion himself accepted the whole thing in the days when he still belonged to the church, before he invented his heresy" (Tertullian, *Against Marcion,* 4.4).

Before Vincent, earlier classic writers had spoken of the wholeness and universality of the church in several interrelated ways: "It is called Catholic then because it extends over all the world . . . teaches universally and completely one and all the doctrines which ought to come to men's knowledge . . . brings into subjection to godliness the whole . . . and because it universally treats and heals the whole class of sins which are committed by soul or body, and possesses in itself every form of virtue which is named, both in deeds and words, and every kind of spiritual gifts" (Cyril of Jerusalem, *Catech. Lect.* 18.23). By the time of

Vincent (430s AD), the core consensual definition of catholicity hinges on these three factors: full consent, doctrinal wholeness, and universal mission.

Fullness of Consent to the Whole of Apostolic Teaching

First, the church is celebrated as universal (*katholikē*) with respect to the fullness of consent given to the whole of catholic truth (Tertullian, *Prescription Ag. Her.* 20–28). Wherever there is wholehearted consent to ancient apostolic teaching, there the whole church is becoming embodied.

To say, "I believe in the holy *catholic* church," means that one believes in the same teaching of the same *ekklēsia* that true believers have received since apostolic times and in all the places where that faith has been truly received (Tertullian, *Ag. Marcion* 4.3–5). "That which was from the beginning, which we have heard, which we have seen with our eyes, which we have looked at and our hands have touched—this we proclaim" (1 John 1:1; Severus, Catena, Cramer, *CEC* 106).

Wholeness of Received Doctrine

Second, that teaching is catholic which embraces all that is necessary for salvation. As the churches of the late second century faced heretical challenges, the term catholic increasingly took on the added nuance of "wholeness of received doctrine." The church is celebrated as universal with respect not only to the completeness of its consensual reception but to the wholeness of its doctrine. By this mark the believer today can be assured that the church in our time endeavors to teach the same fully adequate doctrine that the apostles received from Christ and seeks to do so in relation to emergent or changing cultural contexts.

Teachers of catholic truth are distinguished from schismatic word manipulators who teach only some broken piece of the truth of the whole. The church is catholic because consent to this whole truth has been given from ancient times by all those of every age and culture who share life in Christ. The church does not extol one favorite doctrine in one locale and a different doctrine in another according to local preference or partisanship but the whole counsel of God everywhere (Tertullian, *Prescription Ag. Her.* 20–28). By its doctrinal wholeness and sensible equilibrium, catholic truth is easily distinguished from the imbalances and discrepancies so evident in heresy—evident, that is, to anyone who has been wisely grounded in apostolic teaching.

Catholicity Requires Mission to All Cultures

Third, the church is catholic because her mission is universally addressed to all cultures. The church is celebrated as universal with respect to human cultures, for she is not tied or finally indebted to any one condition of humanity, being "gathered from all classes" and "of every nation" (Ursinus, *Comm. Heid. Catech.*:289).

Peter's vision of the mission of the church to the nations still pervades the cross-cultural Christian imagination: "I now realize how true it is that God does not show favoritism" but accepts those from every nation who "fear him and do what is right" (Acts 10:34, 35; Chrysostom, *Hom. on 1 Cor.* 8.4). Current egalitarian attempts to embody an "inclusive community" only faintly echo the ancient call to catholicity, because they so evidently lack historical awareness inclusive and respectful of past human cultures. This is particularly evident in faddist modern circles.

The mark of catholicity is that characteristic of the church that makes God's good news available to all and requires the church to patiently be heard by anyone who desires to listen (Augustine, *Letters*, FC 18:92). The people of the old covenant were born as progeny of Abraham. It was very difficult for one not born of a Jewish mother to become a Jew. Yet the Hebrew prophets looked for a time in which the covenant would be extended to all the nations, the Gentiles. That time came following the resurrection of Jesus.

Catholicity does not imply that the church's Eucharist is indiscriminately offered to all, including those who have not consented to her teaching or not undertaken her discipline. To offer baptism or Holy Communion to the impenitent would be to ignore discipline as essential to the nature and task of the church.

Those who enter the church by baptism do not thereby pretend to cease having a particular ethnic identity or race or culture or social class, though baptism brings one into a reborn and transmuted relation to all other races, ethnic identities, cultures, and classes. No one is required first to be baptized as a European or Asian in order to become a Christian. Christian baptism and community existed for several centuries before the cultural and national formation began of what we know today as Europe, which gained growing cohesion only after Charlemagne (after 800 AD). By that time the catholic nature of the church had been celebrated in prayers and confessed in baptism for many centuries.

Catholicity with Respect to Time and Place

Catholicity According to the Whole Scope of Time

The church embraces believers spread out over the past, present and future. To the church catholic belong all who have ever believed, now believe, and all who ever will believe in the saving work of the triune God. The church is celebrated as a whole community embracing all times. As far back as human time remembers (as with Adam, Eve, and Abel), some anticipating form of God's called out people have existed within human history through the flow of time. That is the temporal aspect of catholicity.

The church existed in the form of anticipatory belief before Abraham: "Hence there were besides, and before Abraham, other worshippers of the true God, whose priest Melchizedek was," all of whom belonged to the "one true Church of all times" (Ursinus, *Comm. Heid. Catech.*:290). Similarly forward in time yet unrealized: "And surely I am with you always, to the very end of the age" (Matt. 28:20).

The church is celebrated as universal with respect to its durability, transcending all specific, fleeting historical events and cultures, "because it will endure throughout every period of the world" (Ursinus, *Comm. Heid. Catech.*:290).

Catholicity According to Location Throughout the World

Since sent to every culture, the church is celebrated as universal with respect to place. Hence the church is catholic because it is not confined to any single local identity or culture, but dispersed over the entire globe.

In this respect the church is distinguished from the people of the old covenant. They received the inheritance of a particular *land*. The church is not a land but a fellowship that transcends all national and regional identities, all particular places (Augustine, *Answer to Letters of Petilian* 2.33–75). For this reason Paul is said to have preached to the "utmost bounds of the west" (Clement of Rome, *Corinth* 5), as far as anyone could imagine. "I hope to see you in passing as I go to Spain" (Rom. 15:23; Cyril of Jerusalem, *Catech. Lect.* 17.26). Early Syriac tradition finds Thomas in India.

The apostles were commissioned to make disciples of all nations, to baptize, and to teach all that Christ has commanded, with the promise that Christ would himself attend these ministries. "And this gospel of the kingdom will be preached in the whole world as a testimony to all nations" (Matt. 24:14; Chrysostom, *Hom. on Matt.* Hom. 75.2). The risen Lord empowered the church by the sending of the Spirit and commanded recipients to "be my witnesses in Jerusalem, and in all Judea and Samaria, and to the ends of the earth" (Acts 1:8).

It would be a mark of a false church if it failed to proclaim the word everywhere to all who would hear, just as much as if it failed to baptize in the triune name or teach the whole counsel of God. By that failure one could easily tell that the church was not acting "according to the whole" (*kath'olou*), hence not "catholic." Paul understood that "faith comes from hearing the message, and the message is heard through the word of Christ" (Rom. 10:17). This is why "their voice has gone out into all the earth, their words to the ends of the world" (Rom. 10:18, quoting Ps. 19:4). This need not be taken woodenly to mean that the church must be physically present in every square inch of the world, but as an aspiration and hope to be actualized in due time by the power of the Spirit.

The Donatists were rigorists in Numidian Africa who turned away from accountability to the general ecumenical church practice on the neuralgic question of penitential discipline after the persecutions. Augustine challenged them by asking them to explain why Christ "should suddenly be found surviving only in the Africans, and not in all of them? The Catholic Church exists indeed in Africa, since God willed and ordained that it should exist throughout the whole world. Whereas your party, which is called the party of Donatus, does not exist in all those places in which the writings of the apostles, their discourse, and their actions, have been current" (Augustine, *Letters* 49.3). Donatism did not pass the test of catholicity, however profound its beliefs were in other respects.

Since it is by definition worldwide, the church is constantly coming into being in particular historical situations. The church is celebrated as universal precisely with respect to its utterly variable locality, and the boundless particularity of its coming into being. Wherever Christian belief comes into community expression, the church exists in that place

Hence, *the church is rightly called catholic insofar as it does not cease to be universal in scope, even while planting itself concretely within a particular local community.* The universal church expresses itself as a particular congregation when local believers assemble to share the good news, hear the word of scripture interpreted, and share in fellowship with the living Lord. The local church may, while holding to catholic teaching, adapt to local conditions without losing its catholicity (Leo IX, *Symbol of Faith*, SCD 343–50).

Tolerance, Perpetuity, and Fallibility

All the features described above display catholicity when taken together. But has the one, holy, catholic church ever actually come into being, appeared in actual history, in this classic sense of the term catholic? Has an actual "catholic ethos" ever emerged to express the ideally envisioned catholicity of the whole church? Never since Pentecost has the church been wholly lacking in catholic ethos, though the level of responsiveness of particular communities of faith to the wholeness of the Holy Spirit varies widely from time to time. The church's catholicity does not depend upon its ability to express every aspect of every culture in every place, but rather upon expressing the apostolic teaching in every place it finds a hearing.

Adaptability, Tolerance, and Centeredness
as Evidences of Catholicity

The notion of catholicity was from the outset destined to have complementary layers of meanings. Three additional nuances of the term catholic are recurrently interwoven in Christian history: cross-cultural adaptability, the temperament of patient tolerance, and centered orthodoxy.

The word *catholic* has fittingly taken on the meaning of inclusive, *cross-cultural adaptability*. Since orthodoxy is called and sent into every cultural context, it has at its best become exceptionally adept at movement from one language to another, one political sphere to another, one economic system to another, without feeling a compulsive need to subvert each and every culture it enters (Eusebius, *HCCC* 3:71–154).

Out of this history of cultural adaptability, the adjective *catholic* has recurrently taken on the meaning of *a temperament of patient tolerance*. Since the church is called and sent into every cultural context, it has engendered tolerance toward cultural varieties wherever it has remained most true to its catholic mission. Admittedly the church at times has been intolerant and unfair toward some, but just to that extent has it lacked the characteristic of catholicity that remains a mark of the true church (Eph. 4:2; Chrysostom, *Hom. on Eph.* 9.4.1–3; Phil. 4:6).

Meanwhile outspoken advocates of hypertolerance and the rhetoric of absolute relativism have committed demeaning acts of intolerance, chauvinism, and cultural ethnocentrism—sometimes in the very name of toleration. The deeper source of the church's tolerance, however, is not Enlightenment optimism about human nature or Stoic assumptions about the universality of reason or simplistic egalitarianism or the abstract visions of utopian idealism. Rather catholic tolerance is grounded directly in the gospel of God's love for all. It is gentle and patient because it seeks to reflect God's own gentleness and patience (Gal. 5:23; Eph. 4:32; Col. 3:12; 1 Tim. 6:11).

Precisely amid this history of adaptability and caring tolerance, the adjective *catholic* has steadily borne the meaning of *centered orthodoxy*. The catholicity of the church does not move from culture to culture simply by cheap accommodation, but by being itself, by sustaining its own distinctive identity and norms while entering empathically even into what might otherwise seem to be alien cultural situations. The history of orthodoxy is not characterized by cultural rigidity, but astonishing flexibility and openness to cultural variety (Matt. 28:19; John 4; Acts 1:8).

Catholicity does not imply vagueness or indecisiveness. It remains the guardian of its own sacred deposit of truth (Council of Lyons II, 461–66; Vincent of Lérins, *Commonitory*, 21–25). Hence catholicity does not mean simply all those who call themselves Christian regardless of their lack of other tests of the church such as holiness and apostolicity. It is a mistake to yield the term *catholic* to a particular group or tradition or political party or denomination, as if it is an idea that pious Christians might get along without. As *evangelical* is a term that deserves to be reclaimed by the orthodox liturgical traditions, so *catholic* is a term that deserves to be reclaimed by evangelical traditions (Baxter, *The True Catholick*).

It is not uncommon for accommodators of culture who reject classic consensual Christian teaching to desire nevertheless to use the church instrumentally to legitimize their own idiosyncratic biases. When the *ekklēsia* allows itself to be used in this fashion, it is not being catholic and is not contending for the catholic faith. Those who assert personal opinions as if they were consensual catholic teaching abuse catholicity. Subjective experiences or individual opinions can never be the sole criterion of catholicity unless informed by consensual teachings that meet scriptural tests. It is a deceptive use of *catholic* that takes advantage of the good-will of a proximately tolerant and adaptable church to superimpose upon that idea teachings that are inimical to the church.

Whether the Mark of Catholicity May Be Found in a Separate Church Body

This note is written especially for readers who have struggled with whether their own tradition meets the tests of oneness, holiness, catholicity, and apostolicity I have been discussing. Specifically some may have difficulty imagining how or why I could remain committed to my own received church tradition, given the features of consensual Christianity I have described.

This question may be put to anyone of any denomination: Is it even possible that a particular church body or denomination could display the essential mark of catholicity? Though I am seeking honestly to present the ancient ecumenical tradition within the postmodern situation, it would be foolish to deny that I view these issues through the lens of a matrix of particular church traditions. I wish here to make a modest comment on my own particular church tradition, which I identify in a somewhat lighthearted way under the hyphenated phrase Ancient Ecumenical-Anglican-Wesleyan (or more straightforwardly in the lower case "catholic evangelical"), without any pretense that it is normative for other traditions.

Despite occasional myopias of the Anglican evangelical tradition (like excessive optimism, doctrinal latitudinarianism, compulsive pragmatism, class insensitivities, and recurrent softheadedness) it has one feature that I particularly value: irenic-conserving realism. Wherever revolutionary fanaticism approaches, it finds itself nurtured by a deeply ingrained conservative instinct that tempers the wildness of revolutionary fantasies. It seeks change incrementally rather than abruptly or coercively. The broad flow of English political history may be described as a series of compromises and halfway measures that moderated problems gradually but seldom resolved them completely, that made modest adjustments but resisted absolute, abstract, rationalistic, and radical visions of total change (Edmund Burke, *Reflections on the Revolution in France*; J. H. Blunt, *Reformation of the Church of England*). Continuity and free consent and diversity have been highly valued in this tradition (F. W. Puller, *Continuity of the English Church; Our Place in Christendom*; F. Hall, *Historical Position of the Episcopal Church*). This has kept the English Reformation relatively more in touch with its patristic, catholic, and medieval roots than that of the continental Reformed tradition.

There remained within the Anglican *eirēnikon* (the way of peacemaking between many parties) a deep commitment to catholicity, held together especially by a common tradition of prayer (*BCP*; J. Wand, ed., *The Anglican Communion*; More and Cross, eds. *Angl.*; S. Niell, *Anglicanism*). The assumption was that theological differences that did not require a break with the liturgy would run their own course and find fitting resolution through the guidance of the Spirit. By this means the rule of prayer (*lex orandi*) would fittingly correspond with the rule of faith (*lex credendi*). There remained much room for varied opinions, and on the whole a spirit of comparative toleration was engendered. Excessive elasticity (latitudinarianism tending toward indifferentism) was always the peril of the English Church spirit. But the unity of the great diversity was premised on the assumption that the Holy Spirit has remained at work to preserve and unite the church and overrule exaggerated loyalties and providentially hedge the ways of sin. The Vincentian appeal to antiquity and catholicity became the shaping principle of the Anglican reformation (Hall, *DT* 8:230).

If this tradition has been strong in emphasizing unity, antiquity, freedom, diversity, and toleration, it has at times become less robust in rigorous exegesis and systematic teaching of Christian doctrine. It has simultaneously fostered both the growth of the modern ecumenical spirit and the gradual deterioration of ancient ecumenical teaching. This tradition has welcomed and encouraged historical biblical criticism and scientific inquiry, but itself has fallen prey to modern chauvinism and base accommodations to modernity. Although the Anglican ethos has intermittently sought to walk the way of holiness and taught Christian perfection and the assurance of the Spirit, it has seldom shown the sort of strength in classic Christian teaching that has been so characteristic of the Reformed tradition of dissenting Protestantism or of Eastern Orthodox or Roman Catholic traditions. My own Wesleyan evangelical branch of the Anglican tradition, despite many failures, still forms a useful bridge between evangelical Protestants and faithful Catholics, while maintaining deep theological and disciplinary affinities with the Eastern Church tradition. The Anglican evangelical tradition remains quietly very catholic and ecumenical in teaching and discipline, holding to the teaching of scripture, the primitive church, the rule of faith summed up in the creeds and affirmed by the undisputed Ecumenical Councils (J. Wesley, *Letter to C. Middleton*, *WJW* 10:1–79; R. T. Davidson, ed., *The Lambeth Conferences*), and to the Reformation teaching of justification by grace through faith. Its modest claim to share in the church catholic is nothing other than that Word and Sacrament have not been abandoned, nor have ancient conciliar formulations. Its method has remained intuitively Vincentian even when Vincent had been largely forgotten, stressing consensual themes of the faith of ancient conciliar Christianity, tending until recently to regard special fads and specializations and doctrinal systems as passing developments lacking official standing or absolute authority. Like Anglicans, the Wesleyan families of evangelicals have never been quite willing to sanction a single partisan viewpoint in theology, yet have continued to affirm the Apostles' Creed and celebrate a predominantly Cranmerian (which is largely an ancient catholic) liturgy and a hymnody that much of Christendom continues to sing.

When I despair over modern Protestant quasi-apostasies and dilutions, I have imagined myself walking ambivalently down the road toward Rome or Alexandria or Antioch, but in more realistic moments I feel deeply grateful to have been nurtured by my own church tradition, which effectively bequeathed to me some of the essential marks of catholicity even while bearing many scars and warts of pietistic individualism. I hope this low-keyed, critical celebration of my own church tradition does not annoy Lutherans or Baptists or Roman Catholics or charismatics who may have their own reasons for feeling uneasy about such reasoning. My purpose here remains steady: that of articulating a classic ecclesiology wherein each of these valued partners in dialogue might see their own tradition as rooted in the ancient ecumenical tradition.

The Promise of Perpetuity, Imperishability, Indefectibility

God will not be left without witnesses in the world (Acts 14:17). The one, holy, universal church is promised imperishable continuance, even if particular churches or local bodies or denominations may fail or atrophy. Her future finally is not left to human willing or chance, but to grace.

Many branches of the seasonally changing vine may drop off or become dysfunctional and atrophy, but the church itself will be preserved till the end of the age (Heidegger, *Med.* 26.11). The destiny of the church is eternally secure. Though individuals may fall, and even whole communities lose their bearings during particular periods, the church will be preserved (John 16:6, 13; Augustine, *Tractates on John* 99.4). "One holy Christian church will be and remain forever" (Augsburg *Conf.* 7).

Meanwhile the church continues to be vulnerable to those hazards that accompany historical existence generally. The Holy Spirit does not abandon the church amid these earthly struggles but supplies that grace of perseverance by which the church is enabled to remain Christ's living body even while being challenged by forgetfulness, heresy, apostasy, persecution, and schism. The church will be preserved to "proclaim the Lord's death until he comes" (1 Cor. 11:26).

Against the church "the gates of hell shall not prevail" (Matt. 16:18; Luke 1:33; 1 Tim. 3:15). This means that the church will *never decline into total forgetfulness*, because guided by the Spirit, who is promised always to accompany and remind the church (John 14:16; Matt. 23:20; Basil, *On the Holy Spirit* 18.46–47), even when the church fails to listen. The church insofar as she is guided by the Spirit does not fall entirely away from the fundamental truth or into irretrievable error. She is preserved by grace, not by human craft or design (Matt. 7:25).

Despite temporary apostasies, it is unthinkable that God would allow the church finally to become absolutely and continuously apostate or to lose all touch with the righteousness that Christ has once for all bestowed upon her. "For you have been born again, not of perishable seed, but of imperishable, through the living and enduring word of God. For 'All men are like grass,' " but " 'the word of the Lord stands forever.' And this is the word that was preached to you" (1 Pet. 1:23–25; Bede, *On 1 Pet.* 1.23; Calvin, *Comm.* 22:57–60). The promise of indefectibility is not addressed to a particular congregation or denomination or generation or family of churches or passing period of history, but rather the whole church to preserve her from fundamental error in the long course of history—to the end (Matt. 28:20; *Longer Catech.*, Eastern Orthodox Church, 271).

It is promised to the called out people of God that they shall endure until the end of time. Insofar as the faithful are sustained by pure Word and Sacrament, adhering to the "faith once delivered," their sacrifice is received by God as faultless (Ambrose, *Six Days of Creation* 4.2, 7; Chrysostom, *Two Homilies on Eutropius* 52; *Confession of Dositheus* 10–12). The church "does not err, so long as it relies upon the rock Christ, and upon the foundation of the prophets and apostles" (Second Helvetic *Conf.*, *CC*:143). Though particular assemblies may lapse, relapse, or collapse, because of the Spirit's guidance the elect people of God "cannot wholly wander away or fall from salvation" (F. Burmann, *Synopsis Theologiae* 7.1.25), for all those called will not be allowed to err at the same time.

It seems unlikely that God would create the church at great cost only to let it fall finally into permanent or irremediable error. God's final victory at the end of history is a teaching of the power of the Holy Spirit, and not merely of the self-sufficiency or wisdom of the church as such (Calvin, *Inst.* 4.1). Jesus promised that the Holy Spirit would remain steadily present to "teach you all things and will remind you of everything I have said to you" (John 14:26). That community which is being called by the Holy Spirit will not be found falling irretrievably into apostasy. That would make it impossible for all subsequent generations to hear the good news. Yet this does not imply that the church is secure from making mistakes or errors of judgment.

Always some seed of faith remains buried in the ashes even of the most divided and corrupt church. Yet wherever Word and Sacrament are being transmitted and delivered, they are never without some effect, for "my word" shall "not return to me empty, but will accomplish what I desire" (Isa. 55:11), says the Lord (Second Helvetic *Conf. CC*:148; 1 Kings 19:18; Rev. 7:4, 9; Jerome, *Comm. on Is.* 15.16). The foundation is standing sure and the Lord knows who are his (2 Tim. 2:9), as we have recently rediscovered in the church in China during the Cultural Revolution, and Russia after the failed coup of 1991.

Fallibility Within the Historic Church

Redemption occurs through a process in which sinners are brought into a sphere in which long-habituated sins can be gradually reconciled and transformed (Luke 5:31; Bede, *Hom. on Gospels* 1.21). It is fallible and sinful persons who are the recipients of God's saving grace—for the healthy do not need a physician (Mark 2:17). As long as the church exists within the conditions of the history of sin, the church will be prone to being distorted and will be vulnerable to some who wish to use it for their own purposes. Until the consummation of salvation history, when the incurably wicked will be cut off from the living vine, the called out people will be subject to temptation (Ps. 37).

To flee from the scene of human failures would be to flee from the church's own direct arena of mission. Insofar as it is truly the body of Christ living in faith, hope, and love under the life-giving power of the Spirit, the church can never become absolutely or finally corrupted (Matt. 16:18).

Among diseases of the history of sin that continue to challenge, tempt, and plague the church and resist its full growth are the partisan spirit that would divide it, the heretical spirit that would lead it to distort or forget apostolic teaching, the antinomian spirit that turns Christian liberty into libertinism, the legalistic spirit that would turn grace into law, and the contemptuous spirit that would treat grace as a determinant of nature. Despite these challenges—which are permitted by a kind providence to strengthen the church and enable it to grow stronger—the body lives on, the vine sends forth new shoots, the Spirit enlivens and heals, the Head continues to guide and order the whole organism (John 15:1–5; Col. 1:18; Irenaeus, *Ag. Her.* 3.20.2).

The continuing renewal of the worshiping community never comes by avoiding or excluding sinners, for their redemption is the reason the church exists. Clean-hands purists of all periods tend to flee the task of serving sinners, unlike Jesus who mixed it up with the best and worst of them, ate and drank with those most despicable and rejected, and finally identified with all sinners on the cross.

The Consent of the Whole Laity as
Evidence of Catholicity

Caucus-oriented special interest politics, which so harmfully pervades modern church life, tends to undermine the spirit of catholicity in the church. While the caucus is fixated upon particular special interests, catholicity is struggling to embody the whole and ensure the health of the commonweal. The caucus mentality has gained temporary political purchase precisely amid an ethos in which catholicity was being outwardly praised but practically neglected.

The ecumenical councils and major consensual teachers attest ultimate victory of the church as a gift of grace to the whole church in due time (Council of Nicaea I, *SCD* 54; Athanasius et al., *To the Bishops of Africa* 1–6; Basil, *Letters* 114, 13; Gregory of Nazianzus, *On the Great Athanasius*, *Orat.* 21; Cyril, *Letters* 39, 76). The patristic exegetes assented to the councils as evidence of the assent of the whole church. It is this universal consent that is said to be reliable, and finally assured when tested by general lay assent over time.

The consent of the whole *laos* is given as an evidence and external criterion of the ecumenical hope. The Holy Spirit does not introduce novel, postapostolic doctrine through the conciliar process, but rather acts to illuminate and guard from error the ancient and continuing apostolate. This effort is not mechanically forced by the Spirit, but works in a normal human manner through debate, inquiry, parliamentary deliberation, voting, and the apparatus of policy formation (Acts 28:23; Chrysostom, *Hom. on Acts* 55; Merrill, *ACE*:249).

Pascal pictured Christianity as a thousand times having appeared to be "on the point of universal destruction, and every time that it has been in this condition, God has raised it up by some extraordinary stroke of his power" (*Pensées*, in Jacobs, *SCF*:377). Each seeming defeat readies the community for a deeper level of understanding. Each apparent victory readies the community for a deeper level of conflict.

Today, amid the failures of modern ecumenism, the moral catastrophes of broadcast ministries, the growing secularization of the church—all embarrassing, persistent facts—it would seem that the church is once again profoundly imperiled. But just in the midst of these facts, the Spirit works quietly to restore the church to its intrinsic oneness, holiness, universality, and apostolicity.

The Fourth Mark: Apostolicity

The church is not a group of people groping for a philosophy of life congenial to modern conditions, but a living body already being shaped by apostolic teaching. Holding steady to that teaching is a principal mark of the authenticity of the church.

Apostolicity is intrinsically interwoven with the other marks of the church: Only that church that is one can be catholic. Only that church that is united in the one mission of the one Lord can be apostolic. Lacking that holiness which is fitting to the obedience of faith, one finds neither apostolicity nor catholicity. Only that church that is formed by the apostolic memory is united in one body with the Lord.

The Sent Ones

The church is apostolic insofar as it retains, guards, and faithfully transmits its apostolic mission. Those sent by the Son are the apostolate. As Christ was sent by the Father, the apostles were sent by the Son and empowered by the Spirit, The continuing apostolate is still being sent (John 20:21; Cyprian, *Treatises* 1; Lactantius, *Of the Manner in Which the Persecutors Died* 1,2).

"As the Father has sent me, I am sending you" (John 20:21). "When the time had fully come, God sent his son" (Gal. 4:4). Jesus is the model of the *apostle*, the one sent. "Therefore, holy brothers, who share in the heavenly calling, fix your thoughts on Jesus, the apostle" (Heb. 3:1). Jesus is apostle in the sense of being commissioned and authorized by God the Father and sent into the world (Luther, *Lectures on Heb*).

The time of the apostolate begins with the resurrection and ends only with the Lord's return. The commission is to make disciples, baptizing and teaching "to the very end of the age," knowing that the Son is "with you always" by the power of the Spirit (Matt. 28:19, 20), who will "guide you into all truth" (John 16:13) and empower the apostolic mission (Acts 1:8).

The church does not merely *have* a mission; it *is* a mission—the historical embodiment of the mission of the Son through the Spirit. The church does not elicit mission, but rather mission elicits, awakens, and empowers the church. God's mission (*missio dei*) embraces all that the church is and does in its life in the world. This called out community has a key role to play in the history of the emerging reign of God (Matt. 13; 2 Tim. 1:1–14; Heb. 12:22–28).

The Calling and Sending of the Twelve

After praying to the Father, the Son called to himself those whom he wished to assist him in his work. He sent them to preach the good news of the kingdom (Mark 3:13–19; Matt. 10:1–42; Jerome, *Comm. on Matt.* 1.9.37), first to Israel, and then to all nations (Rom. 1:16). The Spirit was promised to supply them with gifts of ministry (Matt. 28:16–20; Mark 16:15; John 20:21–23; Eph. 4). They were confirmed in their mission on the day of Pentecost (Acts 2:1–26), in accord with Christ's promise that they would receive power when the Spirit came, and would be his witness to the ends of the earth (Acts 1:8).

Jesus' call to discipleship is best viewed in relation to his last Supper with his disciples, which constituted a new covenant, a new exodus, a new People of God. The narratives of Jesus' call to discipleship (Mark 1:16–20; Matt. 4:18–22) were formed in the pattern of Yahweh's call of persons to special mission under the old covenant (Abraham, Moses, David, leaders and prophets; Gen. 22:15; Exod. 19:3; 2 Kings 3:10–13; Joel 2:32).

The calling of the apostles was sealed and confirmed by the resurrection. Only after the earthly ministry was completed could the apostles be duly authorized and commissioned to attest Christ's work, illumined by his resurrection (Matt. 28:18–20; Acts 1:8; Chrysostom, *Hom. on Acts 2*). The term *apostle* was applied not exclusively to the Twelve but also to Barnabas (1 Cor. 9:5, 6), Junias and Andronicus (Rom. 16:7), Apollos (1 Cor. 4:6, 9), and others, yet it was typically exemplified by the Twelve.

The very purpose of the coming together of the community is in order that they may be fully prepared to be sent. They come together to receive grace, and scatter to declare grace. They gather to hear the Word of God's reconciling love for the fallen world, and depart to embody that love within that world. The church exists for the purpose of the apostolate. The faithful now scattered in the world are to be finally gathered in the world to come (Ezek. 34:11–16; Matt. 26:31; John 16:17–33; *Didache* 9–10).

Apostolic Authorization

Jesus did not passively wait for a miscellany of disciples to choose him. He actively called and selected them. The relation he established with them was not characteristically focused upon his interpretation of Torah as such (as was typical of the relation of rabbi and disciple) but upon his person. He formed the disciples into a unique community of persons in communion with his distinctive divine-human personhood (Irenaeus, *Ag. Her.* 3.preface, 1). He transferred his authority to the apostles in amazingly direct terms: "He who listens to you listens to me; he who rejects you rejects me" (Luke 10:16; cf. John 15:20).

The institution of apostolic emissaries reported by Luke (6:13; 9:10–12; 22:3, 14, 47; Acts 6:2; Arator, On the Acts 1) had its roots in the Old Testament (2 Chron. 17:7–9). The Greek verb *apostello* translates the Hebrew *shalach* (to send). A *shaliach* is the directly authorized agent of another, assigned to a specific task, authorized to engage precisely in a special service or mission (Mark 3:14; 6:7; 11:11; Matt. 10:1–5; 11:1).

The Twelve were chosen by Jesus, prepared by him, and sent by him. They accompanied him throughout his journeys, and were initiated by him into the mysteries of the coming kingdom (Mark 3:34). Some accompanied him to the Mount of Transfiguration. They were present at the farewell paschal meal.

The number twelve had special significance analogous to the twelve tribes descending from the twelve patriarchs (Matt. 19:28; Acts 26:7) whose restoration was expected in the messianic time. The twelve patriarchs prefigured the new community of faith, the new covenant, the restoration of Israel. When Judas, one of the original Twelve, fell away, he was quickly replaced so that the number of first-generation apostles would again be complete (Acts 1:12–26). The Twelve were sent out to proclaim the coming kingdom, heal, cleanse lepers, drive out demons (Mark 6:7–13; Matt. 10:5–8).

Accurate Remembering as a Defining Mark of the Church

Apostolicity remains a defining mark of the church of each generation (Council of 680, Rome; Leo IX, *Symbol of Faith*, SCD 347; Council of Lyons II, SCD 464–68). The most direct way to test the evidence of whether the attestors bear true or false witness is by asking whether their testimony is apostolic, whether it teaches what the apostles taught (Gal. 1:8, 9; Jerome, *Letters* 84). Those who purport to be Christian teachers but bear testimony contrary to apostolic teaching fail to display a distinctive mark that defines the church. An alleged *ekklēsia* that lacks the mark of apostolicity might continue to live parasitically off of the vital residual wisdoms of the apostolic tradition while ignoring that tradition practically (Irenaeus, *Ag. Her.* 3.1–4).

The apostolic witness is described by Paul as the pillar and ground of the truth (1 Tim. 3:15), i.e., God's own appointed means of upholding Christian truth in the world. Christ entrusted the keys of discipline to the apostles and their successors, authorized their great commission, and sent the Spirit to empower their mission (Matt. 16:19; Tertullian, *Prescription Ag. Her.* 20, 32). That church is apostolic which "has been transmitted to us by the Apostles and their duly consecrated successors" (*Eastern Orthodox Catechism* 194).

None were chosen in the first generation of the apostolate without having accompanied Jesus personally during his entire earthly journey (Acts 1:21, 22), and without having met the risen Lord, and without being personally commissioned by him to testify to him (Luke 24:48; Acts 13:31; 2:32; 3:15; 10:39–43). These elements were considered constitutive of the first generation of the apostolate, whose recollection subsequent generations of the apostolate would scrupulously transmit.

Eyewitness Testimony Requires Faithful, Accurate Transmission

Accurate recollection of apostolic testimony was understood to be ensured by the guidance of the Holy Spirit. Subsequent generations of witnesses are perennially pledged and bound to recall accurately the salvation event as received (Gal. 1:19, 20; 1 Thess. 2:7; Ambrosiaster, *Comm. on Paul*, 1 Cor. 9:1, 2). A direct eyewitness to an unrepeatable event depends upon the Spirit to conserve and sustain the integrity and truthfulness of the previous eyewitnesses.

All Christian testimony and experience stands in this spirit-led succession (Origen, *First Principles*, preface). The disciples at second hand (non-eyewitnesses) do not receive a new, separable, improved, or different revelation but attest to the original revelation centered on the events of cross and resurrection and upon personal meeting with the one mediator. The task of the apostolic successor is not to improve upon the message or embellish it or add to it one's own spin or personal tilt or idiosyncratic twist, but rather simply to remember and attest it accurately, credibly, intelligibly, contextually.

To assist in correct remembering, the Holy Spirit has enabled the apostolic testimony to be written down in a canonically received body of writings ecumenically received by lay consent as normative apostolic teaching. Amid each cultural variation, subsequent apostolic witnesses are solemnly pledged and bound to the apostolic canon as norm of Christian teaching. By the end of the first century, that norm included at least the four gospels and the Pauline letters. Paul made a distinction between his own opinions, which were to be duly considered, and those received from the apostles, which were to be obeyed (1 Cor. 1:1; 4:1–7; 7:12, 40).

Antiquity and Apostolicity

Antiquity and apostolicity are closely intertwined criteria (Vincent of Lérins, *Commonitory*, 27–33). For how could the apostolic message be adequate if it only reached back a generation, lacking eyewitness roots? To be apostolic, the apostolic tradition must date back to the written record of the earliest eyewitnessing attestors of God's own coming. The authenticity of this testimony is preserved by the Spirit through canon and scriptural preaching and through disciplined sacramental integrity.

The appeal to apostolicity is by definition an appeal to antiquity in the Christian tradition. The appeal to novelty is forever tempted to *hairesis*, an alternative choice different from the prevailing apostolic tradition (Tertullian, *Prescription Ag. Her.* 4–6; Vincent of Lérins, *Comm.* 4–10). Contrary to modern assumptions, that which is closest to apostolic testimony is truest, since Christianity is grounded in eyewitness testimony (Tertullian, *Ag. Marcion* 4.5).

Paul viewed his own apostolate as inseparable from the pre-Pauline tradition, as is evident from his own admonition: "But even if we, or an angel from heaven, should preach to you a gospel contrary to that which we preached to you, let him be accursed" (Gal. 1:8). Paul did not invent a new gospel. His gospel was an clarification of pre-Pauline teaching of the Jerusalem church, which he viewed as the binding norm for his own mission and proclamation (Gal. 1:13–20; 2:2; 1 Cor. 11:23–29; 15:5). He delivered to the Corinthians the tradition he had received from the pre-Pauline apostolate: that Christ died for our sin, was buried, was raised, and appeared "to all the apostles." "Last of all, as to one untimely born, he appeared also to me. For I am the least of the apostles, unfit to be called an apostle, because I persecuted the church of God" (1 Cor. 15:7–9). Though Paul did not accompany Jesus throughout his earthly ministry, he did meet him personally on the road to Damascus. Paul understood himself to be an apostle directly called by the risen Lord (Gal. 1:1; Cassiodorus, *Sum. of Gal.* 1.1.1). Paul's apostolate was specifically directed to the Gentiles, whereas the pre-Pauline apostolate had been largely addressed to the Jews (Acts 15). The apostles affirmed Paul's commission to the Gentiles (Gal. 2:7). Paul demonstrated his loyalty to the Jerusalem church by collecting for its poor (Rom. 15:26–28; 1 Cor. 16:1–3; Ambrosiaster, *Comm. on Paul 2* Cor. 8:1–7) and by returning for major feast days (Acts 18:21; 20:16).

Adaptability Without Dilution

The apostolate guards the original testimony without ceasing to apply it meaningfully to the context of local and prevailing conditions. Contemporary preaching must occur in a particular language using available culture-specific symbol systems, yet without ceasing to affirm the original apostolic teaching (2 Cor. 4:7–12; Origen, *OFP* 4.1).

As with catholicity, apostolicity does not imply a lack of adaptability to varied culture formations. Rather it is the opposite: a willingness to enter into the ever-changing language of a given human culture in time and proclaim the unchanging gospel. The proficiency of the apostolic tradition is precisely its ability to meet, flexibly confront, and dialogue with different cultures, to become all things to all men and women on behalf of Christ. Apostolicity is not incapable of responsiveness, but attests a living body of Christ that inhabits each new form of cultural life emergent in human history (Eph. 2:19—3:1).

Because histories change people, and because the apostolic testimony must be attested in ever-new historical situations, it is a necessary feature of the apostolic tradition that it both guard the original testimony and make it understandable in these new cultural settings (Irenaeus, *Ag. Her.* 3.3).

Apostolicity and Succession

Intrinsically connected with the idea of apostolicity is that of succession, since the church is a historical community flowing through time yet sustaining its identity in Christ through time. The affirmation of apostolicity does not specifically require or supply a particular theory of how that apostolicity is transmitted intergenerationally, but it must be transmitted in a reliable way (Didache 11.1, 2; 13.2; 15.1).

From the day of Pentecost onward the disciples "continued steadfastly in the apostles' doctrine and fellowship" (Acts 2:42). The implication is that the continuing church holds the same doctrines that the apostles taught, as witnesses chosen, claimed, and addressed personally by the Lord (2 Tim. 1:12–14). The early church teachers challenged the heretics to produce their own lists of direct succession of *episkopoi* in such a way as to make it clear that their predecessors were in direct succession to the apostles who accurately reported the events of God's saving work in the Son. The principle: That which is truest in Christian teaching is closest in time and spirit to the apostles. What is later tends to be distorted or adulterated by subsequent spin (Tertullian, *Ag. Praxeas* 2, 20).

This apostolic teaching is sufficient for salvation, and remains pertinent to each successive historical period without addition, modification, or imagined improvement. The church is apostolic insofar as it stands in historic continuity with this primitive *ekklēsia* (Eph. 2:20; Rev. 21:14; Matt. 16:18; Jerome, *Ag. Jovian* 1.26; Augustine, *Exposition on Psalms*, Ps. 86; Gregory the Great, *Moralia on Job* 28.5).

Succession and Canon

Christianity adopted from Judaism the practice of defining a canon, which means simply a list of sacred writings that are consensually received by the worshiping community as authorized teaching and reliable recollections of the history of revelation (Irenaeus, *Ag. Her.* 3.2.2–4; Tertullian, *Prescription Ag. Her.* 19; Eusebius, *CH* 5.20.6; Synod of Laodicea). "They are read in congregations so that they may be believed, but they would not be read unless they were believed" (Augustine, *City of God*, 22.8).

Problems of interpretation emerged when alternative interpreters used the
same words of scripture but with different, nonconsensual meanings. This necessitated a conciliar process that sorted out consensual meanings from arbitrary
interpretations (Athanasius, *Defense of the Nicene Council*). A criterion had to be
found to show that the heretics had no legitimate right to distort the scriptures
(Tertullian, *Prescription Ag. Her.* 15–19; cf. Irenaeus, *Ag. Her.* 1.8–10), though
each of their distortions would prove providential in clarifying the mind of the
believing church. The core criterion was liturgical: the baptismal formula as
summarily explicated in the rule of faith and further interpreted by ecumenical
conciliar consent, all of which were finally accountable to the written word of
apostolic testimony.

The church hears the testimony to the resurrection only through the apostolic
tradition. There is no other pathway back to the risen Lord that might bypass
the apostles and their faithful successors (Jude 17). There is no apostolic witness without the church's canon and transmission of apostolic writings. Credible
church traditions emerge only as applications and interpretations of the apostolic
witness.

It is primarily the whole consenting church, not discrete individuals alone, that
succeeds the apostles and embodies apostolicity. It is the whole church catholic
and not merely a fragment of it that is the temple of the Spirit, built on the foundation of the apostles (Eph. 2:20; Marius Victorinus, *Epis. to Eph.* 1.2.20).

The ancient Christian exegetes consensually taught that the most condensed
expression of apostolic teaching was the ancient baptismal confession that could
be traced directly to Christ himself (Matt. 28:19–20; Irenaeus, *Ag. Her.* 3.preface;
Tertullian, *Prescription Ag. Her.* 20, 21). This became the core of *the rule of faith*
that later became the received text of the Apostles' Creed.

In order to authenticate this core, it was found useful to clarify the unbroken succession of overseers in the "mother churches," especially in Rome and
Antioch, where believers from all over had gathered early under Pauline and
Petrine leadership (Hegisippus, in Eusebius *CH* 4.22.1–3; Irenaeus, *Ag. Her.* 3.3;
5.20.1), and in Alexandria where the apostolic teaching harkened back to the
Markan tradition. "And so the churches, many and great as they are, are identical with that one primitive Church issuing from the Apostles, for from them they
are all derived. So all are primitive and all apostolic, while all are one. And their
unity is proved by the peace they share" (Tertullian, *Prescription Ag. Her.* 20).
Since the apostles had a unified witness, subsequent church unity depends on
their unity, blessed by Christ himself. This concern for historic succession was intensified by the challenge of Gnosticism in the second century, which threatened
to rob the church of her distinctive baptismal language and add strange views to
her sacred texts (Apostolic Constitutions 7.4.4).

Shepherding the Historic Succession

The apostles passed this ministry to the next generation, and that generation
passed it to the next, and so on, to fulfill this ministry in each succeeding historical
situation in perpetuity and without interruption until the Lord's return. The
necessity of some sort of succession to the apostles grows out of the continuing
temporal nature of the apostolic commission, which is promised to extend "to the
very end of the age" (Matt. 28:20; Origen, *Ag. Celsus* 5.12). It assumes the finitude
and physical death of all particular personal witnesses.

It might seem that the authentication of the ministry of any succeeding generation would depend entirely upon the faithfulness and accountability and accurate testimony of generations bridging from the original Twelve. This leads to the

anxiety that each generation of Christian memory might be only one generation from extinction. But this anxiety tends to forget the promise of the Spirit and to remember only human forgetfulness. Rather, the continuity depends upon the continuing calling and awakening work of the Spirit.

The apostolate does not seize this testimony as if a matter to be constantly remolded in human hands. It only speaks in response to God's own speech, learning obedience by suffering as did the Son (Heb. 5:8; Phil. 2). "No one takes this honor upon himself; he must be called by God, just as Aaron was. So Christ also did not take upon himself the glory of becoming a high priest. But God said to him, 'You are my Son,' " who "although he was a son, he learned obedience from what he suffered" (Heb. 5:4, 5, 8; Chrysostom, *On Epis. to Heb.* 8.3; Calvin, *Comm.* 22:116–19).

The linear act of historical succession as such does not of itself suffice to guarantee authentic testimony, otherwise every minister ordained in the historical succession of the apostles would have been faithful to the apostolic witness, and this is not the case (Augustine, *Correction of the Donatists, NPNF* 1 4:633–51). Rather, to the historical succession must be added the grace of accurate recollection and obedience to the original apostolic testimony, and the grace-enabled determination to guard and transmit it without novel accretions or substitutions. An ambassador duly authorized and sent on behalf of an official authority who changes the message en route, who revises, innovates, or substitutes or supposedly improves upon the meaning of the original message so that it means something else, is not a faithful ambassador (Gal. 1:1–10; 2 Cor. 5:20).

What the apostolate is to the universal church, the eldership (*presbuteroi*) is to the regional and local church, typically assuming the *episkopos* as a type or paradigm of the shepherding Christ (John 10:1–16; 1 Tim. 3:2; 1 Pet. 2:25; Ignatius, *Trallians* 2.1; 3.1; *Magnesians* 2; 6.1; *Smyrnaeans* 8.1). Every genuine local expression of the Christian community is a refraction that mirrors the whole body of Christ in time and eternity (Ignatius, *Magnesians* 3.2; *Rom.* 9:1).

Ordination and Apostolicity

The received means of passing on an intergenerational ministry is by the laying on of hands with prayer by the power of the Spirit. This is a mark of apostolicity typically enacted ritually by the tactile laying on of hands in due order. Its practice requires the due transmission of apostolic teaching. The act of ordination points beyond itself to the promise of transmitting the sacred deposit of faith to succeeding generations (2 Tim. 1:14; Irenaeus, *Ag. Her.* 3.4).

This guarding and transmitting activity is entrusted typically to the *episkopoi* (Ignatius of Antioch, *Eph.* 6; Hooker, *LEP* 7.4). This is why the apostasy of a bishop is so heartrending for the whole laity. The *presbuteroi* (elders) have specific responsibilities in implementing this discipling locally under the guidance of the *episkopos*. It is finally to the whole lay apostolate that the transmitting action is committed, of whom the *episkopoi* are representative servants voluntarily pledged to sustain apostolic teaching.

In ordination the church prays for grace to transmit the apostolic witness as promised, according to the canon of scripture. Just as healthy parents may give birth to a genetically disabled or impeded child, so may the church inadvertently ordain defective ministers.

If it happens that the word is not preached adequately or the sacraments duly offered to the people, the apostolic ministry has thereby been temporarily but never irreversibly defaulted. If the apostolicity of the church becomes at some particular time gravely defective, the Spirit may be earnestly importuned to revive the church in apostolic teaching. John the Baptist's maxim pertains: "And do not think you can say to yourselves, 'We have Abraham as our father.' I tell you that out of these stones God can raise up children for Abraham" (Matt. 3:9; Chrysostom, *Hom. on Matt.* 11).

Reservations Concerning Historic Succession

Apostolicity is viewed by most Protestants as an indispensable mark of the church in the sense of the pure preaching of the word. Yet many reject the linear historic succession of the episcopacy as an indispensable mark on the grounds that the New Testament appears to regard elders and bishops as the same office (Acts 20:17, 28; Titus 1:5, 7; 1 Tim. 3:1, 8; 1 Pet. 5:1; Didache 15). Timothy was ordained by presbyters (1 Tim. 4:14). As late as Jerome, the patriarch of Alexandria was consecrated by presbyters: "For even at Alexandria from the time of Mark the Evangelist until the episcopates of Heraclas and Dionysius the presbyters always named as bishop one of their own number chosen by themselves . . . For what function, excepting ordination, belongs to a bishop that does not also belong to a presbyter?" (Jerome, *Epist.* 146.1).

Paul admonished the elders of Ephesus, "Keep watch over yourselves and all the flock of which the Holy Spirit has made you overseers. Be shepherds of the church of God, which he bought with his own blood" (Acts 20:28). "And the things you have heard me say in the presence of many witnesses entrust to reliable men who will also be qualified to teach others" (2 Tim. 2:2). He instructed Timothy that the *episkopos* must be "able to teach," able to "take care of God's church," "not be a recent convert," and must guard the deposit of faith and pass it on by appointing elders to maintain and proclaim it (1 Tim. 3:2–7; 2 Tim. 1:14; Titus 1:5–9). While a succession of teaching is clearly commended, it remains controverted as to whether it is a demonstrable linear historic succession. Reformed interpreters view apostolic succession more in terms of contemporary obedience than linear historic succession: "The church maintains continuity with the apostles and with Israel by faithful obedience to [Christ's] call" (United Presbyterian Church Confession of 1967, *BOConf.* 2, a, 1).

Ignatius of Antioch viewed the ministry of *episkopoi* as belonging to the essence of the church and as based upon dominical and apostolic authority (*Trallians* 2, 3; *Eph.* 5, 6) and the validity of Eucharist as dependent upon the authenticity and continuity of episcopal oversight (*Smyrnaeans* 8; cf. Cyprian, *On the Unity of the Church*). Eusebius sought to trace the lines of apostolic succession, but found or left some matters doubtful (Eusebius, *CH* 1.1, 3.4; cf. Kirk, *The Apostolic Ministry*). The accounts given by Irenaeus and Eusebius correspond plausibly with what we know of the developing organization of the community at the time of Paul (Rom. 12:6–8; 1 Cor. 12:29–30; 1 and 2 Timothy, Titus).

Irenaeus was confident that "We are in a position to enumerate those who were by the apostles instituted bishop in the churches, and the successions of these men to our own times. . . . The blessed apostles, then, having founded and built up the church [at Rome], committed into the hands of Linus the office of the episcopate. Of this Linus, Paul makes mention in the Epistles to Timothy. To him succeeded Anacletus; and after him, in the third place from the apostles Clement was allotted the bishopric, who had seen the blessed apostles, and had associated with them, and had the preaching of the apostles still echoing in his ears, and their tradition before his eyes. . . . To this Clement there succeeded Evarestus. Alexander followed Evarestus; then sixth from the apostles, Sixtus was appointed. . . . And this is most abundant proof that there is one and the same vivifying faith which has been preserved in the church from the apostles until now" (Irenaeus, *Ag. Her.* 3.3.2, 3). Irenaeus attested that he himself had seen and met Polycarp, who lived to be very old, who departed this life in martyrdom "having always taught the things which he had learned from the apostles, and which the Church has handed down" (*Ag. Her.* 3.3.4).

Of the perennial vitality of the apostolic tradition, the Anglican theologian Francis Hall wrote, "Nowhere in human history can we find any parallel to the uninterrupted maintenance in many lands, through twelve or thirteen centuries, of a working polity so complex and delicately adjusted, and yet so well determined and coherent, as this one is. And at the end of four additional centuries its sway is still as complete as ever in three-fourths of Christendom" (*DT* 8:153).

Those who challenge historic episcopal succession point to "the heresy of popes like Liberius and Honorius, which was condemned by the Council of Constantinople in 680, and to the infamies of popes like John IX, XIII, XXII, and Alexander VI" (Banks, *MCD*:294).

Although subject to abuse and corruption, the principle of historic succession has proven to be enormously valuable in the history of the church, especially in times of persecution and social upheaval. Those who especially remember its abuses do well also to remember its times of courage and capacity for *marturia*. Those who best celebrate its normative character also recognize its corruptibility.

Apostolicity as a Bulwark Against Ideological Corruption

Apostolicity itself is a critical principle that brings its own acid "hermeneutic of suspicion" to modern ideological critics. What is apostolic we let the apostles tell us; we do not tell the apostles. If the record of their testimony is fundamentally defective, there is no way that the church can begin to learn the truth, for the truth about Christ is attested only by original eyewitnesses and their trustworthy attestors, and these are called the apostolate.

Contemporary witnesses are called to assess every subsequent testimony by its correspondence with the original testimony of the apostles. The working premise is that the Holy Spirit would not allow a truly debilitating or defective testimony to be transmitted to the whole church (Chrysostom, *Hom. on the Statues, NPNF* 1 9:331).

When criticism is working speculatively, as if historians could be the final judges and arbiters of the documents of testimony rather than the text being the judge and constrainer of the interpreter, then there is danger that pretentious criticism may set itself between the apostolic testimony and contemporary hearers. At times this seems to imply that the laity can meet the apostles only if introduced by a prosecutorial guild of professional historians who are predisposed to deny their credentials. This premise has led to the temporary expanding employment of a knowledge elite, but hardly to improved historical inquiry. Good textual inquiry does not lord it over the texts but is called to listen to them.

Does modern historical criticism represent a devastating challenge to the principle of apostolicity? Briefly answered, no. When criticism is working well, so that an orthodox skepticism places in question the speculations of the historical critics, there is nothing to fear from historical inquiry into the tradition of transmission of apostolic testimony. There is only the task of improving historical inquiry and bringing it closer to the facts of the Incarnate, risen Lord and his body the Church.

Questions of Petrine Leadership

The charge given to the whole apostolate was culminated and focused particularly upon Peter ("the rock"), who from the outset seems to have been principal spokesman for the Twelve (Mark 8:29; Matt. 18:21; Luke 9:5; 12:41; John 6:67, 68; Cyril of Alex. *Comm. on John* 4.4). Regularly listed first among the apostles (Mark 3:16–19; Matt. 10:1–4; Luke 6:12–16; Acts 1:13), Peter was chief among witnesses to the resurrection (1 Cor. 15:5). In crucial references, Peter appears to be called to a special role of leadership in the apostolate (Matt. 16:13–19, Luke 22:29–32; John 21:15–17; Augustine, Sermon 229). That Peter was leader of the Twelve seems clear from Paul's references to him and from many other New Testament references. Paul carried out the mission to the Gentiles that Peter led and interpreted (Acts 10–15).

The Meaning of Matthew 16:13–19

This passage is found in all ancient manuscripts. That the text has Palestinian provenance seems implied in the Aramaic tone of its language (Simon bar Jonah, and the metaphors of binding and loosing). Simon was doubtless first called by the Aramaic form Kepha, and only later by the Greek form Cephas, which was Paul's usual designation of him (Gal. 1:18; 2:7–14; 1 Cor. 1:12; 3:22).

The "rock" to which Jesus referred in giving Simon the surname Peter was the revelation that he acknowledged when he confessed; "You are the Christ, the Son of the living God" (Matt. 16:16). Jesus observed that "flesh and blood has not revealed this to you, but my Father who is in heaven" (Matt. 16:17). "Now this name of Peter was given him by the Lord, and that in a figure, that he should signify the Church. For seeing that Christ is the rock (Petra), Peter is the Christian people. For the rock (Petra) is the original name. Therefore Peter is so called from the rock; not the rock from Peter; as Christ is not called Christ from the Christian, but the Christian from Christ," as if to say " 'upon this Rock' which you have confessed . . . 'will I build my Church.' I will build you upon Myself, not Myself upon you" (Augustine, *Sermons on NT Lessons* 26). In being given a new name by Jesus, Simon Peter was given a new apostolic role as "rock," as first confessor of God's singular revelation. Receiving a new name in biblical reference implied receiving a new life, a new identity, a new calling, a new responsibility.

To have stability in space and durability in time the church must be built upon a firm confessional rock—the truth revealed. That rock is the revelation Peter attested. Even the gates of hell will not prevail against this revelation, Jesus promised. The *ekklēsia* is thus protected by the Spirit not from temporary uncertainty but from ultimate defection. Christ himself is finally the foundation, the rock, upon which the church is built.

The Historic Importance of Peter for Orthodox, Catholics, and Protestants

Why Peter, and not another? The answer can only lie in the mystery of God's own choosing. The same question can be asked of Israel or Moses or Abraham or Jeremiah—why these and not others? The Hebraic answer is simply that Yahweh chose them. The *why* remains a gracious mystery.

It was specifically to Peter that Jesus said, "Simon, Simon, Satan has asked to sift you as wheat. But I have prayed for you, Simon, that your faith may not fail. And when you have turned back, strengthen your brothers" (Luke 22:32). Having been tested, in due course Peter did strengthen the faith of the other apostles.

Before this occurred, the divine economy permitted the trial of Jesus to become a temptation to shake the faith of all the disciples. In Jesus' prayer that Peter's faith not fail, the narrative seems to suggest that the future of the whole apostolate in some sense hinged upon steadiness like that of Peter. Peter was kept by the Son's intercession from falling permanently.

Peter is recalled in the New Testament as leading the apostles in the preaching of the gospel, in courage to face persecution, in the disciplining of erroneous faith and practice, and in the mission beyond Palestine (Acts 1:15–26; 2:14–40; 5:1–11; 8:14–25; 9:32–42). No leadership decision of Peter's was more far-reaching than his baptism of the family of Cornelius, the Gentile centurion in Caesarea (Acts 10:1–48; Chrysostom, *Hom. on Acts* 23.10.35), wherein the mission of the church to Gentiles was first established as a precedent. Peter played the leading role at the Apostolic Council in Jerusalem presided over by James (Acts 15), where the decision was made not to impose circumcision on Gentile Christians. Even in the conflict between Peter and Paul in Antioch, where Paul says he "opposed him to his face, because he was clearly in the wrong" (Gal. 2:11), still it was not Barnabas whom Paul rebuked but Peter, thereby once again indicating his role as leader of the apostolate (Schmaus, *Dogma* 4:33–40).

The Historic Position of Rome and the Reformation Critique

Rome was the crossroads of the known world. It was understandable that the diverse communities of faith spread out among many nations would look to the leadership in Rome for normative patterns accountable to the apostolic tradition. There can be little doubt that from the days of Peter and Paul, the church at Rome was exercising wide influence on the church in other locations (Irenaeus, *Ag. Her.* 3.3). Both Peter and Paul had led and instructed the Roman church, and according to tradition both were martyred in Rome. Rome was the only apostolically founded church in the western Mediterranean, and the one that maintained an unsullied apostolic tradition, in close consultation with the bishops of Alexandria and Antioch.

It is not surprising that the Roman bishop would be looked to for guidance of the whole church in a manner parallel to the way each bishop guided a diocesan church. Ecclesial disputes were referred to Rome, Alexandria, and Antioch for settlement just as legal questions of empire were referred to the civil authorities. Matthew 16:18 was viewed in the west as granting authority to the successors of Peter.

By the time of the Reformers, church leadership was accountable to the written word of apostolic testimony. The power of the keys was assumed to be the pardon announced in the preaching of the gospel. The universal priesthood of Christ was understood to be shared by all believers, whose representatives are ordained ministers. Where the gospel is rightly preached and the Sacrament duly administered there is the one true church (Augsburg Confession; Thirty-nine Articles).

Unity and Succession as a Recurrent Tension

As long as the first generation apostles were alive they held the church together by their unified witness. Although they spread in all directions, their testimony was believed to be substantively the same, and they themselves constituted the center of authority for teaching and community. "There is no contradiction or absurdity in Holy Scripture" (Methodius, *On the Resurrection*, 1.9), since the Spirit preserved the unity of the testimony left by the apostles.

As the apostles gradually died, the need for a clear, cohesive teaching authority was increasingly felt. More attention had to be given to the transgenerational guardianship of the sacred testimony to Jesus' life, death, and resurrection.

In ancient Israel when there was only one temple, the high priest represented the unity of the covenant people of God. After the Babylonian captivity, worship in the synagogues became more diffused and localized. The struggle between the primitive unity of the covenant people and the diaspora synagogues' diversity was destined to be played out again in Christianity.

Novatian was a presbyter at Rome who laid claim to being the valid Roman bishop. The resulting disruption intensified the necessity of making sure that rival bishops not compete in the same jurisdiction. Conciliar decisions gradually came to express legitimate authority to coordinate the policies of metropolitan sees and patriarchates under varying conditions.

Cyprian (c. 200–258), bishop of Carthage, established the view that each bishop within his own jurisdiction has full authority of episcopal leadership, yet all bishops are to maintain a coordinated, cooperative, mutually respectful collegial relationship whose unity had dominical grounding in the Lord's calling of Peter (*Treatises* 1.4). He saw the cultural diversity of the church as brought into unity by episcopal guardianship. If so, that unity would have to resist alternative doctrinal pretentions—i.e., heresies (*Letters* 55.24,51.24, 39).

Heresy as Novelty

The need for firm governance was increased by the emergence of early divisive heresies, notably those of Gnosticism, Docetism, and Marcionism. Heresies were considered to be of recent formation, unable to trace their origin to the apostles (Irenaeus, *Ag. Her.* 3.4). A heretical view will "proclaim by its diversity and contrariety that it originates neither from an Apostle nor from an apostolic man; for the Apostles would not have diverged from one another in doctrine; no more would the apostolic man have put out teaching at variance with that of the Apostles. . . . This test will be applied to those churches of a later date, which are daily being founded" (Tertullian, *Prescription Ag. Her.* 32, 36).

Gnosticism had its chief influence in the middle of the second century, claiming to pass on the secret knowledge of salvation through mystical knowers who viewed themselves as guardians of secret traditions of sayings of Jesus. The consensual church answered the gnostics that all saving memories concerning Jesus were known to the apostles and were not furtively passed on by erratic or idiosyncratic secret knowers. Against the Gnostics, the catholics were able to trace their succession in each visible seat of ecclesiastical authority back to the apostles, often within the living memory of the rememberers, or through a series of known successions over several generations. The reliable memory of the events surrounding Jesus was thought to be adequately known and remembered by the bishops, not by secretive groups like the gnostics.

In response to gnostic secrecy, Irenaeus argued that the church had from its beginnings publicly set forth a historically demonstrable succession of overseers in a given locale as a means of ensuring reliable teaching. The teaching of historic succession hinges upon the basic assumption that God came into history in the flesh. Christianity does not speak of a redemption taking place apart from history in an esoteric circle of initiates. The verifiable historical succession of Christian leaders was, for Irenaeus, an implication of historical revelation and the scandal of particularity, stressing public, visible transmission reaching through intergenerational succession (Irenaeus, *Ag. Her.* 2.3).

The Written Word as Defense Against Heresy

In baptism the rule of faith was learned by heart, seldom written down, and confessed by the mouth. The prototypes of the Apostles' Creed were memorized baptismal formulae and hymns and summarizing confessional statements (*COC* 2:3–27). These had received generally accepted form by the middle of the second century. Meanwhile the lists of received apostolic writings began to circulate, and by the fourth century were consensually defined (*SCD* 1–40).

These became the bulwark of the church's defense against heresy. Those who did not accept the rule of faith and the canon of sacred apostolic teachings, and who were not under the discipline of authorized leaders in an open, visible, established succession, were not to be considered reliable teachers of ecumenical Christian teaching. By the time of Irenaeus and Tertullian we have a reasonably settled rule of faith, a body of documents widely received as apostolic testimony, and authorized lists of succession of bishops.

PART IV

HUMAN DESTINY

*The future is not an optional topic for classic Christian
teaching. It is intrinsic to all its other aspects.*

—Irenaeus, *Ag. Her.* 5, I

HERE WE CONSIDER WHAT IT MEANS TO CONFESS Christian faith
regarding such essential and weighty subjects as the future of history,
the resurrection of the body, the return of Christ, the Christian hope, the
final judgment, the communion of saints, and the life everlasting. This traditional
order highlights the final hope that frames all finite thoughts and contextualizes
all human acts. Our modest aim: to state accurately the classic consensus on
these huge questions.

Already we have delved into numerous subjects pertaining to the end (*eschaton*)
of history, but now, following the sequence of the Apostles' Creed and the earliest
baptismal confessions (Profession of the Presbyters of Smyrna, c. 180, Irenaeus,
c. 190, Interrogatory Creed of Hippolytus, c. 215, Nicaea, 325, Constantinople,
381), we come to last things. The pinnacle location of issues of death, personal
survival, and final judgment at the end of the sequence of confessional teachings
does not suggest that these matters are less essential, but all the more decisive.
Their climactic last position among the articles of faith does not imply their triviality, but their finality.

All things in Christian teaching point to a coming consummation. All the vital
energies of the doctrines, moral teachings, and liturgies of classic Christianity
focus finally on events yet to come that will illumine all present life.

Human life attains its final end not in this life but in a future as yet unpossessed. The truest, fullest blessedness does not appear in temporal life, but in
eternal life to come (Titus 1:2; Ambrose, *Of the Christian Faith* 5.17.215–16; 3:7;
Baxter, *The Saints' Eternal Rest*). The drama of human rebellion in history comes
to full recognition only in its last scene. The symphony is not played out until its
last note.

9

LAST THINGS: DEATH AND PERSONAL SURVIVAL

HUMAN BEINGS ARE NOT ASKED whether they wish to be born. They are asked to live according to God's will between birth and death.

Before birth we have no opportunity to choose. After death there is no further opportunity to choose. Having been made without our free choice, we come to a final accounting only as a result of our actual free choices (Heb. 10:26–31; Clement of Alex., *Strom.* 2.13.56–57). We do not reach our final destination without some self-determined choice on our part (Tertullian, *On the Soul* 42, 51–53). Whether mercifully or abruptly or ambivalently, death ends the choosing process enmeshed in time.

Now "we share in his sufferings in order that we may also share in his glory" (Rom. 8:17). Yet even now the faithful "with unveiled faces all reflect the Lord's glory" and "are being transformed into his likeness with ever-increasing glory" (2 Cor. 3:18). Therefore let the faithful "exchange 'glory for glory', becoming greater through daily increase" (Gregory of Nyssa, *On Perfection*). The Holy Spirit is gradually coming "to dwell in the disciples, measuring himself out to them according to their capacity to receive" (Gregory of Nazianzus, *Theol. Orat.* 5.26).

The End of History

God's design is not yet consummated, though its consummation has been anticipatively revealed. The study of its consummation is the last major theme and the crowning reflection of classic consensual exegesis.

The study of eschatology (from *eschaton*, end) is the critical discipline that considers all things that pertain to the life to come insofar as they are revealed by scriptural testimony as most commonly beheld through the eyes of generations of consensual interpreters. A notoriously difficult and enigmatic subject, it is not only the capstone of classical Christian teaching, but may rightly be regarded as its foundation stone, the final premise that informs and shapes all other questions of scriptural reasoning (Benedictus Deus, *SCD* 530–31; Belgic *Conf.* 37).

How All Judgments Within History Are Affected by Its End

Eschatological reasoning inquires into how creatures who, having their beginning in God, and having fallen and received redemption in God, have their final destiny and end in God.

Eschatology builds upon and completes all anteceding theological inquiries. It brings the whole to a fitting conclusion. It embraces all those difficult issues that have to do with *what is yet to be*. It asks on the basis of apostolic testimony: What yet lies ahead, both for personal life and for the cosmos? A major constituent of classic Christian teaching concerns the future in which God's consummating promises are yet to be finally fulfilled and aptly vindicated (1 Cor. 3:22; Gal. 5:5).

A presumed account of Christianity that did not mention its future-tense hope would be grossly deficient. The expected End says something decisive about God: that God will vindicate justice beyond this present sphere—and about the world: that all human motives will come under fair, omniscient divine judgment (Ps. 35:24–27; 1 Pet. 4:17; Bede, *On 1 Pet.* 4.17).

The glory of God's kingdom is already dawning, yet awaits ultimately to be fulfilled and made completely present. "I consider that our present sufferings are not worth comparing with the glory that will be revealed in us," for which "the creation waits in eager expectation" (Rom. 8:18, 19; Irenaeus, *Ag. Her.* 5.32.1). Meanwhile, amid human folly God makes even "human wrath" to praise the divine majesty (Ps. 76:10). The great lengths and strands of providence await a completing event. If so it is foolish to speak of suffering or social justice without reference to the future of God's mercy and justice. No small amount of Christian ethical teaching is directly tied to the promise of the justice of God in the end of history. There is enduring moral relevance for the here and now in the inquiry into the future life.

Living Between the Times of Christ's Coming and Coming Again

The central feature of Jewish expectation of the end was the general resurrection accompanied by judgment and separation of just and unjust. "Multitudes who sleep in the dust of the earth will awake: some to everlasting life, others to shame and everlasting contempt" (Dan. 12:2). This expectation was decisively transformed by the history of Jesus (Dan. 12:2; Matt. 25:46; Acts 24:15; 2 Pet. 2:9).

What lies between now and the end is the subject of a vast constellation of indeterminate theological perplexities sometimes called the last things (*ta eschata*) or *consummatione saeculi, sunteleia aionos,* or eschatology. These terms point to scriptural references to "the last days" (Isa. 2:2), or "the last time" (*eschatos ton chronon,* Oecumenius, *Comm. on 1. Pet.* 1.20), or "the last hour" (*eschate hora,* 1 John 2:18; Augustine, Letter 199.7). The "last days," according to Old Testament prophecy, are the days immediately preceding the final messianic coming and the consummation of world history as presently known (Mic. 4:1; cf. Acts 2:17; John 6:40; Clement of Alex., *Instr.* 1.6).

The New Testament writers had witnessed the messianic coming of the Son in Jesus Christ. In his resurrection the end of history had been already anticipatively recognized. They continued to expect the "last days" (*eschatai hemerai*) as those that would come to fulfillment in the coming again of the Lord in the end time (2 Tim. 3:1; *Bede, On 1 Pet.* 1.5). The time from now to the end was called the present age. The reality that would dawn after the consummation of all things was called the age to come. "This age" (*olam hazzeh, aion houtos*) was distinguished from "the coming age" (*olam habba, aion mellō, aiōnis tois eperchomenois,* Chrysostom, *Hom. on Eph.* 2.7). Those who resist the work of the Holy Spirit will find no peace "either in this age or in the age to come" (Matt. 12:32; cf. Luke 18:30; Gal. 1:4; Col. 1:26; Augustine, Sermon 71.12.20).

The New Testament understands the salvation event to be both occurring in the present by faith and awaiting future consummation. Life is now being lived in between the time of the Savior's incarnate life and the Savior's return (2 Thess. 2; Rev. 1:1–8; Bede, *Expl. of the Apoc.* 1.1–2).

The New Testament teaching of the future is set in an apocalyptic framework that looks toward a final revelation (*apokalupsis*, manifestation, appearing), a coming yet to be revealed (Luke 12:2; 17:30; Rom. 16:25; 1 Pet. 5:1; Gal. 3:23; Oecumenius, *Comm. on Apoc.* 1.1–2; 21.2, 26). Much of the apocalyptic literature anteceding the New Testament looked toward a messianic era of earthly fulfillment whose focal point would be a New Jerusalem (Dan. 9; Joel 3; Zech. 14; Heb. 12:22; Rev. 21:2). The messianic age would be a preparation for the consummation of all things.

The faithful already live anticipatively in the new age by faith in the resurrected Lord (Rom. 6). Eternal life is viewed as already present (1 Tim. 6:12; 1 John 5; Chrysostom, *Hom. on 1 Tim.* 17). Believers are already presently sharing in the coming reign of God. Nonetheless, amid continuing history there still remains this period "between the times" in which the reign of God has been inaugurated yet not consummated as expected in the last days. In commending to Timothy both physical training and godliness, Paul instructed him to be simultaneously accountable for the "promise for both the present life and the life to come" (1 Tim. 4:7–8; Basil the Great, *On Holy Spirit* 14.33).

Life Everlasting: An Article of the Creed

The Apostles' Creed confesses belief in "the communion of saints, the resurrection of the dead, and the life everlasting." The Nicene-Constantinopolitan Creed concludes, "We look for the resurrection of the dead and the life of the world to come" (*CC*:24–25, 33). Only from this final vantage point may the structure of the rule of faith be fully grasped and affirmed.

These last articles of baptismal confession deal with the end and meaning of the whole of human history. This includes the end and meaning of the future of every discrete human person and of the natural history of the cosmos (Rom. 8:18–27; Augustine *on Romans* 53). The subject is not exhausted by asking what happens to an individual person beyond the grave, or even to human history generally. It also encompasses the cosmos, incorporeal spiritual creatures (angelic and demonic powers), and nonrational creatures (Gregory of Nyssa, *The Great Catechism* 5, 6).

Protestant teaching on the end time summed up "the four Last Things: death, the resurrection of the dead, the final judgment, and the end of the world" (Quenstedt, *TDP* 4; Schmid, *DT*:625; cf. Ecclesiasticus 7:40). A similar organization of classic points had been earlier found in medieval scholastic theology: "the four last things of man are Death, Judgment, Heaven . . . and Hell" (Pohle,

DT 12:2). These topics are ordered around a chronological premise that took a systematically-formed conception: death and the abode of the dead, the general resurrection, Christ's coming again, final judgment, the end of the world, and eternal life.

An extended form of the same sequence would include a more sweeping trajectory that we will pursue in what follows. The classic ecumenical consensus has tended to arrange these topics in this approximate order: the relation of sin and death; the death of the just and unjust; life after death, personal survival; the intermediate state of the just and unjust; the general resurrection; the glorified, spiritual body; the future return of Christ; signs of his coming; the Lawless One; millennialism; the last judgment; the separation; the consummation; the new city of God; the new heaven and the new earth; the eternal destiny of the wicked; hell as separation from God; theories of afterlife; the destiny of those who heard no good news; the communion of saints; eternal life; the dwelling of the righteous; the vision of God; and the praise of the triune God. This is our trajectory ahead.

Modesty in Reasoning About the Future

Time-bound human reasoning is ill equipped to speak of what is not yet. No human eye can penetrate the future. Reason only makes conjectures. Passion and imagination may dream or imagine a future condition. Present reasoning proceeds on the basis of assumptions about time and space that cannot be easily transferred or applied to eternity.

Jesus' own self-constrained modesty about the time of his return stands as an example to the faithful of eschatological modesty (Matt. 24:36; Mark 13:23; Acts 1:6, 7; Gregory the Great, *Letters, To Eulogius*, SCD 248). When the disciples met the risen Lord, they asked him, "Lord, are you at this time going to restore the kingdom to Israel?" He answered in his last words to them on earth as reported by Luke, "It is not for you to know the times or dates the Father has set by his own authority" (Acts 1:6, 7; Irenaeus, *Ag. Her.* 5.30.3). Calvin thought it "rash to inquire into matters unknown more deeply than God allows us to know" (*Psychopannychia*, RD:695).

Eschatology may be taught falsely so as to detract from the importance of this life or trivialize historical existence or foster the illusion of escape from human responsibility. But rightly conceived, the teaching of the end of history is a teaching about the momentous meaning of history. The promise of the future is rightly taught as impinging upon the present (1 Cor. 15:51–58).

Paul quoted Isaiah 64:4, " 'No eye has seen, no ear has heard, no mind has conceived what God has prepared for those who love him,' but God has revealed it to us by his Spirit" (1 Cor. 2:9). Biblical revelation concerning the future employs metaphors from time and space reality to point to that which lies beyond time and space. The purpose of scriptural testimony to the future life is not to describe in detail what will happen as if with scientific certainty, but to console, encourage, and engender hope in what God is providing in the future, and faithfulness in this world (2 Pet. 3:11; Gregory of Nazianzus, *Orat.* 7, 18). "The Bible uses the earthly, human categories of time and space not primarily to describe literally *where* we will be and *how* we will exist 'after time,' but to describe symbolically *who* we will be. It is not primarily interested in the 'furniture of heaven' or the 'temperature of hell,' but in *people* and whether they will be together with or separated from God" (Guthrie, *CD*:386). We learn about the future divine-human relation by thinking analogically about what God has done in the past and is doing now. Hope is attached to the One whom we have come to know personally in the history of revelation. Faith remains confident in the completion of what remains unfulfilled but anticipated in the history of redemption. It hopes for clarity in what remains stubbornly ambiguous (Chrysostom, *Hom. on 1 Cor.* 34).

Why So Little Is Known of the Future

Why does God's revelation leave us so much in the dark on such an important subject?

There is a providential reason why finite reasoning is left walking by faith rather than by sight: "It is the glory of God to conceal a matter" (Prov. 25:2). The study of the future remains, according to God's wisdom, a matter of the simple meekness of faith, not the pretense of convoluted knowledge. The study of the end time is a probationary study in which the limits of all human knowing are on trial. The prototypical sin of humanity was the attempt to penetrate forbidden knowledge (Gen. 2:17). Knowledge of the future retains this prohibition as long as human consciousness is enmeshed in time.

Faith is called to live by hope, content to live with what we cannot know by sight, searching the scripture for what has been graciously revealed. The study of the future holds extraordinary blessing: "Blessed is the one who reads the words of this prophecy, and blessed are those who hear it and take to heart what is written in it" (Rev. 1:3). The blessing does not consist in the fact that the human mind might certainly know what will happen, but in the living hope that amid not knowing, it may learn to trust the Giver of history. "Dear friends, now we are children of God, and what we will be has not yet been made known. But we know that when he appears, we shall be like him" (1 John 3:2; Augustine, *Trin.* 15.16.26).

The key: The reasoning of the faithful about the future arises out of personal meeting with the risen Lord. The vision of eternal life is an expression of sharing in Christ's own life, death, resurrection, and exaltation.

Consensus Still in Formation

Endtime questions, despite their importance, remain less consensually matured in their details than other articles of the creed. Though most other subjects of theology have been explored with reasonably full adequacy in the twenty centuries of their long development, there has not yet formed a definitive ecumenical eschatology on many particulars. Many theories remain and compete. Where long-standing differences remain on eschatology between adventists, amillennialists, and other views, we will point to the differences without pretending to have found their resolution.

My aim: to state as accurately as possible the mind of the believing church. Yet I find it a more daunting challenge in these questions. I caution the reader that the consensus is not at points so firm as elsewhere. Though Trinitarian and Christological doctrines received detailed conciliar attention, common points of eschatological teaching were broadly affirmed but not explicitly developed. They appear regularly as points of exegesis and preaching and liturgy, but not as precisely worked out conciliar formulae.

It took considerable time for varied exegetical positions to form on some questions of eschatology: whether there is or is not an intermediate state, whether the coming of Christ is before or after the millennium, whether death ends all possibility of coming to faith. Among early controverted themes were Origen's speculations on universal grace and the eternality of the soul; Augustine's amillennial vision of the church as *City of God*; Gregory the Great's advocacy of purgatory; and the medieval sacraments of penance and unction. The Reformation provided a refreshing exegetical basis for doctrines of the future life, while much of the substance of the earlier tradition remained intact.

The Gospel Transcends Despair Over
the Human Future

Why not limit our imperfect energies to political change and economic development? Too often, in despair, the modern world has reduced the vision of the human future to political regulation or economic interest or social planning or ecological anguish.

Even supposing that a wonderful future society might actually emerge from coordinated political effort, what could incontestably guarantee its permanence? Would the best conceivable society last for more than a generation? Wouldn't the proneness to sin find a way to undermine it? Suppose that such a utopian society, if now impossible, is even achieved in a fourth or fifth millennium—that gives little comfort to those who have already suffered in previous millennia. If the payoff of future hope is a this-worldly society yet to come for others, how does this hope impinge morally upon our present suffering and sacrifice to help it come about? Throughout such probing, classic Christian teaching remains realistic about the capacity of humanity for sin such as might destroy the planet. Yet that realism is set in the context of hope that God's purpose will be fulfilled even under the worst scenarios of human folly. The worst modern fantasies are hardly more horrible than those of ancient apocalyptic imagination.

Christian teaching about the future does not have to do merely with human wish projections, philosophical speculations, rational arguments, or humanistic hopes. Rather it speaks of *a future that has already met us* in Jesus Christ (Bede, *On 1 Pet.* 1.13). It was an expectation planted long before New Testament times that God is acting throughout the whole of human history so as to reveal how the divine promises were in due time to be fulfilled:

"Concerning this salvation, the prophets, who spoke of the grace that was to come to you, searched intently and with greatest care, trying to find out the time and circumstances to which the Spirit of Christ in them was pointing when he predicted the sufferings of Christ and the glories that would follow. It was revealed to them that they were not serving themselves but you, when they spoke of the things that have now been told you by those who have preached the gospel to you by the Holy Spirit sent from heaven" (1 Pet. 1:10–12; Ambrose, *Letters to Laymen* 66). As early Christian preachers searched scripture to discern the grounds of their hope in the fulfillment of God's promises, so do believers today, who look forward to God's justice and holy love becoming clear in future history and finally at the end of history.

Future questions are traditionally viewed from within the sure frame of reference of the work of the Holy Spirit. God the Spirit continues to work to remake the whole of creation into the new creation begun in the Son (Theodoret, *Comm. on 2 Cor.* 5.17.317). Christology looks backward toward the Son's coming and forward to the Son's coming again. Pneumatology looks backward in time to the once-for-all self-offering of the Son on the cross and forward in time to the full application of God's promise in the Parousia through the power of the Holy Spirit.

Meanwhile, the Spirit's converting and sanctifying work is still reliably in process. Faith looks expectantly to its full consummation (Gregory of Nyssa, *On the Christian Mode of Life* FC 58:142). The believer united with Christ by faith looks ahead to a fuller union with Christ in eternity. The history of sin cannot be the last word about humanity. The unfolding story of human history is not yet over. The Spirit still has work to do to complete the Son's mission.

Future Questions Arise Inevitably Out of
Finite Human Existence

Reflection on the future is not unique to Jews and Christians, but found generally in human consciousness. Wherever human life is being lived, it is drawn toward the two most persistent human questions: whence and whither?

Is there an end toward which nature and history are moving? It seems absurd to conscious beings that life could be so full of value and meaning and then end suddenly, abruptly, and absolutely with death. What remains? Why are we here? Can we reliably know anything about the future? Are our hopes merely projections of our human needs and fleeting passions? Do future hopes distort present responsibilities?

No one lives without some modicum of hope. The history of religions is filled with texts expressing hope beyond death. To pretend to be a religion without any teaching of the future life is oxymoronic. There abides in human consciousness "an indestructible instinct of the resurrection" even among those who deny it with their lips (Cyril of Jerusalem, *Catech. Lect.* 18.5). Gregory of Nyssa argued that the persistence of future questions in human life points to the plausibility of personal survival (Gregory of Nyssa, *The Great Catechism* 5). Even where brutally suppressed by a police state, the expectation of final judgment does not disappear, but tends to emerge ever more strongly (Solzhenitsyn, *The Gulag Archipelago*).

Although agnosticism about personal survival may be occasionally found in human cultures, the belief in personal survival beyond death is found in virtually all nations of all historical periods and all stages of civilization. It is thus argued as a premise of human consciousness by virtue of its universality and persistence in human history (2 Cor. 4:13–18; Chrysostom, *Hom. on Cor.* 9.3). Any view that possesses such general reasonable assent must be received attentively as a plausible premise until disproved. Arguably any view so recurrent is likely to emerge out of the very constitution of human nature.

Death and Personal Survival

Life is threatened each day by potential sickness and accident, against which we pay dearly to try to insure ourselves. Our earthly lives are lived in the swift interval between birth and death (Donne, *Meditations*; Shakespeare, *Sonnets*). A bit of me dies when I lose a friend, when "the bell tolls." The loss of anything of high value may serve as a courier of the prospect of death.

"In the midst of life we are encompassed by death," said an eleventh-century hymn (*media vita in morte sumus*, Notker, Duffield, *Latin Hymns*:140). Luther turned this maxim around: "If you hear the Law, it will say in the language of the ancient chant: 'In the midst of life, we are in death.' But the Gospel and faith invert this, and sing, 'In the midst of death, we are in life' " (Luther, *On Genesis* 6.206).

Few have expressed the pathos of human vulnerability more ironically than Chrysostom: "Nothing is weaker than human affairs. Whatever term therefore one may employ to express their insignificance it will fall short of the reality; whether he calls them smoke, or grass, or a dream or spring flowers, or by any other name; so perishable are they, and more naught than nonentities" (Chrysostom, *Eutropius*, *NPNF* 1 9:250).

Facing death is the universal human condition. David said to Solomon, "I am about to go the way of all the earth" (1 Kings 2:2). Paul wrote: "Death passed upon all" (Rom. 5:12; Eusebius, *Proof of the Gospel* 7.1). As we are born without being asked, so do we die. All die: parents die, children die, the children of children will die. Nothing is more certain in life than that it will come to an end (Aphrahat, *Demonstrations, Of Death*, NPNF 2 13:402–9). Each one's last act is already foreknown. "It is appointed for mortals to die once" (Heb. 9:27). The universality of death of human beings is interpreted in the light of salvation history from Adam to Christ: Death is "a consequence of their federal relation to the first Adam, that they may rise again with the second Adam" (Harries, *TM*:279; cf. Rom. 5:12–17; Irenaeus, *Ag. Her.* 3.22.3).

Awareness of Death Deepens Life's Significance

It is precisely because this life is so finitely limited that it becomes more important. As the sick man's prognosis is shortened, the value of his remaining days tends to be heightened. Now is our only time to act, to decide, to affect our families and cultures. Hence it becomes important to "be very careful then how you live— not as unwise but as wise, making the most of every opportunity" (Eph. 5:15; Chrysostom, *Hom. on Eph.* 18.5.15–17; cf. Col. 4:5). No moment, once gone, can be replaced or retracted. One's loving, believing, and one's very being as a person is chosen ever anew with each moment (S. Kierkegaard, *Either/Or* 2).

Suppose every moral decision were forever subject to endless revision. Would not all moral seriousness thereby be infinitely postponable? If there were no death, it seems difficult to conclude that there could be much significance to historical life, since life's significance as decision hinges on its limitation in time. If so, oddly enough, death is what makes life meaningful, for this life is morally serious only if it ends (Ambrose, *On Belief in the Resurrection* 2.124; Frankl, *The Doctor and the Soul*).

The equation is precise: Those who take life seriously take death seriously. Those who take death seriously take life seriously. Where death is avoided, life is avoided. Only one who has accepted the reality of death is prepared to accept life (John 12:24; 2 Cor. 5:11– 15).

Death Ends the Period of Probation of the Will

God gives us only this fleeting time upon earth to make decisions, to shape our own responsive existence, to hear and respond to the divine address, to live for or against the good in each moment (Josh. 24:15; Origen, *Exhortation to Martyrdom* 17). When we die, the time for deciding is past (Gen. 27:2–3). The burden of freedom is lifted; the wealth of freedom spent.

Nature does not permit life without death. Only if a kernel of wheat falls to the ground and dies does it produce many seeds (John 12:24; Theodore of Mopsuestia, *Comm. on John* 5.12.24). Death ends the condition of pilgrimage through the world and inaugurates the consummation, excluding further temporal choices. "Night is coming, when no one can work" (John 9:4; Chrysostom, *Hom. on John* 5.2; cf. Matt. 26:42; 25:13). Human life is in this way analogous to the falling of a tree: "in the place where it falls, there will it lie" (Eccles. 11:3). No one can "obtain after death that which he has neglected to secure here" (Augustine, *Enchiridion* 110; cf. Cyprian, *Letter to Demetrius* 25).

The test that absolutely requires us to face our finitude is simply daily living. From beginning to end we are called to acknowledge our lives as existing under limitation. This is a test that lasts not an hour but a lifetime. Death is the last event in the probation that constitutes life. Life puts every person to this test.

We try to avoid death. At funeral parlors the cosmetics lie thick. We apply euphemisms to every aspect of the finality of death. These days "death has replaced sex as the subject too obscene for polite society" (Guthrie, *CD*:377).

The Living Soul

Through time and accident, the body becomes worn, ravaged, diseased, dysfunctional, and damaged to the point where the soul (i.e., life) no longer can continue to be expressed through it. At the point where the last evidence of aliveness irreversibly leaves the body, we say that a person is dead.

Death is the cessation of finite, natural, bodily life caused by the separation of the soul from the body (Augustine, *CG* 13.6). "When death severs soul from body, the body lies completely still and passive, just like a workman's tools after he has gone away and left them lying" (Nemesius, *On the Nature of Man, NPNF* 2 4:226). Death is seen as a type of separation from God, first in sin, then in the cessation of physical life, and finally in the last judgment if unredeemed.

Soul (*nephesh*) is the life principle of the unified person. Soul is not a part of the body, but intrinsic to the temporal life of the body (Athanasius, *Contra Gentes* 2.30). The language of modernity prefers to speak reflexively of "self" rather than "soul" as the unifying center of personal life. Classically viewed, the soul is not a separable part of the person alongside the body, but the very aliveness of the living person in dialogue with God, oneself, and other selves. This is what "separation of the soul and body means: the cessation or rupture of the previous relation to the environment and the community" (Kasper, *CCF*:336). Irreversible unrelatedness is the basic primitive meaning of *sheol*. By way of contrast, the faithful dead are being united with their Lord in a communion of saints. The soul-body interface that in its original creation was intended to continue without end, now, due to sin, must face death.

It belongs to the soul to live. The very definition of the *nephesh* is "that which is alive," that by which one becomes a "living being" (Gen. 2:7). In death the soul does not cease with the cessation of the body. The soul continues to live by virtue of the powers that belong to its nature.

Life is precisely that which distinguishes the living plant from the shell of a plant that does not have those capacities, hence is a dead organism. Creatures participate in life to the degree that they have vigor, soundness, ebullience, and vivacity consonant with their creaturely potentialities (Isa. 38:1–6; Jerome, *Comm. on Isa.* 11.381–3). What Christ came to bestow is not bare existence but abundant life, "life to the full" (*zōēn perisson*, John 10:10; Augustine, *Tractates on John* 45.15).

Soul Is That Which Makes the Body Alive

The Genesis account of creation made a fundamental distinction between the body as such and that which makes the body alive: First, "the Lord God formed the man from the dust of the ground," and only then "breathed into his nostrils the breath of *life*, and the man became a living being [nephesh, soul]" (Gen. 2:7, italics added; Augustine, *On Gen. Ag. the Manichaeans* 2.7.8). The difference between dust and life is the breath of God (Augustine, *On Gen. Ag. the Manichaeans* 2.8,10). To be formed of dust into plastic existence is not yet the same as becoming a living being by being breathed upon by God. This very dust created as body "returns to the ground it came from" awaiting resurrection, while in death "the spirit returns to God who gave it" (Eccles. 12:7; Lactantius, *DI* 2.13; John Cassian, *Conference* 8.25.3).

The body has mass, magnitude, density, weight, solidity, and physical form. That which animates the body (the breathing Spirit of God enabling *nephesh*, *psuchē*) has none of these. For life itself has no mass. Life weighs nothing. Life cannot be measured. Life cannot be touched or moved like an object from one place to another (Ps. 39:4–6).

The living person possesses attributes that cannot be reduced to measurable material entities of consciousness, imagination, reason, or desire. No computer can track them exhaustively. The computer itself is their creature and artifact. The functions of the self-transcending soul (willing, reasoning, imagining, thinking) are distinguishable from bodily functions (nutrition, respiration, blood circulation, muscular motion, reproduction). These are not reducible to physical properties or empirical descriptions. The soul does not have physical dimension in the same sense as the body, and to look for it is to misunderstand one's eyes (Nemesius, *On the Nature of Man*, LCC 4:224; Calvin, *Inst.* 3.25.6).

From Dust to Dust: Awaiting Resurrection

The word-picture of the dust of creation returning to the dust of death is portrayed at the close of Ecclesiastes, where "the dust returns to the ground it came from" whereas "the spirit returns to God who gave it" (Eccles. 12:1, 5–7; Augustine, *Letters* 143). Death is understood in scripture in three distinguishable forms: physical, spiritual, and eternal.

Physical (temporal) *death* consists in the permanent cessation of bodily life caused by the separation of the soul from the body (Augustine, *CG* 13.6; Clement of Alex., *Stromata* 7). It is the condition in which all vital functions cease permanently until the resurrection. To die is to cease to live, to lose vital power, to expire, to perish. The physical body is resolved into its constituent elements by death. By physical death the tabernacle of the soul's earthly home is dissolved. The tents are stricken, and the soul leaves the body. Once the blood congeals and *rigor mortis* sets in, it is clear that the animating *psuchē* has left the body.

In addition, however, there are in scripture other figurative and typic uses of the term death:

Spiritual death is the fall from grace caused by sin. Grace through faith is victorious over spiritual death even in this life by means of the new birth, so that even while temporal death is occurring, it is being transformed into a spiritual blessing (Chrysostom, *Hom. on the Statues* 5.9). Meanwhile, this side of final resurrection, physical death remains as an effect of the history of sin. God has wisely allowed it within the moral order of the cosmos.

Eternal death is the final state of separation from God, sometimes called "the second death" (Rev. 2:11; 20:6; 21:8), "everlasting destruction," being "shut out from the presence of the Lord" (2 Thess. 1:9), or "destruction" (Gal. 6:8; Phil. 3:19). In the death of his Son, God enables the faithful to escape the second death of eternal separation.

At death the body returns to the earth to await the resurrection. The still living soul does not have to proceed to some particular place to be judged but stands already in the presence of the omnipresent God (Luke 16:20–25; Heb. 9:27; Sulpitius Severus, *Life of St. Martin*, FC 7:113). At the moment of death, the time of deliberating and willing is over, the time of preparation and trial complete. Paul assumed that this side of death the faithful continue "to remain in the body," whereas to die is "to depart and be with Christ" (Phil. 1:20–23; Origen, *OFP* 2.11.5). One cannot speak in this way without implying some sort of personal survival after the death of the body. The living soul does not end with death, though the soul suffers the loss of the body. The continuity of personal life is clearly taught in Luke 23:43; 16:19–31, and Revelation 14:13.

By Sin Comes Death

It should not surprise those who have voluntarily participated in a history of sin and contributed to it their own twisted actions and their consequences should be subject to the moral requirement that accompanied all human life east of Eden: those who sin "surely die" (Gen. 2:17).

The Letter of James states the correlation precisely: "Then, after desire has conceived, it gives birth to sin; and sin, when it is full-grown, gives birth to death" (James 1:15). "There are three stages in temptation. The first is suggestion, the second is experiment, and the third is consent" (Bede, *Concerning the Epis. Of James* 1.15).

Does this mean that human life would have continued had humanity not fallen into sin? This is a hypothetical question that forgets the stubborn historical fact that all persons we have ever met have sinned, but it must nonetheless be answered on the basis of the sacred text: yes, humanity was originally created to remain alive to forever reflect God's goodness. Other corporeal creatures were destined by nature to die, but humanity in its God-created intent is different, being made in the image of God. Prior to the fall, soul and body were created to be forever united.

To some this seems an awkward point of classic Christian teaching: that God does not will death in humans. Humans do through sin. Without sin humanity made in God's image would have transcended the general law of natural death (Gen. 2, 3). The tree of life symbolically points toward an originally intended eternal continuity in fellowship with God. This moot point is something like the question of whether the Son would have become incarnate had humanity not sinned. There is no clear answer in scripture. What we know is that sin did occur as an act of free volition, and with sin death. After generations of experience with death, human death still appears to reason to be somehow contrary to the appropriate ordering of creation, as we see in the philosophical works of Leibniz (*Theodicy*) and Kant (*Fundamental Principles of the Metaphysics of Morals*).

From scripture we can learn (unless we stop up our ears to both good and bad news) that our first parents were endowed with bodily immortality prior to sin (Council of Mileum, canon 1), but lost this through sin (Council of Orange, 2.1). "For the wages of sin is death" (Rom. 6:23; cf. 1 Cor. 15:21, 22). The intrinsic connection between sin and death was recognized by all ancient Christian writers, following the firmly established Hebraic tradition (Job 14:1, 2; 16:22; Pss. 89:48; 90:10; Eccles. 7:2; 8:8).

The surprising inference: death is not morally natural to humanity, or to God's original purpose in human creation, although death is permitted by God as a consequence of sin.

The inevitability of death is an inexorable consequence of Adam's fall but not of Adam's creation. Physical death is not the natural result of the original or intended human condition, but the result of spiritual death through sin (Rom. 4:25). But God has provided a remedy even for the deadly consequences of sin.

Through One Man Death Reigned in All

The history of sin began when man and woman (not one without the other) sought to play God. The biblical pictogram for this is reaching for the tree of life on their own by willful grasping, against the divine prohibition. Together as male and female, humanity freely chose the one action whose consequence was foreknown by them to be death. Equally man and woman broke the order of creation. If woman was first in yielding to temptation, man was first in following (Gen. 3:6; Chrysostom, *Hom. on Genesis* 16, *FC* 74:207–21).

Hence it is said that the cause of death is sin. Paul explained that "sin entered the world through one man, and death through sin, and in this way death came to all men, because all sinned" (Rom. 5:12). The fall is a federal act, involving all humanity. It was "through the disobedience of the one man the many were made sinners" (Rom. 5:19; Origen, *Comm. on Rom.* 5.19). For "by the trespass of the one man, death reigned through that one man" (Rom. 5:17; Ambrosiaster, *Comm. on Paul*, Rom. 5.17; cf. 1 Cor. 15:21). Without this premise, much in classic Christian teaching is made more difficult to understand.

The primordial command was unequivocally clear, with no ambiguities: "You are free to eat from any tree in the garden, but you must not eat from the tree of the knowledge of good and evil, for when you eat of it you will surely die" (Gen. 2:17; Augustine, *CG* 13.23). The resulting judgment and its basis are also clear: "To dust you will return," because you "ate from the tree about which I commanded you, 'You must not eat of it'" (Gen. 3:19; Theodoret, *On Incarnation* 6.1). Death is the ordered and fitting expression of the holiness of God dealing with human sin (Ps. 90:7, 11; Calvin, *Inst.* 2.8.59). Death is described as a curse (Gal. 3:13), a just judgment upon sin (Rom. 1:32), "the last enemy to be destroyed" (1 Cor. 15:26; Chrysostom, *Hom. on Cor.* 39.6). Death is not the primordial will of God, but only consequent to sin. Hence one cannot say that human death was made by God (Wisd. of Sol. 1:13).

If God had been attentive only to justice, lacking mercy, God would have imposed the sentence of death immediately upon the heels of the first sin. Mercifully God has determined to restrain sin to allow time for repentance (Rom. 5:17; 1 Cor. 15:45; 2 Tim. 1:10; Heb. 2:14). Had God executed punishment in Eden immediately, there would have been no human history. Because mercy restrained justice, the history of humanity, in its glory and wretchedness, has proceeded.

The Death of Believers

Readiness to Die

The time of death is unknown. "No man knows when his hour will come" (Eccles. 9:12). Death is certain, time is short, "for we were born only yesterday and know nothing, and our days on earth are but a shadow" (Job 8:9; cf. 9:25). Death ends each and every capacity to exercise freedom within the conditions of time. The prudent person is always prepared for death (Eccles. 9:10; Didymus the Blind, *Comm. on Eccles.* 273–278; Rev. 22:1; Ps. 90:12). "So you must be ready" (Matt. 24:44). "Be dressed ready for service and keep your lamps burning, like men waiting for their master to return from a wedding banquet, so that when he comes and knocks they can immediately open the door for him" (Luke 12:35, 36; Cyril of Alex., *Comm. on Luke*, Hom. 92).

Those who live well have no fear to die (Clementina, *Recog.* 5). Believers do not fear death but sin (Chrysostom, *Concerning the Statues 5.1–6*). The faithful are called to live "godly lives in this present age, while we wait for the blessed hope—the glorious appearing of our great God and Savior, Jesus Christ" (Titus 2:12, 13; cf. Rom. 12:11–14; 2 Pet. 3:11; Cyril of Jerusalem, *Catech. Lect.* 15.2,3), remembering our vulnerability to death—*memento mori*—to ready ourselves for death and live life in awareness of the limited time God has given us (Ps. 90).

The Death of Believers

Those united with Christ by faith understand that his death is the pattern for their death (Athanasius, *On the Incarnation of the Word* 2.20–32). Though he resisted the prospect of death like any ordinary human being, in dying, Jesus freely yielded his spirit into his Father's hands (Luke 23:46; Cyril of Alex., *Comm. on Luke,* Hom. 153). Not seeking death, he trusted God the Father to raise him to new life. Though we follow our natural instinct by resisting death, we are being given the opportunity each day to offer up our lives to God symbolically, or if need be to be ready to die for the truth, confident that we shall live as Christ lives (Calvin, *Inst.* 2.10.14; 3.24, 25).

Death when viewed as a natural process appears as our "last enemy." Viewed under grace it has lost its sting (1 Cor. 15:26). The believer has "crossed over from death to life" (John 5:24). Death for Christian believers is transformed into a penalty whose sting is dissipated (1 Cor. 15:56; Cyril of Jerusalem, *Catech. Lect.* 3.11–12). "If we die with him, we will also live with him" (2 Tim. 2:11).

Death brings its own form of comfort to those who have suffered much. For death ends all temporal suffering, all complicity in sin, and all future burdens of decision making (Rev. 14:13; Andrew of Caesarea, *Comm. on Apoc.* 14.13). In dying, the fertile human capacity for rebellious willing ceases.

The Westminster Confession recapitulated for Protestants the classic Christian teaching of death succinctly: "The bodies of men, after death, return to dust, and see corruption; but their souls (which neither die nor sleep), having an immortal subsistence, immediately return to God who gave them. The souls of the righteous, being then made perfect in holiness, are received into the highest heavens, where they behold the face of God in light and glory, waiting for the full redemption of their bodies" (22.1).

Grace in Dying

Every day the faithful are called to choose anew the way of dying to the world and living to God. Each day offers the opportunity to hand ourselves over in the complete consecration of all our redeemed powers to God's care (Cyprian, *Treatises* 5). In dying, the faithful are enacting in reality what they earlier did once for all in their baptism: "I die every day—I mean that" (1 Cor. 15:31). Ignatius of Antioch in facing death wrote: "I am truly in earnest about dying for God. . . . I am his wheat, ground fine by the lions' teeth to be made purest bread" (Ignatius, *Romans* 4). Without a glimmer of morbidity or despair, when faced with death by a totalitarian power, Ignatius was ready to say to his persecutors, "Allow me to receive the pure light. When I reach it, I shall be fully a man" (Ignatius, *Romans* 6.2).

Death in believers is made subservient to their sanctification, so that even death serves the interests of the coming reign of God. The recollection that life ends in death has the beneficial effect of drawing the faithful completely away from idolatries and toward trust in God. In this way death is taken up even into the economy and quiet ordering of grace (Cyprian, *Treatises* 1). Death itself is viewed as a final passage to the presence of the living God.

Death brings to consummation the sanctification of those prepared by faith to receive it, that in death they may become "the spirits of the righteous made perfect" (Heb. 12:23). That the faithful are glorified in death means "(1) full and accomplished sanctification, the body of sin and death having been laid aside; (2) transportation by the angels to heaven; (3) immunity from the miseries of this life; (4) the fruition of heavenly joy and glory; (5) the praising and lauding of God and Christ; and (6) the longing for and expectation of full glorification, both by the restoration of its own body, and by God's final deliverance of the Church" (J. Altingius, *Methodus Theologiae didacticae*:119).

The Passage of Faithful Death

Death is like a departure from this life to another. In his last communication with Timothy, Paul was clearly expecting an abrupt end to his life: "For I am already being poured out like a drink offering, and the time has come for my departure [*analuseos*, unmooring, unloosing]. . . . Now there is in store for me the crown of righteousness, which the Lord, the righteous Judge, will award to me on that day" (2 Tim. 4:6, 8; Augustine, *Tractates on John* 3.10).

As the *tent* of this body is put aside (2 Pet. 1:14), the spirit returns to God (Luke 23:46; Acts 7:59). "For while we are in this tent, we groan and are burdened, because we do not wish to be unclothed but to be clothed with our heavenly dwelling so that what is mortal may be swallowed up by life" (2 Cor. 5:1–4; Chrysostom, *Hom. on Cor.* 10.3). In the resurrection the perishable is "clothed with the imperishable" (1 Cor. 15:53; Augustine, Sermon, Feast of Ascension 264.6).

Meanwhile this side of death the believer is being abundantly fed at the Lord's Table, that the spiritual body born in baptism may be nourished toward eternal life, finally to be raised up on the day of his coming (Chrysostom, *Baptismal Instructions* ACW 31:150–152). Each service of Word and Sacrament, of meeting with the risen Lord, is an occasion for preparation of the final meeting with the Lord in death and the ensuing life eternal.

Death for believers is transformed from labor to a *rest* (Rev. 14:13), and from affliction to *relief* (2 Thess. 1:7). In Christ death is no more to be feared than sleep followed by a blessed awakening.

Immortality

Job's question remains a perennial human query: "If a man dies, will he live again?" (14:14). Our limited purpose remains to state the classic Orthodox-Catholic-Reformed consensus on this point, even if that consensus has been challenged by modern critics. The unfeigned, accurate, straightforward delineation of the reasoning of the classic position will go far in answering many legitimate questions of critics.

In the absolute sense, God "alone is immortal [*athanasian*]" (1 Tim. 6:16; Augustine, *Confessions* 12.11.11). This does not imply that human creatures cannot be given a share in God's eternal being. It merely affirms that God is the only one who has immortality as a necessary attribute (Calvin, *Inst.* 3.25). God alone necessarily exists. All other beings have a borrowed or derived or dependent existence. Such is as true of the created human soul as of the body. To affirm personal survival after death is not to imply that the survivors were uncreated. Christian hope is not fixed upon the indestructibility of the natural soul of individual human beings, but God's redemptive power (Lactantius, *DI*, 3.12–13).

With this qualification, Christianity affirms that creaturely human life survives bodily death. The human body is mortal, but the vital center of human selfhood is still destined for life with God when all the cells of the body have long decayed (Cyprian, *Treatises* 7). Eternal life with God is not claimed by Christians as a right but as a part of the divine economy of salvation that by grace allows unimpeded and unending communion with God (Lactantius, *DI* 3.13). "To those who by persistence in doing good seek glory, honor and immortality [*aphtharsian*], he will give eternal life" (Rom. 2:7).

Life beyond death is not an intrinsic human possession such that sinners might boast of their achievement. Rather the life that God gives, God may choose to sustain. This sustenance occurs not by natural durability or merit but by grace. Humanity in God's image is endowed with the gift of immortality from God's hand, not as an autonomous natural quality (Gen. 1:26, 27; Ambrose, *Belief in the Resurrection* 2.22).

The term *immortality* has a place in Christian vocabulary only if qualified to mean that the living soul created in the image of God does not die with physical death and awaits the resurrection for its new form of embodiment. The Christian understanding of the future life centers more on God's resurrecting mercy than on the bare notion of autonomous individual survival. ·

Israel's Hope of Immortality

Against the view that there is no Old Testament hope for personal survival or immortality, classic Christian exegetes have been attentive to numerous allusions that assume continuing life after death. Job expressed a confident expectation of a future vision of God: "And after my skin has been destroyed, yet in my flesh I will see God" (Job 19:26). The translation of Enoch (Gen. 5:24) and Elijah (2 Kings 2:11) point to life with God beyond the grave. The people of God are being gathered to a place that is to the spirit what the grave is to the body (Pope, *Compend.*, 3:376), "the place appointed for all the living" (Job 30:23). When Abraham "breathed his last," he was "gathered to his people" (Gen. 25:8; cf. Gen. 25:17; Num. 20:24).

The psalms exude confidence in the expectation of communion with God after death, when flesh fails (Ps. 73:23–28), when one awakens after death, where "in righteousness I will see your face" (Ps. 17:15). "God will redeem my life from the grave; he will surely take me to himself" (Ps. 49:15). The heart of Israel's hope of personal survival hinged on its faith in the steadfast covenant love of God, who would never abandon the faithful, even in the grave: "My body will also rest secure, because you will not abandon me to the grave, nor will you let your Holy One see decay" (Ps. 16:10). Who can read the psalms plausibly with the assumption that the writers knew nothing of a future life?

There were stern warnings in the Old Testament against consulting the dead or "familiar spirits," or persons thought to be able to summon the dead and speak with them (Lev. 19:31; Deut. 18:11; Isa. 8:19). These warnings, far from denying the impossibility of such communications, warn against their potentiality for idolatry, and mark Israel off from idolatrous nations. ·

By the intertestamental period the late Judaic hope of personal survival had found a more explicit voice: "But the souls of the righteous are in the hand of God, and no torment will ever touch them," for "their hope is full of immortality" (Wisd. of Sol. 3:1, 4; cf. 3:15, 16; 15:3, 4).

The Doctrine of Immortality Through Resurrection in the New Testament

It is common in the history of revelation for certain teachings to be revealed gradually through historical experience. The Davidic, prophetic, and Wisdom teachings of immortality could only be adequately made clear after the resurrection of Jesus Christ, who having "destroyed death" has "brought life and immortality [*aphtharsia*] to light through the gospel" (2 Tim. 1:10; Augustine, *Sermons* 4.1). "For the perishable must clothe itself with the imperishable, and the mortal with immortality [*athanasia*]" (1 Cor. 15:53; Ambrose, *On Belief in the Resurrection* 2.53–75).

That souls of believers survive death is apparent in such passages as Matthew 10:28 and Luke 23:43. Jesus is "the resurrection and the life. He who believes in me will live, even though he dies, and whoever lives and believes in me will never die" (John 11:25; Augustine, *Comm. on John, NPNF* 1 7:270–78). Those who welcome God's own coming in faith have already passed from death to life (2 Cor. 5:1; John 5:24; Augustine, *Tractates on John* 22.6).

Jesus understood that Abraham was yet living, and he repeated this point in his parable of the Rich Man and Lazarus (Sister Macrina, *On the Soul and the Resurrection, NPNF* 2 4:447–48). When the beggar of Jesus' parable died, "the angels carried him to Abraham's side. The rich man also died and was buried. In hell, where he was in torment, he looked up and saw Abraham far away, with Lazarus by his side" (Luke 16:22, 23), and spoke to him. "Abraham's bosom" was another term for the resting place of the pious dead. The parable suggests that the souls of the righteous enter immediately after death into a state of happiness, and the souls of the unjust are by their behavior separated from the divine presence. That souls of unbelievers survive death is taught in Matthew 11:21–24; Romans 2:5–11; 2 Corinthians 5:10. Jesus taught that "even Moses showed that the dead rise, for he calls the Lord the God of Abraham, the God of Isaac, and the God of Jacob. He is not the God of the dead, but of the living, for to him all are alive" (Luke 20:37, 38).

We have established that consensual Christian teaching holds a distinct view of the decisive meaning of death and of personal survival after death through the resurrection. This leaves, however, a knotty set of ambiguities with respect to what is happening in the time between death and resurrection, called the intermediate state.

The Intermediate State

It is speculative to apply categories of time to the intermediate period between death and resurrection. "God sees not time lengthwise but obliquely . . . before God it is all in one heap" (Luther, *Comm. Peter and Jude*). Calvin thought it "neither lawful nor expedient to inquire too curiously concerning our souls' intermediate state. Many torment themselves overmuch with disputing as to what place the souls occupy" (*Inst.* 3.25.6). The intermediate state is distinguished from the present state of life, on the one hand, and the final resurrected state, on the other.

What becomes of the soul after death? Is the soul conscious? However intriguing, these questions hardly admit of precise consensually received conclusions, but they remain important to those who face death, hence are a recurrent concern of pastoral care, particularly care of the bereaved.

There is some difference of opinion as to whether the souls of the righteous pass into an intermediate state between death and final judgment, or stand immediately in the presence of the Lord. Principal alternatives may be envisioned as follows:

AGREED	CONTROVERTED	AGREED
The Present State	An Intermediate State	The Final State
Ending in death of believer and unbeliever	Sleeping or awaiting or	Heaven/Hell
	No Intermediate State	
	Directly to bliss	

Christians differ in the way they interpret the pertinent texts, but most affirm that we may rest content that after death the believer is in the hands of God awaiting resurrection. The prevailing interpretation: *The souls of the just are conscious of their joy in the presence of Christ after death and before resurrection. The souls of the unjust are conscious of their absence from the glory of the Lord after death and before resurrection.* Both enter immediately after death into an intermediate state of awaiting final judgment.

Particular and General Judgment

The judgment of the individual soul is traditionally called particular judgment, posited as occurring immediately after death, as distinct from general judgment at the end of this-worldly history (Tho. Aq., *ST* supp. Q69.2). Thomas Aquinas (*SCG* 4.96) argued that immediately after death the soul receives a just retribution for what it has done in this life by becoming immediately aware of its destiny awaiting resurrection day (cf. Council of Lyons II, *SCD* 464). The end-time judgment awaits the event in which the resurrected body is rejoined to the soul. The posited time between them is called the intermediate state.

PARTICULAR JUDGMENT	GENERAL JUDGMENT
Immediately upon death	The last judgment
Soul	Resurrected body
Singly	Together
Separately	Common

Every person shall "appear before the judgment seat of Christ, that each one may receive what is due him for the things done while in the body, whether good or bad" (2 Cor. 5:10; Fulgentius, *On the Forgiveness of Sins* 2.6.1; cf. Rom. 2:6; Rev. 20:12–13; 22:12). Immediately after death, according to much classic exegesis, there is a particular judgment, wherein the soul becomes aware of its final destiny (Augustine, *Tractates on John*, 49.10).

Scriptures that refer to the saints coming immediately into the presence of the Lord after death are commonly considered under the topic of particular judgment, as distinguished from those events of divine general judgment that occur at the end of the world. The destiny of each individual soul is therefore known immediately after death, but the final sentence upon the unjust is not executed until the last day (Augustine, *The Soul and Its Origin* 2.4).

Ursinus summarized the distinction, "There are two degrees in the consummation of eternal life. The one is when the souls of the righteous, being freed from the body, are *immediately* carried into heaven; for in death they obtain a deliverance from all the evils of this life. The other is that greater and more glorious degree to which we shall attain in the *resurrection* of our bodies, when we shall ascend into heaven perfectly redeemed and glorified, and see God as he is" (Ursinus, *Comm. Heid. Catech.*:323, italics added).

Particular judgment is usually thought to be anticipatory of final judgment and individually administered. All are "destined to die once, and after that to face judgment" (Heb. 9:27).

The Intermediate State of the Righteous

The spirits of believers at death are with God. They are the "spirits of the righteous made perfect" whose names are "enrolled in heaven" (Heb. 12:22, 23). Alive and conscious (Matt. 22:32; Luke 16:11; 1 Thess. 5:10), they enjoy a state of rest and blessedness (Rev. 6:9–11). "The spirit returns to God who gave it" (Eccles. 12:7; Augustine, Letter 143). The souls of the righteous dead appear to enter upon this state immediately, according to Luke 16:22 and Revelation 14:13 (see also Phil. 1:23; 1 Thess. 4:17; Council of Lyon, *SCD* 457, 464; Benedict XII, Benedictus Deus *SCD* 530).

Protestant formularies teach that the souls of faithful, forgiven, and undefiled believers (saints) immediately after death are with Christ. The soul "after this life, shall be immediately taken up to Christ its head." It is also taught that "this my body, raised by the power of Christ, shall again be united with my soul, and made like the glorious body of Christ" (*Heid. Catech.*, Q 57). "We believe that the faithful, after bodily death, go directly unto Christ" (Second Helvetic *Conf.*, 26).

That the righteous after death have not yet received glorified resurrection bodies is suggested in 1 Thessalonians 4:16 and in 1 Corinthians 15:52, where an interval is assumed between Paul's time and the time of the Lord's return with the rising of the dead in Christ (Chrysostom, *Hom. on 1 Thess.* Hom. 7; Luther, *Comm. on 1 Cor.* 15, *LW* 28: 191–213).

That believers at death enter paradise immediately seems implied in the words spoken to the thief on the cross. Jesus promised the thief that "today you will be with me in paradise" (Luke 23:43). Paradise is the garden of return, the resting place of the pious dead. The text seems incompatible with any notion that consciousness ends in death or that the soul is destroyed in death (Calvin, *Inst.* 3.25.6).

Justin Martyr taught that souls after death enjoy bliss in the interval between death and general resurrection (*Dialogue with Trypho* 80; Irenaeus, *Ag. Her.* 5.31). Tertullian thought that martyrs entered heaven immediately upon death to behold the beatific vision (*On the Soul* 55; Ambrose, *On Belief in the Resurrection* 20–44; similarly Origen, Eusebius, and Gregory of Nazianzus).

In the Eastern church confessions it is declared that at death souls "depart immediately either to joy, or to sorrow and lamentation; though confessedly neither their enjoyment, nor condemnation are complete. For, after the common resurrection when the soul shall be united with the body, with which it had behaved itself well or ill, each shall receive the completion of either enjoyment or of condemnation" (*Conf.* of Dositheus, 18). Having died, but awaiting general resurrection, "The souls of the righteous are in light and rest, with a foretaste of eternal happiness; but the souls of the wicked are in a state the reverse of this." The fullness of happiness is not posited as being experienced immediately upon death, because "the perfect retribution according to works shall be received by the perfect man after the resurrection of the body and God's last judgment" (*Longer Catech.*, Eastern Orthodox Church, 372, II, p. 503; 2 Tim. 4:8; 2 Cor. 5:10).

In due course the Western medieval scholastic teaching came to distinguish five realms of afterlife: heaven for the just; hell for the unjust (Hades is alternatively construed by some to have two divisions, one for the just—paradise, Abraham's bosom—and the other for the unjust); *limbus infantum* for unbaptized infants (who miss the beatific vision due to their implication in unransomed hereditary sin, though they remain innocent of actual sin, and capable of a natural beatification); *limbus patrum*, where the Old Testament fathers and believing ancients await resurrection; and afterlife purgation, where the imperfect faithful are cleansed and fitted for heaven (Fourth Lateran Council, *SCD* 429; Council of Lyons I, *SCD* 457; Benedict XII, *SCD* 531, 535).

Please note that many of the definitions in this section remain to some degree controverted, hence can hardly be called ecumenically received teachings. Nonetheless, I will attempt to state what I take to be the prevailing view.

At death, the *believer* is not separated from Christ, but from the body. Paul drew this distinction (2 Cor. 5:6–8; Jerome, Hom. 63 on Ps.; cf. Phil. 1:19, 20):

At home in the body	Away from the body
Away from the Lord	At home with the Lord.

"Away from the body" suggests separation of the soul from the body in death. The consensual reading of these texts has drawn the conclusion that the souls of the pious dead are with the Lord. To be absent from the body is to be present to the Lord.

Similarly: "I desire to *depart and be with Christ,* which is better by far; but it is more necessary for you that I remain in the body" (Phil. 1:23, italics added; Ambrose, *On the Benefit of Death* 3.8). Even though Paul wished to be immediately with Christ upon his death, he believed it to be for the church's good that he "remain in the body." This could hardly have been said without the expectation of an immediate joy in the presence of the Lord at death (Calvin, *Inst.* 3.25.6). Nothing, exclaimed Paul, shall separate us from the love of Christ—"neither death nor life," "neither the present nor the future" (Rom. 8:38).

Paradise is a garden metaphor alluding to the restoration of conditions that prevailed in the garden of Eden (Gen. 2:8 ff.). Paradise at times is used as a synonym for heaven or an allusion to a type of heaven (Luke 23:43; 2 Cor. 12:2–4; Rev. 2:7).

The Intermediate State of the Just and Unjust

Already in the Old Testament there was posited a difference between the future condition of the just and unjust. The general resurrection of the just and unjust will bring to a decisive culmination whatever intermediate state is posited. Though the just hoped for deliverance from Sheol, no such hope would be thought possible for the unjust.

Though Sheol is usually translated "hell," it did not have reference to eternal punishment in its earlier development. Sheol is variously portrayed as a place of darkness or silence (Ps. 94:17) or forgetfulness (Ps. 88:12), separated from God's presence (Ps. 6:5), lacking awareness of earthly memories (Eccles. 9:5, 6, 10). In Job's gloomiest picture he expected to "go to the place of no return, to the land of gloom and deep shadow, to the land of deepest night, of deep shadow and disorder, where even the light is like darkness" (Job 10:21, 22; cf. Isa. 14:15–20). As the light of revelation increased, the expectation of the future life was set in greater readiness for the full disclosure of the final things in the ministry of Jesus Christ, which is even yet awaiting final confirmation at the end of history.

Those who have died in disbelief await final judgment under conditions of separation from God or alienation (Tertullian, *On the Soul* 56). Those who "do not obey the gospel" will be "shut out from the presence of the Lord" (2 Thess. 1:8, 9; Chrysostom, *Hom. on Rom.* 31.4–5). The souls of the wicked are pictured in a state of alienation resulting from their guilt as they await the resurrection and general judgment when they will be finally separated from God's holiness through their own recalcitrant decision (Benedict XII, *Benedictus Deus SCD* 530–31). Insofar as they have consciousness, it is portrayed as loss of joy for not being allowed to enter into the presence of God (Luke 13:28; 16:28). They are portrayed as in prison, under guard, being held for the day of judgment (2 Pet. 2:9; Hippolytus, *Ag. Plato* 1).

Consciousness and the Sleep of the Soul After Death

Scripture portrays believers as engaged in a conscious life in dialogue, in communion with God immediately after death (2 Cor. 5:8; Phil. 1:23; Rev. 6:9; 20:4). The soul after death has "a purely spiritual life accompanied by full consciousness, and determined as to happiness or unhappiness by the result of the particular judgment held immediately after death" (Pohle, *DT* 12:7). The premise of a conscious intermediate state is found in the transfiguration narrative (Luke 9:28–36; Proclus, *Orat.* 8), the words of Christ to the dying thief (Luke 23:39–43), and the notion of the communion of saints (2 Cor. 13:14; Rev. 8:3, 4).

The soul after death is not characteristically viewed in the New Testament as remaining in a totally unconscious or unresponsive state, though it is fitting to view it metaphorically as a sleeping state or soul-sleep. Note that sleep does not necessarily imply unconsciousness. The saints united with the Lord are described as those who sleep in Jesus: "so we believe that God will bring with Jesus those who have fallen asleep in him" (1 Thess. 4:14; Augustine, *Tractates on John* 49.9.1–2). Accordingly, life in Christ after death and before resurrection is like a sleeping place, a *koimeterion*, from which we derive our word cemetery.

Luther regarded the condition of faithful souls after death as "a deep strong, sweet sleep," considering "the coffin as nothing other than our Lord Jesus' bosom or *Paradise*, the grave as nothing other than a soft couch of ease or rest" (Luther, *Christian Songs, Latin and German, for Use at Funerals*, WML 6:287). This is why the early Christians called their places of interment "not places of burial or graveyards, but *coemeteria*, sleeping chambers, *dormitoria*, houses of sleep" (Luther, *Gospel Sermon, Twenty-fourth Sunday After Trinity*, SML 8:372). The dead are spoken of metaphorically as sleeping (Dan. 12:2; Matt. 9:24; John 11:1; 1 Cor. 11:30; 15:51; 1 Thess. 4:14), but here the language of analogy is not intended to be applied literally (Chrysostom, *Baptismal Instructions*, 3).

10

THE END OF HUMAN HISTORY

The General Resurrection of the Dead

The Hebraic tradition viewed the human person as grounded in the earth yet capable of transcendence, a single composite reality of inspirited body, so closely woven that it was unthinkable that one could be a person without a body of some sort. The New Testament makes frequent reference to the "resurrection of the dead" (Matt. 22:31; Luke 20:35; Acts 4:2), so as to underscore the expected event as corporate experience as well as corporeal, viewed as participation in the risen Lord.

The Resurrection of the Body

It is an article of the creed to "believe in the resurrection of the body" (*SCD* 6). "We look forward to the resurrection of the dead and the life of the world to come" (Creed of the 150 Fathers). The confession recurs in virtually every form of the ancient rule of faith. The Faith of Damasus confessed explicitly, "We believe that cleansed in his death and in his blood we are to be raised up by him on the last day in this body with which we now live" (*SCD* 15; cf. Creed of the Council of Toledo, *SCD* 20). On his return, the Lord is expected to call the dead from the grave to be raised up by the power of God. "I tell you the truth, a time is coming and has now come when the dead will hear the voice of the Son of God and those who hear will live" (John 5:25; Tertullian, *On the Resurrection of the Flesh* 37; Chrysostom, *Hom. on John* 39.2).

Early preaching consisted in "proclaiming in Jesus the resurrection of the dead" (Acts 4:2). What Paul preached could be summarized simply as "Jesus and the resurrection" (Acts 17:18). To deny the resurrection according to Jesus, would be tantamount to having little knowledge of scripture (Matt. 22:29). It was the defining error of the Sadducees against which Jesus actively taught (Mark 12:18–23; Luke 20:27–33; Acts 23:6–8).

Resurrection (*anastasis*, a standing up again, *egersis*, being raised up) is defined in the Eastern Orthodox *Longer Catechism* as that "act of the almighty power of God, by which all bodies of dead men, being reunited to their souls, shall return to life, and shall thenceforth be spiritual and immortal" (366). "For if they define death as the separation of soul and body, resurrection surely is the re-union of soul and body" (John of Damascus, *OF* 4.27). "All men shall rise again with their own bodies" (Fourth Lateran Council). Resurrection is the act of God by which the human bodies of all times and places, just and unjust alike, though reduced to dust, shall be restored to the souls from which they were separated by death, to be united for eternity in either nearness or distance from God (Pearson, *Creed*, art. 11).

The Just and the Unjust

The key text is from John— "Do not be amazed at this, for a time is coming when all who are in their graves will hear his voice and come out—those who have done good will rise to live, and those who have done evil will rise to be condemned" (John 5:28, 29; Tertullian, *On the Resurrection of the Flesh* 37–38). When this call comes, all will hear, though dead (Gregory of Nyssa, *The Great Catechism* 16).

Some passages of scripture appear to speak only of a resurrection of the just (Isa. 26:19; Luke 14:14). Yet Daniel expected the multitudes now dead to "awake: some to everlasting life, others to shame" (Dan. 12:2).

When Paul stood before the earthly governor Felix, he did not hesitate to point out that all finally must be accountable to the heavenly judge, for there will be "a resurrection of both the righteous and the wicked" (Acts 24:15). This is unambiguously affirmed in the "Athanasian" Creed (Quiquncue): "whence he will come to judge all living and dead: at whose coming all men will rise again with their bodies, and will render an account of their deeds; and those who have behaved well will go to eternal life, those who have behaved badly to eternal fire".

All nations are included (Matt. 25:32); "great and small" (Rev. 20:12) will stand before the final judge. The intention of the phrase in the psalm "the wicked will not stand in the judgment" (Ps. 1:5) is that those who are wicked will appear but will be unable to stand upright in the final judgment (Aphrahat, *Demonstrations, Of Death*).

"I Am the Resurrection"

Jesus not only taught but was the resurrection. From his risen presence the disciples learned what to expect of the end of history. Similarly the coming general resurrection is already being anticipatively experienced in the present by those whose lives are hid in Christ. "I am the resurrection and the life. He who believes in me will live, even though he dies; and whoever lives and believes in me will never die" (John 11:25, 26).

Jesus' resurrection (*anastasis*) illumines both our own present risen life of faith and our future resurrection—both "the 'first resurrection' from the death of sin to the life of righteousness, and the 'second resurrection' or call back from physical death to life." (Wollebius, *RDB*:181, quoting Rev. 20:6). "If the Spirit of him who raised Jesus from the dead is living in you, he who raised Christ from the dead will also give life to your mortal bodies through his Spirit, who lives in you" (Rom. 8:11).

Anastasis is the defining event of the gospel narrative. It had been repeatedly anticipated in many Old Testament promises showing the power of God to renew life and restore lost possibilities: Joseph was raised from the pit. Isaac was raised up from virtual death and given life by God's providence. Abraham was poised to follow the command to sacrifice Isaac who was again raised up. The return from Babylon (Ezek. 37), the taking up of Enoch (Gen. 5:24), Elijah and the son of the woman of Zarephath (1 Kings 17:21), Elisha and the Shunammite's son (2 Kings 4:34) were all regarded by ancient Christian exegetes as anticipatory types of the coming resurrection of the Son, and ultimately of all the just and unjust (Methodius, *Of the Resurrection*). Noah's salvation from the great flood and Moses' exodus were viewed, in the light of Jesus' resurrection, as a kind of baptism, a resurrection. These ancient narratives formed the background of interpretation of New Testament accounts of the daughter of Jairus (Mark 5:41), the widow of Nain (Luke 7:15), Lazarus (John 11), and those who arose at the burial of Jesus (Matt. 27:52).

The expectation of the general resurrection of the body is a distinctive teaching of Judaism and Christianity. Resisting dualisms, it honors the body as integral to human nature. The resurrection *locus classicus* of Hebrew scripture is enunciated amid the patient suffering of Job: "I know that my Redeemer lives, and that in the end he will stand upon the earth. And after my skin has been destroyed, yet in my flesh I will see God. I myself will see him with my own eyes—I, and not another" (Job 19:25–27; Jerome, *To Pammachius* 30). "That Christ rose is the peculiar faith of Christians" (*Leiden Synopsis,* 51.3).

How Immortality and Resurrection Correlate

The event of resurrection and the idea of immortality have often been contrasted in modern Christian teaching. But in ancient exegesis there is a close link between them: In the resurrection the dead will rise "again at the end of the world and become immortal" (*Eastern Orthodox Catechism*:92).

The life that one receives in creation is made mortal through the consequences of sin. The person is deprived of life in time by bodily death. The body in this temporal life is given as a provisional housing for the person through creation (2 Cor. 5:1–5). Congruently but differently: the life that one receives by resurrection is made immortal through the consequences of grace. In the Genesis account soul was created after body, following the generation of the body, adapting itself to the body. In the end, the process is reversed: the body becomes adapted to the spirit, following after the soul, as the glorified body (1 Cor. 15:42; Didymus the Blind, *Comm. on Paul*, 15:10).

Thomas Aquinas provided a classic summary of patristic reasoning why, upon rising, there will be no dying again: Resurrection is required to accomplish God's purpose for humanity because "man's ultimate perfection demands the reunion of soul and body," for the human person without body is missing something essential, hence "a natural desire rises within the soul for union with the body; its will cannot be utterly stilled until it be reunited with the body, in other words, until man rises from the dead." (Tho. Aq., *Compend. of Theology* 151). Thomas argued the congruity of resurrection with immortality in this way: "It is against the nature of the soul to be without the body. But nothing that is against nature can be lasting. Therefore the soul will not be forever without the body. Thus the immortality of the soul seems to require the resurrection of the body" (Tho. Aq., *SCG* 4, 79). Those who rise by Christ's merit will suffer death no more, because by his passion he has "repaired the deficiencies of nature which sin had brought upon nature" in death (*SCG* 4, 82). "We ought to be judged, and if need be punished, in the composite human nature in which we have done good or ill" (Hall, *DT* 10:150). The mortal person is given life anew through the new correspondence of body with soul in the resurrection of the dead. The body is given a glorified form through the resurrection (Tho. Aq., *SCG* 4, 82.7).

Immortality Brought to Light Through the Gospel of the Resurrection

The hope of immortality is not denied in classic Christianity but viewed in the light of the resurrection. Immortality means deathlessness, immunity to death, not being subject to death or to any corrupting influence that might lead to death. The resurrection of Jesus provided for Christian faith the hope of imperishable life, the death of death, the hope of eternal life (Origen, *OFP*:181–85).

The true teaching of immortality has been brought to light through the gospel of grace. "This grace was given us in Christ Jesus before the beginning of time, but it has now been revealed through the appearing of our Savior, Christ Jesus, who has destroyed death and has brought life and immortality [*aphtharsian*] to light through the gospel" (2 Tim. 1:9–10). Through grace we arise again and "abide immortal" (Athanasius, *Ag. Arians* 2.75). "In Christ's death, death died. Life dead slew death; the fullness of life swallowed up death; death was absorbed in the body of Christ" (Augustine, *Tractates on John* 12.11). The soul is life and cannot die because life cannot lack itself (Augustine, *Immort. Of Soul*, 9.16). In destroying death, Christ brought the hope of imperishable life to light and transmuted the hypothesis of the immortality of the soul, not negating the hope of immortality, but viewing it now in the light of the gospel of the resurrection (Augustine, *Trin.*, *FC* 45:382–87).

Those who set immortality and resurrection in direct opposition, as if contraries, have misplaced the correlation between them enabled by grace. By this gospel, Christians have been born "into a living hope through the resurrection of Jesus Christ from the dead, and into an inheritance that can never perish [*kleronomian apartharton*], spoil or fade—kept in heaven for you, who through faith are shielded by God's power" (1 Pet. 1:3–4; Hilary of Arles, *Intro. Comm. on 1 Pet.* 1.4). "For you have been born again, not of perishable seed, but of imperishable, through the living and enduring word of God" (1 Pet. 1:23). The new birth by faith through grace offers imperishable life (Bede, *On 1 Pet.* 1.23). "There is a first birth, in the descent of Adam, which is mortal and therefore corruptible, but there is also a later birth which comes from the Spirit and the ever-living Word of God" (Didymus the Blind, *Comm. on 1 Pet.* 1.23). The resurrection thereby confirmed the perennial human hope for immortality by transforming it into the assurance that through Christ the future life transcends death and corruption (Augustine, *CG*, *FC* 14:457–549).

Death Overcome

Attitudes toward death were changed by the resurrection. Prior to Jesus' resurrection, "all wept for the dead as though they perished. But now that the Savior has raised His body, death is no longer terrible," for believers truly "know that when they die they are not destroyed, but actually begin to live, and become incorruptible through the Resurrection" (Athanasius, *Incarn. of the Word* 27).

Athanasius offered as sufficient evidence of this radical change the incontestable historical fact that *courageous women were empowered to martyrdom without fear*. Every Christian who had lived through the Diocletian persecution (AD 303–305, as had Athanasius himself) knew this to be a fact. It was especially harsh in Alexandria. This example was offered to show the courage of these women: their laughter at the fires of their own persecution. The martyred women who shared in Christ's resurrection learned to "despise even what is naturally fearful," he attested, as those persons from India who handle fire, touching it but unafraid, as stubble enclosed in asbestos no longer needs to dread the fire (Athanasius, *Incarn. of the Word* 27, 44). It is likely that the great bishop of Alexandria had personally ministered to such women.

Celebration of the Body

There is in Jewish and Christian hope of the resurrection of the dead no contempt for the body, nor is there an idealization of the disembodied soul. For what is it that is valued and raised anew but the body?

Hence the body is greatly honored in Christianity (Rom. 6:19; 12:1; 1 Cor. 6:19, 20; 9:27), not only in the incarnation, which is the coming of God in the flesh, but the resurrection as well, which is the reuniting of the human body-soul composite for an eternal destiny near to or separated from God (Justin Martyr, *On the Resurrection* 7).

That the Lord affirms the body is evident in the incarnation, where he assumed not only a human soul but a body. The body of Christ has extraordinary importance in Christianity. His body was offered as a sacrifice on the cross. The Supper is a participation in his body (John 6:35–40). Ultimately our very bodies are to be redeemed. "Offer your bodies as living sacrifices" (Rom. 12:2). "Do you not know that your bodies are members of Christ himself?" (1 Cor. 6:15).

The whole body is understood as set apart for service, as a temple. The Spirit is at work to renew and sanctify the hands (Eph. 4:28), the mouth (Eph. 4:29), the tongue (1 Pet. 3:15), the eyes (Ps. 119:37), the ears (James 1:19), for all the "parts of your body" are "instruments of righteousness" (Rom. 6:13).

The Christian hope risks distortion if stated as if it were essentially a hope for the soul's escape from the prison of the body into a purely spiritual realm. Christianity hopes for the renewal of the whole person, where I will again be myself, will live again in my glorified body (Ignatius, *Smyrna* 2–9). It is the body revivified that rises in the resurrection. "It is precisely the substance of this our flesh but without sin, which will rise again" (Formula of Concord, 548).

Manichaean teaching of matter as evil is rejected by resurrection teaching. Calvin regarded it as a Manichaean error to think that the flesh, being unclean, cannot rise again, as if to imagine that what is infected with the taint of sin could not be divinely cleansed (Calvin, *Inst.* 3.25). The body is the temple of the Holy Spirit. Though the seat of unruly affections, pride, and vanity, the body rightly understood is a divine gift that may in turn be completely consecrated.

The body as such is not treated as an encumbrance but as essential to humanity when viewed within the economy of salvation. "It is not the body, but the corruptibility of the body, which is a burden to the soul" (Augustine, *CG* 13.16; cf. 1 Cor. 6:19; Rom. 8:20–23; Gal. 5:17). "Man is so constituted by nature that every line of the spirit's receptivity and expression is conditioned and accomplished by the use of matter; and no evidence exists that the supernatural elevation of human nature hereafter will bring this law to an end" (Hall, *DT* 10:162).

The resurrection is of the body, but not simply this natural body of flesh, as if it could be spiritlessly restored, for "flesh and blood cannot inherit the kingdom of God, nor does the perishable inherit the imperishable" (1 Cor. 15:50). Rather God is preparing a body suitable to the conditions of eternity in the divine presence (Rufinus, *Comm. on Apostles' Creed* 40).

"If there is a natural body, there is also a spiritual body" (1 Cor. 15:44). Spiritual body does not mean body made out of spirit but body completely enlivened by spirit, just as the present body is indwelt and empowered by the soul (1 Cor. 15:44–46). "Paul teaches not the resurrection of physical bodies but the resurrection of persons, and this is not in the return of the 'fleshly body,' that is, the biological structure, an idea which he expressly describes as impossible ('the perishable cannot become imperishable'), but in the different form of the life of the resurrection" (Ratzinger, *IC*: 277).

The Same Person

Since it is the whole person that God loved and redeemed, the restored whole person is promised as a future hope in Jewish and Christian teaching (Tertullian, *Apology* 48–50).

Resurrection is the complete and final restoration of the whole person. Only on the premise of this restoration is one able to complete humanity's intended eternal destiny of closeness to God (Origen, *OFP* III.6).

"Resurrection is the restoration of the same human body to life in the same substance, less mortality" (Bucanus, *ITLC* 37.2, Heppe, *RD*:701). If the notion of "same body" is not sustained, the resurrection risks being diluted into the notion of a resurrection into a different body (Irenaeus, *Ag. Her.* 5.32). "If the soul did not resume the same body, there would be no resurrection, but rather the assumption of a new body" (Tho. Aq., *ST* supp., Q79.1). The glorified body is not a different body, but a different form of the same body. "We shall arise, clothed not in air or some other flesh, but in the self-same [now-glorified flesh] in which we live, exist, and move" (Eleventh Council of Toledo). Final judgment would make little sense if "new bodies were to be brought before the judgment seat" (Calvin, *Inst.* 3.25.7, cf. Augustine, *Ag. Adimantus* 121.5). "For He did not raise the soul without the body but the body along with the soul; and not another body but the very one that was corrupt" (John of Damascus, *OF* 4.27).

Whether the Atomistic Dissolution of the Body Confounds the Resurrection

Does this imply that precisely the same cells and molecules that once constituted our body will be regathered and recomposed? No. For even in earthly existence, there is no such continuity. The body is constantly changing materially, and has been doing so since infancy (Gregory of Nyssa, *On the Making of Man* 27–30). Yet its basic features have continuity, due to their genetic coding. The DNA molecules provide a unique, specific code for every individual that stamps each one as distinctive. There is no precise molecular sameness between the grain of wheat buried in the ground and the harvest gathered the next summer, but there is clearly continuity in the intergenerational organism (Sister Macrina, *On the Soul and the Resurrection, NPNF* 2 4:446).

Metabolically, "the human body changes its material composition every seven years or so. Hence there can be no absolute bodily identity even in this life" (Pohle, *DT* 12:141). The Pauline teaching of the "same body" does not require a restoration even more fixed and absolute than ordinary metabolic changes require. God will find fit means to guarantee the sameness of the body without construing this as precisely the same cellular identity. The identity of the person will remain, as one person may survive several physical bodies metabolically during a given lifetime. "The human beings that rise again are the identical human beings who lived before, though their vital processes are performed in a different way" (Tho. Aq., *Compend. of Theology* 155).

Even while the physical body is being dissolved through time and death, the glorified body will live on, having been given life in baptism, fed by the Eucharist, and clothed in glory at the last day (Cyril of Jerusalem, *Catech. Lect.* 18.7). "For just as, not existing before I was born, I knew not who I was, and only existed in the potentiality of fleshly matter, but being born, after a former state of nothingness, I have obtained through my birth a certainty of my existence; in the same way, having been born, and through death existing no longer, and seen no longer, I shall exist again just as before I was not, but was afterwards born. Even though fire destroy all traces of my flesh, the world receives the vaporized matter, and though dispersed through rivers and seas, or torn in pieces by wild beasts, I am laid up in the storehouses of a wealthy Lord" (Tatian, *Orat. Ag. the Greeks* 6).

Lacking Resurrection, Is There Moral Absurdity?

If one posits a history full of injustice without a resurrection, the power of evil would appear greater than the power of God, and a major defect would persist in the economy of salvation (Tertullian, *The Resurrection of the Flesh* 41–49). Resurrection is a necessary link in the moral chain of divine promises (John of Damascus, *OF* 4.27).

"Why do the wicked live on, growing old and increasing in power?" asked Job (21:7). There is a moral embarrassment in providence if this question is forever postponed and never dealt with finally (Gregory of Nyssa, *On the Making of Man* 21). At some point the serious moral consciousness must posit a future life in which justice is better done than in ordinary history (Tho. Aq., *SCG* 4.79).

"You must charge God with lack of justice, if there be not judgment and recompense after this world." How could God be righteous if murderers go forever unpunished? No one who presides over the games crowns the athlete while he is striving, but "waits till he has seen how every competitor finishes" (Cyril of Jerusalem, *Catech. Lect.* 18.4).

The Resurrection Analogy of a Living Organism from a Dying Seed

The body that dies becomes subject to the decomposition of its constituent parts, abandoned to the general laws of matter. Can an identity be preserved amid this disintegration? Paul answered with a metaphor: "But someone may ask, 'How are the dead raised? With what kind of *body* will they come?' How foolish! What you sow does not come to life unless it dies. When you sow, you do not plant the body that will be, but just a *seed*, perhaps of wheat or of something else. But *God gives it a body* as he has determined, and to each kind of seed he gives its own body" (1 Cor. 15:35–38, italics added). The seed must be buried to come alive. It must pass into a certain sort of decay and dissolution in order that the seed may then disengage from its old form and begin to sprout. Similarly our bodies die, that by dying they may enter at length into a new life.

The body of the seed dies but the principle of life in the seed remains ready to come alive once buried (*Longer Catech.*, Eastern Orthodox Church, 367). Though there is a vast change, the former identity is not destroyed. The changed form does not imply a breach of organic continuity or a transubstantiation of matter into spirit or the transmigration of souls from one body to another, for it is the same *soma* that is "delivered from its present subjection to the animal *psuchē*, and is subjected to the higher *pneuma*" (Hall, *DT* 10:151). The flesh that cannot inherit incorruption has reference to the intrinsic limitations of the present physical *soma*. Though the body cannot of itself inherit incorruption, it can put on incorruption in the form of being clothed with the imperishable when raised by the power of God (1 Cor. 15:50–54).

The sister of Gregory of Nyssa, Macrina, was his key teacher on the resurrection. What happens in the resurrection, she said, is: "*the return of human nature to its primal condition.* Originally we also were, in a sense, a full ear, but we were withered by the torrid heat of sin; and then on our dissolution by death the earth received us. But in the spring of the resurrection the earth will again display this naked grain of our body as an ear, tall, luxuriant, and upright" (Sister Macrina, *On the Soul and the Resurrection*, italics added).

We Shall Be Like Him

Paul was confident that the risen faithful would be like the risen Lord, our risen bodies like his risen body, no longer subject to death (1 Cor. 15:50–58).

The Risen, Glorified Body

If the new body is more glorious, it is unreasonable to grieve inordinately over the loss of the old body. "So will it be with the resurrection of the dead. The body that is sown is perishable, it is raised imperishable; it is sown in dishonor, it is raised in glory; it is sown in weakness, it is raised in power; it is sown a natural body, it is raised a spiritual body" (1 Cor. 15:42, 43).

"With what kind of body will they come?" (1 Cor. 15:35). What are the properties of the resurrection body? Our Lord's risen body reveals the pattern of the resurrection body, for "our citizenship is in heaven. And we eagerly await a Savior from there, the Lord Jesus Christ, who, by the power that enables him to bring everything under his control, will transform our lowly bodies so that they will be *like his* glorious body" (Phil. 3:20, 21, italics added).

The transfiguration narrative anticipated the type of the glorified body, where Jesus' "face shone like the sun, and his clothes became as white as the light," and "there appeared before them Moses and Elijah, talking with Jesus" (Matt. 17:2; cf. Luke 9:29).

That the risen body is spiritual does not imply that it has become so etherealized as to be no longer a body. It will be distinguishable from what it now is, yet without the unneeded digestive-reproductive functions of the animal economy.

The notion of a spiritual body remains a mystery even when best explained. From scripture we may learn as much as we need to know.

Endowments of the Glorified Body

The risen (glorified-spiritual) body is being endowed with all that is requisite for life in the presence of the holy God. The vision of God is finally beheld only through the transformed eyes of the resurrected body (1 John 3:2; 1 Cor. 13:12).

God is able to renew the body so as to make it a fit temple for the glorified spirit. The risen body will enjoy a bliss and perfection and beauty that reflects its joyful participation in the completeness and beauty of God (Tho. Aq., *ST* supp., 3, Q83–85). The risen body "will be perfectly purged of all earthly lees and dregs, all senses rendered purer, all movements and actions more perfect, and because they will be removed from the necessities of this animal life, sleep, rest, food, drink, medicines, clothes, etc., and because they will be perfectly subject to the Holy Spirit, and their souls regenerated" (Riisen, 18.24, in Heppe, *RD*:708). It is promised to be consummately radiant, agile, fine, and not subject to suffering (Tho. Aq., *Compend. of Theology* 168).

The risen body will not die, because it is "raised imperishable" (1 Cor. 15:42). "There will be no more death or mourning or crying or pain, for the old order of things has passed away" (Rev. 21:4). The risen body will be capable of reflecting the glory of God, because it is "raised in glory" (1 Cor. 15:43) able to praise God without distraction, knowing no weariness or fainting.

In its glorified state, the soul will be given as much or greater excellence than existed in humanity before the fall. The community of the resurrection experiences understanding without error, light without shadow, wisdom without ignorance, reason without obscurity, memory without forgetfulness, volition without depravity, joy without sorrow, and pleasure without pain. In the state of innocence Adam and Eve were not by nature intrinsically prone to sin. So in the state of glory the renewed humanity will not be inclined toward sin (J. Wesley, *WJW* 6:241–52).

These inferences are drawn from scripture texts on the resurrection body of the faithful, and inferences from the narratives of the risen Lord. There is less to go on with respect to the risen bodies of the unjust. They will be cast from God's presence. Apart from God they will lack these qualities of glory, brilliance, perfection of powers, and spirituality. More than this the wisdom of God has not revealed (John of Damascus, *OF* 37).

Resurrection as New Creation

What Abraham said of Yahweh is pertinent to resurrection hope: nothing is too hard for the Lord (Gen. 18:14; cf., Jer. 32:17, 27). God is just as able to restore the unity of the person as God is able to create the person in the first place. "God created us out of nothing; why should He not be able to reawaken that which is destroyed?" (Cyril of Jerusalem, *Catech. Lect.* 18.6). Though above reason, resurrection is not contrary to reason, any more than is creation contrary to reason.

Resurrection is a new creation. Those who believe that the world has been created and exists in all its complexity do not find it impossible that the resurrection can occur in all its complexity. "Why should any of you consider it incredible that God raises the dead?" (Acts 26:8; Chrysostom, *Hom. on Acts* 52)—if God is able to create all that is from nothing? "It is more difficult to give a beginning to what does not exist than to recall into existence what has once existed" (Minucius Felix, *To Octavius* 34).

When Paul preached the resurrection in Athens, Luke's account notes that "some of them sneered" (Acts 17:32). When he proclaimed it before the provincial governor, he was thought to be insane (Acts. 26:8). Upon its first report the disciples "did not believe the women, because their words seemed to them like nonsense" (Luke 24:11; cf. John 20:25; Matt. 28:17).

"Although the resurrection of the dead is beyond [the power of] nature, and [understanding it] is beyond [the capacity of] corrupt reason, it is not contrary to nature, or right reason. Right reason indeed teaches both that the dead can be raised, and that they must be. The former is learned from God's omnipotence and the latter from his justice" (Wollebius, *RDB*:182). The final cause or purpose of the resurrection is "the revelation of the justice and mercy of God; justice in the raising of the wicked for condemnation; and mercy in the raising of the righteous for eternal life" (Wollebius, *RDB*:182, 183; cf. Tho. Aq., *ST* supp., Q79).

Sex and Food in the Glorified Life

Since there is no degeneration of risen bodies, there is no need for generation. The sexual functions of copulation and birth giving are no longer required. The Lord seems to have settled the question for Christian teaching by saying, "When the dead rise, they will neither marry nor be given in marriage; they will be like the angels in heaven" (Mark 12:25).

Every soul will be reunited with its own body. There will remain a distinction of sexes, yet without the exercise of sexual function (Matt. 22:30; Augustine, *CG* 22.17; *Leiden Synopsis* 51.37). One's sexual identity in the resurrection remains intrinsically an aspect of one's personal identity. The notion that women will be changed into men was consistently refuted, for the One "who created both sexes will restore both" (Augustine, *CG* 22.17).

In this life we need food and drink to nurture the earthly body, to prevent it from deteriorating and allow it to grow. But in the risen life there is nothing to cause the glorified body to deteriorate or tend toward corruption (*SCG* 4, 83). When Christ ate and drank after his resurrection, he did so "not out of necessity, but to establish the truth of His resurrection" (Tho. Aq., *SCG* 4, 82.19).

The Return of Christ

At the end of history, the Son is expected to return to earth. The biblical texts suggest that Christ will return in a glorious, public, sudden, and visible manner. It is an article of faith that Christ, having ascended into heaven, "is coming to judge the living and the dead" (Apostles' Creed, *SCD* 2).

Parousia

With Jesus' resurrection the question arose as to whether the coming age had arrived. A new era had been inaugurated, yet he was expected to come again to complete his saving work begun in his earthly ministry. There is good reason despite form-critical skepticism to conclude that Jesus himself expected and taught of his return (*parousia*, Calvin, *Inst.* 2.16.17; O. Cullmann, *The Early Church*:143–65).

All New Testament writers looked forward to the consummation of the kingdom of God that was inaugurated in the ministry of Jesus. At the Last Supper he said, "I will not drink again of the fruit of the vine until that day when I drink it anew in the kingdom of God" (Mark 14:25). Paul wrote to Corinth, "Whenever you eat this bread and drink this cup, you proclaim the Lord's death until he comes" (1 Cor. 11:26). The faithful are called to "eagerly wait for our Lord Jesus Christ to be revealed" (1 Cor. 1:7).

The expectation of his return impressed itself deeply upon the minds of Jesus' followers. His return is not a supplementary footnote, but a recurrent subject of searching discourse by both Jesus and the apostles. The Fourth Gospel recalls his last teaching: "If I go and prepare a place for you, I will come back and take you to be with me" (John 14:3; Cyril of Alex., *Comm. on John* 9).

In the Same Personal Way

Before his farewell meal, he reminded the disciples that they would "see the Son of Man coming on the clouds of the sky, with power and great glory." Having come first in weakness and humility, he would come again in power. His personal coming would be visible as an event in history that "all the nations" would be able to behold (Matt. 24:30), not an imaginary or fantastic or invisible event. "We do not know what is coming to us. But we know Who is coming" (Evanston Assembly Message, *WCC*, *CC*:581).

Immediately after his ascension two heavenly messengers announced, "He will come back *in the same way* you have seen him go into heaven" (Acts 1:11, italics added; Augustine, *Tractates on John* 21.13.2–4). This suggests that his future coming will be, like the incarnation and ascension, personal and visible (Rev. 1:7; 19:11–16). His personal resurrection and ascension is to be completed by his personal return to judge. This return will signify a final victory over the powers of evil yet remaining in history, a victory he promises to share with his called out people. The victory marks the consummation of history, and of the history of revelation.

From Above

"Let no one, therefore, look for the Lord to come from earth, but out of Heaven" (John of Damascus, *OF* 4.26). The descent will be from "the clouds" just as the ascension was into the clouds.

God's glory is often said to appear in clouds (Exod. 16:10; 19:9; Num. 12:5; 2 Chron. 5:13). At his transfiguration a cloud overshadowed him (Matt. 17:5), and at his ascension a cloud received him (Acts 1:9). So his final return will be from clouds of divine majesty and glory in a way that can be beheld by all. "Look, he is coming with the clouds, and every eye will see him" who is called "the Alpha and the Omega" (Rev. 1:7, 8).

Parousia Defined

Several complementary terms were used to point to this event. First and foremost, his return is called the Parousia, literally, presence (1 Cor. 15:23; 1 Thess. 2:19; 2 Pet. 1:16), sometimes translated as "second coming" or return. This does not imply a simple repetition of an event that has already occurred. Rather, it is the consummation of what was begun in the incarnation.

This coming or presence is also called his *epiphaneia*, appearance (2 Thess. 2:8; 1 Tim. 6:14; 2 Tim. 4:1, 8), or his *phanerōsis*, manifestation: "For you died, and your life is now hidden with Christ in God. When Christ, who is your life, appears, then you also will appear with him in glory" (Col. 3:3, 4). This coming will constitute a final *apokalypsis* or unveiling, removing all that now obstructs our temporal beholding of Christ (2 Thess. 1:7; 1 Cor. 1:7; 1 Pet. 1:7). The last day will finally disclose that the meaning of all history has from the outset been hidden in Jesus Christ, the Alpha and Omega of history (Rev. 1:8; 22:13; Calvin, *Inst.* 2.15–16; 4.18.20).

In this final appearance, the servant (*doulos*) form of the body of Christ will be glorified. His coming as incarnate Lord ended in his sacrificial action of atonement. So his final return will not be to repeat the cross, but to declare God's glory to all creation. "Now at His first coming when Christ came to *be judged*, He appeared in the form of *weakness*. Therefore at the second coming, when He will come *to judge*, He will appear in the form of *glory*" (Tho. Aq., *ST* supp., Q90.2, italics added).

His Appearing: Past, Present, Future

In the past tense, *Christ appeared in his earthly ministry that ended on the cross.* The appearance of the incarnate Lord came to a climactic end in his sacrificial death and resurrection: "But now he *has appeared* once for all *at the end of the ages* to do away with sin by the sacrifice of himself" (Heb. 9:26, italics added).

In the present tense, in the period between ascension and Parousia, Christ is *currently appearing in heavenly intercession* for humanity: "For Christ did not enter a man-made sanctuary that was only a copy of the true one; he entered heaven itself, *now to appear* for us in God's presence. Nor did he enter heaven to offer himself again and again, the way the high priest enters the Most Holy Place every year with blood that is not his own. Then Christ would have to suffer many times since the creation of the world" (Heb. 9:24–26, italics added).

In the future tense, Christ "*will appear a second time, not to bear sin, but to bring salvation to those who are waiting for him*" (Heb. 9:28b; Origen, *Hom. on Lev.*

9.9.3). The same person who suffered on the cross will come again at the end of history. "So Christ was sacrificed once to take away the sins of many people, and he will appear a second time" (Heb. 9:28a).

The Time of His Coming

The Purposeful Uncertainty of the Hour of Judgment

The ironic parallelism of death and judgment is deftly captured by orthodox Lutheran John Gerhard: "Just as death is certain, but the hour of death is uncertain, so it is certain that the final judgment will at some time follow, but the hour of judgment is uncertain" (*LT* 19:274).

Why purposefully uncertain? "As Christ would have us to be certainly persuaded that there shall be a day of judgment, both to deter all men from sin, and for the greater consolation of the godly in their adversity: so will he have that day unknown to men, that they may shake off all carnal security, and be always watchful, because they know not at what hour the Lord is coming" (Westminster *Conf.* 33.3; cf. Ambrose, *On Chr. Faith* 4.17). "For what He refused to tell the apostles, He will not reveal to others" (Tho. Aq., *ST* supp., Q77.3). "He scatters the fingers of all calculators and bids them be still" (Augustine, *CG* 18.53).

Paul in his early letters expected an early return of the Lord (1 Thess. 4:13–5:10; 2 Thess. 1:7–10; 2:1–12), but by the time of his later letters this sense of imminence seems to recede, and the Lord's return is envisaged as a fuller cosmic event (Col. 1:12–20; Theodoret, *Epis. to Eph.* 1:10) that might be delayed. He gradually focused more upon the certainty of the consummation than the time, calling hearers to work and not merely to wait. In Crete and Ephesus he urged Timothy and Titus to work toward establishing the *ekklēsia* on the assumption that it must be prepared to have an extended intergenerational future before the consummation. Against a completely realized eschatology, the notion that the day of the Lord has already happened is specifically repudiated by Paul (2 Thess. 2:2).

The Rhetoric of Foreshortening

That is imminent which hangs over, threatens, projects over (*imminens*), appears as if it could happen at any time. The root word does not mean it is certain to come soon, but that its coming could be at any time, including the next moment. The sweeping consequence of final judgment is rhetorically reinforced by the metaphors of imminence, but this does not necessarily mean simple temporal nearness.

With this in mind, the sacred texts employ the prophetic rhetorical device of foreshortening the future so as to view it from the standpoint of eternity, as if a thousand years were but a day. Jesus employed the prophetic rhetoric of an imminent end, yet at the same time made it clear that the specific time of the end was known only to the Father (Mark 13:32). Even in his last letters Paul still expected the imminent return, though he was aware that he might not live to experience it.

Those who asked too curiously about "*When?*" were reproved. They were taught rather to be ready at any time. The day is known only to God. "It is not for you to know the times or dates the Father has set by his own authority" (Acts 1:7). "No one knows about that day or hour" (Mark 13:32). The faithful are called to leave to God the time and manner of "the day of the Lord" (1 Cor. 5:5; Phil. 1:6).

This did not imply that there would be no signs indicating the end time, but that short of that time "the Lord wished the time of the future judgment to remain hidden, that men might watch with care so as not to be found unprepared" (Tho. Aq., *Compend. of Theology*, ch. 242). With the Turk nearing Vienna, the papacy falling away, and the world "cracking on all sides," Luther confessed his intuition "that the world will not endure a hundred years" (*Table Talk*). Yet five centuries later, we know that these events, as portentous as they seemed, were yet to bear fruits of the Spirit that would themselves become a part of the larger, more patient economy of providence.

The blessed hope turns into a macabre vision when the hyperreligious drift into cynically, almost eagerly, waiting for God to destroy the first creation, as if there were something virtuous in beholding destruction. It is not intended that a preoccupation with his return will lead the faithful to undervalue his first coming or his cosmic creation, or to fixate on the details of his return so as to neglect the significance of his incarnate life and atoning death or mission to the fallen world. To "compute the times" is "to wish to know what He himself said that no one can know" (Hugh of St. Victor, *SCF*:452).

Since prophecy is only fully understood at the point of its fulfillment (1 Pet. 1:11), these consummating events may not be clearly recognizable until they are already in the process of happening. Meanwhile we are instructed to "not believe every spirit, but test the spirits to see whether they are from God, because many false prophets have gone out into the world" (1 John 4:1). The crucial test is the simple confession of Jesus Christ as incarnate Lord. "The spirit of the anti-christ, which you have heard is coming and even now is already in the world" is precisely characterized by the failure to acknowledge Jesus as God's own coming (1 John 4:2, 3).

Signs of His Coming

Though uncertain as to time, the approach of the day of his coming will be accompanied by signs. Even if the signs may take an extended period for their fulfillment, the coming itself will be sudden and largely unexpected (Mark 13:36; Luke 21:34, 35; Matt. 24:42–44).

Signs of the Times to Precede the General Judgment

The descriptions of the signs of the end usually include a series of tribulations—wars, famines, earthquakes, persecutions, and apostasy, and the emergence of massive forces opposing Christ (*Longer Catech.*, Eastern Orthodox Church, 234). It seems clear from history generally, however, that these signs are reasonably frequent in ordinary history, hence belong to the structure of this dying world—ascension to Parousia. There have always been natural disasters and outrages against oppressed peoples. These signs exhort us to be aware of our finitude and sin and to be constantly awake to the hope of God's own coming.

The signs that appear as portents of vast disruption in history will recur with greater frequency and intensity as the end approaches (*Barnabas* 4.4). Several key passages portray these signs, especially Matthew 24, Mark 13, and Luke 21, as well as Paul's letter to the Thessalonians and the Book of Revelation. Virtually all the signs that appear in Mark 13 and Matthew 24 recur among the woes of the Apocalypse. It remains debatable among classic exegetes whether or how they may fit together as an overall pattern, and to what extent they are to be literally or metaphorically interpreted.

The actually beheld event of the destruction of Jerusalem became a prevailing archetype for interpreting the general denouement of all things (Dan. 12:1; Matt. 24:21, 22; 2 Pet. 3:9). The desolating sacrilege of Daniel was employed to interpret the destruction of Jerusalem, which was seen as a foreshadowing of all end events (Irenaeus, *Ag. Her.* 5.25; Eusebius, *CH* 3.5–10).

The Universal Preaching of the Gospel: The Calling of the Gentiles

Among other signs of the end were the complementary signs of the calling of the Gentiles and the gathering of the people of Israel. A worldwide dissemination of the gospel is expected among all nations (Mark 13:10; Rom. 11:25). "And this gospel of the kingdom will be preached in the whole world as a testimony to all nations, and then the end will come" (Matt. 24:14); "and you will be my witnesses in Jerusalem, and in all Judea, and Samaria, and to the ends of the earth" (Acts 1:8). All the nations will be given an opportunity to enter the kingdom (Acts 15:14; Rom. 9:24–26; Eph. 2:11–20) before the final judgment. God will not allow the historical process to end until all societies have an opportunity to respond to the news of God's mercy (Origen, *Ag. Celsus* 2.13).

This does not imply that the end must await the literal conversion of every single living person, but that the gospel must be preached, the testimony given, the offer of forgiveness extended to all before the end, and that there will be believers found throughout the world (John of Damascus, *OF* 4.26; Chrysostom, *Hom. on Matt.* 76).

The Gathering of Israel

Both Testaments attest a future return or restoration of Israel (Zech. 12:10; 13:1; 2 Cor. 3:15, 16). The gathering of Israel had been elaborately promised by the Old Testament prophets (Isa. 1:24–27; 60:15–22; Jer. 3:12–18; Ezek. 20:40–42; Amos 9:11–15; Mic. 7:18–20; Zeph. 3:19, 20; Zech. 8:1–9).

The hope of the gathering of God's people is found as early as the Deuteronomic covenant, that "when you and your children return to the Lord your God and obey him with all your heart and with all your soul according to everything I command you today, then the Lord your God will restore your fortunes and have compassion on you and gather you again from all the nations where he scattered you. Even if you have been banished to the most distant land under the heavens, from there the Lord your God will gather you and bring you back. He will bring you to the land that belonged to your fathers, and you will take possession of it" (Deut. 30:2–5; John of Damascus, *OF* 4.26).

During the dispensation of the gospel God will continue gathering his people until the fullness (*pleroma*, the full number of the elect) of the Gentiles has come into the kingdom. The sequence was rehearsed by Jerome: "When the multitude of nations will come in, then this fig-tree [Israel], too, will bear fruit, and all Israel will be saved" (Jerome, *Comm. on Habakkuk* 3.17).

All Israel Will Be Saved

God has not rejected his beloved people of covenant (Rom. 11:1). A remnant of Israel has been chosen by grace (11:6) through whom "salvation has come to the Gentiles" (11:11). Out of Israel has come "riches for the world" (11:12). Even though the hearts of some were hardened to the good news (11:7), Israel continues to be loved by God (11:28), "for God's gifts and his call are irrevocable" (11:29). God is using Israel's hardening of heart as the precise instrument to catapult the gospel beyond Jerusalem to the ends of the earth.

The hardening heart of Israel is always only partial and temporary, not absolute or unending. "Israel has experienced a hardening in part until the full number of the Gentiles has come in. And so *all Israel will be saved*" (Rom. 11:25, 26, italics added; Irenaeus, *Ag. Her.* 4.2.7). "If the part of the dough offered as first-fruits is holy, then the whole batch is holy; if the root is holy, so are the branches. If some of the branches have been broken off, and you, though a wild olive shoot, have been grafted in among the others, and now share in the nourishing sap from the olive root, do not boast" (Rom. 11:16–18; Clement of Alex., *Strom.* 6.15; Wollebius, *RDB*:180, 181).

Ironic Juncture of Extreme Depravity and the Pretense of Security

Paul's last known communication to Timothy declared, "There will be terrible times in the last days. People will be lovers of themselves, lovers of money, boastful, proud, abusive, disobedient to their parents, ungrateful, unholy, without love, unforgiving, slanderous, without self-control, brutal, not lovers of the good, treacherous, rash, conceited, lovers of pleasure rather than lovers of God—having the form of godliness but denying its power" (2 Tim. 3:1–5; Augustine, *Sermons* 229U). All these are signs of God's coming judgment.

In the last days the world will be inundated with defiant wickedness (Matt. 24:12, 37–39; Luke 17:28–30). The air will be poisoned by deceit. Under these conditions the perishing will live under a "powerful delusion" that will cause them to "believe the lie" (2 Thess. 2:11). This depravity is to be accompanied by a pretense of extreme security, as in the days of Noah, and of Lot (Luke 17:26, 28). "While people are saying, 'Peace and safety,' destruction will come on them suddenly" (1 Thess. 5:3; Origen, *Comm. on Matt.* 56).

The Appearance of False Prophets

Jesus taught that at the end "many false prophets will appear and deceive many people. Because of the increase of wickedness, the love of most will grow cold, but he who stands firm to the end will be saved" (Matt. 24:11, 12). "Watch out that no one deceives you. For many will come in my name, claiming, 'I am the Christ,' and will deceive many" (Matt. 24:5).

False teachers will not only promote error but attempt to make error the standard teaching of the gathered community of faith. Attempts of the faithful to correct this error will call forth ridicule, contempt, and persecution. Every heresy has sought to make itself official teaching. In the end these efforts are expected to reach their most intense form in a "great apostasy" that will precede the Lord's coming again.

Persecutions of the godly are to be expected (Mark 13:9; Rev. 11:7; 12:4; 13:7; 17:6; 18:24; 20:4). "Then you will be handed over to be persecuted and put to death, and you will be hated by all nations because of me. At that time many will turn away from the faith, and will betray and hate each other" (Matt. 24:9, 10). This does not imply that each act of persecution is an indicator of an imminent end, but that each persecution points anticipatively toward the final end when God's justice will be consummated. "In the last days scoffers will come, scoffing and following their own evil desires. They will say, 'Where is this "coming" he promised? Ever since our fathers died everything goes on as it has since the beginning of creation.' But they deliberately forget that long ago by God's word the heavens existed and the earth was formed out of water and by water" (2 Pet. 3:3–5; Oecumenius, *Comm. on 2 Pet.* 3.4).

The Lawless One

The lawless one will appear just before the final judgment. "And then the lawless one [*anomos*] will be revealed, whom the Lord Jesus will overthrow" (2 Thess.

2:8). "The coming of the lawless one will be in accordance with the work of Satan displayed in all kinds of counterfeit miracles, signs and wonders, and in every sort of evil that deceives those who are perishing" (2 Thess. 2:9, 10; Augustine, *CG* 20.19.4).

The lawless one is the son of perdition who will devise a rebellion so oppressive as to be distinguished as *the* rebellion (*he apostasia*, 2 Thess. 2:3), where he will seek to be viewed as the equivalent of God, demanding worship of himself in the temple. "Don't let anyone deceive you in any way, for that day will not come until the rebellion occurs and the man of lawlessness is revealed, the man doomed to destruction. He will oppose and will exalt himself over everything that is called God or is worshiped, so that he sets himself up in God's temple, proclaiming himself to be God" (2 Thess. 2:3, 4; Chrysostom, *Hom. on 2 Thess.* 3).

All that restrains this lawlessness is the patient mercy of the triune God. "And now you know what is holding him back, so that he may be revealed at the proper time. For the secret power of lawlessness is already at work; but the one who now holds it back will continue to do so till he is taken out of the way" (2 Thess. 2:6, 7). Both Chrysostom and Augustine regarded the Roman Empire as a form of this restraining influence (Chrysostom, *Hom. on Thess.* 4; Augustine, *Tractates on John* 29.8).

What Second Thessalonians referred to as the man of sin and lawless one is the same one whom John called the *antichristos* or pseudo-Christ (1 John 2:18, 22; 4:3), the archenemy of humanity who in the last days will be inspired by Satan to deceive the nations and persecute the saints (2 Thess. 2:3–12; 2 John 4; Matt. 24:5, 24; Hippolytus, *Treatise on Christ and Antichrist*).

The time of apostasy reaches its culmination in the Antichrist, portrayed in Revelation 13 as a blasphemous beast. Many false teachers were called "anti-Christs"—those who embodied a spirit in opposition to Christ (1 John 2:18, 22; 2 John 7; Athanasius, *LCHS* 2.9) at loose already in the world (1 John 4:3). These are a collective designation for apostates and false teachers who gather under a single head, a prototypical Antichrist (Dan. 7:25; *Barnabas* 4.4–13).

Prototypical apostates have in various periods been identified by various interpreters as the singular Antichrist: Nero and Valerian particularly in the Roman period (Commodianus, *Instructions* 41; Lactantius, *DI* 6. 17; Athanasius, *Hist. Arians* 77; Jerome, *Comm. on Dan.* 7.8), Genseric in the Vandal period, Mohammed after the Arab conquest, the Cathari and Albigenses in the Middle Ages, the corrupted papacy by Reformation writers, and in the modern period notably Hitler, Stalin, and Mao.

The aggressive denial of Jesus as the Christ is the key characteristic of the Antichrist (1 John 2:22; 4:3; 2 John 7; Hippolytus, *Fragments of Commentaries, Daniel*). The Antichrist concentrates in himself the whole history of apostasy (Cyprian, *Letters* 51). Though a mystical number (666) is attached to his name, Irenaeus warned that the number is capable of being fitted to many names so it is unwise to draw rash conclusions from the number (Irenaeus, *Ag. Her.* 5.28–30). "The Abomination of Desolation is the image of the emperor which he set up in Jerusalem; so will it be in the days of Antichrist, who will set up his image in all the churches of the world" (Hippolytus, *Comm. on Matt.*; cf. Eusebius, *Demonstration of the Gospel* 8.2; 3.7).

Disturbances in Nature and History

The apocalyptic prophecies of Mark 13 (cf. Matt. 24 and Luke 21) are taken by ancient exegetes to refer to the end events. They are expected to include famines and earthquakes as "the beginning of birth pains" (Matt. 24:7, 8), the obscuring of sun and moon by the brightness of his glory, the falling of stars from heaven, with the powers of heaven being shaken (Matt. 24:27–29), eclipses, changes in the heavens, and other extraordinary natural disturbances (Origen, *Comm. on Matt.* 39–56; Tertullian, *Ag. Marcion* 3.3).

Unrestrained sedition, famine, and pestilence are signs of the end. "You will hear of wars and rumors of wars, but see to it that you are not alarmed. Such things must happen, but the end is still to come. Nation will rise against nation, and kingdom against kingdom" (Matt. 24:6, 7; Luke 21:9–11). "When these things begin to take place, stand up and lift up your heads, because your redemption is drawing near" (Luke 21:28).

However ambiguous may be the struggle between the kingdom of God and the kingdoms of the world within history, at the end of history God's glory and judgment will be made fully clear to all. Meanwhile "we wait for the blessed hope— the glorious appearing of our great God and Savior, Jesus Christ" (Titus 2:13). Paul felt deep affinity with "all who have longed for his appearing" (2 Tim. 4:8).

Alpha and Omega

The end time will reveal that the Word spoken in Jesus' life and death was the Word spoken from the beginning of history, and will be the same Word spoken at the end of history (John 1:1–3; Rev. 22:13). With this consummation what was already a completed work on the cross in justification will become a completed work in the continuing body of Christ in sanctification. All other historical powers will be judged in the light of the last power.

The first and last letters of the Greek alphabet (alpha and omega) were used to symbolize the beginning and end. Christ is the Alpha and Omega of all things (Rev. 22:13), the one "who is, and who was, and who is to come, the Almighty" (Rev. 1:8). The consummation brings to final fulfillment what was begun in creation and having fallen was renewed in the incarnation.

Countering Simplistic Historical Optimism

However debatable may be the references to the final abomination, Antichrist, and lawlessness, they sharply resist the illusion of an ever-increasing, progressive, immanentally developing justice growing naturally from within history itself (John of Damascus, *OF* 4.26). Such naïveté about history contradicts too much historical experience. The New Testament rather is braced for a period of tribulation at the end when the faithful will be under unprecedented attack (Mark 13:3–23; 2 Thess. 2:1–3; Rev. 12:13–18).

Fallen human nature does not change within the deadly clutches of the history of sin, even though history itself is replete with change. Even the most impressive technological "advances" (nuclear energy, microchips, medicine, scientific experimentation, globalization) can be distorted by the self-assertive will, no matter how well intended. Far from decreasing evil, technology may tend to increase and complicate the power of evil. The past century has shown that it is folly to imagine that greater scientific knowledge will eliminate sin.

Instead of moving toward a benign utopia, the history of sin is moving toward a cataclysmic struggle out of which will come, by grace, a cosmic transformation—a new heaven and a new earth. Only after this ordeal can it be announced that "the kingdom of the world has become the kingdom of our Lord and of his Christ" (Rev. 11:15).

The Heavenly Colony

The present church is viewed by analogy as a colony of citizens in a faraway land whose loyalties and affections remain closely attached to their future home, for "our citizenship is in heaven. And we eagerly await a Savior from there," who "will transform our lowly bodies so that they will be like his glorious body" (Phil. 3:20; Marius Victorinus, *Comm. on Phil.* 3.21).

In this alienated world the full life of the community of faith is as yet incompletely realized. Her essential unity is fragmented. Her holiness is stained by apostasy. Her apostolicity is racked by heresies. Her catholicity is blocked from full presence in all the world. These conditions may last until "the end of the age" (Matt. 13:40), while in the interim wheat and tares grow tangled together (Matt. 13:30).

But on that day the Lord himself will come to free and save the beleaguered faithful. The church is actively awaiting that day, able to survive its darkest hours because of that hope. The faithful community desires his coming, fervently expects it, rejoices that God has promised to complete his purpose in history and make his victory finally known throughout the world.

Ethical Imperatives Embedded in the Parousia Expectation

All exhortations concerning the end are intended to have a practical, ethical meaning: to call persons to current responsibility. Whatever we do now will stand under the judgment of God at the end. All injustices that occur in ongoing history are in the process of being finally brought to correction in the presence of the holy God at the last day (2 Pet. 3:10–12; 1 John 3).

We are therefore to be prudent and watchful, for we know not on what day the Lord comes (Matt. 24:42). He will come unexpectedly, as a thief in the night (Matt. 24:43; 1 Thess. 5:1, 2), with the suddenness and unexpectedness of a flash of lightning (Matt. 24:27, 39, 44). The prayer of the early Christian communities, "Come O Lord" (1 Cor. 16:22; Rev. 22:20; *Didache* 10:6), was a prayer for justice.

Each hearer is called to live life *as if* the final day were overhanging: "Now learn this lesson from the fig tree: As soon as its twigs get tender and its leaves come out, you know that summer is near. Even so, when you see all these things, you know that it is near, right at the door" (Matt. 24:32–34; cf. Mark 13:30; Luke 21:32). He shall come "to present her to himself as a radiant church, without stain or wrinkle or any other blemish, but holy and blameless" (Eph. 5:27).

After gathering the faithful from the world over (Mark 13:27), he will lead them to the throne of the Father in heaven. The church will be presented in her perfected form after the removal of unworthy members. Angelic agents "will weed out of his kingdom everything that causes sin and all who do evil" (Matt. 13:41, 42).

All creation is viewed as awaiting this consummation. "The creation waits in eager expectation for the sons of God to be revealed," when "the creation itself will be liberated from its bondage to decay and brought into the glorious freedom of the children of God" (Rom. 8:19–21). There is an intimate link between the groaning of creation and the groaning of the faithful, for "we ourselves, who have the first-fruits of the Spirit, groan inwardly as we wait eagerly for our adoption as sons, the redemption of our bodies" (Rom. 8:23).

The Millennial Hope

The expectation of a messianic earthly reign of a thousand years was much debated before the time of Jesus in the writings of late Judaic apocalypticism. It held a strong conviction that the world as we know it is being readied for the consummation of God's purpose (1 Enoch 91, 93; Pss. of Solomon 17–18; 2 Esdras 7:28 ff.; 12:34; Apocalypse of Baruch 29:1–8).

Though Jesus did not condone the idea of a coercive political kingdom, he did lead his disciples to expect a spiritual kingdom sharply distinguishable from the kingdoms of this world. The New Testament actively employed vibrant images from the Jewish apocalyptic tradition to interpret its own messianic history. Crucial among these was the metaphor of a thousand-year reign in which Satan would be bound.

The millennium (a thousand years) is the time when the Messianic Deliverer is expected to reign on earth (Isa. 2:3; Dan. 7:14; Zech. 14:9). In this time it is expected that Satan will be restrained (Rev. 20:2), that righteousness and peace will come to the whole world (Isa. 11:3–5; 2:4), and that the fruitfulness of the earth will increase abundantly (Isa. 35:1, 2).

Revelation 20 is the source text for much of the highly symbolic hope. Since the millennial teaching is found preeminently (some say exclusively) in this passage, it should be conceded that it is hazardous to make a symbolic passage the principle of interpretation for all other relatively nonsymbolic passages. The main questions of millennialism hinge on the extent to which the texts point plainly or symbolically to an earthly reign of Christ, and whether that earthly reign will occur before or after his glorious return.

There remains a lack of consensus on interpretation of key millennial passages. The scripture texts admit of different doctrinal formulations, sequences, and explanations. Three views have continued over the centuries to compete as normative interpretations, but the entire discussion that follows has difficulty claiming the kind of firm consensuality over the whole of Christian history that we seek to identify in this study. The three persisting views are:

Realized millennialism holds that the millennium has already occurred or is occurring. *Postmillennialism* holds that the return will occur after the thousand year respite. *Premillennialism* holds that the return will occur before the millennium.

Realized Millennialism

Realized millennialists contend that the millennium is either an already present or an emerging reality. The millennium is now being fulfilled on earth. There is to be no future literal-political earthly kingdom besides the fruits that are already beginning to be borne. Rather the kingdom of God and the kingdoms of this world will continue in a mixed fashion until the Lord's return.

In this view, the presently ongoing millennial age will conclude with Christ's return and judgment. There is in this view resistance to detailed speculative explanations of present history as the fulfillment of specific prophecies.

Augustine discussed Revelation 20:1–10 in some detail in the *City of God* (20.7–14), reasoning by analogy of faith with other passages of scripture that the millennial kingdom is best viewed as the present Christian era wherein the powers of evil are already being restrained and the church being given time to proclaim the gospel. The strongman Satan is being bound up by Christ on the cross and in the descent into the netherworld (Luke 11:21–23; Mark 3:27; Augustine, Sermon 259.2). Ultimately, "to the strong, even the devil is weak"

(Ambrose, *Of the Holy Spirit* 1.intro.2), though penultimately he may be permitted to rage before his final collapse.

During this postresurrection period the gospel is being preached with the hope that Christ will increasingly reign in human hearts. The millennial respite is not to be awaited but has already begun. The church constitutes the proximate firstfruits of the kingdom of God on earth (Augustine, *Enchiridion* 111).

Augustine's view became prototypical for much Western Christianity, both Catholic and Protestant. When the glorious return did not occur in the year AD 1000, the idea of millennium increasingly became viewed symbolically as a long though unspecified period of time. One prevailing interpretation by the Reformers was that the fury of Satan was loosed on the early church during the first three centuries of persecution, after which came the period of Constantine when a relative peace (*pax Romana*) was given, which prevailed for a thousand years, roughly until about AD 1300, when the Ottoman Turkish empire emerged to end that peace (Gerhard, *LT* 20; Schmid, *DT*:651, 652) and the ecclesial establishment became vastly corrupted.

Among different types of realized millennial views were those of Clement of Alexandria, Origen, Dionysius, Tyconius, Augustine, Thomas Aquinas, and much classic Reformation and Counter-Reformation teaching. Consensual Lutheran teaching was well attested by Quenstedt: "Since the second advent of Christ, the general resurrection, the final judgment, and the end of the world are immediately united, and one follows the other without an interval of time, it is manifest that, before the completion of the judgment, no earthly kingdom, and life abounding in all spiritual and bodily pleasure, as the Chiliasts or Millenarians dream, is to be expected" (Quenstedt, *TDP* 4:649).

The term *chiliasm* (from the Greek word for thousand, *chilioi*) was sometimes used to refer to the teaching that focused especially upon sensual indulgence in an earthly kingdom of a thousand years. Eusebius attributed this idea to Cerinthus, a Gnostic of the first century (*CH* 3.28). Among those rejected by the Augsburg Confession for this interpretation were "Papias, Joachim (Abbot of Fiora), the Fanatics and Anabaptists, Casper von Schwenkfeld, and others" (Augsburg 17, 4).

Why Was One Thousand a Sacred Number?

Thomas Aquinas thought that the "thousand years" of Revelation 20:2 referred to "the whole time of the Church in which the martyrs as well as other saints reign with Christ, both in the present Church which is called the kingdom of God, and also—as far as souls are concerned—in the heavenly country; for 'the thousand' means perfection, since it is the cube whose root is ten, which also usually signifies perfection" (*SCG* 4:329; cf. Augustine, *CG* 20.6–8).

Though Protestants generally reject the uncritical identification of the church with the kingdom of God, the same point is made by Protestants such as B. B. Warfield, who held that the millennium was symbolic of the condition of the bliss of the redeemed in heaven, hence not to be interpreted literally as an earthly-historical reign. "The sacred number seven in combination with the equally sacred number three forms the number of holy perfection ten, and when this ten is cubed into a thousand the seer has said all he could say to convey to our minds the idea of absolute completeness" (Warfield, *Biblical Doctrines*:654).

The Critique of Millennialism by Amillennial Teaching

This position is sometimes called amillennialism, suggesting the absence of or lack of interest in the millennium, but the term is a misnomer, since this position does not argue against a millennium but that there is to be expected no future literal, earthly-historical millennium that is not already present in some form. Both pre- and post-millennial positions reject realized millennialism for failing to view the millennium sufficiently seriously as a biblical promise to be literally fulfilled in history.

According to the realized view, the millennium of Revelation 20 is not to be read as a literal thousand years but an indefinite symbolic period of the church age. These exegetes note that the thousand-year reign is not mentioned apart from the most symbolic of all books of the New Testament, the Revelation (Henry, *CWB* 6:1179–81). "The Apocalypse is a prophetic book, full of most abstruse visions, as well as allegorical and quasi-enigmatical forms of speech, difficult to be understood, and therefore to be expounded according to the analogy of the faith, based upon clear and perspicuous Scripture passages" (Hollaz, in Schmid, *DT*:653).

"Sound exegesis requires that the obscure passages of Scripture be read in the light of the clearer ones, and not *vice versa*" (Berkhof, *ST*:715). "It is not proper to construct a dogma alone from a book concerning whose canonicity there has been such extended dissent, and to make it the standard whereby to interpret the plain language of books whose authority is more thoroughly established" (Jacobs, *SCF*:516).

According to this view, premillenarianism depends too much "on the literal interpretation of a highly symbolic passage (Rev. 20:1–6). Among other leading Protestant spokespersons for realized millennialism are A. Kuyper, H. Bavinck, and G. Vos (see also A. Hoekema, *The Bible and the Future*, and Jay Adams, *The Time Is at Hand*) whose orthodoxy is seldom contested. These views are not to be confused with that realized eschatology which argues that Jesus did not expect a future Parousia (C. H. Dodd, *The Parables of the Kingdom*; J. A. T. Robinson, *Jesus and His Coming*).

Postmillennial Teaching

Some postmillennialists have seemed to appear as historical optimists who believe in the triumph of the gospel in human society (S. J. Case, *The Millennial Hope*; H. F. Rall, *Modern Premillennialism and the Christian Hope*). Many have a gradualist and progressive view of the coming kingdom, wherein Christ is gradually coming more and more to reign upon the earth and will come when that process has come to completion. Postmillennialists expect history to get better, not worse.

Postmillennialism means that Christ will return after the gospel has been preached to all and has taken full effect among the nations. The glorious return will occur after the millennial kingdom has been established.

The postmillennial sequence is conceived as follows:

World mission	Kingdom on earth	Christ's Return	Resurrection and Judgment	Eternity

The petition "Thy will be done on earth as it is in heaven" is expected as a growing world-historical condition. It is expected that the will of God will be done on earth either literally for a thousand years or figuratively for a long period of time. The "thousand years" is sometimes (as in realized millennialism) taken symbolically. This position is much like realized millennialism except that the latter does not expect a future earthly reign of Christ distinguishable from the present church age. Among varied representatives of postmillennialism are Joachim of Fiora, Daniel Whitby, Cocceius, Witsius, and Rauschenbusch (Rauschenbusch, *Theology for the Social Gospel*; cf. Hodge, *ST* 3:861–68; Strong, *ST* 3:1010).

Instead of portraying history as progressively improving, opponents of postmillennialism argue that the New Testament tends rather to see the time immediately before the end as one characterized by apostasy, persecution, and suffering (Matt. 24:6–14; 2 Thess. 2:3–12; 2 Tim. 3:1–6; Rev. 13). In the light of human self-assertiveness, it has seemed excessively optimistic to many readers of scripture to assert that an earthly messianic kingdom would directly emerge out of the shambles of the history of sin, or that peace would reign under the present conditions of finite history. To argue that the gospel will permeate society in the present age runs against the grain of those parables of the kingdom that do not look for universal acceptance of Christ in this age. The Augsburg Confession rejected the view that "before the resurrection of the dead, saints and godly men will possess a worldly kingdom" (art. 17).

Premillennial Teaching

The following more complicated sequence is fairly typically envisioned by premillennial teachers (with some variation among interpreters):

Before the Millennium:
Evangelization of the world
Apostasy and tribulation
Antichrist
Armageddon
Parousia (before the millennium, hence premillennial)
First resurrection of dead saints
Transfiguration of living saints
Translation to meet the coming Lord
When the Millennial Kingdom Is Established:
Antichrist slain or restrained
Restoration of Israel
The nations turn to God
Millennial peace
After a Thousand Years:
Satan unrestrained
Satan's final revolt fails
Second resurrection: unjust raised
Last judgment
New heaven and earth
Eternity

Most premillennialists expect a literal fulfillment of the unconditional promises made to Abraham and David. Most current dispensational premillennialists expect Christ to return bodily for an earthly reign of a thousand years or its equivalent. They expect Christ to return before the millennium to institute the kingdom promised to David. "At the close of this age pre-millennialists believe that Christ will return for his church meeting her in the air (this is not the Second Coming of Christ), to establish his kingdom on earth for a thousand years, during which time the promises to Israel will be fulfilled" (C. Ryrie, *The Basis of the Premillennial Faith*:12).

Scriptural Grounds for Positing a First and a
Second Resurrection: Revelation 20

Most references (excepting Rev. 20) assume only one resurrection—that of the just and the unjust (Matt. 25:46; Acts 24:15; cf. Luke 14:14). The key text positing two resurrections is found in John's vision of the saints who "came to life and reigned with Christ a thousand years. (The rest of the dead did not come to life until the thousand years were ended.) This is the first resurrection. Blessed and holy are those who have power over them, but they will be priests of God and of Christ and will reign with him for a thousand years" (Rev. 20:5, 6).

On this ground, premillennialists posit two future resurrections with a thousand years between them (Erickson, *ST* 3:1214 ff.). At the conclusion of the millennium, Satan, having been restrained for a thousand years, will be loosed to make a final assault on the kingdom of God, only to fail: "When the thousand years are over, Satan will be released from his prison and will go out to deceive the nations in the four corners of the earth" (Rev. 20:7, 8).

Realized millennialists interpret this text differently, viewing the "first resurrection" as repentance, faith, baptism, and spiritual regeneration, and the second as the general resurrection. "All the just who live during this time have a first resurrection by Baptism and reign with Christ so long as they are in the state of grace; and they have a second resurrection at the end of the world. Paralleling this is the first death by sin, and the second death in hell" (Trese, *The Creed— Summary of the Faith*; cf. Augustine, *CG* 20.6–7).

Ancient Christian Premillennial Teaching

Irenaeus expressed a premillennial view characteristic of the first three centuries: The present world would endure six thousand years (analogous to the six days of creation), after which there would be a period of suffering and apostasy that would accelerate until the coming of the Antichrist, seated in the temple of God. The entire apostate throng is headed up by the Antichrist, "recapitulating in himself the diabolic apostasy" (Irenaeus, *Ag. Her.* 5.25.1), whereupon Christ will appear, the saints will be resurrected, and the kingdom will be established on earth for another thousand years, the seventh millennium (*Ag. Her.* 5.28.3; 33.2).

This seventh millennium corresponds to the seventh day of creation, when God re-creates the world and the righteous, thus hallowing the last day of the world's week as a millennium of rest and peace. For one day with God is as a thousand years (Ps. 90:4). A new city of God, a new Jerusalem, would then become the center of a new period of peace and righteousness (Matt. 26:29; Irenaeus, *Ag. Her.* 5.33.3, 4). At the end of this thousand-year reign, the final judgment will occur, a new creation will make way for eternity (*Ag. Her.* 5.36.1). The dawning of the eighth day was for the *Letter of Barnabas* analogous to the Christian's Lord's Day, the day on which Christ rose from the dead and ascended into heaven (15.5–9).

Premillennialism was the dominant position among the ante-Nicene Fathers, Justin Martyr (*Dialogue with Trypho* 80.1), the Pastor of Hermas, the *Letter of Barnabas*, Irenaeus (*Against Heresies*), Methodius (*On the Resurrection*), Commodianus (*Instructions* 44, 4), and Tertullian (*Ag. Marcion* 3.24).

By the time of the Decree of Gelasius, AD 493 (*SCD* 161–66), several of the ante-Nicene teachers with premillennialist assumptions were being regarded as inadequate in various ways: Lactantius, Nepos, Commodianus, and Victorinus of Pettau. Among those who earlier had resisted certain aspects of premillennial exegesis were Clement of Alexandria, Dionysius of Alexandria, and Athanasius. Premillennialism was more fundamentally challenged by Origen, Augustine, and the Greek Fathers, who argued that the millennial kingdom had begun with the incarnation. Among Protestant advocates of premillennialism are Bengel, Irving, van Oosterzee, Ellicott, Darby, the Adventists, Christadelphians, Plymouth Brethren, and a host of contemporary evangelical interpreters.

Parousia and Rapture in Dispensationalism

Recent premillennialism has increasingly become wedded to dispensationalism in many evangelical circles (as seen in Darby, Scofield, and Gaebelein, but with some exceptions such as R. H. Gundry and G. E. Ladd). Dispensationalists may divide the return of Christ into two events that occur in different spheres: his coming for the saints (the rapture—in the air) and his coming with the saints (the day of the Lord—on the earth).

The first of these is the Parousia, his coming *for* the saints (1 Thess. 4:15, 16), which results in the rapture of the saints, when Christ does not come to the earth but remains in the upper air, when both those who have died in the Lord and living saints are caught up to meet the Lord in the air. Key text: "For the Lord himself will come down from heaven, with a loud command, with the voice of the archangel and with the trumpet call of God, and the dead in Christ will rise first. After that, we who are still alive and are left will be caught up [*harpagesometha*, seized, snatched] together with them in the clouds to meet the Lord in the air" (1 Thess. 4:16, 17). By this means the faithful will be united with the coming Lord and transformed into the same resurrected state as the heavenly communion of saints. A sudden removal of the faithful connected with the Lord's coming is suggested in Matthew 24:40–41 (= Luke 17:34, 35), where of two men in the field, one shall be taken and the other left, and of two women grinding, one is taken and the other left.

This coming is followed, according to many dispensationalists, by a seven-year period in which the signs of the end occur (the gathering of Israel, the great tribulation, and the Antichrist). After this interval is another coming of the Lord *with* the saints in which he returns to earth.

Those who object argue that it is doubtful that the texts intend to refer to two distinct comings, because Parousia and "day of the Lord" are used interchangeably (2 Thess. 2:1, 2, 8; 2 Pet. 3), and because the coming of the Lord at which the elect are gathered is represented as following the tribulation (Matt. 24:29–31; Berkhof, *ST*:696); hence it is argued that the second coming is a single event.

Social Implications of Millennial Tendencies

There are often ethical-political-ideological tendencies and implications in each of these alternative millennial theories. Postmillennialism, as typified by Arminian-Wesleyan and social gospel exegesis, has taken a more transformationist view of the civil and political order, tending to see the church as actively engaged in the responsibility to change society in conformity with the divine claim. The political tendency is toward active transformation of society from injustice to justice as an act of eschatological accountability. Premillennialism, as typified by much recent Reformed dispensational exegesis, tends toward a more realistic ordering of politics toward the restraint of evil that is not likely to diminish until the Lord's return.

Realized millennialism, as typified by Augustinian exegesis, has tended to identify the millennial kingdom with the church herself, and her sacramental life as the extended incarnation of Christ in history. The political tendency is toward a closer linkage of an established church with state protection. Postmillennialism blends more easily with Arminian synergism, whereas premillennialism blends more easily with Calvinism's stress on the divine decrees.

Postmillennialism held sway during the period of nineteenth-century optimism, and tended to recede with the disillusionment of utopian idealism after World War I. Postmillennialism has flourished in periods in which the church seemed to be succeeding in its worldwide mission, and receded in periods in which that mission seems to be faltering.

Against the historical optimism of postmillennial gradualists (who expect history to get better), the relative historical pessimism of pre-millennialism holds that the millennium will begin with a sudden cataclysmic event only after history has seriously deteriorated. Christ will come only when things get maximally worst. Premillennialists expect history to get a lot worse before it gets any better. Only after Christ personally comes will there be millennial peace, universal harmony in nature and history.

Which position is correct? There is no ecumenical consensus. The Vincentian method arguably points more toward realized millennialism than its alternatives, but not with much confidence (for other views, see G. Ladd, *The Blessed Hope*; M. Erickson, *Contemporary Options in Eschatology*; L. E. Froom, *The Conditionalist Faith of Our Fathers*). The "already/not yet" tension in the texts accounts for much of the potential for diverse interpretation (Phil. 3:12; 2 Thess. 2:7; 1 John 3:2; Rev. 2:25).

General Judgment

In the Apostles' Creed the community of faith confesses that Christ "shall come to judge the quick and the dead." The Nicene-Constantinopolitan Creed affirms, "He shall come again with glory to judge both the quick and the dead" (Creed of the 150 Fathers). The Eastern Form of the Apostles' Creed confesses the one who, having ascended, "comes in glory to judge the living and the dead, of whose kingdom there will be no end" (Cyril of Jerusalem, *Catecheses*, SCD 9).

At his "coming all men shall rise again with their bodies, and shall give account for their own works" (Quicunque Creed). This is the concluding event of world history. What happens "after" final judgment is not history, but a new creation. By this event the remedial dispensation is ended. There is no more time for choosing, only for the consequences of choosing.

The Final Crisis

The topics ahead are: the last assize, the mediatorial judge, the universality of judgment, the charge, inquiry, sentence, and execution of sentence. These teachings comprise the doctrine of the last judgment. They are familiar to all who have sung the hymns of the church, joined in its liturgy, read its poetry, and heard its sacred texts read in worship.

Krisis (judgment) implies a crossroads: a discrimination, a separation, a parting of the ways (John 12:31; Heb. 9:27). It is to such a final juncture that every person comes on the last day (Augustine, *CG* 20.27–30; Sulpitius Severus, *Life of St. Martin*).

"The last judgment is the judicial act by which on the last day, immediately upon the resurrection of the dead, Christ in great majesty and glory will pronounce sentence on all men, will separate the elect from the reprobate, and adjudge the former to life eternal, the latter to unquenchable fire" (Bucanus, *IT* 28, 4; in Heppe, *RD*:703). God will "judge the peoples with equity." For "he comes, he comes to judge the earth. He will judge the world in righteousness and the peoples in his truth" (Ps. 96:13).

On the last day there will be a full disclosure of the character and destiny of each free moral agent, and a decisive separation between the just and unjust. Who is making the judgment? The only one capable of making it. This judge is the searcher of all hearts, who "holds in his hand your life and all your ways" (Dan. 5:23), who knows intimately "everyone's heart" (Acts 1:24).

It is difficult to imagine any Christian teaching more universally received than this. It is rejected chiefly by those who, having abandoned scriptural teaching, cherish the delusions of modern optimism. In this final court, sin is understood in its essence simply as unresponsiveness to God's saving mercy revealed in history.

The Word of God is "sharper than any double-edged sword," penetrating "even to dividing soul and spirit, joints and marrow; it judges the thoughts and attitudes of the heart. Nothing in all creation is hidden from God's sight. Everything is uncovered and laid bare before the eyes of him to whom we must give account" (Heb. 4:13).

Coming, Sitting, Gathering, Separating

Four active verbs characterize the judging work of the Son as portrayed in the parable of the last judgment. "When the Son of Man *comes* in his glory, and all the angels with him, he will *sit* on his throne in heavenly glory. All the nations will be *gathered* before him, and he will *separate* the people one from another as a shepherd separates the sheep from the goats" (Matt. 25:31, 32, italics added).

The sequence of classical Christian reasoning follows along this same order: Parousia, the Judgment Seat, the Gathering for Judgment, and the Judgment itself.

The essential event of final judgment is a just separation of those who are to be with God eternally from those who are to be sent away from God's presence (Irenaeus, *Ag. Her.* 5.27).

The Time of Judgment

When? Judgment follows the general resurrection of the just and unjust. The dead are raised in order to be judged. "Therefore judge nothing before the appointed time; wait till the Lord comes. He will bring to light what is hidden in darkness and will expose the motives of men's hearts. At that time each will receive his praise from God" (1 Cor. 4:5, 6).

The final judgment in effect records the judgment that persons have already passed upon themselves by their conscience and their present relation to the Redeemer. "Whoever does not believe stands condemned already" (John 3:18).

The discerning conscience is already racing toward judgment: "The sins of some men are obvious, reaching the place of judgment ahead of them; the sins of others trail behind them" (1 Tim. 5:24).

Judgment is portrayed not merely as a rational idea or mythical construct but an event. It is pictured as happening on a particular "day of judgment" (John 5:28, 29; 2 Pet. 3:7), "that day" (Matt. 7:22; 2 Tim. 4:8), "when his righteous judgment will be revealed" (Rom. 2:5). "For he has set a day when he will judge the world with justice by the man he has appointed" (Acts 17:31).

How long is a day? Serious interpreters differ: Lactantius thought the "day" would last a thousand years (*Div. Inst.* 7.24). Thomas Aquinas thought that "the divine power will bring it about that in an instant everyone will be apprised of all the good or evil he has ever done" (*Compend. of Theology*, 244). However long, "God will bring every deed into judgment, including every hidden thing, whether it is good or evil" (Eccles. 12:14).

Judgment Entrusted to the One Who Was Judged

The decisive event is overseen by the triune God (Heb. 12:23; Rom. 2:5; Ps. 98:9)—whose judgment is sometimes ascribed to the Father (John 8:50; Acts 17:31; 1 Pet. 2:23) or to the Spirit (John 16:8), but most often portrayed as being personally administered by the God-man, Christ himself (Matt. 25:31, 32; Acts 10:42; Phil. 2:10), who knows our infirmities through his own experience (Heb. 2:18).

The Father "has entrusted all judgment to the Son" (John 5:22). The Father does not judge apart from the Son, but only in and through the Son (Hilary, *Trin.* 7.20). Mercifully, it is by true man (the Son of man who has fully shared the human condition, being tempted in every way) that humanity is judged. The theandric mediator is "the one whom God appointed as judge of the living and the dead" (Acts 10:42), to whom the Father has given "authority to judge because he is the Son of Man" (John 5:27).

This judge mercifully bears in his own body the marks of his passion for the adjudged. This judge is the man on the cross who has already been condemned for the sins of the world. Only God could reason in this way: It is he who "suffered under Pontius Pilate" who "shall come to judge." It is uniquely fitting that the same God-man who came to save humanity from sin should be the judge of sin. We are judged by one who can empathize with our human condition and can understand the obstacles that make our lives so imperfect.

The mercy of the final judge is wholly just, and the justice of the judge incomparably merciful. Lacking either infinite mercy or justice, it could not be God's judgment. These attributes are not contradictory but complementary, and best recognized as complementary on the cross. They are to be eternally united by insurmountable wisdom on the last day (Chrysostom, *To the Fallen Theodore*). The judgment will be final and unchangeable, with no appeal. After the last day there is no more time.

The faithful have no need to dread the final judgment. For "we are not to come before any other Judge than he who is our Advocate and who has taken our cause in hand" (Calvin, *Geneva Catechism*, Q87). The comfort of final judgment is "that in all affliction and persecution I may await with head held high the very Judge from heaven who has already submitted himself to the judgment of God for men and has removed all curse from me" (*Heid. Catech.*, Q 52). Paul was confident that there was in store for him "a crown of righteousness, which the Lord, the righteous Judge, will award to me on that day" (2 Tim. 4:8).

The saints and martyrs and confessors—and indeed, all believers—will in some sense sit and judge empathically with Christ by concurrence (Matt. 19:28; 1 Cor. 6:2, 3; Rev. 20:4; Tho. Aq., *ST* supp., Q89.1; Wollebius, *RDB*:185). "Those will judge with Him—sitting with the judge, as it were—who adhered to Him more than others"—the apostles—and "those who follow in the footprints of the Apostles" (Tho. Aq. *SCG* 4, ch. 96; Wisd. of Sol. 3:7 f.).

Individual Judgment

The Decisive Moral Significance of Final Judgment for Present Choices

Why final? Any judgment short of final judgment would risk being incomplete, hence unjust. After one dies, one's influence continues. The deceased lives on in memory, reputation, progeny, and in the "projects on which he had set his heart." For "no action can be fully assessed before it is finished and its results are evident." "A full and public verdict cannot be pronounced and sentence passed while time rolls on its course" (Tho. Aq., *ST* 3a, Q59.5).

This is why there must be a final judgment at the end of history, and not only at many points within history. The effects of a given life are not known at the time of death. The evil consequences initiated by Hitler and Stalin continue to plague the world long after they are gone, and in generations yet unborn. It is therefore reasonable that the final judgment be rendered only after all accounts of all historical agents are in, namely, at the end time. Good and evil deeds "continue to extend their influence throughout all time as a stone thrown into the water creates successive and ever widening circles" (Jacobs, *SCF*:530). These influences are only known by God's omniscience, hence only revealed at the final judgment.

The incomparable justice of God requires a final judgment, for in this life many if not most evils remain unjudged or crudely judged (Pss. 103:10; 92:7; Luke 6:24, 25; Rom. 9:22). If justice is inadequately fulfilled in this present life, surely another life, another sphere, another city is required to perfect it, as even Kant rightly reasoned. Kant rightly concluded that some future judgment was rationally required by the disparity between conscience and historical injustice (*Prolegomena to the Metaphysics of Morals*). He argued that ethics is "not really the doctrine of how to make ourselves happy but of how we are to be *worthy* of happiness" (*Critique of Practical Judgment* 2.2.5).

Thus only the end of history could be the proper time for final judgment when all things are "brought to their end" (Tho. Aq., *ST* supp., Q88.1). We intuitively hypothesize from conscience that more fitting and impartial justice must somehow follow, even if we cannot now behold it.

We weary the Lord by repeatedly asking, "Where is the God of justice?" (Mal. 2:17). Scripture rather points us toward a final judgment beyond history wherein God will answer all human queries about the course of justice (Chrysostom, *Hom. on the Statues*).

Whether God Acts Justly by Leaving Time for Repentance

Suppose God had provided no time for repentance, and no time for grieving over the consequences of sin—would the world be a better place? There must be some learning time between sin and judgment if God is to provide time for the consequences of sin to be experienced and duly grieved over (2 Pet. 3:9). Sometimes it takes a very long time for the consequences of sin to be realized and corrected.

Suppose the contrary, that God might have created a world in which no time whatever was provided between sin and its punishment. That would have reduced sin drastically, but would have given less opportunity for the free playing out of conscience and responsibility. God apparently opted for the conditions of freedom that now prevail in human creation—human self-determination that has repercussions in succeeding generations. Without positing the very freedom that risks falling into sin, human existence would be reduced to involuntary determinism. The person would hardly be distinguishable from a billiard ball, lacking the capacity for the self-determination and divine-human dialogue that God permits and desires through prayer.

How Conscience Anticipates Final Judgment

These conditions make it necessary to conclude that the full and adequate judgment of sin cannot rightly occur before death, and that final judgment cannot occur before the end of history. The forms of judgment of sin that do occur before death are often roughly conceived and prejudicially framed. Hence this-worldly justice, however important, cannot be finally or irreversibly decisive for the eternal destiny of the person in the presence of God.

Much modern consciousness, to the contrary, following Hegel, Schelling, Marx, and Nietzsche has insisted on viewing moral judgment as entirely immanental within historical processes. The classical Christian consensus viewed final judgment as distinguishable from the continuing judging activity of God in and through history. God is at work within history as Judge, but that work in itself must be completed beyond history if the apparent absurdities of history are to become meaningful.

So conscience awaits final judgment (Acts 24:25). Meanwhile in time our own moral self-awareness compels us constantly to pass judgment on our own actions to assess their rightness or culpability. We may be either too harsh on ourselves or too lenient, but the all-merciful One who judges us finally in the end will judge according to an omniscient justice higher than conscience. This justice has already been demonstrated on the cross.

The correspondence between conscience and final judgment is set forth in this powerful testimony from John's epistle: "This then is how we know that we belong to the truth, and how we set our hearts at rest in his presence whenever our hearts condemn us. For God is greater than our hearts, and he knows everything. Dear friends, if our hearts do not condemn us, we have confidence before God" (1 John 3:19–21).

The Moral Meaning of Freedom Vindicated at the End

There is no meaningful freedom in a moral universe without positing some sort of final accountability and judgment. This makes each person responsible to the Giver of life for the consequences of his or her personal decisions. Jews and Christians know with moral certainty that they will be judged, not what the outcome will be, which is in God's hands. In this way the certainty of final judgment impinges powerfully upon current moral behavior, and upon conscience. It may cause discomfort, as it did in the case of Felix when Paul "discoursed on righteousness, self-control and the judgment to come" (Acts 24:25).

The conclusion of the drama of a personal history remains unknown until after this life is closed. What could be more dramatic? "Man knows not his own end" (Eccles. 9:12).

No further appeal can be made after history's last act. There is no time for another scene. Heaven and earth will pass away, but the final word on that day will not pass away. The audience of the drama is finally all who have ever lived in history, gathered together on the final day (Nicene Creed, *SCD* 54; Lateran Council, *SCD* 255; Council of Toledo XI, *SCD* 287).

Those Who Still Love Darkness Are
Hardly Ready for the Light

The work of judging is best viewed in relation to the primary mediatorial work of the Redeemer. Christ "did not come to judge the world, but to save it" (John 12:47). This does not imply that Christ has no judging functions, as is evident from the next verse: "There is a judge for the one who rejects me and does not accept my words; that very word which I spoke will condemn him at the last day" (John 12:48).

Luther commented: "A physician says to a sick man: 'I want you to get well, I cannot save your life; but I want to help to do it.' But if the sufferer will not allow this or accept his services as doctor, the latter says: 'Now I will not talk to you as your doctor, but, because you compel me, I must be your judge and say: You are going to die' " (*EA* 48:294).

Though God desires the salvation of all, God does not coerce the will of the unjust to accept divine mercy. "This is the verdict: Light has come into the world, but men loved darkness instead of light because their deeds were evil" (John 3:19). "For judgment I have come into this world" (John 9:39), yet judgment as such is never the primary purpose of his coming but the consequence of ignoring his saving activity (John 3:17; Mark 4:12; Isa. 6:9).

Individual Judgment: Each One According to Deeds

Conscience is the inward bar of judgment. All rational persons are already "a law for themselves, even though they do not have the law, since they show the requirements of the law are written on their hearts, their consciences also bearing witness, and their thoughts now accusing, now even defending them" (Rom. 2:15, 16). What happens penultimately in conscience happens ultimately in final judgment: "For we must all appear before the judgment seat of Christ, that each one may receive what is due him for the things done while in the body, whether good or bad" (2 Cor. 5:10).

No one can serve as conscience for another. Finally each conscience is called to account, one by one. All are accountable for the moral use of whatever capacities are given them, not merely to themselves, but to the Giver of these gifts (Tho. Aq., *ST* 3 supp., Q89; Pearson, *EC*:300–304).

"Each of us will give an account of himself to God" (Rom. 14:10, 12). Basil thought it "likely that by an inexpressible power, every deed we have done will be made manifest to us in a single moment, as if it were engraved on a tablet" (Basil, *Comm. on John* 1.18). It will then be clear to all whether one is prepared to live in the presence of God. "In the day when God shall judge, each one's conscience will bear witness to him, and his thoughts will accuse and defend him" so that all merits and demerits will be seen at a single glance (Tho. Aq., *ST* supp., Q87; Job 8:22). "A kind of divine energy will come to our aid, so that we shall recall all of our sins to mind" (Augustine, *CG* 20).

Whether God Remembers Forgiven Sin

That the judgment of all unrepented sin will be visible and will appear to all is taught for these reasons: for the glory of God, that the justice and mercy of God may be manifested; that the promises of God may be fulfilled; that the godly may be exalted and Christ glorified; and that all things may be fitly judged before the conclusion of history (Gerhard, *LT* 18, 35; *Leiden Synopsis* 51, 55).

But those who live in Christ have discovered that their sins are already blotted out, cast into the depths of the sea, remembered no more by God (Isa. 43:25; Jer.

31:34; Ezek. 18:22). Their sins have already been removed as far as is east from west (Ps. 103:12).

What has been already forgiven will not be called to account on the last day (Turretin, *ITE* 22.6.17). "For it is the part of an advocate not to publish, but to cover" (Jacobs, *SCF*:525). In him there is no condemnation (Rom. 8:1). Whoever "hears my word and believes him who sent me has eternal life and will not be condemned" (John 5:24).

Those whose lives are hid in Christ will stand in this judgment without spot or wrinkle (Eph. 5:27). The father receives the prodigal without making a long list of wayward behaviors (Luke 15:20). If the godly recall their own sin, it will be to praise God's mercy.

The Full Disclosure of Mixed Motives

The final divine investigative judgment focuses on the moral truth left unrecognized amid historical ambiguities. Thomas astutely reasoned, "A judicial investigation is not necessary unless good and evil actions are intermingled. When good is present without admixture of evil, or evil without admixture of good, discussion is out of place." (Tho. Aq., *Compend. of Theology*, 243). Hence both the perfectly good and perfectly wicked are judged without further inquiry. But if some have faith but lack charity, or in cases where faith and charity are diluted by excessive attachments, an examination of complex circumstances is required by divine justice.

Because feelings and motives affect conduct, especially when formed into reinforced habits and cherished dispositions, these are fit matters to be subjected to judgment (1 Cor. 4:5; *Longer Catech.*, Eastern Orthodox Church, 231). The purpose of examination is not that the judge may receive new information, for all things are already known by God. Rather the investigative judgment clearly makes known to each person why each is judged as a whole faithful or unfaithful, the former rejoicing in God's mercy and the latter acceding to God's justice.

Sins of Omission and Commission

Not only deeds are judged but words, which have such powerful effects in human relationships. Those who write or speak words (including the many of this book) will "give account on the day of judgment for every careless word they have spoken" (Matt. 12:36; cf. James 3:2).

Both what we do and what we neglect doing are subject to final judgment. For the habits we willfully neglect to amend, we remain responsible. For our negligence by which others are harmed, we are responsible. The entire range of conduct and character of every human being is subject to investigative judgment—every word, thought, and deed (Matt. 12:36, 37).

But on the last day, love will cover a multitude of sins (1 Pet. 4:8), for love is the pivotal feature of the Redeemer and the redeemed character. Acts of mercy to the defenseless will be recognized by the Just One, even if unrecognized by those who did them (Matt. 25).

The Judicial Process

Due judicial process consists in being fairly brought into a just court for the purpose of being charged, having one's cause fairly examined, being judged, receiving sentence, and having the sentence executed. All these elements are embedded in the narratives of the last judgment (Matt 25:37).

The Standard of Judgment:
According to One's Deeds in the Body

The measure by which judgment proceeds is the holy will of God, equitably administered "according to what they had done, as recorded in the books" (Rev. 20:12). The metaphor of accurate records in detailed books is employed in scripture to portray the accuracy of the final accounting of those being judged (Rev. 20:12; cf. Ps. 50:21).

Some have greater responsibility, having received greater gifts; others less (Matt. 11:21–24; Rom. 2:12–16). The measure of light and truth granted will impinge upon final judgment. Those who have not heard the gospel will be judged by the law of their own nature, their conscience guided by their reason, and the law written in their hearts (Rom. 2:14, 15). Those who have Moses and the prophets are to be judged by a different standard than those without them (Matt. 11:24; Luke 12:48; 16:29), for "all who sinned under the law will be judged by the law" (Rom. 2:12). Those who have heard the Gospel will be judged "according to the Gospel," the good news of God's own righteousness in which they may share by faith.

Final judgment focuses upon whether one has been responsive or not to the gifts of God actually offered within the flow of time (Hugh of St. Victor, SCF:464). The judgment finally comes down to whether one has or has not responded trustingly to God's grace. The righteousness that saves is not "a righteousness of my own that comes from the law, but that which is through faith in Christ—the righteousness that comes from God and is by faith" (Phil. 3:9).

Judged According to, Not on Account of, Deeds

Divine mercy does not imply that good works are finally of no importance to God. The apostolic teaching is that all will be judged according to their works as they are fruits of faith, not on account of their works apart from faith (Wollebius, RDB:184). "This explains in part the truth of the seemingly opposed propositions that our works cannot save us, and that we are to be judged and finally rewarded according to them. We are to be judged according to rather than on account of deeds" (non propter, sed secundum opera, Hall, DT 10:179).

The pivot remains: Did faith become active in love? Did the reception of God's mercy express itself in deeds of mercy? Were the poor relieved, was charity shown toward all, were enemies forgiven? Faith is the engendering source and works the expression of the Christian life, assuming that your work is "produced by faith, your labor prompted by love, and your endurance inspired by hope" (1 Thess. 1:3). The faithful are justified "by faith without the merit of works, and with the evidence of works" (Pope, Compend., 3:417).

Those who depart do so not merely by divine predetermination, but more so because of their own recalcitrant will. "A man reaps what he sows. The one who sows to please his sinful nature, from that nature will reap destruction; the one who sows to please the Spirit, from the Spirit will reap eternal life" (Gal. 6:7, 8).

The sinner is understood as the author of his own character, reaping the fruit of his own choices. Character molds destiny. Human freedom is divinely aided. But that does not diminish its quality as freedom. All self-determining beings are given grace adequate for taking free steps toward repenting and believing. It is the ongoing, growing direction of the character that makes the judgment irreversible, a crystallization due to moral choice, not coercion (Origen, OFP 2.10). This does not deny social or genetic or biological or cultural determinants, but focuses upon one's own free response to all conceivable determinants.

The fundamental decision in a court is finally described simply: guilty or not guilty. Only two classes of response finally are provided: left or right, blessed or cursed. The sentence is either, "Come, you who are blessed by my Father, take your inheritance," or "Depart from me, you who are cursed" (Matt. 25:34, 41). The just are taken up into Christ's presence, while the unjust depart from Christ's presence.

Whether Judgment Is Event or Symbol

The picture of final judgment, by rough analogy with earthly courts, is a strong metaphor that intends to communicate the essence of a process that cannot be adequately pictured or imagined since it transcends time. The trumpet sounding, the Lord's coming in the twinkling of an eye, the judge and the judgment, the separation of sheep and goats, the new Jerusalem—these are the "sound words" by which our inadequate perceptions are rightly oriented, despite their limitations.

Though symbolic language is constantly utilized by scripture to point to the final judgment, it would be a vast miscalculation to view final judgment as a non-event or to reduce it to merely metaphorical status (Irenaeus, *Ag. Her.* 5.35). Nor is it wise to view final judgment as a continuing, immanental-historical process, as distinguished from an event effectively consummating history. Final judgment is an event that only God can enact. It is not reducible to our judgment of ourselves, hence not to be psychologized, politicized, or subjectivized. "Too late do they believe in eternal punishment who were unwilling to believe in eternal life" (Cyprian, *To Demetrian* 24).

The courtroom scene is not to be taken so woodenly that its figurative elements cannot be proportionally interpreted. The books to be opened on the last day are not literal books made with paper and ink; rather, the book of life is Christ in whom the faithful are hid (Phil. 4:3; Rev. 5:1–9; 13:8).

The judgment complete, the Lord will lead his own into glory, where they will reign with him forever (Council of Toledo XI, *SCD* 287). With the final judgment, the history of salvation comes full circle in the mode of eternal fulfillment. The work of the Holy Spirit in sanctifying what was begun in creation has come to completion. What was begun for the believer on the day of baptism, and what was begun for the church on the day of Pentecost, will have come to full consummation, the kingdom established (Matt. 25:34–40), the power of evil bound (Rev. 20:1–3).

How do the faithful prepare in time for final judgment? Each time the believer meets the living Lord in Word or Sacrament, the memory of Christ's death is being kept until he comes. The faithful have Christ's own word that he will raise those up on the last day who share in his body and blood by faith.

Three events of transformation exceed our understanding: creation, redemption, and consummation. The mode of each transformation remains a mystery of the triune God. To recall the promises of scripture regarding the consummation is not to forget its mystery.

Consummation: The End of the Age

History is not like Penelope's tapestry, constantly being rewoven and constantly undone, in eternal recurrence. Nor is it like the myth of Sisyphus, who rolled the stone uphill only to have it roll forever down again. Rather Jews and Christians understand that history is characterized by the revelation of meaning through events in a linear trajectory that leads toward a final consummation, not the absurdity of eternal repetition.

End of the Age (Consummatio Saeculi)

"The things concerning Me have an end" (Luke 22:37). The final moment is a vanishing point in which all the rays of creation converge, only to become a new beginning point.

After judgment comes the end of this world, according to Jewish and Christian expectation, and the beginning of the future age. The present state is transcended, not to end the world as such, but to make a new world out of the old, a new heaven and new earth that will not pass away (Isa. 65:17). "For this world in its present form is passing away" (1 Cor. 7:31).

The entire visible creation, implicated in the history of sin, is hastening toward a *krisis* in which its present form shall be dissolved and renewed. One who confesses the beginning of the world's existence must necessarily look toward its final transformation (Gregory of Nyssa, *On the Making of Man* 23). In the consummation God will be "all in all" (1 Cor. 15:28). "Creation itself will be liberated from its bondage to decay" (Rom. 8:21). All things will be reconciled in him (Col. 1:20). God has promised to reestablish or gather up all things (literally re-head, sum up all things, *anakephalaiōsasthai ta panta*) in Christ (Eph. 1:10).

"Heaven and earth will pass away, but my words will never pass away" (Matt. 24:35). The earth and heavens "will perish, but you remain; they will all wear out like a garment, like clothing you will change them and they will be discarded. But you remain the same, and your years will never end" (Ps. 102:26, 27). "The heavens have now their working-day clothes on; but then they will put on their Sunday robes" (Luther, in Jacobs, *SCF*:534).

The Renewed Destiny of the Cosmos

The purpose of God in redemption is not merely to prolong creation quantitatively, but to redeem and perfect it qualitatively. This consummation has begun irreversibly in Jesus Christ. The consummation does not come by human action, political strategy, revolutionary planning, or evolution, but by God's own completing activity. This does not mean that God's kingdom lacks political consequences, or that there is therefore no need for peacemakers or the struggle for justice in history. Rather it means that however imperfect is our own struggle for peace and justice, it will be perfected by God's own peace and justice finally beyond history. "Since the world was, in a way, made for man's sake, it follows that, when man shall be glorified in the body, the other bodies of the world shall also be changed to a better state" (Tho. Aq, *ST* supp., Q74.1). On the assumption that the "dwelling should befit the dweller," Thomas argued that the world was made to be humanity's dwelling, so that when humanity is renewed, "the world will be likewise" (Tho. Aq., *ST* supp., Q91.1).

The regeneration of the human person takes place within the cosmic-historical context in which God's plan is to renovate to its original unfallen condition. This final renovation is described in Paul's letter to Romans, chapters 4–8, and in the apostolic preaching of Acts, where Christ is expected to "remain in heaven until the time comes for God to *restore everything*" (Acts 3:17–21, italics added).

Believers do not simply pray for destruction, but the restoration of God's will in creation. The earth was not simply demolished or destroyed in substance by the flood, but renewed with a rainbow promise. Similarly but on a more grand scale, "this world in its present form is passing away" (1 Cor. 7:31) to make way for a cleansing and a new setting-in-order (Rom. 8:19–22; Rev. 21:1; Pope, *Compend.* 3:424). Yet this renovation requires a complete negation of all that has gone awry, not merely a rearranging of its present broken qualities (Ps. 102:26, 27; Isa. 51:6; Matt. 24:35; 2 Pet. 3:7, 10, 12). The scriptural metaphors here are "vanish like smoke," "be dissolved," "melt," "burn," "pass away," and "be no more" (Wollebius, *RDB*:188; Schmid, *DT*:655). Is there something ecologically dangerous in the idea that the world is transitory? The answer is yes, if one systematically forgets that the transitory is also profoundly valuable, and the gift of God the Creator, given for human stewardship. But such forgetfulness would be a grotesque distortion of the intention of the Christian doctrine of creation.

Augustine held the balance correctly: "The form passes away but not the nature" (commenting upon 1 Cor. 7:31, in *CCF*:350). Those who focus upon the end of the world without a new beginning distort the text. Those who rejoice in a new beginning without awareness of an end shrink the text. It is both a consummation and a new beginning. "Behold, I make all things new" (Rev. 21:5). "Then I saw a new heaven and a new earth, for the first heaven and the first earth had passed away, and there was no longer any sea. I saw the Holy City, the new Jerusalem, coming down out of heaven from God, prepared as a bride beautifully dressed for her husband. And I heard a loud voice from the throne saying, 'Now the dwelling of God is with men, and he will live with them. They will be his people, and God himself will be with them and be their God. He will wipe every tear from their eyes. There will be no more death, or mourning or crying or pain, for the old order of things has passed away' " (Rev. 21:1–4).

The Dross Consumed

The mode of the destruction of the old era is portrayed in scripture as fire. "The heavens will disappear with a roar; the elements will be destroyed by fire, and the earth and everything in it will be laid bare" (2 Pet. 3:11; Tho. Aq., *ST* supp., Q74.3). There is a moral connection between this verse and the next: "Since everything will be destroyed in this way, what kind of people ought you to be. You ought to live holy and godly lives as you look forward to the day of God" (2 Pet. 3:12).

Fire is the most active of all the elements, tending "to consume the corruptible" (Tho. Aq., *SCG* 4:348). Gerhard's conclusion: "Whether the fire be truly corporeal, material and visible, or incorporeal, immaterial and invisible, we leave unsettled (although we incline to the latter), and we earnestly pray God not to reveal this to us by knowledge gained from experience" (Gerhard, in Jacobs, *SCF*:536). Those who miss the ironic wit of Gerhard are not awake.

As the first deconstruction and renovation of the world came by flood, the final purification will occur by fire (Isa. 66:15; Commodianus, *Instructions* 65). To say that the world was "destroyed" by the flood, however, means not that all life ended but that a new beginning was made— life with God is resuming according to God's original will, similarly in the case of the "new earth." "By these waters also the world of that time was deluged and destroyed. By the same word the present heavens and earth are reserved for fire, being kept for the day of judgment and the destruction of ungodly men" (2 Pet. 3:7).

What is destroyed is ungodliness, not creation as such. This is not simple annihilation but purification and transformation. Fire is the consistent biblical symbol of the cleansing, purifying, sanctifying power of God's holiness and justice. The fire of God's holiness against sin is not to be quenched (Matt. 23:33; Mark 9:48). Fire is appointed for cleansing and renewing the world, not merely for annihilation (Irenaeus, *Ag. Her.* 5.36.1). The physical analogy is exact: "Combustion does not annihilate but only redistributes and rearranges particles of matter" (Jacobs, *SCF*:534).

11

THE COMMUNION OF SAINTS AND THE LIFE EVERLASTING

T HE SYMPHONY OF THEOLOGY is poised to celebrate its last reprise. The drama of history, having reached its resolution, is quickly drawing to a certain kind of close, which is itself a new age, remembering, "The Maker of time . . . is not subject to Time" (Gregory of Nazianzus, *Orat.* 39.12).

The Communion of Saints

Eternal life with God brings an incomparable interpersonal blessing: communion with God amid the communion of the saints with God and with all who mirror God's holy love (Luke 23:43; John 12:26; Phil. 1:23). This celebrating community embraces both the living faithful and the faithful departed who now enjoy eternal life with God (Rev. 14:1–4).

The Blessing of Fellowship Embraces the Past, Present, and Future Faithful

The church is a fellowship among the faithful now living, but it extends far wider to embrace also all who have died in faith, as well as all those yet unborn who will come to faith. Some remain pilgrims in history, while others having died in the Lord are already joyfully beholding "clearly God Himself triune and one, as He is" (Council of Florence, *DS* 693).

From Christ "the whole body, joined and held together by every supporting ligament, grows and builds itself up in love, as each part does its work" (Eph. 4:16; Jerome, *Epis. to Eph.* 2.4.16). The faithful form a society, a "people" (*laos*, Rev. 19:4; 21:3; cf. Rom. 9:25; 2 Cor. 6:16; 1 Pet. 2:9, 10), a kingdom (Matt. 25:34; Rev. 1:6), a city (Heb. 11:10, 16; 12:22; Rev. 3:12; 21:2), a bonded community that lives in communion with those of all ages who hunger for righteousness (Ps. 118:63; Tho. Aq., *ST* supp., Q21.2). These themes harmonize in the day by day common praise of the community of celebration.

There is a special union between the faithful on earth and in heaven, enabled by their mutual communion with the one Head, and with each other, a communion sustained by prayer, faith, hope, and love (*Longer Catech.*, Eastern Orthodox Church, 262). The Westminster divines summarized, "All saints that are united to Jesus Christ their head, by his Spirit and by faith, have fellowship with him in his graces, sufferings, death, resurrection and glory: and being united to one another in love, they have communion in each other's gifts and graces" (Westminster 26.1).

The common Christian confession of "the communion of saints" (*hagion koinonian*) is found in the Apostles' Creed and in most forms of the primitive rule of faith ecumenically received (Faustus of Riez, Caesarius of Arles, *SCD 6*). "Saints" refers to all baptized believers whose walk attests their faith in the power of the resurrection. It designates the common bond uniting all members of Christ's church in heaven and earth, within and beyond history, in a real communication of spiritual riches (Irenaeus, *Ag. Her.* 5.27). It

The Communion Is with God and Humanity in God

The community or fellowship (*koinonia*) of the saints is a recurrent theme of the New Testament that points both to communion with God and communion with all who share God's life: "We proclaim to you what we have seen and heard, so that you also may have fellowship *with us*. And our fellowship is *with the Father*, and *with his Son*, Jesus Christ" (1 John 1:3, italics added; cf. 2 Cor. 13:14; Ambrose, *Of the Holy Spirit* 1.12.131). The Son prayed to the Father that the whole community of faith "may be one, as we are one" (John 17:11; Cyril of Alex., *Comm. on John* 11.9).

The unity that was manifest at Pentecost is "the first fruits of that perfect union of the Son with his Father, which will be known in its fulness only when all things are consummated by Christ in his glory. The Lord who is bringing all things into full unity at the last is he who constrains us to seek the unity which he wills for his Church on earth here and now" (New Delhi Message, *WCC*). One baptism unites all the faithful in their diversity of callings. All are baptized into one body (1 Cor. 12:13; Ambrosiaster, *Comm. on Paul*, 1 Cor. 12:13).

Though the union between the saints in heaven is complete and unalloyed, the pilgrim union of saints on earth is mixed, flawed, and imperfect. Thus "there is an union, partly perfect and partly imperfect, between the saints in heaven and the saints below upon earth" (Joseph Hall, *Works*, 7:261). The unity felt within time is linked mysteriously to the unity of the saints experienced in eternity.

While the spiritual combat of the pilgrim church continues on earth, the worshiping community knows itself as "already set at liberty" and "is now in heaven, and triumphs over all those things overcome, and rejoices before the Lord. Yet these two churches have, notwithstanding, a communion and fellowship between themselves" (Second Helvetic Confession). The communion of saints beyond history unites and shares in Christ's intercession for the church militant within history (Gregory I, *Moralia* 12; *Dialogues* 2; Tho. Aq., *ST* supp., Q71–73). This living communion is acknowledged in prayer in acts of Christian worship.

Eucharistic Communion

The communion of saints is portrayed as an already present heavenly community of angelic praise joined with the assembly of redeemed men and women: "But you have come to Mount Zion, to the heavenly Jerusalem, the city of the living God. You have come to thousands upon thousands of angels in joyful assembly, to the church of the first-born, whose names are written in heaven. You have come to God, the judge of all men, to the spirits of righteous men made perfect, to Jesus the Mediator" (Heb. 12:22–24a; Chrysostom, *Epis. to Heb.* 32.3–4). At the Lord's Table in churches around the present world this eternal fellowship is joined and celebrated.

For this reason the Eucharist is called a holy communion. There the faithful commune with Christ and with each other. "Because there is one loaf, we, who are many, are one body, for we all partake of the one loaf" (1 Cor. 10:17; Augustine, Easter Sunday Sermon 227), feeding on Christ's broken body and shed blood by which vital communion with him enables the faithful to be vitally united with each other. "For the bread of God is he who comes down from heaven and gives life to the world" (John 6:33; Cyril of Alex., *Comm. on John* 3.6).

From the outset the disciples are portrayed as continuing in the apostles' teaching and in fellowship with each other, breaking bread, and in prayer, confessing their faults, exhorting one another, sharing all things (Acts 2:42–44; Rom. 12:4, 5; 1 Cor. 12:12; Eph. 4:15, 16).

A Community of Full Disclosure

Full disclosure of all things characterizes this community when it is most fully being itself. In this world and flesh, we now depend upon frail words to reveal partly yet partly conceal our thoughts and feelings. Then we will not need words to let ourselves be known. The full clarity of our being will simply shine forth and achieve direct understanding (1 Cor. 8:2–3; Chrysostom, *Hom. on Cor.* 20.2–3; Gal. 4:9).

If to know is to love, then we will fully love, for we will fully know, knowing even as we are known (1 Cor. 13:12b). The Eucharist prepares us for this uniting and knowing by bringing us into unity with Christ and the neighbor. "Brother lives within his brother, none have secrets to conceal; Heart and mind and will and purpose, one throughout and one within" (Peter Damian, *Ad perennis vitae fontem*, Jacobs, *SCF*:549).

God knows all events in a single cohesive act of consciousness, in contrast to the forms of finite knowing possible for creatures under the conditions of time. (John 17:24; Eph. 1:4; 2 Tim. 1:9). Divine omniscience implies that God grasps all time as if it were a single whole—now: "With the Lord a day is like a thousand years, and a thousand years are like a day" (2 Pet. 3:8; Ps. 90:4).

God's way of experiencing time is in radical simultaneity in which past, present, and future co-inhere without being imprisoned as finite minds are in the succession of moments from past to present to future. Unlike mortals who live in time, God always was (Gen. 21:23) and will be (Deut. 5:23). God's constancy "does not change like shifting shadows" (James 1:17; Didymus the Blind, *Comm. on James* 1.17). God embraces time in the fullest sense, whereas we experience time only in its fleeting mode of constant disappearance. Through prayer by grace the faithful participate in God's knowing embrace of time. Time belongs to the created order, as distinct from the divine essence. With the world, time was created. Before time, nothing was but God. "There was no time, therefore, when you had not made anything, because you have made time itself" (Augustine, *Conf.* 11.14). Eternal life points to a regenerate life fit for life in the presence of the eternal, living God (John 5:24).

The Destiny of Those Unaware of the Gospel

God takes "no pleasure in the death of the wicked, but rather that they turn from their ways and live" (Ezek. 33:11). Are there undisclosed possibilities that might await those of cultures who may have never had adequate chance to hear the gospel? What of those utterly ignorant of God's coming?

Compassionate Christian teaching has often searched for insights into scripture texts by which their plight might be fairly understood. It is fitting here to assess the poignant reasoning of classic Christianity with regard to those who have had no opportunity to come to the truth, as to whether or in what sense they may have a share in life eternal.

The New Testament was addressed primarily to those who are able to hear the gospel. It does not often focus speculatively on what might be the possible destiny of those who never have had such an opportunity. In intent every human is addressed by the gospel. Scripture teaches that God antecedently (before their fall and before their voluntary sin) wills the salvation of all (Eph. 1:1–9; Clement, *Instr.* 1.9; Tertullian, *Ag. Marcion* 2.4–17; John of Damascus *OF* 4.19–21).

The faithful pray for some way of grasping God's deeper intention for those who fall short of the glory of God. God seeks continually to offer forgiveness and life, "if the fundamental disposition which they develop in their earthly probation has not nullified the moral possibility of their benefiting by it" (Hall, *DT* 10:50). Some outside the covenant (the centurion, the woman of Syrophoenicia, Mark 7:26; Matt. 8:5) showed a quality of life and faith of which Christ himself approved.

Those who lived before Christ can only be justly judged according to their responses to the preparing and common grace given them. Abraham appears in Luke 16:19–31 to be present in eternity with the saints (Augustine, Sermon 41.4). According to Paul, so do the righteous of Israel of every generation who remain faithful to the covenant (Rom. 11). Gentiles who have not heard of God's coming will be judged fairly by the incomparably just Judge according to the light given them (Rom. 2:6–16). All humanity is offered sufficient grace to enable each to respond rightly to whatever opportunities are made possible within the conditions of a broken history. The crucial question is whether in meeting these situations they might have developed a nascent predisposition for faith such as the Letter to Hebrews ascribes to Abel (Heb. 11:4; Ephrem, *Comm. on Heb.* 11.4).

It is a house of "many mansions" that the Lord is preparing for the faithful (John 14:2). Although the Lord has sheep "not of this fold" (John 10:16; Augustine, Sermon 138.5), their identity is not revealed to us. What we do know is that we have been given a choice to respond to the truth. There is immense diversity among the actual histories of persons who hear and respond to the gospel and vast variety in the levels of capacity that various cultures and personal dispositions allow. There is not in the real world a simple equality of opportunity to hear God's good news in Jesus Christ, however much it intends to reach out for all. Some of these many mansions may remain opaque to our view (Chrysostom, *Hom. on John* 73).

The Final State of the Unjust

The Meaning of Hell

It is only with tears that the subject of hell is contemplated by those who reach out daily in love for sinners (Lausanne Covenant).

Hell expresses the intent of the holy God to destroy sin completely and forever. Hell says not merely a temporal no but an eternal no to sin. The rejection of evil by the holy God is like a fire that burns on, a worm that dies not (Heb. 12:29; Mark 9:44–48; Aphrahat, *Demonstrations*).

Hell is especially for those who think they are too good to be helped by God. Hell is to be forever without God, against God. This is why the good news carries with it a stern warning: If you chose in time to live without God, you thereby choose eternally to be without God. Hell is where the unjust get their just dessert. Hell is the final state of those who are not in the book of life (Rev. 20:11–15), where "the light of the world does not shine" (Hippolytus, *Ag. Plato* 1). Hell is a place for those who vainly imagine themselves to be good but are not. Jesus is ready to receive into his eternal presence those who honestly know themselves to be sinners, who have turned to trust in God's mercy.

The Plain Meaning of Bleak Words

One who perpetually has chosen the settled disposition of unfaith against faith, and the godless love of self instead of the selfless love of God, lacking that faith that is active in the works of mercy, will continue after death in a similar self-chosen condition of radical, final separation from the divine presence. Exclusion from the presence of God is the central meaning of hell. Whoever "disowns me before men, I will disown him before my Father in heaven" (Matt. 10:33; Chrysostom, *Hom. on Matt.*, Hom. 34.3). "The teaching, in brief, is that unrepented sin is a fatal barrier to eternal life" (Hall, *DT* 10:195).

In Matthew's version of the parable of sheep and goats, Jesus concluded with these words to those who remained totally unresponsive (i.e. dead) to grace and love: "Depart from me, you who are cursed, into the eternal fire prepared for the devil and his angels," Whereupon they "will go away to eternal punishment" (Matt. 25:41, 46; Chrysostom, *Hom. on Matt.*, Hom. 79.2).

The stark words "eternal punishment" and "eternal fire" have withstood numerous attempts at generous reinterpretation, but they remain obstinately in the received text (Jerome, *Ag. Rufinus*, FC 53:109). The text remains resilient against our attempts to soften it. Every mitigating theory is wrecked on these words, which are "not as doubtful or ambiguous as represented; and even if they were, the rule is to interpret the obscure by the plain" (Banks, *MCD*:362). The problem is not that the words are obscure, but that they are all too plain (Augustine, *CG* 21.23; Kierkegaard, *On Self-examination*).

Those who refuse the mercy of God the Son thereby choose to have no share in fellowship with the Father (Matt. 25:41; Origen, *Comm. on Matt.* 73; Calvin, *Inst.* 3.23). Scriptures describe the eternal condition of the ungodly as one of infinite distance from God (Fourth Lateran Council, *SCD* 429). Those who die in original sin or grave personal sin, being separated from God's righteousness, have chosen to be permanently isolated from God's goodness. This is hell—the non-blessedness of life without God, against God (Quicunque Creed, *SCD* 40; Council of Valence 3, 321). "Our merciful Lord never pronounced, nor ever will pronounce, a sentence more terrible than this: to be without God in eternity is Hell. 'Depart from Me'. . . . No profounder mystery is in the Apocalypse than the hallelujahs which are uttered over the demonstrations of the Divine wrath as they proceed from judgment to judgment in their direful procession" (Pope, *Compend.* 3:420, 422).

Sin matters to God. The holy God detests injustice and evil. Creation is a moral order in which those who break God's rules break themselves. Those who persist in sin find themselves eternally alienated from the divine goodness. They bring upon themselves the penalty of having no share in that everlasting life of love of those who inhabit God's kingdom.

Thus the Psalm concludes: "The face of the Lord is against those who do evil, to cut off the memory of them from the earth" (Ps. 34:17). Each one through the mystery of human choice finally either receives and welcomes the glory of God's presence or rejects it and passes into outer darkness (Chrysostom, *Hom. on Phil.* 6). No one but God is capable of judging those inner motives that decide the outcome.

Speaking of Hell: Some Common Misjudgments

Mischievous ideas have attached themselves to popular notions of hell. Because many have been repulsed by Christianity as a result of these dubious assumptions, it is worthwhile to correct at least four them:

1. There is no ecumenically received scriptural authority for the view that God arbitrarily or pretemporally predestines persons to hell without their own choosing or cooperation or without the benefit of conscience and common grace.

2. There is no scriptural warrant for the view that metaphors like the fire and the worm must be taken literally. It would be impossible at the same instant to take both of those metaphors literally, since one would cancel out the other.

3. There is only limited scriptural legitimacy for the view that hell is a physical fire that works directly upon the physical body. Such views are speculative and may be expressed in ways abhorrent to the character of God. Those who assert them as orthodox are challenged to show that such views have been received by a consensus of trusted historic exegetes.

4. There is insufficient scriptural warrant for the assertion that those who have not had a fair chance to hear the gospel are consigned peremptorily or irreversibly to eternal punishment. God is not without means of judging fairly whether they have responded to whatever measure of grace and light they may have been given (Matt. 11:21–24; 25:34, 41; Rom. 2:12–16; 2 Cor. 5;10).

The Constructive Intent of Sobering Analogies

Luther wryly commented that no picture of hell could be as bad as the reality (*Sermon on John* 2:3, WLS 2:626). We may imagine we are spared by the use of metaphors, yet these very metaphors only point toward the more final and serious reality.

The scriptural analogies come from bodily experiences that express despair and horror over evil—the burning of flesh, the "blackest darkness" (Jude 13), "weeping, and gnashing of teeth" (Matt. 8:12; 22:13), "unquenchable fire" (Matt. 3:12; Mark 9:43), an undying worm gnawing at the heart (Isa. 66:24). "By such expressions the Holy Spirit certainly intended to confound all our senses with dread" (Calvin, *Inst.* 3.25.12). If such metaphors sicken the stomach, that is their intended purpose—to spur to repentance, faith, and holiness. If the rhetoric comforted the hearer, it would not fulfill its intended function (Thomas Browne, *Religio Medici* 1:58).

The teaching of hell rightly calls to mind the dignity of human freedom and the high cost of its abuse. "They perish because they refused to love the truth" (2 Thess. 2:10; Cyril of Jerusalem, *Catech. Lect.* 15.14–15).

Those who ascribe their misdeeds constantly to the demonic powers may be playing a deadly game of pretending to "free men from fault" by taking away their very freedom of the will (Jerome, *Apology Ag. Rufinus* 2.7). "They never are free from punishment who in this life did not wish to be free from sin" (Hugh of St. Victor, *SCF*:469).

Whether Fire Is a Metaphorical Reference: Such Fire as God Would Know

This general observation on sobering analogies leads toward a specific application: burning by fire, which is one of the most intense forms of pain, as nurses in hospital burn units testify. The image of fire is frequently used in scripture as a metaphor to point to the ultimate destruction of all that is inconsistent with the holiness of God. If the metaphor is intended to disturb, it reaches its mark (Luke 17:29; James 3:6). It calls us to live so that we need not fear it (Luke 12:5; Rom. 13:3).

Ambrose wrote that hell is "neither a gnashing of the bodily teeth, nor a perpetual bodily fire, nor a bodily worm", but "a quality known to God" (Ambrose, *Comm. on Luke* 7.204). The everlasting fire of scripture could not be a "material fire like our fire, but *such fire as God would know*" (John of Damascus, *OF* 4.27, italics added). It is less a material than a spiritual fire. We know little of it except that it exists (Augustine, *CG* 20.16). "The nature of that everlasting fire is different from this fire of ours, which we use for the necessary purposes of life, and which ceases to burn unless it is sustained by the fuel of some material. But that divine fire always lives by itself" (Lactantius, *DI* 7.21) since it arises out of the nature of God whose holiness is underived, who is incomparably alive.

Though figurative, such metaphors intend accurately to convey truthful ideas and meanings, especially the dreadful reality of loss of God as an irreversible consequence of sin (Heb. 12:29; Mark 9:44–48). The goodness of God guarantees that scripture would not unnecessarily "alarm his moral creatures with groundless fears, or to represent the consequences of sin as more dreadful than they really are" (Wakefield, *CT* 2:642). There has been a disproportional emphasis on the literal interpretation of figurative expressions implying a flood of vindictiveness on the part of God. Undisciplined fantasies of the zealous have ended in misleading caricatures (Irenaeus, *Ag. Her.* 5.9–17).

The overreaction of modern optimism to these descriptions is understandable, even if undiscriminating. Hell has been seized upon as a cheap ploy for discrediting all ancient cosmologies. Yet for no period more than the modern period, with its addicted babies, genocides, and weeping forests, does the concept of hell retain its special existential significance. When unwarranted speculations are taken away from it, the classic Christian teaching of hell has much yet to say precisely to the moral dilemmas of modern consciousness.

If salvation is analogous to light, then darkness serves as its antonym. Fire suggests an eternal casting away of sin. The destiny of sin is to burn and to be completely cast away from God's own life—as far as imaginable (Isa. 26:11; Heb. 10:27; Jude 7; Clement of Alex., *Strom.* 2.13.56–57). These hellish images were not intended to be taken as physiological or empirical descriptions, but as expressive of the infinite distance between God's holiness and sin (Council of Lyons II, *SCD* 464).

The word *Gehenna* comes from the valley of Hinnom (Neh. 11:30), a bleak valley near Mount Zion long associated with idolatrous rites such as passing children through the fires of Moloch (Jer. 7:31; 32:35; 2 Kings 23:10; 2 Chron. 28:3; 33:6). There "perpetual fires were kept burning in this valley for consuming dead bodies of criminals and carcasses of animals and the refuse of the city." Hence Gehenna came to signify *a place where wickedness comes to its end* (Hughes, *CF*:210; cf. 2 Esdras 7:36). One gets the impression from scripture that the holiness of God is consuming sin, burning it away forever, as in a holocaust, a completely burned offering (Heb. *olah kalil, holokautōma*). The rejection of sin by the holy God appears to be complete and never ceasing.

The *Christian Topography* of Cosmas Indicopleustes (c. AD 547) pictured hell in the center of the earth. But Chrysostom had long before advised: "Do not inquire where Hell is, but how to escape it" (Chrysostom, *Hom. on Rom.* 31.5). With the loss of the geocentric conception of Ptolemaic science, the metaphors of above and below had to be recast in less spatially oriented terms. Hades is not merely the physical location in which this eternal distancing takes place, but more so the condition of distance itself: exclusion from the presence of God.

The Injustice of Unremedied Sin

Most of the core teaching of final separation came from the lips of Jesus himself, so cannot easily be set aside as if it were an ancillary tradition. It is hard to think of any Christian teaching that has stronger biblical precedent and greater traditional consensus than the teaching of afterlife justice (Jude 7; 2 Thess. 1:9; Mark 9:43; Matt. 13:42; Ignatius of Antioch, *To the Ephesians* 16.2; Justin Martyr, *Apology* 2.9; Fourth Lateran Council, *DS* 429), yet it remains controversial.

Classic Christian teaching argues that final separation is necessary because neither scripture nor rational moral justice can finally condone the victory of the unjust. It is largely those who persist in an optimistic account of human sin who "do not clearly apprehend the enduring effect of unremedied sin, and therefore cannot perceive the justice of everlasting punishment" (Hall, *DT* 10:195).

The more problematic alternative is to suppose that there is finally no justice—ever. No remedy for evil deeds done in history. This is a premise that thoughtful moral agents find repulsive. This is even more difficult to make consistent with all else that we know about God than the premise of hell. So it is not an evasion of the subject of hell to pursue the consequences of the injustice of unremedied sin.

Augustine found an entry point to sharpen the question: Is it fair that a sin committed in a short time could result in separation from God eternally? Some argue that an endless punitive act would be incompatible with the justice and love of God, for it would be unjust for God to allow never-ending punishment for crimes or offenses committed under conditions of finitude. Is it disproportional to mete out eternal punishment for sins committed in time?

Augustine answered by noting a common precedent of criminal law: A rape that takes minutes may have consequences for a lifetime. A murder that takes only an instant is an irreparable damage (*CG* 20, Tho. Aq., *ST* 1–2, Q87.3.1). So it is with the disobedience of humanity, as typified in scripture by Adam and Eve, whose wages were understood as death for the entire ensuing history of sin. Remember that all sin is finally against not only creatures but the Creator, not simply against oneself or one's neighbor but against the Giver of freedom (Ps. 51:4).

If the consequences of sin extend beyond an individual's finite life, then it is not morally scandalous for the punishment of sin also to extend beyond one's finite life. God's moral order prevails even where human emotions resist it. To permit suffering as a penalty for abusing freedom is not inconsistent with God's goodness and mercy. To fail to discipline misbehavior is to invite more of it. Classic Christian teaching holds that even a briefly committed evil deed may have lasting consequences.

The intent of God in creation is primordially to "desire everyone to be saved and to come to the knowledge of the truth" (1 Tim. 2:4). Classic exegetes recognized a crucial distinction, however, between God's antecedent will to save all and the consequent will of God to deal justly with the ramifications of free human choices. In this way the premise of hell is seen as an expression of the completion of the purpose of God, not a breakdown of that purpose (Cyprian, *Letters*; Calvin, *Inst.* 3.25). God foreknew, but did not predetermine the choices of the unjust that lead to separation (Council of Quiersy, *SCD* 316, 317).

There is no way to avoid the next subject—Satan—since this takes us directly to the Bible's way of picturing the way we got in this predicament.

Satan

Biblical reasoning about the human future is incomplete if it lacks reference entirely to the demonic powers, and more particularly to Satan (the adversary, accuser, hater) or the Devil (*diabolos*, calumniator, accuser, *daimonion*, demon), Lucifer, the supreme embodiment of evil, the superpersonal adversary of humanity (Lactantius, *DI* 3.29; Tertullian, *On the Soul* 20; Jerome, *Ag. Rufinus*).

The Deceiver

Satan is the primordial adversary to God. The root meaning is one who plots furtively against another. In the Old Testament, Satan is an angelic being hostile to God, the chief of the fallen angels (Luke 4:1–4; Ephrem, *Comm. on Tatian's Diatessaron* 4.4–5; Calvin, *Inst.* 1.14.15–18). The devil fell by pride and envy and became stubbornly determined to corrupt the world by deception (*Letter of Barnabas*, 19–21; Gregory of Nyssa, *The Great Catechism* 6–24).

This deceiver seeks to destroy truth while seeming to defend it (Athanasius, *Life of Antony*; Tertullian, *Ag. Praxeas* 1). Satan has become through deception the god of this world (Irenaeus, *Fragments* 46, *ANF* 1:575), the author of countless idolatrous imitations of faith (Tertullian, *Prescription Ag. Her.* 38–40) and pretensions to divinity (Tertullian, *Of the Crown* 7).

The serpent that seduced Eve is an expression of an act of the adversary. Satan came in the form of a serpent in that context. By this means "death entered the world" (Wisdom 2:24). Satan was tormentor of Saul (1 Sam. 18:10), deceiver of the prophets (1 Kings 22:21–23), and tempter of Job permitted by God to test the faithful (Jerome, *Ag. Jovinianus* 2). The devil is portrayed as tempting Jesus to abandon his ministry even before he began it (Mark 1:13; Luke 4:1–13), pretending to be the master of the world (Matt. 4:8, 9). The enmity between the coming reign of God and the demonic powers is dramatically seen in the response to the Son made by persons possessed by demonic powers. Satan tempted Peter, for whom the Lord prayed that he might overcome temptation (Luke 22:31–32).

Satan continues to deceive the world and draw the faithful toward despair, testing faith at every vulnerable soft spot (Rev. 12:10–12; Tertullian, *Spectacles* 23; Oecumenius, *Comm. on Apoc.* 20.7–8). Satan remains "filled with fury because he knows his time is short" (Rev. 12:12; Tertullian, *Spectacles* 16). "And the angels who did not keep their positions of authority but abandoned their own home—these he has kept in darkness, bound with everlasting chains for judgment on the great Day. In a similar way, Sodom and Gomorrah and the surrounding towns gave themselves up to sexual immorality and perversion" (Jude 6; 7; Oecumenius, *Comm. on Jude 7*). "For the demons, inspired with frenzy against humans by reason of their own wickedness, pervert their minds, which already incline downwards, by various deceptive scenic representations, that they may be disabled from rising to the path that leads to heaven." If it were possible, "they would without doubt pull down heaven itself with the rest of creation. But now this they can by no means effect, for they have not the power" (Tatian, *Address to the Greeks* 16).

The Power of Satan Bound

The power of Satan is already broken by the Son, who "saw Satan fall like lightning from heaven" (Luke 10:18; Cyril of Alex., *Comm. on Luke,* Hom. 64). The strong man Satan is being bound. The success of the seventy-two gospel witnesses over the demons was taken as evidence of their impending demise (Luke 10:17). Satan has become the "creditor" for human sin, who became wounded by his own bite, whose power is renounced in baptism (Ambrose, *Letters* 41.7).

The more explicit account of the angels' fall is in Revelation 12, which describes the devil's persecution of the church under the metaphor of a woman "clothed with the sun" (Rev. 12:1). "And there was war in heaven. Michael and his angels fought against the dragon, and the dragon and his angels fought back. But he was not strong enough, and they lost their place in heaven. The great dragon was hurled down—that ancient serpent called the devil, or Satan, who leads the whole world astray. He was hurled to the earth, and his angels with him" (Rev. 12:7–9; Oecumenius, *Comm. on Apoc.* 12.7–9).

The devil is not evil by created nature but by choice. He is called apostate because he was not wicked from the outset of God's creation, but became so by the exercise of his freedom. "He alone is called wicked by preeminence," yet not so as to imagine that he is wicked by nature (Chrysostom, *Hom. on Power of Demons* 2.2). "The Devil and other wicked spirits were created by God good by nature, but they became evil of their own accord" (Fourth Lateran Council, *CC*:57). Because fallen angels are posited as rational creatures, they too are destined to be judged (Matt. 8:29; 1 Cor. 6:3; 2 Pet. 2:4; Chrysostom, *Hom. on Cor.* 16.5).

He is a destroyer of life from primordial times (John 8:44), a murderer from the beginning (Augustine, *Tractates on John* 42.11). "He is the father of falsehood because he generated it and was the first to use it by speaking to Adam when he substituted certain words in place of others" (Theodore of Mopsuestia, *Comm. on John*. 3.8.44). As primordial Deceiver he is able temporarily to play the role of prince of this world (John 14:30), yet his power is already being overcome and judged by the suffering Messiah (John 16:11; Cyril of Alex., *Comm. on John* 10.12; Luther, *Answer to the Goat, LW* 39:123–24). At the last judgment he will depart with the unjust into a lake of fire (Matt. 25:41). The believer's sure defense is in attesting the merit of Christ's death, an attestation of one willing to die for its truth (Rev. 12:11).

A pungent series of Jesus' parables—the tares, the net, the marriage feast, the wise and foolish virgins, the talents, the pounds—focuses upon opportunities forever lost, trust abused, final exclusion and rejection. Without the theme of ultimate exclusion from the presence of the holy God, these parables lose their force.

It is not merely later church teaching but Jesus himself and the apostle Paul who constantly remind hearers that there are sins that exclude one from the kingdom of God (Matt. 5:29–30; 10:28; 23:15, 33; 1 Cor. 6:9–10; Gal. 5:20, 21; Eph. 5:5). The demonic agents have by self-determination become habitually conditioned to say no to God, so much so that finally "their disordered will shall never be taken away from them" (Tho. Aq., *SCG* 4.93). God does not primordially desire that any creature should be lost, but consequent to their own choice, God gives creatures the freedom that has the consequence of complete separation from the joy of the presence of God (1 Thess. 1:9; Rom. 1:10; 1 John 2:17; 1 Tim. 6:9; Augustine, *Ag. Julian* 2.9.32).

Life Everlasting

Finally, the victorious conclusion of the creed sings out: "I believe in the life everlasting [*zōon aiōnion*; Lat. *vitam aeternam*]" (*SCD* 6). The life in which we participate is everlasting, for "while it has a beginning, it will have no end" (Ursinus, *Comm. Heid. Catech.*:319). "When that which is perfect is come, then that which is in part shall be done away" (1 Cor. 13:10).

As "God always was, and always is, and always will be," so it follows that life with God is eternal. This means: "God always Is. For was and will be are fragments of our time . . . What time, measured by the course of the sun is to us, eternity is to the everlasting" (Gregory of Nazianzus, *Orat.* 38.7).

Eternal Life

The destiny of the righteous is eternal life in and with God. The prevailing scriptural term for the final state of the blessed is "eternal life." This life is transmuted into a future life of glory that does not reach full expression until the general resurrection, final judgment, and the final destiny of the faithful (Cyril of Jerusalem, *Catech. Lect.* 18.28–32).

The destiny of the just is called simply "life," or "eternal life," "the life which is life indeed" (1 Tim. 6:19; Matt. 18:8; 7:14; Augustine, *Letters* 130.2.3). "Whoever hears my word and believes him who sent me has eternal life and will not be condemned; he has crossed over from death to life" (John 5:24; Augustine, *Tractates on John* 22.6). The living God permits the new life with God to continue without ceasing. "In short, as Christ begins the glory of his body in this world with manifold diversity of gifts, and increases it by degrees, so also he will perfect it in heaven" (Calvin, *Inst.* 3.25.10).

Eternal life brings to completion the work of grace begun in this life, where one is delivered from sin, its roots and consequences, fulfilling God's purpose in creation, redemption, and consummation (Hilary, *Trin.* 6:43–49; Calvin, *Inst.* 4.16, 17). The transformation begun in faithful baptism does not come to nothing but lives on. The spiritual life begun in penitent faith, imparted in spiritual rebirth, and grown by sanctifying grace lives on by completing grace. The characteristic feature of eternal life is the complete and unending enjoyment of life with God.

Eternal Life Already Experienced in the Present

The best indication of the future of life with God is the life with God already enjoyed now in the celebrating community. "Dear friends, now we are children of God, and what we will be has not yet been made known. But we know that when he appears, we shall be like him, for we shall see him as he is" (1 John 3:2; Augustine, *Trin.*, 15.1.26; Tho. Aq., *ST* supp., Q92). The future of faith is "we shall be like him," in relation to the Father as the Son is to the Father. Already faith shares in the life that has come from God in the Son, but then we participate fully.

Eternal life is already enjoyed (John 3:36; 1 John 5:11, 12; Bede, *On 1 John* 5.11–12). It is in full measure what is already experienced as the life of faith, hope, and love. "As I now feel in my heart the beginning of eternal joy, I shall after this life possess complete bliss, such as eye hath not seen, nor ear heard" (*Heid. Catech.* Q58). The gifts of grace received in this life are firstfruits. The full harvest is to come abundantly in eternity (Rom. 8:23; Eph. 1:13, 14).

"Eternal life begins here, in our hearts; for when we begin to believe in Christ, after we have been baptized, then, according to faith and the Word, we are liberated from death, from sin, and from the devil. Therefore we have the beginning of life eternal and its first fruits in this life, a sort of mild foretaste; we have entered the lobby; but soon, divested of this flesh, we shall fully appreciate all" (Luther, *Sermons on the Psalms*, Ps. 45:6).

The Heavenly Abode of the Righteous

The Greek root word for heaven (*ouranos*) points to the endless expanse of sky lifted up above the earth. It is seen as an immeasurable vault or ceiling or unimpeded space. The same ordinary words for the sky, the upper atmosphere in Hebrew and Greek refer to the heavens, to the exalted abode of God (Luke 24:51; Augustine, Sermon 242.6).

In Christian teaching, heaven is both a place and a condition of eternal rest and joy in the Lord. It is "to be present with the Lord" (2 Cor. 5:8; Chrysostom, *Hom. on Cor.* 10.4). Heaven is where the blessed clearly see God and incomparably enjoy the blessings of divine glory (Matt. 5:12; 6:20; Luke 6:23; 1 Pet. 1:4; Chromatius, *Tractate on Matt.* 17.9.2–3).

Heaven is represented as a secure lodging of unutterable glory, joy, and peace (Cyril of Alex., *Fragment* 172, Reuss, *MKGK* 209). Its most prominent features are tranquillity, holiness, light, beholding, happiness, and the presence of the Lord. What happens in heaven is full and endless participation in God's own goodness and happiness. Those "whose names are written in heaven" have "come to God." They are "the spirits of righteous men made perfect" (Heb. 12:23).

Jesus promised his disciples: "I am going there to prepare a place for you. And if I go and prepare a place for you, I will come back and take you to be with me that you also may be where I am" (John 14:2, 3; Cyril of Alex., *Comm. on John* 9). In the New Jerusalem the glorified saints will dwell in the bodies restored to them at the resurrection (Rev. 21:2; Irenaeus, *Ag. Her.* 5.35).

Knowing and Seeing Fully

The faithful will see God's face (Rev. 22:4; Primasius, *Comm. on Apoc.* 22.4). "Now I know in part; then I shall know fully, even as I am fully known" (1 Cor. 13:12; Chrysostom, *Hom. on Cor.* 34.2). "Blessed are the pure in heart, for they will see God" (Matt. 5:8; Chromatius, *Tractate on Matt.* 17.6.3–4). Christ prayed that the faithful would "behold my glory" (John 17:24; Leo, *Sermons* 95). Now we see God's glory as if in a mirror but then "face to face" (1 Cor. 13:12).

There is an intimacy in these images, like the joy of the child looking into the face of a mother. To see God is to be infinitely happy (Clement of Alex., *Stromata* 7.10). The saints, seeing God, do not see all that God sees, but behold the One who beholds all (Tho. Aq., *ST* supp., Q92.3).

This beholding takes place through the light of glory (Council of Vienne, *SCD* 475) and is sustained eternally without interruption (*Faith of Damasus, SCD* 16; Quicunque Creed, *SCD* 40; Leo IX, *Symbol of Faith, SCD* 347). The faithful live in the light of God's countenance (Num. 6:25, 26; Ps. 67:1).

The faithful are set apart for holiness not only "while on their pilgrimage" through time but "especially after their death, when all reflective vision being done away, they behold clearly the Holy Trinity, in whose infinite light they know what concerns us" (Creed of Dositheus, 8).

The biblical images are ecstatic: "No eye has seen, no ear has heard, no mind has conceived what God has prepared for those who love him" (1 Cor. 2:9, Isa. 64:4; Chrysostom, *Hom. on Cor.* 7.5–6). "The city does not need the sun or the moon to shine on it, for the glory of God gives it light, and the Lamb is its lamp. The nations will walk by its light, and the kings of the earth will bring their splendor into it. On no day will its gates ever be shut, for there will be no night there" (Rev. 21:23–25; Apringius of Beja, *Tractate on the Apoc.* 21.24–26).

The blessed faithful behold in heaven what they believed by faith on earth. A deeper knowing of God will be given to the saints, greater than the fragmentary knowing of this life (John 17:3; 1 Cor. 13:12). Faith is transformed into knowledge by meeting God face to face. "Now this is eternal life: that they may know you, the only true God, and Jesus Christ, whom you have sent" (John 17:3; Cyril of Alex., *Comm. on John* 11.15). The intellect is directly illumined by the light of glory (Gregory of Nyssa, *The Life of Moses*, CWS:111 ff.).

This beholding has already begun in the faithful, "who with unveiled faces all reflect [as in a mirror] the Lord's glory, are being transformed into his likeness with ever-increasing glory" (2 Cor. 3:18; Chrysostom, *Hom. on Cor.* 7.5). Peter wrote to the far away faithful: "Though you have not seen him, you love him; and even though you do not see him now, you believe in him and are filled with an inexpressible and glorious joy, for you are receiving the goal of your faith, the salvation of your souls" (1 Pet. 1:8, 9; Oecumenius, *Comm. on 1 Pet.* 1.8). In ways beyond present knowing, the glorified body will adapt to this beholding,

The Bliss of Hope Fulfilled in Perfect Willing

Those who perfectly behold the life of God eternally experience perfect enjoyment of the will. "Therefore, whoever is happy seeks nothing which does not belong to that in which true beatitude consists" (Tho. Aq., *SCG* 4, 92). If a joy could be imagined in which one is completely and permanently delivered from all evil, so as to share fully in the abundant good of the One who is incomparably good, that is the joy of heaven (Leo, *Sermons*, 21). "Final redemption restores what had been lost in the fall"—the full exercise of the free will to celebrate and reflect the divine good endlessly (John of Damascus, *OF* 4.27).

Only an eternal happiness that cannot end is absolute felicity, for all other modes of happiness are aware of their impending finite ending. "Here is possession displacing hope's desire, even as vision displaces faith's belief. . . . Then is our happiness complete, for the highest delight rises from our being united with what fits us best" (Tho. Aq., *Sentences* 1.1.1).

Words cannot express the heights of this joy. The enjoyment of the presence of God is a "joy unspeakable" (1 Pet. 1:8). Eternal life is a treasure that does not fail, that moth and rust cannot corrupt (Luke 12:33), a "crown of glory that will never fade away" (1 Pet. 5:4) "There the righteous dwell from the beginning, not ruled by necessity, but enjoying always the contemplation of the blessings which are in their view, and delighting themselves with the expectation of others ever new, and deeming those ever better than these" (Hippolytus, *Ag. Plato* 1).

Heaven is a very musical place (Hildegard of Bingen, *Symphonia*:43). The righteous are "hymned by the angels" (Hippolytus, *Ag. Plato* 1). Everyone there is singing God's praise.

The Absence of Negative Obstacles
(Privative Blessings)

The blessings of eternal life with God are sometimes divided into negative and positive blessings. Under negative or "privative blessings" are considered all that is promised to be absent from heaven. There will be freedom from temptation and evil. "The privative blessings are the absence of sin and of the causes of sin, viz., the flesh inciting, the devil suggesting, and world seducing" (Quenstedt; in Schmid, *DT*:661). In eternal life with God there is no inordinate desire, no sin, and no consequent pain, sorrow, sickness and death that come from them.

Absent from heaven will be mental aberrations, neuroses, moral depravity, all influences of the wicked, who "shall cease from troubling" (Job 3:17). Absent from heaven is the temptation that characterizes the body-soul interface under conditions of finitude. Finite freedom is now no longer made vulnerable to anxiety and guilt. Because there is now freedom from temptation, there is freedom from the possibility of sinning. In heaven there is no constant struggle with sin or even the inclination to sin.

The glorified bodies of the celestial city are promised freedom from the drivenness of sex, guilt, fear, and anxiety (Rev. 7:16; 1 Cor. 6:13; Matt. 22:30; 1 Cor. 15:42, 43; Augustine, *Contra Julian* 5.61). "Never again will they hunger; never again will they thirst. The sun will not beat upon them, nor any scorching heat" (Rev. 7:15, 16; Tyconius, *Comm. on Apoc.* 7.16).

The Heavenly Rest of the Righteous

The Letter to the Hebrews described the final state of the just as "entering their rest" (Heb. 4:1–6) from the warfare of the struggle that is required by the conditions of embodied time. It is a rest from the contradictions of human existence under bondage to sin.

This tranquility is not inaction, but unfettered vitality. The quality of life is raised not lowered in spiritual energy, being free of sin. It is more a rest of singing than sleeping, more a life of praise than sloth (Rev. 14:3; Oecumenius, *Comm. on Apoc.* 14.1–5).

For after final judgment the consequences of sin no more affect the faithful. They will have been freed from all that might detract the soul from God, without the tears or pain or limitations that come from sin. God will "wipe every tear from their eyes. There will be no more death or mourning or crying or pain, for the old order of things has passed away" (Rev. 21:4; Oecumenius, *Comm. on Apoc.* 21.3–5).

In this rest there is neither "pain, nor corruption, nor care, nor night, nor day measured by time . . . no numerous wanderings of stars, no painfully-trodden earth, no abode of paradise hard to find; no furious roaring of the sea" (Hippolytus, *Ag. Plato* 2). "For then the outer man will be the peaceful and unblemished possession of the inner man; then the mind, engrossed in beholding God, will be hampered by no obstacles of human weakness" (Leo, *Sermons* 95).

Freedom for Life (Positive Blessings)

The privative blessings of freedom from sin just described are complemented by "positive blessings" of freedom for life in the presence of God, and all that is uniquely present to the glory of God's holiness.

Each human faculty is incomparably blessed in God's presence: The *soul* is blessed with eternal life. The knowing capacity of the rational *mind* is blessed with enlightenment (1 Cor. 13:9–12). The *will* is blessed with rectitude and happiness (Ps. 17:15; Eph. 4:25; 5:27). The glorified *body* is blessed by the right ordering of appetitive powers. The *imagination* is blessed with the thought of the complete security of future blessedness without interruption (John 16:22). This is a happiness that none can take away, for it is eternal union with God (*Longer Catech.*, Eastern Orthodox Church, 380).

The awesome fact of death that had appeared to be so overwhelming becomes itself the transition into incomparable freedom, victory, and the eternal happiness of the just (1 Cor. 15:54–57). The souls of the faithful would be withered by the holiness of God were it not that the grace of God gives strength to recognize and accept the happiness that lives eternally in God's presence.

The Glorified Bodies of Saints

The spiritual body (*soma pneumatikos*) risen by faith through grace into eternal life is promised the full recovery of the condition of humanity prior to the fall: "To him who overcomes, I will give the right to eat from the tree of life, which is in the paradise of God" (Rev. 2:7). These amazing implications follow, as explained by Paul in 1 Corinthians 15: The glorified body, free from death, is characterized by immortal incorruption (*aphtharsia*, immunity from dissolution). The perishable has become clothed "with the imperishable, and the mortal with immortality" (1 Cor. 15:53), now beyond any feeling of discomfort or death, having put on incorruption (Rev. 21:4). Even the scars of the martyrs will enhance, not mar, the glory of their risen bodies (Augustine, *CG* 22.19; Tho. Aq., *ST*, supp., Q82.1.5).

The risen body, freed from the darkness of guilt and sin, is characterized by clarity, brightness, *glory* (*doxa*), by which the "righteous will shine like the sun in the kingdom of their Father" (Matt. 13:43) because they fully reflect the glory of God. This same glory was anticipatively beheld by the disciples in the transfiguration (Mark 9:2).

The new creation of the risen body, freed from infirmities, is characterized by agility and *power* (*dunamis*), by which the body will move with complete ease wherever directed by the soul, as typified by Christ's body in the resurrection (Tho. Aq., *ST*, supp., Q84.1).

Insofar as freed from time-space encumbrances, the risen body is to empirical eyes fully empowered by the Spirit, hence, spiritual, invisible—now characterized by subtlety, by which the soul, being filled with the divine *pneuma*, "assumes into itself the life of the body and raises it to its own level," so that "the body becomes absolutely subject to the spirit" (Tho. Aq., *ST*, supp., Q83.2). When these changes occur, "then the saying that is written will come true: 'Death has been swallowed up in victory'" (1 Cor. 15:54; Augustine, *Sermons for Easter* 233.4).

The Heavenly Gift

It seems contrary to the teaching of justification by faith through grace to say that the just receive heaven as a reward, if by reward is meant that upon which one has a claim due to autonomous human effort. The just have no claim upon final blessedness by which they might assert that it is just that they receive it.

Yet heaven is promised and given the faithful as the gracious consequence of their repentance, faith, and responsive works of love, and in this sense is called a reward not for works but for trusting in God's good work (Luke 6:23; 35; 2 Tim. 4:14; Cyprian, *Letters*; Calvin, *Inst.* 3.18).

There will be differences in heavenly rewards as taught in the parable of the talents (Matt. 25:21–23) and of the pounds (Luke 19:16–19; Cyril of Alex., *Comm. on Luke*, Hom. 129). The principle is, "From everyone who has been given much, much will be demanded, and from the one who has been entrusted with much, much more will be asked" (Luke 12:48; Augustine, *On Grace and Free Will* 3). Some apparently will be saved barely, "but only as one escaping through the flames" (1 Cor. 3:15; Chrysostom, *Hom. on Cor.* 7.11).

Each celestial celebrant will reflect the divine goodness in a different and individuated way (Irenaeus, *Ag. Her.* 5.36.2; Clement of Alex., *Stromata* 6.13). Though each individual shares in the same salvation, the refracted glory will not be monotone, but varied (Chrysostom, *To the Fallen Theodore*). "The sun has one kind of splendor, the moon another and the stars another, and star differs from star in splendor. So will it be with the resurrection of the dead" (1 Cor. 15:41, 42; Jerome, *Ag. Pelagians* 16; Clement of Alex., *Stromata* 6.14). "So there will also be many degrees of splendor and glory in yonder life, as St. Paul teaches in 1 Cor. 15:40; and yet all will be alike in the enjoyment of the same eternal blessedness and delight, and there will be but *one* glory for all, because we shall all be the children of God" (Luther, *Sermons on Romans*; *WLS* 2:622).

Each receives the recompense appropriate as judged by God's wisdom (Matt. 16:27; Chrysostom, *Hom. on Matt.*, Hom. 55.5). "The man who plants and the man who waters have one purpose, and each will be rewarded according to his own labor" (1 Cor. 3:8). "Whoever sows sparingly will also reap sparingly" (2 Cor. 9:6; *Martyrdom of Polycarp* 40; Ignatius of Antioch, *To Polycarp* 1.3; Tertullian, *Scorpiace* 6). If God is just, there are no injustices in heaven. Where seeming discrepancies or inequities may appear, they are not to be explained by human merits, but by the free grace of God (*Decretum Unionis*, *SCD* 693). "But just as small vessels can be as full as larger vessels (though the latter contain more), so everyone in heaven will be wholly fulfilled and wholly at peace" (Kasper, *CCF*:345). "There will be no envy on account of unequal glory, because one love will govern all" (Augustine, *Tractate on John* 67.3). "And thus one will have a gift less than another in such a way that he also has the gift that he does not wish for more" (Hugh of St. Victor, *SCF*:475). The glory each one reflects is measured by the strength of the love one has for God.

Marriage Feast of the Lamb

All whose lives are hid in Christ are being gathered from around the world (Mark 13:27). The dross having been burned away, the faithful will be ready to be received by their Lord (Matt. 13:41, 42). The church will be "prepared as a bride beautifully dressed for her husband" (Rev. 21:2; Augustine, *CG* 20.17), being welcomed into the city of God (Rev. 21:8–10).

The key event of the Revelation of John is the marriage supper of the Lamb (Rev. 19:7–10; Oecumenius, *Comm. on Apoc.* Rev. 19.7–10;), a messianic banquet in which the bride, the church, is dressed in the wedding garment, being now clothed in the righteousness of the bridegroom, Christ.

In the new heaven and earth (Rev. 21:1) at its focal center, the new Jerusalem (21:9–11), God and the Lamb are being worshiped through the Spirit. There "the dwelling of God is with men, and he will live with them. They will be his people, and God himself will be with them and be their God." (21:34; Primasius, *Comm. on Apoc.* 21.27).

Amen to the Glory of the Lord

Triune Praise

The echoes resound eternally in the celebration of the triune God. Nothing brings more delight to the communion of saints. God is one, indivisible, the giver of all and redeemer of all. The work begun in creation, having fallen and been redeemed, is being consummated according to God's promise.

That God the Father is Creator does not prevent the faithful from celebrating the Son through whom "all things were made, and without him nothing was made that has been made" (John 1:3), and the Spirit who is the Eternal One through whom the creative Word speaks. The Father is truly God.

The work of redemption is the proper work of the Son, who is sent by the Father's will and empowered by the Spirit to do all things necessary for the work of redemption. Before all ages the Son was begotten of the Father as light comes from light. The Son has come to save us from sin. The Son is truly God.

The work of consummation, completion, and sanctification is the work of the Spirit, of whom Christ said that this is the One "whom the Father will send in my name" (John 14:26). The Spirit dwells within us to enable us to conform to Christ's likeness. The Spirit is truly God.

The mystery of the triune God is that God is Father, God is Son, and God is Spirit, and that God is one. Yet we do not say that there is one Person in God, but three Persons, and we do not say that there are three gods, but one God. "Now this is the Catholic faith, that we worship one God in Trinity and Trinity in unity" (*Quicunque vult*). "What the Father is to us and gives to us, He is and gives through the Son, in the Holy Spirit; no one has the Father except in the Son, and no one confesses the Son except in the Holy Spirit" (Pieper, *WCB*:56–57; cf. Gregory of Nazianzus, *Orat.* 31).

Classic Christian teaching is offered as a modest gift in order to shed light on baptism and communion. Its intent is that we may know "for what purpose each of the holy mysteries of Baptism is performed, and with what reverence and order you must go from Baptism to the Holy Altar of God, and enjoy its spiritual and heavenly mysteries; that your souls being previously enlightened by the word of doctrine" may receive the gifts offered by God (Cyril of Jerusalem, *Catech. Lect.* 18.32).

From Credo *to* Amēn

The ancient prayer of the church sums up the whole range of classic Christian teaching: "Glory be to the Father, and to the Son, and to the Holy Ghost; as it was in the beginning, is now and ever shall be, world without end. Amen" (*Divine Liturgy of James, Early Liturgies*; *BCP*; cf. Rev. 21:6; 22:13; Augustine, *Trin.* 7.4–6).

The *amēn* (meaning "truly, certainly") to which we come at last in the ancient baptismal creed is more than a period (*SCD* 2). It is an act of whole body-soul unity, of trust, of confirmation. As the creed begins with "I believe" (*credo*), it ends with, "Yes, so be it," "verily," "I confirm it" (*amēn*). Jesus Christ himself is personally God's own "Amen" (Rev. 3:14). "For no matter how many promises God has made, they are 'Yes' in Christ. And so through him the 'Amen' is spoken by us to the glory of God" (2 Cor. 1:20).

EPILOGUE

GENERAL CONSENT OF THE LAITY AS THE PRINCIPLE OF LEGITIMACY

Three Conclusions on Why Historic Consensus Is Vital to Doctrinal Definition

I offer three conclusions drawn from all that we have been through. Each deserves a brief explanation of why we have been engaged in this effort. They are:

- *consensual teachings are readily identifiable textually*
- *consensual authority is grounded in general lay consent*
- *consensus clarification is useful*

These conclusions are testable by any lay believer.

Consensual Teachings Are Readily Identifiable Textually

This summary of classic Christian teaching has sought to identify a viable consensus of what Christians have always believed. It is based on respected texts known to have continuous authority for the worshiping community. Even on points where multiple voices have competed for legitimacy, there has been a discernible consensus.

Through it all, Scripture has remained the primary source, ground, and criterion of Christian teaching. The consensual interpreters of Scripture we have examined in this exploration all have intended help the reader of scripture integrate its wisdom into a cohesive pattern of convictions. They do not intend to coerce belief, but to point to a believing community.

Those quoted have sought to communicate the scripture narrative as a whole as the saving Word of God. Skeptical or exotic interpreters who have presumed themselves to be the judges of the authenticity of canonical scripture have been far less pertinent to this study, since their views have not found consent generally in historic Christian teaching. These challenges may be clever but they are not proved to be always wise according to scripture as viewed by the ecumenical consensus.

What follows is a reflection for both lay and professional readers on how consensual Christian teaching has been formed and corroborated. My task is to plainly set forth the most common way that classic Christianity has sought to understand the integral wisdom of sacred scripture as a cohesive interpretation of Christian truth. This cohesion has often been called "systematic theology," a discipline that functioned adequately before its exponents insisted that they could improve upon the classic tradition from stem to stern.

This epilogue is not meant only for professionals as a defense of this method or ploy to fashion a new method. Rather it is the oldest method in Christian reasoning. And it is a practical summary for lay Christians who want to examine the classic texts themselves for their truthfulness. This is for the laity who wonder how they might assess the extent to which spokespersons are faithfully representing Christian truth.

The Work of Listening: On Assessing Proximate Consensus

The first task has been to listen carefully to the ecumenical councils themselves. They mark the boundaries of the broadest and deepest ocean of Christian consensus. This is where contested questions on prophetic and apostolic testimony have been most thoroughly debated and for most settled biblically and consensually.

The second task has been listening to the decisions of those regional councils that have gained widest intergenerational consent.

Third, beyond these council decisions, we have been listening to those few most widely revered teachers who have through the most generations and widest variety of cultures been most commonly received as able to express accurately the mind of the believing church. While difficult, this task has not proved impossible.

Among these there are eight widely recognized "great doctors of the church" that rise to the top of anybody's list—anybody, that is, who knows the original texts. They are the acknowledged master teachers of historic Christianity who have warranted the reputation of speaking reliably for classic Christianity: Athanasius, Basil, Gregory of Nazianzus, John Chrysostom, Ambrose, Augustine, Jerome, and Gregory the Great.

These voices have been tested by laity for over fifteen hundred years of Christian worship and critical thought. If we are thinking sociologically of an example of a longitudinal study of the vetting extensive of an authoritative voice, there is none to match this extensive vetting process. It has been rigorous and selective for most of two millennia. That it has proven to be a reliable process is evident from the fact that it has been so frequently and ceaselessly been relied upon.

These are the voices that are featured here most often. These writers are highly accessible. Much of their work has been adequately translated into dozens of languages.

In addition to these eight doctors of the church, we have been listening to those consensual interpreters of scripture who have shown relatively more cultural openness, more awareness of the varied interpretations of scripture text configurations in different cultural-historical situations (notably, Clement, Origen, Eusebius, Lactantius, Ephrem, Cyril of Alexandria, John of Damascus and others). These we commonly valued among the classic exegetes. As a result, we have witnessed the enormous cultural flexibility and variability of classical Christian teaching. We have beheld the unique ability of orthodoxy to enter into various cultural settings and speak in different languages without losing its apostolic identity.

These consensual exegetes have only formative, not normative value. They themselves never cease to remind their readers that scripture is to be received as normative authority, and that the consensual tradition of exegesis derives from scripture. The salient question has been throughout: "what does the text of canonical scripture actually say?" The consensual exegetes have no reason to pit tradition against scripture, as we so often do in the modern period. Rather their work is invariably offered as servants of the truth declared in scripture.

The Irenic Intent

Classic Christianity has the peacemaking intent of uniting the body of Christ in the truth of Christian teaching. This unity is truth-driven. Its passion is always conciliatory, unless it is asked to distort the whole scriptural narrative. The task of the consensus bearer is modest and humbling: Just keep your own opinions and preferences in the background. Listen for consensus that lasts intergenerationally.

The aim of consensus-bearing is to state the widest agreement possible that derives strictly from the voices of the apostolic tradition in their beautiful two millennia of varieties—East-West, African-Asian, Roman and Antiochene and Genevan—of cultural experience, exegesis, and pastoral care.

The Danger of Hypertolerance

The irenic task is best accompanied by a realistic, calm, reasoned critical effort—a discerning spirit, a constant vigilance for recognizing points at which faith is misshapen, where false teachers, "feigning faith," offer "something like a deadly drug" steeped in "honeyed wine" (Ignatius, *Trallians* 6). These drugs are rampant in religious communities desperate to accommodate to popular cultural assumptions.

A no-boundaries absolute toleration advocate could not expect to be taken seriously by lay Christian consent over any long term. When classic Christian teaching loses the capacity to discern the difference between false and true teaching (between orthodoxy and aberations), it looses its credibility with the worshiping community. Those who too quickly concede an implicit orthodox intent for any and all the historic heresies, whether Arian, Pelagian, atheist or Epicurean, have forfeited their ability to speak for classic Christian truth.

Unblemished and polluted fish are caught in the same net in the call to decision. As long as the church remains a *corpus mixtum*, we will find persons who come to church, partake of its sacraments, hear its word, and even are paid salaries to provide its leadership, being duly ordained to preach its word and administer its baptism and communion, who yet have not learned its most simple and widely received consensual teachings, such as triunity, incarnation, atonement, resurrection, and the indwelling of the Spirit. Thus it behooves those committed to the apostolic faith to remain attentive to where the true word is being made false by twisted interpretations, however well intended (Hippolytus, *Refutation of All Her.*; Simon Patrick, *A Brief Account of the New Sect of Latitudinarians*). Given the persistence of human self-deception, the faithful are seldom surprised to find heresy mixed inconspicuously with orthodoxy, false with true teaching side by side in the same pew singing the same hymns. This makes the irenic and critical tasks all the more urgent and imperative.

Core Consensual Teachers

Those teachers who deserve our closest attention are those who have been most widely recognized over long periods of time. They have proven to be able wisely to grasp the truth of Christian teaching for many different generations. They have been most attentive to the Spirit's address through the written word of the sacred texts. They best represent the broadest consent of the Christian laity of all times and cultures. This is why we have listened most often to these eight designated voices most widely received by the whole church for the longest period of time as consensual interpreters of the apostles—persons with well-known names and recognized gifts—the four great doctors of the East: Athanasius, Basil, Gregory of Nazianzus, and Chrysostom; and of the West: Ambrose, Augustine, Jerome, and Gregory the Great.

There are many others that are cited as reliable consensual teachers, but these eight are known to seldom lead one astray. Known to whom? Twenty centuries of believers of all continents. Hence they are remembered everywhere as useful and truthful teachers of classic Christianity. What I have found is what so many others have found: these eight are with few exceptions consensually reliable clarifiers of the mind of the believing church.

That does not mean that the "eight great" never made mistakes or misjudgments. One may occasionally find in Augustine an idea that has not been consensually received, such as the fixed number of the elect or a traducian view of the transmission of the human soul by parents to children. At times one may find in these eight a testy spirit, such as in Athanasius and Jerome, to whom we owe so much even amid their testiness. But the history of lay consent is more indebted to these eight exegetes than any since the apostles. All assumed those prior church council decisions that have been repeatedly accepted as received teaching concerning the truth of God's revelation. The extensive tradition of recognition of these and several other figures established itself early through conciliar decisions themselves. By AD 495, the Gelasian decretal universally commended as consensual teaching not only the canons of Nicaea, Ephesus, and Chalcedon "to be received *after* those of the Old or New Testament, which we regularly accept. . . . *and in the same way* the works of Gregory of Nazianzus, Basil, Athanasius, Chrysostom, Theophilus, Cyril of Alexandria, Hilary, Ambrose, Augustine, Jerome and Prosper. Also the epistle of the blessed Leo" and "the decretal epistles" (*SCD* 165). That early list included all the then extant ecumenical councils and the great doctors of the church, plus several others whom we have most quoted often.

Vincent of Lérins noted that the Council of Ephesus (AD 431) had specifically cited as ecumenically reliable witnesses the four leading bishops of Alexandria: Peter, Athanasius, Theophilus, and Cyril, plus the "stars of Cappadocia"—Basil, and the two Gregorys (Nazianzus and Nyssa), and among Western bishops Cyprian, Felix I, Julius I, and Ambrose (*Comm.* 30). Amid doctrinal challenges, the faithful were to be fortified by "the public reading aloud of quotations from the Fathers" such as Athanasius, Theophilus, and Cyril. "Let the standard of antiquity be maintained throughout" (Leo, *Letters* 129). It is no secret. The church knows the voices of those who are her greatest teachers of the sacred text over the longest period of time.

The fifth ecumenical council (Constantinople II, AD 553) determined to "hold fast to the decrees of the four councils, and in every way follow the holy Fathers, Athanasius, Hilary, Basil, Gregory the Theologian, Gregory of Nyssa, Ambrose, Theophilus, Chrysostom of Constantinople, Cyril, Augustine, Proclus, Leo and the writings on the true faith." These are among the teachers most often referenced in orthodox teaching. "The Church is taught indeed by the Life-giving Spirit, but through the medium of the holy Fathers and Doctors whose rule is acknowledged to be the Holy and Oecumenical Synods" (*Conf.* of Dositheus 12).

Testing Consensuality

Their own firmest intention is neglected when their own creativity or imagination is preferred to the revealed word of sacred scripture. What characterized them all was steady attentiveness to the written word. Many of the core consensual teachers had memorized large portions of scripture (notably Didymus the Blind, Jerome, Augustine and Cyril of Alexandria). When Augustine is preferred to Paul, Augustine himself is being abused.

I have personally tested these voices again and again, sometimes against each other and more often with each other. This has required years of study and comparative analysis. There is no other way to make such a test. Those who doubt that such a consensus can exist must go through something like this lengthy learning process before an informed judgment can be made.

Legitimate authority needs to be tested repeatedly to retain its legitimacy. It is always proper to ask the toughest questions to presumed authorities. But when these voices repeatedly radiate the spirit that comes from the center of the worshiping community, the faithful learn anew to trust them on most points and become surprised only when they occasionally misstep, as they sometimes do (and when they do, they are assessed by the wider consensus).

Each of these consensual teachers understood themselves to be strongly guided by the previous prevailing ecumenical consensus. They assumed that the Spirit was guiding the church into all truth (John 16:13; Didymus the Blind, *On the Holy Spirit* 22). Such guidance was occurring not merely individualistically, immediately, privately, or directly, but rather through the media of the written word and the consensual teaching tradition, reasonably assessed, corporately celebrated, and experientially tested (Augustine, *Tractates on John* 96.4).

I do not ask readers to trust me on my own authority, but rather on the plausible wisdom found in scripture tested by centuries of consensus. Constantly assess the alleged consensual judgments reported here by means of the whole narrative of scripture. There may be some readers who will trust me less if I trust sacred texts of any kind. That is called intolerance. Regarding them, I pray that they will listen to the arguments carefully and assess them fairly and reasonably. I am willing to see these arguments tested according to conscience and reason and common sense. Arguments from scripture cannot be tested if the sacred text is already presupposed to be of no avail.

Am I forever fallible in my studied judgment of this supposed consensuality? Of course. This is precisely why I have written this book: I am asking my reader

to test my own fallibility. I solicit your admonition as to where I may have mis-
perceived the gist of the broadest classic consensus. I hope others will admonish
me to see more clearly where my own cultural assumptions or historical myopias
or class biases may have misguided me.

We need each other to balance and amend private judgment, hoping that those
to whom are given the treasured guardianship tasks of teaching and testimony in
the church do not lead the church astray. The punitive promises here are tough
on offenders. Those who fail to be specific in undertaking this admonition, who
too readily dismiss consensual teaching, tend to rule themselves out of the arena
of trustability within the believing community.

Systematic theology began in the tradition of the catena, the stringing of
chains of authoritative comments of the most widely consensual early Christian
writers on a given theme or text. The earliest forms of systematic theology were
tested by their correspondence to the ecumenical consensus.

Regrettably the steady preoccupation of modern historical theology has instead focused on how Christian teaching has constantly been modifying, always
shifting, rather than the many ways it has remained stable and centered. Hence
much more is known by modern historians of the alternatives to consensus than
of the continuities within those developments. A huge literature exists on the varieties of competitive Christian teachings, and a very small literature on centrist
orthodox consent.

The Unity Sought in Christian Teaching

I want to speak primarily of the deep continuities embracing apostolic Christian
teaching of all periods and cultures. Consensual teaching is less about how
Christian teaching has changed than how it has steadily remained the same.
To fail to search for that which unifies the variety is just as egregious an error
as to fail to acknowledge differences within the developing traditions. By
the many references in the embedded notes I have tried to show that a core
unity is actually there textually and not merely an imagined projection. Each
one of the references remains open to challenge as to its context and alleged
consensuality.

The unity of classic Christian teaching is not that of any one teacher's invention. It is the unity known at the Lord's Table. It is the unity shared in baptism,
the unity embodied by those who receive exceedingly varied gifts of the one
Spirit. This unity is being made visible in fragmented ways, and refracted in
beautiful multicolored forms and cultures, through brilliant examples of consensual definition of Christian teaching of all ages. Baptized into this one baptism,
confessing one faith in the one Lord, these attestors are being brought into one
company of the faithful of all ages to confess the apostolic faith and to break the
one bread (Eph. 4:3–5).

To summarize my first conclusion: *The texts documenting the classic consensus
are accessible, well known, and exhaustively vetted for orthodoxy.* Classic Christian
teaching prefers to reference only those texts most obviously consensual and
least subject to quibbling as to their orthodoxy, and most pertinent to the subject
being discussed. This implies a respectful resistance to texts that do not meet
the criteria of consensuality and orthodoxy. This especially requires listening
carefully to the councils, ecumenical and regional, then to the great doctors of
the church, and finally to the key teachers that have survived many centuries of
the vetting process. This is what we have done.

Consensual Authority Is Grounded in General Lay Consent

The jury is the faithful laity over the whole two-millennia stretch of the time of the church. The jury is the communion of saints.

The principle of general lay consent does not ignore or circumvent cultural differences. Rather it celebrates those differences and the unity of the body of Christ that embraces them.

The Apostolic Consensus in the First Generation

The apostles themselves had a fully formed and sufficient vision of the Lord's teaching. But that did not prevent Peter and Paul from earnest debate on Jewish legal practices which led directly to a further refined consensus. There were tensions of culture and language between the proclamations of Mark and John and between James and Paul that have required all subsequent adherents of apostolic teaching to search for their common ground. But were these styles constitutive of fundamental doctrinal differences? The apostles were firmly convinced that the Spirit was leading them into a common faith, not divergent doctrines (John 17:20–26; Cyprian, *The Lord's Prayer* 30; Simon Patrick, *A Discourse About Tradition,* 1683).

It was not the unique or peculiar features of any one apostle's teaching—such as the justification teaching of Paul or the logos Christology of John—that defined the consensus, but rather the consensus emerged out of the Spirit-led recollections of the eyewitness apostles as their teachings were embraced in a convergence. Apostolic consensus did not develop out of a democratic group-think process groping after the best available humanistic solutions to problems or feelings. Rather it lived out of the worshiping community that wholeheartedly consented to the Lord's teaching under the guidance of the Spirit.

By the end of the first century there was a remarkably unified consensual testimony to God's saving activity based upon the leading apostolic witness (Peter, Paul, and the four Gospel writers). Key points commonly shared by second-century interpreters of the apostolic teaching were summarized by C.H. Dodd:

> the Old Testament canon was essential to the interpretation of the New;
> the words of Christ were accurately recalled by the Apostles by the power of the Spirit and had binding authority;
> faith was attached to the Son, who being of the very nature of God, became flesh, sharing our human condition even unto death, was raised from the dead and ascended into heaven to intercede for sinners in the presence of the Father;
> the indwelling Spirit was enabling the mission of the Son, distributing gifts for the upbuilding of the community of faith;
> and the Son would come again in the last days.

(*CC; COC* 2; Dodd, *The Apostolic Teaching and Its Developments*)

The Primitive Rule of Faith

By the end of the first century the baptismal formula (Matt. 28:19b) was taken to be an established summary of the essence of faith (Ignatius, *Philadelphians* 7–9,

Irenaeus, *Ag. Her.* 3.17). It drew together common points of consent in a brief way that could be memorized and confessed from the heart by any believer. By this simple confession the mass of material in sacred scripture was by common assent tightened, unified, its complexity organized, and reliably transmitted.

The Apostles' Creed is the western form of the received text of the consensual memory of the earliest baptismal confession, which developed as a summary exposition of the baptismal formula of Matthew 28:19 (*Didache* 7.1; Justin Martyr, *Apology* 1.61). Irenaeus regarded the rule of faith as the "canon of truth which he received in his baptism" (Irenaeus, *Ag. Her.* 1.9.4; 1.10:1; Tertullian, *On Baptism* 11; *Prescription Ag. Her.* 14; Clement of Alex., *Stromata* 8.15; Cyprian, *Epistles* 69.7; 70.2).

As early as Ignatius (*Magnesians* 11; *Eph.* 7; *Trallians* 9) and Justin (*Apology* I.13, 31, 46; *Dialogue with Trypho* 85), and even earlier in Matthew and Paul, there is a fixed formula for baptismal confession. By the middle of the second century a fixed form of the rule of faith or creed appears to have been in use at Rome. The twelve spare phrases of the Old Roman Symbol appear to be direct descendants of the easily memorizable original baptismal confession that derives from the earliest Pauline and Petrine decades of the Roman church. The Old Roman Symbol, whose earliest extant text is that of Marcellus (AD 337), understood itself to be apostolic in origin and already for many generations (perhaps two and a half centuries) received as such by general consent, hence antedating Marcellus by faithful memory that harks back through ten momentous generations stretching back toward Peter and Paul. If something might have been slightly misremembered, it seems unlikely that it would have been the concise strictly memorized baptismal formula assumed to be the core of the apostolic tradition, the central rule of faith.

The burden of proof reasonably remains on the shoulders of critics who imagine that vast or substantive changes occurred in the baptismal formula. They have the duty of offering plausible reasons why such changes would have been so necessary as to revise the revered apostolic teaching (Hippolytus, *The Apostolic Tradition*; Tertullian, *Prescription Ag. Her.* 12–23). Such arguments have not been forthcoming.

The Conciliar Tradition of General Consent to the Rule of Faith

Though a competitive apocryphal literature later emerged, it was thought especially heinous to lie about the authorship of pseudoapostolic writings such as in the case of The Gospel of Thomas, or pretend that they were actually written by the apostles (Council of Braga II, *SCD* 245; Duns Scotus, *Sentences*, Prologue Q1.6 ff.; Q2.14). The original apostolic testimony was ecumenically considered to have been reliably delivered through the guidance of the Spirit to the church and consensually received as true, and sufficient for salvation (Second Antiochean Formula; Creed of the 150 Fathers, Orthodox Confession of 1643; *Conf.* of Dositheus, 2).

It is this baptismal rule of faith that was constantly referred to as the standard by which other questions were clarified by the ecumenical councils. The Creed of Caesarea of AD 325 showed that the faith confessed then was regarded as the same as that of the apostles, since it concluded with the striking assertion that "we have thought all this in heart and soul ever since we knew ourselves, and we now so think and speak in truth, being *able to show by evidence* and to convince you that we in past times so believed and preached accordingly" (Eusebius, in Socrates, *CH* 1.8, italics added). By AD 431 it was consensually defined that no one within orthodox teaching has acquired the right "to declare or at any rate to compose or devise a faith other than [*heteran*] that defined by the holy fathers who with the Holy Spirit came together at Nicaea" (Ecumenical Council, Ephesus, *SCD* 125). All of these variants referred to the same essential triune confession embedded in Matthew 28:19. On this point of continuity, media favorites like John Dominic Crossan and Marvin Meyer and Bart D. Ehrman have tendentiously represented the formation of orthodoxy to millions.

Seven ancient ecumenical councils are generally recognized by Orthodox, Catholic, Lutheran, Reformed, Anglican, and most Protestant traditions as representing the mind of the believing church: Nicaea, AD 325; Constantinople I, 381; Ephesus, 431; Chalcedon, 451; Constantinople II, 553; Constantinople III, 680–681; Nicaea II, 787. In addition to these seven the Western medieval consensual tradition regarded as ecumenical five Lateran councils (1123, 1139, 1179, 1215, 1512–17), Lyons I and II (1245, 1274), Vienne (1311–12), Constance (1414–18), and Ferrara-Florence (1438–39), and the post-Reformation Roman tradition recognizes Trent (1545–63), Vatican I (1870), and Vatican II (1962–66). Coptic, Syriac, and Armenian traditions recognize the first three.

With few exceptions believers today agree: "If it be asked *who is to decide* whether the decrees of a Council can be proved from Scripture, we can only reply that this is for the whole Church, clergy and laity, throughout the world, to decide; and that in the case of the first six Councils, *the whole Church has decided*.

The Ecumenical Council's Authority Grounded
in General Lay Consent

The authority of the ecumenical councils is grounded in general lay consent under the guidance of the Spirit based on the written word. What makes the general councils reliable is the presence of the Holy Spirit assisting in the interpretation of the apostolic witness.

The ecumenical council that gathered at Chalcedon declared its intention to "make no new exposition" but merely to take away all ambiguity by the consent of the whole church in a "united exposition and doctrine." "This is the orthodox faith; this we all believe; *into this we were baptized*, into this we baptize," (Chalcedon, Session 2, italics added; this formula was widely received in both eastern and western traditions). The councils were pledged to "not move an ancient boundary stone set up by forefathers" (Prov. 22:28). For it was not merely human ingenuity that spoke in the councils but "the Spirit himself of God" confirmed by general lay consent (Ecumenical Councils, Ephesus, *Letter of Cyril to John of Antioch*).

Since the ancient ecumenical councils were "*constituted by universal consent,* one who rejects them does not overthrow them but himself" (Gregory I, *Letters* 1.25, italics added). At the time of Gregory's writing, there had been only four synods of general lay consent, which he summarized so concisely that it has become a standard formula: "The Nicene, in which Arius, the Constantinopolitan, in which Macedonius, the First Ephesian, in which Nestorius, and the Chalcedonian, in which Eutyches and Dioscorus, were condemned" (Gregory I, *Letters* 4.28).

How the Patristic Conciliar Tradition Was
Received in the Reformation

This tradition of general lay consent continued and was received in the Reformation by the repeated acceptance of the three creeds (Apostles', Nicene, and Athanasian [*Quicunque vult*]) as evidenced in the *Augsburg Apology,* the Smalcald Articles,

Melanchthon's Thesis of 1551 (The Three Chief Symbols, *BOC*:17–23, and the Thirty-nine Articles). "The three creeds, Nicene Creed, Athanasian Creed, and that which is commonly called the Apostles' Creed, ought thoroughly to be received and believed; for they may be proved by most certain warrants of holy scripture" (Thirty-nine Articles 3).

Melanchthon followed the earlier Reformers in arguing that Protestant teaching was grounded in a genuinely "Catholic association, which embraces *the common consensus of prophetic and apostolic doctrine*, together with the belief of the true church. Thus in our Confession we profess to embrace the whole doctrine of the word of God, to which the church bears testimony, and that in the sense which the symbols show" (*CR* 24.398, italics added). He condemned as novel whatever might clash with the most ancient consensual symbols of the church (*symbola accepta*; *Loci*, *LCC* 19.19–20).

The Whole Laity Through Extensive Time
Is the Consenting Community

When a consensual council or regional synod seeks to clarify or better articulate the faith once for all delivered to the saints, in effect it is proposing an interpretation to the remembering church and humbly asking the church of subsequent generations for steady confirmation of that interpretation, not as if it were new, but on the assumption that it is apostolic.

A local or regional body may contribute to the attempt to define the larger consensual ecumenical teaching, but not without the subsequent intergenerational consent of the whole church.

Yet no one should assume that absolute unanimity is required for ecumenical consent; otherwise no question would ever be closed, and a single heretic or tiny cadre of objectors would be an absolute obstacle to ecumenical teaching and unity in Christ.

Some symbols have been so widely and repeatedly reaffirmed (such as the Apostles', Nicene, and Quicunque Creeds) that they have gained renowned prestige as truly expressing the mind of the believing church for all times and places. They cannot be overturned by an alleged future consensus without a radical denial of the faith of ancient Christianity and an absurd claim that the ancient church was irreversibly apostate.

The spiritually well-formed Christian believer does not act without the consent of the community of faith. Nothing is done on private cognizance or autonomous judgment. Cyprian promised "to do nothing on my own private opinion, without your advice and without the consent of the people" (Cyprian, *Epistle* 4, 5). The supervising guardians of the church (*episkopoi*) were pledged not to "do anything without the *consent of all*" (Apostolic Canons 34, Synod of Trullo, italics added; cf. Council of Constance).

The Laity as Jury

The check against the abuse of councils is the laity. The whole laity (not theologians or bishops alone) remain in effect the jury for the councils. Their verdict may take decades or even centuries to render and reaffirm.

The assessment of this ministry of the Spirit, says Paul, must "not use deception," nor "distort the word of God. On the contrary, by setting forth the truth plainly we commend ourselves to *every man's conscience* in the sight of God" (2 Cor. 4:2, 3, italics added). This Pauline appeal to conscience lies "open unto all that they may test our actions" (Chrysostom, *Hom. on 2 Cor. 8*). "By doing all things in the light, we become the light itself, so that it 'shines' before others, which is the particular quality of light" (Gregory of Nyssa, *On Perfection*, FC 58:103).

The "subsequent consent" of the church reserves for the whole body of Christ the right and duty critically to review a controverted Christian teaching as to its apostolicity. If the freedom of the church to criticize is limited, the Spirit grieves. A modern council claiming to be ecumenical must stand under this critical judgment. This is why no teaching is catholic unless at the same time apostolic.

The second conclusion in summary: *consensual authority is grounded in general lay consent to apostolic teaching.* The apostles themselves had a fully formed and sufficient vision of the Lord's teaching. They were not in continuing competitive disagreement on the core of Christian teaching. Their shared encounter with Jesus drew them toward unity of witness from the outset. From this was derived the primitive rule of faith that was aptly summarized in the baptismal confession. The authority of the ecumenical councils is grounded in general lay consent under the guidance of the Spirit based on the written word. The tradition of general lay consent established in the patristic period continued and was largely received in the confessional and liturgical practices of the Reformation. The check against the abuse of councils is the whole laity over the whole of time. They remain in effect the jury for the councils, even if their decisions may have taken decades or even centuries to become ecumenically confirmed. This is the democratic and populist aspect of the formation of classic Christian teaching.

Consensus Clarification Is Feasible

Consensus is not intrinsically unattainable, because it has a long history of being attained. The records of that history are found in the texts of the councils and consensual teachers. Though neglected, consensus clarification is entirely feasible, but more accurately recognized only within long time frames. Classic Christian teaching appeals to consensual exegesis.

Consensus Is Recognized Only Within Long Time Frames

The apostolic teaching does not change with time. It is a fixed canon. No one adds or subtracts from it (Rev. 22:18–19). Jesus Christ is "the same yesterday, today, and forever." So "Do not be led away by divers and strange teachings" (Heb. 13:8). The deposit is rock hard, like Peter (*petros*, the Rock), who was called to guard apostolic teaching.

The risen Lord who is always the same meets us within changing time. *It is not he who time changes, but he who changes time.*

The laity is stretched out over twenty centuries and is still growing. It seems at first glance that this longevity encompasses too many cultures to pretend that there is any viable consensus among believers. But this is the unmistakable miracle: there *is* a consensus. It can only seen through large portions of time. So those who see only small hunks of time, like the present, are likely to miss it altogether. It is a picture that can only be seen through a wide-frame historical lens.

Meanwhile general consensus is often misunderstood as absolute unanimity. Whatever occurs in history is imperfect. The church occurs in history, so its consent is always imperfect. Perfectionistic views of absolute consensus always fail to grasp the need for daily repentance. Exaggerated hopes prevent the recognition of roughhewn durable forms of working consensus that have been articulated repeatedly and lived out culturally.

These consensual achievements are known because they have a conspicuous textual history of authority in the worshiping community. Consensus is already a fact. What we have not adequately explained is why that fact is so persistent, yet so ignored by historians. It is a datum hard to see if you have blinders on or glasses that filter out the brilliance of its radiance.

Lay Consent a Protestant Principle

The principle of general lay consent is firmly embedded in the confessions of the Protestant Reformation. According to the Augsburg Confession, "nothing is taught in our churches concerning articles of faith that is contrary to the Holy Scriptures *or what is common to the Christian church*" (CC:79). Augsburg cautioned against ecclesial burdens "introduced contrary to the *custom of the universal Christian church*" (Augsburg, BOC:105, italics added).

The objection of the Reformers to medieval Catholicism was not that it had grown too old, but that it was much too new and mistakenly innovative. It had invented "an unprecedented novelty" in relation to apostolic testimony. Sadly, the novelty was introduced precisely through leaders appointed to guard the tradition, who "under pretext of the power given them by Christ, have not only introduced new forms of worship and burdened consciences with reserved cases and violent use of the ban, but have also presumed to set up and depose kings" (Augsburg *Conf.*, CC:98).

The congregational tradition more directly assumed a due process of lay consent that is entered into "not only expressly by word of mouth, but by sacrifice; by hand writing, and seal; and also sometimes by silent consent, without any writing, or expression of words at all" (Cambridge Platform, CC 391).

Ecumenical consent is intrinsically multigenerational. That differs from the modern notions of experiential consent stemming from Schleiermacher, where consent depends primarily upon contemporary feelings of individuals. This tends to block out reasoned voices of the past generations. Classic Christian consent runs at times against the streams of both pietistic and liberal theology, both of which are in search of a contemporary constructive theology on the basis either of personal experience or social context.

The Apostolic Faith Does Not Change Through Time

The notion finally must be rejected that there is a substantive change of Christian teaching through time by which the apostolic teaching changes from one meaning to an entirely different meaning contradictory to that offered by the apostles. The church remains guardian of the Word made flesh in Jesus Christ as handed down to each succeeding generation with the same sense and meaning throughout the apostolic tradition, beheld through its movement into and through varied cultural experiences.

The work of the Spirit through changing history has brought the church to a more complete perception of the truth of the gospel. But this does not change the truth being perceived. The gains of one generation can be lost by the neglect of another. The principle of lay consent hinges not on the consent of a single generation but the general consent of all generations of Christian laity of all times and place.

Greater light may yet be shed by the written word upon present and future generations, but the light shed will come from the gospel, not so as to revise its truth. Clearer conceptions of its truth are always possible. But the light and truth that will thereby come will not be shining directly from the historical situation but from the truth of the revealed Word. The revealed Word is itself the crucial event to be investigated (Cyril of Alex, *On the Incarnation* 709; Easter Homily 1.6). The event concerns a person, truly human, truly God. That Word does not change or improve.

Meanwhile the ancient Adversary is always appearing as an angel of light, seeming to bear the truth while advancing human illusions. The true faith is "defended with the best results, when a false opinion is condemned even by those who have followed it" (*Tome of Leo*). This means: Those who have come through and beyond the temptations of the heterodoxies are those best able to defend against them. Paul, Cyprian, Jerome, and Augustine are examples.

Paul instructed Timothy to guard what had been committed to him (1 Tim. 6:20). Vincent commented that Christian teaching consists in "what you have received, not what you have thought up; a matter not of ingenuity, but of doctrine; not of private acquisition, but of public Tradition; a matter brought to you, not put forth by you, in which you must be not the author but the guardian, not the founder but the sharer, not the leader, but the follower." The *ekklēsia* is not seeking to discover a new word for each culture but proclaim the truth of the most primitive gospel ever anew, so that "by your expounding it, may that now be understood more clearly which formerly was believed even in its obscurity" (Vincent of Lérins, *Comm.* 22.27). It is tampering with the evidence to pretend to improve upon apostolic testimony itself, although our perceptions of the apostolic witness may improve or worsen.

This does not imply that there can be no progress in church teaching. Vincent argued that there is progress, but true progress is not change. True progress is an advance in understanding of that which has been given fully in the deposit of faith (*Comm.*, 23.28).

The great doctors of the church stood as daily overseers of the church's liturgy and pastoral care and preaching at a particularly crucial time of its early formation—just after the martyr church had winnowed away much dross. We listen to them because the more we know scripture, we realize that they understood how the consenting community reads and compares the interconnected sense of the varied texts of scripture.

The Spirit is Quietly Helping the Formation of General Ecumenical Consent

The classic exegetes view the Spirit as working within the process of the recollection, accurate transmission, and fit interpretation of scripture, not above it. The Spirit does not abandon each reader to his own private self-assertive preference or egocentric interpretation. Scripture is read with prayer for illumination and humility.

This is fairly analogous to the method of science, in which *the general consent of the community of experimenters is more reliable than the particular judgment of one experimenter*. Similarly in democratic theory, the consensus of the body politic is less likely to be tilted, hence closer to truth, accuracy, and consistency, than is individual or autocratic leadership (Vincent of Lérins, *Comm.* 27–33).

Some cannot get it out of their minds that the appeal to consensus seems like merely an abandonment of truth claims. Consensus formation seems like "just counting votes." What if a bad candidate is elected? Sadly, many bad doctrinal candidates have been elected for short periods of time. But in longer time frames the winnowing process has shown the weaknesses of the bad candidates, and given a new opportunity for the worshiping community to do better.

The consensus sought is not an agreement of human voices on God. It is a work of the Spirit creating the unity of the body of Christ. The Spirit and the written word are constantly resisting ill effects which may be left as residues of unwise teachers. Admittedly some periods of church history have adhered inordinately to temporarily imbalanced views. Yet such imbalances are in the long run always being constantly tested by general lay consent.

How the Holy Spirit Has Used and Constructively Transmuted Heterodoxies

The problem of heresy is precisely this: the testimony of scripture may be skewed by the sophistries of human wisdom and the deceptiveness of sin. If there is no corrective effort accurately to identify the apostolic witness as classically and consensually interpreted, then any person on any day might presume to be tempted to hold entirely different and even contradictory senses of scripture as true.

Within the orthodox consensus it was remembered with gratitude that the Holy Spirit has a cheerful history of working through and beyond heterodoxies to clarify consensual teaching. This is why heresy should be studied as carefully as orthodoxy. Classic Christian teaching cannot be studied without the examination of heresy. In order to answer heterodoxy, orthodoxy must read their texts, understand them, study them more carefully and critically than do the advocates of heterodoxy themselves.

Some who falsely claim to have a right to the apostolic witness while distorting it must be answered patiently and confidently. They can be shown how they themselves may have undermined that very right (Tertullian, *Prescription Ag. Her.* 19–32).

It is the nature of heresy to exaggerate some ancillary aspect of the truth into false proportion so as to neglect the appropriate balance of apostolic teaching. Hence there is by definition always some fragment of truth even in the most noxious heresies. Heretics are not beyond the range of providence. But to become tolerant of these imbalances is imprudent.

The African and Asian Contributions to Pre-European Christianity

To say that everyone equally lacks sufficient experience to search for irenic ecumenical wisdom may become an excuse to evade the task altogether. I am a male trying to write for both women and men in the faith, a North American attempting to articulate a consensus of Christian teaching that accurately embraces believers of all continents, races, classes, and nations. I would cease being catholic and evangelical if that were not my aim. That calls for genuine, not false, humility.

That means that I have been called to listen all the more empathically for the lost accents, trying especially to hear the neglected and silenced voices of the Christian past and present. If I wrote an alleged compendium of classic Christianity without listening to Phoebe Palmer or Sister Macrina or Clare of Assisi or Teresa of Avila, I would be more likely to mislead than if I had listened to them as carefully as I actually have over many years. So with the great African tradition of Christian teaching from the Markan tradition to Origen and Cyprian through Athanasius and Augustine. So with the great early Eastern tradition from Polycarp to John of Damascus.

The classic Christian consensus would have been immeasurably impoverished without very early and very influential African and Asian voices. From my own self-perception, I feel myself to be a tough minded critic of my own Euro-American culture based on the ground of values that I have learned from Africans and Asians that predate the West. The durable consensus is far more indebted to classic African and Asian texts of the first millennium than to later European teachers. The pyramid of sources (see Introduction) shows that. The classic ecumenical consensus was maturely formed well before the formation of Europe. There was not even anything recognizable or looking like a cohesive "Europe" in any meaningful literary or cultural sense when Athanasius was writing in Egypt or Cyprian in North Africa or Chrysostom was teaching in Antioch or Ephrem writing poetry in Syria.

It is worth noting that the majority of the eight doctors of the church were from Africa and Asia: Athanasius likely came from a family in middle Egypt. Augustine was African (from inland Numidia), not European. Basil, Gregory of Nazianzus, and Chrysostom were all from the ancient Near East, not Europe. That leaves Jerome, who though born at Strido, spent much of his adult life in the Near East, and Gregory the Great, who as a Roman diplomat was more of a world Christian than any of the other seven, having served for an extended time in Byzantium and earnestly desired to go as a missionary to England, and Ambrose, who spent most of his life in political leadership, first as governor, then bishop. Only the credulous can imagine that these eight teachers were primarily or consciously "European" when a cohesive literate Europe had not even yet emerged, and would not palpably be defined until after Charlemagne.

The seven ecumenical councils were held in the East, not Europe. They were held in Constantinople, Nicaea, Ephesus, and Chalcedon—all beyond the pale or on the far edge of what we today call Europe.

If so, it cannot be claimed without qualification that early ecumenical Christianity was predominantly Western or European. The "West" was its belated outcome, not its premise or reality. This is no small point. It is pursued further in my 2008 book on *How Africa Shaped the Christian Mind* (InterVarsity Press). Classic Christian teaching was clearly influenced more by Africa in scriptural interpretation and the East in dogmatic definition than by texts from Europe or "the West." This study commends a further democratization, internationalization, demasculinization, and cultural pluralization of the process of ecumenical consensus. These correctives are already occurring, however slowly.

Minority Voices in Ecumenical Consent

The early ecumenical councils did not ignore the voices of the poor and the marginalized Cretans or Persians and certainly not of many women of faith who were making their witness in the church of the persecution and in desert asceticism. Such councils could not have gained wide lay consent or been received without the concurrence of the poor or without women or without the dispossessed or without the slaves, bond servants, and second-class citizens of the world. These beloved believers were at the same time becoming through baptism citizens of the emergent international community of faith manifesting itself through Word and Sacrament.

The ordained leaders were often confirmed by the consenting laity without whose agreement they had no power to oversee apostolic teaching. Hence it was never a sure bet whether a particular council would be accepted or not. Some were not. It often took a century or more for a firm consensus to be established by general lay consent. Sometimes local synods made questionable judgments that had to be appealed and rescinded. In those cases the larger *laos* was saying to the leaders of those regional councils: "Sorry, you got it wrong—that was not the shared mind of the believing church."

It seems fatuous to argue that women were so powerless or immobilized or despairing or lacking in identity and influence that they failed wholly to affect that general consensus. This would be to neglect the decisive role of women in the domestic order, in serving ministries, and in the life of prayer. Those who think that way are thinking almost exclusively of political power, as distinguished from the many other forms of power. Note the steady influence of Monica upon Augustine, of Paula upon Jerome, of his mother Nonna upon Gregory of Nazianzus, and of his sister Macrina upon Gregory of Nyssa. Note also as a crucial case in point the decisive influence of the empress Irene in the iconoclastic controversy leading to the judgment of the seventh Ecumenical Council of Nicaea. Note also that the witness of women was especially poignant during the periods of persecutions, as seen in the intrepid history of women saints from Perpetua following.

It is the Spirit who finally guarantees the valid transmission of the apostolic tradition through the general consent of the laity. Both women and men of the laity found that they could count on the Spirit over time to bring the gospel to light and to remember rightly and guide the church into all truth.

The people (*laos*) must finally give or not give consent to the views of the theologians and councils. They do this with their feet and bodies, by general lay consent. It is hardly a perfect instrument of political expression, but it works steadily and surely over time. There is no received apostolic tradition without an intergenerational community of recipients: female and male, of all continents.

Herein lies the power of the people in the Christian structure of authority. It is not a formal vote taken at particular intervals. But it is a vote, even if by the pocketbook or by the silent withholding of consent. Thus there remains a resilient populist element in the Christian structure of authority that, though it must not be overstated, should not be neglected.

Summary of the third conclusion: *Though neglected, consensus clarification is entirely feasible, but more easily recognized only within long time frames.* Consensus is not intrinsically unreachable, because it has a long history of being reached. The records of that history are found in the texts of the councils and consensual teachers. These achievements are known because they have a conspicuous textual history of authority in the worshiping community. This community has learned that heterodoxy may serve the truth by having the unexpected effect of further refining rough and incomplete orthodox consensual exegesis. Less well known, but increasingly recognized is the fact that the most durable consensus is far more indebted to minority and neglected voices, such as classic African and Asian texts of the first millennium, than to later European ideas.

POSTLUDE

ON THEO-COMIC
PERCEPTION

T HERE IS A COMEDIC CONTRADICTION that inheres in the study of God. It is the same contradiction that clings to human existence whenever decisions are required. Reflection on the holy life inevitably reveals the comic, since the seriousness of being human invites perception of our absurdities.

Classic Christianity offers to humanity a volatile, lively spirit of comic discernment. It was not formally listed among the gifts of the Spirit because it is not formal and does not belong on a list. But the gifted in faith are seldom without it. Among the most comic representatives of Christian teachers are Tertullian, Chrysostom, Jerome, Augustine, Luther, and above all Kierkegaard. Most wearisome on this scale are maybe Proclus and Photius, both of Constantinople, although there is surely someone to challenge me on both counts.

Comic consciousness sees through each unexpected reversal of human pride. Comedy glimpses refractions of God's own delight in creation. It lightens the burden of human existence. It is especially welcome amid unventilated God-talk.

We who love and pursue God, but don't miss taking pleasure in the details, we are bipeds who dream of eternity. Playing God, yet with masks showing our life as bums, clowns, and louts—yet bums who can say from the heart, "*Deo gloria*"; clowns who mime the posture of Superman; louts who cannot help but conceive of the idea of perfect being. We are awed by the final judgment, but a little less so than about the brakes on our car. Inheritors of large brains, we cannot balance our bank accounts. Living souls puzzled by death. We are such creatures who take up pen and ink and scribble bold sentences about God, who breathe polluted air as we ponder the ineffable Spirit; who use the name of God most often to intensify cursing, yet still pray to One whom we name Almighty.

It is because humanity is a paradox that the human study of God remains a continuing irony strewn with both blood and flowers. The healthier the study of God, the more candid it is about its own finitude, the stubborn limits of its own knowing, its own charades, masks, and broken mirrors.

Comedy sees tragedy from the viewpoint of its resolution. This is why Kierkegaard knew that humor was, of all stages of consciousness, the nearest to Christianity with its absolute paradox: God made flesh (to relish his discernment, see my 2004 appraisal of *The Humor of Kierkegaard*, Princeton University Press).

That is why the disciplined study of God is best experienced from within a light-hearted, caring community that laughs at its own soberest undertakings. Those whose faith offers the corrective love of admonition to others give a great gift. But the gift is best wrapped in the brightly colored tissue of hope, in an atmosphere where comic lightness about the pretended gravity of our words abounds.

An Invitation to Partners in Dialogue

Lactantius held Plato responsible for leading Ambraciotes to suicide by his errant counsel (Lactantius, *DI*, *FC* 49:214). The unclear or ambivalent writer remains partly responsible for inadvertent but understandable misinterpretations of his words, for which he will be accountable on the last day. Since my life has been fixed on writing for over fifty years, I have a lot to answer for. So I expect to be held thoroughly accountable for this work, first by human auditors, but more so by the single divine auditor.

Nothing would please me more than that this textual study might be followed by a rigorous phase of criticism that would argue for or against its principal thesis: that there is indeed a consensus of classic Christian teaching, and a distinct method of consensual exegesis. This would invite others to do a more thorough job of validating or invalidating this thesis.

Hence my invitation to lay and professional readers is: I welcome thoughtful and informed partners in dialogue who will identify the consensus in different ways, helping me to see where I may have lost ecumenical equilibrium. I ask only that the corrections be documented textually. In this sport, no one makes points without texts that are open to anyone's examination.

There have been challenges at every turn of this historic struggle for consensus. Many points are left to be further challenged and reexamined. My attempt tries to identify that general ecumenical consent that has been reasonably confirmed during the whole course of Christian teaching. I hope it will not be long before any misjudgments and imbalances of my argument may be rightly pruned and duly amended by appeal to general consent.

This invitation is not made out of despair of consensuality, but out of hope for its ever clearer recognition. The laity have waited too long for unapologetic classic Christian reasoning. The classic consensus has been silently waiting through a series of tedious modernities to become better defined. I am now past my seventy-fifth birthday—still budding and sprouting and rooting. The task of classic Christian teaching asks for grace to articulate something that can be spoken only after much lived human experience, study, meditation, and historical listening to different voices in various accents and languages. When I was a young theologian, my energy and imagination were matched by enormous deficits of historical depth, exegetical mellowing, and personal maturing. If I had rashly attempted a systematic classic Christian theology at age thirty-five (in 1966—at a time when both culture and religion were threatening to spin out of control) it would have been a disaster. If the lengthy careers of Augustine, Luther, Wesley, or Barth had ended at age thirty-five, there would have remained far less to remember, and we would have had now only fragments of their life work.

A last note on why I have recast the whole work, once presented as *Systematic Theology* but now as Classic Christianity: When I wrote the three-volume *Systematic Theology*, I was hoping to be a part of rescuing the academic discipline of systematic theology by regrounding it in classic sources. Now I have a much more humble and important task—communicating to the laity the essential teaching of classic Christianity. The faithful laity truly love classic Christianity. They have been singing and praying it for centuries. They are entirely at home with it, and homesick when deprived of it.

ABBREVIATIONS AND
REFERENCES

AAS	*Acta Apostolicae Sedis,* official record of papal statements. Vatican: Rome, 1909–.
ACC	*An American Catholic Catechism.* Edited by G. J. Dyer. New York: Seabury, 1975.
Acc.	According to
ACE	*Aspects of Christian Experience.* Stephen M. Merrill. Cincinnati, OH: Walden and Stone, 1882.
ACW	*Ancient Christian Writers: The Works of the Fathers in Translation.* Edited by J. Quasten, J. C. Plumpe, and W. Burghardt. 44 vols. New York: Paulist Press, 1946–.
ADC	*The Atonement of the Death of Christ.* H. D. McDonald. Grand Rapids, MI: Baker, 1985.
AEG	*Ante-Nicene Exegesis of the Gospels.* Edited by Harold D. Smith. 6 vols. London: SPCK, 1925.
AF	*The Apostolic Fathers.* Edited by J. N. Sparks. New York: Nelson, 1978.
AFT	*Agenda for Theology.* Thomas C. Oden. San Francisco: Harper & Row, 1979.
Ag.	Against
AHS	*Activities of the Holy Spirit.* Edmund J. Fortman. Chicago: Franciscan Herald, 1984.
Alex.	Alexandria
AMW	*After Modernity. . . . What?—Agenda for Theology.* Thomas C. Oden. Grand Rapids, MI: Zondervan, 1989.
ANF	*Ante-Nicene Fathers.* Edited by A. Roberts and J. Donaldson. 10 vols. 1885–96. Reprint, Grand Rapids, MI: Eerdmans, 1979. Book and chapter or section number, followed by volume and page number.
Angl.	*Anglicanism: The Thought and Practice of the Church of England.* Edited by P. E. More and F. L. Cross. London: SPCK, 1935.
APD	*The Apostolic Preaching and Its Developments.* C. H. Dodd. New York: Harper, 1954.
Apol.	Apology
Apos. Const.	*Apostolic Constitutions,* or *Constitutions of the Holy Apostles. ANF,* vol. 7.
Apost.	*Apostolic Constitutions,* or *Constitutions of the Holy Apostles. ANF,* vol. 7.
APT	*Apologetic and Practical Treatises.* Tertullian. Edited by C. Dodgson. Oxford: Parker, 1854.
ARI	*An Address on Religious Instruction.* Gregory of Nyssa. *LCC* III, pp. 268–326.
Ari.	*The Arians.* In *Works of John Henry Cardinal Newman.* Edited by Joseph Rickaby. Westminster, MD: Christian Classics, 1977.
Arndt	*A Greek-English Lexicon of the New Testament and Other Early Christian Literature.* W. F. Arndt and F. W. Gingrich. From W. Bauer, 1953. Chicago: University of Chicago Press, 2000.

Aspects   *Some Aspects of Contemporary Greek Orthodox Thought.* F. S. B. Gavin. Milwaukee, WI: Morehouse, 1923.

AST   *Abstract of Systematic Theology.* James Peitigru Boyce. 1887. Reprint, Louisville, KY: n.p., n.d.

Ath.   *St. Athanasius.* In *Works of John Henry Cardinal Newman.* Edited by Joseph Rickaby. 2 vols. Westminster, MD: Christian Classics, 1977.

ATW   *After Therapy What? Lay Therapeutic Resources in Religious Perspective.* Finch Lectures by Thomas C. Oden, with Responses by N. Warren, K. Mulholland, C. Schoonhoven, C. Kraft, and W. Walker. Edited by Neil C. Warren. Springfield, IL: Thomas, 1974.

BC   **1** *The Book of Concord.* 1580. Edited by T. G. Tappert. Philadelphia: Muhlenberg, 1959. **2** *Basic Christianity.* John Stott. Grand Rapids, MI: Eerdmans, 1964.

BCP   *Book of Common Prayer.* 1662. Royal Breviar's edition. London: SPCK, n.d.

BCSP   *The Beginnings of Christology: A Study of Its Problems.* Willi Marxsen. Philadelphia: Fortress, 1969.

BDC   *The Biblical Doctrine of the Church.* William Robinson. St. Louis, MO: Bethany, 1946.

Bever.   *Institutes of the Christian Religion.* John Calvin. Translated by Henry Beveridge. 2 vols. London: Clarke, 1953.

BHT   *The Bible in Human Transformation.* Walter Wink. Philadelphia: Fortress, 1973.

Bk.   Book

BMW   *The Bible in the Modern World.* James Barr. London: SCM, 1973.

BOC   *The Book of Concord.* 1580. Edited by T. G. Tappert. Philadelphia: Muhlenberg, 1959.

BOConf.   *The Book of Confessions.* New York: United Presbyterian Church, 1966. Part I of *The Constitution of the United Presbyterian Church.* No page references, only section numbers.

BPR   *Book of Pastoral Rule.* Gregory the Great. *NPNF* 2 10.

BQT   *Basic Questions in Theology.* Wolfhart Pannenberg. 3 vols. Philadelphia: Westminster, 1970–73.

Brief Expl.   *Brief Explanation of the Ten Commandments, Creed, and Lord's Prayer.* Martin Luther. In *WML*, vol. 2, pp. 351–286.

BSG   *The Birth of the Synoptic Gospels.* Jean Carmignac. Translated by Michael J. Wrenn. Chicago: Franciscan Herald, 1987.

BTL   *A Black Theology of Liberation.* James H. Cone. Philadelphia: Lippincott, 1970.

BW   *St. Anselm: Basic Writings.* Translated by S. N. Deane. LaSalle, IL: Open Court, 1966.

BWA   *Basic Works of Aristotle.* Edited by R. McKeon. New York: Random House, 1941.

C of E   Church of England

Catech.   Catechism or catechetical

Catech. Lect.   *Catechetical Lectures.* Cyril of Jerusalem. *NPNF* 2 7. *FC* 61, 64.

CC   *Creeds of the Churches.* Edited by John Leith. Richmond, VA: John Knox, 1979.

CCC   *Creeds, Councils and Controversies.* Edited by J. Stevenson. London: SPCK, 1966.

CCF   *The Church's Confession of Faith.* German Bishops Conference. Edited by Walther Kasper. San Francisco: Ignatius, 1987.

CD   **1** *Church Dogmatics.* Karl Barth. Edited by G. W. Bromiley, T. F. Torrance, et al. 14 vols. Edinburgh: Clark, 1936–69. **2** *Christian Doctrine.* Shirley Guthrie. Atlanta: John Knox, 1969. **3** *Christian Dogmatics.* Johannes Jacobus van Oosterzee. London: Hodder & Stoughton, 1874.

CDG   **1** *The Christian Doctrine of God.* William Newton Clarke. Edinburgh: Clark, 1912. **2** *The Catholic Doctrine of Grace.* G. H. Joyce. London: Burns & Oates, 1920.

CDH   *Cur Deus Homo.* Anselm. Translated by S. N. Deane. LaSalle, IN: Open Court, 1966.

CDisc.   *Christian Discourses.* Søren Kierkegaard. Oxford: Oxford University Press, 1952.

CDJR *The Christian Doctrine of Justification and Reconciliation.* Albrecht Ritschl. Edited by H. R. Mackintosh. London, 1900.

CDS *The Christian Doctrine of Salvation.* G. B. Stevens. Edinburgh: Clark, 1909.

CD&ST *Christian Doctrine and Systematic Theology.* Augustus Schultze. Bethlehem, PA: Times Publishing, 1909.

CEJC *The Christology of Early Jewish Christianity.* Richard N. Longenecker. London: SCM, 1970.

CER *Commentary on the Epistle to the Romans.* Martin Luther. Translated by T. Mueller. Grand Rapids, MI: Zondervan, 1954.

CF **1** *The Christian Faith in the Doctrinal Documents of the Catholic Church.* Edited by J. Neuner and J. Dupuis. Rev. ed. New York: Alba House, 1982. **2** *Christian Foundations.* Henry Maldwyn Hughes. London: Epworth, 1951. **3** *The Christian Faith.* Claude Beaufort Moss. New York: Morehouse-Gorham, 1944. **4** *The Christian Faith.* Olin Curtis. Grand Rapids, MI: Kregel, 1971.

CFS *Cistercian Fathers Series.* 44 vols. Kalamazoo, MI: Cistercian Publications, 1968–.

CG **1** *City of God.* Augustine. *NPNF* 1 2. **2** *The Christ of the Gospels.* William West Holdsworth. London: Kelly, 1911.

CGTC *Cambridge Greek Testament Commentary.* Cambridge: Cambridge University Press.

CH *Church History.* Eusebius of Caesarea. *NPNF* 2 1. *FC* 19, 29.

Ch. Dogmatic Constitution on the Church (*Lumen Gentium*), *Doc. Vat. II.*

CHC *Commentary on the Heidelberg Catechism.* Zacharius Ursinus. Cincinnati, OH: Bucher, 1851.

ChF *The Christian Faith.* Friedrich Schleiermacher. Edinburgh: Clark, 1928.

Chr. Christian, Christians

ChrD **1** *Christian Dogmatics.* Edited by Carl E. Braaten and Robert W. Jensen. 2 vols. Philadelphia: Fortress, 1984. **2** *Christian Doctrine.* J. S. Whale. London: Collins, 1957.

ChrF **1** *The Christian Faith.* Olin A. Curtis. New York: Methodist Book Concern, 1905. **2** *The Christian Faith.* Friedrich Schleiermacher. Edinburgh: Clark, 1928.

Clem. II "An Anonymous Sermon, Commonly Called Clement's Second Letter." *LCC* 1, pp. 183–90.

CLRC *Courtenay Library of Reformation Classics.* 5 vols. Appleford, Abingdon, Berkshire, England: Sutton Courtenay Press, n.d.

CLT *A Compendium of Luther's Theology.* Edited by H. T. Kerr. Philadelphia: Westminster, 1953.

C&M *The Church and the Ministry.* Charles Gore. 4th ed. London: Longmans, Green, 1910.

CMM *The Catechism of Modern Man: All in the Words of Vatican II.* Boston: St. Paul Editions, 1967.

CNT *Christology of the New Testament.* Oscar Cullmann. Philadelphia: Westminster, 1959.

COC *Creeds of Christendom.* Edited by P. Schaff. 3 vols. New York: Harper, 1919.

COD *Conciliorum Oecumenicorum Decreta.* Freiburg: Herder, 1962.

Comm. **1** *Commentary.* **2** *Calvin's Commentaries.* John Calvin. 22 vols. Grand Rapids, MI: Baker, 1981. Originally printed for the Calvin Translation Society, Edinburgh. **3** *Commentaries.* Bede. In *Complete Works.* Edited by J. Giles. 12 vols. London, 1843–44. See *MPL* 90–95. **4** *Commonitory.* Vincent of Lérins. *NPNF* 2 11. *LCC* 7.

Common Catech. *The Common Catechism.* Edited by Johannes Feiner and Lukas Vischer. New York: Seabury, 1975.

Compend. **1** *Compendium.* **2** *Compendium of Christian Theology.* William Burt Pope. 3 vols. New York: Phillips & Hunt, n.d. **3** *Compendium of Theology.* Thomas Aquinas. New York: Herder, 1947.

Concl. Unsci. Post. *Concluding Unscientific Postscript.* Søren Kierkegaard. *Translated by* David Swenson. Princeton, NJ: Princeton University Press, 1941.

Conf. Confession(s)

Conf.	*Confessions*. Augustine. *LCC* 7. *NPNF* 1 1. *FC* 21.
CPHS	*The Church in the Power of the Holy Spirit*. Jürgen Moltmann. San Francisco: Harper & Row, 1967.
CPWSF	*Standard Edition of the Complete Psychological Works of Sigmund Freud*. 24 vols. London: Hogarth, 1953–.
CQLS	*Commentaria in Quator Libros Sententiarum*. In *Works of Bonaventure*. Translated by Jose de Vinck. 5 vols. Patterson, NJ: St. Anthony Guild, 1960–70.
CR	*Corpus Reformatorum: Huldreich Zwinglis sämmtliche Werke; Johannis Calvini Opera; Philippi Melanchthonis Opera*. Edited by C. G. Bretschneider and H. E. Bindseil. Halle: Halis Saxonium, 1834–60.
Crit. Pract. Reason	*Critique of Practical Reason. Immanuel Kant. LLA.*
CS	*Christ the Savior*. Reginald Garrigou-Lagrange. London: Herder, 1950.
CSCT	*A Complete System of Christian Theology*. Samuel Wakefield. New York: Carlton & Porter, 1862.
CSEL	*Corpus Scriptorum Ecclesiasticorum Latinorum*. Vienna: Tempsky, 1866.
CSK	*The Cell of Self-Knowledge: Seven Early English Mystical Treatises (including Divers Doctrines, Katherine of Seenes, and Treatise of Contemplation, Margery Kempe)*. Edited by E. G. Gardner. New York: Duffield, 1910.
CSS	*Cistercian Studies Series*. 68 vols. Kalamazoo, MI: Cistercian Publications, 1968—.
CT	**1** *Corpus Theologiae*. Johannes Henricus Heidegger. Zurich, 1700. **2** *Christian Theology*. Adam Clarke. Salem, OH: Schmul, 1990. **3** *Christian Theology*. Millard J. Erickson. Grand Rapids, MI: Baker, 1983. **4** *Essentials and Non-essentials of the Christian Faith*. John M. Shaw. Edinburgh: Clark, 1928. **5** *A Complete System of Christian Theology*. Samuel Wakefield. New York: Carleton and Porter, 1862. **6** *Christian Theology*. Jonathan Weaver. Dayton, OH: United Brethren Publishing, 1900. **7** *Christian Theology*. Emery H. Bancroft. Edited by Ronald B. Majors. Grand Rapids, MI: Zondervan, 1976.
CTC	*Christianae Theologiae Compendium*. Johannes Wollebius. Edited by Ernst Bizer. Neukirchen, 1935. English translation by John Beardslee, in *RDB*.
CTP	*Contemporary Theology and Psychotherapy*. Thomas C. Oden. Philadelphia: Westminster, 1967.
CUP	*Concluding Unscientific Postscript*. Søren Kierkegaard. Translated by David Swenson. Princeton, NJ: Princeton University Press, 1941.
CV	*Christus Victor*. Gustaf Aulen. New York: Macmillan, 1958.
CVL	*The Commonitory of Vincent of Lérins*. With an Appendix by Bishop Beveridge on Consent of the Church. Baltimore, MD: Joseph Robinson, 1847.
CWB	*A Commentary on the Whole Bible*. Matthew Henry. 6 vols. Iowa Falls, IA: World Bible Publishers, n.d.
CWEI	*Collected Writings*. Edward Irving. 5 vols. 1864–65.
CWI	*The Church of the Word Incarnate*. Charles Journet. London: Sheed and Ward, 1954. References are to vol. 1 unless otherwise noted.
CWMS	*Complete Writings of Menno Simons*. Edited by John C. Wenger. Scottdale, PA: Herald, 1956.
CWS	*Classics of Western Spirituality*. Edited by Richard J. Payne, et al. 30 vols. Mahwah, NJ: Paulist Press, 1978–. Volumes unnumbered.
CWST	*Complete Works of St. Teresa*. Teresa of Avila. Edited by E. Allison Peers. 3 vols. London: Sheed and Ward, 1946.
DC	*Doctrines of the Creed*. Oliver C. Quick. London: Nisbet, 1938.
DCC	*Documents of the Christian Church*. Edited by H. Bettenson. New York: Oxford University Press, 1956.
DCF	*A Defence of the Catholic Faith Concerning the Satisfaction of Christ Against Faustus Socinus*. Hugo Grotius. 1617. Translated by F. H. Foster. London: Draper, 1889.
DF	*Doctrina Foederum sive Systema Theologiae didacticae et elencticae*. Johannes Braun. Amsterdam, 1588.

DG   *The Doctrine of God.* Herman Bavinck. Carlisle, PA: Banner of Truth, 1977.

DI   *Divine Institutes.* Lactantius. *ANF* 7. *FC* 49.

Dir. Ec.   *Directory on Ecumenism.* Secretariat for Promoting Christian Unity. Rome: Vatican, 1967.

Div. Inst. *Divine Institutes.* Lactantius. *ANF* 7. *FC* 49.

Div. Names *Divine Names.* Dionysius (Pseudo-Dionysius). Translated by C. E. Rolt. London: SPCK, 1975.

DL   *The Divinity of Our Lord.* H. P. Liddon. London: Rivingtons, 1875.

DNF   *Defensio Fidei Nicaenae.* George Bull. 1685. 2 vols. Oxford: Parker, 1851.

Doc. Vat. II *The Documents of Vatican II.* Edited by W. M. Abbott. New York: Guild, 1966.

Doct.   Doctrine

Dogm.   Dogmatic, Dogmatics

Dogm.   *Dogmatics.* Emil Brunner. Philadelphia: Westminster, 1962. (*The Christian Doctrine of the Church, Faith, and Consummation,* unless otherwise indicated.)

DS   *Enchiridion Symbolorum, Definitionum et Declarationum de Rebus Fidei et Morum.* Compiled by H. Denzinger. 1854. Continued by C. Bannwart, et al. Berlin: Herder, 1922.

DSWT   *Doctrinal Standards in the Wesleyan Tradition.* Thomas C. Oden. Grand Rapids, MI: Francis Asbury, 1988.

DT   **1** *Dogmatic Theology.* Francis Hall, 10 vols. New York: Longmans, Green, 1907–22. **2** *Dogmatic Theology.* Joseph Pohle. Edited by Arthur Preuss. 12 vols. St. Louis, MO: Herder, 1922. **3** *Doctrinal Theology of the Evangelical Lutheran Church.* Heinrich Schmid. 3d ed. Minneapolis, MN: Augsburg, 1899.

DUCC   *Dictionnaire universel et complète des Conciles.* Translated by J. P. Migne. Paris: Aux Ateliers Catholiques du Petit-Montrouge, 1847.

DWC   *The Doctrine of the Work of Christ.* Sidney Cave. Nashville, TN: Cokesbury, 1937.

EA   *Martin Luthers sämmtliche Werke.* Frankfurt and Erlangen, 1826–57. Erlanger Ausgabe, volume number followed by page number.

EC   **1** *An Exposition of the Creed.* John Pearson. 1659. Edited by Edward Burton. London, 1833. **2** *Evangelical Christology.* Bernard Ramm. Nashville, TN: Nelson, 1985. **3** *The Essentials of Christianity.* Henry Clay Sheldon. New York: Doran, 1922.

Ec.   Decree on Ecumenism (*Unitatis Redintegratio*). *Doc. Vat. II.*

Eccl.   Ecclesiastical

ECD   *Early Christian Doctrines.* J. N. D. Kelly. New York: Harper, 1959.

ECF   *Early Christian Fathers.* Edited by H. Bettenson. London: Oxford University Press, 1969.

ECW   *Early Christian Writers: The Apostolic Fathers.* Translated by Maxwell Staniforth. London: Penguin, 1968.

ED   *Elements of Divinity.* Thomas N. Ralston. New York: Abingdon, 1924.

EDQ   *Eighty-three Different Questions.* Augustine. *FC* 70.

EF   *The Evangelical Faith.* Helmut Thielicke. 3 vols. Grand Rapids, MI: Eerdmans, 1974–82.

EH   *Ecclesiastical History.* Eusebius of Caesarea. *FC* 19, 29.

EHCM   *The End of the Historical-Critical Method.* Gerhard Maier. St. Louis, MO: Concordia, 1977.

EL   *Everyman's Library.* New York: Dutton, 1910–.

Elem.   Elementa theologiae dogmaticae. Francois Xavier Schouppe. Brussels: Goemaere, 1863.

ENTT   *Essays in New Testament Themes.* Ernst Käsemann. Studies in Biblical Theology, no. 41. London: SCM, 1964.

EP   *The Epistle of St. Paul to the Colossians.* Joseph J. Rickaby. London: n.p., 1921.

Epist.   Epistle(s)

EPT	*Essays Philosophical and Theological.* Rudolf Bultmann. New York: Macmillan, 1955.
ERD	*Essays, Reviews, and Discourses.* Daniel Whedon. New York: Phillips & Hunt, 1887.
ESS	*Exercitationes sacrae in symbolum. Sacred Dissertations.* Hermann Witsius. Translated by D. Fraser. Utrecht, 1694. Edinburgh: Fullerton, 1823.
ET	English translation
ETA	*Examen Theologicum Acroamaticum.* David Hollaz (or Hollatz). 1707. Leipzig: Brietkopf, 1763.
Evang.	Evangelical
EVO	*Episcopacy and Valid Orders in the Primitive Church.* Darwell Stone. London: Longmans, 1926.
Exhort.	Exhortation
Expos.	Exposition.
FC	*The Fathers of the Church: A New Translation.* Edited by R. J. Deferrari. 95 vols. Washington, DC: Catholic University Press, 1947–.
FEF	*The Faith of the Early Fathers.* Edited by William A. Jurgens. 3 vols. Collegeville, MN: Liturgical Press, 1970–.
FER	*The Fathers for English Readers.* 15 vols. London: SPCK, 1878–90.
FGG	*From Glory to Glory: Texts from Gregory of Nyssa's Mystical Writings.* Translated by H. Musurillo. Crestwood, NY: St. Vladimir's Seminary Press, 1979.
FNTC	*The Foundation of New Testament Christology.* Reginald H. Fuller. New York: Scribner, 1965.
F&T	*Fear and Trembling and Sickness unto Death.* Søren Kierkegaard. Translated by W. Lowrie. Princeton, NJ: Princeton University Press, 1968.
FTCT	*Francisci Turretini Compendium Theologiae.* Leonardus Riisen. Amsterdam, 1695.
GA	*Grammar of Assent.* In *Works of John Henry Cardinal Newman.* Edited by Joseph Rickaby. Westminster, MD: Christian Classics, 1977.
GC	*Of God and His Creatures* (an abbreviated translation of *Summa Contra Gentiles*). Thomas Aquinas. Translated by Joseph Rickaby. Westminster, MD: Carroll, 1950.
Gk.	Greek
GLNT	*Greek-English Lexicon of the New Testament.* J. H. Thayer and C. Grimm. Grand Rapids, MI: Zondervan, 1965.
GRA	*God, Revelation, and Authority.* Carl F. H. Henry. Waco, TX: Word, 1976.
GWC	*God Was in Christ.* Donald M. Baillie. London: Faber & Faber, 1956.
Harmony	*Harmony of the Evangelists.* John Calvin, *Commentaries* 16, 17. See *Comm.*
HB	*The Historian and the Believer.* Van A. Harvey. New York: Macmillan, 1966.
HC	*History of the Councils.* K. J. von Hefele. 5 vols. Edinburgh: Clark, 1872–96.
HCCC	*The History of the Church from Christ to Constantine.* Eusebius. Translated by G. A. Williamson. New York: New York University Press, 1966.
HCS	*A History of the Cure of Souls.* J. T. McNiell. New York: Harper, 1951.
HCT	*The Student's Handbook of Christian Theology.* Benjamin Field. New York: Methodist Book Concern, 1887.
HCTIS	*Historical Criticism and Theological Interpretation of Scripture.* Peter Stuhlmacher. Translated by Roy Harrisville. Philadelphia: Fortress, 1977.
Heb.	Hebrew
Heid.	Heidelberg
Her.	Heresies
Hex.	*Hexaemeron*
Hist.	History
Hom.	*Homily* or *Homilies*
HP	*Hope and Planning.* Jürgen Moltmann. New York: Harper & Row, 1971.

HPC	*A Harmony of Protestant Confessions.* Edited by Peter Hall. London: Shaw, 1842.
HPEC	*Hymnal, Protestant Episcopal Church.* New York: Church Pension Fund, 1916.
HS	**1** *The Holy Spirit.* Alasdair Heron. Philadelphia: Westminster, 1983. **2** *The Holy Spirit: Growth of a Biblical Tradition.* G. T. Montague. New York: Paulist Press, 1976. **3** *The Holy Spirit.* John F. Walvoord. Grand Rapids, MI: Zondervan, 1958.
IAIA	*Juliana of Norwich: An Introductory Appreciation and an Interpretative Anthology.* Edited by P. Franklin Chambers. New York: Harper, 1955.
IBC	*Interpretation: A Bible Commentary for Teaching and Preaching.* 17 vols. Louisville, KY: Westminster John Knox, 1987–.
IBHJ	*I Believe in the Historical Jesus.* 1. Howard Marshall. Grand Rapids, MI: Eerdmans, 1977.
IBHS	*I Believe in the Holy Spirit.* Yves Congar. 2 vols. New York: Seabury, 1983.
IC	*Introduction to Christianity.* Joseph Ratzinger. New York: Herder & Herder, 1970.
ICD	*Introduction to Christian Doctrine.* T. E. Jessop. New York: Nelson, 1960.
ICNT	*Images of the Church in the New Testament.* Paul S. Minear. Philadelphia: Westminster, 1960.
ICT	*Introduction to Christian Theology.* Lectures at Duke Divinity School. Jürgen Moltmann. Edited by Douglas Meeks. Durham, NC: Duke Divinity School, 1968 (mimeographed).
Incarn.	Incarnation
Inst.	Instruction
Inst.	**1** *Institutes of the Christian Religion.* John Calvin. *LCC* 20–21. References are by book and chapter number, sometimes followed by section number. **2** *The Instructor.* Clement of Alexandria. *ANF* 2.
Intro.	Introduction
ITE	*Institutio Theologiae elencticae.* Francis Turretin. Utrecht and Amsterdam, 1701.
ITLC	*Institutiones Theologicae seu Locorum Communium Christianae Religionis.* Guillaume Bucanus. Geneva: Le Preux, 1609. ET: *Institutions of the Christian Religion.* London: George Snowden, 1606.
IW	*The Inspired Word.* Luis Alanso Schoekel. New York: Herder & Herder, 1965.
JGM	*Jesus—God and Man.* Wolfhart Pannenberg. Philadelphia: Westminster, 1968.
JJW	*The Journal of John Wesley.* Edited by N. Curnock. 8 vols. London: Epworth, 1938.
JN	*Jesus of Nazareth.* Günther Bornkamm. London: Hodder & Stoughton, 1960.
JWO	*John Wesley.* Edited by Albert C. Outler. *LPT.* New York: Oxford University Press, 1964.
KC	*Kerygma and Counseling.* Thomas C. Oden. San Francisco: Harper & Row, 1978.
KJK	*Das Kruez Jesu und die Krise der Evangelischen Kirche.* S. Findeisen, H. Frey, and W. Johanning. Bad Liebenzell: Verlag der Liebenzeller Mission, 1967.
KJV	King James Version, 1611.
KM	*Kerygma and Myth: A Theological Debate with Contributions by Rudolf Bultmann, et al.* Edited by H. W. Bartsch. London: SPCK, 1957.
LACT	*Library of Anglo-Catholic Theology.* 83 vols. Oxford: Parker, 1841–63.
Lat.	Latin
LC	*A Compendium of Luther's Theology.* Edited by H. T. Kerr. Philadelphia: Westminster, 1943.
LCC	*The Library of Christian Classics.* Edited by J. Baillie, J. T. McNeill, and H. P. Van Dusen. 26 vols. Philadelphia: Westminster, 1953–61.
LCF	*The Later Christian Fathers.* Edited by H. Bettenson. Oxford: Oxford University Press, 1970.
LCHS	*Letters of St. Athanasius Concerning the Holy Spirit, to Serapion.* Translated by C. R. B. Shapland. New York: Philosophical Library, 1951.
Lect.	Lecture(s)

LEP   *Of the Laws of Ecclesiastical Polity.* Richard Hooker. 2 vols. New York: Dutton, 1960–63.

LF   *A Library of Fathers of the Holy Catholic Church.* Edited by E. B. Pusey, J. Kebel, J. H. Newman, and C. Marriott. 50 vols. Oxford: Parker, 1838–88.

LG   *The Living God.* Vol. 1 of *Systematic Theology.* Thomas C. Oden. San Francisco: Harper & Row, 1987.

LH   *The Latin Hymn-Writers.* S. W. Duffield. New York: Funk & Wagnalls, 1889.

LibT   *Liberation Theology.* Leonardo and Clodovis Boff. San Francisco: Harper & Row, 1986.

Lit.   Constitution on the Sacred Liturgy (*Sancrosantum Concilium*). *Doc. Vat. II.*

Literal   *Literal Interpretation of Genesis.* Augustine. CWS.
Interp. of
Gen.

LLA   *Library of Liberal Arts.* Edited by Oskar Piest. Indianapolis, IN: Bobbs-Merrill, 1951–.

LMJ   *The Life and Ministry of Jesus.* Vincent Taylor. Nashville, TN: Abingdon, 1955.

Loci   *Loci Communnes Theologici.* Melanchthon. *LCC* 19., pp. 18–154.

Loeb   *Loeb Classical Library.* 506 vols. Edited by T. E. Page, et al. Cambridge, MA: Harvard University Press, 1912–.

LPT   *Library of Protestant Thought.* Edited by John Dillenberger. 13 vols. New York: Oxford University Press, 1964–72.

LT   **1** *Loci Theologici.* Martin Chemnitz. 1591. 3 vols. Frankfurt: Hoffmann, 1606. **2** *Loci Theologici.* John Gerhard. 1610–21. 22 vols. Tübingen: n.p., 1762–87.

LTJM   *The Life and Times of Jesus the Messiah.* Alfred Edersheim. Grand Rapids, MI: Eerdmans, 1953.

Luth. Sym.   *Introduction to Lutheran Symbolics.* J. L. Neve. Burlington, IA: German Literary Board, 1917.

LW   *Luther's Works.* Edited by J. Pelikan and H. T. Lehmann. 54 vols. St. Louis, MO: Concordia, 1953–.

LWHG   *The Life and Works of Hugo Grotius.* London: Grotius Society, 1925.

LXX   Septuagint (Greek Old Testament)

Mand.   *Mandates.* Pastor of Hermas.

MB   *The Doctrine of the Mystical Body of Christ According to the Principles of Theology of St. Thomas Aquinas.* Joseph Anger. Translated by John J. Burke. New York: Benziger, 1931.

MC   *On the Meaning of Christ.* John Knox. New York: Scribner, 1947.

MCD   *A Manual of Christian Doctrine.* John S. Banks. Edited by J. J. Tigert. Nashville, TN: Lamar & Barton, 1924.

MCT   **1** *Manual of Christian Theology.* Nathaniel Burwash. 2 vols. London: Horace Marshall, 1900. **2** *A Manual of Catholic Theology.* Matthias Joseph Wilhelm. Edited by T. B. Scannell. New York: Benziger, 1908–9.

MD   *Meditations and Devotions.* In *Works of John Henry Cardinal Newman.* Edited by Joseph Rickaby. Westminster, MD: Christian Classics, 1977.

Med.   *Medulla Theologiae Christianiae.* Johann Heinrich Heidegger. Tiguri: Gessner, 1696.

Med.   *The Mediator.* Emil Brunner. Philadelphia: Westminster, 1947.

Metaphy.   Metaphysics

MH   **1** *Methodist Hymnal.* Nashville, TN: United Methodist Publishing, 1966. **2** *The Methodist Hymnal.* Nashville, TN: Methodist Publishing, 1939.

MHD   *A Manual of the History of Dogma.* Bernhard John Otten. 2 vols. London: Herder, 1917–18.

Mir.   *Essays on Miracles.* In *Works of John Henry Cardinal Newman.* Edited by Joseph Rickaby. Westminster, MD: Christian Classics, 1977.

Mis.   Decree on the Church's Missionary Activity (*Ad Gentes Divinitus*). *Doc. Vat II.*

Mix.	*Discourses to Mixed Congregations.* In *Works of John Henry Cardinal Newman.* Edited by Joseph Rickaby. Westminster, MD: Christian Classics, 1977.
MLS	*Martin Luther: Selections from His Writings.* Edited by John Dillenberger. New York: Doubleday, 1961.
MMIS	*Moral Man and Immoral Society.* Reinhold Niebuhr. New York: Scribner, 1960.
MPG	*Patrologia Graeca.* Edited by J. B. Migne. 162 vols. Paris: Migne, 1857–76. Volume number followed by column number.
MPL	*Patrologia Latina.* Edited by J. B. Migne. 221 vols. Paris: Migne, 1841–65. Volume number followed by column number. General Index, Paris, 1912.
MPNTC	*A Modern Pilgrimage in New Testament Christology.* Norman Perrin. Philadelphia: Fortress, 1974.
MS	*The Ministry of the Spirit.* A. J. Gordon. Philadelphia: American Baptist Publication Society, 1894.
MTEC	*Mystical Theology of the Eastern Church.* Vladimir Lossky. London: Clarke, 1957.
MTM	*More Than Man: A Study in Christology.* Russell F. Aldwinkle. Grand Rapids, MI: Eerdmans, 1976.
MWS	*Ministry of Word and Sacrament: An Enchiridion.* Martin Chemnitz. 1595. St. Louis, MO: Concordia, 1981.
Myst.	Mystical, mystery
NA	*The Nature of the Atonement.* J. M. Campbell. Cambridge: Macmillan, 1856.
NB	*The New Birth.* John Wesley. Edited by T. Oden. San Francisco: Harper & Row, 1984.
NBD	*The New Bible Dictionary.* Edited by J. D. Douglas, et al. London: InterVarsity, 1962.
NDM	*The Nature and Destiny of Man.* Reinhold Niebuhr. 2 vols. New York: Scribner, 1941, 1943.
NE	*A New Eusebius: Documents Illustrative of the History of the Church to A.D. 337.* Edited by J. Stevenson, based on B. J. Kidd. London: SPCK, 1957.
NEB	New English Bible
NIV	New International Version
NJ	*The Names of Jesus.* Vincent Taylor. London: Macmillan, 1953.
NLG	*A New Language for God?* Alvin F. Kimel, Jr. Shaker Heights, OH: Episcopalians United, 1990.
NPNF	*A Select Library of the Nicene and Post-Nicene Fathers of the Christian Church.* Edited by H. Wace and P. Schaff. 1st series, 14 vols. 2d series, 14 vols. New York: Christian, 1887–1900. References are by title, book or chapter, subsection, and *NPNF* series number, volume, and page number.
NQHJ	*A New Quest for the Historical Jesus.* James M. Robinson. Naperville, IL: Allenson, 1959.
NR	Declaration on the Relationship of the Church to Non-Christian Religions (*Nostra Aetate*). *Doc. Vat. II.*
NRSV	New Revised Standard Version
NT	New Testament
NTDC	*New Testament Doctrine of Christ.* A. E. J. Rawlinson. London: Longmans, Green, 1926.
NTI	*New Testament Introduction.* Donald Guthrie. Downers Grove, IL: InterVarsity, 1971.
NTT	1 *New Testament Theology.* W. Beyschlag. 2 vols. London, 1893. 2 *New Testament Theology.* Donald Guthrie. Downers Grove, IL: InterVarsity, 1981.
NUNT	*Explanatory Notes upon the New Testament.* John Wesley. Naperville, IL: Allenson, 1958.
NUOT	*Explanatory Notes upon the Old Testament.* 3 vols. John Wesley. Salem, OH: Schmul, 1975.
OBP	*On Becoming a Person.* Carl R. Rogers. Boston: Houghton Mifflin, 1961.

OC	*The Origin of Christology.* C. F. D. Moule. London: Cambridge University Press, 1977.
OCD	*Outlines of Christian Dogma.* Darwell Stone. New York: Longmans, Green, 1900.
OCETW	*On Christianity: Early Theological Writings.* Friedrich Hegel. New York: Harper, 1948.
OCT	*An Outline of Christian Theology.* William Newton Clarke. Edinburgh: Clark, 1913.
ODCC	*The Oxford Dictionary of the Christian Church.* Edited by F. L. Cross. Revised by F. L. Cross and E. A. Livingstone. Oxford: Oxford University Press, 1974.
OED	*Oxford English Dictionary.*
OF	*On the Orthodox Faith.* John of Damascus. *NPNF* 2 9. *FC* 37.
OFP	**1** *On First Principles.* In *Origen: Selected Works.* Translated by Rowan Greer. *CWS.* New York: Paulist Press, 1979. **2** *On First Principles.* Origen. Translated by G. W. Butterworth. Gloucester, MA: Peter Smith, 1973.
ONTC	*The Origins of New Testament Christology.* 1. Howard Marshall. Downers Grove, IL: InterVarsity, 1976.
OO	*Omnia Opera.* Francisco Suarez. 29 vols. Paris: Ludovicum Vivès, 1856–78.
OOT	*Outlines of Theology.* Archibald Alexander Hodge. Grand Rapids, MI: Eerdmans, 1928.
Orat.	Oration(s)
OSCF	*On the Sacraments of the Christian Faith.* Hugh of St. Victor. Cambridge, MA: Mediaeval Academy of America, 1951.
OT	Old Testament
OTR	*Of True Religion.* Augustine. Chicago: Henry Regnery, 1959. *LCC* 6 unless otherwise noted.
OUED	*Oxford Universal English Dictionary.* Edited by C. T. Onions. 10 vols. Oxford: Oxford University Press, 1937.
PACP	*Plain Account of Christian Perfection.* John Wesley. London: Epworth, 1952.
PC	**1** *The Person of Christ.* Vincent Taylor. London: Macmillan, 1958. **2** *The Person of Christ.* David F. Wells. Westchester, IL: Crossway, 1984.
PCMT	*The Place of Christ in Modern Theology.* A. M. Fairbairn. New York: Scribner, 1900.
PF	*Philosophical Fragments.* Søren Kierkegaard. Princeton, NJ: Princeton University Press, 1962.
PG	*Preparation for the Gospel.* Eusebius. 2 vols. Grand Rapids, MI: Baker, 1981.
Phi.	J. B. Phillips New Testament in Modern English.
Phil. Frag.	*Philosophical Fragments.* Søren Kierkegaard. Princeton, NJ: Princeton University Press, 1985.
Phil.	Philosophy
Philokal.	*The Philokalia.* Compiled by Nikodimos of the Holy Mountain and Makarios of Corinth. Edited by G. E. H. Palmer, et al. 3 vols. London: Faber & Faber, 1979–84.
PJC	*The Doctrine of the Person of Jesus Christ.* H. R. Mackintosh. New York: Scribner, 1931.
PPH	*The Power of the Poor in History.* Gustavo Gutiérrez. Maryknoll, NY: Orbis Books, 1983.
PPJC	*Person and Place of Jesus Christ.* P. T. Forsyth. London: Independent Press, 1930.
PPS	*Parochial and Plain Sermons.* In *Works of John Henry Cardinal Newman.* Edited by Joseph Rickaby. 8 vols. Westminster, MD: Christian Classics, 1977.
PPSW	*Phoebe Palmer: Selected Writings.* Edited by Thomas C. Oden. Sources of American Spirituality Series. Mahwah, NJ: Paulist Press, 1988.
Pray.	*The Prayers of Catherine of Siena.* New York: Paulist Press, 1984.
Prescript.	Prescription
Princip.	*De Principiis.* Origen. *ANF* 4, pp. 239–384; cf. OFP.
Proslog.	*Proslogium.* Anselm. Translated by S. N. Deane. In *BW.*
Prov.	Providence

PS	*Personal Salvation*. Wilbur Tillett. Nashville, TN: Barbee & Smith, 1902.
PSG	*Philosophers Speak of God*. Edited by Charles Hartshorne and William L. Reese. Chicago: University of Chicago Press, 1953.
PT	*The Protestant Tradition*. J. S. Whale. Cambridge: Cambridge University Press, 1955.
PW	*Practical Works*. Richard Baxter. 23 vols. London: James Duncan, 1830.
RAH	*Revelation as History*. Edited by Wolfhart Pannenberg. New York: Macmillan, 1968.
RD	*Reformed Dogmatics*. Heinrich Heppe. Translated by G. T. Thomson. London: Allen and Unwin, 1950.
RDB	*Reformed Dogmatics: Seventeenth-Century Reformed Theology Through the Writings of Wollebius, Voetius, and Turretin*. Edited by John W. Beardslee III. Grand Rapids, MI: Baker, 1965.
RDL	**1** *Revelations of Divine Love*. Julian [Juliana] of Norwich. Translated by M. L. del Mastro. New York: Doubleday, 1977. **2** *Revelations of Divine Love*. Julia of Norwich. Edited by Francis Beer. Heidelberg, 1978.
Relig.	Religion
RMT	*The Resurrection and Modern Thought*. W. J. S. Simpson. London: Longmans, Green, 1911.
RMWC	*Radical Monotheism and Western Culture*. H. Richard Niebuhr. New York: Harper, 1960.
RNT	*Redating the New Testament*. J. A. T. Robinson. Phildelphia: Westminster, 1976.
RO	*Radical Obedience: The Ethics of Rudolf Bultmann*. Thomas C. Oden. Philadelphia: Westminster, 1966.
RPR	*Readings in the Philosophy of Religion*. Edited by John Mourant. New York: Crowell, 1954.
RR	*A Rahner Reader*. Karl Rahner. Edited by G. A. McCool. Greenwich, CT: Seabury, 1975.
RSV	Revised Standard Version
SA	*The Structure of Awareness*. Thomas C. Oden. Nashville, TN: Abingdon, 1968.
Sacr.	Sacrament
SCD	*Sources of Christian Dogma (Enchiridion Symbolorum)*. Edited by Henry Denzinger. Translated by Roy Deferrari. New York: Herder, 1954.
SCDoc.	*System of Christian Doctrine*. Isaak A. Dorner. Edinburgh: Clark, 1898. References are to vol. 4 unless otherwise indicated.
SCF	**1** *A Summary of the Christian Faith*. Henry E. Jacobs. Philadelphia: General Council of Publications, 1905. **2** *On the Sacraments of the Christian Faith*. Hugh of St. Victor. Cambridge, MA: Medieval Academy of America, 1951.
SCG	*On the Truth of the Catholic Faith, Summa Contra Gentiles*. Thomas Aquinas. 5 vols. Garden City, NY: Doubleday, 1955–57. Referenced by book, chapter, and page number.
SD	**1** *The Sickness unto Death*. Søren Kierkegaard. Princeton, NJ: Princeton University Press, 1954. **2** *Sermons on Subjects of the Day*. In *Works of John Henry Cardinal Newman*. Edited by Joseph Rickaby. Westminster, MD: Christian Classics, 1977.
SDF	*The Sayings of the Desert Fathers*. Translated by Benedicta Ward. London: Mowbray, 1975.
Sent.	*Sentences of Peter Lombard. Commentaria in Quator Libros Sententiarum*. In *Works of Bonaventure*. Translated by Jose de Vinck. 5 vols. Patterson, NJ: St. Anthony Guild, 1960–70.
Serm.	Sermon(s)
SFG	*De Substantia Foederis Gratuiti*. Gaspar Olevianus. Geneva, 1585.
SGL	*A Shewing of God's Love*. Julia of Norwich. Edited by Anna Maria Reynolds. London: Sheed and Ward, 1974.
SHD	*Textbook of the History of Doctrines*. Reinhold Seeberg. Grand Rapids, MI: Baker, 1952. Unless otherwise noted, all references are to vol. 1.
Sim.	*Similitudes*. Pastor of Hermas. 2.

SL   *Luthers Werke—Luthers Bibliothek.* 30 vols. St. Louis ed. St. Louis: American Lutheran Union, Missouri Synod, 1859–76.

SL   *The Spirit of Life.* Luis M. Bermejo. Gujarat, India: Gujarat Sahitya Prakish, 1987.

SLT   *Systema Locorum Theologicorum.* Abraham Calovius. 12 vols. in 4. Wittenberg: Johann Roehner, 1655–77.

SML   *Sermons of Martin Luther.* Edited by J. N. Lencker. 8 vols. Grand Rapids, MI: Baker, 1988.

SN   *Sermon Notes.* In *Works of John Henry Cardinal Newman.* Edited by Joseph Rickaby. Westminster, MD: Christian Classics, 1977.

Sol. Dec. Solid Declaration. Part II of the Formula of Concord. *BOC,* pp. 501–636.

SSM   *The Spirit of Spanish Mystics.* Edited by Kathleen Pond. New York: Kennedy, 1958.

ST   **1** *Summa Theologica.* Thomas Aquinas. Edited by English Dominican Fathers. 3 vols. New York: Benziger, 1947. References include part, subpart, question number, volume, and page number of the Benziger edition. See *STae* for the Blackfriars edition. **2** *Systematic Theology.* Louis Berkhof. Grand Rapids, MI: Eerdmans, 1962. **3** *Systematic Theology.* S. Gamertsfelder. Harrisburg, PA: Evangelical Publishing House, 1952. **4** *Systematic Theology.* C. Hodge. 3 vols. Reprint, Grand Rapids, MI: Eerdmans, 1986. **5** *Systematic Theology.* J. Miley. Reprint, Peabody, MA: Hendrickson, 1989. **6** *Systematic Theology.* Miner Raymond. 3 vols. Cincinnati, OH: Hitchcock & Walden, 1877–79. **7** *Systematic Theology.* Lewis Sperry Chafer. 8 vols. Dallas, TX: Dallas Seminary Press, 1947. **8** *Systematic Theology.* A. H. Strong. 1907. 3 vols. in one. Reprint, Old Tappan, NJ: Revell, 1979. **9** *Systematic Theology.* Thomas O. Summers. Edited by J. J. Tigert. 2 vols. Nashville, TN: Methodist Publishing House South, 1888. **10** *Systematic Theology.* Paul Tillich. 3 vols. Chicago: University of Chicago Press, 1951–63.

STae   *Summa Theologiae: Latin Text and English Translation.* Thomas Aquinas. Edited by T. Gilby and T. C. O'Brien. Blackfriars edition. 60 vols. New York: McGraw-Hill, 1964–76.

STC   *Syntagma Theologiae Christianae.* Amandus Polanus von Polansdorf. Hannover: Marnium, 1610.

STCC   *Social Teachings of the Christian Churches.* Ernst Troeltsch. 2 vols. New York: Macmillan, 1931.

STCR   *Systematic Theology of the Christian Religion.* James O. Buswell. Grand Rapids, MI: Zondervan, 1962.

Strom.   *Stromata, or Miscellanies.* Clement of Alexandria. *ANF* 2.

SW   *John Calvin: Selections from His Writings.* Edited by John Dillenberger. Missoula, MT: Scholars Press, 1975.

SWML   *Selected Writings of Martin Luther.* Edited by T. Tappert. 4 vols. Philadelphia: Fortress, 1967.

Syst. Theol. **1** *Systematic Theology.* Charles Hodge. 3 vols. 1877. Reprint, Grand Rapids, MI: Eerdmans, 1968. **2** *Systematic Theology.* John Miley. 2 vols. New York: Eaton & Mains, 1892. **3** *Systematic Theology.* Miner Raymond. 2 vols. Cincinnati, OH: Hitchcock & Walden, 1877. **4** *Systematic Theology.* A. H. Strong. 1907. 3 vols. in one. Reprint, Old Tappan, NJ: Revell, 1979. **5** *Systematic Theology.* Thomas O. Summers. 2 vols. Nashville, TN: Methodist Publishing House South, 1888. **6** *Systematic Theology.* Paul Tillich. 3 vols. Chicago: University of Chicago Press, 1951–63.

Syst.   Systematic

TAA   *Treatises Against the Anabaptists and Against the Libertines.* John Calvin. Edited by B. W. Farley. Grand Rapids, MI: Baker, 1982.

TAG   *The Transactional Awareness Game.* Thomas C. Oden. San Francisco: Harper & Row, 1977.

TAPT   *St. Thomas Aquinas' Philosophical Texts.* Edited by Thomas Gilby. London: Oxford University Press, 1951.

TATT   *St. Thomas Aquinas' Theological Texts.* Edited by Thomas Gilby. London: Oxford University Press, 1955.

TC	**1** *Training in Christianity*. Søren Kierkegaard. Princeton, NJ: Princeton University Press, 1941. **2** *Theologia Christiana*. Benedictus Pictet. Geneva, 1696. **3** *The Church*. Hans Küng. New York: Doubleday, 1976.
TCBM	*The Truth of Christmas—Beyond the Myths: The Gospels of the Infancy of Christ.* Rene Laurentin. Petersham, MA: St. Bede's Publications, 1985.
TCGNT	*A Textual Commentary on the Greek New Testament*. Bruce M. Metzger. New York: United Bible Societies, 1971.
TCI	*Theological Compendium Improved*. Amos Binney, with Daniel Steele. New York: Phillips & Hunt, 1875.
TCL	*Translations of Christian Literature*. Edited by S. Simpson and L. Clarke. London: SPCK, 1917–.
TCNT	Twentieth-Century New Testament
TDNT	*Theological Dictionary of the New Testament*. Edited by G. Kittel. Translated by G. W. Bromiley. 9 vols. Grand Rapids, MI: Eerdmans, 1964–74.
TDOT	*Theological Dictionary of the Old Testament*. Edited by G. J. Botterweck and H. Ringgren. 5 vols. Grand Rapids, MI: Eerdmans, 1975.
TDP	*Theologia Didactico-Polemica*. Friedrich Quenstedt. 4 parts in 1 vol. Wittenberg: J. L. Quenstedt, 1691.
TEV	Today's English Version
TF	*The Trinitarian Faith*. Thomas F. Torrance. Edinburgh: Clark, 1988.
TFE	*Truth, Freedom and Evil*. Anselm of Canterbury. Translated by Jasper Hopkins and Herbert Richardson. New York: Harper & Row, 1967.
TFR	*Commentary on True and False Religion*. Huldreich Zwingli. *WZ* 3, pp. 43–343.
TGI	*The Truth of God Incarnate*. Edited by Michael Green. Grand Rapids, MI: Eerdmans, 1977.
TGS	*Theology of God—Sources*. Edited by K. Kehoe. New York: Bruce, 1971.
Theol.	Theology, theological
Tho. Aq.	Thomas Aquinas
TI	**1** *Theological Institutes*. Richard Watson. Edited by John M'Clintock. 2 vols. New York: Carlton & Porter, 1850. **2** *Theological Investigations*. Karl Rahner. 23 vols. London and New York, 1961–92.
TIR	*Trinity, Incarnation, and Redemption*. Anselm of Canterbury. Translated by Jasper Hopkins and Herbert Richardson. New York: Harper & Row, 1969.
TJC	*The Titles of Jesus in Christology*. Ferdinand Hahn. London: Lutterworth, 1969.
TKG	*Theology and the Kingdom of God*. Wolfhart Pannenberg. Edited by R. J. Neuhaus. Philadelphia: Westminster, 1971.
TLC	*Theology of the Living Church*. L. Harold DeWolfe. New York: Harper, 1953.
TM	*A Handbook of Theology: Homiletical Manual of Christian Doctrine*. John Harries. London: Kelly, 1903.
TNC	*The Two Natures in Christ*. Martin Chemnitz. Translated by J. A. O. Preus. St. Louis, MO: Concordia, 1971.
TNT	**1** *Theology of the New Testament*. Rudolf Bultmann. 2 vols. New York: Scribner, 1952. **2** *An Outline of the Theology of the New Testament*. Hans Conzelmann. Philadelphia: Fortress, 1983. **3** *A Theology of the New Testament*. George E. Ladd. Grand Rapids, MI: Eerdmans, 1974. **4** *The Theology of the New Testament*. George B. Stevens. Edinburgh: Clark, 1908.
TPA	*Theologia Positiva Acroamatica*. John Frederick Koenig. 1664. Rostock: Joachim Wild, 1687.
TPW	*Taylor's Practical Works*. Jeremy Taylor. 2 vols. London: Bohn, 1854.
Tracts	*Tracts and Treatises*. John Calvin. 3 vols. Grand Rapids, MI: Eerdmans, 1958.
Trent	*The Canons and Decrees of the Council of Trent*. Edited by H. J. Schroeder. Rockford, IL: TAN, 1978.
Trin.	Trinity

TSD	*Theologia Scholastica Didactica.* J. H. Alsted. Hanover, 1618.
TWS	*Theology in the Wesleyan Spirit.* Albert C. Outler. Nashville, TN: Tidings, 1975.
UEMA	*The Universities of Europe in the Middle Ages.* Hastings Rashdall. 3 vols. Oxford: Clarendon, 1895.
U&R	*Unity and Reform: Selected Writings of Nicholas de Cusa.* Edited by John P. Dolan. Notre Dame, IN: University of Notre Dame Press, 1962.
US	*Oxford University Sermons.* In *Works of John Henry Cardinal Newman.* Edited by Joseph Rickaby. Westminster, MD: Christian Classics, 1977.
UTS	*Universae Theologiae Systema.* Caspar Brochmann. 1633.
v.	verse
Vat.	Vatican
VCOS	*On the Virgin Conception and Original Sin.* Anselm. *TIR.*
Vis.	*Visions.* Pastor of Hermas.
Vlg.	Vulgate
Vulg.	Vulgate
WA	*Weimarer Ausgabe. Dr. Martin Luthers Werke, Kritische Gemsamtausgabe,* 127 vols. Weimar: Verlag Hermann Böhlau, 1883–. References give volume number followed by page number.
WAS	*What Augustine Says.* Edited by Norman L. Geisler. Grand Rapids, MI: Baker, 1982.
WCB	**1** *What Catholics Believe.* Josef Pieper. New York: Pantheon, 1951. **2** *World Christian Books.* Edited by John Goodwin. London: Lutterworth, 1954–.
WCC	World Council of Churches
Werke	*Huldreich Zwingli's Werke.* Edited by M. Schuler and J. Schulthess. 8 vols. Zurich: Schulthess, 1828.
WF	*Word and Faith.* Gerhard Ebeling. London: SCM, 1963.
WHNS	*A Collection of Hymns for the Use of the People Called Methodists, with a New Supplement.* London: Wesleyan Conference Office, 1876. Referenced by hymn number.
WHS	*The Work of the Holy Spirit.* Abraham Kuyper. New York: Funk & Wagnalls, 1900.
WIB	*Works of Isaac Barrow.* 3 vols. New York: Riker, 1845.
WJE	*The Works of Jonathan Edwards.* 2 vols. Carlisle, PA: Banner of Truth Trust, 1974.
WJW	*Works of the Reverend John Wesley.* Edited by Thomas Jackson. 14 vols. London: Wesleyan Conference Office, 1872.
WJWB	*The Works of John Wesley.* Edited by Frank Baker. Bicentennial ed. 8 vols. Nashville, TN: Abingdon, 1975–. (Formerly published by Oxford University Press.)
WL	*The Word of Life.* Vol. 2 of *Systematic Theology.* Thomas C. Oden. San Francisco: Harper & Row, 1989.
WLS	*What Luther Says.* Edited by E. Plass. 3 vols. St. Louis, MO: Concordia, 1959.
WML	*Works of Martin Luther: An Anthology.* Philadelphia ed. 6 vols. Philadelphia: Muhlenberg, 1943.
WNUUD	*Webster's New Universal Unabridged Dictionary.* 2d ed. New York: World Publishing, 1983.
Works	**1** *Complete Works of John Bunyan.* 4 vols. London: Virtue & Yorston, n.d. **2** *Works of John Fletcher.* 4 vols. Salem, OH: Schmul, 1974. **3** *Works of John Owen.* 16 vols. Reprint, Carlisle, PA: Banner of Truth, 1965. **4** *Works of Thomas Goodwin.* 12 vols. Edinburgh: Nichol, 1861–66. **5** *Works of Andrew Fuller.* 8 vols. Charlestown, MA: Collier, 1820–25.
WT	*Waterbuffalo Theology.* Kosuko Koyama. Maryknoll, NY: Orbis Books, 1974.
WZ	*The Latin Works of Huldreich Zwingli.* Translated by S. M. Jackson. 3 vols. Philadelphia: Heidelberg, 1929.

INDEX

Rufinus, xvii, 10, 11, 171, 188, 189, 229, 284, 521, 599, 691, 791

Rule of faith (regula fidei), 9, 118, 181–82, 184, 186, 208, 222, 284, 292, 446, 503–4, 506, 633, 743, 748, 749, 757, 764, 769, 787, 824, 849–51, 852, 853, 854. See also Baptism; Creeds and creedal prototypes

Russian Catechism, 247, 248, 249, 268, 284, 300, 368, 390, 391, 423, 450, 455, 484

Ruth, 294

Sabbath day service, 183, 459

Sabellianism, 260, 521, 524

Sacraments, 320, 715, 717–18, 736

Saints: communion, 718, 823–27; as community of believers, 670; derivation, 660; as elect, 662, 692, 699, 800; examples, 682; exemplary women, 682; glorified bodies, 834, 836, 837; paradoxical uprightness, 679; Pelagian view, 676; spiritual body, 837; three traditions of the church, 692; unattainability of perfect love, 681–85; warning not to attribute divine attributes to finite creatures, 684–85

Salvation, 561–82; as analogous to light, 829; apostolic teaching and, 756; assurance, through witness of the Spirit, 645–49; benefits, 607; Christianity and, 244; church's intercession for humanity, 738–39; conditional efficacy, 423; confession of sin and, 570, 579–82; consummation and, 769; conversion